EU LAW

EU LAW

Text, Cases, and Materials

FOURTH EDITION

Paul Craig
and
Gráinne de Búrca

OXFORD
UNIVERSITY PRESS

OXFORD

UNIVERSITY PRESS

Great Clarendon Street, Oxford OX2 6DP

Oxford University Press is a department of the University of Oxford.
It furthers the University's objective of excellence in research, scholarship,
and education by publishing worldwide in

Oxford New York

Auckland Cape Town Dar es Salaam Hong Kong Karachi
Kuala Lumpur Madrid Melbourne Mexico City Nairobi
New Delhi Shanghai Taipei Toronto

With offices in

Argentina Austria Brazil Chile Czech Republic France Greece
Guatemala Hungary Italy Japan Poland Portugal Singapore
South Korea Switzerland Thailand Turkey Ukraine Vietnam

Oxford is a registered trade mark of Oxford University Press
in the UK and in certain other countries

Published in the United States
by Oxford University Press Inc., New York

British Library Cataloguing in Publication Data

Data available

Library of Congress Cataloging in Publication Data

Data available

Typeset by Newgen Imaging Systems (P) Ltd., Chennai, India
Printed in Great Britain by Ashford Colour Press Ltd, Gosport, Hants

ISBN 978–0–19–927389–8

3 5 7 9 10 8 6 4

For Anita and Ciaran
P.P.C.

Do mo mháthair agus i gcuimhne m'athar
G. de B.

PREFACE TO THE FOURTH EDITION

Since the third edition of this textbook was published in 2002, no major new EU Treaty has entered into force. However, this five-year period has brought some of the liveliest and most controversial constitutional activity since the process of European integration began in the 1950s. Following an unexpected and novel set of processes, the Treaty establishing a European Constitution (CT) was signed in 2004, but the ratification of the Treaty was halted in its tracks by the negative outcome of the French and Dutch referenda in 2005. As this book goes to press, negotiations on a 'Reform Treaty' which is based very significantly on the provisions of the abandoned CT are ongoing, and it seems possible that such a Treaty may be signed over the next year. This book contains an analysis of many of the key provisions of the CT, which should prove all the more relevant if the Reform Treaty does indeed come to life in the next few years.

In addition to these significant constitutional developments, there has also been the usual range of important EU judicial decisions, legislation, policy developments and scholarly commentary. In particular, EU activity under the Second and Third Pillars continues to grow apace, not least in response to the rise in terrorist activity since 11 September 2001. The fourth edition endeavours to reflect and analyse as many of these important developments as possible.

The structure and content of this edition has been changed in various substantial ways. Four new chapters have been added on the following topics: New Forms of Governance, EU International Relations Law, the Area of Freedom, Security and Justice, and EU Citizenship. Several other chapters have been amalgamated or streamlined in order to make room for the new additions without adding to the length of the book. We have also continued to pursue our general aim of enhancing the comprehensibility and accessibility to students of complex material in the way the chapters are organized, presented, and written.

We are indebted to Jacqueline Senior, Joanna Godfrey, Nicola Haisley, and the OUP team for their great efficiency, professionalism, and help in the preparation of this edition. We are delighted to continue our collaboration with Kate Elliott who, as always, has done a wonderful job as copyeditor. Sincere thanks are also due to Rémy Bonneau, Muhseen Abdoolraman, Cristian Oro-Martinez, Anna Hachmeister, and Fiona D'Souza for their excellent research assistance, and in particular to Michal Golabek for his excellent and extensive work on Chapter 6. Finally, warm thanks are due to our friends and colleagues Marise Cremona and Bruno de Witte for their help and advice on various parts.

The book has been written on the basis of the law as it stood on 1 April 2007.

Paul Craig
Gráinne de Búrca

Paul Craig, QC, FBA is Professor of English Law at St John's College, Oxford.
Gráinne de Búrca is Professor of Law, Fordham University Law School.

OUTLINE TABLE OF CONTENTS

DETAILED CONTENTS

TABLE OF ABBREVIATIONS

AC	Appeal Cases
ACT	Advance Corporation Tax
AFSJ	Area of Freedom, Security and Justice
All ER	All England Law Reports
Am. Econ. Rev.	*American Economic Review*
Am. J Comp. L	*American Journal of Comparative Law*
ANEC	European Association for the Co-ordination of Consumer Representation in Standardization
Antitrust B	*Antitrust Bulletin*
Antitrust LJ	*Antitrust Law Journal*
Bull. EC	Bulletin of the European Communities
BYIL	*British Yearbook of International Law*
CA	English Court of Appeal
CAP	Common Agricultural Policy
CATS	Comité de l'Article Trente Six
CCP	Common Commercial Policy
CDE	*Cahiers de Droit Européen*
CDP	Common Defence Policy
CEE	Charges of Equivalent Effect
CEN	European Committee for Standardization
CENELEC	European Committee for Electrotechnical Standardization
CFI	Court of First Instance
CFSP	Common Foreign and Security Policy
CJEL	*Columbia Journal of European Law*
CLJ	Cambridge Law Journal
CLP	*Current Legal Problems*
CMLR	Common Market Law Reports
CMLRev.	*Common Market Law Review*
Col. LR	*Columbia Law Review*
COREPER	Committee of the Permanent Representatives (of the Member States)
Cornell L Rev.	*Cornell Law Review*
CT	Constitutional Treaty
CYELS	*Cambridge Yearbook of European Legal Studies*
D & R	Decisions and Reports of the European Commission of Human Rights
Dec.	Decision
DG	Directorate General
Dir.	Directive
EAGGF	European Agricultural Guidance and Guarantee Fund
EC	European Community
ECB	European Central Bank

ECHR	European Convention on Human Rights
ECOFIN	Council of Ministers for Economics and Finance
ECommHR	European Commission on Human Rights
ECtHR	European Court of Human Rights
ECJ	European Court of Justice
ECLR	*European Competition Law Review*
ECOSOC	Economic and Social Committee
ECR	European Court Reports
ECSC	European Coal and Steel Community
EC Treaty	European Community Treaty
ECU	European Currency Unit(s)
EDA	Exclusive Distribution Agreement
EDC	European Defence Community
EEA	European Economic Area
EEC	European Economic Community
EELR	*European Environmental Law Review*
EFA Rev.	*European Foreign Affairs Review*
EFTA	European Free Trade Association
EHRLR	*European Human Rights Law Reports*
EHRR	European Human Rights Reports
EJIL	*European Journal of International Law*
EJML	*European Journal of Migration and Law*
ELJ	*European Law Journal*
ELRev.	*European Law Review*
EMI	European Monetary Institute
EMU	Economic and Monetary Union
ENP	European Neighbourhood Policy
EP	European Parliament
EPA	Exclusive Purchasing Agreement
EPC	European Political Co-operation
ERPL	*European Review of Public Law*
ERTA	European Road Transport Agreement
ESCB	European System of Central Banks
ESDP	European Security and Defence Policy
ETSI	European Telecommunications Standards Institute
EU	European Union
EuConst	*European Constitutional Law Review*
EUMC	European Monitoring Centre on Racism and Xenophobia
EUP	*European Union Politics*
Euratom	European Atomic Energy Community
Europol	European Police Office
Fordham Int. LJ	*Fordham International Law Journal*
FRA	Fundamental Rights Agency
GATS	General Agreement on Trade in Service

GATT	General Agreement on Tariffs and Trade
GNP	Gross national product
Harv. Int. LJ	*Harvard International Law Journal*
Harv. LR	*Harvard Law Review*
Hastings I & Comp. LJ	*Hastings International and Comparative Law Journal*
HL	House of Lords
HRLJ	*Human Rights Law Journal*
ICCPR	International Covenant on Civil and Political Rights
ICESCR	International Covenant on Economic, Social and Cultural Rights
ICLQ	*International and Comparative Law Quarterly*
ICR	Industrial Cases Reports
ICRC	International Convention on the Rights of the Child
IGC	Intergovernmental Conference
IJEL	*Irish Journal of European Law*
ILJ	*Industrial Law Journal*
ILO	International Labour Organization
IR	Irish Reports
JCMS	*Journal of Common Market Studies*
JEPP	*Journal of European Public Policy*
JHA	Justice and Home Affairs 'Pillar'
Jnl. Cons. Policy	*Journal of Consumer Policy*
J Pol. Econ.	*Journal of Political Economy*
JSWFL	*Journal of Social Welfare and Family Law*
JWTL	*Journal of World Trade Law*
LIEI	*Legal Issues of European Integration*
LQR	*Law Quarterly Review*
LS	*Legal Studies*
MCA, MCAS	Monetary Compensatory Amount(s)
MEQR	Measures having Equivalent Effect to a Quantitative Restriction
Mich. LR	*Michigan Law Review*
MJ	*Maastricht Journal of European and Comparative Law*
MLR	*Modern Law Review*
MTF	Mergers Task Force
NATO	North Atlantic Treaty Organization
Notre Dame LRev.	*Notre Dame Law Review*
NWJ Int. L and Bus.	*North Western Journal of Law and Business*
NYULRev.	*New York University Law Review*
OECD	Organization for Economic Co-operation and Development
OEEC	Organization for European Economic Co-operation
OJ	Official Journal of the European Communities
OJLS	*Oxford Journal of Legal Studies*
OLAF	Office Européen de Lutte Anti-Fraude (European Anti-Fraud Office)
OMC	Open Method of Co-ordination

PJCC	Police and Judicial Co-operation in Criminal Matters
PL	*Public Law*
PNR	Passenger Name Record
QB	Queen's Bench Reports
Reg.	Regulation
SDA	Selective Distribution Agreement
SEA	Single European Act
SIS	Schengen Information Service
SMEs	Small and Medium-sized Enterprises
So. Cal. L Rev.	*Southern California Law Review*
SPA	Social Policy Agreement
SPS	Agreement on the Application of Sanitary and Phytosanitary Measures
Summit	European Council Meeting
TBT	Agreement on Technical Barriers to Trade
TEU	Treaty on European Union ('Maastricht Treaty')
TN	Nice Treaty
ToA	Treaty of Amsterdam
TRIPS	Agreement on Trade-Related Intellectual Property Rights
U Chic. Legal Forum	*University of Chicago Legal Forum*
UN	United Nations
Vand. L Rev.	*Vanderbilt Law Review*
VAT	Value Added Tax
WEU	Western European Union
WLR	Weekly Law Reports
WTO	World Trade Organization
Yale LJ	*Yale Law Journal*
YBEL	*Yearbook of European Law*

ACKNOWLEDGEMENTS

Grateful acknowledgement is made to all the authors and publishers of copyright material which appears in this book, and in particular to the following for permission to reprint material from the sources indicated:

BASIC BOOKS, a member of Perseus Books LLC for extracts from R. H. Bork: *The Antitrust Paradox: A Policy at War with Itself* (1978), copyright © 1978 Basic Books, Inc.

BLACKWELL PUBLISHERS for extracts from P. Dankert: 'The EC—Past, Present and Future' in L. Tsoukalis (ed.): *The EC—Past, Present and Future* (Basil Blackwell, 1983); extracts from *Modern Law Review*, A. Arnull: 'The use and abuse of Article 177', *MLR* 52 (1989); W. Bishop: 'Price discrimination under Article 86: Political economy in the European Court', *MLR* 44 (1981); A. McGee and S. Weatherill: 'The evolution of the single market-harmonization or liberalisation', *MLR* 53 (1990); and F. Snyder: 'The Effectiveness of European Community Law', *MLR* 56 (1993); extracts from *European Law Journal*, P. Kirchhof: 'The Balance of Powers between National and European Institutions' *ELJ* 5 (1999); and J. Scott and D. Trubek: 'Mind the Gap: Law and New Governance in the EU' *ELJ* 8 (2002); extract from J. Pelkmans: 'The new approach to technical harmonization and standardization', *JCMS* 25 (1987); and extract from J. Vickers: 'Abuse of Market Power', *The Economic Journal* 115 (2005).

CAMBRIDGE UNIVERSITY PRESS: for extracts from J.H.H. Weiler: *The Constitution of Europe: Do the New Clothes have an Emperor?* (CUP, 1999); and extract from A. Moravcsik: 'Negotiating the Single European Act: National Interests and Conventional Statecraft in the European Community' in *International Organization* 45 (1991).

CONTINUUM INTERNATIONAL PUBLISHING GROUP LTD, The Tower Building, 11 York Road, London for extracts from M. Holland: *European Integration from Community to Union* (Pinter, 1993); J. Lodge: introduction, and 'EC Policymaking: Insitutional Dynamics', and from S. Mazey & J. Richardson: 'Pressure Groups and Lobbying in the EC', in J. Lodge (ed): *The European Community and the Challenge of the Future* (Pinter, 1993); and W. Wessels: 'Administrative Interaction', in W. Wallace (ed.): *The Dynamics of European Integration* (RSIA/Pinter 1990).

dE WITTE, BRUNO for extract from B. de Witte: 'Setting the Scene—How did Services get to *Bolkestein* and Why?' *EUI Working Paper LAW 2007/20* (2007).

HART PUBLISHING LTD for extracts from P. Koutrakos: *EU International Relations Law* (Hart, 2006); M. P. Maduro: *We the Court, The European Court of Justice and the European Economic Constitution* (Hart, 1998); and R. Wesseling: *The Modernisation of the EC Antitrust Law* (Hart, 1985).

HARVARD LAW REVIEW for extract from W. Comanor: 'Vertical price-fixing, vertical market restrictions, and the new antitrust policy', in *Harvard Law Review* 98 (1985), copyright © 1985 Harvard Law Review Association.

JOHNS HOPKINS UNIVERSITY PRESS for extract from Wayne Sandholz and John Zysman: '1992: Recasting the European Bargain', in *World Politics* 42:1 (1989), copyright © 1989 Center of International Studies, Princeton University.

KLUWER LAW INTERNATIONAL for extracts from T. Heukels and A. McDonnell (eds.): *The Action for Damages in Community Law* (Kluwer Law International, 1997); and for extracts from *Common Market Law Review*, G. Bebr: 'The Existence of a genuine dispute: An indispensable precondition for the jurisdiction of the Court under Article 177 EEC Treaty?', *CMLR* 17 (1980); M. Cremona, 'The Union as a Global Actor: Roles, Models and Identity', *CMLR* 41 (2004); D. Curtin: 'Scalping the Community Legislator: Occupational Pensions and "Barber"', *CMLR* 27 (1990); C.-D. Ehlermann: 'The international market following the Single European Act', *CMLR* 24 (1987); G. Gaja: 'New developments in the continuing story: The relationship between EEC Law and Italian Law', *CMLR* 27 (1990); R. Gosalbo Bono, 'Some Reflections on the CFSP Legal Order', *CMLR* 43 (2006); B. Hawk: 'System Failure: Vertical restraints and the EC Competition Law', *CMLR* 32 (1995); H. Rasmussen: 'Remedying the crumbling EC Judicial system', *CMLR* 37 (2000); S. Weatherill: 'After Keck: Some thoughts on how to clarify the clarification', *CMLR* 33 (1996); and E. White: 'In search of the limits to Article 30 of the EEC Treaty', *CMLR* 26 (1989).

KORAH, VALENTINE for extract from V. Korah: 'The Rise and Fall of Provisional Validity—The Need for a Rule of reason in EEC Antitrust', in *NWJ Int. L and Bus.*, 320 (Northwestern University School of Law, 1981).

MANCHESTER UNIVERSITY PRESS for extract from P. K. Armstrong and S. Bulmer: *The Governance of the Single European Market* (1998).

NOMOS VERLAGSGESELLSCHAFT for extracts from R. Dehousse: 'Completing the Internal Market: Institutional constraints and challenges', in R. Bieber, R. Dehousse, J. Pinder, and J. Weiler (eds.): *One European Market?* (1988).

OXFORD UNIVERSITY PRESS for extracts from P. P. Craig: 'Britain in the European Union', in J. Jowell & D. Oliver (eds.): *The Changing Constitution* (6th edn., OUP, 2007); E. Denza: *The Intergovernmental Pillars of the European Union* (OUP, 2002); A. Estella: *The EU Principle of Subsidiarity and its Critique* (OUP, 2002); N. MacCormick: *Questioning Sovereignty* (OUP, 1999); S. Peers: *EU Justice and Home Affairs Law* (OUP, 2006); J. Peterson and M. Shackleton (eds.): *The Institutions of the European Union* (OUP, 2006); T. Prosser: *The Limits of Competition Law: Markets and Public Services* (OUP, 2005); F. Snyder: 'EMU Revisited: Are We Making a Constitution? What Constitution Are We Making?', in P. Craig and G. de Búrca (eds.) *The Evolution of EU Law* (OUP, 1999); A. Stone-Sweet: *The Judicial Construction of Europe* (OUP, 2004); N. Walker (ed.): *Europe's Area of Freedom, Security and Justice* (OUP, 2004); H. Wallace, W. Wallace and M. Pollack (eds.): *Policy-Making in the European Union* (OUP, 2005); J. H. H. Weiler: 'The Judicial Après-Nice', in G. de Búrca and J. H. H. Weiler (eds.): *The European Court of Justice* (OUP, 2001); and R. Whish: *Competition Law* (5th edn., OUP, 2003); and for extracts from *Year Book of European Law*, G. de Búrca: 'The Principle of Proportionality and its Application in EC Law', *YBEL* 13 (1993); G. F. Mancini and D. T. Keeling: 'From CILFIT to ERT: The constitutional challenge facing the European Court', *YBEL* 11 (1991); J. Weiler: 'The Community System: the Dual Character of Supranationalism', *YBEL* 1 (1981); and R. Whish and B. Sufrin: 'Article 85 and the Rule of Reason', *YBEL* 7 (1987).

PEARSON EDUCATION LTD for extract from D. Curtin: 'The Constitutional Structure of the Union: A Europe of Bits and Pieces', in *The Common Market Law Review*, published by Kluwer.

PENGUIN BOOKS LTD for extracts from Christopher Johnson: *In with the Euro, Out with the Pound* (Penguin, 1996), copyright © Christopher Johnson 1996; Dennis Swann: *The*

Economics of the Common Market (7th edn., Penguin, 1992), copyright © Dennis Swann 1970, 1992; and Stephen Weatherill and Paul Beaumont: *EU Law: The Essential Guide* (3rd edn., Penguin, 1999), copyright © Stephen Weatherill & Paul Beaumont 1999.

REED ELSEVIER (UK) LTD for extracts from F. Jacobs: 'Is the Court of Justice of the European Communities a Constitutional Court?'; and M. Westlake: *The Commission and the Parliament: Partners and Rivals in the European Policy-Making Process* (Butterworths, 1994).

RODRIGUES, MARIA JOÃO for extract from M. João Rodrigues: 'The Open Method of Coordination as a New Governance Tool' in M. Telò (ed.), 'L'evoluzione della governance europa,' Special Issue of *Europa/Europe*, Rome, No. 2–3, 2001.

SWEET & MAXWELL LTD for extracts from *Law Quarterly Review*, P. P. Craig: 'Compensation in Public Law', *LQR* 96 (1980); from *European Competition Law Review*, S. Bishop, A. Lofaro and F. Rosati: 'Turning the Tables: Why Vertical and Conglomerate Mergers are different', *ECLR* (2006); J. de Azevedo and M. Walker: 'Market Dominance: Measurement, Problems and Mistakes', *ECLR* (2003); P. Lugard and L. Hancher: 'Honey, I Shrunk the Article! A Critical Assessment of the Commission's Notice on Article 81 (3) of the EC Treaty', *ECLR* (2004); D. Ridyard: 'Essential facilities and the obligation to supply competitors' *ECLR* (1996); and from *European Law Review*, C. Barnard: 'Fitting the remaining pieces into the Goods and Persons jigsaw', *ELR* 26 (2001); J. S. Chard: 'The economics of the application of Article 85 to selective distribution systems', *ELR* 7 (1982); L. Gormley and J. de Haan: 'The democratic deficit of the European Central Bank', *ELR* 21 (1996); C. Harlow and R. Rawlings: 'Accountability and Law Enforcement: The Centralized EU Infringement Procedure', *ELR* 31 (2006); H.-C. von Heydebrand u. d. Lasa: 'Free movement of foodstuffs, consumer protection and food standards in the European Community: Has the Court of Justice got it wrong?', *ELR* 16 (1991); K. Lenaerts and T. Corthaut: 'Of Birds and Hedges: The Role of Primacy in Invoking Norms of EU Law', *ELR* 31 (2006); J. F. M. Martin & O. Stehmann: 'Product Market Integration versus Regional Cohesion in the Community', *ELR* 16 (1991); P. Pescatore: 'The Doctrine of "Direct Effect": An Infant Disease of Community Law', *ELR* 8 (1983); R. Schutze: 'Co-operative Federalism Constitutionalised: The Emergence of Complementary Competances in the EC Legal Order', ELR 31 (2006); and D. Wyatt: 'Foglia (No. 2): The Court denies it has jurisdiction to give advisory opinions', *ELR* 7 (1982).

JOHN WILEY & SONS LTD: extracts from A. G. Toth: 'A Legal Analysis of Subsidiarity' and J. Steiner: 'Subsidiarity under the Maastricht Treaty', from D. O'Keeffe & P. M. Twomey (eds.): *Legal Issues of the Maastricht Treaty* (Chancery Press, 1994), copyright © 1994 John Wiley & Sons Ltd.

THE YALE UNIVERSITY LAW JOURNAL COMPANY and WILLIAM S. HEIN COMPANY for extracts from J. Weiler: 'The Transformation of Europe', *The YaleLJ* Vol. 100 (1991).

Every effort has been made to trace and contact copyright holders prior to publication. If notified, the publisher will undertake to rectify any errors or omissions at the earliest opportunity.

TABLE OF CASES

European Court of First Instance

Cases from other jurisdictions

Belgium

European Court & Commission of Human Rights

United States

Commission and Council Decisions

TABLE OF TREATIES, EUROPEAN LEGISLATIVE INSTRUMENTS, AND NATIONAL LEGISLATION

EC Directives

EC Decisions

National Legislation

France

Germany

Ireland

TABLE OF EQUIVALENCES REFERRED TO IN ARTICLE 12 OF THE TREATY OF AMSETRDAM

A. TREATY ON EUROPEAN UNION

Previous numbering	New numbering	Previous numbering	New numbering
TITLE I	TITLE I	TITLE VI (***)	TITLE VI
Article A	Article 1	Article K.1	Article 29
Article B	Article 2	Article K.2	Article 30
Article C	Article 3	Article K.3	Article 31
Article D	Article 4	Article K.4	Article 32
Article E	Article 5	Article K.5	Article 33
Article F	Article 6	Article K.6	Article 34
Article F.1 (*)	Article 7	Article K.7	Article 35
		Article K.8	Article 36
TITLE I	TITLE II	Article K.9	Article 37
Article G	Article 8	Article K.10	Article 38
		Article K.11	Article 39
TITLE III	TITLE III	Article K.12	Article 40
Article H	Article 9	Article K.13	Article 41
		Article K.14	Article 42
TITLE IV	TITLE IV	TITLE VIA (**)	TITLE VII
Article I	Article 10	Article K.15 (*)	Article 43
		Article K.16 (*)	Article 44
TITLE V (***)	TITLE V	Article K.17 (*)	Article 45
Article J.1	Article 11		
Article J.2	Article 12	TITLE VII	TITLE VIII
Article J.3	Article 13	Article L	Article 46
Article J.4	Article 14	Article M	Article 47
Article J.5	Article 15	Article N	Article 48
Article J.6	Article 16	Article O	Article 49
Article J.7	Article 17	Article P	Article 50
Article J.8	Article 18	Article Q	Article 51
Article J.9	Article 19	Article R	Article 52
Article J.10	Article 20	Article S	Article 53
Article J.11	Article 21		
Article J.12	Article 22		
Article J.13	Article 23		
Article J.14	Article 24		
Article J.15	Article 25		
Article J.16	Article 26	(*) New Article introduced by the Treaty of Amsterdam	
Article J.17	Article 27	(**) New Title introduced by the Treaty of Amsterdam	
Article J.18	Article 28	(***) Title restructured by the Treaty of Amsterdam	

B. TREATY ESTABLISHING THE EUROPEAN COMMUNITY

Previous numbering	New numbering	Previous numbering	New numbering
PART ONE	PART ONE	Article 20 (repealed)	—
Article	Article 1	Article 21 (repealed)	—
Article 2	Article 2	Article 22 (repealed)	—
Article 3	Article 3	Article 23 (repealed)	—
Article 3a	Article 4	Article 24 (repealed)	—
Article 3b	Article 5	Article 25 (repealed)	—
Article 3c (*)	Article 6	Article 26 (repealed)	—
Article 4	Article 7	Article 27 (repealed)	—
Article 4a	Article 8	Article 28	Article 26
Article 4b	Article 9	Article 29	Article 27
Article 5	Article 10		
Article 5a (*)	Article 11	CHAPTER 2	CHAPTER 2
Article 6	Article 12	Article 30	Article 28
Article 6a	Article 13	Article 31 (repealed)	—
Article 7 (repealed)	—	Article 32 (repealed)	—
Article 7a	Article 14	Article 33 (repealed)	—
Article 7b (repealed)	—	Article 34	Article 29
Article 7c	Article 15	Article 35 (repealed)	—
Article 7d (*)	Article 16	Article 36	Article 30
		Article 37	Article 31
PART TWO	PART TWO		
Article 8	Article 17	TITLE II	TITLE II
Article 8a	Article 18	Article 38	Article 32
Article 8b	Article 19	Article 39	Article 33
Article 8c	Article 20	Article 40	Article 34
Article 8d	Article 21	Article 41	Article 35
Article 8e	Article 22	Article 42	Article 36
		Article 43	Article 37
PART THREE	PART THREE	Article 44 (repealed)	—
TITLE I	TITLE I	Article 45 (repealed)	—
Article 9	Article 23	Article 46	Article 38
Article 10	Article 24	Article 47 (repealed)	—
Article 11 (repealed)	—		
		TITLE III	TITLE III
CHAPTER 1	CHAPTER 1	CHAPTER 1	CHAPTER 1
Section 1 (deleted)	—	Article 48	Article 39
Article 12	Article 25	Article 49	Article 40
Article 13 (repealed)	—	Article 50	Article 41
Article 14 (repealed)	—	Article 51	Article 42
Article 15 (repealed)	—		
Article 16 (repealed)	—		
Article 17 (repealed)	—		
Section 2 (deleted)	—	(*) New Article introduced by the Treaty of Amsterdam	
Article 18 (repealed)	—	(**) New Title introduced by the Treaty of Amsterdam	
Article 19 (repealed)	—	(***) Title restructured by the Treaty of Amsterdam	

Previous numbering	New numbering	Previous numbering	New numbering
CHAPTER 2	CHAPTER 2	TITLE IV	TITLE V
Article 52	Article 43	Article 74	Article 70
Article 53	—	Article 75	Article 71
Article 54	Article 44	Article 76	Article 72
Article 55	Article 45	Article 77	Article 73
Article 56	Article 46	Article 78	Article 74
Article 57	Article 47	Article 79	Article 75
Article 58	Article 48	Article 80	Article 76
		Article 81	Article 77
CHAPTER 3	CHAPTER 3	Article 82	Article 78
Article 59	Article 49	Article 83	Article 79
Article 60	Article 50	Article 84	Article 80
Article 61	Article 51		
Article 62 (repealed)	—	TITLE V	TITLE VI
Article 63	Article 52	CHAPTER 1	CHAPTER 1
Article 64	Article 53	SECTION 1	SECTION 1
Article 65	Article 54	Article 85	Article 81
Article 66	Article 55	Article 86	Article 82
		Article 87	Article 83
CHAPTER 4	CHAPTER 4	Article 88	Article 84
Article 67 (repealed)	—	Article 89	Article 85
Article 68 (repealed)	—	Article 90	Article 86
Article 69 (repealed)	—	Section 2 (deleted)	—
Article 70 (repealed)	—	Article 91 (repealed)	—
Article 71 (repealed)	—		
Article 72 (repealed)	—	SECTION 3	SECTION 2
Article 73 (repealed)	—	Article 92	Article 87
Article 73a (repealed)	—	Article 93	Article 88
Article 73b	Article 56	Article 94	Article 89
Article 73c	Article 57		
Article 73d	Article 58	CHAPTER 2	CHAPTER 2
Article 73e (repealed)	—	Article 95	Article 90
Article 73f	Article 59	Article 96	Article 91
Article 73g	Article 60	Article 97 (repealed)	—
Article 73h (repealed)	—	Article 98	Article 92
		Article 99	Article 93
TITLE IIIA (**)	TITLE IV		
Article 73i (*)	Article 61	CHAPTER 3	CHAPTER 3
Article 73j (*)	Article 62	Article 100	Article 94
Article 73k (*)	Article 63	Article 100a	Article 95
Article 73l (*)	Article 64	Article 100b (repealed)	—
Article 73m (*)	Article 65	Article 100c (repealed)	—
Article 73n (*)	Article 66	Article 100d (repealed)	—
Article 73o (*)	Article 67	Article 101	Article 96
Article 73p (*)	Article 68	Article 102	Article 97
Article 73q (*)	Article 69		

Previous numbering	New numbering	Previous numbering	New numbering
TITLE VI	TITLE VII	TITLE VII	TITLE IX
CHAPTER 1	CHAPTER 1	Article 110	Article 131
Article 102a	Article 98	Article 111 (repealed)	—
Article 103	Article 99	Article 112	Article 132
Article 103a	Article 100	Article 113	Article 133
Article 104	Article 101	Article 114 (repealed)	—
Article 104a	Article 102	Article 115	Article 134
Article 104b	Article 103		
Article 104c	Article 104	TITLE VIIA (**)	TITLE X
		Article 116 (*)	Article 135
CHAPTER 2	CHAPTER 2		
Article 105	Article 105	TITLE VIII	TITLE XI
Article 105a	Article 106	CHAPTER 1 (***)	CHAPTER 1
Article 106	Article 107	Article 117	Article 136
Article 107	Article 108	Article 118	Article 137
Article 108	Article 109	Article 118a	Article 138
Article 108a	Article 110	Article 118b	Article 139
Article 109	Article 111	Article 118c	Article 140
		Article 119	Article 141
CHAPTER 3	CHAPTER 3	Article 119a	Article 142
Article 109a	Article 112	Article 120	Article 143
Article 109b	Article 113	Article 121	Article 144
Article 109c	Article 114	Article 122	Article 145
Article 109d	Article 115		
		CHAPTER 2	CHAPTER 2
CHAPTER 4	CHAPTER 4	Article 123	Article 146
Article 109e	Article 116	Article 124	Article 147
Article 109f	Article 117	Article 125	Article 148
Article 109g	Article 118		
Article 109h	Article 119	CHAPTER 3	CHAPTER 3
Article 109i	Article 120	Article 126	Article 149
Article 109j	Article 121	Article 127	Article 150
Article 109k	Article 122		
Article 109l	Article 123	TITLE IX	TITLE XII
Article 109m	Article 124	Article 128	Article 151
TITLE VIA (**)	TITLE VIII	TITLE X	TITLE XIII
Article 109n (*)	Article 125	Article 129	Article 152
Article 109o (*)	Article 126		
Article 109p (*)	Article 127	TITLE XI	TITLE XIV
Article 109q (*)	Article 128	Article 129a	Article 153
Article 109r (*)	Article 129		
Article 109s (*)	Article 130		
		TITLE XII	TITLE XIV
		Article 129b	Article 154
(*) New Article introduced by the Treaty of Amsterdam		Article 129c	Article 155
(**) New Title introduced by the Treaty of Amsterdam		Article 129d	Article 156
(***) Title restructured by the Treaty of Amsterdam			

Previous numbering	New numbering	Previous numbering	New numbering
TITLE XII	TITLE XVI	PART FIVE	PART FIVE
Article 130	Article 157	TITLE I	TITLE I
		CHAPTER 1	CHAPTER 1
		SECTION 1	SECTION 1
TITLE XIV	TITLE XVII	Article 137	Article 189
Article 130a	Article 158	Article 138	Article 190
Article 130b	Article 159	Article 138a	Article 191
Article 130c	Article 160	Article 138b	Article 192
Article 130d	Article 161	Article 138c	Article 193
Article 130e	Article 162	Article 138d	Article 194
		Article 138e	Article 195
TITLE XV	TITLE XVIII	Article 139	Article 196
Article 130f	Article 163	Article 140	Article 197
Article 130g	Article 164	Article 141	Article 198
Article 130h	Article 165	Article 142	Article 199
Article 130i	Article 166	Article 143	Article 200
Article 130j	Article 167	Article 144	Article 201
Article 130k	Article 168		
Article 130l	Article 169	SECTION 2	SECTION 2
Article 130m	Article 170	Article 145	Article 202
Article 130n	Article 171	Article 146	Article 203
Article 130o	Article 172	Article 147	Article 204
Article 130p	Article 173	Article 148	Article 205
Article 130q (repealed)	—	Article 149 (repealed)	—
		Article 150	Article 206
TITLE XVI	TITLE XIX	Article 151	Article 207
Article 130r	Article 174	Article 152	Article 208
Article 130s	Article 175	Article 153	Article 209
Article 130t	Article 176	Article 154	Article 210
TITLE XVII	TITLE XX	SECTION 3	SECTION 3
Article 130u	Article 177	Article 155	Article 211
Article 130v	Article 178	Article 156	Article 212
Article 130w	Article 179	Article 157	Article 213
Article 130x	Article 180	Article 158	Article 214
Article 130y	Article 181	Article 159	Article 215
		Article 160	Article 216
PART FOUR	PART FOUR	Article 161	Article 217
Article 131	Article 182	Article 162	Article 218
Article 132	Article 183	Article 163	Article 219
Article 133	Article 184		
Article 134	Article 185		
Article 135	Article 186		
Article 136	Article 187		
Article 136a	Article 188		

Previous numbering	New numbering	Previous numbering	New numbering
SECTION 4	SECTION 4	CHAPTER 3	CHAPTER 3
Article 164	Article 220	Article 193	Article 257
Article 165	Article 221	Article 194	Article 258
Article 166	Article 222	Article 195	Article 259
Article 167	Article 223	Article 196	Article 260
Article 168	Article 224	Article 197	Article 261
Article 168a	Article 225	Article 198	Article 262
Article 169	Article 226		
Article 170	Article 227	CHAPTER 4	CHAPTER 4
Article 171	Article 228	Article 198a	Article 263
Article 172	Article 229	Article 198b	Article 264
Article 173	Article 230	Article 198c	Article 265
Article 174	Article 231		
Article 175	Article 232	CHAPTER 5	CHAPTER 5
Article 176	Article 233	Article 198d	Article 266
Article 177	Article 234	Article 198e	Article 267
Article 178	Article 235		
Article 179	Article 236	TITLE II	TITLE II
Article 180	Article 237	Article 199	Article 268
Article 181	Article 238	Article 200 (repealed)	—
Article 182	Article 239	Article 201	Article 269
Article 183	Article 240	Article 201a	Article 270
Article 184	Article 241	Article 202	Article 271
Article 185	Article 242	Article 203	Article 272
Article 186	Article 243	Article 204	Article 273
Article 187	Article 244	Article 205	Article 274
Article 188	Article 245	Article 205a	Article 275
		Article 206	Article 276
SECTION 5	SECTION 5	Article 206a (repealed)	—
Article 188a	Article 246	Article 207	Article 277
Article 188b	Article 247	Article 208	Article 278
Article 188c	Article 248	Article 209	Article 279
		Article 209a	Article 280
CHAPTER 2	CHAPTER 2		
Article 189	Article 249		
Article 189a	Article 250		
Article 189b	Article 251		
Article 189c	Article 252		
Article 190	Article 253		
Article 191	Article 254		
Article 191a (*)	Article 255		
Article 192	Article 256		

(*) New Article introduced by the Treaty of Amsterdam
(**) New Title introduced by the Treaty of Amsterdam
(***) Title restructured by the Treaty of Amsterdam

Previous numbering	New numbering	Previous numbering	New numbering
PART SIX	PART SIX	Article 231	Article 304
Article 210	Article 281	Article 232	Article 305
Article 211	Article 282	Article 233	Article 306
Article 212 (*)	Article 283	Article 234	Article 307
Article 213	Article 284	Article 235	Article 308
Article 213a (*)	Article 285	Article 236 (*)	Article 309
Article 213b (*)	Article 286	Article 237 (repealed)	—
Article 214	Article 287	Article 238	Article 310
Article 215	Article 288	Article 239	Article 311
Article 216	Article 289	Article 240	Article 312
Article 217	Article 290	Article 241 (repealed)	—
Article 218 (*)	Article 291	Article 242 (repealed)	—
Article 219	Article 292	Article 243 (repealed)	—
Article 220	Article 293	Article 244 (repealed)	—
Article 221	Article 294	Article 245 (repealed)	—
Article 222	Article 295	Article 246 (repealed)	—
Article 223	Article 296		
Article 224	Article 297	FINAL PROVISIONS	FINAL PROVISIONS
Article 225	Article 298	Article 247	Article 313
Article 226 (repealed)	—	Article 248	Article 314
Article 227	Article 299		
Article 228	Article 300		
Article 228a	Article 301		
Article 229	Article 302		
Article 230	Article 303		

(*) New Article introduced by the Treaty of Amsterdam
(**) New Title introduced by the Treaty of Amsterdam
(***) Title restructured by the Treaty of Amsterdam

THE DEVELOPMENT OF
EUROPEAN INTEGRATION

1. INTRODUCTION

EU law is a complex and fascinating subject of study. This book aims to illuminate the EU legal and constitutional processes, and to depict some dimensions of the dynamic relationship between the substantive aims and policies of the European Community and Union, their institutions and procedures, and the constituent Member States. It is important for students of law to situate legal doctrine in its historical and political context, and this book seeks to do so. It also aims to illustrate the strongly dynamic nature of the EU polity, whose policies, institutional structures, and membership have been in a continuous and vibrant process of development and expansion for several decades now.

This chapter examines the history of the European Union, describing some of the major political events which contributed to shaping its legal and constitutional structure, and the various Treaty reforms, beginning with a thumbnail sketch of some theories of integration offered to explain its evolution. The focus then shifts to the four major Intergovernmental Conferences that have taken place since 1985—those which led to the Single European Act, and to the Maastricht, Amsterdam, and Nice Treaties—and explains the significant legal reforms brought about by each of the Treaties adopted. The Chapter concludes by considering the Constitutional Treaty and the future direction of Treaty reform.

In this book, reference will be made to the 'European Community' to describe the three Communities which were originally established in the 1950s, even though, until the amendments made by the Treaty on European Union (TEU) in 1993, the European Coal and Steel Community (ECSC, which expired in 2002), the Economic Community (EEC), and the Atomic Energy Community (Euratom) were, properly speaking, the 'Communities'. After the TEU, the EEC was renamed the European Community, whereas the ECSC and the Euratom retained their original titles, but it is likely that the title European Community will continue to be used to refer to all three collectively.

2. THEORIES OF INTEGRATION: A BRIEF OVERVIEW

The development of European integration has been broadly described in a simplified and linear way: a number of relatively distinct periods or phases of the integration process have been identified, and different theories have emerged to explain the various phases, beginning with the *functionalism* of the 1950s.[1] At this stage there was a belief that European integration would best be furthered by focusing initially on discrete economic sectors which could be managed efficiently and technocratically by supranational institutions, away from the fray of politics. Following the move from the sectoral Coal and Steel Community to the broader Economic Community in the late 1950s, *neofunctionalist* theory emerged as an alternative way of explaining the developing integration process—perhaps most famously described by Haas in the 1960s.[2] Functionalist and neofunctionalist theory are briefly described in the following extract.

J. Lodge, The European Community and the Challenge of the Future[3]

Functionalism starts from the premise that by promoting functional cooperation among states it may be possible to deter them from settling disputes over competition for scarce resources aggressively. The logic behind the approach is to prevent war not negatively—by keeping states apart—but positively by engaging them in cooperative ventures ... to establish functionally specific agencies, initially in what were then seen as non-contentious areas like welfare. These were to transcend national boundaries and be managed by rational technocrats (not swung by the vagaries of political ideology and power-hungry political parties) owing allegiance to a functionally specific organization not to a given nation state.... Their tasks will cover those areas of the economy essential to running military machines.

Neofunctionalists have a common starting point with functionalists in their attachment to the collective pursuit of mutually beneficial goals leading to enhanced economic prosperity.... They argue that competitive economic and political elites mediate in the process and not only become involved in it but become key players.... Neofunctional integration sees integration as a process based on spill-over from one initially non-controversial, technical sector to other sectors of possibly greater political salience, involving a gradual reduction in the power of national government and a commensurate increase in the ability of the centre to deal with sensitive, politically charged issues.

The assumptions and predictions of neofunctionalism were in turn challenged by what has been described as the intergovernmentalist phase of the Community in the 1970s, during which the supranational political EC institutions appeared to lose initiative and influence, and the interests of individual Member States—most clearly symbolized by the so-called Luxembourg veto—dominated the process.

Neofunctionalist arguments were challenged by *neo-realist*[4] and *neo-rational* accounts, amongst which *liberal intergovernmentalism* emerged as a particularly prominent theory,[5] presenting States rather than supranational institutions as the key actors in the integration process, seeking essentially to pursue their own respective preferences and to protect their sphere of power. These theories were applied to the renewed dynamism and deepening of the integration process in the 1980s, with the signature of the Single European

---

[1] D. Chryssochoou, *Theorizing European Integration* (Sage, 2001).
[2] E.B. Haas, *Beyond the Nation State* (Stanford University Press, 1964).
[3] (Pinter, 1993), Introduction, xix.
[4] R. Keohane, *Neo-Realism and Its Critics* (Columbia University Press, 1986).
[5] A. Moravcsik, 'Preferences and Power in the European Community: A Liberal Intergovernmental Approach' (1993) 31 *JCMS* 473 and *The Choice for Europe* (UCL Press, 1999).

Act (SEA)[6] and the Intergovernmental Conferences (IGCs) of the early 1990s leading to the Maastricht Treaty, although the events of this period also generated counter-claims of a *neo-federalist* revival.

From the late 1980s on, the supranationalism–intergovernmentalism dichotomy which underpinned the debate between the two major integration theories of neofunctionalism and neo-realism has been questioned by literature which sees the EU as a system of *multi-level or network governance*.[7] Rather than focusing debate principally on whether it is Member State governments or Europe's supranational institutions which drive the integration process, increasing attention has been paid to the wide range of actors and institutions involved at different levels in law-making and policy-making within the European Union. Thus we see a broader concept of institutions in use,[8] and a focus which goes beyond national and supranational actors and institutions to include the subnational, infra-national, public, and private entities which participate in the system of governance. A range of alternatives to or variants on the dominant integration theories is emerging,[9] and new debates and divisions are replacing the traditional intergovernmental–supranational/neofunctionalist–neo-realist polarities, such as those between 'rationalist' approaches, which view decision-making as being driven by the pursuit of material interests by strategic actors, and 'constructivist' approaches, which lay more emphasis on the influence of norms, ideas, and principles in the process of integration.[10]

3. EUROPEAN INTEGRATION: THE BACKGROUND

Most contemporary accounts of European integration begin with the aftermath of the Second World War, and the desire for a lasting peace in Europe. After the destruction and ruin of the war years, and the climate of nationalism which preceded them, many hoped for a new model

---

[6] W. Sandholtz and J. Zysman, '1992: Recasting the European Bargain' (1989) 42 *World Politics* 1; G. Garrett, 'International Cooperation and Institutional Choice: The European Community's Internal Market' (1992) 46 *International Organization* 533.

[7] See, e.g., M. Jachtenfuchs, 'Theoretical Perspectives on European Governance' (1995) 1 *ELJ* 115 and 'The Governance Approach to European Integration' (2001) 39 *JCMS* 245; G. Marks, L. Hooghe, and K. Blank, 'European Integration since the 1980s: State-centric Versus Multi-level Governance' (1996) 34 *JCMS* 341; B. Kohler Koch (who uses the term 'penetrated governance' rather than multi-level governance), 'The Evolution and Transformation of European Governance' (Institute for Advanced Studies, Vienna: Political Science Series No. 58, 1998); K. Armstrong and S. Bulmer, *The Governance of the Single European Market* (Manchester, 1998); S. Hix, 'The Study of the European Union II. The "New Governance" Agenda and its Rival' (1998) 5 *JEPP* 38; I. Bache and M. Flinders (eds.), *Multi-level Governance* (Oxford University Press, 2004). On networks see, e.g., T. Börzel, 'Policy Networks: A New Paradigm for European Governance?', EUI, Working Paper RSC 97/19; K. Ladeur, 'Towards a Legal Theory of Supranationality—The Viability of the Network Concept' (1997) 3 *ELJ* 33.

[8] On the relevance of institutionalist theory to the EU see K. Armstrong, 'The New Institutionalism', in P. Craig and C. Harlow (eds.), *Lawmaking in the European Union* (Kluwer, 1998); G. Schneider and M. Aspinwall (eds.), *The Rules of Integration: Institutionalist Approaches to the Study of Europe* (Manchester University Press, 2001).

[9] See, e.g., T. Doleys, 'Member States and the European Commission: Theoretical Insights from the New Economics of Organization' (2000) 7 *JEPP* 532; A. Branch and J.C. Øhrgaard, 'Trapped in the Supranational–Intergovernmental Dichotomy: A Reply to Reply to Stone Sweet and Sandholtz' (1999) 6 *JEPP* 123; M. Pollack, 'International Relations Theory and European Integration' (2001) 39 *JCMS* 221. For an account of the relationship between theories of integration and discourses of democracy in the EU see P. Craig, 'The Nature of the Community: Integration, Democracy and Legitimacy', in P. Craig and G. de Búrca (eds.), *The Evolution of EU Law* (Oxford University Press, 1999), ch. 1.

[10] See the introduction to the special issue of the *Journal of European Public Policy* on the subject by T. Christiansen, K.E. Jørgensen, and A. Wiener, 'The Social Construction of Europe' (1999) 6 *JEPP* 528, and more generally T. Checkel, 'The Constructivist Turn in International Relations Theory' (1998) 50 *World Politics* 324.

of political co-operation in Europe. This important point in the story of modern European integration, however, should be considered in a much longer time-frame. Ideas of European unity were articulated long before the arrival of the twentieth century, including the call in 1693 by a prominent English Quaker, William Penn, for a European Parliament and the end of the state mosaic in Europe.[11]

During the war, the Resistance movement had strongly supported the idea of a united Europe, to consolidate the spirit of co-operation of the war years and replace the destructive forces of national chauvinism.[12] However, despite the urgings of federalists such as Altiero Spinelli, the movement for integration faltered after the war, especially after the electoral defeat in the UK of Churchill, who had been a strong proponent of European unity. Promptings towards greater European co-operation, however, came from other sources. Faced with the onset of the cold war and with Europe's severe post-war economic problems, the USA in 1947, the same year in which the General Agreement on Tariffs and Trade (GATT) was signed in an effort to liberalize world trade,[13] announced its so-called Marshall Plan to provide financial aid for Europe. The USA required an organization to administer the programme. This became, in 1948, the Organization for European Economic Co-operation (OEEC) and in 1960, the Organization for Economic Co-operation and Development (OECD). Although essentially intergovernmental, the OEEC required a degree of institutionalized co-ordination and co-operation between the European States which received aid, and provided useful experience for the more developed forms of co-operation and integration to come.[14]

Further examples of early co-operation in defence and other matters are evident in the 1948 Brussels Treaty between France, the UK, and the three Benelux countries, the North Atlantic Treaty Organization (NATO), signed in 1949, and the Western European Union (WEU), created in 1954, which was itself based on the earlier Brussels Treaty. On the economic side, Belgium, the Netherlands, and Luxembourg had signed the Benelux Treaty in 1944, establishing a customs union between them. Developments in the direction of political union were stalled by the UK when, after the 'Congress of Europe' was convened at The Hague in 1948 to draw up proposals for European unity, the UK insisted on an intergovernmental organization which would not compromise state sovereignty. What emerged was the Statute on the Council of Europe, signed in 1949, providing for a Committee of Ministers and a Parliamentary Assembly. The latter had few powers beyond making recommendations to the Committee of Ministers, a twice-yearly meeting of the foreign ministers of the signatory States. However, the Council of Europe became involved in many cultural, economic, and scientific activities, and collaborates with various other international organizations including the EU. Probably its best-known achievement was the adoption of the European Convention on Human Rights (ECHR), which was signed in 1950 and came into force in 1953. The Convention established a Commission and subsequently a Court of Human Rights, which were merged into a single court when the 11th Protocol to the ECHR was ratified by all of the Council of Europe Member States and came into force in 1998. Further, the Council of Europe's Social Charter was signed in 1961 and came into force in 1965, and, although lacking the stronger legal enforcement mechanisms of the Human Rights Convention, it has been important in the field

[11] See D. Urwin, *The Community of Europe: A History of European Integration* (2nd edn., Longman, 1995), tracing many of the arguments for various forms of European co-operation and unity before the onset of the Second World War.

[12] W. Lipgens (ed.), *Documents of the History of European Integration* (European University Institute, 1985).

[13] The GATT 1947 was replaced in 1994, after the very lengthy Uruguay Round negotiations, and the World Trade Organization came into force in 1995.

[14] M. Holland, *European Integration From Community to Union* (Pinter, 1993), 23.

of social and economic rights, complementing the focus on civil and political rights in the ECHR.[15]

Given the failure to convince Britain to participate in more concrete moves towards European integration, the French foreign minister, Robert Schuman, who was a strong supporter of integration, proposed the pooling of Franco-German coal and steel resources under a single High Authority, with the option for other European States to participate. The plan had been drafted by Jean Monnet, a committed federalist. The plan was not only economically inspired, but represented an attempt to restabilize relations between France and Germany after the war, to allay French fears about any German military threat, and to bind them within a limited framework of peaceful co-operation in order to avert rivalry over coal production.[16] The Schuman proposal led to the setting-up of the European Coal and Steel Community (ECSC), with a limited life-span of fifty years, to expire in 2002. This was the first significant step towards European integration going beyond intergovernmentalism, establishing a supranational authority whose independent institutions had the power to bind its constituent member States.

The ECSC Treaty was signed in 1951 by France, Germany, Italy, and the three Benelux countries, to establish a common market in coal and steel. Four institutions were set up: a High Authority, made up of nine independent appointees of the six Member State governments, to be the main executive institution with decision-making power and responsibility for implementing the aims of the Treaty; an Assembly made up of national parliaments' delegates with mainly supervisory and advisory powers; a Council made up of one representative of each of the national governments, with a consultative role and some decision-making powers, and the task of harmonizing the activities of the States and the High Authority; and finally a Court of Justice of nine judges. Since the High Authority could adopt binding decisions by a majority, it was a supranational authority, but its influence was countered in areas in which its decision was not final by the Council, which represented the Member States' interests. The balance of power between the High Authority (later named the Commission after the 1965 Merger Treaty) and the Council was different under the ECSC Treaty from under the later EEC Treaty, with a stronger supranational element and a weaker intergovernmental element. The ECSC was a significant development. For its proponents, it was not merely about coal and steel, but represented a first step towards European integration.[17]

However the period between 1951 and 1957 was a mixed one for European integration. France, rather than agree to German rearmament within NATO as the USA had suggested, proposed in its 1950 Pleven plan the setting-up of a European Defence Community (EDC) with a European army, a common budget, and joint institutions. The EDC Treaty was signed in 1952 by the six ECSC States, with Britain refusing to participate, but progress towards ratification was slow. It was argued that, if there was to be a European army, a common European foreign policy would also be needed, and accordingly plans for a European Political Community were drawn up. The 1953 draft statute which emerged represented a serious effort at designing a European federation, including a co-ordinated foreign policy and eventual economic integration. However, these developments were stopped in their tracks when France, which had been wary of German remilitarization, finally submitted the EDC Treaty to its national assembly, where the proposal to debate its ratification was rejected.[18] This resulted

---

[15] See Ch. 11.

[16] Holland, n. 14 above.

[17] F. Duchêne, *Jean Monnet: The First Statesman of Interdependence* (Norton, 1994), 239, quoting Monnet's comments from 1952.

[18] According to J. Pinder, *The Building of the European Union* (3rd edn., Oxford University Press, 1998), this defeat was due to a combination of nationalists and Stalinists in the French National Assembly in 1954.

in a major setback for the integration process and the shelving of the plans for both defence and political union. It would be thirty-nine years before the Member States would ratify another Treaty—that signed at Maastricht in 1992—purporting to establish a 'European Union'.

4. THE EEC AND EURATOM TREATIES

Yet moves towards integration were not halted. After a conference of foreign ministers of the six States in Messina in Italy in 1955, agreement on moving in the direction of economic integration was reached. A committee chaired by Paul-Henri Spaak, then Belgian Prime Minister and another strong advocate of integration, in 1956 published its report which contained the basic plan for what became the European Atomic Energy Community (Euratom) and the European Economic Community (EEC). This time, although the Treaties may have been politically motivated, the focus was specifically economic.

The economic impetus for the 1957 Treaties was made clear, and the explicit political objectives of the earlier draft European Political Co-operation (EPC) Treaty were avoided. The primary Treaty objectives were to establish a common market, to approximate the economic policies of the Member States, to promote harmonious development of economic activities throughout the Community, to increase stability and raise the standard of living, and to promote closer relations between the Member States. Barriers to trade were to be abolished and a common customs tariff was to be set up, undistorted competition was to be ensured, national economic and monetary policies were to be progressively co-ordinated, and fiscal and social policies gradually harmonized. Unlike in the ECSC there was to be no temporal limit on the existence of the Treaty. The Parliamentary Assembly and the Court of Justice were to be shared with the ECSC,[19] but there was to be a separate Council of Ministers and executive authority, the Commission. It was not until the Merger Treaty of 1965 that these institutions were merged and shared by the three Communities.[20] An Economic and Social Committee with advisory status was set up, to be shared with the Euratom Community.

The location of the Community institutions, a task which under the Treaty fell to the Member States, was a matter of some dispute. The Assembly of the ECSC had been located in Strasbourg, with the High Authority, the Council, and the Court of Justice in Luxembourg. Now the Council, the Commission, their respective staffs, as well as the Economic and Social Committee and the Committee of the Regions, are based in Brussels. The Court of Justice, the Court of First Instance, the Court of Auditors, and the European Investment Bank are however based in Luxembourg. The Parliament continues to have its seat in Strasbourg, with its secretariat in Luxembourg and certain sessions and committee meetings in Brussels. These seats were finally formalized by a Protocol attached to the EC Treaty by the Treaty of Amsterdam, which also determines the seats of some newer institutions.

The common market was to be established over a transitional period of several stages, during which tariff barriers would be removed and a common external customs tariff set up. There were to be common policies in agriculture and transport, free movement of workers, companies, the self-employed, goods, and services, and strict control of anti-competitive practices in the various States. A European Social Fund was established to improve employment

---

[19] This was decided in the Convention on certain Institutions common to the European Communities, signed on the same day as the EEC and Euratom Treaties in 1957.

[20] This Treaty was repealed and replaced, without any substantive amendments, by Art. 9 of the Treaty of Amsterdam signed in 1997.

opportunities, and an Investment Bank to give loans and guarantees and to help less developed regions or sectors. A European Development Fund for overseas countries and territories of some of the Member States was also established.

The Commission was not accorded the same degree of legislative autonomy under the EEC Treaty and Euratom Treaties as it had been under the ECSC Treaty, and the Council was given the power of approval of most Commission legislative proposals. However, the Commission was given a very important position as the initiator of all legislation and overall 'watchdog' of the Treaties, as well as having certain decision-making powers of its own and being the negotiator of international agreements on behalf of the Community.

Voting in the Council was weighted, greater weight being given to the larger Member States than to the smaller, to reflect differences in population size. However voting procedure varied according to the nature of the issue. In a very few instances voting was by simple majority, in many other matters by qualified majority, and in yet others unanimity was required. The issue of voting in Council is significant for the development of the Community since, crudely speaking, it influences whether intergovernmentalism, the interests of each of the Member States, or supranationalism, the overall interest of the Community, has greater sway.

The Parliamentary Assembly which, although it called itself the Parliament, was not officially so named until the adoption of the Single European Act 1986, had few powers under the original Treaty provisions. It had a consultative role in legislation, but was largely a supervisory body whose powers involved questioning the Commission and receiving its annual report. It also possessed, as under the ECSC Treaty, a strong but never-used power of censure, despite the tabling of many motions of censure over the years, including one shortly before the dramatic resignation of the Commission in 1999.[21]

5. THE EEC TREATY TO THE SINGLE EUROPEAN ACT

There were important and interesting developments in the period between the EEC Treaty and the Single European Act 1986, (SEA).

(a) THE GEOGRAPHICAL REACH OF THE COMMUNITY: ENLARGEMENT

One such development was the enlargement of the Community. The UK in the 1950s had chosen to remain outside the EEC, and instead in 1960 set up the European Free Trade Association (EFTA) with six other States: Norway, Sweden, Austria, Switzerland, Denmark, and Portugal. In 1961, after a change of policy, the UK made its first application for Community membership. De Gaulle, who viewed Britain's place as being within the Commonwealth rather than as part of continental Europe, vetoed the application, and again after a second application in 1967. It was not until after De Gaulle's resignation that Britain's application for membership was finally accepted, together with those of Ireland and Denmark, in 1973.

---

[21] See 58–64 for fuller discussion. For further accounts see K. Bradley, 'The Institutional Law of the EU in 1999' (1999/2000) 19 *YBEL* 547, 584; D. Dinan, 'Governance and Institutions 1999: Resignation, Reform and Renewal' (2000) 38 *JCMS* 25; A. McMullan, 'Political Responsibility for the Administration of Europe: the Commission's Resignation' (1999) 54 *Parliamentary Affairs* 703.

Norway, whose application had also been accepted, failed to ratify the Treaty of Accession after a national referendum voted against Community membership. In 1981 the Community expanded again when Greece became a member. Greenland, however, finally left the Community in 1985 after obtaining a degree of internal legislative independence from Denmark, and Spain and Portugal became members in 1986.

(b) COMMUNITY DECISION-MAKING: INTERGOVERNMENTALISM AND SUPRANATIONALISM

The geographic reach of the Community may well have expanded between the EEC Treaty and the SEA. This period was however marked by tensions between an intergovernmental view of the Community, championed initially by President de Gaulle of France but not necessarily shared by other Member States, and a more supranational perspective espoused initially by Walter Hallstein, the Commission President. These strains surfaced in various ways during this period.

(i) *The Luxembourg Accords*

The tension erupted into a crisis in 1965, when the time came under the transitional provisions of the Treaty for the Council of Ministers to move to qualified-majority voting, rather than the unanimous voting which had been in force until then. De Gaulle objected to an important institutional reform proposal made by the Commission, which was combined with a proposal to resolve a conflict over agricultural policy, for the Community to raise its own resources from agricultural levies and external tariffs, instead of being funded by national contributions. He strenuously objected to the 'federalist logic' of the proposal[22] and, after a failure to reach a compromise in the Council, France refused to attend any further Council meetings and adopted what became known as the 'empty-chair' policy. This lasted for seven months, from June 1965 until January 1966, after which a settlement was reached, which became known as the Luxembourg Compromise or the Luxembourg Accords.

These Accords, which were to have considerable impact on the direction and pace of Community development over the next two decades, were essentially an agreement to disagree over voting methods in the Council. While the French asserted that even in cases which provided for majority decision-making, discussion *must* continue until unanimity was reached whenever important national interests were at stake, the other five Member States declared instead that in such circumstances the Council would 'endeavour, within a reasonable time, to reach solutions which can be adopted by all'.[23] Each acknowledged that there was a divergence of views on how to proceed in the event of a total failure to reach agreement.

In practice, it seems that for many years the French view in effect prevailed. States endeavoured to reach agreement in their meetings, and the effect of pleading the 'very important interests' of a State was treated as a veto, which the other Member States would respect. Recourse to qualified-majority voting became the exception rather than the norm. The 'return to intergovernmentalism', as some have termed it, with primacy being accorded to an individual Member State's wish even if it was against that of the majority, affected the dynamics of decision-making in the following years. The shift of power away from the Commission

[22] Pinder, n. 18 above, 12.
[23] Bull. EC 3–1966, 9.

towards the Council also diluted the role of the Parliament, which exercised supervisory powers over the Commission. There was a consequential emphasis on COREPER, the Committee of Permanent Representatives, established under Article 207 EC, which prepared the agenda for Council meetings, and undertook much of the negotiation between Commission and Council on Commission legislative initiatives.

While the Community was experiencing internal crises, it began nonetheless to find its voice on the international stage as a single entity rather than as six Member States. This could be seen in the GATT negotiations of 1967, and in the signing of the Yaoundé Convention between the EEC and eighteen African States in 1963, which was intended to offer preferential treatment in importation to developing countries.

(ii) *The Emergence of the EPC, European Council, and Comitology*

The Luxembourg Accords enhanced Member State power by according States a *de facto* veto which, even if it was not exercised, cast a shadow over Council deliberations and impacted on the shape of resulting Community legislation. The period between the EEC Treaty and the SEA also saw other developments that enhanced Member State power over decision-making.

Intergovernmental co-operation in foreign policy had begun again in 1970, when the Davignon Report recommended the holding of quarterly meetings of the foreign ministers of the Member States, as well as the establishment of a permanent political secretariat. This became an essentially intergovernmental forum for co-operation in foreign policy, without any developed institutional structure. A second report in 1973 recommended its continuation as a form of co-operation, and it became known as European Political Co-operation (EPC). EPC was successful in enabling the Community to be represented as one voice in other international organizations in which all of the Member States participated, but also represented a move towards intergovernmentalism.

In 1974 the European Council was established to regularize the practice of holding summits. This body consisted of the heads of governments of the Member States, with the President of the Commission attending its bi-annual meetings. The European Council's 'summitry' provided the Community with much-needed direction, but represented to some a weakening in the supranational elements of the Community. The European Council was not within the framework created by the Treaties, and it was not until the Single European Act that it was recognized in a formal instrument. The EPC and European Council enabled Member State interests at the highest level to impact on matters of political or economic concern, and their decisions, while not formally binding, would normally constitute the frame within which binding Community initiatives would be pursued.

The Member States also assumed greater control over the detail of Community secondary legislation, through the creation of what became known as Comitology. The details will be considered below.[24] Suffice it to say for the present that this enabled Member States to have a voice and influence over the content of secondary Community legislation in a way that had not been envisaged in the original EEC Treaty.

The trend within the Community from early supranationalism towards greater intergovernmentalism from the time of the Luxembourg Compromise until the adoption of the Single European Act 1986 has been the subject of much comment.

---

[24] See 118–123.

P. Dankert, The EC: Past, Present and Future[25]

The dialectics of co-operation or integration have also continued to dominate the process of European unification—to an increasing extent—ever since 25th March 1957. It has been a continuous 'to and fro' for years, as can be seen from the course of development of the Community institutions. The Council of Ministers, which was originally intended to be a Community body, has now become largely an intergovernmental institution thanks to the famous Luxembourg Agreement, which, under French pressure, put an end to the majority decisions which the Council was supposed to take according to the Treaty on proposals submitted by the European Commission. This rule that decisions could only be taken unanimously had the effect of gradually transforming the Commission into a kind of secretariat for the Council which carefully checked its proposals with national officials before deciding whether or not to submit them. This in turn has a negative effect on the European Parliament which can only reach for power, under the Treaty, via the Commission. The move towards intergovernmental solutions for Community problems reached its peak—after frustrated attempts such as the Fouchet plan at the beginning of the 60s—in the creation of the European Council, the EPC and the EMS.

(iii) *Countervailing Trends: EP Direct Elections, Resources, Budgets, and the ECJ*

It would however be mistaken to think of this period as one in which all developments enhanced the intergovernmental dimension of the Community. There were also trends in the other direction, which strengthened the supranational dynamic of the Community, or should have done so, although, as in the case of direct elections to the EP, the initial outcome was more equivocal.

In 1976, *direct elections to the Parliament* were finally agreed by the Member States, and the first elections took place in 1979. This event ought to have represented a significant development for the Community since the Parliament would become the first Community institution with a direct democratic mandate of sorts, but the elections were not an unqualified success.

M. Holland, European Integration From Community to Union[26]

Transnational party cooperation was at a rudimentary level and the decision to run each of the nine European elections independently and according to national electoral rules did little to persuade voters that the elections were any different from their respective national elections. The election issues were not European ones, but reflected national concerns and parochialism: as a result, turnout was disappointingly low, averaging just 62 per cent … the United Kingdom having the lowest figure at 32.6 per cent.… Faced with this apparent popular disinterest, the first direct elections failed to provide the anticipated springboard for accelerated integration; rather, as the Community entered the 1980s, the popular legitimacy and future development of the Community came into question and a renewed trend towards more modest intergovernmental cooperation emerged.

[25] L. Tsoukalis (ed.), *The EC: Past, Present and Future* (Basil Blackwell, 1983), 7.
[26] N. 14 above, 42.

The equivocal impact of EP direct elections was further underlined by the fact that the Parliament's role in the legislative process at this time was meagre, to say the least: it only had a right to be consulted, and then only when a specific Treaty article so provided.

The supranational dimension to the Community was more unequivocally enhanced by developments relating to *resources and the budget*. In 1969 agreement was reached on funding from the Community's own resources rather than from national contributions, and on the expansion of the Parliament's role in the budgetary process.[27] The political significance of these issues, which were brought about in the first budgetary Treaty of 1970 and the Own-Resources Decision of the same date, lies in the financial independence achieved by the Community and in the strengthening of the Parliament's desired role as a decision-maker.[28] By 1975, the date by which the Community budget was required to be financed entirely from its own resources, a second budgetary treaty had been agreed, with further increases in the Parliament's budgetary role.[29] While these developments gave the Community greater financial independence, there were nonetheless serious disagreements between the Member States as to the use of such resources, more especially because a very significant proportion was used to fund the controversial Common Agricultural Policy.

The *judicial contribution* to the supranational dynamic of the Community was especially important in this period. We shall see later that often when the Community's political processes were less active or in crisis, the Court contributed to its legal development and to the process of integration in a variety of ways. Thus, the ECJ sanctioned a broad reading of Article 308 EC, thereby enhancing the Community sphere of competence.[30] It used the doctrine of direct effect in the 1960s and 1970s to make more effective Community policies, which either the Member States or the Community institutions were failing to implement.[31] It was in the 1970s, too, that the Court triggered a policy of 'negative integration' and influenced the Commission in its subsequent single-market strategy by interpreting very broadly Article 28 EC, on the abolition of non-tariff barriers to the free movement of goods.[32] The principle of the supremacy of Community law over national law served to reinforce these judicial strategies.[33]

(iv) *The Road to the SEA*

Notwithstanding the countervailing tendencies described in the previous section, the 1960s and 1970s were often referred to as a period of political stagnation or malaise in the Community, with the Commission having considerable difficulty in securing agreement in the Council to its proposals. The result was that the attainment of Treaty objectives was often significantly delayed.

---

[27] Arts. 272–273 EC were amended to reflect the Parliament's increased budgetary powers, which also shifted from Council to Parliament the symbolically important task of adopting the budget.

[28] The Community's own resources would hence come from agricultural levies, from customs duties on products from outside the Community, and from a maximum of 1 per cent Value Added Tax (VAT), applied to an assessment basis determined uniformly for the Member States.

[29] A Court of Auditors was also established by the 1975 Treaty to oversee Community revenue and expenditure, and in 1992, following amendments made by the TEU, it acquired official status as the fifth Community institution.

[30] J. Weiler, 'The Transformation of Europe' (1991) 100 *Yale LJ* 2403, 2431–2453. For further discussion of Art. 308 see Ch. 3.

[31] Ch. 8.

[32] Case 120/78 *Rewe-Zentral AG* v. *Bundesmonopolverwaltung für Branntwein* [1979] ECR 649. See Ch. 19.

[33] Ch. 10.

The existence of this malaise is reflected in the continuing flow of reports during this period that attested to the need for institutional reform, combined with a change of approach from the key institutional players. This is exemplified by the Tindemans Report in 1974–1975; that of the 'Three Wise Men' in 1978,[34] both of which recommended strengthening the supranational elements of the Community and diminishing the impact of intergovernmentalism, but neither was acted on; the Genscher–Colombo plan, put forward by the foreign ministers of Germany and Italy, prompted the European Council to issue a 'Solemn Declaration on European Union' in 1983, but nothing more concrete materialized;[35] radical reform was suggested by the European Parliament in 1984 in a 'Draft Treaty on European Union', but it was largely ignored.

Finally, however, after the Fontainebleu European Council summit of 1984, two committees were set up to look at the question of Treaty revision and further political integration. The first was the Adonnino Committee on a people's Europe, to consider the issue of furthering a European identity,[36] and the second was the Dooge Committee to look at questions of political reform. Although the Dooge Report, which again included strong reform proposals, was not itself acted upon, the 1985 European Council in Milan agreed, voting for the first time by majority only, to convene an intergovernmental conference under what was then Article 236 of the EEC Treaty, now Article 48 TEU, to discuss treaty amendment. What emerged from the meetings of the working parties within the intergovernmental conference became the Single European Act (SEA). The reasons why the Member States were willing to accept Treaty reform at this juncture will be considered more fully below.[37]

6. THE SINGLE EUROPEAN ACT

In 1985 the British Commissioner, Lord Cockfield, drew up on behalf of the Commission a precise timetable for the completion of the internal market, known as the 'White Paper', setting out a long list of the barriers which would have to be removed before a deadline of 1992.[38] The Single European Act represented a political commitment to this deadline by the Member States.

(a) INSTITUTIONAL CHANGES

The SEA may not have been as far-reaching as the reforms advocated by reports in the 1970s and 1980s, but it nonetheless made a number of significant institutional reforms. The most important of these changes enhanced the EP's power in the legislative process, through the creation of the new legislative 'co-operation' procedure, Article 252 EC, which made the EP a real player in the Community's legislative process for the first time, thereby transforming Community decision-making, more especially because it was applied to the new harmonization procedure in Article 95 described below.[39] The EP was also given a veto over the accession of new Member States and over the conclusion of agreements with associate States.

[34] For an official summary of the report see Bull. EC 11–1979, 1.5.2.
[35] See Bull. EC 6–1983, 1.6.1.
[36] See COM(84)446 Final.
[37] See 609–612.
[38] COM(85)310.
[39] See 111–112.

The SEA made other institutional changes. It gave a legal basis to European Political Co-operation and formal recognition to the European Council, although not within the Community treaties. A Court of First Instance (CFI) was created to assist the Court of Justice. Lastly, the so-called 'comitology' procedure, under which the Council delegates powers to the Commission on certain conditions, was formally included within Article 202 EC.[40]

(b) SUBSTANTIVE CHANGES

The substantive changes made by the SEA were equally important. First, Article 18 EC set out the internal market aim of 'progressively establishing the internal market over a period expiring on 31 December 1992', and defined the internal market as 'an area without internal frontiers in which the free movement of goods, persons, services and capital is ensured'.

Secondly, qualified-majority voting by the Council was introduced into a range of areas which had previously provided for unanimity. Most important in this respect was the new Article 95 (ex Article 100a). This was added by way of derogation from the 'harmonizing' provision of Article 94, which required unanimity in the Council when adopting directives to approximate national measures affecting the establishment or functioning of the common market, while Article 95 instead allowed for qualified majority when adopting measures to achieve the internal market objectives of Article 18. Article 95 was especially significant, since the unanimity requirement of Article 94 had been a serious obstacle to the passage of harmonization measures that were required for completion of the internal market.[41]

Thirdly, the SEA added new substantive areas of Community competence, some of which had already in fact been asserted by the institutions and supported by the Court, without any express Treaty basis. The additions covered co-operation in economic and monetary union, social policy, economic and social cohesion,[42] research and technological development, and environmental policy.[43] Title III of the SEA, which governed European Political Co-operation outside the Community framework, was subsequently repealed and replaced by the TEU.

(c) REACTION AND ASSESSMENT

When it was signed in 1986, the Single European Act represented the most important revision of the Treaties since they were first adopted, and it heralded a revival of the Community momentum towards integration which has continued at a breathless pace since then.

The initial response to the SEA was nonetheless mixed, some seeing it as an important and a positive step forward for the Community after a period of sluggishness, while others saw it as a setback for the integration process. Thus Pescatore, formerly a judge on the Court of Justice, argued that the Act was fundamentally deceptive, that it ignored all the Community's achievements to date, and implied that the common market project begun in 1957 had to be started all over again.[44] Others, however, having observed the Act in operation for some years, compared the apparent weakness of its provisions with a more optimistic assessment of what it, together with the Commission's White Paper,[45] actually brought about.

---

[40] For further discussion of the committee procedures see Ch. 4.
[41] See Ch. 17.
[42] This policy concerned reducing the disparities between various parts of the EU.
[43] Various Community environmental measures were passed on the basis of Art. 94 EC before the adoption of the Single European Act, and the Council had adopted Environmental Action Programmes since 1973.
[44] P. Pescatore, 'Some Critical Remarks on the Single European Act' (1987) 24 *CMLRev.* 9.
[45] White Paper on the Completion of the Internal Market, COM(85)310.

J. Weiler, The Transformation of Europe[46]

Clearly, the new European Parliament and the Commission were far from thrilled with the new act.

And yet, with the hindsight of just three years, it has become clear that 1992 and the SEA do constitute an eruption of significant proportions. Some of the evidence is very transparent. First, for the first time since the very early years of the Community, if ever, the Commission plays the political role clearly intended for it by the Treaty of Rome. In stark contrast to its nature during the foundational period in the 1970s and early 1980s, the Commission in large measure both sets the Community agenda and acts as a power broker in the legislative process.

Second, the decisionmaking process takes much less time. Dossiers that would have languished and in some cases did languish in impotence for years in the Brussels corridors now emerge as legislation often in a matter of months.

For the first time, the interdependence of the policy areas at the new-found focal point of power in Brussels creates a dynamic resembling the almost forgotten predictions of neo-functionalist spillover. The ever-widening scope of the legislative and policy agenda of the Community manifests this dynamic.

The SEA thus helped to 'kick-start' the process of fulfilling the Community's economic objectives, more especially through the new Article 95 that became the vehicle for the passage of the Commission's programme for completion of the internal market. Moreover, while the SEA was characterized primarily by its 'single market' aims, and while the new provisions on regional policy, the environment, and research might be regarded as merely secondary or supportive, the reality was nonetheless that these changes created autonomous Community competence in these fields. This thereby served to reinforce the views of those who conceived of the single market project in terms of 'a true common marketplace, which, because of the inevitable connection between the social and the economic in modern political economies, would ultimately yield the much vaunted "ever closer union of the peoples of Europe" '.[47] The debate between those on different sides of the political spectrum, between a neo-liberal conception of the EU and the 'European social model', indeed remains as lively today as ever.

7. THE MAASTRICHT TREATY: THE BIRTH OF THE EUROPEAN UNION

The momentum which gave rise to and which was generated by the SEA continued after its adoption. The committee chaired by Jacques Delors on Economic and Monetary Union presented a report in 1989 setting out a three-stage plan for reaching EMU. The European Council decided to hold an intergovernmental conference on the subject, and, significantly, to hold at the same time a second intergovernmental conference (IGC) on political union, apparently in order to balance economic integration with political integration.

On the basis of the IGC negotiations, a draft Treaty was presented by the Luxembourg presidency of the European Council in 1991. After various revisions, the Treaty on European Union

---

[46] N. 30 above, 2454.
[47] *Ibid.*, 2458.

(TEU) was eventually signed by the States in Maastricht in February 1992.[48] It was however rejected by Denmark in a referendum, but after several 'concessions' were secured by the Danish Government a second referendum yielded a narrow majority in favour of ratification. When the last obstacle, a challenge before the German Federal Supreme Court to the constitutionality of ratification,[49] was cleared, the Treaty entered into force in November 1993. Undoubtedly, the popular profile of the Community was raised more by the 'Maastricht' debate than by any previous development in the Community's history.

The most striking feature of the TEU, apart from the detailed provisions on EMU, was the institutional change it brought about, establishing the 'three-pillar' structure for what was henceforth to be the European Union, with the Communities as the first of these pillars and the EEC Treaty being officially renamed the European Community (EC) Treaty.

There were originally seven titles in the TEU: Title I included the 'common provisions' which set out the basic objectives of the TEU. Titles II, III, and IV covered the 'first pillar' amendments to the EEC, ECSC, and Euratom Treaties respectively. Title V created the Second Pillar of the Common Foreign and Security Policy (CFSP), Title VI the Third Pillar of Justice and Home Affairs (JHA), and Title VII contained the final provisions. In addition there were various protocols to the Treaty and declarations adopted by the Member States. The Amsterdam and Nice Treaties leave this basic Union edifice largely as it was, despite the amendment and restructuring of the Second and Third Pillars, and the addition of a new Title VII to allow for closer/enhanced co-operation between Member States (the final provisions thus becoming Title VIII).

(a) THE RATIONALE FOR THE THREE-PILLAR STRUCTURE

It is important at the outset to understand the rationale for the Three-Pillar structure. The most important factor was that the Member States wished for some established mechanism through which they could co-operate in the areas of Common Foreign and Security Policy and Justice and Home Affairs. Setting up *ad hoc* meetings to discuss such matters is cumbersome, time-consuming, and involves heavy 'transaction costs', more especially as the number of players expands.

The Member States were however unwilling to subject these areas to the normal supranational methods of decision-making that characterized the Community Pillar, with all that this entailed for the central role of the Commission and ECJ. This was especially so, given that the Second and Third Pillars concerned important and sensitive areas of policy hitherto considered to be at the core of national sovereignty. The Member States therefore devised a decision-making structure that was more intergovernmental, in which the primary reins of power were retained firmly in their own hands, with the other Community institutions having either no role or one that was much reduced by way of comparison with the Community Pillar.

(b) TITLE I: THE COMMON PROVISIONS

The common provisions of the TEU set out the basic aims and principles of the newly created 'Union' and, although made expressly non-justiciable, they contained some high rhetoric on solidarity between States, closeness to the citizen, respect for national identities and for

---

[48] For a commentary on the Treaty 'From Conception to Ratification' see R. Corbett, *The Treaty of Maastricht* (Longman, 1993).

[49] See Cases 2 BvR 2134/92 and 2159/92 *Brunner v. The European Union Treaty* [1994] 1 CMLR 57, discussed in Ch. 10.

human rights, as well as a provision to safeguard the *acquis communautaire*—the body of Community law built up over the years.[50]

The objectives of the Union, which were to be achieved 'while respecting the principle of subsidiarity as defined in Article 3b EC', included the promotion of 'balanced and sustainable' economic and social progress, through the creation of an area without internal frontiers, the strengthening of economic and social cohesion, and the establishment of EMU including a single currency. The Union's international identity was to be asserted 'through the implementation of a common foreign and security policy including the eventual framing of a common defence policy, which might in time lead to a common defence'. Citizenship of the Union was to be established and close co-operation on justice and home affairs was to be developed. These common provisions were not subject to the jurisdiction of the European Court of Justice (ECJ), although the Court in subsequent judgments cited several of these provisions, and some of these have since been rendered justiciable by the Amsterdam Treaty.

(c) TITLES II—IV: CHANGES TO THE COMMUNITY TREATIES[51]

(i) *Institutional Changes*

The most significant institutional change made by the Maastricht Treaty was the increase in the Parliament's legislative involvement, by the introduction of the so-called co-decision procedure, Article 251 EC. This further increased the EP's powers in the legislative process by allowing it to block legislation of which it disapproved if it was subject to this procedure.[52] The Parliament was also given the right to request the Commission to initiate legislation and the power to block the appointment of the new Commission.

There were other significant institutional changes. Article 7 EC placed the Court of Auditors on a footing equal to that of the other four institutions (Council, Commission, Parliament, and Court of Justice); Article 8 provided for both a European System of Central Banks (ESCB) and a European Central Bank (ECB); Article 195 made provision for a Parliamentary Ombudsman; and Article 263 established a 'Committee of the Regions'.

(ii) *Substantive Changes*

The TEU also brought about numerous substantive changes,[53] which cannot be discussed in detail here. Suffice it to say that the principal changes were as follows.

(1) The aims of the Community as defined in Article 2 EC were amended to include reference to EMU, as well as environmental concerns, convergence of economic policies, social protection, economic and social cohesion, and to emphasize not just balanced expansion but also 'sustainable' growth and 'quality of life' in addition to a raised standard of living.

[50] C. Delcourt, 'The Acquis Communautaire: Has the Concept had its Day?' (2001) 38 *CMLRev.* 829; Codification of the Acquis Communautaire, COM(2001)645.

[51] Fewer changes, principally some of the institutional amendments and the citizenship amendments, were made to the ECSC and Euratom Treaties.

[52] See 113–117.

[53] There were numerous protocols attached to the TEU. For criticism of some of the Protocols, 'tearing holes, of varying sizes, in the acquis communautaire veil', see D. Curtin, 'The Constitutional Structure of the Union: A Europe of Bits and Pieces' (1993) 30 *CMLRev.* 17.

(2) Article 3 EC, which set out the range of Community activities, in addition to listing some of these new aims and expanding on some existing activities, also included policies on research and technological development, trans-European networks, health protection, education, 'the flowering of cultures', development co-operation, consumer protection, energy, civil protection, and tourism.

(3) Article 5 EC established the principle of subsidiarity, which is intended to delineate the spheres in which action is best taken at Community level and national level.

(4) A concept of European citizenship was introduced, Articles 17–21. The list of rights formally associated with EU citizenship is limited, but the ECJ has, as will be seen, given an expansive interpretation to these provisions.[54]

(5) There were new provisions on economic and monetary union, Articles 98–124, which included a detailed timetable for the different stages of monetary union, Articles 116–124.[55] It was to be these provisions that laid the foundations for the introduction of the single currency.

(6) Further areas of competence were added and existing areas expanded, with new titles added to the Treaty in areas such as culture, public health, consumer protection, trans-European networks, and development co-operation, and significant modifications made in relation to the titles on, for example, the environment.

(d) TITLE V, PILLAR TWO: COMMON FOREIGN AND SECURITY POLICY

The Second and Third Pillars of the Union created by the TEU remained apart from the Community institutional and legal structure, and are characterized by a more intergovernmental and less supranational decision-making structure. The Second Pillar concerned the 'Common Foreign and Security Policy' and the Third Pillar, prior to the Amsterdam Treaty, concerned co-operation in 'Justice and Home Affairs'. However, these Pillars were not entirely disconnected from the Community, since they involved the Community institutions and, in particular, the Council to a certain extent.

The field of Common Foreign and Security Policy is now covered by Articles 11–28 TEU, and the current provisions will be explicated below.[56] Suffice it to say for the present that the original formulation in the TEU provided that the Council was to define 'common positions' based on the agreement of the Member States, to which the States had to then ensure their national policies conformed.[57] On the basis of guidelines from the European Council, the Council of Ministers could decide that a certain matter should be the subject of a 'joint action' and, in a departure from the consensus-based intergovernmental approach of the two new Pillars, it could specify which matters were to be decided by qualified majority.[58] This was significant because, with certain limited exceptions, Member States are committed to joint actions in the conduct of their activities.

The Commission was to be 'fully associated' with the work carried out in CFSP and could, as could any Member State, refer any question or submit proposals to the Council or request

---

[54] See Ch. 23.

[55] J. Pipkorn, 'Legal Arrangements in the Treaty of Maastricht for the Effectiveness of the Economic and Monetary Union' (1994) 31 *CMLRev.* 263.

[56] See Ch. 6.

[57] Art. J.2 TEU.

[58] Art. J.3 TEU.

the convening of an extraordinary Council meeting.[59] The EP was to be consulted by the Presidency 'on the main aspects and the basic choices' of the CFSP and its views to be taken into consideration. The Parliament could ask questions of the Council and make recommendations, as well as hold an annual debate on progress in these areas of policy.[60]

(e) TITLE VI, PILLAR THREE: JUSTICE AND HOME AFFAIRS

The original formulation of the Justice and Home Affairs Pillar under Articles K.1–K.9 TEU governed policies such as asylum, immigration, and 'third country' nationals, which have, since the Treaty of Amsterdam, ToA, been integrated into the EC Treaty. However, it also included and still today covers co-operation on a range of international crime issues and various forms of judicial, customs, and police co-operation, including the establishment of a European Police Office (Europol) for exchanging information.[61]

The Council of Ministers again was given the role of adopting joint positions and drawing up agreements on the basis of Member State or Commission initiatives, acting unanimously except on matters of procedure or when implementing joint actions or agreed conventions.[62] Again, the Commission was to be 'fully associated' and the Parliament was to be informed, its views to be 'duly taken into consideration', and it could question or recommend matters to the Council.[63] A Co-ordinating Committee, which became the notorious and secretive K-4 committee, was set up to help the Council, which, like the Political Committee under CFSP, had a role similar to that of COREPER under the EC Treaty. The European Council did not have the same powerful leadership role under the JHA Pillar as under the CFSP Pillar.

(f) REACTION AND ASSESSMENT

The TEU, like the SEA before it, was extensively analysed and criticized. The obscurity and secrecy of the negotiation processes, the complexity of the new 'Union' structure, the mixed bag of institutional reforms, the borrowing of Community institutions for the intergovernmental pillar policy-making, and the many opt-outs and exceptions (the 'variable geometry') attracted much critical comment. The perceived loss of unity and coherence of the Community legal order and the likely effect on the *acquis communautaire*, which had bound all Member States to the same body of legal rules and principles, is addressed in the following extract.

D. Curtin, The Constitutional Structure of the Union: A Europe of Bits and Pieces[64]

The result of the Maastricht summit is an umbrella Union threatening to lead to constitutional chaos; the potential victims are the cohesiveness and the unity and the concomitant power of a legal system painstakingly constructed over the course of some 30 odd years.... And, of

---

[59] Arts. J.8(3)–(4), and J.9.
[60] Art. J.7.
[61] Art. K.1 TEU.
[62] Art. K.3 TEU.
[63] Arts. K.4(2) and K.6.
[64] N. 53 above, 67.

course, it does contain some elements of real *progress* (co-decision and powers of control for the European Parliament, increased Community competences, sanctions against recalcitrant Member States, Community 'citizenship', EMU etc.) but a *process* of integration, if it has any meaning at all, implies that you can't take one step forward and two steps backwards at the same time. Built into the principle of an 'ever closer union among the peoples of Europe' is the notion that integration should only be one way.

It must be said, at the heart of all this chaos and fragmentation, the unique *sui generis* nature of the European Community, its true world-historical significance, is being destroyed. The whole future and credibility of the Communities as a cohesive legal unit which confers rights on individuals and which enters into their national legal systems as an integral part of those systems, is at stake.

With hindsight, it is evident that the 'variable geometry', differentiation, or flexibility, which appeared in several forms in the TEU[65] and which was perceived as undermining the cohesiveness and unity of the Community order, is no merely temporary or transitional feature of European integration. The attraction of flexible or differentiated integration has grown, and both the Amsterdam and the Nice Treaties firmly consolidated this trend in the variety of provisions on 'closer cooperation' and 'enhanced cooperation' adopted.[66] The variety of labels describes a range of related ideas, including the possibility that some States may participate in certain policies while other do not, or that some will participate only partially, or possibly at a later date than others.[67] While the disadvantages of variable geometry may be a perceived lack of unity and increasing fragmentation (the dangers of '*à la carte*' integration), the advantages of providing a means for accommodating difference and reaching consensus in the face of strong divergence, for permitting progress—even if qualified—in crucial areas such as EMU or foreign policy which might otherwise be deadlocked, are evidently considered sufficient to outweigh the former.[68]

(g) FURTHER ENLARGEMENT

The Acts of Accession of Norway, Austria, Sweden, and Finland to the European Union were signed at the European Council meeting in Corfu in 1994, but only the last three acceded in 1995 when, for the second time in just over twenty years, a national referendum in Norway yielded a majority opposed to accession.

---

[65] Examples of differentiated integration introduced by the Maastricht Treaty were the UK's opt-out from what was then the Social Policy Chapter, the exemption from defence policy provisions of Member States which were neutral or were not full WEU members, and the option for the UK and Denmark to decide later whether or not to join in the arrangements for Economic and Monetary Union. For discussion of earlier such episodes in the Community's history see C.-D. Ehlermann, 'How Flexible is Community Law? An Unusual Approach to the Concept of "Two Speeds"' (1984) 82 *Mich. LR* 1274.

[66] C-D. Ehlermann, 'Differentiation, Flexibility, Closer Cooperation: The New Provisions of the Amsterdam Treaty' (1998) 4 *ELJ* 246; J. Shaw, 'The Treaty of Amsterdam: Challenges of Flexibility and Legitimacy' (1998) 4 *ELJ* 63; E. Philippart and G. Edwards, 'The Provisions on Closer Co-operation in the Treaty of Amsterdam: The Politics of Flexibility in the European Union' (1998) 37 *JCHS* 87; H. Bribosia, 'Les coopérations renforcées au lendemain du traité de Nice' [2001] *Revue du droit de l'Union européenne* 111.

[67] For some typologies see J. Usher, 'Variable Geometry or Concentric Circles: Patterns for the EU' (1997) 46 *ICLQ* 243 and A. Stubb, 'Differentiated Integration' (1996) 34 *JCMS* 283. More generally see G. de Búrca and J. Scott (eds.), *Constitutional Change in the EU: From Uniformity to Flexibility* (Hart, 2000) and B. de Witte, D. Hanf, and E. Vos (eds.), *The Many Faces of Differentiation in EU Law* (Intersentia, 2001).

[68] For an examination of the likely centripetal or centrifugal effects on the Union see A. Kolliker, 'Bringing Together or Driving Apart the Union?: Towards a Theory of Differentiated Integration' (2001) 24 *WEP* 125.

On a related note, in 1991 an Agreement on the European Economic Area (EEA) between the EC and EFTA was made, providing for free-movement provisions similar to those in the EC Treaty, similar competition policy and rules, as well as 'close co-operation' in a range of other policy fields. The Agreement came into force at the beginning of 1994. Initially, the ECJ held that the first EEA Agreement was incompatible with the EC Treaty,[69] but after various amendments establishing an EFTA Court without any connection with the ECJ, the ECJ upheld its compatibility with the EC Treaty.[70]

8. THE TREATY OF AMSTERDAM

The aims of the 1996 IGC were more modest than those of the TEU, and the Amsterdam Treaty was declared to be about consolidation rather than extension of Community powers. The most important matter originally intended for the IGC agenda, preparing the Union for its enlargement eastwards, was largely postponed until the Nice IGC. The ToA was signed in 1997 and came into effect on 1 May 1999.

(a) TITLE I: COMMON PROVISIONS

The common provisions of the TEU were changed in a number of ways. The main changes were as follows.

(1) The principle of openness was added to Article 1 TEU so that decisions within the EU are be taken 'as openly as possible' and as closely as possible to the citizen.

(2) New objectives were listed in Article 2 TEU, including the promotion of a high level of employment and the establishment of the rather intriguingly, if somewhat ambiguously, entitled area of 'freedom, security and justice'. This new area was to be the result of the integration of parts of the former Third Pillar on justice and home affairs into the EC Treaty.

(3) In a move designed to enhance the image and assert the normative foundations of the Union, Article 6 TEU was changed to declare that the Union is founded on respect for human rights, democracy, and the rule of law. Respect for these principles was also made a condition of application for membership of the Union under Article 49 TEU.

(4) Article 6(2) TEU, which declares that the Union shall respect the fundamental rights protected in the European Convention on Human Rights (ECHR) and in national constitutions, was rendered justiciable by an amendment to Article 46 TEU.[71]

(5) A new Article 7 TEU provided that if the Council finds a 'serious and persistent breach' by a Member State of principles set out in Article 6, it may suspend some of that State's rights under the Treaty. A parallel provision now appears in the body of the EC Treaty, in Article 309, permitting the Council, where action has been taken under Article 7 TEU, to suspend other Treaty rights of the Member State in question, voting rights being automatically suspended.

---

[69] *Opinion 1/91* [1991] ECR 6079.

[70] *Opinion 1/92* [1992] ECR I–2821. For an assessment of the operation of the EFTA Court see J. Forman, 'The EEA Agreement Five Years On: Dynamic Homogeneity in Practice and its Implementation by the Two EEA Courts' (1999) 36 *CMLRev.* 751.

[71] See Ch. 11 for a more detailed discussion.

(b) PILLAR ONE: THE COMMUNITY PILLAR

The ToA made a number of changes to the provisions of the EC Treaty. The principal modifications are set out below, and will be developed in the course of subsequent chapters.

(1) The ToA deleted obsolete provisions from the EC Treaty, adapted others,[72] and renumbered all the Articles, titles, and sections of the TEU and the EC Treaty. These attempts at presentational clarification did not reduce the overall complexity of the EU's constitutional structure, but they did remove a considerable amount of 'dead wood', in terms of Treaty Articles that were redundant and enabled a more rational numbering of the remaining Treaty provisions.

(2) In institutional terms, the most important change was the amendment and extension of the co-decision procedure, thus consolidating the role of the EP in the decision-making process and virtually eliminating the co-operation procedure apart from provisions on EMU.[73] The EP's power was further augmented by the amendment to the procedure for appointing the Commission President in Article 214(2) EC, requiring Parliamentary assent.

(3) In substantive terms, new tasks were added to Article 2 EC: promotion of equality between men and women is now mentioned as a task, as is the promotion of a high degree of competitiveness, and the promotion of 'a high level of protection and improvement of the quality of the environment' was listed as an independent goal rather than an incidental requirement of economic growth. Complementing this change, an environmental 'integration clause' was added to Article 6 EC, requiring environmental protection to be integrated into the definition and implementation of all the Community policies and activities. Moreover, economic development was henceforth required to be 'sustainable' as well as balanced and harmonious. Article 5 EC on subsidiarity was not amended, but a Protocol fleshing out the application of the principles of subsidiarity and proportionality, in line with an existing Inter-institutional Agreement and the European Council's 1992 guidelines, was annexed to the EC Treaty.

(4) There were substantive changes that impacted directly on the individual. Thus Article 13 EC introduced a new, broad, anti-discrimination provision, conferring legislative competence on the Community to combat discrimination based on sex, racial or ethnic origin, religion or belief, disability, age, or sexual orientation.[74] Article 255 EC embodied the principle of access to documents, while Article 286 EC dealt with data protection.

(5) The substantive scope of Community power was further increased by the ToA, through the addition of new heads of competence or the modification of existing heads. Thus there was a new title on Employment, Articles 125–130 EC, the aims of which were to be furthered principally by soft-law measures. This title became the prototype for an experimental form of governance, usually referred to as the 'open method of coordination' (OMC), discussed below.[75] Further, following a change of government in Britain in 1997, the UK social policy opt-out was no longer necessary,[76] and consequently the Maastricht 'Social Protocol' was repealed, replaced by an amended version of the Social Policy Agreement incorporated into

---

[72] The General Secretariat of the Council issued an explanatory report on these provisions available at [1997] OJ C353/1.

[73] As far as the ECSC and Euratom Treaties are concerned, similar amendments to the relevant institutional provisions of these Treaties were made by the ToA.

[74] See Ch. 24 for further discussion.

[75] See below, Ch. 5.

[76] C. Barnard, 'The United Kingdom, the Social Chapter and the Amsterdam Treaty' (1997) 26 *ILJ* 275.

Articles 136–143 EC.[77] The title on public health in Article 152 EC was replaced and enhanced, establishing more detailed aims and power for the Council to enact standard-setting measures, while simultaneously claiming to 'fully respect the responsibility of the member States for the organization and delivery of health services and medical care'. The title on consumer protection in Article 153 EC was also slightly amended.

(6) The major structural substantive change was the incorporation into the Community Pillar of a large part of the former Third Pillar on the free movement of persons, covering visas, asylum, immigration, and judicial co-operation in civil matters,[78] now to be found in Title IV, Articles 61–69 EC.[79] The aim of this title and that of the amended Third Pillar, which now covers police and judicial co-operation in criminal matters (PJCC), are similarly described, both being intended to establish 'an area of freedom, justice and security'.[80] Further, the *acquis* of the 1985 Schengen Treaty on the gradual abolition of common border checks was integrated by a Protocol to the ToA into the EU framework.[81] While the new Title IV on the free movement of persons is a part of Community law, the close legal and institutional connection between Community policies and those of the two other Union pillars is, as will be seen below,[82] increasingly evident, thereby highlighting the increasing complexity of the EU constitutional order, and the move away from the relative clarity of the previous Community legal order.

(7) A further substantive innovation was Article 11 EC, which provides that the Council may authorize 'closer cooperation' between Member States. The ToA version of Article 11 contained numerous restrictive conditions, including a bar on closer co-operation in relation to EU citizenship or wherever it would 'affect Community policies, actions or programmes', but these were relaxed by the Nice Treaty and moved from Article 11 into the general conditions for enhanced co-operation in Title VII of the TEU. Article 11 was however never actually used before being amended by the Nice Treaty.

(c) TITLE V, PILLAR TWO: COMMON FOREIGN AND SECURITY POLICY

A number of changes were made to the Second Pillar by the Amsterdam Treaty, although without greatly changing its structure or the nature of institutional involvement since the Maastricht Treaty: the EP's role did not alter, the ECJ remained excluded, and there was only a small change in the Commission's role permitting it to submit implementation proposals. However, a variety of criticisms of the Title as established by the Maastricht Treaty had been voiced, and some were addressed by the ToA. These will be considered in detail below,[83] but can be briefly mentioned here.

(1) The first criticism concerned the lack of an international identity for the CFSP. The Union itself was not formally accorded legal personality by the ToA, as this was opposed by some Member States. The ToA however nominated the Secretary-General of the Council as

---

[77] See Ch. 24.

[78] A new title on customs co-operation was also added in Art. 135 EC.

[79] These provisions were subject to opt-outs and are discussed in greater detail in Ch. 7.

[80] Protocols on the issues of asylum and the crossing of external borders were also annexed to the Treaty, and a number of Declarations on provisions of the new title were adopted.

[81] See Ch. 7.

[82] At 95, 250.

[83] See Ch. 6.

'High Representative' for the CFSP to assist the Council Presidency, which would remain the primary representative of the Union.[84] In a significant amendment, Article 24 TEU conferred power on the Council to 'conclude' international agreements,[85] whenever this was necessary in implementing the CFSP, and these provisions were deemed also to apply to issues falling under the Third Pillar on Police and Judicial Co-operation in Criminal Matters (PJCC).[86]

(2) A second criticism was that the instruments available under the Second Pillar, common positions and joint actions, were obscure and ill-defined, and in practice the Council resorted frequently to declarations. The ToA amendments in Articles 13–15 TEU clarified the meaning of common strategies, joint actions, and common positions.

(3) A third criticism was that the decision-making procedures were ineffective, and that the unanimity requirement made progress difficult. The ToA changed the provisions on voting, and Article 23 TEU represented a partial compromise between those calling for more qualified majority voting and those arguing for maintenance of the primarily intergovernmental, consensual approach.

(4) Fourthly, it was argued that the provisions on financing of action under the CFSP were unsatisfactory. The provisions governing budgetary arrangements were amended by the ToA to provide more guidance on which expenditure was to be charged to the Community rather than Member State budgets, Article 28 TEU.

(d) TITLE VI, PILLAR THREE: POLICE AND JUDICIAL CO-OPERATION IN CRIMINAL MATTERS (PJCC)

A major criticism of the Maastricht Treaty was that many of the policies under the JHA Pillar called for institutional provisions and legal controls that were quite different from the intergovernmental processes established. Unlike the foreign and security policy matters under the Second Pillar, JHA subjects such as immigration, asylum, border controls, and constraints on movement touch on fundamental human rights, and raise issues similar to those arising under the free movement provisions of the EC Treaty. Consequently, it was argued that the need for openness and accountability in this policy field was much greater, requiring a full role for the European Parliament and review jurisdiction for the Court of Justice. Arguments for reform ranged from improving the institutional provisions under the existing JHA to absorbing the Third Pillar entirely into the Community Pillar. Predictably, what emerged in the ToA lay between the two, with parts of JHA being incorporated into EC Title IV, and the remaining Third Pillar provisions being expanded and subjected to a range of institutional controls closer to those under the Community Pillar.

There will be detailed consideration of the Third Pillar in a subsequent chapter.[87] Suffice it to say for the present that the overall aim of the Third Pillar was, according to Article 29 TEU, to provide citizens with a high level of safety within an area of freedom, security, and justice,

---

[84] The Council was also formally given power to appoint a 'special representative' with a mandate in relation to particular policy issues, and a number of such appointments have been made.

[85] J.W. de Zwaan, 'Legal Personality of the European Communities and the European Union' (1999) 30 *Netherlands Yearbook of International Law* 75; K. Lenaerts and E. de Smijter, 'The European Union as an Actor under International Law' (1999/2000) 19 *YBEL* 95 and the editorial comment, 'The European Union: A New International Actor' (2001) 38 *CMLRev.* 825.

[86] Art. 38 TEU.

[87] See Ch. 7.

by developing 'common action' in three areas: police co-operation in criminal matters, judicial co-operation in criminal matters, and the prevention and combating of racism and xenophobia. Particular targets mentioned were terrorism, drug and arms trafficking, trafficking in persons, and offences against children, corruption, and fraud. These aims were to be addressed through: closer co-operation between police forces and customs and other Member State authorities, with the help of Europol; through closer co-operation between judicial and other relevant Member State authorities; and through the approximation of certain criminal laws in the Member States.

Articles 30–31 TEU set out more details on the common actions in relation to police and judicial co-operation. Article 34 TEU specifies the range of available legal instruments which the Council may adopt: common positions, framework decisions, decisions, and conventions. These measures are to be adopted by the Council on an initiative from the Commission or a Member State, but the European Parliament was now given a consultative role in decision-making, with the exception of common positions.[88] The ECJ was also given jurisdiction over certain measures adopted under this Pillar,[89] thereby further eroding the distinction between the Community Pillar and the Third Pillar. The interconnection between the two was further underlined by Article 42 TEU, which contains the amended 'passerelle' provision, providing a procedure whereby issues falling under Pillar Three could be dealt with under Title IV of the EC Treaty. The ToA also made provision for the application of the rules on closer co-operation between groups of Member States to apply in relation to the Third Pillar.[90]

(e) TITLE VII: CLOSER CO-OPERATION

This title, which was introduced by the ToA, while not establishing a 'fourth pillar' set out the general conditions under which Member States could seek to establish closer co-operation between them, using the institutions and mechanisms of the TEU and the EC Treaty alike. Like the provisions on closer co-operation under the Third Pillar and those in Article 11 EC for the first Pillar, it has been replaced and amended in certain respects by the Nice Treaty, and therefore will not be analysed here, but will be discussed below in considering the changes introduced at Nice.

(f) TITLE VIII: FINAL PROVISIONS

Article 46 TEU defines the scope of the ECJ's jurisdiction, which henceforth would extend not only to provisions of the EC Treaties but also, under specified conditions, to Third Pillar measures, to Title VII, to all of the final provisions, Articles 46–53 TEU, and to Article 6(2) of the TEU.

Article 49 provides the procedure for new States to become Members of the Union, replacing previous provisions of the EC, Euratom, and ECSC Treaties, and subjecting applicant States to the requirement of respect for the fundamental principles in Article 6 TEU, on which the European Union is now said to be based. This provision requires the Council to act unanimously after receiving the opinion of the Commission and the assent of the Parliament.[91]

[88] Art. 39 TEU.
[89] Art. 35 TEU.
[90] Art. 40 TEU.
[91] Art. 48 TEU would henceforth govern amendments to the Treaties, replacing Arts. 236 EC, 204 Euratom, and 96 ECSC.

(g) REACTION AND ASSESSMENT

Assessment requires a benchmark, some criterion to measure what was achieved against prior aspirations. The two most salient benchmarks were institutional reform to cope with prospective enlargement and broader concerns about the legitimacy of the EU, which many of the contributions to the IGC leading to the ToA sought to address. Viewed against these benchmarks, the ToA does not score high points. Institutional reform to cope with enlargement was not addressed, thereby necessitating further Treaty reform at Nice a few years later. There was moreover relatively little in the ToA to address broader concerns about the legitimacy of the EU, although the extension of co-decision, the creation of the new Title IV and provisions concerning access to documents, data protection, non-discrimination, and the like were of some relevance in this respect.

The ToA did have more general impact in two respects, although neither corresponded to the primary aspirations of those who embarked on this round of Treaty reform. The ToA eroded the distinction between the Pillars that had been crafted but four years earlier. This was true especially in relation to Pillar Three where, as we have seen, part of the JHA Pillar was carved out and placed in the EC Treaty, albeit subject to a rather special regime therein, while the remainder of Pillar Three, recast as PJCC, became subject, in relative terms at least, to a greater degree of supranational oversight than hitherto.

The other broader consequence of the ToA was to constitutionalize and legitimate mechanisms for allowing different degrees of integration and co-operation between different groups of States. Article 40 TEU, Article 11 EC, and the new Title VII on closer co-operation demonstrated that differentiated integration should no longer be thought of as an aberration within the EC and EU legal order, nor as a temporary solution or a means of gradually easing all Member States into a uniform system.

9. AMSTERDAM TO NICE

(a) AMSTERDAM TO NICE: THE IGC

It is noteworthy that the European Communities existed from 1957 until 1985 without a single IGC, and that, by way of contrast, since the SEA there has been an almost continuous process of amendment.[92] Given that the ToA did not address the EU's institutional structure pending enlargement, a further IGC was inevitable. The IGC was called by the European Council at its Cologne summit in 1999, only two months after the Amsterdam Treaty entered into force, to address the size and composition of the Commission, the weighting of votes in the Council, and the extension of qualified majority voting. The European Council at Feira in 2000 added the issue of enhanced co-operation. The IGC leading to the Nice Treaty, following the practice begun during the Amsterdam IGC, was more transparent than earlier such meetings, with many of the documents being posted on an official IGC website.

Despite this relatively modest agenda, however, the deeper legitimacy issues which had surfaced during the Maastricht IGC could not be avoided when issues of institutional reform were on the table, particularly after the crisis provoked by the Commission's resignation. Thus the questions of 'simplifying' the complex Treaty structure and establishing a basic constitutional

---

[92] B. de Witte, 'The Closest Thing to a Constitutional Conversation in Europe: The Semi-permanent Treaty Revision Process', in P. Beaumont, C. Lyons, and N. Walker (eds.), *Convergence and Divergence in European Public Law* (Hart, 2002), ch. 3.

text, of enhancing the transparency and accountability of the EU institutions and their functioning, and of clarifying the powers of the Union *vis-à-vis* the Member States were also discussed during this period.[93] There were, moreover, the beginnings of a broader constitutional debate in the political sphere, stoked by the speech of Joschka Fischer in mid-2000 to the Humboldt University.[94]

(b) AMSTERDAM TO NICE: THE CHARTER OF RIGHTS

In the meantime, the Cologne European Council in 1999 launched another initiative of major constitutional significance, in establishing a 'body' which included national parliamentarians, European parliamentarians, and national government representatives to draft a Charter of fundamental rights for the EU.[95] This body, which renamed itself a 'Convention', began work early in 2000 and drew up a Charter before the end of the same year. The Convention worked in an unusually open and transparent way, posting documents, materials, and drafts on a specially dedicated website, and holding its meetings openly. The Charter was 'solemnly proclaimed' by the Commission, Parliament, and Council and received political approval of the Member States at the Nice European Council in December 2000,[96] but a decision on its legal status and specifically the question of its possible integration into the Treaties was placed on the so-called 'post-Nice agenda' and postponed until the 2004 IGC.

The Charter was a significant development. In substantive terms, despite criticisms of its content, the document was largely welcomed as a step forward for the legitimacy, identity, and human rights commitment of the EU. In terms of process, the mode by which it was drafted and adopted also attracted positive comment as a considerable improvement on the method by which treaties and other agreements have traditionally been negotiated and drawn up at EU level. The decision to establish the Convention on the Future of Europe was, as we shall see, strongly influenced by the process that led to the Charter of Rights.

10. THE NICE TREATY

The Nice Treaty (TN) was concluded in December 2000 after a notoriously fractious and badly run European Council summit. The Treaty consists of two parts, the first part containing the substantive amendments to the EU and EC Treaties,[97] and the second part containing the transitional and final provisions. There were also four protocols: on enlargement, on the Statute of the Court of Justice, on the financial consequences of expiry of the ECSC Treaty, and on Article 67 EC concerning the transitional provisions of Title IV on the free movement

---

[93] Two special reports had also been requested and received by the Commission during this period—one on the *Institutional Implications of Enlargement* presented by a high-level group chaired by Jean-Luc Dehaene: see www.europa.eu.int/igc2000/repoct99_en.pdf, and the other a study prepared by the European University Institute at Florence on the reorganization of the Treaties, available at www.europa.eu.int/comm/archives/igc2000/offdoc/repoflo_en.pdf. See also A Basic Treaty for the European Union, COM(2000)434 and Adapting the Institutions to Make a Success of Enlargement, COM(2000)34. At the same time, the Commission was preparing its own White Paper on European Governance, COM(2001)428.

[94] *Symposium: Responses to Joschka Fischer*, available at www.iue.it/RSC/symposium/.

[95] G. de Búrca, 'The Drafting of the EU Charter of Fundamental Rights' (2001) 26 *ELRev.* 126.

[96] [2000] OJ C364/1.

[97] [2001] OJ C80/1. The relevant provisions of the Euratom Treaty are amended by Art. 3 of the Nice Treaty and those of the ECSC Treaty by Art. 4 TN; K. Bradley, 'Institutional Design in the Treaty of Nice' (2001) 38 *CMLRev.* 1095; R. Barents, 'Some Observations on the Treaty of Nice' (2001) 8 *MJ* 121.

of persons. Twenty-four declarations, including the important declarations on Enlargement and on the Future of the Union, were also adopted and annexed to the final act of the IGC. The principal changes will be briefly discussed here, although some, such as the reform of the judicial system, will be treated in more detail in the later relevant chapters of this book.

(a) TITLE I: COMMON PROVISIONS

The single change made by the TN to this part of the TEU concerned Article 7, the provision dealing with suspension of the rights of a Member State found to be in serious and persistent breach of the principles of respect for democracy, human rights, and the rule of law. Article 7 as amended provides for more detailed procedures to be followed before a negative determination against a Member State is made, including an opportunity for the Member State to be heard and for an independent report to be made, and it also provides for the possibility of acting where there is a clear *risk* of breach. The Court of Justice is given jurisdiction over the procedural stipulations of Article 7 by Article 46 TEU.

(b) PILLAR ONE: THE COMMUNITY PILLAR

The Nice Treaty made a number of changes to the EC Treaty, in particular relating to the Community's institutional and decision-making structure. The most significant were as follows.

(1) The major political achievement was agreement on the *institutional questions* relevant to enlargement: settling the weighting of votes in the Council, the distribution of seats in the European Parliament, and the composition of the Commission. The crucial institutional changes are contained in the Protocol on Enlargement and Declaration 20 attached to the Nice Treaty.

(2) In terms of *weighted voting in the Council*, the main questions were whether a qualified majority must include a majority of Member States, what the size of a 'blocking minority' should be, and more generally what the specific figures should be for each Member State. The debate on these matters was fierce, with large and medium/small States ranged in opposition. Ultimately, what has been called a 'triple majority'[98] was agreed upon: a decision must command the agreement of a majority of the overall number of Member States, but it must command the agreement of two-thirds of the Members where the Council is not acting on a proposal from the Commission; it must have 169 out of 237 weighted votes, or 258 out of 345 after enlargement, and, finally, where a Member State so requests, the votes in favour must represent 62 per cent of the total population of the EU.

(3) In relation to *seats in the European Parliament*, the key issue was the need to accommodate the new States and the corresponding need to reduce the number of seats held by existing States, since if that were not done the overall number of MEPs would be too large. The solution was to raise the overall ceiling of 700 established by the ToA to 732, with reductions to the number of seats for most Member States except Germany and Luxembourg from the time of the European elections in 2004. Article 2(4) of the Protocol allows for the new ceiling to be temporarily exceeded in certain circumstances in the event of accession.

(4) In relation to *reform of the Commission*, the central issue was whether to persist with the regime of at least one Commissioner from each Member State, or to have a smaller

---

[98] X. Yataganas, 'The Treaty of Nice: The Sharing of Power and the Institutional Balance in the European Union—A Continental Perspective' (2001) 7 *ELJ* 242.

Commission combined with a system of rotation of Commissioners between Member States. The pressure from the smaller Member States resulted in a compromise. The regime of one Commissioner per Member State was retained from 2005 onwards, at least until EU membership reached twenty-seven. After that time the number of members of the Commission will be smaller than the number of Member States, and members will be chosen according to a rotation system on the basis of equality rather than size, this new system becoming operative from the date on which the first Commission takes up its duties following the date of accession of the twenty-seventh Member State.[99] A further change was that the Commission President and the list of Commission members can now be nominated and appointed by qualified majority rather than by common accord, and the President's powers of organization within the Commission were strengthened.

(5) The EP's power was further enhanced by *extension of the co-decision procedure* to a considerable range of Treaty provisions,[100] though not, given firm opposition from certain Member States, to certain areas including taxation or social security, a range of social policy provisions under Article 137, the cohesion policy provisions at least until 2007, and parts of Title IV concerning immigration and asylum, where the introduction of qualified-majority voting was also deferred for many provisions.

(6) The Nice Treaty also made *significant changes to the Court system*, which will be discussed in more detail in Chapters 2 and 13. Suffice it for now to say that the powers of the Court of First Instance (CFI) were significantly strengthened, with provision being made for it to exercise preliminary rulings jurisdiction in certain circumstances; its jurisdiction in direct actions was expanded; and it gained appellate jurisdiction from new judicial panels.

(7) The *provisions on closer co-operation* in Article 11 EC were amended. The substantive conditions for the establishment of enhanced co-operation under Article 11 EC are those set out in Article 43 TEU as amended, but the procedure for authorizing such co-operation is specific to the Community pillar with a stronger role for the Commission and Parliament.

(8) In substantive terms, following the Treaty title on Development Co-operation, a new title on economic, financial, and technical co-operation with third countries was adopted in Article 181a.

(c) TITLE V, PILLAR TWO: CFSP

(1) The principal changes made by the Nice Treaty related to security and defence policy in Article 17 TEU. Most of the provisions referring to the WEU were repealed, and the operational capability of the EU itself was emphasized.

(2) There was an extension of qualified-majority voting by the Council to the appointment of special representatives under Article 23(2) TEU, and to the conclusion of certain international agreements under Article 24 TEU. This extension of majority voting in the conclusion of international agreements is also applied to the parallel provisions of the Third Pillar.

(3) The Nice Treaty also introduced a new provision permitting enhanced co-operation under the Second Pillar, Article 27a TEU. Military and defence matters were excluded by Article 27b TEU, but subject to this caveat enhanced co-operation is available in

---

[99] Protocol on Enlargement, Art. 4(2).

[100] A. Dashwood, 'The Constitution of the European Union after Nice: Law-making Procedures' (2001) 26 *ELRev.* 215.

other areas of the CFSP in relation to the implementation of a joint action or common position, provided that the substantive conditions listed are met, and the proper procedure followed.

(d) TITLE VI, PILLAR THREE: PJCC

(1) There were relatively few changes made to the Third Pillar by the Nice Treaty. A formal Treaty foundation was given to Eurojust, the European judicial co-operation unit, and its role is elaborated in Article 31(2) TEU.

(2) The principal change was however to the provisions on enhanced co-operation in Articles 40, 40a, and 40b TEU. Like the enhanced co-operation provisions of the Second Pillar, these are also subject to the substantive conditions of the umbrella enhanced co-operation provisions in Articles 43–45 TEU. The main effect of the amendments to the Third Pillar is to strengthen the role of the Commission, to which Member States must first direct their request to establish enhanced co-operation, and only if it refuses may the States submit their initiative directly to the Council. The Parliament is also given a consultative role. The Luxembourg-style veto was repealed and replaced by a softer protection for Member States which may request that a matter be referred to the European Council.

(e) TITLE VII: ENHANCED CO-OPERATION

The provisions of Article 43, which were established by the Amsterdam Treaty, have been replaced and (at least in the English version of the TEU) been renamed 'enhanced' rather than 'closer' co-operation. Article 43 now provides:

> Member States which intend to establish enhanced cooperation between themselves may make use of the institutions, procedures and mechanisms laid down by this Treaty and by the Treaty establishing the European Community provided that the proposed cooperation:
>
> (a) is aimed at furthering the objectives of the Union and of the Community, at protecting and serving their interests and at reinforcing their process of integration;
>
> (b) respects the said Treaties and the single institutional framework of the Union;
>
> (c) respects the acquis communautaire and the measures adopted under the other provisions of the said Treaties;
>
> (d) remains within the limits of the powers of the Union or of the Community and does not concern the areas which fall within the exclusive competence of the Community;
>
> (e) does not undermine the internal market as defined in Article 14(2) of the Treaty establishing the European Community, or the economic and social cohesion established in accordance with Title XVII of that Treaty;
>
> (f) does not constitute a barrier to or discrimination in trade between the Member States and does not distort competition between them;
>
> (g) involves a minimum of eight Member States;
>
> (h) respects the competences, rights and obligations of those Member States which do not participate therein;
>
> (i) does not affect the provisions of the Protocol integrating the Schengen acquis into the framework of the European Union;
>
> (j) is open to all the Member States, in accordance with Article 43b.

This is followed by Articles 43a and 43b TEU, which provide respectively that enhanced co-operation should be used only as a last resort when it has been established that the same object-ives cannot otherwise be attained within a reasonable period, and that enhanced co-operation should be open to all Member States at any stage under the conditions provided in the Treaty, and that as many States as possible should be encouraged to take part. Article 44 indicates the relevant institutional provisions to be used in the adoption of decisions within a field of enhanced co-operation, and explains the decision-making procedures and obligations in rela-tion to participating and non-participating States. Such decisions are declared not to be part of the Union *acquis*.

The most significant change brought about by the TN is that only a minimum of eight Member States is necessary to establish enhanced co-operation. Further, some of the stricter conditions of the previous Amsterdam conditions have been relaxed. Thus, enhanced co-operation is no longer prohibited where it may *affect* the *acquis communautaire* or the com-petences and rights of non-participating States. Article 43 now provides, in a more positive vein, that any enhanced co-operation is required to *respect* the *acquis* and the competences and rights of non-participating States. The requirement that enhanced co-operation must not undermine the internal market or economic and social cohesion is, however, a newly added restrictive condition.

(f) ENLARGEMENT

The driving force behind the TN was, as we have seen, to make the institutional changes neces-sary to cope with further enlargement. This was especially pressing because this enlargement was to bring ten further States from Eastern Europe into the EU. The 2004 enlargement saw the following States join the EU: the Czech Republic, Estonia, Cyprus, Latvia, Lithuania, Hungary, Malta, Poland, Slovenia, and Slovakia. Two further countries, Bulgaria and Romania, joined the EU in 2007, making twenty-seven States in all. Negotiations are ongoing with Croatia and Turkey.

The policy of conditionality meant that candidate States were required to adapt their laws and institutions in very significant ways long before any date for accession was set, at a time when they had little or no influence on the making of European laws and policies.[101] The requirements to comply with the 'Copenhagen criteria', which were set by the European Council in 1993, and to adopt the entirety of the Community *acquis*, were a considerable bur-den for these countries.[102]

(g) REACTION AND ASSESSMENT

The aspirations underlying the IGC that led to the Treaty of Nice were limited, the primary aim being to do what had been left undone at Amsterdam, this being the institutional reform necessary in the light of impending enlargement. Viewed from this limited perspective the Treaty of Nice did the job. It produced answers on the key issues of Council voting, distribu-tion of EP seats, and the size of the Commission, even if, as was inevitably the case, there was

---

[101] H. Grabbe, 'A Partnership for Accession? The Implications of EU Conditionality for the Central and East European Applicants', EUI Robert Schuman Centre Working Paper 12/99, and 'How does Europeanization affect CEE Governance? Conditionality, Diffusion and Diversity' (2001) 8 *JEPP* 1013; A. Williams, 'Enlargement of the Union and Human Rights Conditionality: A Policy of Distinction?' (2000) 25 *ELRev*. 601.

[102] See www.europa.eu.int/comm/enlargement/intro/criteria.htm#Accession criteria.

room for debate about whether those answers were 'optimal'. There was nonetheless a lingering dissatisfaction with the outcome.

This was in part procedural. There was much adverse media reaction to the ill-tempered exchanges and the late-night wrangling that accompanied the final stages of the IGC and the European Council meeting in Nice. This undoubtedly added to the pressure to reform the Treaty revision process, and formed part of the impetus for the European Council's decision in 2001 to establish a more open and representative Convention to prepare for the next IGC.

The lingering dissatisfaction was also in part substantive. The Nice Treaty may well have addressed the primary institutional issues, but it was readily apparent that there were substantive issues that were regarded as equally important which were not touched. This was reflected in Declaration 23 on the Future of the Union appended to the Nice Treaty, which called for a 'deeper and wider debate about the future of the European Union', involving a broad range of opinion. The Declaration identified four issues for the 2004 IGC: the 'delimitation of powers' between the EU and the Member States, the status of the Charter of Fundamental Rights, simplification of the Treaties, and the role of the national parliaments. We shall see in the section that follows how discussion concerning these issues led to the Convention on the Future of Europe.

11. THE CONSTITUTIONAL TREATY

(a) FROM NICE TO LAEKEN

Declaration 23 appended to the Nice Treaty explicitly envisaged that the four issues identified would be considered further at the Laeken European Council meeting scheduled for December 2001. The nature of subsequent reform was however transformed during the calendar year 2001. A growing consensus emerged among the major institutional players about two crucial issues.[103]

In terms of the *content of the reform agenda*, it came to be accepted that the four issues left over from the Nice Treaty were not discrete. It came to be recognized that, for example, competences, and the status of the Charter, resonated with other issues concerning the institutional balance of power within the EU, and also with the vertical distribution of authority as between the EU and the Member States. The realization that the issues left over from Nice raised broader concerns coincided with a growing feeling that there should be a more fundamental re-thinking of the institutional and substantive fundamentals of the EU.

In terms of the *reform process*, it came to be accepted that if a broad range of issues was to be discussed, then the result, whatsoever it might be, should be legitimated by a process of input from a broader 'constituency' than hitherto. This momentum was fuelled by dissatisfaction with the traditional process of Treaty reform, dominated by the paradigm of the IGC.

This emerging consensus was duly reflected in the Laeken European Council,[104] which gave formal approval, through the Laeken Declaration, to the broadening of the issues left open post-Nice. These four issues became the 'headings' within which a plethora of other questions were posed, concerning virtually every issue of importance for the future of the EU. The Laeken Declaration also formally embraced the Convention model and established a Convention on the Future of Europe, with a composition designed to enhance the legitimacy of its results.

---

[103] P. Craig, 'Constitutional Process and Reform in the EU: Nice, Laeken, The Convention and the IGC' (2004) 10 *EPL* 653.

[104] Laeken European Council, 14–15 Dec. 2001.

(b) THE CONVENTION ON THE FUTURE OF EUROPE

The Convention was composed of representatives from national governments, national parliaments, the EP, and the Commission. The accession countries were also represented. The Convention was chaired by Valéry Giscard d'Estaing, and there were two vice-chairmen, Giuliano Amato and Jean-Luc Dehaene. The principal executive role in the Convention was undertaken by the Praesidium, which was composed of the chairman, the two vice-chairmen, three representatives of national governments, two from the EP, two from the Commission, and two from national parliaments. The reports, papers, and draft articles were readily available on the Convention's website.[105]

The Convention adopted a three-stage methodology. There was the *listening stage* from March until June 2002, when the main emphasis was on general statements concerning the mission of the Union. This was followed by the *examination stage*, in which Working Groups considered particular topics. This exercise occupied the latter half of 2002. This was central to the attainment of the Convention goals, more especially given that the time limit for the Convention's deliberations was very tight.[106] There was then the *proposal stage*, in which the Convention discussed draft articles of the Constitution, normally on the basis of proposals emanating from the relevant Working Groups.

It is nonetheless important to recognize that the decision to press for a Constitutional Treaty was not pre-ordained. The possibility of a constitutional text was mentioned only at the very end of the Laeken Declaration, in the context of Treaty simplification, and the language was brief and cautious.[107] Many Member States felt that the Convention might be nothing more than a high-level talking shop, which produced recommendations.[108] It was therefore something of a surprise when Giscard d'Estaing, in the Convention opening ceremony, announced that he sought consensus on a Constitutional Treaty for Europe. The Convention, once established, developed its own institutional vision. The idea took hold that the Convention should indeed produce a coherent document, and that this should take the form of a Constitutional Treaty. The defining 'Convention moment', when the idea that a Constitutional Treaty should be drafted by the Convention really took hold, was September 2002. A paper from the Secretariat concerned with Treaty simplification was central in this respect,[109] because the Secretariat went systematically through the options for making the Treaties more accessible, including the possibility of drawing up a Basic Treaty. This laid the embryonic foundations for what was to become Part I of the Constitutional Treaty. Matters then moved rapidly. There was a plenary session on 12–13 September 2002, two days after the Report from the Secretariat.[110] Giscard d'Estaing drew together the imminent reports from the Working Groups with the Secretariat paper, and stated that this made it possible for the Convention to 'reflect on the form of the end product, ie the draft Constitutional Treaty for Europe'.[111]

---

[105] http://european-convention.eu.int.

[106] Working groups were established on: subsidiarity, Charter of Rights, legal personality, national parliaments, competence, economic governance, external action, defence, Treaty simplification, freedom, security and justice, and social Europe. The decision to create the first six groups was taken in May 2002; the remaining five groups were created later in Autumn 2002.

[107] 'The question ultimately arises as to whether this simplification and reorganization might not lead in the long run to the adoption of a constitutional text in the Union', Laeken European Council, n. 104 above, 24.

[108] P. Norman, 'From the Convention to the IGC (Institutions)' (September 2003) *Federal Trust*, 2.

[109] CONV 250/02, Simplification of the Treaties and Drawing up of a Constitutional Treaty, Brussels, 10 Sept. 2002.

[110] CONV 284/02, Summary Report on the Plenary Session—Brussels, 12 and 13 Sept. 2002, Brussels, 17 Sept. 2002.

[111] *Ibid.*, 2.

A Preliminary Draft Constitutional Treaty[112] was duly presented in October 2002.[113] The Draft represented an exercise in outline constitutional architecture. It was premised on the idea of a single Treaty with three parts, the first containing the constitutional principles, the second dealing with Union policies, and the third with general provisions concerning ratification and the like. It was an astute political move, notwithstanding the fact that there was much that was unclear or ambiguous. It was important 'internally', sending a message to the Convention members that progress was being made towards something concrete. It was equally important 'externally', acclimatizing Member States to the fact that something real might indeed emerge from the Convention, while allowing time for their comments to be considered.

The Preliminary Draft Constitutional Treaty thus provided the framework into which the more detailed proposals emanating from Working Groups could be fitted, once they had been considered by plenary sessions of the Convention and transformed into Treaty Articles. The Convention's general three-stage methodology, the listening phase, the examination stage, followed by the proposal stage, did not however apply to institutions and their respective powers. It was felt that these issues were too contentious to be dealt with other than in plenary session. This is reflected in the fact that the title on Institutions was empty in the Preliminary Draft Constitution. It was a 'room' without content. Spring 2003 was therefore taken up with contentious discussions in Convention plenary sessions on these matters, and the Praesidium came to exercise ever greater power over these provisions, more especially as the deadline for delivery of the Convention proposals, June 2003, came closer.[114]

The Draft Treaty Establishing a Constitution for Europe was duly agreed by the Convention in June 2003 and submitted to the European Council in July.[115] Particular provisions of the Constitutional Treaty will be considered in subsequent chapters where relevant. Suffice it to say for the present that the CT was divided into four parts: Part I dealt with the basic objectives and values of the EU, fundamental rights, competences, forms of law-making, institutional division of power and the like; Part II contained the Charter of Rights, which had been made binding by Part I; Part III concerned the policies and functions of the EU; and Part IV contained general and final provisions. There was some debate as to whether the CT should include Part III, which deals with the policies and functions of the EU. Its inclusion prevented the CT from being a relatively short text. However in political terms it was insisted on by States that feared that the CT might otherwise undo complex bargains reached over the years that were embodied in the existing Treaties, and in legal terms it would in any event have been necessary to amend the existing Treaties to bring them into line with the CT.

(c) THE IGC

The Laeken European Council might well have been content for Treaty reform to be considered by a more inclusive body, such as the Convention. The Member States were not however willing to give up entirely the 'normal' reins of power, and it was always envisaged that the Convention document would provide a 'starting point for discussions in the Intergovernmental Conference, which will take the ultimate decisions'.[116]

---

[112] CONV 369/02, Preliminary Draft Constitutional Treaty, Brussels, 28 Oct. 2002.

[113] CONV 378/02, Summary Report of the Plenary Session-Brussels, 28 and 29 Oct. 2002, Brussels, 31 Oct. 2002.

[114] Craig, n. 103 above, 664–669.

[115] CONV 850/03, Draft Treaty establishing a Constitution for Europe, Brussels, 18 July 2003.

[116] Laeken European Council, n. 104 above, 25.

It fell therefore to Italy, which had the Presidency of the European Council in the second half of 2003, to deal with the Draft Treaty. The IGC amended a number of provisions in the Draft Treaty concerned primarily with institutional division of power, but the Member States could nonetheless not agree on a final text in December 2003. The Presidency of the European Council passed to Ireland in 2004, and agreement on the Constitutional Treaty was secured at the European Council meeting in June 2004.[117]

(d) CT (NON-)RATIFICATION AND THE REFORM TREATY

It was however still necessary for the final version of the Constitutional Treaty,[118] CT, to be ratified in accord with the constitutional requirements or choices of each Member State. Fifteen Member States ratified the CT, but progress with ratification came to an abrupt halt when France and the Netherlands rejected it in their referenda.[119] A number of Member States therefore postponed their ratification processes. The European Council in 2005 decided it was best for there to be a time for 'reflection', during which Member States were encouraged to engage in debate about the EU with their own citizens. In 2006 the European Council commissioned Germany, which held the Presidency of the European Council in the first half of 2007, to assess and report on the current state of discussion concerning the CT.

The German Presidency sought agreement in the European Council meeting in June 2007[120] on a scaled-down version of the CT. The meeting agreed to what will be known as the Reform Treaty. An IGC was set up to draft the detailed provisions. The Reform Treaty, RT, will amend the TEU and the EC Treaty. The former will retain its existing name, but the EC Treaty will be renamed the Treaty on the Functioning of the Union. The Union is to have a single legal personality and the word 'Community' is to be replaced throughout by the word 'Union'. The word 'Constitution' has been dropped and there will be other changes to the provisions of the Constitutional Treaty. However, many of the CT provisions concerning matters such as the institution's powers, competences, hierarchy of norms, and the like, are to be carried over to the Reform Treaty, albeit with amendments.

(e) REACTION AND ASSESSMENT

It is difficult in the space available to give a balanced reaction to and assessment of the CT. There is considerable diversity of view on just about every facet of this document. We can nonetheless convey some idea of the principal areas of debate.

There is a discourse as to *whether it was wise for the EU ever to have embarked on this ambitious project.* This was reflected in the jibe 'if it ain't broke, why fix it?' On this view grand constitutional schemes of the kind embodied in the CT were both unnecessary, because the EU could function perfectly well on the basis of the Nice Treaty, and dangerous, because the very construction of such a constitutional document would bring to the fore contentious issues concerning matters such as the range of EU competences, the supremacy of EU law over national law, and the inter-institutional division of power, which were best resolved through less formal mechanisms, as opposed to hard-edged constitutional provisions that invited

---

[117] Brussels European Council, 17–18 June 2004, paras. 4–5.
[118] Treaty Establishing a Constitution for Europe [2004] OJ C316/1.
[119] R. Dehousse, 'The Unmaking of a Constitution: Lessons from the European Referenda' (2006) 13 *Constellations* 151.
[120] Brussels European Council, 21–22 June 2007.

high-profile constitutional controversy. There is force in this view. It should nonetheless be recognized that the four issues left over from the Nice Treaty were not discrete. They raised, both directly and indirectly, broader issues concerning the nature of the EU, its powers, mode of decision-making, and relationship with the Member States and their parliaments. The dissatisfaction with piecemeal IGC Treaty reform, monopolized by the Member States, should moreover not be forgotten. If this traditional process had been adhered to in relation to the broadened reform agenda there would have been a raft of criticism about the 'legitimacy and representativeness deficit' inherent in the classic IGC model.

A related, but distinct, set of issues relates *to the way in which the Convention operated*. Thus some cast doubt on the participatory credentials of the Convention, pointing to the increasing centralization of initiative in the Praesidium, especially in the latter stages of the Convention, which left scant time for deliberation of amendments. This was problematic and did not conform to some 'ideal-type' vision of drafting a Constitution. The Convention did not however exist within an ideal-type world. It conducted its task against the real world conditions laid down by the European Council. Once the European Council reaffirmed the deadline the Praesidium had little choice but to take a more pro-active role, since otherwise the Constitutional Treaty would not have been presented to the European Council in June 2003. The absence of the strict deadline would, moreover, still have required 'someone' to have been pro-active in deciding which amendments should be pursued.[121]

A third area of debate concerned the *content of the CT*. It will come as no surprise to learn that there was significant disagreement as to the content of the CT, judged both overall and in relation to particular provisions. In terms of overall judgement, some were critical about the further federalization which they believed to result from the CT, focusing on, for example, provisions that altered voting requirements in the Council from unanimity to qualified majority; others were equally critical about what they saw as the increased intergovernmentalism in the CT, focusing on, for example, enhanced Member State influence in the provisions concerning the inter-institutional distribution of power, the creation of the long-term Presidency of the European Council, and the like. There were also significant differences of view concerning particular provisions of the CT. Thus, for example, some applauded the distribution of competences in the CT, while others were critical, arguing that the provisions were unclear and uncertain. There was a similar spectrum of views on matters such as the balance between the social and economic dimensions in the CT, and the extent to which the Second and Third Pillars had been successfully integrated into the new, more unified Treaty structure. It is not possible, within the confines of this chapter, to 'resolve' debates on these complex issues. Any 'judgement' is best reserved for later chapters, when the relevant CT provisions are considered in more detail. We should nonetheless retain a sense of overall perspective on the content of the CT. It was a relatively conservative document, and did not extend the EU's power to the same extent as had been done by the TEU or even the SEA.

There has also been a vibrant discourse on *what should happen in the light of the negative referenda in France and the Netherlands*.[122] Some contend that while the rejection of the CT by the French and Dutch voters had little to do with its content, grand constitution-making is neither necessary nor desirable, since there is already a relatively stable constitutional settlement in place. The EU should rather get on with its normal business.[123] Others broadly agree

---

[121] To put this point in perspective: it was common for draft articles of the CT to have 50 or more amendments lodged by members of the Convention.

[122] G. de Búrca, 'The European Constitution Project after the Referenda' (2006) 13 *Constellations* 205.

[123] See, e.g., A. Moravcsik, 'Europe without Illusions: A Category Error' (2005) 112 *Prospect*, available at www.prospectmagazine.co.uk/landing_page.php.

with this diagnosis of the French and Dutch referenda, but maintain that the EU needs some constituent document as it moves forward in the new millennium.[124] Yet others see the rejection of the CT as evidence of a deeper malaise within the EU, which cannot and should not be ignored.[125]

Treaty reform has, as seen above, been started once again with the European Council's agreement in June 2007 to the Reform Treaty, the details of which are to be worked out in an IGC. While the Constitutional Treaty has, in formal terms, been jettisoned, it nonetheless remains the official starting point for the content of the Reform Treaty. Many of the provisions of the CT will therefore be found in the Reform Treaty, some will be modified, others will not. It is too early at the time of writing to pass any judgement on this latest saga of Treaty reform, since the detailed provisions are not available. We should, moreover, not forget that the completed Reform Treaty would still require ratification in all Member States, and while most Member States seek to avoid a referendum, whether justifiably or not, the Reform Treaty must nonetheless be ratified in accord with the constitutional requirements of each State.

12. FURTHER READING

(a) Books

Bond, M., and Feus, K., *The Treaty of Nice Explained* (Federal Trust, 2001)

Chryssochoou, D., *Theorizing European Integration* (Sage, 2001)

Corbett, R., *The Treaty of Maastricht* (Longman, 1993)

Duff, A. (ed.), *The Treaty of Amsterdam* (Sweet & Maxwell, 1997)

Holland, M., *European Integration from Community to Union* (Pinter, 1993)

MacCormick, N., *Who's Afraid of a European Constitution?* (Imprint Academic, 2005)

Monar, J., and Wessels, W., *The European Union after the Treaty of Amsterdam* (Continuum, 2001)

Moravcsik, A., *The Choice for Europe* (University College London Press, 1999)

—— (ed.), *Europe without Illusions* (University Press of America, 2005)

Norman, P., *The Accidental Constitution, The Making of Europe's Constitutional Treaty* (EuroComment, 2005)

O'Keefe, D., and Twomey, P. (eds.), *Legal Issues of the Amsterdam Treaty* (Hart, 1999)

Pinder, J., *The Building of the European Union* (3rd edn., Oxford University Press, 1998)

Winter, J., Curtin, D., Kellermann, A., and De Witte, B., *Reforming the Treaty on European Union: The Legal Debate* (Kluwer, 1996)

---

[124] See, e.g., A. Duff, 'Plan B: How to Rescue the European Constitution', Notre Europe, Studies and Research No. 52, 2006.

[125] See, e.g., L. Siedentop, 'A Crisis of Legitimacy' (2005) 112 *Prospect*, available at www.prospectmagazine. co.uk/landing_page.php.

(b) Articles

Bellamy, R., 'The European Constitution is Dead, Long live European Constitutionalism' (2006) 13 *Constellations* 181

Craig, P., 'Constitutional Process and Reform in the EU: Nice, Laeken, the Convention and the IGC' (2004) 10 *EPL* 653

Curtin, D., 'The Constitutional Structure of the Union: A Europe of Bits and Pieces' (1993) 30 *CMLRev.* 17

De Búrca, G., 'The European Constitution Project after the Referenda' (2006) 13 *Constellations* 205

Dehousse, R., 'The Unmaking of a Constitution: Lessons from the European Referenda' (2006) 13 *Constellations* 151

Duff, A., 'Plan B: How to Rescue the European Constitution', Notre Europe, Studies and Research No. 52, 2006

Walker, N., 'A Constitutional Reckoning' (2003) 13 *Constellations* 140

Weiler, J., 'The Transformation of Europe' (1991) 100 *Yale LJ* 2403

Wouters, J., 'Institutional and Constitutional Challenges for the European Union: Some Reflections in the Light of the Treaty of Nice' (2001) 26 *ELRev.* 342

Yataganas, X., 'The Treaty of Nice: The Sharing of Power and the Institutional Balance in the European Union—A Continental Perspective' (2001) 7 *ELJ* 242

Ziller, J., 'Une constitution courte et obscure ou claire et détaillée? Perspectives pour la simplification des traités et la rationalisation de l'ordre juridique de l'union européenne', EUI Working Papers, Law 2006/31.

2

THE INSTITUTIONS

1. CENTRAL ISSUES

i.   There are five principal institutions mentioned in Article 7 EC entrusted with carrying out the tasks of the Community: the Council, the Commission, the European Parliament, the Court of Auditors, and the Court of Justice. This chapter will consider the role of each institution in the Community and the way in which they interrelate. We shall also consider other important institutions such as the European Council, the Economic and Social Committee, the Committee of the Regions, and agencies. The EC's monetary institutions will, however, be discussed later.[1]

ii. This chapter should not be approached with any preconceptions about the traditional division of governmental functions into categories of legislative, executive, administrative, and judicial. Many of these duties are shared between institutions, thereby rendering it impossible to describe any one of them as the sole legislator or the sole executive. The Community does not therefore conform to any rigid separation-of-powers principle of the sort that has shaped certain domestic political systems.

iii. The pattern of institutional competence within the Community has not remained static. It has altered both as a consequence of subsequent Treaty revisions and as a result of organic change in the political balance of power between the institutions over time, including through the emergence of a web of committees and institutional actors beyond the original 'canonical' institutions.

iv. The implications of the Constitutional Treaty[2] for the institutions will be considered in this chapter. The broader implications of the CT provisions for law-making and the locus of legislative and executive power will be considered in a subsequent chapter.[3]

2. THE COMMISSION

(a) THE COLLEGE OF COMMISSIONERS: APPOINTMENT AND REMOVAL

It is important to understand at the outset that the term 'Commission' connotes both the College of Commissioners and the permanent Brussels bureaucracy which staffs the Commission services.[4] The discussion begins with the former.

---

[1] See Ch. 20.
[2] Treaty Establishing a Constitution for Europe [2004] OJ C310/1.
[3] See 138–142.
[4] N. Nugent, *The European Commission* (Palgrave, 2001); A. Stevens, with H. Stevens, *Brussels Bureaucrats? The Administration of the European Union* (Palgrave, 2001); L. Hooghe, *The European Commission and the*

The method of choosing Commissioners has been altered, with the consequence that the Parliament has more say in the process than hitherto. Under Article 214(2) the Council, meeting as the Heads of State and acting by qualified majority, nominates the person intended to be appointed as President of the Commission. This nomination must be approved by the European Parliament (EP). The Council, acting by qualified majority and by common accord with the nominee for President, adopts a list of proposed Commissioners, drawn up in accordance with the proposals made by each Member State. The President and the other Commissioners are then subject to a vote of approval by the EP. Prospective Commissioners are now subject to scrutiny by the relevant parliamentary committee before being approved by the EP. Once this approval has been secured the Council, acting by qualified majority, appoints the President and Commissioners. The main amendment introduced by the Treaty of Nice, TN, is that the operative Council decisions are reached by qualified majority, whereas previously they were made by common accord. Commissioners hold office for five years, and this term is renewable: Article 214(1) EC.

An individual Commissioner can be compulsorily retired if he or she no longer fulfils the conditions for the performance of his or her duties, or in the event of serious misconduct. This decision is made by the ECJ on application by the Council: Article 216 EC. The difficulty of removing individual Commissioners was, as we shall see, part of the problem leading to the downfall of the Santer Commission. Article 216 was therefore supplemented by Article 217(4), introduced by the TN. It provides that a Commissioner shall resign if the President so requests, after obtaining the approval of the College of Commissioners.

(b) THE COLLEGE OF COMMISSIONERS: COMPOSITION

Article 213(1) provides that Commissioners must be chosen on grounds of their general competence and their independence must not be in doubt. Thus while Commissioners come from the Member States they do not represent their own States. This is further reinforced by Article 213(2), which states that Commissioners must be completely independent in the performance of their duties, and can neither seek nor take instructions from any other body. The Commissioners meet collectively as the College of Commissioners. The Commission operates under the guidance of its President, whose organizational powers have been strengthened by the TN reforms, and the Commissioners take decisions by majority vote.[5]

Article 213, as amended by the Protocol on Enlargement in the TN, stipulates that from 1 January 2005 there shall be one Commissioner from each Member State, and that the Council, acting unanimously, can alter the number of members of the Commission. However, when the Union reaches twenty-seven Member States (it now has) Article 213(1) is further modified, such that the number of Commissioners is less than the number of Member States. It is for the Council acting unanimously to decide on the precise number of Commissioners and, acting on the principle of equality, to adopt a rotation system.

These provisions were the result of differences of view in the Intergovernmental Conference (IGC) leading to the TN, where opinion was divided on whether there should

Integration of Europe (Cambridge University Press, 2002); M. Pollack, *The Engines of European Integration: Delegation, Agency and Agenda Setting in the EU* (Oxford University Press, 2003); A. Smith, (ed.), *Politics and the European Commission: Actors, Independence, Legitimacy* (Routledge, 2004); D. Dimitrakopoulos, (ed.), *The Changing European Commission* (Manchester University Press, 2004); D. Spence, (ed.), *The European Commission* (Harper, 2006).

[5] Art. 219 EC.

continue to be one Commissioner from each State, or whether there should be an upper limit combined with a system of rotation.[6] The argument for the latter view was that Commissioners do not represent their States, and that the operation of a Commission with twenty-seven Commissioners could cross the line between a collegiate body and a deliberative assembly.

The Commissioners have their personal staffs (or cabinets), consisting partly of national and partly of Community officials.[7] There will normally be six officials in these teams, although the President of the Commission may have a larger cabinet. The members of the cabinet perform a variety of functions: they liaise with other parts of the Commission, scrutinize draft regulations and directives, and keep the Commissioner informed about developments in other connected areas. There have however been tensions between the cabinets and the Commission bureaucracy, with the former being regarded as representing national rather than Community interests.

(c) THE COLLEGE OF COMMISSIONERS: DECISION-MAKING

The College of Commissioners operates in four different ways.[8] More important matters are dealt with through meetings of the College, which occur weekly, and the agenda is prepared by the Secretariat-General. These meetings will be preceded by discussion held by the Commissioners' *chefs de cabinet*, who will try to resolve differences in advance of the College meeting. Matters on which the *chefs de cabinet* have agreed will be designated as 'A points', and will not normally require discussion within the College. There may also be meetings of Commission groups, designed to co-ordinate the activities of the Commission. Prodi established five such groups, and this practice has been continued by Barroso, with groups of Commissioners responsible for the Lisbon agenda, external relations, communications, equal opportunities, and competitiveness.

The written procedure is used where 'deliberations in College do not seem to be necessary because all points have been agreed by the relevant DGs and approval has been given by the Legal Service'.[9] The proposal is sent to the Commissioners' cabinets, and if there is no objection within a specified period the decision is made. Any Commissioner can raise objections and request that the measure be considered at a College meeting.

A third mode of decision-making is empowerment, whereby the Commission empowers an individual Commissioner to make a decision, while respecting the principle of collective responsibility.

There is finally the possibility of delegating decision-making to directors-general and heads of service, who act on behalf of the Commission. This procedure is used for routine business.

(d) THE PRESIDENCY OF THE COMMISSION

The Presidency of the Commission is a position of real significance. The holder of this post is clearly *primus inter pares* as compared with the other Commissioners, and the President's

---

6 Presidency Note, CONFER 4813/00, 1 Dec. 2000.
7 Nugent, n. 4 above, ch. 5.
8 *Ibid.*, 94–101.
9 *Ibid.*, 94.

powers were increased as a result of the TN. Article 217 provides that the Commission shall work under the political guidance of its President, who shall decide on its internal organization in order to ensure that it acts consistently, efficiently, and on the basis of collegiality. The responsibilities incumbent on the Commission shall be structured and allocated among the Commissioners by the President, who has power to reshuffle the portfolios. The President will therefore decide upon portfolios within the Commission, but there will be negotiations, often intense, between the Commissioners, the President, and the Member States about 'who gets what'. The President can also, after obtaining the approval of the College, appoint Vice-Presidents from among the Commissioners. We have also seen that the President was given power to remove individual Commissioners.

The President plays an important role in shaping overall Commission policy, in negotiating with the Council and the Parliament, and in determining the future direction of the Community.[10] How much is made of the post will depend on the personality and vision of the incumbent.[11] Jacques Delors had a strong personality and a vision for the Community's development. Many of the broader Community initiatives were in no small measure the result of his leadership within the Commission.[12]

(e) THE COMMISSION BUREAUCRACY

The permanent officials who work in the Commission and who form the Brussels bureaucracy are organized as follows.

Directorates General (DGs) cover the major internal areas over which the Commission has responsibility. There are now DGs for: Agriculture; Competition; Economic and Financial Affairs; Education and Culture; Employment, Social Affairs and Equal Opportunities; Enterprise and Industry; Environment; Fisheries and Maritime Affairs; Health and Consumer Protection; the Information and Media Society; Internal Market and Services; the Joint Research Centre; Justice, Freedom and Security; Regional Policy; Research; Taxation and Customs Union; and Transport and Energy. There are DGs dealing with external relations, including: Development, Enlargement, the EuropeAid-Co-operation Office, External Relations, Humanitarian Aid, and Trade. Financial matters are dealt with by the DGs for Budget and the Internal Audit Service.

There are also units which provide general services across the spectrum of Commission activities. These include: the European Anti-Fraud Office (OLAF),[13] Eurostat, Communication, the Publications Office, the Translation Service, the Legal Service, Personnel and Administration, the Joint Research Centre, and the Secretariat General of the Commission.

There are essentially four layers within the Commission bureaucracy.[14] There is the Commissioner who has the portfolio for that area. Then there is the Director General who is the head of a particular DG. There are Directors. Each DG will have a number of Directorates

---

[10] *Ibid.*, ch. 3.

[11] J. Peterson, 'The Santer Era: The European Commission in Normative, Historical and Theoretical Perspective' (1999) 6 *JEPP* 46.

[12] N. Nugent, 'The Leadership Capacity of the European Commission' (1995) 2 *JEPP* 603.

[13] This office is still at present part of the Commission, although it has an individual independent status for its investigative functions and is significantly more independent than the anti-fraud unit which it replaced. See Commission Dec. 99/352/EC, ECSC, Euratom establishing the European Anti-fraud Office (OLAF) [1999] OJ L136/20.

[14] Nugent, n. 4 above, 138–142; A. Stevens with H. Stevens, n. 4 above, ch. 8.

within it, commonly somewhere between four and six, and each of these Directorates will normally be headed by a Director who is responsible to the Director General. The final part of the administrative organization is the Head of Division or Unit. These are parts of Directorates. Each Division or Unit will have a Head who will be responsible to the relevant Director.

Decisions and draft legislative proposals will normally emanate from a lower part of this hierarchy, upwards towards the College of Commissioners. There will be detailed discussion of the legislative process later.[15] Suffice it to say for the present that a proposal will usually originate within the relevant DG. Outside experts will often be used at this formative stage, and there will be consultation with national civil servants. The draft proposal will then pass up through the DGs to the cabinets of the relevant Commissioners, and on to the weekly meeting held by the *chefs de cabinet*. From there it will proceed to the College of Commissioners, which may accept it, reject it, or suggest amendments. Matters are obviously more complex when a proposed measure affects more than one area, and hence more than one DG may be involved.

It is, moreover, not uncommon for the different DGs involved with a measure to have a 'different angle' on the problem. The term 'multi-organization' has been used to describe the priorities of different parts of the administration.[16] It is for this reason that consultations within the Commission will precede the meeting of the College of Commissioners. Formal meetings will be held by the *chefs de cabinet*, the object being to try to reach agreement before the College convenes. The meeting of the *chefs de cabinet* will receive input from discussion sessions held by the particular member of a cabinet who specializes in the relevant area. In addition there will be informal exchanges between opposite numbers within the bureaucracy at all levels, including the Commissioners themselves, members of differing cabinets, and officials who work in DGs with an interest in a measure. The Secretariat-General will also play an important role in co-ordinating the drafting of legislative initiatives within the Commission as a whole.

The basic principle within the Commission is for positions and promotions to be based upon merit, determined by competitive examination. This meritocratic principle is, however, qualified by the fact that Member States will take a keen interest to ensure that their own nationals are properly represented, particularly in the senior posts. For this reason it has been traditional for an informal quota regime to operate in the allocation of such jobs.[17] Whether this can still survive is more doubtful, given that the Court has held that job allocation should not be predetermined and should be decided on merit.[18] We shall return to this issue when considering reform of the Commission.

There has been much carping over the years about the size of the Brussels bureaucracy. This is largely based on ignorance of the facts. In 2005 the Commission employed only just over 24,000 full-time officials.

[15] See Ch. 4.

[16] L. Cram, 'The European Commission as a Multi-Organisation: Social Policy and IT Policy in the EU' (1994) 1 *JEPP* 194.

[17] Nugent, n. 4 above, 174–176.

[18] Case 105/75 *Giuffrida* v. *Council* [1976] ECR 1395.

(f) POWERS OF THE COMMISSION

The powers of the Commission are set out in Article 211 EC:

> In order to ensure the proper functioning and development of the common market, the Commission shall:
>
> — ensure that the provisions of this Treaty and measures taken by the institutions pursuant thereto are applied;
>
> — formulate recommendations or deliver opinions on matters dealt with in this Treaty, if it expressly so provides or if the Commission considers it necessary;
>
> — have its own power of decision and participate in the shaping of measures taken by the Council and by the European Parliament in the manner provided for in this Treaty;
>
> — exercise the powers conferred on it by the Council for the implementation of the rules laid down by the latter.

A 'bare' reading of Article 211 does little to convey the role played by the Commission in the Community, and it is at the heart of many Community initiatives. The Community is not characterized by any rigid doctrine of separation of powers, and the Commission has legislative, administrative, executive, and judicial powers.

(i) Legislative Power

The Commission plays a central part in the legislative process, the details of which will be discussed below.[19] An outline of the Commission's legislative powers will be given here. The most important is the Commission's right of legislative initiative. It has this right because the common format is for the Treaties to stipulate that the Council and European Parliament will act on a proposal from the Commission when making legislation.[20] This right of initiative places it in the forefront of the development of policy. Although legislative proposals will have to be approved by the Council and, in many circumstances, by the European Parliament, the Commission's right of initiative has enabled it to act as a 'motor of integration' for the Community as a whole. Furthermore, the Commission may exercise influence over the Council in diverse ways.[21] It should be noted, however, that the Council can be the *de facto* source of legislative initiatives, even if the details of these suggestions are then given more concrete form by the Commission.[22]

A second way in which the Commission impacts on the legislative process is that it develops the overall legislative plan for any single year. The agenda-setting aspect of the Commission's work is of real significance in shaping the Community's priorities for the forthcoming year.[23]

The Commission also affects Community policy in a third way, by developing general policy strategies for the Community. This is exemplified by the Commission's White Paper on the Completion of the Internal Market,[24] which shaped the Single European Act. Commission

---

[19] See Ch. 4.

[20] This is qualified most importantly by Art. 67 EC, and by provisions dealing with the Second and Third Pillars. See Chs. 6–7.

[21] S. Schmidt, 'Only an Agenda Setter?: the European Commission's Power over the Council of Ministers' (2000) 1 *EUP* 37.

[22] See 52 below.

[23] See 128–129 below.

[24] COM(85)310.

initiatives under the Presidency of Jacques Delors contributed to the development of Economic and Monetary Union. The Commission's Community Charter of the Fundamental Social Rights of Workers[25] (the Social Charter) was important in the debates about Community social policy. A further example is the Commission White Paper on European Governance.[26]

A fourth way in which the Commission exercises legislative power is through its capacity, in certain limited areas, to enact Community norms without the formal involvement of any other Community institution.[27]

Finally, the Commission exercises delegated legislative power.[28] This is expressly contemplated by the fourth indent of Article 211. The Council will delegate power to the Commission to make further regulations within particular areas.

(ii) Administrative Power

The Commission also has significant administrative responsibilities. Policies, once made, have to be administered. Legislation, once enacted, must be implemented. This will commonly be through shared administration, using national agencies.[29] The Commission will maintain a general supervisory overview, in order to ensure that the rules are uniformly and properly applied within the Member States. There can be difficulties in executing this supervisory role successfully, as will be seen below.[30] It has also become increasingly common for the Commission to exercise direct administrative responsibility for the implementation of certain Community policy.[31]

(iii) Executive Power

The Commission possesses responsibilities of an executive nature. Two are of particular importance: those relating to finance and those concerning external relations.

The Commission plays an important role in the establishment of the Community's budget. It also has significant powers over expenditure, particularly in relation to agricultural support, which takes a substantial share of the Community's annual budget, and structural policy, which is designed, *inter alia*, to assist poorer regions to convert or adjust declining industries and combat long-term unemployment.

The Commission also exercises executive powers in the sphere of external relations. Nugent explains.

N. Nugent, The Government and Politics of the European Union[32]

First, the Commission is centrally involved in determining and conducting the EU's external trade relations. On the basis of Article 133 TEC, and with its actions always subject to Council approval, the Commission represents and acts on behalf of the EU both in formal negotiations, such as those that are conducted under the auspices of the World Trade Organisation (WTO),

---

[25] See Ch. 21 below.
[26] European Governance: A White Paper, COM(2001)428, and The Future of European Union—European Governance: Renewing the Community Method, COM(2001)727.
[27] See 110 below.
[28] See 118–123 below.
[29] P. Craig, *EU Administrative Law* (Oxford University Press, 2006), ch. 3.
[30] See 45–46.
[31] Craig, n. 29 above, ch. 2.
[32] (6th edn., Oxford University Press, 2006), 186–187.

and in the more informal and explanatory exchanges that are common between, for example, the EU and the USA over world agricultural trade, and between the EU and Japan over access to each other's markets.

Second, the Commission has important negotiating and managing responsibilities in respect of the various special external agreements that the EU has with many countries and groups of countries. . . .

Third, the Commission represents the EU at, and participates in the work of, a number of important international organizations. Three of these are specifically mentioned in the TEC: the United Nations and its specialized agencies (Article 302); the Council of Europe (Article 303); and the Organization for Economic Cooperation and Development (Article 304).

Fourth, the Commission has responsibilities for acting as a key point of contact between the EU and non-member States. Over 160 countries have diplomatic missions accredited to the EU. . . . The EU, for its part, maintains an extensive network of diplomatic missions abroad, numbering over 130 delegations and offices, and these are staffed by Commission employees.

Fifth, . . . the Commission is entrusted with important responsibilities with regard to applications for EU membership. Upon receipt of an application the Council normally asks the Commission to carry out a detailed investigation of the implications and to submit an opinion. If and when negotiations begin, the Commission, operating within Council-approved guidelines, acts as the EU's main negotiator, except on showpiece ministerial occasions or when particularly sensitive or difficult matters call for an inter-ministerial resolution of differences. . . .

Finally, the Commission is 'fully associated' with the work carried out under the CFSP pillar of the TEU.

(iv) *Judicial Power*

The Commission possesses two kinds of judicial powers, which are based on the first indent to Article 211.

The Commission brings actions against Member States when they are in breach of Community law.[33] The actions will be brought under Article 226 EC and will assume the form of *Commission* v. *Germany*, etc. Recourse to formal legal action will be a last resort and will be preceded by Commission efforts to resolve the matter through negotiation.

The Commission also acts in certain areas as investigator and initial judge of a Treaty violation, whether by private firms or by Member States. The two most important areas are competition policy[34] and state aids.[35] The Commission's decision will be reviewable by the Community's judiciary, normally by the Court of First Instance (CFI). Notwithstanding the existence of judicial review, the Commission's investigative and adjudicative powers provide it with a significant tool for the development of Community policy.

(g) THE DOWNFALL OF THE SANTER COMMISSION AND SUBSEQUENT REFORM

There had been concern in the EC for some considerable time about fraud and mismanagement, particularly in areas such as the Common Agricultural Policy.[36] This culminated in the

[33] See Ch. 12.

[34] See Chs. 25–27.

[35] See Ch. 28.

[36] D. Spence, 'Plus Ça Change, Plus C'est La Meme Chose? Attempting to Reform the European Commission' (2000) 7 *JEPP* 1.

setting up of a Committee of Independent Experts, under the auspices of the European Parliament and the Commission, with a mandate to deal with fraud, mismanagement, and nepotism. The Committee produced its first report in March 1999,[37] the concluding paragraph of which spoke in terms of it 'becoming difficult to find anyone who has even the slightest sense of responsibility' within the Commission.[38] The Report had an immediate, dramatic effect: the Commission resigned *en bloc*. The principal problem revealed by the Committee's Report was not however fraud by the Commission. It was the difficulty of maintaining control over those to whom power had been contracted out,[39] which is an endemic problem for all systems of public administration.[40]

Romano Prodi, the new Commission President, introduced a new Code of Conduct for Commissioners,[41] and set up the Task Force for Administrative Reform (TFRA). The TFRA produced a White Paper,[42] which was heavily influenced by the valuable recommendations made in the Second Report of the Committee of Independent Experts.[43] The general theme of the White Paper was the need for the Commission to concentrate more on its core functions such as policy conception, political initiative, and enforcing Community law. Steps were to be taken to ensure greater linkage between priorities and resources, and to ensure that the requisite resources existed when new tasks were given to the Commission. Activities would be delegated to other bodies, so as to enable the Commission to concentrate on its core activities.[44] 'Externalisation' was to be used only where it was the most efficient option; it would not be pursued at the expense of accountability; and there would have to be sufficient internal resources to ensure proper control. There was to be a new type of implementing body to be headed by Community staff,[45] and important recommendations were also made about staffing and financial control.

The new Financial Regulation has taken up many of these ideas, thereby providing a constitutional framework for much Community administration.[46] The idea that there should be a new breed of agency to oversee work that has been contracted out has also been accepted,[47] and a number of new such agencies have been created.[48]

(h) THE IMPACT OF THE CT

The Constitutional Treaty was significant for the organization of the Commission in two respects. It provided for the Commission President to be indirectly elected. The European Council, taking account of the elections to the European Parliament, would propose to the EP a candidate for election as Commission President, and the candidate would then be elected by

---

[37] Committee of Independent Experts, First Report on Allegations regarding Fraud, Mismanagement and Nepotism in the European Commission, 15 Mar. 1999, para. 1.4.2.

[38] *Ibid.*, para. 9.4.25.

[39] P. Craig, 'The Fall and Renewal of the Commission: Accountability, Contract and Administrative Organization' (2000) 6 *ELJ* 98.

[40] P. Craig, *Administrative Law* (5th edn., Sweet & Maxwell, 2003), ch. 5; M. Freedland, 'Government by Contract and Private Law' [1994] *PL* 86.

[41] The Formation of the Commission, 12 July 1999. See also Operation of the Commission, 12 July 1999.

[42] Reforming the Commission, COM(2000)200.

[43] Committee of Independent Experts, Second Report on Reform of the Commission, Analysis of Current Practice and Proposals for Tackling Mismanagement, Irregularities and Fraud, 10 Sept. 1999.

[44] Reforming the Commission, n. 42 above, Part I, 6.

[45] *Ibid.*

[46] Council Reg. (EC, Euratom) 1605/2002 of 25 June 2002 on the Financial Regulation applicable to the General Budget of the European Communities [2002] OJ L248/1.

[47] Council Reg. (EC) 58/2003 of 19 Dec. 2002 laying down the Statute for Executive Agencies to be entrusted with certain tasks in the management of Community Programmes [2003] OJ L11/1.

[48] Craig, n. 29 above, ch. 2.

the EP, with provision being made for what was to happen if the candidate did not get the requisite majority in the EP.[49]

The CT also contained provisions concerning the composition of the Commission. Opinion was divided as to whether there should continue to be one Commissioner from each State, or whether there should be an upper limit combined with rotation. The argument for the latter view was that Commissioners do not represent their States, and that a Commission with twenty-five or twenty-seven Commissioners could cross the line between a collegiate body and a deliberative assembly. The Draft CT as it emerged from the Convention opted for a compromise solution in which there would be voting and non-voting Commissioners. This was strongly opposed by the Commission itself, and rightly so, since it would have proven unworkable in practice.

The IGC modified these provisions. Article I–26 CT provided that the first Commission appointed under the CT would have a Commissioner from each Member State, plus the President of the Commission and the Union Minister for Foreign Affairs. After the first term of office, the Commission was to consist of the President and the Minister for Foreign Affairs, and members corresponding to two thirds of the Member States, unless the European Council acting unanimously decided to alter this figure.

(i) ROLE OF THE COMMISSION: CONCLUSION

The Commission has always been the political force most committed to integration, ever seeking to press forward to attain the Community's objectives.[50] It must perforce work with the Council and the EP, and the pace of Community development has not always been steady because of this inter-institutional dimension.[51]

There is literature that sees the Commission's influence as in decline, as exemplified by its relatively low impact on the negotiations leading to the Treaty of Nice and the Constitutional Treaty.[52] A more positive picture has however been advanced by other writers, who focus on the continuing importance of the Commission bureaucracy.[53] The degree of power wielded by the Commission and the best way to explain the extent of Commission influence are therefore debated by political scientists. The following extract presents a spectrum of views.

J. Peterson, The College of Commissioners[54]

If the Commission really was so weak, intergovernmentalist accounts of EU politics ... could be marshalled to explain why. First, it makes little difference who is Commission President.

---

[49] Art. I–27(1) CT.

[50] See, e.g., the Commission's communication prior to the Laeken European Council, The Future of the European Union—European Governance: Renewing the Community Method, COM(2001)727.

[51] See Chs. 1, 4.

[52] H. Kassim and A. Menon, 'EU Member States and the Prodi Commission', in D. Dimitrakopoulos (ed.), *The Changing European Commission* (Manchester University Press, 2004), ch. 5.

[53] See, e.g., L. Hooghe and N. Nugent, 'The Commission Services', in J. Peterson and M. Shackleton (eds.), *The Institutions of the European Union* (2nd edn., Oxford University Press, 2006), ch. 8; T. Christiansen, 'The European Commission: The European Executive between Continuity and Change', in J. Richardson (ed.), *European Union, Power and Policy-Making* (3rd edn., Routledge, 2006), ch. 5; M. Rhinard and B. Vaccari, 'The Study of the European Commission' (2005) 12 *JEPP* 387.

[54] Peterson and Shackleton (eds.), n. 53 above, 98–99. See also D. Rometsch and W. Wessels, 'The Commission and the Council of Ministers', in G. Edwards and D. Spence (eds.), *The European Commission* (Longman, 1994), 203.

Second, the Commission is only powerful when and where national preferences converge. Third, the Commission is only empowered to the extent that member governments want to ensure the 'credibility of their commitments to each other'. There is little dispute, among scholars as well as practitioners, that the Commission has traditionally had little influence over most 'history-making' decisions about the broad sweep of European integration.

In contrast, institutionalist theory, now firmly established as the 'leading theoretical approach in EU studies' . . . paints a portrait of the Commission that is often powerful in day-to-day policy debates. . . . According to this view, policy decisions in complex systems such as the EU are difficult to reverse, and policy often becomes locked into existing paths and 'path dependent'. . . .

Some variants of institutionalism combine insights from rational choice and principal-agent theories. . . . They hold that the principal authorities in EU politics—the member governments themselves—make rational choices to delegate tasks to the EU institutions, which then become their agents in specific policy areas. This body of theory sheds light on the tendency for the EU to make policy by means other than the traditional 'Community method' of legislating, according to which only the Commission can propose. . . .

Increased affinity for new policy modes is . . . reflected in the creation of new regulatory agencies. . . . EU governments increasingly seem to want new kinds of agents—not just the Commission—to whom they can delegate cooperative policy tasks. Usually, however, the Commission retains the job of identifying and seeking to solve coordination problems within policy networks of . . . private actors, consumer and environmental groups, and national and European agencies.

Advocates of multi-level governance as an approach to understanding the EU have long contended that the Commission enjoys a privileged place at 'the hub of numerous highly specialized policy networks of technical experts' even retaining 'virtually a free hand in creating new networks'. . . .

3. THE COUNCIL

(a) COMPOSITION

Article 203 EC states that the Council[55] shall consist of a representative of each Member State at ministerial level who is authorized to commit the government of that State.[56] The members of the Council are, therefore, politicians as opposed to civil servants, but the politician can be a member of a regional government where this is appropriate. Article 204 states that the Council shall meet when convened by the President of the Council on his or her own initiative, or at the request of one of its members, or at the request of the Commission. There are approximately eighty Council meetings per year, most of which take place in Brussels, although in April, June, and October they are held in Luxembourg. These meetings are now more transparent than hitherto, as a result of changes introduced in June 2006.[57]

Council meetings are arranged by subject-matter with different ministers attending from the Member States, and are regulated by the Council's Rules of Procedure.[58] There are at

[55] It has been known as the Council of the European Union since 1993 [1993] OJ L281/18.

[56] M. Westlake and D. Galloway, *The Council of the European Union* (3rd edn., Harper, 2004); F. Hayes-Renshaw and H. Wallace, *The Council of Ministers* (2nd edn., Palgrave, 2006).

[57] Brussels European Council, Presidency Conclusions, 15–16 June 2006, Annex 1.

[58] Council Dec. 2006/683/EC, Euratom of 15 Sept. 2006 adopting the Council's Rules of Procedure [2006] OJ L285/47.

present nine such Council configurations, having been reduced from the much larger number of twenty-two that prevailed in the 1990s. The General Affairs and External Relations Council, GAERC, normally attended by foreign ministers, deals with external relations and many matters concerning general Community policy. The Economics and Finance Council (Ecofin), by way of contrast, is concerned with matters such as the budget, Economic and Monetary Union, and financial markets; finance ministers from the Member States attend this Council. There is a Council dealing with matters concerning Justice and Home Affairs. The other Council configurations deal with sectoral issues: Transport, Telecommunications and Energy; Employment, Social Policy, Health and Consumer Affairs; Agriculture and Fisheries; Competitiveness; Environment; and Education, Youth and Culture. The ministers responsible for these matters within the Member States will attend such meetings. They will be supported by their own delegations of national officials who have expertise in the relevant area. The Commission is invited to attend Council meetings.

(b) PRESIDENCY OF THE COUNCIL[59]

Article 203 EC provides for the Presidency of the Council to be held by each Member State in turn for six months. The position of President of the Council has assumed greater importance in recent years, for a number of reasons.[60] Strong central management has become more necessary in order to combat the centrifugal tendencies within the Council. The growing complexity of the Community's decision-making structure has necessitated more co-ordination between the institutions. The scope of EU power has increased, demanding greater leadership in the Council. The Council's wish to take a more proactive role in the development of Community policy has required initiatives which the President can help to organize. Westlake and Galloway capture the importance of the position when they state that 'the Presidency is neither an institution nor a body, but a function and an office which has become vital to the good working of the Council'.[61]

In more concrete terms the President will, seven months before taking office, set the dates for Council meetings in consultation with the Presidencies preceding and following its term of office.[62] Every eighteen months the three Presidencies due to hold office prepare, in consultation with the Commission, a draft programme of Council activities for that period, which has to be endorsed by the General Affairs and External Relations Council, GAERC.[63] The incoming Presidency establishes, at least one week before taking office, indicative provisional agendas for Council meetings for the next six-month period, based on the eighteen-month programme and after consulting the Commission.[64] During the actual six-month tenure, the President sets the provisional agenda for each Council meeting, which must be sent to other Council members and the Commission at least fourteen days before the meeting.[65] Part A of the agenda covers matters that can be approved without discussion; Part B deals with those matters that require deliberation.[66] The provisional agenda is then formally adopted at the beginning of the Council meeting.[67]

[59] E. Kirchner, *Decision-Making in the European Community: The Council Presidency and European Integration* (Manchester University Press, 1992).
[60] Westlake and Galloway, n. 56 above, ch. 18.
[61] *Ibid.*, 326.
[62] Council Dec. 2006/683/EC, n. 58 above, Art. 1.
[63] *Ibid.*, Art. 2(4).
[64] *Ibid.*, Art. 2(5).
[65] *Ibid.*, Art. 3(1).
[66] *Ibid.*, Art. 3(6).
[67] *Ibid.*, Art. 3(7).

The President may also develop policy initiatives within areas which are of particular concern either to the Council as a whole or to the Member State which currently holds the Presidency. The President will have an important liaison role to play with the Presidents of the Commission and the Parliament, and will represent the Council in discussions with institutions outside the Community. The Treaty imposes certain more particular obligations on the President, in relation to matters as diverse as the Common Foreign and Security Policy and the operation of the European Central Bank. It should moreover be noted that the President of the Council also holds the Chair of the European Council, the importance of which will be considered below.

While the Presidency therefore gives considerable power to the incumbent, the office is not without its stresses and pitfalls.[68] Presidencies must since 1989 draw up their programmes and present them to the Commission and the EP. Six months is a short time within which to get things done. The eyes of the other Member States will be focused, often critically and sharply, on the incumbent to determine the use to which the office has been put during that period. If a country tries to use its Presidency to achieve goals which are felt not to accord with the majority sentiment in the Council and which are too narrowly nationalistic, then the criticism is likely to be particularly harsh.[69]

(c) THE COMMITTEE OF PERMANENT REPRESENTATIVES

Article 207(1) EC states that the work of the Council is to be prepared by the Committee of Permanent Representatives (COREPER), and that it shall carry out the tasks assigned to it by the Council. COREPER is also empowered to adopt procedural decisions in cases provided for in the Council's rules of procedure. It does not, however, have the power to take formal substantive decisions in its own right, and must operate as an auxiliary to the Council,[70] but in practice COREPER 'has evolved into a veritable decision-making factory'.[71]

COREPER is staffed by senior national officials and it operates at two levels. COREPER II is the more important and consists of permanent representatives who are of ambassadorial rank. It deals with the more contentious matters such as economic and financial affairs and external relations. It also performs an important liaison role with the national governments. COREPER I is composed of deputy permanent representatives and is responsible for issues such as the environment, social affairs, the internal market, and transport.

COREPER plays an important part in EC decision-making,[72] in part because it will consider and digest draft legislative proposals that emanate from the Commission, and in part because it helps to set the agenda for Council meetings.[73] The agenda is divided into Parts A and B: the former includes those items which COREPER has agreed can be adopted by the Council without discussion; the latter will cover topics which do require discussion. It has been estimated that approximately 70–80 per cent of all Council decisions prepared by

---

[68] T. Christiansen, 'The Council of Ministers, Facilitating Interaction and Developing Actorness in the EU', in Richardson (ed.), n. 53 above, 155–159.

[69] Westlake and Galloway, n. 56 above, 334–337.

[70] Case C–25/94 *Commission* v. *Council* [1996] ECR I–1469.

[71] J. Lewis, 'National Interests: Coreper', in Peterson and Shackleton, n. 53 above, ch. 14.

[72] J. Lewis, 'The Methods of Community in EU Decision-Making and Administrative Rivalry in the Council's Infrastructure' (2000) 7 *JEPP* 261; D. Bostock, 'Coreper Revisited' (2002) 40 *JCMS* 215; Lewis, n. 71 above, ch. 14.

[73] Council Dec. 2006/683/EC, n. 58 above, Art. 19.

COREPER and/or working groups are then taken formally through the Council as 'A' points.[74] Decision-making within COREPER tends to be consensual, even where the formal voting rules specify qualified majority,[75] and Lewis notes that 'from a Janus-faced perspective, they act as both, and simultaneously, state agents and supranational entrepreneurs'.[76]

A large number of working groups, approximately 250, feeds into COREPER, although this number has diminished somewhat as a result of the reduction in the number of Council configurations. They are the lifeblood of the Council. These groups will examine legislative proposals from the Commission. They will be composed of national experts from the Member States or from the Permanent Representations. Their role in the policy-making process will be examined below.[77]

In addition to these working groups the Council will receive input from specialist committees established under the Treaty and from committees created by Community legislation.[78] There can be 'turf battles' between COREPER and other preparatory bodies, such as the Political and Security Committee and the Economic and Finance Committee.[79]

(d) THE COUNCIL SECRETARIAT

In addition to COREPER the Council also has its own General Secretariat, under the responsibility of a Secretary-General, which provides direct administrative support to it.[80] The Secretariat has a staff of about 2,800, and of these roughly 250 are 'A' grade, diplomatic level. This body will furnish administrative services to the Council itself and also to COREPER and the working parties. It will prepare documentation, give legal advice, undertake translation, process decisions, and take part in the preparation of agendas. It will also work closely with the staff of the President of the Council, helping to smooth conflicts and providing valuable information on the way in which such conflicts may best be resolved. The Secretary-General is an important figure, who is also now High Representative for the EU's foreign and security policy. The Secretary-General is assisted by a Deputy Secretary-General, who is responsible for running the General Secretariat. The Council Secretariat has become of increased importance over the years, especially in relation to EU Foreign and Defence Policy, Treaty negotiation,[81] and legal drafting.[82]

(e) POWERS OF THE COUNCIL

The powers of the Council are described in Article 202 EC, albeit in a rather vague manner:

> To ensure that the objectives set out in the Treaty are attained the Council shall, in accordance with the provisions of this Treaty:
>
> — ensure co-ordination of the general economic policies of the Member States;

---

[74] Christiansen, n. 68, above 162.

[75] Lewis, n. 71 above, ch. 14.

[76] *Ibid.*, 289.

[77] See 132.

[78] Hayes-Renshaw and Wallace, n. 56 above, ch. 3.

[79] Lewis, n. 71 above, 280–281.

[80] Art. 207(2).

[81] D. Beach, 'The Unseen Hand in Treaty Reform Negotiations: The Role and Impact of the Council Secretariat' (2004) 11 *JEPP* 408.

[82] Christiansen, n. 68 above, 164–167.

— have power to take decisions;

— confer on the Commission, in the acts which the Council adopts, powers for the implementation of the rules which the Council lays down. The Council may impose certain
requirements in respect of the exercise of these powers. The Council may also reserve
the right, in specific cases, to exercise directly implementing powers itself. The procedures referred to above must be consonant with principles and rules to be laid down in
advance by the Council, acting unanimously on a proposal from the Commission and after
obtaining the opinion of the European Parliament.

A simple reading of this provision does little to convey the reality of the Council's powers. Explanation is therefore required. The Council exercises an important role in the decision-making process in seven ways.

First and foremost, the Council has to vote its approval of virtually all Commission legislative initiatives before they become law. The vote will be by unanimity, qualified, or simple majority depending upon the particular Treaty Article.[83] Moreover, the draft proposal from the Commission will often be subject to considerable modification as a result of scrutiny by COREPER and the working parties.

Secondly, the Council has become more proactive in the legislative process through the use of Article 208. This states that the 'Council may request the Commission to undertake any studies which the Council considers desirable for the attainment of the common objectives, and to submit to it any appropriate proposals'. The Council has used this power to frame specific proposals which it wishes the Commission to shape into concrete legislation.[84] The Council has also increasingly made use of opinions and resolutions as a way of pressuring the Commission into generating legislative proposals.[85]

Thirdly, the Council can delegate power to the Commission, enabling the latter to pass further regulations within a particular area. It is now common for such delegations of power to be subject to the condition that the Commission action is acceptable to committees staffed by national representatives. This operates as a mechanism whereby the Council can ensure that the detail of the delegated legislation is in conformity with its own wishes.[86]

Fourthly, the increasing complexity of the Community's decision-making process has necessitated greater inter-institutional collaboration between the Commission, the Parliament, and the Council. This assumes various guises, from informal discussions concerning the shape of the legislative agenda to the use of Inter-institutional Agreements.[87]

Fifthly, the Council, together with the EP, plays a major role in relation to the EU's budget, on which many initiatives depend.

Sixthly, it will be the Council that will conclude agreements on behalf of the EC or the EU with non-Member States or international organizations.

Finally, in addition to the Council's powers under Pillar One, the EC Treaty, the Council also has significant powers under Pillars Two and Three. Thus, it will be the Council which takes the necessary decisions for defining and implementing the Common Foreign and Security Policy (CFSP) in the light of the guidelines laid down by the European Council,[88] and

---

[83] For a discussion of the Council's voting requirements see 123–125.

[84] Sir Leon Brittan, 'Institutional Development of the European Community' [1992] *PL* 567.

[85] Nugent, n. 32 above, 193.

[86] Council Dec. 1999/468/EC laying down the procedures for the exercise of implementing powers conferred on the Commission [1999] OJ L184/23; see 118–123.

[87] For a discussion of these agreements see 86–87, 129 below.

[88] Art. 13(3) TEU.

it is for the Council to adopt joint actions.[89] The Council also has important powers under the re-modelled Pillar Three, concerned with police and judicial co-operation in criminal matters.[90]

(f) THE IMPACT OF THE CT

The principal impact of the CT in relation to the Council concerned the Council formations, and who should chair them. There was much jockeying for relative power as between the new European Council President, the President of the Commission, and the Member States. The result was a compromise.[91]

There was to be General Affairs Council, GAC, with the task of ensuring consistency in the work of the different Council formations, and preparing and ensuring follow-up to meetings of the European Council, these latter two functions being done in liaison with the President of the European Council and the Commission. The Foreign Affairs Council, FAC, was to be chaired by the new Union Minister for Foreign Affairs. The European Council was to make a decision concerning the other Council formations. The Presidency of the Council formations was to be held by Member State representatives in the Council on the basis of equal rotation and the CT in effect embodied a 'team system' for the Presidency of Council formations, other than the FAC.

(g) ROLE OF THE COUNCIL: CONCLUSION

The Council represents national interests, and always has. Whether the framers of the original Rome Treaty would have been surprised by the way in which the Commission and Council have interrelated since the inception of the Community is unclear. They hoped that the formation of the EEC would herald an era of greater collaboration in which sectional, national interests would diminish in relation to the collective interests of the Community as a whole. The original decision-making structure of the Community certainly bore testimony to the central role accorded to the Commission, as evident from the range of its powers. To be sure, the Council had to approve legislation, but the Commission was in the driving seat. This was because of the Commission's power to set the legislative agenda, because of its institutional resources for the development of Community policy and because, while Council consent was required for the passage of legislation, unanimity was required for Council amendments to Commission proposals.

It would be wrong to depict the Commission and the Council as perpetually at odds with each other throughout the Community's history.[92] But it would be equally mistaken to view the two institutions as co-existing in perfect harmony. There have been real tensions between the federal pro-integration perspective of the Commission and the more cautious, intergovernmental perspective of the Council. The Treaty framers might have hoped that these tensions would be short-lived.[93] If this was so it was too optimistic a forecast. There have been a

---

[89] Art. 14(1) TEU.

[90] Art. 34 TEU.

[91] Art. I–24 CT.

[92] T. Christiansen, 'Intra-institutional Politics and Inter-institutional Relations in the EU: Towards Coherent Governance?' (2001) 8 *JEPP* 747.

[93] See Ch. 1 above.

number of institutional changes, often initially outside the strict letter of the Treaty, whereby the Council strengthened its own position in relation to that of the Commission. This 'temporal' perspective on decision-making will be charted more fully below.[94] Suffice it to say for the present that the development of a veto power in the Council, the growing importance of COREPER, the creation of committees to oversee the delegation of power to the Commission, and the evolution of the European Council all played a part in this process.

The balance of power within the Community is however dynamic, not static. The institutions' formal powers and the actual way in which they interrelate have altered across time. The SEA was the catalyst for a change of attitude on the part of the Member States as represented in the Council. There was a growing recognition that the threat of the veto, if a measure did not conform to a State's interests, was too negative. The SEA also made the European Parliament a more active force in Community decision-making than it had been hitherto. These developments do not mean that relationships between the Council and the Commission, or for that matter between the Council and the Parliament, will always be smooth. It does mean that the inter-institutional relationships that prevail within the Community have moved on. Thus as Christiansen notes, 'the Council may not (yet) be a supranational institution in its own right, but it has certainly moved on from being purely a site of decision-making and the forum for bargaining among representatives of national governments for which it was originally conceived'.[95] The same point is echoed by Hayes-Renshaw, who states that despite the Council being the EU's intergovernmental institution *par excellence*, it is, in reality, 'a unique blend of the intergovernmental and the supranational'.[96] This conclusion is also evident in the following extract.

F. Hayes-Renshaw and H. Wallace, The Council of Ministers[97]

The Council remains the fulcrum of the decision-making, and legislative process of the EU. This reflects the stubborn determination of member governments in the EU to maximize their involvement in framing the decisions and shaping the legislation that would have a bearing on their polities . . . Yet, to view the importance of the Council as the victory of inter-governmentalism over supranationalism, or to expect the Council to be able to 'run' the EU, is to misunderstand the institutional constellation of the EU. The Council shares and diffuses power between countries, between different kinds of interests and constituencies, and between national and EU levels of governance. The Council cannot act alone, but is dependent on intricate relationships with other EU institutions. Since the mid-1990s, however these relationships have changed a good deal. The European Parliament (EP) has gained considerable power as co-legislator with the Council, the Commission has lost ground in what used to be the classic 'Council-Commission tandem', and the Council has gained a good deal more direct executive power in newer areas of EU collective policy-making. All these factors have made the Council both more interesting as an object of study and more diverse in its ways of operating.

---

[94] See 126–128.
[95] N. 68, 148.
[96] Peterson and Shackleton, n. 53 above, 78.
[97] N. 56 above, 321.

4. THE EUROPEAN COUNCIL[98]

(a) COMPOSITION

The first mention of the European Council within a Treaty came in the SEA. The governing provision is now Article 4 TEU:

> The European Council shall provide the Union with the necessary impetus for its development and shall define the general political guidelines thereof.
>
> The European Council shall bring together the Heads of State or of Government of the Member States and the President of the Commission. They shall be assisted by the Ministers for Foreign Affairs of the Member States and by a Member of the Commission. The European Council shall meet at least twice a year, under the chairmanship of the Head of State or of Government of the Member State which holds the Presidency of the Council.
>
> The European Council shall submit to the European Parliament a report after each of its meetings and a yearly written report on the progress achieved by the Union.

Although Article 4 TEU mentions that the European Council will meet at least twice a year, the Lisbon European Council in 2000 decided that a further meeting would be held each spring, in the context of the EU's newly articulated economic, employment, and cohesion strategy.[99] The reality is that the European Council meets at least twice under each Presidency, therefore at least four times per year. Meetings of the European Council were in the past held in the country holding the Presidency of the Council. They are however now normally held in Brussels.

The European Council is mentioned on other occasions within the TEU. Thus, for example, Article 13 TEU provides that the European Council shall define the principles of and guidelines for the Common Foreign and Security Policy (CFSP). It shall decide on common strategies to be implemented by the Union in areas where the Member States have important interests in common.[100] The European Council is also accorded a role in certain provisions of the EC Treaty, normally in the context of politically sensitive matters, such as co-ordination of the economic policies of the Member States: Article 99(2).

(b) RATIONALE

The European Council has evolved over the years. Meetings of Heads of Government took place during the 1960s, but the decision to institutionalize them came in 1974 at the Paris summit. These meetings continued to be held during the 1970s and 1980s, even though there was no formal remit in the Treaty until the Single European Act.

This leads to the rationale for the European Council, given that Member States' interests are already represented in the Council. It was in part due to disagreements between the Member States themselves. These would normally be resolved through the ordinary Council

---

[98] S. Bulmer and W. Wessels, *The European Council* (Macmillan, 1987); P. de Schoutheete and H. Wallace, *The European Council* (Notre Europe, 2002), available at www.notre-europe.asso.fr; P. Ludlow, *The Making of the New Europe: The European Council in Brussels and Copenhagen 2002* (EuroComment, 2004); P. de Schoutheete, 'The European Council', in Peterson and Shackleton (eds.), n. 53 above, ch. 3.

[99] See pt. 7 of the Lisbon European Council conclusions, 24 Mar. 2000.

[100] See also Art. 17 TEU.

mechanisms, but if the disagreements were particularly severe or on important issues, such as the budget, then resolution might be possible only by intervention at the highest level, through the Heads of Government themselves. The evolution of the European Council was also due to the need for a focus of authority at the highest political level, in order that the general strategy for the EU's development could be planned, and in order that its response to broader world problems could be properly focused.

(c) ROLE

The paucity of Treaty references to the European Council should not lead one to doubt its importance. It plays a central role in setting the pace and shape of Community policy, establishing the parameters within which the other institutions operate. As Schoutheete states, 'management of the Union could not be assured without a top-level institution of this type: the European Council has played a fundamental role in European integration and will continue to do so'.[101] The issues which are commonly considered by the European Council vary, but can be grouped into the following categories.

The *European Council is central to the very development of the Community and Union itself.* Major changes in the Treaties will be preceded by an Intergovernmental Conference (IGC). The catalyst for the establishment of such conferences will normally come from a summit meeting of the European Council. Thus the IGC which laid the groundwork for the SEA was initiated by the summit held in Milan in June 1985. The European Council will not only initiate the IGC. It will also affirm the consequential Treaty changes, as exemplified by the Nice European Council[102] that approved the Nice Treaty, subject to ratification by the Member States. The European Council was, moreover, central to the debates about the Constitutional Treaty that had been drafted by the Convention on the Future of Europe.

The *European Council will often confirm important changes in the institutional structure of the Community.* The final decision on the enlargement of the Parliament following German unification was taken by a summit of the European Council.

The *European Council can provide the focus for significant constitutional initiatives that affect the operation of the Community and Union.* Inter-institutional Agreements between the three major institutions will often be made or finalized at a summit meeting. The Inter-institutional Agreement on Subsidiarity and the Declaration on Democracy, Transparency, and Subsidiarity were made at, or on the fringes of, such European Council meetings.

The *European Council will frequently consider the state of the European economy as a whole.*[103] This is in part because of Treaty provisions concerning closer economic union, which demand growing convergence between national economic policies. It is also because of the centrality of economic issues to the very health and vitality of the Community. For this reason the European Council has, for example, taken initiatives designed to combat unemployment, promote growth, and increase competitiveness (the Lisbon agenda).[104]

Conflict resolution is another issue addressed by the European Council. This was one of the rationales for its evolution, and it continues to be of importance. For example, budgetary matters,

---

[101] N. 98 above, 57.

[102] 8 Dec. 2000.

[103] See, e.g., Luxembourg Extraordinary European Council, 20 Nov. 1997; Stockholm European Council, 24 Mar. 2001.

[104] Lisbon European Council, Presidency Conclusions, 23–24 Mar. 2000; Nice European Council, Presidency Conclusions, 7–9 Dec. 2000; European Council, Presidency Conclusions, 22–23 Mar. 2005.

'who contributes how much, and who gets what financial benefits', continued to cause conflict between the Member States in the early 1980s, and then once again in the later 1980s.

The *European Council plays a role in the initiation or development of particular policy strategies*. Examples of this include the adoption of the Social Charter in 1989; policies aimed to combat problems concerning drugs and terrorism;[105] and the extension of the 'open method of coordination' to a range of social and economic policies.[106]

The *European Council is also central in external relations*. It will, for example, consider important international negotiations, such as those with the World Trade Organization (WTO). It will be the European Council which will issue declarations relating to more general international affairs, whether in relation to the civil war in what was Yugoslavia or the conflicts in Lebanon and Iraq.

The *European Council will also consider new accessions to the Community*. Thus, to take recent examples, the European Council affirmed that Bulgaria and Romania should be admitted to the EU in January 2007, and debated more generally the EU's approach to membership and enlargement.[107]

(d) THE IMPACT OF THE CT

The CT had important institutional implications for the European Council. Some Member States felt that the Presidency should no longer rotate between States on a six-monthly basis, since they believed that this would not work within an enlarged Union, which required greater continuity of policy. This view was advocated by a number of the larger States, but was opposed by some of the smaller States, which felt that the Presidency of the European Council would be dominated by the larger Member States.

The view of the larger Member States predominated in the Constitutional Treaty. It provided that the European Council should elect a President, by qualified majority, for two and half years, renewable once.[108] The European Council was to define the general political directions and priorities of the EU,[109] and the President of the European Council was given increased powers within the Council itself.[110]

(e) ROLE OF THE EUROPEAN COUNCIL: CONCLUSION

The European Council is a classic example of change in the original institutional structure of the Treaty to accommodate political reality. It evolved from a series of *ad hoc* meetings outside the letter of the Treaty to a more structured pattern of summits. Treaty-recognition was originally accorded in the SEA and has been modified by later Treaty amendments.

Yet, as we have seen, the brief mention of the European Council in the TEU does little to convey its real importance in the EU's decision-making process. The reality is that no important developments internally or externally occur without having been considered by the European Council. The concluding resolutions do not have the force of law. Nonetheless the European Council's conclusions provide the framework within which the other institutions consider

---

[105] Brussels Extraordinary European Council, 21 Sept. 2001.
[106] N. 104 above.
[107] Brussels European Council, Presidency Conclusions, 15–16 June 2006, paras. 52–53.
[108] Art. I–22 CT.
[109] Art. I–21 CT.
[110] Art. I–24 CT.

more specific policy issues. In the words of Westlake and Galloway, 'it is no exaggeration to say that, since 1975, most of the major political decisions of the European Community have been taken in the European Council'.[111]

It should, moreover, be recognized that the relations between the European Council and other Community institutions have evolved. The early European Council Summits were viewed with suspicion by the Commission, since they were normally secret and the Commission was usually excluded. Matters are very different today. The European Council has been the institutional mechanism whereby the Commission can secure broad agreement from Member States for major initiatives.[112] The European Council's agenda is prepared by the General Affairs and External Relations Council, GAERC.[113] The Commission President is a member of the European Council, and many of the European Council's initiatives are the result of Commission suggestions that are fed into the agenda prepared by the GAERC. The President of the European Parliament has, since 1988, addressed a plenary session of the European Council.

5. THE EUROPEAN PARLIAMENT

The story of the European Parliament is one of gradual transformation from a relatively powerless Assembly under the 1952 ECSC Treaty to the considerably strengthened institution it represents today.[114] The history is touched upon in Chapter 1, and its role in the legislative processes is examined in Chapter 4. The Assembly was given few powers under the ECSC Treaty and under the original EEC and Euratom Treaties. It was intended to exercise consultative and supervisory powers, but not to play any substantial legislative role.

However, although the elite 'government of technocrats' established under the ECSC Treaty was not replicated in the EEC Treaty, the institutions set up by the latter were not a model of democratic organization. We saw in Chapter 1 how the influence of the Parliament grew, with the two budgetary treaties of 1970 and 1975, and after the transition to direct elections with the 'co-operation' and 'assent' procedures under the Single European Act of 1986 and the 'co-decision' procedure under the TEU in 1992,[115] which was strengthened and extended under the Amsterdam and Nice Treaties.[116] Today, the European Parliament exercises substantial powers of a legislative, budgetary, and supervisory nature.

However, while changes in the legislative process have enhanced the power of the only directly elected European institution, the problems of the EU's democratic legitimacy are not thereby resolved.[117] The problems of secrecy, impenetrability, accountability, and representativeness[118] are not addressed simply by giving added powers to the European Parliament. The

---

[111] Westlake and Galloway, n. 56 above, 177.

[112] *Ibid.*, 179–180.

[113] Council Dec. 2006/683/EC, n. 58 above, Art. 2(2), (3).

[114] R. Corbett, *The European Parliament's Role in Closer Integration* (Palgrave, 1998); D. Judge and D. Earnshaw, *The European Parliament* (Palgrave, 2003); R. Corbett, F. Jacobs, and M. Shackleton, *The European Parliament* (6th edn., Harper, 2005); B. Rittberger, *Building Europe's Parliament, Democratic Representation Beyond the Nation State* (Oxford University Press, 2005).

[115] P. Raworth, 'A Timid Step Forwards: Maastricht and the Democratisation of the European Community' (1994) 19 *ELRev.* 16.

[116] A. Dashwood, 'The Constitution of the European Union after Nice: Law-making Procedures' (2001) 26 *ELRev.* 215.

[117] D. Beetham and C. Lord, *Legitimacy and the EU* (Longman, 1998); C. Lord, *Democracy in the European Union* (Sheffield University Press, 1998).

[118] On transparency, 562–567, and on democratic legitimacy, 133–138.

'*demos*' question is a complex one,[119] and many would argue that national parliaments remain the proper democratic focus of the Community, whatever the powers of the European Parliament may be.[120]

(a) COMPOSITION AND FUNCTIONING

The Parliament sits in Strasbourg, but there is a secretariat based in Luxembourg and certain sessions and committee meetings take place in Brussels to facilitate contact with the Commission and Council.[121]

Article 189 EC provides that the EP shall consist of representatives of the peoples of the States and that the number of MEPs shall not exceed 732.[122] Declaration 20 attached to the Nice Treaty specified the number of seats to be held by each Member State in an EU consisting of twenty-seven States, ranging from ninety-nine seats allocated to Germany to five seats given to Malta.[123]

After much wrangling,[124] a Statute regulating important aspects of the rights and duties of MEPs has been enacted pursuant to Article 190(5) EC.[125] The Statute takes effect from the parliamentary term beginning in 2009 and deals with important matters of principle, *inter alia*: that MEPs shall be free and independent and that agreements concerning the resignation from office of a MEP before the end of the parliamentary term shall be null and void; that they shall be entitled to table proposals for Community acts; and that they can access the EP's files. The Statute also regulates a host of practical matters, relating to pay, insurance, and the like. The issue of pay has been of particular significance, since hitherto this was determined by national rates of pay, which differed markedly as between Member States.

The 'representativeness' of the European Parliament has been criticized because the number of MEPs for each State is not proportionate to population size, and the smaller countries are disproportionately over-represented. Article 190 EC was amended at Amsterdam to provide that if future changes are to be made regarding the number of MEPs, 'the number of representatives elected in each Member State must ensure appropriate representation of the peoples of the States brought together in the Community'. However not everyone would accept that the numbers agreed at the Nice IGC to be elected from current and future Member States constituted such appropriate representation. The number of representatives was reduced for all fifteen states prior to enlargement, except Germany and Luxembourg, which were the biggest and the smallest respectively.

A further cause for concern was that, despite the holding of direct elections since 1979,[126] the uniform electoral procedure originally envisaged was not created.[127] Article 190(4) was however amended by the ToA to provide for the possibility of a uniform procedure in all

---

[119] J.H.H. Weiler, *The Constitution of Europe* (Cambridge University Press, 1999); P. Schmitter, *How to Democratize the European Union . . . And Why Bother?* (Rowman & Littlefield, 2000).

[120] E. Smith, *National Parliaments as Cornerstones of European Integration* (Kluwer, 1996).

[121] Case C–345/95 *France* v. *Parliament* [1997] ECR I–5215, on the holding of plenary sessions in Strasbourg.

[122] This ceiling can be temporarily exceeded in the event of new accessions between 2004–2009: Treaty of Nice, Protocol on Enlargement, Art. 2(4).

[123] Prior to the accession of Bulgaria and Romania the number of MEPs was still 732, but the number of MEPs for most Member States was higher than after these two countries acceded.

[124] Corbett, Jacobs, and Shackleton, n. 114 above, 59–67.

[125] Dec. 2005/684/EC of the European Parliament of 28 Sept. 2005 adopting the Statute for Members of the European Parliament [2005] OJ L262/1.

[126] Dec. 76/787 [1976] OJ L278/1. This Decision was amended by Art. 5 of the ToA.

[127] Corbett, Jacobs, and Shackleton, n. 114 above, 14–16.

Member States, or an electoral procedure based on common principles rather than uniformity. There is now a Decision specifying that MEPs are to be elected on the basis of proportional representation; that elections shall be by direct universal suffrage; and that they shall be secret and free.[128] Member States may set a threshold for the allocation of seats, provided it does not exceed 5 per cent of votes cast at national level.

Like the Commission's, the Parliament's term is five years: Article 190(3). Following the TEU provisions on citizenship, citizens of the Union resident in any Member State gained the right to vote and to stand as candidates in European Parliament elections: Article 19(2) EC. The turnout at EP elections has however been low,[129] which is worrying, given that the traditional EU discourse on democracy relies on the democratic legitimacy of the European Parliament. There is moreover significant disparity in voter turnout as between different Member States.[130]

MEPs sit according to political grouping, rather than nationality, although national parties generally remain together within the larger Parliamentary groupings. There are currently seven political groups, the largest three being, respectively, the centre-right European People's Party (Christian Democrats and European Democrats) with 264 seats after the 2004 elections, the Party of European Socialists with 201, and the Group of the Alliance of Liberals and Democrats for Europe with ninety. The other parties are the Greens/Free Alliance with forty-two MEPs, the Confederal Group of the European United Left-Nordic Green Left with forty-one, Union for Europe of the Nations Group with thirty-four, and the Independence/Democracy Group with twenty-two. There were thirty-two non-attached members.

Article 191 EC deals with European political parties. It provides that the Council 'shall lay down the regulations governing political parties at European level and in particular the rules regarding their funding'.[131] While the absence of properly constituted European-wide political parties has long been regretted by advocates of a genuine European political space, even this small step towards their establishment was not uncontentious.[132]

The Parliament elects its own President, together with fourteen Vice-Presidents, for two-and-a-half-year terms, and collectively they form the Bureau of Parliament. The Bureau is the regulatory body responsible for the Parliament's budget and for administrative, organizational, and staff matters. There are also five 'Quaestors', responsible for administrative and financial matters directly concerning members, who assist the Bureau in an advisory capacity. The 'Conference of Presidents' consists of the President together with the leaders of the various political groups. It is the political governing body of the Parliament. It draws up the agenda for plenary sessions, fixes the timetable for the work of parliamentary bodies, and establishes the terms of reference and size of parliamentary committees and delegations.

The Parliament has twenty standing committees on matters including foreign affairs; development; international trade; budgets; economic and monetary affairs; employment and

---

[128] Council Dec. 2002/772/EC, Euratom of 25 June 2002 and 23 Sept. 2002 amending the Act concerning the election of representatives of the European Parliament by direct universal suffrage, annexed to Dec. 76/787/ECSC, EEC, Euratom [2002] OJ L283/1.

[129] M. Franklin, 'European Elections and the European Voter', in Richardson, n. 53 above, ch. 11.

[130] www.europarl.europa.eu/elections2004/ep-election/sites/en/results1306/turnout_ep/index.html.

[131] Reg. 2004/2003/EC of the European Parliament and of the Council of 4 Nov. 2003 on the regulations governing political parties at European level and the rules regarding their funding [2003] OJ L297/1.

[132] Declaration 11 attached to the TN rather nervously affirms that Art. 191 does not 'imply any transfer of powers to the EC' nor affect national constitutional rules. It also specifies that such European funding may not be used to fund political parties at national level and that it should apply on the same basis to all the political forces represented in the European Parliament.

social affairs; environment, public health, and food safety; industry, research, and energy; internal market and consumer protection; transport and tourism; regional development; agriculture and rural development; fisheries; culture and education; legal affairs; civil liberties; justice and home affairs; constitutional affairs; women's rights and gender equality; petitions; human rights; and security and defence. Sub-committees and temporary committees or committees of inquiry can also be established. The Parliament is helped by a large secretariat of approximately 3,500 staff, headed by a Secretary-General. The committees are vital to the functioning of the EP, since they consider legislative proposals from the Commission and propose amendments thereto.[133] They can also produce their own-initiative reports.[134]

Article 199 EC states that the Parliament is to adopt its own rules of procedure,[135] and Article 190(5) requires it to lay down the regulations and general conditions governing the performance of its Members' duties. These regulations require Council approval by qualified majority, except those concerning taxation of MEPs for which unanimity is required.

(b) POWERS

(i) *Legislative Power*

The legislative process will be considered in detail below.[136] Suffice it to say for the present that the position of the EP in this process has become considerably stronger over time. Prior to the Single European Act 1986 the general rule was that the EP only had a right to be consulted on legislation, and that was only where the particular Treaty article so specified. The SEA introduced the co-operation procedure now enshrined in Article 252 EC, and this brought the EP into the legislative process more fully than hitherto. The co-decision procedure was introduced by the TEU and now applies to the passage of much important Community legislation. This procedure is contained in Article 251 EC and makes the EP a co-equal partner with the Council in the enactment of such legislation.[137] There are also certain areas where the assent of the EP is required for legislation.

The EP's role in the Second and Third Pillars is more limited. In relation to the Common Foreign and Security Pillar the Presidency must however consult the EP on the main aspects and basic choices of that policy, and ensure that the views of the EP are duly taken into consideration. The EP is to be kept regularly informed of developments in foreign and security policy; it may ask questions of the Council and offer recommendations; it also holds an annual debate.[138] The position under the reformed Third Pillar on Police and Judicial Co-operation in Criminal Matters (PJCC) is stronger. The EP has the same rights to be kept informed, ask questions, etc.[139] The EP must however also be consulted by the Council before it adopts measures and, provided the Parliament delivers its opinion within the time limit set,

---

[133] Rules of Procedure of the European Parliament (16th edn., Office for Official Publications of the EC, 2006), rules 42–48, available at www.europarl.europa.eu/omk/sipade3?PROG=RULES-EP&L=EN&REF=TOC.

[134] C. Neuhold, 'The "Legislative Backbone" Keeping the Institution Upright? The Role of the European Parliament Committees in the EU Policy-Making Process', European Integration online Papers, Vol. 5 (2001) No. 10.

[135] N. 133 above.

[136] See Ch. 4.

[137] A. Kreppel, 'What Affects the European Parliament's Legislative Influence? An Analysis of the Success of EP Amendments' (1999) 37 *JCMS* 521.

[138] Art. 21 TEU.

[139] Art. 39(2)–(3) TEU.

the Council may not act until the opinion is received.[140] The EP in addition has a consultative role in the authorization of enhanced co-operation under the Third Pillar, and in the allocation of expenditure of the general TEU title on enhanced co-operation.[141]

The changes in the EP's role in the legislative process, most especially through the co-decision procedure, have brought it from the fringes of the Community to become a major player in the shaping of EC legislation. Its role in this respect has been further enhanced through regular meetings held by Council, Commission, and EP in inter-institutional conferences, devoted either to particular topics or to general common problems, and through the EP's greater contribution to the framing of the overall legislative agenda.

The EP made frequent use of litigation in order to defend its role in the legislative process[142] and to contest the choice of legislative procedure used for a particular measure.[143] The ECJ held, after some hesitation,[144] that the EP could be a plaintiff in annulment proceedings, although only where its prerogatives had been infringed.[145] The Court also famously included the Parliament as a respondent in annulment proceedings even though only the Council and the Commission were mentioned under what was Article 173 at that time.[146]

The various judicial developments were gradually incorporated into the relevant provisions of the EC Treaty following successive Treaty amendments. Thus, for example, Article 230 EC has been amended to provide that the EP has full *locus standi* alongside the Commission, the Council, and the Member States to bring annulment proceedings.

(ii) *Dismissal and Appointment Power*

The Commission's accountability to the Parliament has gradually been strengthened. The EP has always had the power to censure the Commission and require its resignation.[147] This power has never actually been used, though various motions of censure have been tabled, including during the period prior to the resignation of the Santer Commission in 1999.

Since the Maastricht Treaty the EP has also had the right to participate in the Commission's appointment. Article 214(2) EC now provides that the Parliament must approve the nomination of the Commission President.[148] While this does not give the EP the right to choose the Commission President on its own, the largest group in the EP successfully argued in 2004 that the new President should come from a party represented from within its ranks.[149] The President and nominated Commissioners must be subject to a vote of approval by the EP.[150]

---

[140] Art. 39(1) TEU.

[141] Art. 44a TEU.

[142] Case 138/79 *Roquette Frères* v. *Council* [1980] ECR 3333; Case 139/79 *Maizena* v. *Council* [1980] ECR 3393.

[143] See, e.g., Case C–22/96 *European Parliament* v. *Council (Telephonic Networks)* [1998] ECR I–3231; Case C–42/97 *European Parliament* v. *Council (Linguistic Diversity)* [1999] ECR I–869; H. Cullen and A. Charlesworth, 'Diplomacy by Other Means: The Use of Legal Basis Litigation as a Political Strategy by the European Parliament and Member States' (1999) 36 *CMLRev.* 1243.

[144] Case 302/87 *Parliament* v. *Council (Comitology)* [1988] ECR 5616.

[145] Case C–70/88 *Parliament* v. *Council (Chernobyl)* [1990] ECR I–2041; Case C–187/93 *Parliament* v. *Council (Transfer of Waste)* [1994] ECR I–2857.

[146] Case 294/83 *Parti Ecologiste 'Les Verts'* v. *Parliament* [1986] ECR 1339, para. 23.

[147] Art. 201 EC.

[148] S. Hix, 'Executive Selection in the European Union: Does the Commission President Investiture Procedure Reduce the Democratic Deficit?', in K. Neunreither and A. Wiener (eds.), *European Integration After Amsterdam* (Oxford University Press, 2000), 95.

[149] M. Shackleton, 'The European Parliament', in Peterson and Shackleton, n. 53 above, 110.

[150] Art. 214(2) EC.

The relevant committee of the EP will question nominated Commissioners about their expertise and vision in the area for which they are to have responsibility. The 'political muscle' wielded by the EP is exemplified by its success in having three people nominated as Commissioners replaced at the last Commission investiture.

In the case of members of the Court of Auditors, the President of the European Monetary Institute, and the President, Vice-President, and Executive Board of the European Central Bank, the Parliament is to be consulted by the Council and the Member States, but its approval is not required.[151]

(iii) *Supervisory Power*

The EP monitors the activities of the other institutions, principally the Commission, through the asking of oral and written questions[152] and the establishment of committees of inquiry. The longstanding practices permitting the setting-up of committees of inquiry and the right to petition the EP were finally given Treaty status at Maastricht, and are now provided for under Articles 193 and 194 EC.[153]

The TEU also provided for the appointment by the Parliament of an Ombudsman.[154] The Ombudsman is to receive complaints from Union citizens or resident third-country nationals or legal persons, concerning 'instances of maladministration in the activities of the Community institutions or bodies' as well as to 'conduct inquiries for which he finds grounds, either on his own initiative or on the basis of complaints submitted to him direct or through a member of the European Parliament'. The Ombudsman is appointed for the duration of the mandate of the Parliament, and in the case of serious misconduct or non-fulfillment of the conditions of office the Court of Justice (ECJ), at the request of the EP, may dismiss the office-holder

The ECJ and the Court of First Instance (CFI) acting in their judicial role are excluded by Article 195 from the Ombudsman's jurisdiction, and the regulations further prohibit intervention in cases before Courts or questioning the soundness of a Court's ruling. However the major limitation on the Ombudsman's jurisdiction is that only EU and not national institutions are subject thereto. The EU bodies which are subject to the Ombudsman's jurisdiction must supply information requested and give access to files, except where grounds of secrecy are pleaded. The Ombudsman is empowered under Article 195 to conduct own-initiative inquiries, as exemplified by the 1996 inquiry into public access to documents held by a number of Community institutions and bodies.[155] At the conclusion of an investigation the Ombudsman sends a report to the Parliament and to the institution under investigation, and the complainant is informed of the outcome. The Ombudsman has also adopted a number of special reports following the responses of the institutions to his draft recommendation on a complaint, and has advised that his recommendations be adopted by Parliament as resolutions, or on occasion, such as in relation to the need for a Code of Good Administration, that an administrative regulation should be enacted.[156] Under Article 41 TEU

---

[151] M. Westlake, 'The European Parliament's Emerging Powers of Appointment' (1998) 36 *JCMS* 431.

[152] Art. 197 EC.

[153] E. Marias, 'The Right to Petition the European Parliament after Maastricht' (1994) 19 *ELRev.* 169; Report on the deliberations of the Committee on Petitions during the parliamentary year 2004–2005, Rapporteur Michael Cashman, A6-0178/2006.

[154] Art. 195 EC; R Heede, *The European Ombudsman: Redress and Control at Union Level* (Kluwer, 2000); P. Bonnor, *The European Ombudsman: A Novel Rule-source in Community Law* (PhD, EUI, 2001).

[155] [1998] OJ C44/1.

[156] See the website of the Ombudsman for details of these special reports and recommendations: http://ombudsman.europa.eu/home/en/default.htm.

after Amsterdam, the Ombudsman gained jurisdiction over matters falling within the reformed Third Pillar.

The office of Ombudsman is considered to have been a significant success since its introduction, and the office is increasingly seen as a source of administrative norms rather than simply a mediation facility for individual complaints.[157] Reference is made to the Ombudsman in Article 43 of the EU Charter of Fundamental Rights which was proclaimed at Nice in 2000. The Ombudsman has not been deterred by the ambivalent legal status of the Charter, but has referred frequently to the fundamental right to good administration contained in Article 41 of the Charter. The annual Reports from the Ombudsman contain a wealth of valuable information about the nature of the complaints received and the way in which they were dealt with.[158]

(iv) *Budgetary Power*

The EP also has important powers in relation to the budget. The Council has the last word on 'compulsory expenditure', while the EP is dominant in relation to 'non-compulsory expenditure', although decisions in relation to the latter are still made in close collaboration with the Council. The EP has unsurprisingly sought to increase non-compulsory expenditure relative to compulsory expenditure. The procedure for adoption of the budget is complex and is contained in Article 272 EC. It is clear that both the Council and the Parliament have a real say in the budget. It is equally clear that the former is still pre-eminent, although developments since the late 1980s have redressed this balance of power by, for example, increasing the proportion of the budget devoted to non-compulsory expenditure and through the procedures provided in Inter-institutional Agreements. The EP has however used its power over the budget to pressure for more general changes in the inter-institutional allocation of power in the EU, and conflicts have sometimes ended up in the Court.[159]

(c) THE IMPACT OF THE CT

The impact of the CT on the EP was largely positive. The CT capped the number of MEPs at 750, and representation of citizens was to be 'degressively proportional', with a minimum of six MEPs per Member State and a maximum of ninety-six. The more precise allocation was to be in accordance with a European Decision to be made by the European Council on the initiative of and with the consent of the EP.[160] The EP's powers were enhanced, in particular in relation to the passage of legislation where it was said to act jointly with the Council, and the co-decision procedure, re-named the ordinary legislative procedure,[161] was extended to a wider range of Treaty articles than hitherto.

---

[157] P. Bonnor, 'The European Ombudsman: A Novel Source of Soft Law in the EU' (2000) 25 *ELRev.* 39 and Bonnor. n. 154 above. For a defence of the less formal, non-juridical, and flexible nature of his role and procedures, however, see I. Harden, 'A l'écoute des griefs des citoyens de l'Union européenne: la mission du Médiateur européen' [2001] *RTDE* 573.

[158] Annual Report 2005, available at http://ombudsman.europa.eu/report/en/default.htm#20052009.

[159] See, e.g., Case 34/86 *Council v. European Parliament* [1986] ECR 2155; Case 377/87 *European Parliament v. Council* [1988] ECR 4017; Case C–284/90 *Council v. European Parliament* [1992] ECR I–2277.

[160] Art. I–20 CT.

[161] Art. I–34 CT, Art. III–396 CT.

(d) ROLE OF THE EUROPEAN PARLIAMENT: CONCLUSION

The EP has undoubtedly become of greater importance in Community decision-making since the SEA. Its legislative, supervisory and budgetary powers have increased, as has its power over the appointment of the Commission. The extent of the EP's influence appears to be greatest over policy-making decisions encapsulated in primary legislation, and it has less impact on either history-making decisions, as exemplified by Treaty revisions, or policy-implementation, as exemplified by the secondary rules made through Comitology.[162] The change in the EP's power is nonetheless marked.

R. Corbett, F. Jacobs, and M. Shackleton, The European Parliament [163]

The European Parliament's role in the Community's legislative procedure has increased from having, initially, no role whatsoever, to having a consultative role, to being a co-legislator with the Council. Parliament has demonstrated its ability to initiate new legislation in areas of concern to the public, to force substantial amendments to major legislative proposals and to oblige the Council to review important elements of several of the common positions it has adopted.

The European Parliament is not a sovereign Parliament in the sense of its word being final. On the other hand, it is not a Parliament whose powers are in practice exercised to legitimize a government's legislative wishes. It is an independent institution whose members are not bound to support a particular governing majority and which does not have a permanent majority coalition. . . .

The European Parliament is now a clearly identifiable part of an institutional triangle. This fact in itself is remarkable in historical terms. The term 'institutional triangle' was virtually unused two decades ago when most commentators referred to a bicephalous Community made up of the Commission and the Council. Now the argument is rather one about preserving and developing the equal status that the Parliament has won with regard to the other two institutions and of making European electorates aware of the contribution that the Parliament is increasingly making to the content of European laws affecting us all.

This leaves open the reason why the EP has been able to increase its power in this manner. Auel and Rittberger have proffered one explanation.[164] They argued that the driving force was the need to alleviate the legitimacy deficit. Input legitimacy connotes the idea that political choices are legitimate because they reflect the 'will of the people', which is normally identified through the legislature. Output legitimacy captures the idea that the political choices thus made effectively promote the welfare of that community.[165] Transfers of competence from Member States to the EC thereby created an asymmetry between input and output legitimacy, and hence a legitimacy deficit, since the normal mechanism for input legitimacy, through national parliaments, was reduced as increasing numbers of areas were regulated by the EC. One response was to foster closer involvement of national parliaments in Community

---

[162] Shackleton, n. 149 above, 113–118. See also 118–123.

[163] N. 114 above, 237.

[164] K. Auel and B. Rittberger, '*Fluctuant nec Merguntur*. The European Parliament, National Parliaments and European Integration', in Richardson, n. 53 above, 125–129. The argument is developed in more detail in Rittberger, n. 114 above.

[165] F. Scharpf, *Governing in Europe, Effective and Democratic?* (Oxford University Press, 1999), 6–7.

decision-making.[166] Another response to this legitimacy deficit was to increase the power of the EP.

K. Auel and B. Rittberger, The European Parliament, National Parliaments and European Integration[167]

[W]e argued that political elites have—since the SEA—gradually empowered the European Parliament's legislative powers and thus its capacity to influence European policy-making. Even though the decisions by member states to increase the legislative powers of the European Parliament were all but uncontroversial, the introduction and transfer of sectoral policy decisions to the European level triggered what we coined a democratic 'legitimacy deficit': European political elites came to perceive that the centralisation of policy-making tasks at the European level undermined the power of domestic parliaments to control and influence their respective governments in European policy-making. The legislative empowerment of the European Parliament was thus considered to serve as a mechanism to 'compensate' for domestic 'de-parliamentarisation'.

6. COURTS

The Court of Justice (ECJ), the Court of First Instance (CFI), and judicial panels constitute the Community's judicial branch.[168] The Treaty of Nice, TN, amended the division of function between the ECJ and the CFI, following reports and options for reform produced by the judicial organs in the IGC deliberations that led to the TN.[169] The most striking changes were the establishment of a third layer of specialized 'judicial panels' under the CFI and the ECJ, Article 225a, and the conferral on the CFI of the power to hear preliminary rulings in certain areas, Article 225(3).

(a) EUROPEAN COURT OF JUSTICE

Following the TN amendments, the composition of the ECJ and the CFI is governed by Articles 221–225a EC. A Protocol on the Statute of the Court of Justice added by the TN replaced the former protocols and deals with the organization and procedure of the Court. The Statute is now capable of amendment by a unanimous act of the Council rather than by the cumbersome Treaty amendment procedure, Article 245 EC, except for certain fundamental provisions on the status of judges and Advocates General. The Rules of Procedure, which build on the provisions of the Statute, are adopted by the ECJ under Article 223 EC, and must be approved by the Council acting by qualified majority.

---

[166] Auel and Rittberger, n. 164 above, 129–136.

[167] *Ibid.*, 136–137.

[168] R. Dehousse, *The European Court of Justice* (Macmillan, 1998); A. Arnull, *The European Union and its Court of Justice* (2nd edn., Oxford University Press, 2006).

[169] P. Craig, 'The Jurisdiction of the Community Courts Reconsidered', in G. de Búrca and J.H.H. Weiler (eds.), *The European Court of Justice* (Oxford University Press, 2001) 177; H. Rasmussen, 'Remedying the Crumbling EC Judicial System' (2000) 37 *CMLRev.* 1071; A. Arnull, 'Judicial Architecture or Judicial Folly? The Challenge Facing the European Union' (1999) 24 *ELRev.* 316; A. Dashwood and A. Johnston (eds.), *The Future of the Judicial System of the EU* (Hart, 2001). See 494–500 for detailed discussion.

Article 221 as amended by the TN provides that there shall be one judge per Member State. There were therefore twenty-five judges prior to the accession of Bulgaria and Romania. The appointment of all judges is required by Article 223 to be 'by common accord of the Governments of the Member States'.[170] The term of office is six years, but the judges can be reappointed. The appointment of new judges or reappointment of existing judges is staggered, so that there will be a partial replacement of judges every three years.

Article 222 provides that the ECJ is to be assisted by eight Advocates General, and that the number can be raised by unanimous decision of the Council. The qualifications for selection, method of appointment, and conditions of office of the Advocates General (AGs) are the same as for the ECJ judges. The AG's duty is principally 'to make, in open court, reasoned submissions on cases': Article 222. After the TN, the conditions under which an AG's opinion may or may not be required are determined in accordance with the Statute.[171]

The qualifications for selection as a judge or AG of the ECJ require 'persons whose independence is beyond doubt and who possess the qualifications required for appointment to the highest judicial offices in their respective countries or who are jurisconsults of recognized competence': Article 223. The Court elects its President from amongst its own judges and appoints its own Registrar.[172] Certain Member States have appointed academics as judges of the ECJ, whereas others, such as the UK and Ireland, have nominated prominent advocates or existing domestic judges. Advocate General Simone Rozès was appointed in 1981, the first female judge of the ECJ was appointed by Ireland only in 1999, followed by Germany's appointment of a female judge in 2000.[173] A judge or AG who, in the unanimous opinion of the other judges and Advocates General, no longer fulfils the requisite conditions and obligations of office may be removed from office.[174] Judges may not hold any other political or administrative office while they are members of the Court and, apart from their normal replacement, their period of office may terminate on death, resignation, or on removal from office.[175]

The ECJ may sit as a full Court, a 'Grand Chamber', or chambers, in accordance with rules laid down by the Statute.[176] It sits as a full Court either where the case is regarded as exceptionally important, or where the subject-matter warrants, such as in an action for dismissal of the Ombudsman or a Commissioner.[177] The Grand Chamber consists of thirteen judges and is used when a Member State or an institution that is party to the proceedings so requests, and in particularly complex or important cases.[178] The great majority of cases are however heard in chambers of three or five judges,[179] which is vital to the Court's functioning, given its increasing case-load.

The ECJ's jurisdiction is specified in the Treaties, and many of the heads of jurisdiction will be considered within subsequent chapters. Suffice it to say for the present that the main provisions governing its jurisdiction are Articles 226–243 EC, and Article 46 TEU. A number of international agreements, such as the Convention on Jurisdiction and the Enforcement of

---

[170] Art. 224 now provides similarly for the CFI.

[171] Statute of the Court of Justice (Nov. 2005), Art. 20 available at www.curia.europa.eu/en/instit/txtdocfr/index.htm.

[172] Art. 223 EC.

[173] J. Shaw, 'Gender and the Court of Justice', in de Búrca and Weiler (eds.), n. 169 above, ch. 4.

[174] Statute, n. 171 above, Art. 6.

[175] *Ibid.*, Art. 4.

[176] Art. 221 EC.

[177] Statute, n. 171 above, Art. 16.

[178] *Ibid.*

[179] *Ibid.*

Judgments in Civil and Commercial Matters made pursuant to Article 293 EC, concluded between the Member States also confer jurisdiction on the ECJ.[180] The limit placed on the Court's jurisdiction in relation to the Third Pillar and Title IV EC has been criticized, and the Commission has proposed amendment to the latter.[181]

(b) THE COURT OF FIRST INSTANCE

The Court of First Instance (CFI)[182] was established in 1988 pursuant to a Treaty amendment introduced by the Single European Act.[183] Initially the CFI had a derivative and secondary institutional status, and was described in the EC Treaty as being 'attached to the Court of Justice'. Following the TN amendments, however, Article 220 describes the ECJ and the CFI alongside one another, each charged within its respective jurisdiction with the same fundamental task of ensuring that the law is observed in the interpretation and application of the Treaty.

Article 224 provides, following TN amendment, that the CFI shall comprise *at least* one judge per Member State, thus distinguishing it from the ECJ where there will henceforth be only one judge per Member State. There were prior to accession of Bulgaria and Romania twenty-five judges on the CFI. There are no separate Advocates General on the CFI, although any judge may be called upon to perform the task of an AG.[184] The members of the CFI shall be chosen from 'persons whose independence is beyond doubt and who possess the ability required for appointment to high judicial office': Article 224. The CFI elects its own President from amongst its judges and appoints its Registrar.[185]

It sits in chambers of three and five judges, or sometimes as a single judge,[186] and approximately 75 per cent of cases are heard by chambers of three judges. It may also sit as a Grand Chamber or Full Court when the complexity or importance of the case demands it.[187]

There is an appeal to the ECJ within two months from the date of the CFI's decision.[188] The appeal is limited to questions of law, and this covers 'lack of competence of the Court of First Instance, a breach of procedure before it which adversely affects the interests of the appellant as well as the infringement of Community law by the Court of First Instance'.[189]

The rationale for the creation of the CFI was to relieve the burden on the ECJ. It was initially given jurisdiction over staff cases, competition cases brought by individuals against the Community institutions, and certain cases under the ECSC Treaty. Gradually the Council transferred to it other categories of case. The CFI's jurisdiction is now determined by Article 225 EC.

Article 225(1) provides that the CFI has jurisdiction over: most direct actions,[190] with the exception of those allocated to the new judicial panels and the actions listed in Article 51 of

---

180 [1972] OJ L299/32 and [1983] OJ C97/23.

181 COM(2006)346 final.

182 Known in French as the *Tribunal de Première Instance*, which explains the T used before the case number when a case is registered with the CFI.

183 Council Dec. 88/591 [1988] OJ L319/1.

184 Statute, n. 171 above, Art. 49.

185 Art. 224 EC.

186 Council Dec. 1999/291 [1999] OJ L114/52; Statute, n. 171 above, Art. 50.

187 *Ibid.*, Art. 50.

188 *Ibid.*, Art. 56.

189 *Ibid.*, Art. 58.

190 These are: annulment actions, Art. 230; actions for failure to act, Art. 232; damages actions, Arts. 235 and 288; staff cases, Art. 236; and proceedings under contractual arbitration clauses in Art. 238.

the Statute;[191] actions brought by Member States against the Commission; actions brought by Member States against the Council relating to acts adopted in the field of state aid and dumping and acts by which the Council exercises implementing powers; actions based on contracts that confer jurisdiction on the CFI; and trade mark cases. Enforcement actions under Articles 226 and 227 remain under the jurisdiction of the ECJ, although this can be amended through the Statute.

Article 225(2) empowers the CFI to hear actions against decisions of the new judicial panels, and the CFI's rulings can be reviewed by the ECJ only in exceptional circumstances, 'where there is a serious risk of the unity or consistency of Community law being affected'.

Article 225(3) was a significant innovation. Prior to the TN preliminary rulings were the exclusive preserve of the ECJ. Article 225(3) for the first time gave the CFI power to decide on preliminary rulings under Article 234 'in specific areas laid down by the Statute', subject to two kinds of control by the ECJ. The Nice IGC specified in Declarations 12 and 13 that attention should be given as soon as possible to the delineation of such areas, but there has nonetheless been no move to make Article 225(3) a reality by specifying the areas in which the CFI would have power over preliminary rulings.[192]

(c) JUDICIAL PANELS

The establishment of judicial panels is governed by Article 225a, which was added by the TN. The principal rationale for this amendment was to ease the workload on the ECJ and CFI. The proposal to create a system of decentralized or regional Community courts was not taken up,[193] but the creation of a third jurisdictional level below the ECJ and the CFI is the most significant structural reform of the EU judicial system since the establishment of the CFI.

Article 225a provides that specialized judicial panels to determine at first instance 'certain classes of action' or 'proceedings brought in specific areas' may be established by decision of the Council, under a novel decision-making procedure. Decisions of such panels are to be subject to an appeal to the CFI on point of law, or also on matters of fact where so specified in the decision establishing the panel. The qualifications required for appointment to one of these panels are similar to but lower than those for the CFI.

A European Union Civil Service Tribunal has now been created to adjudicate on staff cases.[194]

(d) REFORM OF THE COURT SYSTEM

Reform of the EU Court system was long-awaited and oft-proposed, but reactions to the Nice Treaty amendments to the 'judicial architecture' were rather muted.

---

[191] Statute, n. 171 above, Art. 51, currently reserves to the ECJ actions under Arts. 230 and 232 brought by a Community institution, or by the ECB, against another Community institution or the ECB. It also, subject to certain exceptions, reserves to the ECJ actions under Arts. 230 and 232 brought by a Member State against the EP or Council, or by those institutions acting jointly, and actions under these Arts. brought by a Member State against the Commission under Art. 11a EC.

[192] See 494–500 for further discussion.

[193] H. Rasmussen, 'Remedying the Crumbling EC Judicial System' (2000) 37 *CMLRev.* 1071; J.P. Jacqué and J. Weiler, 'On the Road to European Union: A New Judicial Architecture: An Agenda for the Intergovernmental Conference' (1990) 27 *CMLRev.* 185.

[194] Council Dec. 2004/752/EC, Euratom of 2 Nov. 2004, establishing the European Union Civil Service Tribunal [2004] OJ L333/7.

J.H.H. Weiler, The Judicial Après-Nice[195]

The actual outcome of the Conference in this area too, as with the political institutions, is an inability to break away from the scheme of the original Treaties. At the core of this architecture, and its most important feature by any perspective one may care to adopt, is the Preliminary Reference and the Preliminary Ruling. This procedure has remained substantially unchanged for half a century. A Court of First Instance with new-found dignity, Judicial Panels and all the rest notwithstanding, Europe continues to drive in its rusty and trusted 1950 model with the steering wheel firmly in the hands of the Court of Justice.

Put differently, the IGC was not willing to engage in either profound rethinking or profound re-engineering of the judicial function in view of a much changed polity to the one in which the current system was set.... And yet the context in which the judicial system is situated has changed radically in the last fifty years. The increase of size from six Member States to a potential of twenty-six is really only part of the problem, and possibly not even the most important part. Not a limited jurisdiction over some technical areas but a complex polity with jurisdiction ranging from human rights to monetary policy to difficult aspects of immigration and even citizenship.... And then the Court itself: no longer an instance for dispute settlement, but a judicial giant which has successfully positioned itself at the constitutional centre of Europe, a Europe in which national legal orders suddenly feel under threat.

Space precludes detailed elaboration of the changes that may be made to the EU's judicial architecture, although this will be examined in part when discussing preliminary rulings.[196] Suffice it to say for the present that overhaul of the judicial architecture and the division of jurisdiction between the ECJ and CFI for both direct and indirect actions would be desirable.[197]

(e) THE ADVOCATE GENERAL

The ECJ's decision-making is assisted by the office of AG. The AG is a full member of the Court and participates at the oral stage of the judicial hearing. His or her most important task is to produce a written opinion, the 'reasoned submissions' mentioned in Article 222 EC, for the Court. This opinion is produced before the Court makes its decision. Since the TN amendment to Article 222, it is no longer necessary for an AG to be involved in every case and the Statute determines when the AG's involvement is required.[198]

The written opinion sets out the AG's understanding of the law applicable to the case and recommends to the Court how the case ought to be decided. This opinion does not bind the Court, but is very influential, and in fact is followed by the ECJ in a majority of cases. The AG's opinion is intended to constitute impartial and independent advice, and in practice it tends to be a comprehensive, reasoned account of the law governing all aspects of the case. The style and content of the AG's opinion are virtually always more readable than those of the Court's judgments, and often shed light on the meaning of an obscure judgment.

---

[195] Epilogue, in de Búrca and Weiler (eds.), n. 169 above, 217–218.

[196] See 494–500.

[197] Craig, n. 29 above, ch. 9.

[198] Statute, n. 171 above, Art. 20 provides that where the ECJ 'considers that the case raises no new point of law, the Court may decide, after hearing the Advocate General, that the case shall be determined without a submission from the Advocate General'.

A further function allocated to the First Advocate General following the TN reforms to the Statute of the Court is to propose when the ECJ should, exceptionally, review a decision of the CFI given either under the lower court's new preliminary rulings jurisdiction or in its capacity as appellate court from one of the judicial panels established under Article 225a.[199]

(f) PROCEDURE BEFORE THE COURT

Procedure before the ECJ and CFI is governed by their respective rules of procedure.[200] The procedure before the ECJ takes place in two stages, the written and the oral stages.[201] The written part of the proceedings before the ECJ is far more thorough and more important than the oral. At the written stage, all applications, statements of case, defences, and any submissions or relevant documents are communicated to the parties to the case and to the institutions whose decisions are being contested. The oral stage, by contrast, is limited and short. The *juge-rapporteur*, the judge assigned in a given case, prepares and presents to the Court the 'report for the hearing', which summarizes the facts of the case and the arguments of the parties. Then the legal representatives of the parties may make oral submissions to the Court, followed by submissions of the AG and the hearing of any necessary witnesses or experts. The Court has adopted the practice of asking questions of the legal representatives before it. This has become an important part of the oral stage of proceedings, since it clarifies the issues which the Court considers of particular significance in the case.

While there is an appeal from judicial panels to the CFI and appeals on points of law from decisions of the CFI to the ECJ, there is no further appeal from the judgments of the ECJ, which is the ultimate or supreme court of the EU. However, Member States, Community institutions, and parties may under certain conditions contest a judgment rendered without their being heard, where it is prejudicial to their rights.[202] There is also a mechanism whereby any party with an interest in a particular judgment may apply to the Court to construe the meaning or scope of a judgment which is in doubt,[203] and a method for seeking revision of a judgment within ten years of its being given 'on discovery of a fact which is of such nature as to be a decisive factor' and which was unknown at the time the judgment was given.[204]

It is also clear that the Court, while generally building on its own case law, does not consider itself bound by a strict system of precedent.[205] The ECJ may explain the rationale for its departure from prior case law, but will not always indicate the cases that have been 'overruled'.[206]

(g) STYLE OF THE COURT'S JUDGMENTS

The style of the ECJ's judgments stands in contrast to that of the opinions of the Advocates General. The ECJ's and CFI's judgments are collegiate, representing the single ruling of all of

---

[199] *Ibid.*, Art. 62.

[200] For some of the differences between procedure before the ECJ and the CFI, see N. Brown and T. Kennedy, *The Court of Justice of the European Communities* (5th edn., Sweet & Maxwell, 2000). See also K. Lenaerts, 'The European Court of First Instance: Ten Years of Interaction with the Court of Justice', in D. O'Keeffe and A. Bavasso (eds.), *Judicial Review in EU Law* (Kluwer, 2000), 97.

[201] Statute, n. 171 above, Art. 20.

[202] *Ibid.*, Art. 42.

[203] *Ibid.*, Art. 43; Case 69/85 *Re Wünsche* [1986] ECR 947.

[204] Statute, n. 171 above, Art. 44.

[205] A. Arnull, 'Owning up to Fallibility: Precedent and the Court of Justice' (1993) 30 *CMLRev.* 247.

[206] See, e.g., Cases C–267–268/91 *Keck and Mithouard* [1993] ECR I–6097.

the judges hearing the case.[207] Since there are no dissents or separately concurring judgments, the divergent views of different judges may be contained within the language of the judgment. This can result in a ruling that is ambiguous on matters of importance. Further difficulties can arise because of the multiplicity of languages used before the Court.[208] Moreover, while the AG's opinion generally considers exhaustively all the legal arguments potentially relevant to the case, the Court may prefer not to commit itself on a specific legal issue until another case arises where it is directly necessary for a decision.

(h) THE IMPACT OF THE CT

The CT had less impact on the Community Courts than it had on the other institutions. This is in part because their role within the new constitutional scheme was only considered relatively late in the Convention proceedings, when a Discussion Circle was set up and it worked under severe time constraints. There was little consideration given to the general division of jurisdiction between the ECJ, CFI, and national courts and the Discussion Circle focused on a number of more discrete legal issues. The overall judicial architecture in the CT therefore largely replicated that in the existing Treaties. The CT nonetheless contained an interesting modification relating to the appointment of judges and Advocates General, creating a panel to report on the suitability of candidates for these jobs.[209]

(i) ROLE OF THE COURT: CONCLUSION

The ECJ has, as noted above, various heads of jurisdiction specified in Articles 226–245 EC and Article 46 TEU. Article 220 has however been of especial significance in shaping the Court's sphere of influence. It provides that 'the Court of Justice and the Court of First Instance, each within its jurisdiction, shall ensure that in the interpretation and application of this Treaty the law is observed'.

It will be seen in subsequent chapters how the Court utilized this provision to extend review to cover bodies which were not expressly subject to it,[210] and measures which were not listed in the Treaty.[211] In the name of preserving 'the rule of law' the Court has developed principles of a constitutional nature as part of Community law, which bind the Community institutions and the Member States when they act within the Community sphere.[212]

It is the ECJ, as interpreter of the Treaties, which adjudicates on the limits of Community competence as against the Member States.[213] These issues arise in many guises, in direct challenges to Community action by Member States,[214] in actions between the

---

[207] The fact that decisions of the ECJ may not be unanimous and will require a vote is indicated by the Statute, n. 171 above, Art. 17, which provides that decisions of the Court will be valid only when an uneven number of its members sits in deliberations.

[208] Rules of Procedure of the Court of Justice (Dec. 2005), Arts. 29–31. available at www.curia.europa.eu/en/instit/txtdocfr/index.htm.

[209] Art. III–357 CT.

[210] It subjected the Parliament to judicial review under Art. 230 in Case 294/83, n. 146 above, although it was not included in the Treaty as a body subject to review. Conversely, in Case 70/88, n. 145 above, it allowed Parliament to bring such an action despite not being covered by the Treaty.

[211] Case 22/70 *Commission* v. *Council (ERTA)* [1971] ECR 263.

[212] See Chs. 11 and 15.

[213] See Ch. 3.

[214] Cases 281, 283–285, 287/85 *Germany* v. *Commission (Non-Community Workers)* [1987] ECR 3203; Case C–376/98 *Germany* v. *European Parliament and Council* [2000] ECR I–8419.

institutions,[215] in preliminary references relating to the scope of substantive Community law,[216] or proceedings involving the compatibility of an international agreement with the Treaties.[217]

It has moreover been the ECJ that fashioned seminal principles of the Community legal order, such as direct effect, supremacy, pre-emption, and state liability in damages. These principles have defined the very nature of the Community, constitutionalizing the EC and distinguishing it from other international Treaties. They were especially significant in the years of so-called institutional malaise or stagnation. The Court arguably played a 'political' role through law, attempting to render the Treaty effective when its provisions had not been implemented as required by the Community, and to render secondary legislation effective when it had not been properly implemented by the Member States.[218] This was exemplified by the ECJ's role in the creation of the internal market, requiring the 'negative' removal of national barriers to trade, at a time when progress towards completing the Single Market through positive legislative harmonization was hindered by institutional inaction.[219]

It is therefore important to view the ECJ's role from a dynamic, rather than static, perspective. It was suggested, after the revival of the political processes of integration leading to the SEA, that the Court should thereafter adopt a 'minimalist' role.[220] The reality is that the ECJ has not been a consistently 'activist' Court at all times or in all policy spheres. It may for example simultaneously create new methods of enforcement,[221] while reducing its intervention in an area where the legislative institutions have become more active. The Court is moreover aware of the political environment in which it acts, and its judgments are at times influenced by relatively 'non-legal' arguments made by Member States relating to the potential financial impact of a ruling, or by critical responses from the public or from national and Community sources.[222]

The Court's case law cannot be properly understood without an awareness of its approach to interpretation. This is generally described as purposive or teleological, although not in the sense of seeking the purpose or aim of the authors of a text.[223] The fact that the *travaux préparatoires* to the original Treaties were never published meant these were never used as a source, and this is reflected in the Court's case law.[224] In the case of secondary legislation, although the discussions at Council and Commission meetings are not published, declarations and extracts from the minutes have occasionally been relied on as aids to interpretation

---

[215] Case 22/70 *ERTA*, n. 211 above.

[216] Case C–159/90 *SPUC* v. *Grogan* [1991] ECR I–4685; Cases C–267–268/91 *Keck*, n. 206 above.

[217] See, e.g., *Opinion 1/94 Competence of the Community to Conclude International Agreements Concerning Services and the Protection of Intellectual Property, WTO* [1994] ECR I–5267.

[218] See Ch. 8.

[219] Case 8/74 *Procureur du Roi* v. *Dassonville* [1974] ECR 837; Case 120/78 *Rewe-Zentrale AG* v. *Bundesmonopolverwaltung für Branntwein (Cassis de Dijon)* [1979] ECR 649.

[220] T. Koopmans, 'The Role of Law in the Next Stage of European Integration' (1986) 35 *ICLQ* 925.

[221] See, e.g., Cases C–6 & 9/90 *Francovich and Bonifaci* v. *Italy* [1991] ECR I–5357; Cases C–46 & 48/93 *Brasserie du Pêcheur SA* v. *Germany* and *R.* v. *Secretary of State for Transport, ex p. Factortame Ltd. and others* [1996] ECR I–1029. See Ch. 9.

[222] See, e.g., Case C–262/88 *Barber* v. *Guardian Royal Exchange Assurance Group* [1990] ECR I–1889; Case C–450/93 *Kalanke* v. *Freie Hansestadt Bremen* [1995] ECR I–3051 and Case C–409/95 *Hellmut Marschall* v. *Land Nordrhein Westfalen* [1997] ECR I–6363.

[223] A. Bredimas, *Methods of Interpretation and Community Law* (North Holland, 1978); J. Bengoetxea, *The Legal Reasoning of the European Court of Justice* (Oxford University Press, 1993); T. Koopmans, 'The Theory of Interpretation and the Court of Justice', in D. O'Keeffe and A. Bavasso (eds.), n. 200 above, 45.

[224] See, e.g., Case 149/79 *Commission* v. *Belgium* [1980] ECR 3881, 3890, and the discussion of the use of *travaux préparatoires* and of 'declarations' by Member States by Mayras AG in Case 2/74 *Reyners* v. *Belgium* [1974] ECR 631, 666.

before the Court.[225] However in most cases it has denied the relevance of this material if it does not appear in the text of the legislation itself.[226]

Rather than adopting a narrower historical-purposive approach, the Court tends to examine the whole context in which a particular provision is situated, and gives the interpretation most likely to further what the Court considers that provision sought to achieve. This may be far from a literal interpretation of the Treaty or of the legislation in question, even to the extent of flying in the face of the express language. This aspect of the Court's methodology has attracted criticism, although it has been defended robustly by members of the academic community, by its former personnel, and by some practitioners.

The best known of the Court's early critics was Rasmussen. His thesis was that the Court has sought 'inspiration in guidelines which are essentially political of nature and hence, not judicially applicable. This is the root of judicial activism which may be a usurpation of power'.[227] He did not criticize all 'activism', but rather that which he believed to have lost popular legitimacy. There were mixed reactions to Rasmussen's work from an academic community that had largely been supportive of the Court's strategy.[228] Thus Cappelletti argued that Rasmussen's critique lacked a historical dimension, that any constitutional court should have the courage to enforce its 'higher law' against temporary pressures, and that the ECJ's vision 'far from being arbitrary, is fully legitimate, for it is rooted in the text, most particularly in the Preamble and the first articles of the EEC Treaty'.[229]

A further attack on the Court came from Sir Patrick Neill, in his 'case study in judicial activism', in which he argued that the Court was a dangerous institution, skewed by its own policy considerations and driven by an elite mission.[230] Advocate General Fennelly has however pointed out that the Member States through Treaty revisions have either explicitly or implicitly approved many Court decisions.[231] Advocate General Jacobs, in defence of the Court's 'constitutional' role, argued that it plays an essential role in preserving the balance between the Community and the Member States, and in developing constitutional principles of judicial review.

F. Jacobs, Is the Court of Justice of the European Communities a Constitutional Court? [232]

If then, the Court sometimes performs the task of a Constitutional Court, and if it has developed constitutional principles in its case law, we can understand why, in some quarters, the

---

[225] See, e.g., Case 136/78 *Ministère Public* v. *Auer* [1979] ECR 437, paras. 25–26; Case 131/86 *UK* v. *Council* [1988] ECR 905, paras. 26–27.

[226] See, e.g., Case 38/69 *Commission* v. *Italy* [1970] ECR 47, para. 12; Case 143/83 *Commission* v. *Denmark* [1985] ECR 427; Case 237/84 *Commission* v. *Belgium* [1986] ECR 1247; Case 306/89 *Commission* v. *Greece* [1991] ECR 5863, paras. 6 and 8; Case C–292/89 *Antonissen* [1991] ECR I–745.

[227] H. Rasmussen, *On Law and Policy in the European Court of Justice* (Nijhoff, 1986), 62.

[228] See the book reviews by M. Cappelletti (1987) 12 *ELRev.* 3; J. Weiler (1987) 24 *CMLRev.* 555; A. Toth (1987) 7 *YBEL* 411.

[229] *The Judicial Process in Comparative Perspective* (Clarendon Press, 1989), 390–391.

[230] *The European Court of Justice: A Case Study in Judicial Activism* (European Policy Forum, 1995). See also, T. Hartley, 'The European Court, Judicial Objectivity and the Constitution of the European Union' (1996) 112 *LQR* 95.

[231] N. Fennelly, 'Preserving the Legal Coherence within the New Treaty: The ECJ after the Treaty of Amsterdam' (1998) 5 *MJ* 185, 198.

[232] D. Curtin and D. O'Keeffe (eds.), *Constitutional Adjudication in European Community and National Law* (Butterworths (Ireland), 1992), 25, 32. For further defence of the Court see T. Tridimas, 'The Court of Justice

Court's activities have been misunderstood. The Court has sometimes been criticized as a 'political' Court. Such criticisms are probably based on unfamiliarity with the very notion of constitutional jurisprudence, which, as we have seen, is not familiar in all the Member States, and which requires what may seem novel judicial techniques, different approaches to interpretation, even a different conception of the law. Yet, in the Community system, which is based on the notion of a division of powers, some form of constitutional adjudication is inescapable, if indeed the Community is to be based, as its founders intended, on the rule of law.

It is of course true that all constitutional courts must engage with political issues, but, given the unaccountability of courts, the nature and origin of the 'unwritten' values which they promote should be critically scrutinized, as should the extent to which their decisions seem to depart from what their express powers would appear to allow. It is equally important for such judicial decision-making to be fully reasoned.[233]

The ECJ has overall pursued a policy of legal integration, giving substance to an 'outline' Treaty, thereby enhancing the effectiveness of Community law and promoting its integration into national legal systems. While excessive concentration on the Court should be avoided,[234] its role as an institutional actor in the integration process should nonetheless be recognized. The nature of this role has been considered by political scientists as well as lawyers.

For liberal intergovernmentalists the central message is that states are the driving forces behind integration, that supranational actors are there largely at their behest and that such actors as such have little independent impact on the pace of integration.[235] The supranational institutions are viewed as agents for the Member States, which accord power to such institutions from their own self-interest. Thus the ECJ's powers are rationalised on the ground that the existence of proper adjudicatory mechanisms at the supranational level can prevent prisoner dilemma and free rider problems, thereby removing the possibility that the system will be undermined by States seeking to reap the rewards of membership while trying to avoid their obligations.[236]

The idea that the ECJ can in the preceding sense be regarded as an agent of Member States, with little, if any, independent impact on integration, may well be questioned by lawyers, even if they may disagree as to the nature of this impact. It would, to take but one prominent example, be difficult to rationalize the recent case law on citizenship in simple principal–agent terms, given the ECJ's expansive interpretation of the relevant Treaty articles, often in the face of fierce opposition from the Member States.[237] It is moreover clear that political scientists who have studied the Court in depth often disagree markedly with the tenets of liberal intergovernmentalism. Thus Stone Sweet argues against the view that the Court can be regarded as

and Judicial Activism' (1997) 22 *ELRev.* 199; A. Arnull, 'The European Court and Judicial Objectivity: A Reply to Professor Hartley' (1996) 112 *LQR* 95. See also G. Howe, 'Euro-Justice: Yes or No?' (1996) 21 *ELRev.* 187, 191; A. Albors-Llorens, 'The European Court of Justice: More than a Teleological Court' (1999) 2 *CYELS* 373.

233 U. Everling, 'The ECJ as a Decisionmaking Authority' (1994) 82 *Mich. LR* 1294.

234 T. Koopmans, 'The Future of the Court of Justice of the European Communities' (1991) 11 *YBEL* 15. See also K. Alter and S. Meunier-Aitsahalia, 'Judicial Politics in the European Community' (1994) 26 *Comparative Political Studies* 535, 536.

235 A. Moravcsik, 'Preferences and Power in the European Community: A Liberal Intergovernmentalist Approach' (1993) 31 *JCMS* 473 and 'Liberal Intergovernmentalism and Integration: A Rejoinder' (1995) 33 *JCMS* 611, 623–625.

236 Moravcsik, 'Preferences and Power', n. 235 above, 512–514. Moravcsik accepts that the ECJ has extended its powers beyond those strictly necessary for the attainment of his theory, but does not regard this as undermining his more general thesis.

237 See Ch. 23.

some perfect agent for Member State governments, and contends that ECJ decisions often produce 'unintended consequences' not readily foreseen by those who designed the EC.[238] In the following extract he adverts to the constitutionalization of the EC, through doctrines developed by the ECJ, such as direct effect, supremacy, and pre-emption.

A. Stone Sweet, *The Judicial Construction of Europe*[239]

There are a number of reasons why the constitutionalization of the Rome Treaty generated an expansive logic of its own, entailing an increasing demand for law, rule clarification, and capacities for monitoring and enforcement. From the beginning the central mission of the EC was to create the conditions for the development of the Common Market. Yet impersonal exchange, across jurisdictional boundaries, is problematic for reasons that social scientists have explored at length ... As elsewhere, the success of integration has depended heavily on the extent to which the EC could develop effective organizational capacities: to guarantee property rights, to enforce competition rules, to adjudicate legal claims, to build a European framework for regulating market activities, and so on. At the very least constitutionalization accelerated this process. In my view, one can go further: the ECJ authoritatively reconstituted the Community in ways that linked the demand for and supply of European law and courts to the activities of market actors, and then to all activities governed by EC law. Constitutionalization not only positioned the courts as primary arenas for negative integration; it made them supervisors of positive integration, and creators of a growing corpus of rights which the Court found in the Treaty itself.

... With constitutionalization, the national courts too, developed into privileged sites for deliberation and rulemaking, not least because they are charged with supervising the transposition and implementation of EC law by national authorities....

7. THE COURT OF AUDITORS

The Court of Auditors was established by the second Budgetary Treaty of 1975 and came into operation in 1977, replacing the previously existing Auditor of the ECSC and the Audit Board of the Communities. Since the enactment of the TEU, the Court of Auditors has occupied the status of the fifth Community institution in Article 7 EC. It is now governed by Articles 246–248 EC.

The Court of Auditors consists of one national from each Member State, appointed by the Council by qualified majority after consulting the Parliament; the EP has actively exercised its right of consultation, examining each of the proposed candidates thoroughly. The term of office is for six years renewable, and appointments are staggered. The auditors must belong or have belonged in their country to an external audit body, or they must be 'especially qualified for this office'. Article 247(2) EC, and their independence must be beyond doubt. Articles 247(2) and (4). The conditions of office are strict: members may not engage in any other occupation, paid or unpaid, and even after leaving office they must 'behave with integrity and discretion as regards the acceptance ... of certain appointments or benefits'.[240] A member of the Court of Auditors can be removed from office only by decision of the ECJ.

---

238 A. Stone Sweet, *The Judicial Construction of Europe* (Oxford University Press, 2004), 235.
239 *Ibid.*, 238–239.
240 Art. 247(5) EC.

The general task of the Court of Auditors is to scrutinize the finances of the Community and to ensure sound financial management. The Court is to 'examine the accounts of all revenue and expenditure of the Community' and of bodies set up by the Community, where that is permitted.[241] The Parliament and the Council are to be provided by the Court of Auditors with a statement of assurance (SoA) as to the reliability of the accounts and the legality of transactions and irregularities are to be reported. The annual SoA may be supplemented by sectoral assessments on major areas of Community activity. The Court's audit is to be based on records, but also, if necessary, it can be performed on the spot in the Community institutions and in the Member States, in liaison with the competent national audit body.[242] Following the ToA, the Court was given *locus standi* to bring annulment actions under Article 230 EC, similar to that given the European Central Bank.

The Court of Auditors draws up an annual report,[243] which is adopted by a majority of its members, after the close of each financial year.[244] The report is sent to the other Community institutions and published in the Official Journal together with the replies of the institutions. The Court of Auditors may submit observations on specific questions or adopt special reports.[245] It can also deliver opinions at the request of another institution, as when it is consulted on specific legislative proposals.[246] Internal chambers may be established in order to adopt certain categories of reports or opinions.

The tone of the Court's reports has often been extremely critical. It has been noted that it is sometimes difficult to show that the Court of Auditors and the Commission are 'on the same side', and that the Court of Auditors could easily be accused of being 'anti-Communautaire'.[247] While its relations with the Parliament have been described as 'stable and cooperative',[248] there has been strong criticism of the 'indifference displayed at the Council's highest level to the auditing functions and findings of the European Court of Auditors'.[249] More general assessments of the Court of Auditors vary. Thus, one study suggests that it has an uneasy relationship with the Commission, has come into conflict with the Parliament's budgetary control committee, has been largely ignored by the Council, and remains virtually unknown to most national parliaments, although there have been other more positive appraisals of its evolving institutional role.[250]

8. OTHER COMMUNITY INSTITUTIONS

(a) ECONOMIC AND SOCIAL COMMITTEE

Article 7(2) EC makes provision for an European Economic and Social Committee (EESC) to assist the Council and Commission. It is an advisory body representing various sectional or

---

[241] Art. 248(1) EC.

[242] Art. 248(3) EC.

[243] See, e.g., Court of Auditors, Annual Report concerning the financial year 2005 [2006] OJ C263/1.

[244] Art. 248(4) EC.

[245] See, e.g., Court of Auditors, Special Report 9/2006 concerning translation expenditure incurred by the Commission, the Parliament and the Council [2006] OJ C284/01.

[246] Arts. 279, 280(4) EC.

[247] I. Harden, F. While, and K. Donnelly, 'The Court of Auditors and Financial Control and Accountability in the European Community' (1995) 1 *EPL* 599.

[248] B. Laffan, 'Becoming a "Living Institution": The Evolution of the European Court of Auditors' (1999) 37 *JCMS* 251, 261.

[249] House of Lords Select Committee on the EU, 'The European Court of Auditors: The Case for Reform' (Report No. 12, 2000/2001).

[250] Contrast Harden *et al.*, n. 247 above, with Laffan, n. 248 above.

functional interests.[251] Article 257 has been modified by the TN. In what may be a merely cosmetic amendment, but nonetheless one which acknowledges the increasing salience of 'civil society' in European and national discourse, it now provides that the EESC is to consist of the various components of organized civil society, in particular representatives of producers, farmers, carriers, workers, dealers, craftsmen, professional occupations, consumers, and the general interest.[252] The main members have been workers, who are principally represented by trade unions; employers; and others, such as farmers, consumer groups, and the professions. The EESC has 317 members, rising to 344 with the accession of Bulgaria and Romania.[253] Each country has a specified number of members, the largest being twenty-four and the smallest five. The Council, acting by qualified majority, appoints members of the EESC for four years, on the basis of proposals from the Member States, this term being renewable.[254]

The members of the EESC may not be bound by any mandatory instructions, must be completely independent in the performance of their duties, and must act in the general interest of the Community.[255] The EESC operates via a number of different committees. In certain instances the Treaty stipulates that it must be consulted, and the Commission or Council may consult it on other matters. The EESC may also be consulted by the European Parliament.[256] The Council or Commission may set a time limit, of not less than one month, within which the EESC has to act, and if it does not do so then matters can proceed without its input.

The EESC has not, traditionally, been a particularly influential institution, but its status could be enhanced by the increased institutional attention being paid to the importance of 'civil society' in enhancing EU legitimacy, and by the TN's express recognition of the role of civil society in its composition.[257]

(b) COMMITTEE OF THE REGIONS

This Committee was established by the TEU to represent regional and local bodies,[258] in part to counter the idea that the Community was becoming too centralized.[259] The total number of members is the same as for the EESC, as is the allocation between Member States.

The Council, acting by qualified majority, appoints the members for a renewable four-year term. No member of the Committee can at the same time be an MEP but, following an amendment by the TN, Article 263 specifies that members must be 'representatives of regional and local bodies', with electoral mandates or political accountability to an elected assembly. They must be independent and act in the Community's general interest.

The Council and Commission must consult the Committee of the Regions where the Treaty so specifies. It may be consulted in other instances, in particular where a

---

251 S. Smismans, *Law, Legitimacy and European Governance, Functional Participation in Social Regulation* (Oxford University Press, 2004).

252 See S. Smismans, writing before the Nice Treaty, 'An Economic and Social Committee for the Citizen, or a Citizen for the Economic and Social Committee?' (1999) 5 *EPL* 557.

253 See www.eesc.europa.eu/organisation/how/index_en.asp.

254 Art. 259(1) EC.

255 Art. 258 EC.

256 Art. 262 EC.

257 *The ESC: A Bridge between Europe and Civil Society* (Brussels, 2001); *European Social Dialogue and Civil Dialogue: Differences and Complementarities* (EESC, 2004).

258 Art. 263 EC.

259 N. Roht-Arriaza, 'The Committee of the Regions and the Role of Regional Governments in the European Union' (1997) 20 *Hastings Int. & Comp. LJ* 413.

measure concerns cross-border co-operation; it can also be consulted by the European Parliament.[260]

Three main principles lie at the heart of the Committee's work: subsidiarity, proximity, and partnership.[261] These principles inform its contributions to legislative proposals. They also underpin its general studies[262] and those of a more sectoral nature.[263]

(c) AGENCIES

The role of agencies within the EU is of growing importance.[264] There are at present: nineteen Community agencies, with four more under preparation; three EU agencies connected with Pillar Two: CFSP; and three EU agencies connected with Pillar Three: PJCC. They have no formal basis in the Treaty but were created by secondary legislation, normally under Article 308 EC, although the Commission's policy now is to base such agencies on the relevant Treaty provision governing the area in which they will operate.[265]

They function in a range of areas including vocational training, working and living conditions, health and safety at work, the environment, drugs, medicines, plant varieties, internal market harmonization, translation, anti-racism, air safety, maritime safety, railways, and information security.[266]

The powers of the agencies are however fairly circumscribed. A significant part of the role of most agencies is the gathering of information and the facilitation of co-ordination between the Community and national bodies. Some agencies such as the Office for Internal Market Harmonization, and the European Aviation Safety Agency, have the power to make individual decisions. The agencies do not however have direct regulatory powers, in the sense that they cannot make rules pursuant to the exercise of discretionary power,[267] and the Commission is reluctant to accord them such power.[268]

The existing agencies are relatively independent of the other institutions, although the Council and the Commission play differing parts in the appointment of the heads of the

---

[260] Art. 265 EC.

[261] See www.cor.europa.eu/en/presentation/Role.htm.

[262] See, e.g., Committee of the Regions, *The Regional and Local Dimensions in Establishing New Forms of Governance in Europe* (CoR, 2003); Committee of the Regions, *Strengthening Regional and Local Democracy in the European Union* (CoR, 2004).

[263] See, e.g., Committee of the Regions, *Services of General Interest in Europe* (CoR, 2005).

[264] M. Everson, 'Independent Agencies: Hierarchy Beaters?' (1995) 1 *ELJ* 180; A. Kreher, 'Agencies in the European Community: A Step Towards Administrative Integration in Europe' (1997) 4 *JEPP* 225; M. Shapiro, 'The Problems of Independent Agencies in the United States and the European Union' (1997) 4 *JEPP* 276; R. Dehousse, 'Regulation by Networks in the European Community: The Role of European Agencies' (1997) 4 *JEPP* 246; E. Vos, 'Reforming the European Commission: What Role to Play for EU Agencies?' (2000) 37 *CMLRev.* 1113; E. Chiti, 'The Emergence of a Community Administration: The Case of European Agencies' (2000) 37 *CMLRev.* 309; G. Majone, 'Delegation of Regulatory Powers in a Mixed Polity' (2002) 8 *ELJ* 319; E. Chiti, 'Decentralisation and Integration into the Community Administrations: A New Perspective on European Agencies' (2004) 10 *ELJ* 402; D. Geradin and N. Petit, 'The Development of Agencies at EU and National Levels: Conceptual Analysis and Proposals for Reform', Jean Monnet Working Paper 01/04, NYU School of Law; Craig, n. 29 above, ch. 5.

[265] The Operating Framework for the European Regulatory Agencies, COM(2002)718 final.

[266] See http://europa.eu/agencies/community_agencies/index_en.htm.

[267] Case 9/56 *Meroni & Co. Industrie Metallurgiche SpA v. High Authority* [1958] ECR 133.

[268] Regulatory Agencies, n. 265 above; Draft Interinstitutional Agreement on the Operating Framework for the European Regulatory Agencies, COM(2005)59 final.

respective agencies, and they enjoy varying degrees of financial autonomy. In terms of composition, the administrative boards of the agencies are made up of national representatives and sometimes representatives of relevant organizations, of Commission representatives, and of European Parliament appointees also.[269]

In addition to the agencies described above, there are also executive agencies, which are designed to manage some of the non-discretionary functions that fall within the direct administrative responsibility of the Commission in order to enable the Commission to concentrate on its 'core tasks', while avoiding the problems associated with outsourcing that led to the downfall of the Santer Commission.[270]

9. CONCLUSION

i. None of the EU institutions should be seen as a unitary actor. Although each has its own distinctive identity and role, it should be remembered that the internal structure and composition of each is varied and complex.

ii. The powers of the institutions are formally governed by Treaty provisions, but their actual functioning and interaction are determined by a range of inter-institutional agreements and practices, as well as by significant political developments.

iii. Recent years have witnessed a period of institutional flux, with proposals for reform of the internal working and governance structures of the EU administration, following the resignation of the Santer Commission.

iv. The role of the Court of Justice remains central within the EU institutional framework and in the European legal system more generally. Its jurisdiction is broad, notwithstanding the pillar structure, and recent reforms have enhanced the status and powers of the Court of First Instance.

10. FURTHER READING

Brown, N., and Kennedy, T., *The Court of Justice of the European Communities* (5th edn., Sweet & Maxwell, 2000)

Bulmer, S., and Wessels, W., *The European Council* (Macmillan, 1987)

Corbett, R., *The European Parliament's Role in Closer EU Integration* (Macmillan, 1998)

——, Jacobs, F., and Shackleton, M., *The European Parliament* (6th edn., Harper, 2005)

Craig, P., *EU Administrative Law* (Oxford University Press, 2006)

Dashwood, A., and Johnston, A., *The Future of the Judicial System of the European Union* (Hart, 2001)

De Búrca, G., and Weiler, J.H.H., *The European Court of Justice* (Oxford University Press, 2001)

Dehousse, R., *The European Court of Justice* (Macmillan, 1998)

---

[269] Craig, n. 29 above.
[270] Council Reg. (EC) 58/2003 of 19 Dec. 2002, laying down the statute for executive agencies to be entrusted with certain tasks in the management of community programmes [2003] OJ L11/1; Craig, n. 29 above, ch. 2.

Dimitrakopoulos, D. (ed.), *The Changing European Commission* (Manchester University Press, 2004)

Hayes-Renshaw, F., and Wallace, H., *The Council of Ministers* (2nd edn., Palgrave, 2006)

Hooghe, L., *The European Commission and the Integration of Europe* (Cambridge University Press, 2002)

Nugent, N., *The European Commission* (Palgrave, 2001)

Peterson, J., and Shackleton, M., *The Institutions of the European Union* (2nd edn., Oxford University Press, 2006)

Pollack, M., *The Engines of European Integration: Delegation, Agency and Agenda Setting in the EU* (Oxford University Press, 2003)

Richardson, J. (ed.), *European Union, Power and Policy-Making* (3rd edn., Routledge, 2006)

Smith, A. (ed.), *Politics and the European Commission: Actors, Independence, Legitimacy* (Routledge, 2004)

Spence, D. (ed)., *The European Commission* (Harper, 2006)

Stevens, A., with Stevens, H., *Brussels Bureaucrats? The Administration of the European Union* (Palgrave, 2001)

Wallace, H., Wallace, W., and Pollack, M. (eds.), *Policy-Making in the European Union* (5th edn., Oxford University Press, 2005)

Westlake, M., and Galloway, D., *The Council of the European Union* (3rd edn., Harper, 2004)

INSTRUMENTS AND
COMPETENCE

1. INTRODUCTION

In the previous chapter we examined the institutional actors and their respective powers. In this Chapter, we consider the existence and scope of Community powers and the basic requirements for their lawful exercise. Specific issues relating to instruments and competence in the Second and Third Pillars will be discussed in Chapters 6 and 7 respectively. We will use the terms 'competences' and 'powers' interchangeably, although not everyone would agree that they have the same precise meaning.

2. CENTRAL ISSUES

i.   The EC has a number of *formal legal methods* for developing Community policy: principally regulations, directives, and decisions. These will often be used in conjunction with each other. The foundational provision in an area may, for example, be a directive, and regulations and decisions may supplement it. The EC also has numerous *soft law methods* for developing Community policy. There are a range of *other legal and policy instruments* available under the Second and Third Pillars, which differ from those under the Community Pillar.[1] *Formal and informal law will be used together* to attain EC and EU goals in any particular area.

ii. Community action must satisfy a number of *procedural conditions* in order to be lawful. Community measures must be published, reasons must be given, and there are rights of access to documents.

iii. The Community must act within the *limits of its powers*. It must have a *legal basis* within the Treaties for every legal act it adopts. Delimiting the scope of the EC's internal and external competence is however problematic.

iv. Closely related to the question of the *existence* of Community competence and the adequacy of the legal basis for action is the question of when such competence is properly *exercised*. This issue is governed by the principle of *subsidiarity*, which is set out in Article 2 TEU, Article 5 EC, and in a Protocol to the Treaties. The meaning and application of this concept give rise to problems.

---

[1] See Chs. 6 and 7.

3. INSTRUMENTS

It is important to understand the different types of Community legislation. Article 249 EC is the foundational provision:

> In order to carry out their task and in accordance with the provisions of this Treaty, the European Parliament acting jointly with the Council, the Council and the Commission shall make regulations and issue directives, take decisions, make recommendations or deliver opinions.
>
> A regulation shall have general application. It shall be binding in its entirety and directly applicable in all Member States.
>
> A directive shall be binding, as to the result to be achieved, upon each Member State to which it is addressed, but shall leave to the national authorities the choice of form and methods.
>
> A decision shall be binding in its entirety upon those to whom it is addressed. Recommendations and opinions shall have no binding force.

There is no formal hierarchy between these provisions. It should not therefore be thought that regulations are somehow 'superior' to directives, or vice versa. It is equally important to understand that regulations, directives, and decisions will often be connected in the development of Community policy in a particular area. There may, for example, be a 'foundational' regulation, and directives or decisions may be made pursuant to this. The 'foundational' provision may equally be a directive or a decision.

(a) REGULATIONS

Regulations are binding on, and directly applicable in, all Member States. They must be published in the Official Journal and come into force on the date specified in the particular regulation or, if no such date is specified, on the twentieth day following publication.[2] The power to make regulations may be conferred on the Commission by a Council regulation. This issue will be considered more fully below.[3] In most instances the Treaty leaves open the choice whether to proceed by way of regulation, directive, or decision. Only rarely does it prescribe the necessity of legislating by way of regulation.[4]

It is quite common for an individual to allege that a measure which is called a regulation is really a decision. This arises most commonly when an individual seeks to annul a measure, because Article 230 EC limits the ability of individuals to challenge measures in the form of regulations. The test of whether a measure really is a regulation is one of substance and not form. The fact that the contested act is called a regulation is not therefore conclusive.[5]

It is common to think of regulations as akin to either primary or secondary legislation made by Member States. There is some force in this analogy, since regulations are measures of general application, applicable to all Member States. Moreover, as will be seen,[6] the Court has held that regulations are abstract normative measures, which are not directed towards a particular

---

[2] Art. 254 EC. Regs. which are made under Art. 251 EC must also be signed by the President of the European Parliament and by the President of the Council: Art. 254(1) EC.

[3] See Ch. 4.

[4] See, e.g., Art. 39(3)(d) EC and Art. 89 EC, concerning workers and state aids respectively.

[5] See Ch. 14.

[6] *Ibid.*

named person or persons. While this reinforces the sense that regulations are analogous to domestic legislation, either primary or secondary, one should be cautious about pressing this analogy too far. Many regulations, for example in the agricultural sphere, affect only a very small group of people, and may be operative for only a short period of time. Such regulations may, in this sense, be indistinguishable from measures that would be regarded as administrative or executive acts within national legal systems.

Regulations are said by Article 249 to be 'directly applicable'. Commentators have debated the meaning of this term.[7] We cannot know the intent of those who drafted the Treaty in the absence of the *travaux préparatoires*. It is unclear whether the Treaty framers meant the phrase 'directly applicable' to connote the idea that individuals have rights which they can enforce in their own name through national courts. We shall see that the ECJ has on occasion interpreted directly applicable in this manner.[8]

The term does, however, have another meaning, which is concerned with the way in which international norms enter national legal systems. In some Member States, this must be either by the national system transforming the measure into national law, or by a shorter national act adopting the relevant international act. These methods would be very cumbersome when there were many such international measures to be transferred into national legal systems. The Community passes thousands of regulations. If each one had to be separately incorporated into each national legal system before it could be legally effective then the Community would grind to a halt. The phrase 'directly applicable' within Article 249 obviates this difficulty. It signifies that regulations are to be part of the national legal systems, without the need for transformation or adoption by separate national legal measures.

Member States may nonetheless need to modify their law in order to comply with a regulation. This may be the case where a regulation has implications for different parts of national law. However this does not alter the fact that the regulation itself has legal effect in the Member States independently of any national law, and that the Member States should not pass measures that conceal the nature of the Community regulation.

Case 34/73 **Variola v. Amministrazione delle Finanze**
[1973] ECR 981

The ECJ was asked by a national court whether the provisions of a regulation could be introduced into the legal order of a Member State by internal measures which reproduced the contents of the Community provision 'in such a way that the subject-matter is brought under national law'.

THE ECJ

10. The direct application of a Regulation means that its entry into force and its application in favour of those subject to it are independent of any measure of reception into national law.

By virtue of the obligations arising from the Treaty and assumed on ratification, Member States are under a duty not to obstruct the direct applicability inherent in Regulations and other rules of Community law.

---

[7] See, e.g., J. Steiner, 'Direct Applicability in EEC Law—A Chameleon Concept' (1982) 98 *LQR* 229; A. Dashwood, 'The Principle of Direct Effect in European Community Law' (1978) 16 *JCMS* 229.

[8] See Ch. 8.

Strict compliance with this obligation is an indispensable condition of simultaneous and uniform application of Community Regulations throughout the Community.

11. More particularly, Member States are under an obligation not to introduce any measure which might affect the jurisdiction of the Court to pronounce on any question involving the interpretation of Community law or the validity of an act of the institutions of the Community, which means that no procedure is permissible whereby the Community nature of a legal rule is concealed from those subject to it.

Under Article 177 of the Treaty in particular the jurisdiction of the Court is unaffected by any provisions of national legislation which purport to convert a rule of Community law into national law.

(b) DIRECTIVES

Directives differ from regulations in two important ways. They do not have to be addressed to all Member States; and they are binding as to the end to be achieved while leaving some choice as to form and method open to the Member States. The Community institutions generally have considerable choice whether to legislate by regulations or directives. There are however some Treaty Articles which stipulate that directives must be used.[9]

Directives must be notified to the person to whom they are addressed.[10] There was, prior to the TEU, no duty to publish directives in the Official Journal, even though in practice many were published. Directives which apply to all Member States and those passed pursuant to the co-decision procedure must now be published in the Official Journal.[11] The date of entry into force of directives is the same as that for regulations: either the date specified in the directive or, in the absence of any such date, the twentieth day following that of publication.[12]

The ability to legislate through directives as well as regulations gives the Community valuable flexibility. The direct applicability of regulations means that they have to be capable of being 'parachuted' into the legal systems of all the Member States just as they are. Normally every 't' must be crossed, and every 'i' must be dotted in regulations, since Member States must not tamper with them. If this were the only way to develop Community policy, the legislative process would work very slowly. There might be areas where it was difficult to devise regulations with the requisite specificity, which were suited to immediate impact in the Member States. It should be remembered that the Member States have differing legal systems, some being common law, some civil law, and that there are considerable differences between civil law regimes. There are, in addition, variations in the existing political, administrative, and social arrangements within the Member States.

Directives are particularly useful when the aim is to harmonize the laws within a certain area or to introduce complex legislative change. This is because discretion is left to Member States as to how the directive is to be implemented. It should not however be thought that directives are vague. They are not. The ends which Member States have to meet will be set out in considerable detail. The force of directives has been increased by ECJ rulings. The Court held that directives have direct effect, enabling individuals to rely on them, at least in actions against the State,[13] and that a Member State can be liable in damages for non-implementation of a directive.[14]

[9] See, e.g., Arts. 44, 46(2), 52, 94, 96, 132(1), and 137(2) EC.
[10] Art. 254(3) EC.
[11] Art. 254 EC.
[12] Art. 254(1) and (2) EC.
[13] See 279–284.
[14] See 328–341.

(c) DECISIONS

Decisions are, as stipulated by Article 249 EC, binding in their entirety on those to whom they are addressed. They must be notified to the addressee and take effect when notified to those to whom they are addressed.[15] Decisions which are adopted pursuant to Article 251 must be published in the Official Journal. They take effect from the date specified therein or, in the absence of any such date, on the twentieth day following that of their publication.[16] It is open to the Council to delegate power to the Commission to take decisions.[17] The Community institutions remain free to proceed by way of decision in many areas.[18] There are, however, areas where the Treaty stipulates that decisions should be used, as, for example, with breach of the competition rules[19] or the rules on state aids.[20]

The paradigm of a Community decision may well be one made in the context of competition or state aids, whereby the Commission expresses the formal conclusion of its inquiry in relation to a particular undertaking or Member State. There are however Community decisions that do not fit this paradigm and which do not have a specific addressee or addressees. Decisions may be the chosen method for introducing a new policy area, such as the Socrates programme,[21] or for establishing general procedures, as in the context of the Comitology Decision.[22]

We have already noted that the ECJ will determine whether a measure in the form of a regulation is in substance to be classified in this way. The corollary is that measures labelled as regulations which the Court finds not to be regulations in substance will be regarded as decisions. This issue is of particular importance for annulment actions under Article 230.[23]

(d) RECOMMENDATIONS AND OPINIONS

Article 249 EC states clearly that recommendations and opinions are to have no binding force. While this precludes such measures from having direct effect, it does not immunize them from the judicial process. It is, for example, open to a national court to make a reference to the ECJ concerning the interpretation or validity of such a measure.[24] Article 211 EC gives the Commission a general power to formulate recommendations or deliver opinions on matters dealt with in the Treaty, either where it expressly so provides[25] or where the Commission believes that it is necessary to do so.

(e) OTHER METHODS FOR DEVELOPING POLICY

The categories considered above constitute the principal ways in which policy is developed within the EC, but there are other ways in which this can occur.

[15] Art. 254(3) EC.

[16] Art. 254(1) EC.

[17] Art. 202 EC.

[18] It is, e.g., common for the Commission to respond to requests concerning the detailed application of the CAP by issuing a decision on the matter.

[19] Art. 85(2) EC.

[20] Art. 88(2) EC.

[21] Dec. 819/95 [1995] L87/10.

[22] Dec. 99/468 [1999] OJ L184/23.

[23] See Ch. 14.

[24] Case C–322/88 *Grimaldi* v. *Fonds des Maladies Professionelles* [1989] ECR 4407.

[25] Express provision for making recommendations or opinions is to be found in, e.g., Arts. 77, 97, 105, 133(3), and 151(5) EC.

The Commission has, for example, issued policy guidelines in the area of state aids to indicate how it will exercise its discretion.[26] There are Inter-institutional Agreements made between the Council, Commission, and the European Parliament, and they have been made on topics of constitutional significance such as subsidiarity, transparency, and participation rights.[27]

These measures, together with recommendations and opinions, constitute 'soft law',[28] as opposed to the more formal measures such as regulations, decisions, and directives. The admixture of formal and informal law is a common feature of any legal order. This feature has been positively lauded in the EC, rather than seen as a cause for apology or criticism. Thus the Commission in its *2000 Review of the Internal Market Strategy* included a neat checklist of the legislative and non-legislative measures it intended to take in order to attain the single market.[29] The same readiness to use the full range of policy instruments was apparent in the Nice European Council. In the implementation of the Social Agenda 'all existing Community instruments bar none must be used: the open method of co-ordination, legislation, the social dialogue, the Structural Funds, the support programmes, the integrated policy approach, analysis and research'.[30]

The admixture of formal and informal law, while inevitable, can nonetheless give rise to problems. It may be difficult for those affected to understand what the 'law' actually is in a particular area. Recourse to informal law may also prevent the Council and EP from having effective input into the resulting norms.

(f) THE DUTY TO GIVE REASONS

In addition to the duty to publish and notify Community measures, Article 253 EC establishes another important procedural condition for the lawful exercise of Community powers, *the duty to give reasons*:

> Regulations, directives and decisions adopted jointly by the European Parliament and the Council, and such acts adopted by the Council or the Commission, shall state the reasons on which they are based and shall refer to any proposals or opinions which were required to be obtained pursuant to the Treaty.

It is important to note that Article 253 imposes a duty to give reasons not only for administrative decisions, but also for legislative norms, such as regulations or directives. Many national legal systems do not impose an obligation to furnish reasons for legislative acts, or do so only in limited circumstances. The scope and content of this duty will be examined more fully in the context of judicial review.[31]

---

[26] See Ch. 28.
[27] See 103–104.
[28] K. Wellens and G. Borchardt, 'Soft Law in European Community Law' (1989) 14 *ELRev.* 267; J. Klabbers, 'Informal Instruments before the European Court of Justice' (1994) 31 *CMLRev.* 997; L. Senden, *Soft Law in European Community Law* (Hart, 2004). See also Ch. 5 below.
[29] COM(2000)257 final.
[30] Nice European Council, 7–9 Dec. 2000, Annex 1, para. 28.
[31] See Ch. 15.

(g) THE IMPACT OF THE CONSTITUTIONAL TREATY

The Constitutional Treaty[32] would have had a marked impact on this area, because it introduced for the first time a formal hierarchy of norms for the legal measures promulgated by the EU.[33] These provisions were set out in Title V of Part I of the Constitution, entitled 'Exercise of Union Competence'. The foundational provision was Article I–33(1) CT. It provided that in exercising the competences conferred on it by the Constitution, the Union should use as legal instruments European laws, European framework laws, European regulations, European decisions, recommendations, and opinions.[34]

The Constitution specified two types of *legislative acts*, European laws and European framework laws: Article I–33(1) CT. A European law was a legislative act of general application, which was binding in its entirety and directly applicable in all Member States. This corresponded to a regulation within the present system. A European framework law was a legislative act binding as to the result to be achieved on the Member States to which it was addressed, but left the national authority choice as to the form and means of achieving the result. A European framework law therefore corresponded to a directive in the present system.

Article I–33(1) CT also provided for what were termed *non-legislative acts*. A European regulation was a non-legislative act of general application for the implementation of legislative acts and certain specific provisions of the Constitution. It could either be binding in its entirety and directly applicable in all Member States, or be binding as regards the result to be achieved, on all the Member States to which it was addressed, but leaving the national authorities the choice of form and methods of achieving that result. The Constitution therefore in effect provided for secondary European laws and secondary European framework laws. Article I–32(1) CT also specified a category of European decisions which were non-legislative acts that were binding in their entirety.

The Constitution stipulated in Article I–35 CT the way in which non-legislative acts were to be made: the Council and the Commission should adopt European regulations and decisions in the cases referred to in Articles I–36 and 37 CT and in cases specifically laid down in the Constitution. Article I–36 dealt with 'Delegated European Regulations' and Article I–37 made provision for 'Implementing Acts'.

The overall objective of the provisions on the hierarchy of norms was to clarify the types of legal instruments that could be adopted. It appears, however, that the language of 'law' and 'framework law' will not be preserved in the Reform Treaty, but that nonetheless the general idea of a hierarchy of norms will be retained. These matters will be considered further when assessing the impact of the CT on decision-making in the EU.[35]

4. INTERNAL COMMUNITY COMPETENCE

The discussion thus far has been concerned with the types of measures, both formal and informal, that can be made in order to further the objectives of the relevant Treaty Article. These measures must however be made within the limits of competence accorded by the

---

[32] Treaty Establishing a Constitution for Europe [2004] OJ C316/1.

[33] P. Craig, 'The Hierarchy of Norms', in T. Tridimas and P. Nebbia (eds.), *European Law for the Twenty-First Century, Rethinking the New Legal Order, Volume 1* (Hart, 2004), ch. 5; K. Lenaerts and M. Desomer, 'Towards a Hierarchy of Legal Acts in the European Union? Simplification of Legal Instruments and Procedures' (2005) 11 *ELJ* 744; P. Craig, *EU Administrative Law* (Oxford University Press, 2006), 124–131.

[34] Art. I–38(1) CT stipulated that the choice between these measures should be in accordance with the principle of proportionality, and Art. I–38(2) CT imposed a duty to give reasons when making any of these Union acts.

[35] See below, 138–142.

Treaty. Normally this will be unproblematic: the particular regulation will stipulate the Treaty Article on which it is based. Matters can, however, be more difficult for five reasons.

(a) THE AMBIT OF A TREATY ARTICLE

Treaty Articles may be drafted relatively specifically or they may be framed in more broad open-textured terms. In either case it is always possible for there to be disagreement about the ambit, scope, or interpretation of the relevant Treaty Article, more especially so when it is cast in broad terms. Disagreements of this nature are an endemic feature of adjudication.

This is exemplified by the *Working Time Directive* case.[36] The UK sought the annulment of a directive concerned with the organization of working time. The directive had been adopted by qualified majority pursuant to what was Article 118a of the Treaty,[37] concerned with health and safety. The UK argued that the measure should have been made under either what was Article 100 or 235,[38] which require unanimity in the Council. Article 118a was, the UK contended, not suitable for measures of broad social policy, and provisions concerning working time were insufficiently related to health and safety. The ECJ, save for one small point, rejected the argument and concluded that Article 118a was a sound legal basis for the measure.

(b) SHARED AND COMPLEMENTARY COMPETENCE

The existing Treaty does not contain a neat list demarcating which competences are exclusive to the EC and which are shared, although, as we shall see, the CT has attempted to do this. The reality is that many of the competences are shared rather than exclusive, and in some instances the non-exclusive nature of these powers is made express, especially in relation to the newer competences granted to the EC. It is equally important to recognize that the precise division of competence between the EC and the Member States varies in different subject-matter areas,[39] and that it is often drawn in rather imprecise terms. It may therefore be contestable whether a measure falls within the sphere allocated to the Community or to the Member States, and normally this question falls ultimately to the Court of Justice to decide.

The fact that competence is often shared may be the result of a legislative choice, in the sense that the Community legislature devises the legislation so as to leave room for stricter national measures. It may also be the result of constitutional limits laid down in the relevant Treaty Article.

R. Schutze, Co-operative Federalism Constitutionalised: The Emergence of Complementary Competences in the EC Legal Order[40]

Outside the core areas of European integration, the predominant federalist philosophy of the European Community has always been that of legislative co-operation. For those 'flanking policies', Community legislation would not, ipso facto, exclude stricter national measures that

---

[36] Case C–84/94 *United Kingdom* v. *Council* [1996] ECR I–5755. For a similar argument in the context of Art. 47 see Case C–233/94 *Germany* v. *European Parliament and Council* [1997] ECR I–2405. See also Case C–377/98 *Netherlands* v. *Parliament and Council* [2001] ECR I–7079.

[37] The ToA has now substantially amended this and related Arts. of the EC Treaty: see Arts. 137 and 138 EC.

[38] Now Arts. 94 and 308 EC.

[39] Compare, e.g., the different formulations in Art. 152 (health), Art. 153 (consumer protection), Art. 157 (industry), Arts. 163–173 (research and technological development).

[40] (2006) 31 *ELRev.* 167, italics in the original.

harmoniously supplemented the Community standard. Minimum harmonisaiton would set a mandatory floor and permit upward legislative differentiation. National measures that conformed to Community legislation (and the Treaty) would not be pre-empted. However, recourse to minimum harmonization for legislation adopted under Arts 95 and 308 had been a *legislative* choice. . . .

Since the Single European Act. . . the phenomenon of co-operative federalism has increasingly been 'constitutionalised'. Newly introduced legislative competences have set *constitutional* limits to the legislative powers of the Community legislator in two ways. For a number of policy fields, the Treaty mandated the Community legislator to set minimum requirements only. The method of constitutionally fixing minimum harmonization emerged for the first time with the SEA in relation to environmental and social policy. Subsequent amendments have extended it to the area of consumer protection, the protection of public health, and to visa and asylum matters. . . .

A second variant of constitutionally enshrined co-operative federalism appears with the Maastricht Treaty. Instead of referring to 'minimum' standards, the Treaty characterises the function of the Community legislator as 'complementing' or 'supplementing' national action.

This second variant of complementary competence is commonly found in the newer competences granted to the EC, in areas such as employment policy, public health, social policy, education and vocational training, culture, and consumer protection, and the detailed provisions in these areas can vary. The fact that the Treaty articles are framed in terms of 'complementing' or 'supplementing' national action means that it can be difficult to determine precisely which measures fall legitimately within the EC's competence.

(c) IMPLIED POWERS

The institutions may claim that a particular Treaty Article contains an implied power to make the particular regulation. The notion of implied powers is well known in both domestic and international legal systems. The precise meaning of the phrase 'implied power' is more contestable. It can, as Hartley notes, be given a narrow or a wide formulation:[41]

According to the narrow formulation, the existence of a given power implies also the existence of any other power which is reasonably necessary for the exercise of the former; according to the wide formulation, the existence of a given *objective* or *function* implies the existence of any power reasonably necessary to attain it.

The narrow sense of implied power has been long accepted within the Community.[42] The ECJ is also willing to embrace the wider formulation. This is exemplified by the following cases.

[41] T.C. Hartley, *The Foundations of European Community Law* (5th edn., Oxford University Press, 2003), 106, italics in the original.

[42] Case 8/55 *Fédération Charbonnière de Belgique* v. *High Authority* [1956] ECR 245, 280.

Cases 281, 283–285, 287/85 **Germany v. Commission**
[1987] ECR 3203

[Note ToA renumbering: Art. 118 is now Art. 137]

The Commission made a decision pursuant to Article 118 which established a prior communi-cation and consultation process in relation to migration policies affecting workers from non-EC countries. The Member States were to inform the Commission and other Member States of their draft measures concerning entry, residence, equality of treatment, and the integration of such workers into the social and cultural life of the country. After notification to the Commission of such draft measures there would then be consultation with the Commission and other Member States. A number of States challenged this measure as being *ultra vires* the Commission. Article 118, which concerns collaboration in the social field, did not expressly give the Commission power to make binding decisions. The ECJ held that migration policy in rela-tion to non-Member States could fall within Article 118, to some extent at least, because of the effects of such migration on the employment situation in the EC.

THE ECJ

27. [I]t must be considered whether the second paragraph of Article 118, which provides that the Commission is to act, *inter alia*, by arranging consultations, gives it the power to adopt a binding decision with a view to the arrangement of such consultations.

28. In that connection it must be emphasised that where an Article of the EEC Treaty ... con-fers a specific task on the Commission it must be accepted, if that provision is not to be ren-dered wholly ineffective, that it confers on the Commission necessarily and *per se* the powers which are indispensable in order to carry out that task. Accordingly, the second paragraph of Article 118 must be interpreted as conferring on the Commission all the powers which are neces-sary in order to arrange the consultations. In order to perform that task of arranging consult-ation the Commission must necessarily be able to require the Member States to notify essential information, in the first place to identify the problems and in the second place in order to pinpoint the possible guidelines for any future joint action on the part of the Member States; likewise it must be able to require them to take part in consultation.

Case C–176/03 **Commission v. Council**
[2005] ECR I–7879

The Council enacted a Framework Decision under the Third Pillar, Title VI TEU, that required Member States to prescribe criminal penalties for certain environmental offences. The Commission argued that the measure should have been enacted under Article 175 EC, since it was concerned with the environment. The ECJ found that the principal aim of the Framework Decision was to protect the environment, and that it should have been made under Article 175. It accepted that, as a general rule, neither criminal law, nor criminal procedure fell within Community competence, but then reasoned as follows.

THE ECJ

48. However, [this] does not prevent the Community legislature, when the application of effective, proportionate and dissuasive criminal penalties by the competent national authorities

is an essential measure for combating serious environmental offences, from taking measures which relate to the criminal law of the Member States which it considers necessary in order to ensure that the rules which it lays down on environmental protection are fully effective.

The ECJ has been disinclined to place limits on broadly worded Treaty Articles. It can however do so. In the *Tobacco Advertising* case the ECJ held that a directive relating to tobacco advertising could not be based on Article 95.[43]

Case C–376/98 **Germany v. European Parliament and Council**
[2000] ECR I–8419

[Note ToA renumbering: Arts. 3b, 3(c), 7a, 57(2), 66, 100a, 164
are now Arts. 5, 3(1)(c), 14, 47(2), 55, 95, 220]

Germany sought the annulment of a Directive designed to harmonize the law relating to the advertising and sponsorship of tobacco. The Directive had been based on Articles 57(2), 66, and 100a. Article 100a allows the adoption of harmonization measures for the functioning of the internal market. The ECJ cited Articles 100a, 3(c), and 7a of the Treaty. It then continued as follows.

THE ECJ

83. Those provisions, read together, make it clear that the measures referred to in Article 100a(1)...are intended to improve the conditions for the establishment and functioning of the internal market. To construe that article as meaning that it vests in the Community legislature a general power to regulate the internal market would not only be contrary to the express wording of the provisions cited above, but would also be incompatible with the principle embodied in Article 3b...that the powers of the Community are limited to those specifically conferred on it.

84. Moreover, a measure adopted on the basis of Article 100a...must genuinely have as its object the improvement of the conditions for the establishment and functioning of the internal market. If a mere finding of disparities between national rules and of the abstract risk of obstacles to the exercise of fundamental freedoms or of distortions of competition liable to result therefrom were sufficient to justify the choice of Article 100a as a legal base, judicial review of compliance with the proper legal basis might be nugatory. The Court would then be prevented from discharging the function entrusted to it by Article 164...of ensuring that the law is observed in the interpretation and application of the Treaty.

85. So, in considering whether Article 100a was the proper legal basis, the Court must verify whether the measure whose validity is at issue in fact pursues the objectives stated by the Community legislature...

While there are therefore limits to the use of Article 95, subsequent case law on related subject-matter has shown that the ECJ is willing to accept the use of Article 95 as the legal basis for the enacted measure.[44] This is exemplified by the 2006 *Tobacco Advertising* case,[45] where

---

[43] T. Hervey, 'Up in Smoke? Community (Anti-)Tobacco Law and Policy' (2001) 26 *ELRev.* 101.

[44] Case C–377/98 *Netherlands*, n. 36 above; Case C–491/01 *The Queen* v. *Secretary of State for Health, ex p. British American Tobacco (Investments) Ltd. and Imperial Tobacco Ltd.* [2002] ECR I–11453; Case C–210/03 *R* v. *Secretary of State for Health, ex p. Swedish Match* [2004] ECR I–11893.

[45] Case C–380/03 *Germany* v. *European Parliament and Council*, 12 Dec. 2006.

the ECJ upheld the validity of a revised directive on tobacco advertising, which included, subject to limited exceptions, prohibitions on advertising in the press and radio and constraints on sponsorship by tobacco companies. The Court concluded that this measure could validly be adopted under Article 95 EC, since there were disparities between the relevant national laws on advertising and sponsorship of tobacco products, and these disparities could affect competition and inter-state trade.

(d) ARTICLE 308

The fourth reason there can be difficulties concerning the basis for legislation relates to Article 308 EC. Most Treaty Articles relate to a specific subject-matter area, such as workers or goods. The Treaty also contains broader legislative provisions, such as Articles 94 and 95 EC, concerning harmonization of laws. Article 308 is broader still. It provides that:

> If action by the Community should prove necessary to attain, in the course of the operation of the common market, one of the objectives of the Community and this Treaty has not provided the necessary powers, the Council shall, acting unanimously on a proposal from the Commission and after consulting the European Parliament, take the appropriate measures.

Article 308 has been a valuable legislative power, particularly when the Community did not possess more specific legislative authority in certain areas. Thus the Article was used to legitimate legislation in areas such as the environment and regional policy, before these matters were dealt with through later Treaty amendments. Weiler captures the importance of this provision and the manner in which it was interpreted.

J. Weiler, The Transformation of Europe[46]

> In a variety of fields, including, for example, conclusion of international agreements, the granting of emergency food aid to third countries, and creation of new institutions, the Community made use of Article 235 in a manner that was simply not consistent with the narrow interpretation of the Article as a codification of implied powers doctrine in its instrumental sense. Only a truly radical and 'creative' reading of the Article could explain and justify its usage as, for example, the legal basis for granting emergency food aid to non-associated states. But this wide reading, in which all the institutions partook, meant that it would become virtually impossible to find an activity which could not be brought within the objectives of the Treaty.

Article 308 requires that the power should be used to attain a Community objective. Given, however, the breadth of the Treaty objectives, and given also the ECJ's purposive mode of interpreting Community aims, these 'conditions' have not placed a severe constraint on the Council. They are not however entirely devoid of meaning, as exemplified by *Opinion 2/94*.[47] The case was concerned with the legality of the EC's possible accession to the European Convention on Human Rights (ECHR). The ECJ held that Article 308 could not be used to widen the scope of Community powers beyond the framework created by the EC Treaty taken

---

[46] (1991) 100 *Yale LJ* 2403, 2445–2446.

[47] *Opinion 2/94, Accession of the Community to the European Human Rights Convention* [1996] ECR I–1759. Cf. *Opinion 2/91, ILO Convention 170 on Chemicals at Work* [1993] ECR I–1061.

as a whole. Nor could it be used as the foundation for the adoption of provisions which would, in substance, amend the Treaty without following the necessary amendment procedures. It should also be acknowledged that the ECJ was probably content to reach this conclusion in the instant case, thereby avoiding subjecting itself to the ultimate authority of the European Court of Human Rights.

The most problematic aspect of Article 308 is the condition that the Treaty has not 'provided the necessary powers'. The mere fact that another, more specific, Treaty provision has given a power to make recommendations will not preclude the use of Article 308 to enact binding measures.[48] Nor, it seems, will Article 308 be excluded by the fact that the particular Treaty provisions could be interpreted broadly by using the implied-powers doctrine discussed above.[49] Whether the Treaty has provided necessary powers elsewhere can, however, be of particular significance in two situations.

One is where specific Treaty Articles provide for more extensive involvement of the European Parliament than does Article 308. Article 308 only requires the Council to consult the Parliament, whereas other Treaty Articles give the Parliament greater rights in the legislative process. If the Council is able to proceed via Article 308, there is a danger that this will diminish the European Parliament's role. The ECJ has, therefore, stressed that Article 308 can be used only where no other provision of the Treaty gives the Community institutions the necessary power to adopt the relevant measure. The Court will closely scrutinize the use of Article 308 where it is argued that another more specific Treaty article would afford the European Parliament a greater role in the legislative process.[50]

The other situation in which the choice between Article 308 and a more specific Treaty Article can be of significance is where there are differences in the voting rules under the respective Articles. Article 308 requires unanimity in the Council, whereas many other Treaty provisions demand only a qualified majority.

Cases involving the appropriate boundaries of Article 308 have not infrequently been litigated before the ECJ. Thus in the *Tariff Preferences*[51] case the Commission sought the annulment of a Council regulation concerning tariff preferences for goods from developing countries. The Council argued that, since the purpose of the measures was in reality development aid, they could be adopted only by using Article 308. The Commission contended that Article 113 (now Article 133), which concerned the common commercial policy, could be used, and that this required only qualified-majority voting. In fact the Council did not specify any particular Article of the Treaty in the measures. The ECJ annulled the regulations because of failure to state the legal basis of the measures, and because they could have been adopted under Article 113.

More recently in the *Biotechnology Directive* case, the ECJ ruled that a directive concerning patent protection for such inventions was properly adopted under Article 95 and did not require Article 308 as an additional legal basis.[52] By contrast, in a case concerning a regulation on mutual assistance between national administrative authorities to deal with EC agricultural and customs fraud, the Court upheld the use of Article 308, ruling that Article 95 would be inappropriate in this context.[53]

---

[48] Case 8/73 *Hauptzollamt Bremerhaven* v. *Massey-Ferguson* [1973] ECR 897.

[49] *Ibid.*, para. 4.

[50] Case 45/86 *Commission* v. *Council* [1987] ECR 1493; Case C–350/92 *Spain* v. *Council* [1995] ECR I–1985; Case C–271/94 *European Parliament* v. *Council (Re the Edicom Decision)* [1996] ECR I–1689.

[51] Case 45/86 *Commission* v. *Council* [1987] ECR 1493. See also Case 165/87 *Commission* v. *Council* [1988] ECR 5545; Case C–295/90 *European Parliament* v. *Council* [1992] ECR I–4193.

[52] Case C–377/98 *Netherlands* v. *Parliament and Council*, n. 36 above.

[53] Case C–209/97 *Commission* v. *Council* [1999] ECR I–8067.

(e) COMPETENCE AND THE THREE PILLARS

The existence of the Three Pillars can also lead to difficulties in deciding whether there is competence to enact the contested measure.[54] In the real world there is an increasing overlap between the Pillars, and measures may be adopted under the Community Pillar where the primary objective is to support action taken under the Second or Third Pillar. This can lead to claims that the Community measure did not properly fall within the sphere of the relevant Treaty Article.[55]

Thus in the *PNR* case[56] the European Parliament sought the annulment of a Council decision concluding an agreement between the EC and the USA on the transfer of passenger name record data by air carriers to US government departments. The EP argued, *inter alia*, that the decision could not be based on Article 95 EC, since it was not primarily concerned with the functioning of the internal market, but rather with combating terrorism and serious crime. The ECJ held that Article 95, when read in conjunction with the Data Protection Directive, could not justify the Council decision. Advocate General Léger went further, concluding that the decision was not primarily concerned with the internal market, and hence could not be based on Article 95.[57]

5. EXTERNAL COMMUNITY COMPETENCE

The discussion thus far has been concerned with difficulties of drawing the boundaries of the EU's internal competence. There are equal, if not greater, problems in delineating the sphere of the EU's external competence. This is a complex subject.[58] The ensuing discussion merely highlights some of the principal points in the case law. More detailed discussion can be found in the chapter on external relations.[59]

(a) LEGAL PERSONALITY, LEGAL CAPACITY, AND THE MAKING OF THE AGREEMENT

The EC has always had legal personality.[60] The EU was not expressly given legal personality when it was created, but the effect of Article 24 TEU, which was added by the Treaty of Amsterdam and modified by the Nice Treaty, was to confer upon the Council the capacity to enter international agreements negotiated by the Presidency.[61] This applies to agreements made under the CFSP Pillar, and also to those under the PJCC Pillar.[62]

---

[54] M. Cremona, 'External Relations of the EU and the Member States: Competence, Mixed Agreements, International Responsibility, and Effects of International Law', EUI Working Paper, Law No. 2006/22, 9–15.

[55] See, e.g., Case T–315/01 *Yassin Abdullah Kadi* v. *Council and Commission* [2005] ECR II–3649, paras. 87–135.

[56] Cases C–317–318/04 *European Parliament* v. *Council and Commission* [2006] ECR I–4721.

[57] *Ibid.*, AG Léger, paras. 140–152.

[58] I. Macleod, I. Hendry, and S. Hyett, *The External Relations of the European Communities: A Manual of Law and Practice* (Oxford University Press, 1996); D. McGoldrick, *International Relations Law of the European Union* (Longman, 1997); M. Koskenniemi (ed.), *International Law Aspects of the European Union* (Kluwer, 1998); A. Dashwood and C. Hillion (eds.), *The General Law of EC External Relations* (Sweet & Maxwell, 2000); P. Eeckhout, *External Relations of the European Union: Legal and Constitutional Foundations* (Oxford University Press, 2004).

[59] Ch. 6.

[60] Art. 281 EC.

[61] See above, 22–23.

[62] Art. 38 TEU.

The Treaty lays down the procedure for the negotiation and conclusion of international agreements by the EC.[63] In essence the Commission is the principal negotiator, and the Council concludes the agreement on the basis of the proposal put forward by the Commission, after having consulted the European Parliament. The voting rules in the Council and the extent of the EP's involvement may vary depending on the subject-matter of the agreement.

The choice of the legal basis for a measure adopting an international agreement must be made on objective factors that are amenable to judicial review. If the agreement pursues a twofold purpose, one of which is predominant, then the measure must be founded on a single legal basis, namely that required by the predominant purpose. Where exceptionally there are several objectives pursued simultaneously, none of which predominates, then the measure can be founded on the corresponding legal bases.[64]

(b) EXPRESS EXTERNAL COMPETENCE

There is express external competence in areas stipulated by the Treaty. The number of such areas has expanded with successive Treaty amendments and now includes commercial policy;[65] association agreements;[66] the maintenance of relations between the Community and international organizations such as the UN, the GATT, the Council of Europe, and the OECD;[67] development policy;[68] environmental policy;[69] research and technology;[70] monetary and foreign exchange policy;[71] and economic, financial, and technical co-operation with third countries.[72] There are also Treaty provisions on the fostering of co-operation with third countries and international organizations concerning matters such as education, vocational training, culture, health, and trans-European networks.[73]

The existence of express Community competence is however logically distinct from the issue of whether the Community's competence in these areas is exclusive, and the answer can vary from area to area.

(c) IMPLIED EXTERNAL COMPETENCE AND EXCLUSIVITY

(i) The Early Case Law

It is however clear that even if there is no express grant of competence the Community can have implied external competence. The ECJ held in a series of cases that when Community law created powers within its internal system for the purpose of attaining a specific objective,

---

[63] Art. 300(1) EC.

[64] *Opinion 2/00 Opinion Pursuant to Article 300(6) EC, Cartegena Protocol* [2001] ECR I–9713, paras. 22–23.

[65] Art. 133 EC. See P. Eeckhout and T. Tridimas, 'The External Competence of the Community and the Case-Law of the Court of Justice: Principle Versus Pragmatism' (1994) 14 *YBEL* 143.

[66] Art. 310 EC.

[67] Arts. 302–304 EC.

[68] Art. 181 EC.

[69] Art. 174 EC.

[70] Art. 170 EC.

[71] Art. 111 EC.

[72] Art. 181a EC.

[73] Arts. 149(3), 150(3), 151(3), 152(3), 155(3) EC.

the Community was empowered to enter into the international commitments necessary for attainment of that objective, even in the absence of an express provision to that effect.[74]

The issue of whether external power is exclusive is, as stated above, distinct from the existence of such power: implied external competence can be exclusive or shared.[75] While it is clear that the EC's implied external competence can be shared with the Member States, the ECJ also held that in certain circumstances the EC's implied external power would be exclusive. The precise circumstances where this would be so were however not entirely clear,[76] although the formulations used by the ECJ as to when exclusivity would arise were far-reaching.

Thus in *ERTA* the ECJ held that when the Community acted to implement a common policy pursuant to the Treaty, the Member States no longer had the right to take external action where this would affect the rules thus established or distort their scope.[77] This position was modified in *Kramer*.[78] The ECJ held that the EC could possess implied external powers even though it had not taken internal measures to implement the relevant policy, but that until the EC duly exercised its internal power the Member States retained competence to act, provided that their action was compatible with Community objectives. The scope of exclusivity was thrown into doubt because of the *Inland Waterways* case,[79] where the ECJ held that the EC could have exclusive external competence, even though it had not exercised its internal powers, if Member State action could place in jeopardy the Community objective sought to be attained.

(ii) *The WTO Case, External Competence, and the Limits of Exclusive Competence*

The ECJ however pulled back from the very broad reading of exclusivity contained in the *Inland Waterways* case. In *Opinion 1/94 on the WTO Agreement*[80] the ECJ ruled that certain issues covered by the General Agreement on Trade in Services, GATS, and the Agreement on Trade Related Intellectual Property Rights, TRIPS, were not in the scope of the Common Commercial Policy.[81]

The Commission argued in the alternative that exclusive external competence to conclude GATS and TRIPS resided with the EC, either because it flowed implicitly from Treaty provisions concerning internal competence, or from legislative acts of the EC giving effect to that

---

[74] Case 22/70 *Commission v. Council* [1971] ECR 263; Cases 3, 4, and 6/76 *Kramer* [1976] ECR 1279; *Opinion 1/76 On the Draft Agreement Establishing a Laying-up Fund for Inland Waterway Vessels* [1977] ECR 741; *Opinion 2/91 Re the ILO Convention 170 on Chemicals at Work* [1993] ECR I–1061; *Opinion 2/94*, n. 47 above.

[75] *Opinion 1/03 Competence of the Community to conclude the new Lugano Convention on Jurisdiction and the Recognition and Enforcement of Judgments in Civil and Commercial Matters* [2006] ECR I–1145, paras. 114–117.

[76] M. Cremona, 'External Relations and External Competence: the Emergence of an Integrated Policy', in P. Craig and G. de Búrca (eds.), *The Evolution of EU Law* (Oxford University Press, 1999), 137; A. Dashwood and J. Heliskoski, 'The Classic Authorities Revisited', in Dashwood and Hillion (eds.), n. 58 above, 3.

[77] Case 22/70 *Commission* v. *Council*, n. 74 above.

[78] Cases 3, 4, and 6/76 *Kramer*, n. 74 above.

[79] *Opinion 1/76*, n. 74 above.

[80] *Opinion 1/94 Competence of the Community to Conclude International Agreements Concerning Services and the Protection of Intellectual Property, WTO* [1994] ECR I–5267.

[81] *Ibid.*, paras. 53, 71. Art. 133 was amended by the Treaty of Amsterdam after *Opinion 1/94* to empower the Council expressly to bring agreements on services and intellectual property within the scope of the Art. It was amended again by the Treaty of Nice. In most areas covered by Art. 133 the EC will have exclusive external competence, but there are exceptions where competence is shared: Art. 133(6).

competence, or from the need to make an international agreement in order to attain an internal EC objective.[82] The ECJ rejected this contention.

It held in relation to GATS that exclusive external competence was in general dependent on actual exercise of internal powers, and not their mere existence.[83] The *Inland Waterways* case was distinguished on the ground that the EC's very internal objective could not be attained without the making of an international agreement, and internal EC rules could not realistically be made prior to the conclusion of such an agreement.[84] This rationale did not apply to the subject-matter covered by GATS, since attainment of the Community objective did not necessitate agreement with non-Member States.[85] In relation to TRIPS, the ECJ also concluded that the EC did not have exclusive competence. This was because the international action envisaged was not necessary to attain an internal Community objective, and because the EC, although competent to enact harmonization measures, had not done so to any significant extent.[86]

(iii) *The* Open Skies *and* Lugano *Cases, the* ERTA *Ruling, and Exclusive External Competence*

The *WTO* case limited the instances where the ECJ would be willing to conclude that the EC possessed exclusive external competence: it restricted the *Inland Waterways* ruling in the manner set out above and reasoned from the premise that exclusive external competence was normally dependent on the actual exercise of the EC's internal power, and not merely its existence. This reasoning has been followed in later decisions.[87] Subsequent case law has nonetheless revealed that where the EC has exercised its powers internally, the ECJ is prepared to interpret broadly the circumstances in which this gives rise to exclusive external competence for the EC.

This is apparent from the '*open skies*' litigation, involving Commission actions against a number of Member States.[88] The ruling in *Commission* v. *Germany*[89] can be taken by way of example. The Commission brought an action against Germany under what is now Article 226 EC, alleging that it had infringed the Treaty by concluding bilateral 'open skies' agreements with the USA, on the ground that the EC had exclusive external competence in this area.

The Commission argued that this exclusive competence flowed from the principle laid down in the *Inland Waterways* case as interpreted by the *WTO* judgment. The ECJ disagreed. It accepted that an implied external competence could exist not only where the internal competence had been exercised through the enactment of measures to implement the common policy, but also where the Community measures were adopted only when the international agreement was concluded. This was however subject to the limits articulated in the *WTO* case: the principle applied where the internal competence could only be exercised at the same time as the external competence on the ground that conclusion of an international agreement was

---

82 *Ibid.*, para. 72.

83 *Ibid.*, paras. 77, 88–89.

84 *Ibid.*, paras. 85–86.

85 *Ibid.*, para. 86. The ECJ reached the same conclusion in relation to TRIPS: *ibid.*, para. 100.

86 *Ibid.*, paras. 99–105.

87 See, e.g., *Opinion 2/92 Competence of the Community or one of its Institutions to Participate in the Third Revised Decision of the OECD on National Treatment* [1995] ECR I–521.

88 Case C–466/98 *Commission* v. *United Kingdom* [2002] ECR I–9427; Case C–467/98 *Commission* v. *Denmark* [2002] ECR I–9519; Case C–468/98 *Commission* v. *Sweden* [2002] ECR I–9575; Case C–469/98 *Commission* v. *Finland* [2002] ECR I–9627; Case C–471/98 *Commission* v. *Belgium* [2002] ECR I–9681; Case C–472/98 *Commission* v. *Luxembourg* [2002] ECR I–9741; Case C–475/98 *Commission* v. *Austria* [2002] ECR I–9797.

89 Case C–467/98 *Commission* v. *Germany* [2002] ECR I–9855.

necessary to attain the Community objective and internal rules could not be adopted prior to such an agreement. The ECJ found that this rationale for exclusive external competence was inapplicable to the instant case.[90]

The ECJ then considered the alternative argument advanced by the Commission, to the effect that the EC had exclusive external competence in line with the *ERTA* ruling, because it had exercised its internal competence to some degree within the relevant area. Article 80(2) EC empowered the Council to decide whether and to what extent provision should be made for air transport and the Council had adopted a 'package of legislation' based on this Article. The ECJ held that the *ERTA* ruling could apply to internal power exercised in this manner, and therefore the EC had an implied external competence. It followed that when the EC made common rules pursuant to this power, the Member States no longer had the right, acting individually or collectively, to undertake obligations towards non-Member States, which affected those rules or distorted their scope.[91]

The importance of the judgment lies in its confirmation of the broad reading given to the phrase 'affected those rules or distorted their scope', since it is this that transforms external competence into exclusive external competence.[92] The ECJ, in accordance with prior case law, held that this would be so where the international agreement fell within the scope of the common rules or within an area that was already largely covered by such rules, and this was so in the latter case even if there was no contradiction between the international commitments and the internal rules. EC legislative provisions relating to the treatment of non-Member State nationals, or expressly conferring power to negotiate with non-Member States, gave the EC exclusive external competence. This was so even in the absence of express provision authorizing the EC to negotiate with non-Member States in areas where the EC had achieved complete harmonization, since if Member States were able to conclude international agreements individually it would affect the common rules thus made. Distortion in the flow of services in the internal market that might arise as a result of the bilateral agreement did not, by way of contrast, affect the common rules adopted in the area.

The same general message emerges from the *Lugano* Opinion:[93] implied external competence may be exclusive or shared,[94] but where the EC has exercised its powers internally, then the ECJ will be inclined to conclude that this gives rise to exclusive external competence, whenever such exclusive competence is needed to 'preserve the effectiveness of Community law and the proper functioning of the systems established by its rules'.[95]

(d) SHARED COMPETENCE, MIXED AGREEMENTS, AND CO-OPERATION

Notwithstanding the relatively broad reading given to exclusive external competence, the reality is that many external powers continue to be shared between the Member States and the EC. There are a number of reasons why this is so. It may be because the conditions set out above for the Community's exclusive external competence are not satisfied, where for example the EC has not adopted sufficient internal measures to accord it exclusive external competence.[96]

---

[90] *Ibid.*, paras. 80–90.
[91] *Ibid.*, paras. 101–105.
[92] *Ibid.*, paras. 107–113.
[93] *Opinion 1/03*, n. 75 above.
[94] *Ibid.*, paras. 114–115.
[95] *Ibid.*, para. 131.
[96] *Opinion 1/94*, n. 80 above, paras. 99–105; *Opinion 2/00*, n. 64 above, paras. 45–46.

External competence may also be shared because the EC Treaty does not confer sufficient competence on the EC to ratify the agreement in its entirety, thereby requiring allocation as between the EC and the Member States of the power to conclude the agreement with non-Member States,[97] or where the EC has some competence over the relevant area, but this is limited to laying down minimum requirements, thereby leaving Member States free to apply the rules flowing from the international agreement over and beyond this.[98] A further rationale for shared competence is where the appropriate legal basis for the measure concluding the agreement lays down a legislative procedure different from that which has in fact been followed by the Community institutions.[99]

The fact that external competence is shared requires close co-operation between the Member States and EC when the agreement is negotiated. The fact that participation of the Member States and the EC as parties to the international agreement may give rise to problems of co-ordination when the agreement is interpreted or implemented cannot be used to deny their respective legal rights to participate in the agreement.[100] The Member States and EC do however have a duty to co-operate in the negotiation, conclusion, and implementation of the agreement.[101]

It is possible for an agreement in an area of shared competence to be signed only by the Member States[102] or only by the Community.[103] An international agreement made where there is shared competence and where the EC and Member States are parties is known as a 'mixed agreement'.[104] A mixed agreement will be mandatory in those areas of shared competence where the EC and Member States have different obligations.

6. THE PRINCIPLE OF SUBSIDIARITY

Closely linked to the question of the *existence* of Community competence is the principle of subsidiarity, which is intended to regulate the lawfulness of the *exercise* of Community competence. We shall see, however, that these two are not conceptually as distinct as they may first appear. The centrality of subsidiarity to the Maastricht negotiations is well known. The subsidiarity concept was to be used to defeat those who hoped to increase the federalist leanings of the Community under the TEU. It was one of the symbols used to placate the Tory right wing during those long nights spent debating the TEU at Westminster. The meaning of subsidiarity is, however, far from clear. We can at least be clear about the wording of Article 5 EC:

> The Community shall act within the limits of the powers conferred upon it by this Treaty and of the objectives assigned to it therein.
>
> In areas which do not fall within its exclusive competence, the Community shall take action, in accordance with the principle of subsidiarity, only if and in so far as the objectives of the

---

[97] *Opinion 2/00*, n. 64 above, para. 5.

[98] *Opinion 2/91*, n. 74 above, paras. 16–21.

[99] *Opinion 2/00*, n. 64 above, para. 5.

[100] *Opinion 2/91*, n. 74 above, paras. 19–20; *Opinion 1/94*, n. 80 above, para. 107; *Opinion 2/00*, n. 64 above, para. 41.

[101] *Opinion 2/91*, n. 74 above, paras. 36–37; *Opinion 1/94*, n. 80 above, paras. 108–109; *Opinion 2/00*, n. 64 above, para. 18.

[102] *Opinion 2/91*, n. 74 above, para. 5.

[103] Case C–268/94 *Portugal* v. *Council* [1996] ECR I–6177, paras. 68–77.

[104] D. O'Keeffe and H. Schermers (eds.), *Mixed Agreements* (Martinus Nijhoff, 1983); M. Cremona, 'The Doctrine of Exclusivity and the Position of Mixed Agreements in the External Relations of the European Community' (1982) 2 *OJLS* 393; Cremona, n. 54 above.

proposed action cannot be sufficiently achieved by the Member States and can therefore, by reason of the scale or effects of the proposed action, be better achieved by the Community.

Any action by the Community shall not go beyond what is necessary to achieve the objectives of this Treaty.

(a) THE COMMUNITY MUST ACT WITHIN THE LIMITS OF ITS POWERS

This requirement, in the first paragraph of Article 5, need not detain us for long. It has always been recognized that the Community has competence only within the limited areas in which it has been given power. The extent to which this serves as a limit has, however, been reduced by the expansion of the areas over which the Community has competence. Thus the SEA, the TEU, and the ToA have added significantly to the subject-matter competence of the Community. The ECJ has moreover interpreted the Community's legislative competence broadly through recognition of the implied-powers doctrine, and through the use of Article 308.

(b) THE EXCLUSIVE COMPETENCE OF THE COMMUNITY

Article 5 makes it clear that subsidiarity will have to be considered only in relation to areas which do *not* fall within the exclusive competence of the Community. If an area is within the Community's exclusive competence then there is no legal obligation to apply subsidiarity, although it is in fact taken into account.

The problem is that there is no easy criterion for determining the scope of the Community's exclusive competence. The Treaty is not explicitly framed in these terms, and thus the meaning of this phrase is contestable. The Commission has taken the view that an area falls within the exclusive competence of the Community if the Treaties impose on the Community a duty to act, in the sense that it has sole responsibility for the performance of a particular task.[105] It has argued that there is a 'block' of exclusive powers which are joined by the thread of the internal market, including: free movement of goods, persons, services, and capital; the Common Commercial Policy; competition; the Common Agricultural Policy (CAP); the conservation of fisheries; and transport policy.

Commentators differ considerably, and there are both broad and narrow constructions of the term 'exclusive competence'. Toth provides the argument in favour of the broad view.

A.G. Toth, A Legal Analysis of Subsidiarity[106]

The Court has confirmed time and again . . . that in all matters transferred to the Community from the Member States, the Community's competence is, in principle, exclusive and leaves no room for concurrent competence on the part of the Member States. Therefore, where the competence of the Community begins, that of the Member States ends. From then on, Member States no longer have the power unilaterally to introduce legislation. They can act only within the

---

[105] Bull. EC 10–1992, 116. See *1st Report of Commission on Subsidiarity*, COM(94)533.
[106] In D. O'Keeffe and P.M. Twomey (eds.), *Legal Issues of the Maastricht Treaty* (Chancery, 1994), 39–40.

limits of strictly defined management/implementing powers delegated back to the national authorities by the Community institutions. As the Court of Justice has stated: 'The existence of Community powers excludes the possibility of concurrent powers on the part of the Member States.'[107] Even the fact that during a certain period the Community fails to exercise a competence which has been transferred to it, does not create concurrent competence for the Member States during that period. This principle also follows from, or is closely related to, the doctrine of the supremacy of Community law, which of course is a basic tenet of Community law.

The central feature of this broad view is that the Community's exclusive competence exists in those areas in which the Member States have transferred power to the Community, *irrespective* of whether the Community has actually exercised this power. From this premise Toth concluded that subsidiarity could not apply to any matter covered by the original EEC Treaty, including: the free movement of goods, services, persons, and capital; the Common Commercial Policy; competition; the Common Agricultural Policy; Transport Policy; and the common organization of the fisheries. Toth accepted that the Community did not possess exclusive competence within many of the newer areas in which it had been given some power, such as the environment, economic and social cohesion, education and vocational training, consumer protection, and social policy. This was because the relevant Treaty Articles were framed so as to give the Community more limited powers in these spheres. Community legislation on, for example, the environment or health could however also facilitate the completion of the internal market. This would, for Toth, take such matters outside the remit of subsidiarity.[108]

This view of the term 'exclusive competence' has not gone unchallenged. Steiner adopts a narrower construction.

J. Steiner, Subsidiarity under the Maastricht Treaty[109]

The EC, even at its beginnings, was not concerned with dividing competence between the Community and the Member States, but with sharing powers over a wide range of activity in order to achieve certain common and mutually beneficial objectives. Whilst it was clear that in some areas there would be little scope for action by Member States if the desired goal was to be achieved—a customs union is a necessary prerequisite to a single market—in most areas competence was concurrent. This did not mean that States and the Community could legislate on the same issue at the same time, nor that States' competence in these matters was unrestrained (since they are bound to comply with the rules of the EC Treaty), but that their action would be complementary or supplementary. Once the Community has exercised its powers under the Treaty, to regulate a particular matter within a certain area of activity, clearly States are not free to enact measures which conflict with those rules. As the volume and scope of Community law increase, so will States' powers diminish. But there are few areas of activity in which Member States do not retain some degree of competence. Thus it is not surprising that commentators have had difficulty in identifying areas in which the Community has exclusive competence, nor that the Heads of State refrained from doing so at Maastricht.

One is forced to the conclusion that the only areas in which the Community has exclusive competence for the purposes of Article 3b are those in which it *has already legislated*.... Surely

---

[107] The quotation comes from the *ERTA* case: Case 22/70 *Commission* v. *Council* [1971] ECR 263, 276.
[108] A.G. Toth, 'A Legal Analysis of Subsidiarity', 41.
[109] In O'Keeffe and Twomey (eds.), n. 106 above, 57–58, italics in the original.

the competence of Member States ends, not as Toth suggests, where the competence of the Community begins, but where its powers have been exercised....The fact that the competence to act, even to act comprehensively, has been granted to the Community by the Treaty does not, and surely cannot mean that its competence to act in these areas cannot be subject to the subsidiarity principle. To allow whole areas of activity to escape scrutiny under paragraph 2, simply because the Community has potential competence in these areas, would surely undermine the very purpose for which this provision was intended.

The difference between this view and that advanced by Toth is readily apparent. Steiner's hypothesis is that subsidiarity will be excluded only where the Community has actually exercised its power; only in such areas will the Community have exclusive competence. Even if one favours this view, it should nonetheless be recognized that Community power can be exercised through the passage of formal regulations, directives, etc., *or* through the ECJ's decisions. The principles relating to the free movement of goods have, for example, been implemented in part by Community legislation and in part by seminal Court decisions.[110] It is clear that Steiner's approach would have to be construed so as to capture both modes of exercising Community power, and thus even the narrow formulation of the phrase 'exclusive competence' might not be as narrow as initially thought. This is particularly important, given that legislative and judicial power often interact.

(c) THE SUBSIDIARITY CALCULUS

We can now examine the subsidiarity principle itself. The Community is to take action 'only if and in so far as the objectives of the proposed action cannot be sufficiently achieved by the Member States and can therefore by reason of the scale or effects of the proposed action, be better achieved by the Community'. Article 5(3) adds the further condition that 'any action by the Community shall not go beyond what is necessary to achieve the objectives of this Treaty'. It seems clear that the drafting of Article 5 was influenced by the experience of German law concerning the relationship of the Federal authorities and the *Länder*.[111]

Subsidiarity embraces three separate, albeit related, ideas: the Community is to take action only if the objectives of that action cannot be sufficiently achieved by the Member States; the Community can better achieve the action, because of its scale or effects; if the Community does take action then this should not go beyond what is necessary to achieve the Treaty objectives. The first two parts of this formulation entail what the Commission has termed a test of comparative efficiency:[112] is it better for the action to be taken by the Community or the Member States? The third part of the formulation brings in a proportionality test.

The 1993 Inter-institutional Agreement on Procedures for Implementing the Principle of Subsidiarity required all three institutions to have regard to the principle when devising Community legislation. This was re-confirmed by the Protocol on the Application of the Principles of Subsidiarity and Proportionality attached to the ToA.[113] The Commission must provide in its explanatory memorandum concerning proposed legislation a justification for

---

[110] See Ch. 19.

[111] N. Emiliou, 'Subsidiarity: An Effective Barrier Against the "Enterprises of Ambition"?' (1992) 17 *ELRev.* 383 and 'Subsidiarity: Panacea or Fig Leaf?', in O'Keeffe and Twomey, n. 106 above, ch. 5.

[112] Commission Communication to the Council and the European Parliament, Bull. EC 10–1992, 116.

[113] See G. de Búrca, 'Reappraising Subsidiarity's Significance after Amsterdam', Jean Monnet Working Paper 7/1999, available at www.jeanmonnetprogram.org/.

the measure in terms of the subsidiarity principle (paragraphs 4, 5, and 9 of the Protocol), and submit an annual report on the application of Article 5 (paragraph 9). Amendments by the Council or the European Parliament must likewise be accompanied by a justification in terms of subsidiarity, if they entail more extensive Community intervention (paragraph 11). The form of the Community legislation should be as simple as possible, with a preference for framework directives over regulations (paragraph 6). The Protocol nonetheless confirmed that subsidiarity applied only where the Community did not have exclusive competence, and that the subsidiarity principle did not call into question the powers conferred on the EC, as interpreted by the ECJ (paragraph 3).

It is clear that there will be many areas in which the comparative efficiency calculus comes out in favour of Community action. The idea that matters should be dealt with at the level closest to those affected is fine in principle. The very *raison d'être* of the Community will, however, often demand Community action to ensure the uniformity of *general approach* which is of central importance to the realization of a common market. This is confirmed by the Commission's reports made pursuant to Article 9 of the Protocol.[114] There are moreover difficulties with the general approach embodied in the Protocol.

A. Estella, The EU Principle of Subsidiarity and its Critique[115]

> The truth of the matter is that attempting to define *ex ante* criteria of a general and abstract character for the purpose of limiting central intervention stands little hope of success. The reasons for this limitation are functional and can be found in the nature of modern regulatory problems. The functional interconnection between regulatory areas…makes the task of establishing clear dividing lines difficult. Even in those areas in which there seem to be clear reasons in favour of national, or even regional or local, regulation…it will always be possible to argue that due to the close relationship between these areas and the development of the single market, some Community intervention will always be necessary.

It is however also clear that the very existence of Article 5, and in particular paragraph 3 thereof, will, as is apparent from paragraph 6 of the Protocol, have an impact on the existence and form of Community action. The Commission will consider whether action really is required at Community level, and its reasoning will be found in the recitals or explanatory memorandum.[116] If Community action is required, the Commission will proceed through directives rather than regulations. There will be a greater use of guidelines and codes of conduct.

(d) THE ROLE OF THE COURT

It is clear that questions concerning the interpretation of Article 5 can be adjudicated by the ECJ. The real issue is, therefore, the intensity of the judicial review. The indications are that the ECJ will not lightly overturn Community action on the ground that it does not comply with Article 5.

---

114 Better Lawmaking 1999, COM(1999)562 final, 2.
115 (Oxford University Press, 2002), 113–114.
116 Better Lawmaking 2000, COM(2000)772 final, 4–8, 15–21.

This is apparent in *procedural* terms from *Germany* v. *European Parliament and Council*.[117] The ECJ held that Article 253 EC did not require that Community measures contain an express reference to the subsidiarity principle. It was sufficient that the recitals to the measure made it clear why the Community institutions believed that the aims of the measure could best be attained by Community action.

The difficulty of overturning a measure because of subsidiarity is equally apparent in *substantive* terms from the *Working Time Directive* case.[118] The UK argued that the Directive infringed subsidiarity, since it had not been shown that action at Community level would provide clear benefits compared with action at national level. The ECJ disposed of the argument briskly. It was, said the Court, the responsibility of the Council under Article 118a (now Article 138) to adopt minimum requirements so as to contribute to the improvement of health and safety. Once the Council had found it necessary to improve the existing level of protection and to harmonize the law in this area while maintaining the improvements already made, achievement of that objective necessarily presupposed Community-wide action. A similarly 'light' judicial approach to subsidiarity review is evident in other cases.[119]

There are undoubtedly difficulties with judicial review in this area. If the ECJ continues to be very light touch with its review, it will be open to the criticism that it is effectively denuding the obligation in Article 5 of all content. If, by way of contrast, the ECJ takes a detailed look at the evidence underlying the Commission's claim it will have to adjudicate on what may be a complex socio-economic calculus concerning the most effective level of government for different regulatory tasks. The difficulty of adjudicating on the substantive issue of comparative efficiency would nonetheless be alleviated if the Community courts were to require more from the Commission in procedural terms. The obligation to give reasons could be used to require the Commission to disclose the qualitative and quantitative data that are meant to inform its reasoning pursuant to the Protocol attached to the Treaty of Amsterdam. This would not solve all problems of substantive review, but would provide the Community courts with more to go on, as compared to their present reliance on the exiguous reasoning contained in the Preamble to the contested measure.

7. THE IMPACT OF
THE CONSTITUTIONAL TREATY

We have seen that the existing Treaty contains no specific provisions, other than Article 5 EC, which delimit competences between the Community and the Member States. Delimitation of competence was one of the four issues listed in Declaration 23 appended to the Nice Treaty which were to be considered in future Treaty reform.[120] The matter was duly discussed in the Convention on the Future of Europe.

---

[117] Case C–233/94, n. 36 above, paras. 26–28.

[118] Case C–84/94 *United Kingdom* v. *Council*, n. 36 above , paras. 46–47, 55.

[119] Case C–377/98 *Netherlands* v. *Council*, n. 36 above; Cases C–154–155/04 *The Queen, on the application of Alliance for Natural Health and Nutri-Link Ltd* v. *Secretary of State for Health* [2005] ECR I–6451, paras. 99–108; Case C–491/01 *The Queen* v. *Secretary of State for Health, ex p. British American Tobacco (Investments) Ltd. and Imperial Tobacco Ltd.* [2002] ECR I–11453, paras. 177–185; Case C–103/01 *Commission* v. *Germany* [2003] ECR I–5369, paras. 46–47; Case T-168/01 *GlaxoSmithKline Services Unlimited* v. *Commission*, 27 Sept. 2006, paras. 201–202.

[120] A. von Bogdandy and J. Bast, 'The Union's Powers: A Question of Competence. The Vertical Order of Competences and Proposals for its Reform' (2002) 38 *CMLRev.* 277; G. de Búrca, 'Setting Limits to EU Competences', Francisco Lucas Pires Working Paper 2001/02, available at www.fd.unl.pt/je/wpflp02a.doc.

Four principal forces drove this aspect of the reform process: clarity, conferral, containment, and consideration.[121] The desire for clarity reflected the sense that the existing Treaty provisions on competences were unclear, jumbled, and unprincipled. Conferral captured the idea that the EU should act within the limits of its powers, and that it should be accorded the powers necessary to fulfil the tasks assigned to it by the Treaties. The desire for containment reflected the concern, voiced by the German *Länder* as well as some Member States, that the EU had too much power and that it should be limited. The final factor was consideration of whether the EU should continue to have the powers that it had been given in the past, and a re-thinking of the areas in which the EU should be able to act.

The provisions on competence were contained in Title III of Part I of the Constitution.[122] Article I–11(1) CT retained the central principle that the EU operates on the basis of attributed competence. This was reinforced by Article I–11(2) CT, which stated that the Union must act within the limits of the competences conferred on it by the Member States, and that competences not conferred on the Union remained with the Member States.

Different categories of competence were set out in Article I–12 and the divide between them was the subject of intense debate within the Convention: the EU could have exclusive competence; it could share competence with the Member States; the EU could be limited to taking supporting/co-ordinating action; and there were special categories for EU action in the sphere of economic and employment policy, and the CFSP. The Constitution ascribed particular areas to each of the heads of competence. It also attached concrete consequences in terms of EU and state power to legislate in relation to each head of competence. External competence was dealt with in part in Article I–13(2) CT, which provided that the Union shall have exclusive competence for the conclusion of an international agreement when its conclusion is provided for in a legislative act of the Union, or is necessary to enable the Union to exercise its internal competence, or in so far as its conclusion may affect common rules or alter their scope.[123] This is not the place for detailed exegesis on these constitutional provisions. Suffice it to say for the present that there were real difficulties with these provisions.[124]

The CT also addressed subsidiarity. The subsidiarity principle was reiterated, with some modifications, in Article I–11(3) CT. The principal innovation was the Protocol on Subsidiarity attached to the Constitution.[125] This built on the earlier Protocols, the most important change made by the Protocol attached to the CT being the enhanced role accorded to national parliaments. The Commission was obliged to send legislative proposals to the national parliaments at the same time as to the Union institutions.[126] It was then open to a national parliament, within six weeks, to send the Presidents of the Commission, EP, and Council a reasoned opinion as to why it considered that the proposal did not comply with subsidiarity,[127] which the EP, Council, and Commission had to take into account.[128] Where non-compliance with subsidiarity was expressed by national parliaments that represented one third of all the votes allocated to such parliaments, there was a duty to review the proposal.[129] It was however open to the

---

[121] P. Craig, 'Competence: Clarity, Conferral, Containment and Consideration' (2004) 29 *ELRev.* 323.

[122] Treaty Establishing a Constitution for Europe [2004] OJ C310/1.

[123] The content of Art. I–13(2) CT was in marked contrast to the more cautious recommendations of Working Group VII on External Action, CONV 459/02, Final Report of Working Group VII on External Action, Brussels, 16 Dec. 2002, 4, 16.

[124] Craig, n. 121 above.

[125] CT, Protocol No. 2, On the Application of the Principles of Subsidiarity and Proportionality, Art. 2.

[126] *Ibid.*, Art. 4.

[127] *Ibid.*, Art. 6.

[128] *Ibid.*, Art. 7.

[129] *Ibid.*, Art. 7.

Commission or other relevant institution, after such review, to decide to maintain, amend, or withdraw the proposal, giving reasons for the decision.[130] A legal challenge for non-compliance with subsidiarity could be brought by the Member States, or 'notified by them in accordance with their legal order on behalf of their national Parliament or a chamber of it'.[131]

A division of competence along the preceding lines is likely to be retained in the Reform Treaty, albeit with some modifications.[132]

8. CONCLUSION

i. It is important to stress that EC policy in any particular area will be made by various formal legal norms. A basic regulation can be made more concrete through directives or decisions. The foundational provision may equally well be a directive or even a decision. These formal legal norms will be supplemented by a plethora of soft-law devices.

ii. It is axiomatic that the EC has only the powers ascribed to it, but defining those so as to impose meaningful limits on Community competence is difficult to say the least. Experience from other polities where legislative competence is divided between the centre and state authorities indicates that a neat formulaic solution will not be possible, and this is borne out by the competence provisions in the CT.

iii. The ECJ is often cast as the 'villain' in this regard, by construing Articles 308 and 95 very broadly. It should nonetheless be recognized that the greatest expansion of Community competence has been through successive Treaty revisions. It has been the Member States themselves that have been willing to accord new competences to the EC. The fact that the EC may have been given only limited competence over these areas does not change the substance of this point. In some ways, it reinforces it. The very fact that EC competence is shared, in differing ways in different areas, makes the task of 'limiting' or 'defining' Community competence even more problematic.

9. FURTHER READING

Dashwood, A., and Hillion, C. (eds.), *The General Law of EC External Relations* (Sweet & Maxwell, 2000)

Eeckhout, P., *External Relations of the European Union: Legal and Constitutional Foundations* (Oxford University Press, 2004)

Estella, A., *The EU Principle of Subsidiarity and its Critique* (Oxford University Press, 2002)

O'Keefe, D., and Twomey, P.M. (eds.), *Legal Issues of the Maastricht Treaty* (Chancery, 1994)

Weatherill, S., *Law and Integration in the European Union* (Clarendon Press, 1995)

---

130 *Ibid.*, Art. 7.
131 *Ibid.*, Art. 8.
132 Brussels European Council, 21–22 June 2007.

4

LEGISLATION AND
POLICY-MAKING

1. CENTRAL ISSUES

i. The previous chapter focused on the forms of Community action, and the scope of Community powers. The present chapter will consider the process by which the Community enacts legislation. The legislative procedures under the Community Pillar are complex. They are however becoming simpler, although more could still be done in this respect. It is also necessary to consider in outline the legislative process that applies under the Second and Third Pillars.

ii. There are issues of principle concerning the way in which the Community makes delegated legislation. There is the perennial problem of reconciling the need for the expeditious passage of detailed regulatory norms, with some measure of legislative oversight.

iii. It is equally important to understand the way in which legislation is made in practice. The planning of the overall legislative agenda and the passage of particular regulations or directives involves interaction between Community institutions, interest groups, national parliaments, and national bureaucracies.

iv. There is a rich debate about democracy and legitimacy within the EU. An understanding of the issues involved in this discourse is, as we shall see, a condition precedent for having something meaningful to say about it.

v. We shall also consider the impact of the Constitutional Treaty on the issues considered in this chapter.

2. THE COMMUNITY PILLAR:
INITIATING LEGISLATION

The basic principle under the EC Treaty is that the Commission has the right of legislative initiative. This is because the standard format in Treaty articles empowering the making of regulations, etc., in particular areas is that they should be made on a proposal from the Commission. If the Constitutional Treaty had been ratified this would have been further formalized through Article I–26(2), which enshrined the right of initiative within Part I of the Constitution. The Council and the EP can nonetheless be the indirect catalyst for the initiation of Community legislation.

The Council's power flows from Article 208 EC, which provides that it can request the Commission to undertake any studies which the Council considers desirable for the attainment of the common objectives, and to submit to it any appropriate proposals. The Council has not infrequently made use of this Article to give very specific instructions to the Commission concerning action which it, the Council, believes to be desirable. When this occurs the Commission will, at the very least, feel a strong pressure to bring forward legislation of the type suggested by the Council.

The European Parliament can be the catalyst for the initiation of the legislative process by virtue of Article 192 EC, which provides that the European Parliament may, acting by a majority of its members, request the Commission to submit any appropriate proposal on matters on which it considers that a Community act is required for the purpose of implementing the Treaty. The Parliament in its 1996 IGC report pressed for Article 192 to be modified so that the Commission would have a duty to respond to such Parliamentary initiatives, but was unsuccessful. While the Commission does not accept that it must automatically pursue a matter referred to it under Article 192, its Framework Agreement on relations between the Parliament and Commission signed in 2000 included a provision under which the Commission committed itself to undertake 'a prompt and sufficiently detailed response' to Article 192 requests.[1]

The European Parliament has accepted that it must be cautious in its use of the Article.[2] A request pursuant to Article 192 is based on an own-initiative report from the responsible committee within the EP. Authorization from the Conference of Presidents is required before such a report can be drawn up. The relevant committee must also establish that no such proposal is included in the annual legislative programme, that the preparations of such a proposal have not started or are unduly delayed, or that the Commission has not responded positively to earlier requests from the committee responsible or contained in resolutions adopted by the EP. The EP's resolution must indicate the appropriate legal basis and be accompanied by detailed recommendations and must respect the principle of subsidiarity and the fundamental rights of citizens.

3. THE COMMUNITY PILLAR: LEGISLATIVE PROCEDURES

The distinguishing characteristic of the different legislative procedures that apply within the Community Pillar is, principally, the degree of power afforded to the European Parliament. The European Parliament was given the smallest role in the legislative process in the original Rome Treaty, and all subsequent Treaty modifications have increased this. There are three keys to preserving sanity when seeking to understand these legislative procedures.

First, dispel any thought of identifying a single body as the 'legislature' for the Community as a whole. The players which comprise the legislature vary in the different procedures described below.

---

[1] Framework Agreement on relations between the European Parliament and the Commission, C5–349/2000 [2001] OJ C121/122, para. 4. An action seeking annulment of the Framework Agreement failed in Case T–236/00 R II *Stauner et al.* v. *Parliament and Commission* [2001] ECR II–2943, [2002] ECR II–135. The Agreement was revised in 2005 [2006] OJ C117/123.

[2] Rules of Procedure of the European Parliament (16th edn., Office of Official Publications of the EC, 2007), rules 39, 45.

The second key to emerging mentally intact is to realize that there is no magic formula determining which of these procedures applies in any area of the Treaty. Which legislative procedure applies is dependent on what is specified under any particular Treaty Article.

Finally, while it is easy to lose sight of the wood for the trees, it should be recognized that 'some' measure of order has been instilled into the legislative process as a result of the ToA. The Community institutions were mindful of the complexity of the legislative procedures and its damaging effect on the EC's legitimacy.[3] While the number of legislative procedures was not in itself altered by the ToA, the reality is that much important legislation is now governed by the co-decision procedure in Article 251 EC. The discussion should be read with this firmly in mind.

(a) COMMISSION ACTING ALONE

This is quite rare. The Treaty does, however, accord the Commission a power to make legislation without intervention from the other institutions in some areas. For example,[4] the Commission has power under Article 86(3) to promulgate directives or decisions under this Article, which is concerned with the role of the State in relation to public undertakings. The Commission used this power to enact a directive on the transparency of financial relations between Member States and public undertakings,[5] and a directive on competition as it relates to the telecommunications terminal market.[6] Member States challenged both directives, in part because Commission legislation made under Article 86(3) excludes the States, as represented in the Council, from any formal role in the legislative process. The Member States argued unsuccessfully that a different article of the Treaty should have been used, which would have given them such a role.[7]

(b) COUNCIL AND COMMISSION ACTING ALONE

There are a number of areas where the Council and the Commission can take action without any intervention by the European Parliament. The Council will act on a proposal from the Commission and take the decision in accordance with the voting requirement in the relevant Treaty Article.[8] The Council may choose to consult the Parliament, but does not have to do so. This legislative procedure is used, for example, in relation to aspects of free movement of workers and of capital, economic policy, and the common commercial policy.

(c) COUNCIL, COMMISSION, AND CONSULTATION WITH THE EUROPEAN PARLIAMENT

The original Rome Treaty concentrated power in the Commission and the Council: the former would propose a measure and the latter would vote upon it. The only role for the

---

[3] P. Craig, 'Democracy and Rulemaking within the EC: An Empirical and Normative Assessment' (1997) 3 *ELJ* 105.

[4] The Commission can, e.g., act on its own initiative under Art. 39(3)(d) EC.

[5] Dir. 80/723 [1980] OJ L195/35.

[6] Dir. 88/301 [1988] OJ L131/73.

[7] See Ch. 28.

[8] See, e.g., Arts. 26, 45, 49, 55, 57, 60, 96, 99, 104, 133(2) EC.

European Parliament was a consultative one, and this existed only where specified by a particular Treaty Article.

There are still some areas in which the Parliament is limited in this manner. The Council must wait for the Parliament's opinion. If it does not the measure may be annulled.[9] The Parliament may have to be reconsulted, where there are important changes to the measure, not prompted by the Parliament itself, after the initial consultation and prior to its adoption by the Council.[10] Nonetheless, a bare requirement to consult the European Parliament is all that is required. The Council is not bound to adopt the Parliament's opinion. The legislative process is still dominated by the Council and the Commission in these areas. Particular Treaty Articles can also stipulate that the Committee of the Regions or the Economic and Social Committee should be consulted.

The topics on which the Parliament has only a bare right to be consulted include: Article 13, dealing with measures to combat various forms of discrimination; Article 19, concerning rights to vote and stand in municipal elections; Article 22, reinforcing citizenship rights; Article 67(1), concerning visas, asylum, etc.; Article 89, state aids; Article 93, harmonization of indirect taxation; Article 94, approximation of laws for the functioning of the common market; Article 107(6), provisions relating to the Statute of the European System of Central Banks; Article 128, dealing with guidelines for Member States in relation to their employment policies; Article 175(2), fiscal measures, etc., relating to the environment; Article 21 TEU, concerning the general direction of common foreign and security policy; and Article 39 TEU, dealing with police and judicial co-operation in criminal matters.

(d) COUNCIL, COMMISSION, AND THE CO-OPERATION PROCEDURE WITH THE EUROPEAN PARLIAMENT

It was to be nearly thirty years before the European Parliament attained more prominence in the legislative process. In so far as there was any attempted justification for the limited role accorded to the Parliament it was based on the claim that, since it was originally only indirectly elected, its claim to participate in the legislative process was thereby weakened. This argument was palpably flawed. The indirectly elected Parliament had as strong, or stronger, a democratic claim to participate in the legislative process as any of the other Community institutions. In any event the argument failed even in its own terms after the advent of direct elections. Notwithstanding this obvious fact there was no rush by the other institutions to accord a greater democratic role to the Parliament. Quite the contrary. The attempts by the Parliament to secure an equal role with the Council in the legislative process were studiously ignored in the negotiations that led to the SEA.

What emerged was a good deal less than equal status, although it did at least give the Parliament more power than it had had hitherto. The change brought about by the SEA is now to be found in Article 252 EC. The areas to which it currently applies are mainly concerned

---

[9] Case 138/79 *Roquette Frères* v. *Council* [1980] ECR 3333; Case C–65/93 *European Parliament* v. *Council (Re Generalized Tariff Preferences)* [1995] ECR I–643; Case C–156/93 *European Parliament* v *Commission (Re Genetically Modified Micro-organisms in Organic Products)* [1995] ECR I–2019.

[10] Case C–388/92 *European Parliament* v. *Council* [1994] ECR I–2067; Case C–417/93 *European Parliament* v. *Council (Re Continuation of the TACIS Programme)* [1995] ECR I–1185; Case C–21/94 *European Parliament* v. *Council (Re Road Taxes)* [1995] ECR I–1827. Where the changes are either technical or in accordance with the Parliament's wishes re-consultation may not be necessary: Case 41/69 *ACF Chemiefarma* v. *Commission* [1970] ECR 661; Case 817/79 *Buyl* v. *Commission* [1982] ECR 245; Case C–331/88 *R.* v *Minister of Agriculture, Fisheries and Food and Secretary of State for Health, ex p. FEDESA* [1990] ECR I–4023.

with Economic and Monetary Union,[11] since most other areas to which it applied are now governed by the co-decision procedure described in the following section.

The precise details of the Article 252 co-operation procedure therefore need not concern us here. Suffice it to say that this procedure gave the European Parliament a greater role in the legislative process than hitherto, by according it two readings for measures that came within its ambit, through which it was able to propose amendments,[12] many of which were successfully secured.[13]

The fact that Article 252 now only applies in a limited number of areas should not however lead one to underestimate its significance. When it was originally introduced by the SEA it was used for many of the measures to implement the single market, including Article 95. It had moreover an important effect on the entire legislative process.

M. Westlake, The Commission and the Parliament: Partners and Rivals in the European Policy-Making Process[14]

The Single European Act in general, and the co-operation procedure in particular, represented a major constitutional innovation in the Community system. . . .

First, it was immediately apparent that a badly-administered co-operation procedure could lead to blockages and delays. . . . The Commission's reaction was two-fold: internal reform, and increased inter-institutional co-operation, particularly with the Parliament.

Second, the procedure accords the Commission important gate-keeping functions at various stages in the procedure which frequently involve it in delicate political arbitration. It must draft its proposals with an eye to what will 'play' in Parliament, as well as in the Council. It is involved in the Council deliberations leading to the Common Position. . . .

Third, both the Commission and the Parliament immediately recognised the fundamental importance of the first reading stage. At this point there is no majority requirement, nor any deadline, and Parliament can still hope to influence Council deliberations before a Common Position has coalesced. From the Commission's point of view, parliamentary emphasis on the first reading diminishes the risk of blockage at the second stage and reduces the number of situations where the Commission has to arbitrate between conflicting institutional desires. Clearly, emphasis on the first reading has given Parliament's power of delay fresh significance.

Fourth, and more generally, the co-operation procedure entailed a general change in institutional attitudes, particularly in the Commission and the Council. Parliament's powers in the legislative process were transformed from the weak and essentially unconstructive power of delay to a stronger and potentially constructive role in the drafting of legislation.

---

[11] See, e.g., Arts. 102 and 103 EC.

[12] D. Earnshaw and D. Judge, 'The European Parliament and the Sweeteners Directive: From Footnote to Inter-institutional Conflict' (1993) 31 *JCMS* 1; R. Corbett, 'Testing the New Procedures: The European Parliament's First Experience with its New "Single Act" Powers' (1989) 27 *JCMS* 4.

[13] M. Westlake, *The Commission and the Parliament: Partners and Rivals in the European Policy-Making Process* (Butterworths, 1994), 39.

[14] *Ibid.*, 37–38.

(e) COUNCIL, COMMISSION, AND THE EUROPEAN PARLIAMENT: THE CO-DECISION PROCEDURE

The TEU introduced the co-decision procedure,[15] which prevents a measure being adopted without the approval of the Council and the European Parliament, and emphasizes the reaching of a jointly approved text. The procedure is now set out in Article 251 EC and has become the method for making much important Community legislation.[16] It is now the legislative procedure for much EC legislation, except agriculture, fisheries, taxation, trade policies, competition, and EMU.

If the Constitutional Treaty had been ratified the co-decision procedure would have been re-named the ordinary legislative procedure and the number of areas subject to the procedure would have roughly doubled.

The ToA modified Article 251 so as to expedite the procedure and to strengthen further the position of the EP.[17] Article 251 now reads as follows.[18]

1. Where reference is made in this Treaty to this Article for the adoption of an act, the following procedure shall apply.

2. The Commission shall submit a proposal to the European Parliament and the Council.

   The Council, acting by a qualified majority after obtaining the opinion of the European Parliament,

   — if it approves all the amendments contained in the European Parliament's opinion, may adopt the acts thus amended;

   — if the European Parliament does not propose any amendments, may adopt the proposed act;

   — shall otherwise adopt a common position and communicate it to the European Parliament. The Council shall inform the European Parliament fully of the reasons which led it to adopt its common position. The Commission shall inform the European Parliament fully of its position.

   If, within three months of such communication, the European Parliament:

   (a) approves the common position or has not taken a decision, the act in question shall be deemed to have been adopted in accordance with that common position;

   (b) rejects, by an absolute majority of its component members, the common position the proposed act shall be deemed not to have been adopted;

   (c) proposes amendments to the common position by an absolute majority of its component members, the amended text shall be forwarded to the Council and to the Commission, which shall deliver an opinion on those amendments.

---

[15] A. Dashwood, 'Community Legislative Procedures in the Era of the Treaty on European Union' (1994) 19 *ELRev.* 343.

[16] The procedure now applies in the following areas: Arts. 12, 13(2), 18(2), 40, 42, 44, 46(2), 47, 47(2), 55, 62(1), 62(2)(a), 62(3), 63(1), 63(2)(a), 63(2)(b), 63(3)(b), 65, 71(1), 80(2), 95, 129, 135, 137(1–2), 141, 148, 149(4), 150(4), 151(5), 152(4), 153(4), 156, 157(3), 159(3), 162, 166, 172, 175(1)–(3), 179, 191, 255(2) 280(4), 285(1), 286(2). http://ec.europa.eu/codecision/procedure/legalbasis_en.htm. In certain instances the Council will act by unanimity rather than by qualified majority, e.g. Arts. 42, 47(2), 151(5).

[17] The practical implementation of these reforms was dealt with in the Joint Declaration on Practical Arrangements for the New Co-Decision Procedure [1999] OJ C148/1.

[18] Particular Treaty Arts. may add to the Art. 251 procedure by requiring consultation with the Committee of the Regions and/or the Economic and Social Committee.

3. If, within three months of the matter being referred to it, the Council, acting by qualified majority, approves all the amendments of the European Parliament, the act in question shall be deemed to have been adopted in the form of the common position thus amended; however, the Council shall act unanimously on the amendments on which the Commission has delivered a negative opinion. If the Council does not approve all the amendments, the President of the Council, in agreement with the President of the European Parliament, shall within six weeks convene a meeting of the Conciliation Committee.

4. The Conciliation Committee, which shall be composed of the members of the Council or their representatives and an equal number of representatives of the European Parliament, shall have the task of reaching agreement on a joint text, by a qualified majority of the members of the Council or their representatives and by a majority of the representatives of the European Parliament. The Commission shall take part in the Conciliation Committee's proceedings and shall take all the necessary initiatives with a view to reconciling the positions of the European Parliament and the Council. In fulfilling this task, the Conciliation Committee shall address the common position on the basis of the amendments proposed by the European Parliament.

5. If, within six weeks of its being convened, the Conciliation Committee approves a joint text, the European Parliament, acting by an absolute majority of the votes cast, and the Council, acting by a qualified majority, shall each have a period of six weeks from that approval in which to adopt the act in question in accordance with the joint text. If either of the two institutions fails to approve the proposed act within that period, it shall be deemed not to have been adopted.

6. Where the Conciliation Committee does not approve a joint text, the proposed act shall be deemed not to have been adopted.

7. The periods of three months and six weeks referred to in this Article shall be extended by a maximum of one month and two weeks respectively at the initiative of the European Parliament or the Council.[19]

Given that Article 251 is the method for making much Community legislation, it is important to understand the way in which it operates and its normative underpinnings.

(i) *The Stages within Article 251*

We can begin by making clear the stages that operate within Article 251. The EP has two readings, the first of which occurs when the EP gives its opinion to the Council. There is no time limit for the first reading, either for the EP or the Council. The second reading takes place on the assumption that the Council has not approved all the EP's first-reading amendments, or if it has other amendments of its own, which must be passed unanimously in the Council.[20]

If this happens then the Council communicates its common position to the EP, which then has the option at second reading to approve, reject, or propose amendments to the measure. The EP has imposed limits on the second reading amendments that it will propose: they are only admissible if they seek to restore wholly or in part the EP's first-reading position, or to reach a compromise between the EP and Council, or to amend part of the common position that was not included in the initial proposal, or to take account of a new fact situation.[21]

[19] However Declaration 34 attached to the ToA stated that the institutions should strictly respect the deadlines, and have recourse to these time extensions only where strictly necessary.

[20] Art. 250(1) EC.

[21] European Parliament, *Conciliations and Co-decision, A Guide to how Parliament Co-legislates* (DV/547830EN.doc, 2004), 6.

If the EP suggests amendments not all of which are acceptable to the Council then the Conciliation Committee comes into operation.[22] The EP and Council must approve the joint text from the Conciliation Committee. The co-decision procedure can however be concluded at any of the stages, provided that the EP and Council agree.

The co-decision procedure has been modified in practice through the institutionalization of trialogues.[23] These are informal meetings that precede, and can exist alongside, formal meetings of the Conciliation Committee. They have been common since the mid-1990s. The trialogue contains representatives from the Council, EP, and Commission, normally no more than ten, from each institution. The aim is to facilitate compromise.

(ii) *The Practical Operation of Article 251*

The co-decision procedure in Article 251 has been successful in practice. It has accommodated the differing interests that have a stake in the legislative process.[24] There was an increase by a factor of 2.5 in the number of files dealt with by co-decision in the 1999–2004 Parliamentary session, as compared to the 1993–1999 period.[25]

It is also important to understand that not all the stages of Article 251 will be gone through for any particular Community measure. During the 1999–2004 Parliamentary session 115 co-decision dossiers, 28 per cent, were concluded at first reading; 200 dossiers, 50 per cent, at second reading; and eighty-four dossiers, 22 per cent, through conciliation.[26]

The procedure has been effective in accommodating the interests of the three institutional players. Twenty per cent of the Parliament's second-reading amendments to the Council's common position have been accepted in their entirety during the conciliation procedure, 70 per cent have been the subject of a compromise, and only 12 per cent have been rejected.[27]

The average period for conclusion of a dossier at first reading, from Commission proposal to signature of the act is twelve months; the period for conclusion at second reading is twenty-two months; and twenty-nine months for conclusion where there is conciliation.[28]

(iii) *The Power Dynamics within Article 251*

While most commentators agree that Article 251 has been a success, there is nonetheless more disagreement about the particular 'power dynamics' that operate within this procedure and

---

[22] www.europarl.eu.int/code/default_en.htm.

[23] European Parliament, n. 21 above, 13–15; M. Shackleton and T. Raunio, 'Codecision since Amsterdam: A Laboratory for Institutional Innovation and Change' (2003) 10 *JEPP* 171, 177–179.

[24] A. Dashwood, 'Community Legislative Procedures in the Era of the TEU' (1994) 19 *ELRev.* 343; D. Earnshaw and D. Judge, 'From Co-operation to Co-decision: The European Parliament's Path to Legislative Power', in J. Richardson (ed.), *European Union, Power and Policy-Making* (Routledge, 1996), ch. 6; S. Boyron, 'The Co-Decision Procedure: Rethinking the Constitutional Fundamentals', in P. Craig and C. Harlow (eds.), *Lawmaking in the European Union* (Kluwer, 1998), ch. 7; A. Dashwood, 'European Community Legislative Procedures after Amsterdam' (1998) 1 *CYELS* 25; A. Maurer, 'Co-governing after Maastricht: The European Parliament's Institutional Performance 1994–99', EP Working Paper, POLI 104, 1999; Co-decision, An Analysis Prepared by the Co-decision Service of the Commission, available at http://ec.europa.eu/codecision/institutional /analysis/index_en.htm.

[25] European Parliament, n. 21 above, 4.

[26] *Ibid.*, 7.

[27] A. Dashwood, 'The Constitution of the European Union after Nice: Law-Making Procedures' (2001) 26 *ELRev.* 215, 219.

[28] Co-decision, An Analysis Prepared by the Co-decision Service of the Commission, n. 24 above.

disagreement also about the relative power of the EP under co-decision and other legislative procedures.[29]

It is nonetheless clear that the EP has used its veto power under Article 251 sparingly. This does not of course mean that such power is ineffective. Decision-making under the shadow of the veto was, as we shall see below, common within the Council when the Luxembourg Accords imposed a *de facto* unanimity requirement, notwithstanding that actual use of the veto was relatively rare. So too here, the rare use of the veto by the EP does not alter the fact that the EP must accept the measure if it is to become law. The EP's power is further enhanced in relation to the Council because Article 251 read with Article 250(1) requires unanimity in the Council if the Council wishes to make amendments to a Commission proposal,[30] while requiring only a qualified majority where the Council accepts amendments from the EP.

It is more difficult to generalize about the nature of the amendments that the EP manages to secure. There is research indicating that the EP amendments modify the Commission proposal, but do not significantly alter it.[31] This is to some extent unsurprising, since most important draft legislative proposals will have been discussed in detail with the EP and Council/COREPER before the formal Article 251 procedure was initiated, thereby accommodating diverse opinion at that early stage. Where this dialogic process still leaves major differences of view, the EP and indeed Council may well propose more far-reaching amendments to the formal legislation, as exemplified by the extensive amendments proposed by the EP to the Services Directive, forcing the Commission to modify the measure significantly.[32]

It is also important not to overlook the power of the Commission within the Article 251 procedure. It has the power to withdraw a proposed measure before it is adopted and submit a modified version, or to refuse to proceed again at all if it feels that any measure will be amended in ways to which it is fundamentally averse. These are admittedly rather blunt tools, but useful nonetheless. In any event the Commission has more 'fine-tuned' modes of influence. Thus it will routinely respond in detail to, for example, proposed EP amendments, indicating which it feels able to accept and which not. This will often form the foundation for dialogue between Commission and EP as to what will be acceptable to both players. The Commission moreover has the 'leverage' that EP second-reading amendments in relation to which the Commission has delivered a negative opinion can be accepted by the Council only if there is unanimity.[33]

(iv) *The Normative Foundations of Article 251*

Article 251 has a secure normative foundation. The EP has long been pressing for a co-equal role in the legislative process with the Council. The modifications introduced by the ToA go a

---

[29] G. Tsebelis and G. Garrett, 'Legislative Politics and the European Union' (2000) 1 *EUP* 9; C. Crombez, 'Co-decision: Towards a Bicameral European Union' (2000) 1 *EUP* 363; B. Steunenberg, 'Seeing What you Want to See: The Limits of Current Modelling on the European Union' (2000) 1 *EUP* 368; R. Corbett, 'Academic Modelling of the Co-decision Procedure: A Practitioner's Puzzled Reaction' (2000) 1 *EUP* 373; G. Garrett and G. Tsebelis, 'Understanding Better the EU Legislative Process' (2001) 2 *EUP* 353; R. Corbett, 'A Response to a Reply to a Reaction (I Hope Someone is Still Interested)' (2001) 2 *EUP* 361.

[30] Subject to exceptions in Art. 251(4)–(5).

[31] A. Kreppel, 'Moving beyond Procedure: An Empirical Analysis of European Parliament Legislative Influence' (2002) 35 *Comparative Political Studies* 784.

[32] Proposal for a Dir. of the European Parliament and of the Council, on services in the internal market, COM/2004/2 final/3; EP Committee on the Internal Market and Consumer Protection, Report on the Proposal for a Directive of the European Parliament and of the Council, on services in the internal market, A6-0409/2005, Rapporteur Evelyne Gebhardt; Amended Proposal for a Dir. of the European Parliament and of the Council, on services in the internal market, COM(2006)160 final.

[33] Art. 251(3) EC.

considerable way to achieving this goal. The fact that the Article 251 procedure applies to much important EC legislation is in accord with the proposals of the key players in their submissions to the 1996 IGC, including the EP, the Commission, and the Reflection Group.[34] Many of the points made in the extract from Westlake apply equally to the Article 251 procedure. Institutional attitudes have changed markedly since the early 1980s. The attention placed on democracy and legitimacy in the 1990s has helped to secure a more equal and constructive role for the EP in the legislative process.

(f) COUNCIL, COMMISSION, AND THE EUROPEAN PARLIAMENT: ASSENT

The assent procedure is simplicity itself as compared with those considered above. The Council acts after obtaining the assent of the European Parliament: the act can be adopted only if it has been approved by both the Council and the European Parliament. The assent procedure therefore 'grants Parliament an infinite power of delay and an absolute power of rejection',[35] albeit no formal mechanism for making amendments. In order to render this power more discriminating the Parliament's rules provide for the possibility of an interim report with a draft resolution containing recommendations for modification or implementation of the proposal.[36] The Parliament has also unilaterally introduced a conciliation procedure with the Council.[37]

The assent procedure was introduced by the SEA for important matters such as the expansion of Community membership and association agreements. The areas in which it now applies after the ToA include the following: Article 49 of the TEU, concerning membership of the European Union; Article 105(6) EC, concerning various aspects of the functioning of a European Central Bank; Article 107(5), amendment to the Statute of the European System of Central Banks (ESCB); and Article 161, on certain measures relating to economic and social cohesion.

(g) SUMMARY

i. Co-decision has become the general mode of decision-making for much important Community legislation. It works well in practice, and has a secure normative foundation. It facilitates a discourse between the Commission, EP, and Council, allowing the views of each to be taken into account when fashioning legislation.

ii. It would be desirable to abolish the co-operation procedure. It now applies only to a very few areas, each of which could be subject to co-decision.

iii. If the co-operation procedure were to be abolished, then Community legislation could be rationalized in the following manner. The co-decision procedure would be the general method for the making of legislation, as envisaged by the Constitutional Treaty. In areas of major importance the assent procedure would apply. In areas where Member State interests were particularly strong, the EP would be limited to a consultative role.

---

[34] Craig, n. 3 above.
[35] Westlake, n. 13 above, 96.
[36] *Ibid.* See Rules of Procedure of the European Parliament, n. 2 above, rule 75.
[37] Westlake, n. 13 above, 96.

iv. It should not however be forgotten that, although the co-decision procedure is now dominant, there are still variables that can affect the legislative strategy in any particular area. There is the choice between regulations and directives, between detailed and framework legislation, and the balance between formal law and informal law.

4. THE COMMUNITY PILLAR: DELEGATED LEGISLATIVE POWER

(a) COMITOLOGY: RATIONALE

A moment's thought will indicate why delegation of power to make regulations has been necessary. There are certain areas of Community policy, such as agriculture, which require numerous regulations, often passed quickly to cope with changing market circumstances. If the standard methods of enacting Community measures were to be applied the process would grind to a halt, since the large number of such norms could not be enacted with sufficient speed. This explains why the Council, through a 'parent' regulation, authorized the Commission to enact more specific regulations within a particular area, such as agriculture and competition.

The Council was not, however, willing to give the Commission *carte blanche* to legislate in this manner. It made the exercise of delegated legislative power subject to institutional constraints, in the form of committees through which Member State interests could be represented. This was so for two complementary reasons.

On the one hand, there might be disagreements between the States themselves as to the content of the more detailed norms that should be made. It is common to think that Member States only ever disagree on points of general principle. This is quite mistaken. Often they agree on the general strategy, but disagree on its detailed application. The committee structure to be described below gave the Member States the opportunity for input into the making of the detailed norms.

On the other hand, the Council imposed conditions on the delegation of power to the Commission because of the inter-institutional tensions when the committee structure was created. The Council was wary of the federalizing tendencies of the Commission. It was unsurprising, at a time when the Council perceived the Community in intergovernmental terms, that it should be unwilling to delegate power to the Commission without institutional checks to ensure the formal representation of Member State interests.

The Council's 'solution' was to condition the exercise of delegated power on the approval of a committee composed of representatives of Member States. This system came to be known as Comitology. There was no express warrant for such committees in the original Treaty, and their legality was challenged before the Court. The ECJ upheld the validity of the committee system, reasoning that if the Treaty gave power to the Council to delegate to the Commission, then it could do so subject to conditions.[38]

The SEA modified Article 202 in order to provide a secure foundation for this delegation. The third indent of Article 202 states that the Council can confer on the Commission, in the acts which the Council adopts, powers for the implementation of the rules which the Council lays down. It further stipulates that the Council may impose certain requirements on the exercise of these powers, and that it may reserve the right, in specific cases, to exercise

---

[38] Case 25/70 *Koster* [1970] ECR 1161.

implementing powers itself. The procedures are to be consonant with principles and rules laid down in advance by the Council, acting unanimously on a proposal from the Commission after consulting the European Parliament. The Comitology decision establishing the principles and rules to be followed was adopted by the Council in 1987.[39] This Decision rationalized the committee structure.

The European Parliament was unhappy with the 1987 Decision, because it was excluded from the committee system. This discontent increased as the European Parliament gained a greater say in the passage of 'primary' Community legislation, through extension of the co-decision procedure. The Parliament argued that the committee structure was inconsistent with co-decision. Primary legislation will, as we have seen, often be made under co-decision. This includes the primary legislation pursuant to which power is then delegated to the Commission, subject to the committee system. The exclusion of the Parliament from the passage of this delegated legislation served therefore to undermine the gains that the Parliament had made through the extension of co-decision.[40] Recent amendments to the legislation dealing with Comitology have however, as will be seen below, addressed this issue to some extent.

(b) COMITOLOGY: PROCEDURES

Declaration 31 appended to the ToA called on the Commission to submit to the Council by the end of 1998 proposals to amend the 1987 Comitology Decision. A new Decision was adopted in 1999,[41] and the recitals specified four objectives. There should be greater consistency in the choice of committee procedure; greater involvement of the European Parliament; improvement in the information given to the Parliament; and the committees should be more accessible to the public. The 1999 Comitology Decision has recently been amended.[42] The position is now as follows.

Article 1 of the Decision provides that, except in cases where the basic instrument reserves to the Council the right to exercise implementing powers, these powers shall be conferred on the Commission in accordance with the provisions in the basic instrument.

Article 2 establishes criteria for the choice of committee procedure. Article 2(1) states that the management procedure is to be used for management measures, such as agricultural policy, and for the implementation of programmes with substantial budgetary implications. The regulatory procedure is to be used for measures of general scope designed to apply essential provisions of basic instruments, such as those concerned with health and safety. The advisory procedure is to be used whenever it is felt to be most appropriate. Article 2(2) states that the new regulatory procedure with scrutiny applies where a basic instrument adopted in accordance with the co-decision procedure in Article 251 provides for the adoption of measures of general scope designed to amend non-essential elements of that instrument, *inter alia*, by deleting some of those elements or by supplementing the instrument by the addition of new

---

[39] Dec. 87/373 [1987] OJ L197/33.

[40] The Parliament challenged the 1987 Dec., but the action was held to be inadmissible: Case 302/87 *European Parliament* v. *Council* [1988] ECR 5615; K. St. C. Bradley, 'The European Parliament and Comitology: On the Road to Nowhere?' (1997) 3 *ELJ* 230.

[41] Council Dec. 99/468 laying down the procedures for the exercise of implementing powers conferred on the Commission [1999] OJ L184/23; K. Lenaerts and A. Verhoeven, 'Towards a Legal Framework for Executive Rule-Making in the EU? The Contribution of the New Comitology Decision' (2000) 37 *CMLRev.* 645.

[42] Council Dec. 2006/512/EC of 17 July 2006 amending Dec. 1999/468/EC laying down the procedures for the exercise of implementing powers by the Commission [2006] OJ L200/11.

non-essential elements. Reasons must be given if the criteria for the choice of committee procedure are departed from.[43]

Article 3 lays down the advisory procedure. A committee of an advisory nature assists the Commission. It is composed of representatives of the Member States and chaired by the Commission. The Commission submits a draft of the proposed measure to the committee, and the committee then delivers its opinion. The Commission is not bound by this opinion, although it shall take the 'utmost account' of it.

The management procedure is laid down in Article 4. The composition of the committee is the same as above. The Commission submits a proposal, and the committee then delivers an opinion within a time limit set by the Commission chairman. The committee votes in the same manner as the Council itself,[44] but the Commission has no vote. Under this procedure the Commission adopts measures which 'shall apply immediately'. However, if the measure *is not in accordance* with the opinion of the committee, the Commission must communicate this to the Council. The Commission then *may* defer application of the measure for a maximum period of three months. The Council, acting by qualified majority, can take a different decision within this period. The nub of the management procedure is that the committee, composed of national representatives, must vote against the measure in order for it to be 'kicked back' to the Council.

The regulatory procedure is covered by Article 5. The composition of the committee is the same as above, and the voting is in accordance with that in the Council. The sting in the tail is that the Commission can adopt a measure only *if it is in accord* with the opinion of the committee. If *it is not in accord* with the committee's opinion or *if no opinion* is delivered, then the Commission *must* submit to the Council a proposal relating to the measures to be taken, and *must* inform the EP. The nub of the regulatory procedure is that the measure must be referred back to the Council unless the committee votes in favour of it. If the EP considers that the Commission's proposal, made pursuant to a basic instrument under the co-decision procedure, exceeds the implementing powers provided in that instrument, it shall inform the Council. The Council can, within three months of the date of referral, make clear its opposition to the proposal, in which case the Commission must re-examine it. The Commission can then re-submit the proposal, amend it, or present a (new) proposal. Where the Council, within three months, neither adopts the proposed measure nor indicates its opposition, the Commission shall adopt the proposed act.

The new regulatory procedure with scrutiny is dealt with in Article 5a, introduced in 2006 as an amendment to the 1999 Decision. The catalyst for this reform was belated acceptance of the EP's objection, set out above, to the 1999 Comitology Decision where co-decision applied.[45] The novelty of the regulatory procedure with scrutiny is the greater role accorded to the EP. The essence of the new procedure is as follows. The Commission continues to be assisted by a regulatory committee made up of national representatives.

If the committee delivers a favourable opinion the draft measure is submitted to the EP and Council, which can oppose adoption of the draft because: it exceeds the implementing power in the basic instrument; or because it is not compatible with the aim or content of the basic instrument; or it does not respect the principles of subsidiarity and proportionality. In the

---

43 Case C–378/00 *Commission* v. *European Parliament and Council* [2003] ECR I–937, paras. 51–55; Case C–122/04 *Commission* v. *Council* [2006] ECR I–2001, para. 32.

44 See 123–125 below.

45 Proposal for a Council Dec. Amending Dec. 1999/468/EC laying down the procedures for the exercise of implementing powers conferred on the Commission, COM(2002)719 final, at 2; an amended version of the proposal can be found in COM(2004)324 final

event of such opposition within three months from the Council or the EP the draft is not adopted and the Commission may submit an amended draft of the measure or present a legislative proposal on the basis of the Treaty. If there is no opposition within three months the measure is adopted by the Commission.

If the measures envisaged by the Commission are not in accordance with the opinion of the Committee, or no opinion is delivered, then the Commission submits to the Council a proposal relating to the measures to be taken and forwards it to the EP. If the Council opposes the proposed measure by qualified majority within two months then it is not adopted, and the Commission can then submit an amended proposal or present a proposal for primary legislation. If the Council is minded to adopt the proposed measure then it must be submitted to the EP within two months at the latest. The EP can then decide within four months of having the proposed measure forwarded to it to oppose adoption of the measure on the same grounds as above, *viz.*, that it exceeded the implementing powers provided in the basic instrument, etc. If the EP does oppose the measure then it is not adopted, and the Commission can then submit an amended version or present a proposal for primary legislation. If the EP does not oppose within four months then the measure is adopted by the Commission or Council.[46] The broader impact of Article 5a will be considered in the section on evaluation below.

The objective of making the committee system more accessible to the public is dealt with in Article 7.[47] The principles and conditions on access to documents apply to the committees, and the Commission must publish a list of all the committees which assist it in the exercise of implementing powers. It has now done so.[48] The Commission must, from 2000 onwards, publish an annual report on the working of the committees. Moreover, the references of documents sent to the European Parliament are to be made public.

We have already seen that the EP has a role under the regulatory procedure. It is, in addition, given a right by Article 7(3) to be informed by the Commission of committee proceedings, following arrangements to ensure that the transmission system is transparent and that the information forwarded and the various stages of the procedure are identified. It is to receive committee agendas, voting records, and draft measures submitted to the committees for implementation of primary law made under the co-decision procedure. The EP must also be kept informed when the Commission transmits proposals to the Council. In an agreement made between the EP and the Commission,[49] the latter stated that it will also forward to the EP, at its request, specific draft measures for implementing basic instruments even if they were not adopted under co-decision, where they are of particular importance to the EP. The EP can moreover request access to minutes of committee meetings.[50]

Article 8 allows the EP to indicate by resolution that draft implementing measures, which have been submitted to a committee pursuant to a basic instrument adopted by co-decision, would exceed the implementing powers in that instrument. The Commission *must* re-examine the draft measure. It *may* submit new draft measures, continue with the procedure, or submit a (new) proposal. The Commission must inform the Parliament of what it has done, and provide reasons. The agreement between the EP and the Commission provides that

---

[46] The time limits in Art. 5a can be extended or curtailed: Art. 5a(5), and a basic instrument may provide for a modified procedure in cases of urgency: Art. 5a(6).

[47] Art. 6 of Dec. 99/468, n. 41 above, deals with procedures to be followed in the case of safeguard measures.

[48] Information from the Commission—List of Committees which Assist the Commission in the Exercise of its Implementing Powers [2000] OJ C225/2.

[49] Agreement between the European Parliament and the Commission on procedures for implementing Council Dec. 99/468 [2000] OJ L256/19, para. 2.

[50] Case T–188/97 *Rothmans* v. *Commission* [1999] ECR II–2463.

the resolution must be made within one month of the EP receiving the final draft of the implementing measures. It must also be made in plenary session.[51] Article 8 will in due course be rendered redundant by the new Article 5a. The latter however applies only to measures adopted by co-decision enacted after July 2006, which specify use of the new procedure. Earlier measures adopted by co-decision, which were subject to the regulatory procedure, will have to be amended so as to render the new regulatory procedure with scrutiny applicable.[52]

(c) COMITOLOGY: EVALUATION

There has been a considerable literature on the Comitology regime.[53] Concerns were voiced about the exclusion of the EP, the undemocratic nature of the process, the lack of account-ability and transparency, and the corporatist nature of the process.

The Comitology regime has also been defended most prominently by Joerges and Neyer, who see it in terms of deliberative supranationalism.[54] The essence of the argument is that the national delegates who take part in the committees will often regard themselves as part of a team dealing with a transnational problem. Comitology is portrayed as a network of European and national actors, with the Commission acting as co-ordinator. The national par-ticipants in the deliberative process are willing to call their own preferences into question in searching for a Community solution, and this deliberative mode is said to be borne out by empirical study concerning the operation of Comitology in regulating foodstuffs. This central core of the deliberative supranationalism thesis has force.

There are nonetheless problems with this view of Comitology, which relate to the con-straints placed on consensual deliberation, the role accorded to the EP, and the exclusion from the rule-making process of others who might legitimately wish to have a voice in the content of the resultant rule.[55]

Thus Weiler, while acknowledging the importance of Joerges and Neyer's insights concern-ing the deliberative style of Comitology and the search for solutions that transcend purely national interests,[56] was nonetheless troubled by the decisional autonomy of Comitology. The Commission and the Council may both regard the committees as their agents, whereas the reality is that the committees 'have long lost their allegiance to their controllers and work very much within their own universe for what they perceive to be their function and task'.[57] Committee members may be unaware of 'the profound political and moral choices involved in their determinations and of their shared biases',[58] and the shared understandings that prevail between the committee members may mean that 'moral premises are presumed but

---

[51] N. 49 above, paras. 6–7. The time limit can be shorter in urgent cases.

[52] Statement by the European Parliament, Council and Commission concerning the Council Dec. of 17 July 2006 [2006] OJ C255/1.

[53] C. Joerges and E. Vos (eds.), *EU Committees: Social Regulation, Law and Politics* (Hart, 1999); M. Andenas and A. Türk (eds.), *Delegated Legislation and the Role of Committees in the EC* (Kluwer, 2000); C. Bergstrom, *Comitology, Delegation of Powers in the European Union and the Committee System* (Oxford University Press, 2005); P. Craig, *EU Administrative Law* (Oxford University Press, 2006), ch. 4.

[54] C. Joerges and J. Neyer, 'From Intergovernmental Bargaining to Deliberative Political Processes: The Constitutionalization of Comitology' (1997) 3 *ELJ* 273.

[55] Craig, n. 53 above.

[56] J. Weiler, 'Epilogue: "Comitology" as Revolution—Infranationalism, Constitutionalism and Democracy', in Joerges and Vos (eds.), n. 53 above, 347.

[57] *Ibid.*, 342.

[58] *Ibid.*, 348.

not discussed'.[59] Weiler notes also a tension between the deliberative aspects of Comitology and democratic precepts.[60]

> Finally there is the issue of equality of access. One cannot, in the analytic mode, explain Comitology as a deliberative network, which inevitably suggests that some interests are included and some are excluded and, in the normative mode, not acknowledge that this is a major problem for democracy. Equally, one cannot affirm that this is a problem for democracy and thus endorse proposals which would ensure transparency, openness and equal access, and not acknowledge that such proposals, if they are to be efficient, would destroy, or at least seriously compromise, the conditions which enable a deliberative process.

The introduction of the new Article 5a is undoubtedly important in enhancing the legitimacy of Comitology, since it accords the EP as well as the Council power to veto a measure produced by a Comitology committee. This change did not come about smoothly. It was delayed for some considerable time because the Commission would not accept that a negative vote in the EP actually prevented the measure from being adopted by the Commission.[61] This point of principle is now embedded in Article 5a.

This should not however mask the relative powers of the Council and EP in Comitology that still persist. The Council through its representatives on the regulatory procedure with scrutiny committee is still in the driving seat. It will sit with the Commission and devise the proposed measure. The EP, as well as the Council, is then accorded a formal right to object to the final draft.

It should moreover be noted that the legislative veto can only be exercised on the specified ground, *viz.*, that the measure exceeds the implementing powers in the basic instrument, is not compatible with the aim or content of the basic instrument, or does not respect proportionality or subsidiarity. This can be contrasted with the Constitutional Treaty, Article I–36, which gave a general power of veto to the EP and Council without any such limiting conditions. Richard Corbett, the EP's Rapporteur, believes that the conditions in Article 5a are nonetheless framed so broadly as to permit use of the veto on any occasion.[62] Time will tell whether this is so. The 'test case' would be where the EP objected to a measure because of its content, in the sense that it believed that the matter would be better dealt with in a different manner. The language of Article 5a however requires the EP to show that the measure is not *compatible* with the aim of content or the basic instrument, and the Commission may well be inclined to argue that the EP would have to show such incompatibility before its veto power can be exercised, not merely that the EP would prefer a different solution.

5. THE COMMUNITY PILLAR: THE COUNCIL VOTING REQUIREMENTS

The general principle is that, unless the Treaty specifies to the contrary, voting in the Council is to be by majority.[63] There is provision for the voting rights of a State to be suspended if it seriously and persistently breaches the principles of liberty, democracy, etc., contained in

[59] *Ibid.*, 349.
[60] *Ibid.*, 349.
[61] Report on the draft Council Decision amending Dec. 1999/468/EC, Rapporteur Richard Corbett, A6–0236/2006.
[62] *Ibid.*, 9.
[63] Art. 205(1) EC.

Article 6(1) TEU.[64] The Treaty provides for three different rules on voting: unanimity,[65] simple majority, and qualified majority. Which of these voting rules applies will be specified in the particular Treaty Article under which a measure is enacted.

Qualified-majority voting has been the formal legal norm in many areas since the end of the second stage of the transitional period in 1965, and was extended by the SEA, particularly through the addition of Article 95, which deals with completion of the internal market. A requirement of unanimity now generally applies only to politically sensitive topics,[66] to decisions which are of particular importance for the character of the Community,[67] or where the Council seeks to depart from a proposal from one of the other Community institutions, as described above. It should also be recognized that the veto which flows from the unanimity requirement is a double-edged sword: it can protect state autonomy, but it can equally prevent Union action. Much then depends on whether States feel that they will be more 'vetoed against' than 'exercisers of veto power' themselves.

For some considerable time these formal legal powers were overshadowed by the Luxembourg Compromise. This was the result of a political crisis in the Community in the mid-1960s, and coincided with the shift to qualified-majority voting in the Council.[68] In essence the Compromise provided that when majority voting applied to a topic which concerned the important interests of States, they should attempt to reach a solution acceptable to all, and France added the rider that discussion should continue until unanimity was attained. The Compromise fostered a climate in which majority voting prejudicial to the interests of a particular State was avoided. The 'threat' that a Member State would exercise a *de facto* veto power did not enhance the speed of Community decision-making.

The Luxembourg Compromise was not formally abolished, because it never formally existed in legal terms. However, the climate in the Community post-1986 renders it less likely that States will attempt to use such power.[69] Subsequent Treaty amendments generally required greater use of qualified-majority voting, and reflected a shift in Member States' perceptions about the nature of the Community, which renders it less likely that exclusively national interests will be regarded as a valid rationale for the exercise of a veto.[70] Moreover, Member States acknowledged that there had to be an extension of qualified-majority voting in an expanded Union. Unanimity would often be synonymous with inaction, since one State out of twenty-seven would almost certainly object. The very fact that use of the veto is now less readily accepted than hitherto means that Member States will exert more pressure at other points of the decision-making system, so as to ensure that the measure is acceptable to them. It should also be acknowledged that the Council will search for consensus even where the formal voting rules provide for a qualified majority,[71] and approximately 80 per cent of decisions are taken consensually.

---

[64] Art. 7 TEU, Art. 309 EC.

[65] Abstentions do not prevent the adoption of acts for which unanimity is required: Art. 205(3) EC.

[66] E.g. some matters concerned with employment: Art. 137(2) EC as modified by the TN.

[67] E.g. accession of new Member States: Art. 49 TEU.

[68] See 8–9.

[69] M. Westlake, *The Council of the European Union* (Cartermill, 1995), 91–111.

[70] The approach of the Conservative Government to the beef crisis, which consisted, in part, of refusing to agree to any measure on which unanimity was required under the Treaty, itself provoked a very unfavourable response from other States: M. Westlake, 'Mad Cows and Englishmen—The Institutional Consequences of the BSE Crisis', in N. Nugent (ed.), *The European Union 1996* (Blackwell, 1997), 15–27.

[71] W. Nicoll, 'Representing the States', in A. Duff, J. Pinder, and R. Pryce (eds.), *Maastricht and Beyond, Building the European Union* (Routledge, 1994), 193–194.

The figure now required for a qualified majority is the result of hard-fought battles in the TN between large, medium, and small States. The solution embodied in the Nice Treaty is to be found in the Protocol on Enlargement of the Union, coupled with Declaration 20 on Enlargement, and is posited on a Union with twenty-seven States. The Protocol came into effect on 1 January 2005, at which date Article 205(2) was modified as follows.

The votes accorded to each of the States were 'stretched' to accommodate the new States. The largest States have twenty-nine votes each, the smallest three, with gradations in between.[72] Where the Council acts on a proposal from the Commission a qualified majority is 258 out of 345, cast by a majority of members. Where it does not do so, there is the additional requirement that the votes must be cast by at least two-thirds of the States. The wishes of the larger States were further reinforced by Article 205(4), which allows a member of the Council to request verification that the States constituting the qualified majority represent at least 62 per cent of the population. If this condition is not met then the relevant decision cannot be adopted.

These figures are premised on an EU with twenty-seven Member States. Before the accession of Romania and Bulgaria, the total number of votes in the Council was 321, with 232 being required for a qualified majority.

6. DECISION-MAKING UNDER PILLARS TWO AND THREE

Detailed examination of decision-making under the Second and Third Pillars is provided in separate chapters.[73] It is nonetheless important to have a bare outline of the relevant provisions here. Before doing so it should be noted that decision-making within each of the Pillars is not hermetically sealed. There is an increasing degree of cross-pillar policy-making,[74] and the instruments used to regulate a particular topic may well be based on the Community Pillar, and the Second and/or Third Pillars. This can give rise to problems of considerable legal complexity.[75]

(a) PILLAR TWO: COMMON FOREIGN AND SECURITY POLICY

The European Council and the Council dominate decision-making under Pillar Two which remains very largely intergovernmental in nature. This is unsurprising, given the nature of the subject-matter. The range of instruments that can be used under Pillar Two includes defining the principles and general guidelines for the CFSP; deciding on common strategies; adopting joint actions; adopting common positions; and strengthening systematic co-operation

---

[72] Germany, UK, Italy, and France have 29; Spain and Poland, 27; Romania, 14; Netherlands, 13; Greece, Czech Republic, Belgium, Hungary, Portugal, 12; Sweden, Bulgaria, Austria, 10; Slovakia, Denmark, Finland, Ireland, Lithuania, 7; Latvia, Slovenia, Estonia, Cyprus, Luxembourg, 4; Malta, 3.

[73] See Chs. 6–7.

[74] See, e.g., S. Stetter, 'Cross-pillar Politics: Functional Unity and Institutional Fragmentation of EU Foreign Policies' (2004) 11 *JEPP* 720.

[75] See, e.g., Case T–315/01 *Yassin Abdullah Kadi* v. *Council and Commission* [2005] ECR II–3649, paras. 87–135.

between Member States in the conduct of policy.[76] The meaning of each form of action will be considered in the detailed discussion of the CFSP.[77]

(b) PILLAR THREE: POLICE AND JUDICIAL CO-OPERATION IN CRIMINAL MATTERS (PJCC)

The key provision is Article 34 TEU. It establishes four principal mechanisms for attaining the Union's objectives in this area.[78] The Council acts unanimously on the initiative of any Member State or the Commission.

The Council can adopt a *common position* defining the approach of the Union to a particular matter. It can adopt a *framework decision* for the purpose of approximating the laws and regulations of the Member States. These are like directives: they are binding as to the result to be achieved, but leave choice of form and method to the Member States. They are however expressly stipulated not to entail direct effect. The Council can adopt *decisions* for any purpose consistent with the objectives of this Title.[79] These decisions are binding, but do not have direct effect.[80] The Council may also establish *conventions*, which it can recommend for adoption by the Member States in accordance with their national constitutions. The European Parliament has the right to be consulted in the making of framework decisions, decisions, and conventions.[81]

7. THE REALITY OF COMMUNITY DECISION-MAKING

(a) THE TEMPORAL DIMENSION

The discussion thus far has focused on the legislative procedures. To stop there would, however, give only an imperfect grasp of the Community legislative process. We need to press further to understand the way in which Community decision-making actually works. There are different dimensions to this inquiry, one of which is temporal in nature: the way in which the roles played by the Community institutions in the decision-making process has developed over time. What follows does not purport to be a thorough historical analysis, but rather a thematic one.

A central theme is the development of institutional structures outside the strict letter of the Treaty, as a response to tensions between the Council and Commission, since they embodied different conceptions of the Community.

The Council perceived it principally in intergovernmental terms, and this had both a substantive and a procedural dimension. In substantive terms, the Council was unclear precisely how far it wished to travel down the road of European integration. In procedural terms,

---

[76] Art. 12 TEU.

[77] Ch. 6.

[78] S. Peers, *EU Justice and Home Affairs Law* (2nd edn., Oxford University Press, 2006), ch. 2.

[79] Excluding any approximation of the laws and regulations of the Member States: Art. 34(2)(c) TEU.

[80] The Council, acting by qualified majority, adopts the implementing measures needed at Union level: Art. 34(2)(c) TEU.

[81] Art. 39(1) TEU. The Council Presidency and the Commission must regularly inform the EP of discussions in areas covered by this Title: Art. 39(2) TEU. The EP may ask questions of the Council, and make recommendations to it: Art. 39(3).

intergovernmentalism connoted the idea that Member States' interests should not readily be sacrificed to the Community good, and that the Council, as representative of those interests, should retain control over the development of Community policy.

The Commission had a more federalist conception of the Community. This, too, had a substantive and a procedural component. In substantive terms, it manifested itself in a commitment to proceed with the attainment of the Community goals as expeditiously as possible, and to move beyond these to other matters that would further the process of integration. In procedural terms, the Commission's vision naturally inclined to the use of majority voting, as dictated by the Treaty in many areas, with the necessary consequence that the interests of a Member State might have to be sacrificed to achieve the greater Community good.

The original Rome Treaty divided power between Council and Commission, but in many respects it placed the Commission in the driving seat as regards the development of Community policy. This is evident from the Commission's right of legislative initiative; from the plethora of other functions which it was given; and from the fact that the voting rules, while requiring Council consent to a measure, also required unanimity for any Council amendment.[82] The message was that, while the Council had to consent to proposed legislation, it was not easy for it to alter the Commission's draft.

The first twenty years or so of the Community were marked by *de facto* changes in the nature of Community decision-making. The unifying theme was the increased dominance of the Council over the Commission, and the limiting of the federalist tendencies within the Commission by the intergovernmental impulses of the Council. Institutional developments outside the strict letter of the Treaty were the vehicle through which this was achieved.

The Luxembourg Accords were one such development. They were the prime example of negative intergovernmentalism: Member States could block measures they disliked which they felt touched their vital interests. Statistics on the number of occasions on which this power was actually used are, of course, only part of the story, since the threat of the veto shaped the very policies which the Commission would put forward.[83]

The Council's intergovernmental orientation also had a more positive side to it. The Luxembourg Accords were fine if the ultimate objective was to veto a measure. But the Member States also desired more finely-tuned tools through which to influence legislation they wished to be enacted. The growing influence of COREPER, the establishment of management and regulatory committees, the increased use of Article 208 EC, and the evolution of the European Council were all features of positive intergovernmentalism. They increased Member States' influence over Community legislation, and did so in complementary ways. COREPER and the management/regulatory committees enabled the Council to have a more formalized input into the detail of the emergent legislation. Article 208 became a useful vehicle whereby the Council could suggest Community action in particular areas, while the European Council became a mechanism which enabled Member States to discuss general issues of Community concern, outside the framework of the Council itself. The results of their deliberations were often 'binding', in the sense of laying down the parameters of future Community action, whether in relation to the size of the CAP budget or the timetable for moves towards closer economic union.

These developments contributed to the Euro-sclerosis that beset the Community during much of the 1970s. This had reverberations for the ECJ's role. This story has been told most

---

[82] Art. 250(1) EC.
[83] K. Neunreither, 'Transformation of a Political Role: Reconsidering the Case of the Commission of the European Communities' (1971–1972) 10 *JCMS* 233.

fully in the important work of Joseph Weiler.[84] He explains how impediments to the attainment of Community objectives through the political process led to the growing importance of normative supranationalism. The doctrines of direct effect, the supremacy of Community law, and pre-emption were central in this respect. They allowed the ECJ to develop EC law, notwithstanding the difficulties of securing the passage of the required regulations and directives through the legislative process.[85]

Many of the institutional developments which occurred outside the strict letter of the Treaty have now been accorded *de jure* status by their inclusion in Treaty revisions. The management and regulatory committee structure attained a more secure footing by the revisions to Article 202 EC. The European Council was also recognized by the SEA, and now has its foundations in Article 4 of the TEU. COREPER was accorded a more formal status in Article 207. It should however be noted that matters have changed since the 1970s and that the divide between institutions that are supranational and those that are intergovernmental is not as sharp as it might once have been.[86]

(b) THE INTER-INSTITUTIONAL DIMENSION

(i) *Planning the Legislative Agenda*

The institutional reforms in the SEA had a mixed impact on Community decision-making. In one respect they expedited decision-making by extending qualified-majority voting, as exemplified by Article 95 EC. In another respect however the SEA made the legislative process more complex. The Parliament now had power through the co-operation procedure. It was another institutional player whose views had to be accommodated.[87] It became clear that there would have to be more inter-institutional co-operation in planning the overall legislative programme.[88]

The system now operates as follows. The Commission on entering office will publish a five-year programme, setting out the strategic objectives for that period at a relatively high level of generality. Thus the programme for 2005–2009 focused on prosperity, solidarity, and security.[89]

The annual planning cycle begins with the Annual Policy Strategy (APS), which is designed to integrate decisions about priorities and resources more closely together. This identifies early in the previous year the policy priorities for the following year and the implications that this has for resource allocation.[90] The APS is discussed with the Council and European Parliament, and will normally be modified as a result of this dialogue.

The revised APS then forms the basis for the Commission's more detailed work programme for a particular year,[91] which will list the legislative and non-legislative measures to be

---

[84] J. Weiler, 'The Community System: The Dual Character of Supranationalism' (1981) 1 *YBEL* 267 and 'The Transformation of Europe' (1991) 100 *Yale LJ* 2403, 2412–2431.

[85] P. Craig, 'Once Upon a Time in the West: Direct Effect and the Federalization of EEC Law' (1992) 12 *OJLS* 453.

[86] See 53–54, 56–58.

[87] See 112.

[88] Westlake, n. 13 above, 19–21.

[89] Strategic Objectives 2005–2009: Europe 2010, A Partnership for European Renewal, Prosperity, Solidarity, and Security, COM(2005)12 final.

[90] Annual Policy Strategy for 2007, Boosting Trust through Action, COM(2006)122 final.

[91] Commission Legislative and Work Programme 2007, COM(2006)629 final.

introduced to attain the objectives agreed in the modified APS. This is presented to the Council and EP, normally in November.

Each Directorate General establishes Annual Management Plans (AMPs) on the basis of the preceding framework in order to show how it will contribute towards the attainment of the Commission's overall work programme for that year. Each DG will also present an Annual Activity Report (AAR), which mirrors the AMP in the sense of monitoring how far objectives have been realized.

The cycle ends with Synthesis Reports by the Commission which, *inter alia*, assess policy progress, the way in which resources were used, and proposals for remedying deficiencies revealed in the individual reports from the DGs.[92]

Inter-institutional co-operation also occurs through the Conference of Presidents.[93] This is chaired by the President of the Parliament in a non-voting capacity, and composed of the leaders of the political groups, each of which has a vote weighted in accordance with the numerical strength of that group in the Parliament. This body meets twice or three times per month, and, *inter alia*, prepares the agenda for the EP. The Commission will normally attend, and it, as well as the Council, will have the opportunity to make suggestions about the agenda.

(ii) *Inter-institutional Agreements*

An important vehicle for more formal inter-institutional co-operation is the Inter-institutional Agreement or Declaration.[94] These form what has been termed 'a sort of constitutional glue'[95] for the Community, as exemplified by the 1993 Inter-institutional Agreement on Subsidiarity, and the 1993 Inter-institutional Declaration on Democracy, Transparency, and Subsidiarity. Such agreements have also been made in relation to, for example, budgetary discipline, codification, implementation of the budget, and Comitology, and they often form the basis for subsequent hard law. Thus the Inter-institution Declaration on Democracy, Transparency, and Subsidiarity was the catalyst for legislation on transparency in the Commission and Council.[96]

(iii) *The Making of Particular Policies*

The discussion thus far has focused on the differing ways in which the institutions interact in the formulation of *general* legislative policy. It is now time to consider the ways in which the institutions interact in the making of a *particular* piece of legislation.

The content of legislative proposals will normally have been flagged in the Commission's legislative agenda.[97] The precise content will be the result of interaction between the Commission, interest groups, national experts, and senior civil servants. The Commissioner will assume overall responsibility for a proposal within his or her area. It will have been fashioned by the relevant Directorate General. When those directly involved with the proposed measure have given their approval, the draft will be sent to the cabinet of the Commissioner.

---

[92] Policy Achievements in 2005, COM(2006)124 final; Synthesis of the Commission's Management Achievements in 2005, COM(2006)277 final.

[93] R. Corbett, F. Jacobs, and M. Shackleton, *The European Parliament* (6th edn., Harper, 2005), 117–119.

[94] J. Monar, 'Interinstitutional Agreements: The Phenomenon and its Dynamics after Maastricht' (1994) 31 *CMLRev.* 693.

[95] Westlake, n. 13 above, 101.

[96] Council Dec. 93/731 [1993] OJ L340/43; Commission Dec. 94/90 [1994] OJ L46/58.

[97] Sir Leon Brittan, 'Institutional Development of the European Community' [1992] *PL* 567.

When the Commissioner is satisfied with the draft it will then be submitted to the College of Commissioners. Legislative proposals, once formulated, require the endorsement of the whole Commission. The College of Commissioners will normally meet weekly.[98]

> There is no single way in which decisions are taken. In practice teams of relevant commissioners can be delegated to act on behalf of the College; brain storming can be used; or a written procedure adopted whereby urgent and/or uncontroversial proposals are deemed adopted if no objection is lodged within a specified time to the dossier and draft proposal, normally a week.... Only routine matters are delegated to individual commissioners who are then empowered to act within the confines of a very narrow remit on the Commission's behalf: recurrent agricultural regulations are adopted in this way.

The role of groups of national experts, civil servants, and interest groups in this process of policy-formation is an interesting one. The framing of the proposal will involve close collaboration with a wide variety of groups. This occurs before the proposal begins its formal legislative journey. Bureaucracies at national and Community level may well become more interlocked, or *engrenage*.

W. Wessels, Administrative Interaction[99]

> By participating in Community decision-making the national civil servants gain 'access' to and 'influence' on EC decision-making and implementation, thus also increasing their weight inside their respective national systems. The same general cost–benefit calculation applies to Community officials who gain access and influence on 'national' domains by opening their policy cycles to the national colleagues—although traditional federalists and supranationalists would argue that this is an unacceptable loss in autonomy and independence of the EC bureaucracy. This cost–benefit analysis by civil servants (*mutatis mutandis* by heads of State, ministers and interest groups, but not by national parliamentarians) creates a major dynamic for European integration leading not to a transfer of loyalty by national officials to a new centre but to cooperation of officials into a new system of shared government. This stage of State evolution is characterized by an increasing degree of cooperation, in vertical terms between different governmental levels, and in horizontal terms, among several groups of actors. The 'multi-level' interactions of civil servants of several national and international administrations thus reinforce trends towards specific forms of the 'sharing' or 'fusion' of powers between 'bureaucrats and politicians' which non-EC-related studies have identified.

National civil servants are not the only group that has input into policy-formation. Interest groups have, not surprisingly, concentrated increasing resources on the Community. Given that the maxim of lobbyists is to 'shoot where the ducks are' we should therefore expect interest groups to organize themselves at a European level.[100] Successful lobbying is dependent upon developing good advance intelligence; watching the national agenda; maintaining good

---

[98] J. Lodge, 'EC Policymaking: Institutional Dynamics', in J. Lodge (ed.), *The European Community and the Challenge of the Future* (2nd edn., Pinter, 1993), 11.

[99] W. Wallace (ed.), *The Dynamics of European Integration* (RISIA/Pinter, 1990), 230.

[100] See, e.g., S.P. Mazey and J.J. Richardson, *Lobbying in the EC* (Oxford University Press, 1992); R.H. Pedler and M.P.C.M. van Schendelen (eds.), *Lobbying the European Union: Companies, Trade Associations and Issue Groups* (Dartmouth, 1994).

links with national administrations; maintaining close contacts with Commission officials; presenting rational arguments; being co-operative; developing a European perspective; not gloating when successful; and not ignoring the implementation process.[101] Many Euro-associations have been formed to foster this process, but the Commission's attitude towards them is ambivalent.

S. Mazey and J. Richardson, Pressure Groups and Lobbying in the EC[102]

There are many examples of the Commission helping to resource these associations and of individual officials 'massaging' the developmental process within the associations (via direct funding and via 'soft' money, for example financing conferences etc.). Thus much of the Commission's activity—particularly at the service level—is very supportive of Euro-associations. Yet, when faced with the day-to-day pressures of initiating and formulating policy proposals which will actually work in the twelve Member States, Commission officials regularly by-pass the Euro-associations. The reasons for this are two-fold. First . . . the associations are of necessity broad in their interests. Commonly, the national industries being represented by the associations have quite different traditions, different structures, and above all, different and *competing* interests. For example, the financial services sector is quite different in Britain and Germany. This means that a European-level regulatory regime which would suit the British would probably not suit the Germans. As with governmental coalitions, the associations have to devise compromise policies—often referred to by the Commission as 'lowest common denominator policies'—which are so general as to be of little practical use to officials. Moreover, the associations often lack the necessary expertise so needed by Commission officials. Thus, it is very common for officials to develop links with individual national associations . . . and to develop links with individual firms as a means of securing reliable technical information quickly.

The Commission has developed its own principles to govern its dealings with interest groups. It distinguishes between profit- and non-profit-making organizations. It may consult such groups on an *ad hoc* basis or through an advisory committee. It uses Green Papers and the like as a mechanism for eliciting their views. The Commission also demands certain standards from such groups, relating to their dissemination of EC information, their behaviour, and the way in which they represent themselves.

Interest-group pressure at the Community level is to be expected. This does not mean we should be complacent. Profit-making groups outnumber non-profit-making groups by a very significant margin, and their resources are much larger. The costs of organizing at the European level may be especially onerous for the voluntary/non-profit-making sector. Powerful groups are likely to make their voices heard irrespective of whether formal participatory rights exist, but this is not obviously so for those with less financial muscle.

Once a Commission proposal has been formulated *it will make its way to the Council, and normally to the European Parliament*, where the latter has a legislative role in the area. We shall begin by considering the way in which the Council deals with the proposal.

---

[101] S.P. Mazey and J.J. Richardson, 'Pressure Groups and Lobbying in the EC', in Lodge (ed.), n. 98 above, 44.
[102] *Ibid.*, 38–39, italics in the original. See also S. Mazey and J. Richardson, 'Interest Groups and EU Policy-Making: Organizational Logic and Venue Shopping', in J. Richardson (ed.), *European Union, Power and Policy-Making* (3rd edn., Routledge, 2006), ch. 12.

COREPER is of crucial importance. Before any measure is seen by the Council, it will have been thoroughly examined by one or more working groups that assist COREPER, as well as by COREPER I or II. These working groups are composed of national officials and experts from the Member States, plus a member of the Commission. They may be permanent or *ad hoc.* There may be 250 such groups at any one time.[103] These working groups will examine the Commission proposal and prepare a report. This will indicate the areas on which agreement has been reached ('Roman I points') and all other points ('Roman II points'). The latter will then be discussed within COREPER. Points agreed by the working group will normally be accepted by COREPER, with debate focusing on those issues where consensus has not yet been attained. Reference back to the working group may occur.

COREPER continues to be important when proposed measures have been tabled before the Council, since it sets the Council's agenda. Issues on which there is agreement within COREPER will be placed on the 'A list' and will be adopted without discussion. If agreement within COREPER has not been possible then such issues will be placed on the 'B list', indicating that debate and decision by the Council are required. Members of COREPER will attend Council meetings as advisers to their national ministerial representatives. It is moreover COREPER that will negotiate with the EP should the Conciliations Committee be convened pursuant to the co-decision procedure.

The modifications in the decision-making process since the SEA have increased the importance of the Council Presidency. It is the Office of the Presidency that co-ordinates the meetings of the different sectoral Councils. Who participates depends on the subject-matter: on some occasions foreign ministers will attend, on others it will be the minister responsible for a particular sectoral area, such as agriculture. The President mediates conflicts between the Member States, between the Member States and the Commission, and between the Council and the Parliament.

Amendments to Commission proposals normally require unanimity in the Council.[104] This requirement is applicable when the Council adopts a common position at first reading under the co-decision procedure. It gives the Commission considerable leverage in the passage of legislation. This is because if the Council wishes to make changes to legislation, the only way that it can avoid the unanimity requirement is to negotiate with the Commission. The compromise can then take the form of an amended proposal that can pass by qualified majority. Decisions within the Council will often be reached by consensus. We should not, however, underestimate the importance of the shift to majority voting brought about by the SEA. Weiler captures this when stating that 'reaching consensus under the shadow of the vote is altogether different from reaching it under the shadow of the veto'.[105]

It is to the *role of the Parliament* in the passage of legislation that we should now turn. The main part of the Parliament's legislative work is undertaken by standing committees, which are normally subject-matter-based. The appropriate committee will make the initial draft report on legislation submitted to the Parliament pursuant to Article 251 or 252 EC. The responsibility for drawing up the committee report is given to a *rapporteur*, who will present the draft report to the committee. It will normally have four parts: suggested amendments to the Commission proposal; a Draft Legislative Resolution; an Explanatory Statement; and any relevant Annexes. The committee will advise the MEPs how to vote in the plenary session, and the *rapporteur* will usually act as the committee's spokesperson.

---

[103] F. Hayes-Renshaw, C. Lequesne, and P. Mayor Lopez, 'The Permanent Representations of the Member States to the European Communities' (1989) 27 *JCMS* 119, 132.

[104] Art. 250(1) EC.

[105] 'The Transformation of Europe', n. 84 above, 2461.

The Commission will often have an important arbitral role to play, and will have to 'juggle' matters in the attempt to find a legislative package acceptable to Parliament, the Council, and itself. It may well resort to soft law where it is impossible to secure the passage of a regulation or directive.[106]

8. THE EU, DEMOCRACY, AND DECISION-MAKING[107]

The democratic legitimacy of decision-making within the EU has long been a subject of debate. This has been particularly so since the TEU, as reflected in the institutional reports which led to the 1996 IGC[108] and the rich vein of academic literature.[109] A significant part of this literature is concerned with the Community's 'democratic deficit'. While views differ on this issue, the following account, developed from Joseph Weiler's summary of the democratic deficit,[110] is reasonably representative. It is important to understand that the phrase 'democratic deficit' has a number of different features which must be distinguished.

(a) THE NATURE OF THE ARGUMENT

An important critique of Community decision-making is that it is 'unresponsive to democratic pressures'. It is a cardinal feature of democratic regimes that voters can change the government. This is not the case within the EU. Legislative power is divided between the Council, Commission, and Parliament. It is only the Parliament that is directly elected. A change in the Parliament's composition through European elections will not, therefore, necessarily lead to any major shift in EU policy, since it is only one part of the legislature.

---

106 Case C–57/95 *France* v. *Commission (Re Pension Funds Communication)* [1997] ECR I–1627; Cases C–239–240/96 R *United Kingdom* v. *Commission (Re Measures to Assist the Elderly)* [1996] ECR I–4475.

107 The discussion draws in part on P. Craig, 'The Nature of the Community: Integration, Democracy and Legitimacy', in P. Craig and G. de Búrca (eds.), *The Evolution of EU Law* (Oxford University Press, 1999), ch. 1.

108 Craig, n. 3 above; G. de Búrca, 'The Quest for Legitimacy in the European Union' (1996) 59 *MLR* 349.

109 See, e.g., just in terms of books, S. Garcia (ed.), *European Identity and the Search for Legitimacy* (Pinter, 1993); J. Hayward (ed.), *The Crisis of Representation in Europe* (Frank Cass, 1995); A. Rosas and E. Antola (eds.), *A Citizens' Europe, In Search of a New Order* (Sage, 1995); R. Bellamy, V. Bufacchi, and D. Castiglione (eds.), *Democracy and Constitutional Culture in the Union of Europe* (Lothian Foundation Press, 1995); S. Andersen and K. Eliassen (eds.), *The European Union: How Democratic Is It?* (Sage, 1996); R. Bellamy and D. Castiglione (eds.), *Constitutionalism in Transformation: European and Theoretical Perspectives* (Blackwell, 1996); R. Bellamy (ed.), *Constitutionalism, Democracy and Sovereignty: American and European Perspectives* (Avebury, 1996); F. Snyder (ed.), *Constitutional Dimensions of European Economic Integration* (Kluwer, 1996); R. Dehousse (ed.), *Europe: The Impossible Status Quo* (Macmillan, 1997); D. Curtin, *Postnational Democracy, The European Union in Search of a Political Philosophy* (Kluwer, 1997); Craig and Harlow (eds.), n. 24 above; R. Corbett, *The European Parliament's Role in Closer EU Integration* (Palgrave, 1998); J. Weiler, *The Constitution of Europe* (Cambridge University Press, 1999); C. Hoskyns and M. Newman (eds.), *Democratizing the European Union* (Manchester University Press, 2000); B. Laffan, R. O'Donnell, and M. Smith, *Europe's Experimental Union: Rethinking Integration* (Routledge, 2000); F. Mancini, *Democracy and Constitutionalism in the European Union* (Hart, 2000); K. Neunreither and A. Wiener (eds.), *European Integration after Amsterdam, Institutional Dynamics and Prospects for Democracy* (Oxford University Press, 2000); R. Prodi, *Europe As I See It* (Polity, 2000); K. Nicolaidis and R. Howse (eds.), *The Federal Vision, Legitimacy and Levels of Governance in the United States and the European Union* (Oxford University Press, 2001); W. van Gerven, *The European Union, A Polity of States and Peoples* (Hart, 2005).

110 J. Weiler, U. Haltern, and F. Mayer, 'European Democracy and its Critique', in J. Hayward (ed.), *The Crisis of Representation in Europe* (Frank Cass, 1995), 32–33; J. Weiler, 'European Models: Polity, People and System', in Craig and Harlow (eds.), n. 24 above, ch. 1.

A second facet of the democracy deficit argument concerns 'executive dominance'. The transfer of competence to the Community enhances the power of the executive at the expense of parliaments. This is because of the dominance of the Council and European Council in the EU's decision-making process, and the difficulty experienced by national parliamentary bodies in exercising real control over the decisions made in the EU. While the existence of the EP alleviates this problem by providing a directly elected forum at the European level, it does not remove it. This is because of its limited powers; because of lack of voter interest in EP elections; and because of the absence of a developed party system within the EU.

A third feature of the democracy deficit argument is the 'by-passing of democracy argument'. This is applied most frequently to the operation of the complex committee structure, known generally as Comitology. We have seen that many technical, but important, regulations are made by committees established pursuant to a delegation of power to the Commission. Technocrats and national interest groups have dominated this sphere of decision-making to the exclusion of the more regular channels of democratic decision-making, such as the European Parliament and even the Council.

There is, fourthly, what may be termed the 'distance issue'. Many matters have been transferred to Brussels from the nation State, thereby further removing them from the citizen.

A fifth aspect of the democracy deficit can be termed the 'transparency and complexity issue'. Traditionally much of the decision-making of the Community, particularly that of the Council, has taken place behind closed doors. In addition the very complexity of the legislative procedures has meant that it is virtually impossible for anyone, other than an expert, to understand them.

There is, sixthly, the less known 'substantive imbalance issue'. Writers from the left argue that the democratic deficit should also encompass the imbalance between labour and capital, which they claim has been exacerbated by the freeing up of the European market.

There is, finally, the 'weakening of judicial control issue'. A number of legal systems possess courts which have powers, either *ex ante* or *ex post*, over the constitutionality of primary legislation. The transfer of competence to the Community means that such powers are thereby reduced in scope.

(b) EVALUATION: THE EMPIRICAL FRAME OF REFERENCE

We live by and through language. The very language of democratic deficit is powerful in its imagery. It speaks to some base point from which we are deviating, an impression reinforced by the analogy with budget deficit. Democracy cannot however be measured or calibrated in the same way as a budget. Any assessment of the democratic deficit argument must necessarily be partly empirical and partly theoretical. These issues will be addressed in turn. The discussion that follows does not mean that democracy within the EU is incapable of improvement. It does mean that we must be fair when assessing democracy within the EU in comparison to national regimes, and in comparison to what would be the case if the EU did not exist.

The empirical frame of reference is the *status quo ante*. The Community's democratic deficit is adjudged to be so by way of comparison with the position as it would be if matters were still dealt with at the national level. This requires us to assess the reality of decision-making within national polities *and* postulate what the locus of decision-making would be if there were no EU.

(i) *The Comparison with National Polities*

The first step of the argument takes us into familiar territory. Executives tend to be dominant in most modern domestic polities. The degree of dominance varies, but the general proposition nonetheless holds true. The idea that national parliaments really control the emergence or content of legislative norms rarely comports with reality. The force of the 'executive dominance' critique of Community decision-making appears weaker when viewed in this light.[111]

It is, moreover, by no means self-evident that the EP has less power over the content of legislation than do national parliaments. It is common to read general statements that the EP has little real power even now. Empirical evidence for such propositions is wanting. Much important Community legislation is now subject to the co-decision procedure. Statistics show that the EP has had a pretty good strike rate at getting its amendments accepted.[112] It might be argued that these amendments were minor, or ones that the Council was willing to accept. The former can only be tested by a detailed study of the various legislative acts in question. The latter is simply reductionist: of course the Council has to accept the amendments since otherwise the norm will not become law, but this does not prove that the EP exercised no power. The matter can, in any event, be put differently. How many changes which were not executive-sponsored did the legislature in, for example, the UK manage to have incorporated in statutes in any one year?[113]

An understanding of the reality of national decision-making is also of importance when considering the Comitology problem and the 'bypassing of the normal democratic process'. There is a real problem here for the Community. We should, however, be mindful of the fact that the legitimation of secondary norms is an endemic problem for all domestic political systems. The UK, for example, has not satisfactorily resolved the need for the expeditious passage of secondary norms and the need to ensure effective legislative oversight. Indeed, many norms of a legislative nature are not seen by the legislature at all. The Community has moreover endeavoured to alleviate this problem through the reform of the Comitology Decision considered above. These reforms have sought to make the committee procedure more transparent, and have brought the Parliament more fully into the process than hitherto.

(ii) *The Locus of Decision-making if There Were no EU*

The second step of the argument takes us into less familiar terrain. The assumption commonly made is that if the EU did not exist then the matters currently within its competence would be dealt with at national level. Decisions would then be made closer to the people, hence alleviating the 'distance problem', and parliaments would have greater control, hence mitigating the 'executive dominance' problem.

The conclusion does not follow from the premise. The pressures for some form of international co-ordination would still be present, even if the EU never existed. An enduring insight from integration theory is that cross-border flows of goods create international policy

---

[111] It is not fortuitous that the thesis advanced by Andersen and Burns about the erosion of parliamentary democracy applies a theory about that erosion as it operates *within* nation States to the Community: S. Andersen and T. Burns, 'The European Union and the Erosion of Parliamentary Democracy: A Study of Post-Parliamentary Governance', in Andersen and Eliassen (eds.), n. 109 above, ch. 13.

[112] Westlake, n. 13 above, 39; S. Boyron, 'The Co-decision Procedure: Rethinking the Constitutional Fundamentals', in Craig and Harlow (eds.), n. 24 above, ch. 8; Maurer, n. 24 above, 21–29.

[113] It is true that the UK legislature has recently been more active. However the very fact that this has been deemed so worthy of note itself bears testimony to how far commentators have been accustomed to executive dominance of the legislature.

externalities, which in turn create incentives for policy co-ordination.[114] The key issue then becomes not whether States interact, but how. They can do so by *ad hoc* international agreements, involving two or more parties. Some more permanent form of international co-operation will often be preferred in order to reduce the bargaining and transaction costs of *ad hoc* co-ordination. This is especially so when the number of parties becomes larger, and the issues on which they seek to co-ordinate become broader.

The real contrast must, therefore, be between how issues such as 'distance', 'executive dominance', 'transparency', and the like play out as between these differing forms of international co-ordination. There is little room for doubt here: if we apply these criteria then the people fare less well when matters are regulated through a series of *ad hoc* international agreements than they do when they are regulated through a body such as the EU. This is so for a number of reasons. International agreements normally include no forum such as the EP at all. Such agreements are made by the executives, they are run by the executives, and terminated by the executives. National parliaments exercise only minimal control. They may have to give their approval to the agreement, but any parliamentary supervision thereafter will usually be interstitial and marginal at best.[115]

(c) EVALUATION: THE NORMATIVE FRAME OF REFERENCE

We must now consider the theoretical aspect of the democracy deficit argument. The theory is vital, because of the differing meanings of democracy. It is therefore axiomatic that discussion of the deficits of a particular system must be grounded in some more particular conception of democracy. If this is not done then we are testing the system against a criterion which is either not stated or is at best only implicit.

Thus one strand of the democracy deficit critique is based implicitly on the assumption that the EU must be judged by the same normative criteria that are applied to ordinary nation States. It is common to see the argument develop in the following way: national parliaments have certain types of power, and the decision-making structure of the EU is deficient in not according the European Parliament the same degree of power. This will not withstand examination. The EU may not conform to the stereotype of the traditional international agreement, but nor is it a super State in the traditional sense of the term.[116] To reason unthinkingly from the division of power within nation States to the EU is therefore unwarranted.

A more promising approach is to develop the line of argument advanced by Joseph Weiler,[117] and to recognize that different aspects of the EU may best reflect different modes of governance. There are international/intergovernmental facets of Community governance, dealing with fundamental rules of the system and issues of high politics, in which the Member States are the prominent players. There are supranational aspects of the EU, which best

---

[114] A. Moravcsik, 'Preferences and Power in the European Community: A Liberal Intergovernmentalist Approach' (1993) 31 *JCMS* 473, 485; W. Wessels, 'The Modern West-European State and the European Union: Democratic Erosion or a New Kind of Polity?', in Andersen and Eliassen (eds.), n. 109 above, ch. 4; G. Majone, 'The European Community Between Social Policy and Social Regulation' (1993) 31 *JCMS* 153 and 'The Rise of the Regulatory State in Europe' (1994) *West European Politics* 1; Craig, n. 107 above.

[115] This is so even in those countries where national legislation is required to transform rules made pursuant to such international agreements into national law, since executive control over the legislature will mean that this is often unproblematic. The very fact that a large number of such agreements may exist renders it more difficult for parliaments to keep track, and takes such matters out of the purview of the ordinary citizen entirely.

[116] For an interesting discussion of different forms of State and their application to the EU see J. Caporaso, 'The European Union and Forms of State: Westphalian, Regulatory and Post-Modern' (1996) 34 *JCMS* 29.

[117] N. 110 above.

capture governance and legislation under the EC Treaty itself. Member States, combined with the Community institutions, are the main actors in this arena. There are, finally, those aspects of the Community, primarily the making of detailed regulatory norms implementing Community policy, which are best explained in terms of infranationalism. Here the main players tend to be interest groups and bureaucrats, both national and European, which often bypass traditional forms of democratic governance.

Weiler argues that these differing forms of Community governance can best be captured through different models of democracy. He contends that the international facets can be explained through a consociational model of democracy; the supranational aspects of Community governance through some version of Schumpeterian elite democracy or pluralist democracy; and the infranational elements through a neo-corporatist model.

Commentators will undoubtedly have different views on which model of democracy best fits the different aspects of EU governance.[118] This is to be expected. Weiler's general methodology does, nonetheless, free us when thinking about EU democracy from the confines of what is an inappropriate, rigid paradigm of the traditional nation State. If we pursue this general approach then the division of power as it currently exists within the EC itself can be more readily understood and justified.

The Community is built on an institutional balance between the Council, European Parliament, and the Commission, as is evident from, *inter alia*, all the institutional reports leading to the 1996 IGC.[119] It rests on the twofold legitimacy of the Member States, as represented in the Council, and their peoples, as represented in the European Parliament.

The role accorded to the Council in this institutional balance can be defended most fundamentally, because the democratic legitimacy of the Community is founded upon the Member States as well as its peoples. The Council does, in any event, have an indirect democratic mandate, since those who sit on the Council will normally be elected members of their own national executives. The Council's powers can also be sustained on the ground that the Community is based on an international agreement. While it can be accepted that it no longer fits within the paradigm of the standard international agreement, it is a *non sequitur* to conclude that elements of state control are normatively unjustified within such a system.

It is accepted that the European Parliament is deserving of power within the system, by virtue of being directly elected. The gradual extension of the EP's powers in the legislative process bears testimony to this, notwithstanding the fact that it has had to struggle for its powers: the EP 'was born hungry and frustrated and has developed into an habitual struggler'.[120] The generalization of the co-decision procedure to cover much important Community legislation means that the EP has come close to attaining co-equal status with the Council in the legislative process. This is, as the Commission has stated, a natural step in the process of enhancing the democratic legitimacy of the Union, and establishes 'the twofold legitimacy on which the Community is founded, its States and its peoples'.[121] The failure of the EP to obtain a power of legislative initiative *and* its decision not to press for this power at the 1996 IGC are indicative of the limited consequences flowing from the direct democratic mandate. The reasons for this limitation are eclectic. They are in part a reflection of the fact that the EC is not perceived as a State. It is in part because to accord the EP such a power would unbalance the system in its favour *vis-à-vis* the Council. It is in part also because of the perceived need to preserve the unique position of the Commission, so as not to compromise its role as guardian of the Treaties and 'engine room' of the Community.

---

[118] Compare *ibid.*, and Craig, n. 107 above.

[119] Craig, n. 3 above.

[120] M. Westlake, *A Modern Guide to the European Parliament* (Pinter, 1994), 28.

[121] Scope of the Codecision Procedure, SEC(96)1225/4, July 1996, Pt. IIA, para. 1.

The Commission's powers, and its right of legislative initiative, can be seen as helping to ensure that Community policies are directed towards the advancement of the general good laid down in the constituent Treaties, as opposed to narrow sectional self-interests. It is for this reason that the Commission has always opposed any inroad into its right of legislative initiative, believing its 'sole right of initiative to be a fundamental constitutional prerogative vital to the good functioning of the Community's institutional balance and its legislative machinery'.[122] This does not mean that the detailed interpretations of general Community principles or their prioritization are value-free, or that the Commission is free from interest-group pressure. It does mean that the Commission is well placed to consider legislation to attain the general good as laid down in the Treaties. It also means that it conceives of its role in this manner and, at the present stage of the Community's development, that it can fulfil this role better than either the Council or the EP. The members of the Council will often be swayed by relatively short-term considerations relating to the needs of their own Member States. This is less of a problem with the EP, which has not, thus far, divided along generally nationalistic lines. When considered from this perspective the retention of the Commission's right of legislative initiative appears more defensible in normative terms. This is particularly so given the fact that the Commission will engage in detailed negotiations with both the Council and the EP on the annual legislative plan, as well as on specific legislative proposals; and given also the greater control exercised by the EP over the appointment of the Commission.

We can, in the light of this, return to the very first aspect of the democracy deficit argument, which we have not evaluated thus far. This is, as will be recalled, the argument that EU democracy is deficient because those who make the decisions cannot be voted from office. The very fact that legislative power is divided between Council, Commission, and the EP precludes this. There is force in this argument. We must however think through the consequences of this critique.

EU decision-making is posited on institutional balance. If it were felt that the EU could be properly democratic only if the citizens were able to vote out *the body* that exercised legislative power, then this would involve a radical restructuring of the EU. It would not be sufficient for the EP to have some control over the Commission, as it does at present, or to have even greater control. Nor would it suffice for the President of the Commission and the Commissioners to be elected. Nor would it even be sufficient for an elected Commission to become the EU's executive and control the EP. These changes would not meet the critique, because the voters could still not 'vote out' the Member State representatives in the Council. It is doubtful whether the Member States would accede to a system in which their representatives were directly elected, and where they functioned as a 'second chamber' under the control of a directly elected Commission.

9. THE CONSTITUTIONAL TREATY, DEMOCRACY, AND DECISION-MAKING

The impact of the Constitutional Treaty[123] on the institutions was considered above.[124] The CT will not become law, but many of its provisions will be carried over to the Reform Treaty, and the CT's impact on the issues in this chapter should therefore be considered.

---

122   Westlake, n. 13 above, 79. See also J. Fitzmaurice, 'The European Commission', in Duff, Pinder, and Pryce (eds.), n. 71 above, 183–184.
123   Treaty Establishing a Constitution for Europe [2004] OJ C310/1.
124   See above, Ch. 2.

(a) LEGISLATIVE POWER: PRIMARY LEGISLATION

The importance of the institutional balance that has characterized decision-making in the EU thus far was stressed yet again in the documentation to emerge from the Convention.[125] This is readily apparent in relation to the legislative process. The Commission retained in general terms its 'gold standard', the right of legislative initiative.[126] The EP and the Council were said jointly to enact legislation,[127] the co-decision procedure was deemed to be the ordinary legislative procedure for the making of European laws and framework laws,[128] and the reach of this procedure was extended to cover new areas, including agriculture and fisheries, asylum and immigration law, and the structural and cohesion funds. These changes would have been beneficial. It is generally accepted, as seen above, that the co-decision procedure has worked well. The extension of the ordinary legislative procedure to new areas would have been a natural development, building on earlier Treaty reform. The language of 'law' and 'framework law' will not, it seems, be preserved in the Reform Treaty, but the general idea of a hierarchy of norms will be retained.

The CT also modified the definition of qualified majority for voting in the Council and European Council. Article I–25 CT in effect established a double-majority provision. It defined a qualified majority as at least 55 per cent of the members of the Council, comprising at least fifteen of them and representing at least 65 per cent of the EU's population. The blocking minority had however to include at least four Council members, failing which the qualified majority was deemed to be attained. These figures were increased in the relatively rare instances where the EU did not act on a proposal from the Commission or Union Minister for Foreign Affairs.

(b) LEGISLATIVE POWER: DELEGATED REGULATIONS

The EP was also accorded powers in relation to the new breed of 'delegated regulations' established by the Constitutional Treaty. Although these were formally labelled non-legislative acts, they were in effect either secondary European laws, which were binding in their entirety and directly applicable in all Member States, or secondary European framework laws, which were binding as to result, but which left the Member States discretion as to implementation.[129] European laws and framework laws could delegate to the Commission the power to enact delegated regulations to 'supplement or amend certain non-essential elements of the European law or framework law'.[130] The objectives, content, scope, and duration of the delegation had to be defined in the primary laws and framework laws, which had to define the essential elements in the area. Conditions could be attached to the delegation:[131] the European Parliament or the Council could revoke the entire delegation; or the delegated regulation might enter into force only if no objection had been expressed by the European Parliament or the Council within a period set by the law or framework law. There was much to be said in principle for the clearer delineation between primary laws and other legally binding norms.

---

[125] CONV 770/03, Brussels, 2 June 2003, 2.
[126] Art. I–26(2) CT.
[127] Arts. I–20(1) and I–23(1) CT.
[128] Arts. I–34(1) and III–396 CT.
[129] Art. I–33(1) CT.
[130] Art. I–36 CT.
[131] Art. I–36(2) CT.

The schema was advocated by the Commission in its White Paper on European Governance,[132] and in later Communications,[133] with the express hope that it would thereby lead to the demise of the management and regulatory committees that comprise the core of Comitology.

The change would have significantly altered the institutional balance of power in the Community, reducing the power of the Council and EP, and increasing that of the Commission. Comitology committees were created precisely to accord Member States an institutionalized method for input into the content of delegated legislation, with the possibility of formal recourse to the Council, plus some control by the EP. The system embodied in the Constitutional Treaty was based on specification of standards in the primary law, combined with the possibility of control should the draft measure not be to the liking of the EP or Council. The former, specification of standards in the primary law, has limitations, since these will often be at a high level of generality, leaving real regulatory choices to be made through delegated regulations. The latter, the power of the Council and EP to prevent a delegated regulation entering into force if they objected to it, is crucially dependent on an understanding of the nature of the measure, more especially because any decision to object would have to be made within a short period, normally one month. However if Comitology were dismantled, and no other regime were put in place whereby the Council and the EP could become informed about the complex regulatory choices contained in delegated regulations, then it is difficult to see how they would be able to make an informed choice as to whether to object to any such measure.[134]

(c) LEGISLATIVE POWER: SUBSIDIARITY AND NATIONAL PARLIAMENTS

The Constitutional Treaty retained subsidiarity, within Article I–11(3) CT, but the novelty resided in the Protocol attached to the Constitution, which subtly altered the principles contained in earlier such documents.

The important innovation was the enhanced role accorded to national parliaments. The Commission had to send all legislative proposals to the national parliaments at the same time as to the Union institutions. A national parliament, or chamber thereof, could, within six weeks, send the Presidents of the Commission, EP, and Council a reasoned opinion as to why it considered that the proposal did not comply with subsidiarity. The EP, Council, and Commission were obliged to take this opinion into account. Where non-compliance with subsidiarity was expressed by national parliaments that represented one third of all the votes allocated to such parliaments, then the Commission was obliged to review its proposal. The Commission, after such review, could decide to maintain, amend, or withdraw the proposal, giving reasons for the decision. A legal challenge for non-compliance with subsidiarity could be brought by the Member State, or notified by it on behalf of its national parliament or a chamber of it.

It is questionable how far this would have strengthened subsidiarity. The national parliament would have to submit a reasoned opinion as to why it believed that the measure

---

[132] COM(2001)428 final; the White Paper provoked a variety of critical comment, *Symposium: Responses to the European Commission's White Paper on Governance*, available at www.jeanmonnetprogram.org/papers/01.

[133] The Future of the European Union, Renewing the Community Method, COM(2001)727 final.

[134] Craig, n. 53 above, ch. 4.

infringed subsidiarity, and thus why the Commission's comparative efficiency calculus was defective. This would not have been easy. It would have been even more difficult for the requisite number of national parliaments to present reasoned opinions in relation to the same Union measure so as to compel the Commission to review the proposal. Having said this, the Commission would have been likely to take seriously any such reasoned opinion, particularly if it emanated from the parliament of a larger Member State.

(d) THE LOCUS OF EXECUTIVE POWER

The discussion thus far has been concerned with the impact of the Constitutional Treaty on legislative power within the EU. The deliberations concerning executive power were equally significant.[135] The most significant aspect of this debate concerned the Presidency of the Union as a whole. Two main positions can be identified: the single hat view and the separate hats view.

A prominent version of *the 'single hat' view* was that there should be one President for the Union as a whole; the office of President should be connected formally and substantively with the locus of executive power within the Union; and the President of the Commission should hold this office. The Presidency of the European Council should continue to rotate on a six-monthly basis. The real 'head' of the Union would be the President of the Commission, whose legitimacy it was hoped would be increased by his or her election.

A prominent version of *the 'separate hats' view* was that there should be a President of the Commission and a President of the European Council, and that executive power would be exercised by both. It was central to this view that the Presidency of the European Council would be strengthened. It would no longer rotate between States on a six-monthly basis. It was felt that this would not work within an enlarged Union, and that greater continuity of policy would be required. This view was advocated by a number of the larger States, but was opposed by some of the smaller States, which felt that the Presidency of the European Council would be dominated by the larger Member States.

This latter view predominated in the Constitutional Treaty. It provided that the European Council should elect a President, by qualified majority, for two and half years renewable once; that the European Council should define the general political directions and priorities of the EU; and gave the President of the European Council increased powers within the Council itself. It was nonetheless clear that the Commission and its President were still central in this constitutional scheme. The Commission was accorded power to initiate annual and multi-annual programming with the aim of securing inter-institutional agreement, and the Commission President co-operated with the President of the European Council in ensuring the preparation and continuity of the work of the European Council.

The CT also created the post of Union Minister for Foreign Affairs to conduct the EU's foreign and security policy, and ensure consistency in external action. The Minister was to take part in the business of the European Council, preside over the Foreign Affairs Council, and also be a Vice-President of the Commission.[136]

---

[135] P. Craig, 'European Governance: Executive and Administrative Powers under the New Constitutional Settlement' (2005) 3 *I-CON* 407.

[136] Art. I–28 CT. The Reform Treaty will change the name to 'High Representative of the Union for Foreign Affairs and Security Policy'.

(e) THE CONSTITUTIONAL TREATY AND DEMOCRACY

The 'message' that emerged from the Constitutional Treaty concerning democracy within the EU was therefore mixed. Those who hoped that the CT would signal a significant shift to a more parliamentary regime were disappointed. To be sure the power of the EP over primary legislation was increased. However state interests exercised through the Council and European Council were also reinforced through, for example, the creation of the longer-term Presidency of the European Council, and the European Council's retention of ultimate control over the choice of President of the Commission. The reality was therefore that the CT embodied a regime in which executive and legislative powers were shared between the European Council, Council, EP, and Commission. The sharing of such power has been a principal theme of the Community, and in this respect the CT represented continuity with the past, even if the power sharing differed in points of detail.

10. CONCLUSION

i.   Institutional balance between the Commission, Council, and European Parliament has always characterized decision-making within the EU. That balance is dynamic, not static, and it has changed over time.

ii. The increase in the power of the EP has been the principal feature in that institutional dynamic. The generalization of the co-decision procedure has gone a considerable way to affording the EP this co-equal status. The 1999 Comitology Decision has also improved the position of the EP in relation to delegated legislation, as has the 2006 reforms.

iii. The legitimacy of EU decision-making is now founded on the Council, as representing State interests, and the EP as representing the interests of the peoples of Europe. The Commission, which is increasingly accountable to the EP, seeks to ensure that the goals laid down in the Treaties are met.

iv. The fact that the general distribution of legislative authority as it operates in the supranational arena of EC governance can be defended does not mean that the system could not be improved. There is room for improvement in many areas. These include the quality of EU legislation,[137] the role of national parliaments,[138] and citizen participation in EU decision-making.[139]

v.   The Constitutional Treaty is unlikely to enter into force in its present format. The provisions concerning institutions may however be of significance in future Treaty reform.

---

[137] T. Burns, 'Better Lawmaking? An Evaluation of Lawmaking in the European Community', in Craig and Harlow (eds.), n. 24 above, ch. 21. See also Declaration 39 appended to the ToA on the Quality of the Drafting of Community Legislation.

[138] P. Norton (ed.), *National Parliaments and the Role of the European Union* (Frank Cass, 1996); E. Smith (ed.), *National Parliaments as Cornerstones of European Integration* (Kluwer, 1996); H. Schmitt and J. Thomassen (eds.), *Political Representation and Legitimacy in the European Union* (Oxford University Press, 1999); R. Katz and B. Wessels (eds.), *The European Parliament, the National Parliaments and European Integration* (Oxford University Press, 1999).

[139] Craig, n. 3 above; Curtin, n. 109 above.

11. FURTHER READING[140]

Andenas, M., and Türk, A. (eds.), *Delegated Legislation and the Role of Committees in the EC* (Kluwer, 2000)

Anderson, S., and Eliassen, K. (eds.), *The European Union: How Democratic Is It?* (Sage, 1996)

Bellamy, R. (ed.), *Constitutionalism, Democracy and Sovereignty: American and European Perspectives* (Avebury, 1996)

—— and Castiglione, D. (eds.), *Constitutionalism in Transformation: European and Theoretical Perspectives* (Blackwell, 1996)

——, Bufacchi, V., and Castiglione, D. (eds.), *Democracy and Constitutional Culture in the Union of Europe* (Lothian Foundation Press, 1995)

Christiansen, T., and Kirchner, E., *Committee Governance in the European Union* (Manchester University Press, 2000)

Craig, P., and Harlow, C. (eds.), *Lawmaking in the European Union* (Kluwer, 1998)

Curtin, D., *Postnational Democracy, The European Union in Search of a Political Philosophy* (Kluwer, 1997)

Dehousse, R. (ed.), *Europe: The Impossible Status Quo* (Macmillan, 1997)

Hayward, J. (ed.), *The Crisis of Representation in Europe* (Frank Cass, 1995)

Hoskyns, C., and Newman, M. (eds.), *Democratizing the European Union* (Manchester University Press, 2000)

Joerges, C., and Vos, E. (eds.), *EU Committees: Social Regulation, Law and Politics* (Hart, 1999)

Mancini, F., *Democracy and Constitutionalism in the European Union* (Hart, 2000)

Neunreither, K., and Wiener, A. (eds.), *European Integration after Amsterdam, Institutional Dynamics and Prospects for Democracy* (Oxford University Press, 2000)

Nicolaidis, K., and Howse, R. (eds.), *The Federal Vision, Legitimacy and Levels of Governance in the United States and the European Union* (Oxford University Press, 2001)

Prodi, R., *Europe As I See It* (Polity, 2000)

Richardson, J. (ed.), *European Union: Power and Policy-Making* (3rd edn., Routledge, 2006)

Van Gerven, W., *The European Union, A Polity of States and Peoples* (Hart, 2005)

Wallace, W., Wallace, H., and Pollack, M. (eds.), *Policy-making in the European Union* (5th edn., Oxford University Press, 2005)

Weiler, J., *The Constitution of Europe* (Cambridge University Press, 1999)

Westlake, M., *The Commission and the Parliament: Partners and Rivals in the European Policy-Making Process* (Butterworths, 1994)

---

[140] The volume of material on this topic means that only books have been listed here.

5

NEW FORMS OF GOVERNANCE

1. CENTRAL ISSUES

i. The aim of this chapter is not to give a comprehensive overview of 'new governance modes' in the EU, nor to seriously evaluate their functioning, their successes or their failures. Rather it is to give a sense of what the lively, ongoing debate over new forms of governance in the EU is about, and to provide a general account of the apparent shift towards greater use of such forms and modes in recent years. It will also outline some of the reasons which have been suggested for this shift, as well as some of the concerns to which it has given rise.

ii. The language of 'new' or 'alternative' forms of governance in the EU is generally used to refer to a move away from reliance on *hierarchical* modes towards more *flexible* modes as the preferred method of governing. These terms will be explained further in the chapter. Instead of questioning (as many do) whether there is anything new really going on, this chapter suggests that there have been distinct changes in preferred governing modes over the last decade or two in the EU, and it outlines the main contours of those changes.

iii. A number of examples of new governance instruments and methods will be given, in particular the 'new approach to harmonization' and the 'open method of coordination'. A number of other EU governance reform initiatives which are related to the new governance debate will also be discussed, such as the introduction and elaboration of the subsidiarity and proportionality principles, the 'better regulation' initiative and the Commission White Paper on Governance.

2. INTRODUCTION

The previous chapters have introduced the main instruments used by the EU for making law and policy, as well as the main law-making processes by which they are adopted. We have seen that there is a wide range of such instruments and processes, which include binding and non-binding forms of law. In the First Pillar, Article 249 sets out five instruments, three of which are said to be binding (regulations, directives, and decisions) and two of which are not (recommendations and opinions). We have also seen that there is a range of other instruments such as strategies, co-ordination processes, action programmes, declarations, communications, and many others, both binding and non-binding, which are used by the EC to achieve its policy aims. Some of these are listed in the Treaty and some are not. Further, under the Second and Third Pillars there is yet another array of binding and non-binding instruments. The combination of this extensive array of tools and the multiplicity of processes, both formal and informal, for adopting them raises the question of what we mean by 'new' forms of governance.

There has been a lively debate in the EU (and elsewhere) over the last decade about new forms and modes of governance. While some observers are sceptical about the claims of newness and about the argument that anything much has changed, the fact that the debate has been taking place is incontrovertible. For that reason alone, some investigation is warranted. However, there are various other more substantial reasons for assuming that there is something of significance taking place which students and others interested in the governing of the EU should know more about.

In the first place, the EU itself, and the Commission in particular, has in recent years referred expressly to the use of new or 'alternative' regulatory mechanisms and forms of governance.[1] In other words, some of the key EU actors either believe or wish to suggest that there is something distinctive or novel about certain ways of making policy which they intend to pursue, and indeed they have funded extensive research projects on the subject.[2] Secondly, the discussion on new forms of governance is not unique to the EU, and not purely an invention of EU officials, but is part of a broader debate about a shift from 'government' to 'governance' both within States and internationally.[3] Thirdly, while there is undoubtedly some truth in the claim that little if anything is ever really new and that the assertion of novelty is often a rhetorical or strategic device, the very fact that there is a desire to be seen to do something differently usually means that there has been recognition of the inadequacy of past practice, and even a change in rhetoric can lead to more substantive change.

One drawback in seeking to understand the debate and to assess its significance is that the academic and policy literature on new governance in the EU has grown, not only in size but in complexity.[4] There are intense debates over the difference between 'instruments', 'processes', and 'modes', debates over the meaning of 'hard' and 'soft' law, and debates over the meaning of 'law' itself.[5] There are definitions of new governance by reference to actors, instruments, governance attributes,[6] architecture,[7] overall 'modes',[8] or by reference to various combinations of these.[9] There are three-dimensional typologies which distinguish the policy (instruments), politics (actor constellations), and polity (institutional structures) dimensions of new governance

[1] See, e.g., COM(2001)428. Following this White Paper on European Governance, the Commission created a website on the subject of European Governance, with links to its various proposals for reform, including its reports on 'better regulation' and 'better lawmaking'. See http://ec.europa.eu/governance/governance_eu/index_en.htm.

[2] See, e.g., NEWGOV at www.eu-newgov.org/, CONNEX at www.connex-network.org/, and REFGOV at http://refgov.cpdr.ucl.ac.be/, funded under the EU's Sixth Framework Programme for research.

[3] For some notable examples from a vast literature see J. Jordana and D. Levi-Faur (eds.), *The Politics of Regulation Institutional and Regulatory Reforms for the Age of Governance* (Edward Elgar, 2004); A. Héritier, M. Stolleis, and F.W. Scharpf (eds.), *European and International Regulation after the Nation State: Different Scopes and Multiple Levels* (Nomos, 2004); and within the State context R.A.W. Rhodes, *Understanding Governance* (Open University Press, 1997).

[4] For an excellent discussion of the complexity and confusion within the debate see C. Kilpatrick and K. Armstrong, 'Law, Governance and New Governance: The Changing Open Method of Coordination' (2007) 13 *CJEL* 649.

[5] See, e.g., N. Walker and G. de Búrca, 'Reconceiving Law and New Governance' (2007) 13 *CJEL* 519.

[6] J. Scott and D.M. Trubek, 'Mind the Gap: Law and New Approaches to Governance in the European Union' (2002) 8 *ELJ* 1.

[7] C. Sabel and J. Zeitlin, 'Learning from Difference: The New Architecture of Experimentalist Governance in the European Union', European Governance Working Paper, EUROGOV No. C-07-02, 10 May 2007.

[8] H. Wallace, 'An Institutional Anatomy and Five Policy Modes. Policy-Making in the European Union', in H. Wallace, W. Wallace, and M. Pollack (eds.) *Policy-Making in the European Union* (5th edn., OUP, 2005) 49.

[9] See, e.g., C. Knill and A. Lenschow, 'Modes of Regulation in the Governance of the European Union: Towards a Comprehensive Evaluation', European Integration Online Paper No. 7 (2003). Also P. Dabrowksa, *Hybrid Solutions for Hybrid Products: EU Governance of GMOs* (PhD Thesis, EUI, 2006).

modes.[10] The result is a dizzying and often confusing picture for those seeking to grasp the essentials of the debate and a broad overview of what is at stake.

Partly for that reason, this chapter, while acknowledging the inevitable simplification involved in identifying one primary point of analysis for the debate, will emphasize one core and unifying theme, which is *the shift away from hierarchical governance.* In other words, when it comes to the concrete question of what has changed in the EU, and what is distinctive about certain forms of EU governing as compared with others, we suggest that the core of the debate on new governance concerns a move away from hierarchical forms of governing. The concept of hierarchical governing used here implies a number of different things. It implies that policies come from 'above' or from the centre (i.e., they are top-down). It implies that the policies are relatively complete, in the sense that they do not leave much room for discretion on the part of those to whom the policies apply (i.e., they are prescriptive). And it implies that prescriptions are obligatory for those to whom they apply (i.e., they are binding), generally allowing for compulsory legal enforcement.

Within this broad concept of hierarchical governance many of the dimensions and features used by other commentators in their analysis or definitions of new governance are implicated. The emphasis on central governmental *actors* is clearly one, the degree of detail and prescriptive nature of *instruments* is another, and the use of binding measures with reliance on *legal enforceability* is another. Another common description of certain forms of hierarchical governance which refers to the overall style of the governing mode, rather than to actors, instruments, or processes, is the term *command-and-control-type regulation.*

In an influential article on the rise of new governance and its relationship with law in the EU, the 'Classic Community Method' of law-making is identified by Scott and Trubek as a benchmark against which new forms of governance can be measured.[11] They explain this benchmark Classic Community Method as the exercise of legislative power by the EC following the Commission's exercise of its exclusive right of initiative, leading to the adoption of legislation by the Council and Parliament, resulting in a binding uniform rule which is subject to the jurisdiction of the Court of Justice. We can see in this definition the three elements of hierarchical governance which we have set out above: top-down governing by the central institutional actors leading to binding, uniform rules.

New governance modes have, however, also been contrasted, not just with the Classic Community Method, but also with traditional Intergovernmental modes.[12] While very different from the classic Community methods of governing, intergovernmental modes are certainly hierarchical in the top-down sense, albeit privileging state actors and state sovereignty more than supranational EC actors. And while EU intergovernmental decision-making is less likely than Community law-making to lead to detailed prescriptive measures, it does often result in the adoption of binding measures, especially under the Second and Third Pillars, which are obligatory for the Member States.

It should be emphasized, first, that the broad argument that there has been a move away from hierarchical governing in the EU does not mean that there is no longer any reliance on top-down, binding, or detailed legal measures. The Classic Community Method is certainly alive and well, as are many other forms of hierarchical EU governance, intergovernmental and otherwise. A 'move away' implies less reliance, and implies greater reliance on other kinds of

---

[10] O. Trieb, H. Bähr, and G. Falkner, 'Modes of Governance: A Note Towards Conceptual Clarification', European Governance Working Paper, EUROGOV No. N-05-02, 17 Nov. 2005.

[11] Scott and Trubek, n. 6 above.

[12] P. Zysk, *New Governance and New Terrorism in the EU: The Beauty and the Beast* (PhD Dissertation, EUI, 2006).

governing mechanisms, but it does not necessarily mean the disappearance of hierarchical modes, or of other modes which share some of the features of hierarchical governance. Secondly, a 'move away' does not imply that there has in the past been an exclusive reliance on hierarchical governing, but rather it implies that this was officially understood in many instances to be the preferred mode or the more effective mode. There has always been, as indicated at the outset of the chapter, a multiplicity of different instruments and processes of law-making and policy-making in the EU, and not all of these (alone or in combination) could be described as hierarchical. The important point to bear in mind is that the discussion of new forms of governance implies that some shift has occurred, that one mode of governing is no longer assumed to be the preferred or the predominant mode, and that other modes and forms have come to the fore and are increasingly being promoted, tested, and used. Finally, it may be the case that new governance forms are more readily proposed and used in certain areas of policy than others, for a variety of reasons. While there seems to be some empirical evidence for this, with social and environmental policy being two particularly notable fields in this respect—nonetheless the argument we are making is that the tendency to emphasize and promote new forms of governance seems to be a more general one in the EU, and that all policy areas are potentially candidates.

Nevertheless, this description of a shift in emphasis away from hierarchical governance does not yet give any positive indication of what the new forms of governance are. One of the points which this chapter seeks to emphasize is that there is a multiplicity of new or alternative forms of governance being advocated and developed in the EU, some of which exhibit greater continuity with hierarchical modes than others. Overall, however—and again acknowledging the inevitable risk of over-simplification that accompanies any attempt to reduce complexity—we will argue that the shift towards new modes of governance is characterized by a move away from hierarchical governing towards more *flexible* forms of governance. A shift away from hierarchical governance does not mean that the main institutional actors are not centrally involved in policy-making, but rather that they now share that space with other actors, whether States, regional actors, private actors, or others. In other words, policies adopted under new governance modes are not generally created and imposed top-down, but rather those to whom they are to be applied are involved in their shaping and application. Secondly, a move towards more flexible forms of governance does not necessarily mean that there is no legal commitment to the policies which are agreed within these new forms. Some new forms of governance may be wholly voluntaristic, but many others are not. The difference in emphasis between traditional hierarchical forms of governance and alternative governance modes, even when the latter result in binding legal acts, is that there is likely to be greater room for input, adaptation, and revision on the part of those administering the policies or those to whom they are applicable. It also implies that policy-making is less likely to be rigidly prescriptive or difficult to revise.[13]

In giving an overview of the emergence of new forms of governance in the EU, there are a great many different examples which could be given and developments which could be examined. However, given the constraints of space, this chapter will focus on three issues in particular. The first and most specific is the 'new approach to harmonization' which came to

---

[13] For a range of examples of potential new governance modes in the EU see the contributions to G. de Búrca and J. Scott (eds.), *Law and New Governance in the EU and the US* (Hart, 2006), in particular the chapters on environmental law by J. Scott and J. Holder, and by C. Kilpatrick on employment policy. See also T. Hervey and L. Trubek, 'Freedom to Provide Health-care Services within the EU: An Opportunity for a Transformative Directive' (2007) 13 *CJEL* 624, on new governance in EU health-care law.

prominence in the 1980s as part of the EC's Single Market programme, and which exemplifies aspects of the move away from hierarchy and towards greater flexibility.[14]

The second, and undoubtedly the most important in terms of catalyzing the debate on new governance in the EU, is the set of developments that were marked by the EU's adoption of the 'Lisbon Agenda' in 2000.[15] Along with the launch of this broad policy strategy for the EU, a form of policy-co-ordination which became known as the Open Method of Co-ordination (OMC) was explicitly introduced, and this has given rise to a vast literature, much of which is concerned with its analysis as a new mode of governance.[16]

The third, unlike the first two, does not analyse a development within particular policy fields, but rather examines the more general official emphasis on the need for change in the character of EU policy-making over the last decade or so. This emphasis can be discerned in a number of related governance initiatives: (a) the formal introduction of the principles of subsidiarity and proportionality into policy-making by the Maastricht Treaty, and later in the Amsterdam Treaty protocol and subsequent other policy developments;[17] (b) the Commission's 'better regulation' initiative, which reveals the influence of related public management theories which resonate with many aspects of new governance, and also the Commission's White Paper on Governance.

These linked initiatives reveal an ongoing and self-conscious attempt by the EU and its institutional actors to develop what they consider to be improved and more effective methods of regulating and governing, against the backdrop of an assumption that some of their preferred policy methods and legal approaches in the past had not delivered their intended results.[18]

To conclude this introductory section, it can be said that the debate on 'new' forms versus traditional or 'old' forms of governance relies to some extent on a stylized contrast that exaggerates the distinction between various policy-making modes and that conceals the continuities in policy-making over the years. Nevertheless, a stylized contrast can help in clarifying what is at issue in an unquestionably vigorous debate.

3. THE NEW APPROACH TO (TECHNICAL) HARMONIZATION

We will see in subsequent chapters of the book that the early approach to common market harmonization involved attempting to prescribe the desired result through detailed regulation, and that the shortcomings of this approach were recognized before long.[19] These included the length of time it took to secure agreement on detail, the cumbersome nature of the legislative process, and the need for continuous updating of the detail. During the 1980s, the Commission decided, as part of the broader relaunch of the internal market, to adopt a

---

[14] See also Ch. 17 for discussion.

[15] Conclusions of the Lisbon European Council Presidency, 23–24 Mar. 2000. See also the Community Lisbon Programme, COM(2000)330.

[16] For an excellent collection and classification of the extensive OMC literature see the OMC Forum at the EU Center of the University of Wisconsin, Madison: http://eucenter.wisc.edu/OMC/index.htm.

[17] See also Ch. 3 for discussion.

[18] European Governance: A White Paper, COM(2001)428. For analysis see the collection of papers published as part of an online symposium, 'Mountain or Molehill: A Critical Analysis of the Commission White Paper on Governance', Jean Monnet Working Paper 6/01.

[19] See Ch. 17 on the Single Market, Ch. 19 on quantitative restrictions on the free movement of goods, and Ch. 22 on freedom of establishment and services.

'new approach' to harmonization and to the use of standards in removing 'technical barriers to trade'.[20] The main elements of the new approach were set out by the Council in an annex to its resolution adopted in 1985:[21]

> The following are the four fundamental principles on which the new approach is based:—
>   Legislative harmonization is limited to the adoption, by means of Directives based on Article 100 of the EEC Treaty, of the essential safety requirements (or other requirements in the general interest) with which products put on the market must conform, and which should therefore enjoy free movement throughout the Community,
>
>   — the task of drawing up the technical specifications needed for the production and placing on the market of products conforming to the essential requirements established by the Directives, while taking into account the current stage of technology, is entrusted to organizations competent in the standardization area
>   — these technical specifications are not mandatory and maintain their status of voluntary standards
>   — but at the same time national authorities are obliged to recognize that products manufactured in conformity with harmonized standards (or, provisionally, with national standards) are presumed to conform to the 'essential requirements' established by the Directive. (This signifies that the producer has the choice of not manufacturing in conformity with the standards but that in this event he has an obligation to prove that his products conform to the essential requirements of the Directive)
>
> In order that this system may operate it is necessary:— on the one hand that the standards offer a guarantee of quality with regard to the 'essential requirements' established by the Directives, and on the other hand that the public authorities keep intact their responsibility for the protection of safety (or other requirements envisaged) on their territory.

There are several elements to be noted in this new approach to harmonization. The first is that, although directives will continue to be used to set the basic requirements, they are to be limited to the setting of 'essential requirements', which are necessary to ensure public safety and other general interests. In other words, the degree of detail and prescriptiveness in the legislation is to be reduced.

Secondly, the task of setting technical standards for the products which have to meet these essential requirements is to be carried out not by the EC legislative institutions themselves, but by European standardization bodies (which are known as CEN and CENELEC) which act with the agreement of the Commission. Thus we see the devolution of aspects of policy-making to bodies other than the formal EU law-making institutions, in this case to private standard-setting organizations composed of representatives of national standard-setting organizations, which are in turn generally financed by industry and by governments.

Thirdly, the standards set by these bodies are not compulsory, but remain voluntary. However, manufacturers are given an incentive to abide by the standards set because if their products are certified as being in conformity with them, they benefit from the presumption that they meet the essential requirements of the directive and are entitled to enjoy freedom of movement across the EC market. Therefore we see in the new approach to harmonization a certain shift away (even if not entirely) from the three dimensions of hierarchical governance set out earlier: the monopoly of central institutional actors, the degree of prescriptive detail, and the formally compulsory nature of the norms.

---

[20] Technical Harmonisation and Standardisation: A New Approach, COM(1985)19.
[21] [1985] OJ C136/1.

The new approach to harmonization has undergone re-examination and revision on several occasions since its adoption. And although the Commission and others have acknowledged various problems in relation to the process of standard-setting and the standardization bodies,[22] as well as in relation to the national bodies carrying out conformity assessments, nevertheless it seems that the new approach has spread not only to other areas of EC regulation but also to the global regulatory context.[23] Thus the new approach established a form of governance in the area of technical harmonization which, whatever its problems, is considered by the Commission to be 'highly efficient and successful'[24] and has become widespread since its introduction.

This is not to say that the new approach has been an unqualified success in terms of what it set out to do, nor that it does not suffer from a range of deficiencies,[25] but it nonetheless provides a very good example of an early instance of new governance, a form of regulation which moved deliberately away from traditional hierarchical law-making to a more experimental and flexible one. We will return towards the end of the chapter to the question of the shortcomings of new governance in general, and will come back to the problems with the new approach to harmonization in that context.

4. THE LISBON AGENDA AND THE OPEN METHOD OF CO-ORDINATION

In 2000, the European Council at its Lisbon summit introduced a new ten-year set of policy priorities and goals for the EU which have continued to dominate the policy agenda ever since.[26] The overarching aim—the 'new strategic goal'—was to improve the EU's competitiveness and economic performance *vis-à-vis* the United States, and the means by which it was proposed to do so included a range of ambitious policy goals. The goals were along two axes, economic and social. The economic goals included shifting to a 'dynamic, knowledge-based economy' and information society, establishing a European area for research and innovation, developing a business-friendly environment, undertaking further internal-market liberalization reforms, integrating financial markets, and co-ordinating macro-economic policies. The social goals, under the broad umbrella of 'Modernising the European Social Model and Building an Active Welfare State', included training and education for the knowledge society, developing an active employment policy, modernizing social protection (i.e., pension reform), and promoting social inclusion (i.e., anti-poverty measures).

Alongside these two sets of substantive goals, a new policy instrument was introduced under the name of the open method of co-ordination (OMC). In fact, the OMC, which was first named in the Lisbon conclusions, drew to a considerable extent on two existing policy-co-ordination processes introduced into the EC Treaty at Maastricht and Amsterdam,

---

[22] Efficiency and Accountability in Standardization under the New Approach, COM(1998)291. See also Council Conclusions of Mar. 2002 on Standardisation [2002] OJ C66/01.

[23] The 'global approach' involves the adoption of Mutual Recognition Agreements, and is based on similar principles to the new approach. See http://ec.europa.eu/enterprise/newapproach/index_en.htm.

[24] Enhancing the Implementation of the New Approach Directives, COM(2003)240.

[25] H. Schepel, *The Constitution of Private Governance* (Hart, 2005).

[26] There was a mid-term review and re-launch in 2005 of what has become known in various terms as the 'Lisbon Strategy', the 'Lisbon Agenda', or the 'Lisbon Programme': Working Together for Growth and Jobs: A New Start for the Lisbon Strategy, COM(2005)24, and Presidency Conclusions of the Spring European Council, Brussels 2005.

in the field of economic and employment policy respectively. The European Council Conclusions at Lisbon described the new method as follows:

Libson European Council[27]

PUTTING DECISIONS INTO PRACTICE: A MORE COHERENT AND SYSTEMATIC APPROACH

Implementing a new open method of coordination

37. Implementation of the strategic goal will be facilitated by applying a new open method of coordination as the means of spreading best practice and achieving greater convergence towards the main EU goals. This method, which is designed to help Member States to progressively develop their own policies, involves:

— fixing guidelines for the Union combined with specific timetables for achieving the goals which they set in the short, medium and long terms;
— establishing, where appropriate, quantitative and qualitative indicators and benchmarks against the best in the world and tailored to the needs of different Member States and sectors as a means of comparing best practice;
— translating these European guidelines into national and regional policies by setting specific targets and adopting measures, taking into account national and regional differences;
— periodic monitoring, evaluation and peer review organised as mutual learning processes.

38. A fully decentralised approach will be applied in line with the principle of subsidiarity in which the Union, the Member States, the regional and local levels, as well as the social partners and civil society, will be actively involved, using variable forms of partnership. A method of benchmarking best practices on managing change will be devised by the European Commission networking with different providers and users, namely the social partners, companies and NGOs.

The four elements set out above comprise the key features of the OMC, although the exact nature of each element (guidelines, measured against indicators/benchmarks, translated into local policies, accompanied by learning-oriented monitoring and evaluation) varies depending on the policy area in question, and comprises a range of sub-elements. Thus the instrument or tool in itself is quite a general and flexible one which can be adapted to fit different policy requirements.

The origins and broader significance of the new policy instrument are discussed below, in an extract from a paper by the woman who is generally credited with being the architect of the OMC, and who was adviser to the Portuguese Presidency of the EU in the lead-up to the Lisbon Council.

M. João Rodrigues, The Open Method of Coordination as a New Governance Tool[28]

The political construction of Europe is a unique experience. Its success has been dependent on the ability to combine coherence with respect for diversity and efficiency with democratic

---

[27] Lisbon European Council, Presidency Conclusions, 23–24 Mar. 2000.
[28] In M. Telò (ed.), 'L'evoluzione della governance europea', Special Issue of 'Europa/Europe', Rome, No. 2–3, 2001, 96.

legitimacy. This entails using different political methods depending on policies and the various institutional processes. For good reasons, various methods have been worked out which are placed somewhere between pure integration and straightforward co-operation.

. . .

Policies aimed at building the single market, such as monetary policy or competition policy are, logically, based on a stricter method of coordination in relation to the principles to be observed. However, there are other policies which concentrate more on creating new skills and capacities for responding to structural changes. They involve learning more quickly and discovering appropriate solutions. Such policies have resulted in the formulation of strategic guidelines at European level for coping with structural change and which are more open to national diversity.

As a matter of fact the main source of inspiration of the open method of coordination was that of the Luxembourg process regarding European employment strategy. This method was created to overcome a strong political difficulty identified in the preparation of the special European Council of Luxembourg on employment in 1997, because it was impossible to adopt a common target for unemployment reduction, as a counterpart of the common targets for inflation, deficit and debt reduction. But, under the political pressure of this Summit, it became possible to adopt common qualitative guidelines instead. After that, a process was organized whereby Member States emulate each other in applying them, stimulating the exchange of best practices, and defining specific targets while taking account of national characteristics. The European Commission presents the proposal of European guidelines, organises the follow-up and can make recommendations to Member States. Despite some difficulties, the results obtained have been stimulating and encouraging as it is proved by the current National action plans for employment adopted by all Member States. Three years later, the definition of the open method of coordination was expressly undertaken during the preparation of Lisbon European Council in order to develop the European dimension in new policy fields, namely information society, research, enterprise policy, education and fighting social exclusion. . . .

A. The purpose of the open method of coordination is not to define a general ranking of Member States in each policy but rather to organise a learning process at European level in order to stimulate exchange and the emulation of best practices, and in order to help Member States improve their own national policies.

B. The open method of coordination uses benchmarking as a technique but it is more than benchmarking. It creates a European dimension by defining European guidelines and it encourages management by objectives by adapting these European guidelines to national diversity.

C. The open method of coordination is a concrete way of developing modern governance using the principle of subsidiarity.

D. The open method of coordination can foster convergence on common interest and on some agreed common priorities while respecting national and regional diversities. It is an inclusive method for deepening European construction.

E. The open method of coordination is to be combined with the other available methods depending on the problem to be addressed. These methods can range from integration and harmonisation, to co-operation. The open method of coordination itself takes an intermediate position in this range of different methods. It is an instrument to be added to a more general set of instruments.

. . .

The open method of coordination can also become an important tool to improve transparency and democratic participation.

Following the Lisbon summit, as indicated by João Rodrigues, the OMC was extended to a broad range of policy areas beyond those initially proposed. In this context, one important point which has often been made is that there is no one single OMC: it is a 'cookbook' of recipes, with variants on a theme, rather than a single recipe.[29] Indeed, since the formal introduction by Lisbon of the OMC as a distinct policy instrument (or cookbook!), many OMC-like processes or elements of the OMC process have been applied to a wide range of EU policies and issue areas.

Apart from the two pre-existing areas of economic policy co-ordination and the European employment strategy, OMCs were introduced also in the field of social exclusion, pensions, and health-care, and similar mechanisms were introduced in the fields of research, education, enterprise, and the information society. Some combination of broad common guidelines with local or national elaboration, reporting obligations, peer review, feedback, and development of best practices, can be found in many areas of EC and EU policy.

Coming back to our introductory discussion of the EU's move away from hierarchical governance towards new forms of governance, the three elements identified there can clearly be seen in the architecture of the OMC as it was introduced by the Lisbon summit. The first is the shift away from central, top-down governing. At least as it was envisaged at Lisbon, we can see that the OMC was intended to involve a 'fully decentralised approach in line with the principle of subsidiarity in which the Union, the Member States, the regional and local levels, as well as the social partners and civil society, will be actively involved, using variable forms of partnership'.[30] While the extent to which OMC processes have been participatory and decentralized has been seriously questioned, there are clearly areas in which participation has been more extensive than others.[31]

The second element we can see is the move away from the adoption of complete prescriptive policies. In this sense, the OMC architecture is premised on the setting of general guidelines or goals, and these are to be translated into national plans by state and regional actors. Once again, it is evident from a critical perspective that the greater the number and the more detailed the nature of the objectives, targets, and indicators set, the less flexible and the less of a departure from traditional hierarchical governance the particular OMC instrument will be. However, at least as far as its design is concerned, the OMC is clearly intended to promote flexibility and openness, and to facilitate interaction between levels of governance in framing and developing policies.

The third element is the absence of, or a significantly reduced role for, binding instruments and compulsory legal enforcement. While within some of the Treaty-based co-ordination processes, and particularly in the case of economic policy co-ordination, binding rules and legal enforcement do play a role,[32] nonetheless in most of the OMCs and OMC-like processes, legally enforceable or binding norms are scarcely present, or they have a much less prominent role.

Like the new approach to harmonization discussed above, the vast literature generated by the OMC contains much that is critical. Criticism has focused on the empirical question whether the OMC has 'delivered', and whether it can be said to have policy-steering effects.[33]

[29] J. Zeitlin, 'Introduction: The Open Method of Coordination in Question', in J. Zeitlin and P. Pochet with L. Magnusson (eds.), *The Open Method of Coordination in Action: The European Employment and Social Inclusion Strategies* (P.I.E.-Peter Lang, 2005), citing Belgian Minister Frank Vandenbroucke.

[30] Lisbon European Council, n. 27 above, para. 38.

[31] For critical discussion of the role of civil society in OMC inclusion processes see K. Armstrong, 'Tackling Social Exclusion Through OMC: Reshaping the Boundaries of EU Governance', in T. Börzel and R. Cichowski (eds.), *The State of the Union: Law, Politics and Society* (Oxford University Press, 2003), 170 and 'Inclusive Governance? Civil Society and the OMC', in S. Smismans (ed.), *Civil Society and Legitimate European Governance* (Edward Elgar, 2005).

[32] W. Schelkle, 'Hard Law in the Shadow of Soft Law in EU Economic Governance' (2007) 13 *CJEL*, forthcoming.

[33] See, e.g., M. Citi and M. Rhodes, 'New Modes of Governance in the EU: Common Objectives versus National Preferences', European Governance Papers No. 07/01 (2007); A. Moravcsik, 'In Defence of the Democratic Deficit: Reassessing Legitimacy in the EU' (2002) 40 *JCMS* 603.

Other criticisms have focused on the normative question whether it lives up to the language of inclusiveness and participation in its original Lisbon design,[34] or whether the use of this instrument has mainly operated as a bureaucratic means of adjusting to the new reality of economic and monetary union.[35] Others have launched a more full-fronted challenge to the method as a whole—questioning its empirical effectiveness and cautioning about its impact on the EU institutional balance, and on democracy, rights, and the rule of law in general.[36]

We shall return to some of these criticisms at the end of the chapter. For now, the significance of the OMC is in the fact that it was a policy instrument specifically designed and introduced as an alternative to hierarchical, prescriptively detailed, and binding law-making. It was intended as a more flexible instrument which would simultaneously facilitate a degree of policy co-ordination and yet also accommodate diversity between the States. And despite its shortcomings and failures in delivering on the strategic goals of the Lisbon summit, OMC-like processes, or processes with some of the features of OMC continue to be adopted in a whole range of very different policy fields, and not only in the original fields identified for this purpose at Lisbon.

To mention only a few, these range from broad 'Second and Third Pillar' fields like anti-terrorist policy,[37] to more focused internal market issues such as GMO regulation,[38] to very specific and nationally sensitive policies such as the integration and naturalization of third-country nationals.[39] An OMC process (or similar process) seems to be proposed in a range of contexts. Sometimes it appears to be proposed to overcome a political blockage where agreement on some more conventional measure cannot be found; sometimes it is proposed where formal or legal competence is lacking; and sometimes it seems to be proposed because it is considered to be the most suitable instrument for achieving the policy goals in question.

5. GENERAL EU GOVERNANCE REFORM INITIATIVES

The sections above have given two specific examples of what may be considered to be new forms of governance in the EU. The first was a relatively early example of an 'alternative' governance mechanism, viz. the new approach to technical harmonization adopted as part of the Single Market programme in the 1980s. The second was the introduction of a new policy tool at the time of the launch of the EU's Lisbon Agenda, namely the Open Method of Co-ordination.

This section, rather than giving another example of a specific instrument or process, outlines a number of more general legal developments and official reform initiatives over the last decade or so which resonate with, or reflect elements of, the shift in the preferred mode of governance from hierarchical to more flexible modes. The first of these is the introduction and development of the principles of subsidiarity and proportionality into EU law and policy.

---

[34] See, e.g., S. Smismans, 'New Modes of Governance and the Participatory Myth', European Governance Paper 06/01 (2006).

[35] D. Chalmers and M. Lodge, 'The Open Method of Coordination and the European Welfare State', Discussion Paper 11/2003, CARR, London School of Economics.

[36] V. Hatzopoulos, 'Why the Open Method of Coordination is Bad for You: A Letter to the EU' (2007) 13 *ELJ* 309.

[37] Zysk, n. 12 above.

[38] Dabrowska, n. 9 above.

[39] See Communication on Immigration, Integration and Employment, COM(2003)336, discussing a 'reinforced coordination process' in this field; A Common Agenda for Integration: Framework for integration of third-country nationals in the European Union, COM(2005)389.

(a) SUBSIDIARITY AND PROPORTIONALITY

We have seen in Chapter 3 that the term 'subsidiarity' was first introduced into the EC Treaties by the Maastricht Treaty, and that it was inserted into Article 5 EC, together with the principle of conferred powers and the proportionality principle, for a variety of reasons. Amongst these reasons appears to have been a general concern that the EC should not regulate 'unnecessarily': either that it should not take action at all where it was not warranted, and that even where action of some kind might be warranted, care should be taken that it was not unnecessarily intrusive.

The guidelines developed in relation to the subsidiarity and proportionality principles, which were initially contained in the European Council Conclusions at Edinburgh in 1992 and which led to the subsequent adoption of an inter-institutional agreement on the application of subsidiarity and proportionality, were eventually adopted as primary Treaty law in a protocol annexed by the Amsterdam Treaty to the EC Treaty.[40] A number of extracts from that Protocol are set out below. The extracts given do not focus on the specific (and narrow) legal definition of subsidiarity (i.e., whether Community action should be taken in the first place), but instead on those parts which offer guidelines on what kind of action should be taken. Although the principles of subsidiarity and proportionality from a legal perspective are conceptually distinct, the Protocol arguably—and usefully—blurs the line between them.

Protocol on the application of the principles of subsidiarity and proportionality

1. In exercising the powers conferred on it, each institution shall ensure that the principle of subsidiarity is complied with. It shall also ensure compliance with the principle of proportionality, according to which any action by the Community shall not go beyond what is necessary to achieve the objectives of the Treaty.

. . .

4. For any proposed Community legislation, the reasons on which it is based shall be stated with a view to justifying its compliance with the principles of subsidiarity and proportionality; the reasons for concluding that a Community objective can be better achieved by the Community must be substantiated by qualitative or, wherever possible, quantitative indicators.

. . .

6. The form of Community action shall be as simple as possible, consistent with satisfactory achievement of the objective of the measure and the need for effective enforcement. The Community shall legislate only to the extent necessary. Other things being equal, directives should be preferred to regulations and framework directives to detailed measures. Directives as provided for in Article 249 of the Treaty, while binding upon each Member State to which they are addressed as to the result to be achieved, shall leave to the national authorities the choice of form and methods.

7. Regarding the nature and the extent of Community action, Community measures should leave as much scope for national decision as possible, consistent with securing the aim of the measure and observing the requirements of the Treaty. While respecting Community law, care should be taken to respect well established national arrangements and the organisation and

---

[40] G. de Búrca, 'Reappraising Subsidiarity's Significance after Amsterdam', Jean Monnet Working Paper 7/1999, available at www.jeanmonnetprogram.org/.

working of Member States' legal systems. Where appropriate and subject to the need for proper enforcement, Community measures should provide Member States with alternative ways to achieve the objectives of the measures.

...

9. Without prejudice to its right of initiative, the Commission should:

— except in cases of particular urgency or confidentiality, consult widely before proposing legislation and, wherever appropriate, publish consultation documents;

— justify the relevance of its proposals with regard to the principle of subsidiarity; whenever necessary, the explanatory memorandum accompanying a proposal will give details in this respect. The financing of Community action in whole or in part from the Community budget shall require an explanation;

Several features of the Protocol are noteworthy for present purposes. First, the general tenor of all of the provisions set out above suggests a move away from hierarchical governance, as we have defined it earlier in the chapter. The very essence of the subsidiarity and proportionality principles is restraint as regards the need for regulation and restraint in both the form and the content of regulation.

Secondly, paragraphs 6–9 in particular introduce a range of guidelines on the form and nature of action. Thus, the form of action is to be as 'simple' as possible; where legislation is chosen directives are to be preferred to regulations, and framework directives are to be preferred to detailed measures. In other words, the guidelines propose that the degree of prescriptiveness of legislation should be reduced. While directives, as we know, are binding as to their aim, they leave greater room for discretion in their implementation than other measures such as regulations. This point is emphasized further in the recommendation that directives should ideally be 'framework' in nature rather than being detailed measures.

Thirdly, there is an emphasis on leaving room for 'lower' levels of governing to have as much scope for action as possible, although in the Protocol it is only Member States rather than regions or other actors which are mentioned. Nevertheless, this is consistent in a broad sense with a shift away from hierarchical governance, and away from the dominance of centralized, top-down EU action. Further, the provision in paragraph 9 for the Commission to consult extensively before proposing legislation demonstrates a concern for the involvement of other actors in law-making, even if the formal initiative still rests with the Commission.

Finally, even though the two measures listed in paragraph 6—directives and regulations—are legally binding, these are suggested as options only where the Community has decided to 'legislate', and paragraph 7 appears to envisage other possibilities by referring in general terms to 'Community measures' which leave as much scope for national decision as possible. In a related sense, even though the Protocol refers to the need for proper enforcement, it does not specifically refer to judicial enforcement.

Thus the Protocol on subsidiarity and proportionality, albeit in a muted way, clearly reflects the promotion of a move away from hierarchical governance in the sense set out earlier in the chapter. There is an emphasis away from centrally-dominated, detailed prescriptive legislation, and reference is made instead to the need for broad consultation, to the desirability of leaving greater space for national action, and to the desirability of facilitating alternative ways of achieving broadly agreed aims.

As with the other initiatives discussed above, it is difficult to appraise the relative success or failure of the efforts to promote a culture of subsidiarity within EU policy-making. At one level, the requirement to justify the relevance of proposals with regard to the principle of subsidiarity has led to the insertion of a formalistic 'subsidiarity recital' in most legislation, and more generally there has been much scepticism about the operation of subsidiarity as a principle.[41]

Yet if we focus on a different aspect of the issue, it is undoubtedly true that an increasing number of framework directives—as well as many other less prescriptive forms of EC action—have been adopted in important policy fields in recent years, such as water quality, air quality, waste management, eco-design requirements, discrimination in employment, health, and safety of workers, and electronic communications, with proposals for framework directives pending in other important fields such as that of services of general interest. It may be that the choice of instrument is increasingly being made in consciousness of—even if not always in deference to—the kind of guidance given in the Amsterdam protocol.

(b) BETTER REGULATION AND THE COMMISSION'S WHITE PAPER ON GOVERNANCE

The EU's 'better regulation' initiative has its origins in the same guidelines on subsidiarity and proportionality adopted at Edinburgh in 1992, but this initiative addresses other and more specific issues such as overall simplification of the legislative environment,[42] conducting regulatory impact assessments (in particular on business),[43] and the use of alternatives to regulation. This latter aspect is of particular interest in the context of assessing the move to new forms of governance.

According to the Commission, the better regulation initiative is based on three key lines: (i) promoting the design and application of better regulation tools at the EU level; (ii) working more closely with Member States to ensure that better regulation principles are consistently applied throughout the EU; and (iii) reinforcing constructive dialogue between stakeholders and all regulators at EU and national levels.

In 2003, the European Parliament, Council, and Commission published an Inter-Institutional Agreement on better law-making, in which they focused on a number of different issues. Amongst them was the need for greater transparency of the formal law-making process, as well as the need for respect for the subsidiarity and proportionality principles and for democracy. One section of the Agreement focuses specifically on 'alternative methods of regulation', and in particular the practices of 'co-regulation' and 'self-regulation':

European Parliament, Council and Commission Interinstitutional Agreement on Better Law-making (2003)[44]

Use of alternative methods of regulation

16. The three Institutions recall the Community's obligation to legislate only where it is necessary, in accordance with the Protocol on the application of the principles of subsidiarity

---

[41] G. Davies, 'Subsidiarity: The Wrong Idea, in the Wrong Place, at the Wrong Time' (2006) 43 *CMLRev.* 63, who argues that 'subsidiarity ... serves primarily as a masking principle, presenting a centralizing polity in a decentralizing light'; A. Estella, *The Principle of Subsidiarity and its Critique* (Oxford University Press, 2004).

[42] See, e.g., Simplifying and Improving the Regulatory Environment, COM(2002)278; First Progress Report on the Strategy for Simplification of the Regulatory Environment, COM(2006)689; Strategic Review, COM(2006)689; Implementing the Community Lisbon programme: A strategy for the simplification of the regulatory environment, COM(2005)535.

[43] See Action Programme for Reducing Administrative Burdens in the EU, COM(2007)23; SEC(2007)84 on Impact Assessment.

[44] [2003] OJ C321/01.

and proportionality. They recognise the need to use, in suitable cases or where the Treaty does not specifically require the use of a legal instrument, alternative regulation mechanisms.

17. The Commission will ensure that any use of co-regulation or self-regulation is always consistent with Community law and that it meets the criteria of transparency (in particular the publicising of agreements) and representativeness of the parties involved. It must also represent added value for the general interest. . . .

— *Co-regulation*

18. Co-regulation means the mechanism whereby a Community legislative act entrusts the attainment of the objectives defined by the legislative authority to parties which are recognised in the field (such as economic operators, the social partners, non-governmental organisations, or associations). This mechanism may be used on the basis of criteria defined in the legislative act so as to enable the legislation to be adapted to the problems and sectors concerned, to reduce the legislative burden by concentrating on essential aspects and to draw on the experience of the parties concerned.

. . .

20. In the context defined by the basic legislative act, the parties affected by that act may conclude voluntary agreements for the purpose of determining practical arrangements. The draft agreements will be forwarded by the Commission to the legislative authority. In accordance with its responsibilities, the Commission will verify whether or not those draft agreements comply with Community law (and, in particular, with the basic legislative act).

At the request of *inter alia* the European Parliament or of the Council, on a case-by-case basis and depending on the subject, the basic legislative act may include a provision for a two-month period of grace following notification of a draft agreement to the European Parliament and the Council. During that period, each Institution may either suggest amendments, if it is considered that the draft agreement does not meet the objectives laid down by the legislative authority, or object to the entry into force of that agreement and, possibly, ask the Commission to submit a proposal for a legislative act.

21. A legislative act which serves as the basis for a co-regulation mechanism will indicate the possible extent of co-regulation in the area concerned. The competent legislative authority will define in the act the relevant measures to be taken in order to follow up its application, in the event of non-compliance by one or more parties or if the agreement fails. These measures may provide, for example, for the regular supply of information by the Commission to the legislative authority on follow-up to application or for a revision clause under which the Commission will report at the end of a specific period and, where necessary, propose an amendment to the legislative act or any other appropriate legislative measure.

— *Self-regulation*

22. Self-regulation is defined as the possibility for economic operators, the social partners, non-governmental organisations or associations to adopt amongst themselves and for themselves common guidelines at European level (particularly codes of practice or sectoral agreements). As a general rule, this type of voluntary initiative does not imply that the Institutions have adopted any particular stance, in particular where such initiatives are undertaken in areas which are not covered by the Treaties or in which the Union has not hitherto legislated. As one of its responsibilities, the Commission will scrutinise self-regulation practices in order to verify that they comply with the provisions of the EC Treaty.

23. The Commission will notify the European Parliament and the Council of the self-regulation practices which it regards, on the one hand, as contributing to the attainment of the EC Treaty objectives and as being compatible with its provisions and, on the other, as being satisfactory in terms of the representativeness of the parties concerned, sectoral and geographical cover and

the added value of the commitments given. It will, nonetheless, consider the possibility of putting forward a proposal for a legislative act, in particular at the request of the competent legislative authority or in the event of a failure to observe the above practices.

There are, once again, a number of noteworthy features for the purposes of this chapter, in this description of co-regulation and self-regulation.

Thus, as far as co-regulation is concerned, while a legislative framework is initially adopted by the EC, the 'attainment of the objectives' is entrusted to the relevant stakeholders in the field. Those actors then draw up voluntary agreements which are notified to the Commission. Thus we see a departure from the three elements of hierarchical governance identified earlier: law-making is not to be a top-down process involving only the central government actors; details are not prescribed in the framework legislative act but are left to the stakeholders to flesh out; and the agreement adopted by the stakeholders is voluntary. As far as enforcement is concerned, it seems that the framework legislation will make provision for 'follow-up' in the event of non-compliance or failure of the agreement, and that such follow-up can ultimately involve a formal enforcement option if the Commission reports to this effect and proposes an amendment to the legislative act or another legislative measure. Further, we can see that the formal legislative process remains a default policy-making option too, where this is provided for in the framework legislation and where the voluntary agreement fails to meet the objectives of the latter. Thus co-regulation is here envisaged as a kind of alternative regulation in the shadow of traditional law-making.

Self-regulation, a more radically decentralized option, is defined as the adoption by the relevant economic or other actors of common guidelines at European level. It clearly involves a move away from centralized top-down regulation and from the adoption of prescriptive, binding norms. One question is whether it involves any form of EU governance at all, 'new' or otherwise. The answer to this would seem to be that in areas in which the EC has competence to act but chooses to promote or permit self-regulation instead, the Commission retains a role in scrutinizing self-regulatory practices to check whether they are compatible with EU law requirements. It will report to the other EU law-making institutions on the representativeness of the parties involved and the 'value' and coverage of the commitments made. Further, as in the case of co-regulation, formal legislation remains a default option in the event of failure to follow the practices agreed.

While there does not yet seem to have been extensive use of co-regulation or self-regulation, the Commission has begun to propose or facilitate these in a number of areas, such as in the field of internet safety[45] and mobile phone safety[46] in relation to children, and in other audio-visual sectors. A self-regulation agreement has also been adopted by the European Advertising Standards Alliance and approved by the Commission.[47] The main critique in relation to this particular form of EU governance concerns its effectiveness, but there is on the other hand no evidence that more hierarchical forms of regulation are effective or feasible for the kinds of areas in which co-regulation or self-regulation is being proposed.

The better regulation initiative subsequently formed a part of the Commission's broader governance reform agenda in the late 1990s. In 2001, following several years of consultation

[45] See http://ec.europa.eu/information_society/activities/sip/index_en.htm.
[46] See http://ec.europa.eu/information_society/activities/sip/public_consultation/mobile_agreement/index_en.htm.
[47] See www.easa-alliance.org/.

and discussion on the need for reform of EU governance,[48] the Commission adopted its White Paper on European Governance. This document drew on a large array of working papers and background documents.[49] The Commission made a series of recommendations on how to enhance democracy in Europe and increase the legitimacy of the institutions. Although it is a rather broad-ranging and in some respects unfocused document, many of the issues with which it deals are related to the kind of governance reforms being discussed in this chapter. Extracts from the relevant parts are included below:

European Governance: A White Paper[50]

There needs to be a stronger interaction with regional and local governments and civil society. Member States bear the principal responsibility for achieving this. But the Commission for its part will:

- Establish a more systematic dialogue with representatives of regional and local governments through national and European associations at an early stage in shaping policy.
- Bring greater flexibility into how Community legislation can be implemented in a way which takes account of regional and local conditions.

. . .

The Commission will:

- Promote greater use of different policy tools (regulations, "framework directives", co-regulatory mechanisms).
- Simplify further existing EU law and encourage Member States to simplify the national rules which give effect to EU provisions.

. . .

A complementary response at EU level is needed in three areas to build a better partnership across the various levels:

Involvement in policy shaping. At EU level, the Commission should ensure that regional and local knowledge and conditions are taken into account when developing policy proposals. For this purpose, it should organise a systematic dialogue with European and national associations of regional and local government, while respecting national constitutional and administrative arrangements . . .

. . .

Greater flexibility. Local conditions can make it difficult to establish one set of rules that covers the whole of the Union, without tying up the legislation in excessive complexity. There should be more flexibility in the means provided for implementing legislation and programmes with a strong territorial impact, provided the level playing field at the heart of the internal market can be maintained.

The Commission is also in favour of testing whether, while respecting the existing Treaty provisions, the implementation of certain EU policies could be better achieved by target-based,

---

[48] For an earlier stage of the governance reform discussion stimulated by the Commission see N. Lebessis and J. Paterson, 'Evolution in Governance: What Lessons for the Commission? A First Assessment', European Commission Forward Studies Unit, 1997.

[49] See http://ec.europa.eu/governance/index_en.htm for the relevant documentation.

[50] COM(2001)428.

tripartite contracts. Such contracts should be between Member States, regions and localities designated by them for that purpose, and the Commission.... The area of environmental policy might be a candidate for this pilot approach. Furthermore, the Commission has already committed itself to a more decentralised approach in future regional policy.[51]

...

BETTER POLICIES, REGULATION AND DELIVERY

The European Union's policies and legislation are getting increasingly complex. The reluctance of Council and European Parliament to leave more room for policy execution to the Commission means that legislation often includes an unnecessary level of detail....

The level of detail in EU legislation also means that adapting the rules to technical or market changes can be complex and time-consuming. Overall the result is a lack of flexibility, damaging effectiveness....

...

The European Union will rightly continue to be judged by the impact of its regulation on the ground. It must pay constant attention to **improving the quality, effectiveness and simplicity of regulatory acts**. Effective decision-making also requires the combination of different policy instruments (various forms of legislation, programmes, guidelines, use of structural funding, etc.) to meet Treaty objectives. In making full use of the Treaty, the Commission could also make proposals to take the Union's objectives forward through enhanced co-operation.

Achieving improvements depends on seven factors.

- First, proposals must be prepared on the basis of **an effective analysis** of whether it is appropriate to intervene at EU level and whether regulatory intervention is needed....
- Second, **legislation is often only part of a broader solution** combining formal rules with other non-binding tools such as recommendations, guidelines, or even self-regulation within a commonly agreed framework. This highlights the need for close coherence between the use of different policy instruments and for more thought to be given to their selection.
- Third, the **right type of instrument** must be used whenever legislation is needed to achieve the Union's objectives:
  — The **use of regulations** should be considered in cases with a need for uniform application and legal certainty across the Union. This can be particularly important for the completion of the internal market and has the advantage of avoiding the delays associated with transposition of directives into national legislation.
  — So-called **'framework directives'** should be used more often. Such texts are less heavy-handed, offer greater flexibility as to their implementation, and tend to be agreed more quickly by Council and the European Parliament. Whichever form of legislative instrument is chosen, **more use should be made of 'primary' legislation limited to essential elements** (basic rights and obligations, conditions to implement them), leaving the executive to fill in the technical detail via implementing 'secondary' rules.
- Fourth, under certain conditions, implementing measures may be prepared within the **framework of co-regulation**. Co-regulation combines binding legislative and regulatory action with actions taken by the actors most concerned, drawing on their practical expertise. The result is wider ownership of the policies in question by involving those most affected by implementing rules in their preparation and enforcement. This often achieves better compliance, even where the detailed rules are non-binding.

[51] Second Cohesion Report, COM(2001)21 final.

Thus, in the White Paper we see the Commission's focus on a range of related issues, all of which reflect aspects of a move—or rather a proposed move—away from hierarchical. There is an emphasis on the need to involve actors other than the main EU legislative organs, as well as on reducing the degree of detail and prescriptiveness of legislation. There is also an emphasis on the need for a mixture of policy instruments, including the traditional Community method, but also a range of others like tripartite contracts,[52] and including some of the 'alternative regulatory methods' we have seen above, such as the co-regulation, the OMC, recommendations, and guidelines.

The White Paper initiative, and in particular the document itself, has been criticised on numerous grounds, on the basis that ultimately very little was said, few concrete proposals for change emerged, and in some ways the Commission appeared to be primarily concerned with defending its own role. Nevertheless, as can be seen from the extracts above, the White Paper embodies and advances several of the themes and proposals which originated in the subsidiarity and proportionality guidelines, and subsequently in the regulation initiative. It clearly manifests the thinking of the Commission on the issue of governance reform.

6. APPRAISING THE MOVE TOWARDS NEW FORMS OF GOVERNANCE

Two issues will be briefly addressed below. First, we will consider various possible reasons which have been offered for the rise of new governance methods in the EU, i.e., for the shift in emphasis away from hierarchical modes towards more flexible modes of governance. Secondly, we will briefly mention some of the main critiques and defences of new governance.

J. Scott and D. Trubek, Mind the Gap: Law and New Governance in the EU[53]

Why do we see increasing use of New Governance in the EU?

As the papers in this volume show, 'new governance' covers a number of very disparate mechanisms each of which has its own particular history. Most, if not all, have emerged as pragmatic forms of accommodation between emerging needs of the Union and available mechanisms for policy making. While detailed histories of all these mechanisms are not available, six factors seem to explain the new governance trend.

a. Increasing complexity and uncertainty of the issues on the agenda

New governance can be seen as a way of coping with complex problems under conditions of uncertainty and thus the trend to new governance may well reflect the increasing salience of such complex problems on the Union's agenda. We can see this within the Union's traditional

---

[52] See A framework for target-based tripartite contracts and agreements between the Community, the States and regional and local authorities, COM(2002)709. The environmental field has been identified as one of the primary areas for the development of tripartite contracts or agreements. In 2003, three pilot project initiatives for tripartite agreements in Birmingham (UK), Lille (France), and Pescara (Italy) on urban mobility, air quality, and management of green spaces respectively, were granted support from the Commission.

[53] N. 6 above.

areas of competence as well as in some of the newer areas it is engaging with. Thus, for example, the unexpected complexities involved in 're-regulation' under the Single Market led to the emergence of the comitology system, and as the Union moves into new areas such as employment and social exclusion it starts to tackle problems that have stymied many Member States for years and for which no easy or uniform solution exists.

b. Irreducible diversity

Not only are many of the problems the Union is now dealing with highly complex; they also may simply not allow for uniform solutions. This is certainly true of many of the issues confronted by the European Employment Strategy (EES) OMC. The underlying systems of industrial relations and social protection of the fifteen Member States vary tremendously, and there is rarely one solution that will work effectively in all these diverse settings. . . .

c. New approaches to public administration and law

The trend to new governance has undoubtedly been influenced by developments in the fields of public administration and law. One can see elements of some of the practices we are calling new governance in domestic administrative law and public administrative practice in Europe and the United States. In these fields, there has been a growing recognition of the limits of traditional top-down regulatory approaches, and repeated calls for things like power sharing, participation, management by objectives, and experimentation.

d. Competence 'creep'

Some of the new approaches may have been adopted to deal with areas where legal authority for EU level action is limited or non-existent. This may well be true of some of the areas to be covered by future OMCs. While the EES has a treaty base, there is no explicit treaty base for such areas as social exclusion and pensions. In such cases, new governance may or may not be the best available approach to policy making, but it may be the only way the Union can play a role in a particular domain.

e. Legitimacy

New Governance often reflects an effort to secure legitimacy for EU policy making. The social dialogue seems to solve some of the democratic deficit problems in the area it covers by essentially delegating law making authority to representatives of the parties to be affected by these laws. . . .

f. Subsidiarity

[W]hile the pressure [suggested above] may well have impelled the Union towards new approaches had there been no independent subsidiarity doctrine, the strength of this doctrine and the political forces behind it certainly added impetus to the trend.

A slightly different, although broadly complementary, account of the reasons for the rise (or, to use their terms, the 'explosion') of new governance forms in the EU is given by Sabel and Zeitlin. They provide an account of new governance in the EU as a form of experimentalism, and explain it in terms of an architecture with four key features: first, the setting of framework goals by the EU institutions and the States; secondly, freedom on the part of lower-level authorities or units to pursue those goals as they see fit; thirdly, a requirement that these lower-level authorities report regularly on their performance and participate in some form of mutually comparative peer-review; and fourthly, periodic review of the framework goals and of the processes by those who established them. Below, they summarize the range of fields in which this new governance architecture is to be found, and suggest some of the main reasons for the rapid expansion:

C. Sabel and J. Zeitlin, Learning from Difference: The New Architecture of Experimentalist Governance in the European Union[54]

Given the growing recognition of the need to learn from diversity in order to harmonize, coordinate, and revise regulatory rules without imposing an unworkable uniformity, the new architecture took shape roughly between the mid-1980s and 2000, i.e. between the Single European Act and the Lisbon Summit. For purposes of exposition, and with no pretension to taxonomic comprehensiveness or precision, we can say that the architecture was elaborated more or less independently in three domains: re-regulation of privatized network infrastructure, public health and safety, and social solidarity [The authors also refer to Justice and Home Affairs as a fourth domain]. . . .

From roughly the turn of the millennium onwards, as we will see, the new architecture became available not only as a response to catastrophic breakdowns in regulatory capacity (food safety, maritime safety/pollution) or the threat of these (financial market supervision), but also as a means for unblocking rule making in domains that had become stalemated by struggles between proponents of (traditional) centralization and (traditional) decentralization (competition policy, state aid). In this most recent period, innovations associated with one of the three originating domains of the new architecture are more and more often proposed for others (such as OMCs in occupational health and safety and fundamental rights or councils of national regulators attached to agencies in drug authorization and maritime safety—to mention only examples that we discuss below.) This suggests that the actors perceive commonalities to the problems arising in the three domains, and for that reason are confident that variants of the problem-solving architecture that address these commonalities in one setting can be adapted to address them in others.

Notice that the possibility or scope conditions for experimentalist governance are distinct and much broader than the historical contexts from which the new architecture emerged in particular policy sectors and in the EU more generally. The possibility conditions for experimentalist governance are arguably quite minimal: strategic uncertainty, meaning that policy makers recognize that they cannot rely on their strategic dispositions (e.g. more market vs. more plan) to guide action in a particular domain (or equivalently that they do not know *how* to achieve their declared goals); and a multi-polar or polyarchic distribution of power, in which no single actor has the capacity to impose her own preferred solution without taking into account the views of the others. . . . Together these conditions open up the possibility for transforming distributive bargaining into deliberative problem-solving through the institutional mechanisms of experimentalist governance.

Thus, while Scott and Trubek emphasize the complexity of problems, the need to accommodate diversity, the lack of legal powers, the search for new ways of making policy-making more legitimate, and the political influence of the subsidiarity concept as reasons which explain the increasing adoption of new governance mechanisms, Sabel and Zeitlin focus additionally on actual or potential crisis (the breakdown of regulatory authority) as well as the existence of uncertainty about how to address problems in a situation of mutual interdependence. It is certainly true that we can readily perceive from sources such as the Lisbon conclusions that there

---

[54] European Governance Working Paper, EUROGOV No. C-07-02, 10 May 2007.

was a great deal of uncertainty about how to tackle a variety of the EU's social and economic problems, while documents such as the White Paper on Governance clearly reveal the anxiety of the Commission and other EU institutional actors in relation to the EU's perceived legitimacy and in relation to the effectiveness of its regulatory capacity and performance.

However, a better understanding of the likely triggering factors and 'scope conditions' for new governance does not necessarily provide a guide to the likely success of new governance methods in addressing complex social and economic problems in the EU context where other methods of regulation have proven inadequate. In this respect, the verdict on the performance of new modes of governance has been mixed. For many critics, the fundamental question is one of effectiveness, in particular since it is difficult to point to or to prove particular concrete results for some of the softer policy instruments, including the OMC.[55] There have been other related criticisms of new governance, for example that it is merely a new bureaucratic exercise to cover for inaction or to conceal another agenda.[56] Others however take the view that given the admitted inadequacy and unworkability of command-and-control-type regulation in so many of the relevant fields, criticisms of new governance for not yet demonstrating adequate results are both misdirected and premature. Further, many of the virtues of new governance methods are arguably in the novel processes, and not just in their policy outcomes: the virtues of greater participation, for example, or, in somewhat more substantive terms, the virtues of knowledge-creation and experimentation as goods in themselves; or the virtues of reflexivity and revisability in the face of changing circumstances.

A separate set of critiques focus less on the ineffectiveness of new governance mechanisms and more on the assumption that they will have an adverse impact on a range of constitutional interests: on the institutional balance in the EU, on the rule of law, on fundamental rights, and on democracy itself.[57] Again, as with the results-based critique, a first response to this criticism is that it is simply premature, and that there is no evidence of such impact. A more fundamental and challenging response is the suggestion that new governance modes may well necessitate some productive reconceptualization of settled understandings of 'the institutional balance', legal values and even of democracy, in particular in the non-state context of the EU.[58]

7. CONCLUSIONS

i.   The topic of new governance modes in the EU is, as we have seen, a lively and contested one. There are some who question the very existence of the phenomenon and deny that any real change has occurred, and many others who acknowledge the rise of new regulatory methods but who view these developments with scepticism or with distrust.

ii. It is difficult to deny, however, that there has been a concerted emphasis in the EU over the past two decades in particular on the need to reform governance in ways which depart from traditional, hierarchical forms of law-making and policy-making. Specific

---

[55] See, e.g., Citi and Rhodes, n. 33 above; Moravcsik n. 33 above. For strong counter-arguments see J. Zeitlin, 'The Open Method of Coordination in Action: Theoretical Promise, Empirical Realities, Reform Strategy', in Zeitlin and Pochet with Magnusson, n. 29 above.

[56] Chalmers and Lodge, n. 35 above.

[57] For a composite critique based on all of these see Hatzopoulos, n. 36 above.

[58] For a version of some of these arguments see C. Sabel and W. Simon, 'Epilogue', in de Búrca and Scott, n. 13 above. More generally see the essays contained in the special issue of the *Columbia Journal of European Law* (2007) vol. 13.

regulatory initiatives such as the 'new approach' and the OMC, as well as broader governance-reform initiatives such as the better regulation strategy and the operationalization of the principles of subsidiarity and proportionality attest to this.

iii. The verdict on the significance and impact of new governance modes is mixed, but for the most part, given the long-term and iterative nature of many new governance forms, it is too early to be able to assess such developments from the point of view of their policy results. Nevertheless, the rise of 'new', 'alternative' or 'experimentalist' governance methods has unquestionably given rise to a whole range of interesting and complex new research questions, as well as a set of challenges to traditional conceptions of law and legal regulation.

8. FURTHER READING

Note: the literature on new governance is vast, and for that reason the list of further reading includes only a selective range of electronic resources, books, and journal issues, in particular those with some legal focus, and it does not list any individual papers or articles.

Newgov at www.eu-newgov.org/

Connext at www.connex-network.org/

Refgov at http://refgov.cpdr.ucl.ac.be/

Omc Forum at http://eucenter.wisc.edu/OMC/index.htm

Special issue of the *European Law Journal* (2002) Vol. 8

Special issue of the *Columbia Journal of European Law* (2007) Vol.13

Special issue of the *Journal of European Public Policy* (2004) Vol. 11

De Búrca, G., and Scott, J. (eds.), *Law and New Governance in the EU and the US* (Hart, 2006)

Kohler-Koch, B., and Eising, R. (eds.), *The Transformation of Governance in the European Union* (Routledge, 1999)

Zeitlin, J., Pochet, P., with Magnusson, L. (eds.), *The Open Method of Coordination in Action: The European Employment and Social Inclusion Strategies*, (P.I.E.-Peter Lang, 2005)

EU INTERNATIONAL
RELATIONS LAW

1. CENTRAL ISSUES

i.   The EU for some years has attempted to strengthen and highlight its international role and identity. However, the complex and fragmented framework governing its international relations, consisting of three pillars and a myriad of differently configured powers, instruments, and institutional actors, is a hindrance to this endeavour.

ii.   The EC has international legal personality, and most observers now accept that the EU does too, even if this is not explicit in the Treaties.

iii.   The law governing the EC's external competence is a complicated body of doctrine developed by the ECJ. While the express external powers of the EC under the Treaty were few, the Court early on gave a wide interpretation of the Community's implied powers, sowing the seeds for what has become known as the principle of parallelism of internal and external powers.

iv.   Two important legal questions dominate this doctrine. The first is whether a given external power exists and the second is whether it is exclusive to the Community or shared with the Member States. While the ECJ has consistently answered the first in very broad terms, it has grown more cautious in relation to the second. Since *Opinion 1/94* on the WTO agreements, the ECJ has interpreted many of the EC's external powers as being shared with the Member States. At the same time, it has gradually given a less expansive reading to the scope of the EC's common commercial policy (CCP).

v.   The existence of many shared competences has led to the phenomenon of 'mixed agreements', involving the participation of both sets of actors in the negotiation, conclusion, and implementation of agreements. While this has problematic consequences in terms of efficiency and visibility for international partners, it has been praised as a unique feature of the EC's federalism, and an important source of practical co-operation between the Community and the Member States.

vi.   Apart from the many areas of EC external competence, the EU also enjoys external powers now under the Second and Third Pillars, in the common foreign and security policy (CFSP) and the area of police and judicial co-operation in criminal matters (PJCC). Given the overlaps in subject-matter between the three pillars, as seen recently in cases concerning counter-terrorism economic sanctions, a range of legal issues arises. These include the appropriate legal basis for action, the proper delimitation of the scope of each pillar, and the organization of co-operation across pillars.

vii. The ECJ has played an active role in EU international relations. It has played a key role in determining the existence, scope, and nature of the EC's and increasingly the EU's competences. It has treated international agreements (including mixed agreements) as acts of the EC which are subject to the full range of its jurisdiction. It has confirmed that international agreements are a binding and integral part of the EC legal order, and that, in principle, they may enjoy direct effect. However, it has consistently ruled that provisions of the WTO Agreements may not be invoked before European courts.

2. INTRODUCTION: THE EU AS AN INTERNATIONAL ACTOR

The European Union has begun to emerge as a significant global actor. While it enjoys substantially more influence in some fields than others, as a general matter the EU has developed a substantial network of relations through which it acts to influence international affairs. More specifically, the EU is the world's largest trading power and a major donor of development aid and humanitarian assistance. It has been described as a civilian[1] or normative power.[2] This reflects the fact that the means it deploys are—of necessity, given its lack of military capacity—economic, diplomatic, and political rather than coercive in nature. In other words, EU relies primarily on 'soft power' on the global stage.[3]

In 2001, the Laeken Declaration of the European Council, which set the stage for the drafting of the Constitutional Treaty, referred in rather self-important and bombastic tones to the EU's role as an international actor:

Europe's new role in a globalised world[4]

What is Europe's role in this changed world? Does Europe not, now that is finally unified, have a leading role to play in a new world order, that of a power able both to play a stabilising role worldwide and to point the way ahead for many countries and peoples? Europe as the continent of humane values, the Magna Carta, the Bill of Rights, the French Revolution and the fall of the Berlin Wall; the continent of liberty, solidarity and above all diversity, meaning respect for others' languages, cultures and traditions. The European Union's one boundary is democracy and human rights. The Union is open only to countries which uphold basic values such as free elections, respect for minorities and respect for the rule of law.

...A power seeking to set globalisation within a moral framework, in other words to 'anchor it in solidarity and sustainable development'.

Lofty aspirations aside, the EU plays many different roles at the same time, and its international identity is complex and composite. In positive terms, it can be described as flexible and multifaceted; in negative terms, as fractured and confused. In the extract below, five different roles of the EU are identified.

---

[1] F. Duchêne, 'Europe's Role in a World Peace', in R. Mayne (ed.), *Europe Tomorrow: Sixteen Europeans Look Ahead* (Fontana, 1972).
[2] I. Manners, 'Normative Power Europe: A Contradiction in Terms?' (2002) 40 *JCMS* 235.
[3] J. Nye, *Soft Power. The Means to Success in World Politics* (Public Affairs, 2004)
[4] Conclusions of the Laeken European Council, Dec. 2001.

M. Cremona, The Union as a Global Actor: Roles, Models and Identity[5]

(i) Laboratory and model. The success of the Community, and now the Union, in establishing a functioning regional integration arrangement ('RIA') and a workable institutional structure, and in opening regional markets, has led to the characterization of the Union as a model of regional economic integration. It may also be seen as a laboratory for experiments in a deeper form of integration. . . .

(ii) Market player. It is as an active player in the global market that the Union has played its first and still most high-profile role. From the start of its existence as a customs union, the European Community has been involved in developing a trade policy through autonomous and contractual instruments, and in multilateral fora, in order to defend and promote its interests. . . .

(iii) Rule generator. . . . One of the distinctive features of the EU's network of partnerships, associations and cooperation agreements is the way in which they have served to export regulatory norms. These may range from detailed commitments in relation to the approximation of laws in line with EU models, to less specific commitments, the introduction of a functioning system of competition or intellectual property law, for example. . . .

(iv) Stabilizer. If one were to categorize the Union's developing role in the sphere of foreign policy it would, I think, be as a 'stabilizer'. In constructing its (international) identity the Union presents itself as a force for stabilization, not only within the borders of Europe, but more widely. . . .

(v) Magnet and neighbour. . . . Enlargement has enabled the Union to achieve some of its aims of stabilization and unification within Europe . . . [T]he Union has been prepared actively to use its attraction and the incentive of membership as a policy instrument in its own right. . . .

The constitutional structure of EU international relations law is fragmented. EU foreign relations are regulated by norms arising from at least three different legal orders, including the national, the international, and the EU legal order with its varied pillar structure.[6] The overall picture has been described as a multi-level-constitution of EU foreign relations,[7] and in more critical terms as Byzantine in nature.[8] Overall, we shall also see that it is a picture dominated much more by case law than by treaty provisions or other positive legal sources.[9]

3. EXTERNAL CAPACITY AND COMMUNITY COMPETENCE

(a) INTERNATIONAL LEGAL PERSONALITY

According to Article 281 EC the Community 'shall have legal personality'. We shall see in Chapter 10 that this provision formed a central part of the argument of the ECJ for the

---

[5] (2004) 41 *CMLRev.* 553.

[6] M. Krajewski, 'European Foreign Policy and Constitution' (2004) 23 *YBEL* 435.

[7] D. Thym, 'Reforming Europe's Common Foreign and Security Policy' (2004) 10 *ELJ* 5; R. Wessel, 'The Multilevel Constitution of European Foreign Relations', in N. Tsagourias (ed.), *Transnational Constitutionalism: International and European Models* (Cambridge University Press, 2006).

[8] M. Mendez, Note on Cases C–317 and 318/04 *European Parliament* v. *Council (PNR)* [2006] ECR I–4721 (2007) *ECLRev.* 127.

[9] B. de Witte, 'Too Much Constitutional Law?', in M. Cremona and B. de Witte (eds.), *EU Foreign Relations Law: Constitutional Fundamentals* (Hart, forthcoming).

autonomy and supremacy of the EC legal system.[10] Given the ambiguity of the phrase in Article 281, Article 282 specifies:

> In each of the Member States, the Community shall enjoy the most extensive legal capacity accorded to legal persons under their laws; it may, in particular, acquire or dispose of movable and immovable property and may be a party to legal proceedings.

It is notable however that there is no mention of *international* personality in either provision. In this sense the EC Treaty differs from both the Coal and Steel Treaty and the Euratom Treaty, each of which made express reference to international legal capacity.[11] This makes it all the more striking that the ECJ in the early ERTA (AETR, to use the French acronym) case nonetheless interpreted Article 281 as granting the EC international legal personality

---

Case 22/70 **Commission v. Council (AETR/ERTA)**
[1971] ECR 263

[Note ToA renumbering: Art. 210 is now Art. 281]

Five out of six Member States of the EEC and a number of other European States which were not EEC members signed a 1962 European Agreement concerning the work of crews of vehicles engaged in international road transport (AETR), but it did not enter into force and negotiations were resumed in 1967. Similar work undertaken at EC level had resulted in the adoption of Council Regulation 543/69 standardizing driving and rest periods of drivers. A year after the adoption of this Regulation, the Member States concluded the negotiations on a new European Agreement (AETR) with other States. The Commission brought an action for the annulment before the ECJ of all legal consequences of the Council proceedings which had led to the adoption of the AETR. The Commission argued that Article 71 (ex Article 75) EC, conferring power on the EC to implement the common transport policy, applied to external relations just as to domestic matters, otherwise the full effect of the provision would be jeopardized. The ECJ ruled that it must first decide whether the power to conclude the AETR was vested in the Community or in the Member States.

THE ECJ

12. In the absence of specific provisions of the Treaty relating to the negotiation and conclusion of international agreements in the sphere of transport policy—a category into which, essentially, the AETR falls—one must turn to the general system of Community law in the sphere of relations with third countries.

13. Article 210 provides that 'The Community shall have legal personality'.

14. This provision, placed at the head of Part Six of the Treaty, devoted to 'General and Final Provisions', means that in its external relations the Community enjoys the capacity to establish contractual links with third countries over the whole field of objectives defined in Part One of the Treaty, which Part Six supplements.

---

[10] Case 6/64 *Costa* v. *ENEL* [1964] ECR 585.

[11] Art. 6(2) ECSC Treaty provided: '[i]n international relations, the Community shall enjoy the legal capacity it requires to perform its functions and attain its objectives'. The EURATOM Treaty provides in Art. 101(1) that '[t]he Community may, within the limits of its powers and jurisdiction, enter into obligations by concluding agreements or contracts with a third State, an international organization or a national of a third State'.

The ECJ thus extrapolated from the statement of legal personality to conclude that the Community's external capacity covers the 'whole extent of the field of the objectives defined in Part One'. However, it distinguished the broad notion of capacity from actual legal authority or competence to enter into an international agreement in a given circumstance. Capacity means that there is the potential for the EC to act, whereas legal authority must be found in the specific conferral of power in another provision of the Treaty.

While the division of powers between the Member States and the EC is a matter of Community law, the international capacity of the EC is governed by public international law. Under international law, the EC enjoys the right to be represented and to receive the representatives of third States and organizations, the right to conclude treaties, the right to submit claims or to act before an international court or judge, the right to become party to international conventions, and the right to enjoy immunities.

The position of the EU is more problematic. There is no provision akin to Article 281 EC in the EU Treaty. Further, when the Maastricht Treaty was being signed, a number of Member States explicitly requested that the EU should not have legal personality. Moreover since the ECJ's jurisdiction over the EU Treaty is limited, there has been no opportunity for an ERTA-style case to clarify or settle the issue. EU law therefore left the question of legal personality unresolved, which meant that the answer would have to be found in public international law.

From the perspective of international law, three factors are particularly relevant here. The first is the manner in which the EU's objectives are worded in the Treaty and the way in which the EU presents itself; and the second is the behaviour of the EU in practice, in particularly in the Second Pillar on foreign and security policy. The third relevant factor is the similarity of the question to that which came before the International Court of Justice in the 1949 *Reparation for Injuries* case, where the ICJ acknowledged that the United Nations, because it was entrusted by its members with certain functions, duties, and responsibilities, was to be considered an international person.[12] These three factors provide considerable support for the proposition that the EU is an international legal person.[13] And even though the arguments to be made against the international legal personality of the EU have not changed over the last decade, there has been a rise in the international activities and practice of the EU *qua* EU, including most notably the conclusion of international agreements under Articles 24 and 38 TEU. These developments will be discussed further below.

(b) THE NEED FOR A LEGAL BASIS AND THE LIMITS OF EXTERNAL COMMUNITY COMPETENCE

Given its foundation on the principle of conferred powers, the Community may act only when there is a legal basis for action provided in the Treaties.[14] The choice of legal basis determines the procedures by which secondary measures are adopted and the participation of the EC institutions in decision-making.[15] The importance of choosing the correct legal base and

---

[12] *Reparation for Injuries Suffered in the Service of the United Nations* [1949] ICJ Rep. 174, 179–180.

[13] J. Klabbers, 'Presumptive Personality: The European Union in International Law', in M. Koskenniemi (ed.), *International Law Aspects of the European Union* (Kluwer Law International, 1998); J.W. de Zwaan, 'Legal Personality of the European Communities and the European Union' (1999) 30 *Netherlands Yearbook of International Law*.

[14] See Ch. 3.

[15] On external relations and legal basis see D. Chalmers, 'Legal Base and the External Relations of the European Community', in N. Emiliou and D. O'Keeffe (eds.), *The European Union and World Trade Law after the GATT Uruguay Round* (Wiley, 1996); P. Koutrakos, 'Legal Basis and Delimitation of Competence', in Cremona and de Witte, n. 9 above.

the consequences of not doing so were highlighted in *Opinion 2/00*, which concerned the EC's signature of the Cartagena Protocol to the Convention on Biological Diversity:

Opinion 2/00 (Re Cartagena Protocol)
[2001] ECR I–9713

THE ECJ

5. The choice of the appropriate legal basis has constitutional significance. Since the Community has conferred powers only, it must tie the Protocol to a Treaty provision which empowers it to approve such a measure. To proceed on an incorrect legal basis is therefore liable to invalidate the act concluding the agreement and so vitiate the Community's consent to be bound by the agreement it has signed. That is so in particular where the Treaty does not confer on the Community sufficient competence to ratify the agreement in its entirety, a situation which entails examining the allocation as between the Community and the Member States of the powers to conclude the agreement that is envisaged with non-member countries, or where the appropriate legal basis for the measure concluding the agreement lays down a legislative procedure different from that which has in fact been followed by the Community institutions.

6. Invalidation of the measure concluding the agreement because of an error as to its legal basis is liable to create, both at Community level and in the international legal order, complications which the special procedure of a prior reference to the Court, laid down in Article 300(6) EC, is specifically designed to forestall. . . .

. . .

The ECJ then referred to its case law on the 'objective' choice of legal basis,[16] which specifies that where a measure has more than one purpose, where one purpose is incidental and the other predominant, it should be based on a single legal basis rather than two, but added that where, however, the objectives were inseparably linked, more than one legal basis could be used.[17]

If an international agreement is found to have been concluded by the Community on the wrong legal basis, the measure concluding the agreement will be invalidated. But in order to protect third parties and to comply with the Vienna Convention on the Law of Treaties, the ECJ ruled in *France v. Commission* that such agreements are nonetheless to be binding on the Community.[18] The Community is required to act again, using the correct legal basis this time.[19] However, if the Court finds that the Community had no competence to adopt the decision concluding the agreement, and no competence to enter the agreement itself, this is obviously not possible.

The issue arose in the *Passenger Name Records* (PNR) case in which the Parliament challenged both the Council's conclusion of an agreement with the US on the processing and transfer of PNR data, and a Decision adopted by the Commission determining that the US Bureau of Customs and Border Protection provided an adequate level of protection of PNR data under the Data Protection Directive.[20] The PNR Agreement was concluded on the basis of Article 95 EC which was also the legal basis for the Data Protection Directive. The Court took the view that although the data would be initially collected by airlines in the course of an

---

[16] See Ch. 3, n. 64.
[17] *Opinion 2/00 (re Cartagena Protocol)* [2001] ECR I–9713.
[18] Case C–327/91 *France v. Commission* [1994] ECR I–3641, para. 25.
[19] Case C–94/03 *Commission v. Council (Rotterdam Convention)* [2006] ECR I–1.
[20] Dir. 95/46/EC [1995] OJ L281/31.

activity falling within the scope of Community law (sale of an airplane ticket), the further use of the data would be for the purpose of safeguarding public security in combating terrorism. And since the use of data for public security purposes was expressly excluded from the scope of the Directive, in part because the Directive had been based on the internal-market provision of Article 95, the Court ruled that both acts fell outside the scope of EC competence.[21] As a result, the EC was required to denounce the agreement within a specific period of time, and in accordance with the relevant rules of international law.[22]

(c) EXPRESS AND IMPLIED COMPETENCE

Since the foundation of the EEC, there have been two Treaty provisions which expressly provide for the conduct of international relations by the Community. These are Article 133 (ex Article 113) on the common commercial policy (CCP) and Article 310 (ex Article 238) on the conclusion of agreements 'establishing an association' with the Community. The EC was also empowered to maintain relations with other international organizations, in particular the Council of Europe, the OECD, and the organs and specialized agencies of the UN. Further express treaty-making powers were added by the Single European Act in the fields of research, technological development, and the environment, and subsequently by the Treaty on the European Union in the fields of development co-operation and economic and monetary policy.

While these were undoubtedly significant powers, the ECJ apparently took the view that the Community would not be able to develop a sufficiently strong international presence on the basis of these express powers alone. This seems to be the logic underpinning its ruling in *ERTA*, where the Court sought to avoid the prospect of unco-ordinated external representation of the EC by its Member States in fields in which they had adopted common internal policies.

Case 22/70 **Commission v. Council (AETR/ERTA)**
[1971] ECR 263

[Note ToA renumbering: Art. 113 is now 133, Art. 114 has been repealed,
Art. 238 is now Art. 310, Arts. 74 and 75 are now Arts. 70 and 71 respectively)

Having ruled that the EC had capacity to enter into international agreements with third countries the Court turned to the question of the EC's legal authority or competence, and specifically whether it had competence to sign the AETR Agreement:

THE ECJ

16. Such authority arises not only from an express conferment by the Treaty—as is the case with Articles 113 and 114 for tariff and trade agreements and with Article 238 for association

---

[21] See also para. 54 of the judgment which refers to the fact that Art. 3(2) of the Dir. excludes from the Dir.'s scope the processing of personal data in the course of an activity which falls outside the scope of Community law, such as activities provided for by Titles V and VI TEU, and in any case processing-operations concerning public security, defence, state security, and the activities of the State in areas of criminal law. The *PNR* case also raises a fundamental issue of cross-pillar activities of the Union and problems of demarcation of the legal base. This will be discussed further below.

[22] Cases C–317 and 318/04 *European Parliament* v. *Council (PNR)*, n. 8 above; for comment see Mendez, n. 8 above.

agreements—but may equally flow from other provisions of the Treaty and from measures adopted, within the framework of those provisions, by the Community institutions.

. . .

23. According to Article 74, the objectives of the Treaty in matters of transport are to be pursued within the framework of a common policy.

24. With this in view, Article 75 (1) directs the Council to lay down common rules and, in addition, 'any other appropriate provisions'.

25. By the terms of subparagraph (a) of the same provision, those common rules are applicable 'to international transport to or from the territory of a Member State or passing across the territory of one or more Member States'.

26. This provision is equally concerned with transport from or to third countries, as regards that part of the journey which takes place on Community territory.

27. It thus assumes that the powers of the Community extend to relationships arising from international law, and hence involve the need in the sphere in question for agreements with the third countries concerned.

28. Although it is true that Articles 74 and 75 do not expressly confer on the Community authority to enter into international agreements, nevertheless the bringing into force, on 25 March 1969, of Regulation No 543/69 of the Council on the harmonization of certain social legislation relating to road transport (OJ L 77, p. 49) necessarily vested in the Community power to enter into any agreements with third countries relating to the subject-matter governed by that regulation.

29. This grant of power is moreover expressly recognized by Article 3 of the said regulation which prescribes that: 'The Community shall enter into any negotiations with third countries which may prove necessary for the purpose of implementing this regulation'.

30. Since the subject-mater of the AETR falls within the scope of Regulation No 543/69, the Community has been empowered to negotiate and conclude the agreement in question since the entry into force of the said regulation.

According to the Court, the fact that by the time the contested decision was taken by the Council on the international road transport agreement, a common policy on social aspects of road transport had already been adopted by the EC made it possible to imply external powers on the part of the Community. Conversely, the Court ruled that until the internal rules had been adopted, those powers remained vested in the Member States.[23]

In the subsequent *Kramer* case concerning fisheries conservation, the ECJ reiterated this dimension of the *ERTA* judgment. It ruled that EC legal authority 'arises not only from an express conferment by the Treaty, but may equally flow *implicitly* from other provisions of the Treaty, from the Act of Accession and from measures adopted, within the framework of those provisions, by the Community institutions'.[24] In the context of *Kramer*, the ECJ ruled that, given the EC's internal power to take any measure for the conservation of the biological resources of the sea, the only way to ensure effective and equitable conservation was by a system including also non-member countries. Thus, 'it follows from the very duties and powers which Community law has established and assigned to the institutions of the Community on the internal level that the Community has authority to enter into international commitments for the conservation of the resources of the sea'.[25]

---

[23] Case 22/70 *ERTA* [1971] ECR 263, para. 82.
[24] Cases 3, 4, and 6/76 *Kramer* [1976] ECR 1279, paras. 19–20.
[25] *Ibid.*, para. 30.

There is a subtle difference between the *Kramer* and the *ERTA* rulings. The ERTA principle is based on the actual adoption of internal rules. In *Kramer*, however, the Court reasoned in a somewhat different way, ruling that the Treaty provisions which explicitly confer competence on the internal level in this particular field must, on the grounds of equity and effectiveness, be read as implicitly conferring treaty-making power. This has been described as a 'principle of complementarity' since the external competence of the Community is viewed as necessary to complement its internal competence.[26]

Even after *Kramer*, doubts persisted whether the Community enjoyed international competence in the absence of *either* express conferral of external powers *or* the actual adoption of common internal rules. *Opinion 1/76* was the final ambitious step in this expansive articulation of the implied powers doctrine.

Opinion 1/76 (European Laying-up Fund for Inland Waterway Vessels)
[1977] ECR 741

The subject of this Opinion was the legal competence of the EC to sign an international agreement establishing a European laying-up fund for inland waterway vessels. The aim of the proposed scheme was to eliminate disturbances arising from surplus carrying capacity for goods by inland waterway in the Rhine and Moselle basins. This objective could not have been fully achieved by establishment of common EC transport rules under Article 71 EC, because of the traditional participation of Swiss vessels, therefore Switzerland was brought into the scheme by means of the international agreement. The Court elaborated further on the scope of the implied treaty-making powers of the Community.

THE ECJ

3. [A]uthority to enter into international commitments may not only arise from an express attribution by the Treaty, but equally may flow implicitly from its provisions. The Court has concluded *inter alia* that whenever Community law has created for the institutions of the Community powers within its internal system for the purpose of attaining a specific objective, the Community has authority to enter into the international commitments necessary for the attainment of that objective even in the absence of an express provision in that connection.

4. This is particularly so in all cases in which internal power has already been used in order to adopt measures which come within the attainment of common policies, it is, however, not limited to that eventuality. Although the internal Community measures are only adopted when the international agreement is concluded and made enforceable, as is envisaged in the present case by the proposal for a regulation to be submitted to the Council by the Commission, the power to bind the Community vis-à-vis third countries nevertheless flows by implication from the provisions of the Treaty creating the internal power and in so far as the participation of the Community in the international agreement is, as here, necessary for the attainment of one of the objectives of the Community.

This case has been described as endorsing the principle of parallelism, according to which the external competence of the Community mirrors its internal competence.[27] The upshot is

---

[26] See A. Dashwood, 'The Classic Authorities Revisited', in A. Dashwood and C. Hillion (eds.), *The General Law of EC External Relations* (Sweet & Maxwell, 2000).

[27] T. Tridimas and P. Eeckhout, 'The External Competence of the Community and the Case-Law of the Court of Justice: Principle versus Pragmatism' (1994) 14 *YBEL* 143.

that the EC has competence to enter into an international agreement in a given domain provided that (i) the Treaty confers *internal* competence on the EC in that domain for the purpose of attaining a specific objective, and (ii) participation of the Community in the agreement in question is *necessary* for the attainment of that objective. In other words, for the Community to have external competence in a certain field, it is not necessary for it to have *exercised* its internal competence in that field. Instead, the very existence of such internal competence is sufficient.

Finally, we shall also see in Chapter 11 how the Court in *Opinion 2/94* on accession of the EC to the ECHR made it clear that there are other limits to the implied external competence of the Community.[28] The Court in that case ruled, in relation to the subject of human rights protection, that where entry into an international agreement would have fundamental institutional implications for the EC and would modify its own system of protection, this would fall outside the external competence of the Community.

(d) EXCLUSIVE COMMUNITY COMPETENCE

Once the existence of Community competence is established, the next important question is whether it is exclusive competence, or whether it is shared with the Member States. Exclusivity means that the competence has been completely transferred by Member States to the Community and that there is no concurrent Member State competence.[29]

The ECJ established the exclusive nature of the Community's competence as regards the common commercial policy in *Opinion 1/75* as far as the conclusion of international agreements is concerned,[30] and similarly in *Donckerwolcke* as far as the adoption of autonomous or unilateral legislative acts is concerned.[31]

The Court based its assertion of exclusivity on two main factors. The first was the threat which concurrent powers would pose to mutual trust within the Community and thus to the coherence and effectiveness of the defence of Community commercial interests *vis-à-vis* non-member countries. The second was the risk of distortion of competition within a single market brought about by different commercial and trading policies, given the varying degrees of economic strength of the different Member States. Its reasoning here has been described as 'a characteristic mixture of pragmatism and (again) the link between external and internal trade policy'.[32] The same reasoning was echoed in the Court's judgment on the establishment of the common fisheries policy.[33] It follows from this case law that if a particular issue is deemed to fall within the scope of these policies—CCP or fisheries—the Community's competence will be exclusive.

We see that in the early case law, the claim of exclusivity of external competence was linked by the ECJ to the autonomy of the Community legal order *vis-à-vis* the Member State. The very existence of implied powers in these cases is closely tied by the Court to their exclusive nature.[34] At the same time, the doctrine of pre-emption was developed, according to which

---

[28] *Opinion 2/94 on Accession by the Community to the ECHR* [1996] ECR I–1759, See Ch. 11, sect. 8(d)(i).

[29] D. O'Keeffe, 'Exclusive, Concurrent and Shared Competence', in Dashwood and Hillion, n. 26 above.

[30] *Opinion 1/75 (Understanding on a Local Cost Standard)* [1975] ECR 1355.

[31] Case 41/76 *Donckerwolcke* [1976] ECR 1921.

[32] M. Cremona, 'External Relations and External Competence. The Emergence of an Integrated Policy', in P. Craig and G. de Búrca, *The Evolution of EU Law* (Oxford University Press, 1999), ch. 4.

[33] Case 804/79 *Commission* v. *UK* [1981] ECR 1045, paras. 17 and 18. This case in fact established exclusivity with regard to Art. 102 of the Act of Accession.

[34] See Cremona, n. 32 above, who argues that this is a stage during which the 'classic' form of pre-emption theory was developed by the Court. EC competence was seen as *either* exclusive or concurrent. Concurrent

once the Community had exercised its powers either internally or externally, and the field was thus 'occupied', the Member States were precluded from acting. The rationale was that unilateral action by individual Member States would be incompatible with the unity of the market and the uniform application of Community law. While the ECJ has now moved a considerable distance from this position, and the norm is now one of shared powers between the Community and the Member States in the external field, it is necessary, in order to understand this complicated area of law, to trace the journey taken by the Court to reach the current position.

Case 22/70 Commission v. Council (AETR/ERTA)
[1971] ECR 263

[Note ToA renumbering: Art. 5 is now Art. 10]

THE ECJ

17. In particular, each time the Community, with a view to implementing a common policy envisaged by the Treaty, adopts provisions laying down common rules, whatever form these may take, the Member States no longer have the right, acting individually or even collectively, to undertake obligations with third countries which affect those rules.

18. As and when such common rules come into being, the Community alone is in a position to assume and carry out contractual obligations towards third countries affecting the whole sphere of application of the Community legal system.

19. With regard to the implementation of the provisions of the Treaty the system of internal Community measures may not therefore be separated from that of external relations.

20. Under Article 3(e), the adoption of a common policy in the sphere of transport is specially mentioned amongst the objectives of the Community.

21. Under Article 5, the Member States are required on the one hand to take all appropriate measures to ensure fulfilment of the obligations arising out of the Treaty or resulting from action taken by the institutions and, on the other hand, to abstain from any measure which might jeopardize the attainment of the objectives of the Treaty.

22. If these two provisions are read in conjunction, it follows that to the extent to which Community rules are promulgated for the attainment of the objectives of the Treaty, the Member States cannot, outside the framework of the Community institutions, assume obligations which might affect those rules or alter their scope. . . .

. . .

31. These Community powers exclude the possibility of concurrent powers on the part of Member States, since any steps taken outside the framework of the Community institutions would be incompatible with the unity of the Common Market and the uniform application of Community law.

Following *ERTA*, the ECJ indicated that there were a number of other contexts in which Community competence would be exclusive.

---

competence at that stage meant 'distinct, discrete compartments for the EC and the Member States' and did not include the concept of complementary action by both the EC and the Member States in the same field, unless the Member States were acting under a form of authorization from the Community.

The *first*—a now very limited example—was where internal powers could only be effect-ively exercised *at the same time* as external powers. The Court ruled in *Opinion 1/76* that exclusive external powers could arise at the moment of being exercised, even without there having been any prior exercise of internal powers, so long as internal competence could be effectively exercised only at the same time as external competence,[35] and so long as the con-clusion of the international agreement was necessary in order to attain objectives of the Treaty that could not be attained by unilateral rules.[36] However, this rather convoluted instance has effectively been restricted to the facts of *Opinion 1/76*.[37] In later cases, it is clear that the ECJ has reverted to the less expansive stance that the adoption of internal legislation is generally a prerequisite for the exclusivity of implied powers.[38]

The *second* context articulated by the ECJ was where the agreement falls into an area which is already largely covered by Community rules. The Court ruled that external Community competence will be exclusive where rules have been adopted in other areas of EC law apart from common policies (such as the common transport policy in *ERTA*) and particularly in areas where harmonizing legislation has been adopted.[39] The Court relied in making this argument on the ubiquitous Article 10 EC, which has been so extensively used in expanding on the effectiveness of EC law.[40]

Thus in *Opinion 2/91* on the International Labour Organization's Convention No 170 (which *inter alia* regulated safety in the use of chemicals at work), the ECJ based its argument for exclusive competence in part on the fact that in all areas of policy corresponding to the objectives of the EC Treaty, Article 10 EC requires Member States to facilitate the achievement of the Community's tasks and to abstain from any measure which could jeopardize the attain-ment of the objectives of the Treaty.[41] The Court ruled that even though there was no actual contradiction between the rules of the Convention and the provisions of EC directives in the same field, the general area covered by the Convention was one which to a large extent had been covered by progressive Community rules, such as that Member States could not under-take commitments in this field outside the scope of the Community. In other words, no contradiction between rules was necessary in order to deprive Member States of compe-tence—the mere fact of the existence of Community rules on broadly the same subject-matter was sufficient. The Court however drew back in part from this extensive holding on the facts of the case by ruling that competence was not actually exclusive in the given context, since both the EC rules and the ILO Convention laid down *minimum standards* only, so that there was nothing to prevent Member States from fully complying with EC law.[42]

The *third* and *fourth* possible examples of exclusive Community competence respectively were referred to in the ECJ's *Opinion 1/94*, in which it ruled on the competence of the EC to

---

[35] *Opinion 1/76 (European Laying-up Fund for Inland Waterway Vessels)* [1977] ECR 741, paras. 4 and 7; *Opinion 1/94 (WTO Agreement: GATS and TRIPS)* [1994] ECR I–5267, para. 85.

[36] See, in particular, in the series of open skies cases Case C–467/98 *Commission* v. *Denmark* [2002] ECR I–9519, para. 57; *Opinion 1/94*, n. 35 above, para. 89.

[37] The case—on the laying-up fund for inland waterway vessels—allegedly involved a situation in which the achievement of the Treaty objective required the prior conclusion of an international agreement and could not be attained by adopting internal rules.

[38] *Opinion 1/94*, n. 35 above, paras. 88–89.

[39] *Opinion 2/91 on the ILO Convention* [1993] ECR I–1061, paras. 10–11.

[40] See Chs. 8–10.

[41] *Opinion 2/91*, n. 39 above, para.10; See also *Opinion 1/03 on the Lugano Convention* [2006] ECR I–1145, para. 119.

[42] *Opinion 2/91*, n. 39 above, para. 18.

conclude two of the WTO agreements, namely the General Agreement on Trade in Services (GATS) and the Agreement on Trade-related Intellectual Property Rights (TRIPS):

Opinion 1/94 on the WTO Agreements (GATS and TRIPS)
[1994] ECR I–5267

95. Whenever the Community has included in its internal legislative acts provisions relating to the treatment of nationals of non-member countries or expressly conferred on its institutions powers to negotiate with non-member countries, it acquires an exclusive external competence in the spheres covered by those acts.

96. The same applies in any event, even in the absence of any express provision authorizing its institutions to negotiate with non-member countries, where the Community has achieved complete harmonization of the rules governing access to a self-employed activity, because the common rules thus adopted could be affected within the meaning of the AETR judgment if the Member States retained freedom to negotiate with non-member countries.

On the other hand, despite articulating these two additional grounds for exclusive competence,[43] the Court in *Opinion 2/94* also ruled that the risk that bilateral agreements would lead to distortions in the flow of services in the internal market did not provide grounds for exclusive EC competence. This was because there was nothing in the Treaty to prevent the EU institutions from arranging, in the common internal rules laid down by them, concerted action in relation to non-member countries or from prescribing the approach to be taken by the States in their external dealings.[44] Ultimately, since the two situations outlined in paragraphs 95 and 96 (treatment of nationals of non-EU countries, and issue-areas which have been completely harmonized, respectively) clearly did not cover all service sectors, competence to conclude the GATS was shared between the Community and the Member States.[45]

Opinion 2/94 represented the first high-profile shift by the Court away from its expansive case law on the exclusive nature of the EC's implied external competence. The line of case law from *ERTA*, including *Kramer* and *Opinions 1/75, 1/76*, and *2/91* had all been in the direction of widening the sphere of external Community competence and extending its exclusive nature. *Opinion 2/92*, which followed shortly after *Opinion 1/94*, also adopted a more measured tone in relation to exclusivity.

Opinion 2/92 (OECD Decision on National Treatment)
[1995] ECR I–521

31. In that regard, the Court has consistently held, most recently in Opinion 1/94 . . . , that the Community's exclusive external competence does not automatically flow from its power to lay down rules at internal level. As the Court pointed out in the AETR judgment . . . , the Member States whether acting individually or collectively, only lose their right to enter into obligations with non-member countries as and when there are common rules which could be affected by such obligations.

---

[43] See also Case C–467/98 *Commission* v. *Denmark*, n. 36 above, paras. 83–84, and *Opinion 1/03*, n. 41 above, para. 122.

[44] *Opinion 1/94*, n. 35 above, paras. 78–79; Case C–467/98 *Commission* v. *Denmark*, n. 36 above, paras. 85–86; *Opinion 1/03*, n. 41 above, para. 123.

[45] *Opinion 1/94*, n. 35 above, paras. 95–96.

In keeping with the often complex and technical tone of the case law, it is evident that the determination of whether a given field has been completely or exhaustively occupied is far from clear, and requires a definition of the relevant field. In *Opinion 2/92 (OECD)* itself, for example, the Court ruled that the internal measures adopted by the EC had not covered all the fields of activity to which the OECD decision was related, and that the EC enjoyed exclusive competence only in areas where internal common rules had been adopted.

In *Opinion 1/94* and, more recently in its *Open Skies* rulings,[46] the ECJ purported to summarize the various situations—set out above—in which the Community has so far been held to have exclusive competence. Apart from the lack of clarity in their scope and the debate they have generated, these situations are, according to the Court in *Opinion 1/03* on the Lugano Convention 'only examples, formulated in the light of the particular contexts with which the Court was concerned'.[47] Having restated its previous case law, however, the ECJ went on to set out more general guidelines on how to determine whether the Community's competence in a given instance is exclusive.

Opinion 1/03 (Lugano Convention)
[2006] ECR I–1145

THE ECJ

124. It should be noted in that context that the Community enjoys only conferred powers and that, accordingly, any competence, especially where it is exclusive and not expressly conferred by the Treaty, must have its basis in conclusions drawn from a specific analysis of the relationship between the agreement envisaged and the Community law in force and from which it is clear that the conclusion of such an agreement is capable of affecting the Community rules.

125. In certain cases, analysis and comparison of the areas covered both by the Community rules and by the agreement envisaged suffice to rule out any effect on the former (see Opinion 1/94...; Opinion 2/92..., and Opinion 2/00...).

126. However, it is not necessary for the areas covered by the international agreement and the Community legislation to coincide fully. Where the test of 'an area which is already covered to a large extent by Community rules' (Opinion 2/91...) is to be applied, the assessment must be based not only on the scope of the rules in question but also on their nature and content. It is also necessary to take into account not only the current state of Community law in the area in question but also its future development, insofar as that is foreseeable at the time of that analysis (see, to that effect, Opinion 2/91...).

127. That that assessment must include not only the extent of the area covered but also the nature and content of the Community rules is also clear from the Court's case-law referred to in paragraph 123 of the present opinion, stating that the fact that both the Community rules and the international agreement lay down minimum standards may justify the conclusion that the Community rules are not affected, even if the Community rules and the provisions of the agreement cover the same area.

...

---

[46] Case C–466/98 *Commission v. United Kingdom* [2002] ECR I–9427; Case C–467/98 *Commission v. Denmark*, n. 36 above; Case C–468/98 *Commission v. Sweden* [2002] ECR I–9575; Case C–469/98 *Commission v. Finland* [2002] ECR I–9627; Case C–471/98 *Commission v. Belgium* [2002] ECR I–9681; Case C–472/98 *Commission v. Luxembourg* [2002] ECR I–9741; Case C–475/98 *Commission v. Austria* [2002] ECR I–9797.

[47] *Opinion 1/03*, n. 41 above, para. 121.

133. It follows from all the foregoing that a comprehensive and detailed analysis must be carried out to determine whether the Community has the competence to conclude an international agreement and whether that competence is exclusive. In doing so, account must be taken not only of the area covered by the Community rules and by the provisions of the agreement envisaged, insofar as the latter are known, but also of the nature and content of those rules and those provisions, to ensure that the agreement is not capable of undermining the uniform and consistent application of the Community rules and the proper functioning of the system which they establish.

Notably, these guidelines still appear to give a relatively broad interpretation to the circumstances in which EC competence will be exclusive on the ground that the internal rules adopted by the Community may be 'adversely affected by' an international agreement.

(e) SHARED COMPETENCE

Despite the extensive and doctrinally intricate case law on the scope of exclusive competence, the reality is that by far the greatest part of the EC's external competence is joint or shared in nature.

With a view to providing a systematic analysis, MacLeod, Hendry, and Hyett have identified five specific situations of joint or shared competence.[48] The *first* is where this appears from the Treaty Article conferring power on the Community. Examples include agreements within the framework of the EMU, development co-operation, and technical co-operation, where Member States have retained their competence to negotiate in international bodies and to conclude international agreements.[49] The Court has ruled that this means the Member States may enter commitments themselves *vis-à-vis* non-Member States either collectively or individually, or jointly with the EC.[50] They may exercise their retained powers either 'collectively in the Council or outside it', and where they act collectively they may adopt acts 'not in their capacity as members of the Council, but as representatives of their governments, and thus collectively exercising the powers of the Member States'.[51]

The *second* situation is where the Community has a power to adopt common internal rules which has not yet been exercised. An example was the case of the common fisheries policy during the transitional period.

The *third* is where an agreement covers both matters falling within Community competence and matters within Member States' competence. The Court ruled to this effect in *Opinion 1/78 (Natural Rubber Agreement)* when it decided that although the field covered by the agreement in question was within the exclusive competence of the EC under Article 133, the financing of this area remained within the competence of the Member States.[52] Since this was a central element of the agreement and the participation of the Member States was required, competence was deemed to be shared.

The *fourth* situation is where the Community's competence derives from the existence of internal 'minimum rules' where Member States are entitled to maintain higher standards which will not 'affect' the scope of internal EC rules, as we saw in the case of *Opinion 2/91* on ILO Convention

---

[48] I. MacLeod, I. D. Hendry, and S. Hyett, *The External Relations of the European Communities* (Clarendon Press, 1996), 63–64.

[49] See Arts. 111(5) EC, 174(4) EC, and 181 EC.

[50] See, e.g., Case C–316/91 *European Parliament* v. *Council* [1994] ECR I–625, on the Lomé Convention.

[51] Cases C–181 and 248/91 *European Parliament* v. *Council and Commission* [1993] ECR I–3685, para. 12.

[52] *Opinion 1/78 (International Agreement on Natural Rubber)* [1979] ECR 2871.

No. 170. The *fifth* situation includes certain fields where Community and Member State competence can co-exist without either displacing the other. An example is the case of intellectual property, where the nature of the rights created at the Community level, such as the Community trade mark, is such that they do not replace national-level intellectual property rights.

Where competence is shared between the Member States and the EC, the ECJ has ruled that each is under a duty of close co-operation due to the requirement of unity in the international representation of the Community.[53]

(f) CONCLUSION

It is evident from the discussion above that the constitutional core of EU international relations law has been shaped entirely by the ECJ, and that it centres on the notions of capacity, competence, and exclusivity. It is a complex, difficult, and detailed case law which does little to assist the clarity and comprehensibility of the EU's international role either for other actors on the global stage or, indeed, for students! Nonetheless, the basic foundations of the doctrine initially laid down in *ERTA* remain in place, as is evident from the recent *Opinion 1/03* on the Lugano Convention.

4. AREAS OF EXTERNAL ACTION UNDER THE EC TREATY

Following this overview of the general constitutional principles underpinning external EC action, we turn now to the EC Treaty foundations of some of the most important external policies.

(a) THE COMMON COMMERCIAL POLICY (CCP)

The most important of the Treaty Articles governing the EU's CCP are Articles 131 and 133 EC. Article 131 EC sets the aims of the policy:

> By establishing a customs union between themselves Member States aim to contribute, in the common interest, to the harmonious development of world trade, the progressive abolition of restrictions on international trade and the lowering of customs barriers.
>
> The common commercial policy shall take into account the favourable effect which the abolition of customs duties between Member States may have on the increase in the competitive strength of undertakings in those States.

Article 133(1) EC further describes the measures to be adopted in the framework of this policy:

> The common commercial policy shall be based on uniform principles, particularly in regard to changes in tariff rates, the conclusion of tariff and trade agreements, the achievement of uniformity in measures of liberalisation, export policy and measures to protect trade such as those to be taken in the event of dumping or subsidies.

---

[53] *Opinion 1/94*, n. 35 above, para. 108. See the discussion of mixed agreements below.

The mode of decision-making for the CCP is a distinctive and unusual one under the EC Treaty. Following a proposal from the Commission, the Council adopts the legislation by qualified majority, and there is no role provided for the European Parliament.

The CCP covers both unilateral measures adopted by the Community institutions (such as protective measures) and conventional measures negotiated with third countries and international organizations (trade agreements). The Court in an early case ruled that the proper functioning of the customs union justifies a wide interpretation of Article 133 and of the powers which it confers.[54] As we have seen in other chapters on the single market and on the free movement of goods, the Member States of the EEC established a customs union with the aim of building a common market which formed the very basis of the Community. The link between the common commercial policy and the common market may explain many of the developments in this field, including the Commission's and the ECJ's determination to establish and expand exclusive EC competence in the early years.[55]

Opinion 1/75, dealing with an OECD Understanding on export credits, laid down the foundations for the scope and nature of the CCP. Here the Court defined the scope of the CCP very broadly by reference to the external trade policy of a State,[56] ruling that it was a field which developed progressively through a combination of internal and external measures without any priority of one kind over the other.[57] The ECJ then turned to the nature of this policy competence, and ruled that the defence of the Community's common interest, the need to prevent distortions of competition between undertakings, and the principle of Member State loyalty to the EC and its institutions meant that competence must be exclusive.[58]

However, although the ECJ has continued to confirm the exclusivity of EC competence in the CCP, it has not interpreted this exclusivity strictly. The Court left some scope for gradual implementation of the CCP, during which period the Member States were not precluded from acting, provided that their activities were regulated by Community law. In *Donckerwolcke* the ECJ ruled that the Member States could deviate from CCP rules, albeit only under 'specific authorization' by the Community.[59]

The Court's dynamic construction of the scope of the CCP was particularly important in the 1970s when there was a tendency towards a more regulatory and less liberalizing approach to international trade. This move involved also taking the concerns of developing countries more seriously into account. In *Opinion 1/78* on the International Agreement on Natural Rubber, the ECJ emphasized the complex objectives of commodities agreements of this kind, and ruled that the EC must be able to avail itself of 'more elaborate means' to further the development of international trade.[60] This meant that the CCP could not be restricted only to the traditional aspects of external trade, and that 'the Treaty . . . does not form a barrier to the possibility of the Community's developing a commercial policy aiming at a regulation of the world market for certain products rather than at a mere liberalization of trade'.[61] Ultimately

---

[54] Case 8–73 *Hauptzollamt Bremerhaven* v. *Massey-Ferguson GmbH* [1973] ECR 897, para. 4.

[55] M. Cremona, 'EC External Commercial Policy after Amsterdam: Authority and Interpretation within Interconnected Legal Orders', in J.H.H. Weiler (ed.), *Towards a Common Law of International Trade? The EU, the WTO and the NAFTA* (Oxford University Press, 2000).

[56] P. Koutrakos, *EU International Relations Law* (Hart, 2006), 34 to the effect that this comparison makes the EC's trade policy competence appear potentially unlimited.

[57] *Opinion 1/75 (Understanding on a Local Cost Standard)* [1975] ECR 1355.

[58] For critique of some of these arguments see P. Eeckhout, *External Relations of the European Union. Legal and Constitutional Foundations* (Oxford University Press, 2004), 15.

[59] Case 41/76 *Donckerwolcke*, n. 31 above, para. 32.

[60] *Opinion 1/78*, n. 52 above.

[61] *Ibid.*, paras. 43–53.

the Court ruled that the EC had exclusive competence in substantive terms to enter the agreement, but that the role of the Member States in financing the agreement meant that their involvement was also required.

This approach towards trade agreements pursuing developmental aims was confirmed in the *General System of Preference* judgment,[62] in which the GSP system was said to reflect a new concept of international trade relations in which development played a major role and which fell within the scope of Article 133 EC.

The international trade policy picture changed again after 1986, when the GATT contracting parties initiated a new round of multilateral trade negotiations, the Uruguay Round, which included in its agenda for the first time trade in services, trade-related aspects of intellectual property rights, and trade-related investment measures. These issues, together with the former GATT, were brought together in a single agreement establishing the World Trade Organization signed in Marrakesh in 1994. Since the Commission considered that the Community had exclusive competence to sign the final agreement, but the Member States did not wish to give up their powers in this respect, the Court was asked for its opinion. In *Opinion 1/94*, the ECJ decided in the first place that all WTO agreements on trade in goods fell within the Community's commercial policy competence. It then turned to trade in services and concluded that this area could not immediately, and as a matter of principle, be excluded from the scope of Article 133.[63] However, it then considered that it must take into account the definition of trade in services in the GATS.

Opinion 1/94 (WTO Agreement: GATS and TRIPS)
[1994] ECR I–5267

THE ECJ

43. Under Article I(2) of GATS, trade in services is defined, for the purposes of that agreement, as comprising four modes of supply of services: (1) cross-frontier supplies not involving any movement of persons; (2) consumption abroad, which entails the movement of the consumer into the territory of the WTO member country in which the supplier is established; (3) commercial presence, i.e. the presence of a subsidiary or branch in the territory of the WTO member country in which the service is to be rendered; (4) the presence of natural persons from a WTO member country, enabling a supplier from one member country to supply services within the territory of any other member country.

44. As regards cross-frontier supplies, the service is rendered by a supplier established in one country to a consumer residing in another. The supplier does not move to the consumer's country; nor, conversely, does the consumer move to the supplier's country. That situation is, therefore, not unlike trade in goods, which is unquestionably covered by the common commercial policy within the meaning of the Treaty. There is thus no particular reason why such a supply should not fall within the concept of the common commercial policy.

45. The same cannot be said of the other three modes of supply of services covered by GATS, namely, consumption abroad, commercial presence and the presence of natural persons.

---

62 Case 45/86 *Commission* v. *Council* [1987] ECR 1493.
63 *Opinion 1/94*, n. 35 above, paras. 36–41.

46. As regards natural persons, it is clear from Article 3 of the Treaty, which distinguishes between 'a common commercial policy' in paragraph (b) and 'measures concerning the entry and movement of persons' in paragraph (d), that the treatment of nationals of non-member countries on crossing the external frontiers of Member States cannot be regarded as falling within the common commercial policy. More generally, the existence in the Treaty of specific chapters on the free movement of natural and legal persons shows that those matters do not fall within the common commercial policy.

47. It follows that the modes of supply of services referred to by GATS as 'consumption abroad', 'commercial presence' and the 'presence of natural persons' are not covered by the common commercial policy.

Community competence over cross-border services was thus held to be exclusive, but the Member States in principle retained their competence over other modes of supplying services.[64] The Court also ruled that transport services were to be regarded as not falling into the CCP and that they remained implied powers under the EC chapter on transport, and thus shared between the EC and its Member States.[65] It also ruled to the same effect for much of the TRIPs Agreement. Consequently, since the Community and its Member States were jointly competent to conclude both GATS and TRIPs, the whole WTO Agreement was concluded as a 'mixed agreement'.

Opinion 1/94 was an important opinion which marked the end of the expansion of EC competence under the CCP, as well as the end of the period of judicial activism with regard to the EC's exclusive competence. Recent cases have confirmed this and indicated that trade measures will not necessarily be perceived as trade or commercial policy measures if they pursue other objectives such as environmental policy.[66]

The Treaty of Amsterdam confirmed the position articulated in *Opinion 1/94* while providing for a possible future decision by the Council to extend the scope of the CCP. A new paragraph 133(7) was added to permit the Council to extend it to include intellectual property negotiations. The Treaty of Nice represented a further stage in the evolution of the field, bringing the most radical revision to the CCP provisions since the inception of the EC Treaty in 1957.[67] The first important change was an explicit reference to the need to ensure the compatibility of external agreements with internal policies and rules, under the joint responsibility of the Council and the Commission. On the scope of the CCP, one of the most significant changes is its extension to cover the negotiation and conclusion of agreements on trade in services and commercial aspects of intellectual property, although exclusive competence is ruled out in this respect. Transport is clearly excluded from the CCP, and investment is still not explicitly included within Article 133. There is also now provision for exceptions to the exclusive nature of EC competence under the CCP, in so far as agreements relating to trade in cultural and audiovisual services, educational services, and social and human health services are said to fall within the shared competence of the Community and the Member States. These provisions however only cover *agreements*, so that unilateral measures will continue to fall under the respective internal Treaty provisions, even when trade with third countries is involved.[68]

---

[64] For a critique of the Court's reasoning in relation to the movement of persons see Eeckhout, n. 58 above, 30.
[65] These powers could become exclusive under the conditions set in Case 22/70 *ERTA*, n. 23 above.
[66] *Opinion 2/00*, n. 17 above.
[67] M. Cremona, 'A Policy of Bits and Pieces? The Common Commercial Policy After Nice' (2002) 4 *CYELS* 61.
[68] *Ibid.*, 83.

(b) ASSOCIATION, PARTNERSHIP, AND CO-OPERATION

Article 310 EC provides:

> The Community may conclude with one or more States or international organisations agreements establishing an association involving reciprocal rights and obligations, common action and special procedure.

Apart from the CCP, the power to conclude Association Agreements was the only express external relations power of the EC until the Single European Act. The first Association Agreements were concluded with Greece and Turkey, and with the African, Carribean, and Pacific (ACP) countries under the Yaoundé Convention, a few years after the entry into force of the EEC Treaty.[69] Many others have followed since. The Association Agreements concluded with the States of central and eastern Europe were known as 'Europe Agreements', and took account of the fact that these States were likely soon to become EU members. These agreements have been extensively invoked before the Court, which has consistently ruled that, like other international agreements, they form an integral part of the Community legal order and that it enjoys broad jurisdiction over their provisions.[70]

The Treaty itself provides no indication of what an association should involve apart from the skeletal provisions of Article 310. The initial association agreements in fact included measures covering the entire subject-matter of the Treaty.[71] Amongst the most important of the Association Agreements currently in force are the agreements with the ACP countries, most recently the Contonou Agreement, which provides for free trade in most goods, as well as equality in establishment, and significant aid. Other important Association Agreements include the European Economic Area Agreement, the stabilization and association agreements with certain countries of the Western Balkans, and the Euro-Mediterranean Agreements.

The EU also concludes other agreements which are similar to Association Agreements but which provide for less intensive forms of integration or which cover a narrower range of fields. Examples are the co-operation and partnership agreements concluded with the countries of the ex-Soviet Union, now members of the Commonwealth of Independent States (CIS), and interregional co-operation agreements with the countries of Latin America, South-East Asia, and the Arab States.

(c) DEVELOPMENT POLICY, TECHNICAL CO-OPERATION, AND HUMANITARIAN AID

There was no explicit legal basis in the EC Treaty relating to these three fields until the Maastricht Treaty was adopted. However, they were developed on the basis of other EC external policies including commercial policy and association, as well by using the residual powers provision in Article 308.

---

[69] See [1963] OJ L26/296; [1964] OJ L27/3685; and [1964] OJ L93/1430.

[70] Case C–63/99 *Głoszczuk;* Case C–235/99 *Kondova;* Case C–257/99 *Barkoci and Malik* [2001] ECR I–6557; Case C–268/99 *Jany* [2001] ECR I–8615; Case C–162/00 *Land Nordrhein-Westfalen* v. *Pokrzeptowicz-Meyer* [2002] ECR I–1049.

[71] See for more detailed analysis S. Peers, 'EC Frameworks of International Relations: Co-operation, Partnership and Association', in Dashwood and Hillion, n. 26 above; K. Lenaerts and E. De Smijter, 'The European Community's Treaty Making Competence' (1996) 16 *YBEL* 1.

We saw in *Opinion 1/78* that the ECJ accepted the use of trade instruments with a development dimension, although it ruled that the provision of financing by Member States would result in an agreement of the kind at issue being 'mixed'.[72] Following that case, the association and trade legal bases of the Treaty were used for many agreements concluded with developing countries. The Court in the *Bangladesh* case ruled that the EC did not have exclusive competence in the field of humanitarian aid, and that Member States were not precluded from exercising their competence collectively within the Council or outside it.[73] In *Parliament* v. *Council* (*Lomé IV*) the Court further ruled that the EC competence in the field of development was not exclusive, and that Member States were accordingly entitled to enter into commitments themselves. Finally the ECJ ruled that the competence to implement the EC's financial assistance was shared by the EC and its Member States.[74]

The Maastricht Treaty subsequently inserted an independent EC Treaty basis for development policy in Articles 177 and 178, and the Nice Treaty later provided a legal basis for 'financial and technical cooperation' with third States in Article 181(a) EC. In both of these areas, Community policy is expressly required to contribute to the general objective of developing and consolidating democracy and the rule of law, and to that of respecting human rights and fundamental freedoms.

(d) EXTERNAL ENVIRONMENTAL ACTION

Environmental policy is an example of a field in which internal and external activities are often so closely linked that EC internal competence would be rather limited in effect without its external counterpart.[75] This is reflected in the fact that as soon as an explicit environmental policy title was inserted into the EC Treaty by the SEA, provision was made for (shared) external competence in Article 174(4).

One of the most contentious issues has been the overlap between environmental measures and the CCP. In *Greece* v. *Council* the Court accepted that a regulation establishing uniform rules regarding the conditions under which agricultural products likely to be contaminated may be imported into the Community from non-member countries fell within the CCP.[76]

Ten years later, in *Opinion 2/00*[77] the Court had to decide whether the Cartagena Protocol to the Convention on Biological Diversity was principally an environmental agreement, principally a trade agreement, or one which was inextricably concerned with both. The ECJ decided on the first option, i.e. that the Protocol was concerned principally with environment rather than trade. It also held that the Community's external environmental powers are not confined to the arrangements referred to in Article 174(4), but extend to all areas of Community environmental law making.

Opinion 2/00 was an important ruling in the same vein as *Opinion 2/94*,[78] in that it marked a decisive step for the Court in demarcating not only the limits of the exclusive external competence of the EC, but also the substantive limits of the scope of the CCP. The Court clearly did not wish the more recent Treaty Articles creating new legal bases for EC external action to

---

[72] *Opinion 1/78*, n. 52 above.

[73] Cases C–181 and 248/91, n. 51 above, paras. 14–16.

[74] Case C–316/91 *European Parliament* v. *Council*, n. 50 above.

[75] See D. Thieme, 'European Community External Relations in the Field of the Environment' (2001) 10 *European Environmental Law Review* 252.

[76] Case C–62/88 *Greece* v. *Council* [1990] ECR I–1527.

[77] *Opinion 2/00*, n. 17 above.

[78] *Opinion 2/94*, n. 28 above.

be swallowed up by a catch-all interpretation of Article 133 EC, and it decisively rejected the assumption which the Commission appeared to have made for many years, i.e. that the CCP takes priority over all other areas of Community competence.[79] In the final analysis the Court ruled that the EC's conclusion of the Protocol must be founded on a single legal basis, specific to environmental policy.

Its approach in *Opinion 2/00* can be contrasted with that which it adopted in the *Energy Star* case, in which it held that an agreement with the US on the co-ordination of energy-efficient labeling programmes for office equipment was a trade measure which required Article 133 as a single legal base.[80] The decisive factors for the Court in the latter case were that the instrument had a direct impact on trade in office equipment and only an indirect and distant effect on the environment, such that the trade objective was predominant.

A recent case falling between the poles of predominant environmental competence and predominant trade competence respectively is that concerning the Rotterdam Convention on international trade in hazardous chemicals.[81] The ECJ here took the view that the agreement should be concluded using a dual legal basis, with Article 133 EC for the CCP and Article 175(1) for environmental policy.

(e) EXTERNAL DIMENSIONS OF INTERNAL POLICIES

While the external dimension to many internal policies was initially developed on the basis of Article 308 EC and using the implied powers doctrine, later amendments to the Treaty provided express powers in the areas of education,[82] vocational training,[83] culture,[84] and public health,[85] in which the Community is explicitly required to foster co-operation with third countries and international organizations. Other areas providing for co-operation with third countries are those of trans-European networks under Article 155(3) EC and research under Article 70.

Implied competences exist also with regard to certain internal market measures which are not covered by the CCP, such as unilateral external action in the area of services. In such fields there is scope for EC involvement on the basis of the internal market provisions of the Treaty.[86] In the area of social policy, Article 118 was held to confer competence to conclude international agreements, even though the Community's internal legislative competence in the field was defined in rather subsidiary terms. Such external competence, as we have seen from *Opinion 2/91*,[87] becomes exclusive where there is Community legislation which could be affected by the provisions of the international agreement.

Further, the operation of the single currency and of monetary union requires international co-operation. Article 111 EC provides for the conclusion of international agreements on an exchange-rate system for the Euro in relation to non-Community currencies.[88]

---

[79] *Opinion 2/00*, n. 17 above, para. 35; A. Dashwood, 'Commentary on Opinion 2/00, Cartagena Protocol on Biosafety, 6 December 2001' (2002) 39 *CMLRev.* 353, 367.

[80] Case C–281/03 *Commission* v. *Council* [2002] ECR I–12049. See also Case C–94/03 *Commission* v. *Council*, n. 19 above.

[81] Case C–94/03, n. 19 above.

[82] Art. 149(3) EC.

[83] Art. 150(3) EC.

[84] Art. 151(3) EC.

[85] Art. 152(3) EC.

[86] Eeckhout, n. 58 above, 123.

[87] *Opinion 2/91*, n. 39 above.

[88] For controversy over whether the EC or the ECB (with its own separate legal personality) has external competence in this field see C. Zilioli and M. Selmayr, 'The External Relations of the Euro Area: Legal Aspects'

With regard to Title IV of the EC Treaty on 'Visas, Asylum and Immigration and Other Policies Related to the Free Movement of Persons' there is, on the basis of *ERTA* reasoning, clearly an implied competence to conclude agreements over the whole area. The EC has exercised this in its negotiation of readmission agreements of illegal immigrants, and by integrating migration issues into its overall relations with third countries.[89] Finally, the ECJ held in *Opinion 1/03* that the EC had exclusive competence to conclude the Lugano Convention on jurisdiction and the recognition and enforcement of judgments in civil and commercial matters, a subject-matter which is also covered by Title IV of the Treaty.[90]

5. EXTERNAL POWERS UNDER THE EU TREATY

We have examined the emergence of the EU's Second and Third Pillars in Chapter 1, and Chapter 7 examines some further aspects of the Third Pillar's area of freedom, security, and justice. The focus of the present section is on the law which has emerged from the externally-focused policies under these two Pillars.

(a) THE SECOND PILLAR: THE SCOPE OF THE COMMON FOREIGN AND SECURITY POLICY

The Treaty itself refers to the scope of the CFSP in very wide terms, as covering 'all areas of foreign and security policy'. Article 2 of the TEU also refers to the CFSP, declaring that the Union has among its objectives:

— to assert its identity on the international scene, in particular through the implementation of a common foreign and security policy including the progressive framing of a common defence policy, which might lead to a common defence, in accordance with the provisions of Article 17.

The objectives of the CFSP are listed in Article 11 TEU. These are:

— to safeguard the common values, fundamental interests, independence and integrity of the Union in conformity with the principles of the United Nations Charter,
— to strengthen the security of the Union in all ways,
— to preserve peace and strengthen international security, in accordance with the principles of the United Nations Charter, as well as the principles of the Helsinki Final Act and the objectives of the Paris Charter, including those on external borders,
— to promote international cooperation,
— to develop and consolidate democracy and the rule of law, and respect for human rights and fundamental freedoms.

(1999) 36 *CMLRev.* 273; C.W. Herrmann, 'Monetary Sovereignty over the Euro and External Relations of the Euro Area: Competences, Procedures and Practice' (2002) 7 *EFA Rev.* 1, 23.

[89] See, e.g., the re-admission agreements with Hong Kong, Sri Lanka, Macao, Albania: respectively SEC(2003)255, [2004] OJ L143/97, COM(2004)92.

[90] *Opinion 1/03*, n. 41 above.

Article 17 TEU provides that the CFSP is to include all questions relating to the security of the Union, including the progressive framing of a common defence policy, which might lead to a common defence.

The scope of the CFSP is thus potentially extremely broad,[91] and is described in terms both of its objectives and of the instruments supplied to achieve those objectives. These instruments include *principles and general guidelines* (which can include matters with defence implications), *common strategies* in areas where the Member States have important interests in common (both to be adopted by the European Council), *decisions* necessary for defining and implementing the CFSP, *joint actions* which address specific situations where operational action by the Union is deemed to be required, and *common positions* which define the approach of the Union to a particular matter of a geographical or thematic nature (adopted by the Council). Other instruments which contribute to building the CFSP are: *information and consultation* on any matter of foreign and security policy of general interest and *international agreements*.

The TEU provided for the Union to be served by a 'single institutional framework'. This means that the Community institutions and the European Council now have among their tasks the elaboration of the CFSP. There is an inherent tension built into this construction. On the one hand, the institutions are required to ensure the consistency and the continuity of the activities carried out in order to attain the Union's objectives. On the other hand, they must do this while respecting and building upon the *acquis communautaire*, and Article 47 provides further that nothing in the EU Treaty shall affect the TEC or the subsequent Treaties and Acts modifying or supplementing them.

There is clearly an overlap of competence between the Second Pillar area and the external policies of the EC.[92] Given that the Second Pillar covers 'all areas of foreign and security policy', there is no reason for economic aspects to be excluded. However, since the differences between the procedures, the powers of the institutions, the guarantees for individuals, and the nature of EC law (in particular its direct effect and arguably also its primacy) and other areas of EU law are so important, the question of the borderline between the CFSP and Community powers is crucial.

The limits of the Member States' powers when acting outside the scope of the Communities were initially addressed by the Court in cases pre-dating the creation of the CFSP, when the conduct by Member States of their foreign policies was subject to 'European political cooperation' (EPC) regulated by the SEA. In *Centro-Com*, concerning action by the Member States pursuant to a UN Sanctions Regulation against Serbia and Montenegro, the ECJ ruled that the Member States' powers 'must be exercised in a manner consistent with Community law'.[93] Even if they had foreign and security objectives, measures the effect of which was to restrict the export of products could not be treated as falling outside the scope of the CCP, but had to respect the provisions of the CCP. Applied to the CFSP context, the ruling in this case indicates that, even when acting within the scope of the CFSP, the Member States must respect EC law.

Secondly, the ECJ drew a limit to the scope of the CFSP, indicating that although it applies in principle to all areas of foreign and security policy, it does not cover areas where there is Community competence, such as the CCP. The subsequent *Airport Transit Visas* case suggests

---

91 For an overview of activities see R. Dover, 'The EU's Foreign, Security, and Defence Policies', in M. Cini (ed.), *European Union Politics* (Oxford University Press, 2007).

92 R. Baratta, 'Overlaps Between European Community Competence and European Union Foreign Policy Activity', in E. Cannizzaro (ed.), *The European Union as an Actor in International Relations* (Kluwer, 2002).

93 Case C–124/95 *R. v. HM Treasury and Bank of England, ex p. Centro-Com* [1997] ECR I–81, para. 25.

that this is so not only in relation to exclusive Community competence, but also to shared competence.[94]

In the recent *Kadi* and *Yusuf* cases, on the other hand, the CFI cautioned against the converse risk, i.e. the overreaching of the Community Pillar and its encroachment onto the terrain of the CFSP. The cases—which are on appeal to the ECJ at the time of writing—concerned the Community's competence to impose 'smart' economic sanctions on individuals pursuant to a UN Resolution.[95] The EC had based its measure on the residual powers clause of the EC in Article 308, together with Articles 60 and 301 EC. The Commission argued to the CFI that the fight against international terrorism fell within the objectives of the EC mentioned in Articles 2 and 3 EC, thus bringing the measure within the scope of Article 308, but the Court rejected this. In the CFI's view, although it was undoubtedly the aim of the EC Treaty to put an end to past conflict in Europe through ever closer union, that was without any reference to a common foreign and security policy, which fell exclusively within the objectives of the TEU. Although the CFI accepted that an objective of the EU might inspire action by the EC within the sphere of competence of the latter, it could not be the basis for this kind of action under Article 308. If the EC could always take action to achieve the objectives of the EU, this would deprive many provisions of the TEU of their ambit and effect.[96] Ultimately, however, the CFI ruled on a different ground that these particular economic sanctions had been properly adopted under the EC Treaty, and the case is on appeal to the ECJ at the time of writing.

(b) THE SECOND PILLAR: THE CONSTITUTIONAL NATURE OF THE CFSP

We have seen in Chapter 1 how the CFSP emerged from a history of intergovernmental co-operation between the States on foreign policy matters. The TEU's provisions were perceived as a codification, with only minor adjustments, of the earlier EPC. But the systemic differences between the two led to the gradual detachment of the CFSP from EPC practice.

The EU Treaty clearly provided that the Member States were under an obligation to support the Union's external and security policy actively and unreservedly, in a spirit of loyalty and mutual solidarity. They were further required to work together to enhance and develop their mutual political solidarity and to refrain from any action contrary to the interests of the Union or likely to impair its effectiveness as a cohesive force in international relations. All of these duties were laid down as legal obligations of a binding nature. While some of the failures of the CFSP and the discord between Member States on high-profile situations like the Iraq war suggest a very mixed record, in fact the CFSP system has enabled a reasonable amount of progress to be made towards the co-ordination of national foreign policies on a range of issues. This is despite the fact that no formal mechanism of supranational enforcement of the various obligations of solidarity and loyalty has been established.

As we have seen above, a clear separation of the Union legal system from the Community legal system is impossible. Cross-fertilization between the two systems has taken place and is well exemplified in the *Pupino* ruling. The ECJ there held that the principle of loyal co-operation, which is contained in Article 10 EC as far as the Community Pillar is concerned, applies also

---

[94] Case C–170/96 *Commission v. Council* [1998] ECR I–2763. Although it concerned the delimitation between the First and the Third Pillars, the reasoning is applicable by analogy here.

[95] Case T–306/01 *Yusuf and Al Barakaat v. Council and Commission* [2005] ECR II–3533; Case T–315/01 *Kadi v. Council and Commission* [2005] II–3649.

[96] *Ibid.*, para. 156.

to the Member States when they act within the scope of Union powers.[97] This arguably re-inforces the obligation of co-operation also with regard to the CFSP.

From a constitutional point of view, CFSP instruments are undoubtedly legal in nature, but their exact legal nature is somewhat different from that of the legislative instruments adopted under the Community Pillar. It has been argued that CFSP instruments are best understood as 'international law decisions' which nonetheless bear a close affinity to Community law in that they are binding upon both Member States and the EU institutions, and are adopted by the Council as the major decision-making body under both the EC and the CFSP legal orders.[98] Finally, although this characterization would undoubtedly be disputed by some, it has been suggested that there are reasons to believe that the core features of supranational Community law are not entirely absent from the law of the CFSP:

R. Gosalbo Bono, Some Reflections on the CFSP Legal Order[99]

Nowadays, even the sacrosanct Community principles of direct effect and primacy over the law of the Member States cannot be said to be completely alien to the CFSP legal order. As regards the principle of direct effect, the practice has started, especially in the EU's fight against terrorism, to insert unconditional obligations in common positions which relate to physical and legal persons as opposed to governments. . . . As regards the principle of primacy, joint actions and common positions are legally binding upon Member States which are under a duty to abide by them 'actively' and 'unreservedly' (Art. 11(2) TEU); . . . . Finally, although the CFSP objectives do not fall within the exclusive competence of the Union, there is no legal obstacle to an application of the principles of the *AETR* case law to the CFSP.

(c) THE THIRD PILLAR: THE EXTERNAL DIMENSION OF POLICE AND JUDICIAL CO-OPERATION IN CRIMINAL MATTERS

This Third Pillar of the EU is the least substantial in scope, due in part to the amendments made by the Treaty of Amsterdam in transferring a significant part of its original subject-matter to the Community Pillar.[100] Its current objectives are described as: preventing and combating crime and organized crime, in particular terrorism; trafficking in persons and offences against children; illicit drug trafficking and illicit arms trafficking, corruption, and fraud. These objectives are to be pursued by a range of means including (1) closer co-operation between police forces and customs authorities in the Member States, (2) closer co-operation between judicial authorities of the Member States, and (3) approximation of rules on criminal matters in the Member States.

The legal basis for the external dimension of this Pillar is in Article 38, which provides that the agreements referred to in Article 24 (i.e. CFSP agreements) may cover matters falling under this Title. Thus the Union may negotiate and conclude agreements with third countries or international organizations.[101] Moreover, Article 37 TEU provides that within international

---

97 Case C–105/03 *Pupino* [2005] ECR I–5285.

98 R. Gosalbo Bono, 'Some Reflections on the CFSP Legal Order' (2006) 43 *CMLRev.* 337, 378.

99 *Ibid.*

100 See Ch. 7.

101 The Union began to exercise its contractual powers in this field in 2003 by concluding three agreements: two with the US on extradition and mutual legal assistance respectively, and one with Iceland and Norway on the application of certain provisions of the EU Convention on Mutual Assistance in Criminal Matters of 2000.

organizations and at international conferences, Member States shall defend the common positions adopted under the provisions of Title VI TEU. A number of other Articles within the Third Pillar assimilate the external representation and co-ordination of Member States' actions in this field to that of the CFSP. Finally, some of the important agencies set up on the basis of Title VI TEU—in particular Europol and Eurojust—have been vested with their own powers to conclude agreements with third countries and international organizations.[102]

(d) CROSS-PILLAR INTERACTIONS AND THE ECONOMIC DIMENSIONS OF SECURITY

It could be said that EU external relations law contains a greater number of mechanisms aimed at preventing interaction between the different pillars rather than promoting their harmonious coexistence.[103] On the other hand, foreign policies based on the First, Second, and Third Pillars necessarily overlap and conflicts over the proper legal basis arise. The European Security Strategy of 2003 marked an important shift in its attempt to make strategic use of all the external policies of the EU.[104] Although primarily a political document, it has potentially important consequences for the mainstreaming of security concerns, and particularly counter-terrorist action in the post-9/11 era, into other foreign policy activities including development co-operation and association agreements. Nonetheless, this strategy also raises a number of legal questions similar to those we have seen above in the interaction between the EC's common commercial policy and Member State foreign policies in the case of economic sanctions, and similar to those which have arisen in the case of 'dual-use' goods.

Dual-use goods are products which can be used for both civil and military purposes, and they are regulated by two different constitutional systems: The Community rules apply in relation to their civil use, and Member State rules apply with regard to questions of national security. They fall within the scope of the 'public security' exception in Article 30 EC which, according to the ECJ in the *Aime Richardt* case, covers both a Member State's internal and external security.[105] The EU regime for export control was established in 1994. It was based on two pillars: the EC regulation laid down the procedural requirements for the export of dual-use goods, while the CFSP decision listed the relevant dual-use goods and sensitive destinations. The latter was therefore outside the jurisdiction of the Court. According to its critics, this arrangement hindered the effectiveness and uniformity of the system, and relegated EC law to the rank of administrative implementation of a CFSP decision, and subordinated it to the dominance of the intergovernmental CFSP.[106]

However, in the subsequent *Werner* and *Leifer* cases, the ECJ ruled that measures the effect of which was to prevent or restrict the export of certain products could not be treated as falling outside the scope of the common commercial policy on the ground that they had foreign policy and security objectives.[107] Given that the CCP is a field of exclusive Community

---

[102] Europol has already concluded a wide range of bilateral operational or strategic agreements with other States and international organizations.

[103] See in particular Art. 47, discussed below.

[104] European Security Strategy: A Secure Europe in a Better World, Annex to the Presidency conclusions of Dec. 2003.

[105] Case C–367/89 *Criminal proceedings against Aime Richardt and Les Accessoires Scientifiques SNC* [1991] ECR I–4621.

[106] Eeckhout, n. 58 above, 191.

[107] Case C–70/94 *Fritz Werner Industrie-Ausrustungen GmbH v. Federal Republic of Germany* [1995] ECR I–3189; Case C–83/94 *Criminal proceedings against Peter Leifer and Others* [1995] ECR I–3231.

competence, the Member States could act only on the basis of a specific authorization. Following these rulings the EU changed its approach and the dual-use goods system operates now solely on the basis of the EC regulation, and national measures regarding export controls must operate within the limits set by this regulation.[108]

The imposition of economic sanctions by the Union was organized differently. Even before the Treaty provided for a specific mechanism, the EU proceeded by following an EPC decision on the appropriateness of particular sanctions, while the relevant substantive rules were contained in an EC regulation adopted under Article 133 EC.[109] The Maastricht Treaty established an inter-pillar mechanism in Article 301 EC which provides that:

> Where it is provided, in a common position or in a joint action adopted according to the provisions of the Treaty on European Union relating to the common foreign and security policy, for an action by the Community to interrupt or to reduce, in part or completely, economic relations with one or more third countries, the Council shall take the necessary urgent measures.

This is supplemented by Article 60 EC which states that the Council may where necessary take urgent measures on the movement of capital and payments regarding the third countries in question. The EC has on numerous occasions adopted a range of economic sanctions of various kinds, including trade embargoes, financial sanctions, and other prohibitions on lending or investment.[110]

We shall see in Chapter 11 that the operation of sanctions has raised questions about their compatibility with the fundamental rights regime in the EU. In the *Bosphorus* case, the ECJ upheld the compatibility of sanctions imposed by an EC regulation in implementation of a UN Security Council resolution with the right to property and the freedom to pursue a commercial activity, and its approach was broadly upheld in a later challenge before the European Court of Human Rights.[111]

More recently, so-called 'smart sanctions' directed against particular persons and organizations, rather than against States or regimes, have come to prominence. These sanctions raise additional human rights concerns, including the right to a fair hearing and to an effective judicial remedy. However, as we shall again see in Chapter 11, the CFI in the cases of *Yusuf*, *Kadi*, *Hassan*, and *Ayadi* has ruled that since these sanctions are mandated by the UN Security Council, they cannot be reviewed for compatibility with fundamental rights, but only indirectly for compatibility of the Security Council measures with *ius cogens* norms.[112] On the other hand, where the sanctions are imposed under 'autonomous' EU measures, rather than UN-mandated ones, the human rights standards protected under EU law have been held by the CFI to be applicable.[113]

---

[108] Reg. 1334/2000 [2000] OJ L159/1.

[109] Before the EPC emerged in the 1980s, Member States adopted sanctions following the so-called 'Rhodesia doctrine' on the basis of Art. 297 EC, which provides for Member States to consult each other with a view to acting together the steps needed to prevent the functioning of the common market being affected by the necessity to adopt such measures.

[110] P. Koutrakos, *Trade, Foreign Policy & Defence in EU Constitutional Law* (Hart, 2001), 69.

[111] Case C–84/95 *Bosphorus Hava Yollari Turizm ve Ticaret AS v. Minister for Transport, Energy and Communications* [1996] ECR I–3953, and subsequently App. no. 45036/98, *Bosphorus v. Ireland*, judgment of the ECtHR of 30 June 2005. See Ch. 11, nn. 206–209 and text.

[112] Case T–306/01 *Yusuf*, n. 95 above; Case T–315/01 *Kadi*, n. 95 above, on appeal to the ECJ Case C–402/05 P; Case T–253/02 *Ayadi v. Council* [2006] ECR II–2139; Case T–49/04 *Hassan v. Council and Commission* [2006] ECR II–52.

[113] Case T–228/02 *Organisation des Modjahedines du peuple d'Iran v. Council*, 12 Dec. 2006. See further Ch. 11, n. 26.

Thus while the dual-use goods example suggests a move from the dominance of the CFSP over the EC Pillar to the converse, where the EC Pillar (the CCP) predominates, the example of economic sanctions indicates a possible evolution towards a more integrated cross-pillar approach.

6. THE CONCLUSION OF INTERNATIONAL AGREEMENTS BY THE EU AND OTHER FORMS OF EU INTERNATIONAL PRACTICE

We have seen above that the EC has enjoyed international legal personality since its creation, and that the EU's legal personality has developed gradually through its practice in international relations, sanctioned by successive Treaty amendments. International agreements are the most important form of external law-making by the EU. Both the EC and the EU Treaties contain provisions on the exercise of this power. The international practice of the EC and EU however also includes participation in international organizations. Both forms of international activity have important ramifications internally, as well as internationally through the creation of obligations which may entail international responsibility.

(a) PROCEDURES FOR CONCLUDING AGREEMENTS UNDER THE EC AND EU TREATIES

A general procedure for the exercise of treaty-making powers is provided in Article 300 EC. This provision organizes the division of tasks between the institutions and stipulates the various voting procedures. Article 300(1) provides:

> Where this Treaty provides for the conclusion of agreements between the Community and one or more States or international organisations, the Commission shall make recommendations to the Council, which shall authorise the Commission to open the necessary negotiations. The Commission shall conduct these negotiations in consultation with special committees appointed by the Council to assist it in this task and within the framework of such directives as the Council may issue to it.

The first step of the procedure is thus the negotiation of an agreement, which is, in principle, the task of the Commission. It is generally the Commission which initiates the whole enterprise, albeit under the general political leadership of the European Council. The directives which form the basis for the Commission's actions are informally known as 'negotiating mandates'. These tend to be rather general in nature, although the Council sometimes specifies the result which is sought and the margins of the concessions which the Commission is permitted to make.

The second stage of the procedure is the conclusion of the agreement. Here the power is with the Council. Article 300(2) begins:

> Subject to the powers vested in the Commission in this field, the signing, which may be accompanied by a decision on provisional application before entry into force, and the

conclusion of the agreements shall be decided on by the Council, acting by a qualified majority on a proposal from the Commission.

A qualified majority is required for the opening of the negotiations, as well as for the signing and conclusion of an agreement.[114] However, in both cases there are two exceptional cases in which unanimity is required. The first is when the agreement covers a field for which unanimity is required for the adoption of internal rules. The second is when it concerns an Association Agreement referred to in Article 310.

In the case of an agreement which is part of the Common Commercial Policy, the procedure is further modified and involves a specialized committee. Article 133 provides:

> Where agreements with one or more States or international organisations need to be negotiated, the Commission shall make recommendations to the Council, which shall authorize the Commission to open the necessary negotiations. The Council and the Commission shall be responsible for ensuring that the agreements negotiated are compatible with internal Community policies and rules.
>
> The Commission shall conduct these negotiations in consultation with a special committee appointed by the Council to assist the Commission in this task and within the framework of such directives as the Council may issue to it. The Commission shall report regularly to the special committee on the progress of negotiations.

Similar committees may be appointed to assist the Commission in the negotiation of other types of agreements.[115] They are aimed to ensure control by Member States of the direction of the negotiations.

Further, the procedure and the role played by the Community institutions may also be limited in the case of agreements concerning monetary or foreign exchange regime matters. According to Article 111(3) EC it is for the Council to decide on the arrangements for the negotiation and conclusion of agreements. It shall do so by a qualified majority on a recommendation from the Commission and after consulting the European Central Bank. The Commission is to be 'fully associated with the negotiations'.

Although Article 300 refers to 'agreements', the ECJ ruled in *Opinion 1/75* ruled that this notion is to be construed broadly as referring to 'any undertaking entered into by entities subject to international law which has binding force, whatever its formal designation'.[116] The intention of the parties to give the document binding force will be decisive. In *France* v. *Commission*, concerning the EC–US antitrust agreement on the application of competition laws, the Court made clear that the Commission could not adopt a binding document of this kind together with another international actor, outside the procedure provided for in Article 300.[117] However, where it is clear throughout negotiations that the intention of the parties is not to enter into legally binding commitments, the adoption by the Commission together with an international partner of 'Guidelines' is not precluded by Article 300.[118]

---

[114] All of these acts take the form of decisions or sometimes regs.

[115] The Article 133 Committee is purely advisory and is limited to giving assistance in the negotiation of trade agreements, Case C–61/94 *Commission* v. *Germany (International Dairy Arrangement)* [1996] ECR I–3989, para. 14.

[116] *Opinion 1/75*, n. 57 above, 1359–1360; Case C–327/91 *France* v. *Commission*, n. 18 above.

[117] *Ibid.*; Case C–189/97 *European Parliament* v. *Council* [1999] ECR I–4741.

[118] Case C–233/02 *French Republic* v. *Commission (Guidelines on Regulatory Co-operation and Transparency Concluded with the USA)* [2004] ECR I–2759.

Within the framework of the CFSP, the EU can engage in contractual relations within that policy by virtue of Article 24 TEU. Article 24 provides:

> 1. When it is necessary to conclude an agreement with one or more States or international organisations in implementation of this title, the Council may authorise the Presidency, assisted by the Commission as appropriate, to open negotiations to that effect. Such agreements shall be concluded by the Council on a recommendation from the Presidency.
> 2. The Council shall act unanimously when the agreement covers an issue for which unanimity is required for the adoption of internal decisions.
> 3. When the agreement is envisaged in order to implement a joint action or common position, the Council shall act by a qualified majority in accordance with Article 23(2).
> 4. The provisions of this Article shall also apply to matters falling under Title VI. When the agreement covers an issue for which a qualified majority is required for the adoption of internal decisions or measures, the Council shall act by a qualified majority in accordance with Article 34(3).
> 5. No agreement shall be binding on a Member State whose representative in the Council states that it has to comply with the requirements of its own constitutional procedure; the other members of the Council may agree that the agreement shall nevertheless apply provisionally.
> 6. Agreements concluded under the conditions set out by this Article shall be binding on the institutions of the Union.

Article 38 TEU declares these provisions applicable also to matters falling within the scope of the Third Pillar on Police and Judicial Co-operation in Criminal Matters (PJCC).

It was initially unclear on whose behalf the agreements based on Article 24 were signed: whether for the Member States acting together or the EU.[119] Practice has however made clear that it is the latter. Council decisions providing for signature state clearly that 'the President of the Council is hereby authorized to designate the person(s) empowered to sign the Agreements on behalf of the European Union, subject to their later conclusion'.[120] Consequently, the EU is described in all these agreements either as a Participating Party, or a Contracting Party.[121] As regards the legal nature of these agreements, Council decisions concluding them generally contain a provision to the effect that '[t]he Presidency of the Council is hereby authorized to designate the person empowered to sign the Agreement in order to bind the European Union'. It is clear from Article 24 TEU and from provisions normally contained in such international agreements that they are binding on the Member States as well as on the institutions of the EU.

(b) MIXED AGREEMENTS

Mixed agreements are by now a very common phenomenon, and an integral part of the legal landscape so long as both the Community and its Member States each retain treaty-making capacity.[122] Mixed agreements are agreements to which both the Community and the

---

[119] S. Marquardt, 'The Conclusion of International Agreements under Art 24 of the Treaty on European Union', in V. Kronenberger (ed.), *The EU and the International Legal Order: Discord or Harmony?* (Asser Press, 2001).

[120] See, e.g., Art. 1(1) of Council Decision of 6 June 2003 concerning the signature of the Agreements between the EU and the USA on extradition and mutual legal assistance in criminal matters [2003] OJ L181/25.

[121] It should be noted that some may still refuse to attribute these agreements to the EU as a distinct entity. See, e.g., the 'Report on Legal Personality of the European Union', 2001/2021 (INI), submitted by the European Parliament, comparing these agreements to a 'joint venture' in private law.

[122] The literature on mixed agreements is vast. See, for instance, D. O'Keeffe and H.G. Schermers (eds.), *Mixed Agreements* (Kluwer, 1983); J. Heliskoski, *Mixed Agreements as a Technique for Organizing the International Relations of the European Community and its Member States* (Kluwer, 2001).

Member States are contracting parties on the basis that their joint participation is required, because not all matters covered by the agreement fall exclusively within Community competence or exclusively within Member State competence. A mixed agreement will also be used in a case where competence over the subject-matter of the agreement is shared between the Member States and the EU. Mixed agreements form an integral part of Community law and are binding on both the institutions of the Community and the Member States.

Discussions of mixity, as with many aspects of EU external relations, tend to be rather intricate and confusing. Rosas has proposed a detailed typology of mixed agreements on the basis of the nature of the competence involved.[123] He distinguishes between parallel and shared competence. Parallel competence implies that the Community's participation in an agreement is just like that of any other contracting party and has no direct effect on the rights and obligations of Member States.

Shared competence on the other hand entails some division of rights and obligations contained in the agreement. He subdivides shared competence into (i) co-existent competence, where an agreement contains some provisions falling under the exclusive competence of either the EC or the Member States, so that the agreement can be divided into separate parts; and (ii) concurrent competence where the agreement in question forms a whole which cannot be divided into separate parts. Rosas also proposes a distinction between obligatory and optional mixity, although it is one which is difficult to apply in practice. Indeed, it has been suggested that any attempt to classify mixed agreements risks over-simplifying the phenomenon, since the practice is extremely complicated and involves the interaction of a range of external Community powers and a variety of international agreements.[124]

The ECJ has not generally attempted any detailed delineation of areas of competence in the context of mixed agreements. Once exclusive competence is ruled out, the Court generally turns its attention to how best to organize the joint participation of the Community and the Member States. One additional reason for its unwillingness to address the exact scope of the respective competences of States and Community has been the dynamic and evolving nature of Community competence.[125] In its *Ruling on the compatibility with the Euratom Treaty of Member State participation in the Convention on the Physical Protection of Nuclear Materials, Facilities and Transports*, the ECJ held that the division of competence with regard to implementation of the agreement was to be resolved on the basis of the same principles that govern the division of powers concerning the negotiation and conclusion of agreements.[126] The Court emphasized that the duty of co-operation must be observed in all in three stages of external action, i.e. in negotiation, conclusion, and execution of mixed agreements.[127] Further, responsibility for the performance of mixed agreements also follows their respective competences.[128] And the Court has also ruled that whatever difficulties there may be in managing mixed agreements, these difficulties do not provide a reason for altering the classification of competence, or for arguing that it should be exclusive.[129]

As far as negotiation is concerned, the division of competence under a mixed agreement does not, generally, influence participation in negotiations. While the practice is decided on a

---

[123]　A. Rosas, 'The European Union and Mixed Agreements', in Dashwood and Hillion, n. 26 above.

[124]　Eeckhout, n. 58 above, 191.

[125]　*Ruling 1/78 Euratom (Nuclear Materials)* [1978] ECR 2151, para. 35.

[126]　*Ibid.*, para. 36.

[127]　See also Case C–25/94 *Commission v. Council (FAO Agreement)* [1996] ECR I–1469, para. 48.

[128]　See however the suggestion by Jacobs AG that there might be a case for joint liability at the international level in Case C–316/91 *Parliament v. Council*, n. 50 above, para. 69 of his opinion.

[129]　*Opinion 1/94*, n. 35 above, para. 107; *Opinion 2/00*, n. 17 above, para. 41.

case-by case-basis, it is accepted that the Commission may act as a sole negotiator for the whole agreement according to the mandate given to it by the Council. This was the case for the WTO Agreement where the Council stated that 'in order to ensure the maximum consistency in the conduct of the negotiations, it was decided that the Commission would act as a sole negotiator on behalf of the Community and the Member States' and that the decision authorizing the Commission to open the negotiations 'does not prejudge the question of the competence of the Community or the Member States on particular issues'.[130] In general, the 'common statement' is agreed by consensus and the Commission presents it when competence is exclusive, whereas the Presidency presents the agreed position for matters falling under shared competence.

The phenomenon of mixity has attracted a range of views, with some regarding it as a necessary evil which is rendered all the more problematic by the enlargement of EU membership, while others have praised it as a 'near-unique contribution to true federalism':

J.H.H. Weiler, The External Legal Relations of Non-Unitary Actors: Mixity and the Federal Principle[131]

Mixed agreements, especially when they do not specify the demarcation line between Community and Member States, diffuse at a stroke the explosive issues of the scope of Community competences (and treaty making power) and the parameters of the preemptive effect. It may be thus employed illegally . . . even in those cases where the Community should act alone. It is not easy to assess the practice. From the legal point of view this particular practice must be condemned since it is a breach of the principle of preemption-exclusivity. It also prevents, naturally, the consolidation by virtue of parallelism of wider Community treaty-making power. But preemption does not operate in a legal vacuum. One purpose of the doctrine of preemption in general is to induce, even force, the Member States to act in a Community framework. Preemption is designed for situations where there is an objective necessity for action. By precluding unilateral Member State activity (or joint non-Community action), it is hoped that the objective necessity will force the Member States into joint *Community* action. In some cases the reluctance of the Member States to allow exclusive Community action might be so great— especially if this could mean, say a de facto confirmation of the ever-growing scope of the Common Commercial Policy—that they would prefer not to act at all. It may be that the mixity is the best compromise between the Community exclusivity and no action at all. Since most mixed agreements do not specify the demarcation between Community and Member State competences, this issue is left murky though it can surface again in the implementation of the mixed agreement, its amendment, termination, and/or breach. Mixity may also have advantages, even in this 'false' situation, from the international point of view in terms of voting or other rights in multilateral contexts. In conclusion, one can say that this type of mixity is a symptom of the cleavage between legal doctrine and political power which at present seems unavoidable.

(c) THE ROLE OF THE EUROPEAN PARLIAMENT

Although the power of the European Parliament has been consistently expanding in external relations, it has done so only in small steps.[132] The Parliament's role in treaty-making remains

---

130 *Opinion 1/94*, n. 35 above, 5282.

131 In J.H.H. Weiler, *The Constitution of Europe: Do the New Clothes Have an Emperor?* (Cambridge University Press, 1999).

132 S. Krauss, 'The European Parliament in EU External Relations' (2000) 5 *EFA Rev.* 215; D. Thym, 'Parliamentary Accountability of EU External Relations', in Cremona and de Witte, n. 9 above.

limited. It is called upon to act only at the stage of conclusion of agreements, which considerably reduces its opportunity for influencing their content.[133] However, a range of informal procedures and mechanisms have been created to compensate for this, in order to enable the Parliament to be 'regularly and fully informed' and so that its views can be taken into account.[134]

Formally speaking, Article 300(3) EC provides as a general rule only for *consultation* of the Parliament before an agreement is concluded. And in the case of common commercial policy agreements under Article 133, no provision is made for any kind of participation by the Parliament. The arguments given for this restrictive approach to parliamentary participation tend to be pragmatic, pointing in particular to the length of the process for negotiating and concluding international agreements, and in particular in the case of mixed agreements. As against this, however, the provision in Article 300(3) for Parliament to deliver its opinion within a time limit set by the Council should provide an answer to this concern.[135]

Yet the limits on Parliament's role are even more striking when we consider that the provision for simple consultation applies to cases where the agreement covers a field for which the co-decision or co-operation procedure is required for the adoption of internal rules. Both of these procedures recognize the importance of parliamentary participation in internal policy-making by providing for a substantial or co-equal role, and yet in the field of external relations the Parliament—which is the EU institution with the most plausible claim to direct democratic legitimacy—has a marginal role.

However, by way of exception to this generally limited role, Article 300(2) EC provides that agreements entailing the amendment of an act adopted under the co-decision procedure require the *assent* of the European Parliament before they are concluded, although it is not obvious what logic lies behind this differentiation. Parliament's assent must also be obtained in three further cases: (i) association agreements referred to in Article 310, (ii) other agreements which establish a specific institutional framework by organizing co-operation procedures, and (iii) agreements having important budgetary implications for the Community.[136] This last category of agreements has given rise to problems of interpretation, in particular around the issue of when budgetary implications can be said to be 'important'.[137]

(d) THE MEMBER STATES' DUTY OF SINCERE CO-OPERATION

Although there is no explicit Treaty provision which specifies that the Member States must not enter into negotiations and conclude international agreements which would deviate from the position taken by the Community, it seems that the supremacy of EC law, together with Article 10 EC, effectively requires States to abstain from any such action or from enacting any rules which would conflict with EC norms.

---

[133] Eeckhout, n. 58 above, 183 for a democracy-based critique of the omission of the European Parliament from the conclusion of international agreements, especially those negotiated under the Second and Third Pillars.

[134] This was done previously under the so-called Luns-Westerterp procedure and at present under the Framework Agreement on relations between the European Parliament and the Commission, CS-0349/2000, [2000] OJ C121/122, as revised by EP Dec. 2005/2076 (ACI).

[135] Koutrakos, n. 56 above, 144.

[136] Also in this case the Council and the European Parliament may, in an urgent situation, agree upon a time limit for the assent.

[137] Case C–189/97 *European Parliament* v. *Council*, n. 117 above, for discussion as to what the appropriate point of comparison should be for weighing the amount of expenditure under a given agreement.

It will be recalled that Article 10 requires Member States to facilitate the achievement of the Community's tasks and to abstain from any measure which could jeopardize the attainment of the Treaty objectives. This 'duty of sincere co-operation' applies whether the Community's competence is exclusive or shared. The implications of this provision have been held to mean that when the EC institutions envisage taking Community action, and once they adopt a decision authorizing the Commission to negotiate a multilateral agreement, the Member States are under a duty, if not to abstain from action, at the very least to co-operate closely with the Community institutions in order to 'facilitate the achievement of the Community tasks and to ensure the coherence and consistency of the action and its international representation'.[138] If on the other hand they negotiate, conclude, ratify, or implement bilateral or multilateral treaties concerned with the same issues, without co-operating or consulting with the Commission, they will be in breach of EC law.

(e) CO-OPERATION WITHIN INTERNATIONAL ORGANIZATIONS

The EC Treaty expressly provides for the establishment of relations with other international entities. Article 302 EC refers to the maintenance of all appropriate relations with the organs of the United Nations and of its specialized agencies, and more generally with 'all international organizations'. The maintenance of such relations is the task of the Commission. Other Treaty provisions mention the Council of Europe and the OECD as well as 'appropriate' or 'competent' international organizations in the context of the EMU, education, culture, public health, and the environment. Article 111(4) EC also makes specific provision for the Council to decide on the position of the Community and its representation, at the international level, in relation to issues concerning economic and monetary union. And in the context of the CFSP, Article 19(1) TEU provides that the 'Member States shall coordinate their action in international organizations and at international conferences'.

In *Opinion 1/76*, the ECJ ruled that the powers of the Community to enter international agreements include a power, within the scope of EC competence, to enter agreements establishing international organizations.[139] This was further implicitly confirmed by *Opinion 1/94* where Community participation in the Agreements establishing the World Trade Organization was approved. Community participation can either take the form of full membership, as in the WTO example,[140] or it may take the form of observer status, as in the case of the ILO. In many instances, as in the WTO case, the EC participates in the organization alongside its Member States. If membership of the organization in question is open only to States, then the Member States will adopt a common position on the issue for which the Community is competent, and they must act jointly in the Community's interest in accordance with their general duty of co-operation.[141]

---

[138] Case C–266/03 *Commission* v. *Luxembourg (Inland Waterways Agreement)* [2005] ECR I–4805; Case C–433/03 *Commission* v. *Germany (Inland Waterways Agreement)* [2005] ECR I–6985.

[139] *Opinion 1/76*, n. 35 above; S. Marchisio, 'EU's Membership in International Organisations', in Cannizzaro, n. 92 above; R. Frid, *The Relations between the EC and International Organizations—Legal Theory and Practice* (Kluwer, 1995).

[140] Other examples include the Food and Agriculture Organization and the European Bank for Reconstruction and Development. In some cases the EC has joined a pre-existing international organization, whereas in other cases it has participated in the agreement creating a new organization.

[141] See *Opinion 2/91*, n. 39 above, paras. 1–5.

7. THE EU AND INTERNATIONAL LAW

In international law the Community and the Union are separate entities. In the discussion of international personality we saw that both the EC and the EU may be the subject of rights and obligations arising under international agreements. However, since the ECJ's jurisdiction over the Second Pillar is extremely limited, the Court has so far only ruled on the relationship between EC law and international law.

(a) INTERNATIONAL AGREEMENTS CONCLUDED BY THE COMMUNITY ARE BINDING UPON IT AND ARE PART OF EC LAW

Article 300(7) EC applies the international law principle of *pacta sunt servanda* within EC law by providing that agreements concluded under the conditions set out in that Article shall be binding on the institutions of the Community and on the Member States.[142] The Court has consistently held since the *Haegeman* ruling that once an agreement enters into force, its provisions form an 'integral part' of Community law.[143]

(b) THE COMMUNITY LEGAL SYSTEM IS AN AUTONOMOUS LEGAL ORDER

When the EC has become a party to an organization or an agreement setting up bodies whose powers may conflict with those of the Community institutions, the Court has been particularly insistent on defending the autonomy of the Community legal order. In *Opinion 1/76*, the ECJ ruled out the possibility of establishing a special tribunal composed of six judges from the ECJ and one judge from Switzerland, on the ground that ECJ judges might face a conflict of jurisdiction or allegiance to two different bodies.[144]

A similar ruling was given in relation to provisions of the proposed EEA Agreement in *Opinion 1/91*.[145] The proposed conferral of jurisdiction upon a new EEA Court, which would have been composed of three judges from the ECJ and three from EFTA States, was held to be incompatible with Community law. So was the fact that the agreement had the effect of introducing into the Community legal order a large body of legal rules which would be juxtaposed with a corpus of identically-worded Community rules, with all the problems of interpretation and consistency that would follow. This was said to conflict with Article 220 EC[146] and, more generally, with the very foundations of the Community.[147] A similar approach can be seen in

---

[142] Eeckhout, n. 58 above, 276.

[143] Case 181/73 *Haegeman* [1974] ECR 449, para. 5; *Opinion 1/91 (EEA Agreement I)* [1991] ECR 6079, para. 37.

[144] *Opinion 1/76*, n. 35 above.

[145] *Opinion 1/91*, n. 143 above.

[146] Art. 220 sets out the basic task and role of the ECJ by providing: '[t]he Court of Justice and the Court of First Instance, each within its jurisdiction, shall ensure that in the interpretation and application of this Treaty the law is observed'.

[147] Following renegotiation of the agreement, and the replacement of the earlier proposed EEA Court with an EFTA Court consisting only of judges from the EFTA countries, with more limited jurisdiction, the ECJ upheld the compatibility of the revised Agreeement with the EC Treaty: *Opinion 1/92 (EEA Agreement II)* [1992] ECR I–2821.

Opinion 1/00 on the agreement establishing a European Common Aviation Area where, although ultimately it upheld the compatibility of the agreement with the EC Treaty, the Court ruled:

> The preservation of the autonomy of the Community legal order requires therefore, first, that the essential character of the powers of the Community and its institutions as conceived in the Treaty remain unaltered...
>
> Second, it requires that the procedures for ensuring uniform interpretation of the rules of the ECAA Agreement and for resolving disputes will not have the effect of binding the Community and its institutions, in the exercise of their internal powers, to a particular interpretation of the rules of Community law referred to in that agreement... [148]

The exclusive jurisdiction of the ECJ is confirmed by Article 292 EC, in accordance with which the Member States undertake not to submit a dispute concerning the interpretation or application of the EC Treaty to any method of settlement other than those provided for in the Treaty. The breach of this obligation formed basis of the *Sellafield* case brought by the Commission against Ireland:

Case C–459/03 **Commission v. Ireland**
[2006] ECR I–4635

Ireland instituted proceedings against the UK before the international arbitral tribunal provided for under the United Nations Convention on the Law of the Sea (UNCLOS), in relation to the failure to protect the marine environment with regard to the operation of the MOX plant situated on the Irish Sea coast. The Commission as a result brought proceedings against Ireland under Article 226 EC for violation of the obligation in Article 292 EC. The ECJ ruled that the breach related to an area of shared external competence, and that the matters covered by the relevant UNCLOS provisions were to a large extent already regulated by Community measures. It ruled further that UNCLOS had been concluded by the Community, and continued:

THE ECJ

123. The Court has already pointed out that an international agreement cannot affect the allocation of responsibilities defined in the Treaties and, consequently, the autonomy of the Community legal system, compliance with which the Court ensures under Article 220 EC. That exclusive jurisdiction of the Court is confirmed by Article 292 EC, by which Member States undertake not to submit a dispute concerning the interpretation or application of the EC Treaty to any method of settlement other than those provided for therein (see, to that effect, Opinion 1/91... and Opinion 1/00...).

124. It should be stated at the outset that the Convention precisely makes it possible to avoid such a breach of the Court's exclusive jurisdiction in such a way as to preserve the autonomy of the Community legal system.

125. It follows from Article 282 of the Convention that, as it provides for procedures resulting in binding decisions in respect of the resolution of disputes between Member States, the system for the resolution of disputes set out in the EC Treaty must in principle take precedence over that contained in Part XV of the Convention.

---

[148] *Opinion 1/00 on the establishment of a European Common Aviation Area* [2002] ECR I–3493.

126. It has been established that the provisions of the Convention in issue in the dispute concerning the MOX plant come within the scope of Community competence which the Community exercised by acceding to the Convention, with the result that those provisions form an integral part of the Community legal order.

127. Consequently, the dispute in this case is indeed a dispute concerning the interpretation or application of the EC Treaty, within the terms of Article 292 EC.

128. Furthermore, as it is between two Member States in regard to an alleged failure to comply with Community-law obligations resulting from those provisions of the Convention, this dispute is clearly covered by one of the methods of dispute settlement established by the EC Treaty within the terms of Article 292 EC, namely the procedure set out in Article 227 EC.

Ultimately, the ECJ ruled that Ireland had violated its obligation to respect the exclusive nature of the ECJ's jurisdiction to resolve disputes concerning the interpretation and application of provisions of Community law, and that such a violation involved a manifest risk of adverse effects on the jurisdictional order laid down in Treaties and on the autonomy of the Community legal system.

(c) THE EFFECT OF OTHER RULES OF INTERNATIONAL LAW AND OF INTERNATIONAL AGREEMENTS TO WHICH THE MEMBER STATES ARE PARTY

Article 300(7) EC mentions only agreements which have been concluded by the Community, and makes no reference to other rules of international law. However, the Court has acknowledged the binding nature of such other rules.

In *Poulsen* it ruled that the EC must respect international law in the exercise of its powers,[149] and specifically that it was required to comply with the rules of customary international law when adopting a regulation suspending the trade concessions resulting from an agreement concluded with a non-member country. In *Racke* the ECJ held that the rules of customary international law concerning the termination and the suspension of treaty relations by reason of fundamental change of circumstances (*rebus sic stantibus*) are binding upon the Community institutions and form part of the Community legal order.[150] And in a ruling concerning the *International Dairy Agreement*, the Court referred for the purpose of interpretation to the general rule of international law requiring the parties to any agreement to show good faith in its performance.[151] The ECJ has also ruled that agreements entered by the Community bind the Member States by virtue of their duties under Community law and not international law, since they are not contracting parties.[152]

As regards international agreements to which the Community is not a party, but which are binding on the Member States, Article 307 EC specifies that, in the case of agreements concluded *before* 1 January 1958 (or, for acceding States, before the date of their accession), between one or more Member States on the one hand, and one or more third countries on the other, the rights and obligations arising shall not be affected by the provisions of the EC

---

[149] Case C–286/90 *Anklagemyndigheden* v. *Poulsen and Diva Navigation* [1992] ECR I–6019, para. 9.

[150] Case C–162/96 *Racke GmbH & Co.* v. *Hauptzollamt Mainz* [1998] ECR I–3655, para. 46.

[151] Case C–61/94 *Commission* v. *Germany*, n. 115 above, para. 30.

[152] Case C–239/03 *Commission* v. *France (Etang de Berre)* [2004] ECR I–9325, para. 26.

Treaty. The ECJ has clarified further the conditions for the application of Article 307 in various cases. In *T. Port*, it ruled:

> Thus, for a Community provision to be deprived of effect as a result of an international agreement, two conditions must be fulfilled: the agreement must have been concluded before the entry into force of the Treaty and the third country concerned must derive from it rights which it can require the Member State concerned to respect.[153]

The Community itself is not bound by such previous agreements. Article 307 contains only a duty on the part of the EC institutions not to impede the performance of the obligations of Member States which stem from such a prior agreement which confers rights on third countries.[154]

Further, to the extent that such agreements are not compatible with the EC Treaty, the ECJ has ruled that the Member State or States concerned are under an obligation to take all appropriate steps to eliminate the incompatibilities established. The case below illustrates that the fact that a Member State encounters difficulties in bringing its obligations to a third State in line with its obligations under EC law does not release the State from its obligation to adjust, and where necessary to denounce the conflicting agreement.[155]

Case C–84/98 **Commission v. Portugal**
[2000] ECR I–5215

[Note ToA renumbering: Art. 234 is now Art. 307]

Following its accession to the EC in 1986 Portugal was required to adjust its prior agreement with the Federal Republic of Yugoslavia (FRY), so as to respect Regulation 4055/86 on the freedom of maritime transport services between Member States and third countries. Portugal raised four arguments which it claimed prevented it from modifying its obligations, and the Court dismissed each in turn. The final argument is addressed in the extract below:

THE ECJ

39. In this case, the Portuguese Government has not succeeded in adjusting the contested agreement by recourse to diplomatic means within the time-limit laid down by Regulation No 4055/86.

40. It must be borne in mind that the Court has already held that, in such circumstances, in so far as denunciation of such an agreement is possible under international law, it is incumbent on the Member State concerned to denounce it (see, to that effect ... *Commission* v *Belgium* [1999] ...).

41. However, the Portuguese Government denies any failure to fulfil its obligations. ...

...

49. Finally, the Portuguese Government contends, in essence, that, with regard to pre-Community conventions concluded between a Member State and a third country, although

---

[153] Cases C–364–365/95 *T. Port GmbH & Co.* v. *Hauptzollamt Hamburg-Jonas* [1998] ECR I–1023, para. 61.
[154] Case 812/79 *Attorney General* v. *Juan C. Burgoa* [1980] ECR 2787, para. 9.
[155] See also Case C–170/98 *Commission* v. *Belgium* [1999] ECR I–5493; Case C–62/98 *Commission* v. *Portugal* [2000] ECR I–5171; Case C–84/98 *Commission* v. *Portugal* [2000] ECR I–5215.

Article 234 of the Treaty imposes the obligation to take all appropriate steps to eliminate any incompatibility between a rule of the convention and a Community rule, that provision is not indifferent to the legal consequences and political costs flowing from that obligation. Cases where a convention must be denounced under Article 234 of the Treaty arise only exceptionally and in extreme circumstances. Such denunciation would involve a disproportionate disregard of the interests linked to its foreign policy as compared with the Community interest. Moreover, the Commission should have referred to that provision in the statement of the reasons for a request for a pre-Community convention to be adjusted or denounced....

[*The ECJ went on to conclude that it was not impossible, in the case at hand, for Portugal to respect the rights of the FRY since the agreement itself enabled the parties to denounce it.*]

58. Furthermore, although, in the context of Article 234 of the Treaty, the Member States have a choice as to the appropriate steps to be taken, they are nevertheless under an obligation to eliminate any incompatibilities existing between a pre-Community convention and the EC Treaty. If a Member State encounters difficulties which make adjustment of an agreement impossible, an obligation to denounce that agreement cannot therefore be excluded.

59. As regards the argument that such denunciation would involve a disproportionate disregard of foreign-policy interests of the Portuguese Republic as compared with the Community interest, it must be pointed out that the balance between the foreign-policy interests of a Member State and the Community interest is already incorporated in Article 234 of the Treaty, in that it allows a Member State not to apply a Community provision in order to respect the rights of third countries deriving from a prior agreement and to perform its obligations thereunder. That article also allows them to choose the appropriate means of rendering the agreement concerned compatible with Community law.

. . . .

61. In those circumstances, it must be held that, by failing either to denounce or adjust the contested agreement so as to provide for fair, free and non-discriminatory access by all Community nationals to the cargo-shares due to the Portuguese Republic, as provided for in Council Regulation (EEC) No 4055/86, the Portuguese Republic has failed to fulfil its obligations under Articles 3 and 4(1) of that regulation.

In case of the GATT 1947, the ECJ ruled in the *International Fruit Company* case that the Community was bound by its provisions, notwithstanding the fact that it was not a party to it. The Court declared that the EC had assumed the functions inherent in the tariff and trade policy in their entirety on the expiry of the transitional period, and since this was an area governed by the GATT, the provisions of that agreement bound the Community.[156]

8. THE LEGAL EFFECT OF INTERNATIONAL AGREEMENTS IN THE EC LEGAL ORDER

One of the major legal topics within EC external relations has been the question of what effect international agreements have within the EC legal order. We have seen above that international agreements entered into by the EC have been held to be an integral part of the EC legal order,[157] and are binding upon the Community in accordance with Article 300(7). And we

---

[156] Cases 21–24/72 *International Fruit Company NV* v. *Produktschap voor Groenten en Fruit* [1972] ECR 1219, paras. 14–18.
[157] See n. 143 above.

shall see in Chapter 8 that in the case of most forms of binding EC law, the Court has held that they are in principle capable of having direct effect.

When it comes to international agreements, the question whether they can have direct effect concerns the capacity for such agreements to be directly invoked and enforced not only within the legal orders and before the courts of the Member States, but also within the EC legal order and before the ECJ. Arguments may be made both for and against the direct effect of international agreements. On the one hand, as treaties concluded with other States or international organizations, they can be viewed as traditional international agreements binding only the States or organizations which signed them, and having no specific effect on individuals and no automatic 'self-executing' quality. On the other hand, as agreements entered into by the Community, they can be viewed as sharing some of the key characteristics of EC law, and in particular could be capable of direct effect and enforcement by individuals whenever sufficiently precise and unconditional. Opting broadly for the approach which would integrate agreements made by the Community into the law of the Member States, the Court held that international agreements can, *under certain circumstances*, be directly effective.

We shall see, however, that in the field of international agreements a range of more political considerations comes into play, and the question whether or not the provisions of a particular agreement have direct effect is not determined solely by reference to the legal criteria first developed in *Van Gend en Loos*.

The issue which dominated this area of law for many years and has generated a vast academic literature, namely whether the provisions of the General Agreement on Trade and Tariffs (GATT) 1947 and the successor World Trade Organization (WTO) agreements can have direct effect, was first raised several decades ago.

Cases 21–24/72 **International Fruit Company v. Produktschap voor Groenten en Fruit** [1972] ECR 1219

A Dutch court made a preliminary reference to the ECJ, asking whether it had jurisdiction to rule on the validity of Community regulations in relation to a provision of international law and if so whether the regulations in question were contrary to the GATT.

THE ECJ

7. Before the incompatibility of a Community measure with a provision of international law can affect the validity of that measure, the Community must first of all be bound by that provision.

8. Before invalidity can be relied upon before a national court, that provision of international law must also be capable of conferring rights on citizens of the Community which they can invoke before the courts. . . .

18. It therefore appears that, in so far as under the EEC Treaty the Community has assumed the powers previously exercised by Member States in the area governed by the General Agreement, the provisions of that agreement have the effect of binding the Community.

19. It is also necessary to examine whether the provisions of the General Agreement confer rights on citizens of the Community on which they can rely before the courts in contesting the validity of a Community measure.

20. For this purpose, the spirit, the general scheme and the terms of the General Agreement must be considered.

The Court concluded from various aspects of the GATT, including the 'great flexibility of its provisions', the possibilities of derogation, and the power of unilateral withdrawal from its obligations, that it was 'not capable of conferring on citizens of the Community rights which they can invoke before the courts'. In other words, in terms of the criteria for direct effect laid down in earlier cases, the provisions of GATT were insufficiently precise and unconditional in the sense that they permitted the obligations contained therein to be modified, and they allowed for too great a degree of flexibility. The ECJ was unwilling to accord direct effect to international obligations of this nature, no doubt also because they were normally invoked to challenge the legality of EC legislation.[158]

In the later *Polydor* case, the Court was confronted with a provision of a free trade agreement between the Community and Portugal before Portugal had joined the Community.[159] Here the ECJ ruled that a provision of the trade agreement on free movement of goods, although it was worded identically to a provision of the then EEC Treaty (now Article 28), was not to be interpreted in the same way and should not be given direct effect, since the agreement with Portugal did not have the same aim or purpose as the EEC Treaty of establishing a single market.

In *Kupferberg*,[160] however, the ECJ ruled that a different provision of the Portuguese free trade agreement did have direct effect, since the provision was unconditional, sufficiently precise, and its direct application was within the *purpose* of the agreement. It is notable that, unlike in the GATT cases, the effect of declaring the trade agreement in *Kupferberg* to be directly effective was to extend the scope of Community rules rather than to challenge or invalidate them. Similarly, the ECJ has held that provisions of the earlier Lomé Convention governing relations between the EC and the African, Caribbean, and Pacific States were directly effective, where it was national rather than EC legislation which was being challenged for incompatibility with the Convention.[161]

It should be noted that in paragraph 8 of the *International Fruit* judgment (above), the Court appeared to equate direct effect with the possibility of review of legality, and to rule out the latter unless the former were present. However, in the later *Nakajima* case, the Court distinguished between the 'direct effect' of the provisions of an international trade agreement on the one hand, and the possibility of invoking those provisions before the ECJ to claim that EC legislation was incompatible with them on the other.[162] However, in *Germany* v. *Commission*, the ECJ made clear that a GATT provision could be invoked for the purposes of alleging the incompatibility of an EC measure in two circumstances only: (1) where the Community *intended* to implement that particular obligation, or (2) where the Community measure being challenged expressly referred to the particular GATT provision.[163]

---

[158] This was confirmed in various cases after *Kupferberg* including Case 9/73 *Schluter* v. *Hauptzollamt Lörrach* [1973] ECR 1135; Case C–469/93 *Amministrazione delle Finanze dello Stato* v. *Chiquita Italia* [1995] ECR I–4533.

[159] Case 270/80 *Polydor Ltd. and RSO Records Inc.* v. *Harlequin Record Shops Ltd. and Simons Records Ltd.* [1982] ECR 329.

[160] Case 104/81 *Hauptzollamt Mainz* v. *C.A. Kupferberg & Cie KG* [1982] ECR 3641; G. Bebr, 'Agreements Concluded by the Community and their Possible Direct Effect: From International Fruit Company to Kupferberg' (1983) 20 *CMLRev.* 35.

[161] See Case C–469/93 *Chiquita*, n. 158 above.

[162] Case C–69/89 *Nakajima* v. *Council* [1991] ECR I–2069, paras. 28–29. For this purpose, according to the Court, the provisions need only be binding on the Community. However, in the case in question the ECJ ruled that the Community anti-dumping rules in issue did not conflict with the Anti-Dumping Code adopted under the GATT. See also Case 70/87 *Fediol* v. *Commission* [1989] ECR 1781, and compare Case C–76/00 P *Petrotub SA and Republica SA* v. *Council* [2003] ECR I–79.

[163] Case C–280/93 *Germany* v. *Commission* [1994] ECR I–4873, and see Case C–76/00 P *Petrotub*, n. 162 above, in which a Council reg. was annulled for incompatibility with the GATT/WTO anti-dumping code.

Nonetheless, despite this restrictive approach, the ECJ in other cases has applied the obligation of harmonious interpretation—i.e. the principle that EC law should be interpreted in the light of international law and of binding international agreements,[164] to provisions of GATT and other WTO agreements such as that on Trade-Related Intellectual Property Rights (TRIPs).[165] This has the consequence of enhancing their effectiveness in certain circumstances, albeit not normally when they are being invoked to challenge EC measures.

Following the establishment of the WTO and the adoption of the new GATT in 1994, it was argued that in view of the changed provisions and the more effective means of dispute settlement and enforcement under the new system, the premises on which the GATT 1947 had been held to lack direct effect no longer applied.[166] Having avoided addressing the question of the legal effect and enforceability of the WTO agreements in a series of cases before the ECJ and the CFI, the ECJ finally confronted it directly.

Case C–149/96 **Portugal v. Council**
[1999] ECR I–8395

Portugal brought an action for annulment of a 1996 Council Decision, arguing *inter alia* that the Decision was in breach of the WTO rules, including provisions of GATT 1994. Portugal argued that the case did not raise the problem of direct effect, but rather 'the circumstances in which a Member State may rely on the WTO agreements before the Court for the purpose of reviewing the legality of a Council measure'. The ECJ began by indicating that it was only where an international agreement did not itself settle the question of the effects which its provisions would have within the legal orders of the contracting parties that it would fall to be decided by the courts.

THE ECJ

36. While it is true that the WTO agreements, as the Portuguese Government observes, differ significantly from the provisions of GATT 1947, in particular by reason of the strengthening of the system of safeguards and the mechanism for resolving disputes, the system resulting from those agreements nevertheless accords considerable importance to negotiation between the parties.

[*The ECJ examined the dispute-settlement rules of the WTO, and noted that although they provided for withdrawal of any measures found to be incompatible with WTO rules, they also allowed for compensation to be paid instead as a temporary measure where withdrawal would be impracticable. And if a member of the WTO failed to comply with a recommendation made by the dispute resolution body, that member would be requested to enter negotiations with the other party to the dispute 'with a view to finding mutually acceptable compensation'. The Court continued:*]

40. Consequently, to require the judicial organs to refrain from applying the rules of domestic law which are inconsistent with the WTO agreements would have the consequence of

---

[164] Case C–61/94 *Commission* v. *Germany*, n. 115 above, para. 52; Case C–341/95 *Safety Hi-Tech* v. *S & T Srl* [1998] ECR I–4355, para. 20; Case C–286/90 *Poulsen*, n. 149 above, para. 9.

[165] Case C–53/96 *Hermès International* v. *FHT Marketing Choice* [1998] ECR I–3603; Cases C–300 and 392/98 *Dior* v. *Tuk Consultancy* [2000] ECR I–11307; Case C–245/02 *Anheuser-Busch Inc.* v. *Budjovický Budvar, národní podnik* [2003] ECR I–10989, paras. 54–57.

[166] See, e.g., Case T–228/95 R *S. Lehrfreund Ltd.* v. *Council and Commission* [1996] ECR II–111, para. 28, and many cases which followed. There is also a vast and specialized academic literature on this subject.

depriving the legislative or executive organs of the contracting parties of the possibility afforded by Article 22 of that memorandum of entering into negotiated arrangements even on a temporary basis.

41. It follows that the WTO agreements, interpreted in the light of their subject-matter and purpose, do not determine the appropriate legal means of ensuring that they are applied in good faith in the legal order of the contracting parties.

42. As regards, more particularly, the application of the WTO agreements in the Community legal order, it must be noted that, according to its preamble, the agreement establishing the WTO, including the annexes, is still founded, like GATT 1947, on the principle of negotiations with a view to 'entering into reciprocal and mutually advantageous arrangements and is thus distinguished, from the viewpoint of the Community, from the agreements concluded between the Community and non-member countries which introduce a certain asymmetry of obligations, or create special relations of integration with the Community, such as the agreement which the Court was required to interpret in *Kupferberg*.

43. It is common ground, moreover, that some of the contracting parties, which are among the most important commercial partners of the Community, have concluded from the subject-matter and purpose of the WTO agreements that they are not among the rules applicable by their judicial organs when reviewing the legality of their rules of domestic law.

44. Admittedly, the fact that the courts of one of the parties consider that some of the provisions of the agreement concluded by the Community are of direct application whereas the courts of the other party do not recognise such direct application is not in itself such as to constitute a lack of reciprocity in the implementation of the agreement (*Kupferberg*, paragraph 18).

45. However, the lack of reciprocity in that regard on the part of the Community's trading partners, in relation to the WTO agreements which are based on 'reciprocal and mutually advantageous arrangements and which must *ipso facto* be distinguished from agreements concluded by the Community, referred to in paragraph 42 of the present judgment, may lead to disuniform application of the WTO rules.

46. To accept that the role of ensuring that those rules comply with Community law devolves directly on the Community judicature would deprive the legislative or executive organs of the Community of the scope for manoeuvre enjoyed by their counterparts in the Community's trading partners.

47. It follows from all those considerations that, having regard to their nature and structure, the WTO agreements are not in principle among the rules in the light of which the Court is to review the legality of measures adopted by the Community institutions.

The ECJ then ruled that the neither of the two conditions established in the *Nakajima* and *Germany* cases[167] was fulfilled, and so it could not review the legality of the Council Decision in the light of the WTO rules. A number of factors were thus cited by the ECJ as arguments against the direct judicial enforceability of the WTO agreements.

First, the Agreements themselves do not specify precisely what their own methods of enforcement are to be, given that compensation is permitted in certain circumstances as an alternative to direct enforcement, and that there is scope for negotiation over the recommendations of the WTO dispute-settlement bodies.

Secondly, the ECJ took the view that the WTO was still founded on the principle of mutually advantageous negotiations, rather than on clearly and precisely binding legal commitments of the kind to be found in other international agreements entered by the Community. Such other agreements, according to the Court, include those involving an 'asymmetry of

---

[167] See nn. 162 and 163.

obligations', where a guarantee of clear legal enforcement by the EC is given regardless of the lack of direct reciprocity in the relationship with the other party—e.g., the previous Lomé agreements with the ACP States, as well as those involving special relationships of integration with the Community, such as the Portugal free trade agreement in *Kupferberg* or the Europe Association agreements.[168] In other words, lack of reciprocity in obligations and commitments under an international agreement has not in itself been sufficient reason for the ECJ to deny the direct applicability of such an agreement. However, the Court was unwilling to accord such legal effect within the EC legal order to the WTO agreements, given the particular kind of lack of reciprocity in *enforcement* which this would involve—i.e. the Community's Courts giving effect to the obligations contained in these broad-ranging multilateral trade agreements while the other trading partners could enjoy the full 'scope for manoeuvre' expressly permitted under them. The ECJ also commented that the lack of reciprocity in terms of willingness to recognize the direct applicability of the WTO agreements could lead to 'disuniform application of WTO rules'.

The Court's judgment generated another avalanche of academic commentary, much of which conceded that while the legal reasoning was less than convincing, the political motivation for the ruling is relatively obvious.[169] For some, this motivation is regrettable,[170] for others it is entirely pragmatic and even laudable, given growing criticisms of the WTO system for privileging trade liberalization over other social and environmental values.[171]

Since the *Portugal* ruling, the ECJ and CFI have in many cases resisted attempts to narrow the potential scope of the judgment. The ECJ ruled out any remaining uncertainty over the direct effect of provisions of the GATT,[172] and confirmed the application of the *Portugal* ruling in this respect to other WTO agreements such as those on Trade Related Intellectual Property Rights (TRIPS)[173] and on Technical Barriers to Trade (TBT).[174] The CFI also rejected a series of creative legal arguments including attempts to rely on Article 307 EC,[175] or on the principle of *pacta sunt servanda*,[176] and to invoke provisions of the WTO agreements in the context of actions for damages.[177] A number of unsuccessful attempts was also made to invoke the

---

[168] N. 70 above.

[169] For one example see S. Peers, 'Fundamental Right or Political Whim? WTO Law and the ECJ', in G. de Búrca and J. Scott (eds.), *The EU and the WTO: Legal and Constitutional Issues* (Hart, 2001), 111, 120–122.

[170] See, e.g., G. Zonnekeyn, 'The Status of WTO Law in the Community Legal Order: Some Comments in the Light of the Portuguese Textiles Case' (2000) 25 *ELRev*. 293; S. Griller, 'Judicial Enforceability of WTO Law in the EU' (2000) 3 *JIEL* 441. A longstanding advocate of the justiciability and direct effect of the GATT/WTO Agreements has been E.-U. Petersmann, 'The Dispute Settlement System of the World Trade Organization and the Evolution of the GATT Dispute Settlement System since 1948' (1994) 31 *CMLRev*. 1157 and 'Proposals for a New Constitution for the European Union: Building Blocks for a Constitutional Theory and Constitutional Law of the EU' (1995) 32 *CMLRev*. 1123.

[171] A. Rosas (2000) 37 *CMLRev*. 797.

[172] Case C–307/99 *OGT* v. *Hauptzollamt Hamburg-St. Annen* [2001] ECR I–3159.

[173] Cases C–300 and 392/98 *Dior*, n. 165 above; Case C–89/99 *Schieving-Nijstad* v. *Groeneveld* [2001] ECR I–5851, paras. 51–55; Case C–245/02 *Anheuser-Busch*, n. 165 above, paras. 54–57; Case T–279/03 *Galileo International Technology LLC* v. *Commission* [2006] ECR II-1291.

[174] Cases C–27 and 122/00 *The Queen* v. *Secretary of State for the Environment, Transport and the Regions, ex p. Omega Air Ltd and others* [2002] ECR I–2569.

[175] Case T–2/99 *T-Port GmbH* v. *Council* [2001] ECR II–2093; Case T–3/99 *Bananatrading GmbH* v. *Council* [2001] ECR II–2093. For pre-*Portugal* v. *Council* cases attempting to use Art. 307 EC in the context of the GATT see Cases C–364 and 365/95 *T-Port*, n. 153 above, discussed in sect. 7(c) above.

[176] Case T–383/00 *Beamglow Ltd*. v. *Parliament, Council and Commission* [2005] ECR II–5459.

[177] Case T–18/99 *Cordis Obst und Gemüse Großhandel* v. *Commission* [2001] ECR II–913; Case T–30/99 *Bocchi Food Trade International* v. *Commission* [2001] ECR II–943; Case T-52/99 *T. Port* v. *Commission* [2001] ECR II–981.

Nakajima and *Germany* doctrine,[178] in order to rely on the effects of the ruling of a dispute settlement panel within the WTO system,[179] specifically by arguing that the EC intended to implement or execute a particular WTO obligation following a dispute-settlement process.[180] A similar attempt was rejected by the ECJ in *Biret*, but significantly the Court (unlike the CFI from which the appeal was brought) left open the possibility that a provision of the WTO agreements, including as in this case the Agreement on Sanitary and Phytosanitary Standards (SPS), might be capable of being invoked to challenge the legality of an EC measure in the context of an action for damages, following the expiry of the reasonable period for compliance with its ruling set by a WTO dispute-settlement body.[181]

In contrast to its reluctance to permit the general judicial enforceability of the WTO agreements, the ECJ has been more willing to recognize the enforceability of other international agreements, even broad multilateral agreements, which do not involve special relations of integration with the EU. In the *Biotechnology* case, the ECJ declined to rule on whether the Rio Convention on Biological Diversity had created directly effective individual rights in the narrow sense, but confirmed its broader invocability by declaring that, unlike the WTO Agreements, the Biodiversity Convention was 'not strictly based on reciprocal and mutually advantageous arrangements' and that courts could therefore review the Community's compliance with the obligations contained therein.[182] Moreover in the case of a regional environmental agreement, the ECJ ruled that the Protocol for the protection of the Mediterranean sea against pollution from land-based sources, and a later amended Protocol which had been signed by the EC and approximately 21 other States in the region, was directly effective.[183]

The ECJ in *Racke* ruled that provisions of the EEC–Yugoslavia co-operation agreement of 1980 were directly effective, and could be invoked along with provisions of customary international law to challenge the legality of an EC regulation.[184] Similarly, in a series of cases involving various Europe Association Agreements, the ECJ declared their provisions on freedom of establishment and the free movement of workers to be directly effective.[185] These judgments follow the pattern of similar rulings in which the Court has recognized the direct effect of various provisions of association or co-operation agreements with third countries,[186] as well as the provisions of secondary decisions adopted by association councils or bodies set up under those agreements.[187] Agreements of this sort fall within the category of those setting

---

[178] See nn. 162 and 163. The Commission recently argued that the *Nakajima* exception should be abolished, or treated as an aspect of the obligation of harmonious interpretation with international law, but the Advocate General rejected the argument and the ECJ did not address it: Case C–313/04 *Franz Egenberger GmbH Mölkerei und Trockenwerk* v. *Bundesamt für Landwirtschaft und Ernährung* [2006] ECR I–6331.

[179] Case T–18/99 *Cordis*, n. 177 above; Case T–30/99 *Bocchi*, n. 177 above; Case T–52/99 *T. Port*, n. 177 above.

[180] Case T–19/01 *Chiquita Brands International, Inc.* v. *Commission of the European Communities* [2005] ECR II–315, paras. 83–171.

[181] Case C–94/02 P *Etablissements Biret et Cie SA* v. *Council* [2003] ECR I–10565, paras. 54–68. For commentary see M. Mendez, 'The Impact of WTO Rulings in the Community Legal Order' (2004) 29 *ELRev.* 517; A. Thies, (2004) 41 *CMLRev.* 1661.

[182] Case C–377/98 *Netherlands* v. *Council* [2001] ECR I–7079.

[183] Case C–213/03 *Syndicat professionnel coordination des pêcheurs de l'étang de Berre et de la region* v. *EDF* [2004] ECR I–7357, paras. 31–47.

[184] Case C–162/96 *Racke*, n. 150 above.

[185] N. 70 above.

[186] For a small sample see Case C–18/90 *Onem* v. *Kziber* [1991] ECR I–199; Case C–179/98 *Belgium* v. *Mesbah* [1999] ECR I–7955 on the EEC–Morocco Co-operation Agreement; Case C–103/94 *Krid* v. *WAVTS* [1995] ECR I–719; Case C–113/97 *Babahenini* v. *Belgium* [1998] ECR I–813 on the EEC–Algeria Co-operation Agreement; Case C–37/98 *Savas* [2000] ECR I–2927 on the EC–Turkey Association Agreement.

[187] There are dozens of cases on these issues. For a small selection see Case 12/86 *Demirel* v. *Stadt Schwäbisch Gmünd* [1987] ECR 3719; Case C–192/89 *Sevince* [1990] ECR I–3461; Case C–237/91 *Kus* [1992] ECR I–6781;

up 'special relations of integration' with the EC of the kind referred to by the ECJ in paragraph 42 of its ruling in *Portugal* v. *Council.*

9. THE ROLE OF THE ECJ IN EU INTERNATIONAL RELATIONS

It is clear from the above discussion of the ECJ's approach to the effect of international agreements in the EC legal order, as well as its approach to the nature and breadth of EC competence and the scope of the CCP in the early years, that the Court has played an active and at times activist role in EU external relations. Below, a broader overview of the Court's role in the important and expanding field of international relations will be provided.

(a) PRE-EMPTIVE JURISDICTION: THE ADVISORY OPINION PROCEDURE OF ARTICLE 300(6)

The most distinctive source of ECJ jurisdiction in the field of international relations is the advisory opinion procedure provided for in Article 300(6) EC.[188]

The European Parliament, the Council, the Commission or a Member State may obtain the opinion of the Court of Justice as to whether an agreement envisaged is compatible with the provisions of this Treaty. Where the opinion of the Court of Justice is adverse, the agreement may enter into force only in accordance with Article 48 of the Treaty on the European Union.

The fact that a Treaty amendment is required in the case of a negative opinion indicates clearly that the Court's opinions are binding on the institutions. In its first Opinion, the ECJ outlined the rationale for this advisory procedure, and indicated that the scope of the questions which can form the subject of the request is very broad, and includes questions concerning the competence of the EC to enter the agreement:

Opinion 1/75 (Understanding on a Local Cost Standard)
[1975] ECR 1355

[Note ToA renumbering: Art. 228 is now Art. 300]

THE ECJ

The compatibility of an agreement with the provisions of the Treaty must be assessed in the light of all the rules of the Treaty, that is to say, both those rules which determine the extent of the powers of the institutions of the Community and the substantive rules.

and in more recent years Cases C–317 and 369/01 *Abatay* [2003] ECR I–12301, paras. 58–59; Case C–373/02 *Öztürk* [2004] ECR I–3605, paras. 37–68; Case C–136/03 *Dörr* [2005] ECR I–4759, paras. 58–69; Case C–230/03 *Sedef* [2006] ECR I–157, para. 33.

[188] And Arts. 103–105 of the European Atomic Energy Community Treaty. While there is no formal Opinion provided by an Advocate General, they are nevertheless heard in closed session. For instance, in the proceedings on *Opinion 1/03*, n. 41 above, 8 Advocates General were heard.

> It is the purpose of the second subparagraph of Article 228 (1) to forestall complications which would result from legal disputes concerning the compatibility with the Treaty of international agreements binding upon the Community. In fact, a possible decision of the Court to the effect that such an agreement is, either by reason of its content or of the procedure adopted for its conclusion, incompatible with the provisions of the Treaty could not fail to provoke, not only in a Community context, but also in that of international relations, serious difficulties and might give rise to adverse consequences for all interested parties, including third countries.
>
> For the purpose of avoiding such complications the Treaty had recourse to the exceptional procedure of a prior reference to the Court of Justice for the purpose of elucidating, before the conclusion of the agreement, whether the latter is compatible with the Treaty. This procedure must therefore be open for all questions capable of submission for judicial consideration, either by the Court of Justice or possibly by national courts, in so far as such questions give rise to doubt either as to the substantive or formal validity of the agreement with regard to the Treaty.

There is no time limit for the submission of a request under Article 300(6). Moreover, as we have seen earlier in this chapter, the term 'agreement' has been interpreted broadly so as to include 'any undertaking entered into by entities subject to international law which has binding force, whatever its legal designation'.[189] On the other hand, the ECJ indicated in its *Opinion 2/94* on accession to the ECHR that the purpose of the agreement envisaged must be known before the Court is in a position to give an opinion.[190] The Court ruled that it was not necessary that the Council should already have adopted a decision to open negotiations, but the Court would need sufficient information concerning the specific arrangements envisaged, such as the proposed mechanism for judicial control under the ECHR. Since no such information was provided for the purpose of *Opinion 2/94*, the Court ruled that it could not give its opinion on that point.

Once an agreement is signed, the Court is precluded from continuing with an Article 300(6) procedure, although it remains an 'envisaged agreement' until 'the Community's consent to be bound by the agreement is finally expressed' through its conclusion by the Council.[191] In *Opinion 3/94*, however, the ECJ did not give an opinion even though the agreement had not yet been concluded, because the Court decided that since the preventive function of the procedure could no longer be achieved, there was no point in responding, and the party which had requested an opinion would instead have to seek annulment of the decision to conclude the agreement.[192]

Finally, the ECJ has ruled that once the legal basis on which the Community may act has been established, it is beyond the Court's jurisdiction to engage in a more precise delineation of competence, and in particular the Article 300(6) procedure is not intended to resolve the difficulties associated with the implementation of an envisaged agreement where competence is shared.[193]

---

[189] *Opinion 1/75*, n. 57 above.

[190] *Opinion 2/94*, n. 28 above.

[191] Eeckhout, n. 58 above, 230.

[192] *Opinion 3/94 (Banana Framework Agreement)* [1995] ECR I–4577.

[193] *Opinion 2/00*, n. 17 above, paras. 17–18.

(b) JURISDICTION OF THE ECJ OVER INTERNATIONAL AGREEMENTS UNDER OTHER EC TREATY PROCEDURES

International agreements entered into by the EC may form the subject-matter of a reference for a preliminary ruling on a point of interpretation or validity under Article 234 EC. In the first example of such a reference, the ECJ ruled in *Haegeman* that the Community's Association Agreement with Greece was, in so far as the Community was concerned, an act of the institutions within the meaning of Article 234 EC.[194] Therefore, the provisions of the Agreement formed an integral part of Community law and the Court had jurisdiction to give preliminary rulings on their interpretation. In addition to agreements concluded by the Community the Court has asserted its jurisdiction to interpret other acts such as decisions of bodies (like the Turkey–EC Association Council) set up under an agreement[195] as well as non-binding recommendations made under an international agreement.[196]

Unsurprisingly, international agreements and other provisions of international law have been held to be amongst the rules of law to be taken into account in assessing the validity of Community measures. This is clear from the *International Fruit Company* case, which has been discussed above in relation to the direct effect of international agreements, but which is an important case on EC external relations more generally.[197] Effectively, by treating international agreements in principle in the same way as internal EC acts, the Court was able to broaden its jurisdiction and permit itself to hear actions for annulment and actions for damages brought on the basis of international agreements. Further, the Court has jurisdiction to give a ruling in the event that Member States fail to fulfil their obligations under an international agreement.[198]

The grounds for annulment of an agreement alleged to violate the Treaty are the same as for internal acts, in accordance with Article 230 EC: i.e. lack of competence, infringement of an essential procedural requirement, infringement of the Treaty or of any rule of law relating to its application, or misuse of powers. Thus the alleged infringement may arise from the procedure followed for the conclusion of an international agreement,[199] or in the substantive provisions of the agreement,[200] or the agreement may be *ultra vires* in the sense that the Community lacked competence to conclude it.[201]

Since international agreements concluded by the Community are binding upon it, a violation of their provisions may, in principle, form the basis for an action in damages under Article 288 EC. Thus far, however, no such action has been successful. Most of the cases brought have been based on the alleged violation of WTO law, and the ECJ has consistently held that the provisions of the WTO agreements do not form part of the rules by which the ECJ and CFI review the legality of acts adopted by the Community institutions, they do not enable individuals to rely on their provisions before the courts, and their infringement will not give rise to non-contractual liability on the Community's part.[202]

---

[194] Case 181/73 *Haegeman*, n. 143 above, paras. 4–6.
[195] Case C–192/89 *Sevince*, n. 187 above.
[196] Case C–188/91 *Deutsche Shell* [1993] ECR I–363.
[197] Koutrakos, n. 56 above, 193.
[198] *Opinion 1/91*, n. 143 above, para. 38.
[199] See, e.g., Case C–327/91 *France* v. *Commission*, n. 18 above.
[200] Case C–122/95 *Germany* v. *Council* [19989] ECR I–973.
[201] Cases C–317 and 318/04 *European Parliament* v. *Council (PNR)*, n. 8 above.
[202] See nn. 172–181.

Finally, as we shall see in Chapter 12, the Commission may initiate an infringement procedure under Article 226 (and other Member States may do so under Article 227) when it considers that one of the States has failed to respect the obligations contained in an international agreement of the Community This is true also with regard to the WTO agreements even though, as we saw in *Portugal* v. *Council*,[203] they are not among the rules which Member States may invoke to claim the illegality of the Community acts.

(c) THE ECJ AND MIXED AGREEMENTS

Although the Court's first ruling on the interpretation of international agreements in the *Haegeman* case concerned a mixed agreement, that fact seemed to play no part in the Court's assessment of its jurisdiction in that case.[204] The mixed nature of the agreement was invoked for the first time in *Demirel*, concerning the EC–Turkey Association Agreement:

> Since the agreement in question is an association agreement creating special, privileged links with a non-member country which must, at least to a certain extent, take part in the Community system, Article 238 must necessarily empower the Community to guarantee commitments towards non-member countries in all the fields covered by the Treaty. Since freedom of movement for workers is, by virtue of Article 48 et seq . of the EEC Treaty, one of the fields covered by that Treaty, it follows that commitments regarding freedom of movement fall within the powers conferred on the Community by Article 238. Thus the question whether the Court has jurisdiction to rule on the interpretation of a provision in a mixed agreement containing a commitment which only the Member States could enter into in the sphere of their own powers does not arise.[205]

While this passage seems to suggest that the Court's jurisdiction over mixed agreements covers all issues, with the exception of matters which fall within the exclusive competence of the Member States, it has been argued that in fact the judgment does not address the question of the ECJ's jurisdiction in cases where the relevant provisions of an international agreement have been concluded on the basis of the Member States' powers.[206]

An opportunity for clarification of this point arose in *Hermès*, in which a preliminary reference was made to the ECJ on a question concerning the interpretation of Article 50 of the TRIPS Agreement, concerning the power of judicial authorities to order provisional measures to prevent certain infringements of intellectual property rights.[207] One of the objections raised was that the dispute concerned the application of national trade mark law. The Court replied that it did indeed have jurisdiction, since:

> [W]here a provision can apply both to situations falling within the scope of national law and to situations falling within the scope of Community law, it is clearly in the Community interest that, in order to forestall future differences of interpretation, that provision should be interpreted

---

[203] Case C–268/94 *Portugal* v. *Council* [1996] ECR I–6177.

[204] P. Koutrakos, 'The Interpretation of Mixed Agreements under the Preliminary Reference Procedure' (2002) 7 *EFARev.* 25.

[205] Case 12/86 *Demirel*, n. 187 above.

[206] A. Dashwood, 'Preliminary Rulings on the Interpretation of Mixed Agreements', in D. O'Keeffe and A. Bavaso, *Liber Amicorum in Honour of Lord Slynn of Hadley* (Kluwer Law International, 2000), i, 171.

[207] Case C–53/96 *Hermès International*, n. 165 above.

uniformly, whatever the circumstances in which it is to apply … In the present case, as has been pointed out in paragraph 28 above, Article 50 of the TRIPS Agreement applies to Community trade marks as well as to national trade marks.

Since the provision applied also to Community trade marks, the Court ruled that it had jurisdiction to provide an interpretation of the Article.

Some of the questions which persisted after *Hermès* were addressed by the ECJ in its ruling in *Parfums Christian Dior*, in which Article 50 of the TRIPS Agreement was again at issue. Having repeated various aspects of the ruling in *Hermès* including the paragraph above, the ECJ went on to extend further the scope of its jurisdiction to rule on Article 50:

Cases C–300 and 392/98 **Parfums Christian Dior**
[2000] ECR I–11307

[Note ToA renumbering: Art. 177 is now Art. 234]

THE ECJ

36. In that regard, the Member States and the Community institutions have an obligation of close cooperation in fulfilling the commitments undertaken by them under joint competence when they concluded the WTO Agreement, including TRIPs (see, to that effect, Opinion 1/94 …).

37. Since Article 50 of TRIPs constitutes a procedural provision which should be applied in the same way in every situation falling within its scope and is capable of applying both to situations covered by national law and to situations covered by Community law, that obligation requires the judicial bodies of the Member States and the Community, for practical and legal reasons, to give it a uniform interpretation.

38. Only the Court of Justice acting in cooperation with the courts and tribunals of the Member States pursuant to Article 177 of the Treaty is in a position to ensure such uniform interpretation.

39. The jurisdiction of the Court of Justice to interpret Article 50 of TRIPs is thus not restricted solely to situations covered by trade-mark law.

This is a strong and broad assertion of the Court's jurisdiction with regard to the TRIPS Agreement, and the implications and shortcomings of the judgment have given rise to comment:

P. Koutrakos, EU International Relations Law[208]

[T]he judgment in *Dior*, as a whole, constitutes a significant advancement in the construction of the role of the Court of Justice in EC international relations. On the one hand, it appears to define the twin principles governing the status of the mixed agreements within the Community legal order, namely the jurisdiction of the Court of Justice over their interpretation and the duty of close cooperation imposed upon Community institutions and Member States

---

[208] (Hart, 2006), 201.

over their application. On the other hand, both these principles are constructed in very broad terms. Whilst not atypical in the case law on EC international relations, the absence of a clearer line of reasoning is regrettable. This is all the more so as the limits of the Court's jurisdiction are so ill-defined. Its general formulation in *Dior* is a case in point. In principle, the role of the Court appears to be confined to the definition of the obligations assumed by the Community. In practice, in the light of the Court's reluctance to allocate competences within the context of mixed agreements, it appears that only in areas clearly falling within the exclusive competence of the Member States would it be precluded from exercising its jurisdiction.

This broad jurisdiction of the Court was confirmed in two subsequent sets of infringement proceedings brought by the Commission against Member States, involving the Berne Convention for the Protection of Literary and Artistic Works[209] and the Convention for the protection of the Mediterranean sea respectively.[210] The Court ruled that mixed agreements had the same status within the EC legal order as purely Community agreements 'insofar as the provisions fall within the scope of Community competence', and it repeated that when they ensure compliance with commitments arising from an agreement entered into by the EC, the Member States are fulfilling an obligation in relation to the EC which has assumed responsibility for its performance.[211] In both cases, the ECJ found the subject-matter of the agreements to be largely governed by EC law, and it ruled that there was a clear Community interest in compliance by the Member States and the Community with the commitments entered into.

Thus, as Koutrakos notes above, the ECJ has construed its jurisdiction over mixed agreements very broadly, and it seems that only where a particular area falls clearly within the exclusive competence of the Member States under a mixed agreement will the Court decline to interpret or enforce it.

(d) THE ECJ AND THE CFSP

As we saw above, the CFSP was created to include all areas of foreign and security policy within its scope. The possibility of conflict with parallel parts of Community external competence was thus clear. Article 2 TEU arguably envisages this by listing amongst the EU's objectives:

> [T]o maintain in full the *acquis communautaire* and build on it with a view to considering to what extent the policies and forms of cooperation introduced by this Treaty may need to be revised with the aim of ensuring the effectiveness of the mechanisms and the institutions of the Community.

The key provision aimed at preventing the encroachment of the CFSP on Community law is Article 47 TEU which provides:

> Subject to [the provisions specifically aimed at amending the three existing Treaties, and the final provisions of the TEU], nothing in this Treaty shall affect the Treaties establishing the European Communities or the subsequent Treaties and Acts modifying or supplementing them.

---

[209] Case C–13/00 *Commission* v. *Ireland (Berne Convention)* [2002] ECR I–2943.
[210] Case C–239/03 *Commission* v. *France*, n. 152 above.
[211] *Ibid.*, paras. 25–26.

In contrast to the expansive jurisdiction which the ECJ has construed for itself within the Community Pillar, Article 46 TEU expressly excludes the CFSP from the jurisdiction of the Court. Some of the likely reasons for this jurisdictional exclusion are set out in the following extract:

E. Denza, The Intergovernmental Pillars of the European Union[212]

The first reason was that EPC, and the CFSP instruments are essentially short-term in character, and potentially both wide-ranging and sensitive. Unlike treaties, the texts agreed by the Member States are not designed to establish a permanent framework of mutual legal obligations between Contracting Parties but to condition a collective approach to a specific overseas crisis, a catastrophe, or a change of regime or to impose collective discipline on a particular multilateral negotiation. They are often overtaken by events, and in this case the practice is for the Member States to renegotiate or even to ignore them. . . .

The second reason concerned the nature and the record of the ECJ. The judges appointed to the Court have not generally come to their task from a background of public international law, and they have over the years elaborated doctrines—particularly in the sphere of the external relations of the European Communities—which lay much more emphasis on the integrationist purpose of the Treaties and less on presuming a minimum derogation from individual sovereign powers than a tribunal of international lawyers would have done. The UK was particularly sensitive to this fear that the ECJ might warm excessively to its task . . . [C]oncern remained that certain ECJ doctrines—emphasizing for example the exclusive nature of Community external powers to the detriment of pre-existing national powers—might find their way into the CFSP.

Despite the jurisdictional exclusion, however, the Court has derived a certain limited scope for judicial supervision from Articles 46 and Article 47 TEU.[213] In the *Airport Transit Visas* case the Court defined its role as being to ensure that acts which fall under the TEU do not encroach upon the powers conferred by the EC Treaty on the Community. The Court ruled that it had jurisdiction to review the content of a measure adopted outside the scope of the Community Pillar, in order to ascertain whether it affected the powers of the Community and to annul the measure if it appeared that it should have been based on a provision of the EC Treaty instead.[214] The ECJ effectively used this power in a subsequent case concerning the possible enforcement of EC environmental law through criminal penalties.[215]

There has however been sustained criticism of the lack of judicial control over the law adopted within the CFSP, in particular on account of the likely consequences for individuals.[216] In contrast to the scenario envisaged by Denza, above, an increasing number of CFSP and

---

[212] (Oxford University Press, 2002), 311–312.

[213] It has also been argued that since the provisions of the EU Treaty are a matter of legal obligation under international law, the Member States could, in theory, bring an action against one another before the International Court of Justice: see M.-G. Garbagnati Ketvel, 'The Jurisdiction of the European Court of Justice in Respect of the Common Foreign and Security Policy' (2006) 55 *ICLQ* 77.

[214] Case C–170/96 *Commission* v. *Council*, n. 94 above, paras. 16–17. Although the case concerned a measure adopted under the provisions of the Third rather than the Second Pillar of the TEU, there is no reason why the interpretation of Art. 47 TEU would not be equally applicable to the CFSP.

[215] Case C–176/03 *Commission* v. *Council* [2005] ECR I–7879.

[216] P. Eeckhout, 'Does Europe's Constitution Stop at the Water's Edge? Law and Policy in the EU's External Relations' (2005) *Walter van Gerven Lectures*, Leuven.

Third Pillar measures have a legislative or quasi-legislative character, and the present limitation of judicial review has been described as 'patently insufficient from the perspective of the rule of law'.[217] Perhaps in a partial response to such critiques, the ECJ has read its jurisdiction somewhat more broadly than the Treaty text suggests. As we shall see in Chapter 14, the ECJ ruled in the *Segi/Gestoras Pro-Amnistia* case that, despite the text of Article 35(1) EU which does not mention common positions among the acts which can form the object of a preliminary ruling, the right to make a reference to the Court of Justice for a preliminary ruling exists in respect of all measures adopted by the Council, whatever their nature or form, which are intended to have legal effects in relation to third parties.[218] In the cases in question, the contested common positions had been adopted on a dual legal basis, under both the Second and Third Pillars.

10. COHERENCE, CONSISTENCY, AND CO-OPERATION IN THE GOVERNANCE OF EU INTERNATIONAL RELATIONS

One of the key aims of the EU's foreign policy is to co-ordinate a variety of different external activities. As we have already noted, some overlap in competences is inevitable, given that the CFSP covers 'all areas of foreign and security policy'. While not the only or even the most important aspect of foreign policy, consistency is nonetheless a significant goal in the external relations of an entity like the EU which is a relative newcomer to the international scene and which still lacks a coherent and recognizable international identity. In order to establish and shape its international role more effectively, the EU needs to ensure co-ordination on a number of different levels. Below, we will consider some of the different dimensions of this task. Co-ordination needs to be pursued first, in the international representation of the EU, secondly, across the different activities and pillars of the EU, and, thirdly, between the Member States and the EU. Finally, we will consider the significance of co-ordination in the context of one important new area of EU foreign policy: the neighbourhood policy.

(a) INTERNATIONAL REPRESENTATION AND THE EU

In order to perform their tasks under the Treaties, the Community and the Union have developed extensive diplomatic relations with other subjects of international law. Almost all States have established diplomatic missions to the Communities (which have been renamed Representative Missions to the European Union), and the Communities maintain relations through Commission 'delegations' in more than 150 States and international organizations. They enjoy customary privileges and immunities under international law. Their task is to communicate the views and to represent the interests of the Communities as a whole. However, in formal terms they receive instructions from and report to the Commission alone.[219] As far as international organizations are concerned, Article 302 EC provides that it shall be for the Commission to ensure the maintenance of all appropriate relations with the

---

[217] *Ibid.*
[218] Case C–355/04 P *Segi and others* v. *Council*, 27 Feb. 2007; Case C–354/04 P *Gestoras Pro Amnistía and others* v. *Council*, 27 Feb. 2007.
[219] MacLeod, Hendry, and Hyett, n. 48 above, 216–219.

organs of the United Nations and its specialised agencies, and with 'all international organisations'.[220]

Several provisions of the TEU aim at organizing the representation of the interests of the Union internationally. Article 18 TEU provides that in matters which come within the scope of the Common Foreign and Security Policy, the Union is represented by the Presidency which is also responsible for the implementation of CFSP decisions. When necessary the Presidency expresses the position of the Union in international organizations and in international conferences. In its duties the Presidency is assisted by the Secretary-General of the Council (who also exercises the function of High Representative for the CFSP) and, if necessary, by the next Member State to hold the rotating Presidency. Moreover, the Council may, whenever it deems it necessary, appoint a special representative with a mandate in relation to particular policy issues. The Commission is to be fully associated with the tasks of the Presidency.

Article 19 TEU requires Member States to co-ordinate their action in international organizations and at international conferences as well as to uphold EU common positions in such fora. In international organizations and at international conferences where not all the Member States participate, those which do take part have particular duties: they are required to uphold EU common positions and to keep the others informed of any matter of common interest. The Member States which are also members of the UN Security Council are required to 'concert' their practice and to keep the other Member States fully informed. Those Member States which are permanent members of the Security Council must, in the execution of their functions, ensure the defence of the positions and the interests of the Union.

Article 20 provides for the co-operation of the diplomatic and consular missions of the Member States and the Commission delegations in third countries and international conferences, and their representations to international organizations, in ensuring that the common positions and joint actions adopted by the Council are complied with and implemented. This co-operation is to take form of an exchange of information, carrying out joint assessments and contributing to the implementation of the EU's common positions and joint actions.

(b) THE REQUIREMENT OF COHERENCE ACROSS PILLARS AND POLICIES

The longstanding division in foreign policy between high politics (e.g., matters of war and peace) and low politics (e.g., economic and other more 'technical' matters) is arguably legally reflected in the pillar structure of the EU. Within the context of globalization, however, the reality of political and economic interaction prevails over this kind of formal delineation. Perhaps it is this mismatch between the constitutional framework and the practical reality of EU international relations that has kept the theme of 'coherence' at the centre of EU attention, such that it has been described as 'the true recurrent theme of European foreign policy'.[221]

The need for coherence is expressed in Article 3 TEU which requires the Union to 'ensure the consistency of its external activities as a whole in the context of its external relations, security, economic and development policies'. It is the role of the 'single institutional framework' to ensure the desired consistency and coherence, and it is the Council and the Commission which have particular responsibility in this regard.

---

[220] To this end, two liaison offices have been established in Geneva and New York by the General Secretariat of the Council.

[221] P. Gauttier, 'Horizontal Coherence and the External Competences of the European Union' (2004) 10 *ELJ* 23, 25.

However, to summarize the argument of a recent commentator, this legal attempt to ensure greater coherence has had mixed results.[222] In his view, first, while it is arguable that the single institutional framework has allowed for some political progress to be made, the goal articulated by Article 3 TEU has had the effect of increasing the pressure placed by the Council on the Commission, without necessarily delivering significant results. Secondly, the 'common strategy', one of the new CFSP legal instruments which was to aim at greater overall unity and some kind of harmonization has rarely been used. Thirdly, the creation and reinforcement of the role of the Secretary General/High Representative has improved the effectiveness of the CFSP, but has also introduced a degree of competition with the Commissioners responsible for external relations. Fourthly, the power to conclude agreements which conferred on the Union an embryonic international legal personality was only a partial compromise, which 'does not shelter the Union from repeated risks of incoherence and inter-institutional and inter-pillar bickering'.[223]

(c) CO-ORDINATION BETWEEN THE MEMBER STATES AND THE EU: CO-OPERATION AND COMPLIANCE

The effectiveness of EU external activities also depends on whether the EU manages to ensure the co-operation and, where necessary, the compliance of its Member States. The duty of loyal or sincere co-operation has its written basis in Article 10 EC within the Community legal order, but its application has been said to go beyond the EC Treaty and to include the other pillars of the Union.[224]

The broader application of this obligation is reinforced by Article 11(2) of the TEU according to which the Member States are under a duty to support the Union's external and security policy 'actively and unreservedly in a spirit of loyalty and mutual solidarity'. Moreover, the Member States are to work together to enhance and develop their mutual political solidarity. They are required by the TEU to refrain from any action which is contrary to the interests of the Union or likely to impair its effectiveness as a cohesive force in international relations, and the Council is required to ensure compliance with these principles.

Initially, the ECJ used Article 10 EC together with other provisions to pressurize the institutions and the States to act in the defence of the Community's interests.[225] It ruled that Member States were required to facilitate the achievement of the Community tasks and to abstain from any measure which could jeopardize the attainment of the objectives of the Treaty. Further, the Court has emphasized that this 'duty of genuine cooperation is of general application and does not depend either on whether the Community competence is exclusive or on any right of the Member State to enter into obligations towards non-member countries'.[226] The Article 10 obligation to comply with Community law imposes a legal constraint on the Member States in their external action in both substantive and procedural terms. In substantive terms, Article 10 has been held to require Member States to facilitate the application of Community law and thus not to give effect to a bilateral agreement falling outside the field of application of the

---

[222] *Ibid.*, 35.

[223] *Ibid.*

[224] On its application to the Third Pillar see Case C–105/03 *Pupino*, n. 97 above, para. 42.

[225] See, e.g., Case 22/70 *ERTA*, n. 23 above; Cases 3, 4, and 6/76 *Kramer*, n. 24 above; *Opinion 2/91*, n. 39 above; *Opinion 1/94*, n. 35 above.

[226] See Case C–433/03 *Commission* v. *Germany*, n. 138 above, para. 64; Case C–266/03 *Commission* v. *Luxembourg*, n. 138 above, para. 58.

Treaty, where giving effect to it would impede the application of a right conferred by Community law, and would undermine the supremacy of EC law.[227]

The *Open Skies* cases provides a further example in which, although the agreements concluded by the Member States fell largely outside exclusive Community competence, the Member States' treaty-making powers in the field were said by the ECJ to be constrained by the need to comply with the EC Treaty rules on the right of establishment.[228]

In procedural terms, three noteworthy issues can be mentioned. *First*, in two recent cases concerning Luxembourg and Germany respectively, the Court ruled that not only are the Member States precluded from individual action when a Community agreement exists, but they are also subject to special duties of action and abstention, in particular where the Commission has submitted proposals to the Council which represent the point of departure for concerted Community action.[229]

Secondly, the need for consistency in the international representation of the Community became a particularly salient issue at the time of the Uruguay Round negotiations which led to the establishment of the WTO. The ECJ expressly referred to this in *Opinion 1/94*, in which the Commission claimed to be the sole spokesperson for the Community and the Member States. According to the argument of the Commission, this was necessary to secure the effective implementation of the WTO agreements. Despite acknowledging these concerns, the Court ruled that the allocation of competence could not be influenced by them,[230] but it also ruled that where the subject-matter of an agreement fell within shared EC Member State competence, it was essential to ensure close co-operation between them both in the process of negotiation and conclusion, and in the actual fulfilment of the commitments entered. That obligation to co-operate was said to flow from the requirement for unity in the international representation of the Community.[231]

Thirdly, as we have seen above, the Court held in the *Sellafield* case that Ireland was in breach of the duty of co-operation by instituting dispute settlement proceedings against the UK under UNCLOS, in relation to matters which fall within Community competence, without consulting the Commission.[232]

Finally, it has been argued that the unity of the international presence of the EU and its Member States which is achieved through this kind of co-operation may be greater than the unity resulting from the exclusive competence of the Community, since it operates also when the Member States are exercising their own competences.[233]

(d) THE MAKING OF AN INTEGRATED FOREIGN POLICY: EUROPEAN NEIGHBOURHOOD POLICY

We will conclude the discussion on forms of co-ordination of EU foreign policy with a brief discussion of the relatively recently developed European Neighbourhood Policy (ENP). The

---

[227] Case 235/87 *Matteucci* v. *Communaute francaise de Belgique et al.* [1988] ECR 5589, at 5611–5612.

[228] Case C–487/98 *Commission* v. *Denmark* [2002] ECR I–9519, paras. 122–139. See also M. Cremona, 'External Relations of the EU and the Member States: Competence, Mixed Agreements, International Responsibility and the Effects of International Law', FIDE Report, 2006.

[229] Case C–266/03 *Luxembourg*, n. 138 above, para. 60; Case C–433/03 *Germany*, n. 138 above, para. 66.

[230] *Opinion 1/94*, n. 35 above, para. 107.

[231] *Ibid.*, para. 108. The ECJ also referred to *Opinion 1/78*, n. 52 above, paras. 34–36, and *Opinion 2/91*, n. 39 above.

[232] Case C–459/03 *Commission* v. *Ireland (Sellafield)* [2006] ECR I–4635; see also the opinion of Poiares Maduro AG.

[233] M. Cremona, 'Defending the Community Interest: the Duties of Cooperation and Compliance', in Cremona and de Witte, n. 9 above.

ENP has been described as 'a particularly developed expression of a policy designed to meet the challenge of ensuring coherence between the three EU pillars'.[234]

The ENP is a new type of integrated foreign policy instrument directed towards the EU's neighbouring countries.[235] It emerged from the so-called 'Wider Europe' initiative to exploit the momentum arising from the 2004 'big bang' enlargement and the expansion of EU borders.[236] Its objective is the creation of a framework for increasing stability and security in the European neighbourhood. Given that it operates through a matrix of legislative and soft law measures, it constitutes a challenge not only to the pillar structure but also to the instruments which are now available to the EU:

> The ENP, as an alternative mechanism designed to offer coherent policy-making in the cross-pillar context of relations with the EU's strategically important neighbours, does not rely on new instruments but rather offers a way of integrating existing instruments via 'soft' frameworks (European Council and Council Conclusions and Commission policy papers among others).[237]

The neighbourhood policy attempts to be comprehensive in so far as it integrates related components from all three pillars of the Union's present structure. It provides for economic development and closer economic integration, co-operation in energy, transport, environment, health sectors, visas and border controls (from the First Pillar), political stability and regional conflict prevention, co-operation in the fight against the proliferation of WMD (the Second Pillar), and co-operation in the fight against organized crime and terrorism (the Third Pillar). Its overarching objectives include security-building as well as the promotion of human rights and the rule of law. It purports to offer a means for an enhanced and more focused policy approach on the part of the EU, drawing on the main instruments which are available to the EU and its Member States.[238]

The ENP operates through Action Plans, which are based on prior country reports prepared by the Commission with the contribution of the High Representative, and drafted in collaboration with the partner States. The Action Plans do not seek to replace the existing contractual links between the neighbouring countries and the EU, such as the Partnership and Co-operation Agreements, and the Euro-Mediterranean Agreements. Rather they identify key actions in a limited number of fields which need to be addressed as a particularly high priority, and they set up a clear time horizon for addressing these different priorities. They are approved by the respective Co-operation or Association Councils, but they do not have legally binding effect, remaining essentially a soft law instrument. It has been argued that,

> [T]he non-legally binding nature of the ENP, also an essential feature of the pre-accession strategy, prevents long competence discussions and 'pillar politics' from stalling and undermining policy development and coherence. While not legally binding, each AP makes it clear that the

---

[234] M. Cremona and C. Hillion, 'L'Union fait la force? Potential and Limitations of the European Neighbourhood Policy as an Integrated EU Foreign and Security Policy', EUI Working Paper 2006/39.

[235] Initially it included three regional groups of countries: the Eastern European countries, the Western Balkans, and the Southern Mediterranean. Later, Azerbaijan and Georgia were included in the process in addition to two, Egypt and Lebanon, with which talks are continuing.

[236] Wider Europe—Neighbourhood: A New Framework for Relations with our Eastern and Southern Neighbours, COM(2003)104; European Neighbourhood Policy—Strategy Paper, COM(2004)373.

[237] Cremona and Hillion, n. 234 above.

[238] COM(2004)373, 8.

deepening of the existing relationship is subject to the neighbour's fulfilment of the *commitments* set out in the Action Plan.[239]

Implementation of the Action Plans is monitored by the bodies set up under the Partnership and Co-operation Agreements or Association Agreements, and through sub-committees dealing with those sectors or issues.[240]

11. INTERNATIONAL RELATIONS IN THE CONSTITUTIONAL TREATY

The final issue we will examine is the provision made for international relations within the Treaty establishing a Constitution for Europe, many aspects of which seem likely to be contained in the future Reform Treaty. It was evident from early on in the constitutional process that the desire to enhance the external role of the EU was a significant part of the motivation for enacting a new constitutional settlement.[241] The concern with Europe's role in the world was ultimately strongly reflected in the text of the Constitutional Treaty adopted. Three principal dimensions of achieving the objective of stronger external unity, representation, and capacity for action can be identified.

The *first* is the strengthening of the EU's international identity, given the complex and fragmented nature of the EC's current international representation, and the resulting lack of clarity for third States and other actors. The Constitutional Treaty was to replace the existing Treaties. The new EU was to have legal personality[242] and to replace as a single actor on the international scene the current EC and EU, including by succeeding to all rights and obligations of the EC and the EU. The 'pillar structure' would formally disappear and all of the provisions relating to the external policies which are currently located in different parts of the Treaties were to be grouped in a single Title covering all aspects of the Union's external action, and subjected to a set of broad common objectives.[243] The Union would also have been required to respect these principles when developing and implementing different areas of its external action, including the external dimensions of internal policies.[244]

The institutional innovations in the CT aimed to match this integrated approach. The permanent President of the European Council, who would have been appointed for a period of up to five years, was to chair and drive forward the work of the European Council.[245] However, it was to be the job of the EU Minister for Foreign Affairs to conduct the Union's CFSP and to act also as Vice-President of the Commission, in order to ensure the consistency of the whole of the EU's external action.[246] This double-hatting was seen as one of the major achievements

---

[239] Cremona and Hillion, n. 234 above. A new type of legally binding relationship has however been envisaged, which would take the form of a 'European neighbourhood agreement' or 'enhanced agreement' to replace the existing agreements between the Union and the relevant neighbours. See C. Hillion, 'Mapping-Out the New Contractual Relations between the European Union and Its Neighbours: Learning from the EU–Ukraine "Enhanced Agreement"' (2007) 12 *EFARev.* 169.

[240] See Reg. 1638/2006 of the European Parliament and of the Council of 24 Oct. 2006 laying down general provisions establishing a European Neighbourhood and Partnership Instrument [2006] OJ L310/1.

[241] G. de Búrca, 'The EU Constitution: In Search of Europe's International Identity', Fourth Walter Van Gerven Lecture (Europa Law Publishing, 2005).

[242] Art. I–7, Treaty Establishing a Constitution of Europe [2004] OJ C310/01.

[243] See the objectives set out in Art. I–3(4) for the EU's 'relations with the wider world'.

[244] Art. III–293.

[245] Art. I–22.

[246] Art. I–28.

of the CT in the field of external relations, but it also raised concerns about the loyalty of the person, given that conflicts between the Council and the Commission are common. Moreover, it would have reinforced the dominance of the executive branch. The Foreign Minister was to preside over the Foreign Affairs Council and to be assisted by a European External Action Service. This would have been the first time that the Treaties provided for the Commission to ensure the external representation of the EU with the exception of the CFSP.

A *second* dimension of the CT's focus on external relations was the objective of strengthening the EU's capacity for unified action, and the effectiveness of its international action and instruments in all fields of foreign policy and external actions. In addition to the creation of the Foreign Minister and the inclusion of the CFSP under the general umbrella of external action, a number of other rather ambiguous changes were made to the CFSP. The current range of CFSP policy instruments (in particular common strategies, common positions, and joint actions) were to be replaced by one instrument, the European decision, which was to be a binding but 'non-legislative' act. This simplification would probably have been a superficial one, given the fact that in practice there would continue to be several different versions of the act entitled 'decision', each with different legal consequences.[247] Unanimity was to remain the rule under the CFSP, however, although qualified-majority voting was to be extended to cover cases where the Council acted on a proposal of the Foreign Minister following a special request from the European Council, except for European Security and Defence Policy (ESDP) matters. The provisions on ESDP were extended under the CT and the goal of a European common defence clearly articulated. Other noteworthy changes included an updating of the 'Petersberg Tasks',[248] a 'solidarity clause' in response to new threats,[249] and the possibility for a closer group of Member States to move more rapidly than others on certain questions. This would have included permitting the Council to entrust the implementation of a military task to a group of Member States, the establishment of a European Armaments, Research, and Military Capabilities Agency,[250] and the possibility for 'permanent structured co-operation' in defence.[251]

Notably, the European Parliament's role in the CFSP was barely altered, and the field was to remain largely outside judicial control. The important exceptions to this however were that the Court was to be given jurisdiction to review the legality of European decisions providing for restrictive measures against natural or legal persons,[252] and that it was to be given jurisdiction to rule on the compatibility of international CFSP agreements with the Constitution.[253] The Court would have continued to police the borderline between the CFSP and other external policies.

Further, the provisions on the Common Commercial Policy were clarified. The CCP's scope was to be extended to include all foreign direct investment and was clearly categorized as an exclusive competence. Decision-making would have been simplified, although qualified-majority voting was not applied across the whole field. The Constitution would have retained the principle of parallelism established by the Nice Treaty for trade in services, trade aspects of intellectual property, and foreign direct investment, and unanimity would apply when a trade agreement included provisions for which unanimity is required for the adoption of

---

[247] M. Cremona, 'The Draft Constitutional Treaty: External Relations and External Action' (2003) 40 *CMLRev.* 1347, 1358.

[248] See Art. III–309(1).

[249] Arts. I–43 and III–329.

[250] Arts. I–41(3) and III–311.

[251] Arts. I–41(6) and III–312. See J. Howorth, 'The European Draft Constitutional Treaty and the Future of European Defence Initiative: A Question of Flexibility' (2004) 9 *EFARev.* 483.

[252] Art. III–376.

[253] Art. III–325.

internal rules.[254] The role of the European Parliament in the CCP was to be substantially increased: it would have been informed on the progress of negotiations and would have to give its assent for the conclusion of agreements.

One other important modification was that all international agreements (except monetary agreements) were to be negotiated and concluded following the same procedure in which the work would be divided between the Commission and the Minister for Foreign Affairs (responsible for agreements that exclusively or principally relate to the CFSP). The CT also expanded the role of the European Parliament, which would have to give its assent when the agreement concerned an area which was subject to the legislative co-decision procedure. This would have been much broader than at present. Decision-making would have remained subject to the rule of parallelism (i.e., that qualified-majority voting would apply, except when unanimity was required for the adoption of an EU act). Unanimity would always have applied in the case of association and pre-accession agreements providing for economic, financial, or technical co-operation.

A *third* and more specific dimension of the changes made by the Constitutional Treaty to EU international relations was simply the move formally to constitutionalize EU external relations. In the first Article of the CT, the Union is called on to 'exercise on a Community basis the competences [the Member States] confer on it'.[255] It has been noted that although this was an odd phrase, given that the Community would no longer exist, it nevertheless implied that 'all Union competences will carry certain *communautaire* characteristics, such as the potential for direct effect, and primacy over national law'.[256] The CT also attempted to codify some of the most important principles of external relations law derived from the Court's case law. The doctrine of implied powers appeared in the provision which states that the Union may conclude international agreements where the Constitution so provides, but also 'where the conclusion of an agreement is necessary in order to achieve, within the framework of the Union's policies, one of the objectives referred to in the Constitution, or is provided for in a legally binding Union act or is likely to affect common rules or alter their scope'.[257] The other example of this 'rather misguided' attempt to codify the complex case law can be found in Article I–13(2) on the exclusive external competences, which arguably confused the issue of implied powers with that of exclusive competence.[258] It has been argued that these attempts to encapsulate the ECJ's jurisprudence were less than successful, given the complexity of the Court's case law and the inevitability that any meaningful interpretation of the new CT provisions would require reference to the previous jurisprudence.[259]

Finally, the CT also codified and categorized the list of express external competences of the Union, and indicated in Article I–13 which were exclusive and which shared. The Constitution would also have introduced a new, specific legal basis for the Neighbourhood Policy.[260] Last but not least, as we will see in Chapter 11, explicit provision was made for the accession by the EU to the ECHR.[261] At the time of writing, it seems likely that the envisaged Reform Treaty will contain many of the provisions on international relations which would have come into force if the CT had been ratified. However, there are certain notable changes in the approach of the

[254] QMV would not have applied to agreements concerning trade in cultural and audiovisual services and to agreements in the field of social, education, and health services.

[255] Art. I–1.

[256] Cremona, n. 247 above, 1351.

[257] Art. III–323.

[258] B. de Witte, 'The Constitutional Law of External Relations', in I. Pernice and M. Poiares Maduro (eds.), *A Constitution for the European Union: First Comments on the 2003 Draft of the European Convention* (Nomos, 2004).

[259] *Ibid.*, 101.

[260] Art. I–57.

[261] Art. I–9.

proposed Reform Treaty. One is that the provisions governing the CFSP will not be placed together with the other provisions on external relations, but will continue to be dealt with under a separate title and a separate Treaty. Another is that the Foreign Minister will not be given the title 'Minister' but will be referred to as a High Representative. These are in part symbolic but also significant changes.

12. CONCLUSIONS

i. The area of external relations has received particular attention in recent years, as the EU strives to assert its presence on the world stage.

ii. One of the crucial issues for the conduct of EU international relations, given the complex, multi-level, and multi-pillared nature of its constitutional structure, is effective co-ordination across many dimensions and levels. This includes co-ordination across pillars and policies, co-ordination between the EU/EC and the Member States, and co-ordination at the level of international representation.

iii. With the enlargement of the EU to twenty-seven members, the problem of co-ordinating the international relations of the EU, the problem of effective international law-making (given the need, amongst other things, for domestic ratification of mixed agreements), and the ambition of presenting a single face to the outside world become ever more challenging.

iv. The relevant provisions of the Constitutional Treaty reflected the desire to strengthen and streamline the framework for conducting EU external relations and, although the CT did not come into force, it seems likely that many of these provisions will be contained in the proposed future Reform Treaty.

13. FURTHER READING

Cannizzaro, E. (ed.), *The European Union as an Actor in International Relations* (Kluwer, 2002)

Dashwood, A., and Hillion, C. (eds.), *The General Law of EC External Relations* (Sweet & Maxwell, 2000)

Denza, E., *The Intergovernmental Pillars of the European Union* (Oxford University Press, 2002)

Eeckhout, P., *External Relations of the European Union. Legal and Constitutional Foundations* (Oxford University Press, 2004)

Hill, C., and Smith, M., *International Relations and the European Union* (OUP, 2005)

Koskenniemi, M. (ed.), *International Law Aspects of the European Union* (Kluwer Law International, 1998)

Koutrakos, P., *EU International Relations Law* (Hart, 2006)

MacLeod, I., Hendry, D., and Hyett, S., *The External Relations of the European Communities* (Clarendon Press, 1996)

Smith, K., *European Union Foreign Policy in a Changing World* (Polity Press, 2003)

Wessel, R.A., *The European Union's Foreign and Security Policy: A Legal Institutional Perspective* (Kluwer Law International, 1999)

7

THE AREA OF FREEDOM, SECURITY, AND JUSTICE

1. CENTRAL ISSUES

i. The Area of Freedom, Security, and Justice (AFSJ) comprises Title VI TEU, which is the Third Pillar, and Title IV EC.

ii. The subject-matter dealt with by these provisions is important and politically sensitive. Thus Title VI TEU covers police and judicial co-operation in criminal matters, while Title IV EC is concerned with Visas, Asylum, Immigration, and Judicial Co-operation in Civil Matters.

iii. The EU's involvement in what is now known as the AFSJ pre-dates the TEU, but it was that Treaty which laid the Treaty foundations for involvement in this area. These were then modified significantly by the Treaty of Amsterdam. Section 2 of this chapter provides an overview of these developments.

iv. It is important to be clear about the rationale for the AFSJ. The 'official view' is that the policies that make up the AFSJ were 'compensatory measures' made necessary by Community provisions on the free movement of persons, although commentators differ as to how far this provides a full explanation for EU involvement. This will be considered in Section 3.

v. The Treaty provisions dealing with the AFSJ are complex, and so too is the decision-making process that applies to Title VI TEU and Title IV EC. These matters are considered respectively in Sections 4 and 5 of the chapter.

vi. The ECJ's powers under Title VI TEU and Title IV EC differ, and its powers in both areas are different from those normally applicable in the Community Pillar. The difficulties that this gives rise to, and the ECJ's response, are discussed in Section 6.

vii. Section 7 examines in more depth two topics that come within the AFSJ, asylum, and police and judicial co-operation, while Section 8 examines the impact of the Constitutional Treaty.

2. A BRIEF OVERVIEW

The development of the Area of Freedom, Security, and Justice (AFSJ)[1] was considered in Chapter 1. It may nonetheless be helpful to recapitulate briefly the principal developments in this area.[2]

Intergovernmental co-operation to combat matters such as terrorism, cross-border crime, and external frontiers did not begin with the Maastricht Treaty. Numerous mechanisms for co-operation pre-dated the TEU. Thus, for example, the Trevi Group was created in 1975 by the Rome European Council in order to co-ordinate the fight against terrorism, and its mandate was extended in 1985 to encompass serious international crimes such as drug trafficking, bank robbery, and arms trafficking. A further prominent example is the Schengen Agreement 1985, designed to remove border controls among the participating States, which was supplemented by the Schengen Implementing Convention 1990.

It was nonetheless the TEU that formalized EU competence over such matters, by creating the Three–Pillar structure. The general rationale for this structure was that the Member States wished for some established mechanism through which they could co-operate in the areas of Common Foreign and Security Policy and Justice and Home Affairs. Setting up *ad hoc* meetings to discuss such matters is cumbersome, time-consuming, and involves heavy 'transaction costs', more especially as the number of players expands. The Member States were however unwilling to subject these areas to the normal supranational methods of decision-making that characterized the Community Pillar, with all that this entailed for the central role of the Commission and ECJ. This was especially so, given that the Second and Third Pillars concerned sensitive policy areas, hitherto considered to be at the core of national sovereignty. The Member States therefore devised a decision-making structure that was more intergovernmental, with the other Community institutions having either no role or one that was much reduced by comparison with the Community Pillar.

The original formulation of the Justice and Home Affairs Pillar under Articles K.1 to K.9 TEU governed policies such as asylum, immigration, and 'third country' nationals, which have, since the Treaty of Amsterdam, ToA, been integrated into Title IV EC. However, it also included and still covers co-operation on a range of international crime issues and various forms of judicial, customs, and police co-operation.[3]

The Council of Ministers was given the role of adopting joint positions and drawing up agreements on the basis of Member State or Commission initiatives, acting unanimously except on matters of procedure or when implementing joint actions or agreed conventions.[4] The Commission was to be 'fully associated' and the Parliament was to be informed, its views to be 'duly taken into consideration', and it could question or recommend matters to the Council.[5] A Co-ordinating Committee, which became the notorious and secretive K-4 committee, was set up to help the Council, which had a role similar to that of COREPER under the

---

[1] K. Hailbronner, *Immigration and Asylum Law and Policy of the European Union* (Kluwer, 2000); E. Guild and C. Harlow (eds.), *Implementing Amsterdam: Immigration and Asylum Rights in EC Law* (Hart, 2001); E. Denza, *The Intergovernmental Pillars of the European Union* (Oxford University Press, 2002); N. Walker (ed.), *Europe's Area of Freedom, Security and Justice* (Oxford University Press, 2004); S. Peers, *EU Justice and Home Affairs Law* (2nd edn., Oxford University Press, 2006); H. Toner, E. Guild, and A. Baldaccini, *Whose Freedom, Security and Justice? EU Immigration and Asylum Law and Policy* (Hart, 2007).

[2] For detailed treatment see Peers, n. 1 above, ch. 2.

[3] Art. K.1 TEU.

[4] Art. K.3 TEU.

[5] Arts. K.4(2) and K.6.

EC Treaty. The European Council did not initially have the same powerful leadership role under the JHA Pillar as under the CFSP Pillar.

A major criticism of the Maastricht Treaty was that many of the policies under the JHA Pillar called for institutional provisions and legal controls different from the intergovernmental processes established. Topics such as immigration, asylum, border controls, and constraints on movement touch on fundamental human rights, and raise issues similar to those under the free movement provisions of the EC Treaty. Consequently, it was argued that the need for openness and accountability in this policy field was much greater, requiring a full role for the European Parliament and jurisdiction for the ECJ. Arguments for reform ranged from improving the institutional provisions under the existing JHA to absorbing the Third Pillar entirely into the Community Pillar.

Predictably, what emerged in the Amsterdam Treaty lay between the two, with parts of JHA being incorporated into EC Title IV and the remaining Third Pillar provisions being subjected to institutional controls closer to those under the Community Pillar. Further, the *acquis*[6] of the 1985 Schengen Treaty on the gradual abolition of common border checks was integrated into the EU framework by a Protocol to the ToA. The various parts of the Schengen *acquis* were, as provided for by the Amsterdam Treaty, assigned by the Council, under the jurisdiction of the Court, to the appropriate EC or EU Treaty basis. In the absence of such assignment, they were to be based on the Third Pillar on Police and Judicial Co-operation in Criminal Matters (PJCC).

The overall aim of the Third Pillar is, according to Article 29 TEU, to provide citizens with a high level of safety within an area of freedom, security, and justice, by developing 'common action' in three areas: police co-operation in criminal matters, judicial co-operation in criminal matters, and the prevention and combating of racism and xenophobia. These aims were to be addressed through closer co-operation between police forces, customs authorities, and judicial authorities, and through the approximation of certain criminal laws in the Member States. The general aim of Title IV EC is, according to Article 61 EC, the creation of an area of freedom, security, and justice by the adoption of measures to deal with matters such as asylum, border controls, and visas. There were relatively few changes made to the Third Pillar by the Nice Treaty. A formal Treaty foundation was given to Eurojust, the European judicial co-operation unit. The principal change was however to the provisions on enhanced co-operation in Articles 40, 40a, and 40b TEU.[7]

The Area of Freedom, Security, and Justice is thus comprised of the Third Pillar, Title VI TEU, and Title IV EC. There is some variable geometry in these areas, in the sense that some States have opt-outs.[8] Thus in relation to Schengen the UK and Ireland are not bound by the *acquis*, but can opt in to all or part of Schengen, subject to a decision in favour by the Council acting with unanimous approval of the Schengen States,[9] and special, rather complicated provision is also made for Denmark. Norway and Iceland, two countries which participate in the

---

[6] This *acquis*—roughly meaning the accumulated body of law—includes the Schengen Treaty itself and its implementing Convention, as well as decisions and declarations adopted by its Executive Committee, and other acts of implementation. See P.J. Kuijper, 'Some Legal Problems Associated with the Communitarization of Policy on Visas, Asylum and Immigration under the Amsterdam Treaty and Incorporation of the Schengen Acquis' (2000) 37 *CMLRev.* 345; S. Peers, 'Caveat Emptor: Integrating the Schengen Acquis into the European Union Legal Order' (1999) 2 *CYELS* 87.

[7] See above, 29–30.

[8] Peers, n. 1 above, 55–64.

[9] The position of the UK and Ireland with regard to border controls is also protected by another Protocol on the application of Art. 14 EC.

Nordic passport union with Sweden, Denmark, and Finland, but which are not EU members, also participate on a different basis in the Schengen system,[10] and there are complex provisions relating to new Accession States.[11] In relation to Title IV EC the UK and Ireland have an opt-out with certain possibilities for subsequently opting in,[12] and Denmark has a complex partial opt-out.

A further layer of complexity was added to the provisions that govern this topic by the Prum Convention.[13] It was made in 2005 by Belgium, Germany, France, the Netherlands, Luxembourg, Austria, and Spain, in order to increase cross-border co-operation in combating terrorism, cross-border crime, and illegal immigration. While it clearly entails closer co-operation on these issues, it was not adopted in accordance with the provisions on closer co-operation in the Nice Treaty. There are however moves by the Justice and Home Affairs Council to render the provisions of the Convention applicable to all Member States through Council decisions.

3. RATIONALES

It is clear therefore that the AFSJ covers both Title VI TEU and Title IV of the EC Treaty. This brief overview tells us however relatively little about the rationales for the creation of the AFSJ.

We can begin by considering the official rationale. The following extract from the Council's website on Justice and Home Affairs links the need for the AFSJ to free movement of persons *and* to the inherently trans-border impact of matters such as immigration and organized crime.

Justice and Home Affairs Council[14]

When the Member States negotiated the Treaty on European Union, they drew up a list of areas of common interest. This ambitious list includes matters relating to asylum, immigration, controls at the Union's external frontiers, drugs, international fraud, civil and criminal justice, customs cooperation and police cooperation, particularly against international crime and terrorism . . . Why did they decide on such cooperation? What needs did it meet?

The creation of an area of free movement of persons must be accompanied by flanking measures to strengthen external frontiers and asylum and immigration policies

One of the prime objectives of the construction of Europe was to create a large European economic market. . . . In that area without internal frontiers, goods, capital and services were to move about and be exchanged freely and without obstacles. However the fourth freedom, the free movement of persons, gave rise to problems different from those caused by the free movement of goods: problems of the internal security of each State.

Lifting the frontiers between Member States to permit people to pass freely cannot take place to the detriment of the security of the population, of public order and of civil liberties. To obviate this, flanking compensatory measures were adopted.

---

[10] See Council Dec. 2000(29)EC [2000] OJ L1/51 and Council Dec. 2000(777)EC [2000] OJ L309/29.

[11] Peers, n. 1 above, 60–62.

[12] These provisions are set out in a separate Protocol on the position of the UK and Ireland. See, for discussion, the UK House of Lords Select Committee *Report on UK Participation in the Schengen Acquis*, 9 Mar. 2000.

[13] J. Ziller, 'Le traité de Prum: Une vraie-fausse coopération renforcée dans l'Espace de sécurité de liberté et de justice', EUI Working Paper, Law, 2006/32.

[14] Available at www.consilium.europa.eu.

Strengthening the External Frontiers

By doing away with the frontiers between Member States, the latter were deprived of an important national instrument for controlling and filtering the entry and identity of persons and ensuring internal security within their territory. A person present in one State can cross the frontiers of another state without hindrance ... To ensure the same level of security without that tool, controls at the external frontiers, ie between a Member State of the Union and a third state, need to be strengthened....

....

The strengthening of the Union's external frontiers, a measure to compensate for the disappearance of internal frontiers, therefore requires increased cooperation between the interior and justice ministries and, more particularly, the police forces, customs and immigration services.

Immigration and the nationals of third states

Freedom of movement of persons is designed for the citizens of the European Union, ie those holding the nationality of one of the Member States. In an area without frontiers, what happens in the case of nationals of third States legally present in the territory of one of the Member States? ... These are just some of the new questions to which cooperation in the field of justice and home affairs must provide answers.

Looked at from another angle, the disappearance of internal frontiers also raises the questions of illegal immigration or of illegal residence or employment which the Member States have to resolve together....

Asylum

The Member States have to agree on the very concept of political refugee in order to avoid a confusing situation in which one Member State grants asylum where another refuses it. They have to avoid a situation in which applications are made to several States at the same time. They have to cooperate in discussing the minimum guarantees to be granted to asylum applicants in the event of their expulsion and their rights during examination of an asylum application or an appeal....

The issues of the strengthening of external frontiers, immigration and asylum, which are all linked to the disappearance of internal frontiers, are very sensitive political questions for each State. They are perceived as directly affecting the sovereignty, security and people of those States. Their political culture, their legal systems and their administrative traditions and practices are often very different. That is why concerted action, comprehension and dialogue in the context of the JHA are proving to be fundamental.

Schengen and the free movement of persons

[T]he Amsterdam Treaty ... integrates the Schengen acquis into the European Union framework....

The Member States of the European Union can no longer tackle certain problems in dispersed order, but must combine their efforts

Drugs, organised crime, international fraud, trafficking in human beings and the sexual exploitation of children are all problems of great concern to all the Member States of the European Union. These disorders know no frontiers. The aim of the European Union is to become an area of freedom, security and justice, and not an area for all manner of trafficking.

Drugs

[T]he consumption and trafficking of drugs are linked to other problems, such as large-scale crime or money laundering....

Organized crime

Cases of crime, terrorism and fraud can no longer be dealt with solely in a national framework, especially since the creation of a large European market. . . .

The link between the need for the AFSJ, free movement of persons and the inherently trans-border impact of matters such as immigration, asylum, and organized crime, has been echoed by commentators.

S. Lavenex and W. Wallace, Justice and Home Affairs, Towards a 'European Public Order'?[15]

There were several overlapping rationales for developing common policies within the EU, emerging both from functionalist spill-over from other EU policies, and from new challenges faced by the member states, . . . The requirements of the single market included 'free movement of persons'. Cross-border movements intensified among geographically compact, densely populated countries, as prosperity rose and communication links improved. The success of the 1992 internal market programme in removing controls on goods crossing internal frontiers focused on the remaining controls on people at the EU's internal frontiers. The further surge in border-crossing which the internal market programme encouraged also alerted law enforcement agencies to the need to agree on 'compensatory measures' to maintain public order across the EU for the movement of both the lawful and the unlawful, legal and illegal.

Apart from these functionalist dynamics, new domestic priorities shaped the agenda of evolving cooperation. These included concern about cross-border crime and the international mobility of criminals as well as changing patters of migration. Tightened controls on immigration from the mid-1970s onwards coincide with increasing flows from outside Europe and a global rise in the number of refugees, leading to a surge of asylum seekers arriving in western Europe. . . .

German concerns and anxieties were a driving force in the development of common policies.

The official explanation for the emergence of the AFSJ has nonetheless been contested. It has been argued that the 'compensatory measures rationale' cannot readily explain the *restrictiveness* of the policies adopted in areas such as migration, asylum, and the like, and that the driving force behind AFSJ has in reality been security.

C. Costello, Administrative Governance and the Europeanisation of Asylum and Immigration Policy[16]

[T]he compensatory measures rationale cannot provide an explanation for the restrictiveness of the policies and practices adopted. Bigo . . . goes so far as to describe '[t]he debate on compensatory measures and the security deficit created by the opening of the internal borders [as]

---

[15] In H. Wallace, W. Wallace, and M. Pollack (eds.), *Policy Making in the European Union* (5th edn., Oxford University Press, 2005), 460–461.

[16] In H. Hofmann and A. Türk (eds.), *EU Administrative Governance* (Edward Elgar, 2006), 289–290.

one of the strongest myths of EU self-presentation'. Any internal market rationale is agnostic as to the restrictiveness or otherwise of external barriers, but simply requires the application of common rules. For example, for internal free trade in goods, there must be a common external tariff and commercial policy, but not of any particular restrictiveness. In contrast in relation to the free movement of persons...there are no common immigration rules, but rather a restrictive entry control system. The lie that this system is required by the internal free market movement is revealed in relation to the UK and Ireland's participation in a range of external border control measures without any commitment to the abolition of internal border controls.

It is moreover clear that while the official rationale played a role in the emergence of the AFSJ, this development also provided a 'new' banner through which the legitimacy of the EU could be enhanced. The 1990s was a decade in which the legitimacy of the EU came to be increasingly questioned. The IGC discussions leading to the Amsterdam Treaty were shot through with soul-searching concerning input and output legitimacy. Now to be sure the institutional regime through which the AFSJ was delivered did little to enhance input legitimacy. To the contrary, it created numerous problems in this regard, as will be seen below. It nonetheless served as an appropriate vehicle through which it could be argued that the EU fostered output legitimacy. The initial establishment of the EEC had been justified in large part in terms of outcomes, increased peace, and prosperity. It is therefore neither fortuitous nor surprising that the AFSJ should be justified in similar terms, more especially because fears relating to crime and the like regularly featured high in Eurobarometer polls as to the concerns of EU citizens. Consider in this respect the following extract from the Tampere European Council in 1999.

Tampere European Council[17]

Towards a Union of Freedom, Security and Justice: The Tampere Milestones

1. From its very beginning European integration has been firmly rooted in a shared commitment to freedom based on human rights, democratic institutions and the rule of law. These common values have proved necessary for securing peace and developing prosperity in the European Union. They will also serve as a cornerstone for the enlarging Union.

2. The European Union has already put in place for its citizens the major ingredients of a shared idea of prosperity and peace: a single market, economic and monetary union, and the capacity to take on global political and economic challenges. The challenge of the Amsterdam Treaty is now to ensure that freedom, which includes the right to move freely throughout the Union, can be enjoyed in conditions of security and justice accessible to all. It is a project which responds to the frequently expressed concerns of citizens and has a direct bearing on their daily lives.

3. This freedom should not, however, be regarded as the exclusive preserve of the Union's own citizens. Its very existence acts as a draw to many others world-wide who cannot enjoy the freedom Union citizens take for granted. It would be in contradiction with Europe's traditions to deny such freedom to those whose circumstances lead them justifiably to seek access to our territory. This in turn requires the Union to develop common

---

[17] 15–16 Oct. 1999, 2–3.

policies on asylum and immigration, while taking account the need for a consistent control of external borders to stop illegal immigration and to combat those who organise it and commit related international crimes....

4. The aim is an open and secure European Union, fully committed to the obligations of the Geneva Refugee Convention and other relevant human rights instruments....

5. The enjoyment of freedom requires a genuine area of justice, where people can approach courts and authorities in any Member State as easily as their own....

6. People have the right to expect the Union to address the threat to their freedom and legal rights posed by serious crime... The joint mobilisation of police and judicial resources is needed to guarantee that there is no hiding place for criminals or the proceeds of crime within the Union.

7. The area of freedom, security and justice should be based on the principles of transparency and democratic control....

8. The European Council considers it essential that in these areas the Union should also develop a capacity to act and be regarded as a significant partner on the international scene....

The discussion thus far has highlighted the rationales for the development of the AFSJ. The extent to which the issues dealt with therein relating to immigration, border controls, the fight against organized crime, asylum, and the like can be considered to be a *coherent* package has however been contested by Walker.

N. Walker, In Search of the Area of Freedom, Security and Justice: A Constitutional Odyssey[18]

To begin with, we might speak of a basic *thematic* coherence in the area of FSJ—a fundamental unity of subject matter. Yet unlike many of the major domains of European law such as the internal market... the subject matter assembled under the AFSJ do not form a 'natural' unity in terms of a clearly defined overall project. Although analogies have often been drawn between the '1992' Single Market project and the ASFJ, the two are not comparable in terms of precision and internal consistency. The '1992' project concerned a well-defined set of objectives directed towards a particular *finalité*.... In contrast, the AFSJ, even if part of its initial Maastricht inspiration was the attempt to supply a menu of compensatory measures concerning the control of movements across the EU's external borders and the development of new capacities for the internal monitoring of populations in the light of the supposed 'security deficit' attendant upon the completion of an internal market... has no *finalité* other than continuing adherence to a highly abstract triumvirate of values....

But if there is no clearly defined overall project implicit in the very idea of AFSJ, perhaps there is a kind of *historical* coherence in terms of a tried-and-tested pattern of common treatment.... Here, too, only a weak argument can be made. The Treaties tell us that AFSJ is concerned, on the one hand, under Title IV EC, with 'Visas, Asylum, Immigration and Other Policies Relating to Free Movement of Persons',..., and on the other hand under Title VI TEU with 'Provisions on Police and Judicial Cooperation in Criminal Matters'. Yet we need only look at the variety of government departments under which these policies are traditionally organized

---

[18] In Walker, n. 1 above, 5–7, italics in the original.

in various European states to conclude that history lends no obvious coherence to this enterprise....

Another type of coherence, then, might be *institutional* coherence. Is the AFSJ characterized by a distinctive institutional methodology? Evidently, the answer must again be no.... Under Amsterdam ... there is a clear divide between the communitarized Title IV EC and the more state-centred rump Third Pillar under Title VI EU, even if Title IV EC remains only partly and incrementally communitarized and Title VI EU allows a greater role for EC institutions and instruments than its Maastricht predecessor ...

Strikingly, however, institutional diversification has developed hand-in-hand with a new impetus towards *policy* coherence.... [T]he post-Amsterdam era is clearly marked by an attempt to *construct* a new kind of policy whole out of diverse parts. To begin with, the very coining of the concept of an Area of Freedom, Security and Justice in the Treaty of Amsterdam is a statement of intent to consider the matters under Title IV EC and Title VI EU as a new policy domain, their new institutional separation notwithstanding.... [T]he special Tampere European Council late in 1999 drew upon the new rhetoric and institutional capability in order to launch an explicit and ambitious programme of action to develop a common policy field within and across four general headings—A Common EU Asylum and Migration Policy; A Genuine European Area of Justice; A Unionwide Fight against Crime and Stronger External Action—complete with timetables and milestones.

There is force in this argument. The AFSJ is marked by institutional diversity rather than a distinctive institutional methodology, and the framers of the Amsterdam Treaty did consciously construct a new policy from diverse parts. There is nonetheless also room for disagreement with this thesis, relating to the extent to which the AFSJ is marked by thematic coherence. It is questionable whether the *finalité* of the 1992 internal market project is that much more well-defined than that of the AFSJ. We should remember in this respect that the former is ongoing, notwithstanding the temporal 'end-point' of 1992, and that there is increased contestation as to the balance between the social and the economic in internal market initiatives.[19]

4. TREATY PROVISIONS

The powers accorded to the EU institutions in relation to AFSJ are complex. It is therefore necessary to be clear about these, both in relation to both Title VI TEU and Title IV EC.

(a) TITLE VI TEU: POLICE AND JUDICIAL CO-OPERATION IN CRIMINAL MATTERS

The Third Pillar is now concerned with police and judicial co-operation in criminal matters. Article 29 TEU is the principal empowering provision.

Without prejudice to the powers of the European Community, the Union's objective shall be to provide citizens with a high level of safety within the area of freedom, security and justice by developing common action among the Member States in the fields of police and judicial cooperation in criminal matters and by preventing and combating racism and xenophobia.

---

[19] See Ch. 17.

> That objective shall be achieved by preventing and combating crime, organised or other-
> wise, in particular terrorism, trafficking in persons and offences against children, illicit drug
> trafficking and illicit arms trafficking, corruption and fraud, through:
>
> — closer cooperation between police forces, customs authorities and other competent
>   authorities in the Member State, both directly and through the European Police Office
>   (Europol), in accordance with the provisions of Articles 30 and 32;
> — closer cooperation between judicial and other competent authorities of the Member
>   States, including cooperation through the European Judicial Cooperation Unit ('Eurojust'),
>   in accordance with the provisions of Articles 31 and 32;
> — approximation, where necessary, of the rules on criminal matters in the Member States,
>   in accordance with the provisions of Article 31(e).

The powers contained in Article 29 TEU are qualified, in formal terms at least, by Article 33 TEU, which provides that Title VI shall not affect the exercise of the responsibilities incumbent upon Member States with regard to the maintenance of law and order and the safeguarding of internal security.

Articles 30–31 TEU set out more details on the common actions in relation to police and judicial co-operation respectively. It is for the Council to lay down the conditions under which the competent authorities referred to in Articles 30 and 31 may operate in the territory of another Member States in liaison and agreement with the authorities of that State.

Four areas of action are identified in relation to police co-operation in Article 30(1) TEU. They relate broadly to prevention, investigation, and detection; storage and exchange of information; training, research, and equipment; and investigation of organized crime. The Council was charged with promoting co-operation in these areas through Europol, the European Police Office which was introduced by the Maastricht TEU and finally formally established in 1999 after the Europol Convention was ratified by all Member States in 1998.[20]

Article 31(1) TEU specifies five areas where judicial co-operation in criminal matters should occur: facilitating proceedings and enforcement of decisions; facilitating extradition between Member States; ensuring compatibility in the rules applicable in the Member States in order to improve such co-operation; preventing conflicts of jurisdiction between Member States; and the establishment of minimum rules relating to the constituent elements of criminal acts and penalties in the fields of organized crime, terrorism, and illicit drug trafficking. Article 31(2) provides that the Council is to encourage co-operation through Eurojust by: enabling the latter to facilitate proper co-ordination between Member States' national prosecuting authorities; promoting support for Eurojust for criminal investigations in cases of serious cross-border crime; and facilitating close co-operation between Eurojust and the European Judicial Network.

Article 34(1) TEU imposes a procedural obligation on Member States to inform and consult one another within the Council with a view to co-ordinating their action in the areas covered by Title VI, and to that end they must establish collaborations between the relevant departments of their administrations.

Article 34(2) TEU is of particular importance, since it specifies the range of legal instruments which the Council may adopt, acting unanimously on the initiative of any Member State or the Commission. The European Parliament must be consulted before any such measure is adopted, with the exception of common positions.[21] Thus the Council can adopt

---

[20] For the Europol Convention see [1995] OJ C316/2.
[21] Art. 39(1) TEU.

common positions, which define the Union's approach to a given matter. It can adopt *framework decisions* for the purpose of approximation of the laws and regulations of the Member States. These are similar in character to EC directives, in that they are binding upon the Member States as to the result to be achieved, but leave the Member States with discretion as to the form and methods of implementation. Framework decisions are however explicitly stated not to have direct effect. The Council can also adopt *decisions* for any purpose consistent with the objectives of Title VI, excluding any approximation of the laws and regulations of the Member States. These decisions are binding, but once again they are said not to have direct effect. The Council, acting by qualified majority, is to adopt measures necessary to implement those decisions at the level of the Union. The final type of instrument specified in Article 34(2) is *conventions*, which the Council can recommend to the Member States for adoption in accordance with their constitutional requirements.[22]

The ECJ now has jurisdiction over certain measures adopted under the Third Pillar. Article 35 TEU established a preliminary reference procedure similar, though not identical, to that of Article 234 EC. Thus Article 35(1) TEU provides that the ECJ has jurisdiction, subject to the conditions below, to give preliminary rulings on the validity and interpretation of framework decisions and decisions, and on the interpretation of conventions, and on the validity and interpretation of the measures implementing them. This is however operative only if a Member State accepts this jurisdiction of the ECJ, and if it does so the Member State can then specify either that a preliminary reference can be sent by any court or tribunal against whose decisions there is no judicial remedy, or by any national court or tribunal.[23]

Further, Article 35(6) TEU gives the ECJ jurisdiction to review the legality of framework decisions and decisions at the suit of a Member State or the Commission, on the same grounds as those in Article 230 EC. However this jurisdiction is restricted, in that it cannot review the legality or proportionality of 'operations carried out by the police or other law enforcement services of a Member State or the exercise of the responsibilities incumbent upon Member States with regard to the maintenance of law and order and the safeguarding of internal security'.[24]

Finally, the Court was given jurisdiction in disputes between Member States concerning the interpretation or application of any legal acts adopted under Article 34(2), or between the Commission and a Member State concerning the interpretation or application of a Convention adopted under Article 34, if the Council cannot first resolve the dispute.[25]

Article 37 deals primarily with the international dimension of the Third Pillar issues. It provides in essence that Member States are obliged to defend common positions adopted under Title VI within international organizations and at international conferences they attend. It also more importantly renders applicable the provisions of the CFSP Pillar on the respective positions of the Council Presidency, the Secretary-General, the Council, and the Commission in relation to the representation of the Union, particularly in international fora. These provisions are found in Article 18 TEU. They stipulate that the Presidency shall represent the Union, that it shall be responsible for implementation of decisions taken under this Title, and shall in principle express the position of the Union in international organizations and international conferences. The Presidency is assisted by the Secretary-General of the Council, and

---

[22] Art. 34(2) TEU states that, unless they provide otherwise, conventions shall, once adopted by at least half of the Member States, enter into force for those Member States. Measures implementing conventions are adopted by the Council by a majority of two-thirds of the contracting parties.

[23] Art. 35(3) TEU.

[24] Art. 35(5) TEU.

[25] Art. 35(7) TEU.

the Commission is to be fully associated with these tasks. It is open to the Council, whenever it deems it necessary, to appoint a special representative with a mandate for a particular policy issue. Article 19 TEU specifies in more detail the role of Member States in international organizations and at international conferences. Article 38 TEU continues the linkage between the Second and Third Pillars, stipulating that the provision of the CFSP[26] under which the Council is given the power to conclude international agreements negotiated by the Presidency is also applicable to the Third Pillar.

Article 40 TEU sets out the conditions for enhanced co-operation with a view to achieving the objectives of the Third Pillar. Like the enhanced co-operation provisions of the Second Pillar, these are also subject to the substantive conditions of the umbrella enhanced co-operation provisions in Articles 43–45 TEU.

The final Article of Title VI, Article 42 TEU, reinforces both symbolically and legally the linkage between the Third Pillar and Title IV EC. It contains the amended 'passerelle' provision linking the Title with the EC Treaty Title on the free movement of persons, and provides a procedure whereby issues under the former may be dealt with under the latter.

> The Council, acting unanimously on the initiative of the Commission or a Member State, and after consulting the European Parliament, may decide that action in areas referred to in Article 29 shall fall under Title IV of the Treaty establishing the European Community, and at the same time determine the relevant voting conditions relating to it. It shall recommend the Member States to adopt that decision in accordance with their respective constitutional requirements.

(b) TITLE IV EC: VISAS, ASYLUM, IMMIGRATION, AND OTHER POLICIES RELATED TO FREE MOVEMENT OF PERSONS

The second limb of the AFSJ is to be found in Title IV EC. The key enabling provision is Article 61 EC, which provides as follows.

> In order to establish progressively an area of freedom, security and justice, the Council shall adopt:
>
> (a) within a period of five years after the entry into force of the Treaty of Amsterdam, measures aimed at ensuring the free movement of persons in accordance with Article 14, in conjunction with directly related flanking measures with respect to external border controls, asylum and immigration, in accordance with the provisions of Article 62(2) and (3) and Article 63(1)(a) and (2)(a) and measures to prevent and combat crime in accordance with the provisions of Article 31(e) of the Treaty on European Union;
>
> (b) other measures in the fields of asylum, immigration and safeguarding the rights of nationals of third countries, in accordance with the provisions of Article 63;
>
> (c) measures in the field of judicial cooperation in civil matters as provided for in Article 65;
>
> (d) appropriate measures to encourage and strengthen administrative cooperation, as provided for in Article 66;

---

[26] Art. 24 TEU.

(e) measures in the field of police and judicial cooperation in criminal matters aimed at a high
     level of security by preventing and combating crime within the Union in accordance with
     the provisions of the Treaty on European Union.

Article 64 EC is analogous to Article 33 TEU, and states that Title IV shall not affect the
exercise of responsibilities incumbent on Member States with regard to the maintenance of
law and order and the safeguarding of internal security. Article 64(2) also provides a mechanism for dealing with an emergency situation in a particular Member State which is
confronted with 'a sudden inflow of nationals of third countries'.

Articles 62, 63, 65, and 66 EC flesh out the details of Article 61. Thus Article 62 EC expands
on Article 61(a). The Council is required, within a period of five years after the entry into force
of the Amsterdam Treaty, to adopt measures to ensure, in compliance with Article 14 EC, the
absence of controls on persons, whether they are Union citizens or nationals from third countries, when crossing internal borders. It is also required to adopt measures on the crossing of
external borders, in order to establish standards and procedures to be followed by Member
States in carrying out checks on persons at such borders, rules on visas for those intending to
stay no more than three months, and measures setting out the conditions under which
nationals from third countries have the freedom to travel within the territory of the Member
States during a period of no more than three months.

Article 63 EC builds on Article 61(b). The Council is obliged, once again within the five-
year period post the Amsterdam Treaty, to adopt measures concerning four related areas. The
first is asylum and the measures to be adopted, which must be in accordance with the Geneva
Convention of 1951 and the Protocol of 1967 on the status of refugees, relate to criteria for
deciding which State should be responsible for considering an asylum application; minimum
standards on the reception of asylum seekers in Member States; minimum standards on
whether third country nationals are refugees; and minimum standards on procedures in
Member States for granting or withdrawing refugee status. The second area on which the
Council must adopt measures concerns refugees and displaced persons. The third concerns
immigration policy so far as it relates to, on the one hand, conditions of entry and residence
and standards on procedures for the issue by Member States of long-term visas and residence
permits, including those for family reunion, and, on the other hand, illegal immigration and
illegal residence. The final area dealt with by Article 63 EC concerns measures defining the
rights and conditions under which nationals of third countries who are legally resident in a
Member State may reside in another Member State.

Article 65 EC expands on Article 61(c), dealing with judicial co-operation in civil matters
having cross-border implications in so far as necessary for the proper functioning of the
internal market. The measures to be adopted include improvements to, and simplification of,
the system for cross-border service of judicial and extrajudicial documents, co-operation in
taking evidence, and the recognition and enforcement of foreign judgments. Article 65 also
empowers the making of measures to promote the compatibility of the conflict of laws' and
jurisdiction rules of the Member States, and the elimination of obstacles to the good functioning of civil proceedings, if necessary by promoting the compatibility of civil procedure
rules in the Member States.

Article 66 EC builds on Article 61(d), by imposing a general obligation on the Council to
ensure co-operation between the relevant departments of Member State administrations
covered by Title IV, and between those departments and the Commission.

The measures adopted pursuant to Articles 62–66 are made under the procedure laid down in Article 67 EC. This is a complex provision, with a number of qualifications and exceptions.[27] The essence of the scheme is as follows. During a transitional period of five years following the entry into force of the Amsterdam Treaty, the general rule was that the Council acted unanimously on a proposal from the Commission or on the initiative of a Member State after consulting the EP, although as the transitional period drew to a close it was the Commission that made the majority of new proposals.[28] After this period, Article 67(2) EC provided that the Council should act on proposals from the Commission, but that the Commission must examine any request made by a Member State that it should submit a proposal to the Council. Article 67(2) further provided that the Council, acting unanimously after consulting the EP, should take a decision with a view to providing for all or parts of the areas covered by Title IV to be governed by the co-decision procedure in Article 251. This power was acted on in 2004 and the co-decision procedure complete with qualified-majority voting in the Council became the norm for most measures, except legal migration, family law, and some asylum issues.[29]

The ECJ's preliminary rulings jurisdiction over Title IV is limited to national courts from which there is no judicial remedy, and it has no jurisdiction over certain free movement measures concerning law and order and internal security.[30] There is power pursuant to Article 67(2) EC for the Council, acting unanimously with the consent of the EP, to adapt the provisions relating to the powers of the ECJ. The Commission has proposed that the preliminary ruling jurisdiction under Article 68 EC should be brought into line with the general regime under Article 234,[31] but its proposal has not thus far been acted on.

5. DECISION-MAKING

An understanding of the formal Treaty powers in any given area is necessary, but not sufficient. It has to be complemented by awareness of the decision-making process and the actors that participate therein.

(a) THE EUROPEAN COUNCIL

It is fitting to begin with the role of the European Council. We have already touched on the important contribution it made in this area through the Tampere European Council. There is little doubt that the European Council played a central role in 'constructing' the AFSJ and imbuing it with the political authority that comes from a meeting of the heads of state.

---

[27] Peers, n. 1 above, 22–29.

[28] *Ibid.*, 23.

[29] Council Dec. 2004/927/EC of 22 Dec. 2004 providing for certain areas covered by Title IV of Part Three of the Treaty establishing the European Community to be governed by the procedure laid down in Art. 251 of that Treaty [2004] OJ L396/45; S. Peers, 'Transforming Decision-Making on EC Immigration and Asylum Law' (2005) 30 *ELRev.* 283.

[30] See Art. 68 EC.

[31] Adaptation of the provisions of Title IV establishing a European Community relating to the jurisdiction of the Court of Justice with a view to ensuring more effective judicial protection, COM(2006)346.

Tampere European Council[32]

> The European Council is determined to develop the Union as an area of freedom, security and justice by making full use of the possibilities offered by the Treaty of Amsterdam. The European Council sends a strong political message to reaffirm the importance of this objective and has agreed on a number of policy orientations and priorities which will speedily make this a reality.

The European Council set out in some detail the four principal components of the AFSJ. The Common EU Asylum and Migration Policy dealt with matters such as partnership with countries of origin, the development of a common European asylum system, fair treatment for third country nationals, and management of migration flows. The second component was a Genuine European Area of Justice, embracing matters such as better access to justice in Europe, mutual recognition of judicial decisions, and greater convergence in civil law. The Union-wide Fight against Crime constituted the third part of this schema, dealing with issues such as crime prevention at EU level, improving co-operation against crime and action against money laundering. The final component, less well-defined than the preceding three, was concerned with Stronger External Action.

The Tampere programme featured frequently in subsequent European Council meetings, although the aspects highlighted in such meetings were often influenced by the prevailing political priorities, whether those were concerns about illegal immigration or the fight against terror. Thus in the Seville Summit in 2002 the European Council was determined 'to speed up the implementation of all aspects of the programme adopted in Tampere for the creation of an area of freedom, security and justice in the European Union',[33] and it gave particular attention to asylum and immigration. This same theme was reiterated a year later at the Thessaloniki Summit in 2003, where the European Council noted the top political priority ascribed to migration, and stated that 'there is a marked need for a more structured EU policy, which will cover the whole spectrum of relations with third countries'.[34] It considered in detail the emerging regime dealing with illegal immigration, external borders, the return of illegal migrants, co-operation with third countries, asylum, and the integration of third country nationals lawfully residing in the EU. It was the Madrid bombings and the fight against terror which cast a shadow over the Brussels European Council in March 2004.[35] They led the European Council to issue a Declaration on Combating Terrorism and to create the post of Counter-terrorism Co-ordinator for the EU.

The Tampere programme has now been superseded by the Hague programme, devised primarily by the Justice and Home Affairs ministers and adopted by the European Council in 2004. The salience of recent political events emerges clearly in the following extract.

---

[32] N. 17 above, 1.
[33] Seville European Council, 21–22 June 2002, 7.
[34] Thessaloniki European Council, 19–20 June 2003, 3.
[35] Brussels European Council, 25–26 Mar. 2004.

Brussels European Council, Area of Freedom Security and Justice: The Hague Programme[36]

14. The security of the European Union and its Member States has acquired a new urgency, especially in the light of the terrorist attacks in the United States on 11 September 2001 and in Madrid on 11 March 2004.

The citizens of Europe rightly expect the European Union, while guaranteeing respect for fundamental freedoms and rights, to take a more effective, joint approach to cross-border problems such as illegal migration and trafficking in and smuggling of human beings, as well as to terrorism and organized crime.

15. Five years after the European Council's meeting in Tampere, when it agreed on a programme which laid the foundation for important achievements in the area of freedom, security and justice, it is time for a new programme to enable the Union to build on these achievements and effectively meet the new challenges it will face. To this end, it adopted a new multi-annual programme for the next five years, to be known as the Hague Programme, which is attached to these conclusions.

The details of the Hague programme are contained in Annex I to the European Council's conclusions. These provisions build on and develop the Tampere programme, placing particular emphasis on timely implementation of the measures. The Commission was invited to present an Action Plan in 2005 through which the aims of the programme could be translated into concrete actions, and was invited also to present to the Council a yearly report or scoreboard on the implementation of the Hague programme. We see here evidence of the symbiotic relationship between European Council and Commission, discussed earlier in the context of the institutions and their powers.[37] The approval of the European Council provides a more general framework for the development of EU policy in a particular area, with concrete initiatives being developed by the Commission within this overall framework, which thereby influence the very framework itself. The Action Plan was duly presented in 2005. It followed the taxonomy of the Hague programme and listed a whole raft of measures designed to take further each particular aspect of that programme.[38]

The European Council has continued to pay close attention to the Hague programme in subsequent summits. Thus the Brussels European Council in December 2006 took stock of the implementation of the Hague programme and 'reiterated its commitment to the further development of the area of freedom, security and justice'.[39] Attention was focused once again on implementation and the possibility of 'improving decision-making and action in the area of freedom, security and justice on the basis of the existing Treaties',[40] with considerable emphasis being placed on 'intensifying operational cooperation between competent authorities of the Member States'.[41] The European Council is therefore an important player in this area, reflecting the overall political significance of the issues addressed by the AFSJ.

---

[36] 4–5 Nov. 2004, 4.

[37] See above, Ch. 2.

[38] Council and Commission Action Plan implementing the Hague Programme on strengthening freedom, security and justice in the European Union [2005] OJ C198/1.

[39] 14–15 Dec. 2006, para. 16.

[40] *Ibid.*, para. 19.

[41] *Ibid.*, para. 20.

(b) THE COUNCIL

The role of the Council, and more specifically the Justice and Home Affairs Council, is equally significant. It should be remembered that the Council is the institution formally charged with adopting the measures specified in Title VI TEU and Title IV EC.[42] The volume of JHA business has increased markedly over the years, with the consequence that the JHA Council meets on average almost once per month with 'long agendas, comprising both proposals for decisions with legislative impact and coordination of national policies across a range of areas'.[43] Approximately 40 per cent of the documents that go through the Council relate to JHA,[44] and in excess of 500 decisions relating to JHA issues were made by the Council between May 1999 and December 2003.[45]

This volume of complex business requires a significant support structure, which serves moreover to bring together initiatives under Title VI TEU and Title IV EC. The normal regime of support for the Council has therefore been modified. There are essentially three layers of support beneath the Justice and Home Affairs Council. COREPER provides the highest level of support, meeting weekly and setting the agendas for JHA meetings. The lowest level is composed of working groups of specialists, which operate in all major areas of AFSJ policy. There are therefore such groups on matters ranging from police co-operation to migration, from expulsion to judicial networks, and from asylum to substantive criminal law.

There are however also groups which operate between COREPER and the working parties. In relation to Title VI TEU there is the Article 36 Committee, also known as CATS (*Comité de l'Article Trente Six*). This nomenclature flows from Article 36 TEU, which provides for a Co-ordinating Committee to be established consisting of senior officials. In addition to its co-ordinating role it is to give opinions to the Council, either on its own initiative or at the request of the Council, and it is to contribute, without prejudice to the role of COREPER, to the preparation of the Council's discussions on Title VI issues. In relation to Title IV EC there is SCIFA, the Strategic Committee on Immigration, Frontiers and Asylum, SCIFA + which includes national heads of border control, a Committee on Civil Law Matters, and a High Level Working Group on Asylum and Migration.[46] The following extract provides insight into the working of CATS, the Article 36 Committee.

F. Hayes-Renshaw and H. Wallace, The Council of Ministers[47]

Article 36 provides only that the committee consist of 'senior officials' from each of the Member States. In practice, the members are mainly drawn from the national ministries of justice, although some come from the national interior ministries, depending on how such matters are dealt with in the member state in question. The Commission is required to be 'fully associated with the work' of the Committee, and Commission officials attend all the meetings of the CATS, which is convened about once a month. . . .

---

[42] In Case C–257/01 *Commission* v. *Council* [2005] ECR I–345, the ECJ upheld the retention of implementing powers by the Council in the context of certain Title IV measures even though the reasons given by the Council were 'general and laconic': para. 53

[43] F. Hayes-Renshaw and H. Wallace, *The Council of Ministers* (2nd edn., Palgrave, 2006), 45.

[44] *Ibid.*, 45.

[45] J. Monar, 'Justice and Home Affairs', in L. Miles (ed.), *The European Union: Annual Review of the EU 2003/2004* (Blackwells, 2004), 117–133.

[46] Lavenex and Wallace, n. 15 above, 468.

[47] N. 43 above, 86–87.

Although not unfamiliar with intergovernmental cooperation, JHA officials' experience of European integration is much less ingrained than that of many of their colleagues in the national administrations, particularly those in the foreign, agricultural and finance ministries. As a result, there was a certain initial reluctance to move beyond informal dialogue and exchanges of information to a more formal, institutionalized process of common actions and harmonized legislation. However, inside observers now speak of the growth of a harmonization reflex in certain areas and, where this is unrealistic or unnecessary, given the very different judicial backgrounds and criminal law systems with which the members of the committee and working parties are familiar, a recognition of the need to cooperate and coordinate to the extent possible.

The working groups that feed into the intermediate committees are also of considerable importance. Aden has argued that such bodies have considerable autonomy in the development of policy, especially in the fields of police and judicial co-operation.

H. Aden, Administrative Governance in the Fields of EU Police and Judicial Co-operation[48]

From the perspective of administrative governance, this means that there are structural limits for political steering. Administrative governance strategies are only to a lesser extent politically defined. Instead they result from the 'necessities' perceived by the relevant administrative actors themselves. The Justice and Home Affairs Council's work is largely based on working groups in which senior officers from national police and judicial institutions establish practical co-operation as well as exchange their views on specific areas of crime...Policy-making is therefore even more so than in other areas based on the experience of senior officials. The Council meetings themselves concentrate on defining priorities between different propositions made by those working groups. If there are several alternatives their choice is largely determined by the priorities of the political agenda, for example by cross-border crime cases reported by the media. Scientific knowledge only plays a minor role.

(c) THE COMMISSION

The Council and its support structure are therefore central to the development of the AFSJ. So too is the Commission. It is still common to think of the AFSJ as being intergovernmental, with the consequence that the Commission plays only a minor role. The Third Pillar component of the AFSJ is indeed more intergovernmental than the First Pillar, but the Commission nonetheless plays a significant role in the former as well as the latter, and in any event the AFSJ also includes Title IV EC, in which the supranational component is greater, albeit not equivalent to that in other areas of the First Pillar. The 'bottom line' is that the Commission is an important player across the entirety of the AFSJ.

It is the Commission that is the principal source of legislative initiatives relating to AFSJ, and virtually all such measures now emanate from the Commission.[49] The importance of the AFSJ to the Commission's overall programme is underlined by the fact that 17 per cent of all

---

48 In Hofmann and Türk, n. 16 above, 351.
49 Peers, n. 1 above, 23.

legislative proposals relate to this area. A bare glance at the 2005 Action Plan[50] and the Commission's Freedom Security and Justice website[51] reveals the number and diversity of measures that address AFSJ issues. This does not of course mean that it will always be successful in its initiatives, but this is also true of other areas.

The Commission's role is not however confined to initiation of particular legislative proposals. It is, as we have already seen, charged by the Council with the more general strategic role of drawing up the detailed action plan to implement the Hague programme, including the scoreboard to measure progress in this area. The Commission has in this more general strategic capacity produced reports on implementation of the Hague programme,[52] evaluated EU policies in the AFSJ,[53] proffered more general thoughts on the best way of attaining the objectives of the Hague programme,[54] and proposed a framework programme for Fundamental Rights and Justice for the period 2007–2013.[55]

The Commission has, as might be expected, its own 'agenda' when considering the overall architecture of the AFSJ. It advocates, wherever possible, bringing AFSJ decision-making in line with the more general Community method that prevails in the First Pillar. It maintains that the difficulties with decision-making in relation to AFSJ are in large part due to the decision-making process under Title VI TEU, which is characterized by: distinct legal instruments; insufficient powers for the EP in the legislative process; the unanimity requirement that leads to lowest common denominator results; a shared right of initiative with each of the twenty-five Member States that does not favour a true European dimension; a limited role for the ECJ; and lack of formal infringement procedures to ensure proper implementation.[56] The way forward was, said the Commission, to make use of the 'bridging clauses' in Article 42 TEU and Article 67(2) EC so as to bring decision-making closer to the normal Community method.[57]

Implementing the Hague Programme: the Way Forward[58]

By applying the 'Community' method, the following advantages would be obtained:

- increasing the efficiency, the transparency and the accountability of the legislative procedures;

- generalising the Community legislative instruments (Regulations, Directives, Decisions under the current Treaties);

- guaranteeing a 'European dimension' of the legislative proposals through the right of initiative of the Commission and the use of effective impact assessment tools;

- favouring both consensus and high standard achievements through the qualified majority vote;

---

[50] N. 38 above.
[51] http://ec.europa.eu/justice_home/fsj/intro/fsj_intro_en.htm.
[52] Report on the implementation of the Hague programme for 2005, COM(2006)333 final.
[53] Evaluation of EU Policies on Freedom, Security and Justice, COM(2006)332 final.
[54] Implementing the Hague Programme: the Way Forward, COM(2006)331 final.
[55] Establishing for the period 2007–2013 a framework programme on Fundamental Rights and Justice, COM(2005)122 final.
[56] Implementing the Hague Programme, n. 54 above, 12.
[57] *Ibid.*, 13–14.
[58] *Ibid.*, 14.

• ensuring a proper judicial dialogue with national jurisdictions through the preliminary ruling mechanism and monitoring of implementation by the Member States through the infringement procedure.

(d) THE EUROPEAN PARLIAMENT

The role of the European Parliament in the AFSJ has been more limited. It has only a right to be consulted under Title VI TEU, and this was also the case until recently in relation to Title IV EC. The EP's Committee on Civil Liberties, Justice, and Home Affairs has regularly issued reports on AFSJ initiatives, but its impact has been limited, although the situation may well now improve with the introduction of the co-decision procedure for many Title IV EC measures.

S. Peers, EU Justice and Home Affairs Law[59]

[T]he European Parliament had a marginal role during the transitional period, as its power of consultation, already intrinsically weak, was weaker in the particular framework of Title IV, given the requirement of unanimous voting in the Council, the shared power of initiative for member States, and the deference of the Commission to member States. In particular, the Commission, as compared to its normal practice, rarely amended its proposals to take account off the EP's opinion, and Member States showed no interest at all in amending their proposals in light of the EP's views. Several negative votes by the EP against proposals were simply ignored by the Council. The EP's frustration with its position led it to bring proceedings against parts of a Council Directive on family reunion which arguably breach human rights standards, as well as against Council and Commission approval of the transfer of passenger data to US law enforcement authorities, and certain provisions of the EC's asylum procedures directive.

The various changes from 2003 to 2005 in the Title IV institutional framework have meant...that the EP now enjoys co-decision powers as regards civil law (except for family law), visas, borders, freedom to travel legislation (except as regards visa lists and the visa format), asylum, and irregular migration. Legislation concerning legal migration and cooperation between administrations is still subject only to the consultation of the EP. Taken as a whole, this is a fundamental change in the position of the EP, but the impact is only just beginning to be felt, with only one civil law and five borders and visa measures adopted to date using the co-decision procedure.

(e) AGENCIES

The discussion of decision-making in relation to AFSJ would be incomplete if it did not take account of the important role played by agencies. They play an increasingly important role across a wide variety of areas in the EC.[60] Their responsibility within the AFSJ is especially significant.

---

[59] N. 1 above, 26–27.
[60] P. Craig, *EU Administrative Law* (Oxford University Press, 2006), ch. 5.

A distinctive feature of Title VI TEU is that the Treaty articles state that the aims set out in Article 29 TEU should often be attained by the Council acting through agencies. Thus Article 29 specifically makes mention of both Europol and Eurojust, while Article 30(2) TEU requires the Council to promote police co-operation through Europol and Article 31(2) stipulates that the Council should encourage judicial co-operation in criminal matters through Eurojust.

The role of Europol and Eurojust will be considered in more detail below.[61] Suffice it to say for the present that the agreement to set up Europol dates from the Maastricht Treaty. The Europol Convention flowed from a Council act based on what was Article K3 of the TEU.[62] It was ratified by all Member States in October 1998 and Europol became fully operational in July 1999.[63] Its objectives are to enhance effectiveness and co-operation between Member States in dealing with offences that come within Europol's remit.[64] Eurojust was established in 2002 to enhance co-operation between the competent authorities responsible for investigation and prosecution of cross-border and organized crime.[65]

Agencies play a less prominent role in the context of Title IV EC than they do in relation to the Third Pillar. However they are nonetheless being given an increasingly important role. This is exemplified by the creation in 2004 of FRONTEX,[66] which is to co-ordinate co-operation between Member States concerning the management of external borders, assist in the training of border guards, undertake risk assessment, and provide assistance in relation to high technology surveillance systems that can be used on external borders. The timing of the establishment of this agency is not fortuitous. The Eastern enlargement brought increased fears that the EU's borders would become more porous and less secure.

The broader significance of this development is brought out well by Walker. He notes that while the normal constitutional logic of the EU is legislation-centred, this is not the case with prominent areas of the AFSJ, where executive action predominates.

N. Walker, In Search of the Area of Freedom, Security and Justice: A Constitutional Odyssey[67]

While there are many areas of FSJ in which legislation is at the centre of the policy agenda, particularly in Title IV of the EC Treaty, in police and criminal justice co-operation this is far less evidently the case. Clearly, the provisions for approximation of substantive criminal law and compatibility of procedural measures are legislation-centred, but just as, if not more, significant a thrust in the residual third pillar is towards executive action, whether co-operation between existing national measures and operational agencies or the development of new Europe-wide agencies such as Europol and Eurojust. The reasons for this distinctive policy texture are complex. They have to do with the way in which state sovereigntist sensibilities

---

[61] See below, 262–263.

[62] Council Act of 26 July 1995 drawing up the Convention based on Art. K.3 of the Treaty on European Union, on the establishment of a European Police Office (Europol) [1995] OJ C316/1. It can be found at www.europol.eu.int/index.asp?page=legalconv.

[63] Communication concerning the taking up of activities of Europol [1999] OJ L185/1.

[64] Europol Convention, n. 62 above, Art. 2.

[65] Council Dec. 2002/187/JHA of 28 Feb. 2002 setting up Eurojust with a view to reinforcing the fight against serious crime [2002] OJ L63/1.

[66] Council Reg. (EC) 2007/2004 of 26 Oct. 2004 establishing a European Agency for the Management of Operational Cooperation at the External Borders of the Member States of the European Union [2004] OJ L349/1.

[67] N. 1 above, 21–22.

have been most jealous of the more familiar and more symbolically loaded legislation-centred indices of national authority and so have been more permissive and less vigilant of other aspects of policy co-operation. . . . They have also to do with the fact that, by their very nature, those dimensions of internal security policy which are concerned with primary law enforcement—namely police and prosecution—involve tasks of an intrinsically executive or operational character.

What this entails is that notwithstanding state sovereigntist concerns about the Europeanization of internal security, we are arguably witnessing a degree of executive (as opposed to legislative) penetration of national systems and challenges to statist prerogatives, through new agencies and other systems and instruments of co-operation which have persuasive or compulsory consequences for both the national governments involved and the individual citizens affected, that is unmatched in any other area of integration.

(f) DECISION-MAKING ACROSS PILLARS

The discussion thus far has concentrated on the contribution to decision-making in relation to the AFSJ by the actors considered above. A further dimension to the reality of decision-making should also be noted. This is the increasing tendency for policy initiatives to involve measures enacted under more than one pillar.[68] It is, for example, common in the fight against terrorism for measures to be made under all three pillars. This can in turn lead to contestable legal issues as to whether a particular measure could be validly enacted on the Treaty article cited as its foundation.[69]

6. LEGAL DOCTRINE, JUDICIAL TELEOLOGY, AND ITS LIMITS

It is clear from the preceding discussion that the central precepts of Community legal doctrine, fashioned in the context of the First Pillar, are of limited application in the AFSJ. The nature of those limits differs as between Title VI TEU and Title IV EC. Some of these limitations have been discussed above and will be considered in other chapters.[70] It is nonetheless important to reflect on the extent to which the ECJ has felt able to overcome these limitations through creative case law.

(a) TITLE VI TEU AND LEGAL DOCTRINE

Article 34 TEU specifies, as we have seen, the measures that can be adopted to achieve the objectives in Title VI TEU. A distinctive feature of this regime is that Article 34 states expressly that framework decisions and decisions do not have direct effect. The meaning of the phrase

---

[68] See, e.g., S. Stetter, 'Cross-pillar Politics: Functional Unity and Institutional Fragmentation of EU Foreign Policies' (2004) 11 *JEPP* 720.

[69] See, e.g., Case T–315/01 *Yassin Abdullah Kadi* v. *Council and Commission* [2005] ECR II–3649, paras. 87–135.

[70] See Ch. 8 and 14.

'direct effect' is however, as will be seen below,[71] contestable, and it is possible on the basis of the ECJ's case law to adopt either a broad or a narrow definition of direct effect.

The broader definition connotes the capacity of a provision of EC law to be invoked before a national court, which is sometimes referred to as 'objective' direct effect. While the normal consequence of a legal provision being invoked is that it confers a legal right of some kind on the individual who invokes it, this is not, on the broader definition, an essential component of the notion of direct effect. The narrower 'classical' definition of direct effect is usually expressed in terms of the capacity of a provision of EC law to confer rights on individuals which they may enforce before national courts, which is sometimes referred to as 'subjective' direct effect. The degree of difference between the two formulations depends, *inter alia*, on the definition of 'rights' being used. If what is meant is simply the *right to invoke* EC law in a national court to assist one's case, then there is little difference between the narrow and the broad notions of direct effect.

The preclusion of direct effect in the context of framework decisions and decisions clearly must have some meaning, and at the minimum this would mean that the narrow definition of direct effect is not operative in this area. An individual could not therefore claim that a framework decision or a decision conferred a subjective right that could be enforced through national courts. The Community Courts might nonetheless regard this as exhausting the remit of this limitation, with the consequence that the broader definition of direct effect set out above could still be applied in the context of Title VI. This would force the ECJ to demarcate more precisely than hitherto the essential difference between the narrow and broad views of direct effect.

Article 34 however only precludes direct effect in relation to framework decisions and decisions. It could therefore be argued, as Peers does,[72] that direct effect is not excluded with regard to common positions and conventions. There is force in this argument. It might however be difficult for an individual to prove the requisite specificity and clarity of the measure for it to have direct effect, and the ECJ has stated that common positions are not intended to produce legal effects for third parties.[73]

The ECJ is however clearly inclined to give the narrowest interpretation to Treaty provisions that derogate from the normal principles that it has developed. It has therefore held that the principle of indirect effect,[74] whereby national authorities and national courts have an obligation to interpret national law to be in conformity with a directive, also applies to framework decisions under the Third Pillar.

Case C–105/03 **Criminal Proceedings against Maria Pupino**
[2005] ECR I–5283

Pupino was a nursery school teacher and it was alleged that she had mistreated and assaulted children in her care. Italian criminal procedure consisted of two stages, and the general rule was that evidence would only be taken at the second stage. Italian law allowed for exceptions to this general rule in certain instances, but those exceptions did not cover the instant case. The Italian Public Prosecutor nonetheless sought to take evidence from the children at the first

---

[71] See below, 269–270.
[72] Peers, n. 1 above, 33.
[73] Case C–354/04 P *Gestoras Pro Amnistia, Olano and Errasti v. Council*, 27 Feb. 2007, paras. 51–53.
[74] See above, 287–296.

stage, on the ground that given their age and vulnerability they might otherwise forget or repress what had occurred. Pupino opposed this. The Italian court acknowledged that it could not accept the Public Prosecutor's application, since it did not come within the exceptions provided for in Italian law. It nonetheless asked the ECJ whether the national court should interpret Italian law in the light of Community law, this being relevant in the instant case because there was a Council Framework Decision concerning the standing and protection of victims in criminal proceedings. A number of Member States argued that the duty to interpret national law in conformity with EC law did not apply to the Third Pillar. The ECJ disagreed. It noted that framework decisions were binding as to the result to be achieved and continued as follows.

THE ECJ

34. The binding character of framework decisions, formulated in terms identical to those of the third paragraph of Article 249 EC, places on national authorities, and particularly national courts, an obligation to interpret national law in conformity.

35. The fact that, by virtue of Article 35 EU, the jurisdiction of the Court of Justice is less extensive under Title VI of the Treaty on European Union than it is under the EC Treaty, and the fact that there is no complete system of actions and procedures designed to ensure the legality of the acts of the institutions in the context of Title VI, does nothing to invalidate that conclusion.

36. Irrespective of the degree of integration envisaged by the Treaty of Amsterdam in the process of creating an ever closer union among the peoples of Europe within the meaning of the second paragraph of Article 1 EU, it is perfectly comprehensible that the authors of the Treaty on European Union should have considered it useful to make provision, in the context of Title VI of that Treaty, for recourse to legal instruments with effects similar to those provided for by the EC Treaty, in order to contribute effectively to the pursuit of the Union's objectives.

37. The importance of the Court's jurisdiction to give preliminary rulings under Article 35 EU is confirmed by the fact that, under Article 35(4), any Member State, whether or not it has made a declaration pursuant to Article 35(2), is entitled to submit statements of case or written observations to the Court in cases which arise under Article 35(1).

38. That jurisdiction would be deprived of most of its useful effect if individuals were not entitled to invoke framework decisions in order to obtain a conforming interpretation of national law before the courts of the Member States.

[*Some Member States argued that this interpretative obligation did not apply in the Third Pillar because it contained no provision equivalent to Article 10 EC. The ECJ disagreed.*]

. . .

42. It would be difficult for the Union to carry out its task effectively if the principle of loyal cooperation, requiring in particular that Member States take all appropriate measures, whether general or particular, to ensure fulfillment of their obligations under European Union law, were not also binding in the area of police and judicial cooperation in criminal matters, which is moreover entirely based on cooperation between the Member States and the institutions, as the Advocate General has rightly pointed out in paragraph 26 of her Opinion.

43. In the light of all the above considerations, the Court concludes that the principle of conforming interpretation is binding in relation to framework decisions adopted in the context of Title VI of the Treaty on European Union. When applying national law, the national court that is called upon to interpret it must do so as far as possible in the light of the wording and purpose of the framework decision in order to attain the result which it pursues and thus comply with Article 34(2)(b) EU.

44. It should be noted, however, that the obligation on the national court to refer to the content of a framework decision when interpreting the relevant rules of its national law is limited by general principles of law, particularly those of legal certainty and non-retroactivity.

45. In particular, those principles prevent that obligation from leading to the criminal liability of persons who contravene the provisions of a framework decision from being determined or aggravated on the basis of such a decision alone, independently of an implementing law. . . .

It remains to be seen how far other EC law principles concerning matters such as incidental effect, equal and effective remedies, and state liability in damages are applied in the context of the Third Pillar.[75] The application of the supremacy principle in the context of the Third Pillar has yet to be tested before the Community Courts. This issue will be discussed when we analyse the supremacy principle, and the arguments in favour of its application will be considered at that juncture.[76] The difficulties concerning the application of state liability in damages will be considered below.[77]

(b) TITLE VI TEU AND LEGALITY REVIEW

The fact that the ECJ will construe limits to its 'normal powers' narrowly is equally apparent in relation to legality review and the Third Pillar. We have seen that the ECJ has power under Article 35(6) TEU to review the legality of framework decisions and decisions.[78] The ECJ has been creative in its construction of Article 35, as is shown by *Gestoras*.[79]

Case C–354/04 P **Gestoras Pro Amnistia, Olano and Errasti v. Council**
27 February 2007

The Council adopted common position 2001/931 on the basis of Articles 15 and 34 TEU. The common position was passed to implement Resolution 1373 of the UN Security Council, which provided that all states should afford one another assistance relating to criminal proceedings concerning the financing or support of terrorist acts. The annex to the common position contained a list of groups in relation to which Member States should afford each other the widest cooperation in preventing and combating terrorist acts, and the list included Gestoras Pro Amnistia, which claimed compensation for the damage suffered by its inclusion in the list. The ECJ decided that Article 35 TEU conferred no jurisdiction to award damages under Title VI, Pillar Three of the TEU. The applicant argued that it was therefore deprived of all judicial protection, because Article 35 TEU did not allow any direct challenge, or indirect challenge via a preliminary ruling, to a common position. The ECJ disagreed.

---

[75] For an affirmative answer in principle see Peers, n. 1 above, 33. See also K. Lenaerts and T. Corthaut, 'Of Birds and Hedges: The Role of Primacy in Invoking Norms of EU Law' (2006) 31 *ELRev.* 287.

[76] See below, 351–352; Lenaerts and Corthaut, n. 75 above, 289–292.

[77] See below, 255.

[78] The ECJ can also review acts made under the TEU where it is claimed that they should have been passed under the EC Pillar: Case C–170/96 *Commission* v. *Council (Airport Transit Visas)* [1998] ECR I–2763; Case C–176/03 *Commission* v. *Council* [2005] ECR I–7879, para. 39.

[79] See also Case C–355/04 P *Segi, Izaga and Galarraga* v. *Council*, 27 Feb. 2007.

THE ECJ

51. As is clear from Article 6 EU, the Union is founded on the principle of the rule of law and it respects fundamental rights as general principles of Community law. It follows that the institutions are subject to review of the conformity of their acts with the treaties and the general principles of law, just like the Member States when they implement the law of the Union.

[*The ECJ noted that a common position defined the approach of the EU in relation to a particular matter, and was not intended in itself to produce legal effects in relation to third parties.*]

53. Article 35(1) EU, in that it does not enable national courts to refer a question to the Court for a preliminary ruling on a common position but only a question concerning the acts listed in that provision, treats as acts capable of being the subject of a reference for a preliminary ruling all measures adopted by the Council intended to produce legal effects in relation to third parties. Given that the procedure enabling the Court to give preliminary rulings is designed to guarantee observance of the law in the interpretation and application of the Treaty, it would run counter to that objective to interpret Article 35(1) narrowly. The right to make a reference to the Court for a preliminary ruling must therefore exist in respect of all measures adopted by the Council, whatever their nature or form, which are intended to have legal effects in relation to third parties.

54. As a result, it has to be possible to make subject to review by the Court a common position which, because of its content, has a scope beyond that assigned by the EU Treaty to that kind of act. So, a national court hearing a dispute which . . . raises serious doubts whether that common position is really intended to produce legal effects in relation to third parties, would be able, subject to the conditions fixed by Article 35, to ask the Court to give a preliminary ruling. It would then fall to the Court to find, where appropriate, that the common position is intended to produce legal effects in relation to third parties, to accord it its true classification and to give a preliminary ruling.

55. The Court would also have jurisdiction to review the lawfulness of such acts when an action has been brought by a Member State or the Commission on the conditions fixed by Article 35(6).

We see here classic ECJ reasoning to circumvent limits to its review power. It relies on the general principle that the EU is founded on the rule of law to provide the foundation for judicial review of a common position. The nature of a measure is to be judged by its substance, not its form. Hence if a measure bearing the name 'common position' produces legal effects for third parties it goes beyond the role assigned for that kind of measure by the EU Treaty, and the ECJ can therefore accord it its true classification and give a preliminary ruling.

(c) TITLE VI TEU: THE LIMITS OF JUDICIAL CREATIVITY

It would nonetheless be wrong to conclude that the Community Courts can, though creative interpretation, circumvent all limits on its 'normal powers'. Thus in *Gestoras Pro Amnistia*[80] the ECJ held that damages could not be claimed against the EU for losses suffered as the result of a measure adopted under the Third Pillar, since Article 35 TEU conferred no jurisdiction on the ECJ equivalent to Article 288(2) EC.

---

[80] Case C–354/04 *Errasti*, n. 73 above, paras. 44–48.

This raises the interesting related issue as to whether state liability in damages applies in the context of the Third Pillar. This liability is based in part on Article 10 EC, and on reasoning from general principle as to the obligation to provide a remedy that will ensure the more effective protection of the relevant Community right. There is no express exclusion of such liability in Title VI TEU. However the ECJ has closely linked the existence and conditions for state liability in damages to those under Article 288(2) EC, which govern Community liability in damages.[81] The application of state liability principles to the Third Pillar would therefore be open to the objection that the Member States were being subjected to a species of liability that did not attach to the EU itself. This tension would be all the greater where either it was unclear whether the losses flowed from Member State or Community action, or both contributed to the losses suffered.

The Community Courts are also powerless to fill the gap concerning enforcement actions brought by the Commission against Member States. Article 35 TEU contains nothing equivalent to Article 226 EC. The closest provision is Article 35(7) TEU, which enables the ECJ to rule on any dispute between the Commission and Member States concerning the interpretation and application of conventions established under Article 34(2)(d). This only applies to conventions and is a far cry from the general enforcement power accorded to the Commission under Article 226 EC. A factor driving the Commission to communautarize Title VI is, as we have seen, so as to make such enforcement actions available.[82]

The judicial regime in Title VI TEU is also incomplete because it affords no opportunity for individuals to challenge Third Pillar measures directly, since Article 35(6) only gives this power to the Commission and the Member States.

(d) TITLE IV EC: THE LIMITS TO PRELIMINARY RULINGS

In general terms, the normal Community legal regime applies in Title IV EC, subject however to the more limited nature of the preliminary ruling mechanism that applies in this area. We have seen that the Commission has proposed to bring this into line with the normal Article 234 mechanism, but this proposal has, thus far, not been accepted by the Council. The Member States may well be wary of this change, since it could impact on their ability to process asylum applications: if any court or tribunal could request a ruling then this might mean that a large number of cases concerning asylum applicants in the same position could effectively be 'frozen' pending the outcome of the ECJ's ruling, thereby rendering the attainment of 'national targets' for settling asylum applications more difficult.[83] The limitation on Article 234 references is nonetheless regrettable and has been criticized by commentators.[84]

7. ASYLUM, RIGHTS, AND THE AFSJ

It would be impossible within the scope of this Chapter to give even the most limited précis of the many different substantive areas encompassed by the AFSJ. Nor would this be particularly useful, given the complexity and range of the subject-matter. It is nonetheless important to

---

[81] See below, 583–584.
[82] N. 54 above, 13–15.
[83] We are indebted to Cathryn Costello for this point.
[84] Peers, n. 1 above, 53; Costello, n. 16 above, 299–300.

look at some parts of the AFSJ. It is only by doing so that one can begin to understand what it means more concretely to create an 'Area of Freedom, Security, and Justice', and the difficulties of making this a reality. The strategy for the remainder of the chapter is therefore to focus on two such topics.

(a) TREATY PROVISIONS

This section will consider asylum, because of its intrinsic importance and because it is the area where the most comprehensive range of legislative measures has been adopted. Asylum law is, as Peers notes, 'one of the most complex areas of JHA cooperation, although one of the most important'.[85]

Asylum policy is currently based on Article 63(1)–(2) EC, which builds on Article 61(b), set out above.[86] It will be remembered that under Article 63(1) the Council is obliged, within the five-year period post the Amsterdam Treaty, to adopt measures concerning criteria for deciding which State should be responsible for considering an asylum application; minimum standards on the reception of asylum seekers in Member States; minimum standards on whether third country nationals are refugees; and minimum standards on procedures in Member States for granting or withdrawing refugee status. These measures must be in accordance with the Geneva Convention of 1951 and the 1967 Protocol on the status of refugees. Article 63(2) requires the Council to adopt minimum standards for giving temporary protection to displaced persons from third countries who cannot return to their country of origin and for persons who otherwise need international protection. It also requires the Council to promote a balance of effort between Member States in receiving and bearing the consequences of receiving refugees and displaced persons.

The importance attached to this area is apparent from the fact that a Common EU Asylum and Migration Policy was the first of the four broad issues addressed by the Tampere European Council.

Tampere European Council[87]

A Common European Asylum System

13. The European Council reaffirms the importance the Union and Member States attach to absolute respect of the right to seek asylum. It has agreed to work towards establishing a Common European Asylum System, based on the full and inclusive application of the Geneva Convention, thus ensuring that nobody is sent back to persecution, i.e., maintaining the principle of non-refoulement.

14. This System should include, in the short term, a clear and workable determination of the State responsible for the examination of an asylum application, common standards for a fair and efficient asylum procedure, common minimum conditions of reception of asylum seekers, and the approximation of rules on the recognition and content of the refugee status. It should also be completed with measures on subsidiary forms of protection offering an appropriate status to any person in need of such protection. . . .

---

[85] Peers, n. 1 above, 298. See also R. Byrne, G. Noll, and J. Vedsted-Hansen, 'Understanding Refugee Law in an Enlarged European Union' (2004) 15 *EJIL* 355.

[86] See above, 240.

[87] N. 17 above.

15. In the longer term, Community rules should lead to a common asylum procedure and a uniform status for those who are granted asylum valid throughout the Union. The Commission is asked to prepare within one year a communication on this matter.

16. The European Council urges the Council to step up its efforts to reach agreement on the issue of temporary protection for displaced persons on the basis of solidarity between States. The European Council believes that consideration should be given to making some form of financial reserve available in situations of mass influx of refugees for temporary protection. The Commission is invited to explore the possibilities for this.

17. The European Council urges the Council to finalise promptly its work on the system for the identification of asylum seekers (Eurodac).

(b) THE ASYLUM LEGISLATION

The issue covered by Article 63(1)(a) concerning *which State has responsibility for asylum seekers* was addressed by the Dublin Convention, in force from 1 September 1997.[88] This Convention, like the Schengen Convention, was concerned with abolishing internal borders in the EU, and the Dublin Convention was agreed 'because Member States feared that loosening or abolishing internal border checks would lead to an increase in multiple asylum applications'.[89] Some common rules were therefore required to deal with this issue, since otherwise different Member States would take different views as to which State was responsible for handling the application. The Dublin Convention was however criticized both for the substantive criteria adopted to determine which State was responsible for dealing with asylum applications, and because in 1998–1999 only 1.7 per cent of all asylum applications in the EU resulted in the transfer of the asylum-seeker as a result of the Convention rules.[90] A new regulation, the Dublin II Regulation, was therefore adopted in 2003.[91] It altered the criteria from the original Dublin Convention, but did not address 'the argument that the Dublin rules are an expensive waste of time, ultimately applying to only a very small percentage of asylum seekers'.[92] The Member States hoped that the new regime would be more efficacious because of the link with the EURODAC scheme,[93] which required finger-prints from all asylum-seekers over the age of 14 to be transmitted to a central unit, in order to determine whether an asylum-seeker has made multiple applications in the EC. The efficacy of this scheme has however been questioned, since it is dependent on the willingness of border officials to take such finger-prints, when the effect would be the subsequent return of an asylum-seeker to that State.[94]

---

[88] Convention determining the State responsible for examining applications for asylum lodged in one of the Member States of the European Communities—the Dublin Convention [1997] OJ C254/1; K. Hailbronner and C. Thiery, 'Schengen II and Dublin: Responsibility for Asylum Applications in Europe' (1997) 34 *CMLRev.* 957.

[89] Peers, n. 1 above, 318.

[90] *Ibid.*, 319.

[91] Council Reg. (EC) 343/2003 of 18 Feb. 2003 establishing the criteria and mechanisms for determining the Member State responsible for examining an asylum application lodged in one of the Member States by a third-country national [2003] OJ L50/1.

[92] Peers, n. 1 above, 321.

[93] Council Reg. (EC) of 11 Dec. 2000 concerning the establishment of 'Eurodac' for the comparison of finger prints for the effective application of the Dublin Convention [2000] OJ L316/1.

[94] E. Brouwer, 'Eurodac: Its Temptations and Limitations' (2002) 4 *EJML* 231.

The minimum standards on *reception of asylum-seekers*, the issue covered by Article 63(1)(b), was dealt with in a directive in 2003.[95] The Directive sets out minimum procedural and substantive obligations on the State receiving the asylum-seeker.[96] The generally accepted rationale for this aspect of asylum policy is that 'different reception conditions in the EU Member States may be a substantial factor for migratory movements of refugees within the European Union',[97] although Costello has doubted the extent to which distribution of asylum-seekers can be explained on this ground.[98] In any event Peers has questioned the standards laid down in the Directive on the grounds that they are lower than those proposed by the Commission, that they are imprecisely worded, and that they are unlikely to have done much to close the gap between the countries with higher and those with lower standards concerning reception.[99]

The *determination of refugee and subsidiary protection status*, the issue covered by Article 63(1)(c), was also dealt with by directive in 2004.[100] There is general agreement that in relation to refugees the Directive complies with the criteria of the Geneva Convention, and the Directive makes it clear that the 'actors of persecution' do not have to be the State, but can be private parties, if it can be shown that the State is unable or unwilling to provide protection against them. Costello nonetheless cautions that 'asylum systems in the different Member States continue to reach widely divergent results, as evidenced in the different recognition rates for asylum seekers from different countries'.[101]

There has however been considerable disquiet about *procedural standards* and the Asylum Procedures Directive,[102] which was enacted in furtherance of Article 63(1)(d). Hailbronner provides the rationale for such a measure.

K. Hailbronner, Asylum Law in the Context of a European Migration Policy[103]

The harmonization of asylum procedures is of paramount importance for a common asylum system, first, because common or at least similar procedures help to prevent secondary movements, secondly, as a matter of non-discrimination on a European level because asylum seekers upon entry into force of the Dublin Convention are no longer able freely to choose their country of application, and thirdly to enable in the long run a follow-up EC legislative act to the Dublin Convention which defines the Member State responsible for examining an asylum application according to the country in which the asylum seeker has applied for protection. Such a system can work only in a balanced manner, without imposing very different burdens on Member States, if there are no incentives for asylum seekers to choose one country rather than another because of better protection guarantees, shorter asylum procedures, or the

95 Council Dir. 2003/9/EC of 27 Jan. 2003 laying down minimum standards for the reception of asylum-seekers [2003] OJ L31/18.
96 Peers, n. 1 above, 324–327.
97 K. Hailbronner, 'Asylum Law in the Context of a European Migration Policy', in Walker (ed.), n. 1 above, 78.
98 Costello, n. 16 above, 291–292.
99 Peers, n. 1 above, 327.
100 Council Dir. 2004/83/EC of 29 Apr. 2004 on minimum standards for the qualification and status of third country nationals or stateless persons as refugees or as persons who otherwise need international protection and the content of the protection granted [2004] OJ L304/12; Peers, n. 1 above, 327–335.
101 Costello, n. 16 above, 317.
102 Council Dir. 2005/85/EC of 1 Dec. 2005 on minimum standards on procedures in Member States for granting and withdrawing refugee status [2005] OJ L326/13.
103 N. 97 above, 70.

incentive to be able to stay in a country due to lax enforcement of expulsion decisions even after a claim has been rejected.

Space precludes detailed examination of this Directive. Suffice it to say that the Directive has been challenged by the EP[104] and has been strongly criticized by experts. Thus Peers states that 'it is doubtful that any piece of EC legislation has ever been responsible for so many human rights breaches'.[105] Similar thoughts are echoed by Costello.

C. Costello, The European Asylum Procedures Directive in Legal Context[106]

Of all the post-Amsterdam measures in the asylum field, the Procedures Directive has been the most controversial. This is at least partly explained by the context wherein national governments jealously guard their leeway to manipulate asylum procedures, in order to pursue various goals....

The highly qualified and differentiated procedural guarantees in the Procedures Directive are the result, and demonstrate a reluctance to commit to unequivocal procedural standards, or maintain access to asylum within the EU. Thus, the critiques of the Procedures Directive are well-founded. In particular, the variety of procedures permitted reflects an assumption that it is possible to determine the cogency of claims on the basis of generalisations or cursory examination. This runs counter to any informed context-sensitive understanding of the asylum process. In the worst cases under the Procedures Directive, such as the supersafe third country provisions, the generalised assessment entirely substitutes for any individual process. In the Directive, we see the result of a legislative process which should have established clear minimal guarantees, but instead cast a negotiated settlement in law, apparently reinvesting national administrations with discretion that they had lost in some measure due to domestic and ECHR rulings.

(c) CONCLUSION

It is clear, even from this brief overview, that attainment of the AFSJ in relation to asylum policy has been problematic. The difficulties are in part practical, as exemplified by the problems encountered with the Dublin II Regulation and EURODAC. They are in part conceptual, in so far as measures such as the Asylum Procedures Directive raise principled concerns as to EU competence, constitutional law, and compliance with fundamental rights. Underlying these concerns there is a latent ambiguity as to the very meaning of 'AFSJ'. Thus, as Costello notes, the references to 'freedom' and 'security' beg the question whose freedom and whose security is being safeguarded?[107] The Tampere European Council certainly intended the freedom to include that of the asylum-seekers,[108] but the Treaty itself and subsequent legislative developments show that this is to be carefully balanced against the freedom and security of EU citizens 'from the perceived threat of unmanaged migration'.[109]

---

[104] The case is pending: Case C–133/06 *European Parliament* v. *Council* [2006] OJ C108/12.
[105] Peers, n. 1 above, 341.
[106] UNHCR, Research Paper 134 (2006), 34.
[107] Costello, n. 16 above, 290.
[108] N. 17 above, para. 3.
[109] Costello, n. 16 above, 290.

8. POLICING, SECURITY, RIGHTS, AND THE AFSJ

The other area that will be briefly considered is policing and security, which is grounded primarily on Title VI TEU and often takes the form of executive action rather than legislation. It therefore provides an interesting contrast to asylum, which is based on Title IV EC and where the prime mechanism has been Community legislation.

(a) TREATY PROVISIONS

It will be recalled that Article 29 TEU, the foundational provision of Title VI, provides that the 'Union's objective shall be to provide citizens with a high level of safety within the area of freedom, security and justice by developing common action among the Member States in the fields of police and judicial cooperation in criminal matters and by preventing and combating racism and xenophobia'. The objective is to be achieved by preventing and combating crime through: closer co-operation between police forces, customs authorities, and other competent authorities in the Member State, both directly and through Europol; closer co-operation between judicial and other competent authorities of the Member States; and through approximation, where necessary, of the rules on criminal matters in the Member States. Article 30 TEU identifies, as seen above, four areas of action for police co-operation concerning prevention, investigation, and detection; storage and exchange of information; training, research, and equipment; and investigation of organized crime, and Europol is to be one of the main vehicles for achieving these objectives. Article 31(1) TEU specifies five areas for judicial co-operation in criminal matters: facilitating proceedings and enforcement of decisions; facilitating extradition between Member States; ensuring compatibility in the rules applicable in the Member States in order to improve such co-operation; preventing conflicts of jurisdiction between Member States; and the establishment of minimum rules relating to the constituent elements of criminal acts and penalties in the fields of organized crime, terrorism, and illicit drug trafficking. Eurojust is to help foster such co-operation.

The importance of policing and security was reinforced by the Tampere European Council in 1999. The fight against crime was the third of the four broad areas identified by the European Council as part of the AFSJ.

Tampere European Council[110]

C. A Unionwide Fight against Crime

40. The European Council is deeply committed to reinforcing the fight against serious organised and transnational crime. The high level of safety in the area of freedom, security and justice presupposes an efficient and comprehensive approach in the fight against all forms of crime. A balanced development of Unionwide measures against crime should be achieved while protecting the freedom and legal rights of individuals and economic operators.

---

[110] N. 17 above.

The European Council set out in greater detail its thoughts on crime prevention at Union level, with initial priority being accorded to juvenile, urban, and drug-related crime. It also proffered suggestions concerning increased co-operation against crime through, *inter alia*: the establishment of joint investigative teams to combat terrorism and trafficking in drugs and people; the creation of a European Police Chiefs' Operational Task Force to exchange, in co-operation with Europol, experience, information, and best practice; the strengthening of Europol and Eurojust; and the creation of a European Police College to train senior police officers. The European Council suggested moreover the offences that should be considered initially for approximation of Member States' criminal laws, and placed special emphasis on action against money laundering.

(b) POLICE AND CUSTOMS OPERATIONS BY NATIONAL AUTHORITIES

The objectives laid down in Title VI, as glossed by the Tampere European Council, have been developed by the Council and Commission. Thus, as Peers states,[111] national police and customs co-operation has been advanced by: requiring or encouraging the harmonization of national law and policy; facilitating co-ordination between national law enforcement authorities; and allowing, subject to certain conditions, the law enforcement authorities in one Member State to undertake operations in another. The range and complexity of the measures are daunting. The following extract, which concerns harmonization and facilitation of national law, conveys an idea of the range of hard and soft law devices used in just one area, drug use.

S. Peers, EU Justice and Home Affairs Law [112]

EU measures against narcotic drugs have been developed in the framework of successive multi-annual Action Plans. Over the years, EU action has included further measures concerning substantive criminal law, particularly harmonizing the law concerning drug precursors, drug trafficking and synthetic drugs. Specific anti-drug measures concerning the harmonizing of policing have comprised Resolutions or Recommendations on: coordination between police and customs regarding combating drugs; drug statistics; drug indicators; generic classification of new synthetic drugs; drug abuse in prisons; investigation methods...; cooperation between national authorities; training of drugs law enforcement officers and guidelines for taking samples of seized drugs. A Joint Action addresses customs/business cooperation against drug trafficking.

Non-policing measures have included Resolutions and Recommendations on the recreational use of drugs, prevention and reduction of health-related harm associated with drug dependence, the incorporation of drug prevention in the school curriculum, inclusion of substance abuse in the university curriculum, drug dependency and national health care, the role of families and road accidents. The EC has also established an agency monitoring the use of narcotic drugs, and its health funding programmes address drug-related issues.

There are also mechanisms for joint operations and investigations between national law enforcement agencies and customs authorities. These have however been criticized as

---

[111] Peers, n. 1 above, 524–535.
[112] *Ibid.*, 525–526.

suffering from a lack of specific rules on public accountability, and because of the absence of minimum standards concerning matters such as liability for police action.[113]

(c) EU BODIES

The objectives of Title VI are, as we have seen, also to be attained through the efforts of EU bodies, notably Europol and Eurojust. Articles 30–31 TEU expressly mandate the Council to promote police and judicial co-operation through Europol and Eurojust respectively.

The agreement to set up Europol dates from the Maastricht Treaty. The Europol Convention[114] flowed from a Council act based on what was Article K3 of the TEU.[115] It was ratified by all Member States in October 1998 and Europol became fully operational in July 1999. Its objectives are to enhance effectiveness and co-operation between Member States in dealing with offences that come within Europol's remit.[116] It has important tasks concerning the collection and provision of information:[117] it is to facilitate exchange of information between Member States; obtain, collate, and analyse information and intelligence; notify competent authorities within Member States of information of concern to them; aid investigations in Member States by forwarding relevant information to them; and maintain a computerized information system. Europol can also give advice on investigations, and provide assistance through advice and research in relation to training, crime prevention methods, organization and equipment, and forensic police methods. Co-ordination and co-operation between Europol and national police forces is also accorded a high prominence.

Eurojust was established in 2002 to enhance co-operation between the competent authorities responsible for the investigation and prosecution of cross-border and organized crime.[118] It has competence in relation to crimes that fall within Europol's jurisdiction and other crimes specifically listed.[119] Its objectives are to stimulate and improve co-ordination between the competent authorities of the Member States concerned with investigation and prosecution of these crimes; to improve co-operation between such authorities by facilitating the execution of international mutual legal assistance and implementation of extradition requests; and otherwise to support Member States' authorities in order to render their prosecutions and investigations more effective.[120] Eurojust will normally act through its national members, but can also in certain circumstances act as a College. In either eventuality, the twin themes of information provision coupled with co-operation/co-ordination dominate the more detailed delineation of its tasks. In addition Eurojust shall,[121] *inter alia*, give assistance in order to improve co-operation between the national authorities; ensure that the Member States' authorities inform each other of investigations and prosecutions of which it has been informed; assist such authorities at their request concerning the best possible co-ordination of investigations and prosecutions; and co-operate and consult with the European Judicial Network.

---

113 *Ibid.*, 535.
114 N. 62 above.
115 *Ibid.*
116 Europol Convention, n. 62 above, Art. 2.
117 *Ibid.*, Art. 3.
118 Council Dec. 2002/187/JHA of 28 Feb. 2002 setting up Eurojust with a view to reinforcing the fight against serious crime [2002] OJ L 63/1.
119 *Ibid.*, Art. 4.
120 *Ibid.*, Art. 3.
121 *Ibid.*, Art. 6(b)-(g).

We have seen that the Tampere European Council called for the establishment of a European Police College, and this was duly established in 2000,[122] its principal task being the training of senior police officers. The European Council also favoured the creation of an Operational Task Force of Police Chiefs, and this was created in 2000, although it had no formal legal foundation. It now meets within the framework of Europol with regard to operational matters, and in the JHA Council for issues of a more strategic nature.[123]

(d) INFORMATION, POLICING, AND SECURITY

It is readily apparent from the discussion thus far that information, its collation, sharing, and analysis are regarded as central in pursuing the policing and security objectives in Title VI. A considerable range of initiatives have therefore been devoted to information in this broad sense. Thus there are specific provisions dealing with exchange of information in areas such as customs, drugs, football security, terrorism, passenger data,[124] and immigration.[125]

The most controversial such measure is the Data Retention Directive,[126] which requires Member States to compel telecommunications operators to retain 'traffic and location data' for the entire population. This does not cover the actual content of the communication, but the Directive is nonetheless far-reaching and covers internet communications as well as more traditional forms of telephony. The object of the Directive, as specified in Article 1, is to assist the 'investigation, prosecution and detection of serious crime, as defined by each Member State in its national law'. It is for national law to determine the conditions of access to the data, subject to compliance with the European Convention of Human Rights and tests of necessity and proportionality.[127]

In addition to these individual measures, there are also more general EU information systems.[128] There is the system managed by Europol, described above. The Schengen Information System (SIS) is for the use of national police, customs, and border control authorities in order to make checks on those crossing external borders or within the Schengen States; it is also used by immigration officers in relation to third country nationals when dealing with matters such as visas. There is also a Customs Information System (CIS), which is designed to assist in preventing, investigating, and prosecuting serious contraventions of national customs law.

There are provisions on EU data protection, but their adequacy has been questioned. Thus Peers has argued that the Europol, SIS, and CIS Conventions 'make no serious attempt to strike the balance'[129] between the practical demands of law enforcement and the individual's right to check the accuracy of such data, since the Conventions 'give maximum discretion to

---

[122] Council Dec. 2000/820/JHA of 22 Dec. 2000, Establishing a European Police College (Cepol) [2000] OJ L336/1.

[123] Peers, n. 1 above, 542; T. Bunyan, 'The EU's Police Chief Task Force (PCTF) and Police Chiefs Committee', available at www.statewatchorg/news/2006/mar/pcf.pdf.

[124] Cases C–317 and 318/04 *European Parliament* v. *Council and Commission (PNR)* [2006] ECR I–4721, annulling a Dec. on the processing and transfer of personal data to the USA from air passenger records.

[125] Peers, n. 1 above, 542–544.

[126] Dir. 2006/24/EC of the European Parliament and of the Council of 15 Mar. 2006 on the retention of data generated or processed in connection with the provision of publicly available electronic communications services or of public communications networks and amending Dir. 2002/58/EC [2006] OJ L105/54; P. Breyer, 'Telecommunications Data Retention and Human Rights: The Compatibility of Blanket Traffic Data Retention with the ECHR' (2005) 11 *ELJ* 373.

[127] *Ibid.*, Art. 4.

[128] Peers, n. 1 above, 547–551.

[129] *Ibid.*, 555.

law enforcement authorities with no indication of circumstances in which personal data must or may be released to an individual'.[130] The system is therefore dependent on supervisory bodies the efficacy of which is open to question, and there is little by way of rules on transparency or parliamentary accountability to oversee such bodies.

(e) CONCLUSION

This brief account of policing and security as one part of the AFSJ reveals similar concerns to those encountered in the discussion of asylum: effectiveness and the impact on rights, combined with the additional concern relating to the complexity of the material.

The *effectiveness* of the initiatives has been touched on in the previous discussion. It has been raised more generally by Fijnaut,[131] who asks the central question whether the EU measures have 'added value' in terms of increasing security within the EU. This is, he readily accepts, a question that is difficult to answer, in part because of the relative paucity of detailed studies on EU criminal activity.[132] Fijnaut identifies a second factor that renders an answer to the question difficult.

C. Fijnaut, Police Cooperation and the Area of Freedom, Security and Justice[133]

The second reason why the added value of police co-operation in terms of increased safety and protection from organized crime cannot presently be determined . . . is that there is no, or hardly any, research being carried out on how this co-operation actually operates and what effects it has on the problems of crime. . . .

Thus, in fact, almost nothing can be said about the way in which Europol functions in practice. The annual reports from this service do indicate that it was, in past years, involved in one way or another in hundreds of investigations in the Member States of the EU, but what this involvement represented in practice, what added value was gained from these investigations, what effects these investigations had on the problem of organized crime and so on are all questions which an outsider cannot in fact answer in the absence of scholarly research. . . .

The direct co-operation between police services of the Member States at the national level in the fight against (organized) crime is just as difficult to assess as their mutual co-operation through Europol. Throughout the EU, there is, to the knowledge of the author, no research in which this form of co-operation is systematically examined. . . .

The impact of policing and security provisions on *individual rights* is an endemic problem for any polity. The EU's powers are not primarily operational, and therefore some of the difficult problems between rights and security in Member States do not arise in relation to the EU. There are nonetheless real tensions in this respect. This is exemplified by the issues concerning privacy and data protection that are engaged by the Data Retention Directive, and by the EU's response to terrorism through the use of 'smart/targeted sanctions' leading to seizure of financial assets, leaving those affected in a difficult position where they contest the correctness of their inclusion on the relevant list.

---

[130] *Ibid.*, 555.

[131] C. Fijnaut, 'Police Cooperation and the Area of Freedom, Security and Justice', in Walker (ed.), n. 1 above, 267.

[132] *Ibid.*, 268–269.

[133] *Ibid.*, 270–271.

The *complexity* of the subject-matter is a further problem in this area. This flows in part from the plethora of measures, hard and soft law, that govern policing and security, which render it difficult for even experts to keep abreast of the field. This problem is compounded by the relative lack of transparency which, as Fijnaut notes, is particularly undesirable for matters so politically sensitive as terrorism, organized crime, and immigration.[134] There is moreover the conceptual and doctrinal complexity that flows from the fact that there can be significant overlap between the Third Pillar and the other two Pillars. Thus measures adopted in the fight against terrorism have often been based on both the Second and Third Pillars,[135] and these measures may well include standard EC regulations as well as common positions, framework decisions, and the like. The interplay more generally between Title VI TEU and the Community Pillar can lead to significant conceptual complexity.[136]

9. THE IMPACT OF THE CONSTITUTIONAL TREATY

The status of the Constitutional Treaty[137] was considered above.[138] The impact of the CT on the AFSJ was significant,[139] and the general approach is preserved in the impending Reform Treaty. The areas covered by Title VI TEU and Title IV EC were brought together as Chapter IV of Part III of the CT. The pre-existing distinction between the three Pillars was abolished and the AFSJ was brought into a common institutional framework. This meant that: qualified-majority voting would become the norm in this area; the EP's power would be enhanced though the application of the ordinary legislative procedure; which was the successor to the co-decision procedure; the CT's regime of European laws and European framework laws would apply to the AFSJ; and the ECJ's jurisdiction would be extended to all aspects of the AFSJ. The Commission would have the right of legislative initiative.[140]

There were however still some exceptions to the application of the new 'unitary' regime in the context of the AFSJ. Thus there were some areas where unanimity in the Council was required and the EP's rights were limited to consultation,[141] and other areas where unanimity in the Council was combined with consent of the EP.[142] Moreover, while the ECJ's standard jurisdiction was applicable to the AFSJ, it could not review the validity or proportionality of operations carried out by the police or other law-enforcement services of a Member State, or the exercise of responsibilities incumbent on Member States with regard to the maintenance of law and order and the safeguarding of internal security.[143]

The CT also amended the substantive scope of the provisions concerned with matters such as immigration, asylum, criminal law, and police and judicial co-operation.[144] Thus, to mention but a few such examples, immigration and asylum policies were to be 'common', rather

---

[134] *Ibid.*, 267.
[135] See, e.g., Case C–354/04 P, *Gestoras Pro Amnistia*, n. 73 above.
[136] Peers, n. 1 above, 510–523; Fijnaut, n. 131 above, 258–267.
[137] [2004] OJ C310/1.
[138] See above, 31–36.
[139] Art. I–42 CT; Arts. III–257–277 CT.
[140] Some measures could however be made on the initiative of a quarter of the Member States: Art. III–264 CT.
[141] See, e.g., Art. III–266(3) CT: emergency situation resulting from influx of nationals from third countries.
[142] See, e.g., Art. III–274(1) CT: creation of European Public Prosecutor.
[143] Art. III–377 CT.
[144] Peers, n. 1 above, 86–89.

than, as at present, concerned with setting minimum standards;[145] provision was made for the creation of a European Public Prosecutor;[146]and the focus for judicial co-operation in criminal matters was mutual recognition.[147]

10. CONCLUSION

i. The nature of the topics comprised in the AFSJ and the volume of measures, both hard law and soft law, that have been enacted bear testimony to its overall importance within the EU polity.

ii. The distinctive nature of the AFSJ stems ultimately from the Member States' unwillingness for the normal Community method to be applied. The distinction between the 'intergovernmental' AFSJ and the 'supranational' Community Pillar should not be overplayed, more especially because developments since the Amsterdam Treaty have blurred that distinction. It nonetheless remains the case that in relative terms the Member States retain greater power under the AFSJ than they do in relation to the generality of issues dealt with under the Community Pillar, although the relevant provisions of the Constitutional Treaty indicated the willingness of the Member States to bring the AFSJ closer into line with decision-making in other areas.

iii. It is little surprise, given the nature of the subject-matter, that many of the measures enacted have proven controversial. There have, as we have seen, been problems concerning effectiveness, complexity, compliance with fundamental rights,[148] and accountability.

iv. The EU bears responsibility in this respect, but so too do the Member States. The measures enacted are dependent in the last resort on what the Member States will accept, and 'all Member States have a contradictory stance regarding closer integration: recognizing the logic that rising cross-border movement and crime requires responses that override the boundaries between national jurisdictions, while resisting the adjustments in national practices and the public concessions of sovereignty that this entails'.[149]

11. FURTHER READING

(a) Books

Denza, E., *The Intergovernmental Pillars of the European Union* (Oxford University Press, 2002)

Guild, E., and Harlow, C. (eds.), *Implementing Amsterdam: Immigration and Asylum Rights in EC Law* (Hart, 2001)

---

[145] Art. III–265 CT.

[146] Art. III–274 CT.

[147] Art. III–270 CT.

[148] See also Case C–540/03 *European Parliament* v. *Council (Family Reunification)* [2006] ECR I–5769, challenging parts of the Family Reunification Dir. The challenge failed on the facts, but the ECJ held that it was incumbent on Member States to apply the relevant provisions in a manner consistent with fundamental rights, which were binding on Member States when they implemented Community rules: paras. 104–105; Case C–303/05 *Advocaten voor de Wereld VZW* v. *Leden van de Ministerraad*, 3 May 2007, concerning the legality of the European Arrest Warrant.

[149] Lavenex and Wallace, n. 15 above, 479.

Hailbronner, K., *Immigration and Asylum Law and Policy of the European Union* (Kluwer, 2000)

Peers, S., *EU Justice and Home Affairs Law* (2nd edn., Oxford University Press, 2006)

—— and Rogers, N., *EU Immigration and Asylum Law* (Martinus Nijhoff, 2006)

Toner, H., Guild, E., and Baldaccini, A. (eds.), *Whose Freedom, Security and Justice? EU Immigration and Asylum Law and Policy* (Hart, 2007)

Walker, N. (ed.), *Europe's Area of Freedom, Security and Justice* (Oxford University Press, 2004)

(b) Articles

Byrne, R., Noll, G., and Vedsted-Hansen, J., 'Understanding Refugee Law in an Enlarged European Union' (2004) 15 *EJIL* 355

Costello, C., 'Administrative Governance and the Europeanisation of Asylum and Immigration Policy', in H. Hofmann and A. Turk (eds.), *EU Administrative Governance* (Edward Elgar, 2006), ch. 9

Hailbronner, K., 'European Immigration and Asylum Law after the Amsterdam Treaty' (1998) 35 *CMLRev.* 1047

Lavenex, S., and Wallace, W., 'Justice and Home Affairs, Towards a "European Public Order"?', in H. Wallace, W. Wallace, and M. Pollack (eds.), *Policy Making in the European Union* (5th edn., Oxford University Press, 2005), ch. 18

Monar, J., 'Justice and Home Affairs in the Treaty of Amsterdam: Reform at the Price of Fragmentation' (1998) 23 *ELRev.* 320

Peers, S., 'Caveat Emptor: Integrating the Schengen Acquis into the European Union Legal Order' (1999) 2 *CYELS* 87

—— 'EU Immigration and Asylum Law: Internal Market Model or Human Rights Model?', in T. Tridimas and P. Nebbia (eds.), *EU Law for the Twenty-First Century: Rethinking the New Legal Order, Vol. I* (Hart, 2004), 345

THE NATURE AND EFFECT OF
EC LAW: DIRECT EFFECT
AND BEYOND

1. CENTRAL ISSUES

i.   The doctrine of 'direct effect' of EC law applies in principle to all binding Community law including the EC Treaties, secondary legislation, and international agreements. The most problematic issues concern EC directives and international agreements.[1]

ii. The meaning of direct effect remains contested. In a broad sense it means that provisions of binding EC law which are clear, precise, and unconditional enough to be considered justiciable can be invoked and relied on by individuals before national courts. There is also a 'narrower' or classical concept of direct effect which is defined in terms of the capacity of a provision of EC law to *confer rights* on individuals.

iii. While directives can be enforced directly by individuals against the State after the time limit for their implementation has expired (vertical direct effect), resulting where necessary in the disapplication of conflicting domestic law, the ECJ has ruled that they cannot of themselves impose obligations on individuals (no horizontal direct effect).

iv. However, other legal mechanisms have been developed by the Court to give effect to directives which have not properly been implemented or are not being properly applied. First, there is a broad obligation on national courts to interpret domestic law, as far as possible, in conformity with directives (indirect effect), after the time limit for their implementation has expired. Secondly, during the period after adoption of a directive but before the time limit for implementation has expired, all organs of the State, including courts, must refrain from adopting any measure or interpretation liable seriously to compromise the result prescribed by the directive. Thirdly, a directive can in certain cases be legally invoked in proceedings between private parties (incidental effect) so long as the directive does not in itself impose a legal obligation on one of the parties.

---

[1] The legal effect of international agreements is considered in Ch. 6, 206–213.

2. THE AMBIGUOUS CONCEPT OF
DIRECT EFFECT: A GUIDE

The topic dealt with in this chapter is central to the study of EU law. It has been developed by the ECJ and its jurisprudence has become more complex over the years. The discussion in this section is therefore designed to help the reader navigate through the difficult waters that lie ahead. Or, if you prefer a different metaphor, regard this section as programme notes to render the scenes of a complex play more readily understandable. This is all the more so since, as will be apparent, the story is still unfolding.

(1) The starting point is the distinction between *public and private enforcement*. Law can be enforced either through a public arm of government, which is accorded power to bring infringers to court, or through actions brought by private individuals, or an admixture of the two. The Treaty embodied an express mechanism for public enforcement in Article 226, allowing the Commission to sue Member States before the ECJ for breach of Community law. This compulsory jurisdiction was itself unusual, since most international treaties contained no such mechanism. There are however limits to this mode of enforcement: the Commission did not have the institutional capacity to prosecute more than a tiny fraction of all possible infringements; the remedy under Article 226 was weak; and the Article could not be used against private individuals.[2]

(2) The ECJ therefore took the bold step of legitimating *private enforcement by holding that Treaty Articles could, subject to certain conditions, have direct effect, such that individuals could rely on them before their national courts and challenge inconsistent national action, thereby bringing individuals into the Community legal order.* The domestic effect of an international treaty has traditionally been a matter to be determined in accordance with the constitutional law of each State party to that treaty. In countries which adopt a largely dualist approach to international law, international agreements do not of themselves give rise to rights or interests which citizens can invoke before national courts. Instead, the provisions of such treaties bind only the States at an intergovernmental level and, in the absence of implementation, cannot be directly domestically enforced by citizens.[3] Since the texts of the EC Treaties made no reference to the effect which their provisions were to have, the original Member States may not have envisaged that the provisions of these Treaties would be treated any differently, in domestic terms, from those of other international treaties. The ECJ nonetheless held that the EEC Treaty was different from other treaties and that individuals could derive rights from its provisions that could be enforced at national level.

(3) So far so good. The development may have been bold, but it does not seem as if there is anything too complex thus far. This is not quite so, since there is *academic and judicial uncertainty about the exact meaning of the term direct effect.*[4] It is possible on the basis of the ECJ's

---

[2] P. Craig, 'Once upon a Time in the West: Direct Effect and the Federalization of EEC Law' (1992) 12 *OJLS* 453.

[3] D. Wyatt, 'New Legal Order or Old' (1982) 7 *ELRev.* 14.

[4] See the earlier discussion of differences in meaning between the terms 'direct applicability' and 'direct effect', which the ECJ used interchangeably: T. Winter, 'Direct Applicability and Direct Effects' (1972) 9 *CMLRev.* 425; Warner AG in Case 131/79 *Santillo* [1980] ECR 1585, 1608–1609; P. Eleftheriadis, 'The Direct Effect of Community Law: Conceptual Issues' (1996) 16 *YBEL* 205; Case C–253/00 *Muñoz* v. *Frumar Ltd.* [2002] ECR I–7289, Geelhoed AG.

case law to adopt either a broad or a narrow definition of direct effect.[5] The broader defin-ition, which can arguably be derived from *Van Gend en Loos*, can be expressed as *the capacity of a provision of EC law to be invoked before a national court*.[6] This is sometimes referred to as 'objective' direct effect.[7] While it is true that the normal consequence of a legal provision being invoked, as in *Van Gend en Loos* itself, is that it confers a legal right of some kind on the indi-vidual who invokes it, this is not, on the broader definition, an essential component of the notion of direct effect. If on the other hand the narrower 'classical' definition of direct effect is adopted, it is usually expressed in terms of the *capacity of a provision of EC law to confer rights on individuals which they may enforce before national courts*. This is sometimes referred to as 'subjective' direct effect. The degree of difference between these formulations depends how-ever on the definition of 'rights' being used. If what is meant is simply the *right to invoke* EC law in a national court to assist one's case,[8] then there is little difference between the narrow and the broad notions of direct effect.[9] In many other cases, however, the ECJ has gone beyond the simple reference to a right to invoke, and has indicated that an individual litigant can rely before a national court on the substantive right, such as the right to be free from discrimin-ation based on nationality.[10] Moreover if the 'conferral of rights on individuals' involves entitlement to a particular remedy[11] or the imposition of a corresponding duty or liability on another party,[12] then there may well be a relevant difference between the broad and the nar-row definitions. In reality, the ECJ seems to use the language of 'conferral of rights' in the con-text of direct effect in several different senses. Thus even the narrow definition of direct effect in subjective terms as 'the conferral of individual rights' is not particularly precise, given the ambiguity in the notion of 'rights'. The ambiguity in the meaning of direct effect is not however of purely academic interest. It has, as will be seen below, important practical implications.[13]

(4) We shall return to this issue in due course. Let us for the present take up the thread of the story concerning direct effect. The next stage was reasonably predictable. *The ECJ, having*

---

[5] For various analyses see S. Prechal, 'Does Direct Effect Still Matter?' (2000) 37 *CMLRev.* 1047 and also *Directives in EC Law* (2nd edn., Oxford University Press, 2005); M. Lenz, D.S. Tynes, and L. Young, 'Horizontal What? Back to Basics' (2000) 25 *ELRev.* 509; C. Hilson and T. Downes, 'Making Sense of Rights: Community Rights in EC Law' (1999) 24 *ELRev.* 121.

[6] In Case 26/62 *Van Gend en Loos* [1963] ECR 13 the ECJ ruled that Art. 12 should be interpreted 'as pro-ducing direct effects and creating individual rights', thus implying that the latter followed from, but was not necessarily a condition for, the former.

[7] W. van Gerven, 'Of Rights, Remedies and Procedures' (2000) 37 *CMLRev.* 501; D. Edward, 'Direct Effect, the Separation of Powers and the Judicial Enforcement of Obligations', in *Scritti in Onore di Giuseppe Federico Mancini, II, Diritto dell'Unione Europea* (Guiffré, 1998), 423.

[8] See, e.g., Case C–63/99 *Gloszczuk* [2001] ECR I–6369; Case C–257/99 *Barkoci and Malik* [2001] ECR I–6557; Case C–235/99 *Kondova* [2001] ECR I–6427; Case C–268/99 *Jany* [2001] ECR I–8615; Case C–327/02 *Panayotova* [2004] ECR I–11055, para. 18.

[9] A related question, if the narrower 'subjective' definition is adopted, concerns *who* can invoke the rights conferred by a directly effective provision of law. See Cases C–87–89/90 *Verholen* [1991] ECR I–3757; Case C–72/95 *Kraaijeveld* [1996] ECR I–5403, paras. 57–60; Cases C–240–244/98 *Océano Grupo Editorial* v. *Rocio Murciano Quintero* [2000] ECR I–4491, discussed below at n. 112 and text; Case C–230/97 *Awoyemi* [1998] ECR I–6781.

[10] For an early example see Case 57/65 *Lütticke* v. *Hauptzollamt Sarrelouis* [1966] ECR 205 on Art. 90 EC.

[11] See for discussion Prechal, n. 5 above; M. Ruffert, 'Rights and Remedies in European Community Law: A Comparative View' (1997) 34 *CMLRev.* 307; Van Gerven, n. 7 above.

[12] See the arguments of Hilson and Downes, n. 5 above, who apply a Hohfeldian analysis to the language and judgments of the ECJ in this field.

[13] Thus, e.g., the ECJ has held that even though dirs. do not give rise to rights between private parties they can nonetheless be invoked in certain ways before national courts: 284–300.

established that Treaty Articles could in principle have direct effect, then expanded the concept in two related ways: the conditions for direct effect were subtly loosened and direct effect thus modified was applied to regulations and decisions as well as Treaty Articles.

(5) The *judicial focus then shifted to directives.* Many commentators and indeed national courts doubted whether directives could have direct effect, since the very nature of directives did not meet the original conditions for direct effect laid down in *Van Gend.* The ECJ nonetheless held that directives were capable in principle of direct effect. It however also held that directives were only capable of *vertical direct effect,* meaning that they could only be raised against the State or a state entity. They were not capable of having *horizontal direct effect,* in the sense that they could not impose obligations on a private party. The reasons for this ruling were, as will be seen, controversial and remain so.

(6) It is from this point on that the story becomes more complex. *On the one hand, the vertical/horizontal distinction required the ECJ and national courts to differentiate between state entities and non-state entities. On the other hand, the ECJ fashioned certain new ways in which provisions of Community law could impact on national law.* Thus it created the doctrine of 'indirect effect' which meant that, even if directives did not have horizontal direct effect, national courts were under an interpretive obligation to construe national law to be in conformity with directives. It also fashioned what has been termed the concept of 'incidental horizontal effects', whereby a directive can preclude reliance on a provision of national law that is inconsistent with the provisions of the directive even in an action between private parties. This is premised on the primacy of Community law and entails a distinction between a directive having an 'exclusionary' impact, which in effect connotes the idea that the directive 'knocks out' or 'excludes' inconsistent national law; and a directive having a 'substitution' effect, which connotes the idea that the directive will in itself mandate certain novel EC legal consequences within the national legal order.[14] The tenability of this distinction is however questionable, as will be seen from the subsequent discussion. It has in any event rendered this body of law considerably more difficult than hitherto.

(7) The story recounted in outline here and in detail in the remainder of the chapter is still continuing. The end point remains to be seen. What is apparent is that direct effect, in the classic 'subjective' sense of the capacity of a provision of EC law to confer rights on individuals which they may enforce before national courts, is increasingly seen as but one way for Community law to impact on national law. On this view classic direct effect, indirect effect, and incidental horizontal effect provide different ways in which Community law can impact on national legal systems.[15] This development has moreover been further driven by the desire to exert judicial control over framework decisions made in the Third Pillar, which are specifically said to lack direct effect. The ECJ has nonetheless held that this does not preclude indirect effect being accorded to these measures.[16]

(8) We shall evaluate the overall impact of these developments at the end of this chapter. For the present we turn to the foundations of direct effect laid down in the seminal decision in *Van Gend en Loos.*

---

[14] See, e.g., Case C–244/98 *Océano Grupo,* n. 9 above, paras. 26–39, Saggio AG; Case C–287/98 *Luxemburg* v. *Linster* [2000] ECR I–6917, paras. 57–90, Leger AG.

[15] See, e.g., K. Lenaerts and T. Corthaut, 'Of Birds and Hedges: The Role of Primacy in Invoking Norms of EU Law' (2006) 31 *ELRev.* 287.

[16] Case C–105/03 *Pupino* [2005] ECR I–5285, paras. 34–48.

3. THE DIRECT EFFECT OF TREATY PROVISIONS

(a) FOUNDATIONS: *VAN GEND EN LOOS*

The ECJ first articulated its doctrine of direct effect in 1963 in what remains the most famous of all of its rulings.

Case 26/62 NV Algemene Transporten Expeditie Onderneming van Gend en Loos v. Nederlandse Administratie der Belastingen
[1963] ECR 1

[Note ToA renumbering: Art. 12 is now Art. 25, Art. 169 is now Art. 226, Art. 170 is now Art. 227, and Art. 177 is now Art. 234 EC]

The Van Gend en Loos company imported a quantity of chemicals from Germany into the Netherlands. It was charged with an import duty which had allegedly been increased (by changing the tariff classification from a lower to a higher tariff heading) since the coming into force of the EEC Treaty, contrary to Article 12. On appeal against payment before the Dutch Tariefcommissie, Article 12 was raised in argument and two questions were referred to the ECJ under Article 177 EC. The first was 'whether Article 12 of the EEC Treaty has direct application within the territory of a Member State; in other words, whether nationals of such a State can, on the basis of the Article in question, lay claim to individual rights which the courts must protect'. Observations were submitted to the ECJ by the Belgian, German, and Netherlands governments. Belgium argued that the question was whether a national law ratifying an international Treaty would prevail over another law, and that this was a question of national constitutional law which lay within the exclusive jurisdiction of the Netherlands court. The Netherlands government argued that the EEC Treaty was no different from a standard international Treaty, and that the concept of direct effect would contradict the intentions of those who had created the Treaty.

THE ECJ[17]

To ascertain whether the provisions of an international treaty extend so far in their effects it is necessary to consider the spirit, the general scheme and the wording of those provisions.

The objective of the EEC Treaty, which is to establish a Common Market, the functioning of which is of direct concern to interested parties in the Community, implies that this Treaty is more than an agreement which merely creates mutual obligations between the contracting states. This view is confirmed by the preamble to the Treaty which refers not only to governments but to peoples. It is also confirmed more specifically by the establishment of institutions endowed with sovereign rights, the exercise of which affects Member States and also their citizens. Furthermore, it must be noted that the nationals of the states brought together in the Community are called upon to cooperate in the functioning of this Community through the intermediary of the European Parliament and the Economic and Social Committee.

In addition the task assigned to the Court of Justice under Article 177, the object of which is to secure uniform interpretation of the Treaty by national courts and tribunals, confirms that the states have acknowledged that community law has an authority which can be invoked by their

---

[17] [1963] ECR 1, 12–13.

nationals before those courts and tribunals. The conclusion to be drawn from this is that the Community constitutes a new legal order of international law for the benefit of which the states have limited their sovereign rights, albeit within limited fields, and the subjects of which comprise not only Member States but also their nationals. Independently of the legislation of Member States, Community law therefore not only imposes obligations on individuals but is also intended to confer upon them rights which become part of their legal heritage. These rights arise not only where they are expressly granted by the Treaty, but also by reason of obligations which the Treaty imposes in a clearly defined way upon individuals as well as upon the Member States and upon the institutions of the Community. . . .

The wording of Article 12 contains a clear and unconditional prohibition which is not a positive but a negative obligation. This obligation, moreover, is not qualified by any reservation on the part of states which would make its implementation conditional upon a positive legislative measure enacted under national law. The very nature of this prohibition makes it ideally adapted to produce direct effects in the legal relationship between Member States and their subjects.

The implementation of Article 12 does not require any legislative intervention on the part of the states. The fact that under this Article it is the Member States who are made the subject of the negative obligation does not imply that their nationals cannot benefit from this obligation. . . .

It follows from the foregoing considerations that, according to the spirit, the general scheme and the wording of the Treaty, Article 12 must be interpreted as producing direct effects and creating individual rights which national courts must protect.

In addition the argument based on Articles 169 and 170 of the Treaty put forward by the three governments which have submitted observations to the court in their statements of case is misconceived . The fact that these Articles of the Treaty enable the Commission and the Member States to bring before the court a state which has not fulfilled its obligations does not mean that individuals cannot plead these obligations, should the occasion arise, before a national court. . . .

A restriction of the guarantees against an infringement of Article 12 by Member States to the procedures under Article 169 and 170 would remove all direct legal protection of the individual rights of their nationals. There is the risk that recourse to the procedure under these articles would be ineffective if it were to occur after the implementation of a national decision taken contrary to the provisions of the Treaty.

The vigilance of individuals concerned to protect their rights amounts to an effective supervision in addition to the supervision entrusted by Articles 169 and 170 to the diligence of the Commission and of the Member States.

Van Gend en Loos was a ground-breaking judgment. The strong submissions made on behalf of the three governments (half of the Member States at the time) which intervened indicate that the concept of direct effect of Treaty provisions, understood as the *immediate enforceability by individual applicants of those provisions in national courts*, probably did not accord with the understanding of those States of the obligations they had assumed when they became parties to the EEC. They argued that international treaties were really just a compact between States and did not give rise to rights that individuals could enforce in their national courts. They also contended that the sole method of enforcing Community law was through an action under what is now Article 226, brought by the Commission. The ECJ nonetheless held that Treaty Articles could have direct effect.

It *reasoned partly from the text of the Treaty*. It pointed to the Preamble which makes reference to citizens as well as to States, and argued that the preliminary-ruling procedure established in what is now Article 234 envisaged that parties before national courts could plead and rely on points of EC law. The ECJ pointed also to the fact that citizens were envisaged as having a role to play under the Treaties through the medium of the European Parliament. This textual 'evidence' for direct effect is not particularly strong. The ECJ's argument based on Article 234 is nonetheless interesting and subtle. We do not have the *travaux préparatoires*, and hence we do not know what the Treaty framers had in mind with this provision. If however individuals could never invoke EC law in national courts through Article 234 then it could only ever be used if the parties to the case were both public bodies, and there is nothing in the wording of Article 234 to indicate any such limitation. The very existence of Article 234 therefore lent force to the argument that individuals could at the very least invoke Community law at national level and challenge inconsistent national action. It was therefore unsurprising that the ECJ should replay this same argument when it justified the direct effect of directives.[18]

The ECJ's *reasoning was however principally characterized by a vision of the kind of legal community that the Treaties seemed designed to create.* The case provides an early example of the ECJ's teleological methodology, which involves the Court reading the text—and the gaps in the text—of the Treaty in such a way as to further what it determines to be the underlying and evolving aims of the Community enterprise as a whole.[19] The ECJ's vision for the EEC was very different from that advanced by the Member States.

The ECJ held that the Community was not to be regarded as simply a compact between States; it was also concerned with the peoples of those States. The famous language of a 'new legal order of international law' was designed to legitimate the conclusion that the EEC was different from other international treaties, in that individuals could derive rights from the EEC Treaty, even if that was not normally the case. There was clearly an element of circularity in this argument. The very decision as to whether direct effect did or did not exist was itself of crucial importance in deciding whether the EEC Treaty really could be regarded as distinct from other international treaties. Major constitutional developments are however not infrequently characterized by such reasoning.

The ECJ also rejected the other argument of the Member States. It held that public enforcement of EEC law through the Commission via Article 226 did not preclude private enforcement via direct effect. Thus the Court developed the concept of direct effect principally in view of the kind of legal system which it considered necessary to carry through the ambitious economic and political programme outlined in the Treaties. The ECJ considered a strong enforcement method was needed to ensure that Member States complied with the provisions to which they had agreed. Automatic internalization of Treaty rules within national legal systems would clearly strengthen the effectiveness of Community norms as well as aiding the Commission in its Article 226 enforcement function by involving individuals and all levels of the national court system directly in their implementation.[20] Consider in this respect the view of Pierre Pescatore, a former judge of the Court.

P. Pescatore, The Doctrine of 'Direct Effect': An Infant Disease of Community Law[21]

It appears from these considerations that in the opinion of the Court, the Treaty has created a Community not only of States but also of peoples and persons and that therefore not only Member States but also individuals must be visualised as being subjects of Community law.

---

[18] See below, 279–281.
[19] See Ch. 1.
[20] Craig, n. 2 above; see also Ch. 12.
[21] (1983) 8 *ELRev.* 155, 158.

This is the consequence of a democratic ideal, meaning that in the Community, as well as in a modern constitutional State, Governments may not say any more what they are used to doing in international law: *L'Etat, c'est moi*. Far from it; the Community calls for participation of everybody, with the result that private individuals are not only liable to burdens and obligations, but that they have also prerogatives and rights which must be legally protected. It was thus a highly political idea, drawn from a perception of the constitutional system of the Community, which is at the basis of *Van Gend en Loos* and which continues to inspire the whole doctrine flowing from it.

(b) THE CONDITIONS FOR DIRECT EFFECT: BROADENING THE CONDITIONS

The ECJ in *Van Gend en Loos* established the initial conditions to be met before a Treaty Article could be deemed to have direct effect. It established the requirement, familiar from international law, that a provision be essentially 'self-executing'. Thus the criteria which were met by Article 25 EEC and which enabled it to have direct effect were that it was: *clear, negative, unconditional, containing no reservation on the part of the Member State, and not dependent on any national implementing measure*. The development of direct effect in subsequent years was however characterized by the broadening and loosening of these initial conditions.

The condition that the Treaty Article should be *clear and unconditional, containing no reservation on the part of the Member States*, was qualified within a few years of the *Van Gend* ruling. The ECJ made it clear that the existence of Member State discretion to, for example, prevent the free movement of goods on grounds laid down in what is now Article 30 EC did not preclude the direct effect of Article 28, since the cases coming within Article 30 were exceptional and did not undermine the force of the clear obligation contained in what is now Article 28.[22] Similarly in *Van Duyn*[23] the ECJ rejected the argument that what is now Article 39(3), which allows limitations on the free movement of workers on grounds of public policy, public security, or public health, prevented Article 39 from having direct effect, because 'the applications of these limitations is subject to judicial control'.[24] The idea that direct effect could apply even where the Member States possessed discretion, on the ground that the exercise thereof could be controlled by the courts, represented a significant juridical shift in thinking about direct effect.

The *idea that direct effect was precluded where further measures were required at national level* was also modified. The ECJ's strategy was to fasten on the *basic principle* that governed the relevant area, and provided that this was deemed to be sufficiently certain, it would accord it direct effect, notwithstanding the absence of implementing measures at Community and national level. Thus Article 43 EC, for example, provided that restrictions on freedom of establishment of Community nationals in States other than that of their nationality were to be abolished 'within the framework of the provisions set out below'. The framework in question was to have included a general programme and a set of directives to liberalize the activities of employed and self-employed persons, but few of these had been adopted by the time the *Reyners* case arose in 1973.

---

[22] Case 13/68 *SpA Salgoil* v. *Italian Ministry of Foreign Trade* [1968] ECR 453.
[23] Case 41/74 *Van Duyn* v. *Home Office* [1974] ECR 1337.
[24] *Ibid.*, para. 7.

Case 2/74 **Reyners v. Belgium**
[1974] ECR 631

[Note ToA renumbering: Arts. 52, 54, and 57 are now Arts. 43, 44, and 47 respectively]

Jean Reyners was a Dutch national who obtained his legal education in Belgium, but was refused admission to the Belgian Bar (as *avocat*) solely on the ground that he lacked Belgian nationality. He challenged the relevant Belgian legislation before the Conseil d'Etat, which referred several questions to the ECJ, including the question whether Article 52 was directly effective in the absence of implementing directives under Articles 54 and 57. The Belgian government argued that Article 52 merely laid down a principle that was to be complemented by secondary legislation, and that it was not for the Court to exercise a discretionary power reserved to the legislative institutions of the Community and the Member States.

THE ECJ

24. The rule on equal treatment with nationals is one of the fundamental legal provisions of the Community.

25. As a reference to a set of legislative provisions effectively applied by the country of establishment to its own nationals, this rule is, by its essence, capable of being directly invoked by nationals of all the other Member States.

26. In laying down that freedom of establishment shall be attained at the end of the transitional period, Article 52 thus imposes an obligation to attain a precise result, the fulfilment of which had to be made easier by, but not made dependent on, the implementation of a programme of progressive measures.

27. The fact that this progression has not been adhered to leaves the obligation itself intact beyond the end of the period provided for its fulfilment....

...

29. It is not possible to invoke against such an effect the fact that the Council has failed to issue the directive provided for by Articles 54 and 57 or the fact that certain of the directives actually issued have not fully attained the objective of non-discrimination required by Article 52.

30. After the expiry of the transitional period the directives provided for by the Chapter on the right of establishment have become superfluous with regard to implementing the rule on nationality, since this is henceforth sanctioned by the Treaty itself with direct effect.

Thus the ECJ determined that, despite the slow pace of harmonization of national laws in this field, the Treaty could be directly invoked by individuals in order to challenge obvious instances of nationality discrimination against them. The basic principle of non-discrimination was deemed to be directly effective, even though the conditions for genuine freedom of establishment were far from being achieved. Whereas many cases on direct effect concern the enforcement of obligations against a Member State which has failed properly to implement Community requirements, the *Reyners* case shows the Court employing direct effect to compensate for insufficient action on the part of the *Community* legislative institutions.

A similar use of direct effect to 'trigger' the proper implementation of a Treaty provision can be seen in the second *Defrenne* judgment,[25] which relaxed further the original *Van Gend en Loos* criteria for direct effect. While in *Reyners*, the terms of Article 43 seemed to envisage

---

[25] Case 43/75 *Defrenne* v. *Société Anonyme Belge de Navigation Aérienne* [1976] ECR 455.

further implementing measures, Article 141 in *Defrenne* appeared to lack sufficient precision to be directly enforced by a national court. Article 141 at that time required States to ensure 'the application of the principle that men and women should receive equal pay for equal work'.[26] Unlike the Treaty provisions in *Van Gend* and *Costa*, Article 141 did not impose a very precise negative obligation on the Member States. The term 'principle', for example, is not very specific, nor were the terms 'pay' and 'equal work' defined. It was also evident that neither the Commission nor the States considered that provision to be directly effective or legally complete.[27] What the Court did, however, was to identify and isolate the *principle* of Article 141 at the time, that of equal pay for equal work, rather than to focus on the fact that there might be cases, unlike the one at hand, involving complex factual questions regarding 'work of equal value' concerning jobs which were different in nature.

The Court's concern in such cases seems to have been to ensure that the Community's aims were not ignored either by reluctant Member States or by sluggish Community institutions, during the years of so-called legislative sclerosis which followed the Luxembourg Accords.[28] If a national court was unsure of the exact meaning of the relevant provision, the ECJ was more than willing to clarify its scope in a preliminary ruling under Article 234.

The original conditions for direct effect have therefore been loosened in the years since *Van Gend en Loos*, although there are still cases where the ECJ finds that a Treaty Article does not have direct effect.[29] The current position can be summarized as follows: *a Treaty Article will be accorded direct effect provided that it is intended to confer rights*[30] *on individuals and that it is sufficiently clear, precise, and unconditional.*[31] This criterion clearly leaves the Community Courts with considerable room for manoeuvre.

4. THE LEGAL EFFECTS OF REGULATIONS AND DECISIONS

The principal forms of legislative action which the Community may adopt are set out in Article 249 EC. In legal terms, the most important are regulations and directives, although there are also many softer forms of law provided for in the Treaty, or which have evolved in practice. The EC—and now EU—also has competence to enter into agreements with countries outside the EU. A further important source of Community law is the 'general principles' of law drawn by the ECJ from the common traditions and constitutional rules of the Member States,[32] and from international agreements and conventions to which all are party.[33]

It will be seen in the discussion which follows that virtually all binding forms of Community law have been deemed by the ECJ to be capable of direct effect, and that, while

---

[26] See further Ch. 24 on Equal Treatment for the inclusion of 'work of equal value' in the amended Art. 141.

[27] See Trabucchi AG in Case 43/75 *Defrenne*, n. 25 above, 485.

[28] See Ch. 1.

[29] Case T–191/99 *Petrie* v. *ALLS I/CDFL* [2001] ECR II–3677, paras. 34–35; Art. 255 was not unconditional and required further implementation before it could be relied upon for a precise result; Case 126/86 *Zaera* v. *Institutio Nacionale de la Seguridad Social* [1987] ECR 3697, paras. 10–11, the promotion of accelerated living standards in Art. 2 did not confer rights on individuals.

[30] Subject to the preceding discussion, at 269–271.

[31] Pescatore, n. 21 above, 176–177; Van Gerven AG suggested that the test for direct effect is whether a provision of Community law is 'sufficiently operational' to be applied by a court: Case C–128/92 *Banks* v. *British Coal* [1994] ECR I–1209, 1237; Lenaerts and Corthaut, n. 15 above, 311.

[32] See Ch. 15.

[33] Case 11/70 *Internationale Handelsgesellschaft* [1970] ECR 1125.

other types of non-binding or soft law are not said to have direct effect, they are influential in other ways and may have what has become known as indirect or interpretative effects.[34]

(a) REGULATIONS

We saw in *Van Gend* that the textual basis in the EC Treaty for the conclusion that Treaty provisions could have direct effect was not compelling. However, Article 249 of the Treaty provides that a regulation 'shall be binding in its entirety and directly applicable in all Member States'. Policy considerations aside, this language seems to envisage that regulations, at least, will immediately become part of the domestic law of Member States, without needing transposition. If they are immediately part of the domestic law of Member States there is no reason why, so long as their provisions are sufficiently clear, precise, and relevant to the situation of an individual litigant,[35] they should not be capable of being relied upon and enforced by individuals before their national courts.[36]

The direct effect of regulations was affirmed in the *Slaughtered Cow* case, where the ECJ chastised the Italian government for choosing a method of implementing a regulation which cast doubt on the legal nature and direct applicability of that measure. It held that all methods of implementation were contrary to the Treaty, 'which would have the result of creating an obstacle to the direct effect of Community Regulations and of jeopardizing their simultaneous and uniform application in the whole of the Community'.[37] More recently in *Muñoz*[38] the ECJ stated that 'owing to their very nature and their place in the system of sources of Community law, regulations operate to confer rights on individuals which the national courts have a duty to protect'.

A national measure enacted with the intention of giving effect to a regulation will however not necessarily be invalid. In *Amsterdam Bulb*, the ECJ ruled that it is only if a national measure alters, obstructs, or obscures the direct effect or nature of the Community regulation that it will constitute a breach of Community law.[39] The concern seems to be that if a Member State's implementation of a regulation conceals the fact that it is indeed a Community regulation, it could have adverse consequences for the EC since the particular qualities of Community law, for example that it takes priority over conflicting national law, that there must be adequate remedies for breach, that it may be subject to different methods of interpretation, may be ignored. Further, the ECJ was clearly concerned that Member States might adversely affect the content of the regulation through their implementing measures. Nonetheless, in *Amsterdam Bulb* the ECJ accepted that States could provide in national legislation for appropriate sanctions which were not provided for in the regulation, and could continue to regulate various related issues which were not covered in the regulation. Indeed, in some cases a regulation may positively *require* national implementing measures.[40]

---

[34] See, e.g., Case 322/88 *Salvatore Grimaldi* v. *Fonds des Maladies Professionelles* [1989] ECR 4407.

[35] See Case C–403/98 *Azienda Agricola Monte Arcosu* v. *Regione Autonoma della Sardegna* [2001] ECR I–103 in which the provisions of a reg. were not sufficiently precise and therefore could not be directly relied upon. Compare Case C–278/02 *Herbert Handlbauer GmbH* [2004] ECR I–6171, paras. 24–35.

[36] See Geelhoed AG's discussion of the relationship between the direct applicability of provisions of a reg. and their direct effect in terms of the capacity of individuals to invoke and derive rights from those provisions in Case C–253/00 *Muñoz*, n. 4 above.

[37] Case 39/72 *Commission* v. *Italy* [1973] ECR 101, para. 17.

[38] In Case C–253/00 *Muñoz*, n. 4 above, para. 27.

[39] Case 50/76 *Amsterdam Bulb BV* v. *Produktschap voor Siergewassen* [1977] ECR 137.

[40] Case C–403/98 *Azienda Agricola Monte Arcosu*, n. 35 above, para. 26.

(b) DECISIONS

Under Article 249 EC a decision is to be 'binding in its entirety upon those to whom it is addressed'. Unlike a regulation, a decision will not normally be a general measure but an individual one which is directed to a specific addressee or addressees.[41]

The ECJ in *Grad* had little hesitation in holding that decisions, too, could be directly effective, despite the fact that Article 249, unlike in the case of regulations, made no reference to their 'direct applicability'.[42] In an often-repeated phrase, the Court ruled that it did not follow from this 'that other categories of legal measures mentioned in that Article can never produce similar effects', and it relied on the principle of *effet utile* or effectiveness to conclude that decisions could in suitable cases be invoked by individuals before national courts.[43]

Returning to our earlier discussion of the narrower and the broader conceptions of direct effect, the ECJ in this judgment discussed direct effect in terms of the right of an individual to 'invoke the obligation' created by a decision before a national court (the broad notion of invocability), but also spelt out in some detail the substance of that obligation (the more precise notion of conferral of rights).

5. THE LEGAL EFFECTS OF DIRECTIVES

(a) DIRECT EFFECT OF DIRECTIVES

(i) *The Foundations:* Van Duyn *and* Ratti

The key reason given by the Court for the direct effect of Treaty provisions was that the fundamental aims of the Treaty and the nature of the system it was designed to create would be seriously hampered if its clear provisions could not be domestically enforced by those they affected. The explanation for the direct effect of regulations was more straightforwardly textual: Article 249 specifically provided for their direct applicability, from which the Court deduced that they had the capacity to be invoked by individuals before national courts and to confer rights on them. In the case of decisions, the ECJ took the view that, since they were intended to be binding upon addressees, there was no reason why they should not be directly enforced before a national court where their provisions were sufficiently clear.

The position of directives under the Treaty is somewhat different. Under Article 249, a directive 'shall be binding as to the result to be achieved, upon each Member State to which it is addressed, but shall leave to the national authorities the choice of form and methods'. Unlike that of regulations or decisions, national implementation of directives is specifically envisaged by the Treaty. Its rationale may be explained as follows.

The directive is one of the main 'instruments of harmonization' used by the Community institutions to bring together or co-ordinate the disparate laws of the Member States in various fields. Sometimes the provisions of a directive represent a compromise between Member States on a complex or sensitive matter and in respect of which certain discretionary options are left open to States. Eventual implementation need not be uniform in every Member State, although the actual aim of the directive must be properly secured in each.

---

[41] See the discussion in Ch. 3, indicating the various types of EC dec. which are used, some of which are individual in nature and addressed to particular parties, but others of which are general in nature and without addressees.

[42] Case 9/70 *Franz Grad* v. *Finanzamt Traunstein* [1970] ECR 825.

[43] *Ibid.*, para. 5.

From this description, it appears that some of the criteria for direct effect laid down in the early case law are missing. A directive may well leave some discretion to the Member States; it will always require further implementing measures; and if it sets out its aim only in general terms, it may not be sufficiently precise to allow for proper national judicial enforcement. It was therefore difficult to reconcile the original criteria for direct effect—precision, unconditionality, the absence of discretion, and the absence of a need for implementing measures—with the particular nature of directives.

However, the aims of legal integration and effectiveness which underpinned the ECJ's original articulation of the notion of the direct effect of Treaty provisions can be equally applied to the case of directives. Many important areas of Community policy rely, in accordance with the Treaty, for their practical realization on the proper implementation of Community directives. If States fail or refuse to implement or apply such measures properly, those Community policies will suffer. The ECJ therefore sought to promote the legal effectiveness of directives even in the absence of their implementation. It held that directives could in principle have direct effect. It gave three reasons for this, two in *Van Duyn*, and the third in *Ratti*.

Case 41/74 **Van Duyn v. Home Office**
[1974] ECR 1337

[Note ToA renumbering: Arts. 48, 177, and 189 are now
Arts. 39, 234, and 249 respectively]

THE ECJ

12. [I]t would be incompatible with the binding effect attributed to a directive by Article 189 to exclude, in principle, the possibility that the obligation which it imposes may be invoked by those concerned. In particular, where the Community authorities have, by directive, imposed on Member States the obligation to pursue a particular course of conduct, the useful effect of such an act would be weakened if individuals were prevented from relying on it before their national courts and if the latter were prevented from taking it into consideration as an element of Community law. Article 177, which empowers national courts to refer to the Court questions concerning the validity and interpretation of all acts of the Community institutions, without distinction, implies furthermore that these acts may be invoked by individuals in the national courts. It is necessary to examine, in every case, whether the nature, general scheme and wording of the provision in question are capable of having direct effects on the relations between Member States and individuals.

The first reason given by the ECJ is functional: directives are binding and will be more effectively enforced if individuals can rely on them than if they cannot.

The second reason is textual: Article 177, now Article 234, allows national courts to refer questions concerning any Community measure to the ECJ, including directives, and this implied that such acts could be invoked by individuals before national courts.

The third rationale, articulated in the *Ratti* case,[44] is the estoppel argument: Member States were precluded by their failure to implement a directive properly from refusing to recognize its binding effect in cases where it was pleaded against them. The idea here is that the Member State should have implemented the directive, and that if it had done so then the individual would

---

[44] Case 148/78 *Pubblico Ministero v. Tullio Ratti* [1979] ECR 1629, para. 23.

have been able to rely on the national implementing law. Given that the Member State had in that sense committed a wrong by failing to implement the directive, it could not therefore rely on that wrongdoing so as to deny the binding effect of the directive itself after the date for implementation had passed. Where necessary, a conflicting national law should be disapplied.[45]

(ii) *Subsequent Application: Sufficiently Clear and Precise Provisions of a Directive*

The net effect of these rulings was that directives were capable in principle of having direct effect. The key issue was whether the particular provision of the directive relied on was sufficiently clear and exact to be capable of being applied directly by a national court, and this could vary as between different provisions of a directive.

In *Van Duyn* itself, Directive 64/221 allowed Member States to take measures restricting the movement of non-nationals on grounds such as public policy, without defining the permissible range of public-policy concerns. The ECJ ruled that by providing that measures taken on public-policy grounds had to be based on the personal conduct of the individual, the directive had limited the discretionary power conferred on States. The obligation imposed was clear, precise, and legally complete.[46]

In most, though not all,[47] later cases the ECJ ruled that the existence of discretion would not necessarily prevent a directive from being directly relied upon by an individual. This would be true for example where a Member State has fully exercised its discretion on implementation,[48] or where the State has chosen not to exercise a particular discretionary option,[49] or where a clear and precise obligation can be separated out from other parts of a directive,[50] or a clear obligation of result can be identified.[51] Occasionally, a provision initially held by the ECJ to be incapable of direct effect has been held in a later case to be sufficiently clear to impose an obligation on the Member State.[52]

More controversially, in *Kortas*, the ECJ ruled that the possibility for a Member State to derogate from a harmonizing directive under Article 95(4) EC did not prevent the directive having direct effect, nor preclude an individual from relying directly on its provisions, *even in the situation where* a Member State had sought permission for such a derogation and the Commission had unreasonably failed to respond to its request.[53]

---

[45] Case C–462/99 *Connect Austria Gesellschaft für Telekommunikation GmbH v. Telekom-Control-Kommission and Mobilkom Austria AG* [2003] ECR I–5197, para. 40.

[46] See also Case C–72/95 *Kraaijeveld*, n. 9 above, para. 59; Case C–287/98 *Linster*, n. 14 above, paras. 37–39, where the existence of discretion in a dir. did not preclude a national court from examining whether the discretion had been exceeded. Contrast Case C–365/98 *Brinkmann* [2000] ECR I–4619.

[47] A recent example is Case C–157/02 *Rieser Internationale Transporte GmbH v. Autobahnen- und Schnellstraßen-Finanzierungs-AG (Asfinag)* [2004] ECR I–1477.

[48] Case C–441/99 *Riksskatteverket v. Gharehveran* [2001] ECR I– 7687.

[49] Case C–303/98 *SIMAP v. Valencia Sindicatode Médicos Asistencia Pública* [2000] ECR I–7963; Cases C–453 and 462/02 *Finanzamt Gladbeck v. Linneweber* [2005] ECR I–1131. See also Case C–76/97 *Tögel* [1998] ECR I–5357 and Case C–241/97 *Försäkringsaktiebolaget Skandia* [1999] ECR I–1951, where the existence of exceptions did not prevent the provisions of a dir. from being directly effective.

[50] Case C–346/97 *Braathens Sverige AB v. Riksskatteverket* [1999] ECR I–3419; Case C–292/02 *Meiland Azewijn BV v. Hauptzollamt Duisburg* [2004] ECR I–7905; Cases C–465/00, 138–139/01 *Rechnungshof v. Österreichischer Rundfunk* [2003] ECR I–4989. For comment see C.D. Classen (2004) 41 *CMLRev.* 1377.

[51] Case C–476/01 *Criminal proceedings against Felix Kapper* [2004] ECR I–5205, for the example of the obligation of mutual recognition of driving licences.

[52] Compare Case C–236/92 *Comitato di Coordinamento per la Difesa della Cava v. Regione Lombardia* [1994] ECR I–483 with Case C–365/97 *Commission v. Italy* [1999] ECR I–7773.

[53] Case C–319/97 *Kortas* [1999] ECR I–3143. The ECJ held that an action against the Commission for breach of its obligations under Art. 232 EC was the appropriate remedy.

(iii) *Direct Effect: Time Limits for Implementation*

The result of *Van Duyn, Ratti*, and subsequent case law is that although Article 249 does not declare directives to be directly applicable, so that they do not automatically become part of national law upon adoption, they may produce 'similar effects' to regulations after the time limit for their implementation has expired and the State has not properly implemented them.[54]

The ECJ has however made clear that directives may have an impact even before the implementation period has passed. Thus in *Inter-Environnement Wallonie* it held that although States are not obliged to implement a directive before the period for its transposition has expired, they must, during that period, *refrain* from adopting any measures liable to compromise seriously the result prescribed by the directive.[55] Moreover in the curious *Mangold* case,[56] discussed below,[57] the ECJ told the national court that it must '*set aside* any provision of national law which may conflict with Community law, even where the period prescribed for transposition of that directive has not yet expired'.[58]

The vertical direct effect of directives has also been bolstered by the ruling in *Marks & Spencer*, which declared that even after a Member State has implemented a directive correctly into national law, an individual can continue to rely directly on the provisions of the directive against the State so long as it is not being properly *applied* in practice.[59]

(b) THE VERTICAL/HORIZONTAL DISTINCTION

The ECJ had thus far expanded the ambit of direct effect. In the *Marshall* case it however held that the direct effect of a directive could not be pleaded against an *individual*, but only against the State.[60]

Case 152/84 **Marshall v. Southampton and South-West Hampshire
Area Health Authority (Teaching)**
[1986] ECR 723

[Note ToA renumbering: Arts. 189 and 191 are now Arts. 249 and 254 respectively]

Helen Marshall was dismissed after 14 years' employment by the respondent health authority on the ground that she had passed 60, and the Authority's policy required female employees to retire at 60 and male employees at 65. National legislation imposed no obligation on women to retire at 60 but neither did it prohibit employers from discriminating on grounds of sex in retirement matters. Marshall argued however that her dismissal violated the 1976 Equal

---

[54] Case 8/81 *Becker* v. *Finanzamt Münster-Innenstadt* [1982] ECR 53; Case C–141/00 *Ambulanter Pflegedienst Kügler GmbH* v. *Finanzamt für Körperschaften I in Berlin* [2002] ECR I–6833, paras. 52–60.

[55] Case C–129/96 *Inter-Environnement Wallonie ASBL* v. *Région Wallone* [1997] ECR I–7411.

[56] Case C–144/04 *Mangold* v. *Helm* [2005] ECR I–9981, paras, 76–78, emphasis added; see for a comment on the case Editorial [2006] 43 *CMLRev.* 1.

[57] See below, 291, 411–412.

[58] Case C–144/04 *Mangold*, n. 56 above, paras. 76–78.

[59] Case C–62/00 *Marks & Spencer plc* v. *Commissioners of Customs & Excise* [2002] ECR I–6325, paras. 22–28; M. Ruffert (2003) 40 *CMLRev.* 729; S. Drake (2003) 28 *ELRev.* 418.

[60] Moreover, a dir. even if pleaded by an individual only against the State, cannot of itself result in the imposition of a civil obligation on another individual: Case C–201/02 *Wells* v. *Secretary of State for Transport, Local Government and the Regions* [2004] ECR I–723, paras. 57–58.

Treatment Directive, and the Court of Appeal referred to the ECJ for a ruling as to whether she could rely on the provisions of the Directive against the Health Authority. Advocate General Slynn suggested in his opinion that to give 'horizontal effect' to directives by allowing them to impose obligations directly on an individual would 'totally blur the distinction between directives and regulations' established by the Treaty.[61]

THE ECJ

48. With regard to the argument that a directive may not be relied upon against an individual, it must be emphasized that according to Article 189 of the EEC Treaty, the binding nature of a directive, which constitutes the basis for the possibility of relying on the directive before a national court, exists only in relation to 'each Member State to which it is addressed'. It follows that a directive may not of itself impose obligations on an individual and that a provision of a directive may not be relied upon as such against such a person.

A number of differing rationales have been suggested as to why directives should only have vertical and not horizontal direct effect.

The reason given by the ECJ in *Marshall* was *textual*: Article 249 stipulates that the binding effect of a directive is to exist only as against the State(s) to which it is addressed. There are however two difficulties with this argument.

On the one hand, it is debatable in textual terms. The wording of Article 249 merely signifies that a Member State is only bound by a directive if mentioned therein as being bound, by way of contrast to regulations that bind all Member States. It says nothing one way or the other as to whether, if a particular Member State is bound by a directive, it may also impose an obligation on a private individual.

On the other hand, the Court's unusual textual faithfulness in this context and its emphasis on the addressee of directives contrasts with its approach to the direct effectiveness of certain Treaty Articles which, like directives, are also explicitly addressed only to the Member State. Article 141, for example, is addressed only to the Member States, providing that States are to ensure the application of the principle of equal pay for male and female workers. In the first *Defrenne* case, however, the ECJ dismissed the argument that Article 141 could be relied upon only as against the State. It held that since 'Article 119 is mandatory in nature, the prohibition on discrimination between men and women applies not only to the action of public authorities, but also extends to all agreements which are intended to regulate paid labour collectively, as well as to contracts between individuals'.[62]

A *rule of law* argument has also been put against the horizontal direct effect of directives. Thus Advocate General Slynn in *Marshall* was concerned about the fact that directives were not at that time required, until after the Maastricht Treaty, to be notified or published in the Official Journal.[63] The great majority of directives were however published and the requirement of publication is now contained in Article 254 EC. Moreover, all directives contain a time limit for their implementation, thus reducing the basic rule-of-law concern.

A third argument is that *horizontal direct of directives would erode the distinction between regulations and directives*. This is, so the argument goes, because directives would thereby have legal impact even though they had not been implemented in the Member States, thereby eroding

---

61 [1986] ECR 723, 734.

62 Case 43/75 *Defrenne*, n. 25 above. See also Case C–281/93 *Angonese v. Cassa di Risparmio di Bologna* [2000] ECR I–4134, paras. 32–36.

63 Case 152/84 [1986] ECR 723, 734; See also Case C–192/89 *Sevince v. Staatssecretaris van Justitie* [1990] ECR I–3461, para. 24.

the distinction between regulations, which are directly applicable, and directives, which are not. The argument is however problematic. In so far as it has force it is equally true of vertical direct effect of directives. To accord direct effect to directives does not however in reality erode the distinction between regulations and directives. The key distinction between the two instruments is that Member States are intended to have choice as to form and methods of implementation for directives. Giving direct effect to directives, whether vertical or horizontal, is not intended to undermine this. It is not intended to take away this choice. It is merely expressive of the fundamental proposition that if such implementing measures have not been enacted within the required time then the binding ends stipulated in the directive can still be enforced, provided that they are sufficiently certain, precise, etc.

The final argument adduced against horizontal direct effect is *legal certainty*. Directives, even where their core aim or principle is clear and susceptible to judicial enforcement, often leave much to be fleshed out in national implementing measures. However, the counter-argument is that this may equally be true of the 'vertical' direct effect of directives, and it may also be true of Treaty Articles which share similar characteristics of breadth and flexibility, yet it has not prevented the ECJ from pursuing a strategy of maximum legal effectiveness in respect of the latter. Moreover, even if directives were to be capable of horizontal direct effect this would only apply if the relevant provisions really were sufficiently clear, precise, and unconditional.

The 'doctrinal rule' that directives cannot have horizontal direct effect necessarily leads to discrimination between the private and public sectors.[64] The ECJ has nonetheless continued to insist on the formal requirement that directives should have vertical direct effect only, and not horizontal direct effect, despite widespread academic criticism and numerous opinions given by Advocates General in favour of full horizontal direct effect. The ruling in *Marshall* was confirmed ten years afterwards in the *Dori* case, with the support of all but one of the Member States which intervened before the Court.[65]

The ECJ has at the same time developed a number of doctrinal devices which have reduced the impact of there not being horizontal direct effect of directives. This strategy of seeking to enhance the domestic enforcement of directives in a range of different ways, despite its formal insistence on the 'no horizontal direct effect for directives' rule, has been evident in the Court's rulings ever since the *Marshall* case. It is to these strategies that we now turn.

(c) EXPANDING VERTICAL DIRECT EFFECT: A BROAD CONCEPT OF THE STATE

The first strategy was to expand the notion of a 'public body' against which directives could be enforced. In *Marshall* itself, having ruled out the direct enforceability of a directive against an individual, the Court concluded that the complainant could nevertheless rely on the provisions of this Directive as against the Health Authority, since it could be regarded as an organ of the State:[66]

49. In that respect it must be pointed out that where a person involved in legal proceedings is able to rely on a directive as against the State he may do so regardless of the capacity in

[64] R. Mastroianni, 'On the Distinction Between Vertical and Horizontal Direct Effect of Directives: What Role for the Principle of Equality?' (1999) 5 *EPL* 417.

[65] Case C–91/92 *Dori* v. *Recreb Srl* [1994] ECR I–3325; Case C–201/02 *Wells*, n. 60 above, para. 56. For a strong critique see J. Coppel, 'Rights, Duties and the End of Marshall' (1994) 57 *MLR* 859.

[66] See also Case C–438/99 *Jiménez Melgar* v. *Ayuntamiento de Los Barrios* [2001] ECR I–6915, paras. 32–33.

which the latter is acting, whether employer or public authority. In either case it is necessary to prevent the State from taking advantage of its own failure to comply with Community law....

51. The argument submitted by the United Kingdom that the possibility of relying on provisions of the directive against the respondent *qua* organ of the State would give rise to an arbitrary and unfair distinction between the rights of State employees and those of private employees does not justify any other conclusion. Such a distinction may easily be avoided if the Member State concerned has correctly implemented the directive into national law.[67]

The Court's justification for allowing the 'vertical' direct effect of directives against organs of the State is not based upon the responsibility of the particular state organ (such as a Health Authority) for failure to implement the directive pleaded. Further, the Court has held that not only courts, but even state organs and domestic administrations which play no part in the formal implementation of European legislation, are bound to apply the provisions of directives in practice, something which has been referred to as 'administrative direct effect'.[68] The extent to which this takes place in practice is difficult to determine, since the relative paucity of litigation on the question could be interpreted as evidence in either direction. In *Costanzo*, which involved the tendering procedure for award of public contracts, the question was whether a regional authority, the Municipality of Milan, was bound directly by the provisions of a directive where the relevant national legislation was incompatible with the Directive.

Case 103/88 **Fratelli Costanzo SpA v. Comune di Milano**
[1989] ECR 1839

THE ECJ

30. It is important to note that the reason for which an individual may, in the circumstances described above, rely on the provisions of a directive in proceedings before the national courts is that the obligations arising under those provisions are binding upon all the authorities of the Member States.

31. It would, moreover, be contradictory to rule that an individual may rely upon the provisions of a directive which fulfil the conditions defined above in proceedings before the national courts seeking an order against the administrative authorities, and yet to hold that those authorities are under no obligation to apply the provisions of the directive and refrain from applying provisions of national law which conflict with them. It follows that when the conditions under which the Court has held that individuals may rely on the provisions of a directive before the national courts are met, all organs of the administration, including decentralized authorities such as municipalities, are obliged to apply those provisions.

The broad interpretation of what constitutes an organ of the State for the purposes of enforcement of directives seems at odds with the refusal to extend their direct enforceability to relations between non-state entities and individuals. Further, although the ECJ elaborated somewhat on the Community meaning of the State or public body for the purposes of the

---

[67] Case 152/84 *Marshall*, n. 63 above.

[68] See B. de Witte, 'Direct Effect, Supremacy and the Nature of the Legal Order', in P. Craig and G. de Búrca (eds.), *The Evolution of EU Law* (Oxford University Press, 1999), ch. 5; Cases C–246–249/94 *Cooperativa Agricola Zootecnica S. Antonio* v. *Amministrazione delle Finanze dello Stato* [1996] ECR I–4373.

enforceability of directives, it has been criticized for failing in key decisions to provide adequate guidance on a complex issue.[69] The *Foster* case, decided in 1990, remains the primary ruling on the matter.

Case C–188/89 A. Foster and Others v. British Gas plc
[1990] ECR I–3313

The plaintiffs were employed by British Gas, whose policy it was to require women to retire at 60 and men at 65. British Gas was at the time a nationalized industry with responsibility for and a monopoly of the gas-supply system in Great Britain. The plaintiffs sought to rely on the provisions of the 1976 Equal Treatment Directive, and the House of Lords asked the ECJ whether British Gas was a body of the kind against which the provisions of the Directive could be invoked.

THE ECJ

18. On the basis of those considerations, the Court has held in a series of cases that unconditional and sufficiently precise provisions of a directive could be relied on against organizations or bodies which were subject to the authority or control of the State or had special powers beyond those which result from the normal rules applicable between individuals.

19. The Court has accordingly held that provisions of a directive could be relied on against tax authorities (the judgments in Case 8/81 *Becker* [1982] ECR 53, Case 221/88 *ECSC* v. *Busseni* [1990] ECR I–495), local or regional authorities (judgment in Case 103/88 *Costanzo* [1989] ECR 1839), constitutionally independent authorities responsible for the maintenance of public order and safety (judgment in Case 222/84 *Johnston* v. *Chief Constable of the RUC* [1986] ECR 1651), and public authorities providing public health services (judgment in Case 152/84 *Marshall* [1986] ECR 723).

20. It follows from the foregoing that a body, whatever its legal form, which has been made responsible, pursuant to a measure adopted by the State, for providing a public service under the control of the State and has for that purpose special powers beyond those which result from the normal rules applicable in relations between individuals, is included in any event among the bodies against which the provisions of a directive capable of having direct effect may be relied upon.

It is evident from paragraph 20 of *Foster* that the Court considered a company in the position of British Gas to be an organ of the State. However, it is not entirely clear what kind of control the State must have over a body in order for it to be one which, constitutionally speaking, represents the power of the State.[70] *Foster* provides no authoritative definition, but merely indicates that a body which has been made responsible for providing a public service under the control of the State is *included* within the Community definition of a public body. Subsequent case law initially left it in the hands of national courts to apply the loose criteria

---

[69] D. Curtin, 'The Province of Government: Delimiting the Direct Effect of Directives in the Common Law Context' (1990) 15 *ELRev*. 195; E. Szyszczak, 'Foster v. British Gas' (1990) 27 *CMLRev*. 859.

[70] In Case C–419/92 *Scholz* v. *Opera Universitaria di Cagliari* [1994] ECR I–505, the case proceeded on the 'common ground' that the University of Cagliari was an emanation of the State. See R. White, 'Equality in the Canteen' (1994) 19 *ELRev*. 308.

articulated in *Foster*,[71] but the ECJ in a number of recent cases ruled that a particular body clearly satisfies those criteria for the purposes of invoking a directive against it.[72]

(d) 'INDIRECT EFFECT': DEVELOPMENT OF THE PRINCIPLE OF HARMONIOUS INTERPRETATION

(i) *The Principle of Harmonious Interpretation: The Obligation to Interpret National Law in Conformity with Directives*

The second way in which the ECJ encouraged the application and effectiveness of directives, despite denying the possibility of direct horizontal enforcement, was by developing a principle of harmonious interpretation which requires national law to be interpreted 'in the light of' directives. The Court thereby sought to ensure that directives would be given some effect despite the absence of proper implementation. The *Von Colson* case is a leading authority.

Case 14/83 **Von Colson and Kamann v. Land Nordrhein-Westfalen**
[1984] ECR 1891

The ECJ ruled that the Equal Treatment Directive on which the plaintiffs relied in their claim of unlawful sex discrimination was not sufficiently precise to guarantee them a specific remedy of appointment to a post, but it went on to rule on what effect the directive's aims might nonetheless have on the interpretation of national law.

[Note ToA renumbering: Art. 189 is now Art. 249]

THE ECJ

26. However, the Member States' obligation arising from a directive to achieve the result envisaged by the directive and their duty under Article 5 of the Treaty to take all appropriate measures, whether general or particular, to ensure the fulfillment of that obligation, is binding on all the authorities of Member States including, for matters within their jurisdiction, the courts. It follows that, in applying the national law and in particular the provisions of a national law specifically introduced in order to implement Directive No 76/207, national courts are required to interpret their national law in the light of the wording and the purpose of the Directive in order to achieve the result referred to in the third paragraph of Article 189.

. . .

28. . . . It is for the national court to interpret and apply the legislation adopted for the implementation of the directive in conformity with the requirements of Community law, in so far as it is given discretion to do so under national law.

---

[71] Case C–343/98 *Collino & Chiappero* v. *Telecom Italia* [2000] ECR I–6659; Cases C–253–258/96 *Kampelmann* v. *Landschaftsverband Westfalen-Lippe* [1997] ECR I–6907, para. 47; Cases T–172 and 175–177/98 *Salamander* v. *Parliament & Council* [2000] ECR II–2487, para. 60.

[72] Case C–157/02 *Rieser*, n. 47 above, paras. 22–29, concerning an Austrian body which had been made responsible for the management of a motorway; Case C–180/04 *Vassallo* v. *Azienda Ospedaliera Ospedale San Martino di Genova* [2006] ECR I–7251, para. 26; Case C–53/04 *Marrosu and Sardino* v. *Azienda Ospedaliera Ospedale San Martino di Genova e Cliniche Universitarie Convenzionate* [2006] ECR I–7213.

The Court in *Von Colson* expressly identified the national courts as organs of the State which are responsible for the fulfillment of Community obligations, and encouraged the German court in question to supplement the domestic legislation, which did not on its face seem to provide an adequate remedy, by reading it in conformity with the Directive's requirement to provide a real and effective remedy. The case also makes clear that the doctrine of harmonious interpretation, or 'indirect effect', does not require the provisions of a directive to satisfy the specific justiciability criteria (clarity, precision, unconditionality) for direct effect.

The principle has been strengthened over time in various ways, with the Court declaring it to be 'inherent in the system of the Treaty', derived from the obligation in Article 10 EC, and an aspect of the requirement of full effectiveness of EC law,[73] which applies not only to national courts, but to all competent authorities called upon to interpret and apply national law.[74]

(ii) *The Obligation applies even in a 'Horizontal' Case between Private Parties*

Von Colson concerned a directive which had been inadequately implemented,[75] and the case was brought against a state employer. Later cases however established that the obligation requires a national court to interpret national law in the light of an inadequately implemented or a non-implemented directive *even in a case against an individual*, thus side-stepping in a certain way the prohibition on horizontal direct effect.

The *Marleasing* case concerned a 'horizontal' situation involving two private parties before a domestic court, where the interpretation of national law in the light of an unimplemented directive would not impose penal liability on any party, but was likely to affect its legal position in a disadvantageous way.[76]

Case C–106/89 **Marleasing SA v. La Comercial Internacionale de Alimentacion SA** [1990] ECR I–4135

[Note ToA renumbering: Arts. 5 and 189 EC are now Arts. 10 and 249]

The plaintiff company brought proceedings against La Comercial to have the defendant company's articles of association declared void as the company was created for the sole purpose of defrauding and evading creditors, including itself. The provisions of the relevant Council Directive did not include this 'lack of cause' as a ground for the nullity of a company, whereas certain provisions of the Spanish Civil Code provided for the ineffectiveness of contracts for lack of cause. The Spanish court referred the case to the ECJ, asking whether the Council Directive could have direct effect between individuals so as to preclude the declaration of nullity of a company on grounds other than those set out in the Directive. Advocate General Van

---

[73] Case C–160/01 *Mau* [2003] ECR I–4791, para. 34; Cases C–397–403/01 *Pfeiffer* v. *Deutsches Rotes Kreuz, Kreisverband Waldshut eV* [2004] ECR I–8835, para. 114.

[74] Case C–218/01 *Henkel KGaA* [2004] ECR I–1725, para. 60.

[75] See also Case C–421/92 *Habermann-Beltermann* v. *Arbeiterwohlfahrt, Bezirksverband* [1994] ECR I–1657.

[76] Case C–106/89 *Marleasing SA* v. *La Comercial de Alimentacion SA* [1990] ECR I–4135, confirmed in many subsequent cases; G. Betlem, 'The Principle of Indirect Effect of Community Law' (1995) 3 *ERPL* 1; M. Amstutz, 'In-Between Worlds: *Marleasing* and the Emergence of Interlegality in Legal Reasoning' (2005) 11 *ELJ* 766.

Gerven's opinion argued that the obligation to interpret a provision of national law in conformity with a directive applied whenever the provision in question was to any extent open to interpretation in accordance with methods recognized by national law.[77]

THE ECJ

7. However, it is apparent from the documents before the Court that the national court seeks in substance to ascertain whether a national court hearing a case which falls within the scope of Directive 68/151 is required to interpret its national law in the light of the wording and the purpose of that directive in order to preclude a declaration of nullity of a public limited company on a ground other than those listed in Article 11 of the directive.

8. In order to reply to that question, it should be observed that, as the Court pointed out in its judgment in Case 14/83 *Von Colson and Kamann* v. *Land Nordrhein-Westfalen* [1984] ECR 1891, paragraph 26, the Member States' obligation arising from a directive to achieve the result envisaged by the directive and their duty under Article 5 of the Treaty to take all appropriate measures, whether general or particular, to ensure the fulfilment of that obligation, is binding on all the authorities of Member States including, for matters within their jurisdiction, the courts. It follows that, in applying national law, whether the provisions in question were adopted before or after the directive, the national court called upon to interpret it is required to do so, as far as possible, in the light of the wording and the purpose of the directive in order to achieve the result pursued by the latter and thereby comply with the third paragraph of Article 189 of the Treaty.

This judgment confirmed that an unimplemented directive could indeed be relied on to influence the interpretation of national law in a case between individuals.

(iii) *The Obligation applies to all National Law, and not only to Legislation Implementing a Directive*

A second point which *Marleasing* clarified, which had been implicit but not explicit in *Von Colson*, was that the obligation of harmonious interpretation applies even in a case where the national law *predates* the directive and has no specific connection with the directive. In *Marleasing* itself there was no domestic implementing legislation which could be interpreted in the light of the Directive, but only domestic law which pre-dated the Directive and was not intended to implement it. This point was confirmed and extended in subsequent cases, most recently in *Pfeiffer* where the ECJ ruled that the obligation of interpretation applies to the national legal system as a whole, and not only to specific legislation.[78]

(iv) *The Obligation of Interpretation is Strong, but does not require a* Contra Legem *Interpretation of National Law*

Debate has continued over the question how strongly national courts are being encouraged to interpret otherwise clear provisions of national law so as to comply with the terms of a directive.[79]

---

[77] *Ibid.*, 4146.

[78] Cases C–397–403/01 *Pfeiffer*, n. 73 above, para. 115.

[79] Cases 262/88 *Barber* v. *Guardian Royal Exchange* [1990] ECR 1889, 1937, Van Gerven AG; Cases C–63–64/91 *Jackson* v. *Chief Adjudication Officer* [1992] ECR I–4737, para. 29, AG's Opinion; Case C–271/91 *Marshall* v. *Southampton and South West-Hampshire Area Health Authority* [1993] ECR I–4367, para. 10, AG's Opinion, that EC law could not compel the national court to give an interpretation *contra legem*. See also Case C–168/95 *Luciano Arcaro* [1996] ECR I–4705, discussed in more detail below.

Even if, as Advocate General Van Gerven suggested in *Marleasing*, it remains essentially a matter for resolution in accordance with national principles of interpretation, the Treaty-derived obligation on national courts to take all measures possible to comply with Community law clearly alters and constrains the interpretive discretion they would otherwise have under national law alone. After *Marleasing*,[80] the ECJ did not noticeably retreat from its strong encouragement to interpret domestic law in conformity with directives, but in general left it to national courts (and other relevant authorities) to decide whether an interpretation in conformity with a directive was possible,[81] or whether it would result in a *contra legem* reading.[82]

In *Wagner-Miret*, the Court accepted that the Spanish legislation in question could not be interpreted in such a way as to give effect to the result sought by the applicants,[83] and similarly in *Dori*,[84] *El Corte Inglés*,[85] *Evobus Austria*,[86] and *Alcatel Austria*[87] the limits of interpretation articulated by the national court or apparent in the terms of the legislation were accepted by the ECJ.

However by way of contrast, on occasion, as in *Pupino*, even though the ECJ defers to the ultimate assessment of the national court, the judgment expressly suggests that an interpretation in conformity with the directive or framework decision seems possible.[88] The *Coote* ruling equally demonstrates the ECJ's readiness to articulate a strong interpretation obligation and to provide firm guidance to the national court.[89] While the Court in *Coote* did not specify exactly how the British court should interpret domestic sex discrimination legislation, it gave a clear indication that when interpreting that law in the light of the Equal Treatment Directive, the national court should read it in the light of the obligation imposed by the Directive to introduce measures to protect workers who are victimized after the employment relationship has ended, by the refusal of the employer to provide a reference.[90]

---

[80] In the case itself, despite declaring that national courts must read national law in conformity with a relevant dir. only 'in so far as possible', the ECJ went on to rule that the Spanish court was *precluded* from interpreting national law in a way which did not comply with the provisions of the dir.

[81] In the *Connect Austria* case, which involved litigation between a company and a State regulatory authority (i.e. a vertical situation), the ECJ ruled that since it was impossible to construe the national implementing legislation in conformity with the dir., the dir. should be directly enforced against the State by means of disapplying conflicting national law: Case C–462/99 *Connect Austria*, n. 45 above, paras. 38–42.

[82] See Case C–365/98 *Brinkmann* [2000] ECR I–4619, para. 41; Betlem, n. 76 above, suggests that the ECJ gave a *Marleasing*-style mandatory ruling also in Case C–177/88 *Dekker* v. *Stichting Vormingscentrum voor Jong Volwassenen* [1990] ECR I–3941 which came close to requiring an interpretation of national law *contra legem*. See also the ECJ's comment in Case C–300/95 *Commission* v. *United Kingdom* [1997] ECR I–2649, in effect dismissing the Commission's argument that the UK courts should not interpret domestic law *contra legem* in order to comply with Community law.

[83] Case C–334/92 *Wagner Miret* v. *Fondo de Garantía Salarial* [1993] ECR I–6911, para. 22. See also Case C–131/97 *Carbonari* v. *Università degli Studi di Bologna* [1999] ECR I–1103, paras. 48–50.

[84] Case C–91/92 *Dori*, n. 65 above, para. 27.

[85] Case C–192/94 *El Corte Inglés* v. *Cristina Blázques Rivero* [1996] ECR I–1281, para. 22.

[86] Case C–111/97 *Evobus Austria* v. *Niederösterreichischer Verkehrsorgination* [1998] ECR I–5411, paras. 18–21.

[87] Case C–81/98 *Alcatel Austria* v. *Bundesministerium für Wissenschaft und Verkehr* [1999] ECR I–7671, paras. 49–50. Contrast Case C–76/97 *Tögel*, n. 49 above, para. 28.

[88] See also Case C–105/03 *Pupino*, n. 16 above, paras. 47–49.

[89] Case C–185/97 *Coote* v. *Granada Hospital* [1998] ECR I–5199. See also Case C–168/00 *Leitner* v. *TUI Deutschland* [2002] ECR I–2631, Tizzano AG; Case C–60/00 *Carpenter* v. *Home Secretary* [2002] ECR I–6279, para. 41, Stix Hackl AG.

[90] *Ibid.*, paras. 18–27. Note that the Sex Discrimination Act in question, although it predated the Dir., was nonetheless intended to implement it, but the industrial tribunal had ruled that the provisions of the Act did not regulate behaviour after the contract of employment had ended.

More generally, even if the Court has left the application of the interpretive obligation in particular factual circumstances largely to the national courts,[91] it has regularly emphasized the strength of the obligation in general. Thus in *Pfeiffer*, which concerned the application of the Working Time Directive to emergency medical services, the ECJ ruled that 'the principle of interpretation in conformity with Community law thus requires the referring court to do whatever lies within its jurisdiction, having regard to the whole body of rules of national law' to ensure that a directive is effective.[92]

(v) *The Positive Obligation of Harmonious Interpretation applies only after the Time Limit for Implementation of the Directive has Expired*

It was for some time unclear whether the obligation to interpret national law in conformity with a directive arose *before* the time limit for implementation of the directive expired.[93] The *Ratti* case indicated that a directive can only be directly enforced (i.e. can only have vertical direct effect) when the time limit for implementation has expired.[94] However, the ECJ in *Inter-Environnement Wallonie* had also ruled that Member States are under a negative obligation to *refrain*, during the period after adoption of a directive but before the time limit for implementation has expired, 'from taking any measures liable seriously to compromise the result prescribed by the directive',[95] even though (apart from the circumstances of the curious ruling in *Mangold*[96]) they are under no positive obligation to disapply conflicting national law before the expiry of the time limit.[97]

A number of Advocates General had argued that the obligation of harmonious interpretation should apply before the expiry of the time limit for implementation,[98] and this also seemed to be implicit in the ECJ's ruling in *Pupino*.[99] However, in *Adeneler*, the ECJ finally addressed the point directly and ruled that:

> [W]here a directive is transposed belatedly, the general obligation owed by national courts to interpret domestic law in conformity with the directive exists only once the period for its transposition has expired.[100]

---

91 See, however, Case C–408/01 *Adidas-Salomon AG and Adidas Benelux BV* v. *Fitnessworld Trading Ltd.* [2003] ECR I–12537, paras. 15–22, which suggests that the obligation of interpretation may be stronger where the national court is interpreting legislation which was specifically intended to implement the dir.

92 Cases C–397–403/01 *Pfeiffer*, n. 73 above, para. 118; S. Prechal [2005] 42 *CMLRev.* 1445.

93 M. Klamert, 'Judicial Implementation of Directives and Anticipatory Indirect Effect: Connecting the Dots' (2006) 43 *CMLRev.* 1251, arguing that prior to the expiry of the implementation period the interpretation obligation should be considered to be based only on Art. 10 EC, whereas after the period has expired it should be based on the legal supremacy of the dir. itself pursuant to Art. 249 EC, with different legal consequences flowing from each.

94 Case 148/78 *Ratti* [1979] ECR 1629.

95 Case C–129/96 *Inter-Environnement Wallonie*, n. 55 above, para. 45, Case C–157/02 *Rieser*, n. 47 above, para. 66.

96 Case C–144/04 *Mangold*, n. 56 above.

97 Case C–156/91 *Hansa Fleisch Ernst Mundt* [1992] ECR I–5567, para. 20; Case C–157/02 *Rieser*, n. 47 above, para. 67. For the same 'obligation to refrain' as it applies to the transitional period for the coming into force of provisions contained within a dir., see Case C–316/04 *Stichting Zuid-Hollandse Milieufederatie* v. *College voor de toelating van bestrijdingsmiddelen* [2005] ECR I–9759, para. 42.

98 See Case 80/86 *Kolpinghuis Nijmegen* [1987] ECR 3969, para. 32; Betlem, n. 76 above, 11–12; Case C–156/91 *Hansa Fleisch*, n. 97 above, para. 23, Jacobs AG, concerning a Decision; Case C–106/89 *Marleasing*, n. 76 above, para. 9, AG's Opinion; Case C–144/04 *Mangold*, n. 56 above, paras. 117–120, Tizzano AG; Case C–313/02 *Wippel* v. *Peek & Cloppenburg* [2004] ECR I–9483, paras. 59–63, Kokott AG.

99 Case C–105/03 *Pupino*, n. 16 above.

100 Case C–212/04 *Konstantinos Adeneler et al.* v. *Ellinikos Organismos Galaktos (ELOG)* [2006] ECR I–6057, para. 116.

However, the Court went on to rule that the general *Inter-Environnement Wallonie* obligation on the State to refrain, even before expiry of the time-limit, from any measures liable to compromise the result sought by the directive includes a corresponding negative interpretative obligation on national courts as organs of the State:

> It follows that, from the date upon which a directive has entered into force, the courts of the Member States must refrain as far as possible from interpreting domestic law in a manner which might seriously compromise, after the period for transposition has expired, attainment of the objective pursued by that directive.[101]

(vi) *The Obligation of Harmonious Interpretation and Criminal Liability*

The obligation of harmonious interpretation cannot result in the imposition or aggravation of criminal liability on an individual, but it may result in other adverse repercussions for the individual.

Apart from the *contra legem* limit, the other main restriction on the interpretive obligation is the principle of non-retroactivity of penal liability articulated by the ECJ in *Kolpinghuis Nijmegen*.[102] In this case, the Dutch prosecution authorities sought to use the provisions of an unimplemented EC Directive against the defendant.[103] The ECJ, after reiterating the principle of interpretation in paragraph 26 of *Von Colson*, declared that:

> [T]he obligation on the national court to refer to the content of the directive when interpreting the relevant rules of its national law is limited by the general principles of law which form part of Community law and in particular the principles of legal certainty and non-retroactivity . . . a directive cannot, of itself and independently of a law adopted for its implementation, have the effect of determining or aggravating the liability in criminal law of persons who act in contravention of the provisions of that directive.[104]

(vii) *The Obligation of Harmonious Interpretation and Non-criminal Liability*

There has however been more debate about the relationship between the duty of harmonious interpretation and non-criminal liability. Consider the ruling in the *Arcaro* case.[105] The ECJ, having reiterated the obligation of harmonious interpretation, ruled:

> However, that obligation of the national court to refer to the content of the directive when interpreting the relevant rules of its own national law reaches a limit where such an interpretation

---

[101] *Ibid.*, para. 123.

[102] Case 80/86 *Kolpinghuis Nijmegen*, n. 98 above.

[103] This principle was later extended by the ECJ to the case of regs., despite the fact that regs. as a general matter do not require implementation: Case C–60/02 *Criminal proceedings against X* [2004] ECR I–651, paras. 54–64.

[104] *Ibid.*, paras. 13–14. The ruling was confirmed in subsequent cases including Cases C–74 and 129/95 *Criminal Proceedings against X* [1996] ECR I–6609. It was also applied in the context of the criminal proceedings against the Italian prime minister in Cases C–387, 391, and 403/02 *Criminal proceedings against Silvio Berlusconi et al.* [2005] ECR I–3565, which was not a case about harmonious interpretation, but about disapplication of conflicting national law and direct reliance by the State on the dir. against the defendant. See however the opinion of Kokott AG, in which she reached a different conclusion from the ECJ.

[105] Case C–168/95 *Luciano Arcaro* [1996] ECR I–4705.

leads to the imposition on an individual of an obligation laid down by a directive which has not been transposed, or, more especially, where it has the effect of determining or aggravating, on the basis of the Directive and in the absence of a law enacted for its implementation, the liability in criminal law of persons who act in contravention of that directive's provisions (see *Kolpinghuis Nijmegen*, cited above).[106]

The case was concerned with criminal liability. The Court seemed however to suggest a narrowing of the principle of interpretation by reference to its impact on an individual, even if that impact does not amount to the imposition or aggravation of *criminal* liability. The *Arcaro* ruling suggests that where an interpretation of national law in the light of a directive amounts to 'the imposition on an individual of an obligation laid down in the directive',[107] it goes too far and is neither permitted nor required by EC law.[108] This implies that a distinction has to be made between the 'imposition of an obligation' on an individual party, which is not permitted, and the creation of other kinds of legal disadvantage or detriment for that party falling short of a legal obligation, which is permitted.[109]

However in *Centrosteel*, Advocate General Jacobs suggested that the ruling in *Arcaro* should be read in the context of the criminal proceedings in which the case had arisen.[110] He argued:

> In summary, I am of the opinion that the Court's case law establishes two rules: (1) a directive cannot *of itself* impose obligations on individuals in the absence of proper implementation in national law; (2) the national courts must nevertheless interpret national law, as far as possible, in the light of the wording and purpose of relevant directives. While that process of interpretation cannot, of itself and independently of a national law implementing the directive, have the effect of determining or aggravating criminal liability, it may well lead to the imposition upon an individual of civil liability or a civil obligation which would not otherwise have existed.

His first point reiterates the ban on direct horizontal effect, and the second point, while ruling out the interpretation of non-implementing national law in such a way as to aggravate or determine an individual's criminal liability, does not rule out an obligation on national courts to interpret non-implementing national law in such a way as to aggravate or determine an individual's *civil* liability, or to impose a legal obligation on such an individual. While the ECJ in *Centrosteel* did not refer to *Arcaro* or to the debate about the limits of the interpretation obligation, it gave a strong ruling directing the Italian court to interpret national law in conformity the directive.

---

[106] *Ibid.*, para. 42. See also Case C–105/03 *Pupino*, n. 16 above, paras. 45–47.

[107] For various possible interpretations of this phrase see P. Craig, 'Directives: Direct Effect, Indirect Effect and the Construction of National Legislation' (1997) 22 *ELRev.* 519.

[108] In Case C–106/89 *Marleasing*, n. 76 above, Van Gerven AG argued that an interpretation of national law in the light of a dir. in a way which would impose a 'civil penalty' upon an individual would contravene the principles of legal certainty and non-retroactivity, but the ECJ did not discuss the question.

[109] Hilson and Downes, n. 5 above, use Hohfeld's conceptual scheme, and contrast the notion of legal *obligation* with that of legal *disability*. Others suggest a notion of 'passive' horizontal direct effect which does not amount to a 'positive obligation': J. Stuyck and P. Wytinck (1991) 28 *CMLRev.* 205. See further below for the idea of 'exclusionary effect' which does not amount to 'substitution'.

[110] Case C–456/98 *Centrosteel* v. *Adipol* [2000] ECR I–6007, paras. 31–35, Jacobs AG. See however the more cautious Opinion of Colomber AG in Cases C–392 and 422/04 *i-21 Germany GmbH and ISIS Multimedia Net GmbH & Co. KG* v. *Bundesrepublik Deutschland* [2006] ECR I–8559, paras. 87–91.

Case C–456/98 **Centrosteel v. Adipol**
[2000] ECR I–6007

Centrosteel (an Italian company) claimed for payment of money under a commercial agency contract with the defendant Adipol (an Austrian company). The latter argued that the contract was void because of Centrosteel's failure to comply with the Italian legal requirement of compulsory registration of commercial agents. Centrosteel relied on Directive 86/653 on self-employed commercial agents, the only requirement of which for the validity of an agency contract was that a written document be drawn up, and which had been interpreted in the earlier *Bellone* case[111] as precluding a law such as the Italian registration requirement. Since Centrosteel and Adipol were private parties, and the directive had not been implemented at the time their dispute arose, to permit Centrosteel to rely directly on the Directive against Adipol would have amounted to giving it a form of horizontal effect. After noting that certain Italian courts had already, following the *Bellone* ruling, begun to change their case law relating to the invalidity of agency contracts in the light of the EC Directive in order to conform with the Directive's requirements, the ECJ continued:

THE ECJ

19. In those circumstances, the answer to be given to the questions referred must be that the Directive precludes national legislation which makes the validity of an agency contract conditional upon the commercial agent being entered in the appropriate register. The national court is bound, when applying the provisions of domestic law predating or post-dating the said Directive, to interpret those provisions, so far as possible, in the light of the wording and purpose of the Directive, so that those provisions are applied in a manner consistent with the result pursued by the Directive.

The implications of the ECJ's ruling were that Adipol would be under a legal obligation to pay the amount due under the contract with Centrosteel. If Italian law were not read in the light of the Directive, however, and if the agency contract were rendered void for violation of Italian registration law, Adipol would not be under this obligation. This kind of effect has been referred to as the 'exclusionary effect' of a directive: i.e., it prevents conflicting national law from being enforced, but it does not amount to a 'substitution effect' since it is the commercial contract and not the Directive itself which imposes obligations on the parties.

In the *Océano* case decided the same year,[112] the Court did not follow the more radical suggestion of Advocate General Saggio to give this kind of 'exclusionary effect' to directives in all cases by means of a duty on national courts to 'invoke' unimplemented directives and to 'disapply' conflicting national law without necessarily substituting provisions of EC law.[113] Instead, the ECJ focused on the obligation of harmonious interpretation.

---

[111] Case C–215/97 *Bellone* v. *Yokohama* [1998] ECR I–2191.

[112] Cases C–240–244/98 *Océano Grupo*, n. 9 above; J. Stuyck, (2001) 38 *CMLRev.* 719.

[113] The Advocate General was proposing something close to horizontal direct effect, which he argued was already implicit in ECJ case law such as *CIA Security* and *Ruiz Bernaldéz*, discussed below, namely a duty on national courts to give effect to unimplemented dirs. by refusing to apply any conflicting rules of national law, even in cases concerning disputes between individuals. He referred to this in para. 37 of his opinion in *Océano* as the 'exclusionary effect' of unimplemented dirs.—i.e. the fact that they are a superior source of EC law means that national courts are obliged to give them precedence over conflicting national law. For similar arguments see Lenz, Tynes, and Young, n. 5 above.

Cases C–240–244/98 Océano Grupo Editorial v. Rocio Murciano Quintero
[2000] ECR I–4491

The case involved proceedings between two private parties—an action brought by Océano before a Barcelona court for payment owed to it under a contract by the defendant Murciano Quintero. The question was whether the Barcelona court had jurisdiction over the case according to a jurisdiction clause in the contract. While Spanish law was not entirely clear as to whether such a jurisdiction clause should be treated as unfair or not, the EC Unfair Contract Terms Directive—which had not at the time been implemented into Spanish law—regarded it as unfair. Having cited *Marleasing* and *Dori*, the ECJ continued as follows.

THE ECJ

31. Since the court making the reference is seised of a case falling within the scope of the Directive and the facts giving rise to the case postdate the expiry of the period allowed for transposing the Directive, it therefore falls to that court, when it applies the provisions of national law outlined in paragraphs 10 and 11 above which were in force at the material time, to interpret them, as far as possible, in accordance with the Directive and in such a way that they are applied of the court's own motion.

32. It is apparent from the above considerations that the national court is obliged, when it applies national law provisions predating or postdating the said Directive, to interpret those provisions, so far as possible, in the light of the wording and purpose of the Directive. The requirement for an interpretation in conformity with the Directive requires the national court, in particular, to favour the interpretation that would allow it to decline of its own motion the jurisdiction conferred on it by virtue of an unfair term.

This ruling does not declare that the Spanish court *must* decline jurisdiction by reading national law in the light of the Directive's requirements, but indicates that it should 'favour' that interpretation if it is possible. While such an interpretation of national law would not impose a legal obligation on Océano, it would deprive that company of any existing right under national law to enforce the consumer contract before the Barcelona court. Thus the defendant would benefit from the terms of the Directive even though it had not been implemented, and the plaintiff company would suffer a legal disadvantage or disability, albeit not in the form of a legal obligation directly imposed by the Directive.

The *Coote*, *Océano*, *Centrosteel*, and *Pfeiffer* judgments indicate that the harmonious interpretation requirement is alive and well, and that when the circumstances are suitable, the ECJ will give firm guidance to a national court about how it should 'harmoniously' interpret national law even when this results in the imposition on a private party of civil liability *under national law*.

It remains unclear, however, whether the ECJ shares the view expressed by Advocate General Jacobs in *Centrosteel* that an interpretation of national law in the light of a directive may indeed result in the imposition of a legal obligation on an individual which would not otherwise have existed,[114] or whether the Court prefers the more limited approach which it adopted in *Wells* in relation to the direct effect of a directive, rather than its indirect interpretative effect. The position of the ECJ in *Wells* was that, while an unimplemented directive may

---

[114] See n. 110 above.

result in 'adverse repercussions' for an individual, it cannot result in the imposition of any legal obligation on him or her.[115] While Advocate General Jacobs in *Centrosteel* shared this view as to the limits on the direct effect of a directive, he took a different approach to indirect effect, arguing that the interpretation of national law in the light of a directive may well result in the imposition of a legal obligation on an individual. It remains to be seen whether or not the ECJ adopts this stronger formulation for indirect effect.

(e) INCIDENTAL HORIZONTAL EFFECTS

The third and closely related development which has lessened the impact of the *Marshall/Dori* no-horizontal-direct-effect-of-directives rule is a line of case law which permits the use of unimplemented directives in certain cases between private parties. This development, which is most strikingly evident in the *CIA Security*[116] and *Unilever Italia*[117] cases, is complex and confusing.

Like the cases concerning indirect interpretive effect discussed above, it is often difficult to distinguish these cases, in convincing conceptual terms, from direct horizontal effect. It brings us back also to the distinction suggested at the outset of the Chapter between the broader concept of direct effect which entails the invocability of EC law, and a narrower concept which relates to the conferral of subjective rights on individuals. The following cases suggest that directives can have a limited form of horizontal effect when they do not directly impose legal obligations on individuals.

Case C–194/94 **CIA Security International SA v.
Signalson SA and Securitel SPRL**
[1996] ECR I–2201

CIA Security brought proceedings against the defendants before the Belgian commercial courts asking for orders requiring them to cease unfair trading practices. CIA argued that the two companies had libelled it by claiming that the alarm system which it marketed had not been approved as required under Belgian legislation. CIA agreed that it had not sought approval but argued that the Belgian legislation was in breach of Article 28 EC and had not been notified to the Commission as required by Directive 83/189 on technical standards and regulations. The national court asked the ECJ whether the Directive was sufficiently clear and precise to be directly effective before the national court, and whether a national court should refuse to apply a national measure which had not been communicated as required by the Directive. The ECJ began by ruling that the national regulation should indeed have been notified under the Directive.

THE ECJ

44. [A]rticles 8 and 9 of Directive 83/189 lay down a precise obligation on Member States to notify draft technical regulations to the Commission before they are adopted. Being, accordingly, unconditional and sufficiently precise in their content, those articles may be relied on by individuals before national courts.

---

[115] Case C–201/02 *Wells*, n. 60 above, paras. 56–57.
[116] Case C–194/94 *CIA Security International SA v. Signalson SA and Securitel Sprl* [1996] ECR I–2201.
[117] Case C–443/98 *Unilever Italia SpA v. Central Food SpA* [2000] ECR I–7535.

> 45. It remains to examine the legal consequences to be drawn from a breach by Member States of their obligation to notify and, more precisely, whether Directive 83/189 is to be interpreted as meaning that a breach of the obligation to notify, constituting a procedural defect in the adoption of the technical regulations concerned, renders such technical regulations inapplicable so that they may not be enforced against individuals.

The Court ruled that part of the aim of the Directive was to protect the free movement of goods by preventive control,[118] and that it would enhance the effectiveness of that control to provide that a breach of the obligation to notify would render the un-notified domestic regulation inapplicable to individuals.[119] The ECJ did not mention *Dori* or *Marshall* and did not (unlike the Advocate General) directly advert to the fact that this was a case between private parties.

However, although CIA would rely on the Directive primarily as against the application of the State's technical regulation on the requirement of approval of alarm systems, the outcome of such reliance in the proceedings against the two defendants before the national court could presumably be that the defendants may be found liable for unfair trading. Thus, the case gives some effect to the provisions of a directive in proceedings between individuals, and it may have relieved the plaintiff of a domestic legal obligation. Further, although it did not of itself impose a legal obligation on the defendants, it removed from them the protection of the national technical regulation and exposed them to potential liability under other provisions of national law.

In other words, this is the kind of 'exclusionary' effect referred to by Advocate General Saggio in the *Océano* case:[120] the directive is invoked in a case between individuals to preclude the application of a conflicting provision of national law, and the result is that one of the parties to the case is subject to a legal liability or disadvantage to which it would not have been subject had the offending national law been applied.[121]

The issue of indirect horizontal reliance on directives in disputes involving private parties is also apparent in other cases.[122] The crucial factor in these horizontal cases is that one party suffers a legal detriment and the other party gains a legal advantage from the terms of an unimplemented directive.[123] The common factor, shared also by the *Océano*, *Centrosteel*, and *Pfeiffer* cases on indirect effect discussed above, seems to be that the directive does not *of itself* impose an obligation on another individual, and that the obligation is imposed by some other provision of national or private law. This is evident in the following cases.

---

[118] This factor was used to limit the application of the *CIA Security* ruling in the later case of Case C–226/97 *Lemmens* [2000] ECR I–3711.

[119] Contrast Case C–235/95 *AGS Assedic Pas-de-Calais* v. *François Dumon* [1998] ECR I–4531, paras. 32–33, and Case 280/87 *Enichem Base* v. *Comune di Cinisello Balsamo* [1989] ECR 2491, paras. 22–24 in which the obligation imposed on Member States by various dirs. to notify the Commission of national rules could not be invoked by individuals in order to challenge national legislation.

[120] Case C–244/98 *Océano Grupo*, n. 14 above.

[121] One explanation offered for what was at the time a surprising outcome in the case was that it concerned an action to enforce a public-law obligation under Belgian trade practices legislation, to prevent a breach of statutory duty by the defendants, rather than merely resolving a private-law dispute. See J. Stuyck (1996) 33 *CMLRev.* 1261 and J. Coppel (1997) 26 *ILJ* 69. See also P.J. Slot (1996) 33 *CMLRev.* 1035, 1049, suggesting something similar to Saggio AG's 'exclusionary effect' distinction.

[122] See also Case C–441/93 *Panagis Pafitis* v. *Trapeza Kentrikis Ellados AE* [1996] ECR I–1347.

[123] For a somewhat different view, which sees the cases as being about 'disguised vertical direct effect' in which a private party is precluded from benefiting from the State's substantive breach of an EC dir., see M. Dougan, 'The "Disguised" Vertical Direct Effect of Directives' (2000) 59 *CLJ* 586.

Ruiz Bernáldez[124] concerned criminal proceedings against the defendant for causing an accident while driving drunk, in which he was ordered to pay reparation for the damage to property caused. The Spanish criminal court referred to the ECJ the question whether the national insurance rules, which absolved the insurance company from any obligation to pay, were compatible with Directive 72/166 on motor vehicle insurance. The ECJ ruled that the Directive required an insurer to compensate third-party victims of car accidents, and that an insurer could not rely on national statutory provisions or contractual clauses to refuse to compensate such victims.[125] Thus a legal obligation to compensate the third party, which may not have existed under domestic law alone, could be derived from the Directive and imposed directly on the insurer. The enforcement of the Directive therefore removed or 'excluded' an exemption provided under national law for the insurance company, and it was national law rather than the Directive which imposed the obligation to pay.[126]

In the case of *Smithkline Beecham*,[127] in which a private party sought an injunction under national law to restrain the defendant from marketing its toothpaste, the ECJ ruled that Directive 76/768 on cosmetics precluded the application of national law restricting certain forms of toothpaste marketing. This resulted in the enforcement between private parties of a directive containing substantive rules on the marketing of cosmetics so as to remove a conflicting national law. The plaintiff was disabled from relying on national law and the defendant thereby gained the benefit of the prohibition in the directive.

The same general pattern is apparent in the *Unilever Italia* case, which also involved Directive 83/189.[128]

Case C–443/98 **Unilever Italia SpA v. Central Food SpA**
[2000] ECR I–7535

The Directive was invoked to prevent the enforcement of a national regulation which, although properly notified, had been adopted in breach of a standstill clause under the Directive. The contract was for delivery of a quantity of olive oil, and the olive oil delivered by the plaintiff was labelled in a way which complied with EC law, but not with the contested Italian labelling legislation. Thus it was a case where reliance by one party on the terms of the Directive in order to have national law disapplied would result in the imposition of contractual obligations on the defendant, which would not have been imposed had the national law been applied. Jacobs AG, having discussed the *CIA Security* ruling, argued that the offending national legislation should not be rendered unenforceable in private contractual proceedings of this kind. He contended that such unenforceability would give rise to considerable legal uncertainty, and that it would

---

[124] Case C–129/94 *Criminal Proceedings Against Rafael Ruiz Bernáldez* [1996] ECR I–1829. It has been argued that this case is better understood as one on indirect effect: S. Drake, 'Twenty Years after Von Colson' (2005) 30 *ELRev.* 329.

[125] Note that the insurer was not actually party to the case: Stuyck, n. 121 above, 1272 argues that, because proceedings were brought by the State, the Court permitted a dir. to confer rights on an individual which would generate obligations for other individuals.

[126] See n. 124 above for an argument that the case really involved indirect interpretative effect.

[127] Case C–77/97 *Österreichische Unilever GmbH* v. *Smithkline Beecham* [1999] ECR I–431.

[128] For an extensive discussion of this interesting Dir. see S. Weatherill, 'Compulsory Notification of Draft Technical Regulations: The Contribution of Directive 83/189 to the Management of the Internal Market' (1996) 16 *YBEL* 129; S. Weatherill, 'A Case Study in Judicial Activism in the 1990s: the Status before National Courts of Measures Wrongfully Un-notified to the Commission', in D. O'Keeffe and A. Bavasso (eds.), *Judicial Review in EU Law* (Kluwer, 2000), 481.

be unjust since it would penalize individuals for the State's failure. He argued further that breach of the Directive's standstill clause was different from a breach of the notification requirement and should not lead to the unenforceability of national regulations. It seems that the AG had doubts about the *CIA Security* ruling itself, and was seeking to narrow the relevance and applicability of the ruling.[129] The ECJ however disagreed and did not address the arguments of the Advocate General.[130] Having recalled in paragraphs 40–43 its reasoning in *CIA Security* about the aim of Directive 83/189 and why it should render unenforceable any national regulations adopted in breach thereof, the Court continued:

THE ECJ

45. It is therefore necessary to consider, secondly, whether the inapplicability of technical regulations adopted in breach of Article 9 of Directive 83/189 can be invoked in civil proceedings between private individuals concerning contractual rights and obligations.

46. First, in civil proceedings of that nature, application of technical regulations adopted in breach of Article 9 of Directive 83/189 may have the effect of hindering the use or marketing of a product which does not conform to those regulations.

47. That is the case in the main proceedings, since application of the Italian rules is liable to hinder Unilever in marketing the extra virgin olive oil which it offers for sale.

48. Next, it must be borne in mind that, in *CIA Security*, the finding of inapplicability as a legal consequence of breach of the obligation of notification was made in response to a request for a preliminary ruling arising from proceedings between competing undertakings based on national provisions prohibiting unfair trading.

49. Thus, it follows from the case-law of the Court that the inapplicability of a technical regulation which has not been notified in accordance with Article 8 of Directive 83/189 can be invoked in proceedings between individuals for the reasons set out in paragraphs 40 to 43 of this judgment. The same applies to non-compliance with the obligations laid down by Article 9 of the same directive, and there is no reason, in that connection, to treat disputes between individuals relating to unfair competition, as in the *CIA Security* case, differently from disputes between individuals concerning contractual rights and obligations, as in the main proceedings.

50. Whilst it is true, as observed by the Italian and Danish Governments, that a directive cannot of itself impose obligations on an individual and cannot therefore be relied on as such against an individual (see Case C–91/92 *Faccini Dori* [1994] ECR I–3325, paragraph 20), that case-law does not apply where non-compliance with Article 8 or Article 9 of Directive 83/189, which constitutes a substantial procedural defect, renders a technical regulation adopted in breach of either of those articles inapplicable.

51. In such circumstances, and unlike the case of non-transposition of directives with which the case-law cited by those two Governments is concerned, Directive 83/189 does not in any way define the substantive scope of the legal rule on the basis of which the national court must decide the case before it. It creates neither rights nor obligations for individuals.

52. In view of all the foregoing considerations, the answer to the question submitted must be that a national court is required, in civil proceedings between individuals concerning contractual rights and obligations, to refuse to apply a national technical regulation which was adopted during a period of postponement of adoption prescribed in Article 9 of Directive 83/189.

The 'public law' rationale suggested to explain earlier cases does not help in this case, which concerned a dispute between private parties where one sought to impose contractual obligations

---

[129] See his subsequent Opinion in Case C–159/00 *Sapod Audic* v. *Eco Emballages SA* [2002] ECR I–5031, para. 62.
[130] S. Weatherill, 'Breach of Directives and Breach of Contract' (2001) 26 *ELRev.* 177.

on another. True, the labelling legislation challenged here was a public regulation, but the plaintiff was seeking to have that set aside rather than enforced against the defendant.

The ECJ attempted in two ways to distinguish this case from the prohibited 'horizontal direct effect' cases such as *Dori* and *Marshall*. The first was by emphasizing the particular nature and aims of Directive 83/189 and the rationale outlined in *CIA Security* for declaring national rules which breach this Directive to be unenforceable.[131] Its second and more important argument, for general purposes, was that the Directive itself creates no individual rights and imposes no obligations on individuals.[132] This is the now familiar 'exclusionary effect' argument: that the Directive can be invoked in cases between individuals in order to have national law disapplied, so long as the Directive does not create new law, new rights, or new obligations to be applied. Rather it leaves a 'void' which is filled by other provisions of national law—and, in this case, of national contract law. We shall evaluate this argument in more detail below.

(f) STATE LIABILITY IN DAMAGES FOR NON-IMPLEMENTATION OF A DIRECTIVE

One final and important way for an individual to enforce the provisions of a directive despite the prohibition on horizontal direct effect is to sue the State in damages, pursuant to the famous *Francovich* ruling of the ECJ, for loss caused by the State's failure to implement a directive.[133] Rather than attempting to enforce the directive against the private party on whom the obligation would be imposed if the directive were properly implemented, the individual instead can bring proceedings for damages against the State. The significance of *Francovich* will be discussed in fuller detail in the next chapter. Suffice it to say in this context that the ruling has provided a further incentive for Member States to implement directives properly and on time.

6. DIRECTIVES AND THE EFFECT OF COMMUNITY LAW: AN EVALUATION

The ECJ's jurisprudence concerning the nature and impact of EC law on national law has become increasingly complex over the years, more especially in relation to directives. The Court's rationalization of the tension between the no-horizontal-direct-effect rule on the one hand, and the *Marleasing-Centrosteel-Mangold* and *CIA Security-Unilever* lines of case law on the other, relies on highly refined and questionable distinctions. If the ECJ is determined to promote the effectiveness of directives in a variety of extremely complex legal ways regardless of their proper domestic implementation, the prohibition on horizontal direct effect looks somewhat hollow.[134] It is therefore all the more important to stand back and evaluate the central precepts underlying this case law.

---

[131] For other post-*CIA Security* cases in which various attempts to invoke Dir. 83/189 [1983] OJ L109/8 were made, but without success for the applicants, see Cases C–425–427/97 *Albers* [1999] ECR I–2947; Case C–37/99 *Donkersteeg* [2000] ECR I–10223; Case C–314/98 *Sneller's Autos* v. *Algemeen Directeur van de Dienst Wegverkeer* [2000] ECR I–8633; Case C–278/99 *Van der Burg* [2001] ECR I–2015.

[132] The ECJ here may have been seeking to avoid acknowledging rights for individuals which they could use in seeking damages from the State under the *Francovich* doctrine. See n. 133 below and Ch. 9 for further discussion.

[133] Cases C–6 and 9/90 *Francovich and Bonifaci* v. *Italy* [1991] ECR I–5357.

[134] Dougan, n. 123 above; Weatherill, n. 130 above.

(a) LEGAL CERTAINTY, HORIZONTAL DIRECT EFFECT, AND INDIRECT EFFECT

It may be helpful to ground the subsequent discussion by having the following simple paradigm in mind. The Chief Executive Officer, CEO, of a company consults the in-house legal counsel about what the company should do in the following circumstances. There is a Community directive on some aspect of equality, which either has not been implemented by the relevant State, or there are doubts as to whether the implementation is properly in accord with the demands of the directive. The CEO wishes to know whether the company should follow the relevant national law or the directive. She wishes to do what is legally correct and to avoid litigation with employees.

If directives had horizontal direct effect the task of the in-house legal counsel would be relatively straightforward. The lawyer would compare the relevant national law and the directive. He would identify inconsistencies. In so far as there were any, he would decide whether the provisions of the directive were sufficiently precise, clear, and unconditional to give rise to direct effect. Assuming that they were, he would then advise the CEO to follow the directive, and tell her that the supremacy of Community law meant that inconsistent national law would be trumped by the directive.

Consider by way of contrast the task facing the in-house legal counsel under the present law. Directives do not have horizontal direct effect. He would nonetheless still have to identify any possible inconsistencies between national law and the directive, but having done so the best answer that he could give to the CEO as to which law the company should follow is that this would depend on whether a national court would feel able to interpret the national law to be compatible with the directive. It is unlikely that he could give more than a rough guess in this respect, depending on the nature of the inconsistencies that exist.

There is a certain tension and paradox in all this. The ECJ has tended in the post-*Marshall* case law to deny horizontal direct effect to directives on grounds of legal certainty for defendants.[135] It is however arguable that indirect effect creates considerably greater problems for courts and litigants alike.

The national court has to tread the ever-difficult line of deciding how far it can 'interpret' national law to be in conformity with the directive, without thereby crossing the line between interpretation and judicial re-writing of legislation. The potential private defendant will often simply not know the answer to this without resort to litigation. The legal uncertainty facing the legal adviser to the CEO has been made more difficult by developments within the doctrine of indirect effect. Remember in this respect that: the provision of the directive does not need to be precise and unconditional in order to be subject to the doctrine of indirect effect; the duty of harmonious interpretation now demands that national courts consider all national law in deciding whether compatibility with the provisions of the directive can be attained; and the extent to which indirect effect can lead to the imposition of non-criminal obligations, as opposed to 'adverse repercussions', on defendants is still unclear, as is the line betwixt the two. The reality at present is that legal uncertainty about the effectiveness and applicability of an unimplemented directive—and correspondingly about the validity of conflicting national law—in any given situation is extremely high.

---

[135] See, e.g., Case C–201/02 *Wells*, n. 60 above, para. 56.

(b) PRIMACY, EXCLUSION, AND SUBSTITUTION

The ECJ has consistently refused to depart from the clear *Marshall/Dori* rulings that a directive cannot be invoked by an individual so as to impose a direct obligation on another individual. Yet cases such as *CIA Security*, *Unilever Italia*, *Panagis Pafitis*, and *Smithkline Beecham* demonstrate that directives which contain substantive rules and requirements directly affecting the legal position of the parties can be enforced horizontally between the parties, provided that this can rationalized in terms of an exclusionary, rather than substitutionary, effect. This argument must be carefully evaluated. The distinction has thus far been articulated principally in the Opinions of Advocates General and in the academic literature, but it seems to underlie the ECJ's jurisprudence on incidental horizontal effect.

Let us recall the central idea. Directives can, even in actions between private parties, have an 'exclusionary' impact, excluding inconsistent national law. This is said to flow from the primacy of Community law. The result in the instant case is then said to be justified on the basis of the national law that subsists in the absence of that part of national law that has been excluded by the directive. This is distinguished from a 'substitution' effect, which connotes the idea that the directive will in itself mandate certain novel legal consequences within the national legal order, where it contains no such provisions. This can, so the argument goes, occur in actions against the State only where the conditions for direct effect have been met. This distinction is however problematic in conceptual terms, since it at one and the same time 'proves too little' and 'proves too much'. This is so for four reasons.

First, the very determination of whether a case is to be regarded as one of 'exclusion' or 'substitution' can be problematic. The characterization of a case as being one of 'exclusion' and not 'substitution' is dependent on the identification of some 'default rule' of the national legal system that will govern the matter, once the provision that is inconsistent with the directive is excluded. Whether such a default rule exists and its content may be contentious, depending upon the level of abstraction at which the issue is framed.[136] The more broadly the issue is framed the more likely you are to find some national default rule, but the more difficult it becomes to mask the reality that a new rule is being substituted within the national legal system.

Secondly, the argument 'proves too little' when considered from the perspective of the parties to the case, and especially the private defendant, since the distinction between 'exclusion', combined with the residual application of national law, and 'substitution', entailing the application of 'new' rules derived from the directive, conceals more than it reveals. The reality is that in both instances it is the directive that mandates the outcome, and this constitutes a new legal status quo within the national legal system. From the perspective of the private party it matters not whether this is conceptualized in terms of 'modification' of national rules or imposition of 'new' EC rules.

Thirdly, the argument 'proves too little' when considered from the perspective of the national legal system. It is premised on the unspoken assumption that to 'exclude' that part of a national law that is inconsistent with a directive is somehow less intrusive or less dramatic than 'substitution' of something new within the national legal order. There is no reason why this has to be so. Consider the structure of legal rules. They will normally contain a core provision that will then be qualified or conditioned by other provisions. Contract rules may, for example, be premised on a core idea of freedom to contract, which is then qualified in a variety of ways by more specific rules concerning unfair consumer terms, illegality,

---

[136] See, e.g., Cases C–240–244/98 *Océano Grupo*, n. 9 above, para. 39, Saggio AG who talks of the exclusion of the incompatible rule being filled by application by 'analogy or recourse to general principles of national law if those national provisions comply with the principles on which the directive is based'.

misrepresentation, and the like. It cannot be assumed that the impact of exclusion of one such rule for inconsistency with a directive, coupled with the application of the remainder of national contract law, will be any less far-reaching for that legal system than the substitution/introduction of a legal concept which that system did not hitherto possess. It might be, but it equally well might not, depending on the nature and importance of the rules respectively excluded or substituted.

Fourthly, the argument also 'proves too much'. The exclusionary effect of a directive is, as we have seen, said to be based on the primacy of Community law. It is however unclear why, if this is the foundational premise, it should not also demand the substitution/introduction of rules from the directive, even where no relevant provisions currently exist within the national legal order. This is of course precisely what direct effect, including vertical direct effect, of directives coupled with primacy does demand. If primacy really is the driving imperative then it is unclear why it should not also demand substitution even in horizontal cases. The essential thrust behind the primacy argument, and the way it is commonly put, is in terms of hierarchy: the superiority of EC law is said to demand exclusion. Yet if it is normative hierarchy that drives the argument, it is unclear why it should not also demand substitution, where this is required to effectuate the directive in the national legal order. This is more especially so because it may be fortuitous, depending on the structure of rules within a legal system, whether the case should be characterized as one of exclusion or substitution.

7. GENERAL CONCLUSIONS

i. While some have argued that EC law should simply be applicable law, capable of use in national courts as the 'law of the land', it remains the case that different kinds of EC law enjoy different kinds of domestic legal effect.

ii. Most provisions of EC law can be invoked by individuals before national courts when they satisfy basic conditions of justiciability: this is known as 'direct effect'. Normally, though not always, this means that they are capable of conferring rights on individuals.

iii. The position of directives is very complicated. They can be directly invoked by individuals before national courts against a state body, or indirectly invoked against a State or private party in order to secure an interpretation of national law in conformity with their provisions. And they can be directly invoked in proceedings against other individuals (horizontally) only in circumstances where they do not of themselves impose an obligation on a private party.

iv. The principle that national law should be interpreted in the light of EC law is a broad one. It applies not only to directives, but also to EC Treaty provisions, to general principles of EC law, to international agreements entered by the EC, and to other forms of non-binding EC law.

8. FURTHER READING

(a) Books

Prechal, S., *Directives in EC Law* (2nd edn., Oxford University Press, 2005)

Prinssen, J., *Direct Effect: Rethinking a Classic of EC legal Doctrine* (Europa Law Publishing, Hogendrop Papers, 2002)

(b) Articles

Betlem, G., 'The Principle of Indirect Effect of Community Law' (1995) 3 *ERPL* 1

—— 'The Doctrine of Consistent Interpretation: Managing Legal Uncertainty' (2002) 22 *OJLS* 397

Coppel, J., 'Rights, Duties and the End of Marshall' (1994) 57 *MLR* 859

—— 'Horizontal Direct Effect of Directives' (1997) 28 *ILJ* 69

Craig, P., 'Once upon a Time in the West: Direct Effect and the Federalization of EEC Law' (1992) 12 *OJLS* 453

Curtin, D., 'The Province of Government: Delimiting the Direct Effect of Directives in the Common Law Context' (1990) 15 *ELRev.* 195

De Witte, B., 'Direct Effect, Supremacy and the Nature of the Legal Order', in P. Craig and G. de Búrca (eds.), *The Evolution of EU Law* (Oxford University Press, 1999) 177

Dougan, M., 'The "Disguised" Vertical Direct Effect of Directives' (2000) 59 *CLJ* 586

Drake, S., 'Twenty Years after "Von Colson": The Impact of "Indirect Effect" on the Protection of the Individual's Community Rights' (2005) 30 *ELRev.* 329

Eleftheriadis, P., 'The Direct Effect of Community Law: Conceptual Issues' (1996) 16 *YBEL* 205

Griller, S., 'Judicial Enforceability of WTO Law in the EU' (2000) 3 *JIEL* 441

Hilson, C., and Downes, T., 'Making Sense of Rights: Community Rights in EC Law' (1999) 24 *ELRev.* 121

Klamert, M., 'Judicial Implementation of Directives and Anticipatory Indirect Effect: Connecting the Dots' (2006) 43 *CMLRev.* 1251

Lenz, M., Tynes, D.S., and Young, L., 'Horizontal What? Back to Basics' (2000) 25 *ELRev.* 509

Mastroianni, R., 'On the Distinction Between Vertical and Horizontal Direct Effect of Directives: What Role for the Principle of Equality?' (1999) 5 *EPL* 417

Pescatore, P., 'The Doctrine of "Direct Effect": An Infant Disease of Community Law' (1983) 8 *ELRev.* 155

Prechal, S., 'Does Direct Effect Still Matter?' (2000) 37 *CMLRev.* 1047

Ross, M., 'Effectiveness in the EU Legal Order: Beyond Supremacy to Constitutional Proportionality' (2006) 31 *ELRev.* 476

Ruffert, M., 'Rights and Remedies in European Community Law: A Comparative View' (1997) 34 *CMLRev.* 307

Tridimas, T., 'Black, White, and Shades of Grey: Horizontality of Directives Revisited' (2002) 21 *YBEL* 327

Van Gerven, W., 'The Horizontal Direct Effect of Directive Provisions Revisited: the Reality of Catchwords', in T. Heukels and D. Curtin (eds.), *Institutional Dynamics of European Integration, Liber Amicorum for Henry Schermers* (Martinus Nijhoff, 1994)

—— 'Of Rights, Remedies and Procedures' (2000) 37 *CMLRev.* 501

Weatherill, S., 'Breach of Directives and Breach of Contract' (2001) 26 *ELRev.* 177

Winter, T., 'Direct Applicability and Direct Effects' (1972) 9 *CMLRev.* 425

Wyatt, D., 'New Legal Order or Old' (1982) 7 *ELRev.* 147

9

THE APPLICATION OF EC LAW:
REMEDIES IN NATIONAL COURTS

1. CENTRAL ISSUES

i. The ECJ has developed the 'effectiveness of EC law' as a legal principle, which includes an obligation on national courts to ensure they give adequate effect to EC law in cases arising before them. In recent years, the Court has emphasized the principle of effective judicial protection as a *fundamental right*, drawing support from the ECHR.

ii. Neither the EU Treaties nor Community legislation lay down a general scheme of substantive or procedural law governing remedies for the enforcement of EC law. However, sectoral legislation addressing remedial issues exists in various EU law fields,[1] and there have been moves towards more ambitious harmonization and co-ordination projects in civil, commercial, and criminal law.[2]

iii. Early ECJ case law emphasized a principle of national autonomy and primary responsibility in the field of remedies, whereby EC law would be given effect at domestic level in accordance with the procedures and rules established by national law. The Court also ruled that EC law did not require national courts to provide new remedies. The principle of national procedural autonomy was qualified by two requirements: that national procedures and rules should be applied to rights arising from national law and EC law in the same way (equivalence), and that they should not render the exercise of EC rights impossible in practice (practical possibility).

iv. The ECJ later emphasized a stronger and generally applicable requirement of adequacy and effectiveness in the domestic enforcement of EC law, derived from Article 10 EC. The

---

[1] Three representative examples are in the fields of public procurement, environmental law, and intellectual property. For recent developments in these fields see COM(2006)195 on revision of the procurement remedies dirs, Dir. 2004/95 on environmental liability [2004] OJ L143/56, and Dir. 2004/48 on enforcement of intellectual property rights [2004] OJ L195/16.

[2] Art. 65 EC governs the adoption of measures concerning judicial co-operation in civil matters and suggests promoting the compatibility of the rules on civil procedure in the various Member States. Arts. 29–31 EU govern the harmonization of criminal law measures: see generally the 2005 Council and Commission Action Plan on Implementing the Hague Programme on Strengthening Freedom Security and Justice in the EU [2005] OJ C198/1. On proposals to harmonize in the field of contract law, including on the issue of remedies, see COM(2003)68, COM(2004)651, and COM(2005)456. On the possibility of adopting criminal law sanctions within the EC Pillar see the important judgment in Case C–176/03 *Commission* v. *Council* [2005] ECR I–7879, and the Commission's response COM(2005)583. On EU civil procedure more generally see the special issue of the *EBLRev* (2006) 17(3).

Court in some cases even required national courts to make available a particular type of remedy (reparation, interim relief, etc.), regardless of whether this would be available under national law.

v. The most famous judgment in which the ECJ ruled that EC law requires national courts to provide a *specific* form of remedy is *Francovich*, in which the principle of state liability to provide compensation for breach of EC law was introduced. The scope of this EC 'right to reparation' from the State was subsequently expanded and clarified, and a parallel principle of *individual* liability to compensate for breaches of EC law, at least in the field of competition law, was introduced.

vi. A synthesis of the case law indicates that while the principle of national procedural and remedial autonomy and competence remains important, the qualifications of equivalence and effectiveness are powerful doctrinal tools directing national courts to undertake a case-by-case appraisal of national rules. National courts are expected to engage in a context-specific proportionality analysis of any restrictive provisions of national law and to disapply these whenever necessary to give effect to EC law.

2. THE PRINCIPLE OF NATIONAL PROCEDURAL AUTONOMY

(a) WHERE NO RELEVANT RULES OF EC LAW EXIST, THE NATIONAL LEGAL SYSTEM DETERMINES THE PRIMARY CONDITIONS UNDER WHICH RIGHTS GRANTED BY EC LAW ARE TO BE PROTECTED

Early in its case law the ECJ ruled that it was for the national legal system to determine how the interests of a person adversely affected by an infringement of Community law were to be protected. Only a very basic degree of guidance was provided in these cases.[3]

Case 33/76 **Rewe-Zentralfinanz eG and Rewe-Zentral AG v. Landwirtschaftskammer für das Saarland**
[1976] ECR 1989

[Note: Art. 5 EC is now Art. 10]

The applicant companies applied for a refund, including interest, of charges they had paid in Germany for import inspection costs, which had been imposed in violation of the Treaty. The national time limit for contesting the validity of national administrative measures had passed, and the case was referred to the ECJ to see whether Community law required that they be granted the remedy sought.

---

[3] Case 6/60 *Humblot* v. *Belgium* [1960] ECR 559; Case 13/68 *Salgoil* v. *Italian Ministry for Foreign Trade* [1973] ECR 453.

THE ECJ[4]

Applying the principle of cooperation laid down in Article 5 of the Treaty, it is the national courts which are entrusted with ensuring the legal protection which citizens derive from the direct effect of the provisions of Community law.

Accordingly, in the absence of Community rules on this subject, it is for the domestic legal system of each Member State to designate the courts having jurisdiction and to determine the procedural conditions governing actions at law intended to ensure the protection of the rights which citizens have from the direct effect of Community law, it being understood that such conditions cannot be less favourable than those relating to similar actions of a domestic nature . . .

. . . In the absence of such measures of harmonisation the right conferred by Community law must be exercised before the national courts in accordance with the conditions laid down by national rules.

The position would be different only if the conditions and time-limits made it impossible in practice to exercise the rights which the national courts are obliged to protect.

This is not the case where reasonable periods of limitation of actions are fixed.

Perhaps a better term than 'national procedural autonomy' is 'procedural competence'[5] or 'primary national procedural responsibility', since the case clearly emphasized the responsibility of the Member States, where there are no relevant Community rules, for determining the procedural conditions under which Community rights are to be protected.[6] The ECJ then imposed two 'Community' requirements on any national conditions:[7] first, the principle of *equivalence* or non-discrimination, meaning that the remedies and forms of action available to ensure the observance of national law must be made available in the same way to ensure the observance of Community law; and, secondly, the principle of *practical possibility*, meaning that national conditions and procedures should not make the exercise of the right impossible in practice.

(b) THERE IS NO OBLIGATION TO 'CREATE NEW REMEDIES'?

Subject to these two requirements, the procedures and remedies for breach of Community law were primarily a matter for the Member States. In the absence of harmonization or the creation of Community rules, the States were not required to provide remedies which would not be available under national law. In *Rewe-Handelsgesellschaft Nord* v. *Hauptzollamt Kiel* (the 'butter-buying cruises' case), the ECJ was asked whether a trader had a right under EC law to require a national court to compel his third party competitor to comply with

---

[4] [1976] ECR 1989, 1997.

[5] This has been suggested by numerous authors including W. van Gerven, M. Dougan, and C. Kakouris. See also J. Delicostopoulos, 'Towards European Procedural Primacy in National Legal Systems' (2003) 9 *ELJ* 599.

[6] See also Case 45/76 *Comet BV* v. *Produktschap voor Siergewassen* [1976] ECR 2043; Case 179/84 *Bozetti* v. *Invernizzi* [1985] ECR 2301.

[7] See, for criticism of the conflation of 'procedures' and 'remedies' in discussion of this subject and for a query whether the appropriate term should be national *remedial* autonomy rather than national *procedural* autonomy, C. Kilpatrick, 'The Future of Remedies in Europe', in C. Kilpatrick, T. Novitz, and P. Skidmore (eds.), *The Future of Remedies in Europe* (Hart, 2000), 1, 4.

EC obligations.[8] The Court ruled:

> [I]t must be remarked first of all that, although the Treaty has made it possible in a number of instances for private persons to bring a direct action, where appropriate, before the Court of Justice, it was not intended to create new remedies in the national courts to ensure the observance of Community law other than those already laid down by national law. On the other hand the system of legal protection established by the Treaty, as set out in Article 177 in particular, implies that it must be possible for every type of action provided for by national law to be available for the purpose of ensuring observance of Community provisions having direct effect, on the same conditions concerning the admissibility and procedure as would apply were it a question of ensuring observance of national law.[9]

New national remedies did not therefore have to be created, although existing national remedies must not render the exercise of the right impossible in practice.[10]

In one particular branch of case law concerning the repayment of charges levied in breach of EC law, however, the Court effectively insisted that a right to repayment must in principle be available under national law, on the basis that this flowed directly from the nature of the substantive provisions of EC law in question.[11] In *San Giorgio* the Court ruled:

> 12. In that connection it must be pointed out in the first place that entitlement to the repayment of charges levied by a member state contrary to the rules of Community law is a consequence of, and an adjunct to, the rights conferred on individuals by the Community provisions prohibiting charges having an effect equivalent to customs duties or, as the case may be, the discriminatory application of internal taxes. Whilst it is true that repayment may be sought only within the framework of the conditions as to both substance and form, laid down by the various national laws applicable thereto, the fact nevertheless remains, as the court has consistently held that those conditions may not be less favourable than those relating to similar claims regarding national charges and they may not be so framed as to render virtually impossible the exercise of rights conferred by Community law.[12]

It has been argued that this line of case law concerning unlawfully levied charges involves the ECJ imposing a particular remedy,[13] or perhaps insisting, as a matter of Community law, upon the availability of a specific remedy within national legal systems.[14]

---

[8] Case 158/80 *Rewe-Handelsgesellschaft Nord mbH* v. *Hauptzollamt Kiel* [1981] ECR 1805.

[9] *Ibid.*, para. 44.

[10] In Case 309/85 *Barra* v. *Belgium* [1988] ECR 355 the Court considered that national legislation restricting repayment of a fee which had been charged in breach of Community law would render the exercise of Community rights impossible in practice. See also Case C–62/00 *Marks & Spencer* v. *Commissioners of Customs and Excise* [2002] ECR I–6325.

[11] See, e.g., Case 199/82 *Amministrazione delle Finanze dello Stato* v. *San Giorgio* [1983] ECR 3595; Case C–192/95 *Comateb* v. *Directeur Général des Douanes et Droits Indirects* [1997] ECR I–165. There is an extensive case law on the topic of recovery of unlawfully levied charges, and in particular on the question of the compatibility with EC law of different versions of the defence of 'passing on': see n. 180 below.

[12] Case 199/82 *San Giorgio*, n. 11 above.

[13] M. Dougan, 'Cutting your Losses in the Enforcement Deficit: A Community Right to the Recovery of Unlawfully Levied Charges?' (1998) 1 *CYELS* 233.

[14] The national legal system nonetheless still retains some discretion in deciding on the exact system for repayment of charges: Cases C–10–22/97 *Ministero delle Finanze* v. *IN.CO.GE.'90 Srl* [1998] ECR I–6307, para. 28. where the ECJ rejected the Commission's argument about the appropriate national remedy.

At the same time, even in these cases the Court continued to emphasize the primary role of the national legal system in laying down the conditions governing the grant of such a remedy, so long as they satisfied the principles of equivalence and practical possibility. As Advocate General Warner said in the case of *Ferwerda*:[15]

> To that one might object that, if so, there will be a lack of uniformity in the consequences of the application of Community law in the different Member States. The answer to that objection is … that this Court cannot create Community law where none exists: that must be left to the Community's legislative organs.

3. FURTHER REQUIREMENTS OF COMMUNITY LAW: PROPORTIONALITY, ADEQUACY, AND EFFECTIVE PROTECTION

(a) PROPORTIONALITY, ADEQUACY, AND EFFECTIVENESS OF NATIONAL RESPONSES

The 'recovery of charges' cases generally involve either an individual seeking to recover from the State the cost of charges which it has imposed in breach of EC law, or the State's attempt to recover money which it has wrongfully paid in breach of EC law. But the issue of national responses to the breach of EC law by *individuals* has also arisen. Some of these cases, such as *Sagulo* and *Heylens* below, raise questions of the compatibility with Community law of heavy penalties imposed by a Member State for relatively minor administrative breaches by persons enjoying rights under Community law.[16] Others, such as *Von Colson*, concern the adequacy and deterrent effect of national penalties for serious breaches by companies or individuals of fundamental rules of Community law.[17]

In *Sagulo*, the ECJ ruled that while Member States were entitled to impose reasonable penalties for infringements of administrative requirements governing EC residence permits by migrant workers, the penalties must not be disproportionate to the offence in question and must not constitute an obstacle to the exercise of fundamental EC rights such as freedom of movement.[18] On the other hand, Member States are *required* by EC law—more specifically by Article 10 EC—to take 'all effective measures to sanction conduct which affects the financial interests of the Community'.[19] Moreover the States may impose criminal penalties even where Community legislation provides only for civil sanctions, as long as any such penalties imposed satisfy the principle of equivalence and are 'effective, proportionate and dissuasive'.[20]

---

[15] Case 265/78 *Ferwerda* v. *Produktschap voor Vee en Vlees* [1980] ECR 617, 640. Here the Court accepted that the systematic application of the principle of legal certainty could make it practically impossible for the authorities to recover money granted in breach of an EC reg.

[16] Where the penalty is imposed by the State under legislation which of itself is in breach of EC law, the penalty is automatically also invalid, and no question of its proportionality arises: Case C–13/01 *Safalero Srl* v. *Prefetto di Genova* [2003] ECR I–8679.

[17] See also Case 68/88 *Commission* v. *Greece* [1989] ECR 2965.

[18] Case 8/77 *Sagulo, Brenca, and Bakhouche* [1977] ECR 1495, paras. 12–13. See also Case 77/81 *Zuckerfabrik Franken* [1982] ECR 681.

[19] Case C–186/98 *Nunes and de Matos* [1999] ECR I–4883.

[20] *Ibid.*

In *Von Colson*, the Court was asked to rule on the compatibility with EC law of national sanctions designed to remedy breaches by an employer (or the State) of rights enjoyed by individuals under the Equal Treatment Directive 76/207.[21] The plaintiffs had been discriminated against on grounds of sex in applying for posts as prison workers, but they were told that they were only entitled, by way of remedy, to 'reliance loss' (e.g., the costs of travel to the interview), and not compensation or appointment to the post. The ECJ ruled:

> 23. Although ... full implementation of the directive does not require any specific form of sanction for unlawful discrimination, it does entail that that sanction be such as to guarantee real and effective judicial protection.
>
> ...
>
> 28. It should, however, be pointed out to the national court that although Directive No 76/207/EEC, for the purpose of imposing a sanction for the breach of the prohibition of discrimination, leaves the Member States free to choose between the different solutions suitable for achieving its objective, it nevertheless requires that if a Member State chooses to penalize breaches of that prohibition by the award of compensation, then in order to ensure that it is effective and that it has a deterrent effect, that compensation must in any event be adequate in relation to the damage sustained and must therefore amount to more than purely nominal compensation such as, for example, the reimbursement only of the expenses incurred in connection with the application.

Von Colson thus added the more robust requirement of *adequacy and effectiveness* of national remedies to the established principles of practical possibility, and equivalence or non-discrimination,[22] and to the requirement of proportionality of penalties. Later rulings such as *Johnston*,[23] *Heylens*,[24] and *Panayotova*[25] confirmed that this requirement to provide adequate and effective remedies was a general one, extending beyond sex discrimination law. In *Heylens*, a Belgian football trainer's diploma was refused recognition by the French authorities where he worked, and the ECJ, drawing on the right to an effective judicial remedy in Articles 6 and 13 of the European Convention on Human Rights, ruled:

> [S]ince free access to employment is a fundamental right which the Treaty confers individually on each worker in the Community, the existence of a remedy of a judicial nature against any decision of a national authority refusing the benefit of that right is essential in order to secure for the individual effective protection for his right.[26]

According to the Court, the right to effective judicial review also generally requires the giving of reasons for decisions which curtailed or denied a Community right, and must enable the person affected 'to defend that right under the best possible conditions'.[27]

---

[21] Case 14/83 *Von Colson and Kamann* v. *Land Nordrhein-Westfalen* [1984] ECR 1891.

[22] For cases in which national procedural rules on security for costs were found to be indirectly discriminatory, not as compared with equivalent Community law claims, but in relation to traders from other Member States, see Case C–43/95 *Data Delecta* [1996] ECR I–4661, para. 12; Case C–323/95 *Hayes* v. *Kronenberger* [1996] ECR I–1711, para. 13.

[23] Case 222/84 *Johnston* v. *Chief Constable of the RUC* [1986] ECR 1651. See also Cases C–87–89/90 *Verholen* v. *Sociale Verzekeringsbank* [1991] ECR I–3757, para. 24, concerning national rules on standing.

[24] Case 222/86 *UNECTEF* v. *Heylens* [1987] ECR 4097.

[25] Case C–327/02 *Panayotova* v. *Minister voor Vreemdelingenzaken en Integratie* [2004] ECR I–11055.

[26] Case 222/86 *Heylens*, n. 24 above, para. 14.

[27] *Ibid.*, para. 15. See also, on the right to judicial review, Case C–228/98 *Dounias* v. *Ypourgio Oikonomikon* [2000] ECR I–577, paras. 64–66; Case C–424/99 *Commission* v. *Austria* [2001] ECR I–9285; Case C–1/99 *Kofisa Italia* [2001] ECR I–207; Case C–226/99 *Siples* [2001] ECR I–277.

In *Coote*,[28] the Court underscored a specific dimension of the right to effective judicial protection, ruling that the principle of *access to judicial control* must extend also to retaliatory measures adopted by an employer in reaction to an equal treatment claim.[29] In *Schneider*, the ECJ ruled that the requirement of effective judicial protection in the Equal Treatment Directive was fully satisfied by the existence of an action for state liability before the civil courts, even if a parallel action before the administrative courts was limited in terms of the factual review which could be carried out.[30]

In a different context,[31] in *Upjohn*, the ECJ ruled also on the standard of review required, indicating that EC law did not oblige the national legal system to provide a judicial review procedure under which national courts would be competent to substitute their assessment of the facts and the scientific evidence found for that of the national decision-making body, provided that those courts were empowered effectively to apply the principles of EC law when conducting judicial review.[32] Moreover in *Evans* the Court concluded that a system of national redress which provided for a combination of administrative review, arbitration (so long as each of these provided appropriate procedural rights to the claimant), and appellate judicial review for motor accident compensation claims would satisfy the requirement of effective protection.[33]

(b) EFFECTIVE PROTECTION VERSUS 'NO NEW REMEDIES': EARLY TENSIONS

The shift from the *non-discriminatory* application of national rules, and from the minimal-sounding requirement that EC rights should not be rendered *impossible in practice* to the more positive requirement that they be given *adequate and effective* protection, brought certain tensions to light.

In *Rewe-Handelsgesellschaft Nord* v. *Hauptzollamt Kiel*[34] the Court declared that the Treaty had not intended to create new remedies in national courts, nor to require those courts to create new remedies, and that national provisions could be applied as long as they complied with the principles of equivalence and practical possibility. However, two developments had already undermined the significance of the 'no new remedies' statement: first, in the recovery-of-charges cases, the provision of a certain type of remedy was held to be a necessary adjunct to the substantive EC right; and secondly when a national rule or principle rendered the exercise of a Community right impossible in practice, that rule would have to be set aside.

This tension was vividly highlighted in *Factortame I* in which the ECJ, drawing on its earlier *Simmenthal* ruling,[35] strongly emphasized the effectiveness requirement, and insisted on its priority over principles of UK law. In legal terms this went no further than previous rulings of the Court, but the results in *Factortame I* were dramatic. The national rule in question was a

---

[28] See Case C–185/97 *Coote* v. *Granada Hospitality Ltd.* [1998] ECR I–5199, in which an employer had refused to provide references for an employee, in retaliation for proceedings brought against it under the Dir.

[29] See also Case C–253/00 *Muñoz* v. *Frumar* [2002] ECR I–7289.

[30] Case C–380/01 *Gustav Schneider* v. *Bundesminister für Justiz* [2004] ECR I–1389.

[31] The relevance of the varying factual contexts and the different substantive sectors in which the ECJ has ruled on the remedial requirements of national law is a dimension which clearly merits further analysis: see C. Kilpatrick *et al.*, n. 7 above, P II, 'Sectoral Approaches to EC Remedies', and M. Dougan, *National Remedies Before the Court of Justice* (Hart, 2004).

[32] Case C–120/97 *Upjohn* v. *The Licensing Authority* [1999] ECR I–223, paras. 33–36.

[33] Case C–63/01 *Evans* v. *Secretary of State for the Environment and the Motor's Insurer's Bureau* [2003] ECR I–14447.

[34] Case 158/80 *Rewe-Handelsgesellschaft Nord mbH* v. *Hauptzollamt Kiel* [1981] ECR 1805, para. 44.

[35] Case 106/77 *Amministrazione delle Finanze dello Stato* v. *Simmenthal SpA* [1978] ECR 629.

principle which, according to the House of Lords, prohibited absolutely the grant of the particular remedy sought. Therefore, the impact of requiring the principle of effectiveness of Community law to be given priority over the national rule was to require the grant of a remedy in novel circumstances, where it had not been previously available under national law.

Case C–213/89 R. v. Secretary of State for Transport, ex parte Factortame Ltd. and Others
[1990] ECR I–2433

[Note ToA renumbering: Art. 5 is now Art. 10]

Factortame and other companies, whose directors and shareholders consisted mainly of Spanish nationals, were incorporated under UK law and operated fishing vessels registered as British vessels under British law. The 1988 Merchant Shipping Act was introduced to require all fishing vessels to register anew, and the applicants did not satisfy the new registration conditions. They argued that these conditions, including a 75 per cent. nationality requirement for directors and shareholders, breached Community law, and they sought interim relief pending final judgment. When the case reached the House of Lords it was held that interim relief was precluded both by the common law rule prohibiting the grant of an interim injunction against the Crown and by the presumption that an Act of Parliament is in conformity with EC law until a decision on its compatibility has been given. However, the House of Lords referred the case to the ECJ to see if interim relief was required as a matter of EC law.

THE ECJ

13. The House of Lords ... found in the first place that the claims by the appellants in the main proceedings that they would suffer irreparable damage if the interim relief which they sought were not granted and they were successful in the main proceedings were well founded. However, it held that, under national law, the English courts had no power to grant interim relief in a case such as the one before it. . . .

  . . .

17. ... [T]he preliminary question raised by the House of Lords seeks essentially to ascertain whether a national court which, in a case before it concerning Community law, considers that the sole obstacle which precludes it from granting interim relief is a rule of national law, must disapply that rule.

  . . .

19. In accordance with the case-law of the Court, it is for the national courts, in application of the principle of cooperation laid down in Article 5 of the EEC Treaty, to ensure the legal protection which persons derive from the direct effect of provisions of Community law. . . .

20. The Court has also held that any provision of a national legal system and any legislative, administrative or judicial practice which might impair the effectiveness of Community law by withholding from the national court having jurisdiction to apply such law the power to do everything necessary at the moment of its application to set aside national legislative provisions which might prevent, even temporarily, Community rules from having full force and effect are incompatible with those requirements, which are the very essence of Community law (judgment of 9 March 1978 in Case 106/77 *Simmenthal* [1978] ECR 629).

21. It must be added that the full effectiveness of Community law would be just as much impaired if a rule of national law could prevent a court seised of a dispute governed by

Community law from granting interim relief in order to ensure the full effectiveness of the judgment to be given on the existence of the rights claimed under Community law. It follows that
a court which in those circumstances would grant interim relief, if it were not for a rule of
national law, is obliged to set aside that rule.

The emphasis in *Factortame* is on the requirement of effectiveness of EC law, rather than on
the primary role of national procedural law which was emphasized in early rulings. The ECJ
left it to the House of Lords to specify the conditions under which interim relief should be
granted in a given case,[36] but made clear that a rule which prohibited absolutely the grant of
interim relief would be unacceptable. We will see below that later cases involving a strong
'effectiveness' ruling by the ECJ have further reduced the significance and scope of the 'no new
remedies' rule.[37]

4. DEVELOPMENT OF THE 'EFFECTIVENESS' REQUIREMENT

(a) PHASE 1: A STRONG INITIAL REQUIREMENT

A stream of cases from the early 1990s onwards highlighted the tension between the emphasis
on national procedural responsibility and autonomy, and the requirement that national
remedies—particularly in the context of EC directives whose provisions expressly require the
availability of adequate judicial remedies—must secure the effectiveness of Community
rights.

In *Dekker*, the applicant sought damages before the Dutch courts against an employer who,
in breach of the EC Equal Treatment Directive, refused to employ her on grounds of her
pregnancy. Citing its *Von Colson* judgment on the Directive's requirement of effective judicial
protection, the ECJ ruled that to subject a claim for redress to a requirement of 'fault' on the
part of the employer, a defence of justification or other ground of exemption, would undermine the Directive.[38] The provisions of the Equal Treatment Directive requiring access to a
judicial remedy may account in part for the strength of the ruling.[39] Nonetheless, the judgment marked a further dilution of the principle of national procedural autonomy, especially
since the national rule did not discriminate between situations involving Community law and
those involving domestic law, and the requirement of fault might not render the exercise of
the Community right 'impossible' in practice.

In *Cotter and McDermott*, the Irish Supreme Court considered that the payment to married
women of social welfare benefits for dependents which had previously been paid to married
men but denied to married women in breach of EC sex discrimination law would offend

---

[36] The precise conditions under which interim relief against a provision of national law which implemented
Community law should be available were later specified by the ECJ in Cases C–143/88 and 92/89 *Zuckerfabrik
Süderdithmarschen* [1991] ECR I–415; Case C–334/95 *Kruger GmbH* [1997] ECR I–4517.

[37] See nn. 65–73 below, and accompanying text.

[38] Case C–177/88 *Dekker* v. *Stichting voor Jong Volwassenen (VJV) Plus* [1990] I–ECR 3941, para. 26.

[39] See however in the different context of recovery of unlawful charges Case C–188/95 *Fantask A/S* v.
Industriministeriet [1997] ECR I–6783, the ECJ ruled that a principle of national law, under which a claim for
the recovery of charges levied for a long time in breach of EC law would be dismissed if neither the national
authorities nor the applicants were aware of their unlawfulness, made it excessively difficult to obtain a remedy
for the breach.

against the national legal principle prohibiting unjust enrichment.[40] On a reference to the ECJ, however, the Court ruled that to permit reliance by the national authorities on the prohibition against unjust enrichment would allow them to use their own unlawful conduct to undermine the effect of the Directive.[41] The desire to prevent the State profiting from its own wrong seems to have played as much a part in the Court's reasoning as the desire not to weaken the effectiveness of the Directive.[42]

Then in *Emmott*, the applicant sought retrospective payment of a disability benefit for the period in which Council Directive 79/7 (on sex discrimination in social security) had remained unimplemented in Ireland.[43] She had been told by the government department that no decision could be made in her case pending the ECJ's ruling in *Cotter and McDermott*, but when she finally applied for judicial review of the decisions relating to her benefits the department pleaded that her delay in initiating proceedings constituted a bar to the action. Having set out the principle of national procedural autonomy and the conditions of equivalence and practical possibility, the ECJ then ruled that given the 'particular nature of directives', a Member State could not, where an individual sought to rely on the provisions of a directive, invoke against that individual a national time limit for bringing proceedings until the directive was properly implemented.[44]

On this key point, as we shall see below, the *Emmott* ruling was subsequently confined largely to the facts of the case, by emphasizing the misleading conduct of the national authorities.[45] However, the ECJ gave robust remedial rulings in a number of other kinds of discrimination cases,[46] and more generally, it seemed after *Factortame I*, *Cotter*, and *Emmott*, that the requirement that remedies for breach of Community law should be effective had become much stronger and had modified considerably the basic notion of national procedural autonomy and competence. The deference implicit in earlier rulings was replaced by an expectation that national courts would be creative in deciding which national rules should be disapplied in order to enforce EC law more effectively.

A consequence of this creativity was a greater degree of uncertainty for both national courts and litigants. In *Marshall II*, below, the complainant was faced with a domestic statutory ceiling on awards of compensation for discrimination in breach of EC law. The question was whether the national court should ignore or override the statutory limit even though it did not render the exercise of her right 'practically impossible'.

---

[40] Case C–377/89 *Cotter and McDermott* v. *Minister for Social Welfare* [1991] ECR I–1155.

[41] *Ibid.*, para. 21.

[42] Contrast Case 68/79 *Hans Just I/S* v. *Danish Ministry for Fiscal Affairs* [1980] ECR 501, in which the State was not obliged to repay taxes it had imposed in breach of Community law, if that would unjustly enrich a trader who had passed on the cost of the tax to third parties. See also Cases C–192–218/95 *Comateb* v. *Directeur Général des Douanes et Droits Indirects* [1997] ECR I–165; Case C–453/99 *Courage Ltd.* v. *Crehan* [2001] ECR I–6297, para. 30; Cases C–295–298/04 *Manfredi* v. *Lloyd Adriatico Assicurazion SpA et al.* [2006] ECR I–6619. The difference in the way the unjust enrichment argument was treated in these cases on the one hand and in *Cotter* on the other is not always easy to understand.

[43] Case C–208/90 *Emmott* v. *Minister for Social Welfare* [1991] ECR I–4269.

[44] *Ibid.*, paras. 21 and 23.

[45] Interestingly, the Commission seems to try to revive *Emmott* and to give it a broader reading in one of its 2003 Communications: COM(2002)725 on Better Monitoring of the Application of Community Law, fn. 36.

[46] In several discrimination cases the Court specified that, following the disapplication of an offending national law and pending the adoption of non-discriminatory rules, the appropriate interim remedy would be to level upwards to the existing EC rule. See, e.g., Case 286/85 *McDermott and Cotter* v. *Minister for Social Welfare and Attorney-General* [1987] ECR 1453; Case C–33/89 *Kowalska* v. *Freie und Hansestadt Hamburg* [1990] ECR I–2591, para. 20; Case C–18/95 *Terhoeve* v. *Inspecteur van de Belastingdienst Particulieren* [1999] ECR I–345, para. 57.

Case C–271/91 **Marshall v. Southampton and South West Hampshire Area Health Authority II**
[1993] ECR I–4367

Following the ECJ ruling in Case 152/84 *Marshall (No. 1)*,[47] the case was remitted to the Industrial Tribunal, which assessed compensation at £18,405 including a sum of £7,710 by way of interest. Under UK legislation, however, the maximum amount of compensation which could be awarded was £6,250, and it was unclear whether the Industrial Tribunal had power to award interest. The House of Lords asked the ECJ whether such an applicant was entitled to full reparation for the loss sustained, and whether Article 6 of Directive 76/207 could be relied on to challenge national legislation limiting the amount of compensation to be awarded.

THE ECJ

23. As the Court held in Case 14/83, *Von Colson and Kamann v. Land Nordrhein-Westfalen* [1984] ECR 1891, paragraph 18, Article 6 does not prescribe a specific measure to be taken in the event of a breach of the prohibition of discrimination but leaves Member States free to choose between the different solutions suitable for achieving the objective of the Directive, depending on the different situations which may arise.

24. However, the objective is to arrive at real equality of opportunity and cannot therefore be attained in the absence of measures appropriate to restore such equality when it has not been observed. As the Court stated in paragraph 23 in *Von Colson*, cited above, those measures must be such as to guarantee real and effective judicial protection and have a real deterrent effect on the employer.

25. Such requirements necessarily entail that the particular circumstances of each breach of the principle of equal treatment should be taken into account. In the event of discriminatory dismissal contrary to Article 5(1) of the Directive, a situation of equality could not be restored without either reinstating the victim of discrimination or, in the alternative, granting financial compensation for the loss and damage sustained.

26. When financial compensation is the measure adopted in order to achieve the objective indicated above, it must be adequate, in that it must enable the loss and damage actually sustained as a result of the discriminatory dismissal to be made good in full in accordance with the applicable national rules.

. . .

30. It also follows from that interpretation that the fixing of an upper limit of the kind at issue in the main proceedings cannot, by definition, constitute proper implementation of Article 6 of the directive, since it limits the amount of compensation *a priori* to a level which is not necessarily consistent with the requirement of ensuring real equality of opportunity through adequate reparation for the loss and damage sustained as a result of discriminatory dismissal.

31. With regard to the second part of the second question relating to the award of interest, suffice it to say that full compensation for the loss and damage sustained as a result of discriminatory dismissal cannot leave out of account factors, such as the effluxion of time, which may in fact reduce its value. The award of interest, in accordance with the applicable national rules, must therefore be regarded as an essential component of compensation for the purposes of restoring real equality of treatment.

---

[47] See Ch. 8.

Here, two national rules governing remedies—a substantive rule imposing a ceiling on damages and a jurisdictional rule concerning the power to award interest—had to be disapplied by the national court in order to provide an effective remedy for breach of EC law.

Marshall II contrasts with earlier case law of the Court, in particular the decisions in *Humblet*[48] and *Roquette*.[49] In those cases the ECJ had ruled that it was for the Member States to decide whether or not to award interest on the reimbursement of sums wrongly levied under Community law, whereas in *Marshall II* it was not open to the Member State to refuse to pay interest. While later cases like *Sutton* narrowed the scope of *Marshall II* in some respects, by treating compensation for dismissal as distinct from repayment of social security arrears,[50] other cases like *Evans* have affirmed and extended it by declaring that where compensation or restitution is required by a particular directive, national law must not exclude factors such as the effluxion of time which affect the value of the compensation or restitution.[51]

(b) PHASE 2: A PARTIAL JUDICIAL RETREAT

Immediately after *Marshall II*, the ECJ seemed to pull back from the boldness of its rulings in the *Dekker, Factortame I, Emmott*, and *Marshall II* line of cases.

In *Steenhorst-Neerings*, an action for retrospective payment of several years of disability benefits was brought by the applicant, covering the period when the Directive on sex discrimination in social security had not been properly implemented into Dutch law.[52] Dutch law however provided that such benefits should not be payable retroactively for more than one year. The ECJ distinguished the case from *Emmott*, despite the apparent similarities between the two. It ruled that the one-year period for retroactive payment was not a time-limit for bringing proceedings, and did not operate (as in *Emmott*) as absolute bar to bringing an action, in order to protect the finality of administrative decisions. Instead, it satisfied the twin conditions of equivalence and practical possibility:

> 23. On the other hand, the aim of the rule restricting the retroactive effect of claims for benefits for incapacity for work is quite different from that of a rule imposing mandatory time-limits for bringing proceedings. As the Government of the Netherlands and the defendant in the main proceedings explained in their written observations, the first type of rule, of which examples can be found in other social security laws in the Netherlands, serves to ensure sound administration, most importantly so that it may be ascertained whether the claimant satisfied the conditions for eligibility and so that the degree of incapacity, which may well vary over time, may be fixed. It also reflects the need to preserve financial balance in a scheme in which claims submitted by insured persons in the course of a year must in principle be covered by the contributions collected during that same year.

The legal circumstances in *Steenhorst-Neerings* were clearly similar to those in *Emmott*, where a plaintiff who had been prevented from claiming a right under Community law, in circumstances of sex discrimination, now confronted a restriction which substantially

---

[48] Case 6/60, n. 3 above.

[49] Case 26/74 *Société Roquette Frères v. Commission* [1976] ECR 677.

[50] Case C–66/95 *R. v. Secretary of State for Social Security, ex p. Eunice Sutton* [1997] ECR I–2163.

[51] Case C–63/01 *Evans*, n. 33 above, paras. 67–71.

[52] Case C–338/91 *Steenhorst-Neerings v. Bestuur van de Bedrijfsvereniging voor Detailhandel, Ambachten en Huisvrouwen* [1993] ECR I–5475.

reduced the effectiveness and extent of the available remedy. The broader principle articulated in *Emmott*, that a Member State cannot rely on domestic procedural restrictions to limit an applicant's claim to rights under a directive until that directive has been properly implemented, was abandoned.

Confirming the trend of *Steenhorst-Neerings*, the ECJ in *Johnson II* ruled that 'the solution adopted in *Emmott* was justified by the particular circumstances of that case, in which a time-bar had the result of depriving the applicant of any opportunity whatever to rely on her right to equal treatment under the directive'.[53] Advocate General Jacobs in his opinions in *BP Supergas*[54] and *Denkavit International*[55] suggested that the fact that the State itself was at fault in *Emmott* and had led the applicant to make the error in question was highly significant.[56] The Court itself continued to limit the scope of *Emmott* along these lines in *Texaco A/S*,[57] *Fantask A/S*,[58] *BP Supergas*,[59] and *Spac*.[60] The *Levez* case also supports this rationale for *Emmott*, since the ECJ there acknowledged that an otherwise reasonable legislative limit on the retroactivity of a claim for damages could be rendered inapplicable by the improper conduct of the defendant employer.[61]

Steenhorst-Neerings represented a retreat not only from *Emmott*, but also from the principle of adequacy of compensation for sex discrimination established in *Marshall II*. This was reinforced in *Johnson II*, where the Court ruled that, even where the concerns of the State to ensure administrative convenience and financial balance were not in issue, a provision restricting to one year the retroactive effect of a claim for a non-contributory incapacity benefit was compatible with Community law.[62] In the *Sutton* case concerning social security benefits, the ECJ had to deal directly with the scope of its ruling in *Marshall II*, and confined it further by introducing a distinction between dismissal on grounds of sex, and the discriminatory denial of social security benefits.

Case C–66/95 R. v. Secretary of State for Social Security, ex parte Eunice Sutton
[1997] ECR I–2163

The applicant successfully challenged the refusal to grant her an invalid care allowance under national law, on the basis that this contravened Directive 79/7 on equal treatment in social

---

53 Case C–410/92 *Johnson v. Chief Adjudication Officer* [1994] ECR I–5483, para. 26. See also Cases C–114–5/95 *Texaco A/S v. Havn* [1997] ECR I–4263, para. 48; Case C–90/94 *Haahr Petroleum v. Havn* [1997] ECR I–4085, paras. 51–52.

54 Case C–62/93 *BP Supergas v. Greece* [1995] ECR I–1883, paras. 55–59, Jacobs AG.

55 Case C–2/94 *Denkavit International BV v. Kamer van Koophandel en Fabrieken voor Midden-Gelderland* [1996] ECR I–2827, para. 74, Jacobs AG.

56 See also, in his extra-judicial capacity, F. Jacobs, 'Enforcing Community Rights and Obligations in National Courts: Striking the Balance', in J. Lonbay and A. Biondi (eds.), *Remedies for Breach of EC Law* (Wiley, 1997), 25 at 29; M. Hoskins, 'Tilting the Balance: Remedies and National Procedural Rules' (1996) 21 *ELRev.* 365.

57 Cases C–114–115/95 *Texaco*, n. 53 above.

58 Case C–188/95 *Fantask A/S*, n. 39 above. See also Case C–88/99 *Roquette Frères v. Direction des Services Fiscaux du Pas-de-Calais* [2000] ECR I–10465.

59 J. Coppel, 'Time up for Emmott?' (1996) 25 *ILJ* 153.

60 Case C–260/96 *Ministero delle Finanze v. Spac* [1998] ECR I–4997, para. 31.

61 Case C–326/96 *Levez v. Jennings Ltd.* [1998] ECR I–7835, para. 34. For a similar ruling concerning action by a public contracting authority in relation to a tendering process, where an otherwise reasonable time limit could be applied in such a way as to violate the requirement of an effective remedy, see Case C–327/00 *Santex SpA v. Unita Socio Sanitaria Locale n. 42 di Pavia* [2003] ECR I–1877.

62 Case C–410/92 *Johnson*, n. 53 above. See also Case C–394/93 *Alonso-Pérez v. Bundesanstalt für Arbeit* [1995] ECR I–4101. Contrast Case C–246/96 *Magorrian and Cunningham v. Eastern Health and Social Services*

security. She was awarded arrears of benefit, but was refused interest because national law did not provide for the payment of interest on social security benefits. On a reference to the ECJ, she argued that Article 6 of Directive 79/7 was almost identically worded to Article 6 of Directive 76/207 in *Marshall II*, both being concerned with equal treatment, and that interest should therefore be awarded just as in the earlier case.

THE ECJ

23. That interpretation cannot be adopted. The judgment in *Marshall II* concerns the award of interest on amounts payable by way of reparation for loss and damage sustained as a result of discriminatory dismissal. As the Court observed in paragraph 31 of that judgment, in such a context full compensation for the loss and damage sustained cannot leave out of account factors, such as the effluxion of time, which may in fact reduce its value. The award of interest, in accordance with the applicable national rules, must therefore be regarded as an essential component of compensation for the purposes of restoring real equality of treatment.

24. By contrast, the main proceedings concern the right to receive interest on amounts payable by way of social security benefits. Those benefits are paid to the person concerned by the competent bodies, which must, in particular, examine whether the conditions laid down in the relevant legislation are fulfilled. Consequently, the amounts paid in no way constitute reparation for loss or damage sustained and the reasoning of the Court in its judgment in *Marshall II* cannot be applied to a situation of that kind.

. . .

27. . . . Amounts paid by way of social security benefit are not compensatory in nature, with the result that payment of interest cannot be required on the basis either of Article 6 of Directive 76/207 or of Article 6 of Directive 79/7.

Sutton suggests that the requirements imposed by EC law on the availability of national remedies may depend on the nature of the right at stake and on the kind of Community measure which has been breached.[63] Payment of arrears of social security benefits was distinguished from 'compensation for loss or damage', so that there was no requirement of full or adequate compensation for the former under national law.

Finally, even if there is a requirement of adequate compensation for damage caused by a breach of a particular directive, such as the Equal Treatment Directive, this does not necessarily mean that a ceiling on damages will always be impermissible. A maximum upper limit on damages is acceptable in certain cases, such as a case of sex discrimination in access to employment, for example, where the claimant would not have been successful in obtaining the job even in the absence of discrimination, so that the loss sustained is more limited.[64]

Board [1997] ECR I–7153, and Case C–78/98 *Preston* v. *Wolverhampton Healthcare NHS Trust* [1999] ECR I–3201.

[63] The cases concerning repayment of sums wrongly paid are instructive in this respect, since not all repayment cases are subject to the same analysis. Contrast some of the cases concerning unduly paid agricultural subsidies with those concerning improperly paid state aid: compare, e.g., Case C–24/95 *Land Rheinland-Pfalz* v. *Alcan Deutschland* [1997] ECR I–1591 on state aid with Case C–298/96 *Öhlmühle Hamburg* v. *Bundesanstalt für Landwirtschaft und Ernährung* [1998] ECR I–4767 and Case C–366/95 *Landbrugsministeriet—EF-Direktoratet* v. *Steff-Houlberg Export* [1998] ECR I–2661 on agricultural subsidies.

[64] Case C–180/95 *Draehmpaehl* v. *Urania Immobilienservice* [1997] ECR I–2195. The judgment is now reflected in Art. 6(2) of the amended Equal Treatment Dir., as an exception to the rule that there can be no prior upper limit on damages set by national law.

(c) PHASE 3: A ROBUST REQUIREMENT THAT CERTAIN REMEDIES MUST BE MADE AVAILABLE

Despite the ECJ's draw-back from the full implications of cases like *Emmott* and *Marshall II* however, there certainly has not been any *general* retreat from the robust requirement of adequate and effective national remedies.

In *Metallgesellschaft & Hoechst*, in which the plaintiffs challenged the imposition of advance corporation tax (ACT) on subsidiaries whose parent companies were not resident within the Member State, the ECJ ruled that it was for the national court to classify the nature of an action brought, whether as an action for restitution or an action for compensation for damage.[65] The national court argued that it was not clear whether English law even provided for restitution for damage arising from loss of the use of sums of money where no principal sum was due, but the ECJ responded that in an action for restitution, the principal sum, due was precisely the amount of interest which would have been generated by the sum, use of which was lost as a result of the premature levy of the tax. In other words, the very substance of the plaintiffs' claim was the interest which would have accrued had they not been subject to discriminatory advance taxation. The ECJ ruled:

> Consequently, Article 52 of the Treaty entitles a subsidiary resident in the United Kingdom and/or its parent company having its seat in another Member State to obtain interest accrued on the ACT paid by the subsidiary during the period between the payment of ACT and the date on which MCT became payable, and that sum may be claimed by way of restitution.[66]

This case suggests a further *Factortame*-type erosion of the 'no new remedies' rule since, although restitution was not a remedy unknown to the English legal system, the ECJ brushed aside the national court's argument that restitution might not be available in these circumstances by characterizing the claim as damage flowing directly from the breach of Article 43. On the question whether full compensation equal to the sum claimed by the plaintiffs had to be paid, the ECJ referred to the difference between *Marshall II* (in which interest was held to be an essential component of compensation to restore equality of treatment) and *Sutton* (in which interest was deemed not to be an essential component of the right to obtain arrears of benefits), and deemed *Metallgesellschaft* to be analogous to *Marshall II*, with interest as an essential component of the claim.

The case is a robust ruling in the tradition of *Johnston I* and *Marshall II*, and is joined in that respect by the later judgments in *Courage*,[67] *Manfredi*,[68] and *Muñoz*.[69] In *Courage*, the ECJ ruled that a right of action in damages against another party for breach of Article 81 EC must in principle be available to an individual before national courts.[70] In *Manfredi*, which similarly concerned damages for breach of EC competition law, the Court ruled that injured parties must be able to seek compensation not only for actual loss, but also for loss of profit.[71] In *Muñoz*, the full effectiveness of the EC rules on quality standards was held by the ECJ to require that a civil action based on non-compliance with these rules should be

---

[65] Case C–410/98 *Metallgesellschaft & Hoechst* v. *Inland Revenue* [2001] ECR I–4727.
[66] *Ibid.*, para. 89.
[67] Case C–453/99 *Courage*, n. 42 above.
[68] Cases C–295–298/04 *Manfredi*, n. 42 above.
[69] Case C–253/00 *Muñoz*, n. 29 above.
[70] Case C–453/99 *Courage* v. *Crehan*, n. 42 above, paras. 25–28.
[71] Cases C–295–298/04 *Manfredi*, n. 42 above, para. 100.

available.[72] In these cases, the Court focused primarily, not on the procedural autonomy of the national legal system, but instead on the nature or importance of the substantive Community right at issue (for example, non-discrimination under Article 43 EC in *Factortame* and *Metallgesellschaft*, equal treatment in employment in *Marshall II*, competition law rules in *Courage, Manfredi,* and *Eco Swiss China Time,*[73] and quality standards and fair trading in *Muñoz*).[74]

The Court's choice to emphasize the substantive Community right at issue, in particular where detailed EC legislation on the substance exists, seems to increase the likelihood that it will point to the need to override or disapply a restrictive national rule. Conversely, in cases in which the Court begins by emphasizing the presumptive legitimacy of national remedial systems (such as *Steenhorst-Neerings, Sutton,* and *Johnston II*), such an outcome is correspondingly less likely.

(d) THE BALANCE BETWEEN EFFECTIVE JUDICIAL PROTECTION OF EC RIGHTS AND NATIONAL PROCEDURAL AUTONOMY AND RESPONSIBILITY

Looking at the various strands and phases of case law together, it might be said that while there was an initial retreat following the interventionist approach of *Factortame, Marshall II,* and *Emmott*, a more complex and nuanced 'balance' between different interests is suggested by the case law overall.

The conditions of effectiveness and equivalence must be considered by national courts in deciding whether a national rule or principle could undermine the exercise of a Community right. This approach is well outlined in the cases of *Peterbroeck*[75] and *Van Schijndel*[76] concerning the capacity of national courts to consider points of Community law of their own motion.

Cases C–430–431/93 **Van Schijndel & Van Veen v. Stichting Pensioenfonds voor Fysiotherapeuten**
[1995] ECR I–4705

The applicants argued that the appeal court whose ruling they sought to challenge ought to have considered, if necessary of its own motion, the compatibility of a compulsory Pension

---

[72] Case C–253/00 *Muñoz*, n. 29 above, paras. 30–32. Compare the somewhat different case of Case C–13/01 *Safalero*, n. 16 above, where the ECJ held there was no obligation on a State to permit an affected third party importer to challenge the confiscation of goods held by another, where that third party had the right to bring proceedings for a declaration of incompatibility of the seizure with EC law. Compare also Case C–216/02 *Österreichischer Zuchtverband für Ponys, Kleinpferde und Spezialrassen* v. *Burgenländische Landesregierung* [2004] ECR I–10683.

[73] Case C–126/97 *Eco Swiss China Time Ltd* v. *Benetton International NV* [1999] ECR I–3055; Case C–234/04 *Kapferer* v. *Schlank & Schick* [2006] ECR I–2585, on consumer protection in contract law.

[74] For an argument that the uncertainty in the case law on national judicial protection is attributable to 'an uncertainty regarding the exact content of these rights in need of remedial protection' see T. Eilmansberger, 'The Relationship between Rights and Remedies in EC law: In Search of the Missing Link' (2004) 41 *CMLRev.* 1199.

[75] Case C–312/93 *Peterbroeck, Van Campenhout & Cie.* v. *Belgian State* [1995] ECR I–4599.

[76] Cases C–430–431/93 *Van Schijndel & Van Veen* v. *Stichting Pensioenfonds voor Fysiotherapeuten* [1995] ECR I–4705.

Fund provision with EC competition law. They had not themselves previously raised any point of EC law. Under Dutch law, such a plea involving a new argument could only be made where no examination of facts was required, and the court could not raise such points of law of its own motion. On a reference, the ECJ was asked whether the national court must apply provisions of EC law even where the party to the proceedings had not relied on them. The ECJ began by setting out the basic notion of national procedural autonomy, qualified by the principles of equivalence and practical effectiveness.

THE ECJ

19. For the purposes of applying those principles, each case which raises the question whether a national procedural provision renders application of Community law impossible or excessively difficult must be analysed by reference to the role of that provision in the procedure, its progress and its special features, viewed as a whole, before the various national instances. In the light of that analysis the basic principles of the domestic judicial system, such as the protection of the rights of the defence, the principle of legal certainty and the proper conduct of procedure must, where appropriate, be taken into consideration.

20. In the present case, the domestic law principle that in civil proceedings a court must or may raise points of its own motion is limited by its obligation to keep to the subject matter of the dispute and to base its decision on the facts put before it.

21. That limitation is justified by the principle that, in a civil suit, it is for the parties to take the initiative, the court being able to act of its own motion only in exceptional cases where the public interest requires its intervention. That principle reflects conceptions prevailing in most of the Member States as to the relations between the State and the individual; it safeguards the rights of the defence; and it ensures proper conduct of proceedings by, in particular, protecting them from the delays inherent in examination of new pleas.

22. In those circumstances, the answer to the second question must be that Community law does not require national courts to raise of their own motion an issue concerning the breach of provisions of Community law where examination of that issue would oblige them to abandon the passive role assigned to them by going beyond the ambit of the dispute defined by the parties themselves and relying on facts and circumstances other than those on which the party with an interest in application of those provisions bases his claim.

The case states that each national provision governing enforcement of an EC right before national courts must be examined and weighed not in the abstract, but in the specific circumstances of each case, to see whether, taking its purpose into account, it renders the exercise of that right excessively difficult.

In *Van Schijndel*, the principle of judicial passivity was, on the facts, considered by the ECJ to be compatible with the exercise of the Community right. In *Peterbroeck*, by contrast, where similar aims of legal certainty and the proper conduct of procedure underpinned a procedural provision of the Belgian Tax Code preventing both the parties and the court from raising a point of EC law after a sixty-day time period, the application of the rule was found in the particular circumstances of the case to render the exercise of the Community right excessively difficult.[77] While the sixty-day period for raising new pleas was itself reasonable, the particular circumstances of the case were deemed by the ECJ to render the rule objectionable.[78]

---

[77] N. 75 above.

[78] This was apparently because no court or tribunal in the proceedings had had an opportunity to raise the point of EC law so as to make a reference to the ECJ. See also Case C–327/00 *Santex*, n. 61 above, for a case in

The reasoning in the case is somewhat strained,[79] but, together with later cases concerning the role of national courts in raising points of EC law of their own motion, it illustrates well that the determination of the compatibility of a national procedural rule with the Community requirement of effectiveness depends on the precise circumstances of each case.

In *Kraaijeveld*, the ECJ suggested that EC law does not confer a *general* power on national courts to consider points of EC law of their own motion, but that if they have a discretion or obligation to raise points of national law of their own motion they must also apply such discretion or obligation to points of Community law.[80] In *Fazenda Pública*, the Court linked the power and 'in certain cases' the obligation on national courts to make a reference to the ECJ with their power or obligation to raise points of EC law of their own motion.[81]

In *Océano*, the ECJ went further by declaring that the aims of the Unfair Contract Terms Directive would not be ensured if the consumer were obliged to raise the unfair nature of such terms, and that the national court must have power to evaluate terms of this kind of its own motion.[82] The ECJ did not actually specify that national courts *must raise* a specific point of EC law of their own motion, but rather that they *must have the power* to raise it. This formulation, which was stronger than in earlier cases, was linked to the facts of *Océano*, and particularly to the subject-matter of consumer protection law.

A stronger ruling still on the 'own motion' issue was in *Eco Swiss China Time*, in which the ECJ indicated that, in the circumstances of that case concerning review of an arbitration award, the national court *must* raise a point based on breach of Article 81 EC.[83] Once again, the nature of the substantive EC right in question—in this case the fundamental competition rules of the Treaty—was relevant to the Court's conclusion.

The case of *Kühne and Heitz* presents a similarly robust ruling on a related point, concerning the obligation of a national administrative body to re-open a decision which had become final following a national court ruling which was based on a misunderstanding of EC law.[84] This was qualified somewhat in the subsequent *Kapferer* case, however, where the ECJ accepted the principle of *res judicata* and the finality of national judicial proceedings.[85]

The 'balancing' approach to the requirements of equivalence and effectiveness on the one hand, and the *prima facie* principle of national procedural autonomy on the other, introduces a kind of proportionality test for weighing the restrictive effect of a national rule on a particular Community right against the legitimate aim served by that rule, taking into account the specific factual circumstances of the case. As a result, it introduces a considerable degree of uncertainty and unpredictability within national procedural systems, as can be seen from the flow of preliminary references which continue to be sent to the ECJ on these

---

which a plea which would otherwise have been inadmissible on grounds of delay may have to be considered by the national court due to the conduct of the defendant public authority.

[79] G. de Búrca, 'National Remedies for Breach of EC Law: The Changing Approach of the ECJ', in Lonbay and Biondi (eds.), n. 56 above.

[80] Case C–72/95 *Aannemersbedrijf P.K. Kraaijeveld BV* v. *Gedeputeerde Staten van Zuid-Holland* [1996] ECR I–5403.

[81] Case C–446/98 *Fazenda Pública* v. *Camara Municipal do Porto* [2000] ECR I–11435, para. 48.

[82] Cases C–240–244/98 *Océano Grupo Editorial* v. *Rocio Murciano Quintero* [2000] ECR I–4491, para. 26.

[83] Case C–126/97 *Eco Swiss*, n. 73 above, paras. 36–37. This judgment might be understood, however, as being simply based on the principle of equivalence, since national courts were required to permit an application for annulment of an arbitration award on grounds of failure to observe national public policy rules, and Art. 81 EC was deemed by the ECJ to have at least the same status as those national public policy rules. Nonetheless, the ECJ usually leaves the question of equivalence to be determined by the national court, whereas here that decision was taken out of the national court's hands.

[84] Case C–453/00 *Kühne and Heitz* [2004] ECR I–837. For comment see R. Caranta (2005) 42 *CMLRev.* 179.

[85] Case C–234/04 *Kapferer*, n. 73 above. On *res judicata* see also Case C–126/97 *Eco Swiss*, n. 73 above.

questions.[86] Two examples can be drawn from recent lines of case law, one concerning national rules of evidence, the other adding to the extensive existing jurisprudence on time limits.

On evidentiary rules, the *Steffensen*[87] and *Boiron*[88] cases illustrate the intricacy and complexity of the task faced by national courts which are required to engage in the procedural balancing exercise. In *Boiron*, which was a state aid case, the question was whether national rules placing the burden of proof for demonstrating overpayment of competitors on an economic operator were in compliance with the principle of effectiveness. The ECJ followed its usual ruling by declaring that where the national court found that the evidentiary requirement in fact rendered it excessively difficult for the operator to produce the necessary proof, the national court was required 'to use all procedures available to it under national law, including that of ordering the necessary measures of inquiry, in particular the production by one of the parties or a third party of a particular document' to comply with the EC requirement of effective judicial protection.[89]

Steffenson on the other hand concerned a directive on control of foodstuffs which required a second opinion on the analysis of a sample of foodstuffs to be obtained in circumstances such as those of the case, where a manufacturer was being fined for misleading quality-labelling. A second opinion had not been obtained in this case, and the question was whether the sample could be introduced in evidence despite the violation of the Directive's second-opinion requirement. Under German law, evidence obtained by an irregular administrative procedure could nonetheless be admitted in legal proceedings, and evaluated on that basis. The ECJ left it to the national court to decide whether the evidentiary rule was compatible with the principles of equivalence and effectiveness, but gave extensive guidance on the latter, drawing on the jurisprudence of the ECHR concerning the 'adversarial principle' and the right to a fair hearing.[90] *Steffensen* thus introduces yet another crucial factor into the matrix which national courts must consider when weighing the effectiveness of remedies for EC rights against national procedural rules, i.e. whether fundamental rights protected by the ECHR are respected.[91]

On limitation periods, although the general rule established in many cases is that reasonable national limitation periods are compatible with EC requirements, the ECJ in *Manfredi* ruled that a national rule under which the limitation period begins to run from the day on which an anti-competitive agreement or concerted practice was adopted could make it practically impossible to exercise the right to seek compensation for the harm caused, particularly if the limitation period was also a short one and not capable of being suspended.[92] In *Marks & Spencer*[93] and *Grundig Italiana*,[94] the Court ruled that although national legislation reducing the period within which repayment of sums collected in breach of Community law may

---

[86] For an interesting ruling on whether the principle of effectiveness requires national law to provide compensation for the costs associated with bringing a motor insurance claim see Case C–63/01 *Evans*, n. 33 above, on the need to compensate for the effluxion of time. In Case C–472/99 *Clean Car Autoservice GmbH* v. *Stadt Wien* [2001] ECR I–9687, paras. 27–31, the ECJ ruled that where the question of costs was not governed by EC law, it was fully permissible for the national court to apply existing national rules on costs to the preliminary reference procedure.

[87] Case C–276/01 *Joachim Steffensen* [2003] ECR I–3735.

[88] Case C–526/04 *Laboratoires Boiron SA* v. *URSSAF de Lyon* [2006] ECR I–7529.

[89] *Ibid.*, para. 57.

[90] Case C–276/01 *Steffensen*, n. 87 above, paras. 68–79.

[91] See Ch. 11.

[92] Cases C–295–298/04 *Manfredi*, n. 42 above.

[93] Case C–62/00 *Marks & Spencer*, n. 10 above.

[94] Case C–255/00 *Grundig Italiana SpA* v. *Ministero delle Finanze* [2002] ECR I–8003.

be sought is not in itself incompatible with the effectiveness principle, the new limitation period must remain reasonable and must include adequate transitional arrangements. In *Marks & Spencer* the ECJ emphasized that the limitation period must be set in advance and cannot operate retroactively in a way which deprives individuals of the chance of exercising their rights.[95] Moreover in *Grundig Italiana*, the Court gave a very specific ruling on the adequacy of certain transitional arrangements in the field of tax recovery, ruling that a ninety-day transitional limitation period was unreasonable and insufficient, given that it replaced a previous five-year period for preparing and submitting proceedings.[96]

The fact that there is such diversity of time-limits used by different Member States means that the Court generally grants considerable latitude in determining what is reasonable, but it is nonetheless evident that some kind of comparative judgment is made by the ECJ with reference to the practices of other Member States.[97]

(e) CAN THE PLAINTIFF'S CONDUCT AFFECT THE RIGHT TO AN EFFECTIVE REMEDY?

In *Dionysios Diamantis*, the ECJ ruled that a national court may refuse to permit a plaintiff to rely on EC rights if such reliance constitutes an abuse of those rights.[98] The ECJ in *Rechberger* rejected an argument raised by Austria as a defence to an action for damages brought against it for breach of EC law, where that argument was based on the misconduct of a relevant third party.[99] In *Banks*, the ECJ ruled that the failure to take legal action under Article 35 of the ECSC Treaty could not deprive an applicant, under domestic law, of the right to plead the infringement of another directly effective provision of that Treaty.[100] Finally, in *Courage* the Court ruled that an individual could not be prohibited from relying on Article 81 simply because he had been party to an anti-competitive agreement within the meaning of that provision, but that EC law did not prohibit a national rule preventing such a party from relying on his own unlawful actions to obtain damages where he bears significant responsibility for the distortion of competition.[101] And in *Manfredi*, the Court ruled that the requirements of effectiveness and equivalence did not prevent national courts from taking steps to ensure that the protection of EC rights did not entail the unjust enrichment of those claiming them.[102]

The ECJ has also considered the impact of a plaintiff's failure to mitigate losses on the availability and extent of national remedies. In *Metallgesellschaft* the Court dismissed the argument of the UK that the plaintiffs should have refused to comply with the national tax rule which infringed their EC rights and should have relied on the direct effect of EC rights, rather than paying the tax and challenging it afterwards.[103] However, reasonable national rules

---

[95] Case C–62/00 *Marks & Spencer*, n. 10 above, paras. 39–42. See also Case C–30/02 *Recheio-Cash & Carry SA v. Fazenda Publica/Registo Nacional de Pessoas Colectivas* [2004] ECR I–6051, where a 90-day limitation period was reasonable even though applicable to taxes paid at a time when the EC Dir. had not been transposed.

[96] Case C–255/00 *Marks & Spencer*, n. 94 above, paras. 37–42.

[97] Case C–30/02 *Recheio—Cash & Carry*, n. 95 above, para 22.

[98] Case C–373/97 *Dionysios Diamantis* v. *Elliniko Dimosio* [1999] ECR I–1705, paras. 42–44, in which the ECJ however ruled that some of the impugned conduct would not amount to an abuse of rights under the Second Company Dir.

[99] Case C–140/97 *Rechberger* v. *Austria* [1999] ECR I–3499.

[100] Case C–390/98 *H.J. Banks & Co. Ltd.* v. *The Coal Authority* [2001] ECR I–6117, paras. 122–123.

[101] Case C–453/99 *Courage*, n. 42 above, paras. 24 and 36 in particular.

[102] Cases C–295–298/04 *Manfredi*, n. 42 above, para. 99. For further discussion of unjust enrichment see nn. 40–42 above and text.

[103] Case C–397/98 *Metallgesellschaft Ltd.* v. *Inland Revenue* [2001] ECR I–1727, paras. 99–107.

overning the responsibility of parties to show due diligence in mitigating their losses are quite compatible with EC law so long as they are applied equally to claims based on EC law.[104]

5. DEVELOPMENT OF THE 'EQUIVALENCE' PRINCIPLE

While most of the ECJ's case law since *Von Colson* has focused on the concrete implications of the effectiveness principle, attention has also been given to the principle of equivalence.

This is well illustrated by the case law concerning national time limits. Reasonable time limits, as we have seen, have regularly been held by the Court to be compatible with the effectiveness principle,[105] whereas the exact meaning of the equivalence principle remained unclear. *Edis* concerned the repayment of charges which had been paid but were not due under Community law, where national law imposed a time limit of three years for bringing proceedings for repayment for charges of this kind. This was less favourable than the ordinary time limits governing actions between individuals for repayment of sums paid but not due.

Case C–231/96 **Edis v. Ministero delle Finanze**
[1998] ECR I–4951

36. Observance of the principle of equivalence implies, for its part, that the procedural rule at issue applies without distinction to actions alleging infringements of Community law and to those alleging infringements of national law, with respect to the same kind of charges or dues (see, to that effect, Joined Cases 66/79, 127/79 and 128/79 *Amministrazione delle Finanze dello Stato* v. *Salumi* [1980] ECR 1237, paragraph 21). That principle cannot, however, be interpreted as obliging a Member State to extend its most favourable rules governing recovery under national law to all actions for repayment of charges or dues levied in breach of Community law.

37. Thus, Community law does not preclude the legislation of a Member State from laying down, alongside a limitation period applicable under the ordinary law to actions between private individuals for the recovery of sums paid but not due, special detailed rules, which are less favourable, governing claims and legal proceedings to challenge the imposition of charges and other levies. The position would be different only if those detailed rules applied solely to actions based on Community law for the repayment of such charges or levies.

Similar rulings were given in the cases of *Spac*,[106] *Aprile*,[107] *Dilexport*,[108] and *Roquette*,[109] affirming the acceptability of national time limits which were not the most favourable within the national remedial system, but which applied equally to actions based on Community law and 'similar' actions based on national law.

---

[104] This is the case for claims against the Community institutions before the ECJ: see Case T–178/98 *Fresh Marine Company* v. *Commission* [2000] ECR II–3331, para. 121.

[105] On the reasonableness of a 3-month time limit to challenge an interim arbitration award see Case C–126/97 *Eco Swiss*, n. 73 above.

[106] Case C–260/96 *Spac*, n. 60 above.

[107] Case C–229/96 *Aprile* v. *Amminstrazione delle Finanze dello Stato* [1998] ECR I–7141.

[108] Case C–343/96 *Dilexport* v. *Amministrazione delle Finanze dello Stato* [1999] ECR I–579.

[109] Case C–88/99 *Roquette Frères*, n. 58 above.

While the ECJ has frequently stated that it is in principle for the national court to determine the question of equivalence,[110] it has intervened at times to indicate that the application of a particular national rule does not satisfy that principle, or to suggest what other rules of domestic law might usefully provide a comparator for the purposes of considering 'equivalence'. In *Eman and Sevinger*, concerning national remedies for violation of the right to vote in European Parliament elections, the ECJ proposed that the national court 'may usefully refer to the detailed rules for legal redress laid down in cases of infringement of the national rules in the context of elections to the institutions of the Member State'.[111] In *Weber's Wine World*, although the actual application of the equivalence test to the facts of the case and to the national procedural system in general was left to the national court, the ECJ gave a clear ruling about what would be likely to violate the equivalence requirement.[112]

In *Levez*, an employee was seeking damages for arrears in payment which had been denied to her in breach of the equal pay provision of the Treaty. The ECJ had ruled that the two-year limit on arrears of damages in Industrial Tribunal proceedings could not be applied to her on account of the role played by her employer's deception in the delay.[113] However, the UK argued that the time limit should nonetheless apply to her case, because an alternative full remedy before the county court in an action for deceit against her employer and in an action based on the Equal Pay Act had been open to her, so that the exercise of her right was not rendered ineffective in practice. The ECJ accepted the effectiveness point, but went on to consider the requirement of equivalence and gave firm guidance to the national court on how to apply this.

Case C–326/96 **Levez v. Jennings Ltd.**
[1998] ECR I–7835

43. In order to determine whether the principle of equivalence has been complied with in the present case, the national court—which alone has direct knowledge of the procedural rules governing actions in the field of employment law—must consider both the purpose and the essential characteristics of allegedly similar domestic actions (see *Palmisani*, paragraphs 34 to 38).

44. Furthermore, whenever it falls to be determined whether a procedural rule of national law is less favourable than those governing similar domestic actions, the national court must take into account the role played by that provision in the procedure as a whole, as well as the operation and any special features of that procedure before the different national courts (see, *mutatis mutandis*, *Van Schijndel and Van Veen*, paragraph 19).

[*The ECJ rejected the UK's argument that the equivalence requirement was satisfied by the fact that a claim under the Equal Pay Act (which was intended to implement EC law) was comparable to a claim based directly on Article 141 EC, and continued as follows:*]

49. Secondly, it is necessary to consider the possibilities contemplated by the order for reference. It is there suggested that claims similar to those based on the Act may include those

---

[110] Case C–261/95 *Palmisani* v. *INPS* [1997] ECR I–4025, para. 33: Case C–326/96 *Levez*, n. 61 above, para. 39.

[111] Case C–300/04 *Eman and Sevinger* v. *College van Burgemeester en Wethouders van Den Haag* [2006] ECR I–8055.

[112] Case C–147/01 *Weber's Wine World Handels-GmbH* v. *Abgabenberufungskommission Wien* [2003] ECR I–11365.

[113] Case C–326/96 *Levez*, n. 61 above.

linked to breach of a contract of employment, to discrimination in terms of pay on grounds of race, to unlawful deductions from wages or to sex discrimination in matters other than pay.

50. If it transpires, on the basis of the principles set out in paragraphs 41 to 44 of this judgment, that a claim under the Act which is brought before the County Court is similar to one or more of the forms of action listed by the national court, it would remain for that court to determine whether the first-mentioned form of action is governed by procedural rules or other requirements which are less favourable.

51. On that point, it is appropriate to consider whether, in order fully to assert rights conferred by Community law before the County Court, an employee in circumstances such as those of Mrs Levez will incur additional costs and delay by comparison with a claimant who, because he is relying on what may be regarded as a similar right under domestic law, may bring an action before the Industrial Tribunal, which is simpler and, in principle, less costly.

52. Also of relevance here is the fact mentioned by the national court that the rule at issue applies solely to claims for equal pay without discrimination on grounds of sex, whereas claims based on 'similar' rights under domestic law are not limited by the operation of such a rule, which means that such rights may be adequately protected by actions brought before Industrial Tribunals.

53. In view of the foregoing, the answer must be that Community law precludes the application of a rule of national law which limits an employee's entitlement to arrears of remuneration or damages for breach of the principle of equal pay to a period of two years prior to the date on which the proceedings were instituted, even when another remedy is available, if the latter is likely to entail procedural rules or other conditions which are less favourable than those applicable to similar domestic actions. It is for the national court to determine whether that is the case.

This ruling was followed by the ECJ in the later case of *Preston*, where it was asked by the House of Lords for more precise guidance on the EC law criteria for identifying a 'similar' cause of action in domestic law.[114] Essentially the ECJ has developed the same context-specific balancing approach for national courts to assess the 'equivalence' of domestic rules as it did for assessing their 'effectiveness' in *Peterbroeck* and *Van Schijndel*.

In *Dounias*, the ECJ declared that it was for the national court to scrutinize domestic procedures not only to determine whether they were comparable, but also to detect whether there was any inherent discrimination in their *application* in favour of domestic claims.[115] And in *Manfredi*, the Court ruled that if in similar domestic actions it is possible to award specific damages such as exemplary or punitive damages, it must also be possible to award them in actions based on EC rules.[116]

Some have argued that an excessive emphasis on the need for effectiveness of EC rights rather than on the principle of equivalence could actually lead to a reverse form of discrimination in favour of EC law.[117] This notion of genuine equality of remedies for EC rights and for national law rights is also mirrored by another development in ECJ case law which points towards the need for parity between national-level and EC-level remedies for the enforcement of EC rights. In other words, EC law should not demand better enforcement of EC law from

---

[114] Case C–78/98 *Preston*, n. 62 above.

[115] Case C–228/98 *Dounias*, n. 27 above, para. 65. In this case the Court seemed to suggest that the equivalence principle should be considered first, and only then the effectiveness principle: see para. 60.

[116] Cases C–295–298/04 *Manfredi*, n. 42 above, para 99.

[117] See, e.g., Jacobs AG in Cases C–430–431/93 *Van Schijndel*, n. 76 above, and Léger AG in Case C–66/95 *Sutton*, n. 50 above.

the national legal orders than it is prepared to provide itself at European level. Thus in *Upjohn*, the ECJ ruled that Community law did not require the Member States to establish a procedure for judicial review of national decisions revoking marketing authorizations for medicinal products, which involved a more extensive review than that carried out by the ECJ in similar cases.[118] And in *Bergaderm*, in an action for damages brought against the Community before the ECJ, the Court ruled that the conditions under which Member States may incur liability for damage to individuals caused by a breach of Community law could not, in principle, differ from those governing the liability of the Community in similar circumstances.[119]

6. NATIONAL REMEDIES AND EC LAW: SUMMARY

i.   While early ECJ case law emphasized the autonomy and primary responsibility of the national legal system in the absence of Community harmonization of remedies, this approach has yielded over time to a stronger insistence on the effectiveness of Community law, and on effective judicial protection as a fundamental right.

ii. While certain strands of case law—mainly those in which the ECJ focuses on a particular substantive EC law right, usually a right which is specified in EC legislation—seem to require *specific* national remedies to be made available, many other cases continue to emphasize the primary responsibility of the national legal system, subject only to the principles of equivalence and effectiveness.

iii. Over time the Court has developed a detailed balancing approach, which requires the importance of the Community right to be weighed against the scope and purpose of the national rule, taking into account all the circumstances of the case. Although it often gives firm guidance on the requirements of effectiveness and equivalence, the Court generally acknowledges the legitimacy of diverse national rules and the primary role of the national court in assessing these.

7. THE PRINCIPLE OF (STATE) LIABILITY FOR BREACH OF EC LAW

(a) ORIGINS OF THE PRINCIPLE

We have seen that, despite its early 'no new remedies' rule in *Rewe-Handelsgesellschaft*, the ECJ had nonetheless in certain cases declared that a particular kind of national remedy must be made available. Cases such as *San Giorgio* on the repayment of charges,[120] *Factortame I* on interim relief,[121] *Heylens* on judicial review,[122] *Muñoz* on civil remedies,[123] and *Courage* on damages[124] required national courts to ensure the availability of particular remedies in certain

---

[118] See Case C–120/97 *Upjohn*, n. 32 above, para. 33.

[119] Case C–352/98P *Bergaderm* v. *Commission* [2000] ECR I–5291, para. 41, drawing on Cases C–46 and 48/93 *Brasserie du Pêcheur* [1996] ECR I–1029, para. 42. See for a discussion M. de Visser, 'The Concept of Concurrent Liability and its Relationship with the Principle of Effectiveness' (2004) 11 *MJ* 47.

[120] Case 199/82 *San Giorgio*, n. 11 above.

[121] Case C–213/89 *The Queen* v. *Secretary of State for Transport, ex p. Factortame Ltd.* [1990] ECR I–2433.

[122] Case 222/86 *Heylens*, n. 24 above.

[123] Case C–253/00 *Muñoz*, n. 29 above.

[124] Case C–453/99 *Courage*, n. 42 above.

circumstances, even while leaving the specific conditions governing the grant of such remedies to the national legal systems.

However, the most distinctive of the Court's interventionist rulings which required the availability of a particular remedy as a matter of EC law is the *Francovich* judgment. This ruling established the principle of state liability to pay compensation for breach of EC law.

Cases C–6 and 9/90 **Francovich and Bonifaci v. Italy**
[1991] ECR I–5357

[Note ToA renumbering: Art. 5 is now Art. 10]

The applicants brought proceedings against Italy for the government's failure to implement Directive 80/987 on the protection of employees in the event of their employer's insolvency. No steps had been taken pursuant to the Directive to guarantee payment of wages owed by employers, and they argued that the State was liable to pay them the sums owed. The ECJ ruled that although the provisions of the Directive lacked sufficient precision to be directly effective, they nevertheless clearly intended to confer rights of which these individuals had been deprived through the State's failure to implement them.

THE ECJ

29. The national court thus raises the issue of the existence and scope of a State's liability for harm resulting from the breach of its obligations under Community law. . . .

(a) The existence of State liability as a matter of principle

30. It must be recalled first of all that the EEC Treaty has created its own legal system which is an integral part of the legal systems of the Member States and which their courts are bound to apply; the subjects of that legal system are not only the Member States but also their nationals. Just as it imposes obligations on individuals, Community law is also intended to create rights which become part of their legal patrimony; those rights arise not only where they are expressly granted by the Treaty but also by virtue of obligations which the Treaty imposes in a clearly defined manner both on individuals and on the Member States and the Community institutions: see Case 26/62 *Van Gend en Loos* and Case 6/64 *Costa* v. *ENEL*.

. . .

32. Furthermore, it has been consistently held that the national courts whose task it is to apply the provisions of Community law in cases within their jurisdiction must ensure that those rules have full effect and protect the rights which they confer on individuals: see in particular Case 106/77 *Simmenthal* and Case C–213/89 *Factortame*.

33. It must be held that the full effectiveness of Community rules would be impaired and the protection of the rights which they grant would be weakened if individuals were unable to obtain compensation when their rights are infringed by a breach of Community law for which a Member State can be held responsible.

34. The possibility of compensation by the Member State is particularly indispensable where, as in this case, the full effectiveness of Community rules is subject to prior action on the part of the State and consequently individuals cannot, in the absence of such action, enforce the rights granted to them by Community law before the national courts.

35. It follows that the principle of State liability for harm caused to individuals by breaches of Community law for which the State can be held responsible is inherent in the system of the Treaty.

> 36. Further foundation for the obligation on the part of Member States to pay compensation for such harm is to be found in Article 5 EEC, under which the Member States are required to take all appropriate measures, whether general or particular, to ensure fulfilment of their obligations under Community law. Among these is the obligation to nullify the unlawful consequences of a breach of Community law. . . .
>
> 37. It follows from all the foregoing that it is a principle of Community law that the Member States are obliged to pay compensation for harm caused to individuals by breaches of Community law for which they can be held responsible.

Contrasting with its early statement that the Treaty did not intend to create new remedies,[125] the ECJ ruled that the principle of state liability is inherent in the EC Treaty, indicating that an action for compensation against the State for breach of EC law must be available.[126] Another significant feature of *Francovich* at the time was that it required the provision by national courts of a damages remedy for breach of Community measures which lacked direct effect.[127] This represented an important additional move towards enhancing the effectiveness of unimplemented directives,[128] by presenting an alternative remedy for cases where national law could not otherwise be construed compatibly with an unimplemented directive.[129]

Despite the importance of the principle established, however, *Francovich* gave only minimal guidance for the future.[130] Three basic conditions were established for breaches involving a State's non-implementation of a *directive*: the conferment of specific rights,[131] whose content must be identifiable under the directive, upon an individual, and a causal link between the State's breach and damage to the individual.[132] For further conditions, the Court fell back on the familiar principle of national procedural autonomy.[133]

(b) CLARIFYING AND EXTENDING THE PRINCIPLE

The opportunity for many questions to be clarified came in the joined cases of *Brasserie du Pêcheur* and *Factortame III*, in which a series of questions was referred from the German

---

[125] Dougan has argued that while the Court clearly intended to develop a Community system of liability of public authorities and a right to reparation, it did not necessarily intend to create a specific 'Community remedy in damages': see M. Dougan, 'The Francovich Right to Reparation: Reshaping the Contours of Community Remedial Competence' (2000) 6 *EPL* 103.

[126] M. Ross, 'Beyond Francovich' (1993) 56 *MLR* 55; P. Craig, 'Francovich, Remedies and the Scope of Damages Liability' (1993) 109 *LQR* 595.

[127] D. Curtin, 'State Liability under Private Law: A New Remedy for Private Parties' (1992) 21 *ILJ* 74.

[128] See Ch. 8.

[129] See, e.g., Case C–334/92 *Wagner Miret* v. *Fondo de Garantía Salarial* [1993] ECR I–6911; Case C–54/96 *Dorsch Consult Ingenieurgesellschaft mbH* v. *Bundesbaugesellschaft Berlin mbH* [1997] ECR I–4961; Case C–81/98 *Alcatel Austria* v. *Bundesministerium für Wissenschaft und Verkehr* [1999] ECR I–7671; Case C–111/97 *Evobus Austria* [1998] ECR I–5411; Case C–258/97 *Hospital Ingenieure Krankenhaustechnik Planungs-Gesellschaft mbH (HI)* v. *Landeskrankenanstalten-Betriebsgesellschaft* [1999] ECR I–1405; Case C–131/97 *Carbonari* v. *Università degli Studi di Bologna* [1999] ECR I–1103.

[130] For a fundamental challenge to the very concept of state liability see C. Harlow, '*Francovich* and the Problem of the Disobedient State' (1996) 2 *ELJ* 199.

[131] For a case in which it was held that the Dir. did not create such rights see Case C–22/02 *Peter Paul et al.* v. *Bundesrepublik Deutschland* [2004] ECR I–9425.

[132] Cases C–6 and 9/90 *Francovich* [1991] ECR I–5357, paras. 39–40.

[133] *Ibid.*, paras. 42–43.

Bundesgerichtshof and the English High Court respectively. The judgment is long, detailed, and deserves close reading.[134]

Cases C–46/93 and 48/93 **Brasserie du Pêcheur SA v. Germany, and R. v. Secretary of State for Transport, ex parte Factortame Ltd. and Others**
[1996] ECR I–1029

[Note ToA renumbering: Arts. 5, 30, 52, 164, 189, and 215 are now
Arts. 10, 28, 43, 220, 249, and 288 respectively]

The *Factortame* reference arose from the same factual background as *Factortame I* (above) and *II*, in which Spanish fishermen had invoked Article 52 EC to challenge the UK's conditions for registration as a British vessel.[135] They sought damages for losses caused by the UK's breach of the Treaty. At the same time, in a case arising from litigation over Germany's beer purity laws, in which Germany had been found to be in breach of Article 30 EC, a French brewery which suffered losses when it was forced to cease exports to Germany sought compensation from the German State. It was argued before the ECJ that compensation should not be available for breach of directly effective EC law, since national remedies would already be available.

THE ECJ

19. That argument cannot be accepted.

20. The Court has consistently held that the right of individuals to rely on the directly effective provisions of the Treaty before national courts is only a minimum guarantee and is not sufficient in itself to ensure the full and complete implementation of the Treaty. . . . The purpose of that right is to ensure that provisions of Community law prevail over national provisions. It cannot, in every case, secure for individuals the benefit of rights conferred on them by Community law and, in particular, avoid their sustaining damage as a result of a breach of Community law attributable to a Member State. As appears from paragraph 33 of the judgment in *Francovich*, the full effectiveness of Community law would be impaired if individuals were unable to obtain redress when their rights were infringed by a breach of Community law.

. . .

22. It is all the more so in the event of an infringement of a right directly conferred by a Community provision upon which individuals are entitled to rely before the national courts. In that event, the right to reparation is the necessary corollary of the direct effect of the Community provision whose breach caused the damage sustained.
[*The ECJ rejected the German government's argument that a general right to reparation under Community law could be created only by legislation, and defended its own role as interpreter of the Treaty.*]

27. Since the Treaty contains no provisions expressly and specifically governing the consequences of breaches of Community law by Member States, it is for the Court, in pursuance of

---

[134] For some of the many commentaries on the case see N. Emiliou (1996) 21 *ELRev.* 399; Harlow, n. 130 above; J. Convery, 'State Liability in the UK after *Brasserie du Pêcheur*' (1997) 34 *CMLRev.* 603; P. Craig, 'Once More unto the Breach: The Community, the State and Damages Liability' (1997) 105 *LQR* 67; P. Oliver (1997) 34 *CMLRev.* 635.

[135] Case C–221/89 *R. v. Secretary of State for Transport, ex p. Factortame* [1991] ECR I–3905, known as *Factortame II*.

the task conferred on it by Article 164 of the Treaty of ensuring that in the interpretation and application of the Treaty, the law is observed, to rule on such a question in accordance with generally accepted methods of interpretation, in particular by reference to the fundamental principles of the Community legal system and, where necessary, general principles common to the legal systems of the Member States.

28. Indeed it is to the general principles common to the laws of the Member States that the second paragraph of Article 215 of the Treaty refers as the basis of the non-contractual liability of the Community for damage caused by its institutions or by its servants in the performance of their duties.

29. The principle of non-contractual liability of the Community expressly laid down in Article 215 of the Treaty is simply an expression of the general principle familiar to the legal systems of the member states that an unlawful act or omission gives rise to an obligation to make good the damage caused. That provision also reflects the obligation on public authorities to make good damage caused in the performance of their duties.

Rather than drawing only on the principle of effectiveness and on Article 10 EC, as it had done in *Francovich*, the ECJ here located the principle of state liability also in the context of the Treaty provisions on the *Community's* liability under Article 288, which in turn are expressly based on the general principles common to the Member States. This reasoning seems intended to legitimate the development of the principle of state liability, ostensibly deriving it from well-established principles of the national legal orders rather than from the imagination of the ECJ.

Drawing on international law principles, and on its case law under Art 226 EC, the Court ruled that the State is liable whichever of its organs is responsible for the breach and regardless of the internal division of powers between constitutional authorities.[136] In later cases the Court ruled that Member States are not required to change the distribution of powers and responsibilities between public bodies, and that in States with a federal structure, reparation for damage does not have to be provided by the federal State.[137] Equally, in States without a federal structure, reparation for damage caused to individuals can properly be made by a public law body legally distinct from the State, or an autonomous territorial body to which legislative or administrative tasks have been delegated.[138]

In a notable development, the Court ruled in *Köbler* that the principle of state liability applies even to violations of EC law by national courts of last instance. The case concerned the failure of the Austrian Verwaltungsgericht (supreme administrative court) to refer to the ECJ the question whether a long-service increment for university professors, which was restricted to professors who had spent fifteen years at an Austrian university, was contrary to the Treaty provisions on free movement of workers. An earlier ruling of the ECJ on a similar question concerning the Austrian increment had seemed to indicate that it would violate Article 39 EC, but in *Köbler*, the Verwaltungsgericht adopted a new factual classification which it had rejected in the earlier case, i.e. that the increment was a reward for loyalty, and thus could be argued to be justified under Article 39.

---

[136] R. Davis, 'Liability in Damages for a Breach of Community Law: Some Reflection on the Question of Who to Sue and the Concept of "the State" ' (2006) 31 *ELRev.* 69.

[137] Case C–302/97 *Konle* v. *Austria* [1999] ECR I–3099, paras. 61–64.

[138] Case C–424/97 *Haim* v. *Kassenzahnärtztliche Vereinigung Nordrhein* [2000] ECR I–5123, paras. 31–32.

Case C–224/01 **Gerhard Köbler v. Republik Österreich**
[2003] ECR I–10239

33. In the light of the essential role played by the judiciary in the protection of the rights derived by individuals from Community rules, the full effectiveness of those rules would be called in question and the protection of those rights would be weakened if individuals were precluded from being able, under certain conditions, to obtain reparation when their rights are affected by an infringement of Community law attributable to a decision of a court of a Member State adjudicating at last instance.

34. It must be stressed, in that context, that a court adjudicating at last instance is by definition the last judicial body before which individuals may assert the rights conferred on them by Community law. Since an infringement of those rights by a final decision of such a court cannot thereafter normally be corrected, individuals cannot be deprived of the possibility of rendering the State liable in order in that way to obtain legal protection of their rights.

35. Moreover, it is, in particular, in order to prevent rights conferred on individuals by Community law from being infringed that under the third paragraph of Article 234 EC a court against whose decisions there is no judicial remedy under national law is required to make a reference to the Court of Justice.

36. Consequently, it follows from the requirements inherent in the protection of the rights of individuals relying on Community law that they must have the possibility of obtaining redress in the national courts for the damage caused by the infringement of those rights owing to a decision of a court adjudicating at last instance (see in that connection *Brasserie du Pêcheur and Factortame*, cited above, paragraph 35).

The ECJ dismissed a range of arguments by several governments which had intervened against the proposed application of state liability to the conduct of courts of last instance. These included arguments based on the principle of legal certainty, on *res judicata*, on the independence and authority of the judiciary, and on more practical problems like the absence of a competent national court to adjudicate on the conduct of a court of last instance.[139] None of these arguments could justify the complete exclusion of the possibility of state liability for mistaken judicial decisions, according to the ECJ. The Court drew support for its conclusion from the fact that under the ECHR system, state reparation can be obtained for infringements of the Convention stemming from a decision of a national court of last instance.

Köbler was affirmed and reinforced by the ECJ in its subsequent judgment in *Traghetti del Mediterraneo*, where the ECJ condemned Italian legislation which sought substantially to restrict state liability for damage caused by a last instance court.[140]

After *Brasserie du Pêcheur*, and particularly the reasoning in paragraph 22 of that judgment, a further question about the scope of the principle established arose. The question was whether liability to compensate for violation of EC law would be extended beyond state violations to cover also breaches of EC law by *private* parties.[141] The issue was partly addressed by the ECJ in the competition law case of *Courage*. Having first reiterated its famous 'new legal order' reasoning from *Van Gend en Loos*, the ECJ then emphasized the fundamental nature of

---

[139] Case C–224/01 [2003] ECR I–10239, paras. 37–50. For comment on *Köbler* see C. Classen, (2004) 41 *CMLRev.* 813.

[140] Case C–173/03 *Traghetti del Mediterraneo SpA v. Italy* [2006] ECR I–5177.

[141] See Van Gerven AG in Case C–128/92 *Banks v. British Coal* [1994] ECR I–1209, and again extra-judicially in 'Bridging the Unbridgeable: Comunity and National Tort Laws after *Francovich* and *Brasserie*' (1996) 45 *ICLQ* 507, at 530–532.

the prohibition on anti-competitive agreements in Article 81 EC, breach of which would render any such agreement automatically void.

Case C–453/99 **Courage Ltd. v. Crehan**
[2001] ECR I–6297

23. Thirdly, it should be borne in mind that the Court has held that Article 85(1) of the Treaty and Article 86 of the EC Treaty (now Article 82 EC) produce direct effects in relations between individuals and create rights for the individuals concerned which the national courts must safeguard. . . .

. . .

25. As regards the possibility of seeking compensation for loss caused by a contract or by conduct liable to restrict or distort competition, it should be remembered from the outset that, in accordance with settled case-law, the national courts whose task it is to apply the provisions of Community law in areas within their jurisdiction must ensure that those rules take full effect and must protect the rights which they confer on individuals (see *inter alia* the judgments in Case 106/77 *Simmenthal* [1978] ECR 629, paragraph 16, and in Case C–213/89 *Factortame* [1990] ECR I–2433, paragraph 19).

26. The full effectiveness of Article 85 of the Treaty and, in particular, the practical effect of the prohibition laid down in Article 85(1) would be put at risk if it were not open to any individual to claim damages for loss caused to him by a contract or by conduct liable to restrict or distort competition.

27. Indeed, the existence of such a right strengthens the working of the Community competition rules and discourages agreements or practices, which are frequently covert, which are liable to restrict or distort competition. From that point of view, actions for damages before the national courts can make a significant contribution to the maintenance of effective competition in the Community.

28. There should not therefore be any absolute bar to such an action being brought by a party to a contract which would be held to violate the competition rules.

The *Courage* case, bolstered by the subsequent *Manfredi* judgment,[142] is significant in requiring that national law must provide an action for damages against a private party for breach of the Treaty competition law rules, but it remains unclear whether its implications extend beyond the sphere of competition law.[143]

(c) THE CONDITIONS FOR STATE LIABILITY

After affirming and clarifying the basic principle of state liability, the ECJ in *Brasserie du Pêcheur* then elaborated on the conditions for such liability, drawing on Article 288 EC governing liability of the Community institutions. In the Court's words, the conditions under which States incur liability for breach of EC law cannot differ from those governing the liability of the EC in similar circumstances.[144]

---

[142] Cases C–295–298/04 *Manfredi*, n. 42 above.

[143] W. van Gerven, 'Crehan and the Way Ahead' (2006) 17 *EBLR* 269, mentions Arts. 39, 49, and 141 EC, and regs. imposing obligations on individuals as the most likely candidates for future extension of the principle of individual liability. See also S. Drake, 'Scope of Courage and The Principle of "Individual Liability" for Damages' (2006) 26 *ELRev*. 841.

[144] The ECJ also ruled that national law could, if so desired, set stricter conditions for liability: see para. 66.

Cases C–46 and 48/93 **Brasserie du Pêcheur SA v. Germany**
[1996] ECR I–1029

43. The system of rules which the Court has worked out with regard to Article 215 of the Treaty, particularly in relation to liability for legislative measures, takes into account, inter alia, the complexity of the situations to be regulated, difficulties in the application or interpretation of the texts and, more particularly, the margin of discretion available to the author of the act in question.

44. Thus, in developing its case-law on the non-contractual liability of the Community, in particular as regards legislative measures involving choices of economic policy, the Court has had regard to the wide discretion available to the institutions in implementing Community policies.

45. The strict approach taken towards the liability of the Community in the exercise of its legislative activities is due to two considerations. First, even when the legality of measures is subject to judicial review, exercise of the legislative function must not be hindered by the prospect of actions for damages whenever the general interest of the Community requires legislative measures to be adopted which may adversely affect individual interests. Second, in a legislative context characterized by the exercise of a wide discretion, which is essential for implementing a Community policy, the Community cannot incur liability unless the institution concerned has manifestly and gravely disregarded the limits on the exercise of its powers.

46. That said, the national legislature—like the Community institutions—does not systematically have a wide discretion when it acts in a field governed by Community law. Community law may impose upon it obligations to achieve a particular result or obligations to act or refrain from acting which reduce its margin of discretion, sometimes to a considerable degree. This is so, for instance, where, as in the circumstances to which the judgment in *Francovich* relates, Article 189 of the Treaty places the Member State under an obligation to take, within a given period, all the measures needed in order to achieve the result required by a directive. In such a case, the fact that it is for the national legislature to take the necessary measures has no bearing on the Member State's liability for failing to transpose the directive.

47. In contrast, where a Member State acts in a field where it has no wide discretion, comparable to that of the Community institutions in implementing Community policies, the conditions under which it may incur liability must, in principle, be the same as those under which the Community institutions incur liability in the comparable situation.

. . .

51. In such circumstances, Community law confers a right to reparation where three conditions are met: the rule of law infringed must be intended to confer rights on individuals; the breach must be sufficiently serious; and there must be a direct causal link between the breach of the obligation resting on the State and the damage sustained by the injured parties.

. . .

53. . . . Those conditions correspond in substance to those defined by the Court in relation to Article 215 in its case-law on liability of the Community for damage caused to individuals by unlawful legislative measures adopted by its institutions.

. . .

55. As to the second condition, as regards both Community liability under Article 215 and Member State liability for breaches of Community law, the decisive test for finding that a breach of Community law is sufficiently serious is whether the Member State or the Community institution concerned manifestly and gravely disregarded the limits on its discretion.

56. The factors which the competent court may take into consideration include the clarity and precision of the rule breached, the measure of discretion left by that rule to the national or Community authorities, whether the infringement and the damage caused was intentional or

involuntary, whether any error of law was excusable or inexcusable, the fact that the position taken by a Community institution may have contributed towards the omission, and the adoption or retention of national measures or practices contrary to Community law.

57. On any view, a breach of Community law will clearly be sufficiently serious if it has persisted despite a judgment finding the infringement in question to be established, or a preliminary ruling or settled case law of the Court on the matter from which it is clear that the conduct in question constituted an infringement.

In the cases at hand, the ECJ suggested that the national authorities must have known that certain of the German beer designation rules were in breach of Community law, given earlier ECJ rulings to this effect.[145] The Court also indicated that while the existence of a prior ECJ ruling finding an infringement of EC law would indicate that a subsequent similar infringement constitutes a sufficiently serious breach, such a ruling would not be *necessary* to establish a sufficiently serious breach.[146] Similarly, parts of the Merchant Shipping Act 1988's conditions for registration were *prima facie* incompatible with EC law, whereas others might have appeared to be capable of justification.[147] In assessing the question of 'sufficient seriousness' the UK court was encouraged to consider the existing legal disputes over the common fisheries policy, the fact that the Commission had made its attitude known in good time to the UK, and 'the assessments as to the state of certainty of Community law made by the national courts in the interim proceedings brought'.[148] Causation of damage was ultimately a question for the national courts to decide,[149] and, while later rulings confirm this position, the ECJ has nonetheless given legal guidance on causation.[150]

On the crucial question of the *standard* of liability, while the ECJ did not respond directly to a question from the German government on the meaning of 'fault', the Court made clear that the concept of 'sufficiently serious breach' (which arguably carries connotations of fault) was all that could be required by domestic law:[151] This position was strongly affirmed by the *Köbler* and *Traghetti* cases on state liability arising from the action of national courts. In *Köbler* the ECJ ruled that, regard being had to 'the specific nature of the judicial function' and the legitimate requirements of legal certainty,[152] state liability in cases of judicial breach was governed by the same conditions (i.e. conferral of rights on individuals, a sufficiently serious breach, and a causal link between the State's breach and damage to the individual) and by the same standard of liability as any other state violation of EC law. As far as the standard is concerned, liability can only be incurred 'in the exceptional case where the court has manifestly

---

[145] The referring German court, upon receiving the ECJ's ruling in *Brasserie du Pêcheur*, ultimately awarded no damages at all to the plaintiffs even as regards the provisions governing the designation '*Bier*', on the basis that there had been no direct causal connection between Germany's sufficiently serious breach and the damage suffered: see [1997] 1 CMLR 971. See Oliver, n. 134 above, 657; E. Deards (1997) 22 *ELRev*. 620.

[146] Paras. 91–95 of the judgment.

[147] The House of Lords ultimately upheld the finding of the Divisional Court and Court of Appeal that the breach was sufficiently serious to give rise to liability in damages. For the series of domestic judgments on this issue see [1997] *EuLR* 475, [1998] 1 All ER 736, [1999] All ER 640 (CA), [2000] 1 AC 524 (HL), and finally the Div. Ct. ruling in [2001] 1 WLR 942.

[148] Para. 63 of the judgment.

[149] Para. 65. See also Case C–140/97 *Rechberger*, n. 99 above, paras. 72–73; Case C–127/95 *Norbrook Laboratories Ltd.* v. *Ministry of Agriculture Fisheries and Food* [1998] ECR I–1531.

[150] Case C–319/96 *Brinkmann Tabakfabriken GmbH* v. *Skatteministeriet* [1998] ECR I–5255, para. 29.

[151] Cases 46 and 48/93 *Brasserie du Pecheur* [1996] ECR I–1029, paras. 76–79. On this point see also Case C–424/97 *Haim*, n. 138 above.

[152] Case C–224/01 *Köbler*, n. 139 above, para. 53.

infringed the applicable law'.[153] The Court repeated the content of paragraphs 56 and 57 of *Brasserie du Pêcheur*, but added one further indicator of manifest breach by a national court of last instance: non-compliance by the court in question with its obligation to make a reference to the ECJ for a preliminary ruling.

In *Traghetti del Mediterraneo*, Italian legislation sought to restrict state liability arising from damage caused by a last instance court by excluding liability where the infringement was the result of an interpretation of law or an assessment of facts or evidence, and by limiting liability solely to cases of intentional fault and serious misconduct by the national court.[154] The ECJ rejected arguments made by various governments that the impugned legislation struck a fair balance between effective judicial protection on the one hand, and legal certainty and the independence of the judiciary on the other. On the requirement of showing intentional fault and serious misconduct by the national court, the ECJ ruled:

> [A]lthough it remains possible for national law to define the criteria relating to the nature or degree of the infringement which must be met before State liability can be incurred for an infringement of Community law attributable to a national court adjudicating at last instance, under no circumstances may such criteria impose requirements stricter than that of a manifest infringement of the applicable law, as set out in paragraphs 53 to 56 of the *Köbler* judgment.[155]

Similarly, the Court ruled that the exclusion of liability for an interpretation of law or assessment of facts or evidence by the national court of last instance 'would render meaningless' the principle laid down in *Köbler*, since a manifest infringement of EC law could readily arise from either of these two kinds of essential judicial activity, especially when carried out by a court of last instance.[156]

On the facts of *Köbler* itself, the ECJ ruled that although it was normally for the national court to apply the law to the facts of the case, it had enough information in this case to give guidance on whether the conditions for state liability were fulfilled.[157] The issue was whether the Austrian Verwaltungsgericht had 'manifestly infringed' EC law by failing to re-refer the question of the compatibility of a long-service increment with Article 39 EC to the ECJ. The Verwaltungsgericht had initially referred the question to the ECJ, but had subsequently withdrawn it on the suggestion of the ECJ registrar, who assumed it had been resolved in Professor Köbler's favour by the earlier *Schöning-Kougebetopoulou*[158] ruling, which had found a similar long-service increment to be incompatible with Article 39. The Verwaltungsgericht then decided to re-classify the long-service increment as a loyalty bonus under national law, possibly in order to avoid the application of the *Schöning-Kougebetopoulou* ruling. However, taking a benign view of the action of the Verwaltungsgericht in reclassifying the bonus, the ECJ ruled that, in failing to re-refer the question under Article 234,[159] its infringement of EC law was not sufficiently manifest to attract state liability.[160]

---

[153] *Ibid.*, paras. 52–53.

[154] Case C–173/03 *Traghetti del Mediterraneo*, n. 140 above. For discussion, see G. Anagnostaras, 'Erroneous Judgments and the Prospect of Damages' (2006) 31 *ELRev*. 735.

[155] *Ibid.*, para. 44.

[156] *Ibid.*, paras. 34–40.

[157] Case C–224/01 *Köbler*, n. 139 above, para. 101.

[158] Case C–15/96 *Kalliope Schöning-Kougebetopoulou v. Freie und Hansestadt Hamburg* [1998] ECR I–47.

[159] Interestingly, although the provision of EC law violated by the Austrian court was Art. 234 EC, the provision which the ECJ analysed in order to determine whether the first condition of liability (conferral of rights on individuals) was satisfied was Art. 39 EC, on the free movement of workers.

[160] Case C–224/01 *Köbler*, n. 139 above, paras. 121–124.

Guidance on the general notion of a 'sufficiently serious breach' has also been given in other cases. In *British Telecom*,[161] the ECJ agreed that the UK had misimplemented a public procurement directive, but concluded that it did not amount to a sufficiently serious breach. The provision of EC law breached was not clear and precise, the UK's interpretation had been made in good faith and in keeping with the aims and wording of the Directive, and no guidance had been available from past rulings of the Court or the Commission. A similar ruling was given by the ECJ in *Denkavit*, in relation to an incorrect transposition by Germany of a company taxation directive, since almost all other Member States had adopted the same interpretation of the Directive as Germany and there was no existing case law on the provision in question.[162] Other rulings have followed suit.[163]

By contrast, in *Dillenkofer*,[164] concerning Germany's failure to implement the Package Holidays Directive 90/314, the ECJ ruled that *Francovich* had established that non-transposition of a directive within the prescribed time limit *of itself* amounted to a sufficiently serious breach.[165] Similarly in *Lomas*, the refusal of the UK to grant export licences for live sheep to Spain, on the ground that Spanish slaughterhouses were not complying with the terms of an EC directive, constituted a sufficiently serious breach.[166] The UK government argued that its breach of Article 29 EC was justified by the protection of animal welfare, but the Court ruled that the lack of discretion left to Member States under the Directive, the clarity of the Treaty provision breached, and the absence of a properly verified ground of justification pointed to a sufficiently serious breach. In *Evans*, by contrast, the ECJ left it to the national court to decide whether there were defects in the transposition of the Second Motor Insurance Directive, and if so whether those constituted a sufficiently serious breach.[167]

(d) STATE LIABILITY AND THE NATIONAL REMEDIAL FRAMEWORK

While *Brasserie du Pêcheur/Factortame III* provided some guidance on the conditions governing state liability, many issues were left by the Court to be governed by national law subject to the familiar twin principles of equivalence and effectiveness.[168] In other words, while the right to reparation and its core principles and conditions are determined by EC law,[169] the right is provided within the framework of domestic legal systems, with their varying procedural and

---

[161] Case C–392/93 *R. v. HM Treasury, ex p. British Telecommunications plc* [1996] ECR I–1631.

[162] Cases C–283, 291, and 292/94 *Denkavit International* v. *Bundesamt für Finanzen* [1996] ECR I–5063, paras. 51–52.

[163] Case C–319/96 *Brinkmann*, n. 150 above, paras. 30–32; Case C–127/95 *Norbrook*, n. 149 above.

[164] Cases C–178–179, and 188–190/94 *Dillenkofer* v. *Germany* [1996] ECR I–4845, paras. 21–23. For a case involving misimplementation, rather than non-implementation, of the Package Holidays Dir. which also constituted a sufficiently serious breach see Case C–140/97 *Rechberger*, n. 99 above, paras. 51–53.

[165] Cases C–178–179, and 188–190/94 *Dillenkofer*, n. 164 above, paras. 21–23.

[166] Case C–5/94 *R.* v. *Ministry of Agriculture, Fisheries and Food, ex p. Hedley Lomas* [1996] ECR I–2553, paras. 28–29. For other cases of sufficiently serious breach see Case C–118/00 *Larsy* v. *INASTI* [2001] ECR I–5063; Case C–150/99 *Stockholm Lindöpark Aktiebolag* v. *Sweden* [2001] ECR I–493.

[167] Case C–63/01 *Evans*, n. 33 above, paras. 82–88.

[168] For interesting comparative discussions of the procedural conditions prevailing in different Member States see C. Kremer, 'Liability for Breach of EC Law' (2003) 22 *YBEL* 203; H. Xanathi, 'Effective Judicial Protection at the National Level Against Breaches of EC Law' (2005) 5 *EJLR* 409.

[169] See, for a recent reiteration, Case C–300/04 *Eman*, n. 111 above, para. 70.

substantive rules on matters such as time limits, causation, mitigation of loss, and assessment of damages.[170]

In *Brasserie/Factortame* themselves, the ECJ ruled that German law limiting the State's liability in exercising its legislative function, and certain English law requirements such as 'abuse of power' or proof of misfeasance in public office, fell foul of the effectiveness principle, making it 'excessively difficult' to obtain reparation. Concerning the extent of reparation, the Court ruled that, in order to constitute effective protection, 'reparation for loss or damage caused to individuals as result of breaches of Community law must be commensurate with the loss or damage sustained'.[171] This requirement of commensurability is strong, recalling the ruling in *Marshall II*.[172] While reasonable restrictions may be imposed on the extent of damages available, they must satisfy the conditions of equivalence and effectiveness. Rules on mitigation of loss are apparently acceptable, but the total exclusion of loss of profits, or the restriction of damages to certain specific interests such as property, would violate the effectiveness principle.[173] Although the ECJ rejected the German government's request for a temporal limit on the effects of the *Brasserie* ruling, the Court indicated that Germany could take account, within the framework of its *national* law on liability, of temporal concerns such as the principle of legal certainty.[174]

In a trilogy of Italian cases concerning claims arising out of the *Francovich* litigation, the compatibility of national provisions restricting the availability of compensation for the State's prior breach of EC law arose.[175] This breach was the failure to implement Directive 80/987 on the protection of employees following their employer's insolvency. In *Bonifaci and Berto*, the ECJ found various provisions of the legislation limiting the period from which wage claims could be made to be excessively restrictive.[176] In *Palmisani*[177] the applicant was refused compensation under the Italian scheme because she had not brought her claim for compensation until after the time limit set in the Italian legislation, which was one year from the date of its entry into force. The national court referred to the ECJ the question whether this time limit breached the principle of equivalence, since the general time limit for cases of non-contractual liability brought under the Italian Civil Code was five years. The ECJ ruled that while a one-year time limit from the date of entry into force of the measure implementing the

---

[170] In Case C–228/98 *Dounias*, n. 27 above, the exceptional availability of witness evidence in proceedings to establish state liability was deemed compatible with the principles of equivalence and effectiveness. See also Case C–118/00 *Larsy*, n. 166 above.

[171] Cases 46 and 48/93 *Brasserie du Pêcheur/Factortame*, n. 151 above, para. 82.

[172] Case C–271/91 *Marshall* v. *Southampton and South West Hampshire Area Health Authority II* [1993] ECR I–4367.

[173] Cases 46 and 48/93 *Brasserie du Pêcheur*, n. 151 above, paras. 84–88. On mitigation of loss and economic loss in general see Case C–410/98 *Metallgesellschaft*, n. 65 above, para. 91; Cases C–295–298/04, *Manfredi*, n. 42 above. As regards exemplary damages in English law, the ECJ in *Brasserie du Pêcheur* ruled that such an award could not be ruled out in the case of the State's breach of EC law in similar circumstances to those which would give rise to an award in an action founded on domestic law: Cases 46 and 48/93 *Brasserie du Pêcheur*, n. 151 above, para. 89.

[174] *Ibid.*, para. 98.

[175] Cases C–94–95/95 *Bonifaci and Berto* v. *IPNS* [1997] ECR I–3969; Case C–261/95 *Palmisani*, n. 110 above; Case C–373/95 *Maso and Gazzetta* v. *IPNS* [1997] ECR I–4051; see Dougan, n. 125 above.

[176] The Court also ruled that while retroactive application of the measures adopted should be sufficient to ensure adequacy of reparation, this would not necessarily be so if employees could demonstrate otherwise: see Cases C–94–95/95 *Bonifaci and Berto*, n. 175 above, paras. 51–53. See also Case C–373/95 *Maso and Gazzetta*, n. 175 above, paras. 58–59, in which the Court ruled that although national rules against aggregation of benefits were in principle permissible, they could not cover benefits such as jobseekers' allowances which arose after termination of employment and would not have overlapped with the unpaid wages.

[177] Case C–261/95 *Palmisani*, n. 110 above.

directive would not breach the principle of effectiveness, the position in relation to the principle of equivalence was less clear. The Court then distinguished between claims for wages under the national law implementing the directive, and claims for damages for loss caused by the late implementation of the directive which were governed by the Italian compensation scheme set up by the later measure. The latter was established precisely to satisfy the *Francovich* requirement of an action for state liability, and its aim was to compensate individuals for loss caused by the State's failure to implement a directive, whereas the former was intended to provide a particular social security benefit.

For this reason, it might be inappropriate to compare the time limit for actions under the compensation scheme with the time limit for social-security claims in national law, rather than with the ordinary system of non-contractual liability. The latter system, like the *Francovich* right of reparation, was 'intended to guarantee reparation of the loss or damage sustained as a result of the conduct of the perpetrator'. Ultimately, the ECJ left it to the Italian court to decide on the issue of 'equivalence', while suggesting that this principle might have been violated by the legislation at issue.[178]

(e) STATE LIABILITY AS A RESIDUAL REMEDY?

Given that the action for compensation is available for breach of directly effective as well as non-directly effective Community rights, what advantages are there for an individual to choose the EC-mandated action for compensation rather than another existing national remedy?[179]

There is some suggestion in cases like *Société Comateb*[180] and *Sutton*[181] that where a national remedy is unsatisfactory due to the existence of a legitimate national procedural restriction, an action in damages against the State might provide an alternative remedy which is not affected by that particular restrictive national rule. In each case, having conceded that restrictions on the availability of national remedies were potentially legitimate, the ECJ went on to consider the possible liability of the State in damages.[182] One reading of the cases is that they

---

[178] *Ibid.*, para. 39. See also Cases C–52 and 53/99 *ONP* v. *Camarotto* [2001] ECR I–1395. On equivalence, see also Case C–470/04 *N* v. *Inspecteur van de Belastingdienst Oost/kantoor Almelo* [2006] ECR I–7409.

[179] See Oliver, n. 134 above, and Deards, n. 145 above, who question whether the action for damages may be made subsidiary to other national remedies. For a detailed discussion see G. Anagnostraras, 'State Liability and Alternative Courses of Action: How Independent Can an Autonomous Remedy Be?' (2002) 21 *YBEL* 355.

[180] Cases C–192–218/95 *Comateb*, n. 42 above, concerning the principle of unjust enrichment as a barrier to the repayment of charges wrongly levied. There is an extensive case law on repayment of charges and the defence of 'passing on' the cost of charges to consumers. For further discussion see Dougan, n. 13 above. Compare *Comateb*, where the ECJ accepted the compatibility in principle of such an unjust enrichment rule with the effectiveness principle with Case C–147/01 *Weber's Wine World*, n. 112 above, where the ECJ ruled that a *presumption* of unjust enrichment, on the sole basis that the charge was passed on to third parties, would make the exercise of EC rights excessively difficult in practice. For a case on the topic brought by the Commission, rather than by an affected individual, against a Member State see Case C–129/00 *Commission* v. *Italy* [2003] ECR I–14637.

[181] Case C–66/95 *Sutton*, n. 50 above, concerning the non-availability of interest on arrears of social security owed under Dir. 79/7. Similarly in Case C–90/96 *Petrie* v. *Università degli Studi di Verona et Camilla Bettoni* [1997] ECR I–6525, the ECJ ruled that although applicants for teaching posts who had been subject to an unlawful discriminatory condition could not insist that they must be eligible for appointment to these posts under national law, that did not mean that they could not seek compensation under the conditions laid down in *Brasserie du Pêcheur*.

[182] The *Palmisani* case also lends some support to the hypothesis that, e.g., an action for damages against the State for loss caused by the misimplementation of a dir. would also have to include loss caused by the effluxion of time, even where such loss could not be recovered as interest in an action for repayment of arrears under national law.

assume that an action for compensation based on *Francovich* principles may prove to be a more effective remedy than others available under national law. This assumption has, however, been criticized on the basis that an action based on *Francovich* requires the establishment of additional onerous conditions, such as a sufficiently serious breach and causation of loss.[183]

The ECJ on the other hand rejected the opposite assumption in the *Stockholm Lindöpark* case, i.e. it rejected the argument that the availability of a *Francovich*-style action for damages should be precluded by the fact that a separate action under national law could be based on the direct effect of Community law.[184] Moreover in *Wells*, the ECJ left it to the national court to decide which kind of remedy would be available and appropriate for a violation of EC environmental impact assessment law.[185] The Court there ruled that EC law imposed an obligation on Member States to 'nullify the unlawful consequences of a breach of Community law', but that it was for the national court to determine whether a planning consent unlawfully granted could be revoked, or whether instead the individual affected could claim compensation for harm suffered.[186]

According to Prechal, state liability for breach of EC law is 'a sort of residual remedy . . . a second rank alternative' to the direct or indirect effect of EC rights and their enforcement at national level.[187] She argues that EC law may even sometimes require litigants, as a way of mitigating their loss, to rely first on the direct or indirect effect of an EC right before seeking state compensation. In her view, the subsidiary and complementary character of state liability—a kind of 'safety net' where other devices fail—is confirmed by a long line of judgments since *Francovich*. Dougan also argues that the ECJ tends to use state liability as a cure for inadequate domestic remedies.[188] These commentators have questioned, ultimately, whether the tendency of the Court to present state liability as a panacea where national remedies are otherwise lacking might even have the effect of lowering the effectiveness of national protection.

8. CONCLUSIONS

i. In responding to the lack of harmonized Community remedies, the ECJ's intervention to stimulate an incremental degree of national procedural alignment has prompted differing reactions. Some applaud the Court for treading a difficult path between the need to respect national legal autonomy and competence, and the competing need to promote effective enforcement of EC law.[189]

ii. Others caution against the effects of such reactive, *ad hoc*, and haphazard judicial lawmaking and argue for a more systematic, politically legitimate, and carefully considered political approach to the effectiveness of EC law and the creation of a system of Community procedures and remedies.[190] Yet, given the slow pace and difficulty of achieving

---

183 Dougan, n. 125 above.

184 Case C–150/99 *Stockholm Lindöpark*, n. 166 above, para. 35.

185 Case C–201/02 *Wells* v. *Secretary of State for Transport* [2004] ECR I–723.

186 *Ibid.*, paras. 67–69.

187 S. Prechal, 'Direct Effect and State Liability: What's the Difference After All?' (2006) 17 *EBLR* 299.

188 Dougan, n. 31 above, ch. 5; Anagnostraras, n. 179 above.

189 See, e.g., Jacobs, n. 56 above, and as AG in Cases C–430–31/93 *Van Schijndel*, n. 117 above, para. 27, Jacobs AG. For an account of the case law as an insistence on 'European procedural primacy' see J. Delicostopoulos, 'Towards European Procedural Primacy in National Legal Systems' (2003) 9 *ELJ* 599.

190 F. Snyder, 'The Effectiveness of European Community Law' (1993) 56 *MLR* 19, 50–53.

any progress with legislative harmonization or co-ordination in these fields, it has been suggested that incremental reform through the Court's case law may in some respects be desirable.[191]

iii. However, it has also been argued that remedial harmonization may simply be a task for which the ECJ is inherently unsuited.[192] The contribution of the ECJ's case law in most sectors has been described as promoting a form of negative rather than positive harmonization, setting limits and boundaries for national systems rather than prescribing harmonized solutions.[193] Even in sectors such as competition law and state aid, where there is a dense EC legislative framework, judicially-led harmonization has been described as minimum rather than full harmonization.

iv. The Community's lack of legislative activity can be interpreted in different ways. It may be seen to reflect a clear political wish on the part of the Member States and the Council not to harmonize or even co-ordinate domestic procedures in this respect. On the other hand, it may be seen as reflecting the difficulty and complexity of the task which would be involved.[194]

v. It has been suggested that Member States may be particularly resistant to the prospect of Community interference—whether legislative or judicial—with their systems of private law, which reflect implicit but fundamental social and cultural choices.[195] Nonetheless, the intense activity in recent years to activate the EU's 'area of freedom, security and justice', including co-ordination of civil procedural law across the Member States, may indicate a shift in this respect.[196] While remedial 'harmonization' in its strong form may be off the agenda, other more gradual forms of mutual alignment and recognition may well be likely to emerge.

9. FURTHER READING

(a) Books

Dougan, M., *National Remedies before the Court of Justice* (Hart, 2004)

Kilpatrick, C., Novitz, T., and Skidmore, P., *The Future of Remedies in Europe* (Hart, 2000)

Lonbay, J., and Biondi, A. (eds.), *Remedies for Breach of EC Law* (Wylie, 1997)

Ward, A., *Individual Rights and Private Party Judicial Review in the EU* (2nd edn., Oxford University Press, 2007)

(b) Articles

Anagnostaras, G., 'The Allocation of Responsibility in State Liability Actions for Breach of Community Law' (2001) 26 *ELRev.* 139

---

[191] C. Himsworth, 'Things Fall Apart: The Harmonisation of Community Judicial Protection Revisited' (1997) 22 *ELRev.* 291, 307.

[192] Dougan, n. 31 above.

[193] *Ibid.*, chs. 6 and 7.

[194] C. Harding, 'Member State Enforcement of European Community Measures: The Chimera of "Effective" Enforcement' (1997) 4 *MJ* 5.

[195] D. Caruso, 'The Missing View of the Cathedral: The Private law Paradigm of European Legal Integration' (1997) 3 *ELJ* 3; H. Collins, 'European Private Law and the Cultural Identity of States' (1995) 3 *European Review of Private Law* 353.

[196] See the developments mentioned at n. 2 above.

—— 'Erroneous Judgments and the Prospect of Damages: the Scope of the Principle of Governmental Liability for Judicial Breaches' (2006) 31 *ELRev.* 735

Caranta, R., 'Judicial Protection Against Member States: A New Jus Commune Takes Shape' (1995) 32 *CMLRev.* 703

Craig, P., 'Once More unto the Breach: The Community, the State and Damages Liability' (1997) 105 *LQR* 67

Delicostopoulos, J., 'Towards European Procedural Primacy in National Legal Systems' (2003) 9 *ELJ* 599

Dougan, M., 'Cutting your Losses in the Enforcement Deficit: A Community Right to the Recovery of Unlawfully Levied Charges?' (1998) 1 *CYELS* 233

—— 'The *Francovich* Right to Reparation: Reshaping the Contours of Community Remedial Competence' (2000) 6 *EPL* 103

Drake, S., 'Scope of Courage and the Principle of "Individual Liability" for Damages' (2006) 6 *ELRev.* 841

Harlow, C., 'A Common European Law of Remedies', in C. Kilpatrick, T. Novitz, and P. Skidmore (eds.), *The Future of Remedies in Europe* (Hart, 2000)

Prechal, S., 'Member State Liability and Direct Effect: What's the Difference After All?' (2006) 17 *EBLR* 299

Tridimas, T., 'Liability for Breach of Community Law: Growing Up and Mellowing Down?' (2001) 38 *CMLRev.* 301

Van Gerven, W., 'Bridging the Gap between Community and National Laws: Towards a Principle of Homogeneity in the Field of Legal Remedies?' (1995) 32 *CMLRev.* 679

THE RELATIONSHIP BETWEEN EC LAW AND NATIONAL LAW: SUPREMACY

1. CENTRAL ISSUES

i. The doctrine of supremacy of Community law had no formal basis in the EC Treaty, but was developed by the ECJ on the basis of its conception of the 'new legal order'.

ii. The ECJ ruled that the aim of creating a uniform common market between different States would be undermined if Community laws could be made subordinate to the national laws of the various States.

iii. The validity of EC law can therefore, according to the ECJ, never be assessed by reference to national law.[1] National courts are required to give immediate effect to the provisions of directly effective EC law (of whatever rank) in cases which arise before them, and to ignore or to set aside any national law (of whatever rank) which could impede the application of EC law.

iv. The requirement to 'set aside' conflicting national law does not entail an obligation to nullify national law, which may continue to apply in any situation which is not covered by a conflicting provision of Community law.

v. Most national courts do not accept the unconditionally monist view of the ECJ as regards the supremacy of EC law. While they accept the requirements of supremacy in practice, most regard this as flowing from their national constitutions rather than from the authority of the EC Treaties or the ECJ, and they retain a power of ultimate constitutional review over measures of EC law.

2. THE FIRST DIMENSION: SUPREMACY FROM THE ECJ'S PERSPECTIVE

(a) THE FOUNDATIONS: *COSTA*

The EEC Treaty contained no provision dealing with the supremacy of Community law over national law. Nor has any such provision been included in any later Treaty amendment. A

---

[1] However the CFI has held that the EU is bound by Resolutions of the United Nations Security Council: Case T–315/01 *Yassin Abdullah Kadi* v. *Council and Commission* [2005] ECR II–3649.

supremacy clause was incorporated in the Constitutional Treaty and will be considered below. Notwithstanding the absence of any explicit provision in the Rome Treaty, the ECJ enunciated its vision of supremacy in the early years of the Community's existence. It touched on the issue in *Van Gend en Loos*[2] when it stated that the Community constituted a new legal order of international law for the benefit of which the States had limited their sovereign rights, but the ECJ's primary focus was on direct effect. The supremacy doctrine was however at the forefront of the decision in *Costa*.

Case 6/64 **Flaminio Costa v. ENEL**
[1964] ECR 585, 593

[Note ToA renumbering: Arts. 5, 7, 177, and 189
are now Arts. 10, 12, 234, and 249 respectively]

THE ECJ

By contrast with ordinary international treaties, the EEC Treaty has created its own legal system which, on the entry into force of the Treaty, became an integral part of the legal systems of the Member States and which their courts are bound to apply.

By creating a Community of unlimited duration, having its own institutions, its own personality, its own legal capacity and capacity of representation on the international plane and, more particularly, real powers stemming from a limitation of sovereignty or a transfer of powers from the States to the Community, the Member States have limited their sovereign rights, albeit within limited fields, and have thus created a body of law which binds both their nationals and themselves.

The integration into the laws of each Member State of provisions which derive from the Community, and more generally the terms and the spirit of the Treaty, make it impossible for the states, as a corollary, to accord precedence to a unilateral and subsequent measure over a legal system accepted by them on the basis of reciprocity. Such a measure cannot therefore be inconsistent with that legal system. The executive force of Community law cannot vary from one State to another in deference to subsequent domestic laws, without jeopardizing the attainment of the objectives of the Treaty set out in Article 5(2) and giving rise to the discrimination prohibited by Article 7.

The obligations undertaken under the Treaty establishing the Community would not be unconditional, but merely contingent, if they could be called into question by subsequent legislative acts of the signatories....

The precedence of Community law is confirmed by Article 189, whereby a regulation 'shall be binding' and 'directly applicable in all Member States'. This provision, which is subject to no reservation, would be quite meaningless if a State could unilaterally nullify its effects by means of a legislative measure which could prevail over Community law.

It follows from all these observations that the law stemming from the Treaty, an independent source of law, could not, because of its special and original nature, be overridden by domestic legal provisions, however framed, without being deprived of its character as Community law and without the legal basis of the Community itself being called into question.

The transfer by the states from their domestic legal system to the Community legal system of the rights and obligations arising under the Treaty carries with it a permanent limitation of their sovereign rights, against which a subsequent unilateral act incompatible with the concept of the Community cannot prevail.

---

[2] Case 26/62 *NV Algemene Transporten Expeditie Onderneming van Gend en Loos* v. *Nederlandse Administratie der Belastingen* [1963] ECR 1.

The ECJ deploys a number of arguments to justify its conclusion that Community law should be accorded supremacy over national law.[3]

First is the statement that the Treaty created its own legal order which immediately became 'an integral part' of the legal systems of the Member States.

Second, and perhaps more contentious, is the Court's statement of how, in constitutional terms, the Member States created this legal order. This was done, said the Court, by the States transferring to the new Community institutions 'real powers stemming from a limitation of sovereignty'. As in the case of *Van Gend*, the Court made no reference to the constitution of any particular Member State to see whether such a transfer or limitation of sovereignty was contemplated, or was possible in accordance with that constitution.

In its *third* argument, the Court drew on the spirit and the aims of the Treaty to conclude that it was 'impossible' for the Member States to accord primacy to domestic laws. The 'spirit' of the Treaty required that they all act with equal diligence to give full effect to Community laws which they had accepted on the basis of 'reciprocity'. Since the 'aims' of the Treaty were those of integration and co-operation, their achievement would be undermined by one Member State refusing to give effect to a Community law which, as they had agreed, should uniformly and equally bind all. This was a pragmatic and purposive argument rather than a textual one, and an argument which the ECJ has deployed repeatedly: that securing the uniformity and effectiveness of Community law is necessary if the concrete aims set out in the Treaties are to be realized.

The *fourth* argument was that the obligations undertaken by the Member States in the Treaty would be 'merely contingent' rather than unconditional if they were to be subject to later legislative acts on the part of the States.

The only genuinely textual evidence used by the Court was in its *final* argument: that the language of direct applicability in what is now Article 249 would be meaningless if States could negate the effect of Community law by passing subsequent inconsistent legislation. Yet this textual argument is weak, since Article 249 refers only to the direct applicability of regulations, while the Court in *Costa* sought to establish a general principle of the supremacy of *all* binding Community law. Moreover, direct applicability refers to the way in which Community law becomes part of the national legal system without the need for implementing measures, but does not resolve the priority between this law and other forms of national law.

What comes across most strongly is the teleological rather than textual approach in the Court's judgment, with emphasis placed on the aims of the Community and the spirit of the Treaties. The Court's decision was clearly a bold step to support its own conception of the Community legal order by asserting that the States had permanently limited their powers and had transferred sovereignty to the Community institutions.

(b) THE AMBIT: *INTERNATIONALE HANDESLGESELLSCHAFT* AND *SIMMENTHAL*

While the conceptual basis for the supremacy of Community law was set out in *Costa*, the force and ambit of the principle became clearer in later decisions. In the following case, the Court ruled that the legal status of a conflicting national measure was not relevant to the question

---

[3] Several of these arguments were used by the Procureur Général before the Belgian Cour de Cassation in *Minister for Economic Affairs* v. *SA Fromagerie Franco-Suisse 'Le Ski'* [1972] 2 CMLR 330, where he successfully persuaded the court that the supremacy of Community law over Belgian law should be acknowledged.

whether Community law should take precedence.[4] Not even a fundamental rule of national constitutional law could be invoked to challenge the supremacy of a directly applicable Community law.

Case 11/70 Internationale Handelsgesellschaft mbH v. Einfuhr- und Vorratsstelle für Getreide und Futtermittel
[1970] ECR 1125

The applicant argued that a Community regulation under which a deposit would be forfeited if the goods were not exported within the period of time set was contrary to principles of national constitutional law, including freedom of action and of disposition, economic liberty and proportionality.

THE ECJ

3. Recourse to the legal rules or concepts of national law in order to judge the validity of measures adopted by the institutions of the Community would have an adverse effect on the uniformity and efficacy of Community law. The validity of such measures can only be judged in the light of Community law. In fact, the law stemming from the Treaty, an independent source of law, cannot because of its very nature be overridden by rules of national law, however framed, without being deprived of its character as Community law and without the legal basis of the Community itself being called into question. Therefore the validity of a Community measure or its effect within a Member State cannot be affected by allegations that it runs counter to either fundamental rights as formulated by the constitution of that State or the principles of a national constitutional structure.

It will be seen below that this ruling gave rise for some time to a potentially serious conflict in the relationship between the German Constitutional Court and the Court of Justice. While the ECJ has sought to avoid a direct constitutional conflict with a national court,[5] it has never retreated from its claims.

The ECJ faced the opposite kind of argument in *Ciola*, where the Austrian government argued that the principle of primacy should not automatically apply 'to specific individual administrative acts'.[6] The Court dismissed this argument, reaffirming that any provision of national law which conflicted with directly effective Community law should not be applied. Thus the principle of primacy is equally asserted and required by the ECJ whenever directly effective EC law is concerned,[7] and regardless of whether fundamental national constitutional norms or minor administrative acts are at issue.

The ECJ in *Simmenthal* developed further its supremacy doctrine, by making clear that the supremacy of Community law applied irrespective of whether the national law pre-dated or post-dated the relevant Community law. A Community measure rendered inapplicable any

---

[4] See also Case C–473/93 *Commission* v. *Luxembourg* [1996] ECR I–3207, para. 38.

[5] See, e.g., Case C–446/98 *Fazenda Pública* v. *Câmara* [2000] ECR I–11435, paras. 36–38.

[6] Case C–224/97 *Ciola* v. *Land Vorarlberg* [1999] ECR I–2517, para. 24. The government claimed that such automatic application to all administrative acts would undermine the principles of legal certainty and legitimate expectations.

[7] For the application of the *Simmenthal* reasoning and the principle of primacy to the decisions of Association Councils see Case C–65/98 *Eyup* v. *Landesgeschäftstelle* [2000] ECR I–4747, para. 41.

conflicting provision of national law and prevented the adoption of new national law that would conflict with Community law.

Case 106/77 Amministrazione delle Finanze dello Stato v. Simmenthal SpA
[1978] ECR 629

The respondent company, which had imported beef from France into Italy, brought an action before the Pretore claiming repayment of the fees which had been charged to it for a veterinary inspection at the frontier, on the basis that the charge was incompatible with EC law. The ECJ, on a preliminary reference, ruled that such charges were indeed contrary to the Treaty. When the Pretore therefore ordered repayment of the amounts with interest, the Italian fiscal author-ities objected that the national court could not simply refuse to apply a national law which con-flicted with Community law, but must first bring the matter before the Italian Constitutional Court to have the Italian law declared unconstitutional. The Pretore therefore referred the case again to the ECJ, asking whether in these circumstances the national law must be disregarded forthwith without waiting until it was set aside by the appropriate constitutional authority.

THE ECJ

17. Furthermore, in accordance with the principle of the precedence of Community law, the relationship between provisions of the Treaty and directly applicable measures of the institu-tions on the one hand and the national law of the Member States on the other is such that those provisions and measures not only by their entry into force render automatically inapplic-able any conflicting provision of current national law but—in so far as they are an integral part of, and take precedence in, the legal order applicable in the territory of each of the Member States—also preclude the valid adoption of new national legislative measures to the extent to which they would be incompatible with Community provisions.

18. Indeed any recognition that national legislative measures which encroach upon the field within which the Community exercises its legislative power or which are otherwise incompat-ible with the provisions of Community law had any legal effect would amount to a correspond-ing denial of the effectiveness of obligations undertaken unconditionally and irrevocably by Member States pursuant to the Treaty and would thus imperil the very foundations of the Community.

...

21. It follows from the foregoing that every national court must, in a case within its jurisdic-tion, apply Community law in its entirety and protect rights which the latter confers on individ-uals and must accordingly set aside any provision of national law which may conflict with it, whether prior or subsequent to the Community rule.

(c) THE NATIONAL BODIES THAT MUST
APPLY THE SUPREMACY DOCTRINE:
SIMMENTHAL, LARSY, CIF

The cases considered thus far laid the foundations for the supremacy doctrine and determined its ambit. They did not however address a separate issue, this being which national courts could apply the supremacy doctrine. This was of special concern in many civil law countries, where it was often only the Constitutional Court which could, according to national law, declare a national law to be unconstitutional. This issue came before the ECJ in *Simmenthal*, where the Italian tax authorities questioned the Pretore's order awarding the repayment of fees which had been charged under an existing national law, before it had been adjudicated upon by the Constitutional Court.

Case 106/77 **Amministrazione delle Finanze dello Stato v. Simmenthal SpA**
[1978] ECR 629

THE ECJ

21. It follows from the foregoing that every national court must, in a case within its jurisdiction, apply Community law in its entirety and protect rights which the latter confers on individuals and must accordingly set aside any provision of national law which may conflict with it, whether prior or subsequent to the Community rule.

22. Accordingly any provision of a national legal system and any legislative, administrative or judicial practice which might impair the effectiveness of Community law by withholding from the national court having jurisdiction to apply such law the power to do everything necessary at the moment of its application to set aside national legislative provisions which might prevent Community rules from having full force and effect are incompatible with those requirements which are the very essence of Community law.

23. This would be the case in the event of a conflict between a provision of Community law and a subsequent national law if the solution of the conflict were to be reserved for an authority with a discretion of its own, other than the court called upon to apply Community law, even if such an impediment to the full effectiveness of Community law were only temporary.

24. The first question should therefore be answered to the effect that a national court which is called upon, within the limits of its jurisdiction, to apply provisions of Community law is under a duty to give full effect to those provisions, if necessary refusing of its own motion to apply any conflicting provision of national legislation, even if adopted subsequently, and it is not necessary for the court to request or await the prior setting aside of such provision by legislative or other constitutional means.

The clear message from the ECJ was that, even if the Constitutional Court was the only national court empowered to pronounce on the constitutionality of a national law, where a conflict between national law and Community law arose before another national court, that court must give immediate effect to the Community law without awaiting the prior ruling of the constitutional court. This ruling has been affirmed many times. It was of great significance both practically and conceptually. The supremacy of EC law penetrated throughout the national legal system and was to be applied by all national courts in cases that fell within their jurisdiction. It was not necessary for an individual to fight her way through to the national constitutional court. The national court seised of the dispute could itself refuse to apply provisions of national law that conflicted with EC law.

The *Simmenthal* principle was applied and extended in the *Factortame* case.[8] UK law did not at that time allow interim relief to be claimed against the Crown. The ECJ repeated much

---

[8] Case C–213/89 *R. v. Secretary of State for Transport, ex p. Factortame Ltd. and others* [1990] ECR I–2433.

of the *Simmenthal* ruling on the need for effectiveness and for the automatic precedence of directly effective Community law over national law, and then stated:[9]

> It must be added that the full effectiveness of Community law would be just as much impaired if a rule of national law could prevent a court seised of a dispute governed by Community law from granting interim relief in order to ensure the full effectiveness of the judgment to be given on the existence of the rights claimed under Community law. It follows that a court which in those circumstances would grant interim relief, if it were not for a rule of national law, is obliged to set aside that rule.

The *Simmenthal* principle was further extended in *Larsy*, where the ECJ ruled that not only national courts but also the relevant administrative agencies, in this case a national social insurance institution, should disapply conflicting national laws in order to give effect to the primacy of Community law.[10]

(d) IMPACT ON NATIONAL LAW: *SIMMENTHAL* AND *KAPFERER*

We have seen that according to the ECJ a Community measure renders inapplicable any conflicting provision of national law and prevents the adoption of new national law that would conflict with Community law. Two points should be made by way of further clarification.

First, the *Simmenthal* principle does not require the national court to invalidate or annul the provision of national law that conflicts with EC law, but rather to refuse to apply it, and considerations of legal certainty may mean that the inapplicability of the national law will not expose those who relied on it to penalties.[11] This distinction between disapplying and nullifying national law was emphasized in the *IN.CO.GE '90* case. The ECJ rejected the Commission's argument that the incompatibility of EC law with a subsequently adopted rule of national law must render the national rule non-existent.[12]

> It cannot therefore, contrary to the Commission's contention, be inferred from the judgment in *Simmenthal* that the incompatibility with Community law of a subsequently adopted rule of national law has the effect of rendering that rule of national law non-existent. Faced with such a situation, the national court is, however, obliged to disapply that rule, provided always that this obligation does not restrict the power of the competent national courts to apply, from among the various procedures available under national law, those which are appropriate for protecting the individual rights conferred by Community law.

Secondly, it is clear from *Kapferer*[13] that a national court is not always obliged to review and set aside a final judicial decision that infringes Community law. The ECJ recognized the importance of the principle of *res judicata*, whereby judicial decisions which have become

---

9 *Ibid.*, para. 21.
10 Case C–118/00 *Larsy* v. *INASTI* [2001] ECR I–5063, paras. 52–53. See also Case C–198/01 *CIF* v. *Autorita Garante della Concorrenza del Mercato* [2003] ECR I–8055.
11 Case C–198/01 *CIF*, n. 10 above.
12 Cases C–10–22/97 *Ministero delle Finanze* v. *IN.CO.GE '90 Srl* [1998] ECR I–6307, para. 21.
13 Case C–234/04 *Kapferer* v. *Schlanck and Schick* [2006] ECR I–2585.

definitive can no longer be called into question. Community law did not therefore require a national court to disapply domestic rules of procedure conferring finality on a decision, even if to do so would enable it to remedy an infringement of Community law by the decision at issue. The relevant national procedural rules must however comply with the principles of equivalence and effectiveness.[14]

(e) SUPREMACY: THE SECOND AND THIRD PILLARS

The discussion thus far has focused on supremacy in relation to the Community Pillar. It is not entirely clear whether this doctrine is also applicable in relation to the Second and Third Pillars, an issue that is becoming of increasing importance given the volume of material produced particularly under the Third Pillar.

Lenaerts and Corthaut argue that the reasoning in *Costa* used to justify supremacy can be equally applied to the Second and Third Pillars, and that the need to ensure the consistent application of EU law in all States operates with similar force in this area. They set out the basic rule from *Costa* and then continue as follows.

**K. Lenaerts and T. Corthaut, Of Birds and Hedges:
The Role of Primacy in Invoking Norms of EU Law[15]**

The same principle applies in the second and third pillar as well. . . . The same reasons that led the Court in *Costa v ENEL* to proclaim the primacy of EC law are easily transposed to the EU legal order. The EU is similarly established for an indefinite period, and provided with its own organs (actually the same organs as the EC), and, in a functional sense, legal personality. Furthermore, the Union has practical competences, transferred to it by the Member States, allowing the Union to do such diverse things as adopting a common definition of terrorism, imposing sanctions against third states, helping out victims of crime and sending troops and policemen on peacekeeping missions across the Globe after concluding international treaties solely in the name of the Union. As a corollary, it can thus be argued that in those areas the sovereignty of the Member States has been limited. From there it does not take much imagination to submit that the Member States have created a legal order which is binding on them, even if no enforcement mechanism similar to Arts 226 to 228 is available.

. . .

One could think that only provisions of EU law enjoying direct effect could be awarded this type of precedence. . . . This is however not a necessity, even though primacy and direct effect are not entirely unrelated. It appears from *Costa* that the real concern is consistency: to the extent that a national measure is inconsistent with EC law, it cannot be allowed to apply over EC law. But if we take consistency seriously, there is no need for identifying whether a provision confers rights on individuals. The only thing that matters is that EC law, and by extension EU law, puts forward an identifiable result which cannot be thwarted by incompatible national measures. This result may often involve granting rights to individuals, but may also involve an obligation on a government to create the conditions under which rights are granted to individuals, as will almost always be the case with Directives. . . . When it comes to precedence the only question is whether a conflict can be identified. In principle, if that is the case the conflicting

---

[14] See Ch. 9 for discussion of these principles.
[15] (2006) 31 *ELRev.* 287, 289–291.

provision of national law has to yield. This also means, however, that the exclusion only applies to the extent of the conflict.

All this changes, however, when EU law itself grants rights to individuals, which would otherwise not exist in the national legal order. At that stage, we are not merely concerned with removing inconsistencies from the legal order, but with actively imposing a particular burden on an identifiable debtor for the benefit of an identifiable creditor that would otherwise not exist. It is only then that direct effect comes into play ... In those circumstances, it does not suffice to stop the application of inconsistent national law, as EU law must be put in place to fill the gaps in the national legal order. Then it does matter whether the norm relied upon was intended to confer rights upon individuals, and whether it is sufficiently clear, precise and unconditional, because, on the one hand, the norm identifies the object of the benefit claimed and the person who must provide the benefit and, on the other hand, the norm indicates when and under what conditions this right can be deemed to be created in the legal order allowing for the right to be claimed.

Some commentators may disagree with this conclusion. The reasoning does however focus on the right issues. If we are to reach a principled conclusion as to whether supremacy applies to the Second and Third Pillars then it makes good sense to see whether the reasoning in *Costa*, which laid the foundations for supremacy in Pillar One, can be applied by way of analogy. Their reasoning concerning direct effect and supremacy also focuses on the salient issues. Whether a provision is intended to accord rights to individuals, and whether it is sufficiently well-defined to do so, is conceptually distinct from the issue of supremacy. There is therefore nothing odd in principle with an EU norm being regarded as supreme, with the correlative obligation on the national authorities to disapply conflicting national law, even if the norm does not fulfil the conditions for direct effect. Moreover, even if such a norm does not give rise to rights *stricto sensu*, this does not preclude an individual being able to rely on it in order to exclude inconsistent national law.[16] The ECJ was indeed willing to apply the principle of indirect effect to the Third Pillar in *Pupino*.[17] It did not address the issue of supremacy, but this should not be taken as an implicit indication that measures enacted under the Third Pillar do not have primacy over national law. The ECJ was willing to apply principles such as loyal cooperation from the Community Pillar to the Third Pillar, and there is much in its reasoning that sits comfortably with the precepts underpinning the *Costa* case.

(f) CONCLUSION

The supremacy of Community law and the requirement that national courts must ensure its practical effectiveness are thus, as far as the ECJ was concerned, established beyond question in a consistent line of case law.

There are certain provisions of the EC Treaty which some may view as a partial dilution of the supremacy principle, such as Article 307, which relieves Member States of the obligation to ensure the primacy of EC law in certain circumstances,[18] or Article 297, which appears to

---

[16] See above 287–303 for discussion of circumstances in which an individual is able to rely on a norm of Community law before a national court, even where the norm does not have direct effect.

[17] Case C–105/03 *Criminal Proceedings against Maria Pupino* [2005] ECR I–5283. For more detailed discussion see 250–253.

[18] Art. 307 EC, e.g., provides a limited exception to the obligation of Member States to ensure the supremacy of EC law where conflicting state obligations arise from agreements concluded with non-Member States before the entry into force of the EC Treaty: see, e.g., Case C–158/91 *Ministère Public and Direction du Travail et de l'Emploi* v. *Levy* [1993] ECR I–4287; Case C–13/93 *Office Nationale de l'Emploi* v. *Minne* [1994] ECR I–371; Case

carve out an area within which the Member States retain a degree of sovereignty.[19]
Nonetheless, these are provisions of limited scope, and the basic principle of supremacy articulated by the ECJ is a broad and general one.

Nevertheless, this constitutes only one part of the supremacy story. Ultimately, the acceptance and practical application of the primacy of EC law are dependent on the adaptation and
acquiescence of the legal and constitutional orders of the Member States.

J. Weiler, The Community System: the Dual Character of Supranationalism[20]

As in the case of 'direct effect' the derivation of supremacy from the Treaty depended on a
'constitutional' rather than international law interpretation. The Court's reasoning that
supremacy was enshrined in the Treaty was contested by the governments of Member States
in this case and others. Acceptance of this view amounts in effect to a quiet revolution in the
legal orders of the Member States. . . .

It follows that the evolutionary nature of the doctrine of supremacy is necessarily bidimen-
sional. One dimension is the elaboration of the parameters of the doctrine by the European
Court. But its full reception, the second dimension, depends on its incorporation into the constitutional orders of the Member States and its affirmation by their supreme courts. It is relatively easy to trace the evolution of the Community dimension of the doctrine. . . .

As regards the second dimension, the evolutionary character of the process is more complicated. It should be remembered that in respect of the original Member States there was no
specific constitutional preparation for this European Court-inspired development.

3. THE SECOND DIMENSION: SUPREMACY FROM THE PERSPECTIVE OF THE MEMBER STATES

This evolutionary process of acceptance of supremacy noted by Joseph Weiler is still evident
today. There is a continuing tension between national accounts of the character of
Community law and the ECJ's account. Constitutional conflicts continue to arise in specific
cases, and it remains ultimately for national courts to resolve particular cases arising before
them involving a conflict between Community law and national law.[21]

The accommodation so far reached by the courts of various Member States on the issue of
the primacy of Community law will now be examined. For reasons of space, only a small number of the Member States are selected for discussion.[22] It may be helpful to frame the subsequent discussion by distinguishing four more particular issues that can arise in any Member
State concerning the supremacy issue.

C–124/95 R., ex p. Centro-Com Srl v. HM Treasury and Bank of England [1997] ECR I–81; Case C–55/00
Gottardo v. INPS [2002] ECR I–413; J. Klabbers, 'Moribund on the Fourth of July? The Court of Justice on the
Prior Agreements of the Member States' (2001) 26 ELRev. 187 and C. Hillion (2001) 38 CMLRev. 1269.

[19] See, e.g., P. Koutrakos, 'Is Article 297 EC a "Reserve of Sovereignty"' (2000) 37 CMLRev. 1339.
[20] (1981) 1 YBEL 267, 275–276.
[21] M. Claes, The National Courts' Mandate in the European Constitution (Hart, 2006).
[22] A-M. Slaughter, A. Stone Sweet, and J. Weiler (eds.), The ECJ and National Courts: Doctrine and
Jurisprudence (Hart, 1998); K. Alter, Establishing the Supremacy of European Law: The Making of an International
Rule of Law in Europe (Oxford University Press, 2001); N. Walker (ed.), Sovereignty in Transition (Hart, 2003).

i.   The first is whether the Member State accepts the supremacy of Community law, assuming that the EC acts within its proper sphere of competence. The general answer to this question is affirmative, subject to the qualifications flowing from the other three issues.

ii. Assuming an affirmative answer to this first question, the second issue is the conceptual basis on which the Member State accords supremacy to EC law. It may choose to do so because it accepts the ECJ's *communautaire* reasoning in *Costa*, or because of a provision within its own national legal order. For the great majority of Member States the latter rather than the former provides the conceptual foundation for its acceptance of supremacy.

iii. The third important issue is whether the national legal order places limits on its acceptance of Community law supremacy derived from its own national constitution, and/or national fundamental rights. We have seen that the ECJ regards the supremacy of EC law as operating against all species of national law, including the national constitution. On this view any norm of EC law trumps any norm of national law. This proposition is not generally accepted by Member States.

iv. The final issue is known as *Kompetenz-Kompetenz*. It addresses the issue of who has ultimate authority to define the allocation of competence as between the Community and the Member States. The ECJ under Article 220 EC regards this to be its task, whereas virtually all national constitutional or supreme courts determine such questions ultimately by reference to their own national constitutional provisions, although they will treat with respect the ECJ's own view on the matter.

(a) FRANCE

(i) *Case Law and Doctrine*

The French judicial system is divided between the administrative courts and the ordinary courts. In 1970 the supreme administrative court, the Conseil d'Etat, rejected in practice the supremacy of Community law over national law.[23] In *Semoules*,[24] the Conseil d'Etat ruled that, since it had no jurisdiction to review the validity of French legislation, it could not find such legislation to be incompatible with Community law, nor could it accord priority to the latter. This was so notwithstanding the fact that the French Constitution provided for the primacy of certain international treaties over domestic law, since the Conseil d'Etat held that decisions on the constitutionality of legislation were for the Conseil Constitutionnel, the Constitutional Council, to make before the legislation was promulgated.

A doctrinal 'split' occurred when the supremacy of Community law over French law was accepted in 1975 in *Café Jacques Vabres* by the Cour de Cassation,[25] the highest of the ordinary judicial courts, in a case concerning a conflict between Article 90 EC and a later provision of the French Customs Code. Following the suggestion of the Procureur Général, the Cour held that the question was not whether it could review the constitutionality of a French law. Instead, when a conflict existed between an 'internal law' and a properly ratified 'international act' which had thus entered the internal legal order, the Constitution itself accorded priority

---

[23] D. Pollard, 'The Conseil d'Etat is European—Official' (1990) 15 *ELRev.* 267, 268–270 and 'European Community Law and the French Conseil d'Etat' (1992–5) 30 *Irish Jurist* 79.

[24] Decision of 1 Mar. 1968 in *Syndicat Général de Fabricants de Semoules de France* [1970] CMLR 395.

[25] Decision of 24 May 1975 in *Administration des Douanes* v. *Société 'Cafés Jacques Vabre' et Sàrl Weigel et Cie.* [1975] 2 CMLR 336.

to the latter. Respect for the principle of the primacy of international treaties should not be left to the Conseil Constitutionnel to secure, since it was the duty of the ordinary courts before which such problems actually arose to do justice in the case.

It was not until 1989 that the Conseil d'Etat finally abandoned its so-called 'splendid isolation' and decided, in its capacity as an electoral court, to adopt the same position as the Conseil Constitutionnel and the Cour de Cassation.[26]

Raoul Georges Nicolo
[1990] 1 CMLR 173

The applicants were French citizens who brought an action for the annulment of the European Parliament elections in France in 1989, on the ground that the right to vote and to stand had been given to French citizens in the non-European overseas departments and territories of France. It was argued that the French statutory rule under challenge—Act 77–729—was contrary to the EEC Treaty.

COMMISSAIRE FRYDMAN[27]

However, the whole difficulty is then to decide whether, in conformity with your settled case law, you should dismiss this second argument by relying on the 1977 Act alone, without even having to verify whether it is compatible with the Treaty of Rome, or whether you should break fresh ground today by deciding that the Act is applicable only because it is compatible precisely with the Treaty.

In this connection we know that you held, in the famous divisional decision of 1 March 1968, *Syndicat Général des Fabricants de Semoules de France* that an administrative court cannot accord treaties precedence over subsequent legislation which conflicts with them and that this case law applies to Community rules just as much as to ordinary international conventions....

The theoretical foundation of these decisions, which clearly does not take the form of an objection to the principle of the superiority of treaties over statutes, which is expressly stated by Article 55, should rather be sought in your wish to uphold the principle that it is not for the administrative courts to review the validity of legislation....

On the other hand I believe it is possible to take the view that ... Article 55 of itself necessarily enables the courts, by implication, to review the compatibility of statutes with treaties. Indeed, we must attribute to the authors of the Constitution an intention to provide for actual implementation of the supremacy of treaties which they embodied in that provision....

On this basis, therefore, I propose that you should agree to give treaties precedence over later statutes.

... I am aware that the Court of Justice of the European Communities—which, as we know, gives the Community law absolute supremacy over the rules of national law, even if they are constitutional—has not hesitated for its part to affirm the obligation to refuse to apply in any situation laws which are contrary to Community measures.

I do not think you can follow the European Court in this judge-made law which, in truth, seems to me at least open to objection. Were you to do so, you would tie yourself to a supranational

---

[26] Dec. of 20 Oct. 1989 in *Nicolo*. It has been suggested that earlier decisions of the Conseil Constitutionnel, which indicated that it was for the other French courts to ensure that international treaties were applied, acted as a spur to the Conseil d'Etat to reverse its original position. See P. Oliver, 'The French Constitution and the Treaty of Maastricht' (1994) 43 *ICLQ* 1, 10.

[27] [1990] 1 CMLR 173, 177, 178.

way of thinking which is quite difficult to justify, to which the Treaty of Rome does not subscribe expressly and which would quite certainly render the Treaty unconstitutional, however it may be regarded in the political context. . . .

I therefore suggest that you should base your decision on Article 55 of the Constitution and extend its ambit to all international agreements.

The Conseil d'Etat, although it did not expressly adopt the Commissaire's view, appeared to accept the premise underlying that view. It ruled that the French statutory rules were not invalid on the ground that they were 'not incompatible with the clear stipulations of the abovementioned Article 227(1) of the Treaty of Rome'.[28]

By 1989 both the Cour de Cassation and the Conseil d'Etat were therefore willing to accord primacy to Community law over national law, and hence to give an affirmative answer to the first of the issues set out at the beginning of this section.

It was however equally clear that the answer to the second question, the conceptual basis on which supremacy was accorded to Community law, was Article 55 of the French Constitution and not the *communautaire* reasoning of the ECJ in *Costa*. In *Café Jacques Vabres* the Procureur Général tried to persuade the Cour de Cassation to adopt the ECJ's reasoning, and to base the supremacy of Community law on the very nature of the EU legal order. The Cour de Cassation however grounded its decision on Article 55 of the French Constitution. The Conseil d'Etat's ruling in *Nicolo* also rested on Article 55 of the French Constitution, which provides for the superiority of international treaties over national law, and in this case *Commissaire* Frydman discouraged the Conseil d'Etat from subscribing to the ECJ's 'supra-national way of thinking'.

The Conseil d'Etat has also, since *Nicolo*, recognized the primacy of both Community regulations and directives over French statutes, without discussing the theoretical basis for that supremacy,[29] but it has not recognized the primacy of EC law over the Constitution itself.[30] It is therefore reasonably clear that the French courts do not accept the supremacy of Community law over all national law, as stipulated in the ECJ's jurisprudence. This therefore provides the answer to the third of the issues set out earlier. Community law is held to rank above statute, but below the Constitution.

This view is reinforced by the approach taken by the Conseil Constitutionnel in relation to amendments to the French Constitution consequent upon the Maastricht and Amsterdam Treaties. According to the Conseil, in order for the transfer of competences required by these Treaties to be compatible with the French Constitution, the 'essential conditions for the exercise

---

[28] Pollard, n. 23 above, 271, 273–274.

[29] See *Boisdet* [1991] 1 CMLR 3, on a reg. which was adopted after the French law, and *Rothmans and Philip Morris* and *Arizona Tobacco and Philip Morris* [1993] 1 CMLR 253 on a dir. adopted before the French law. For comment see H. Cohen (1991) 16 *ELRev.* 144; P. Roseren, 'The Application of Community Law by French Courts From 1982 to 1993' (1994) 31 *CMLRev.* 315, 342, argues that Art. 55 cannot explain the primacy of Community *secondary* legislation over French law in cases such as *Boisdet* and *Rothmans*.

[30] In *Sarran and Levacher*, Dec. of 30 Oct. 1998, the Conseil d'Etat declared that Art. 55 does not give international treaties a position of precedence over the Constitution itself or over provisions of a constitutional nature. The case did not concern EC law. For discussion See C. Richards, 'Sarran et Levacher: Ranking Legal Norms in the French Republic' (2000) 25 *ELRev.* 192. The Cour de Cassation gave a similar ruling in the *Fraisse* case on 2 June 2000. For discussion of both cases see V. Kronenberger, 'A New Approach to the Interpretation of the French Constitution in Respect of International Conventions' (2000) 47 *NILR* 323. More recently the Conseil d'Etat stated that the supremacy of EC law could not lead, within the national legal order, to calling into question the supremacy of the French Constitution: CE, 3 Dec. 2001, *Syndicat National de l'Industrie de Pharmaceutique*. See, however, CE, 8 Feb. 2007, *Arcelor*.

of national sovereignty' must not be affected.[31] The Conseil Constitutionnel has tended to base its reasoning on the relationship between EU law and national law on Article 88–1 of the French Constitution.[32] It ruled in relation to the Constitutional Treaty that where Treaty amendments contained a clause that ran counter to the French Constitution, called into question constitutionally guaranteed rights and freedoms or adversely affected the fundamental conditions of the exercising of national sovereignty, then authorization to ratify such measures required prior revision of the Constitution.[33]

The Conseil Constitutionnel has, in a series of cases concerning transposition of directives, based the supremacy of Community law on Article 88–1 of the French Constitution, but has made it clear that if a directive conflicts with an express contrary provision of the Constitution then the constitutional requirement to transpose the directive no longer applies and the transposing law cannot enter into force.[34]

(ii) Summary

i. In France, the main initial obstacle to the recognition of supremacy of EC law has been the jurisdictional limitation of the French courts under the Constitution, rather than, as in other Member States, difficulties concerning the fundamental constitutional status of the norms which appeared to conflict with Community law The French courts do now accept, subject to what is said below, the supremacy of Community law over national law.

ii. The primacy accorded to Community law is however 'not by virtue of the inherent nature of Community law as the Court of Justice would have it, but under the authority of their own national legal order'.[35] It is Article 55 or Article 88–1 of the French Constitution that provides the conceptual foundation for the acceptance of supremacy in France.

iii. The French courts do not it seems accept that Community law takes precedence over the Constitution.

iv. There has not been a clear case in the French courts raising the issue of *Kompetenz-Kompetenz*, but the predominant academic view is that this would be regarded as residing in the French courts.

(b) GERMANY

(i) Case Law and Doctrine

Article 24 of the German Constitution allows for the transfer of legislative power to international organizations, but the question raised in the following case was whether Article 24 permitted the transfer to an organization such as the EC, of a power to contravene certain basic principles protected under the Constitution itself.

---

[31] The criteria for determining these essential conditions are not entirely clear, A. Bonnie, 'The Constitutionality of Transfers of Sovereignty: The French Approach' (1998) 4 *EPL* 517; J. Plötner, 'Report on France', in Slaughter *et al.*, n. 22 above.

[32] Which provides that France shall participate in the EC and the EU 'constituted by States that have freely chosen, by virtue of the Treaties that establish them, to exercise some of their powers in common'.

[33] Dec. No. 2004–505 DC, 19 Nov. 2004.

[34] The Conseil Constitutionnel appears to have taken a narrow view of the term 'express constitutional provision': C. Richards, 'The Supremacy of Community Law before the French Constitutional Court' (2006) 31 *ELRev.* 499, 507–508.

[35] B. de Witte, 'Community Law and National Constitutional Values' (1991) 2 *LIEI* 1, 4 and also 'Direct Effect, Supremacy and the Nature of the Legal Order', in P. Craig and G. de Búrca (eds.), *The Evolution of EU Law* (Oxford University Press, 1999).

Internationale Handelsgesellschaft mbH v. Einfuhr- und Vorratstelle für Getreide und Futtermittel
[1974] 2 CMLR 540

The facts are those set out in Case 11/70 before the ECJ.[36] On receiving the ECJ's ruling, the German Administrative Court[37] decided that since Article 24 could not be equated with an amendment of the German Constitution the Federal legislature could not, when ratifying the EEC Treaty, disclaim the observance of elementary basic rights in the Constitution. It also expressed concern that if Community law were given precedence over divergent constitutional provisions, national constitutional law would be eliminated as the highest national check on European legislation that did not have equivalent legal safeguards. Consequently the Administrative Court ruled, in the face of the ECJ's conflicting judgment, that the Community's deposit system breached basic principles of German constitutional law, and it requested a ruling from the Federal Constitutional Court, the Bundesverfassungsgericht (BVerfG). This judgment, known as the 'Solange I' decision (so long as), was given by the BVerfG in 1974.

THE BUNDESVERFASSUNGSGERICHT (BVerfG)[38]

Article 24 of the Constitution deals with the transfer of sovereign rights to inter-state institutions. This ... does not open the way to amending the basic structure of the Constitution, which forms the basis of its identity, without a formal amendment to the Constitution, that is, it does not open any such way through the legislation of the inter-state institution. Certainly, the competent Community organs can make law which the competent German constitutional organs could not make under the law of the Constitution and which is none the less valid and is to be applied directly in the Federal Republic of Germany. But Article 24 of the Constitution limits this possibility in that it nullifies any amendment of the Treaty which would destroy the identity of the valid constitutional structure of the Federal Republic of Germany by encroaching on the structures which go to make it up....

The part of the Constitution dealing with fundamental rights is an inalienable essential feature of the valid Constitution of the Federal Republic of Germany and one which forms part of the constitutional structure of the Constitution. Article 24 of the Constitution does not without reservation allow it to be subjected to qualifications. In this, the present state of integration of the Community is of crucial importance. The Community still lacks a democratically legitimated Parliament directly elected by general suffrage which possesses legislative powers and to which the Community organs empowered to legislate are fully responsible on a political level. It still lacks in particular a codified catalogue of fundamental rights, the substance of which is reliably and unambiguously fixed for the future in the same way as the substance of the Constitution....

Provisionally, therefore, in the hypothetical case of a conflict between Community law and ... the guarantees of fundamental rights in the Constitution ... the guarantee of fundamental rights in the Constitution prevails as long as the competent organs of the Community have not removed the conflict of norms in accordance with the Treaty mechanism.

The highest German court therefore refused to recognize the unconditional supremacy of Community law, because of the possible impact of EC law on basic rights enshrined in the

---

[36] See above 347.
[37] [1972] CMLR 177, 184.
[38] [1974] 2 CMLR 540, 549–550.

German Constitution. It ruled that Article 24 of the Constitution could not cover a transfer of power to amend an 'inalienable essential feature' of the German constitutional structure, such as its protection for fundamental rights. The BVerfG would not abandon its jurisdiction to decide which legislative transfers would alter an unalterable feature of the Constitution, and the protection of fundamental rights in the German Constitution would prevail over Community law in the event of conflict.

In 1986, however, in a case in which an EC import licensing system was challenged despite an ECJ ruling on its validity,[39] the BVerfG delivered its so-called *Solange II* judgment, which qualified the 1974 *Solange I* judgment to a considerable extent. Solange means 'so long as' and it refers to the statement of the BVerfG that so long as the Community had not removed the possible 'conflict of norms' between Community law and national constitutional rights, the German court would ensure that those rights took precedence.

Re Wünsche Handelsgesellschaft
[1987] 3 CMLR 225

Having considered various changes in Community law since the 1974 decision, including the ECJ's development of protection for fundamental rights, the adoption of various declarations on rights and democracy by the Community institutions,[40] and the fact that all EC Member States had acceded to the European Convention on Human Rights, the BVerfG in *Solange II* ruled as follows.[41]

THE BUNDESVERFASSUNGSGERICHT (BVERFG)

In view of these developments, it must be held that, *so long as* the European Communities, and in particular the case law of the European Court, generally ensure an effective protection of fundamental rights as against the sovereign powers of the Communities which is to be regarded as substantially similar to the protection of fundamental rights required unconditionally by the Constitution, and in so far as they generally safeguard the essential content of fundamental rights, the Federal Constitutional Court will no longer exercise its jurisdiction to decide on the applicability of secondary Community legislation cited as the legal basis for any acts of German courts or authorities within the sovereign jurisdiction of the Federal Republic of Germany, and it will no longer review such legislation by the standard of the fundamental rights contained in the Constitution.

The *Solange II* decision rendered a clash between EC law and national law over fundamental rights less likely. It should nonetheless be recognized, as Frowein makes clear, that the court in *Solange II* did not surrender jurisdiction over fundamental rights, but only stated that it would not exercise that jurisdiction as long as the present conditions as to the protection of fundamental rights by the ECJ prevailed.[42] The Federal Constitutional Court preserved its final authority to intervene if real problems concerning the protection of fundamental rights

---

[39] Case 345/82 *Wünsche Handelsgesellschaft v. Germany* [1984] ECR 1995.

[40] See Ch. 11.

[41] *Re Wünsche Handelsgesellschaft*, Decision of 22 Oct. 1986 [1987] 3 CMLR 225, 265.

[42] J. Frowein, 'Solange II' (1988) 25 *CMLRev.* 201, 203–204. See also W. Roth, 'The Application of Community Law in West Germany: 1980–1990' (1991) 28 *CMLRev.* 137.

in Community law arose. It is nonetheless clear that the German courts are reluctant to exercise the jurisdiction which they retain.

This is exemplified by the ruling given by the Federal Constitutional Court concerning a claim that certain Community regulations concerning bananas interfered with the right to pursue a trade and the right to property as protected by the German Constitution. The BVerfG deemed the reference inadmissible.[43] The Constitutional Court stated that it had already declared itself satisfied, in its *Solange II* and *Maastricht* decisions, with the fact that human rights protection within the EC legal order was generally comparable to the level of human rights protection under the German Basic Law. Consequently, constitutional complaints attacking secondary Community law on the basis of German fundamental rights would be inadmissible *ab initio* if they did not argue that the general level of European human rights protection, including ECJ case law since *Solange II*, fell below the necessary level, as compared to German levels of protection.

The most dramatic stage in the story, however, came with the so-called 'Maastricht judgment' of the BVerfG, when the constitutionality of the State's ratification of the Treaty on European Union was challenged.

Brunner v. The European Union Treaty
[1994] 1 CMLR 57

Germany had completed the legislative part of the TEU ratification process in 1992, amending its Constitution, but before the Federal President signed the formal instrument of ratification, constitutional complaints were made to the BVerfG. It decided that ratification was compatible with the Constitution, but it ruled not just on Germany's constitutional competence to ratify the TEU, but also on what the future position would be if the Community attempted to exercise powers which were not clearly provided for in the Treaties. The judgment provoked a great deal of comment.[44] Affirming the sovereignty of the German State, the Constitutional Court made clear that it would not relinquish its power to decide on the compatibility of Community law with the fundamentals of the German Constitution and would continue to exercise a power of review over the scope of Community competence.

THE BUNDESVERFASSUNGSGERICHT (BVᴇʀғG)

13. ... The Federal Constitutional Court by its jurisdiction guarantees that an effective protection of basic rights for the inhabitants of Germany will also generally be maintained as

---

[43] Decision of 7 June 2000; A. Peters, 'The Bananas Decision 2000 of the German Federal Constitutional Court: Towards Reconciliation with the ECJ as regards Fundamental Rights Protection in Europe' (2000) 43 *German Yearbook of International Law* 276; C. Schmid, 'All Bark and No Bite: Notes on the Federal Constitutional Court's "Banana Decision" ' (2001) 7 *ELJ* 95; F. Hoffmeister (2001) 38 *CMLRev.* 791; M. Aziz, 'Sovereignty Lost, Sovereignty Regained: the European Integration Project and the BVerfG', Robert Schuman Centre Working Paper, EUI 2001/31.

[44] For some of the English-language commentaries see M. Herdegen, 'Maastricht and the German Constitutional Court: Constitutional Restraints for an Ever Closer Union' (1994) 31 *CMLRev.* 235; U. Everling, 'The Maastricht Judgment of the German Federal Constitutional Court and its Significance for the Development of the European Union' (1994) 14 *YBEL* 1; M. Zulegg, 'The European Constitution under Constitutional Constraints: The German Scenario' (1997) 22 *ELRev.* 19; J.H.H. Weiler, 'Does Europe Need a Constitution? Reflections on Demos, Telos and the German Maastricht Decision' (1995) 1 *ELJ* 219; N. MacCormick, 'The Maastricht-Urteil: Sovereignty Now' (1995) 1 *ELJ* 259; J. Kokott, 'German Constitutional Jurisprudence and European Integration' (1996) 2 *EPL* 237 and 413.

against the sovereign powers of the Communities and will be accorded the same respect as the protection of basic rights acquired unconditionally by the Constitution, and in particular the Court provides a general safeguard of the essential content of the basic rights. The Court thus guarantees this essential content as against the sovereign powers of the Community as well. . . .

48. There is . . . a breach of Article 38 of the Constitution if an Act that opens up the German legal system to the direct validity and application of the law of the (supranational) European Communities does not establish with sufficient certainty the intended programme of integration. If it is not clear to what extent and degree the German legislature has assented to the transfer of the exercise of sovereign powers, then it will be possible for the European Community to claim functions and powers that were not specified. That would be equivalent to a general enablement and would therefore be a surrender of powers, something against which Article 38 of the Constitution provides protection.

. . .

55. The Federal Republic of Germany, therefore, even after the Union Treaty comes into force, will remain a member of a federation of States, the common authority of which is derived from the Member States and can only have binding effects within the German sovereign sphere by virtue of the German instruction that its law be applied. Germany is one of the 'Masters of the Treaties' which have established their adherence to the Union Treaty concluded 'for an unlimited period' with the intention of long-term membership, but could ultimately revoke that adherence by a contrary act. The validity and application of European law in Germany depends on the application-of-law instruction of the Accession Act. Germany thus preserves the quality of a sovereign state in its own right.

. . .

99. Inasmuch as the Treaties establishing the European Communities, on the one hand, confer sovereign rights applicable to limited factual circumstances and, on the other hand, provide for Treaty amendments . . . this distinction is also important for the future treatment of the individual powers. Whereas a dynamic extension of the existing Treaties has so far been supported on the basis of an open-handed treatment of Article 235 of the EEC Treaty as a 'competence to round off the Treaty' as a whole, and on the basis of considerations relating to the 'implied powers' of the Communities, and of Treaty interpretation as allowing maximum exploitation of Community powers (*effet utile*), in future it will have to be noted as regards interpretation of enabling provisions by Community institutions and agencies that the Union Treaty as a matter of principle distinguishes between the exercise of a sovereign power conferred for limited purposes and the amending of the Treaty, so that its interpretation may not have effects that are equivalent to an extension of the Treaty. Such an interpretation of enabling rules would not produce any binding effects for Germany.

This was a long and powerful judgment which warned the Community institutions and the ECJ that Germany's acceptance of the supremacy of Community law was conditional. The BVerfG emphasized its intention to ensure that the Community did not stray beyond the powers expressly conferred upon it in the Treaties by the Member States. Thus, even if German courts have accepted that, within its proper sphere of application, Community law should be given precedence over national law, the BVerfG asserted its jurisdiction to review the actions of European 'institutions and agencies', which presumably included the ECJ, to ensure that they remained within the limits of their powers and did not transgress the basic constitutional rights of German inhabitants.

Some of the more contentious aspects of the judgment concerned the BVerfG's comments about the nature of national democracy, and about the need for national democratic legitimation to express the 'spiritual, social and political' homogeneity of a people.[45] However, other sections of the judgment appear more open to the possibility that the EU could develop the conditions of political openness and the 'free interaction of social forces, interests and ideas' necessary for full democratic legitimation,[46] so that, presumably, a wider range of powers and competences could be transferred by Germany to the EU without breaching the basic principle of democracy guaranteed by the Constitution.

Since the drama of the Maastricht decision, some more concrete challenges to the supremacy of EC law and to the rulings of the ECJ arose before the German courts in a lengthy, contentious, and much-litigated dispute over the Community's banana import regime.[47] There are however signs that the threat of conflict between the ECJ and the German courts has subsided.

The June 2000 decision of the Bundesverfassungsgericht,[48] which rejected as inadmissible the claim that Community legislation violated German fundamental rights, was hailed as evidence of a renewed co-operative relationship between the two courts, and as an indication that the threat to the supremacy of EC law posed by the terms of the Maastricht judgment had subsided.[49] Commentators, looking at the bananas decision and another decision of the BverfG, suggested that the BVerfG had erected such high hurdles that 'it has become very improbable that the Constitutional Court will exercise its reserve control',[50] or its 'subsidiary emergency jurisdiction'[51] over the compatibility of EC law with the German constitution.[52]

The possibility of conflict between EU law and German constitutional law is nonetheless still present, as exemplified by the decision of the Constitutional Court[53] on the European Arrest Warrant.[54] However on this occasion the principal rationale for the Court's decision was that the national law implementing the Framework Decision on the European Arrest Warrant infringed certain principles of the German Basic law.[55]

(ii) *Summary*

i.   The German courts accept the primacy of Community law in circumstances where there is no conflict with the German Constitution and no issue about whether the Community had competence to act.

---

[45] Paras. 44–46 of the judgment, and the comments of Weiler about the *völkish* nature of this view of the demos, n. 44 above.

[46] Paras. 41–42.

[47] Case C–280/93 *Germany* v. *Commission* [1994] ECR I–4873; Case C–466/93 *Atlanta Fruchthandelsgesellschaft* v. *Bundesamt für Ernährung* [1995] ECR I–3799; Order of the Federal Tax Court, 9 Jan. 1996, 7 EuZW 126 (1996); U. Everling, 'Will Europe Slip on Bananas? The Bananas Judgment of the Court of Justice and National Courts' (1996) 33 *CMLRev.* 401; N. Reich, 'Judge-made Europe à la Carte' (1996) 7 *EJIL* 103.

[48] N. 43 above.

[49] U. Elbers and N. Urban, 'The Order of the German Federal Constitutional Court of 7 June 2000 and the Kompetenz-Kompetenz in the European Judicial System' (2001) 7 *EPL* 21, 32.

[50] F. Hoffmeister (2001) 38 *CMLRev.* 791, commenting also on the *Alcan* decision of the BVerfG on 17 Feb. 2000 EuZW 445 (2000).

[51] Peters, n. 43 above, 281.

[52] For a more critical view see, Schmid, n. 43 above, 106.

[53] Decision of 18 July 2005, 2BvR 2236/04.

[54] Council Framework Dec. 2002/584/JHA of 13 June 2002 on the European arrest warrant and the surrender procedures between Member States [2002] OJ L190/1. The ECJ has now held that this measure is valid: Case C–303/05 *Advocaten voor de Wereld VZW* v. *Leden van de Ministerraad*, 3 May 2007.

[55] It has however been argued by A. Hinarejos Parga (2006) 43 *CMLRev.* 583 that the Court might well have been able to interpret the implementing law to be in conformity with the Basic Law if the Court had used the principle of interpretation, which was held to apply to Pillar Three in Case C–105/03 *Pupino* [2005] ECR I–5285 to the instant case.

ii. The conceptual foundation for this acceptance of supremacy is not the *communautaire* reasoning of the ECJ, but Article 24, now Article 25, of the German Constitution.

iii. The German courts continue to possess jurisdiction where Community law impinges on fundamental rights protected by the German Constitution, but any claimant will have to show that the protection afforded by Community law is generally deficient before the German courts will exercise their jurisdiction.

iv. The German courts also regard themselves as possessing the ultimate *Kompetenz-Kompetenz* to decide whether action taken by the Community falls within the scope of Community competence. The more recent case law indicates however that they would only exercise such power in cases where the competence exercised by a Community institution was clearly in excess of that accorded by the Treaties.

(c) ITALY

(i) *Case Law and Doctrine*

Article 11 of the Italian Constitution permits such limitations of sovereignty as are necessary to an organization which ensures peace and justice between nations. This has formed the basis for the Italian courts' acceptance of the supremacy of Community law, although, as in the case of other Member States, this acceptance has not been unconditional.

Frontini v. Ministero delle Finanze
[1974] 2 CMLR 372

The plaintiff brought proceedings to challenge the applicability of increased agricultural levies, which had been imposed by EC regulation, on the import of meat into Italy. Frontini argued that the regulation was inapplicable in Italy, and the case was transmitted to the Italian Constitutional Court to determine the constitutional legitimacy of the Italian EEC Treaty Ratification Act 1957. That Act made Article 249 of the Treaty, providing for the direct applicability of Community regulations, effective in Italy.

THE COURT[56]

The EEC Treaty Ratification Act 1957, whereby the Italian Parliament gave full and complete execution to the Treaty instituting the EEC, has a sure basis of validity in Article 11 of the Constitution whereby Italy 'consents, on condition of reciprocity with other states, to limitations of sovereignty necessary for an arrangement which may ensure peace and justice between the nations' and then 'promotes and favours the international organizations directed to such an aim'. . . .

. . . It is hardly necessary to add that by Article 11 of the Constitution limitations of sovereignty are allowed solely for the purpose of the ends indicated therein, and it should therefore be excluded that such limitations of sovereignty, concretely laid out in the Rome Treaty, signed by countries whose systems are based on the principle of the rule of law and guarantee the essential liberties of citizens, can nevertheless give the organs of the EEC an unacceptable power to violate the fundamental principles of our constitutional order or the inalienable rights

---

56 [1974] 2 CMLR 372, 384.

of man. And it is obvious that if ever Article 189 had to be given such an aberrant interpretation, in such a case the guarantee would always be assured that this Court would control the continuing compatibility of the Treaty with the above mentioned fundamental principles.

While accepting the direct effect of Community law and confirming Italy's constitutional competence to ratify the EC Treaties, the Constitutional Court in *Frontini* expressed similar reservations to those of the German BVerfG, and confirmed that it would continue to review the exercise of power by the 'organs of the EEC' to ensure that there was no infringement of fundamental rights or of the basic principles of the Italian constitutional order.

Frontini was followed in 1984 by *Granital*,[57] in which the Italian Constitutional Court accepted that, in order to give effect to the supremacy of Community law, Italian courts must be prepared where necessary to disregard conflicting national law and to apply Community law directly. The national law would not be abrogated, but rather ignored in so far as the field in which it operated had been pre-empted by Community law. The national provisions would however survive and still govern the relevant subject-matter in areas beyond the scope of the Community act. However the Italian Constitutional Court was prepared to adjudicate not simply on questions of conflict between specific Community measures and fundamental Italian constitutional rights, but also on the basic question of the division of competence between national law and Community law.[58]

The possibility of conflict was demonstrated in *Fragd*,[59] in which the Italian Constitutional Court considered that a Community measure would not be applied in Italy if it contravened a fundamental principle of the Italian Constitution concerning human rights protection.

G. Gaja, New Developments in a Continuing Story: The Relationship between EEC Law and Italian Law[60]

While the *Frontini* decision by the Constitutional Court has often been viewed as a significant example of the willingness on the part of national courts to subject EEC legislation to constitutional rules concerning the protection of fundamental rights, little has happened so far to justify this evaluation. . . .

In *Spa Fragd* v. *Amministrazione delle Finanze*, the Court examined whether a system, such as that applying to preliminary rulings on validity of Community acts, whereby a declaration of invalidity may not produce any effect in the proceedings before the referring court, is consistent with the constitutional principles on judicial protection. . . . The Constitutional Court's main aim was to try and support the view that, as a matter of Community law, rulings should always have some effects in those proceedings. Possibly as a way of persuading the Court of Justice of the need to accept this solution, the Constitutional Court also viewed the problem from the perspective of the constitutional protection of fundamental rights. The Court said:

. . .

In substance, everyone's right to have a court and judicial proceedings for each dispute would be emptied of its essential content if, when a court doubts the validity of a rule which

---

[57] Dec. 170 of 8 June 1984 in *SpA Granital* v. *Amministrazione delle Finanze*. For an unofficial translation see G. Gaja (1984) 21 *CMLRev.* 756.

[58] R. Petriccione, 'Italy: Supremacy of Community Law over National Law' (1986) 11 *ELRev.* 320.

[59] *Spa Fragd* v. *Amministrazione delle Finanze*, Dec. 232 of 21 Apr. 1989 (1989) 72 RDI.

[60] (1990) 27 *CMLRev.* 83, 93–94.

should be applied, the answer came from the court to whom the question has to be referred that the rule is in fact void, but that this should not be relevant for the dispute before the referring court, which should nevertheless apply the rule that is declared to be void.

Contrary to the State Attorney's view, one could not invoke the primary need for the uniform application of Community law and for certainty of law against the possible violation of a fundamental right.

...

Unlike *Frontini*, the *Fragd* decision shows that the Constitutional Court is willing to test the consistency of individual rules of Community law with the fundamental principles for the protection of human rights that are contained in the Italian Constitution. This significantly widens the way for the exercise by the Constitutional Court of a control which has hitherto been only theoretical.

(ii) *Summary*

i. The Italian courts have accepted the primacy of Community law, subject to the qualifications mentioned below.

ii. The primacy of Community law is based on Article 11 of the Italian Constitution, and not the *communautaire* reasoning of the ECJ.

iii. The Italian courts do not accept that Community law has primacy over the Italian Constitution, and they retain ultimate authority over the issue of whether Community law infringes fundamental rights.

iv. It seems moreover that the Italian courts regard themselves as possessing the ultimate *Kompetenz-Kompetenz*, being prepared in principle to adjudicate on the division of competence between national law and Community law.[61]

(d) THE UNITED KINGDOM

(i) *Case Law and Doctrine*

The central obstacle to acceptance by the UK of the supremacy of EC law is the constitutional principle of parliamentary sovereignty, which in its traditional formulation holds that Parliament has the power to do anything other than to bind itself for the future.[62] This means that if there is a clash between a later and an earlier norm then the latter is taken to be impliedly repealed or disapplied by the former. Moreover, the UK's dualist approach to international law means that international treaties ratified by the UK are not part of the domestic law of the UK, and in order to be enforceable at the domestic level they must be incorporated by an Act of Parliament. In theory therefore the sovereignty principle makes it very difficult for the supremacy of Community law over later Parliamentary legislation to be guaranteed, since the Act of Parliament which incorporates EC law and makes it domestically binding seems vulnerable to any later Act of Parliament which contravenes or contradicts it, expressly or impliedly.

---

[61] P. Ruggeri Laderchi, 'Report on Italy', in Slaughter *et al.*, n. 22 above, ch. 5, points out the procedural problems for Italian courts wishing to exercise a form of *ultra vires* review of Community acts. See also A. Adinolfi, 'The Judicial Application of Community Law in Italy (1981–1997)' (1998) 35 *CMLRev.* 1313, 1314–1325.

[62] P. Craig, 'United Kingdom Sovereignty after *Factortame*' (1991) 11 *YBEL* 221; P. Craig, 'Britain in the European Union', in J. Jowell and D. Oliver (eds.), *The Changing Constitution* (6th edn., Oxford University Press, 2007), ch. 4.

It was nevertheless decided, after the EC Treaties were ratified by the UK in 1972, to give internal legal effect to Community law by means of an Act of Parliament: the European Communities Act 1972, section 2(1) of which provides:

> All such rights, powers, liabilities, obligations and restrictions from time to time created or arising by or under the Treaties, and all such remedies and procedures from time to time provided for by or under the Treaties, as in accordance with the Treaties are without further enactment to be given legal effect or used in the United Kingdom shall be recognized and available in law, and be enforced, allowed and followed accordingly; and the expression 'enforceable Community right' and similar expressions shall be read as referring to one to which this subsection applies.

Section 2(1) makes the concept of direct effect a part of the UK legal system. It deems law which under the EC Treaties is to be given immediate legal effect to be directly enforceable in the UK. Accordingly UK courts, which on the orthodox domestic approach to international law may not directly enforce a provision of an international treaty or a measure passed thereunder, are directed by section 2(1) to enforce any directly effective EC measures. There is no need for a fresh act of incorporation to enable UK courts to enforce each EC Treaty provision, regulation, or directive which according to EC law has direct effect.

Section 2(2) provides for the implementation of Community obligations, even when they are intended to replace national legislation and Acts of Parliament, by means of Order in Council or statutory instrument rather than by primary legislation only. Section 2(4) then provides:

> The provision that may be made under subsection (2) above includes, subject to Schedule 2 to this Act, any such provision (of any such extent) as might be made by Act of Parliament, and any enactment passed or to be passed, other than one contained in this Part of this Act, shall be construed and have effect subject to the foregoing provisions of this section; . . .

The Schedule to which the provision refers sets out a number of powers, such as increasing taxation or legislating retroactively, which cannot be exercised by Order in Council or by delegated legislation, even if they are necessary to comply with a Community obligation. For these powers it seems an Act of Parliament will be needed. But the part of section 2(4) which has received most attention is the clause beginning 'any enactment passed or to be passed', which became prominent when the courts sought a way to reconcile new obligations under Community law with the traditional approach to statutory interpretation. Section 3 of the Act then provides:

> For the purposes of all legal proceedings any question as to the meaning or effect of any of the Treaties, or as to the validity, meaning or effect of any Community instrument, shall be treated as a question of law (and, if not referred to the European Court, be for determination as such in accordance with the principles laid down by and any relevant decision of the European Court or any court attached thereto).

This provision makes the decisions of the ECJ on the meaning and effect of EC law authoritative in UK courts, giving them, to use domestic legal language, the force of precedent.

The leading decision on the relationship between Community law and UK law is *Factortame*, which will be considered below. Prior to that decision the judicial approach varied. The predominant approach, despite early judicial comments to the contrary,[63] was to use

---

[63] *Felixstowe Dock and Railway Company* v. *British Transport and Docks Board* [1976] 2 CMLR 655.

principles of construction to assume that when Parliament enacted the 1972 European Communities Act it intended any ambiguity or inconsistency with EC law to be resolved by giving primacy to EC law,[64] provided that there was no indication that Parliament expressly intended to depart from a provision of Community law, the assumption being that if the latter were to occur then the courts would follow the will of Parliament.[65] Thus where an apparently conflicting provision of English law was capable of being read in conformity with Community law, this was the proper approach to take.[66] In some cases the courts assumed that this approach would only apply where the provision of Community law was directly effective.[67] However in *Litster*,[68] *Pickstone*,[69] and *Webb*[70] the House of Lords was prepared to construe domestic statutes in conformity with EC law which was not directly effective, even where that construction was not in accordance with the literal or *prima facie* meaning of the statutes. This was so even where the national statute was introduced to implement a non-directly effective directive. We can now consider *Factortame*.[71]

Factortame Ltd v. Secretary of State for Transport (No. 2)
[1991] 1 AC 603

The applicants were companies incorporated under UK law, but the majority of the directors and shareholders were Spanish. The companies were in the business of sea fishing and their vessels were registered as British under the Merchant Shipping Act 1894. The statutory regime governing sea fishing was altered by the Merchant Shipping Act 1988. Vessels that had been registered under the 1894 Act had to register under the new legislation. Ninety-five vessels failed to meet the new criteria and the applicants argued that the relevant parts of the 1988 Act were incompatible with, *inter alia*, Articles 52, 58, and 221 of the EC Treaty. The first *Factortame* case[72] was concerned with whether interim relief should be available against the Crown, in order to protect the applicants' financial interests if they were prevented from fishing pending the final judgment. Such relief was not available as a matter of UK law at that time, but the ECJ ruled that the absence of such relief was itself a breach of Community law.[73] This was accepted by the House of Lords in *Factortame (No. 2)*, from which the following extract is taken.

LORD BRIDGE[74]

Some public comments on the decision of the Court of Justice, affirming the jurisdiction of the courts of member states to override national legislation if necessary to enable interim relief to

---

[64] *Shields* v. *E. Coomes (Holdings) Ltd.* [1979] 1 All ER 456, 461.

[65] *Macarthys* v. *Smith* [1979] 3 All ER 325, 329.

[66] *Garland* v. *British Rail* [1983] 2 AC 751, 771.

[67] *Duke* v. *GEC Reliance Ltd.* [1988] AC 618, 638.

[68] *Litster* v. *Forth Dry Dock Co. Ltd.* [1990] 1 AC 546.

[69] *Pickstone* v. *Freemans* [1989] AC 66.

[70] *Webb* v. *EMO* [1993] 1 WLR 49.

[71] For commentaries on the implications of the *Factortame* case for UK constitutional law see Craig, n. 62 above, 252; W. Wade, 'Sovereignty—Revolution or Evolution?' (1996) 112 *LQR* 568; T. Allan, 'Parliamentary Sovereignty: Law, Politics and Revolution' (1997) 113 *LQR* 443. See also D. Nicol, *EC Membership and the Judicialization of British Politics* (Oxford University Press, 2001), ch. 7.

[72] *Factortame Ltd.* v. *Secretary of State for Transport* [1990] 2 AC 85.

[73] N. 8 above.

[74] [1991] 1 AC 603, 658.

be granted in protection of rights under Community law, have suggested that this was a novel and dangerous invasion by a Community institution of the sovereignty of the United Kingdom Parliament. But such comments are based on a misconception. If the supremacy within the European Community of Community law over the national law of member states was not always inherent in the EEC Treaty it was certainly well established in the jurisprudence of the Court of Justice long before the United Kingdom joined the Community. Thus, whatever limitation of its sovereignty Parliament accepted when it enacted the European Communities Act 1972 was entirely voluntary. Under the terms of the 1972 Act it has always been clear that it was the duty of a United Kingdom court, when delivering final judgment, to override any rule of national law found to be in conflict with any directly enforceable rule of Community law. Similarly, when decisions of the Court of Justice have exposed areas of United Kingdom statute law which failed to implement Council directives, Parliament has always loyally accepted the obligation to make appropriate and prompt amendments. Thus there is nothing in any way novel in according supremacy to rules of Community law in those areas to which they apply and to insist that, in the protection of rights under Community law, national courts must not be inhibited by rules of national law from granting interim relief in appropriate cases is no more than a logical recognition of that supremacy.

The acceptance by UK courts of the supremacy of Community law was further evidenced by the *EOC* case, where the House of Lords stated that there was no constitutional barrier to an applicant before any UK court, and not only the House of Lords, seeking judicial review of primary legislation which was alleged to be in breach of Community law.

Equal Opportunities Commission v. Secretary of State for Employment
[1994] 1 WLR 409

[Note ToA renumbering: Arts. 7, 52, and 177 are now Arts. 12, 43, and 234 respectively]

The Equal Opportunities Commission (EOC) considered that the Employment Protection (Consolidation) Act of 1978 on part-time workers was contrary to Community law. In a letter from the Secretary of State for Employment to the EOC, the Secretary refused to accept that the UK was in breach of EC law. The EOC sought judicial review of the Secretary of State's decision. The Secretary of State argued that the English court had no jurisdiction to declare that the UK or the Secretary of State was in breach of any obligations under Community law.

LORD KEITH[75]

The question is whether judicial review is available for the purpose of securing a declaration that certain United Kingdom primary legislation is incompatible with Community law. ... In the *Factortame* series of cases ... the applicants for judicial review sought a declaration that the provisions of Part II of the Merchant Shipping Act 1988 should not apply to them on the ground that such application would be contrary to Community law, in particular Articles 7 and 52 of the EEC Treaty. ... The Divisional Court, under Article 177 of the Treaty, referred to the Court of Justice of the European Communities a number of questions, including the question whether these restrictive conditions were compatible with Articles 7 and 52 of the Treaty. The European

---

[75] [1994] 1 WLR 409, 418–419.

Court ... answered that question in the negative, and although the final result is not reported, no doubt the Divisional Court in due course granted a declaration accordingly. The effect was that certain provisions of United Kingdom primary legislation were held to be invalid in their purported application to nationals of Member States of the European Community, but without any prerogative order being available to strike down the legislation in question, which of course remained valid as regards nationals of non-member States. At no stage in the course of the litigation, which included two visits to this House, was it suggested that judicial review of legislation was not available for obtaining an adjudication upon the validity of the legislation in so far as it affected the applicants.

The *Factortame* case is thus a precedent in favour of the EOC's recourse to judicial review for the purpose of challenging as incompatible with Community law the relevant provisions of the 1978 Act.

While the UK courts have accepted the primacy of Community law, the conceptual foundation for their decisions has varied. In *Factortame (No 2)* Lord Bridge adverted to reasoning used by the ECJ in justifying according primacy to EC law, as exemplified by his reference to supremacy being inherent in the nature of the EC Treaty. Lord Bridge however also premised the UK's acceptance of supremacy on a UK statute, the 1972 European Communities Act.

It was the domestic acceptance of supremacy that was emphasized in *Thoburn*.[76] Laws LJ held that the constitutional relationship between the UK and the EU was not to be decided by the ECJ's jurisprudence: that case law could not itself entrench EU law within national law.[77] The constitutional relationship between the EU and the UK, including the impact of membership of the EU on sovereignty, was to be decided by the common law in the light of any statutes that Parliament had enacted.[78] The common law had, said Laws LJ, modified the traditional concept of sovereignty by creating exceptions to the doctrine of implied repeal. Ordinary statutes were subject to the doctrine of implied repeal. What Laws LJ referred to as 'constitutional statutes', which conditioned the legal relationship between citizen and State in some overarching manner, or which dealt with fundamental constitutional rights, were not subject to the doctrine of implied repeal.[79] The repeal of such a statute, or its disapplication in a particular instance, could only occur if there were some 'express words in the later statute, or by words so specific that the inference of an actual determination to effect the result contended for was irresistible'.[80] The ECA 1972 was regarded as just such a constitutional statute. It contained provisions that ensured the supremacy of substantive Community law in the event of a clash with national law, and was not subject to implied repeal. Laws LJ nonetheless sounded a warning note reminiscent of that from the earlier German jurisprudence, when he stated that:[81]

In the event, which no doubt would never happen in the real world, that a European measure was seen to be repugnant to a fundamental or constitutional right guaranteed by the law of England, a question would arise whether the general words of the ECA were sufficient to incorporate the measure and give it overriding effect in domestic law.

---

[76] *Thoburn* v. *Sunderland City Council* [2003] QB 151.
[77] *Ibid.*, paras. 57–58.
[78] *Ibid.*, para. 59.
[79] *Ibid.*, para. 62.
[80] *Ibid.*, para. 63.
[81] *Ibid.*, para. 69.

The following extract draws together the preceding case law and considers its substantive impact and the way that it can be conceptualized.

P. Craig, Britain in the European Union[82]

The substantive impact of *Factortame, EOC* and *Thoburn* may be described as follows.

First, in doctrinal terms these decisions mean that the concept of *implied repeal*, or *implied disapplication*, under which inconsistencies between later and earlier norms were resolved in favour of the former, will, subject to what is said below, no longer apply to clashes concerning Community and national law....

Second, if Parliament ever does wish to derogate from its Community obligations then it will have to do so *expressly and unequivocally*. The reaction of our national courts to such an unlikely eventuality remains to be seen. In principle two options would be open to the national judiciary. Either they could choose to follow the latest will of Parliament, thereby preserving some remnant of traditional orthodoxy on sovereignty. Or they could argue that it is not open to our legislature to pick and choose which obligations to subscribe to while still remaining within the Community....

Third, the supremacy of EC law over national law *operates in areas where EC law is applicable*, as is made clear from the dictum of Lord Bridge set out above.... The problem being addressed here is often referred to as *Kompetenz-Kompetenz*: who has the ultimate authority to decide whether a matter is within the competence of the EC? The ECJ may well believe that it is the ultimate decider of this issue. However, that national courts may not always be content with this arrogation of authority.

...

Commentators have been divided as to how best to conceptualize the impact of the courts' jurisprudence.

It is possible to rationalize what the courts have done as a species of *statutory construction*.... All would agree that if a statute can be reconciled with a Community norm through construing the statutory words without unduly distorting them then this should be done, more especially when the statute was passed to effectuate a directive. However the species of statutory construction being considered here is more far-reaching. On this view accommodation between national law and EC law is attained through a rule of construction to the effect that inconsistencies *will* be resolved in favour of the latter *unless* Parliament has indicated clearly and ambiguously that it intends to derogate from Community law. The degree of linguistic inconsistency between the statute and the Community norm is not the essential point of the inquiry. Provided that there is no unequivocal derogation from Community law then it will apply, rather than any conflicting domestic statute.... The construction view is said to leave the essential core of the traditional view of legal sovereignty intact, in the sense that it is always open to a later Parliament to make it unequivocally clear that it wishes to derogate from EC law.... This approach is, however, problematic....[83]

A second way to conceptualize what the courts have done is to regard it as a *technical legal revolution*. This is the preferred explanation of Sir William Wade who sees the courts' decisions as modifying the ultimate legal principle or rule of recognition on which the legal system is

---

[82]   Ch. 4 of Jowell and Oliver (eds.), n. 62 above.

[83]   The section of the extract which has been omitted here sets out three specific problems with the 'statutory construction' view, and indicates also that this particular view of the reconciliation of UK parliamentary sovereignty with the supremacy of EC law in the UK has been expressed extra-judicially by Lord Hoffmann and by Laws LJ.

based. On this view the 'rule of recognition is itself a political fact which the judges themselves are able to change when they are confronted with a new situation which so demands'. Such choices are made by the judiciary at the point where the law 'stops'.

There is however a third way in which to regard the courts' jurisprudence. This is to regard decisions about supremacy as being based on *normative arguments of legal principle the content of which can and will vary across time.* . . . On this view there is no *a priori* inexorable reason why Parliament, merely because of its very existence, must be regarded as legally omnipotent. The existence of such power, like all power, must be justified by arguments of principle which are normatively convincing. Possible constraints on Parliamentary omnipotence must similarly be reasoned through and defended on normative grounds. This approach fits well with the reasoning of Lord Bridge in the second *Factortame* case.

(ii) *Summary*

i. Notwithstanding early doubts whether UK courts would be able to accommodate the supremacy of EU law, they have now done so. A clash between national law and EU law will be resolved in favour of the latter. It is however unclear as yet what the UK courts would do if Parliament sought expressly to derogate from a provision of EU law, while still remaining in the EU.

ii. The conceptual foundation for the UK's acceptance of the supremacy of EU law has been primarily the 1972 ECA. There has however been some recognition of the ECJ's own reasoning in this regard.

iii. While the UK does not have a written constitution Laws LJ nonetheless intimated that if EU law were to be repugnant to rights recognized by the UK constitutional order then it might not override the relevant domestic law.

iv. There has been no UK case directly raising the issue of *Kompetenz-Kompetenz*. The decisions according supremacy to EU law are however premised on the assumption that the EU is acting within the scope of its authority. If a real issue of this nature were to arise the UK courts would probably regard themselves as possessing the ultimate *Kompetenz-Kompetenz*, while at the same time according respect to the views of the ECJ on the relevant matter.

(e) POLAND

(i) *Case Law and Doctrine*

The issues posed by the ECJ's supremacy doctrine are also evident in the jurisprudence of the newer accession countries.

Polish Membership of the European Union (Accession Treaty)
K18/04, 11 May 2005

The Polish Constitutional Tribunal considered the constitutionality of Polish membership of the EU. The Tribunal noted that the Polish Constitution did not have a category of 'supranational organization' and that the Accession Treaty between Poland and the EU should be regarded as a form of international agreement. It then continued as follows.

CONSTITUTIONAL TRIBUNAL

7. Article 90(1) of the Constitution authorizes the delegation of competences of State organs only 'in relation to certain matters'. This implies a prohibition on the delegation of all competences of a State authority organ or competences determining its substantial scope of activity, or competences concerning the entirety of matters within a certain field.

8. Neither Article 90(1) nor Article 91(3) authorize delegation to an international organization of the competence to issue legal acts or take decisions contrary to the Constitution, being the 'supreme law of Poland' (Article 8(1)). Concomitantly, these provisions do not authorize the delegation of competences to such an extent that it would signify the inability of the Republic of Poland to continue functioning as a sovereign and democratic State.

. . .

11. Given its supreme legal force (Article 8(1)), the Constitution enjoys precedence of binding force and precedence of application within the territory of the Republic of Poland. The precedence over statutes of the application of international agreements which were ratified on the basis of a statutory authorization or consent granted (in accordance with Article 90(3)) via the procedure of a nationwide referendum, as guaranteed by Article 91(2) of the Constitution, in no way signifies an analogous precedence of these agreements over the Constitution.

[*The Court noted the possibility of conflict or collision between Community norms and the Polish Constitution, and continued as follows:*]

13. Such a collision would occur in the event that an irreconcilable inconsistency appeared between a constitutional norm and a Community norm, such as could not be eliminated by means of applying an interpretation which respects the mutual autonomy of European law and national law. Such a collision may in no event be resolved by assuming the supremacy of a Community norm over a constitutional norm. Furthermore, it may not lead to the situation whereby a constitutional norm loses its binding force and is substituted by a Community norm, nor may it lead to an application of the constitutional norm restricted to areas beyond the scope of Community law regulation. In such an event the Nation as the sovereign, or a State authority authorized by the Constitution to represent the Nation, would need to decide on: amending the Constitution; or causing modifications within Community provisions; or, ultimately, on Poland's withdrawal from the European Union.

14. The principle of interpreting domestic law in a manner 'sympathetic to European law' . . . has its limits. In no event may it lead to results contradicting the explicit wording of constitutional norms or being irreconcilable with the minimum guarantee functions realized by the Constitution. In particular, the norms of the Constitution within the field of individual rights and freedoms indicate a minimum and unsurpassable threshold which may not be lowered or questioned as a result of the introduction of Community provisions.

The approach of the Polish courts is also apparent in the decision of the Constitutional Tribunal concerning the European Arrest Warrant, EAW.[84] The Constitutional Tribunal held that the domestic law giving effect to the EAW was incompatible with Article 55(1) of the Polish Constitution, which prohibited the extradition of a Polish citizen. The Constitutional Tribunal was willing to accept that Article 55(1) should if possible be interpreted to be in conformity with EU law, but nonetheless felt unable to read the legislation giving effect to the EAW as being consistent with Article 55(1). It held that the constitutional prohibition on extradition applied also to the regime of surrender under the EAW. The Constitutional Tribunal acknowledged that the Constitution might well have to be amended in order to ensure compliance with the

---

[84] Polish Constitutional Tribunal, 27 Apr. 2005, No. P 1/05; Noted by D. Leczykiewicz (2006) 43 *CMLRev.* 1181.

EU Framework Decision creating the EAW. The time limit for domestic enactment of this Decision had however passed. The Constitutional Tribunal was therefore willing to defer the cancellation of the binding force of the Polish law implementing the EAW for eighteen months, in order to allow the necessary changes to be made to the Constitution.

(ii) *Summary*

i.   The Polish courts accept the supremacy of EU law over statute, subject to the qualifications below.

ii. The conceptual foundation for this is to be found in provisions of the Polish Constitution, not the *communautaire* reasoning of the ECJ.

iii. The Polish courts do not accept the supremacy of EU law over the Constitution. They also regard national constitutional rights as a minimum that cannot be questioned as the result of a Community provision.

iv. It is also reasonably clear that the Polish courts regard themselves as possessing the ultimate *Kompetenz-Kompetenz*.

v.   The ruling on the EAW indicates the priority accorded to the Polish Constitution. The ruling however also indicates the willingness to bring Polish law into line with the demands of EU law, as evidenced by the way in which the Constitutional Tribunal delayed the cancellation of the national law pending possible amendment of the Constitution.

(f) CENTRAL AND EAST EUROPEAN STATES

The judicial approach in the new Member States from Central and Eastern Europe is not uniform, and space precludes detailed examination of all such case law. The Czech Constitutional Court has, for example, adopted a nuanced approach. The judgment was in many respects 'Euro-friendly', and the Court accepted that EU protection for fundamental rights was in accord with that in the Czech Republic; at the same time it stipulated some limits on its acceptance of the primacy of EU law.[85]

It is nonetheless interesting to reflect more generally on this jurisprudence. Sadurski notes that such countries joined the EU in order, *inter alia*, to provide a secure foundation for democracy and human rights, and points to the paradox that their constitutional courts have resisted the supremacy of EU law on the ground that it might endanger domestic constitutional protection of such rights.[86] In the following extract he seeks to explain the fact that such courts have engaged in reasoning analogous to that of the German courts in the *Solange* cases.

W. Sadurski, 'Solange Chapter 3': Constitutional Courts in Central Europe—Democracy—European Union[87]

The Solange story was well suited to be taken up in Central and Eastern Europe after accession, for two powerful reasons. First, in nearly all post-communist European States, constitutional courts established themselves as powerful, influential, activist players, dictating the

---

[85] Decision Pl. US 50/04; W. Sadurski, ' "Solange Chapter 3": Constitutional Courts in Central Europe—Democracy—European Union', EUI Working Papers, Law No. 2006/40, 6–10.

[86] *Ibid.*

[87] *Ibid.*, 2–4.

rules of the political game for other political actors.... While the powers of the constitutional courts in CEE largely resemble (and often exceed) those of their Western European counterparts, the other branches of CEE States are weaker, more chaotic, disorganized and inefficient compared to those in Western Europe.... Accession to the EU provided those courts with yet another opportunity to reinforce their own powers—an opportunity not to be missed: they could easily ... assert a right to establish and enforce criteria of democracy, rule of law and human rights protection, which would inform the relationship between the European and national constitutional orders. Such a power would further increase their position vis-à-vis the political branches in their countries, by delineating those aspects of the supremacy of European law which they deemed unacceptable, or by dictating the need to carry out constitutional amendments if certain dimensions of supremacy were to be accepted.

The second reason why the Solange story almost begged for a recurrence in CEE stemmed from the strong sovereignty concerns which were felt and expressed in CEE states prior to accession, and persisted after joining the EU. Elsewhere I have described the situation surrounding this concern as a 'sovereignty conundrum': the often perceived irony that almost immediately after the shaking off of the brutal dominance by the Soviet Union (with its doctrine of "limited sovereignty" of Warsaw Pact States) and the recovery of their long-missed independence, these countries should accede to a supranational Community in which traditional, strict sovereignty is found to be obsolete and in which they are asked to transfer much of their sovereignty to supranational institutions.... The constitutional courts thus found themselves in a situation in which the pull towards rephrasing sovereignty-based objections against the supremacy of EU law, in terms of their role as guardians of constitutional values, was irresistible....

4. THE CONSTITUTIONAL TREATY

The ECJ's jurisprudence on supremacy has, as we have seen, been developed in the absence of any supremacy clause in the Treaties. The Constitutional Treaty[88] included such a provision, which looks to be preserved in the impending Reform Treaty, albeit as a Declaration rather than a Treaty Article. Article I–6 CT provided that:

> The Constitution and law adopted by the Union's institutions in exercising competences conferred on it, shall have primacy over the law of the Member States.

This was reinforced by Article I–5(2), which stipulated that Member States should take all appropriate measures, general or particular, to ensure fulfilment of the obligations flowing from the Constitution or resulting from the Union Institutions' acts.

It would however be mistaken to think that Article I–6 would have 'resolved' the supremacy issue in EU law. The wording of Article I–6 was crucially ambiguous.[89] The phrase 'shall have primacy over the law of the Member States' could be interpreted to mean, following the ECJ's jurisprudence, that supremacy operated over all national law, including provisions in a national constitution. It could alternatively be read so as to accord primacy to EU law over national law, but not the national constitution itself. This ambiguity was 'reinforced' when

---

[88] Treaty Establishing a Constitution for Europe [2004] OJ C310/1.

[89] P. Craig, 'The Constitutional Treaty and Sovereignty', in C. Kaddous and A. Auer (eds.), *Les Principes Fondamentaux de la Constitution Européene* (Dossier de Droit Européen No. 15, Helbing & Lictenhahn/Bruylant/LGDJ, 2006), 117–134.

Article I–6 was read in its entirety: the early part of the Article which referred to the EU distinguished between the Constitution and law adopted by the institutions. It would have been perfectly possible to have drafted Article I–6 'symmetrically' so as to read that: 'the Constitution and law adopted by the Union's institutions in exercising competences conferred on it should have primacy over the *constitutions* and law of the Member States', thereby removing the ambiguity that attached to the Article.

Declaration 1 attached to the Constitutional Treaty stated that '[t]he Conference notes that Article I–6 reflects the existing case law of the Court of Justice of the European Communities and the Court of First Instance'. This provided some indirect support for the view that the Member States accepted the jurisprudence of the Community Courts when signing the Constitutional Treaty. The Declaration could not however remove the ambiguity in the meaning of Article I–6. It could only be a tool for interpretation, to reinforce the views of those who wished to interpret it as trumping national constitutions as well as national law.

The ambiguous wording in Article I–6 was probably retained in the Constitutional Treaty, because it would have been difficult to secure agreement if Article I–6 had been drafted expressly so as to include the supremacy of EU law over national constitutions. In many countries the idea that EU law could trump the national constitution would either have required a constitutional amendment before accession to the CT, or would have been regarded as simply not possible at all, on the ground that it would be too invasive of the essential or irreducible elements of national sovereignty.[90]

It should moreover be noted that Article I–6 only accorded primacy to Union law 'in exercising competences conferred on it'. There was nothing in this wording that resolved the issue of *Kompetenz-Kompetenz*. There is no doubt that the ECJ would have had authority, under Article I–29, to pronounce on whether the EU had competence to act or not. This would not however have cloaked such a judgment with supremacy pursuant to Article I–6, since that supremacy only operated when the EU was exercising competences conferred on it, which was the very question in issue. Moreover the wording of Article I–11(2), which was framed in terms of the Union acting within the limits of the competences conferred on it by the Member States, with competences not conferred on the EU remaining with the Member States, did nothing to bolster the claims of the EU to decide on the ultimate boundaries of competence. The wording and tenor of this Article pointed rather to the *Kompetenz-Kompetenz* residing with the Member States.

5. CONSTITUTIONAL PLURALISM

While the debate over whether there is or can be a final judicial arbiter in Europe remains a live one, different versions of constitutional pluralism are increasingly being proposed as a more attractive alternative to the stalemate of nation-State-centred versus EU-centred monism.[91] The following extracts are from the writings of two commentators whose approaches to the

---

[90] The Conseil Constitutionnel in France ruled that the primacy clause of the CT could be accepted without amendment of the French Constitution: n. 33 above. For difficulties with this reasoning see Richards, n. 34 above, 509–513.

[91] See also C. Schmid, 'From Pont d'Avignon to Ponte Vecchio: The Resolution of Constitutional Conflicts between the EU and the Member States through Principles of Public International Law' (1998) 18 *YBEL* 415; M. Kumm, 'Who is the Final Arbiter of Constitutionality in Europe?: Three Conceptions of the Relationship between the German Federal Constitutional Court and the European Court of Justice' (1999) 36 *CMLRev.* 351; N. Walker, 'The Idea of Constitutional Pluralism' (2002) 65 *MLR* 317; N. Walker, 'Late Sovereignty in the European Union', in Walker, n. 22 above, ch. 1; M. Maduro, 'Contrapunctual Law: Europe's Constitutional Pluralism in Action', in *ibid.*, ch. 21.

constitutional relationship between national law and European law have altered somewhat in recent years. Paul Kirchhof, former judge of the Bundesverfassungsgericht and one of the main architects of the *Maastricht* judgment at the time, expresses a more co-operative and pluralist vision of this relationship than some of his earlier views suggested; while Neil MacCormick's proposed analysis is one of 'legal pluralism under international law', in place of his earlier radically pluralist perspective which saw the answer to fundamental constitutional conflict as lying in politics rather than in law.

N. MacCormick, Questioning Sovereignty[92]

The doctrine of supremacy of Community law is not to be confused with any kind of all purpose subordination of Member State law to Community law. Rather, the case is that these are interacting systems, one of which constitutes in its own context and over the relevant range of topics a source of valid law superior to other sources recognized in each of the Member State systems....

On the whole therefore, the most appropriate analysis of the relations of legal systems is pluralistic rather than monistic, and interactive rather than hierarchical. The legal systems of Member States and their common legal system of EC law are distinct but interacting systems of law, and hierarchical relationships of validity within criteria of validity proper to distinct systems do not add up to any sort of all-purpose superiority of one system over another. It follows also that the interpretative power of the highest decision-making authorities of the different systems must be, as to each system, ultimate. It is for the ECJ to interpret in the last resort and in a finally authoritative way the norms of Community law. But equally, it must be for the highest constitutional tribunal of each member State to interpret its constitutional and other norms, and hence to interpret the interaction of the validity of EC law with higher level norms of validity in the given state system....

... The potential conflicts and collisions of systems that can in principle occur as between Community and member States do not occur in a legal vacuum, but in a space to which international law is also relevant. Indeed, it is decisively relevant, given the origin of the Community in Treaties and the continuing normative significance of *pacta sunt servanda*, to say nothing of the fact that in respect of their Community membership and otherwise the states owe each other obligations under international law.... What that signals is that state Courts have no right to assume an absolute superiority of state constitution over international good order, including the European dimension of that good order. This is not the same as saying that they must simply defer to whatever the ECJ considers to be mandated by the European constitution.... But in the event of an apparently irresoluble conflict arising between one or more national courts and the ECJ, there would always on this thesis be a possibility of recourse to international arbitration or adjudication to resolve the matter.

P. Kirchhof, The Balance of Powers between National and European Institutions[93]

European law would lose its roots and its power to grow by being made autonomous and separate from the Member States, whereas in the close interweaving with Member States'

---

[92] (Oxford University Press, 1999), 117–121.
[93] (1999) 5 *ELJ* 225, 227–228, 241.

constitutions it gains its identity in a unitary origin and a unitary future.... [C]onflicts of norms that may arise are not to be avoided or resolved by a conflict of laws provision whereby one takes primacy over the other and norms are rendered non-legal, but through mutual respect and through 'cooperation'.... The ECJ and the constitutional courts each have adjudicatory responsibility of their own for the success of the European legal community.... Accordingly, it is not just 'open skies' that are above these courts of last instance; a system of balance of powers between the European and Member State courts is developing. Whoever seeks to interpret this system of balance and cooperation as a hierarchy is closing off the way laid down in European integration towards a balance of powers within the judicature.... Adjudicating means establishing the culture of measure, of balance, of co-operation, not dominance, subordination and rejection.

6. CONCLUSIONS

i. The supremacy of EC law still clearly retains its 'bi-dimensional' character, despite the monist view of supremacy asserted by the ECJ in *Simmenthal* and *Internationale Handelsgesellschaft.*

ii. While there are exceptions, most notably in the Netherlands,[94] most Member State courts continue to locate the authority of EU law in the national legal order centrally within the national constitution, and not in the jurisprudence of the Court of Justice or in the sovereignty of the EU.

iii. Further, many higher national courts have asserted the ultimate (albeit residual) role of national courts in ensuring that the proper boundaries of EC competence are respected and in protecting rights which are fundamental within the national legal order.[95]

iv. Thus far, while the residual control of national courts has been firmly asserted as a matter of constitutional theory, it has rarely materialized in practice. Nonetheless, it remains as a clear counterpoint to the ECJ's assertion of the autonomy of Community law, and it may influence the ECJ in showing greater sensitivity to national constitutional concerns.[96] It remains to be seen whether the ECJ's upholding of the European arrest warrant[97] gives rise to constitutional conflict with any national courts.

7. FURTHER READING

(a) Books

Alter, K., *Establishing the Supremacy of European Law: The Making of an International Rule of Law in Europe* (Oxford University Press, 2001)

---

[94] M. Claes and B. de Witte, 'Report on the Netherlands', in Slaughter *et al.*, n. 22 above, ch. 6; B. de Witte, 'Do Not Mention the Word: Sovereignty in two Europhile Countries', in Walker (ed.), n. 22 above; L. Besselink, 'Curing a "Childhood Sickness"'? On Direct Effect, Internal Effect, Primacy and Derogation from Civil Rights' (1996) 3 *MJ* 165.

[95] See also the decision of the Danish Supreme Court in *Carlsen* v. *Prime Minister*, judgment of the Højesteret, 6 Apr. 1998 [1999] 3 CMLR 854; K. Høegh, 'The Danish Maastricht Judgment' (1999) 24 *ELRev.* 80, and the decision of the Irish Supreme Court in *Crotty* v. *An Taoiseach* [1987] IR 713.

[96] See, e.g., de Witte, 'Community Law and National Constitutional Values', n. 35 above, and the notion of 'contrapunctual law' in Maduro, n. 91 above.

[97] Case C–303/05 *Advocaten voor de Wereld*, n. 54 above.

Claes, M., *The National Courts' Mandate in the European Constitution* (Hart, 2006)

MacCormick, N., *Questioning Sovereignty* (Oxford University Press, 1999)

Nicol, D., *EC Membership and the Judicialization of British Politics* (Oxford University Press, 2001)

Slaughter, A.-M., Stone Sweet, A., and Weiler, J.H.H. (eds.), *The European Court of Justice and National Courts: Doctrine and Jurisprudence* (Hart, 1998)

Walker, N. (ed.), *Sovereignty in Transition* (Hart, 2003)

(b) Articles

Craig, P., 'Britain in the European Union', in J. Jowell and D. Oliver (eds.), *The Changing Constitution* (6th edn., Oxford University Press, 2007), ch. 4

—— 'National Courts and Community Law', in J. Hayward and A. Menon (eds.), *Governing Europe* (Oxford University Press, 2003), ch. 2

—— 'The Constitutional Treaty and Sovereignty', in C. Kaddous and A. Auer (eds.), *Les Principes Fondamentaux de la Constitution Européene* (Dossier de Droit Européen No. 15, Helbing & Lictenhahn/Bruylant/LGDJ, 2006), 117–134

De Witte, B., 'Direct Effect, Supremacy and the Nature of the Legal Order', in P. Craig and G. de Búrca (eds.), *The Evolution of EU Law* (Oxford University Press, 1999)

Elbers, U., and Urban, N., 'The Order of the German Federal Constitutional Court of 7 June 2000 and the Kompetenz-Kompetenz in the European Judicial System' (2001) 7 *EPL* 21

Everling, U., 'The Maastricht Judgment of the German Federal Constitutional Court and its Significance for the Development of the European Union' (1994) 14 *YBEL* 1

Kumm, M., 'Who is the Final Arbiter of Constitutionality in Europe?' (1999) 36 *CMLRev.* 251

Lenaerts K., and Corthaut, T., 'Of Birds and Hedges: The Role of Primacy in Invoking Norms of EU Law' (2006) 31 *ELRev.* 287

Maduro, M., 'Contrapunctual Law: Europe's Constitutional Pluralism in Action', in N. Walker (ed.), *Sovereignty in Transition* (Hart, 2003), ch. 21

Reich, N., 'Judge-made "Europe à la carte": Some Remarks on Recent Conflicts between European and German Constitutional Law Provoked by the Banana Litigation' (1996) 7 *EJIL* 103

Sadurski, W., ' "Solange Chapter 3": Constitutional Courts in Central Europe—Democracy—European Union', EUI Working Papers, Law No. 2006/40

Schmid, C., 'All Bark and No Bite: Notes on the Federal Constitutional Court's "Banana Decision"' (2001) 7 *ELJ* 95

Walker, N., 'The Idea of Constitutional Pluralism' (2002) 65 *MLR* 317

Weiler, J.H.H., 'The Community System: the Dual Character of Supranationalism' (1981) 1 *YBEL* 267

Zuleeg, M., 'The European Constitution under Constitutional Constraints: The German Scenario' (1997) 22 *ELRev.* 19

11

HUMAN RIGHTS IN THE EU

1. CENTRAL ISSUES

i.   The original three European Community Treaties, signed in the 1950s, contained no provisions concerning the protection of human rights. More than fifty years since the first of the Communities was founded, this position has changed considerably. The Court of Justice has declared that the 'general principles of EC law' include protection for fundamental rights which are part of the common constitutional traditions of the Member States and contained in international human rights treaties on which they have collaborated or which they have signed, and this has been affirmed in the EU Treaty.

ii. Apart from the case law, the EU has begun to develop a range of human rights policies. At the level of internal policy, these are most notably in the field of anti-discrimination law, pursuant to Article 13 of the EC Treaty. At the level of external policy, human rights has played a role in the EC's international trade and development policy, and in its use of 'political conditionality' for candidate Member States, but also in a growing range of 'human rights and democratization' policies and in the common foreign and security policy.[1]

iii. There has also been a series of institutional initiatives in the human rights field. These include the establishment in the Amsterdam Treaty of a sanction mechanism for serious and persistent breaches of human rights in Article 7 TEU, and the establishment in 2002 of an EU Network of Independent Experts on Fundamental Rights to exercise monitoring and advisory functions. In 2007, an EU Fundamental Rights Agency was established to replace the existing EU Monitoring Center against Racism and Xenophobia.

iv. A Charter of Fundamental Rights for the EU was drafted and officially 'proclaimed' in 2000.[2] The Treaty establishing a Constitution for Europe would have given this Charter full legal effect by incorporating it, with some amendments, into Part Two of the Constitution. However, the legal status of the Charter remains uncertain following the non-ratification of the Constitutional Treaty in 2005, and pending further developments to the proposed Reform Treaty, and for now it is best considered as an influential form of soft law.

---

[1] See http://ec.europa.eu/comm/external_relations/human_rights/intro/index.htm#7.

[2] For some of the vast literature on the Charter see (2001) 8(1) *MJ*; E. Eriksen, J.E. Fossum, and A. Menéndez (eds.), *The Chartering of Europe* (Arena Report No. 8/2001), available at http://ec.europa.eu/justice_home/doc_centre/rights/charter/docs/network_commentary_final%20_180706.pdf; K. Feus (ed.), *An EU Charter of Fundamental Rights: Text and Commentaries* (Federal Trust, 2000); EU Network of Independent Experts on Fundamental Rights, *Commentary on the Charter* (June, 2006).

v. These various institutional and policy developments in the human rights field have not silenced the debate as to whether the EU is or is not a significant 'human rights organization,'[3] nor as to whether its attention to human rights protection amounts to more than lip service, or self-serving instrumentalism.[4] In the fields of immigration, asylum, criminal justice, and anti-terrorism in particular, the EU has been sharply criticized for neglecting and undermining human rights concerns.[5]

vi. The decades-old debate over accession by the EC to the European Convention on Human Rights (ECHR) was revived during the drafting of the Constitutional Treaty, and the text of the CT ultimately provided for accession by the EU. Overlapping case law of the two European Courts has kept the issue alive even since the non-ratification of the CT.

2. BACKGROUND

This high political profile in recent years of human rights in the EU context has not been a sudden development. The ECJ's progressive development over many years of a kind of unwritten bill of rights for the Community was gradually given express recognition in the Treaties. In particular, Article 6 TEU declares that respect for fundamental rights and freedoms constitutes one of the basic principles on which the Union is founded, and Article 7 provides a mechanism for sanctioning Member States who violate these principles in a grave or persistent manner. Nevertheless, these and other provisions were grafted on to a set of treaties which, despite the broad range of powers and policies covered, were for a long time largely focused on economic aims and objectives. This legacy remains significant since, despite its constantly changing and expanding nature, the European Union's dominant focus remains an economic one, and the debate over the appropriate scope of its 'human rights role' remains lively and contested even after the adoption of the Charter of Fundamental Rights.

In the early 1950s, at a time when there were great hopes for European integration, proposals for a European Political Community Treaty were drawn up,[6] into which the substantive rights provisions of the ECHR were to be incorporated. However, these proposals were abandoned after the failure to ratify the earlier European Defence Treaty in 1952.[7] Perhaps in reaction to what were perceived to be overreaching integration proposals, the 1957 EEC Treaty was restricted essentially to the aims of economic integration, and—despite the idealistic rhetoric of the three Community treaties, which posited economic integration as a

---

[3] P. Alston, J. Heenan, and M. Bustelo (eds.), *The EU and Human Rights* (Oxford University Press, 1999), in particular ch. 1; and the response by A. von Bogdandy, 'The European Union as a Human Rights Organization: Human Rights and the Core of the European Union' (2000) 37 *CMLRev.* 1307. For a more normative analysis see S. Besson, 'The EU and Human Rights: Towards a Post-National Human Rights Institution' [2006] *HRLRev.* 323

[4] A. Williams, *The Irony of Human Rights in the European Union* (Oxford University Press, 2004). Both Amnesty and Human Rights Watch in recent years have commented critically on the EU's human rights role: 'Amnesty International's Assessment of EU Human Rights Policy: Recommendations to the Irish Presidency', (Amnesty, Jan. 2004), and K. Roth 'Filling the Leadership Void: Where is the European Union?' (Human Rights Watch World Report, 2007).

[5] See, e.g., Amnesty International, 'Human Rights Dissolving at the Borders? Counter-Terrorism and EU Criminal Law' (Amnesty, May, 2005); C. Teitgen-Colly, 'The European Union and Asylum: An Illusion of Protection' (2006) 43 *CMLRev.* 1503.

[6] A.H. Robertson, 'The European Political Community' (1952) 29 *BYIL* 383.

[7] A.H. Robertson, *European Institutions* (2nd edn., Stevens & Sons, 1966), 19–21.

means to better ends rather than as an end in itself—no mention of political union or of human rights was included.[8]

However, the Community before long established itself as a powerful entity the actions of which had considerable impact on many broader political and social issues, and its express policy competences were also extended beyond the economic realm. Further, Community action through the doctrine of direct effect often had effective legal impact on private economic and commercial interests. Economic actors began to claim legal protection for fundamental property and commercial rights which were given specific protection within certain Member State constitutions. Thus the first steps taken by the ECJ in the field of fundamental rights protection concerned economic rights such as the right to property and the freedom to pursue a trade or profession.

The initial trigger for the Court's declaration that fundamental rights formed part of the EC legal order was the challenge posed to the supremacy of Community law by Member State courts which felt that EC legislation was encroaching upon important rights protected under national law. The ECJ's development initially gained the support of the Member States, since protection for these rights was being introduced by the ECJ into Community law as a restraint upon the powers of the Community institutions rather than as a restraint upon Member States.

Since then, however, there has been a considerable expansion of both judicial and legislative activity in the area of human rights protection, including the extension by the ECJ of fundamental-rights review to certain acts of the Member States. Some of these developments have given rise to concerns that the EC is encroaching upon tasks properly performed by national constitutions and by the ECHR. The debate over the drafting of the Charter of Fundamental Rights also illustrated these tensions, with some calling for a stronger and more extensive role for the EU and the ECJ in human rights protection, but others favouring a more limited role for the EU and viewing the Charter as primarily relevant to the EU institutions rather than the Member States.[9] We will return to this subject below.

3. FOUNDATIONS: THE EC BOUND BY 'GENERAL PRINCIPLES OF LAW' INCLUDING HUMAN RIGHTS

The ECJ in an early series of cases initially resisted attempts by litigants to invoke rights and principles recognized by domestic law (such as legitimate expectations, proportionality, and natural justice), and was unwilling to treat them as part of the Community's legal order, even where they were fundamental principles common to the legal systems of most or all Member States.[10] Subsequently, however, the Court's attitude changed.

In 1969 in *Stauder* the Court responded positively to an argument based on the fundamental right to human dignity, which the applicant alleged had been violated by the domestic

---

[8] M. Dauses, 'The Protection of Fundamental Rights in the Community Legal Order' (1985) 10 *ELRev*. 398, 399; P. Pescatore, 'The Context and Significance of Fundamental Rights in the Law of the European Communities' (1981) 2 *HRLJ* 295.

[9] For an example of the latter view see, e.g., the comments of the UK representative who participated in the drafting of the Charter, Lord Goldsmith, 'A Charter of Rights, Freedoms and Principles' (2001) 38 *CMLRev*. 1201 and 'The Charter of Rights—A Brake Not an Accelerator' [2005] *EHRLRev*. 473.

[10] Cases 1/58 *Stork* v. *High Authority* [1959] ECR 17; Cases 36, 37, 38, and 40/59 *Geitling* v. *High Authority* [1960] ECR 423; Case 40/64 *Sgarlata and others* v. *Commission* [1965] ECR 215.

implementation of an EC provision concerning a subsidized-butter scheme for welfare recipients.[11] Having construed the EC measure in a manner consistent with protection for human dignity, the ECJ declared that 'the provision at issue contains nothing capable of prejudicing the fundamental human rights enshrined in the general principles of Community law and protected by the Court'.[12] *Stauder* thus represented a distinct change of approach, introducing the idea of general principles of EC law which include protection for fundamental human rights.[13] The new approach was confirmed and elaborated upon in the famous *Internationale Handesgesellschaft* case, in which the German Constitutional Court was asked to set aside an EC measure concerning forfeiture of an export-licence deposit, which apparently conflicted with German constitutional rights and principles such as economic liberty and proportionality.

Case 11/70 **Internationale Handelsgesellschaft v. Einfuhr- und Vorratstelle für Getreide und Futtermittel**
[1970] ECR 1125

THE ECJ

3. Recourse to the legal rules or concepts of national law in order to judge the validity of measures adopted by the institutions of the Community would have an adverse effect on the uniformity and efficacy of Community law. The validity of such measures can only be judged in the light of Community law. In fact, the law stemming from the Treaty, an independent source of law, cannot because of its very nature be overridden by rules of national law, however framed, without being deprived of its character as Community law and without the legal basis of the Community itself being called into question. Therefore the validity of a Community measure or its effect within a Member State cannot be affected by allegations that it runs counter to either fundamental rights as formulated by the constitution of that State or the principles of a national constitutional structure.

4. However, an examination should be made as to whether or not any analogous guarantee inherent in Community law has been disregarded. In fact, respect for fundamental rights forms an integral part of the general principles of Community law protected by the Court of Justice. The protection of such rights, whilst inspired by the constitutional traditions common to the Member states, must be ensured within the framework of the structure and objectives of the Community. It must therefore be ascertained, in the light of the doubts expressed by the Verwaltungsgericht, whether the system of deposits has infringed rights of a fundamental nature, respect for which must be ensured in the Community legal system.

The ECJ then concluded that there had been no infringement of the rights claimed, since the restriction on the freedom to trade, etc., was not disproportionate to the general interest advanced by the deposit system. When the case returned to the German court, however, the

---

[11] Case 29/69 *Stauder* v. *City of Ulm* [1969] ECR 419.

[12] *Ibid.*, para 7.

[13] For a discussion of the early 'fundamental rights' implicit within the Treaty itself which were developed by the ECJ as general principles of law see D. Shachor-Landau, 'Reflections on the Two European Courts of Justice', in Y. Dinstein *et al.* (eds.), *International Law at a Time of Perplexity* (Martinus Nijhoff, 1989), 792, and for a discussion of the pre- and post-*Stauder* case law at the time see U. Scheuner, 'Fundamental Rights in European Community Law and in National Constitutional Law' (1975) 12 *CMLRev.* 171.

national court concluded that the principle of proportionality enshrined in German constitutional law had indeed been violated by the Community deposit system. The effect of this
and of subsequent cases on the constitutional relationship between Community law and
German law is discussed in Chapter 10, but the case also provides an interesting illustration of
the difficulty facing the ECJ in seeking to assimilate the 'common constitutional principles' of
the Member States as part of the Community legal order. If the ECJ's interpretation of the
requirements of these principles differs significantly from the interpretation of the Member
States which also claim to guarantee their protection, the legitimacy of the Court's adjudication is likely to be called into question.

4. THE RIGHTS PROTECTED WITHIN EU LAW: SOURCES

Since the *Handelsgesellschaft* ruling, the ECJ has continually emphasized the autonomy of
Community 'general principles' of law, while simultaneously stressing that the source of these
general principles is not entirely independent of the legal cultures and traditions of the Member
States. In the case of *Nold*, concerning the drastic impact on the applicant's right to a livelihood
of the Community regulation of the market in coal, the Court indicated that there were two primary sources of 'inspiration' for the general principles of EC law: first, the common national
constitutional traditions, and secondly, international human rights agreements:

Case 4/73 **Nold v. Commission**
[1974] ECR 491

13. As the Court has already stated, fundamental rights form an integral part of the general
principles of law, the observance of which it ensures.

In safeguarding these rights, the Court is bound to draw inspiration from constitutional traditions common to the Member States, and it cannot therefore uphold measures which are
incompatible with fundamental rights recognized and protected by the Constitutions of those
States.

Similarly, international treaties for the protection of human rights on which the Member
States have collaborated or of which they are signatories, can supply guidelines which should
be followed within the framework of Community law.

(a) INTERNATIONAL INSTRUMENTS

As far as international treaties are concerned, the Court has consistently treated the European
Convention on Human Rights as a special source of inspiration for the general principles of
EU law. It has ruled, for example, that EC legislation restricting the powers of Member State
authorities to limit free movement and residence,[14] or legislation concerning the right to

---

[14] As early as in Case 36/75 *Rutili* v. *Minister for the Interior* [1975] ECR 1219, the ECJ described provisions
of secondary EC legislation as specific manifestations of more general fundamental principles of Community
law which could be found in the ECHR.

pursue claims by judicial process, or rights against sex discrimination, or data-protection and privacy, were specific EC law manifestations of general principles contained in the ECHR.[15]

Further, although the ECJ has never said that the ECHR is formally binding upon the EC/EU, nor that its provisions are formally incorporated into EU law,[16] Article 6 TEU expressly refers to the ECHR. In more practical terms, the ECJ—and even the CFI, despite its stronger insistence on the formal 'externality' of the ECHR[17]—routinely refers to the 'special significance' of the Convention as a key source of inspiration for the general principles of EC law.[18]

In this way the Court can continue to claim the autonomy and supremacy of Community law, and, while avoiding the charge of having judicially incorporated the Convention and other international agreements into Community law without Member State consent, it can at the same time point to a strong consensus among the States—all of which are signatories to the ECHR—as regards the foundations of the general principles of Community law. Finally, as we shall see below, by treating the ECHR as a source of inspiration rather than a formally binding, incorporated charter, the ECJ has retained the freedom to 'go beyond' the Convention in recognizing rights as part of EC law—such as the right to lawyer–client confidentiality derived from principles 'common to' Member State laws in *AM & S*[19]—which were not expressly protected in the ECHR.[20]

Apart from the ECHR, the Court occasionally draws—albeit much less frequently—on other regional and international instruments.[21] In *Defrenne* v. *Sabena III*,[22] the Court, deeming the elimination of sex discrimination to be a fundamental Community right, supported its conclusion by noting that 'the same concepts are recognized by the European Social Charter of 18 November 1961 and by Convention No. 111 of the International Labour Organization of 25 June 1958 concerning discrimination in respect of employment and occupation'.[23] In a number of cases, the International Covenant on Civil and Political Rights (ICCPR) has been identified as a source of inspiration for the general principles of EC law, although the ECJ in

---

[15] Case 222/84 *Johnston* v. *Chief Constable of the RUC* [1986] ECR 1651, para. 18; Case C–424/99 *Commission* v. *Austria* [2001] ECR I–9285, paras. 45–47 on access to judicial protection; Case C–13/94 *P.* v. *S. and Cornwall County Council* [1996] ECR I–2143, para. 18; Case C–185/97 *Coote* v. *Granada Hospitality* [1998] ECR I–5199, paras. 21–23 on discrimination; Cases C–465/00, 138 and 139/01 *Rechnungshof* v. *Österreichischer Rundfunk* [2003] ECR I–12489, on privacy and data protection.

[16] For an early discussion see Trabucchi AG in Case 118/75 *Watson and Belmann* [1976] ECR 1185, 1207.

[17] Case T–347/94 *Mayr-Melnhof Kartongesellschaft mbH* v. *Commission* [1998] ECR II–1751, para. 311; Case T–112/98 *Mannesmannröhren-Werke* v. *Commission* [2001] ECR II–729, para. 59, in which the CFI ruled that it had no jurisdiction to 'apply' the ECHR and that it was not part of EC law.

[18] See, e.g., Case C–260/89 *Elliniki Radiophonia Tileorassi AE* v. *Dimotiki Etairia Pliroforissis and Sotirios Kouvelas* [1991] ECR I–2925, para. 41; *Opinion 2/94 on Accession by the Community to the ECHR* [1996] ECR I–1759, para. 33; Case C–299/95 *Kremzow* v. *Austria* [1997] ECR I–2629, para. 14.

[19] Case 155/79 *AM & S Europe Ltd.* v. *Commission* [1982] ECR 1575; Cases T–125 and 253/03 R *Akzo Nobel Chemicals Ltd.* v. *Commission* [2003] ECR II–4771.

[20] This was noted by Warner AG at the time in his opinion in *AM & S*, n. 19 above. Since then, the absence of lawyer–client confidentiality has been found by the ECtHR in a range of cases to contribute to a violation of the right to individual petition under Art. 34, the right to privacy under Art. 8, and the right to a fair trial under Art. 6 of the ECHR.

[21] For an argument that the EU is subject to more extensive human rights obligations under international law than the ECJ has hitherto acknowledged, including under custom and treaties, see T. Ahmed and I. de Jesús Butler, 'The EU and Human Rights: An International Law Perspective' (2006) 17 *EJIL* 771.

[22] Case 149/77 *Defrenne* v. *Sabena* [1978] ECR 1365.

[23] *Ibid.*, para. 26 of the judgment. See also Case 6/75 *Horst* v. *Bundesknappschaft* [1975] ECR 823, 836, where Reischl AG drew on an 'internationally recognized principle of social security as set out in Art. 22(2) of International Labour Convention No. 48 on the Maintenance of Migrants' Pension Rights of 1935'.

the case of *Grant* was surprisingly dismissive of an opinion given by the ICCPR Human Rights Committee.[24]

Somewhat controversially in the *Kadi* and *Yusuf* cases, the Court of First Instance ruled that it could not review the EC's implementation of a UN Security Council resolution freezing the assets of individuals suspected of terrorist involvement for compliance with the general principles of EC law, because although the EC is not directly bound by the UN Charter, it is indirectly bound, by virtue of provisions of the EC Treaty, by obligations under the UN Charter in the same way as the Member States are.[25] However, the CFI ruled that it could indirectly review the UN resolution for compliance with *ius cogens* principles of international law concerning human rights protection.[26]

Moreover in a challenge brought to the EU Family Reunification Directive by the European Parliament, the ECJ—while upholding the Directive—drew not only on the ECHR and the ICCPR but also on the International Convention on the Rights of the Child, and referred in addition to the three Council of Europe human rights instruments which were cited in the Directive itself.[27] This was also the first case in which the ECJ (as compared with the CFI which had regularly cited the Charter) expressly relied on the provisions of the EU Charter of Fundamental Rights, which was politically proclaimed in 2000 and included in the Constitutional Treaty in 2004 but the legal status of which remained ambiguous after the subsequent non-ratification of the CT.[28] We will return to the content and status of the Charter of Fundamental Rights below.

(b) INTERNATIONAL HUMAN RIGHTS TREATIES: FLOOR OR CEILING?

A question which has been raised is whether the international human rights agreements to which all Member States are party should be seen as representing merely a lowest common denominator (a floor), beyond which the ECJ is free to develop higher EU standards of protection, or should they rather be seen as representing the only reliably *common* standard across Member States, and therefore as the highest standard (the ceiling) from which EU general principles can be derived?

The consensus in relation to the ECHR, at any rate, appears to be that it represents a floor rather than a ceiling,[29] and that while the level of protection for rights should not fall below

[24] Case C–249/96 *Grant* v. *South West Trains Ltd.* [1998] ECR I–621, paras. 44–47. For a case involving criminal penalties where the ICCPR was discussed by the CFI see Case T–48/96 *Acme Industry* v. *Council* [1999] ECR II–3089.

[25] Case T–315/01 *Kadi* v. *Council and Commission* [2005] ECR II–3649, paras. 192–208, 221–225; Case T–306/01 *Yusuf and Al Barakaat International Foundation* v. *Council and Commission* [2005] ECR II–3533, paras. 242–258, 272–276. Compare however Case T–228/02 *Organisation des Modjahedines du peuple d'Iran* v. *Council*, 12 Dec. 2006, involving so-called 'autonomous' EU measures which were not mandated by UN Security Council resolutions, and where the CFI found measures to be in breach of the general principles of EU law.

[26] Case T–315/01 *Kadi*, n. 25 above, paras. 226–232; Case T–306/01 *Yusuf*, n. 25 above, paras. 277–283. More specifically, the CFI discussed the impact of the UN Resolution on the right to property and the right to a fair hearing (also the right to effective judicial protection, although the CFI declared that this was not part of *ius cogens*), and found no incompatibility.

[27] Case C–540/03 *European Parliament* v. *Council* [2006] ECR I–5769, paras. 37–39, 57, 107 in particular. The three Council of Europe instruments were the European Social Charter 1961, the Revised European Social Charter, and the European Convention on the legal status of migrant workers 1977.

[28] *Ibid.*, paras. 37–39 and 58.

[29] See, e.g., Lenz AG in Case 137/84 *Ministère Public* v. *Mutsch* [1985] ECR 2681, 2690, on language rights in criminal proceedings, and also Scheuner, n. 13 above, 181.

what is provided by the Convention,[30] EU law can provide more extensive protection. This is the view which prevailed in the drafting of the EU Charter on Fundamental Rights.[31]

More controversial has been the practice in recent years of the EU in relation to other Council of Europe human rights instruments, such as the Convention on Action against Trafficking in Human Beings, in which the EU has insisted on including a 'disconnection clause', which effectively provides that the EU and its Member States, in relations between themselves, will apply the rules of EU law on trafficking in persons, rather than the provisions of the new Convention.[32] This practice has been criticized for undermining the application of human rights conventions of this kind to the EU and to its Member States, and for potentially allowing the application of lower human rights standards—below the floor set by the Council of Europe instrument—instead.[33]

The EU's Network of Independent Experts on Fundamental Rights, established in 2002, has consistently argued for the standards of protection for fundamental rights within EU law (in particular as expressed in the EU Charter) to be 'indexed' to international human rights standards, so as to avoid requiring Member States to choose between their loyalty to EU law and their other international commitments.[34]

(c) NATIONAL CONSTITUTIONAL TRADITIONS

The case law of the Court has drawn far less frequently on national constitutional provisions than on the ECHR and other European and international human rights instruments, despite the symbolic prominence given both by the Court and the EU treaties to the 'common constitutional traditions' of the States. While occasionally the Advocate General in a case has conducted a brief survey of national constitutional provisions, the Court has much more rarely cited any specific constitutional provision.[35]

The reasons are to some extent obvious, in that it is more difficult for the ECJ to assert a 'common' approach where a particular right does not appear in every national constitution, whereas an instrument like the ECHR is supposed to reflect precisely the collectively shared commitments of all Member States. Further, the fear of compromising the doctrinal supremacy of EU law by appearing to defer to a particular national constitutional provision has animated the ECJ's case law ever since *Costa v. Enel*.[36] This is evident in the *Hauer* case, where an EC regulation restricting the applicant's right to plant vines on her land prompted the referring German federal administrative court to declare that an EC regulation which was incompatible with German fundamental constitutional rights would not be applied. We see

---

[30] See the AG in Case C–49/88 *Al-Jubail Fertilizer Co. and Saudi Arabian Fertilizer Co. v. Council* [1991] ECR I–3187, 3230–3231.

[31] See Art. 52(3) of the Charter.

[32] See Art. 40(3) of the Council of Europe Convention on Action Against Trafficking in Human Persons 2005 (CETS no. 197).

[33] See the speech by Serhiy Holovaty, Chairperson of the Parliamentary Assembly of the Council of Europe's Committee on Legal Affairs, to the 26th Conference of European Ministers for Justice, Apr. 2005.

[34] For the Annual Reports and other reports of the Network of Experts see http://ec.europa.eu/justice_home/cfr_cdf/index_en.htm.

[35] See, e.g., Case 17/74 *Transocean Marine Paint v. Commission* [1974] ECR 1063, para. 17, where the Court, after a survey by the AG of the administrative law of several of the Member States, recognized 'the general rule that a person whose interests are perceptibly affected by a decision taken by a public authority must be given the opportunity to make his point of view known'.

[36] Case 6/64 [1964] ECR 585.

the ECJ here seeking to ground its decision both in the 'common constitutional traditions' of the States and in the collective commitments of the ECHR.

Case 44/79 **Hauer v. Land Rheinland-Pfalz**
[1979] ECR 3727

THE ECJ

14. As the Court declared in its judgment of 17 December 1970, Internationale Handelsgesellschaft [1970] ECR 1125, the question of a possible infringement of fundamental rights by a measure of the Community institutions can only be judged in the light of Community law itself. The introduction of special criteria for assessment stemming from the legislation or constitutional law of a particular Member State would, by damaging the substantive unity and efficacy of Community law, lead inevitably to the destruction of the unity of the Common Market and the jeopardizing of the cohesion of the Community.

15. The Court also emphasized in the judgment cited, and later in the judgment of 14 May 1974, Nold [1974] ECR 491, that fundamental rights form an integral part of the general principles of the law, the observance of which it ensures; that in safeguarding those rights, the Court is bound to draw inspiration from constitutional traditions common to the Member States, so that measures which are incompatible with the fundamental rights recognized by the Constitutions of those States are unacceptable in the Community, and that, similarly, international treaties for the protection of human rights on which the Member States have collaborated or of which they are signatories, can supply guidelines which should be followed within the framework of Community law. That conception was later recognized by the joint declaration of the European Parliament, the Council and the Commission of 5 April 1977, which, after recalling the case law of the Court, refers on the one hand to the European Convention for the Protection of Human Rights and Fundamental Freedoms of 4 November 1950.

. . .

17. The right to property is guaranteed in the Community legal order in accordance with the ideas common to the Constitutions of the Member States , which are also reflected in the first Protocol to the European Convention for the Protection of Human Rights. . . .

20. [I]t is necessary to consider also the indications provided by the constitutional rules and practices of the nine member states. One of the first points to emerge in this regard is that those rules and practices permit the legislature to control the use of private property in accordance with the general interest. Thus some constitutions refer to the obligations arising out of the ownership of property (German Grundgesetz, article 14 (2), first sentence), to its social function (Italian Constitution, article 42 (2)), to the subordination of its use to the requirements of the common good (German Grundgesetz , article 14 (2), second sentence, and the Irish Constitution, article 43.2.2*), or of social justice (Irish Constitution, article 43.2.1*). . . .

In *Martinez et al.*, the applicants drew unsuccessfully on the common parliamentary traditions of the Member States, as well as on the principle of freedom of association,[37] in order to challenge the refusal to permit them, as a group of non-aligned MEPs, to register as a political party in order to gain certain privileges, but the CFI did not deny the possibility in principle

---

[37] For other cases on freedom of association see Case C–415/93 *Union Royal Belge des Sociétés de Football Association* v. *Bosman* [1995] ECR I–4921; Case C–325/92 *Montecatini* v. *Commission* [1999] ECR I–4539.

that 'common parliamentary traditions' could form a source of inspiration for the general principles of EC law.[38]

(d) NATIONAL CONSTITUTIONAL TRADITIONS AND THE 'MAXIMUM STANDARD' PROBLEM

The identification of shared underpinnings in establishing the sources of inspiration for EU fundamental rights is, of course, only a first step. If the ECJ were to take a 'lowest common denominator' approach, the risk would be that the Court would give EU recognition only to those rights shared by all (or most) States, and might ignore the protection given by a sole State to a right considered fundamental within that legal order. On the other hand, a 'maximum standard' approach could lead to the contrary situation where one particular Member State's recognition of a specific right, even if shared by no other, would be imposed by the ECJ on the rest of the States through the general principles of EU law.[39]

In *Mannesmannröhren-Werke*, concerning the right to remain silent in the context of competition proceedings, the CFI was dismissive of the 'maximum standard' approach:

> In the field of competition law, the national laws of the Member States do not, in general, recognise a right not to incriminate oneself. It is, therefore, immaterial to the result of the present case whether or not, as the applicant claims, there is such a principle in German law.[40]

In the case of *AM & S*, not all of the Member States were happy with the Court's derivation of a principle of lawyer–client confidentiality from a comparative survey of the laws of the Member States, and the French government in particular argued that the case represented 'an attempt to foist on the Community what was no more than a domestic rule of English law'.[41] However, the Advocate General took the view that a general principle could be distilled from among the various States even if the 'conceptual origin' of the principle and 'the scope of its application in detail' differed as between Member States.[42]

A somewhat similar technique was used by the ECJ in *Omega Spielhallen*, where it chose to abstract from the strong and *particular conception* of human dignity within German law to a more *general concept* of human dignity which could be said to be shared by all the Member States. However, *Omega Spielhallen* was an easier case to decide, in that it did not concern a Member State challenge to the validity of an EC measure, but rather a State seeking an individual derogation from EC free movement rules.[43] To that extent Germany was seeking recognition for its own standards of protection for human dignity, not in order to have it

---

[38] Cases T–222, 327, and 329/99 *Martinez, Gaulle, Front national and Bonino* v. *European Parliament* [2001] ECR II–2823, para. 240.

[39] Compare L. Besselink, 'Entrapped by the Maximum Standard: on Fundamental Rights, Pluralism and Subsidiarity in the European Union' (1998) 35 *CMLRev.* 629 and J. Weiler, 'Fundamental Rights and Fundamental Boundaries', in his *The Constitution of Europe* (Cambridge University Press, 1999), ch. 3.

[40] Case T–112/98 *Mannesmannröhren-Werke*, n. 17 above, para. 84.

[41] See Warner AG in Case 155/79 *AM & S*, n. 19 above, 1575, 1631. Case 17/74 *Transocean Marine Paint*, n. 35 above, provides another example of the recognition by the Court of a general principle of Community law where some, but not all, of the Member States afford protection to the particular right or principle.

[42] *Ibid.*

[43] Case C–36/02 *Omega Spielhallen- und Automatenaufstellungs-GmbH* v. *Oberbürgermeisterin der Bundesstadt Bonn* [2004] ECR I–9609, paras. 34–38. See also Case C–112/00 *Schmidberger* v. *Austria* [2003] ECR I–5659.

imposed on the other Member States, but in order to gain an exemption from free movement principles.

As a general matter, it can be said that the Court is prepared to recognize a particular right as part of the general principles of EU law when several Member States, even if not all of them, expressly recognize that right,[44] and the ECJ has also been more careful than the CFI not to dismiss a State's claim for recognition of a particular right on the basis that it is recognized by that State only.

Finally, even where it might be said that there is general consensus amongst the States that a particular right exists, it seems inevitable that there will not be a consensus as to how that right should be interpreted and 'translated' into a general principle of EU law. For instance, even if all Member States agree that there should be protection for freedom of expression, they are likely to have rather different views on how, in a particular context, it should be protected. National legal systems vary widely, for example, in the degree to which they regulate the nature and content of broadcasting.[45]

To take another example, while all Member States recognize the right to life, a handful of the twenty-nine states including Ireland and Malta continue to maintain extremely restrictive national abortion laws, which in Ireland's case partly reflects the constitutional status of the right to life of the foetus. Another example can be seen in the strong protection given by Germany's *Grundgesetz* to economic rights and to the freedom to pursue a trade or profession, while the constitutions of other States reflect different social priorities. In *Grant* and *D v. Council*, the ECJ relied in part on different national legal conceptions of marriage to deny that there had been any breach of the applicants' rights under the general principles of EC law.[46]

In other words, although the idea of 'common constitutional traditions' as a foundation for the general principles of EU law is an attractive one in principle, it is difficult to avoid the fact that the differences between specific national conceptions of particular human rights are often great. Thus, even if the ECJ accepts the argument of a particular party that a given right should be recognized as part of Community law, the way in which the Court determines the legal scope of that right and the permissible restrictions upon it in the context of the case at hand may well differ from the way it would be applied in a national context, and may disappoint the applicant, as seen in *Hauer*[47] and *Handelsgesellschaft*.[48]

5. CHALLENGES TO EU ACTION: ADJUDICATION OF RIGHTS CLAIMS

The ECJ over time has heard a growing number of challenges to EU legislation in which violation of human rights has been pleaded as a ground. The Court appears increasingly willing to go beyond the minimal citation of human rights provisions, and in particular to discuss the substantive case law of the European Court of Human Rights. Nonetheless, despite this increasing engagement with human rights arguments, the number of cases in which the Court

---

[44] See, e.g., the ECJ's note of caution in Case C–49/88 *Al-Jubail*, n. 30 above, para. 16.

[45] R. Craufurd-Smith, *Broadcasting Law and Fundamental Rights* (Oxford University Press, 1997). For a recent example see Case C–245/01 *RTL Television GmbH* v. *Niedersächsische Landesmedienanstalt für privaten Rundfunk* [2003] ECR I–12489.

[46] Case C–249/96 *Grant*, n. 24 above; Cases C–122 and 125/99 P *D* v. *Council* [2001] ECR I–4319.

[47] Case 44/79 *Hauer* v. *Land Rheinland-Pfalz* [1979] ECR 3727.

[48] Case 11/70 *Internationale Handelsgesellschaft* v. *Einfuhr- und Vorratstelle für Getreide und Futtermittel* [1970] ECR 1125.

has actually annulled the EU legislation impugned remains very low. We shall see below that there has been a greater degree of success in challenging individual administrative acts of the Commission or other EC actors, but that the Court has remained deferential in its review of EU legislation.[49]

(a) CHALLENGES TO LEGISLATION

Although in *Nold*[50] the Court had declared that 'general principles of law' would take precedence, in the event of conflict, over specific Community measures, the ECJ emphasized that in the dispute at hand the right to property and to a trade or profession were far from absolute, and that limitations were justified by the overall objectives of the EC. And in a series of cases concerning property and economic rights which followed, the ECJ continued the approach adopted in *Nold* and *Hauer*, ruling that restrictions on property rights for the promotion of other legitimate interests are acceptable, and that only a disproportionate and intolerable or arbitrary interference will actually render legislation invalid.

In *Bosphorous*, concerning the effects on the applicant's rights of an EC regulation implementing UN-mandated sanctions against the former Yugoslavia, the ECJ ruled that the fundamental interests of the international community could justify restrictions of property or trade rights caused by the impounding of a Yugoslav-owned aircraft leased by the applicant, even where the latter appeared to be entirely uninvolved in any activities of the Yugoslav State.[51] A similar ruling was given by the CFI in the *Yusuf* and *Kadi* cases involving the freezing of assets of individuals by an EC Regulation implementing a UN Security Council Resolution,[52] although in the *Modjahedines* case the CFI ruled that where assets are frozen by the EU authorities (other than where mandated by a UN SC resolution) the right to a fair hearing, the right to be given reasons and the right to effective judicial protection are applicable, even if in restricted form.[53]

In *Booker Aquacultur*, the Court ruled that an EC Directive on the control of fish diseases which failed to require compensation for the compulsory destruction of diseased fish by national authorities did not constitute a disproportionate restriction on the right to property.[54] Similarly, in a range of other challenges to EU measures relying on a variety of trade and property rights claims, the Court has repeatedly emphasized the legitimacy of 'reasonable' restrictions in accordance with the ECHR.[55]

---

[49] For early commentaries on this see A. Clapham, 'A Human Rights Policy for the European Community' (1990) 10 *YBEL* 309, 331; J. Coppel and A. O'Neill, 'The European Court of Justice: Taking Rights Seriously?' (1992) 29 *CMLRev.* 669. For discussion of successful claims invoking fundamental rights against the Community, including against administrative and legislative action, see J.H.H. Weiler and N. Lockhart, ' "Taking Rights Seriously" Seriously: The European Court and its Fundamental Rights Jurisprudence' (1995) 32 *CMLRev.* 51 and 579.

[50] Case 4/73 *Nold* v. *Commission* [1974] ECR 491.

[51] See Case C–84/95 *Bosphorus* v. *Minister for Transport* [1996] ECR I–3953 and also the first instance judgment in Case T–184/95 *Dorsch Consult* v. *Council* [1998] ECR II–667, paras. 87–88.

[52] See Case T–315/01 *Kadi* and Case T–306/01 *Yusuf*, both n. 25 above. However, since the CFI was essentially reviewing the compatibility with human rights of the UN measure, rather than the EC measure (since the EC was treated as having no discretion with regard to the implementation of the Resolution), the CFI's review was based on its reading of the right to property as part of international *ius cogens*.

[53] Case T–228/02 *Modjahedines*, n. 25 above.

[54] Cases C–20 and 64/00 *Booker Aquacultur Ltd. and Hydro Seafood GSP* v. *The Scottish Ministers* [2003] ECR I–7411.

[55] See, e.g., Cases C–37 and 38/02 *Di Lenardo Adriano Srl* v. *Ministero del Commercio con l'Estero* [2004] ECR I–6911; Cases C–453/03, 11, 12, and 194/04 *The Queen, ex p. ABNA Ltd.* v. *Secretary of State for Health and Food*

Even beyond the sphere of property rights, there has been very limited success in challenging EU legislation. In proceedings brought by the Dutch government to challenge the legality of the Biotechnology Directive on the basis that its provisions concerning the patentability of isolated parts of the body violated the right to human dignity and to human integrity, the ECJ responded that the legislative provisions in question ensured full respect for human dignity and integrity.[56] Moreover in a recent challenge by the European Parliament to the EU Directive on family reunion, relying on a range of human rights arguments, the ECJ responded that the Directive did not violate the right to respect for family life or the obligation to have regard to the best interests of the child, and that it left the Member States a sufficient margin of appreciation in implementing the Directive to enable them to comply with such rights.[57]

(b) CHALLENGES TO ADMINISTRATIVE ACTS

In two classes of case in particular—those of staff cases, and competition law proceedings—applicants have enjoyed a greater measure of success in challenging specific EC administrative acts (rather than general legislative measures) for violation of fundamental rights.

(i) *Staff Cases*

In a range of staff and recruitment cases the ECJ has accepted arguments based on pleas such as the violation of freedom of expression,[58] freedom of religion,[59] the right to private life, and non-discrimination,[60] and has required the EU institutions to amend several of their practices.

A notable exception is the case of *D* v. *Council* in which the ECJ ruled that neither the principle of equal treatment, non-discrimination on grounds of sex, nor respect for private and family life was breached by the Council's refusal to recognize a Swedish employee's registered partnership with a same-sex partner (which had a civil status comparable to marriage in Sweden) as equivalent to marriage for the purposes of obtaining an EU staff household allowance.[61] And in *Joël De Bry*, the ECJ ruled that the rights of the defence did not include any obligation on the Commission to give a prior warning to an employee before a staff appraisal.[62]

(ii) *Competition Proceedings*

The area of the Commission's enforcement powers in competition proceedings has been a fertile source of litigation, in which general principles of law and fundamental rights—often the

---

Standards Agency [2005] ECR I–10423; Case C–295/03 P *Alessandrini* v. *Commission* [2005] ECR I–5673; Case C–347/03 *Regione autonoma, Friuli-Venezia Giulia and Agenzia regionale per lo sviluppo rurale (ERSA)* v. *Ministero delle Politiche Agricole e Forestali* [2005] ECR I–3785. On intellectual property see, e.g., Case T 195/00 *Travelex Global and Financial Services Ltd.* v. *Commission* [2003] ECR II–1677.

56 Case C–377/98 *Netherlands* v. *Council and Parliament* [2001] ECR I–7079.
57 Case C–540/03 *European Parliament* v. *Council*, n. 27 above.
58 Case 100/88 *Oyowe and Traore* v. *Commission* [1989] ECR 4285. Compare the unsuccessful outcome in the colourful case of Case C–274/99 P *Connolly* v. *Commission* [2001] ECR I–1611.
59 Case 130/75 *Prais* v. *Council* [1976] ECR 1589.
60 For some examples see Case C–404/92 P *X* v. *Commission* [1994] ECR I–4737; Cases C–122 and 125/99 P *D*, n. 46 above; Case C–191/98 P *Tzoanos* v. *Commission* [1999] ECR I–8223; Case C–252/97 *N* v. *Commission* [1998] ECR I–4871.
61 Cases C–122 and 125/99 P *D*, n. 46 above.
62 Case C–344/05 P *Commission* v. *Joël De Bry* [2006] ECR I–10915.

cluster of rights referred to as 'rights of the defence'[63] including the right to a fair hearing[64] and related principles such as non-retroactivity of penal liability[65]—have frequently been invoked to challenge executive and administrative EC action.

The Commission's powers in competition proceedings are very wide, including the authority to investigate and make searches, as well as to impose severe financial penalties, and affected parties have repeatedly called upon the Court to limit and control their exercise by reference to fundamental legal principles.[66] The relatively early case of *Hoechst* involved a challenge by the applicant company to various decisions of the Commission ordering an investigation into its affairs in the context of suspected anti-competitive practices.

Cases 46/87 and 227/88, **Hoechst AG v. Commission**
[1989] ECR 2859

THE ECJ

12. It should be noted, before the nature and scope of the Commission's powers of investigation under Article 14 of Regulation No 17 are examined, that that article cannot be interpreted in such a way as to give rise to results which are incompatible with the general principles of Community law and in particular with fundamental rights.

. . .

14. In interpreting Article 14 of Regulation No 17, regard must be had in particular to the rights of the defence, a principle whose fundamental nature has been stressed on numerous occasions in the Courts decisions (see in particular the judgment of 9 November 1983 in Case 322/81 Michelin v. Commission [1983] ECR 3461 paragraph 7).

. . .

17. Since the applicant has also relied on the requirements stemming from the fundamental right to the inviolability of the home, it should be observed that, although the existence of such a right must be recognized in the Community legal order as a principle common to the laws of the Member States in regard to the private dwellings of natural persons, the same is not true in regard to undertakings, because there are not inconsiderable divergences between the legal systems of the Member States in regard to the nature and degree of protection afforded to business premises against intervention by the public authorities.

---

[63] For some recent examples see the principle of *non bis in idem* in Case C–397/03 P *Archer Daniels Midland* v. *Commission* [2006] ECR I–4429, and the right of access to documents (specifically to the file containing objections and evidence against a defendant) in Case T–210/01 *GEC* v. *Commission* [2005] ECR II–5575; Cases C–204–219/00 P, *Aalborg Portland A/S et al.* v. *Commission* [2004] ECR I–123.

[64] Case C–185/95 P *Baustahlgewebe* v. *Commission* [1998] ECR I–8417 (on the length of time of proceedings), and compare Cases T–213/95 and 18/96 *SCK & FNK* v. *Commission* [1997] ECR II–1739. Other cases outside the competition field which uphold the right to a fair hearing include Case C–49/88 *Al-Jubail*, n. 30 above (on anti-dumping); Case C–7/98 *Krombach* v. *Bamberski* [2000] ECR II–1935 (in the context of the Brussels Convention); Case T–83/96 *Van der Wal* v. *Commission* [1998] ECR II–545 (on the right of access to documents used in judicial proceedings).

[65] For an important ruling of the ECJ's Grand Chamber on this principle see Cases C–189–213/02 P, *Dansk Rorindustri et al.* v. *Commission* [2005] ECR I–5425.

[66] For selected examples from a long list see Cases 17/74, n. 35 above; Cases 209–215/78 *Van Landewyck* v. *Commission* [1980] ECR 3125; Case 136/79 *National Panasonic* v. *Commission* [1980] ECR 2033; Cases 100–103/80 *Musique Diffusion Française* v. *Commission* [1983] ECR 1825; Case 322/81 *Michelin* v. *Commission* [1983] ECR 3461; Case 5/85 *AKZO Chemie* v. *Commission* [1986] ECR 2585; Case 374/87 *Orkem* v. *Commission*

18. No other inference is to be drawn from Article 8(1) of the European Convention on Human Rights which provides that: 'Everyone has the right to respect for his private and family life, his home and his correspondence'. The protective scope of that article is concerned with the development of man's personal freedom and may not therefore be extended to business premises. Furthermore, it should be noted that there is no case law of the European Convention on Human Rights on that subject.

19. None the less, in all the legal systems of the Member States, any intervention by the public authorities in the sphere of private activities of any person, whether natural or legal, must have a legal basis and be justified on the grounds laid down by law, and, consequently, those systems provide, albeit in different forms, protection against arbitrary or disproportionate intervention. The need for such protection must be recognized as a general principle of Community law.

The Court found on the facts of the case that there had been no breach by the Commission of any of the principles invoked by the applicants. The judgment was criticized on the ground that the Court too rapidly dismissed the argument that the Commission's power of search contravened the right to privacy of the dwelling which is protected in the ECHR, and had overlooked existing case law of the Court of Human Rights (ECtHR).[67] In its subsequent ruling in *Niemietz*,[68] the ECtHR ruled explicitly that the right to respect for private life in Article 8 of the Convention did extend to business premises, and this was later acknowledged by the ECJ in other cases including *Roquette Frères*, even while emphasizing that more extensive interference may be justified under Article 8 ECHR where business or commercial premises are concerned.[69]

Similarly, in relation to the right to a fair trial in Article 6(1) of the ECHR, the decision of the ECJ in *Orkem*,[70] in which it ruled that Article 6 did not confer the right 'not to give evidence against oneself', was at odds with the subsequent ruling of the ECtHR in *Funke*, in which that court indicated that Article 6 protected the right 'to remain silent and not to contribute to incriminating [oneself]'.[71] However in the later *Hüls* judgment of the ECJ—also concerning competition law proceedings—the Court emphasized the significance of the ECHR and of the case law of the ECtHR, ruling that the presumption of innocence applies to competition proceedings which may result in fines.[72] In *Mannesmannröhren-Werke*, where the applicant relied on Article 6 ECHR to challenge the Commission's insistence, on pain of penalty, that it must answer certain questions posed in the course of a competition investigation, the CFI ruled that the applicant 'cannot directly invoke the Convention before the

---

[1989] ECR 3283; Case T–11/89 *Shell* v. *Commission* [1992] ECR II–757; Case T–347/94 *Mayr-Melnhof*, n. 17 above; Case C–185/95 P *Baustahlgewebe*, n. 64 above; Case T–112/98 *Mannesmannröhren-Werke*, n. 17 above.

67 See in particular the *Chappell* case, App. no. 10461/83, Series A, No. 152A, although this case did not resolve the issue.

68 *Niemietz* v. *Germany*, Series A, No. 251 (1992) 16 EHRR 97, para. 31 in particular.

69 Case C–94/00 *Roquettes Frères SA* v. *Commission* [2002] ECR I–9011, para. 29.

70 Case 374/87 *Orkem*, n. 66 above, para. 30 of the judgment. However, the Court did go on to rule that by virtue of the 'rights of the defence' in investigative procedures, the Commission could not compel a company to provide it with answers which might involve an admission of a breach which it was incumbent on the Commission to prove. See also Case C–60/92 *Otto* v. *Postbank* [1993] ECR I–5683. For a case dealing with alleged pressure imposed by the Commission on an applicant to admit to particular allegations in order to have the potential fine reduced see Case T–347/94 *Mayr-Melnhof*, n. 17 above.

71 *Funke* v. *France*, Series A, No. 256A (1993) 16 EHRR 297, para. 44 of the judgment. See W. van Overbeek, 'The Right to Remain Silent in Competition Investigations' (1994) 15 *ECLR* 127.

72 Case C–199/92 P *Hüls* v. *Commission* [1999] ECR I–4287, paras. 149–150.

Community Courts', but at the same time asserted that the general principles of EC law, including the various rights of the defence, provided equivalent protection.[73] Ultimately, however, neither the ECJ nor the CFI found any infringement of the various rights of the defence by the Commission in either *Hüls* or *Mannesmannröhren-Werke*, or in a series of other cases dealing with the presumption of innocence.[74] And in *Danzer*, where the applicants attempted to extend the right against self-incrimination to the context of company law, the CFI ruled that the right did not apply to the requirement on companies under an EC Company Law Directive to disclose their annual accounts.[75]

(c) SUMMARY

i. Although the broad 'sources of inspiration' for the general principles of EC law in national constitutional traditions and international agreements are relatively clear and uncontroversial, the derivation by the ECJ of particular concrete rights from these general sources, and their application to the circumstances of specific cases, is more contested .

ii. Some have argued for the ECJ to develop a 'maximum universal standard' based on the highest level of protection given by any single Member State, while others have warned against the risk of the opposite 'lowest common denominator' approach. While the Court is clearly reluctant to refuse EC law recognition to a principle which is important in a number of Member States, it has never expressly endorsed either a maximalist or a minimalist approach, but has continued on a pragmatic case-by-case basis to identify and interpret particular rights which are pleaded.

iii. While the European Convention on Human Rights is not a formal part of EC law, it is the most common source of reference for fundamental EU rights. The CFI and the ECJ regularly draw on the provisions of the ECHR, and in recent years have made extensive reference to the case law of the Court of Human Rights. The relationship between the two systems, which would have been clarified by the EU Charter of Fundamental Rights and the Treaty establishing a Constitution for Europe, remains legally ambiguous. Other international human rights instruments are occasionally cited, including now the EU Charter itself.

iv. While fundamental rights claims are increasingly frequently made before the CFI and ECJ, they have been more successful in disputes involving individual administrative acts such as in staff cases or occasionally in competition proceedings, than in challenges to legislative policy.

---

[73] Case T–112/98 *Mannesmannröhren-Werke*, n. 17 above, paras. 66–77.

[74] See, e.g., Case C–57/02 P *Acerinox* v. *Commission* [2005] ECR I–6689, paras. 87–89, where use by the Commission of a voluntary admission made earlier to it by an undertaking, to establish an infringement, did not constitute a breach of the privilege against self-incrimination or of other rights of the defence. In Case T–59/02 *Archer Daniels Midland Co.* v. *Commission*, 27 Sept. 2006, the CFI ruled that reliance on an incriminating statement contained in a report compiled by the US FBI did not in the circumstances of the case constitute a violation of the right against self-incrimination or other rights of the defence.

[75] Case T–47/02 *Danzer* v. *Council* [2006] ECR II–1779. The CFI also dismissed a range of other arguments that various rights including protection of business secrets, principles of free competition, property rights and data protection had been infringed, ruling that any restrictions on the rights claimed were clearly justified and not disproportionate.

6. CHALLENGES TO MEMBER STATE ACTION: FUNDAMENTAL RIGHTS

Thus far we have considered the role of human rights as standards for assessing the legality of EU action, and as constraints on the acts of the EU institutions. Over time, however, the ECJ also ruled that fundamental rights are binding not only on the EC institutions but also on the Member States when they are acting within the scope of application of EC law. This development remains contentious, not only because it is not always clear when and whether States are acting 'within the scope of application' of EC law, but also more generally because some of the Member States are resistant to the idea of the ECJ determining standards of human rights protection to be applied to them The various situations in which EC fundamental rights have been held to bind Member States are set out below.

(a) APPLYING PROVISIONS OF EC LEGISLATION BASED ON PROTECTION FOR HUMAN RIGHTS

When applying provisions of EC legislation which are based on protection for human rights, Member States are bound by the general principles of EC law.

In *Rutili* in 1975, the ECJ described provisions of Directive 64/221, which set limits on the restrictions which could be imposed Member States on the free movement of workers, as specific expressions of the more general principles enshrined in the ECHR.[76] The restrictive measures adopted by France in that case therefore had to be examined for compliance with the provisions of the Directive, which in turn reflected provisions of the ECHR.

Similarly in *Johnston* v. *RUC*, the ECJ declared that the requirement of judicial control stipulated in the 1976 Equal Treatment Directive reflected a general principle of EC law derived both from national constitutional traditions and from Articles 6 and 13 of the ECHR, and that the Directive's requirement accordingly had to be interpreted as providing the right to an effective remedy.[77]

The ECJ gave a similar ruling about the relationship between the right to privacy in Article 8 of the ECHR and the EU Data Processing Directive in the *Österreichischer Rundfunk* case. The relevant provisions of the Directive were to be interpreted in the light of the Convention and ECHR case law.[78]

(b) MEMBER STATES AS 'AGENTS'

When acting as 'agents' of EC law, implementing or enforcing EC measures, Member States are bound by the general principles of EC law. In a second stage of development, the ECJ went further and ruled that the Member States are required, when interpreting and implementing Community law, to act and to legislate in a way which respects the rights set out in the ECHR,

---

[76] For comment on this aspect of the case see Trabucchi AG in Case 118/75 *Watson*, n.16 above, 1207–1208.

[77] Case 222/84 *Johnston*, n. 15 above. For similar rulings see Case 222/86 *UNECTEF* v. *Heylens* [1987] ECR 4097; Case C–185/97 *Coote*, n. 15 above. Also on access to court and the ECHR see Case T–111/96 *ITT Promedia NV* v. *Commission* [1998] ECR II–2937.

[78] Cases C–465/00, 138, and 139/01 *Österreichischer Rundfunk*, n. 15 above.

even when the Community measures do not themselves embody the particular right claimed,[79] as was the case in *Rutili, Johnston,* and *Österreichischer Rundfunk.*

In a case brought by the Commission against Germany, challenging Germany's implementation of Regulation 1612/68 on migrant workers whereby a prior condition of adequate housing before family members could install themselves with a migrant worker had been imposed, the ECJ upheld the Commission's challenge and ruled that the Regulation must be interpreted in the light of the requirement of respect for family life in Article 8 of the ECHR.[80] In *Kent Kirk,* the Court ruled that the domestic effect of applying a retroactive provision of an EC fisheries regulation to a UK statutory instrument would violate the principle of non-retroactivity of penal liability enshrined in Article 7 of the ECHR.[81]

The legal position was clearly outlined in *Wachauf,* in which the Court ruled that Member States are bound, when implementing Community law, by all of the same general principles and fundamental rights which bind the Community in its actions.[82] In *Wachauf* this meant that the Member State should endeavour to provide compensation, on the expiry of his tenancy, for a tenant farmer who had discontinued milk production, even though the EC Regulation being implemented did not specifically provide for such compensation.[83]

In both the *Lindqvist* case concerning the Data Protection Directive[84] and the challenge brought by the European Parliament to the Family Reunification Directive,[85] the ECJ emphasized that those Directives did not in themselves violate fundamental rights by leaving discretionary choices to the Member States, because the Directives could not be read as permitting the Member States to use their discretion in such a way as to infringe fundamental rights.

(c) MEMBER STATES DEROGATING FROM MEASURES OF EC LAW

The previous category concerns situations in which Member States are *implementing* EC measures, including where they enjoy room for discretion in implementation. However, Member States are also sometimes permitted by the Treaty or by analogous principles developed by the ECJ to *derogate* from EC rules on public policy or other grounds.

Rutili provides one example of such a situation, but in that case an EC directive, which defined the scope of the derogation, also required the Member States to protect certain rights which are included the ECHR. It was later argued to the Court in a number of cases, however, that whenever the Member States seek to rely on an exception to the operation of Community rules, they are acting within the field of Community law and thus should be bound to respect

---

[79] Case C–219/91 *Criminal Proceedings against Ter Voort* [1992] ECR I–5495, paras. 33–38 on compliance by a Member State with Art. 10 of the ECHR when giving effect to EC Dir. 65/65 on the categorization of medicinal products.

[80] Case 249/86 *Commission* v. *Germany* [1989] ECR 1263.

[81] Case 63/83 *R.* v. *Kent Kirk* [1984] ECR 2689, paras. 21–23. More recently on Art. 7 ECHR and non-retroactivity of penal liability see Cases C–74 and 129/95 *Criminal Proceedings against X* [1996] ECR I–6609; Case C–60/02 *Criminal Proceedings against X* [2004] ECR I–651; Case C–387/02 *Berlusconi et al.* [2005] ECR I–3565.

[82] Case 5/88 *Wachauf* v. *Germany* [1989] ECR 2609, paras. 17–19. See also Case C–292/97 *Karlsson* [2000] ECR I–2737.

[83] On the substance of the right, however, the ECJ in later cases adopted a less expansive approach to compensation as a dimension of the right to property: Cases C–20 and 64/00 *Booker Aquacultur*, n. 54 above; Case C–2/92 *Bostock* [1994] ECR I–955; Case C–313/99 *Mulligan* v. *Minister for Agriculture and Food* [2002] ECR I–5719.

[84] Case C–101/01 *Lindqvist* [2003] ECR I–12971, paras. 84–90.

[85] Case C–540/03 *European Parliament* v. *Council*, n. 27 above, paras. 15–23.

such rights. In *Cinéthèque*,[86] the ECJ initially appeared—against the advice of Advocate General Slynn—to reject this argument, and in *Demirel*, the Court stated firmly that it would not examine the compatibility of national law with fundamental rights or any other general principles of law where the national law lay 'outside the scope of Community law'.[87]

In the *ERT* case, however, the ECJ clarified its stance on derogations from EC law, declaring that it had a duty to ensure that the Member State had adequately respected those fundamental rights which were part of Community law.

Case C–260/89 Elliniki Radiophonia Tileorassi AE (ERT) v. Dimotiki Etairia Pliroforissis and Sotirios Kouvelas
[1991] ECR I–2925

[Note ToA renumbering: Arts. 56 and 66 are now Arts. 46 and 55 respectively]

ERT was a Greek radio and television company which enjoyed exclusive rights under statute, and which sought an injunction from a domestic court against the respondents, who had set up a TV station and begun to broadcast programmes in defiance of ERT's exclusive statutory rights. The defence relied mainly on EC law relating to the free movement of goods and to the rules on competition and monopolies, as well as on the provisions of the ECHR concerning freedom of expression. The ECJ began by repeating its traditional sentences on the sources of inspiration for fundamental rights in EC law, and cited its judgments in *Nold* and *Wachauf*.

THE ECJ

42. As the Court has held (see Cases C–60 & 61/84 *Cinéthèque*, paragraph 25 and Case C–12/86 *Demirel v. Stadt Schwäbisch Gmünd*, paragraph 28), it has no power to examine the compatibility with the European Convention on Human Rights of national rules which do not fall within the scope of Community law. On the other hand, where such rules do fall within the scope of Community law, and reference is made to the Court for a preliminary ruling, it must provide all the criteria of interpretation needed by the national court to determine whether those rules are compatible with the fundamental rights the observance of which the Court ensures and which derive in particular from the European Convention on Human Rights.

43. In particular, where a Member State relies on the combined provisions of Articles 56 and 66 in order to justify rules which are likely to obstruct the exercise of the freedom to provide services, such justification, provided for by Community law, must be interpreted in the light of the general principles of law and in particular of fundamental rights. Thus the national rules in question can fall under the exceptions provided for by the combined provisions of Article 56 and 66 only if they are compatible with the fundamental rights, the observance of which is ensured by the Court.

44. It follows that in such a case it is for the national court, and if necessary, the Court of Justice to appraise the application of those provisions having regard to all the rules of Community law, including freedom of expression, as embodied in Article 10 of the European

---

[86] Cases 60 and 61/84 *Cinéthèque v. Fédération Nationale des Cinémas Français* [1985] ECR 2605, paras. 25–26 in particular.

[87] Case 12/86 *Demirel v. Stadt Schwäbisch Gmünd* [1987] ECR 3719, para. 28. For criticism of the case as an attempt by the ECJ to increase its own jurisdiction and promote its own conception of fundamental rights see Coppel and O'Neill, n. 49 above; for a response see Weiler and Lockhart, n. 49 above.

Convention on Human Rights, as a general principle of law the observance of which is ensured by the Court.

45. The reply to the national court must therefore be that the limitations imposed on the power of the Member States to apply the provisions referred to in Articles 66 and 56 of the Treaty on grounds of public policy, public security and public health must be appraised in the light of the general principle of freedom of expression embodied in Article 10 of the European Convention on Human Rights.

The ruling represents a further extension of the Court's jurisdiction to review compliance with fundamental rights by the Member States when they rely upon derogations from basic Treaty rules, and a further encroachment by the 'general principles of EC law' into the legal systems of the Member States. In the words of two seasoned observers commenting on the *ERT* ruling, 'some of those derogations are bound up with fundamental notions governing the relationship between States and their citizens cannot fail to appreciate the potential incidence of that judgment on national sovereignty'.[88] The subsequent *Familiapress* case clarified that even where a Member State does not rely on one of the Treaty-based public-policy-type derogations, but instead on the broader range of 'public interest justifications' developed by the ECJ for non-discriminatory national measures, the latter measure will be assessed by the ECJ for compatibility with fundamental rights.[89]

Despite arguments made—even by members of the Court itself—to reduce or confine the scope of these rulings,[90] they have been confirmed many times since. In the sensitive field of immigration, for example, there has been a steady stream of rulings concerning the right to family life where States had relied on the public policy or public interest derogation to expel a migrant who was covered by EC law or to refuse some other family benefit. In cases such as *Orfanopoulos*,[91] *MRAX*,[92] *Baumbast*,[93] *Carpenter*,[94] *Akrich*,[95] and *Commission v. Germany*,[96] the Court emphasized the requirements on States to take adequate account of the impact of its proposed action on the right to family life, as protected by Article 8 of the ECHR. Indeed in both *Carpenter* and even more notably in *Akrich*, the ECJ seemed to stretch its previous interpretation of what falls 'within the scope of Community law'.

In *Carpenter*, the Court ruled that the UK's proposal to deport the non-EU-national spouse of a British citizen constituted a potential restriction on the latter's freedom to provide cross-border services, so that the measure fell within the scope of EC law, and was ultimately found by the Court to violate the right to respect for family life.[97] In *Akrich*, which also involved a

---

[88] D. Mancini and D. Keeling, 'From *CILFIT* to *ERT*: The Constitutional Challenge Facing the European Court' (1991) 11 *YBEL* 1, 11–12.

[89] Case C–368/95 *Vereinigte Familiapress Zeitungsverlags- und Vertriebs GmbH v. Heinrich Bauer Verlag* [1997] ECR I–3689. This case clarified an uncertainty which had existed since the *Cinéthèque* ruling, n. 86 above.

[90] F. Jacobs, 'Human Rights in the European Union: The Role of the Court of Justice' (2001) 26 *ELRev.* 331, 337–339. Compare his expansive earlier argument for human rights review of national measures by the ECJ in his opinion as AG in Case C–168/91 *Konstantinidis v. Stadt Altensteig* [1993] ECR I–1191, especially at 1211–1212.

[91] Cases C–482 and 493/01 *Orfanopoulos and Oliveri v. Land Baden-Württemberg* [2004] ECR I–5257, paras. 97–100.

[92] Case C–459/99 *MRAX v. Belgium* [2002] ECR I–6591, paras. 53, 61, and 62.

[93] Case C–413/99 *Baumbast and R. v. Home Secretary* [2002] ECR I–7091, paras. 72–73.

[94] Case C–60/00 *Carpenter v. Home Secretary* [2002] ECR I–6279.

[95] Case C–109/01 *Home Secretary v. Akrich* [2003] ECR I–9607.

[96] Case C–441/02 *Commission v. Germany* [2006] ECR I–3449, paras. 108–113.

[97] Case C–60/00 *Carpenter*, n. 94 above, paras. 37–46.

proposed deportation by the UK of a non-EU-national spouse, the ECJ ruled that although the spouse in this case was not lawfully resident and was therefore not covered by EC law on the free movement of workers or services, the fact that she was married to an EU citizen and returning to the UK from Ireland nonetheless meant that the UK was obliged to ensure due respect for the right to family life.[98]

These cases certainly provide support for the comment made by Mancini and Keeling about the potential incidence of the *ERT* (and *Familiapress*) judgment on national sovereignty, and they illustrate the continued expansion of ECJ review of Member State measures for compatibility with fundamental rights. The same can also be said of *Karner*, in which the ECJ similarly adopted an expansive view of what falls 'within the scope of application of EC law'.[99]

Less controversially, the Court has also confirmed that the protection of human rights *in itself* constitutes a legitimate interest which will justify a restriction on EC free movement rules. In *Schmidberger*[100] and *Omega Spielhallen*[101] Austria and Germany respectively claimed that the precise ground for its derogation from EC free movement rules was the protection of fundamental rights, and the ECJ upheld their respective claims.

Case C–112/00 **Schmidberger v. Austria**
[2003] ECR I–5659

Austria relied on protection for freedom of expression and assembly as a public policy ground to justify the temporary closure of roads (trade routes) between Austria and Italy, in order to allow an environmental demonstration to take place. The ECJ however presented the case as a conflict between two legal interests of equal weight—the freedom of movement guaranteed by the EC Treaty on the one hand, and the freedom of expression and assembly of the demonstrators guaranteed by human rights instruments such as the ECHR on the other—each of which may be restricted in pursuit of other general interest.

THE ECJ

70. In its order for reference, the national court also raises the question whether the principle of the free movement of goods guaranteed by the Treaty prevails over those fundamental rights.

71. According to settled case-law, fundamental rights form an integral part of the general principles of law the observance of which the Court ensures. For that purpose, the Court draws inspiration from the constitutional traditions common to the Member States and from the guidelines supplied by international treaties for the protection of human rights on which the Member States have collaborated or to which they are signatories. The ECHR has special significance in that respect (see, inter alia , Case C–260/89 ERT 1991 ECR I–2925, paragraph 41; Case C–274/99 P Connolly v Commission 2001 ECR I–1611, paragraph 37, and Case C–94/00 Roquette Frères 2002 ECR I–9011, paragraph 25).

---

[98] Case C–109/01 *Akrich*, n. 95 above, paras. 58–60.

[99] Case C–71/02 *Karner* v. *Troostwijk* [2004] ECR I–3025, and for comment see J. Stuyck (2004) 41 *CMLRev.* 1683 and F. De Cecco, 'Room to Move? Minimum Harmonization and Fundamental Rights' (2006) 43 *CMLRev.* 9.

[100] Case C–112/00 *Schmidberger*, n. 43 above.

[101] Case C–36/02 *Omega Spielhallen*, n. 43 above.

72. The principles established by that case-law were reaffirmed in the preamble to the Single European Act and subsequently in Article F.2 of the Treaty on European Union (Bosman, cited above, paragraph 79). That provision states that 'the Union shall respect fundamental rights, as guaranteed by the European Convention for the Protection of Human Rights and Fundamental Freedoms signed in Rome on 4 November 1950 and as they result from the constitutional traditions common to the Member States, as general principles of Community law.'

73. It follows that measures which are incompatible with observance of the human rights thus recognised are not acceptable in the Community (see, inter alia , ERT , cited above, paragraph 41, and Case C–299/95 Kremzow 1997 ECR I–2629, paragraph 14).

74. Thus, since both the Community and its Member States are required to respect fundamental rights, the protection of those rights is a legitimate interest which, in principle, justifies a restriction of the obligations imposed by Community law, even under a fundamental freedom guaranteed by the Treaty such as the free movement of goods.

. . .

76. In the present case, the national authorities relied on the need to respect fundamental rights guaranteed by both the ECHR and the Constitution of the Member State concerned in deciding to allow a restriction to be imposed on one of the fundamental freedoms enshrined in the Treaty.

77. The case thus raises the question of the need to reconcile the requirements of the protection of fundamental rights in the Community with those arising from a fundamental freedom enshrined in the Treaty and, more particularly, the question of the respective scope of freedom of expression and freedom of assembly, guaranteed by Articles 10 and 11 of the ECHR, and of the free movement of goods, where the former are relied upon as justification for a restriction of the latter.

The ECJ then went on to engage in a fairly detailed analysis of the nature and degree of the restriction imposed on the free movement of goods by the measures taken to protection freedom of expression and assembly, and ultimately ruled that it was limited, necessary, and proportionate.[102]

In *Omega Spielhallen*, Germany successfully pleaded the protection of human dignity as a ground for restricting the marketing in Germany of laser games which simulated the killing of human beings. The ECJ agreed that the 'public policy derogation in Article 46 EC permitted the prohibition of commercial exploitation of such games on the basis of the protection of human dignity', which was specifically protected by the German constitution. Having declared that protection for human dignity was also a general principle of EC law, even though particular conceptions of the appropriate level of protection may differ from State to State,[103] the ECJ upheld the national restriction as a proportionate and necessary one.[104]

(d) MEMBER STATES AND SITUATIONS OUTSIDE THE SCOPE OF COMMUNITY LAW

Member States are not obliged to comply with the general principles of EC law in situations which lie 'outside the scope of Community law'. We saw that the ECJ in *Demirel* stated that it would not examine the compatibility with human rights of Member State measures which fall

---

[102] Case C–112/00 *Schmidberger*, n. 43 above, paras. 81–94.
[103] Case C–36/02 *Omega Spielhallen*, n. 43 above.
[104] *Ibid.*, paras. 36–41.

outside the scope of Community law.[105] But at the same time, cases such as *Carpenter* and *Akrich* demonstrate that it is often difficult to predict which situations will be deemed by the ECJ to lie 'outside' and which 'inside' the field of application of EC law for the purposes of human rights review.

In a range of cases involving either 'wholly internal situations' such as *Kremzow*,[106] or situations which are not in any other way governed by EC law such as *Grado and Bashir*[107] and *Annibaldi*,[108] or more controversially in cases such as *Dem' Yanenko*,[109] the ECJ has refused to scrutinize national measures for compatibility with fundamental rights.

A comparison of the *Maurin* and *Steffensen* cases concerning national prosecutions for violation of foodstuff safety and labelling standards highlights the difference in treatment depending on whether a given situation is held to fall within the scope of EC law or not. In *Maurin*, the defendant was prosecuted for selling food products after the expiry of their use-by date.[110] He argued that procedural unfairness in his trial breached his rights of the defence as protected under the ECHR, but the ECJ ruled that the national legislation fell outside the scope of EC law. While there was a directive requiring food products to indicate a sell-by date on their label, there was no Community measure governing the sale of properly labelled food products after the sell-by date, which was the situation in Maurin's case. In *Steffensen*, by comparison, the ECJ required that national evidentiary rules be interpreted in light of the ECHR's right to a fair hearing, and in particular the right to comment effectively on evidence submitted against a defendant, because the EC Directive on official control of foodstuffs was relevant to the prosecution in that case.[111]

(e) THE CHARTER OF FUNDAMENTAL RIGHTS AND THE MEMBER STATES

The legal status of the EU Charter on Fundamental Rights remains uncertain after the non-ratification of the EU Constitutional Treaty.[112] However, the Charter was drafted 'as if' it were to be binding, and Article 51 thereof indicates to whom its provisions are addressed:

> The provisions of this Charter are addressed to the institutions and bodies of the Union . . . and to the Member States only when they are implementing Union law.

---

[105] N. 87 above.

[106] Case C–299/95 *Kremzow*, n. 18 above.

[107] Case C–291/96 *Criminal Proceedings Against Grado and Bashir* [1997] ECR I–5531. This case concerned the position of a national of a Member State in criminal proceedings within another Member State, but since the case did not raise any applicable issue of Community law, the ECJ ruled that it could not consider whether the right to dignity and equality of the non-national had been respected. See also Case C–177/94 *Criminal Proceedings against Perfili* [1996] ECR I–161.

[108] Case C–309/96 *Annibaldi* v. *Sindaco del Commune di Guidoma* [1997] ECR I–7493, concerning regional environmental regulation in Italy.

[109] Case C–45/03 *Oxana Dem'Yanenko*, Order of 18 Mar. 2004. At the time of writing in 2007, the Order was, somewhat surprisingly, still not available on the ECJ's electronic database. In its Order the ECJ refused to rule on the case of a Ukrainian national who, shortly after attempting suicide, had been deported from Italy due to her failure to apply for a residence permit on time. The case concerned an interpretation of the Schengen Implementation Convention, but the ECJ refused to give a ruling on the basis that the Italian court which had made the reference was not a 'court from which there is no judicial remedy' under Art. 68(1) of the EC Treaty. For criticism of the case see J. Baquero Cruz (2004) 8 *Revista de Derecho Comunitario Europeo* 935.

[110] Case C–144/95 *Maurin* [1996] ECR I–2909.

[111] Case C–276/01 *Joachim Steffensen* [2003] ECR I–3735, especially paras. 69–78.

[112] See below, 417–418.

The formulation used in Article 51 appears to reflect only (b) above—i.e. that Member States are bound by fundamental rights when they are *implementing* EC law—and not the broader version that the States are bound whenever they act 'within the scope of application' of Community law. The broader formulation clearly also covers (c) above—cases in which Member States are derogating from EC law—and it is a formulation which has been repeated by the ECJ in many cases, including the landmark *ERT* case.[113] The broader 'within-the-scope-of-application' formulation also seems to cover situations such as that in *Akrich*,[114] which are more difficult to describe as Member States implementing or derogating from EC law. The choice to use a narrower wording in Article 51, however, may have been deliberate. There were strong political voices raised in support of limiting the Charter's applicability as much as possible to the EU and its institutions, and to limiting its relevance for the Member States as much as possible.[115]

Nonetheless, despite the narrow wording of Article 51, the explanatory memorandum to the Charter, which would have been given legal weight by the Constitutional Treaty,[116] purports to explain it more broadly. The explanatory memorandum when dealing with Article 51 draws attention to the unambiguous nature of the *ERT* ruling, and places the *Wachauf and Karlsson* cases,[117] which seem to have influenced the choice of wording in the Charter, in that context.[118] Until the legal fate of the Charter becomes clearer, or until the ECJ has ruled more frequently on its provisions, it will be difficult to know whether the general scope of review of national action in the field of EC law has been reduced, at least in so far as the rights contained within the Charter are concerned. So far, however, there is no indication that the Court is inclined to reduce the scope of its jurisdiction over Member State action for compliance with fundamental rights, and there is every indication that it views the Charter as an affirmation of its case law concerning the sources of human rights as general principles of EC law.[119]

7. EU HUMAN RIGHTS POLICY: POLITICAL AND INSTITUTIONAL DEVELOPMENTS

(a) POLITICAL APPROVAL OF THE ECJ

The Court's approach to acknowledging human rights as part of the 'general principles of EC law' was formally approved by a joint declaration of the Parliament, Council, and Commission in 1977, in which the three institutions also formally committed themselves to ensuring respect for fundamental rights in the exercise of their powers.[120] This joint declaration,

---

[113] N. 88 above.

[114] N. 98 above.

[115] See Lord Goldsmith's comments, n. 9 above. For a more general argument in favour of limiting the scope of the ECJ's review of national measures for compatibility with fundamental rights see Jacobs, n. 90 above, 337–338.

[116] Art. II–112(7) of the Constitutional Treaty would have added a subpara. to the provisions of the Charter to provide, '[t]he explanations drawn up as a way of providing guidance in the interpretation of the Charter of Fundamental Rights shall be given due regard by the courts of the Union and of the Member States'.

[117] See n. 82 above. *Karlsson* involved a relatively simple example of a Member State implementing EU law, and has little or nothing to say about whether other situations fall within the scope of EC or EU law for the purposes of the applicability of the general principles of EC law.

[118] G. de Búrca, 'The Drafting of the EU Charter of Fundamental Rights' (2000) 25 *ELRev*. 331.

[119] On the latter point, see Case C–540/03 *European Parliament* v. *Council*, n. 27 above, para. 38.

[120] [1977] OJ C103/1.

although not legally binding, was symbolically important in indicating that the Community's political institutions supported the Court's derivation of rights from the ECHR and from national constitutional principles.

A range of other non-binding initiatives, declarations, and resolutions on human rights were adopted over the years by the institutions acting together or alone. These included a Joint Declaration of the three institutions in 1986, a range of Declarations and Resolutions on Racism and Xenophobia by the European Council, a Declaration of Fundamental Rights and Freedoms by the European Parliament in 1989, a Community Charter of Fundamental Social Rights, signed by eleven of the then twelve Member States in 1989, as well as lofty references in the preamble to the Single European Act, to the ECHR, to the European Social Charter, and to 'equality and social justice'.

(b) HUMAN RIGHTS AMENDMENTS TO THE TREATIES

Hard legal approval followed these softer instruments with the amendments introduced by the TEU, the ToA, and the Nice Treaty. The various Treaty amendments constituted significant political moves to assert the role of fundamental human rights within the European Union.

First, Article 6(2) of the TEU now provides that the Union 'is founded on' the principles of liberty, democracy, and respect for human rights and fundamental freedoms. Following the ToA, respect for these fundamental principles was also formally listed as a condition of application for membership of the European Union by Article 49 TEU.

Secondly, the ECJ was given jurisdiction not only under the EC Treaty, but under any provision of the other two pillars over which it has been given jurisdiction (primarily Pillar Three), to review the conduct of the European institutions for compliance with these principles.[121] This provision—which came into force only in 1999—expressly legitimated what the Court in practice had been doing for many years in relation to the EC institutions.

Thirdly, Article 7 TEU, which was first introduced by the Amsterdam Treaty, empowers the Council to suspend some of the voting and other rights of a Member State which is found to be responsible for a serious and persistent breach of the fundamental principles in Article 6.[122] Article 7 was amended by the Nice Treaty in 2000 to provide for more detailed and fairer procedures to be followed before a negative determination against a Member State is made, and to include the possibility of acting *before* a breach has occurred, and the ECJ was given jurisdiction over the procedural provisions. The Nice amendments—adopted shortly after Article 7 first came into force—were a result of the controversial Haider affair, which began when a series of diplomatic sanctions was adopted by fourteen of the then fifteen Member States against Austria, in protest against the entry of the far-right Freedom Party into coalition government in Austria in 2000.[123] The sanctions were ultimately lifted after a positive report on the situation in Austria was issued following an *ad hoc* monitoring procedure carried out by a three-person committee appointed by the President of the ECtHR. It was in part as a result of unease over the way the Austrian situation had been handled that the amendments to Article 7 TEU were proposed and adopted. However, despite the symbolism of Article 7, and a number of attempts which have

[121] For an unsuccessful attempt to bring an action directly on the basis of Art. 6 TEU for alleged failure by the Commission to investigate breaches of the application's human rights by the Spanish courts see Case T–337/03 *Bertelli Galvez* v. *Commission* [2004] ECR II–1041.

[122] See Art. 309 EC as amended.

[123] M. Merlingen, C. Muddle, and U. Sedelmeier, 'The Right and the Righteous?: European Norms, Domestic Politics and the Sanctions against Austria' (2001) 39 *JCMS* 59.

been made by the European Parliament to instigate its application, it seems unlikely to have any significant application in practice.[124] Perhaps its most notable achievement to date has been to trigger the establishment of a new institution—an EU-wide network of independent experts to monitor and report on the human rights performance of the Member States.

The final Treaty changes worthy of mention here are those which would have been introduced by the Constitutional Treaty, had it been ratified.[125] Several of these amendments are discussed elsewhere in the chapter, in particular those concerning the incorporation of the Charter of Fundamental Rights and the provision for accession by the EU to the ECHR. Two other relevant changes in particular would have been (i) the addition of some other rights and values to those on which the EU is said to be founded, such as human dignity, and the 'rights of persons belonging to minorities' and (ii) inclusion of the protection of children's rights as an objective of the EU.

(c) NEW HUMAN RIGHTS INSTRUMENTS AND INSTITUTIONS

The first and most important recent development has been the approval of the EU Charter of Fundamental Rights at the Nice European Council in 2000. The Charter will be discussed in more detail below, where we shall see that despite the non-adoption of the Constitutional Treaty which would have given legal status to the Charter, it is nonetheless playing a role in EU law- and policy-making in a number of different ways.

A second significant recent institutional development has been the establishment of an EU network of independent experts on fundamental rights.[126] This was set up by the Commission at the request of the European Parliament in 2002, initially in order to assist the Parliament in assessing whether and how the various rights contained in the Charter were being implemented by the EU *and* by the Member States.[127] In addition to publishing annual reports on the observance of these rights by the EU and Member States, including thematic reports on particular selected topics, the network has published various other detailed reports and opinions on specific issues on its own initiative as well as at the Commission's request,[128] as well as a lengthy commentary on the Charter of Fundamental Rights.

Thirdly, an EU Fundamental Rights Agency was established in 2007 to subsume and replace the existing EU Monitoring Center for Racism and Xenophobia which was set up in 1997.[129] Although there was some controversy during the debate preceding the establishment of the Agency over what powers it should have, and in particular whether these should include monitoring Member States for the purposes of Article 7 TEU, its mandate covers only the collection of information, formulating opinions, highlighting good practices, and publishing thematic reports. It remains to be seen what the relationship of the Agency to the network of independent experts on fundamental rights will be, and whether the network—with the more comprehensive monitoring role it has carved out for itself—will be established on a more permanent basis.

---

[124] For a sharp critique see A. Williams, 'The Indifferent Gesture: Article 7 TEU, the Fundamental Rights Agency and the UK's Invasion of Iraq' (2006) 31 *ELRev*. 3.

[125] J. Dutheil de la Rochère, 'The EU and the Individual: Fundamental Rights in the Draft Constitutional Treaty' (2004) 41 *CMLRev*. 345.

[126] See http://ec.europa.eu/justice_home/cfr_cdf/index_en.htm.

[127] Report on the Situation as regards Fundamental Rights in the European Union (2000), A–5 223/2001.

[128] See http://ec.europa.eu/justice_home/cfr_cdf/list_opinions_en.htm. Topics include ethnic profiling, the responsibilities of Member States in relation to CIA activities and 'extraordinary renditions', the right to conscientious objection.

[129] Council Reg. 168/2007 [2007] OJ L53/1.

Finally, in an externally-oriented institutional initiative, the European Council in 2004 announced the creation of a new post of Personal Representative on Human Rights to the existing Council Secretary-General and High Representative for the CFSP. There have at the time of writing been two such post-holders to date, to raise the profile and pursue the representation of the EU in human rights matters in the foreign policy field.

(d) FUNDAMENTAL RIGHTS AS A SOURCE OF POLICY COMPETENCE

The chapter so far has focused mainly on the jurisprudence of the Court, which established fundamental rights and general principles as a constraint on Community and Member State action, as values they must respect in the course of their other activities. The question remains whether promotion and protection of human rights is itself an objective of the EU, and a source of Community legislative competence.

We shall see below that the official approach to the Community's legal powers in the field of human rights has been at best equivocal. Whenever a potentially expansive new power or legal norm is created, such as the anti-discrimination power in Article 13 EC, or more generally by the adoption of the Charter of Fundamental Rights, there seems to be a countervailing restrictive move on the part of political and institutional actors—e.g. in the insistence on remaining 'within the limits of the powers conferred by the Treaty' in Article 13, and the insistence in Article 51 of the Charter that no new Community task or power has been created by its adoption.

(i) *Limited EC Treaty Powers*

Only a few provisions of the EC Treaty directly address questions of human rights. Articles 177 on development policy and 181a on co-operation with third countries specify that the Community shall contribute to the general objective of developing and consolidating democracy and the rule of law, and to that of respecting human rights and fundamental freedoms.[130] Article 13 gives the EC legislative power to enact laws combating discrimination on a range of grounds, there are several provisions on equal treatment between men and women, and reference to the Geneva Convention on Refugees appears in Article 63 of the EC Treaty on asylum.

In its Opinion on Accession to the ECHR in 1996, in which the ECJ concluded that the EC lacked competence to accede to the ECHR without first amending the EC Treaty, the Court pointed to the Community's lack of 'general power to enact rules on human rights':

Opinion 2/94 on Accession by the Community to the ECHR
[1996] ECR I–1759

[Note ToA renumbering: Arts.130u and 235 EC are now Arts. 177 and 308 EC respectively. Arts. F and J. 1 TEU are now Arts. 6 and 11 respectively, and Art. K. 2 has been replaced]

27. No Treaty provision confers on the Community institutions any general power to enact rules on human rights or to conclude international conventions in this field.

---

[130] For discussion of the scope of the EC's power to address human rights concerns in development policy agreements under Art. 177 at the time see Case C–268/94 *Portuguese Republic* v. *Council* [1996] ECR I–6177.

28. In the absence of express or implied powers for this purpose, it is necessary to consider whether Article 235 of the Treaty may constitute a legal basis for accession.

29. Article 235 is designed to fill the gap where no specific provisions of the Treaty confer on the Community institutions express or implied powers to act, if such powers appear none the less to be necessary to enable the Community to carry out its functions with a view to attaining one of the objectives laid down by the Treaty.

. . .

32. It should first be noted that the importance of respect for human rights has been emphasized in various declarations of the Member States and of the Community institutions. Reference is also made to respect for human rights in the preamble to the Single European Act and in the preamble to, and in Article F(2), the fifth indent of Article J. 1.(2) and Article K. 2 (1) of, the Treaty on European Union. Article F provides that the Union is to respect fundamental rights, as guaranteed, in particular, by the Convention. Article 130u(2) of the EU Treaty provides that Community policy in the area of development cooperation is to contribute to the objective of respecting human rights and fundamental freedoms.

33. Furthermore, it is well settled that fundamental rights form an integral part of the general principles of law whose observance the Court ensures. For that purpose, the Court draws inspiration from the constitutional traditions common to the Member States and from the guidelines supplied by international treaties for the protection of human rights on which the Member States have collaborated or of which they are signatories. In that regard, the Court has stated that the Convention has special significance (see in particular ERT).

34. Respect for human rights is therefore a condition of the lawfulness of Community acts. Accession to the Convention would, however, entail a substantial change in the present Community system for the protection of human rights in that it would entail the entry of the Community into a distinct international institutional system as well as the integration of all the provisions of the Convention into the Community legal order.

35. Such a modification of the system for the protection of human rights in the Community, with equally fundamental institutional implications for the Community and for the Member States, would be of constitutional significance and would therefore be such as to go beyond the scope of Article 235. It could be brought about only by way of Treaty amendment.

In ruling that the Community lacked legislative competence under the Treaties to become a party to the Convention, the ECJ gave some indication of the limits of human rights as a legislative foundation for Community action, although without ruling more specifically on the issue of what other, less fundamental kinds of legislation the Community might be competent to adopt in the human rights field. Paragraph 27 is particularly relevant in this respect, although it merely denies that the Community enjoys power under any particular Treaty provisions to enact *general* rules on human rights.

The Opinion however can be read as agreeing that Article 308 may form the basis for the adoption of specific Community measures for the protection of human rights, so long as they do not amount to an amendment of the Treaty by going beyond the scope of the Community's defined aims and activities. Indeed the regulations on human rights and democratization in development policy and co-operation policy adopted in 1999 were based on Articles 177 and 308 EC respectively,[131] and the regulation establishing the EU Fundamental Rights Agency in 2007 was also based on Article 308.[132]

---

[131] See Regs. 975/1999 and 976/1999 [1999] OJ L120/1 and 8.
[132] N. 129 above.

Ensuring respect for human rights is, however, described by the Court in its Opinion as a 'condition for the lawfulness of Community acts',[133] rather than as an independent objective of the EC. What appeared to place accession to the ECHR beyond the scope of Community competence was not the fact that it would entail concluding an agreement for the protection of fundamental rights, but the fact that the agreement envisaged would bring with it institutional and constitutional changes of such significance as to require a Treaty amendment.[134]

(ii) *Externally Focused Human Rights Policies*

The EU has frequently been criticized for its apparently greater willingness to promote and enforce human rights—through forms of conditionality including the use of negative sanctions[135]—in its external policies than in its internal policies.[136] Unlike the more uncertain situation under the Community Pillar, human rights protection has been readily acknowledged as an objective of the EU common foreign and security policy under the Second Pillar. This is evident from Article 11 TEU, which uses the same language as the provisions on external development and co-operation policy under Articles 177 and 181a EC, in declaring that one of its objectives is 'to develop and consolidate democracy and the rule of law, and respect for human rights and fundamental freedoms'.

A range of instruments has been used in the external context, such as the regular practice since 1995 of including human rights clauses in external agreements dealing with trade, development, and association relationships,[137] as well as the active—and sometimes controversial[138]—use of conditionality in the pre-accession process for new Member States.[139] At the same time, criticism has also been voiced at the fact that, in the external sphere, human rights policy was largely confined to projects funded under the so-called 'human rights and democratization' initiative provided for under one specific part of the EU budget, and was not integrated across the pillars and across the different dimensions of foreign policy.

The criticisms of incoherence and of double standards have increasingly been acknowledged by the Council of Ministers in its EU annual reports on human rights, which it has published since 1999.[140] The EU's external relations website also now emphasizes the various foreign policy instruments which it now claims to use to promote human rights, including guidelines, demarches, common positions, joint actions, consultations, and funding.

Nevertheless, the EU continues to face a range of significant criticisms in relation to its human rights role, with two particular claims recurring. These are, first, that it continues to be

---

[133] See also the subsequent Resolution of the European Parliament on Respect for Human Rights in the EU [1996] OJ C320/36.

[134] For a discussion of various aspects of *Opinion 2/94* see *The Human Rights Opinion of the ECJ and its Constitutional Implications,* Cambridge University CELS, Occasional Paper No. 1 (Cambridge University Press, 1996).

[135] E. Fierro, 'Legal Basis and Scope of the Human Rights Clause in EC Bilateral Agreements' [2001] *ELJ* 41; B. Brandtner and A. Rosas, 'Human Rights and the External Relations of the EC: An Analysis of Doctrine and Practice' (1998) 9 *EJIL* 468.

[136] P. Alston and J. Weiler, 'A Human Rights Agenda for the Year 2000', in Alston *et al.*, n. 3 above; A. Williams, *EU Human Rights Policies: A Study in Irony* (Oxford University Press, 2004).

[137] For a detailed legal analysis see L. Bartels, *Human Rights Conditionality in the EU's International Agreements* (Oxford University Press, 2005).

[138] H. Arikan, 'A Lost Opportunity? A Critique of the EU's Human Rights Policy Towards Turkey' (2002) *Mediterranean Politics* 19.

[139] B. de Witte and G. Toggenburg, 'Human Rights and Membership of the European Union', in S. Peers and A. Ward (eds.), *The EU Charter of Fundamental Rights* (Hart, 2004), 59.

[140] See, e.g., the Annual Report for 2006, para. 4.19 in particular.

a weak actor as far as the promotion of human rights is concerned,[141] and, secondly, that the problem of double standards between what it expects of itself and its members on the one hand, and what it demands of countries outside the EU on the other hand, remains a serious one.[142]

(iii) *Internally Focused Human Rights Policies: Anti-discrimination*

Since 1999 when the EU Annual Human Rights reports were first published, the trend within the reports has been to move from an initially much greater emphasis on foreign and external policy towards a gradually more extensive consideration of the human rights aspects of internal EU policies also, including anti-discrimination policy, social exclusion, combating human trafficking, and gender mainstreaming. The two main reasons usually given for the more extensive emphasis on the external dimension are that there are more severe and more fundamental human rights problems occurring outside the EU than within, and that the EU has only a very limited competence to address human rights issues within its boundaries.[143]

However, in its 2001 Annual Report, the Council declared that the EU was 'committed to intensifying the process of "mainstreaming" human rights and democratization objectives into all aspects of EU external and internal policies', and in both its 2005 and 2006 Annual Reports, the Council presented a chapter on 'thematic issues' which purported to look at both internal and external dimensions of particular topics together.

Undoubtedly the most significant source of EC competence in the field of human rights protection within the EU, apart from the last-resort provision in Article 7 TEU, has been that introduced by the Amsterdam Treaty into Article 13 of the EC Treaty, supplementing the existing range of EU gender equality policies. Article 13 provides that the Community legislature may, within the limits of the Community's powers, take 'appropriate action to combat discrimination based on sex, racial or ethnic origin, religion or belief, disability, age or sexual orientation'. Hitherto, discrimination on grounds of sex and nationality was expressly prohibited by Community law, although the basis for adopting general legislation in these fields was for some time unclear.[144] While the case of *P* v. *S*[145] appeared to suggest that a more general prohibition on discrimination extending beyond sex and nationality to embrace transsexuality and other grounds was *already* part of the 'great value of equality' and one of the fundamental principles underlying EC law, the ECJ in *Grant* v. *South West Trains* beat a hasty retreat from that position.[146]

In *Grant* the Court ruled, in a case concerning an employee who had been refused travel benefits for her same-sex partner, that EC law did not at the time cover discrimination on the basis of sexual orientation. The Court in *Grant* confined the ruling in *P* v. *S* to discrimination based 'essentially' on the sex of the person, which did not, in its view, apply to discrimination on the grounds of sexual orientation of the kind at issue in *Grant*. In making reference to Article 13 EC concerning sexual orientation which was not yet in force at that time, the ECJ

---

[141] Roth, n. 4 above.

[142] Williams, n. 4 above; F. Van den Berghe, 'The EU and the Protection of Minorities: How Real is the Alleged Double Standard?' (2003) 22 *YBEL* 155.

[143] For a challenge to these arguments see Williams, n. 4 above.

[144] See Ch. 24 for discussion of the legislative basis for some of the equal treatment legislation between men and women, and Case C–295/90 *European Parliament* v. *Council* [1992] ECR I–4193 on the appropriate legal basis for legislation concerning nationality discrimination in the field of vocational training.

[145] Case C–13/94 *P* v. *S*, n. 15 above, especially paras. 18–22.

[146] Case C–249/96 *Grant*, n. 24 above. Contrast the Opinion of the AG.

argued that it was not for the Court to extend Community law beyond the scope provided for in the Treaty.[147]

Its more expansive judicial approach to prohibiting discrimination against transsexuals under EC sex equality law, on the other hand, was confirmed in *K.B.* v. *NHS*, where the ECJ drew support from the ECtHR to give a somewhat convoluted ruling on the incompatibility of British law with EC equal pay law.[148] The Court ruled that the inability of a woman to obtain a survivor's pension as the widow of her post-operative transsexual partner amounted to unequal treatment in violation of Article 141 on equal pay between men and women, where that inability was due to the fact that under UK law, a couple whose birth certificates show they are of the same sex could not marry and a birth certificate could not be legally altered to reflect a sex change. Although this did not amount to discrimination between men and women, it did amount to discrimination as between transsexuals (who could not legally marry someone of their original sex) and non-transsexual persons. The complicated logic of the ECJ's ruling seems to proceed in three stages: (i) because the refusal to permit a birth certificate to be altered in these circumstances was a violation of the right to private life under the ECHR,[149] it followed (ii) that the legal condition which prevented her from qualifying for the right to equal treatment under EC law was a violation of the ECHR, and consequently (iii) this brought her case within the scope of EC equal pay law.

However, the more restrictive approach in *Grant* to the issue of sexual-orientation discrimination (as compared with discrimination against transsexuals) was reinforced in the case of *D* v. *Council*, which concerned unequal benefits for an EU employee whose relationship with a same-sex partner had been granted formal status as a registered partnership under Swedish law.[150] While the case on its facts clearly concerns an indirect form of discrimination on grounds of sexual orientation, since traditional marriage with the access to financial benefits which it brings was not open to same-sex couples—just as the legal barrier to marriage in *K.B.* concerned an indirect discrimination of the same kind against transsexuals—the ECJ based its reasoning on an acceptance of the non-equivalence of a traditional marriage and a nationally recognized registered partnership.[151] Further, just as in *Grant*, the ECJ emphasized its own unfitness, as a judicial institution, to bring about a positive change which was more properly to be enacted by legislation.

This clearly represents a retreat from the strong principle of equality as a fundamental right, and a deferential judicial stance in a situation where the exercise of positive legislative competence has been made possible under the Treaty and under staff regulations, but not yet exercised. Further, although no legislative move had been made to give registered partnerships a position equivalent to marriage, an amendment to the Staff Regulations which had not come into force at the time of the case provided for equal treatment of officials irrespective of their sexual orientation.

---

[147] *Ibid.*, paras. 47–48.

[148] Case C–117/01 *K.B.* v. *NHS* [2004] ECR I–541.

[149] The ECtHR had ruled to this effect in *Goodwin* v. *United Kingdom*, App. no. 28957/95 (2002) 35 EHRR 18.

[150] Cases C–122 and 125/99 P *D*, n. 46 above.

[151] For a recent decision of the Ombudsman concerning a complaint against the Commission for failing to commence infringement proceedings against Spain where it had discriminated on the basis of sexual orientation in a family reunification decision see www.ombudsman.europa.eu/decision/en/031687.htm. The Ombudsman did not uphold the complaint.

Cases C–122 and 125/99 P **D v. Council**
[2001] ECR I–4319

36. It is clear, however, that apart from their great diversity, such arrangements for registering relationships between couples not previously recognised in law are regarded in the Member States concerned as being distinct from marriage.

37. In such circumstances the Community judicature cannot interpret the Staff Regulations in such a way that legal situations distinct from marriage are treated in the same way as marriage. The intention of the Community legislature was to grant entitlement to the household allowance under Article 1(2)(a) of Annex VII to the Staff Regulations only to married couples.

38. Only the legislature can, where appropriate, adopt measures to alter that situation, for example by amending the provisions of the Staff Regulations. However, not only has the Community legislature not shown any intention of adopting such measures, it has even (see paragraph 32 above) ruled out at this stage any idea of other forms of partnership being assimilated to marriage for the purposes of granting the benefits reserved under the Staff Regulations for married officials, choosing instead to maintain the existing arrangement until the various consequences of such assimilation become clearer.

It can be argued on the basis of this case that the introduction of positive legislative competence to promote fundamental rights such as the right to be free from arbitrary discrimination has provided the Court with an argument for limiting the judicial development of equality rights as general principles of EC law.

Article 13 EC is not in itself a prohibition on discrimination on grounds which it lists, and, unlike the equal pay provision as between men and women in Article 141 EC, it is not directly effective. Rather it enables the Community to adopt measures to combat discrimination on the grounds listed within the scope of the policies and powers otherwise granted in the Treaty. Prior to the coming into force of Article 13, the European Monitoring Centre for Racism and Xenophobia had been established by a regulation based on Articles 284 and 308 EC,[152] but Article 13 has since facilitated stronger law-making in this field.[153]

Two important measures were adopted in 2000, the first—the Race Directive—to prohibit discrimination on grounds of racial and ethnic origin,[154] and the second, the so-called Framework Employment Directive, covering discrimination in the field of employment on the grounds listed in Article 13 (other than race, ethnic origin, or sex, which are already covered by other legislation): i.e. religion, belief, disability, age, and sexual orientation.[155] While the jurisdictional limitation in Article 13 specifies that the EC can act only within the limits of the Community's powers, Article 3 of the Anti-racism Directive gives it an apparently wide scope, including a prohibition on discrimination in relation to social protection, health care, housing, and education. An action plan to combat racism was adopted in 1998, and in 2000 a broader action programme to combat discrimination on all the grounds listed in Article 13 (other than sex, which is already covered by an action programme) was adopted.[156] The

---

[152] Council Reg. 1035/97 [1997] OJ L151.

[153] M. Bell, *Anti-Discrimination Law and the EU* (Oxford University Press, 2002). Art. 13 was also amended by the Nice Treaty to include a power for the Council to adopt non-harmonizing 'incentive measures' under the co-decision legislative procedure.

[154] Council Dir. 2000/43 [2000] OJ L180/22.

[155] Council Dir. 2000/78 [2000] OJ L303/16.

[156] Council Dec. 2000/750 [2000] OJ L303/23.

Commission has also promoted 'mainstreaming' policies initially in the area of gender, but subsequently in the field of race and disability in particular, with a view to integrating anti-discrimination considerations into other areas of EC policy formation.

While many Member States were initially slow to implement the Anti-discrimination Directives, and the Commission successfully brought infringement proceedings against four Member States for failure in this respect, cases have now begun to come before the ECJ concerning the enforcement of the Directives in domestic law.[157] In *Chacón Navas*, the ECJ ruled that the prohibition against disability discrimination in the Framework Employment Directive did not cover sickness, so that an employer who dismissed an employee after an eight-month absence due to illness did not act contrary to the Directive.[158] More fundamentally, in *Mangold*,[159] a case which echoes the expansive approach of *P* v. *S* to the principle of equal treatment, the Court ruled that although the period for transposing the Framework Employment Directive into national law had not yet expired, the general principle of equal treatment in EC law prohibited a national measure from discriminating arbitrarily on the basis of age:

Case C–144/04 **Mangold v. Rüdiger Helm**
[2005] ECR I–9981

THE ECJ

74. In the second place and above all, Directive 2000/78 does not itself lay down the principle of equal treatment in the field of employment and occupation. Indeed, in accordance with Article 1 thereof, the sole purpose of the directive is 'to lay down a general framework for combating discrimination on the grounds of religion or belief, disability, age or sexual orientation', the source of the actual principle underlying the prohibition of those forms of discrimination being found, as is clear from the third and fourth recitals in the preamble to the directive, in various international instruments and in the constitutional traditions common to the Member States.

75. The principle of non-discrimination on grounds of age must thus be regarded as a general principle of Community law. Where national rules fall within the scope of Community law ... and reference is made to the Court for a preliminary ruling, the Court must provide all the criteria of interpretation needed by the national court to determine whether those rules are compatible with such a principle. ...

76. Consequently, observance of the general principle of equal treatment, in particular in respect of age, cannot as such be conditional upon the expiry of the period allowed the Member States for the transposition of a directive intended to lay down a general framework for combating discrimination on the grounds of age, in particular so far as the organisation of appropriate legal remedies, the burden of proof, protection against victimisation, social dialogue, affirmative action and other specific measures to implement such a directive are concerned.

---

[157] See pending Case C–303/06 *Coleman* v. *Attridge Law* [2006] OJ C237/10.

[158] Case C–13/05 *Chacón Navas* v. *Eurest Colectividades SA* [2006] ECR I–6467.

[159] For a discussion of the surprising approach of the ECJ to the direct effect of this Dir. before the time limit had expired, by drawing on the general principle of equal treatment rather than the specific provisions of the Dir. on age discrimination see Ch. 8.

> 77. In those circumstances it is the responsibility of the national court, hearing a dispute involving the principle of non-discrimination in respect of age, to provide, in a case within its jurisdiction, the legal protection which individuals derive from the rules of Community law and to ensure that those rules are fully effective, setting aside any provision of national law which may conflict with that law

However, adverse reactions to the *Mangold* case may induce the ECJ to return to the more conservative approach to the relationship between the 'general principle of equality' and existing or imminent legislation which it had demonstrated in *Grant* and *D*, as the recent Opinions of the Advocates General in *Palacios de la Villa*[160] and *Lindorfer*,[161] concerning age discrimination, may suggest.

Overall, it can be said that the ECJ's approach to equality, while lauded for many years as a strong and bold approach in the field of sex discrimination, has become somewhat more equivocal and less uniform in strength as the reach of EC equality law has begun to expand. This expansion has come about as a result of the enactment of Article 13, as well as through the impact of ECHR rulings, and most importantly the adoption of the Anti-discrimination Directives with their implicit 'hierarchy' of equality norms.[162]

8. THE EU CHARTER OF FUNDAMENTAL RIGHTS

(a) INTRODUCTION

We have seen in Chapter 1 that the European Council in 1999 launched an initiative to draft a Charter of Fundamental Rights for the EU. This development came after many years of discussion of whether the EU should accede to the ECHR or should have its own Bill of Rights. The novel Convention process by which the Charter was adopted, which became a model for the subsequent Convention on the Future of Europe, produced a draft Charter in less than a year, following a more open and relatively more participative procedure than almost any previous EC or EU initiative.[163] The Charter was solemnly proclaimed by the Commission, Parliament, and Council and was politically approved by the Member States at the Nice European Council summit in December 2000.[164]

The Charter was drafted 'as if' it were to have full legal effect,[165] but the question of its ultimate legal status was left to be decided by the political process following the Nice and Laeken European Council Declarations.[166] These in turn led to the drafting by the Convention

---

[160] Case C–411/05 *Palacios de la Villa* v. *Cortefiel Servicios*, 15 Feb. 2007, Mazák AG, especially paras. 79–100.

[161] Case C–227/04 P *Lindorfer* v. *Council*, 30 Nov. 2006, Sharpston AG, especially paras. 51–58. An earlier Opinion had been given in the same case by Jacobs AG on 27 Oct. 2005, but after the ECJ gave its ruling in *Mangold* a second Opinion was sought to take into account the possible impact of that case (by which stage Jacobs AG had retired and been replaced by Sharpston AG).

[162] M. Bell and L. Waddington, 'Reflecting on Inequalities in European Equality Law' (2003) 28 *ELRev*. 349.

[163] G. de Búrca, 'The Drafting of the EU Charter of Fundamental Rights' (2001) 26 *ELRev*. 126; J. Schönlau, 'Drafting Europe's Value Foundation: Deliberation and Arm-twisting in Formulating the Preamble to the EU Charter of Fundamental Rights', in Eriksen *et al.* (eds.), n. 2 above.

[164] [2000] OJ C364/1.

[165] On the legal nature of the Charter, COM(2000)644. See also L. Betten 'The EU Charter of Fundamental Rights: A Trojan Horse or a Mouse?' [2001] *IJCLLIR* 151.

[166] B. de Witte, 'The Legal Status of the Charter: Vital Question or Non-Issue?' (2001) 8 *MJ* 81; C. McCrudden, 'The Future of the EU Charter of Fundamental Rights', J. Dutheil de la Rochère, 'Droits de

on the Future of Europe in 2004 of the Constitutional Treaty, which incorporated the Charter of Fundamental Rights, with a number of amendments, as Part II of a three-Part constitutional text. In other words, had the Constitutional Treaty been ratified as anticipated in 2005, the Charter of Fundamental Rights would have become the binding centrepiece of a European Constitution. However, since the CT was not ratified, the status of the Charter remains unsettled at least until the proposed Reform Treaty takes further shape. For the moment, it appears to have returned to a pre-CT position, without having been negatively affected by the non-ratification. Instead it is being treated by the EU political institutions and by the Court as an important but non-binding form of legal guidance on the existence and identity of the fundamental rights which are protected as part of EU law. This will be discussed further below.

(b) CONTENT

The mandate originally given by the European Council to the body which first drafted the Charter of Rights was to consolidate and render visible the EU's existing 'obligation to respect fundamental rights' rather than to create anything new, and the sources on which the drafting body should draw were indicated.[167] However, the Charter contains several innovative provisions (e.g., a prohibition on reproductive human cloning) and there are also notable omissions (e.g., protection for the rights of minorities). And while its preamble declares that the EU *recognizes* the rights, freedoms, and principles set out therein, overall the Charter could perhaps best be described as a creative distillation of the rights contained in the various European and international agreements and national constitutions on which the ECJ had for some years already been drawing.

Following its lofty preamble in the name of the 'peoples of Europe',[168] which refers amongst other things to the common and indivisible universal values on which the Union is founded, and to the diversity of cultures, traditions, and identities in Europe, the Charter is divided into seven chapters. The various rights are grouped into six distinct chapters, and the final chapter contains the so-called horizontal clauses or general provisions. The first six chapters are headed: I. Dignity, II. Freedoms, III. Equality, IV. Solidarity, V. Citizens' Rights, VI. Justice.

The foundational rights such as the right to life, freedom from torture, slavery, and execution, are contained in the first Chapter. While these might once have appeared anomalous in a Charter addressed primarily to the institutions of the EU, on the basis that EU powers to infringe such rights remain limited, the gradual moves in the direction of a European defence policy and the growing body of policing, criminal law, and 'anti-terrorism' policies suggest that this is no longer so. Indeed, a recent report of a temporary committee of the European Parliament has suggested that some of the EU institutions (including the Council and Europol) were complicit in concealing the operation of secret CIA detention camps within EU countries and in the practice of 'extraordinary rendition' of individuals for torture.[169]

l'homme: La Charte des droits fondamentaux et au dela', and G. de Búrca, 'Human Rights: The Charter and Beyond', all forming Jean Monnet Working Paper 10/01, www.jeanmonnetprogram.org/papers.

[167] These were specified as the rights contained in the ECHR and those derived from the common constitutional traditions of the Member States, as well as from provisions of the European Social Charter and the Community Charter of Fundamental Social Rights of Workers 'which go beyond mere objectives'. See Conclusions of the Cologne European Council, June 1999.

[168] For an analysis see Schönlau, n. 163 above.

[169] See the Draft Report of the Temporary Committee of 24 Nov. 2006, especially paras. Available at www.europarl.europa.eu/comparl/tempcom/tdip/draft_final_report_en.pdf.

The second Chapter on freedoms also concentrates on basic civil and political liberties to be found in the ECHR, such as liberty, association, expression, property, and private and family life,[170] but contains in addition certain fundamental social rights such as the right to education, the right to engage in work, and the right to asylum, as well as a number of provisions which have gained particular prominence in the EU context, such as the right to protection of data and the freedom to conduct a business.

Chapter III on equality contains a basic equality-before-the-law guarantee, as well as a provision similar (though not identical) to that in Article 13 EC, a reference to positive action provisions in the field of gender equality, protection for children's rights, and some weaker provisions guaranteeing 'respect' for cultural diversity, for the rights of the elderly, and for persons with disabilities.

Chapter IV on solidarity contains certain labour rights and reflects some of the provisions of the European Social Charter which have already been integrated into EC law.[171] This Chapter contains a mixture of fundamental provisions such as the prohibition on child labour and the right to fair and just working conditions, as well as others which have been criticized as insufficiently fundamental to have a place in this Charter, such as the right to a free placement service. Further, this Chapter of the Charter has been particularly criticized because of the weak formulation of many of the rights contained (including some, such as environmental and consumer protection, which are not formulated as rights or freedoms at all), and because of the phrase 'in accordance with Community law and national laws and practices' which follows them and which seems to undermine the content of the guarantee.

Chapter V contains 'citizens' rights', many of which, unlike the other provisions of the Charter, are not universal but are guaranteed only to EU citizens. These include the rights of EU citizenship in Articles 18–22 of the EC Treaty, while the more broadly applicable rights include the right of access to documents and the right to good administration, which is the first to have been judicially cited by the CFI.[172]

Chapter VI, entitled Justice, includes several of the so-called rights of the defence, such as the right to a fair trial, the presumption of innocence, the principle of legality and proportionality of penalties, and the familiar EC right to an effective remedy.

(c) THE 'HORIZONTAL' CLAUSES

The final Chapter VII contains the general clauses which relate to the scope and applicability of the Charter, its addressees, its relationship to other legal instruments, and the 'standard' of protection. The Constitutional Treaty would have made several changes to these horizontal clauses, but as we have seen it has not come into effect, which leaves the Charter for now as it stood when originally drafted in 2000.

Article 51(1) indicates that the Charter is addressed to the institutions and bodies of the EU, and to the Member States, only when they are 'implementing' Union law.[173] A cursory mention of the principle of subsidiarity is made in this context, although its meaning is difficult to discern. Article 51 goes on to specify that the EU and the Member States 'respect the rights, observe the principles and promote the application thereof in accordance with their

---

170 C. McGlynn, 'Families and the EU Charter of Fundamental Rights: Progressive Change or Entrenching the Status Quo?' (2001) 26 *ELRev*. 582.

171 M. Gijzen, 'The Charter: A Milestone for Social Protection in Europe?' (2001) 8 *MJ* 33.

172 Case T–54/99 *max.mobil Telekommunikation Service GmbH* v. *Commission* [2002] ECR II–313, para. 48.

173 For fuller discussion see Section 7(v) above, and nn. 113–119 and text.

respective powers'. This obligation to 'promote' the rights in the Charter contrasts with the rather more negative phrasing of the sentence which follows in Article 51(2), and which asserts that no new power or task for the EC or EU is created by the Charter.[174]

In other words, two different possibilities are presented by the different parts of Article 51. Paragraph (2) presents the Charter simply as a codified or supplemented form of what already exists under ECJ jurisprudence: i.e., a broad set of standards against which EU and Member State action within the scope of existing EU policies and powers is to be judged, and not as a source of or basis for positive action, whereas the obligation to 'promote' the rights suggests something more proactive.[175]

The Constitutional Treaty would have added two further clauses to Article 51, to lock in the more limited reading. On the one hand, Member States in respecting, observing, and promoting the Charter rights under paragraph (1) would have to 'respect the limits of the powers of the Union as conferred on it in the other Parts of the Constitution', and on the other hand paragraph (2) would have confirmed that the Charter did not 'extend the scope of application' of EU law.

Article 52(1), which draws on the jurisprudence of both the ECHR and the ECJ, contains a general 'derogation' clause, indicating the nature of the restrictions on Charter rights which will be acceptable.[176] Any limitation on the exercise of rights and freedoms contained in the Charter must be 'provided for by law' and must respect the *essence* of those rights and freedoms. Limitations must meet the requirements of proportionality and must be 'necessary and genuinely meet objectives of general interest recognized by the Union,[177] or the need to protect the rights and freedoms of others'.

Article 52(2) then addresses the question of overlap between existing provisions of EC law and the new provisions of the Charter, providing that rights recognized by the Charter which are 'based on' the EC or EU Treaties 'shall be exercised under the conditions and within the limits defined by those Treaties'. This seems intended to avoid any potential differences in the interpretation of similarly worded provisions of the Charter and of the EC/EU Treaties, although the phrase 'based on' is perhaps somewhat ambiguous. The explanatory memorandum refers instead to a right which 'results from' the Treaties, and states that the Charter does not alter the system of rights conferred by the Treaties.

The tricky relationship between the ECHR,[178] other international human rights instruments, national constitutional provisions, and the new Charter is addressed in Articles 52(3)

[174] The relevant explanatory note to Art. 51 reads '[p]aragraph 2 confirms that the Charter may not have the effect of extending the competences and tasks which the Treaties confer on the Community and the Union. Explicit mention is made here of the logical consequences of the principle of subsidiarity and of the fact that the Union only has those powers which have been conferred upon it. The fundamental rights as guaranteed in the Union do not have any effect other than in the context of the powers determined by the Treaty.'

[175] Note the speech of Commissioner Vitorino to the European Parliament on 17 Apr. 2002, 'The Future of Fundamental Rights in the EU', in which he argues that the Charter should not be limited by a negative approach, but should have a proactive effect in the promoting of human rights by creating policies related to them.

[176] For criticism see D. Triantafyllou, 'The European Charter of Fundamental Rights and the "Rule of Law": Restricting Fundamental Rights by Reference' (2002) 39 *CMLRev.* 53.

[177] This formulation was criticized by some who saw it as permitting the economic objectives of the EU to be introduced as grounds for limiting the scope of fundamental rights, something which would not be possible under most provisions of the ECHR.

[178] P. Lemmens, 'The Relationship between the Charter of Fundamental Rights of the EU and the ECHR: Substantive Aspects' (2001) 8 *MJ* 49; K. Lenaerts and E. de Smijter, 'The Charter and the Role of the European Courts' (2001) 8 *MJ* 49; and F. Tulkens, 'Towards a Greater Normative Coherence in Europe: The Implications of the Draft Charter of Fundamental Rights of the European Union' (2000) 21 *HRLJ* 329. S. Parmar, 'International Human Rights Law and the EU Charter' (2001) 8 *MJ* 351.

and 53. It seems that during the drafting process, a long and heated debate on the proper relationship of the Charter to the Convention was held, as well as on the question whether a right contained in the Charter should necessarily be interpreted in the same way as a similar or identical right contained in the ECHR, and on the proper relationship of the Court of Justice and the European Court of Human Rights.[179] Article 52(3) relates specifically to the ECHR and is evidently intended to promote harmony between the provisions of the European Convention and those of the Charter, while not preventing the EU from developing more extensive protection than is provided for under the Convention:

> In so far as this Charter contains rights which correspond to rights guaranteed by the Convention for the Protection of Human Rights and Fundamental Freedoms, the meaning and scope of those rights shall be the same as those laid down by the said Convention. This provision shall not prevent Union law providing more extensive protection.

This provision does not specifically address the question of the relationship between the two European Courts, the ECtHR and the ECJ, although it seems likely to be intended to promote deference on the part of the ECJ to the ECtHR. The explanatory memorandum declares that the EU legislator must comply with the standards laid down in the ECHR 'without thereby adversely affecting the autonomy of Community and that of the Court of Justice', but it also indicates that the meaning of the rights are determined in part by the ECtHR.

The Constitutional Treaty would have added four further clauses to Article 52. The first of these, paragraph (4), would have stipulated that the provisions of the Charter derived from national constitutional traditions should be interpreted in harmony with those traditions. Paragraph (6) would have complemented this by stipulating that 'full account' should be taken of national laws and practices as specified in the Charter. Paragraph (7) would have been an interesting amendment in that it sought to give legal weight to the explanatory memorandum to the Charter which was drafted by the secretariat—and which, although it frequently provides a helpful explanation or background to a provision, was not drafted with a view to having legal force.[180]

However, the most contentious and much-debated amendment which the CT would have introduced was that in paragraph (5), which sought to distinguish provisions of the Charter containing 'principles', and to stipulate that provisions containing 'principles' would be 'judicially cognizable' only when they had been implemented by legislative or executive acts of the EU or the Member States, and only in relation to interpretation or rulings on the legality of the latter. Although this amendment was somewhat complicated and unclear, it seems to have been intended to introduce into the Charter some version of the traditional (and often criticized) distinction between negatively-oriented civil and political rights, and positively-oriented economic and social rights, with a view to rendering the latter largely non-justiciable.

Article 53 of the Charter contains a kind of general non-regression clause which is similar in ways to that in Article 53 of the ECHR, and which refers not only to the ECHR but also to national constitutions and international agreements:

> Nothing in this Charter shall be interpreted as restricting or adversely affecting human rights and fundamental freedoms as recognised, in their respective fields of application, by Union

---

[179] See the account of Lord Goldsmith, n. 9 above.
[180] Para. (7) read: '[t]he explanations drawn up as a way of providing guidance in the interpretation of the Charter of Fundamental Rights shall be given due regard by the courts of the Union and of the Member States'.

law and international law and by international agreements to which the Union, the Community or all the Member States are party, including the European Convention for the Protection of Human Rights and Fundamental Freedoms, and by the Member States' constitutions.

It was queried whether the presence of this clause and the absence of a 'supremacy' clause in the Charter guaranteeing the primacy of EC law could call into question the long-established supremacy doctrine.[181] Such a concession seems highly unlikely, even if the general wording of Article 53(3) preserves the existing tension between the autonomy of the EU/EC legal order on the one hand, and the claims of Member States to the authority of their fundamental constitutional provisions on the other.

Finally, Article 54 contains a clause modelled on Article 17 of the ECHR, which provides that no provision of the Charter shall imply the right to engage in any activity aimed at the destruction or excessive limitation of any of the rights contained therein.

(d) CURRENT STATUS

As noted above, despite the blow dealt to the full legal effect of the Charter by the non-ratification of the Constitutional Treaty, which would have included a slightly amended version of the Charter in its second Part, the Charter is not without current legal effect.[182]

A range of institutional actors has made use of its provisions since its adoption. The Commission by an internal decision of 13 March 2001 decided to conduct a form of compatibility review with regard to the Charter, and to consider any legislative proposal connected with the protection of fundamental rights for its compatibility with the provisions of the Charter, *inter alia* by the inclusion of recitals in the legislation mentioning the relevant Charter rights. Four years later, the Commission followed up with a Communication on compliance with the Charter of Rights in legislative proposals,[183] and commissioned an external report on human-rights impact assessment for EU legislative policy proposals.[184] As a general matter, the Commission's practice of citing and having regard to the provisions of the Charter seems unaffected by the failure to ratify the Constitutional Treaty, and in particular by the negative referenda in France and the Netherlands.

The European Ombudsman has also continued to make regular reference to the Charter, to various aspects of the right to good administration, and to the right of access to the Ombudsman in Articles 41–43 thereof, in his speeches and his annual reports. In a speech to the European Parliament on 8 April 2002, he criticized the EU institutions for their failure to observe many of the rights contained in the Charter, in particular in relation to their own recruitment and staff regulations, and declared that 'European citizens have the right to expect the Charter to be followed by those institutions whose presidents solemnly proclaimed it in Nice in December 2000, that is the Council, the Parliament and the Commission'. In a more recent speech in April 2006, the current Ombudsman indicated that the post-Constitutional Treaty debate over the legal status of the Charter had not changed anything in

---

[181] J. Liisberg, 'Does the EU Charter of Fundamental Rights Threaten the Supremacy of Community Law?' (2001) 38 *CMLRev.* 1171.

[182] See n. 119 and text.

[183] COM(2005)172; H. Toner, 'Impact Assessment and Fundamental Rights Protection in EU Law' (2006) 31 *ELRev.* 316.

[184] 'The Consideration of Fundamental Rights in Impact Assessment: Final Report', available at http://ec.europa.eu/justice_home/doc_centre/rights/doc/study_epec_fund_rights_agency_en.pdf.

this respect: '[f]or the European Ombudsman, the principal yardstick to measure compliance with human rights is the Charter of Fundamental Rights'.[185]

Finally, after several years of silence on the Charter, the ECJ eventually followed the practice of so many of its Advocates General and of the CFI[186] by referring approvingly to the Charter as a re-affirmation of the general principles of law common to the Member States. In the course of its judgment on the challenge brought by the European Parliament to the family reunification directive, the ECJ declared:

Case C–540/03 **European Parliament v. Council**
[2006] ECR I–5769

38. The Charter was solemnly proclaimed by the Parliament, the Council and the Commission in Nice on 7 December 2000. While the Charter is not a legally binding instrument, the Community legislature did, however, acknowledge its importance by stating, in the second recital in the preamble to the Directive, that the Directive observes the principles recognised not only by Article 8 of the ECHR but also in the Charter. Furthermore, the principal aim of the Charter, as is apparent from its preamble, is to reaffirm 'rights as they result, in particular, from the constitutional traditions and international obligations common to the Member States, the Treaty on European Union, the Community Treaties, the [ECHR], the Social Charters adopted by the Community and by the Council of Europe and the case-law of the Court ... and of the European Court of Human Rights'.

In a later judgment in *Reynolds Tobacco*, the ECJ confirmed this stance by referring to Article 47 of the Charter on the right to an effective remedy and declaring that 'although this document does not have legally binding force, it does show the importance of the rights it sets out in the Community legal order'.[187] The seal of approval finally given by the Court to the Charter as a significant source of the general principles of EC law confirms that the Charter has definitively entered the constitutional practice of the EU, even if final resolution of its legal status is likely to remain suspended while discussions over the proposed Reform Treaty take place.

9. THE EU AND THE ECHR

(a) ACCESSION BY THE EC/EU TO THE ECHR

We have seen that the question whether the EU—and formerly, the EC—should accede to the European Convention on Human Rights has been a persistent one for many decades, and a question which did not disappear with the drafting of the EU Charter of Fundamental Rights. On the contrary, the Constitutional Treaty pursued a twin-track strategy by both incorporating the entirety of the Charter into Part II, and also by providing in Article I–9 for the EU to

---

[185] See www.ombudsman.europa.eu/speeches/en/2006-04-28.htm.

[186] The first such reference by the CFI was Case T–54/99 *max.mobil Telekommunikation Service GmbH* v. *Commission* [2002] ECR II–313, paras. 48, 57, and there have been many since. For some recent examples see Case T–210/01 *GEC* v. *Commission*, judgment of 14 Dec. 2005, Case T–378/02 R *Technische Glaswerke Ilmenau GmbH* v. *Commission* [2005] ECR II–5575.

[187] Case C–131/03 P *R.J. Reynolds Tobacco Holdings* v. *Commission* [2006] ECR I–7795.

accede to the ECHR. This raises the question why accession by the EU to the ECHR is still considered to be desirable, despite the gradual enhancement of the status of human rights within the EU over the years, and despite the adoption of the EU's own 'bill of rights'.

There are several possible answers. First, is that, as we have seen, the EU—and in particular the ECJ as its judicial branch—has continued to encounter criticism of its human rights role, and scepticism as to whether its commitment to promoting human rights (rather than EU economic and political interests) is genuine. An initial concern has been that the Court has used human rights discourse in an attempt to extend the influence of EC law over areas which should remain the primary concern of the Member States, given their political, cultural, and ideological diversity.[188]

A second concern is that the Court has manipulated the rhetorical force of the language of rights, while in reality merely advancing the commercial goals of the common market, and remaining biased towards 'market rights' instead of protecting values which are genuinely fundamental to the human condition.[189]

A third and opposite concern has also led to criticism of the Court, not because the rights which it favours are market rights rather than human rights, but rather because it has at times been too deferential, stopping short of requiring Member States to observe human rights principles in areas covered by Community law.[190]

A final objection is that the ECJ should not in any case be modelling itself as a European Human Rights Court, since this is not the primary function or purpose it has been allocated under the Treaties, and because another European Court, the ECtHR in Strasbourg, was specifically entrusted by the Member States of the Council of Europe with the task of monitoring their compliance with the commitments of the Convention on Human Rights,[191] The ECtHR was not only established with an express human rights jurisdiction, but has acquired expertise and a moral stature which the ECJ does not yet share. Moreover the ECJ's extension of the Community's competence to require national laws to comply with fundamental rights has also highlighted the possibility of conflict between the pronouncements of the two European Courts.[192] Some have taken the view that any serious conflict of interpretation between the two courts is unlikely,[193] but others—including the Convention on the Future of Europe and the Intergovernmental Conference that followed it—have concluded that accession by the EC to the ECHR, and even to the Council of Europe, should take place.[194] Eventually, at the same time that the EU Constitutional Treaty included a provision for accession by the EU

---

[188] See, e.g., the controversy over the Irish abortion information, Case C–159/90 *SPUC* v. *Grogan* [1991] ECR I–4685, which led to an attempt by the Irish government (which it subsequently sought to qualify by means of a Declaration) to insulate the Irish constitutional prohibition on abortion, and on information and referral services, from the possible impact of Community law: see Protocol 17 of the TEU.

[189] For a combination of both of these concerns see Coppel and O'Neill, n. 49 above. Compare Weiler and Lockhart, n. 49 above.

[190] J.H.H. Weiler, 'The European Court at a Crossroads: Community Human Rights and Member State Action', in F. Capotorti *et al.* (eds.), *Du Droit International au Droit de l'Intégration* (Nomos, 1987), 839–841. Contrast Jacobs, n. 90 above.

[191] See, e.g., the argument of the UK Government in Case 118/75 *Watson*, n. 16 above, 1191.

[192] See, e.g., R. Lawson, 'Confusion and Conflict? Diverging Interpretations of the ECHR in Strasbourg and Luxembourg', in R. Lawson and M. de Bloijs (eds.), *The Dynamics of the Protection of Human Rights in Europe* (Kluwer, 1994); D. Spielman, 'Human Rights Case Law in the Strasbourg and Luxembourg Courts: Inconsistencies and Complementarities', in Alston *et al.* (eds.), n. 3 above.

[193] P. van Dijk and G. van Hoof, *Theory and Practice of the European Convention on Human Rights* (3rd edn., Kluwer, 1998), 21.

[194] A. Clapham, 'Where is the EU's Human Rights Common Foreign Policy?', in Alston *et al.* (eds.), n. 3 above.

to the ECHR, a parallel provision allowing for accession by the EU on the part of the ECHR was added to Article 59 of the ECHR by Protocol No. 14.

The current state of play, therefore, is that while accession is now legally possible from the perspective of the Council of Europe, it is not yet possible from the EU side because of the non-ratification of the Constitutional Treaty. This means that—in view of *Opinion 2/94* of the ECJ—an amendment of the EU or EC Treaty is still necessary before accession can take place.

(b) INDIRECT REVIEW OF EC/EU ACTS BY THE ECtHR

The main practical difference which accession of the EC/EU to the ECHR would make is that the EU institutions would be subject to the review jurisdiction of the European Court of Human Rights, and the ECJ would no longer be the final arbiter of the lawfulness of EU action which is alleged to violate human rights. At present, in the absence of such accession, the situation remains more complex, and the approach of the Court of Human Rights to challenges brought before it against EU action has evolved in recent years.

While the Court of Human Rights will not admit complaints brought *directly* against the EC/EU, since the latter is not a party to the Convention,[195] the Court over the last decade has—in a development of the position taken by the former Commission on Human Rights in *M* v. *Germany*[196]—increasingly entertained indirect complaints against EC and EU acts which are brought against one or all Member States.

In 1999, the ECtHR ruled in *Matthews* v. *UK* that, while the Convention did not preclude the transfer by a State of national competences to an international organization such as the EC, the responsibility of the States for violations of the ECHR would continue even after such a transfer.[197] The case concerned the UK's denial of voting rights in Gibraltar for elections to the European Parliament, but the actual denial—and therefore the violation of Article 3 of Protocol No. 1 to the ECHR—stemmed from a treaty signed by all the Member States of the EU. This treaty was the 1976 Act Concerning the Election of the Representatives of the European Parliament by Direct Universal Suffrage. In other words, the violation resulted from an atypical piece of primary EU law rather than from a British law. According to the ECtHR, however, the fact that the violation stemmed from an EU law did not absolve the UK from responsibility for the violation, since that responsibility derived from the UK having voluntarily entered EC Treaty commitments. The Court ruled ultimately that there had been a violation of the essence of the right to vote, and the case clearly demonstrates that acts will not escape the review of the ECtHR simply because they are adopted by the EC or EU. Rather the Member States continue to retain responsibility for securing the rights protected by the Convention.[198]

Matthews was in some ways an unusual case, because the law which was found to be in violation of the Convention was an international agreement entered into by all EC Member States. It was an agreement which could not be reviewed by the ECJ, and one for which each Member State could plausibly continue to be held responsible. However, in a subsequent

---

[195] For decisions of the previously existing Commission on Human Rights on this and on several related questions see App. no. 13258/87, *Melcher (M)* v. *Germany*, 64 D & R 138; App. no. 21090/92, *Heinz* v. *Contracting States and Parties to the European Patent Convention*, 76 AD & R 125; App. no. 21072/92, *Gestra* v. *Italy*, 80 BD & R 93.

[196] App. no. 13258/87, n. 195 above.

[197] App. no. 24833/94, *Matthews* v. *UK* [1999] BHRC 686, esp. paras. 34–35; R. Harmsen, 'National Responsibility for EC Acts under the ECHR: Recasting the Accession Debate' (2001) 7 *EPL* 625.

[198] See also App. no. 43844/98, *TI* v. *UK* [2000] INLR 211, on the UK's responsibility under the Dublin Convention, an agreement signed between all EU Member States concerning asylum procedures, for continuing to secure ECHR rights.

series of cases involving various EC and EU acts, the ECtHR seemed willing to entertain indirect challenges against a variety of such acts, although in most cases it dismissed the challenge for other reasons. In *Guerin*, for example, where an action was brought against the then fifteen Member States in order to challenge decisions of the EC Commission alleging violation of Articles 6 and 13 of the ECHR, the ECtHR dismissed the application on the ground that Articles 6 and 13 did not cover the rights being claimed, without adverting to the fact that the impugned act was an EC measure.[199]

Subsequently in *Senator Lines*, an action was brought by a German company against the fifteen Member States complaining of a fine imposed by the EC Commission upon it under EC competition law.[200] The company alleged violation of the presumption of innocence and of the right to a fair trial[201] and, although the ECtHR ultimately rejected the complaint, it did so on the basis that Senator Lines was not the victim of any violation, since the fine imposed had not ultimately been enforced and had been quashed by the EC's Court of First Instance. Despite the fact that the main argument made by the respondent governments was that the impugned measure was an act of the EC Commission and not an act of any State within the jurisdiction of the ECHR, the Court of Human Rights made no reference to this.

A similar approach was also taken in the *Segi/Gestoras Pro-Amnistía* and *Emesa Sugar* cases. In *Emesa Sugar*, an action brought by the applicant company before the ECtHR effectively complained of a violation by the European Court of Justice of its right to a fair hearing under Article 6(1) of the ECHR, due to the fact that the applicant had no opportunity to respond to the Advocate General's opinion prior to the ruling by the ECJ.[202] The first argument made both by the respondent Dutch government and by the EC Commission, intervening, was that the ECtHR should declare the application inadmissible, given that it was directed specifically against an act of an EC institution (the ECJ). Once again, however, the ECtHR ignored the argument and instead declared the application inadmissible on a substantive point because it concerned the payment of import duties, which did not fall within the meaning of 'civil rights and obligations' in Article 6(1) of the ECHR.

In *Segi/Gestoras Pro-Amnistía*, an action was brought by two Basque organizations against the then 15 EU Member States to challenge the fact that they had been listed in the annex to an EU CFSP 'Common Position' on combating terrorism.[203] While the Common Position, as an act unanimously adopted under the Second Pillar, has more in common with the international agreement (primary EU law) in *Matthews* than with the Commission fine in *Senator Lines* or the ECJ proceedings in *Emesa Sugar*, the ECtHR once again did not address these matters in considering whether it had jurisdiction to hear the case. Instead, the Court dismissed the application on the basis that the two organizations were not yet 'victims' within the meaning of the Convention, and the Court specifically emphasized the applicability of its case law concerning the status of victim to 'the acts of an international legal order'.[204]

---

[199] App. no. 51717/99, *Guérin Automobiles* v. *les 15 Etats de l'Union Européenne*, judgment of the ECtHR of 4 July 2000.

[200] App. no. 56672/00, *DSR-Senator Lines GmbH* v. *The 15 Member States of the European Union*, admissibility decision of the ECtHR of 10 Mar. 2004.

[201] A challenge to the Commission's decision had earlier been brought before the CFI, but both the CFI and the ECJ had rejected an application for interim relief: Case T–191/98 R *DSR Senator Lines* v. *Commission* [1999] ECR II–2531 and, on appeal, Case C–364/99P R *DSR Senator Lines* v. *Commission* [1999] ECR I–8733.

[202] App. no. 62023/00, *Emesa Sugar* v. *Netherlands*, admissibility decision of the ECtHR of 13 Jan. 2005. The relevant decision of the ECJ is Case C–17/98 *Emesa Sugar* v. *Aruba* [2000] ECR I–665.

[203] App. nos. 6422/02 and 9916/02, *SEGI* v. *The 15 Member States of the EU*, admissibility decision of the ECtHR of 23 May 2002.

[204] *Ibid.*

Thus, although in *Guérin, Senator Lines, Segi,* and *Emesa Sugar,* the ECtHR eventually rejected the admissibility of each of the applications brought against a range of different EU acts (Commission decisions, a Council common position, and an ECJ ruling, respectively), it is significant that in none of the cases did the ECtHR do so on the ground that it lacked jurisdiction to examine violations committed by the EC/EU.

The most important ruling to be given by the ECtHR concerning its jurisdiction over acts of the EC in recent years is the *Bosphorus* case against Ireland.[205] This case was brought by a Turkish company against Ireland for the impounding, without compensation, of an airline which the applicant company had leased from the national airline of the former Yugoslavia. The Irish authorities had impounded the aircraft in reliance on an EC Regulation—following the interpretation of that Regulation by the ECJ on a reference from the Irish Supreme Court[206]—which implemented the UN sanctions regime against the former Yugoslavia during the civil war in the early 1990s. The ECtHR took the view that the alleged violation was committed by Ireland due to the State's compliance with a binding and non-discretionary EC law obligation—in other words, the EC Regulation was the real source of the alleged violation. The ECtHR went on to set out the approach which it should adopt when complaints of this kind were made to it:

Bosphoros v. Ireland, App. no. 45036/98,
Judgment of 30 June 2005

EUROPEAN COURT OF HUMAN RIGHTS

1. The question is therefore whether, and if so to what extent, that important general interest of compliance with EC obligations can justify the impugned interference by the State with the applicant's property rights.

2. The Convention does not, on the one hand, prohibit Contracting Parties from transferring sovereign power to an international (including a supranational) organisation in order to pursue co-operation in certain fields of activity (the M. & Co. decision, at p. 144 and Matthews at § 32, both cited above). Moreover, even as the holder of such transferred sovereign power, that organisation is not itself held responsible under the Convention for proceedings before, or decisions of, its organs as long as it is not a Contracting Party. . . .

3. On the other hand, it has also been accepted that a Contracting Party is responsible under Article 1 of the Convention for all acts and omissions of its organs regardless of whether the act or omission in question was a consequence of domestic law or of the necessity to comply with international legal obligations. . . .

4. In reconciling both these positions and thereby establishing the extent to which State action can be justified by its compliance with obligations flowing from its membership of an international organisation to which it has transferred part of its sovereignty, the Court has recognised that absolving Contracting States completely from their Convention responsibility in the areas covered by such a transfer would be incompatible with the purpose and object of the Convention: the guarantees of the Convention could be limited or excluded at will thereby depriving it of its peremptory character and undermining the practical and effective nature of

---

[205] App. no. 45036/98, *Bosphorus* v. *Ireland* (2006) 42 EHRR 1. For comments on the judgment see S. Douglas Scott (2006) 43 *CMLRev.* 243 and A. Hinarejos Parga (2006) 31 *ELRev.* 251.
[206] Case C–84/95 *Bosphorus* v. *Minister for Transport* [1996] ECR I–3953.

its safeguards (M. & Co. at p. 145 and Waite and Kennedy, at § 67). The State is considered to retain Convention liability in respect of treaty commitments subsequent to the entry into force of the Convention. . . .

5. In the Court's view, State action taken in compliance with such legal obligations is justified as long as the relevant organisation is considered to protect fundamental rights, as regards both the substantive guarantees offered and the mechanisms controlling their observance, in a manner which can be considered at least equivalent to that for which the Convention provides (see the above-cited M. & Co. decision, at p. 145, an approach with which the parties and the European Commission agreed). By 'equivalent' the Court means 'comparable': any requirement that the organisation's protection be 'identical' could run counter to the interest of international co-operation pursued (paragraph 150 above). However, any such finding of equivalence could not be final and would be susceptible to review in the light of any relevant change in fundamental rights' protection.

6. If such equivalent protection is considered to be provided by the organisation, the presumption will be that a State has not departed from the requirements of the Convention when it does no more than implement legal obligations flowing from its membership of the organisation.

However, any such presumption can be rebutted if, in the circumstances of a particular case, it is considered that the protection of Convention rights was manifestly deficient. In such cases, the interest of international co-operation would be outweighed by the Convention's role as a 'constitutional instrument of European public order' in the field of human rights . . .

7. It remains the case that a State would be fully responsible under the Convention for all acts falling outside its strict international legal obligations. The numerous Convention cases cited by the applicant at paragraph 117 above confirm this. Each case (in particular, the Cantoni judgment, at § 26) concerned a review by this Court of the exercise of State discretion for which EC law provided . . . The Matthews case can also be distinguished: the acts for which the United Kingdom was found responsible were 'international instruments which were freely entered into' by it (§ 33 of that judgment) . . .

8. Since the impugned act constituted solely compliance by Ireland with its legal obligations flowing from membership of the EC (paragraph 148 above), the Court will now examine whether a presumption arises that Ireland complied with its Convention requirements in fulfilling such obligations and whether any such presumption has been rebutted in the circumstances of the present case.

The ECtHR went on in paragraphs 159–165 to survey the EU's system of protection for fundamental rights, and to rule that the presumption that Ireland complied with its ECHR obligations did indeed arise, on the basis that the EU provided human rights protection 'equivalent' to that of the ECHR system, and that there was no dysfunction in the EU's control system such as to rebut that presumption in the case at hand.[207]

Two separate Opinions were signed by seven judges in the case, however, expressing certain reservations about the approach of the majority. These Opinions, while concurring with the substantive ruling that no violation of the right to property had occurred, expressed varying views about the approach taken to the 'presumption of compliance' with the ECHR of national acts adopted pursuant to international legal obligations. In particular, they expressed

---

[207] For a critical commentary on the case see K. Kuhnert, 'Bosphorus—Double Standards in European Human Rights Protection?' (2006) 2 *Utrecht Law Review* 177, and for a more approving assessment see C. Costello, 'The Bosphorus Ruling of the ECtHR: Fundamental Rights and Blurred Boundaries in Europe' (2006) 6 *HRLR* 87.

concern about the idea of abandoning a case-by-case review of compliance for a largely abstract review of the organization's general system of 'equivalent protection' for human rights. They also drew attention to the deficiencies in the EU's system of judicial protection due to the limited *locus standi* for private parties before the ECJ, and raised the question whether this amounted to a violation of Article 6(1) of the ECHR.[208]

It is evident from the discussion above that the answer to the question whether and in what circumstances the ECtHR will indirectly review EU action is not straightforward. The position can be summarized as follows. Where an EU act—such as a directive, which was at issue in the case of *Cantoni*[209]—leaves room for implementation choices to Member States, or where it is 'an international agreement freely entered into by the Member State' as in *Matthews*, a challenge can be brought before the ECtHR against the implementing State, which remains responsible for any violation of ECHR obligations. Where however an EU act—as in the case of the regulation in *Bosphorus*—leaves no discretion in implementation to the Member State, the State will be presumed (in the absence of contrary evidence of a dysfunction in control) to have acted compatibly with the ECHR so long as the EU control system overall provides an equivalent level of protection for human rights to that provided by the ECHR. Finally, where an EU act—as in *Senator Lines* or *Emesa Sugar*—is one which is not subject to implementation by the States but is adopted by an autonomous EU institution such as the Commission or the Court, it seems that an applicant will have to bring an action against all of the Member States collectively as the author of the act, and it seems likely (although perhaps not certain[210]) that the ECtHR will apply the presumption of compatibility.

Ultimately, while it has been argued that recent cases demonstrate that a kind of *de facto* accession of the EC to the ECHR has already taken place,[211] it seems equally true—as the concurring ECtHR opinions in *Bosphorus* explicitly said—that recent cases demonstrate the need for *de jure*—accession to take place so that EU acts may directly and unequivocally be subject to full review by the ECtHR. There seems to be no good reason why the EU—unlike the many Member States which have well-established and sophisticated domestic systems for constitutional human rights protection—should benefit from a presumption of compatibility of its acts with the ECHR, and should escape full scrutiny by the Court of Human Rights.

---

[208] The question whether the restricted access of individuals to direct actions before the ECJ under Art. 230 violates the principle of effective judicial protection, including that expressed by Art. 6 of the ECHR, has been raised many times before the CFI and ECJ. See, e.g., Case C–263/02 P *Jégo-Quéré* v. *Commission* [2004] ECR I–3425; Case T–50/00 *UPA* v. *Council* [2002] ECR I–06677; Case T–370/02 *Alpenhain-Camembert-Werk* v. *Commission* [2004] ECR II–2097; Case T–338/02 *Segi* v. *Council* [2004] ECR II–1647; Case C–141/02 P *Commission* v. *T-Mobile Austria* [2005] ECR I–1283; Case T–231/02 *Gonnelli and AIFO* v. *Commission* [2004] ECR II–1051.

[209] App. no. 17862/91, *Cantoni* v. *France*, judgment of the ECtHR of 15 Nov. 1996. The case concerned a claim of violation of Art. 7(1) of the ECHR on retroactivity of criminal liability, due to the allegedly inadequate definition in a provision of the French Public Health Code, which implemented EU Dir. 65/65, of the term 'medical product'.

[210] It is possible, although unlikely, that the ECtHR might refuse to apply the presumption of compatibility in the case of such 'self-executing' EU acts if they are for some reason not subject to adequate review within the EU itself—as was true of the measure at issue in *Matthews*. It is possible also to imagine a non-reviewable Second Pillar Common Position (like that in *Segi*) which does not require any implementation, being treated by the ECJ like the international agreement in *Matthews*. Another possibility, however, is that the ECJ will apply the presumption of compatibility to such self-executing EU acts, but would treat the lack of reviewability as a consideration such as to rebut the presumption of ECHR compatibility.

[211] Harmsen, n. 197 above, 640, 641–642.

(c) MUTUAL INFLUENCE OF THE ECJ AND THE ECtHR IN THE ABSENCE OF ACCESSION

Similar issues and cases tend increasingly to arise before the ECtHR and the ECJ/CFI, given the expansion of the scope of EC law and EC human rights law, and also in view of the growing influence of the Charter of Fundamental Rights. The issue of AIDS testing arose before both the CFI and the ECJ in the form of privacy claims against the Community institutions under Article 8 of the ECHR and, although the CFI dismissed these claims quickly,[212] the ECJ was more cautious and found a breach of the right to privacy in one case.[213]

The potential for differences in interpretation between the two sets of European Courts on the same issue can be seen in a range of earlier cases of the ECJ and ECtHR respectively. Compare, for example, the judgment of the ECtHR in *Open Door Counselling*[214] with the Opinion of the Advocate General in *Grogan*,[215] or the approach of the ECJ in *ERT*[216] with that of the ECtHR in *Lentia v. Austria*,[217] or the decision of the ECJ in *Hoechst*[218] with that of the ECtHR in *Niemietz*;[219] or the ECJ in *Orkem*[220] with the ECtHR in *Funke*,[221] and the subsequent series of ECJ and CFI cases concerning various rights of the defence in EC competition proceedings in *SKC*,[222] *Limburgse Vinyl Maatschappij*,[223] *Baustahlgewebe*,[224] and *Roquette Frères*.[225]

Another recent indication of the potential for conflict arose in the *Emesa Sugar* litigation. In *Emesa Sugar*,[226] the applicant relied before the ECJ on the *Vermeulen* judgment of the ECtHR[227] to argue that the lack of opportunity for it to reply to the Advocate General's Opinion constituted a violation of the right to adversarial proceedings in Article 6(1) of the ECHR. The ECtHR in *Vermeulen* had condemned the lack of opportunity to reply to the

---

[212] See Cases T–121/89 and 13/90 *X* v. *Commission* [1992] ECR II–2195; Case T–10/93 *A* v. *Commission* [1994] ECR II–179. For similarly unsuccessful challenges see Case T–11/90 *H. S.* v. *Council* [1992] ECR II–1869; Case T–176/94 *K* v. *Commission* [1995] ECR SC IA–203, II–261.

[213] Case C–404/92 P, *X*, n. 60 above. For an earlier unsuccessful challenge see, however, Case C–206/89 R *S* v. *Commission* [1989] ECR 2841.

[214] *Open Door Counselling Ltd. and Dublin Well Woman Centre* v. *Ireland*, Series A No. 246 (1992) 15 EHRR 244.

[215] Case C–159/90 *Grogan*, n. 188 above.

[216] Case C–260/89 *ERT*, n. 18 above.

[217] *Informationsverein Lentia* v. *Austria* (1994) 17 EHRR 93. In this case the ECtHR found that the radio and television monopoly of the Austrian Broadcasting Corporation constituted a violation of Art. 10 of the Convention, whereas the ECJ in Case C–260/89 *ERT*, n. 18 above, left the Art. 10 issue to be decided by the national court. See also Case C–23/93 *TV10 SA* v. *Commissariaat voor de Media* [1994] ECR I–4795, concerning Dutch broadcasting restrictions, in which the ECJ referred to its conclusion in an earlier case, Case C–353/89 *Commission* v. *Netherlands* [1991] ECR I–4069, that the maintenance of the pluralism which the broadcasting policy sought to safeguard was precisely what the ECHR was designed to protect. See the similar conclusion of the Commission on Human Rights in its decision of 11 Jan. 1994, App. no. 21472/93, *X* v. *Netherlands*, 76A D & R 129.

[218] Cases 46/87 and 227/88 *Hoechst AG* v. *Commission* [1989] ECR 2859.

[219] *Niemietz* v. *Germany*, n. 68 above. See however the subsequent decision of the ECJ in Case C–94/00 *Roquette Frères*, n. 69 above, citing the later ECHR judgment in *Colas Est* v. *France*, judgment of 16 Apr. 2002.

[220] Case 374/87 *Orkem*, n. 66 above.

[221] *Funke* v. *France*, n. 71 above.

[222] Cases T–213/95 and 18/96 *SCK*, n. 64 above, paras. 56–57.

[223] Cases T–305/94–335/94 *Limburgse Vinyl Maatschappij NV* v. *Commission* [1999] ECR II–931, especially para. 420.

[224] Case C–185/95 P *Baustahlgewebe*, n. 64 above. For discussion of some of these issues see Lenaerts and de Smijter, n. 178 above.

[225] Case C–94/00 *Roquettes Frères*, n. 69 above.

[226] Case C–17/98 *Emesa Sugar*, n. 202 above. For comment see R. Lawson (2000) 37 *CMLRev.* 983.

[227] *Vermeulen* v. *Belgium* [1996] ECHR 19075/91.

426 | HUMAN RIGHTS IN THE EU

submissions of the Procureur Général before the Belgian Cour de Cassation under Article 6(1), but the ECJ ruled that the role of the Advocate General in the context of EC proceedings was different in key respects, so that there was no violation of Article 6(1).[228] The apparently conflicting case law of the ECHR was not, according to the ECJ, transposable to the situation of the Advocate General.[229]

However, the subsequent ruling of the ECtHR in the case of *Kress*[230] seemed to imply that the case law might indeed apply also to the situation of a judicial officer such as the EU Advocate General, and this argument was made before the ECJ in the later case of *Kaba*.[231] Advocate General Colomer in *Kaba* dismissed the argument, and in the course of his Opinion he was very critical of the relevant case law of the ECtHR,[232] but the ECJ did not address the issue and decided the case on a different ground. Interestingly, when *Emesa Sugar* subsequently brought its case for violation of the right to a fair hearing by the ECJ before the European Court of Human Rights, the ECtHR dismissed the application as inadmissible on the basis that customs duties did not fall within the scope of the right to a fair hearing in Article 6(1).[233] In other words, despite the lurking conflict underpinning the case, both the ECJ and the ECtHR in their different ways sought to avoid giving contradictory rulings, or finding the jurisprudence of the other European Court to be at fault.

What can increasingly be seen is a determination on the part of both sets of European Courts to avoid Conflict in their respective case law, and to demonstrate deference to the approach of the other Court in relation to similar questions arising before them.[234] And while, as we have seen, many approving references to the jurisprudence of the ECtHR are to be found in the case law of the ECJ, the ECtHR also recently referred to the 'strong persuasive value' of an ECJ ruling on the question of sex discrimination in social security in the case of *Stec*.[235]

10. CONCLUSIONS

i. Human rights issues occupy an increasingly high profile within EU law and policy, in particular given the anti-discrimination powers in Article 13 EC and the legislation which has been adopted under it. The sanction mechanism in Article 7 TEU, although unlikely to be used, has added to this profile-raising. New instruments such as human-rights mainstreaming and human-rights impact assessment are being developed by the Council and Commission, and new bodies such as the Network of Independent Experts on Fundamental Rights, and the Fundamental Rights Agency have been established.

ii. The institutional and judicial approval of the EU Charter of Fundamental Rights has given it an ongoing salience even though its ultimate legal status remains undetermined. Although the Charter applies mainly to the EU and its institutions, it is addressed also to the Member States 'when implementing Union law', and it declares that no new power or

---

[228] Case C–17/98 *Emesa Sugar*, n. 202 above.

[229] *Ibid.*, para. 16.

[230] App. no. 39594/98 *Kress* v. *France*, judgment of the ECtHR of 11 June 2001.

[231] Case C–466/00 *Kaba* v. *Home Secretary* [2003] ECR I–2219.

[232] *Ibid.*, paras. 104–106. See also the Opinion of Colomer AG in Case C–480/99 P *Plant* v. *Commission* [2001] ECR I–265, especially para. 36.

[233] N. 202 above.

[234] For a case in which the ECtHR drew support from the human rights approach of the EU by looking not at the ECJ's jurisprudence but at the provisions of the Charter of Fundamental Rights see App. no. 28957/95, *Goodwin* v. *United Kingdom*, n. 149 above, para. 100, on the right of transgendered persons to marry.

[235] App. nos. 65731/01 and 65900/01, *Stec* v. *United Kingdom* (2006) 43 EHRR 47, para. 58.

task for the EU is created by its provisions. Nonetheless, all addressees are expressly required to promote the rights contained therein.

iii. The complex but co-operative relationship between the ECJ and the European Court of Human Rights is increasingly highlighted both by the number of cases before the CFI and the ECJ in which ECHR jurisprudence is cited and followed, and by the growing number of cases coming before the ECtHR which indirectly challenge EU measures, including the important recent *Bosphorus* judgment. The ongoing attempts by the two European judiciaries, and by the EU Charter, to promote harmony and to avoid conflict between the two systems, do not resolve all of the concerns. The question of accession by the EC/EU to the ECHR, despite the failure of the CT, remains very much on the agenda.

11. FURTHER READING

(a) Books and Collections

Alston, P., Bustelo, M., and Heenan, J. (eds.), *The EU and Human Rights* (Oxford University Press, 1999)

Williams, A., *EU Human Rights Policies: A Study in Irony* (Oxford University Press, 2004)

(b) Articles

Besselink, L., 'Entrapped by the Maximum Standard: On Fundamental Rights, Pluralism and Subsidiarity in the European Union' (1998) 35 *CMLRev.* 629

Coppell, J., and O'Neill, A., 'The European Court of Justice: Taking Rights Seriously?' (1992) 12 *Legal Studies* 227

Douglas Scott, S., 'The Charter of Fundamental Rights as a Constitutional Document' [2004] *EHRLR* 37

Goldsmith, T., 'A Charter of Rights, Freedoms and Principles' (2001) 38 *CMLRev.* 1201

Lenaerts, K., and De Smijter, E., 'A Bill of Rights for the EU' (2001) 38 *CMLRev.* 273

Von Bogdandy, A., 'The EU as a Human Rights Organization' (2000) 37 *CMLRev.* 1307

Weiler, J., 'Fundamental Rights and Fundamental Boundaries', in N. Neuwahl and A. Rosas (eds.), *The EU and Human Rights* (Kluwer, 1995)

—— 'Does the EU Truly Need a Charter of Rights?' (2000) 6 *ELJ* 95

—— and Lockhart, N., ' "Taking Rights Seriously" Seriously: The European Court and its Fundamental Rights Jurisprudence' (1995) 32 *CMLRev.* 51, 579

ENFORCEMENT ACTIONS AGAINST MEMBER STATES

1. CENTRAL ISSUES

i. Amongst the tasks entrusted to the Commission by Article 211 EC is that of ensuring the proper application of Community law. The main component of the Commission's task in ensuring this is to monitor Member State compliance and to respond to non-compliance.

ii. The Treaty provides for various enforcement mechanisms[1] involving judicial proceedings against the Member States, which are brought either by the Commission or—much less frequently—by a Member State. Article 226 establishes the general enforcement procedure, giving the Commission broad power to bring enforcement proceedings against Member States which it considers to be in breach of their obligations under Community law.[2]

iii. The enforcement procedure functions in part as an elite means for resolving disputes involving Member States amicably without recourse to litigation, in part as a channel for individuals to complain to the Commission about breaches of EC law, and in part as an 'objective' law enforcement tool by the Commission.[3] It has also been described as a legal mechanism for enhancing the accountability of the different actors involved, in particular the Member States and the Commission.[4]

iv. As the number of infringement cases continues to rise, with the expansion of both EU policies and membership, the general enforcement mechanism has come under increasing

---

[1] See, e.g., Art. 88(2) on state aid and Art. 95(4) on internal market measures. Under Art. 237 the Board of the European Investment Bank and the Council of the European Central Bank have powers similar to those of the Commission under Art. 226. Art. 298 provides for an enforcement procedure where Member States have relied on Art. 297 to derogate from fundamental Community rules: see Case C–120/94 R *Commission* v. *Greece* [1994] ECR I–3037.

[2] The infringement procedure under Art. 88 of the Coal and Steel Treaty (which expired at the end of 2002) gave considerably more power to the Commission (then called the High Authority), which was empowered to record the failure of a State to fulfil its obligations, without first bringing the case before the ECJ. However, the State itself could then bring the matter before the Court: Arts. 141–142 Euratom mirror Arts. 226–227 EC.

[3] For a discussion of the tensions between all three dimensions see R. Rawlings, 'Engaged Elites: Citizen Action and Institutional Attitudes in Commission Enforcement' (2000) 6 *ELJ* 4.

[4] C. Harlow and R. Rawlings, 'Accountability and Law Enforcement: The Centralized EU Infringement Procedure' (2006) 31 *ELRev.* 447.

strain.[5] Various attempts have been made to address the problem of overload and delay. The Commission has begun to emphasize preventive mechanisms and alternative methods of resolution, to prioritize certain kinds of breach, and to identify cases involving widespread, general, or persistent breaches. As of 2005, environmental cases continued to make up almost one quarter of the number of cases open.

v.   The pecuniary penalty mechanism of Article 228, which was created in the 1990s, allows the Commission to request the ECJ to impose a penalty payment on a Member State which has failed to comply with a previous judgment pursuant to Article 226. Although the number of judgments involving penalty payments remains small, both the early case law and the gradually expanding use by the Commission of Article 228 have begun to give shape to the procedure.

2. THE FUNCTION AND OPERATION OF THE INFRINGEMENT PROCEDURE

Article 226 provides:

> If the Commission considers that a Member State has failed to fulfil an obligation under this Treaty, it shall deliver a reasoned opinion on the matter after giving the State concerned the opportunity to submit its observations.
>
> If the State concerned does not comply with the opinion within the period laid down by the Commission, the latter may bring the matter before the Court.

(a) NATURE AND FUNCTION OF THE PROCEDURE

The Commission initiates Article 226 proceedings either in response to a complaint from someone in a Member State or on its own initiative. Since it has no investigation service, complaints are brought on the basis of information gained from diverse sources, e.g. through the press, from European Parliament questions or petitions, or increasingly through modern technological sources such as databases indicating when Member States have failed to notify their implementation of a directive.

The Commission has repeatedly stated in its annual reports over the last ten or fifteen years that complaints from citizens constitute a significant source for the detection of infringements, and has suggested that the Article 226 procedure thus contributes towards creating a more participatory Community in which citizens can play a role in law enforcement.[6] In 1999 a standard complaint form was designed for individuals to use.[7] Nonetheless, the Commission has equally emphasized the fact that the enforcement procedure is not intended primarily to provide individuals with a means of redress, but rather is an 'objective' mechanism for ensuring state compliance with EC law.[8] Indeed, the Commission has regularly

---

5   For a useful overview see R. Munoz, 'The Monitoring of the Application of Community Law: The Need to Improve the Current Tools and an Obligation to Innovate', Jean Monnet Working Paper 04/2006.

6   For the Commission's Annual Monitoring Reports see http://ec.europa.eu/community_law/eulaw/index_en.htm.

7   [1999] OJ C119/5.

8   See, e.g., *13th Annual Report* [1996] OJ C303/8.

cautioned against over-emphasizing the role of individuals, pointing to its own discretion in deciding whether to commence infringement proceedings, emphasizing the bilateral rather than trilateral nature of the procedure,[9] and identifying the primary objective as that of bringing offending Member States into line rather than satisfying individual interests.[10]

Given the Commission's ambivalent attitude, it is not surprising to find that the role actually played by individual complainants is imprecise and varying. On the one hand, the individual has no say in determining whether or not the Commission actually initiates proceedings against a Member State.[11] On the other hand, since the establishment of the Ombudsman's office, individuals have regularly made complaints about the Commission's procedures, leading to pressure from the Ombudsman on the Commission to make changes and improvements to its practices.[12] After the Ombudsman's own-initiative investigation into the Commission's enforcement procedures in 1996,[13] the Commission ceased its previous practice of failing to inform complainants when a case had been terminated, began to make more frequent use of press releases, and to place more information about the various formal stages of the infringement procedure on the internet. In 2002, the Commission issued a communication to the European Parliament on relations with individual complainants, outlining the changes it had made, including the publication of a consolidated version of its internal procedural rules governing relations with complainants.[14] The Commission also listed its administrative commitments to complainants, including a commitment to deal with any case arising out of a complaint within a year of receipt of the latter.[15]

A major source of frustration for individual complainants has been the difficulty in obtaining access to documents related to the infringement proceedings, but their attempts to obtain access by means of complaints to the Ombudsman or through the European Courts have not met with much success.[16] The Commission has invariably the invoked exception to the EC transparency rules governing 'inspections, investigations and audits',[17] and these have largely been upheld by the Ombudsman[18] and by the Courts. In *Petrie*, the CFI underscored the bilateral nature of infringement proceedings in upholding the refusal of access to documents:

> So far as concerns the applicants' argument that proceedings under Article 226 EC seeking to establish the facts relating to the infringements of Community law complained of must

---

[9] COM(2002)141.

[10] *18th Annual Report*, COM(2001)309.

[11] See Case 247/87 *Star Fruit* v. *Commission* [1989] ECR 291; Case T–182/97 *Smanor* v. *Commission* [1998] ECR II–271.

[12] For some recent examples see complaints no. 146/2005(GG), no. 3317/2004(GG), no. 956/2004(PB), and no. 289/2005(WP)GG, which resulted in a Special Report to the European Parliament on 30 May 2006. All reports and draft recommendations to the Commission are available on the Ombudsman website: www. ombudsman.europa.eu.

[13] See 303/97/PD, reported in the Ombudsman's Annual Report for 1997. See R. Mastroianni, 'The Enforcement Procedure under Article 169 of the EC Treaty and the Powers of the European Commission: Quis Custodiet Custodes?' (1995) 1 *EPL* 535; P. Kunzlik, 'The Enforcement of EU Environmental Law: Article 169, the Ombudsman and the Parliament' (1997) 6 *EELR* 46 and more recently Harlow and Rawlings, n. 4 above.

[14] COM(2002)141, OJ [2002] C 244/5. See also, in the same year, the Commission Communication on Better Monitoring of Community Law, COM(2002)725.

[15] *Ibid*. In 2006 however, the Ombudsman sent a special report to the European Parliament arising out of a complaint made to him against the Commission, due to the Commission's unjustified failure to deal with a particular complaint within the promised one-year deadline: see the special report of 30 May 2006, www. ombudsman.europa.eu.

[16] See below 441, nn. 80–81, and text.

[17] See now Art. 4(2) of Reg. 1049/2001 [2001] OJ L145/43, governing access to documents.

[18] See, e.g., the Ombudsman's decisions on Complaints 2821/2004/OV and 3732/2005/JMA.

respect the audi alteram partem principle, it must be noted that individuals are not party to proceedings concerning failure to fulfil obligations and for that reason cannot invoke rights to a fair hearing involving application of the audi alteram partem principle.[19]

However, the Commission's 'aloof, unresponsive and negative' attitude towards citizen complainants, as well as its 'practically unlimited discretion' and tendency towards arbitrariness have come in for sharp criticism,[20] and even the Ombudsman has been criticized, at earlier stages, for wasting the opportunity to push for stronger administrative and citizen-friendly reforms.[21]

Harlow and Rawlings have recently analysed the evolution of the infringement procedure—and the implicit models of accountability on which it is premised—through three phases: an initial diplomacy phase shaped largely by the Commission, a subsequent more judicialized phase influenced by the jurisprudence of the Court but still dominated by the Commission's negotiatory approach, and a third more clearly legalized phase following the enactment of a provision for pecuniary penalties against States. They note, however, that sitting somewhat uncomfortably alongside the bilateral and elite conceptions of the infringement procedure favoured by the Court and the Commission there exists a more participatory conception, which is championed by the Ombudsman and the Parliament as well as by many citizens:

Carol Harlow and Richard Rawlings, Accountability and Law Enforcement: The Centralized EU Infringement Procedure[22]

Söderman [the first EU Ombudsman] portrays the 'citizen who complains' as a 'party in the administrative procedure', who ought to be recognised as such and should enjoy all the procedural safeguards of EC law together with (subject to legal confidentiality) access to the file in accordance with the right to good administration contained in Art.41 of the European Charter of Fundamental Rights. This tripartite analysis, with the Commission presented as arbitrator between two parties, contrasts significantly with the view of Court and Commission of an elite procedure confined to two parties: Commission and Member State. . . .

But just how far can such an approach sensibly go, given the evident need for an efficient procedure and for the Commission to retain effective control of decisions? One need not be an apologist for the Commission to appreciate that complainants are self-selecting and that their concern to vindicate the rule of law is commonly a product of private interest, even if, in some of the cases discussed above, a strong measure of public interest is joined. The dissonance between a Commission policy of stopping at the point of voluntary compliance and a natural concern among complainants with the effects of past infringements is an obvious flashpoint.

---

[19] Case T–191/99 *Petrie* v. *Commission* [2001] ECR II–3677, para. 70. See also Case T–105/95 *WWF* v. *Commission* [1997] ECR II–313; Case T–309/97 *Bavarian Lager Company* v. *Commission* [1999] ECR II–3217.

[20] Rawlings, n. 3 above; L. Krämer, 'Monitoring Application of Community Law', submission to the Hearing of the European Parliament (Committee on Legal Affairs), Feb. 2006, available at www.europarl.europa.eu/comparl/juri/hearings/20060223/kraemer_en.pdf.

[21] Rawlings, n. 3 above.

[22] (2006) 31 *ELRev.* 447.

(b) OPERATION OF THE PROCEDURE

The infringement procedure can be divided into four distinct stages:

1. Negotiations at the initial *pre-contentious stage* give the Member State the occasion to explain its position and the opportunity to reach an accommodation with the Commission.

2. If the matter is not clarified or resolved informally between the two at this stage, the state will be *formally notified* of the specific infringement alleged by means of a letter from the Commission. The State is usually given two months to reply, except in cases of urgency, and the Commission normally decides within a year either to close a case or to proceed.

3. If, after negotiation with the State, the matter has not been resolved, the Commission may proceed to the stage of issuing a *reasoned opinion*. The reasoned opinion sets out clearly the grounds on which the alleged infringement rests, and marks the beginning of the time period within which the Member State must comply, if it is to avoid the final stage.

4. The final stage is *referral* of the matter by the Commission *to the Court of Justice.*

The Commission clearly continues to value and to affirm the 'elite co-operation' dimension of the infringement procedure which enables disputes over enforcement to be resolved at the pre-contentious stage, or even after the formal stage has begun, without actual recourse to the Court. During the mid-1990s, however, following a change of practice by the Commission concerning the issue of letters of formal notice, the number of referrals to the Court rose rapidly.[23] However, they subsequently stabilized again,[24] leading the Commission to remark on the efficient handling of proceedings, and to suggest that 'in many cases the pre-litigation examination of complaints is enough to prompt the Member States to put the situation right'.[25]

In its 2002 communication on Better Monitoring, the Commission emphasized a range of 'complementary mechanisms' for resolving instances of Member State non-compliance, such as problem-solving networks like the internal market SOLVIT network, national mediation, and even national judicial proceedings. Secondly, the Commission emphasized a range of mechanisms of infringement-prevention and management, such as interpretative communications, promotion of peer pressure, notification obligations, transparency campaigns, providing training, exchanges of information and practice, and so-called 'package meetings' with Member States. These are all apparently intended to help Member States with compliance so that the need for recourse to formal infringement proceedings is correspondingly reduced. Thirdly, the Commission introduced a number of criteria for it to follow in prioritizing particular kinds of infringement, beginning with infringements that 'undermine the foundations of the rule of law', secondly infringements that undermine the 'smooth functioning of the EC legal system', and thirdly the incorrect transposition or non-transposal of directives.

In other words, the centralized EC enforcement mechanism of Article 226 is supposed to be just one mechanism, and usually a last-resort and carefully targeted mechanism, after other strategies to encourage compliance have failed, and after negotiation and constructive

---

[23] See the *13th* and *14th Annual Reports* for 1995 and 1996 [1996] OJ C3031 and [1997] OJ C3321 respectively.

[24] See the *16th, 17th*, and *18th Annual Reports* for 1998, 1999, and 2000, COM(1999)301, COM(2000)92, and COM(2001)309 respectively.

[25] See the discussion of statistics in COM(2002)725, Commission Communication on Better Monitoring of the Application of Community Law.

intervention have not succeeded. Quite apart from the drastically limited time and resources of the Commission, there are pragmatic and political reasons for it to exercise political discretion and not to pursue every known Member State breach to judgment. As Rawlings has noted, 'Commission discretion allows, and scarce resources dictate, an ordered policy of selective enforcement'.[26] Finally, it is important to remember that enforcement actions successfully brought before the ECJ do not necessarily lead to compliance, even with the additional deterrent of the pecuniary penalty procedure of Article 228 EC.

3. THE RELATIONSHIP BETWEEN THE 'PUBLIC' AND THE 'PRIVATE' ENFORCEMENT MECHANISMS

The early rulings of the ECJ which established the principle of direct effect made clear that the public enforcement procedures of Articles 226 and 227 (then Articles 169 and 170) provide merely one amongst several legal mechanisms for ensuring the application of Community law. According to the ECJ in *Van Gend en Loos*:[27]

> The vigilance of individuals concerned to protect their rights amounts to an effective supervision in addition to the supervision entrusted by Articles 169 and 170 to the diligence of the Commission and of the Member States.

Advocate General Roemer in the case argued that the preliminary rulings procedure and the infringement procedure are fundamentally distinguished by the fact that in a preliminary reference from a national court under Article 234, the ECJ will give only a ruling on the interpretation of Community law, leaving it for the national court to spell out the implications of that ruling in the particular case; whereas in proceedings under Article 226 or 227 (ex Article 169 or 170) the ECJ will pronounce directly on the compatibility of a Member State's conduct with Community law.[28] In *Mölkerei-Zentrale* the ECJ ruled that proceedings brought by an individual were intended to protect individual rights in a specific case, whereas Commission enforcement proceedings were intended to ensure the general and uniform observance of Community law.[29] This meant that the two kinds of proceedings 'have different objects, aims and effects, and a parallel may not be drawn between them'.[30] Despite the attempts to maintain a clear distinction between the outcome of a preliminary ruling and an enforcement action, however, it is evident from *Van Gend en Loos* and from many subsequent decisions that the ECJ in the context of its preliminary rulings interpretive jurisdiction does often effectively declare whether a Member State is in breach of EC law.[31]

Nevertheless, the two procedures continue to be treated in legal terms as quite distinct. Quite recently, the ECJ rejected the UK's argument that infringement proceedings by the Commission should be deemed inadmissible on the basis that national judicial

---

[26] Rawlings, n. 3 above, 26.
[27] [1963] ECR 1, 13.
[28] *Ibid.*, 25.
[29] Case 28/67 *Mölkerei-Zentrale Westfalen v. Hauptzollamt Paderborn* [1968] ECR 143, 153.
[30] *Ibid.*
[31] Ch. 13.

proceedings were pending:

> The existence of the remedies available through the national courts cannot prejudice the bringing of an action under Article 226 EC, since the two procedures have different objectives and effects[32]

In similar vein, the ECJ has ruled that 'the direct effect of a Community provision, and hence the ability of individuals to enforce it before national courts, [is] no defence to a Commission action under Article 226 [ex Article 169] for failure to implement that provision'.[33]

4. THE COMMISSION'S DISCRETION

There has been much debate over the extent of the Commission's discretion to bring proceedings under Article 226. This discretion could be problematic in several ways. One possibility is that the Commission uses its discretion in a way which is excessively lenient or arbitrarily selective with defaulting Member States. Another possibility is that enforcement proceedings could be used unfairly or oppressively, if there are insufficient constraints on the Commission in terms of time and procedure.

It is clear that, in view of the multiple roles of the Commission under the Treaty, there may be political and other reasons leading it to exercise its discretion against bringing infringement proceedings, even where it is undeniable that a Member State is in blatant violation of EC law.[34] The language of paragraph 2 of Article 226 clearly suggests that, once it has issued a reasoned opinion indicating a breach by a Member State, the Commission has broad discretion whether or not to bring the matter before the ECJ. And even though paragraph 2 uses mandatory language with respect to the decision to issue a reasoned opinion (the Commission 'shall' deliver a reasoned opinion where it considers a State has failed to fulfil a Treaty obligation), there is agreement on the fact that this language (especially the subjective term 'considers') leaves the Commission with discretion whether and when to issue a reasoned opinion.[35]

As to the *manner* in which the Commission exercises its discretion in bringing proceedings, the Court has repeatedly made clear that, as far as the substantive reasons for bringing an enforcement action are concerned, proceedings are entirely 'objective'. This apparently means that the Court will examine only whether the infringement alleged by the Commission does in fact exist, and will not look into the Commission's motives for bringing the action.[36] In the

---

[32] Case C–508/03 *Commission* v. *United Kingdom* [2006] ECR I–3969, para 71.

[33] Case 29/84 *Commission* v. *Germany* [1985] ECR 1661, para 29. See also Case 102/79 *Commission* v. *Belgium* [1980] ECR 1473; Case 168/85 *Commission* v. *Italy* [1986] ECR 2945.

[34] P. Craig, 'Once Upon a Time in the West: Direct Effect and the Federalization of EEC Law' (1992) 12 *OJLS* 453, 456.

[35] A. Evans, 'The Enforcement Procedure of Article 169 EEC: Commission Discretion' (1979) 4 *ELRev.* 442, 445.

[36] See, e.g., Case C–200/88 *Commission* v. *Greece* [1990] ECR I–4299, para. 9. For another example see the AG's opinion in the *Open Skies* case, dismissing the argument that the Commission's action should be inadmissible on the ground of misuse of procedure, since it had brought this set of infringement proceedings against 8 Member States primarily in order to pressurize the Council to open negotiations with the USA: Cases C–466–476/98 *Commission* v. *United Kingdom et al.* [2002] ECR I–9855, para. 29, Tizzano AG.

following case, the UK argued that there was a political motive behind the Commission's action, and that it was seeking to bypass the procedures set up under a directive:

Case 416/85 **Commission v. United Kingdom**
[1988] ECR 3127

9. That argument cannot be upheld. In the context of the balance of powers between the institutions laid down in the Treaty, it is not for the Court to consider what objectives are pursued in an action brought under Article 169 of the Treaty. Its role is to decide whether or not the Member State in question has failed to fulfil its obligations as alleged. As the Court held in Case 7/68 *Commission* v. *Italy* [1968] ECR 423, an action against a Member-State for failure to fulfil its obligations, the bringing of which is a matter for the Commission in its entire discretion, is objective in nature.

Conversely, the *absence* of a specific motive or interest on the Commission's part in bringing proceedings against a Member State will not affect the admissibility of the enforcement proceedings either.[37] The Commission acts 'in the general interest', according to the Court, and does not have to have a specific interest, because 'Article 226 is not intended to protect that institution's own rights'.[38]

States have enjoyed greater success in arguing that there are *procedural* constraints, such as reasonable time limits, on the Commission's discretion. In an early case, the Court ruled that the Commission's choice of moment to initiate proceedings could not affect their admissibility.[39] However, despite some initial reluctance,[40] the ECJ subsequently ruled that there were certain constraints on the Commission's discretion as far as the *length* of time taken by the Commission to bring proceedings in respect of a particular infringement was concerned. In a case in which the Netherlands argued that a period of more than five years for bringing infringement proceedings from the time the first letter was sent to it by the Commission was excessive, the ECJ ruled that although Article 226 deliberately laid down no particular time-limit for bringing proceedings, excessive delay might nonetheless be prejudicial:

It is true that in certain cases the excessive duration of the pre-litigation procedure laid down by Article 169 is capable of making it more difficult for the Member State concerned to refute the Commission's arguments and of thus infringing the rights of the defence. However, in the instant case, the Netherlands Government has not proved that the unusual length of the procedure had any effect on the way in which it conducted its defence.[41]

More recently, however, the Court rejected an argument by the UK that, given the length of time which had passed since the particular events which were the subject of the infringement proceedings, the proceedings brought by the Commission would violate the principle of legal certainty and the acquired rights of individuals who had been affected by those earlier events.[42]

[37] Case C–431/92 *Commission* v. *Germany* [1995] ECR I–2189, paras. 19–22.
[38] Case C–394/02 *Commission* v. *Greece* [2005] ECR I–4713, paras. 15–6.
[39] Case 7/68 *Commission* v. *Italy* [1968] ECR 423, 428.
[40] Case 7/71 *Commission* v. *France* [1971] ECR 1003, paras. 5–6.
[41] Case C–96/89 *Commission* v. *Netherlands* [1991] ECR I–2461, para. 16.
[42] Case C–508/03, n. 32 above. See also Case C–475/98 *Commission* v. *Austria* [2002] ECR I–9797.

Restrictions have also been imposed on the Commission's discretion regarding when to refer a matter to the Court *after* the issuing of a reasoned opinion, rather than on its discretion in commencing the infringement proceedings in the first place. Clearly, requiring a response to a reasoned opinion within an excessively short period of time is just as likely to affect the ability of a Member State to exercise its rights of defence as is excessive delay in commencing proceedings. In proceedings against Ireland, the ECJ referred to the Commission's 'regrettable behaviour' and reprimanded it for the short time it had allowed the State for compliance with the reasoned opinion. However, the Commission's action was nevertheless admissible since, despite the short time period, the Commission had in fact awaited Ireland's reply before referring the matter to the Court:

> The Court is compelled to state its disapproval of the Commission's behaviour in this regard. It is indeed unreasonable, as Ireland has pointed out, to allow a Member State five days to amend legislation which has been applied for more than 40 years and which, moreover, has not give rise to any action on the part of the Commission over the period which has elapsed since the accession of the Member State in question. Furthermore, it is clear that there was no particular urgency.[43]

The ECJ later ruled that proceedings brought by the Commission against Belgium were inadmissible due to the shortness of the time allowed for responding to the letter of formal notice and the reasoned opinion.[44] The Court ruled that a reasonable period must be allowed, although very short periods could be justified in circumstances of urgency or where the Member State was fully aware of the Commission's views long before the procedure started.[45] A period of four months to respond to a reasoned opinion was adequate where a Member State had three years' prior notice of the Commission's view.[46] And in a case against Austria the ECJ rejected the argument that a period of seven days for responding to a formal letter and fourteen days for responding to a reasoned opinion were too short, accepting that these periods were justified by the urgency of the complaint and the particular circumstances of the case.[47]

The Court's unwillingness to require the Commission, other than in a case in which the rights of the defence may be prejudiced, to initiate Article 226 proceedings within a reasonable time contrasts with its approach to the action under Article 232 (ex Article 175) EC.[48] Proceedings under Articles 232 are brought against one of the Community institutions (rather than against a Member State) for failure to take action required by the Treaty. In the case of proceedings against a Community institution, the ECJ has held that the party bringing the action is required to do so within a reasonable period, even though Article 232 makes no mention of any time limit.[49]

The desire of the ECJ not to place too many fetters on the Commission's discretion under Article 226 is further revealed by the Court's response to actions for 'failure to act' brought by

---

[43] Case 74/82 *Commission* v. *Ireland* [1984] ECR 317, para. 12.

[44] Case 293/85 *Commission* v. *Belgium* [1988] ECR 305.

[45] *Ibid.*, para. 14 of the judgment. See also Case C–56/90 *Commission* v. *United Kingdom* [1993] ECR I–4109; Case C–333/99 *Commission* v. *France* [2000] ECR I–1025.

[46] Case C–473/93 *Commission* v. *Luxembourg* [1996] ECR I–3207.

[47] Case C–328/96 *Commission* v. *Austria* [1999] ECR I–7479.

[48] See also Art. 148 Euratom.

[49] Case 59/70 *Netherlands* v. *Commission* [1971] ECR 639, paras. 14–18. The case in fact concerned the parallel provisions of the Coal and Steel Treaty, which is no longer in existence, but the reasoning is presumably equally applicable to Art. 232 EC.

non-privileged parties against the Commission under Article 232 EC, which have attempted to require the Commission to initiate infringement proceedings under Article 226. The Court has consistently refused to admit such actions. Consistently with its 'bilateral' rather than trilateral conception of the infringement procedure, the ECJ in *Star Fruit* rejected an attempt by a company to use Article 232 to require the Commission to commence infringement proceedings against France:

> It is clear from the scheme of Article 169 of the Treaty that the Commission is not bound to commence the proceedings provided for in that provision but in this regard has a discretion which excludes the right for individuals to require that institution to adopt a specific position.[50]

Further, the Court has dismissed actions for annulment directed by an individual litigant against a 'decision' by the Commission not to commence proceedings against a Member State, again on the basis that this was a matter within the Commission's discretion and that the action sought—the adoption of a reasoned opinion—would not be susceptible in any case to an action for annulment.[51]

Although the lack of a role for individuals in the initiation and conduct of enforcement proceedings has provoked considerable adverse comment,[52] we have seen above that the Commission's discretion in this respect may not be entirely unjustified.[53]

F. Snyder, The Effectiveness of European Community Law[54]

[NB Arts. 169, 170, and 171 are now Arts. 226, 227, and 228 respectively]

The main form of dispute settlement used by the Commission is negotiation, and litigation is simply a part, sometimes inevitable but nevertheless generally a minor part, of this process. The Commission's view of litigation thus differs substantially from that of the European Court. In order to understand why this is so, we need to consider the role of the Commission in the Community litigation system.

Put simply, it is a distinctive role. The Commission has complete discretion in bringing infringement proceedings against Member States under Article 169; it is a necessary intermediary in actions by one Member State against another under Article 170; it will ... be entitled under the amended Article 171 to request the Court to impose a lump sum or penalty payment on Member States which have failed to comply with a previous judgment by the Court; ... Consequently the Commission can use litigation as an element in developing longer-term strategies. Instead of simply winning individual cases, it is able to concentrate on establishing basic principles or playing for rules.

---

[50] Case 247/87, n. 11 above, para. 11. Compare Case C–107/95 P *Bundesverband der Bilanzbuchalter* v. *Commission* [1997] ECR I–947.

[51] Case C–87/89 *Sonito* v. *Commission* [1990] ECR I–1981; Case T–201/96 *Smanor* v. *Commission* [1997] ECR II–1081; Case T–182/97 *Smanor*, n. 11 above. In the latter two cases the applicant wanted the Commission to bring infringement proceedings against France as a basis for its own *Francovich* action against the State, having already failed before the French courts in an action for damages.

[52] See E. Szyszczak, 'L'Espace Sociale Européenne: Reality, Dreams or Nightmares?' [1990] *German Yearbook of International Law* 284, 300.

[53] See n. 26 above; Harlow and Rawlings, n. 4 above; and extract, above, 431; J. Weiler, 'The Community System: The Dual Character of Supranationalism' (1981) 1 *YBEL* 267, 299.

[54] (1993) 56 *MLR* 19, 30.

The Commission itself has imposed certain administrative constraints on its own discretion. For example, from 1989 onwards it decided to bring immediate infringement proceedings against a defaulting State as soon as the time limit for implementation of a directive had passed.[55] And from 1990 on, the Commission began to issue letters of formal notice as a matter of routine whenever Member States had not 'notified national measures implementing Directives which are due for implementation'.[56] Further, we have seen that the Commission undertook to codify its own internal rules governing relations with individual complainants in response to pressure from the Ombudsman.[57] It is likely, indeed, that both the supervisory role of the European Parliament and the administrative role of the Ombudsman have functioned as a positive influence on the Commission's conduct in the infringement procedure, and have strengthened the mechanisms and forms of accountability of the Commission within that process.

5. THE REASONED OPINION

(a) FUNCTION

The reasoned opinion which the Commission is required to issue and to notify to a Member State forms an important part of the pre-judicial procedure under Article 226, and provides the Member State concerned with a measure of protection. Together with the letter of formal notice the reasoned opinion (sometimes followed by a supplementary reasoned opinion[58]) is the official means by which the Commission communicates to the State the substance of the complaint against it, and specifies a time period within which the violation of Community law must be remedied. It is aimed to provide the Member State with a clear statement of the case against it, and to 'ensure respect for the principles of natural justice'.[59]

(b) FORM AND CONTENT

The obligation to provide reasons is a requirement of general importance in Community law, and Article 254 of the Treaty expressly requires regulations, directives, and decisions to state the reasons on which they are based. Article 226 extends this requirement to opinions issued by the Commission under the enforcement procedure. Although the reasoning requirement in EC law constitutes an 'essential procedural requirement' breach of which constitutes a ground for annulment of a measure under Article 230, the Commission's opinion under Article 226 is not subject to an action for annulment because it does not have binding effect.[60] According to Advocate General Lagrange in an early case:

> No formalism must be demanded of this document, since, as I have said, the reasoned opinion is not an administrative act subject to review by the Court of its legality.[61]

---

[55] *7th Annual Report* [1990] OJ C232/6.

[56] *8th Annual Report*, n. 3 above, at 7(e).

[57] COM(2002)141, n. 14 above.

[58] See, e.g., Case C–354/99 *Commission* v. *Ireland* [2001] ECR I–7657; Case C–155/99, *Commission* v. *Italy* [2001] ECR I–4007.

[59] Evans, n. 35 above, 446.

[60] Case 48/65 *First Lütticke Case* (*Alfons Lütticke GmbH* v. *Commission*) [1966] ECR 19.

[61] Case 7/61 *Commission* v. *Italy* [1961] ECR 317, 334, 336.

However, although a reasoned opinion may not be the subject of a direct action for annulment, a Member State which is the subject of such an opinion may contest the lack of adequate reasoning in a different way, by raising the matter before the ECJ if and when the enforcement proceedings reach that stage.[62] In an early case in which Italy challenged the legal form and content of the reasoned opinion, the ECJ replied:

> The opinion referred to in Article 169 of the Treaty must be considered to contain a sufficient statement of reasons to satisfy the law when it contains—as it does in this case—a coherent statement of the reasons which led the Commission to believe that the State in question has failed to fulfil an obligation under the Treaty.[63]

This means that the Commission is not obliged in its reasoned opinion to address or to answer every argument made by the Member State at the pre-litigation stage, nor to indicate what steps should be taken by the State to remedy the alleged breach.[64] Further, the initial letter of formal notice need not meet particularly strict requirements, since the reasoned opinion is the crucial document which sets out the complaint to which the Member State must respond. Nonetheless, the essence of the complaint must be the same in the formal letter,[65] the reasoned opinion, and in the Commission's application to bring the case before the ECJ.[66] But so long as the Commission sets out clearly in the reasoned opinion the grounds on which it has relied in concluding that the State has violated Community law, and the particular complaints which will form the subject-matter of the proceedings,[67] the reasoning requirement will be satisfied.

Given that the reasoned opinion is intended to operate as a procedural protection for the Member State, the Commission is not entitled to amend the substantive content of its submission when the case comes to be heard before the Court, even if both parties wish the Court to consider other aspects of the State's conduct which took place after the date of the reasoned opinion.[68] In such a case, the Commission cannot amend its complaint to include a fresh objection after the reasoned opinion has been issued, but must initiate the entire Article 226 procedure again. This requirement that the content of the reasoned opinion be essentially the same as (although not necessarily in every respect identical to[69]) the submissions contained in the Commission's application to the Court has been reiterated many

---

[62] In Case C–191/95 *Commission* v. *Germany* [1998] ECR I–5449; Case C–272/97 *Commission* v. *Germany* [1999] ECR I–2175; and Case C–198/97 *Commission* v. *Germany* [1999] ECR I–3257, the ECJ dismissed several challenges by Germany to the reasoned opinion, on the ground that it had been adopted by the College of Commissioners without having the text of the opinion before them. The ECJ said that it was sufficient for the Commissioners to have available to them, at the time, the information on which the decision to commence proceedings had been based.

[63] Case 7/61 *Commission* v. *Italy* [1961] ECR 317, 327.

[64] Case C–247/89 *Commission* v. *Portugal* [1991] ECR I–3659, para. 22.

[65] For a case in which an allegation of breach of Art. 10 EC was not admitted by the Court, because the formal letter had not referred to it, see Case C–371/04 *Commission* v. *Italy* [2006] ECR I–10257.

[66] See Case C–191/95 *Commission* v. *Germany* [1998] ECR I–5449, para. 54; Case C–365/97 *Commission* v. *Italy* [1999] ECR I–7773, para. 26.

[67] Case C–328/96 *Commission* v. *Austria* [1999] ECR I–7479, paras. 39–41, where part of the Commission's complaint was ruled inadmissible for failure to specify this.

[68] Case 7/69 *Commission* v. *Italy* [1970] ECR 111, where Italy had enacted a law, after the date of the reasoned opinion, intended to remedy the alleged violation. Although both Italy and the Commission wished the Member State to take into account the impact of the new law (which the Commission considered to be inadequate to cure the breach), the ECJ refused to do so.

[69] See, e.g., Case C–433/03 *Commission* v. *Germany* [2005] ECR I–6985, paras. 28–29.

times.[70] However, it will not be sufficient for the Commission when the matter comes before the Court simply to refer in its application to 'all the reasons set out in the letter of formal notice and the reasoned opinion'. Rather the application itself must contain a statement of the grounds on which it is based.[71]

On the other hand, where enforcement proceedings brought by the Commission have been found by the ECJ to be inadmissible on the ground that the Commission's application is based on an objection different from that in the reasoned opinion, the Commission is not obliged to recommence the entire pre-litigation procedure but may lodge a fresh application before the Court based on the same objections as the reasoned opinion originally issued.[72] And where EC legislation on which the reasoned opinion was based has been amended prior to the case coming before the ECJ, this does not necessarily mean the Commission has to withdraw the action or issue a new reasoned opinion, so long as the obligations under the amended measure correspond to those arising under the original legislation.[73]

There is one circumstance in which the Court will accept an application made by the Commission which is not the same as it was under the reasoned opinion, and that is where the change *limits* what is contained in the reasoned opinion rather than expanding it in a way which could disadvantage the respondent State.[74] And finally, an extension of the subject-matter of the dispute to events which took place *after* the reasoned opinion is acceptable in so far as they are of the same kind and constitute the same conduct as the events to which the opinion referred,[75] or only if the later evidence is not being used to establish a specific violation, but rather to support the argument that the other violations alleged are part of a general and persistent pattern.[76] This can be seen with particularly notable effect in a case brought against Ireland for general and persistent breach of the EC Waste Directive.[77]

The Commission is also not prohibited from responding, during the hearing before the Court, to arguments and defences raised by the respondent Member State, even where it has not made those points in the reasoned opinion itself.[78] And the Member State cannot complain of a breach of the right to a fair hearing by the fact that the Commission, in its application to the ECJ, does not take account of facts or defences put forward by the Member State after the expiry of the period set by the reasoned opinion.[79]

(c) CONFIDENTIALITY OF THE REASONED OPINION

In a number of cases, individual complainants who had sought to persuade the Commission to bring proceedings against a Member State and who were disappointed by the Commission's

---

[70] See, e.g., Case 232/78 *Commission* v. *France* [1979] ECR 2729; 124/81; Case 166/82 *Commission* v. *Italy* [1984] ECR 459 and more recently Case C–350/02 *Commission* v. *Netherlands* [2004] ECR I–6213.

[71] Case C–43/90 *Commission* v. *Germany* [1992] ECR I–1909, paras. 7–8. See also Case C–52/90 *Commission* v. *Denmark* [1992] ECR I–2187.

[72] Case C–57/94 *Commission* v. *Italy* [1995] ECR I–1249.

[73] Case C–365/97, n. 66 above; Case C–275/04 *Commission* v. *Belgium* [2006] ECR I–9883; Case C–203/03 *Commission* v. *Austria* [2005] ECR I–935.

[74] See Case C–191/95 *Commission* v. *Germany* [1998] ECR I–5449, and for a similar judgment under Art. 228 EC see Case C–177/04 *Commission* v. *France* [2006] ECR I–2461.

[75] Cases 42/82 *Commission* v. *France* [1983] ECR 1013, para. 20; Case C–113/86 *Commission* v. *Italy* [1988] ECR 607, para. 11; Case C–236/05 *Commission* v. *United Kingdom* [2005] ECR I–10819, paras. 12–17.

[76] Case C–494/01 *Commission* v. *Ireland* [2005] ECR I–3331, paras. 35–37, discussed below at nn. 115–116 and text.

[77] *Ibid.*

[78] Case 211/81 *Commission* v. *Denmark* [1982] ECR I–4547, para. 16.

[79] Case C–3/96 *Commission* v. *Netherlands* [1998] ECR I–3931.

ultimate failure or refusal to do so, subsequently sought to obtain disclosure of the reasoned opinion and of other documentation relevant to the investigative proceedings. Yet, despite an initial setback for the Commission in the *WWF* case,[80] neither the Community Courts nor even the Ombudsman[81] has been prepared to require disclosure or to censure non-disclosure of a reasoned opinion, a draft reasoned opinion, or indeed of any documents relating to the investigative stage of the infringement procedure.

In *WWF*, the CFI ruled, in relation to a Commission investigation into possible breaches of EC law, that:

> In this regard, the Court considers that the confidentiality which the Member States are entitled to expect of the Commission in such circumstances warrants, under the heading of protection of the public interest, a refusal of access to documents relating to investigations which may lead to an infringement procedure, even where a period of time has elapsed since the closure of the investigation.[82]

Similarly, in the *Bavarian Lager* case the Court ruled, in the context of a draft reasoned opinion which was not ultimately sent by the Commission to the Member State under investigation, that since the procedure was still at the stage of investigation at the time, the Member States were entitled to expect confidentiality from the Commission.[83] Finally, in *Petrie*, which concerned a request for access to a range of documents including letters of formal notice and reasoned opinions, the CFI ruled:

> This requirement of confidentiality remains even after the matter has been brought before the Court of Justice, on the ground that it cannot be ruled out that the discussions between the Commission and the Member State in question regarding the latter's voluntary compliance with the Treaty requirements may continue during the court proceedings and up to the delivery of the judgment of the Court of Justice. The preservation of that objective, namely an amicable resolution of the dispute between the Commission and the Member State concerned before the Court of Justice has delivered judgment, justifies refusal of access to the letters of formal notice and reasoned opinions drawn up in connection with the Article 226 EC proceedings on the ground of protection of the public interest relating to inspections, investigations and court proceedings, which comes within the first category of exceptions in Decision 94/90.[84]

Access to Commission documents is now governed by Regulation 1049/2001, and the Commission has continued to rely successfully on the exception in Article 4(2) thereof, governing 'protection of the purpose of inspections, investigations and audits' to refuse access to documents relating to infringement proceedings. Nevertheless, even though it is not required to and cannot be compelled to do so, the Commission now does occasionally publish its reasoned opinions, in particular in cases where the State itself does not wish for it to remain confidential.

---

[80] See Case T–105/95, n. 19 above, in which the CFI restricted the Commission's ability to rely on a particular exception to the obligation to provide access to documents as a mandatory general exception rather than an individual discretionary one.

[81] See n. 18 above.

[82] *Ibid.*, para. 62.

[83] Case T–309/97 *Bavarian Lager*, n. 19 above, para. 46.

[84] Case T–191/99 *Petrie*, n. 19 above, para. 68.

6. WHY IS AN ENFORCEMENT ACTION ADMISSIBLE AFTER THE BREACH IS REMEDIED?

Article 226 sets out the conditions which must be satisfied before the Commission may initiate enforcement proceedings in the Court. If the Commission has not issued a reasoned opinion or has not given the Member State concerned a period of time within which to cure the alleged infringement, the action will not be admissible. On the other hand, once those conditions have been fulfilled and the period laid down by the Commission for compliance has expired without any action being taken by the Member State, it is no answer for that State to assert, when the case is heard before the ECJ, that the breach has since been remedied.

The question for the ECJ is whether the Member State was in breach at the time the Commission initiated proceedings before the Court. The Court's approach here contrasts with its approach to actions brought against a Community institution for failure to act, just as it did concerning the issue of delay in initiating proceedings.[85] In proceedings against the European Parliament under Article 232 for failure to act, the ECJ held that the action was devoid of purpose once the institution in question had acted to remedy its default.[86] Yet where proceedings have been brought under Article 226 by the Commission against Member States, such actions have been declared admissible by the Court even though the State in question had remedied its breach by that time. Several reasons have been offered to explain why enforcement actions may be admissible after the infringement has been cured.

In the first place, the Commission argues that it has a continued interest in bringing the action, not least to prevent States from undermining infringement proceedings by bringing their illegal conduct to an end just before judgment is rendered, and possibly re-commencing that same conduct again afterwards.[87] Secondly, it is important for the Court to be able to rule on the legality of breaches of short duration, since these may be no less serious than longer breaches.[88] However, if the effects of a specific infringement have actually come to an end before the expiry of the period set out in the reasoned opinion,[89] the action before the ECJ will be inadmissible even if the Commission fears that a similar breach is likely to occur again in the future.[90] A third reason for giving judgment even after the breach has been remedied is in order to establish the basis for liability on the part of a defaulting Member State.[91] An individual's action for redress before the national courts—which has been cited by the Commission as 'one of the best ways of combating recidivism'[92]—could derive considerable assistance from a prior finding of the ECJ that the Member State in question had acted in violation of Community law.[93] A prior finding by the ECJ of an infringement is likely to be an

---

[85] See above, 436–437.

[86] Case 377/87 *Council* v. *Parliament* [1988] ECR 4017. The position, however, might be different if it were likely that some party might later wish to seek redress from the institution in question for loss caused by the illegal failure to act.

[87] See Lagrange AG in Case 7/61 *Commission* v. *Italy* [1961] ECR 317 at 334.

[88] See Lenz AG in Case 240/86 *Commission* v. *Greece* [1988] ECR 1835, 1844.

[89] Retroactive legislation to 'cure' an earlier breach will not be accepted by the ECJ: Case C–221/03 *Commission* v. *Belgium* [2005] ECR I–8307.

[90] E.g., Case C–362/90 *Commission* v. *Italy* [1992] ECR I–2353; Case C–525/03 *Commission* v. *Italy* [2005] ECR I–9405.

[91] Case 240/86, n. 88 above, para. 14; Case C–168/03 *Commission* v. *Spain* [2004] ECR I–8227, para. 24

[92] COM(2002)725 on Better Monitoring of the Application of Community Law.

[93] For discussion of the principle of state liability to an aggrieved individual for breach of EC law, following Cases C–6 and 9/90; *Francovich and Bonifaci* v. *Italy* [1991] ECR I–5357; see Ch. 9.

effective means, even if not a necessary one, of showing the illegality of state action when damages are sought for loss caused by that action.[94]

7. TYPES OF BREACH BY MEMBER STATES OF COMMUNITY LAW

Article 226 is very general in its description of a Member State violation for the purposes of enforcement proceedings. The Commission must simply consider that a State 'has failed to fulfil an obligation under this Treaty'. This may include actions as well as omissions on the part of States, failure to implement directives, breaches of specific Treaty provisions or of other secondary legislation, or of any rule or standard which is an effective part of Community law. Cases involving breaches by Member States in the sphere of the Community's external relations have come before the Court in recent years.[95]

An interesting and unusual example of breach of an EC Treaty provision can be seen in a case brought against Ireland for having brought dispute-settlement proceedings involving the interpretation of EC law against the UK, in relation to the MOX nuclear recycling plant in the UK, to a tribunal under the International Convention of the Law of the Sea, rather than before the ECJ.[96] According to the ECJ, 'a breach of this nature involves a manifest risk that the jurisdictional order laid down in the Treaties and consequently the autonomy of the Community legal system may be adversely affected'.[97]

Certain kinds of breach are far more often the subject of infringement proceedings than others, and the following examples illustrate some of the sorts of breaches with which the cases are concerned.

(a) BREACH OF THE OBLIGATION OF CO-OPERATION UNDER ARTICLE 10 EC

Case 96/81 **Commission v. Netherlands**
[1982] ECR 1791

The Commission brought proceedings against the Netherlands alleging failure to implement certain bathing water directives and claiming that the Dutch Government had failed to provide information on its compliance with the provisions of one directive, as required by the terms of directive itself. The Commission argued that due to the failure to supply this information, it was entitled to presume that the respondent State had failed to implement the necessary national measures. The breach identified in the application to Court by the Commission was not

---

[94] See the attempt in Case T–182/97 *Smanor* v. *Commission* [1998] ECR II–271 to obtain an enforcement ruling from the ECJ for this precise purpose.

[95] E.g. the 'Open Skies' cases: C–466–476/98 *Commission* v. *United Kingdom et al.* [2002] ECR I–9855; Case C–13/00 *Commission* v. *Ireland* [2002] ECR I–2943. Also Case C–433/03 *Commission* v. *Germany* [2005] ECR I–6985 on failure to consult the Commission before ratifying a waterways agreement with Romania, which was then a non-Member State.

[96] Case C–459/03 *Commission* v. *Ireland* [2006] ECR I–4635.

[97] *Ibid.*, para. 154.

however 'failure to comply with the duty to provide information' but rather 'failure to fulfil the obligation to implement the directive'.

THE ECJ

6. It should be emphasized that, in proceedings under Article 169 of the EEC Treaty for failure to fulfil an obligation, it is incumbent upon the Commission to prove the allegation that the obligation has not been fulfilled. It is the Commission's responsibility to place before the Court the information needed to enable the Court to establish that the obligation has not been fulfilled, and in doing so the Commission may not rely on any presumption.

However, although the Commission cannot rely on a presumption of breach where a Member State fails to provide information on compliance,[98] the ECJ has ruled that once the Commission has produced sufficient evidence to show that the Member State appeared to be violating Community law it is incumbent on the State not simply to deny the allegations, but to contest the information produced in a substantive way.[99] Further, even though the burden of proof lies with the Commission to show breach, where the complaint is of inadequate transposition of a directive it is not necessary for the Commission actually to demonstrate the harmful effects of the transposing legislation.[100]

In the bathing water case above, the EC went on to say that all Member States had an obligation under Article 10 EC to facilitate the achievement of the Commission's tasks, including that of monitoring compliance with the Treaty. This particular mode of infringement is frequently invoked by the Commission in enforcement actions where Member State authorities refuse or fail to respond to its requests for information.[101] Clearly, if a Member State is not willing to respond at the pre-litigation stage of an investigation by the Commission for the purposes of infringement proceedings, it will be very difficult for the Commission to ascertain whether or not there has been a breach by the State. The Commission's attempt to find a way round this is to initiate separate enforcement proceedings on the basis of a breach of the obligation of co-operation.[102]

(b) INADEQUATE IMPLEMENTATION OF COMMUNITY LAW

In many cases, the cause of the Commission's complaint is not the complete failure to transpose or to implement Community legislation, but rather its inadequate implementation.

---

[98] Case C–217/97 *Commission* v. *Germany* [1999] ECR I–5087; Case C–221/04 *Commission* v. *Spain* [2006] ECR I–4515.

[99] Case 272/86 *Commission* v. *Greece* [1988] ECR 4875, para. 21; Case C–508/03, n. 32 above, para. 80.

[100] Case C–392/96 *Commission* v. *Ireland* [1999] ECR I–5901.

[101] Case 240/86, n. 88 above.

[102] For other cases on Art. 10 see, e.g., Case C–35/88 *Commission* v. *Greece* [1990] ECR I–3125; Case C–48/89 *Commission* v. *Italy* [1990] ECR I–2425; Case C–374/89 *Commission* v. *Belgium* [1991] ECR I–367; Case 272/86, n. 99 above.

Case 167/73 **Commission v. France**
[1974] ECR 359

[Note ToA renumbering: Art. 48 is now Art. 39]

The French legislature had failed to repeal a provision of the French Code du Travail Maritime under which a certain proportion of the crew of a ship was required to be of French nationality. This nationality requirement was contrary to Community law, but the French Government claimed that directions had been given verbally to the naval authorities to treat Community nationals as French nationals, and that this was sufficient to comply with Community law.

THE ECJ

40. It appears both from the argument before the Court and from the position adopted during the parliamentary proceedings that the present state of affairs is that freedom of movement for workers in the sector in question continues to be considered by the French authorities not as a matter of right but as dependent on their unilateral will.

41. It follows that although the objective legal position is clear, namely, that Article 48 and Regulation No 1612/68 are directly applicable in the territory of the French Republic, nevertheless the maintenance in these circumstances of the wording of the Code du Travail Maritime gives rise to an ambiguous state of affairs by maintaining, as regards those subject to the law who are concerned, a state of uncertainty as to the possibilities available to them of relying on Community law.

42. This uncertainty can only be reinforced by the internal and verbal character of the purely administrative directions to waive the application of the national law.

In the case of directives, which are not directly applicable, it is always incumbent on the Member States to implement them fully. Even where directives are vertically directly effective or can be given indirect domestic effect in another way, this does not reduce the obligation on the State to implement them properly. Article 249 EC provides that the manner and form of implementation of directives are a matter for each Member State to decide, but this has not prevented the ECJ from reviewing the adequacy of the chosen method of implementation. According to the Court, the freedom of a Member to decide on the manner of implementation:

> [D]oes not however release it from the obligation to give effect to the provisions of the directive by means of national provisions of a binding nature.... Mere administrative practices, which by their nature may be altered at the whim of the administration, may not be considered as constituting the proper fulfilment of the obligation deriving from that directive.[103]

A further objection to a Member State's reliance on such 'whimsical' administrative practices is that, quite apart from their uncertainty and alterability, they lack the appropriate publicity to constitute adequate implementation.[104] However, the ECJ does not always condemn a Member State which has failed to adopt any specific measures to implement a directive, as is evident from the following case in which the Commission brought enforcement

---

[103] Case 96/81 *Commission* v. *Netherlands* [1982] ECR 1791, para. 12.
[104] Case 160/82 *Commission* v. *Netherlands* [1982] ECR 4637.

proceedings against Germany for failure to implement Directives 77/452 and 77/453 governing the right of establishment and freedom to provide services for nurses.

Case 29/84 **Commission v. Germany**
[1985] ECR 1661

[Note ToA renumbering: Art. 189 is now Art. 249]

17. The German Government does not deny that mere administrative practices, which by their nature can be modified as and when the administration pleases and which are not publicized widely enough, cannot be regarded as a proper fulfilment of the obligation imposed on the Member States by Article 189 of the Treaty, as the Court has consistently held. However, the government claims that that principle cannot be applied in this instance because the administrative practice in question cannot be changed as and when the administration pleases and it has been given sufficient publicity. . . .

[*After summarizing the Commission's counter-argument, the ECJ ruled as follows:*]

22. Faced with those conflicting views, the Court considers it necessary to recall the wording of the third paragraph of Article 189 of the Treaty, according to which a directive is binding, as to the result to be achieved upon each Member State to which it is addressed, but leaves to the national authorities the choice of form and methods.

23. It follows from that provision that the implementation of a directive does not necessarily require legislative action in each Member State. In particular the existence of general principles of constitutional or administrative law may render implementation by specific legislation superfluous, provided however that those principles guarantee that the national authorities will in fact apply the directive fully and that, where the directive is intended to create rights for individuals, the persons concerned are made fully aware of their rights and, where appropriate, afforded the possibility of relying on them before the national courts.

In subsequent judgments the ECJ added to this by ruling that proper transposition was particularly important for individuals to know their rights when those on whom the directive in question conferred rights were nationals of *other* Member States.[105]

However, in proceedings brought by the Commission against the UK for improper implementation of the Product Liability Directive 85/374, the ECJ made an interesting use of the 'indirect effect' of directives—i.e. the obligation on national courts to construe domestic law in accordance with a relevant directive[106]—to dismiss the Commission's application. Whereas the Commission argued that the UK was in breach of the Directive because national courts would be required to interpret national law *contra legem* in order to conform with its requirements, the ECJ simply ruled that there was nothing to suggest that the UK courts would not, if called upon to do so, interpret the relevant national law—the Consumer Protection Act—in the light of the wording and purpose of the Directive so as to give effect to its aim.[107]

---

[105] See Case C–365/93 *Commission v. Greece* [1995] ECR I–499, para. 9; Case C–96/95 *Commission v. Germany* [1997] ECR I–1653, paras. 34–35; Case C–162/99 *Commission v. Italy* [2001] ECR I–541.

[106] Case C–300/95 *Commission v. United Kingdom* [1997] ECR I–2649.

[107] Contrast Case C–338/91 *Steenhorst-Neerings* [1993] ECR I–5475, in which the ECJ ruled that where a Member State had not implemented a dir. properly, the capacity of national courts to read apparently inconsistent national legislation in a way which conformed with the un-implemented dir. would not absolve the Member State from the obligation to implement properly.

Finally, where national legislation has been the subject of different judicial interpretations, some of which are consistent with and others inconsistent with EC law, the ECJ has ruled that at the very least such legislation must be insufficiently clear to comply with EC law.[108]

(c) BREACH OF A POSITIVE OBLIGATION TO ENSURE THE EFFECTIVENESS OF COMMUNITY LAW

In furtherance of its policy of encouraging Member States to take active steps to ensure the effectiveness of Community law, the Court has declared that Article 10 EC is breached if a Member State fails to penalize those who infringe Community law in the same way as it penalizes those who infringe national law, and in a way which is 'effective, proportionate and dissuasive'.[109]

Secondly, a Member State may be in breach of the Treaty where it fails to prevent action by other parties which is frustrating Community objectives, even if there is no discrimination or double standards of the kind suggested in the case above. Thus in proceedings brought by the Commission against France, the ECJ found that in failing to take adequate steps to prevent violent and disruptive protests by French farmers which were hindering the free movement of agricultural goods, the Member State was in breach of its obligations under the Treaty.[110]

(d) GENERAL AND PERSISTENT BREACHES

The Commission has at times used the infringement procedure to monitor Member State implementation of a particular law or set of laws, and in some cases to challenge relatively minor breaches where they are part of a pattern of inadequate implementation and compliance in practice.[111] And even when legislation is properly implemented, a State may be held in breach if an administrative practice infringes EC law, at least in circumstances where the practice in question is consistent and general.[112] In cases of this kind, according to the ECJ, the Member State's failure to fulfil obligations can be established only by means of 'sufficiently documented and detailed proof of the alleged practice of the national administration and/or courts', which is different from the kind of evidence usually required when the breach concerns the terms of national legislation.[113]

In a landmark case against Ireland in 2005, described by one commentator as 'pathbreaking',[114] the Court ruled that a general administrative practice could actually be deduced from a selected number of individual infringements, so that a finding of 'general and persistent breach' could be made against the State.[115] The Commission brought proceedings against Ireland citing twelve individual complaints relating to waste disposal which allegedly violated

---

[108] Case C–129/00 *Commission* v. *Italy* [2003] ECR I–14637, para. 33.

[109] Case 68/88 *Commission* v. *Greece* [1989] ECR 2979; Case 143/83 *Commission* v. *Denmark* [1985] ECR 427, paras. 8–10.

[110] Case C–265/95 *Commission* v. *France* [1997] ECR I–6959. For a case which is somewhere on the borderline between this and the cases referred to in the previous footnote see Case C–60/01 *Commission* v. *France* [2002] ECR I–5679 and the comment by B. Kurcz and K. Zieleskiewicz (2002) 39 *CMLRev.* 1443.

[111] See Case C–365/97, n. 66 above, and the comment by J.C. van Haersolte (2002) 39 *CMLRev.* 407.

[112] Case C–494/01, n. 76 above; Case C–441/02 *Commission* v. *Germany* [2006] ECR I–3449.

[113] Case C–441/02, n. 112 above. In this case the ECJ found that the Commission had not proven that the German practice of making expulsion orders against EU citizens was sufficiently consistent and general, rather than being merely a series of isolated cases: paras. 51–53.

[114] P. Wenneras, 'A New Dawn for Commission Enforcement under Articles 226 and 228 EC' (2006) 43 *CMLRev.* 31.

[115] Case C–494/01, n. 76 above.

the Waste Directive, and argued that these were examples which illustrated breaches of a more general nature.[116] The Commission sought judgment not only on the twelve specific complaints but also on the general and persistent nature of the deficiencies in Ireland's implementation of the Directive. Ireland challenged this claim, arguing that the twelve complaints in the reasoned opinion definitively delimited the subject-matter of the action against it. The ECJ however supported the Commission's stance and declared, on the basis of an examination of the individual complaints brought, that Ireland was generally and persistently failing in its obligation to implement the provisions of the Directive correctly.[117] In terms of proof, the ECJ ruled that once the Commission had adduced sufficient evidence (of individual complaints) to show a persistent and repeated practice of breach, it was up to the State to challenge in detail the evidence provided and the consequences flowing from it.

(e) ACTION BY THE COURTS OF A MEMBER STATE

Failure by a Member State's judiciary to comply with Community law has never formed the basis of an Article 226 judgment against that State, even though the action of national courts is often implicated in a particular breach.[118] Yet the Court has always said that Member States are responsible even for actions and inaction on the part of constitutionally independent organs of the State, and we have seen recently that the ECJ ruled that a State may be liable in damages to individuals for breaches of EC law committed by national courts of last instance.[119] Nonetheless, the ECJ has not yet directly addressed the question whether a national court could be the subject of infringement proceedings under Article 226,[120] and it has been suggested that the Commission has deliberately sought to avoid such politically sensitive cases.[121]

In 2004, however, the Commission took the unprecedented step of issuing a reasoned opinion against Sweden, citing the failure of its supreme courts to make references to the ECJ under Article 234 and the absence of any law or regulation governing the procedure for making preliminary references.[122] It seems that, although the Swedish government has proposed to introduce procedural legislation in an attempt to resolve the case politically before it is referred to the ECJ, it is far from being accepted within Sweden that there has in fact been any violation of EC law by the Swedish courts.[123]

8. STATE DEFENCES IN ENFORCEMENT PROCEEDINGS

Although Member States have not lacked ingenuity or resourcefulness in providing reasons to justify their failure to fulfil Treaty obligations,[124] the ECJ has not been very receptive to such arguments. In one case in which an intervening Member State put forward a defence on behalf

---

[116] *Ibid.*, para. 20.

[117] *Ibid.*, paras. 127, 139, 170, 171, 193.

[118] See, e.g., Case C–129/00, n. 108 above.

[119] See Case C–224/01 *Köbler* [2003] ECR I–10239. See Ch. 9 for discussion.

[120] See however the view of Warner AG in Case 30/77 *R. v. Bouchereau* [1977] ECR 1999, 2020.

[121] Rawlings, n. 3 above.

[122] Document number C(2004)3899 of 7 Oct. 2004, relating to infringement proceedings 2003/2161.

[123] U. Bernitz, 'Controlling Member State Courts under EU Law' (2005), available at www.law.harvard.edu/students/orgs/hela/papers/.

[124] See, e.g., Case C–353/96 *Commission v. Ireland* [1998] ECR I–8565.

of the State against which infringement proceedings had been brought, the intervention was rejected as inadmissible and the ECJ found a breach of EC law.[125] Many 'defences' have been unsuccessfully pleaded in infringement proceedings. There is, however, nothing to prohibit Member States from introducing surprise defences which they did not raise in the pre-litigation procedure, even though the Commission certainly cannot introduce surprise complaints in the same way.[126] Further, the fact that a Member State's infringement has had 'no adverse effects' is not a defence to infringement proceedings.[127]

(a) *FORCE MAJEURE*

On many occasions, States have invoked difficulties in their parliamentary procedures, or problems with the separation of powers within their systems, to explain delay in compliance with EC law, but these have consistently been rejected by the ECJ. It has ruled on the one hand that a State is responsible for breach 'whatever the agency of the State whose action or inaction is the cause of the failure to fulfil its obligations, even in the case of a constitutionally independent institution',[128] and on the other hand that 'a Member State may not plead provisions, practices or circumstances existing in its internal legal system in order to justify a failure to comply with obligations and time limits laid down in Community directives'.[129] The ECJ did however agree that *force majeure* could be pleaded in a case where a bomb attack presented 'insurmountable difficulties', rendering compliance with the Treaty impossible.[130]

(b) LACK OF INTENTIONAL WRONGDOING BY THE STATE

The Court has been similarly dismissive of arguments by Member States that they were not at fault, or were not deliberately delaying or opposing EC law. Its response to such pleas has been to declare that 'the admissibility of an action based on Article 169 [now 226] of the Treaty depends only on an objective finding of a failure to fulfil obligations and not on proof of any inertia or opposition on the part of the Member State concerned'.[131] Similarly, the Court has rejected the relevance of arguments that the Member State's breach was 'minor',[132] or that it was the result of 'excusable error'.[133] The Court looks only to see whether or not the infringement

---

[125] Case C–13/00, n. 95 above, where the UK intervened to argue that the breach alleged constituted a violation of international law obligations and not of EC law.

[126] Case C–414/97 *Commission* v. *Spain* [1999] ECR I–5585.

[127] Case C–150/97 *Commission* v. *Portugal* [1999] ECR I–259; Case C–36/05 *Commission* v. *Spain* [2006] ECR I–10313.

[128] Case 77/69 *Commission* v. *Belgium* [1970] ECR 237, para. 15.

[129] E.g., Case 280/83 *Commission* v. *Italy* [1984] ECR 2361, para. 4; Case 160/82, n. 104 above; Case 215/83 *Commission* v. *Belgium* [1985] ECR 1039; Case C–298/97 *Commission* v. *Spain* [1998] ECR I–3301; Case C–326/97 *Commission* v. *Belgium* [1998] ECR I–6107.

[130] Case 33/69 *Commission* v. *Italy* [1970] ECR 93, para. 16. However, even in this case the Court was not satisfied that the bomb attack rendered compliance excessively difficult by the time proceedings were brought. See also Case 70/86 *Commission* v. *Greece* [1987] ECR 3545; Case C–334/87 *Greece* v. *Commission* [1990] ECR I–2849, para. 11, for a definition of *force majeure* in other circumstances.

[131] Case 301/81 *Commission* v. *Belgium* [1983] ECR 467, para. 8.

[132] Case C–43/97 *Commission* v. *Italy* [1997] ECR I–4671.

[133] Case C–385/02 *Commission* v. *Italy* [2004] ECR I–8121, para. 40.

has taken place as alleged, and the breach need not involve any deliberate infringement or moral wrongdoing on the part of the Member State.[134]

(c) THE COMMUNITY MEASURE ON WHICH THE INFRINGEMENT PROCEEDINGS ARE BASED IS ILLEGAL

Case 226/87 **Commission v. Greece**
[1988] ECR 3611

[Note ToA renumbering: Arts. 90, 169, 170, 173, and 175 are now
Arts. 86, 226, 227, 230, and 232]

A year after adopting a decision under Article 90 EC declaring Greek legislation on public-sector insurance to be incompatible with the Treaty, when Greece had taken no action to amend the legislation, the Commission brought infringement proceedings before the ECJ. The Greek Government contested the lawfulness of the Commission's initial Article 90 decision.

THE ECJ

14. The system of remedies set up by the Treaty distinguishes between the remedies provided for in Articles 169 and 170, which permit a declaration that a Member State has failed to fulfil its obligations, and those contained in Articles 173 and 175, which permit judicial review of the lawfulness of measures adopted by the Community institutions, or the failure to adopt such measures. Those remedies have different objectives and are subject to different rules. In the absence of a provision of the Treaty expressly permitting it to do so, a Member State cannot therefore plead the unlawfulness of a decision addressed to it as a defence in an action for a declaration that it has failed to fulfil its obligations arising out of its failure to implement that decision.

It therefore seems that it is not possible for a Member State to plead the illegality of an earlier Community decision addressed to it in order to resist judgment against it in Article 226 proceedings for failure to comply with that decision. The rationale is that if the Member State objected to the decision, it had the opportunity at the time of bringing a direct action for its annulment under Article 230. However, a plea of illegality might be a defence to an action under Article 226 where the Community measure was so gravely flawed as to be legally 'non-existent', or where the earlier measure was not a decision addressed to the Member State in question, but a regulation the illegality of which might not have been apparent to the Member State until the Commission brought enforcement proceedings.[135] It may also be possible for

---

[134] See however Case C–146/89 *Commission* v. *United Kingdom* [1991] ECR I–3533, in which the Court was sufficiently impressed by the 'exemplary conduct' of the UK in later voluntarily remedying its breach to order each party to bear its own costs.

[135] See Mancini AG in Case 204/86 *Commission* v. *Greece* [1988] ECR 5323, 5343–5345; Case 226/87 *Commission* v. *Greece* [1988] ECR 3611, 3617. For an unsuccessful attempt to plead the illegality of a dir. (rather than a dec.) which the State had failed to implement see Case C–74/91 *Commission* v. *Germany* [1992] ECR I–5437.

the illegality of the decision to be pleaded in an extreme case where the decision infringes a principle of a constitutional nature.[136]

(d) OTHER MEMBER STATES ARE ALSO IN BREACH

This ground has been pleaded numerous times by Member States, without success.[137] The idea that the obligation to comply with Community law is a reciprocal one which depends on full compliance by other Member States has long been rejected by the ECJ. Since *Van Gend en Loos*[138] the ECJ has been determined to distinguish Community law from traditional forms and principles of international law,[139] in which the reciprocity principle has a much more central role. However, this has not deterred Member States from continuing to raise the concept of reciprocity in their defence in EC infringement proceedings.[140]

9. ARTICLE 227

In addition to the Commission's enforcement power under Article 226, Article 227 of the EC Treaty provides a means for any Member State to initiate an action against another State which it considers to be in breach of the Treaty.[141] Article 227 provides:

> A Member State which considers that another Member State has failed to fulfil an obligation under this Treaty may bring the matter before the Court of Justice.
>
> Before a Member State brings an action against another Member State for an alleged infringement of an obligation under this Treaty, it shall bring the matter before the Commission.
>
> The Commission shall deliver a reasoned opinion after each of the States concerned has been given the opportunity to submit its own case and its observations on the other party's case both orally and in writing.
>
> If the Commission has not delivered an opinion within three months of the date on which the matter was brought before it, the absence of such opinion shall not prevent the matter from being brought before the Court.

Unlike under Article 226, the Member State bringing the action does not first have to contact the Member State which is the subject of the complaint. Instead the matter must first be brought by the complainant State before the Commission. The procedure thereafter is similar to that under Article 226, except that in the case of Article 227 both States must be heard and given a chance to make oral and written submissions before the Commission gives its reasoned opinion. Given that Article 227 provides a mechanism for Member States rather than the Commission to bring another State before the ECJ, it seems the complainant State may bring the case to the ECJ even where the Commission takes the view that there is no breach.

Article 227 has very rarely been used, no doubt because of the ill-will it could occasion (and reflect) between Member States, and because of their preference for resolving disputes by

---

[136] Cases 6 and 11/69 *Commission* v. *France* [1969] ECR 523; Case 70/72 *Commission* v. *Germany* [1973] ECR 813; Case 156/77 *Commission* v. *Belgium* [1978] ECR 1881.

[137] See, e.g., Case C–146/89, n. 134 above.

[138] Case 26/62 [1963] ECR 1.

[139] See Case 52/75 *Commission* v. *Italy* [1976] ECR 277, para. 11.

[140] For a recent example see Case C–266/03 *Commission* v. *Luxembourg* [2005] ECR I–4805.

[141] See also Art. 142 Euratom.

political means.[142] Where political solutions fail, however, States have occasionally had recourse to this mechanism. In 1978 France, with the support of the Commission, successfully brought proceedings against the UK over a fishing dispute.[143] In 1995 Belgium, without the support of the Commission but with the support of four other Member States, brought an unsuccessful action against Spain in relation to its 'rules of origin' requirements for Rioja wine.[144] And in 2000, Spain brought an action against the UK on account of the way in which the UK extended voting rights in European Parliament elections to residents of Gibraltar.[145] The Commission encouraged the two States to resolve the dispute amicably and declined to issue a reasoned opinion, 'given the sensitivity of the underlying bilateral issue',[146] but the ECJ ultimately upheld the conduct of the UK and found against Spain.

10. ARTICLE 228: THE PECUNIARY PENALTY

The provision for a penalty payment to be imposed against a Member State which has failed to comply with a previous enforcement judgment of the Court was first introduced into Article 228 EC by the Treaty on European Union in 2002. It was intended to give teeth to the infringement procedure, and to provide a sharper incentive for Member States to comply with ECJ rulings against them. Prior to the existence of the penalty payment option, the only way provided under Article 228 to 'enforce' compliance with a judgment against a Member State under Article 226 was by bringing the State before the ECJ again for another declaratory ruling.

Article 228 now provides:

> 1. If the Court of Justice finds that a Member State has failed to fulfil an obligation under this Treaty, the State shall be required to take the necessary measures to comply with the judgment of the Court of Justice.
>
> 2. If the Commission considers that the Member State concerned has not taken such measures it shall, after giving that State the opportunity to submit its observations, issue a reasoned opinion specifying the points on which the Member State concerned has not complied with the judgment of the Court of Justice.
>
> If the Member State concerned fails to take the necessary measures to comply with the Court's judgment within the time-limit laid down by the Commission, the latter may bring the case before the Court of Justice. In so doing it shall specify the amount of the lump sum or penalty payment to be paid by the Member State concerned which it considers appropriate in the circumstances.
>
> If the Court of Justice finds that the Member State concerned has not complied with its judgment it may impose a lump sum or penalty payment on it.
>
> This procedure shall be without prejudice to Article 227.

---

[142] In 1984 the procedure was set in motion by the Commission in response to a complaint from France against the Netherlands, which led to a reasoned opinion by the Commission: see Case 169/84 *Cofaz* v. *Commission* [1986] ECR 391, para. 6.

[143] Case 141/78 *France* v. *United Kingdom* [1979] ECR 2923.

[144] Case C–388/95 *Belgium* v. *Spain* [2000] ECR I–3121.

[145] Case C–145/04 *Spain* v. *United Kingdom* [2006] ECR I–7917. The UK's action had been a response to the judgment of the European Court of Human Rights in App. no. 24833/94, *Matthews* v. *United Kingdom*, ECHR 1999–I.

[146] Case C–145/04, n. 145 above, para. 32.

No upper limit to the amount of penalty is specified,[147] and the Court is not bound to follow the proposal of the Commission. There is no mechanism for collection of the payment should a Member State refuse to comply,[148] and there is no power to seek an injunction[149] or to order a Member State to take specific action.[150] The Court has also indicated that it has no jurisdiction under Article 228 to require Member States to comply with its judgment within a specified period of time.[151]

Initially it seemed that, unlike a declaratory judgment under Article 226 which would be given by the ECJ even where the Member State had complied with the Commission's reasoned opinion before judgment, as long as the State had not complied before the expiry of the period laid down in the reasoned opinion, the ECJ would not impose a periodic penalty in circumstances where the Member State had apparently complied before the date of the Article 228 judgment.[152] However, with the introduction of lump sum payments to penalize a state breach which continues between the date of the initial Article 226 judgment and the date of the Article 228 judgment the practice has changed, and judicial proceedings will not now be withdrawn just because a State has belatedly complied.[153] On the other hand, it is clear that the success of Article 228 cases depends largely on the quality of the evidence submitted by the Commission, and the continuing saga of Italian employment discrimination against foreign-language lecturers demonstrates the invidious effects for individual complainants (who, as we have seen, are in no sense parties to the case) when the Commission fails to bring sufficient evident to prove its allegations.[154]

After a slow start, Commission is gradually making more use of the procedure for proposing pecuniary penalties,[155] invoking it most frequently in cases involving serious and persistent breaches, and particularly in the sphere of environmental policy.[156] The Commission also now publishes, in an annex to its annual reports on monitoring the application of EC law, a list of Article 226 judgments with which individual Member States have not yet complied, together with an indication of what action it is taking (under Article 228 or otherwise) against those States. And although the number of judgments actually given remains very low, the Court of Justice has handed down a number of significant rulings which are gradually giving

[147] Art. 229, which provides for the imposition of penalties by the Court under regs. adopted by the Council and the Parliament, also specifies that the Court's jurisdiction under such legislation may be unlimited.

[148] For a critical analysis see M. Theodossiou, 'An Analysis of the Recent Response of the Community to Non-compliance with Court of Justice Judgments: Art. 228' (2003) 27 *ELRev.* 25.

[149] Although the Court has power to order injunctive measures in interim proceedings under Art. 243, it does not have these powers under Art. 228, when giving judgment in infringement proceedings.

[150] See Case C–105/02 *Commission* v. *Germany* [2006] ECR I–9659, paras. 44–45.

[151] Case C–473/93 *Commission* v. *Luxembourg* [1996] ECR I–3207, paras. 51–52. However, in Case C–291/93 *Commission* v. *Italy* [1994] ECR I–859, para. 6, the ECJ ruled that, although Art. 228 did not specify the period within which a judgment must be complied with, the interest in the immediate and uniform application of Community law required compliance as soon as possible.

[152] See Case C–119/04 *Commission* v. *Italy* [2006] ECR I–6885, concerning the long-running complaint about nationality discrimination against foreign-language university lecturers, where the Court did not impose the penalty requested by the Commission on the basis that Italy appeared to have substantially complied by the date the Court examined the facts. In fact it has been argued that Italy had not at all complied with the previous judgment, and that the law it had introduced in purported compliance with that earlier judgment had left the affected individuals in a worse position than they had been under the original discriminatory employment conditions. See H. Rodgers, *Parliament Magazine*, Feb. 2007.

[153] Case C–304/02 *Commission* v. *France* [2005] ECR I–6263, and the Commission's memo SEC(2005)1658.

[154] N. 152 above.

[155] For criticism of its under-use see European Parliament resolution on the Commission's 21st and 22nd Annual Reports on monitoring the application of Community law (2003 and 2004), P6_TA(2006)0202.

[156] For a pending environmental case see also Case C–503/04 *Commission* v. *Germany*, action brought by the Commission on 7 Dec. 2004.

shape to the penalty payment procedure. Many of the cases involve breaches which by their nature are not susceptible to immediate or easy resolution, such as improving the quality of bathing waters or maintaining a system of fisheries inspection and monitoring which is capable of ensuring that conservation regulations are observed in practice. However, when the period of time over which the Member State's breach persists becomes excessive, the Court seems willing to impose the sharper incentive of a penalty payment.

Initially in 1996 and 1997 the Commission published a memorandum on the application of the Treaty provision, and a method of calculation for penalties.[157] In these documents the Commission argued that the amount should reflect the aim of the sanction, i.e. to secure effective compliance with EC law as quickly as possible, and that the most appropriate means of achieving this aim would be a *periodic* penalty running from the date of service of the ECJ's judgment. In the Commission's view, penalties should always be deterrent and never purely symbolic. The daily penalty should be calculated on the basis of three criteria: (1) the seriousness of the infringement (including not only failure to comply with an ECJ judgment, but also the seriousness of the original infringement in terms of both effects and symbolism), (2) its duration, and (3) the need to ensure that the penalty itself is a deterrent to further infringements. The method of calculation should involve a uniform flat-rate amount per day of delay to penalize the violation of the principle of legality, multiplied by factors reflecting the seriousness of the infringement and its duration,[158] and by a factor representing the ability of the Member State to pay and the number of votes it has in the Council. This initial approach was amended and supplemented by the Commission in a memorandum in 2005, following a number of rulings by the Court, in particular on the issue of lump sum payments.[159] While these had not been ruled out in its initial guidelines, the Commission had clearly expressed a strong preference for periodic penalties, and in practice a lump sum penalty had never been proposed to the Court.

The Court itself, ever since its first ruling on the pecuniary penalty,[160] has repeatedly emphasized that while it agrees with much of the guidance published by the Commission, it is not bound by the Commission's advice.[161] In a case against Spain concerning non-compliance with a judgment concerning the quality of bathing water, for example, the Court rejected the Commission's proposal to impose a *daily* penalty on Spain, and instead imposed an annual penalty to be assessed on an ongoing basis so as to reflect the progress towards compliance effected by Spain.[162] This was because of the nature of the breach, and in particular the difficulty of showing, until a considerable period of time after the fact, that the quality of bathing water did conform to the limit values set by EC law.[163] And in a case against France involving inadequate implementation of the Products Liability Directive, the Court rejected the Commission's guidelines for calculating the coefficient relating to the duration of the infringement.[164]

---

[157] See [1996] OJ C242/6 and [1997] OJ C63/2. For discussion see Theodossiou, n. 148 above.

[158] See the Commission's internal decision on the 'duration coefficient' in PV(2001) 1517/2 of 2 Apr. 2001.

[159] SEC(2005)1658.

[160] Case C–387/97 *Commission* v. *Greece* [2000] ECR I–5047. For comment see L. Borszak, 'Punishing Member States or Influencing Their Behaviour or *Iudex (non)* Calculat?' (2001) 13 *JEL* 235 and C. Hilson (2001) 3 *Env. LR* 131.

[161] *Ibid.*, paras. 87–89. Although the Court did rule against Greece and imposed a penalty, it reduced the amount of the periodic penalty payment proposed by the Commission.

[162] Case C–278/01 *Commission* v. *Spain* [2003] ECR I–14141. For comment see M. Ruffert (2004) 41 *CMLRev.* 1387.

[163] The Court did similarly in Case C–304/02, n. 153 above, varying the periodic penalty proposed by the Commission and imposing it on a half-yearly rather than a daily basis, to allow progress towards compliance to be measured.

[164] Case C–177/04, n. 74 above.

More fundamentally, the Court in 2004 imposed the first lump sum penalty payment on a Member State for a longstanding violation, even though the Commission had not recommended this.[165] The case, in which sixteen other Member States intervened, was brought against France for non-compliance with a judgment dating from 1991 concerning the monitoring and implementation of EC rules on fisheries conservation. Four of the intervening Member States supported the possibility of imposing a lump sum penalty concurrently with a periodic penalty, on the basis that the lump sum payment was a complementary deterrent measure. The twelve other States, however, put forward several arguments based on the Treaty text as well as on policy and principle, against the concurrent imposition of both penalties. The Court dismissed all of these arguments:

Case C–304/02 **Commission v. France**
[2005] ECR I–6263

80 The procedure laid down in Article 228(2) EC has the objective of inducing a defaulting Member State to comply with a judgment establishing a breach of obligations and thereby of ensuring that Community law is in fact applied. The measures provided for by that provision, namely a lump sum and a penalty payment, are both intended to achieve this objective.

81 Application of each of those measures depends on their respective ability to meet the objective pursued according to the circumstances of the case. While the imposition of a penalty payment seems particularly suited to inducing a Member State to put an end as soon as possible to a breach of obligations which, in the absence of such a measure, would tend to persist, the imposition of a lump sum is based more on assessment of the effects on public and private interests of the failure of the Member State concerned to comply with its obligations, in particular where the breach has persisted for a long period since the judgment which initially established it.

82 That being so, recourse to both types of penalty provided for in Article 228(2) EC is not precluded, in particular where the breach of obligations both has continued for a long period and is inclined to persist.

The Court took the view that the absence of any Commission guidelines for the imposition of a lump sum penalty did not lead to any violation of the principle of legal certainty, nor did the fact that the Commission had not proposed the imposition of a lump sum penalty in this particular case present any obstacle to the imposition of such a penalty by the Court. The ECJ rejected the argument that it needed 'political legitimacy' to impose a financial penalty not suggested by the Commission, and declared that the financial penalties to be imposed should be decided upon 'according to the degree of persuasion needed in order for the Member State in question to alter its conduct'.[166] The rights of defence of the Member State were not affected by its being unable to put forward arguments against a lump sum, in the Court's view, because the Article 228(2) procedure was to be viewed as a method of enforcement of the earlier judgment, following a finding, based on *inter partes* proceedings, that a breach of EC law persisted.[167]

---

[165] Case C–304/02, n. 153 above. In a subsequent case against France where once again, the Commission had requested only a periodic penalty and not a lump sum, the ECJ considered whether a lump sum should nonetheless be imposed, but concluded that it should not: Case C–177/04, n. 74 above.

[166] Case C–304/02 *Commission* v. *France*, n. 153 above, paras. 90–91.

[167] *Ibid.*, para. 93.

Interestingly, especially in view of the extensive counter-arguments made by several Member States against the power of the Court to impose a lump sum penalty where it had not been proposed by the Commission in accordance with pre-established criteria, the ECJ's reasoning on the amount of the lump sum penalty was minimal in the extreme. The Court simply stated in two brief paragraphs that:

> 114 In a situation such as that which is the subject of the present judgment, in light of the fact that the breach of obligations has persisted for a long period since the judgment which initially established it and of the public and private interests at issue, it is essential to order payment of a lump sum (see paragraph 81 of the present judgment).
>
> 115 The specific circumstances of the case are fairly assessed by setting the amount of the lump sum which the French Republic will have to pay at EUR 20 000 000.

Following the case, the Commission amended its original guidelines, referring not only to the desirability of a lump sum payment where Member States have delayed considerably in compliance, but also to the principle of proportionality and equal treatment of the Member States, which had been emphasized by the ECJ in other Article 228 judgments,[168] as well as the need for sanctions to be foreseeable.[169] On lump sum payments, the Commission indicated that it would henceforth propose at least a minimum lump sum payment to the Court in *every* Article 228 case, to reflect 'the principle that any case of persistent non-compliance . . . in itself represents an attack on the principle of legality'.[170]

The Commission made a range of other recommendations in its follow-up memorandum, e.g. proposing that distinct sanctions could be imposed for distinct infringements within the context of a single case, to allow for greater precision and adaptability. Drawing on the Spanish bathing water and French fisheries cases, it also proposed to allow for adjustment of sanctions to reflect partial or gradual compliance, and for periods such as six months or a year, rather than only daily penalties. A procedure to allow for the suspension of penalties after appropriate verification of compliance with conditions set down by the Court was also suggested. Several other guidelines were laid down, including factors which would aggravate or mitigate the seriousness of a breach for the purposes of calculating the penalty due. However, shortly after the fisheries judgment imposing both a lump sum and six-monthly period penalty upon it, France challenged the decision made by the Commission pursuant to that judgment.[171] The Commission in its decision claimed that France was continuing its failure to comply fully with the original judgment under Article 226 and should pay the periodic penalty. In an action for annulment lodged before the Court of First Instance, France has claimed that the Commission lacked competence to impose the periodic penalty, that it erred in its assessment that the State's breach continued, and that in any case the penalty imposed was too high.[172]

It is evident that the Article 228 mechanism, although slow to develop and to take shape, now represents the sharp end of the overall enforcement procedure, with a distinctly less diplomatic and more formal legal flavour than the Article 226 stage. However, it is also evident that the burden is on the Commission to marshall the appropriate evidence against the

---

[168] Case C–378/97 *Commission* v. *Greece* [2000] ECR I–5047; Case C–278/01, n. 162 above.

[169] SEC(2005)1658.

[170] *Ibid.*, para 20. Since then the Commission has begun to request lump sum penalties: see, e.g., Case C–219/06 *Commission* v. *Luxembourg*, action brought on 12 May 2006.

[171] Case T–139/06 *France* v. *Commission*, action brought on 12 May 2006.

[172] *Ibid.*

Member State before the ECJ, and that a failure to do so in Article 228 proceedings may well undermine the effect of a previous Article 226 judgment against a State.[173]

11. INTERIM MEASURES

Under Articles 242 and 243 EC the ECJ has the power to prescribe interim measures which it considers to be necessary in a case which has been brought before it.[174] Although interim measures may be sought in any case before the ECJ,[175] they may be particularly useful for the Commission to seek at the same time as proceedings under Article 226.

When in Article 226 proceedings a breach is found, the Court simply declares that the Member State has failed to fulfil its obligations, and its ruling does not have any effect on the impugned national rule or provision. Indeed as a general matter, actions before the ECJ do not have suspensory effect.

Article 242 however provides:

> Actions brought before the Court of Justice shall not have suspensory effect. The Court of Justice may, however, if it considers that circumstances so require, order that application of the contested act be suspended.

Article 243 then provides:

> The Court of Justice may in any cases before it prescribe any necessary interim measures.

The Court's Rules of Procedure specify that such interim measures may not be ordered unless there are circumstances giving rise to urgency, as well as factual and legal grounds which establish a *prima facie* justification for granting the measures sought. The effect of the urgency requirement is that the interim measures requested must be of such a nature as to prevent the injury which is alleged. Further, the Commission must display diligence in response to a complaint made against a Member State if it is seeking interim measures, given the requirement of urgency, and the ECJ may refuse to order such measures if it has not done so.[176]

12. CONCLUSIONS

Reflecting on the use of Article 228 after the first lump-sum judgment against France, together with the Court's willingness to support the Commission's use of Article 226 to pursue 'general and persistent breaches' in the case against Ireland, Wenneras has argued that the Commission 'now possesses a formidable set of tools under Articles 226 and 228 EC to tackle infringements of Community law effectively' and that Member States 'cannot afford to flout Community

---

[173] On the long-running saga of foreign-language lecturers in Italy see Cases C–212/99 *Commission* v. *Italy* [2001] ECR I–4923 and C–119/04 *Commission* v. *Italy* [2006] ECR I–6885, n.152 above.

[174] See also Arts. 39 ECSC, 157–158 Euratom; C. Gray, 'Interim Measures of Protection in the European Court' (1979) 4 *ELRev.* 80; G. Borchardt, 'The Award of Interim Measures by the ECJ' (1985) 22 *CMLRev.* 203; P. Oliver, 'Interim Measures: Some Recent Developments' (1992) 29 *CMLRev.* 7.

[175] See, e.g., the Court's dismissal of Greece's objection to an application for interim measures in the context of Art. 298 enforcement proceedings against it: Case C–120/94 R, n. 1 above.

[176] Case C–87/94 R *Commission* v. *Belgium* [1994] ECR I–1395.

law'.[177] Despite this positive appraisal of some of the more effective enforcement tools which have been developed, it is equally true that the enforcement machinery is under great strain with the expansion of the EU and the continued rise in the number of complaints. According to Munoz, even the supplementary mechanisms which have been introduced to try to cope with the increasing load are inadequate, thus presenting the Commission with two possibilities, '[f]irstly, to implement a filter in order to limit the number of infringement procedures; or secondly, to fight for a drastic reform of tools to control the application of Community law'.[178] While arguing against a policy of selectivity and filtering, and in favour of a more fundamental reform of the enforcement tools to allow for 'a more genuinely reactive mechanism', he suggests that selectivity and filtering is nonetheless the most likely immediate future direction to be taken.

i. Some of the main criticisms of the enforcement procedure over the years, including its lack of effectiveness, the lack of an adequate role for individual complainants, and the elite and unresponsive attitude of the Commission, have gradually been addressed. The penalty payment procedure under Article 228, and the development of a procedure for pursuing 'general and persistent breaches' has begun to tackle aspects of the effectiveness problem; and pressure from the Ombudsman and the European Parliament has encouraged the Commission to follow somewhat more regular and transparent administrative procedures including in its dealings with individual complainants.

ii. Despite the various reforms, the overall enforcement mechanism continues to be divided into distinct phases: parts of it operating in a bilateral and diplomatic dispute-resolution mode, parts of it according to a more formal, judicially-monitored sanction procedure, and parts of it as a quasi-administrative complaints procedure.

iii. The main challenge for the enforcement procedure at present is the pressing risk of overload, despite the array of preventative, alternative and supplementary mechanisms proposed by the Commission. Unless a more thoroughgoing reform and buttressing of the enforcement mechanism is undertaken, it seems likely that its accessibility to individual complainants will continue to shrink, and that the Commission will move increasingly towards prioritizing certain categories of breach.

13. FURTHER READING

(a) Books

Gil Ibáñez, A., *The Administrative Supervision and Enforcement of EC Law* (Hart, 1999)

Schermers, H., *Judicial Protection in the European Union* (6th edn., Kluwer, 2002)

Tallberg, J., *European Governance and Supranational Institutions: Making States Comply* (Routledge, 2003)

(b) Articles

Borchardt, G., 'The Award of Interim Measures by the European Court' (1985) 22 *CMLRev.* 203

---

[177] Wenneras, n. 114 above.
[178] Munoz, n. 5 above.

Evans, A., 'The Enforcement Procedure of Article 169 EEC: Commission Discretion' (1979) 4 *ELRev.* 442

Gray, C., 'Interim Measures of Protection in the European Court' (1979) 4 *ELRev.* 80

Harlow, C., and Rawlings, R., 'Accountability and Law Enforcement: The Centralized EU Infringement Procedure' (2006) 31 *ELRev.* 447

Mastroianni, R., 'The Enforcement Procedure under Article 169 of the EC Treaty and the Powers of the European Commission: Quis Custodiet Custodes?' (1995) 1 *EPL* 535

Munoz, R., 'The Monitoring of the Application of Community Law: The Need to Improve the Current Tools and an Obligation to Innovate', Jean Monnet Working Paper 2006

Rawlings, R., 'Engaged Elites, Citizen action and Institutional Attitudes in Commission Enforcement' (2000) 6 *ELJ* 4

Theodossiou, M., 'An Analysis of the Recent Response of the Community to Non-compliance with Court of Justice Judgments: Art. 228' (2003) 27 *ELRev.* 25

Wenneras, P., 'A New Dawn for Commission Enforcement under Arts. 226 and 228 EC: General and Persistent (GAP) Infringements, Lump Sums, and Penalty Payments' (2006) 43 *CMLRev.* 31

PRELIMINARY RULINGS

1. INTRODUCTION

Article 234 EC, which contains the preliminary ruling procedure, is one of the most interesting provisions of the EC Treaty. There would have been few, at the inception of the Treaty, who guessed its importance in shaping both Community law, and the relationship between the national and Community legal systems. Article 234 (ex Article 177) is very much the 'jewel in the Crown' of the ECJ's jurisdiction. It reads as follows:

> The Court of Justice shall have jurisdiction to give preliminary rulings concerning:
> - (a) the interpretation of the Treaty;
> - (b) the validity and interpretation of acts of the institutions of the Community and of the ECB;
> - (c) the interpretation of the statutes of bodies established by an act of the Council, where those statutes so provide.
>
> Where such a question is raised before any court or tribunal of a Member State, that court or tribunal may, if it considers that a decision on the question is necessary to enable it to give judgment, request the Court of Justice to give a ruling thereon.
>
> Where any such question is raised in a case pending before a court or tribunal of a Member State, against whose decisions there is no judicial remedy under national law, that court or tribunal shall bring the matter before the Court of Justice.

Prior to the Nice Treaty only the ECJ could give preliminary rulings. Article 225(3) now accords the CFI jurisdiction to give such rulings in specific areas laid down by the Statute of the Court of Justice. If the CFI feels that such a case raises issues of principle which will affect the unity or consistency of EC law it may refer the case to the ECJ. Where the CFI does give a preliminary ruling, its decision may exceptionally be subject to review by the ECJ, under the conditions laid down by the ECJ's Statute, where there is a serious risk that the unity or consistency of EC law will be affected. The power to accord the CFI jurisdiction to give preliminary rulings has not, however, been acted on thus far. The ECJ therefore currently hears all Article 234 cases.

The relationship between national courts and the ECJ is reference-based. It is not an appellate system. No individual has a right of appeal to the ECJ. It is for the national court to make the decision to refer. The ECJ will rule on the issues referred to it, and the case will then be sent back to the national courts, which will apply the Community law to the case at hand.

2. CENTRAL ISSUES

i.   Article 234 has been of seminal importance for the *development of Community law*. It is through preliminary rulings that the ECJ has developed concepts such as direct effect and supremacy.[1] Individuals assert in national courts that their *Member States* have broken a Community provision, which give them rights that they can enforce in their national courts. The national court seeks a ruling from the ECJ whether the particular Community provision has direct effect, and the ECJ is thereby able to develop the concept. Article 234 is also an indirect way of testing the validity of *Community action* for conformity with EC law.[2]

ii. Article 234 has been the mechanism through which national courts and the ECJ have engaged in *a discourse on the appropriate reach of Community law when it has come into conflict with national legal norms*.

iii. Article 234 has been the principal vehicle through which the *relationship between the national and Community legal systems has been fashioned*. The *original* conception of the relationship was *horizontal* and *bilateral*. It was horizontal in that the ECJ and the national courts were separate but equal. They had differing functions, which each performed within its appointed sphere. It was for the national court to decide whether to refer a matter to the ECJ, which the ECJ would then interpret. It was bilateral in the sense that, in principle, the ECJ's rulings were delivered to the particular national court that made the request. In this sense, there was a series of bilateral relationships between the ECJ and each of the national courts.

iv. The relationship has become steadily more *vertical* and *multilateral*. It has become more vertical in that developments have emphasized the fact that the ECJ sits in a superior position to that of the national courts. The verticality of the relationship also manifests itself in a less obvious, but equally important, manner. The ECJ has, in effect, enrolled the national courts as enforcers and appliers of Community law. They are perceived as a central part of a Community-wide judicial hierarchy,[3] with the ECJ sitting at the apex of this hierarchy. The relationship has become more multilateral, in that judgments given in response to the request for a ruling from one Member State are increasingly held to have either a *de facto* or *de jure* impact on all other national courts.

v.   There has been much discussion about *reform of the Community judicial system*.[4] This discourse has been driven by the increased workload on the ECJ and CFI, and by the enlargement of the EU.

3. FOUNDATIONS

(a) TYPES OF PRELIMINARY RULING PROCEDURE

The changes introduced by the ToA mean that there are now three different types of preliminary-ruling procedure.

---

[1] F. Mancini and D. Keeling, 'From *CILFIT* to *ERT*: The Constitutional Challenge Facing the European Court' (1991) 11 *YBEL* 1, 2–3.

[2] See below, 528–530.

[3] Report of the Court of Justice on Certain Aspects of the Application of the Treaty on European Union (1995), paras. 11–15.

[4] See below, 494–500.

The first version of this procedure is contained in Article 234, set out above. This version will continue to apply to all requests for preliminary rulings coming under Pillar One, the EC Treaty, except for those arising under Articles 61–69.

The second species of preliminary ruling operates in the context of Articles 61–69, Title IV EC, which deal with 'Visas, Asylum, Immigration and Other Policies Concerning the Free Movement of Persons'. These matters were, prior to the ToA, dealt with in Pillar Three, concerning Justice and Home Affairs (JHA), but there were criticisms about treating such matters in this way.[5] The ToA brought many important Pillar Three issues within Pillar One. The Article 234 procedure was, however, modified in its application in relation to Title IV. Article 68 stipulates that a preliminary ruling can be sought only by a national court or tribunal against whose decisions there is no judicial remedy in national law.[6] This is as opposed to the 'normal' position under Article 234 whereby any court or tribunal has discretion to seek a reference.[7] The limit placed on the Court's jurisdiction in relation to the Third Pillar and Title IV EC has been criticized,[8] and the Commission has proposed amendment to the latter to bring it into line with the normal Article 234 regime.[9] The ECJ has moreover proposed amendments to its Rules of Procedure for cases concerned with the Area of Freedom, Security, and Justice.[10]

The third species of preliminary ruling was introduced by Article 35 TEU as modified by the ToA. This covers the re-modelled Pillar Three which now deals with 'Police and Judicial Co-operation in Criminal Matters' (PJCC). Article 35 in effect provides that the ECJ shall have jurisdiction to give preliminary rulings on the interpretation and validity of certain measures adopted under this Pillar, but *only if* the Member State accepts the ECJ's jurisdiction by making a declaration. Article 35(3) further provides that a Member State has a choice whether a preliminary ruling can be sought by any court or tribunal or only by such a body against whose decisions there is no judicial remedy in national law.

(b) PROVISIONS WHICH CAN BE REFERRED

A preliminary reference can be made in relation to three types of subject-matter. References may be made concerning *the interpretation of the Treaty*: Article 234(1)(a).[11] This includes all Treaties amending or supplementing the EC Treaty. Particular subsidiary conventions may provide for references to be made to the ECJ. It is through Article 234(1)(a) that the Court has given many of its seminal judgments concerning direct effect and supremacy. The ECJ does not however pass judgment on the validity as such of a national law. It interprets the Treaty.

---

[5] See Ch. 1.

[6] Case C–51/03 *Georgescu* [2004] ECR I–3203; Case C–45/03 *Oxana Dem'Yanenko*, 18 Mar. 2004.

[7] Art. 68(3) also provides that the Council, Commission, or a Member State can request the ECJ to give a ruling on a question of interpretation arising under Title IV, or acts of the institutions based on this Title. Such rulings do not apply to judgments of national courts, etc., which have become *res judicata*.

[8] S. Peers, 'Who's Judging the Watchmen? The Judicial System of the "Area of Freedom, Security and Justice"' (1998) 18 *YBEL* 337; A. Albors-Llorens, 'Changes in the Jurisdiction of the ECJ under the Treaty of Amsterdam' (1998) 35 *CMLRev.* 1273.

[9] On adaptation of the provisions of Title IV of the Treaty establishing the European Community relating to the jurisdiction of the Court of Justice with a view to ensuring more effective judicial protection, COM(2006)346 final.

[10] See below, 495.

[11] Rights and obligations arising from agreements concluded before the entry into force of the Treaty between a Member State and a third country are not affected by the provisions of the Treaty. For a Community provision to be deprived of effect such an agreement must have been concluded before the entry into force of the EC Treaty, and the third country must derive rights from it which it can require the Member State concerned to respect: Cases C–364 and 365/95 *T. Port GmbH & Co. v. Hauptzollamt Hamburg-Jonas* [1998] ECR I–1023.

The consequence of this interpretation may be that a provision of national law is incompatible with EC law, and the supremacy of EC law will mean that there is an obligation on, *inter alia*, national courts to redress the situation. The ECJ itself is nonetheless not directly making any judgment on the validity of national law.[12]

Article 234(1)(b) allows for preliminary references to be made which relate *to the validity and interpretation of acts of the institutions* of the Community. The former covers cases such as *ICC*[13] and *Foto-Frost*,[14] to be considered below, in which the validity of, for example, a Community decision or regulation arises in proceedings before a national court. The latter covers, *inter alia*, those cases where an individual argues that a Community regulation is capable of giving rise to rights that can be enforced in national courts. References can however be made under Article 234(1)(b) irrespective of whether or not the Community provision is directly effective, in order, for example, to clarify the interpretation of the relevant provision. References may also be made in relation to non-binding acts such as recommendations,[15] and certain agreements with non-Member States.[16]

The precise ambit of Article 234(1)(c), which embraces *the interpretation of statutes of bodies established by an act of the Council*, is not so clear. The word 'statute' in Community law normally connotes an instrument which governs the operation of an institution, such as the statute of the ECJ. Such statutes will be acts of the Council, and will therefore fall within Article 234(1)(b). It may well be that, as Hartley suggests, Article 234(1)(c) is designed to limit the scope of Article 234(1)(b) in relation to such statutes.[17]

The ECJ has also held that a preliminary reference may be made in circumstances in which a provision of national law is based on or makes some reference to Community law, even if the consequence is that the ambit of Community law is extended by the national provisions.[18]

There are specific subject-matter limits as to what can be referred under the modified Article 234 procedure which applies to Title IV, Articles 61–69,[19] and to the procedure which operates in the context of Pillar Three.[20]

---

[12] See, e.g., Case C–167/94 R *Grau Gomis* [1995] ECR I–1023; Cases C–37 and 38/96 *Sodiprem Sarl* v. *Direction Générale des Douanes* [1998] ECR I–2039; Cases C–10 and 22/97 *Ministero delle Finanze* v. *IN. CO. GE. '90 Srl* [1998] ECR I–6307; Information Note on References from National Courts for a Preliminary Ruling, [2005] OJ C143/1.

[13] Case 66/80 *International Chemical Corporation* v. *Amministrazione delle Finanze dello Stato* [1981] ECR 1191.

[14] Case 314/85 *Firma Foto-Frost* v. *Hauptzollamt Lübeck-Ost* [1987] ECR 4199.

[15] Case 322/88 *Salvatore Grimaldi* v. *Fonds des Maladies Professionnelles* [1989] ECR 4407.

[16] Case 181/73 *Haegeman* v. *Belgium* [1974] ECR 449; Cases 267–269/81 *Amministrazione delle Finanze dello Stato* v. *Società Petrolifera Italiana SpA and SpA Michelin Italia* [1983] ECR 801; Case C–53/96 *Hermès International* v. *FHT Marketing Choice BV* [1998] ECR I–3603; Cases C–300 and 392/98 *Parfums Christian Dior* v. *Tuk Consultancy BV* [2000] ECR I–11307; T.C. Hartley, *The Foundations of European Community Law* (5th edn., Clarendon Press, 2002), 273–276.

[17] *Ibid.*, 270–271.

[18] See, e.g., Cases C–297/88 and 197/89 *Dzodzi* v. *Belgium* [1990] ECR I–3763; Case C–231/89 *Gmurzynska-Bscher* v. *Oberfinanzdirektion Köln* [1990] ECR I–4003; Case C–28/95 *Leur-Bloem* v. *Inspecteur der Belastingdienst/Ondernemingen Amsterdam 2* [1997] ECR I–4161; Case C–130/95 *Bernd Giloy* v. *Hauptzollamt Frankfurt am Main-Ost* [1997] ECR I–4291; Case C–217/05 *Confederacion Espanola de Empresarios de Estaciones de Servicio* v. *Compania Espanola de Petroleos SA*, 14 Dec. 2006; S. Lefevre, 'The Interpretation of Community Law by the Court of Justice in Areas of National Competence' (2004) 29 *ELRev.* 501.

[19] Art. 68(2): the ECJ has no jurisdiction to rule on any measure, etc., made pursuant to Art. 62(1) concerning the maintenance of law and order, and the safeguarding of internal security.

[20] Art. 35(5) TEU: the ECJ has no jurisdiction to review the validity or proportionality of operations of the police or other law enforcement agencies, or the exercise of the Member States' responsibilities in relation to law and order and internal security.

(c) COURTS OR TRIBUNALS WHICH CAN REFER

Article 234(2) and (3) is framed in terms of courts or tribunals of a Member State which may or must make a reference. It is for the ECJ to decide whether a body is a court or tribunal for these purposes; the categorization under national law is not conclusive.[21] The ECJ will take a number of factors into account when making this determination, including: whether the body is established by law, whether it is permanent, whether its jurisdiction is compulsory, whether its procedure is *inter partes*, whether it applies rules of law, and whether it is independent.[22] The application of these criteria has not however always been straightforward.[23] The *Broekmeulen* case nonetheless provides a good example of the ECJ's reasoning.

Case 246/80 C. Broekmeulen v. Huisarts Registratie Commissie
[1981] ECR 2311

[Note ToA renumbering: Art. 177 is now Art. 234]

The case concerned a Dutch body called the Appeals Committee for General Medicine. It heard appeals from another body, which was responsible for registering those who wished to practise medicine in the Netherlands. Both of these bodies were established under the auspices of the Royal Netherlands Society for the Promotion of Medicine. Although this was a private association, it was indirectly recognized in other parts of Dutch law, and in reality it was not possible to practise without registration. The Appeals Committee was not a court or tribunal under Dutch law, but it did follow an adversarial procedure and allow legal representation. Broekmeulen was of Dutch nationality, but had qualified in Belgium. He sought to establish himself as a doctor in the Netherlands and his application to be registered was refused. The question arose whether the Appeals Committee was a court or tribunal for the purposes of Article 177.

THE ECJ

14. A study of the Netherlands legislation and of the statutes and internal rules of the Society shows that a doctor who intends to establish himself in the Netherlands may not in fact practise either as a specialist, or as an expert in social medicine, or as a general practitioner, without being recognised and registered by the organs of the Society....

15. It is thus clear that ... the Netherlands system of public health operates on the basis of the status accorded to doctors by the Society and that registration as a general practitioner is essential to every doctor wishing to establish himself in the Netherlands as a general practitioner.

---

[21] Case 43/71 *Politi* v. *Italy* [1971] ECR 1039; Case C–24/92 *Corbiau* v. *Administration des Contributions* [1993] ECR I–1277.

[22] Case C–54/96 *Dorsch Consult Ingenieurgesellschaft mbH* v. *Bundesbaugesellschaft Berlin mbH* [1997] ECR I–4961; Cases C–9 and 118/97 *Proceedings brought by Jokela and Pitkaranta* [1998] ECR I–6267; Case C–407/98 *Abrahamsson and Anderson* v. *Fogelqvist* [2000] ECR I–5539; Case C–195/98 *Österreicher Gewerkschaftsbund, Gewerkschaft Öffentlicher Dienst* v. *Republik Österreich* [2000] ECR I–10497; Case C–178/99 *Salzmann* [2001] ECR I–4421; Case C–53/03 *Syfait* v. *GlaxoSmithKline plc* [2005] ECR I–4609.

[23] T. Tridimas, 'Knocking on Heaven's Door: Fragmentation, Efficiency and Defiance in the Preliminary Ruling Procedure' (2003) 40 *CMLRev.* 9, 27–34.

16. Therefore a general practitioner who avails himself of the right of establishment and the freedom to provide services conferred upon him by Community law is faced with the necessity of applying to the Registration Committee established by the Society, and, in the event of his application's being refused, must appeal to the Appeals Committee. The Netherlands Government expressed the opinion that a doctor who is not a member of the Society would have the right to appeal against such a refusal to the ordinary courts, but stated that the point had never been decided by the Netherlands courts. Indeed all doctors, whether members of the Society or not, whose application to be registered as a general practitioner is refused, appeal to the Appeals Committee, whose decisions to the knowledge of the Netherlands Government have never been challenged in the ordinary courts.

17. [I]t should be noted that it is incumbent upon Member States to take the necessary steps to ensure that within their own territory the provisions adopted by the Community institutions are implemented in their entirety. If, under the legal system of a Member State, the task of implementing such provisions is assigned to a professional body acting under a degree of governmental supervision, and if that body, in conjunction with the public authorities concerned, creates appeal procedures which may affect the exercise of rights granted by Community law, it is imperative, in order to ensure the proper functioning of Community law, that the Court should have an opportunity of ruling on issues of interpretation and validity arising out of such proceedings.

18. As a result of all the foregoing considerations and in the absence, in practice, of any right of appeal to the ordinary courts, the Appeals Committee, which operates with the consent of the public authorities and with their cooperation, and which, after an adversarial procedure, delivers decisions which are recognised as final, must, in a matter involving the application of Community law, be considered as a court or tribunal of a Member State within the meaning of Article 177 of the Treaty. Therefore, the Court has jurisdiction to reply to the question asked.

It is necessary that the body making the reference be a court or tribunal of a Member State.[24] This can be problematic in, for example, the context of arbitration. Whether an arbitral court or tribunal can be regarded as an emanation of a Member State will depend on the nature of the arbitration. The fact that the arbitral body gives a judgment according to law, and that the award is binding between the parties, will not, however, be sufficient. There must be a closer link between the arbitration procedure and the ordinary court system in order for the former to be considered as a court or tribunal of a Member State.[25]

(d) COURTS OR TRIBUNALS WHICH MUST REFER

Article 234 draws a distinction between courts or tribunals with a discretion to refer to the ECJ, Article 234(2), and courts or tribunals 'against whose decisions there is no judicial remedy under national law', Article 234(3), which have an obligation to refer, provided that a decision on a question is necessary to enable judgment to be given. The rationale for the duty to refer in Article 234(3) is to prevent a body of national case law that is not in accordance with EC law from being established in any Member State.[26]

---

[24] Case C–355/89 *DHSS (Isle of Man)* v. *Barr and Montrose Holdings Ltd.* [1991] ECR I–3479; Case C–100/89 *Kaefer and Procacci* v. *France* [1990] ECR I–4647.

[25] Case 102/81 *Nordsee Deutsche Hochseefischerei GmbH* v. *Reederei Mond Hochseefischerei Nordstern AG and Co. KG* [1982] ECR 1095; Case C–126/97 *Eco Swiss China Time Ltd.* v. *Benetton International NV* [1999] ECR I–3055; Case C–125/04 *Denuit and Cordenier* v. *Transorient-Mosaique Voyages and Culture SA* [2005] ECR I–923.

[26] Case C–393/98 *Ministerio Publico and Gomes Valente* v. *Fazenda Publica* [2001] ECR I–1327, para. 17; Case C–99/00 *Criminal Proceedings against Lyckeskog* [2002] ECR I–4839, paras. 14–15.

There are two views about the types of bodies covered by Article 234(3). According to the abstract theory, the only bodies which come within this Article are those whose decisions are never subject to appeal. According to the concrete theory, the real test is whether the court or tribunal's decision is subject to appeal in the type of case in question.[27]

Costa[28] suggested that the ECJ favoured the concrete theory. In that case the *giudice concili-atore* (magistrate) made a reference to the ECJ. Although his decisions were capable of being appealed in some instances, there was no such right of appeal in the particular case because the sum involved was relatively small. Notwithstanding this fact, the ECJ treated the national court as one against whose decision there was no judicial remedy in the actual case at hand.

The concrete theory was affirmed in *Lyckeskog*.[29] The ECJ held that decisions of a national appeal court that could be challenged before a national supreme court did not come within Article 234(3), and this was so notwithstanding the fact that the appeal court decision was subject to a prior declaration of admissibility before it could be appealed to the supreme court. If a question concerning the interpretation of EC law arose before the supreme court it would be under an obligation to refer pursuant to Article 234(3), either when examining admissibility or at a later stage.[30]

(e) THE NATIONAL COURT RAISING COMMUNITY LAW OF ITS OWN VOLITION

The issue of whether national courts can be limited by national procedural rules on whether they can raise a matter of EC law appears to be as follows. In *Peterbroeck* the ECJ held that a national procedural rule which prevented a national court from raising a matter of EC law of its own motion concerning the compatibility of a national law with EC law, even where it had not been raised by the person concerned within the specified time, was itself contrary to Community law. It was held that the domestic rule could not be justified on the ground of legal certainty or the proper conduct of procedure.[31] This case was distinguished in *Van Schijndel*.[32] The ECJ held that there was no such obligation on national courts if those courts were required to abandon the passive role assigned to them by the domestic procedural rules by going beyond the ambit of the dispute as defined by the parties themselves.

The ECJ has made it clear that, unless they were granted leave to intervene in the national proceedings, parties other than those mentioned in Article 20 of the Statute of the Court have no rights to intervene in Article 234 proceedings.[33]

4. THE EXISTENCE OF A QUESTION

It is for the national court to decide whether to make a reference. The mere fact that a party before the national court contends that the dispute gives rise to a question concerning the validity of Community law does not mean that the court is compelled to consider that a question

---

[27] Difficulties may also arise in circumstances where the judgment in question can be reconsidered in other proceedings: Case 107/76 *Hoffmann-La Roche* v. *Centrafarm* [1977] ECR 957.

[28] Case 6/64 [1964] ECR 585, 592.

[29] Case C–99/00, n. 26 above.

[30] For discussion within the UK see *Chiron Corporation* v. *Murex Diagnostics Ltd.* [1995] All ER (EC) 88, 93–94; Hartley, n. 16 above, 283–289; F. Jacobs, 'Which Courts and Tribunals are Bound to Refer to the European Court?' (1977) 2 *ELRev.* 119.

[31] Case C–312/93 *Peterbroeck, Van Campenhout & Cie. SCS* v. *Belgium* [1995] ECR I–4599.

[32] Cases C–430–431/93 *Van Schijndel and Van Veen* v. *Stichting Pensioenfonds voor Fysiotherapeuten* [1995] ECR I–4705. See Ch. 9 above for more general discussion of remedies, procedural autonomy, and EC law.

[33] Case C–181/95 *Biogen Inc.* v. *Smithkline Beecham Biologicals SA* [1997] ECR I–357.

has been raised within the meaning of Article 234.[34] The national court may conclude that a reference is not required because the Community Courts have already resolved the issue, because there is no doubt as to the validity of the Community measure, or because a decision on the question is not necessary for the case before the national court.

(a) THE DEVELOPMENT OF PRECEDENT

(i) *Prior ECJ Rulings and National Law in Breach of EC Law*

It is clear that Article 234 is designed to be used only if there is a question to be answered which falls into one of the categories mentioned in Article 234(1). There may be a number of reasons why a 'question' posed by the national court does not necessitate a ruling, the most obvious being that the ECJ has already ruled on the matter.

Cases 28–30/62 Da Costa en Schaake NV, Jacob Meijer NV and Hoechst-Holland NV v. Nederlandse Belastingadministratie
[1963] ECR 31

[Note ToA renumbering: Arts. 12 and 177 are now Arts. 25 and 234]

The facts in the case were materially identical to those in Case 26/62, *Van Gend en Loos*. The questions asked were also materially identical to those posed in the *Van Gend* case.

THE ECJ

The regularity of the procedure followed by the Tariefcommissie in requesting the Court for a preliminary ruling under Article 177 of the EEC Treaty has not been disputed and there is no ground for the Court to raise the matter of its own motion.

The Commission ... urges that the request be dismissed for lack of substance, since the questions on which an interpretation is requested from the Court in the present cases have already been decided ... in Case 26/62, which covered identical questions raised in a similar case.

This contention is not justified. A distinction should be made between the obligation imposed by the third paragraph of Article 177 upon national courts or tribunals of last instance and the power granted by the second paragraph of Article 177 to every national court or tribunal to refer to the Court of the Communities a question on the interpretation of the Treaty. Although the third paragraph of Article 177 unreservedly requires courts or tribunals of a Member State against whose decisions there is no judicial remedy under national law—like the Tariefcommissie—to refer to the Court every question of interpretation raised before them, the authority of an interpretation under Article 177 already given by the Court may deprive the obligation of its purpose and thus empty it of its substance. Such is the case especially when the question raised is materially identical with a question which has already been the subject of a preliminary ruling in a similar case.

When it gives an interpretation of the Treaty in a specific action pending before a national court, the Court limits itself to deducing the meaning of the Community rules from the wording

---

[34] Case C–344/04 *R. on the application of IATA and ELFAA v. Department of Transport* [2006] ECR I–403, paras. 27–28; Case T–47/02 *Danzer and Danzer v. Council* [2006] ECR II–1779, paras. 36–37.

and spirit of the Treaty, it being left to the national court to apply in the particular case the rules which are thus interpreted. Such an attitude conforms with the function assigned to the Court of ensuring unity of interpretation of Community law within the six Member States. . . .

It is no less true that Article 177 always allows a national court, if it considers it desirable, to refer questions of interpretation to the Court again. This follows from Article 20 of the Statute of the Court of Justice, under which the procedure laid down for the settlement of preliminary questions is automatically set in motion as soon as such a question is referred by a national court.

The Court must, therefore, give a judgment on the present application.

The interpretation of Article 12 of the EEC Treaty, which is here requested, was given in the Court's judgment . . . in Case 26/62.

[*The Court then repeated the judgment it had given in the case of* Van Gend en Loos. *It continued as follows.*]

The questions of interpretation posed in this case are identical with those settled as above and no new factor has been presented to the Court.

In these circumstances the Tariefcommissie must be referred to the previous judgment.

The ECJ's approach appears clearly in this extract. The national court is still able, in formal terms, to refer a matter to the ECJ, even where the ECJ has ruled on the issue. However, it is clear that such an application must raise some new factor or argument. If it does not do so, then the Court will be strongly inclined to restate the substance of the earlier case. The existence of an earlier ruling can deprive the national court's obligation to refer 'of its purpose and thus empty it of its substance'. The *Da Costa* case, therefore, initiated what is in effect a system of precedent. These seeds have been developed by the ECJ in later cases:

Case 283/81 **Srl CILFIT and Lanificio di Gavardo SpA v. Ministry of Health**
[1982] ECR 3415

[Note ToA renumbering: Art. 177 is now Art. 234]

The plaintiffs alleged that certain duties imposed by Italian law were in breach of Regulation 827/68. The Italian Ministry of Health urged the Italian Court of Cassation, against whose decisions there was no judicial remedy under national law, not to refer the matter to the ECJ, because the answer to the question was so obvious as to remove the need for a reference. The Court of Cassation decided that this contention was itself an issue of Community law. It therefore requested a ruling from the ECJ on whether the obligation to refer imposed in Article 177(3), was unconditional, or whether it was premised on the existence of reasonable interpretive doubt about the answer which should be given to a question. The ECJ's response to the *acte clair* point will be examined in detail below. The ECJ also gave guidance on the relevance of its prior decisions.

THE ECJ

8. In this connection, it is necessary to define the meaning for the purposes of Community law of the expression 'where any such question is raised' in order to determine the circumstances in which a national court or tribunal against whose decisions there is no judicial remedy under national law is obliged to bring a matter before the Court of Justice.

9. In this regard, it must in the first place be pointed out that Article 177 does not constitute a means of redress available to the parties to a case pending before a national court or tribunal. Therefore the mere fact that a party contends that the dispute gives rise to a question concerning the interpretation of Community law does not mean that the court or tribunal concerned is compelled to consider that a question has been raised within the meaning of Article 177. On the other hand, a national court or tribunal may, in an appropriate case, refer a matter to the Court of Justice of its own motion.

10. Secondly, it follows from the relationship between paragraphs (2) and (3) of Article 177 that the courts or tribunals referred to in paragraph (3) have the same discretion as any other national court or tribunal to ascertain whether a decision on a question of Community law is necessary to enable them to give judgment. Accordingly, those courts or tribunals are not obliged to refer to the Court of Justice a question concerning the interpretation of Community law raised before them if that question is not relevant, that is to say, if the answer to that question, regardless of what it may be, can in no way affect the outcome of the case.

11. If, however, those courts or tribunals consider that recourse to Community law is necessary to decide a case, Article 177 imposes an obligation on them to refer to the Court of Justice any question of interpretation which may arise.

12. The question submitted by the Corte di Cassazione seeks to ascertain whether, in certain circumstances, the obligation laid down by paragraph (3) of Article 177 might none the less be subject to certain restrictions.

13. It must be remembered in this connection that in … *Da Costa* the Court ruled that: 'Although paragraph (3) of Article 177 unreservedly requires courts or tribunals of a Member State against whose decision there is no judicial remedy under national law … to refer to the Court every question of interpretation raised before them, the authority of an interpretation under Article 177 already given by the Court may deprive the obligation of its purpose and thus empty it of its substance. Such is the case especially when the question raised is materially identical with a question which has already been the subject of a preliminary ruling in a similar case.'

14. The same effect, as regards the limits set to the obligation laid down by paragraph (3) of Article 177, may be produced where previous decisions of the Court have already dealt with the point of law in question, irrespective of the nature of the proceedings which led to those decisions, even though the questions at issue are not strictly identical.

15. However, it must not be forgotten that in all such circumstances national courts and tribunals, including those referred to in paragraph (3) of Article 177, remain entirely at liberty to bring a matter before the Court of Justice if they consider it appropriate to do so.

A previous ruling can therefore be relied on even if it did not emerge from the same type of proceedings, and even though the questions at issue were not strictly identical. Provided that the point of law has already been determined by the ECJ, it can be relied on by a national court in a later case, thereby obviating the need for a reference, subject to the qualification in paragraph 15. The national courts were encouraged to rely on the ECJ's prior rulings where the substance of the legal point had already been adjudicated. Those earlier ECJ rulings became, in that sense, precedents for the national courts.

(ii) *Prior ECJ Rulings and the Validity of Community Legislation*

The cases discussed thus far concerned the impact of an earlier ECJ ruling when Member State action has been alleged to violate the Treaty. The ECJ has been even more forceful when the impact of its previous decisions on the validity of Community legislation has been in issue. This is exemplified by the *ICC* case:

Case 66/80 International Chemical Corporation v. Amministrazione delle Finanze dello Stato
[1981] ECR 1191

Council Regulation 563/76 was designed to reduce stocks of skimmed-milk powder. It made the grant of Community aid dependent on proof that the recipient had purchased a certain quantity of such skimmed milk held by an intervention agency. Compliance with this obligation was secured, *inter alia*, by the payment of security that was forfeited if the skimmed-milk was not bought. The plaintiff received the Community aid and paid the security, but did not buy the skimmed milk powder, and hence the national intervention agency did not release the security. In an earlier case the ECJ had found that Regulation 563/76 was invalid, because the price at which the milk powder was to be bought was regarded as disproportionately high.[35] The plaintiff, therefore, took the view that the security could not be forfeited, since it only served to ensure compliance with an obligation (to buy the milk powder), which was invalid. The Italian court requested a ruling on whether the earlier judgment, holding the regulation to be null and void, was effective in any subsequent litigation, or whether such a finding was only of relevance in relation to the court which had originally sought the ruling.

THE ECJ

11. The main purpose of the powers accorded to the Court by Article 177 is to ensure that Community law is applied uniformly by national courts. Uniform application of Community law is imperative not only when a national court is faced with a rule of Community law the meaning and scope of which is to be defined; it is just as imperative when the Court is confronted by a dispute as to the validity of an act of the institutions.

12. When the Court is moved under Article 177 to declare an act of one of the institutions to be void there are particularly imperative requirements concerning legal certainty in addition to those concerning the uniform application of Community law. It follows from the very nature of such a declaration that a national court may not apply the act declared to be void without once more creating serious uncertainty as to the Community law applicable.

13. It follows therefrom that although a judgment of the Court given under Article 177 of the Treaty declaring an act of an institution, in particular a Council or Commission regulation, to be void is directly addressed only to the national court which brought the matter before the Court, it is sufficient reason for any other national court to regard that act as void for the purposes of a judgment which it has to give.

14. That assertion does not however mean that national courts are deprived of the power given to them by Article 177 . . . and it rests with those courts to decide whether there is a need to raise once again a question which has already been settled by the Court where the Court has previously declared an act of a Community institution to be void. There may be such a need in particular if questions arise as to the grounds, the scope and possibly the consequences of the invalidity established earlier.

15. If that is not the case national courts are entirely justified in determining the effect on the cases brought before them of a judgment declaring an act void given by the Court in an action between other parties.

---

[35] See Case 116/76 *Granaria* v. *Hoofdproduktschap voor Akkerbouwprodukten* [1977] ECR 1247.

16. It should further be observed, as the Court acknowledged in its judgments ... in Joined Cases 117/76 and 16/77, *Ruckdeschel and Diamalt*,[36] and Joined Cases 124/76 and 20/77, *Moulins de Pont-à-Mousson and Providence Agricole*,[37] that as those responsible for drafting regulations declared to be void the Council or the Commission are bound to determine from the Court's judgment the effect of that judgment.

17. In the light of the foregoing considerations and in view of the fact that by its second question the national court has asked, as it was free to do, whether Regulation 563/76 was void, the answer should be that that is in fact the case for the reasons already stated in the judgments of 5 July 1977.

The *ICC* case provides further evidence of the ECJ's approach to precedent. The national court has discretion to refer a matter to the Court, even if the latter has already given judgment. However, the ECJ makes it patently clear that, although such a judgment is addressed primarily to the court which requested the original ruling, it should be relied on by other national courts before which the matter arises. The original ruling will, in this sense, have a multilateral and not merely a bilateral effect. A decision of the ECJ will, therefore, have a precedential impact on all national courts within the Community.

While an ECJ ruling on the validity of a Community regulation will have an *erga omnes* effect, the Court has made it clear that national courts cannot themselves find a Community norm to be invalid.

Case 314/85 **Firma Foto-Frost v. Hauptzollamt Lübeck-Ost**
[1987] ECR 4199[38]

A national court inquired whether it had the power to declare invalid a Commission decision, on the ground that it was in breach of a Community regulation on a certain issue.

THE ECJ

13. In enabling national courts against whose decisions there is a judicial remedy under national law to refer to the Court for a preliminary ruling questions on interpretation or validity, Article 177 did not settle the question whether those courts themselves may declare that acts of Community institutions are invalid.

14. Those courts may consider the validity of a Community act and, if they consider that the grounds put forward before them by the parties in support of invalidity are unfounded, they may reject them, concluding that the measure is completely valid. By taking that action they are not calling the existence of the Community measure into question.

15. On the other hand, those courts do not have the power to declare acts of the Community institutions invalid. As the Court emphasised in the judgment ... (Case 66/80, *International Chemical Corporation* ...), the main purpose of the powers accorded to the Court by Article 177 is to ensure that Community law is applied uniformly by national courts. That requirement of uniformity is particularly imperative when the validity of a Community act is in

---

[36] [1977] ECR 1753.

[37] [1977] ECR 1795.

[38] See also Case C–27/95 *Woodspring DC* v. *Bakers of Nailsea Ltd.* [1997] ECR I–1847; Case C–461/03 *Gaston Schul Douane-expediteur BV* v. *Minister van Landbouw, Natuur en Voedselkwalitiet* [2005] ECR I–10513, paras. 15–25; Case C–344/04 *IATA*, n. 34 above, paras. 27–32.

question. Divergences between courts in the Member States as to the validity of Community acts would be liable to place in jeopardy the very unity of the Community legal order and detract from the fundamental requirement of legal certainty.

. . .

17. Since Article 173 gives the Court exclusive jurisdiction to declare void an act of a Community institution, the coherence of the system requires that where the validity of a Community act is challenged before a national court the power to declare the act invalid must also be reserved to the Court of Justice.

18. It must also be emphasised that the Court of Justice is in the best position to decide on the validity of Community acts. Under Article 20 of the Protocol on the Statute of the Court of Justice of the EEC, Community institutions whose acts are challenged are entitled to participate in the proceedings in order to defend the validity of the acts in question. Furthermore, under the second paragraph of Article 21 of that Protocol the Court may require the Member States and institutions which are not participating in the proceedings to supply all information which it considers necessary for the purpose of the case before it. . . .

19. It should be added that the rule that national courts may not themselves declare Community acts to be invalid may have to be qualified in certain circumstances in the case of proceedings relating to an application for interim measures; however, that case is not referred to in the national court's question.

20. The answer to the first question must therefore be that national courts have no jurisdiction to declare that acts of Community institutions are invalid.

The ECJ, in *Atlanta*,[39] provided guidance on the issue of interim relief raised in paragraph 19. Where a national measure is challenged because of the alleged invalidity of the EC regulation on which it was based, the national court can grant interim relief. Certain conditions must however be met. The national court must have serious doubts about the validity of the EC measure, and must have referred the measure to the ECJ for a ruling. The interim relief must be necessary to prevent serious and irreparable damage to the applicant. The national court must take due account of the Community interest.[40] It must moreover respect any decision of the ECJ or CFI already given on the substance of the disputed measure.

(iii) *Prior Rulings and Legal Certainty*

The discussion thus far has been concerned with the effect of a prior ruling of the Community Courts for national courts. It is, as we have seen, for the national court to apply that prior ruling. The ECJ does not however delve into the national legal system and determine the validity of national law. It gives an interpretation of the compatibility of national law with EC law, and it is then for the national court to apply that interpretation within its legal system. The general principle is that the ECJ's ruling establishes the law from the time that it entered into force, and should therefore be applied to legal relationships before the ruling was given. This can however lead to difficulties concerning legal certainty.[41]

---

[39] Case C–465/93 *Atlanta Fruchthandelsgesellschaft mbH* v. *Bundesamt für Ernährung und Forstwirtschaft* [1995] ECR I–3761; Cases C–143/88 and 92/89 *Zuckerfabrik Süderdithmarschen AG* v. *Hauptzollamt Itzehoe* [1991] ECR I–415; Case C–334/95 *Kruger GmbH & Co. KG* v. *Hauptzollamt Hamburg-Jonas* [1997] ECR I–4517.

[40] By considering whether, e.g., the EC measure would be deprived of all effectiveness if it were not implemented immediately.

[41] J. Komarek, 'Federal Elements in the Community Judicial System: Building Coherence in the Community Legal System' (2005) 42 *CMLRev.* 9; R. Caranta (2005) 42 *CMLRev.* 179. Compare Case C–234/04 *Kapferer* v. *Schlanck & Schick GmbH* [2006] ECR I–2585; Cases C–392 and 422/04 *i-21 Germany GmbH and Arcor & Co. KG* v. *Germany* [2006] ECR I–8559.

Case C–453/00 **Kühne & Heitz NV v. Produktschap voor Pluimvee en Eieren**
[2004] ECR I–837

The applicants were exporters of poultry meat to non-member countries. The product was originally classified under one heading of the common customs tariff, on the basis of which the applicants were paid certain export refunds. The Dutch customs authorities then decided that the product should fall under a different classification and demanded reimbursement of the export refunds. The applicants appealed that decision to a Dutch court, which dismissed the appeal. The applicants did not request a preliminary ruling on the matter. In a subsequent decision involving different parties the ECJ made it clear that the re-classification of the product by the Dutch customs authorities was erroneous. The applicants then sought reimbursement of the refunds that they would have received if the Dutch authorities had classified the goods correctly. Under Dutch law administrative bodies could, in principle, reopen a final decision, and could in certain circumstances withdraw the decision. However under Dutch law the finality of an administrative decision would not normally be affected by subsequent judicial decisions, since that could seriously impair legal certainty and give rise to administrative chaos. The ECJ reiterated the general principle that a ruling under Article 234 established the law as it should be understood from the time it entered into force, and that therefore this should be applied by an administrative body to legal relationships before the ruling was given. The issue was whether this should be applied even where the administrative decision had become final.

THE ECJ

24. Legal certainty is one of a number of general principles recognised by Community law. Finality of an administrative decision ... contributes to such legal certainty and it follows that Community law does not require that administrative bodies be placed under an obligation, in principle to reopen an administrative decision which has become final in that way.
[*The ECJ then noted that under Dutch law administrative decisions could, subject to certain conditions, be reopened.*]
26. [T]he circumstances of the main case are the following. First, national law confers on the administrative body competence to reopen the decision ... which has become final. Second, that decision became final only as a result of a judgment of a national court against whose decisions there is no judicial remedy. Third, that judgment was based on an interpretation of Community law which, in the light of a subsequent judgment of the Court, was incorrect and which was adopted without a question being referred to the Court for a preliminary ruling in accordance with the conditions provided for in the third paragraph of Article 234 EC. Fourth, the person concerned complained to the administrative body immediately after becoming aware of that judgment of the Court.
27. In such circumstances, the administrative body concerned is, in accordance with the principle of cooperation arising under Article 10 EC, under an obligation to review that decision in order to take account of the interpretation of the relevant provisions of Community law given in the meantime by the Court. The administrative body will have to determine on the basis of the outcome of that review to what extent it is under an obligation to reopen, without adversely affecting the interests of third parties, the decision in question.

(iv) *Conclusion*

The development of precedent charted above has implications for the relationship between national courts and the ECJ. It modifies the original conception of a horizontal and bilateral relationship. In so far as ECJ rulings have precedential value, they place the Court in a superior position to the national courts. The very existence of a system of precedent is indicative of a shift to a vertical hierarchy between the ECJ and national courts: the ECJ will lay down the legally authoritative interpretation, which will then be adopted by national courts. The creation of precedent serves also to render that relationship less bilateral, and more multilateral, since an earlier ECJ ruling can be relied on by any national court faced with the point of law that has already been decided by the ECJ.

The importance attached to earlier rulings is both reflected in and reinforced by Article 104(3) of the Rules of Procedure,[42] which allows the ECJ to give its decision by reasoned order referring to a previous decision or earlier case law, where a question referred is identical to one that has already been answered or where the answer to the question can be clearly deduced from prior case law. Thus if the national court does refer where there is an existing precedent the ECJ may well give judgment by reasoned order that reiterates its previous ruling.

(b) THE 'ACTE CLAIR' DOCTRINE

A national court may feel that the answer to the issue is so clear that no reference to the ECJ is required. National courts have, in the past, refused to make a reference for this reason.[43] The conditions in which this is legitimate were considered in *CILFIT*:

Case 283/81 Srl CILFIT and Lanificio di Gavardo SpA v. Ministry of Health
[1982] ECR 3415

[Note ToA renumbering: Art. 177(3) is now Art. 234(3)]

The facts were set out above. Where a precedent exists, then the relationship between the ECJ and the national court is as set out in the preceding section. The *acte clair* doctrine may however apply where there is no prior ECJ decision on the point. The extract follows on immediately from that given above.

THE ECJ

16. Finally, the correct application of Community law may be so obvious as to leave no scope for any reasonable doubt as to the manner in which the question raised is to be resolved. Before it comes to the conclusion that such is the case, the national court or tribunal must be convinced that the matter is equally obvious to the courts of the other Member States and to the Court of Justice. Only if those conditions are satisfied may the national court or tribunal refrain from submitting the question to the Court of Justice and take upon itself the responsibility for resolving it.

17. However, the existence of such a possibility must be assessed on the basis of the characteristic feature of Community law and the particular difficulties to which its interpretation gives rise.

---

[42] Rules of Procedure of the Court of Justice, 1 Dec. 2005, available at www.curia.europa.eu/en/instit/txtdocfr/index.htm.
[43] See, e.g., *Re Société des Pétroles Shell-Berre* [1964] CMLR 462.

18. To begin with, it must be borne in mind that Community legislation is drafted in several languages and that the different language versions are equally authentic. An interpretation of a provision of Community law thus involves a comparison of the different language versions.

19. It must also be borne in mind, even where the different language versions are entirely in accord with one another, that Community law uses terminology which is peculiar to it. Furthermore, it must be emphasised that legal concepts do not necessarily have the same meaning in Community law and in the law of the various Member States.

20. Finally, every provision of Community law must be placed in its context and interpreted in the light of the provisions of Community law as a whole, regard being had to the objectives thereof and to its state of evolution at the date on which the provision in question is to be applied.

21. In the light of all those considerations, the answer to the question submitted . . . must be that paragraph (3) of Article 177 of the EEC Treaty is to be interpreted as meaning that a court or tribunal against whose decisions there is no judicial remedy under national law is required, where a question of Community law is raised before it, to comply with its obligation to bring the matter before the Court of Justice, unless it has established that the question raised is irrelevant or that the Community provision in question has already been interpreted by the Court or that the correct application of Community law is so obvious as to leave no scope for any reasonable doubt. The existence of such a possibility must be assessed in the light of the specific characteristics of Community law, the particular difficulties to which its interpretation gives rise and the risk of divergences in judicial decisions within the Community.

The implications of *CILFIT* were considered by a number of commentators. References to Article 177 should now be read as to Article 234.

G.F. Mancini and D.T. Keeling, From *CILFIT* to *ERT*: The Constitutional Challenge Facing the European Court[44]

The correct analysis of *CILFIT* was given by a Danish scholar, Professor Hjalte Rasmussen,[45] who maintains that the judgment was based on an astute strategy of 'give and take'. The Court, recognizing that it could not in any case coerce the national courts into accepting its jurisdiction, concedes something—a great deal in fact, nothing less than the right not to refer if the Community measure is clear—to the professional or national pride of the municipal judge, but then . . . restricts the circumstances in which the clarity of the provision may legitimately be sustained to cases so rare that the nucleus of its own authority is preserved intact (or rather consolidated because it voluntarily divested itself of a part of its exclusive jurisdiction). The objective of the Court is plain: by granting supreme courts the power to do lawfully that which they could in any case do unlawfully, but by subjecting that power to stringent conditions, the Court hoped to induce the supreme courts to use willingly the 'mechanism for judicial cooperation' provided by the Treaty. The result is to eliminate sterile and damaging conflicts and to reduce the risk that Community law might be the subject of divergent interpretations.

Mancini and Keeling therefore saw *CILFIT* as a necessary dialogue between the ECJ and the national courts, with the intent being to rein in the latter. The 'give and take' of *CILFIT*

[44] N. 1 above, 4.
[45] H. Rasmussen, 'The European Court's *Acte Clair* Strategy in *CILFIT*' (1984) 9 *ELRev.* 242.

involved the ECJ accepting the *acte clair* doctrine in principle, but placing significant constraints on its exercise in the hope that national courts would play the game and refuse to refer only when matters really were unequivocally clear.

Some writers were however more sceptical as to whether the conditions laid down in *CILFIT* really did curb the discretion of national courts.

A. Arnull, The Use and Abuse of Article 177[46]

The effect of the *CILFIT* decision, it was argued,[47] would be to enable national judges to justify any reluctance they might feel to ask for a preliminary ruling by reference to a decision of the European Court. Of the factors to be borne in mind by national courts before they concluded that the meaning of a provision of Community law was clear, only the requirement that the different language versions be compared, it was submitted, had any teeth. However, even this requirement was less onerous than it seemed, as comparison of the different language versions would usually be carried out by reference to the version in the judge's own tongue.

[*Arnull examined the practice of the United Kingdom courts that had cited the* CILFIT *decision. He concluded in the following vein.*[48]]

The English cases in which *CILFIT* has been cited and a reference made seem to support Rasmussen's view that the effect of that decision, despite appearances to the contrary, would be to make national courts wary of deciding points of Community law for themselves. However, the English cases where *CILFIT* was mentioned but no reference made show that sometimes the outcome of that ruling has been far less beneficial. They illustrate how it can be used to justify refusing to make a reference where the national court has formed a view as to how the points of Community law at issue should be resolved. Courts in the United Kingdom make far fewer references than courts in other Member States of comparable size.... It is therefore a serious matter when a decision of the European Court is used by the English Courts as a reason for failing to take a step which it might otherwise have been more difficult to avoid.

Others have however argued that the conditions in *CILFIT* are too restrictive, and that more discretion should be left to national courts. Thus Advocate General Jacobs argued that national judges should not have to consider all the official language versions of Community acts.[49] Rasmussen has also advocated relaxation of the *CILFIT* conditions.

H. Rasmussen, Remedying the Crumbling EC Judicial System[50]

The thrust of a *CILFIT II* should be to give the initiative back to the judges of the Member States, trusting them to solve on their own far more questions of interpretation of Community law, including those which are not straightforward. In technical terms, a *CILFIT II* should operate

---

[46] (1989) 52 *MLR* 622, 626.

[47] Arnull is referring to an earlier piece, 'Reflections on Judicial Attitudes at the European Court' (1985) 34 *ICLQ* 168, 172.

[48] N. 46 above, 636–637.

[49] Case C–338/95 *Wiener v. Hauptzollamt Emmerich* [1997] ECR I–6495.

[50] (2000) 37 *CMLRev.* 1071, 1109.

so as to enlarge considerably the scope of the Community acts which are deemed to be *actes clairs*. The job to pin down on paper the demarcation line between those cases which will deserve EC judicial attention ... and those classes of cases which the national judges ought to decide on their own responsibility will not be an easy one, but it is as indispensable as difficult.

Current indications are however that the ECJ is content with the formulation in *CILFIT* and shows no inclination to modify the ruling to any significant degree.[51] It is true that in *Intermodal*[52] the ECJ declined to extend the *CILFIT* conditions, holding that a national court was not required to ensure that the matter was equally obvious to bodies of a non-judicial nature, such as administrative authorities. Subject to that caveat, the ECJ reaffirmed the *CILFIT* condition that before declining to refer a national court must be convinced that the matter was so obvious that there was no scope for any reasonable doubt about the way in which the question should be resolved, and more especially that the matter was equally obvious to other national courts and to the ECJ.[53]

(c) PRECEDENT, *ACTE CLAIR*, SECTORAL DELEGATION, AND THE DEVELOPMENT OF A COMMUNITY JUDICIAL SYSTEM

Opinions may well differ on the rationale for, and success of, the *CILFIT* strategy. The doctrine of precedent, the *acte clair* concept, and sectoral delegation of functions to national courts do, however, have broader ramifications for the development of the Community judicial system

(i) *Precedent*

Let us begin by considering precedent. The *Da Costa* decision was a rational step for the ECJ to have taken. Rasmussen correctly pointed out that the authority of the Court's decisions was thereby enhanced, since they became authoritative rulings for national courts.[54] The relationship between national courts and the ECJ was altered. It was no longer bilateral, where rulings were of relevance only to the national court which requested them. It became multilateral, in the sense that ECJ rulings had an impact on all national courts. The decision in *CILFIT* to reinforce precedent was similarly significant: the ECJ's rulings were to be authoritative in situations where the point of law was the same, even though the questions posed in earlier cases were different, and even though the types of proceeding in which the issue arose differed.

It should moreover be recognized that the development of precedent was largely inevitable. The original bilateral conception of the relationship between the ECJ and national courts, whereby the ECJ's rulings were relevant only for the national court which requested them, was unrealistic. Taken literally it would have meant that a ruling would have to be given, even if the inquiry sought by a national court replicated that in an earlier case that had already been decided by the ECJ. The Court would be 'forced' solemnly to hear the matter, only to reach the

---

[51] Case C–461/03 *Gaston Schul*, n. 38 above, para. 16; Case T–47/02 *Danzer*, n. 34 above, para. 36.
[52] Case 495/03 *Intermodal Transports BV* v. *Staatssecretaris van Financien* [2005] ECR I–8151, para. 39.
[53] *Ibid.*, paras. 38–39.
[54] N. 45 above.

same conclusion as it had done previously. A judicial system could not be supposed to exist on such terms. The ECJ would quickly tire of the waste of time and resources. The national courts would not see the sense of a system which placed pressure on them to allow issues to be litigated again, where the ECJ had already given a considered judgment.

It is true that the regime of precedent means that a national court might misinterpret past ECJ authority. This does not however undermine the rationality of the precedent system, since it leads in aggregate to a more effective regime of Community law. A system of precedent inevitably entails certain 'error costs': the possibility of mistakes by national courts. Precedent does, however, also have substantial 'benefits'. Most fundamentally, national courts become enforcers of Community law in their own right. When the ECJ has decided an issue, national courts apply that ruling without further resort to the ECJ. The national courts are, in this sense, 'enrolled' as part of a network of courts adjudicating on Community law, with the ECJ at the apex of that network. They become 'delegates' in the enforcement of EC law, and part of a broader Community judicial hierarchy. The costs of precedent must therefore be weighed against the benefits. These include the increased volume of Community law which can be litigated, mostly correctly, at any one time, and also the important symbolic advantage which flows from the recognition that the national courts are part of a Community judicial hierarchy. It is therefore unsurprising that the ECJ should have stated in its report for the 1996 IGC that 'national courts are called upon to play a central role as courts with general jurisdiction for Community law'.[55] It should be noted that a study found a high rate of national implementation of ECJ rulings, 96.3 per cent.[56]

(ii) Acte Clair

Let us now move to *acte clair*. The Court in *CILFIT* had a choice. It could have rejected the *acte clair* doctrine in EC law, the view espoused by Advocate General Capotorti.[57] The Court declined to follow this approach, and instead gave the doctrine limited support. Now it might be contended, as seen above, that the real objective was to deal it a death-blow by hedging it around with restrictions or, more moderately, to convince national courts to be responsible when using *acte clair*.

We should, however, distinguish purpose and effect. Even accepting the Mancini/Keeling thesis as to the Court's purpose, the effect is to leave 'clear' cases that fall within these conditions to the national courts. For such cases, the national courts operate once again as the delegates of the ECJ for the application of Community law. The ECJ itself can then utilize its time in resolving more problematic cases. The conditions in *CILFIT* help to ensure that national courts will not readily regard cases as *acte clair* unless they really are free from interpretive doubt, although it is doubtless true that national courts can interpret these conditions rather differently.[58]

The qualified approval given to the concept can nonetheless be regarded as rational, since the cost/benefit analysis discussed in the context of precedent applies equally here. The fact that a national court might, on occasion, misapply the criteria, intentionally or unintentionally, does not render the exercise a failure. These costs have to be balanced against the

---

[55] N. 3 above, para. 15.

[56] S. Nyikos, 'The Preliminary Reference Process: National Court Implementation, Changing Opportunity Structures and Litigant Desistment' (2003) 4 *EUP* 397.

[57] [1982] ECR 3415, 3439.

[58] Tridimas, n. 23 above, 41–44.

benefits: straightforward cases can be disposed of expeditiously by national courts. Moreover, this method of dealing with such cases further emphasizes the role of national courts as but part of a broader judicial hierarchy, with the ECJ at the apex.

There are moreover 'safety' devices built into the system, independently of the conditions in *CILFIT*, so the danger of incorrect constructions made by national courts becoming embedded should not be over-stated. The concern is that a national court might refuse to make a reference, even though the conditions in *CILFIT* were not met. A national court minded to do this intentionally would however now be aware of the possibility of damages liability pursuant to *Kobler*.[59] There is the further possibility that the Member State might be subject to an enforcement action under Article 226.[60] In any event, the matter might still come before the ECJ via a different court from the same legal system, or from a different legal system. It would also be open to the ECJ to correct aberrant interpretations by national courts, in the context of a case on a related point that had come before it, although the implications of this for prior decisions at national level would be subject to *Kühne*.[61]

(iii) *Sectoral Delegation*

This discussion would be incomplete if it did not take into account what is in effect *sectoral delegation of responsibility* to national courts: a conscious choice made by the Community to devolve certain application and enforcement functions to the national courts, as occurred in the context of competition policy.[62]

The rationale for this devolution was instructive. Prior to recent reforms, the Commission was charged with the initial role in the enforcement of competition policy. It did not however possess the resources necessary for this task and therefore called on the national courts. These always played a role in the enforcement of competition law, but this was consciously generalized, so that straightforward competition violations could be dealt with at national level, thereby allowing the Commission and Community Courts to deal with more difficult cases, or those which raised new issues of principle. Such sectoral delegation was facilitated because of the accumulated weight of Community precedent.

(d) SUMMARY

i.   The relationship between national courts and the ECJ has been transformed by the development of precedent, *acte clair*, and sectoral delegation of responsibility.

ii. These developments have made national courts Community Courts in their own right. They can dispose of cases without the need for a further reference to the ECJ. They can do so where there is a Community precedent on the point, where the matter is so clear as to obviate the need for a reference, or where more general responsibility has been delegated to them in a particular area.

iii. The combined effect has been to render the relationship more vertical and multilateral than it was at the inception of the Community.

---

[59] Case C–224/01 *Kobler* v. *Austria* [2003] ECR I–10239.
[60] The Commission issued a reasoned opinion in relation to Sweden in this respect, C(2004)3899.
[61] See above, 473.
[62] See Ch. 25 below.

5. THE DECISION TO REFER: THE NATIONAL COURT'S PERSPECTIVE

The discussion thus far has touched on factors which can influence the national court's decision whether to refer: the existence of an ECJ judgment, and the *acte clair* doctrine. We now consider the more general factors that a national court may take into account when making the decision whether to refer.

There are two criteria that must be satisfied before a reference may be made. The first is that the question must be raised before a court or tribunal of the Member State. However, it has been seen that the *CILFIT* case held that a national court may raise a matter of its own motion, even if this has not been done by the parties.[63] The second general criterion is that the national court must consider that a decision on the question is necessary to enable it to give judgment. *CILFIT* makes it clear that even a national court of last resort must believe that this is so before it is obliged to make a reference. It should also be noted that Article 234 does not provide that the reference must be necessary, but that a decision on the question be necessary to enable the national court to give judgment. The danger of confusing these two issues is brought out in the *Bulmer* case.

The *Bulmer* case shows the *early approach* of the UK courts to the exercise of the discretion accorded to them.

H.P. Bulmer Ltd. v. J. Bollinger SA
[1974] 2 WLR 202

Bollinger made champagne and claimed that the use of the word champagne by makers of cider, in the form of champagne cider, should be prohibited. Bollinger alleged that the use of the word champagne to describe products other than those which came from the Champagne region in France was contrary to Community law. Bollinger asked that this question of Community law should be referred to the ECJ. The judge at first instance refused to make the reference, and Bollinger appealed to the Court of Appeal. Lord Denning emphasized that the discretion whether to refer was for the national court and that it should only do so where the decision on the question was necessary to enable it to give judgment. A reference might not be necessary where there was an existing ECJ judgment on the point or where the matter was *acte clair*.

COURT OF APPEAL: LORD DENNING MR

(2) Guidelines as to the exercise of discretion. Assuming that the condition about 'necessary' is fulfilled, there remains the matter of discretion. . . .

  (i)   The time to get a ruling. The length of time . . . before a ruling can be obtained from the European Court. This may take months and months. . . . Meanwhile, the whole action in the English court is stayed until the ruling is obtained. This may be very unfortunate, especially in a case where an injunction is sought or there are other reasons for expedition. . . .

  (ii) Do not overload the Court. The importance of not overloading the European Court by references to it. If it were overloaded, it could not get through its work. . . .

---

[63] See also nn. 31, 32 above.

(iii) Formulate the question clearly. The need to formulate the question clearly. It must be a question of interpretation only of the Treaty. It must not be mixed up with the facts. . . .

(iv) Difficulty and importance. The difficulty and importance of the point. Unless the point is really difficult and important, it would seem better for the English judge to decide it himself. For in so doing, much delay and expense will be saved. . . .

(v) Expense. The expense of getting a ruling from the European Court. . . .

(vi) Wishes of the parties. The wishes of the parties. If both parties want the point referred . . . the English court should have regard to their wishes, but it should not give them undue weight. The English court should hesitate before making a reference against the wishes of one of the parties, seeing the expense and delay which it involves.

Lord Denning MR decided on the facts that a reference was not needed for a number of reasons.[64] The judgment was not uncontroversial and the guidelines were criticized. Thus Francis Jacobs argued that there were many situations where time and costs would be saved by an early reference and that cases raising important points of EC law could arise where there was little at stake between the parties.[65]

The *Samex* case is more indicative of the *current approach* of the UK courts, which are more ready to refer.

Customs and Excise Commissioners v. ApS Samex (Hanil Fiber Industrial Co. Ltd., third party)
[1983] 1 All ER 1042

An EC regulation allowed Member States to impose quantitative limits on the import of textiles from certain countries outside the EC. The implementation of the import scheme was left to the Member States, who were to issue import licences up to the quota for each year. The defendant made a contract to buy goods from a non-Member State, which stipulated that the goods had to be shipped by a certain date. The Customs authorities discovered that the goods had been shipped outside the relevant dates, and imposed penalties on the defendant. The latter responded by arguing that the Customs authorities were in breach of the Community regulation, and sought a reference to the ECJ. Bingham J considered the guidelines set out by Lord Denning MR in *Bulmer*. He then continued as follows.

HIGH COURT: BINGHAM J

Sitting as a judge in a national court, asked to decide questions of Community law, I am very conscious of the advantages enjoyed by the Court of Justice. It has a panoramic view of the Community and its institutions, a detailed knowledge of the treaties and of much subordinate legislation made under them, and an intimate familiarity with the functioning of the Common Market which no national judge denied the collective experience of the Court of Justice could hope to achieve. Where questions of administrative intention and practice arise the Court of Justice can receive submissions from the Community institutions, as also where relations between the Community and non-Member States are in issue. Where the interests of Member States are affected they can intervene to make their views known. . . .

---

[64] The time and expense involved; the facts had not been fully found; and the point was not a difficult one [1974] 3 WLR 202, 216–217.

[65] F.G. Jacobs, 'When to Refer to the European Court' (1974) 90 *LQR* 486, 492.

Where comparison falls to be made between Community texts in different languages, all texts being equally authentic, the multinational Court of Justice is equipped to carry out the task in a way which no national judge, whatever his linguistic skills, could rival. The interpretation of Community instruments involves very often not the process familiar to common lawyers of laboriously extracting the meaning from words used but the more creative process of supplying flesh to a spare and loosely constructed skeleton. The choice between alternative submissions may turn not on purely legal considerations, but on a broader view of what the orderly development of the Community requires. These are matters which the Court of Justice is very much better placed to assess and determine than a national court.

While UK courts sometimes still refer to the guidelines in *Bulmer* they also tend to be more ready to make a reference. Sir Thomas Bingham MR encapsulates the more modern approach.[66]

[I]f the facts have been found and the Community law issue is critical to the court's final decision, the appropriate course is to refer the issue to the Court of Justice unless the national court can with complete confidence resolve the issue itself. In considering whether it can … the national court must be fully mindful of the differences between national and Community legislation, of the pitfalls which face a national court venturing into what may be an unfamiliar field, of the need for uniform interpretation throughout the Community and of the great advantages enjoyed by the Court of Justice in construing Community instruments. If the national court has any real doubt, it should obviously refer.

6. ACCEPTANCE OF THE REFERENCE: THE ECJ'S PERSPECTIVE

It will then be for the national court to decide whether to make a reference. We now turn to consider how the ECJ perceives its role when an issue is referred by a national court. It will be apparent that the ECJ's approach has altered since the inception of the Community.

(a) THE INITIAL APPROACH, COME ONE, COME ALL

The ECJ's initial approach was very liberal and it would, wherever possible, read the reference so as to preserve its ability to pass judgment on the case.

The ECJ was prepared to *correct improperly framed references*. Thus in *Costa* the ECJ stated that it had power to extract from a question imperfectly formulated by the national court, those questions which really did pertain to the interpretation of the Treaty.[67] This is also exemplified by the *Schwarze* case.

---

[66] *R. v. International Stock Exchange, ex p. Else* [1993] QB 534. See also *Polydor Ltd. v. Harlequin Record Shops Ltd.* [1980] 2 CMLR 413; *R. v. Plymouth Justices, ex p. Rogers* [1982] 3 WLR 1; *R. v. Pharmaceutical Society of Great Britain, ex p. The Association of Pharmaceutical Importers* [1987] 3 CMLR 951; *R. v. HM Treasury, ex p. Daily Mail and General Trust plc* [1987] 2 CMLR 1; *R. v. Secretary of State for the National Heritage, ex p. Continental Television BV* [1993] 2 CMLR 333; *R. v. Ministry of Agriculture, Fisheries and Food, ex p. Portman Agrochemicals Ltd.* [1994] 3 CMLR 18; *Beckmann v. Dynamco Whicheloe MacFarlane Ltd.* [2000] OPLR 245.

[67] Case 6/64 *Costa* v. *ENEL*, n. 28 above.

Case 16/65 **Firma C. Schwarze v. Einfuhr- und**
Vorratsstelle für Getreide und Futtermittel
[1965] ECR 877

[Note ToA renumbering: Arts. 173 and 177 are now Arts. 230 and 234]

Schwarze obtained import licences from the EVSt to import barley. The EVSt fixed the rate of levy which should be paid, pursuant to a Council regulation. The rate of levy was fixed on the basis of a Commission decision. Schwarze argued that the levy rate was too high, and that the Commission decision was illegal. The Finanzgericht therefore submitted a number of detailed questions to the ECJ. France argued that the questions being asked were concerned not with the interpretation of the Treaty, but rather with the validity of Community acts; and that the proper way of challenging such acts was via Article 173, and not via Article 177.

THE ECJ

It appears from the wording of the questions submitted that the Hessisches Finanzgericht is concerned not so much with the interpretation of the Treaty or of an act of a Community institution, as with a preliminary ruling on the validity of such an act under Article 177(1)(b). . . .

In its comments, the government of the French Republic complains that several of the questions submitted call for more than just an interpretation of the Treaty. The Court of Justice would, in answering these alleged questions of interpretation, actually be ruling on points involving not the interpretation of the Treaty but the validity of acts of the EEC institutions.

The contention of the French Republic that Article 177 cannot be used to obtain from the Court a ruling that such an act is null and void is pertinent. That provision does, however, expressly give the Court power to rule on the validity of such an act. Where it appears that the real object of the questions submitted by a national court is a review of the validity of Community acts rather than an interpretation thereof, the Court of Justice must nevertheless decide the questions immediately, instead of holding the referring court to a strict adherence to form which would only serve to prolong the Article 177 procedure and be incompatible with its true nature. Such a strict adherence to form is conceivable in actions between parties whose respective rights must be determined according to strict rules. It would not, however, be appropriate in the very special area of judicial cooperation provided for in Article 177, where the national court and the Court of Justice—each within its own jurisdiction and with the purpose of ensuring a uniform application of Community law—must together and directly contribute to the legal conclusions. Any other procedure would have the result of letting the national courts rule on the validity of acts of the Community.

The ECJ also *commonly rejected claims that a reference should not be accepted because of the reasons for making it, or the facts on which it was based.* The ECJ emphasized that these matters were the domain of the national court. Thus in *Costa* the ECJ stated that Article 234 'is based on a clear separation of functions between national courts and the Court of Justice'. The ECJ was not empowered to 'investigate the facts of the case or to criticise the grounds and purpose of the request for interpretation'.[68] Similarly in *Pierik*,[69] the ECJ reiterated that Article 234 was based on a clear division of function, which precluded it from judging the relevance of the

---

[68] *Ibid.*, 593.
[69] Case 117/77 *Bestuur van het Algemeen Ziekenfonds, Drenthe-Platteland* v. *G. Pierik* [1978] ECR 825.

questions asked, or from determining whether concepts of Community law really were applicable to the case before the national court. The ECJ stressed the point once again in *Simmenthal*,[70] stating that what is now Article 234 was based on a distinct separation of function between national courts and the ECJ, such that the latter did not have jurisdiction to take cognizance of the facts of the case or to criticize the reasons for the reference.

The ECJ's approach during the Community's early development was therefore an open and flexible one. It clearly did not wish to discourage litigants from having recourse to Community law, more especially because it was through Article 234 that the ECJ developed doctrines such as direct effect and supremacy. Nor did the ECJ wish to place obstacles in the path of national judiciaries by refusing to answer questions unless they were perfectly framed. This would not have encouraged national judges to make use of novel legal machinery.

(b) THE ECJ ASSERTS AUTHORITY OVER CASES REFERRED

It is clear, notwithstanding the cases considered above, that the ECJ regards itself as having the ultimate authority to decide whether a reference is warranted or not. The seminal case in this respect is *Foglia*.

Case 104/79 **Pasquale Foglia v. Mariella Novello**
[1980] ECR 745

[Note ToA renumbering: Arts. 95 and 177 are now Arts. 90 and 234]

Foglia made a contract to sell wine to Novello, and the contract stated that Novello would not be liable, *inter alia*, for any taxes levied by the French or Italian authorities which were contrary to EC law. The goods were carried by Danzas, a general transporter. The contract of carriage also contained a clause stipulating that Foglia would not be liable for charges which were contrary to EC law. Danzas in fact paid a French tax, and this was included in the bill submitted to Foglia, who paid the bill including the amount of the disputed tax, notwithstanding the clause in the contract of carriage which would have entitled him not to do so. Foglia then sought to recover this amount from Novello in an action before an Italian court. The latter refused to pay, relying on the clause in her contract with Foglia which stipulated that she would not be liable for any unlawful charge. Novello argued that the charge was contrary to Article 95. The Italian court sought a preliminary ruling whether the French tax was in fact contrary to Community law. The ECJ noted that the pleadings of Foglia and Novello concerning tax discrimination were essentially identical.

THE ECJ

10. It thus appears that the parties to the main action are concerned to obtain a ruling that the French tax system is invalid for liqueur wines by the expedient of proceedings before an Italian court between two private individuals who are in agreement as to the result to be attained and who have inserted a clause in their contract in order to induce the Italian court to give a ruling on the point. The artificial nature of this expedient is underlined by the fact that Danzas did not exercise its rights under French law to institute proceedings over the consumption tax although it

---

[70] Case 35/76 *Simmenthal SpA v. Ministero delle Finanze* [1976] ECR 1871, para. 4.

undoubtedly had an interest in doing so in view of the clause in the contract by which it was also bound and moreover of the fact that Foglia paid without protest that undertaking's bill which included a sum paid in respect of that tax.

11. The duty of the Court of Justice under Article 177 of the EEC Treaty is to supply all courts in the Community with the information on the interpretation of Community law which is necessary to enable them to settle genuine disputes which are brought before them. A situation in which the Court was obliged by the expedient of arrangements like those described above to give rulings would jeopardise the whole system of legal remedies available to private individuals to enable them to protect themselves against tax provisions which are contrary to the Treaty.

The ECJ therefore declined to give a ruling, but the Italian judge was undaunted and referred further questions to the ECJ. He asked, in effect, whether the preceding decision was consistent with the principle that it was for the national judge to determine the facts and the need for a reference.

Case 244/80 **Pasquale Foglia v. Mariella Novello (No. 2)**
[1981] ECR 3045

THE ECJ

12. In his first question the Pretore requested clarification of the limits of the power of appraisal reserved by the Treaty to the national court on the one hand and the Court of Justice on the other with regard to the wording of references for a preliminary ruling and of the appraisal of the circumstances of fact and law in the main action, in particular where the national court is requested to give a declaratory judgment.

...

14. With regard to the first question it should be recalled, as the Court of Justice has had occasion to emphasise in very varied contexts, that Article 177 is based on cooperation which entails a division of duties between the national courts and the Court of Justice in the interest of the proper application and uniform interpretation of Community law throughout all the Member States.

15. With this in view it is for the national court—by reason of the fact that it is seised of the substance of the dispute and that it must bear the responsibility for the decision to be taken— to assess, having regard to the facts of the case, the need to obtain a preliminary ruling to enable it to give judgment.

16. In exercising that power of appraisal the national court, in collaboration with the Court of Justice, fulfils a duty entrusted to them both of ensuring that in the interpretation and application of the Treaty the law is observed. Accordingly the problems which may be entailed in the exercise of its power of appraisal by the national court and the relations which it maintains within the framework of Article 177 with the Court of Justice are governed exclusively by the provisions of Community law.

17. In order that the Court of Justice may perform its task in accordance with the Treaty it is essential for national courts to explain, when the reasons do not emerge beyond any doubt from the file, why they consider that a reply to their question is necessary to enable them to give judgment.

18. It must in fact be emphasised that the duty assigned to the Court by Article 177 is not that of delivering advisory opinions on general or hypothetical questions but of assisting in the

administration of justice in the Member States. It accordingly does not have jurisdiction to reply to questions of interpretation which are submitted to it within the framework of procedural devices arranged by the parties in order to induce the Court to give its view on certain problems of Community law which do not correspond to an objective requirement inherent in the resolution of a dispute. A declaration by the Court that it has no jurisdiction in such circumstances does not in any way trespass upon the prerogatives of the national court but makes it possible to prevent the application of the procedure under Article 177 for purposes other than those appropriate for it.

19. Furthermore, it should be pointed out that, whilst the Court of Justice must be able to place as much reliance as possible upon the assessment by the national court of the extent to which the questions submitted to it are essential, it must be in a position to make any assessment inherent in the performance of its own duties in particular in order to check, as all courts must, whether it has jurisdiction. Thus the Court, taking into account the repercussions of its decisions in this matter, must have regard, in exercising the jurisdiction conferred upon it by Article 177, not only to the interests of the parties to the proceedings but also to those of the Community and of the Member States. Accordingly it cannot, without disregarding the duties assigned to it, remain indifferent to the assessments made by the courts of the Member States in the exceptional cases in which such assessments may affect the proper working of the procedure laid down by Article 177.

. . .

21. The reply to the first question must accordingly be that whilst, according to the intended role of Article 177, an assessment of the need to obtain an answer to the questions of interpretation raised, regard being had to the circumstances of fact and law involved in the main action, is a matter for the national court it is nevertheless for the Court of Justice, in order to confirm its own jurisdiction, to examine, where necessary, the conditions in which the case has been referred to it by the national court.

. . .

25. The reply to the fourth question must accordingly be that in the case of preliminary questions intended to permit the national court to determine whether provisions laid down by law or regulation in another Member State are in accordance with Community law the degree of legal protection may not differ according to whether such questions are raised in proceedings between individuals or in an action to which the State whose legislation is called in question is a party, but that in the first case the Court of Justice must take special care to ensure that the procedure under Article 177 is not employed for purposes which were not intended by the Treaty.

The important point of principle in *Foglia (No. 2)* was that the ECJ would be the ultimate decider of its own jurisdiction. The reasoning is both subtle and dramatic. The judgment begins in orthodox fashion in demarcating the roles of the national court and the ECJ. A few paragraphs later this was transformed: due regard was to be given to the view of the national court as to whether a response was required to a question, but the ultimate decision rested with the ECJ. If, in order to resolve this issue, further and better particulars were required from the national courts, then these must be forthcoming.

Foglia was therefore not simply about hypothetical cases. It was about the primacy of control over the Article 234 procedure, and the nature of the judicial hierarchy, involving Community and national courts, which operates through this Article. The original division of function between national courts and the ECJ may have been separate but equal, as manifested in the idea that the former decide whether to refer, while the latter gives the ruling on the matter placed before it. *Foglia* reshaped that conception. The ECJ was not simply to be a passive receptor, forced to adjudicate on whatever was placed before it. It would assert some control over the suitability of the reference. The decision in the case, concerning the allegedly hypothetical nature of the proceedings, was simply one manifestation of this assertion of jurisdictional control. The ECJ would, in the future, 'make any assessment inherent in the performance of its own duties in particular in order to check, as all courts must, whether it has jurisdiction' (paragraph 19).

The *Foglia* case generated much comment. Bebr argued against the ruling. References to Article 177 should now be read as to Article 234.

G. Bebr, The Existence of a Genuine Dispute: An Indispensable Precondition for the Jurisdiction of the Court under Article 177 EEC Treaty?[71]

In its well-established case law the Court of Justice has always viewed Article 177 as establishing a method of co-operation between the national courts and the Court, based on jurisdictional exclusivity rather than on a hierarchical superiority. Moreover it has systematically refused to review the grounds for questions raised and their relevance to the pending litigation, being obviously anxious to demonstrate that its function is limited to an interpretation of Community rules or to a review of validity of Community acts....[72]

... In this case it took note of several factors from which it inferred that the dispute was fabricated and that, therefore, it lacked jurisdiction....

The fabricated nature of a dispute as a precondition for the admissibility of a referral is a slippery concept, not without dangerous pitfalls. The French government which participated in the preliminary proceedings did not, it may be noted, even contest the jurisdiction of the Court. The Court did so of its own motion. Of course, there may be various shades and degrees to which litigation may appear fabricated. The situation may seldom be clear cut. Litigation in which a private party seeks to obtain a ruling in a test case in which it invokes a directly effective Community rule against a Member State before its own national courts may raise a similar problem; it may also lack the character of a genuine dispute. Who may say with any certainty that the plaintiff entertained the action seriously or whether he merely sought to obtain a decision in a test case which although of negligible interest to him, raised a question of principle?[73]

Not all were however opposed to the decision in *Foglia*. Wyatt argued in favour of the ruling. Wyatt noted that enforcement actions brought by the Commission under Articles 226 and 227 are subject to preliminary objections concerning admissibility.

D. Wyatt, Foglia (No. 2): The Court Denies it has Jurisdiction to Give Advisory Opinions[74]

[A]t bottom the controversy over the Court's decision in *Foglia* v. *Novello* ... turns on the simple question whether or not references to the European Court from national courts are

---

[71] (1980) 17 *CMLRev.* 525, 530–532.

[72] The author quotes examples of this approach including cases such as *Costa*.

[73] Bebr also objected to the *Foglia* ruling because of the difficulties which it would thereby create for the judge in the national courts, and for the implications which it might have for the ambit of direct effect.

[74] (1982) 7 *ELRev.* 186, 187–188, 190, italics in the original.

subject, before the European Court, to the same preliminary objections as to admissibility as any other claim upon the part of private parties, Member States, or Community institutions, to invoke the Court's jurisdiction. If they are not, then the guardians of the European Court's judicial functions, indeed of its very jurisdiction, within the framework of Article 177 EEC, are national courts, rather than the Court itself. It is not impossible that the draftsmen of the Treaty should have ordained such a thing. Simply improbable, in view of the departure from principle which it would involve: superior courts are invariably entrusted with the competence to determine their own jurisdiction.

[*Wyatt demonstrated*, inter alia, *differing ways in which the ECJ determined various jurisdictional issues, such as whether the body making the reference was a court. Later he referred to the reasoning in* Foglia (No. 2), *in which the ECJ emphasized that it had no jurisdiction to give advisory opinions.*]

While the Court must be able to place as much reliance as possible upon assessments by national courts of questions referred, it must, it insisted, be in a position to make *itself* any assessment inherent in the performance of its own duties, in particular in order to *check*, as all *courts* must, whether it had jurisdiction. In exercising its *jurisdiction* under Article 177, the Court was bound to consider, not only the interests of the parties to the proceedings, but also the interests of the Community, and of the Member States....

The Court's reasoning is convincing. It affirms its right to determine its own jurisdiction, and contrasts its own essentially judicial functions, with the delivery of advisory opinions. The distinction between a judgment and an advisory opinion is that the former affects the legal position of the parties to a dispute; the latter has no such effect. The capacity to give a *judgment* itself characterises the organ in question as a *court*. The capacity to give legal advice of course has no such corollary....

(c) CASES WHERE THE ECJ HAS DECLINED JURISDICTION

The principle in *Foglia* lay dormant for some considerable time, and attempts to invoke it were unsuccessful.[75] This fuelled the belief that the case was a one-off, justified by the particular circumstances and unlikely to be repeated. The ECJ however began to use the *Foglia* principle, particularly from the 1990s onwards.[76] The cases fall into a number of categories.

The *hypothetical nature of the question* provides one example.[77] There are a number of reasons for refusing to give such rulings. They are, in part, practical, since it would be a waste of judicial resources to give a ruling in an hypothetical case because the putative problem may never in fact transpire.[78] There are also conceptual problems. If a case really is hypothetical it may be unclear precisely who should be the appropriate parties to the action, and the relevant arguments may not be put. Moreover, if the hypothetical problem actually becomes 'concrete',

---

[75] Case 261/81 *Walter Rau Lebensmittelwerke* v. *De Smedt Pvba* [1982] ECR 3961; Case 46/80 *Vinal SpA* v. *Orbat SpA* [1981] ECR 77; Case C–150/88 *Eau de Cologne and Parfumerie-Fabrik Glockengasse No. 4711 KG* v. *Provide Srl* [1989] ECR 3891.

[76] For earlier case law see Case 126/80 *Salonia* v. *Poidomani and Giglio* [1981] ECR 1563; Case C–368/89 *Crispoltini* v. *Fattoria Autonoma Tabacchi di Città di Castello* [1991] ECR I–3695.

[77] Case C–467/04 *Criminal Proceedings against Gasparini and others* [2006] ECR I–9199.

[78] The wastage of resources argument will also be of relevance if the problem has become moot, in the sense that it has been resolved. Whether a problem has become moot can itself be contentious. Compare Cases C–422–424/93 *Zabala* v. *Instituto Nacional de Empleo* [1995] ECR I–1567 with Case C–194/94 *CIA Security International SA* v. *Signalson SA* [1996] ECR I–2201.

it may not do so in exactly the form envisaged by the court's judgment, with the corollary that the relevance of that judgment in the light of what has subsequently transpired will be unclear. While there may, therefore, be sound reasons for refusing to give opinions in hypothetical cases, there is also a fine line dividing that type of case from test cases.[79] One function of all legal systems is to enable people to plan their lives with knowledge of the legal implications of the choices they make. Test cases enable individuals to gain such knowledge. That the line between advisory opinions/hypothetical judgments and test cases can be a fine one is exemplified by the facts of the *Foglia* case itself.[80] Moreover, it is clear that the mere fact that parties agree on the interpretation they wish to be accorded to EC law does not, in itself, mean that the dispute is not a real one.[81]

A second reason why the ECJ may not wish to give a ruling is that *the questions raised are not relevant to the resolution of the substantive action in the national court.* Thus in *Meilicke*[82] the action was brought by a German lawyer, who challenged a theory of non-cash contributions of capital developed by the German courts on the ground that it was not compatible with the Second Banking Directive. The ECJ cited *Foglia (No. 2)*, and declined to give a ruling because it had not been shown that the issue of non-cash subscriptions was actually at stake in the main action. In *Corsica Ferries*[83] the ECJ reiterated that it had no jurisdiction to rule on questions that had no relation to the facts or the subject-matter of the main action, and decided that only four of the possible eight questions met this criterion. The same concern with relevance was evident in *Monin*,[84] where the ECJ held that it lacked jurisdiction to answer questions that did not involve an interpretation of Community law required for the decision by the national court. It therefore declined to answer questions placed before it by an insolvency judge, given that this judge would not have to deal with these issues in the insolvency itself. The *Dias* case exemplifies the same general point.[85]

---

[79] Case C–412/93 *Leclerc-Siplec* v. *TFI Publicité and M6 Publicite* [1995] ECR I–179 Jacobs AG; Case C–200/98 *X AB and Y AB* v. *Rikssatteverket* [1999] ECR I–8261.

[80] It is far from self-evident that the *Foglia* case was a hypothetical case in the normal sense of that term. It concerned an actual seller of wine, whose business was being affected by a current French tax which he believed to be contrary to Community law. The ECJ's argument that the issue should have been resolved by a different route will not withstand examination. Danzas had no incentive to litigate in France, even though it initially paid the tax, since it was a general carrier, and it would make no commercial sense for it to start an expensive action which was of no specific concern to its business. Foglia's decision to pay Danzas, even though it could have resisted payment under the contract, is also readily explicable. If Foglia had resisted payment then either Danzas would have accepted this, swallowed the loss, and still not have pursued the claim in France because it would not have been worthwhile; and/or it would have accepted this, but increased the cost of carriage by the amount of the tax for subsequent journeys and passed it on to Foglia. In either eventuality the legality of the tax under Community law would not have been contested. Even if Danzas had resorted to formal litigation with Foglia, this action would probably have been initiated in Italy, since it would have been an ordinary contract action the governing law of which would probably have been Italian. Compare *Foglia* to Case C–379/98 *PreussenElektra AG* v. *Schhleswag AG, in the presence of Windpark Reufenkoge III GmbH and Land Schleswig-Holstein* [2001] ECR I–2099, paras. 38–46.

[81] Case C–412/93 *Leclerc-Siplec*, n. 79 above; Case C–341/01 *Plato Plastik Robert Frank GmbH* v. *Caropack Handelsgesellschaft mbH* [2004] ECR I–4883; Case C–144/04 *Mangold* v. *Helm* [2005] ECR I–9981.

[82] Case C–83/91 *Wienand Meilicke* v. *ADV/ORGA F. A. Meyer AG* [1992] ECR I–4871.

[83] Case C–18/93 *Corsica Ferries Italia Srl* v. *Corpo dei Piloti del Porto di Genova* [1994] ECR I–1783.

[84] Case C–428/93 *Monin Automobiles-Maison du Deux-Roues* [1994] ECR I–1707.

[85] See also Case C–134/95 *Unità Socio-Sanitaria Locale No. 47 di Biella (USSL)* v. *Istituto Nazionale per l'Assicurazione contro gli Infortuni sul Lavoro (INAIL)* [1997] ECR I–195; Cases C–320, 328, 329, 337, 338, and 339/94 *Reti Televisive Italiane SpA (RTI)* v. *Ministero delle Poste e Telecommunicazione* [1996] ECR I–6471; Case C–167/01 *Kamer van Koophandel en Fabrieken voor Amsterdam* v. *Inspire Art Ltd.* [2003] ECR I–10155; Case C–314/01 *Siemens AG Österreich and another* v. *Hauptverband der österreichischen Socialversicherungsträger* [2004] ECR I–2549; Case C–293/03 *Gregorio My* v. *ONP* [2004] ECR I–12013; Case C–152/03 *Ritter-Coulais* v. *Finanzamt Gemersheim* [2006] ECR I–1711.

Case C–343/90 **Lourenço Dias v. Director da Alfandega do Porto**
[1992] ECR I–4673

[Note ToA renumbering: Art. 95 is now Art. 90]

Dias was a van driver who was prosecuted for modifying his imported vehicle in a manner which altered its categorization for tax purposes, without having paid the extra tax. The ECJ was presented with eight detailed questions from the national court concerning the compatibility of the relevant national rules with Article 95. The Portuguese government argued that the sole basis of the dispute was a narrow question concerning its tax system and that none of the questions actually referred dealt with that issue. The ECJ accepted that national courts were *prima facie* in the best position to decide on the need for a reference, and that therefore, in principle, the ECJ was bound to give a ruling when asked. It then qualified this obligation.

THE ECJ

17. Nevertheless, in Case 244/80 *Foglia (No. 2)* . . . paragraph 21, the Court considered that, in order to determine whether it has jurisdiction, it is a matter for the Court of Justice to examine the conditions in which the case has been referred to it by the national court. The spirit of cooperation which must prevail in the preliminary ruling procedure requires the national court to have regard to the function entrusted to the Court of Justice, which is to assist in the administration of justice in the Member States and not to deliver advisory opinions on general or hypothetical questions. . . .

18. In view of that task, the Court considers that it cannot give a preliminary ruling . . . where, *inter alia*, the interpretation requested relates to measures not yet adopted by the Community institutions (see Case 93/78, *Mattheus* . . .), the procedure before the court making the reference . . . has already been terminated (see Case 338/85 *Pardini* . . .) or the interpretation of Community law sought by the national court bears no relation to the actual nature of the case or to the subject-matter of the main action (Case 126/80 *Salonia* . . .).

19. It should also be borne in mind that . . . it is appropriate that, before making the reference to the Court, the national court should establish the facts of the case and settle the questions of purely national law. . . . By the same token, it is essential for the national court to explain the reasons why it considers that a reply to its questions is necessary to enable it to give judgment. . . .

20. With this information in its possession, the Court is in a position to ascertain whether the interpretation of Community law which is sought is related to the actual nature and subject-matter of the main proceedings. If it should appear that the question raised is manifestly irrelevant for the purposes of deciding the case, the Court must declare that there is no need to proceed to judgment.

A third rationale for refusing to take a case may be that *the questions are not articulated clearly enough for the ECJ to be able to give any meaningful legal response.*[86] This should be contrasted with the situation in which the ECJ does tease out the real question from a reference which has been imperfectly formulated.[87] The ECJ will not however alter the substance of the

---

[86] Case C–318/00 *Bacardi-Martini SAS and Cellier des Dauphins* v. *Newcastle United Football Club* [2003] ECR I–905.

[87] Case C–88/99 *Roquette Frères SA* v. *Direction des Services Fiscaux du Pas-de-Calais* [2000] ECR I–10465.

questions referred to it. Governments and the parties concerned are allowed to submit observations under Article 20 of the Statute of the Court. They are notified of the order of the referring court, and hence it would be wrong for the ECJ to alter the substance of the questions referred.[88]

Closely allied to this third rationale is a fourth, where *the facts are insufficiently clear for the Court to be able to apply the relevant legal rules.* It is often thought that the ECJ merely responds in an abstract manner to very generally framed questions under Article 234. This is not so. The Court will normally only be able to characterize the nature of the legal issue if it is presented with a reference which has an adequate factual foundation, as the following case makes clear.

Cases C–320–322/90 **Telemarsicabruzzo SpA v. Circostel, Ministero delle Poste e Telecommunicazioni and Ministerio della Difesa**[89]
[1993] ECR I–393

An Italian court referred two questions to the ECJ concerning the compatibility of national provisions on the distribution of TV frequencies with EC competition law. The national court provided almost nothing by way of explanation for these questions.

THE ECJ

6. It must be pointed out that the need to provide an interpretation of Community law which will be of use to the national court makes it necessary that the national court define the factual and legislative context of the questions it is asking or, at the very least, explain the factual circumstances on which those questions are based.

7. Those requirements are of particular importance in the field of competition, which is characterized by complex factual and legal situations.[90]

8. The orders for reference contain no such details.

9. Although the Court has been provided with some information by the file submitted by the national court and the written observations..., and by the oral observations of the parties at the hearing, that information is fragmentary and does not enable the Court, in the absence of adequate knowledge of the facts underlying the main proceedings, to interpret the Community competition rules in the light of the situation at issue....

10. In those circumstances, there is no need to give a decision on the questions submitted....

The ECJ has incorporated the results of its case law in its Information Note on References from National Courts for a Preliminary Ruling.[91] Paragraph 22 states that the order for reference should contain a statement of reasons which is succinct but sufficiently complete to give the Court a clear understanding of the factual and legal context of the main action. It should include, in particular, a statement: setting out the subject-matter of the dispute and the essential facts; the relevant national law; identify as accurately as possible the Community provisions relevant to the case; the reasons why the national court referred the matter and the relationship

---

88 Case C–235/95 *AGS Assedic Pas-de-Calais* v. *Dumon and Froment* [1998] ECR I–4531.

89 See also Case C–157/92 *Banchero* [1993] ECR I–1085; Case C–386/92 *Monin Automobiles* v. *France* [1993] ECR I–2049; Case C–458/93 *Criminal Proceedings against Saddik* [1995] ECR I–511; Case C–167/94 R *Grau Gomis* [1995] ECR I–1023; Case C–2/96 *Criminal Proceedings against Sunino and Data* [1996] ECR I–1543; Case C–257/95 *Bresle* v. *Préfet de la Région Auvergne and Préfet du Puy-le-Dôme* [1996] ECR I–233.

90 Compare Case C–316/93 *Vaneetveld* v. *Le Foyer SA* [1994] ECR I–763.

91 [2005] OJ C143/01.

between the provisions of EC law and national provisions applicable to the action; and a summary of the parties' arguments where appropriate.

(d) LIMITS OF THE POWER TO DECLINE A CASE

The ECJ has exerted greater control over the admissibility of references than hitherto. It has however also made it clear that it will decline to give a ruling only if the issue of EC law on which an interpretation is sought is manifestly inapplicable to the dispute before the national court, or bears no relation to the subject-matter of that action.[92]

Case C–264/96 ICI Chemical Industries plc (ICI) v. Colmer (HM Inspector of Taxes)
[1998] ECR I–4695

The case concerned the compatibility of UK tax legislation with the rules on freedom of establishment.

THE ECJ

14. The United Kingdom Government has expressed doubts as to the relevance of the first question in determining the issue in the main proceedings. It argues that, even if the Act were found to entail a restriction on freedom of establishment, incompatible with Article 52 of the Treaty, this would have no bearing on the determination of the proceedings. ICI would in any event be denied the tax relief provided for under the Act, since the majority of the companies . . . are resident, not in other Member States, but in non-member countries.

15. According to established case law, it is solely for the national courts before which the proceedings are pending . . . to determine in the light of the particular circumstances of each case both the need for a preliminary ruling to enable them to give judgment, and the relevance of the questions which they submit to the Court. . . . A request for a preliminary ruling from a national court may be rejected only if it manifest that the interpretation of Community law or the examination of the validity of a rule of Community law sought by that court bears no relation to the true facts or the subject matter of the main proceedings.

16. However, that is not the situation in the present case. The House of Lords observes that opinion differs as to the proper construction of section 258(5) . . . one interpretation of which makes it necessary to determine whether the Act is compatible with Article 52 of the Treaty.

(e) SUMMARY

i. The ECJ will decline to take a case under Article 234 in a number of situations. These are where the question referred is hypothetical, where it is not relevant to the substance of the

---

[92] Case C–85/95 *Reisdorf* v. *Finanzamt Köln-West* [1996] ECR I–6257; Case C–118/94 *Associazione Italiana per il World Wildlife Fund* v. *Regione Veneto* [1996] ECR I–1223; Case C–129/94 *Criminal Proceedings against Bernaldez* [1996] ECR I–1829; Case C–446/93 *SEIM—Sociedade de Exportacoa de Materias, Ld* v. *Subdirector-Geral das Alfandegas* [1996] ECR I–73; Case C–266/96 *Corsica Ferries France SA* v. *Gruppo Antichi Ormeggiatori del Porto di Genova Coop. arl* [1998] ECR–3949; Cases C–215 and 216/96 *Bagnasco* v. *BPN and Carige* [1999] ECR I–135; Case C–379/98 *PreussenElektra AG*, n. 80 above, paras. 38–39; Case C–138/05 *Stichting Zuid-Hollandse Milieufederatie* v. *Minister van Landbouw, Natuur en Voedselkwaliktiet* [2006] ECR I–8339; Case C–295/05 *Asemfo* v. *Transformacion Agraria SA*, 19 Apr. 2007.

dispute, where the question is not sufficiently clear for any meaningful legal response, and where the facts are insufficiently clear for the application of the legal rules.

ii. It will, however, only decline to give a ruling if the issue of EC law on which an interpretation is sought is manifestly inapplicable to the dispute before the national court or bears no relation to the subject-matter of that action.

iii. The rhetoric in Article 234 cases will often be phrased in traditional terms: the judgment will speak of the co-operation between national courts and the ECJ and of the fact that it is for the national court to decide whether to refer or not.[93] This language *is* still meaningful. The relationship under Article 234 is a co-operative one.

iv. It is, however, now common for the traditional formula to be supplemented by appropriately drawn caveats which make it clear that the ECJ will not adjudicate if the questions are not relevant, or if they are hypothetical, etc.[94]

v. With changes in the rhetoric have come changes in reality. The co-operation between national courts and the ECJ still exists, but the latter is no longer the passive receptor of anything thrust before it. It has begun to exercise more positive control over its own jurisdiction in the manner redolent of most superior courts.

7. THE DECISION ON THE REFERENCE: INTERPRETATION VERSUS APPLICATION

The preceding discussion has considered whether a reference should be made from the perspective of the national court, and whether the reference should be accepted from the perspective of the ECJ. We now consider the effect of the ECJ's decision when it rules on a reference.

Article 234 gives the ECJ power to interpret the Treaty, but does not specifically empower it to apply the Treaty to the facts of a particular case. The very distinction between interpretation and application is said to characterize the division of authority between the ECJ and national courts: the former interprets the Treaty, the latter apply that interpretation to the facts of a particular case. This distinction is said to differentiate the relationship between national courts and the ECJ from that in a more truly federal, appellate system, where the superior court may well decide the actual case.

Theory and reality have not, however, always marched hand in hand. The dividing line between interpretation and application can be perilously thin, more especially because many of the questions submitted to the Court are, by their nature, very detailed, and are capable of being answered only by a specific response. The more detailed is the interpretation provided by the ECJ, the closer it approximates to application. It is moreover common for the ECJ to give 'guidance' to the national court on how the point of law should be applied in the instant case, and this further diminishes the line between interpretation and application.

Litigants have often argued that the Court should decline to give a ruling because the question posed was not seeking an interpretation, but rather an application, of the Treaty. The ECJ has not been deterred by such objections. Thus in *Van Gend en Loos*[95] it was argued that the

---

[93] See, e.g., Case C–435/97 *World Wildlife Fund (WWF)* v. *Autonome Provinz Bozen* [1999] ECR I–5613.
[94] See, e.g., Cases C–332, 333, and 335/92 *Eurico Italia Srl* v. *Ente Nazionale Risi* [1994] ECR I–711.
[95] Case 26/62 [1963] ECR 1.

question presented concerning the tariff classification of urea-formaldehyde required, not an interpretation of the Treaty, but rather an application of the relevant Dutch customs legislation. The Court rejected the argument, stating that the question related to interpretation: the meaning to be attributed to the notion of duties existing before the coming into force of the Treaty.

A willingness to respond in detail can be perceived in other cases. *Cristini* v. *SNCF*[96] was concerned with the meaning of Article 7(2) of Regulation 1612/68, which provides that a Community worker who is working in another Member State should be entitled to the same 'social advantages' as workers of that State. The question put by the French court was whether this meant that a provision which allowed large French families to have reduced rail fares was a social advantage within the ambit of Article 7(2). Although the ECJ denied that it had power to determine the actual case, in reality it did just that, and responded to the question by stating that the concept of a social advantage included this fare reduction.[97]

Another example of the detailed nature of the ECJ's rulings is *Marleasing*.[98] The ECJ produced a detailed response to the question whether Article 11 of Directive 68/151 was exhaustive of the types of cases in which the annulment of the registration of a company could be ordered. The judgment furnished the national court with a very specific answer, which simply required the Spanish court to execute the ECJ's ruling.

The ECJ's willingness to provide very specific answers to questions serves to blur the line between interpretation and application. It also serves to render the idea of the ECJ and the national courts being separate but equal, each having their own assigned roles, more illusory. The more detailed the ECJ's ruling, the less there is for the national court to do, other than execute the ruling in the instant case. The ECJ will be particularly motivated to provide 'the answer' where it wishes to maintain maximum control over the development of an area of the law, as exemplified by cases concerning damages liability of Member States. Thus the ECJ has furnished 'guidance' to the national court on whether there has been a serious breach for the purposes of the test.[99] It has also gone further, and stated that it has sufficient information to dispose of this aspect of the case in its entirety.[100]

8. REFORM

The 1961 volume of the European Court Reports had 350 pages; the 2003 volume contained 15,132 pages for the ECJ and 6,094 for the CFI. It does not take a mathematical wizard to realize that the 'come one, come all' strategy would lead to practical workload problems for the ECJ. The establishment of the CFI has done something to alleviate the workload, but not enough in the longer term.

The length of time to process a preliminary ruling rose in 2003, but fell slightly in 2004, and more significantly in 2006.[101] The Rules of Procedure were modified to alleviate these

---

[96] Case 32/75 [1975] ECR 1085.

[97] *Ibid.*, para. 19.

[98] Case C–106/89 *Marleasing SA* v. *La Comercial Internacional de Alimentacion SA* [1990] ECR I–4135.

[99] Cases C–46 and 48/93 *Brasserie du Pêcheur SA* v. *Germany, R.* v. *Secretary of State for Transport, ex p. Factortame Ltd.* [1996] ECR I–1029.

[100] Case C–392/93 *R.* v. *HM Treasury, ex p. British Telecommunications plc* [1996] ECR I–1631.

[101] References for preliminary rulings took on average 25 months in 2003 as compared to 24 months in 2002, while appeals took 28 months as compared to 19 months in 2002: Proceedings of the Court of Justice, Annual Report 2003, 9; references for preliminary rulings in 2004 took on average 23 months, direct actions 20 months, and appeals 21 months: Proceedings of the Court of Justice, Annual Report 2004, 12; references for preliminary rulings in 2006 were however down to 19.8 months, with direct actions taking 20 months and appeals taking

difficulties.[102] There is provision for expedited hearings in case of urgency: Article 62a. Preliminary rulings can be given by reasoned order where the ECJ refers to prior case law in certain types of cases: those where the request is identical to a point dealt with by existing case law, or where the answer can clearly be deduced from existing case, or where the answer admits of no reasonable doubt: Article 104(3).[103] The Nice Treaty also enabled a case to be decided without an Opinion from the Advocate General,[104] and this power was used in approximately 30 per cent of cases in 2004, and 33 per cent in 2006.[105]

The length of time to process cases can be especially problematic in certain areas, such as the Area of Freedom, Security, and Justice. The ECJ has therefore proposed a new form of urgent preliminary ruling procedure designed to reduce the time taken for cases involving individual freedom, or those where delay could cause serious and irreparable damage to a fundamental right.[106]

The catalyst for more general discussion of reform was the IGC that led to the Nice Treaty. This was directly concerned with the institutional implications of enlargement, including the effect on the Community Courts. Two important papers were produced which addressed the future shape of the Community's judicial architecture. One was written by those currently in the ECJ and CFI,[107] and will be referred to hereafter as the Courts' paper. The other was produced by a Working Party composed largely of former judges of the ECJ at the behest of the Commission.[108] The Chairman was Ole Due and it will be referred to as the Due Report.

The steep rise in the number of Article 234 references was of particular concern. It was noted in the Courts' paper that 'the constant growth in the number of references for preliminary rulings emanating from courts and tribunals of the Member States carries with it a serious risk that the Court of Justice will be overwhelmed by its case-load'.[109] Both reports considered different ways in which this problem could be tackled.[110]

(a) LIMITING THE NATIONAL COURTS EMPOWERED TO MAKE A REFERENCE

There is a 'precedent' for such reform in Articles 61–69, the new Title IV of the EC Treaty. Article 68 stipulates that a preliminary ruling can be sought only by a national court or tribunal

---

17.8 months: Proceedings of the Court of Justice, Annual Report 2006. The reports are available at www.curia.europa.eu/en/instit/presentationfr/index.htm.

[102] The Rules of Procedure of the Court of Justice of the European Communities of 19 June 1991 [1991] OJ L176/7, as amended, available at www.curia.europa.eu/en/instit/txtdocfr/index.htm.

[103] F. Jacobs, 'Recent and Ongoing Measures to Improve the Efficiency of the European Court of Justice' (2004) 29 *ELRev.* 823, 825. This power was used on 11 occasions in 2003, on 22 occasions in 2004, and on 16 occasions in 2006.

[104] Art. 222 EC; Art. 20 Statute of the Court of Justice.

[105] Proceedings of the Court of Justice, Annual Report 2004, n. 101 above, 13; Proceedings of the Court of Justice, Annual Report 2006, n. 101 above, 3.

[106] Discussion Paper on the treatment of questions referred for a preliminary ruling concerning the area of freedom, security, and justice (25 Sept. 2006); Supplementary Paper (14 Dec. 2006), available at www.curia.eu/en/instit/txtdocfr/index.htm.

[107] The Future of the Judicial System of the European Union (Proposals and Reflections) (May 1999), hereafter FJS.

[108] Report by the Working Party on the Future of the European Communities' Court System (Jan. 2000), hereafter WP.

[109] *Ibid.*, 22. See also T. Kennedy, 'First Steps Towards a European Certiorari?' (1993) 18 *ELRev.* 121.

[110] Rasmussen, n. 50 above; P. Craig, 'The Jurisdiction of the Community Courts Reconsidered', in G. de Búrca and J.H.H. Weiler (eds.), *The European Court of Justice* (Oxford University Press, 2001), ch. 6; J. Weiler, 'Epilogue: The Judicial Apres Nice', in *ibid.*, 215; C. Turner and R. Munoz, 'Revising the Judicial Architecture of

against whose decisions there is no judicial remedy in national law. Notwithstanding this the Courts' paper and the Due Report came down firmly against any general use of this to limit preliminary rulings.[111] This is unsurprising. The ability of any national court to refer to the ECJ has been central to the development of EC law in both practical and conceptual terms.

In practical terms, it has been common for cases raising important points of EC law to have arisen on references from lower level national courts. To limit the ability to refer would result in cases being fought to the apex of national judicial systems merely to seek a reference to the ECJ. The ability of any national court to refer is also a safeguard against the possibility that the court of final resort may be 'conservative or recalcitrant', and hence reluctant to refer.

In conceptual terms, the ability of any national court or tribunal to refer has emphasized the penetration of EC law to all points of the national legal system. It is of course true that even if references were limited to courts of last resort, lower courts would still have the ability to apply existing Community precedent. The fact that any national court can refer however emphasizes that an individual can rely on directly effective Community rights at any point in the national legal system.

(b) A FILTERING MECHANISM BASED ON THE NOVELTY, COMPLEXITY, OR IMPORTANCE OF THE QUESTION

This reform would allow the ECJ 'to concentrate wholly upon questions which are fundamental from the point of view of the uniformity and development of Community law'.[112] The Due Report advocated some constraints of this kind.[113] It suggested that national courts of final resort should be obliged to refer only questions which are 'sufficiently important for Community law', and where there is still 'reasonable doubt' after examination by lower courts. There are two problems with this suggestion.

First, 'national courts and tribunals might well refrain from referring questions to the Court of Justice, in order to avoid the risk of their references being rejected for lack of interest'.[114] This could jeopardize the machinery for ensuring that Community law is interpreted uniformly throughout the Member States.

Secondly, there is another problem that is not mentioned in either report. Those who are in favour commonly point to the USA where the Supreme Court will decide which cases it is willing to hear. The crucial difference is that the US is an appellate system and the EC is a referral system. In the USA if the Supreme Court declines to hear a case there will be a decision on the point of law from a lower-tier federal court or state court. The situation in the EC is markedly different. The national court has not decided the case. It has referred a question, and if the ECJ declines to answer because it is not sufficiently important or novel there is no decision by a Community Court at all. This places the national court in a difficult position. It could attempt to decide the matter of EC law for itself. The national court could alternatively decline to decide the EC point one way or the other. The effect would be that the party who

the European Union' (1999–2000) 19 *YBEL* 1; A. Arnull, 'Judicial Architecture or Judicial Folly? The Challenge Facing the European Union' (1999) 24 *ELRev.* 516; A. Dashwood and A. Johnston (eds.), *The Future of the Judicial System of the European Union* (Hart, 2001).

111 FJS, n. 107 above, 23–24; WP, n. 108 above, 12–13.

112 FJS, n. 107 above, 25. See also Case C–338/95 *Wiener* v. *Hauptzollamt Emmerich* [1997] ECR I–6495, Jacobs AG.

113 WP, n. 108 above, 14–15.

114 FJS, n. 107 above, 25.

sought to rely on the EC point would be unable to do so, and the case would be decided on the assumption that this point was unproven.

(c) THE NATIONAL COURT PROPOSES AN ANSWER TO THE QUESTION

The national court could include in its reference a proposed reply to the question referred. The advantages were said, in the Courts' paper, to be that it would 'lessen the adverse effect of the filtering mechanism on the co-operation between the national court and the Court of Justice, while the proposed reply could at the same time serve as the basis for deciding which questions need to be answered by the Court of Justice and which can be answered in the terms indicated'.[115] A similar proposal was advanced in the Due Report.[116]

This idea has been incorporated in the guidance given to national courts, which states that 'the referring court may, if it considers itself to be in a position to do so, briefly state its view on the answer to be given to the questions referred for a preliminary ruling'.[117]

There are, however, limits to how far this proposal can be taken. Most national courts are not specialists in EC law. It is one thing for the national court to identify a question that is necessary for the resolution of the case. It is another thing to be able to answer it. Higher level national courts may be able to furnish some answer to the question posed. This proposal would nonetheless transform the task of such courts. There would have to be detailed argument before the national court of the EC issues in order to provide the judge with the requisite material from which to give an answer to the question posed.

Nor is it clear that this proposal would in reality relieve much of the ECJ's workload. Even if national courts are required or encouraged to provide an answer, the ECJ still has to give the matter some detailed consideration in order to decide whether the question really can be answered in the terms indicated by the national court.

(d) TOWARDS AN APPELLATE SYSTEM

A more radical option considered in the Courts' paper would transform the system from one which is reference based, to one which is more appellate in nature.[118]

> A more radical variant of the system would be to alter the preliminary ruling procedure so that national courts which are not bound to refer questions to the Court of Justice would be required, before making any reference, first to give judgment in cases raising questions concerning the interpretation of Community law. It would then be open to any party to the proceedings to request the national court to forward its judgment to the Court of Justice and to make a reference for a ruling on those points of Community law in respect of which that party contests the validity of the judgment given. This would give the Court of Justice the opportunity of assessing, at the filtering stage, whether it needed to give its own ruling on the interpretation of Community law arrived at in the contested judgment.

---

[115] FJS, n. 107 above, 25–26.
[116] WP, n. 108 above, 18.
[117] N. 91 above, para. 23.
[118] FJS, n. 107 above, 26.

The Due Report was however strongly opposed to this change, stating that 'such a proposal would debase the entire system of co-operation established by the Treaties between national courts and the Court of Justice'.[119]

If this proposal were to be adopted it would fundamentally alter the current regime from a reference system to an appellate one. This is not an objection in and of itself, but we should nonetheless be cognizant of the change thereby entailed. The national court would give a decision on the case, and it would then be for the parties to 'require' the national court to make a reference to the ECJ. This was acknowledged in the Courts' paper.[120]

> [S]uch a procedure would involve a fundamental change in the way in which the preliminary ruling system currently operates. Judicial co-operation between the national courts and the Court of Justice would be transformed into a hierarchical system, in which it would be for the parties to an action to decide whether to require the national court to make a reference to the Court of Justice, and in which the national court would be bound, depending on the circumstances, to revise its earlier judgment so as to bring it into line with a ruling by the Court of Justice. From the point of view of national procedural law this aspect of the system would doubtless raise problems which could not easily be resolved.

There are a number of *difficulties* with this proposal. To require national courts to decide the point of EC law would be to impose a burden on them which many lower-tier courts would find difficult to discharge. It would be unlikely to relieve the ECJ's caseload, since there would always be an incentive on the losing party to seek a reference to the ECJ.[121] It would seem to involve the overruling of *Foto-Frost*,[122] since the national court might well be adjudicating on the validity of a Community law norm. It is, moreover, unclear in the Court's paper whether the losing party can request or require the national court to refer the matter to the ECJ.[123]

We should also consider the *possible advantages* of this proposal. An appellate system is more characteristic of a developed federal or confederal legal system, and it could be argued that the EC is ready for such a change. National courts have become more familiar with EC law, and it may be time to move towards an appellate regime where the national court gives judgment on the case, subject to appeal to the ECJ. We should not however go down this road on the assumption that it will thereby radically limit the ECJ's caseload.

(e) CREATION OF DECENTRALIZED JUDICIAL BODIES

The ECJ's burden would be eased if decentralized courts were created. This would also bring legal redress physically closer to citizens, who could obtain a preliminary ruling without the necessity of travelling to Luxembourg. The Courts' paper and the Due Report were however concerned that such decentralized courts would jeopardize the uniformity of Community law,[124] and the Due Report was against this option largely for that reason.[125] The Courts' paper sought to meet this concern by allowing a case to go to the ECJ from one of the decentralized courts.

---

[119] WP, n. 108 above, 13.
[120] FJS, n. 107 above, 26.
[121] *Ibid.*, 26.
[122] Case 314/85 *Firma Foto-Frost* v. *Hauptzollamt Lübeck-Ost* [1987] ECR 4199.
[123] FJS, n. 107 above, 26 is ambiguous in this respect.
[124] *Ibid.*, 28; WP, n. 108 above, 21.
[125] *Ibid.*, 21–22.

The creation of regional courts to supplement the existing judicial architecture of the Community has been advocated in the past,[126] but has generally been opposed by the CFI.[127] The suggestion was not taken up in the Nice Treaty. It may however be inevitable at some time in the future. If such courts were to be created they should be part of the Community judicial machinery operating at national or regional level.

(f) THE CFI TO HAVE JURISDICTION TO GIVE PRELIMINARY RULINGS: THE NICE TREATY

Prior to the Nice Treaty only the ECJ could hear cases under Article 234. The ECJ's workload would however be reduced by allowing the CFI to give preliminary rulings. The possibility of conferring such jurisdiction on the CFI was canvassed positively, albeit cautiously, in the Courts' paper.[128] The Due Report was however opposed to this change, except in a limited number of special areas.[129]

There is much to be said for the idea that the CFI should be able to give preliminary rulings. Some Article 234 cases involve indirect challenge to the validity of Community norms, where the non-privileged applicants cannot satisfy the standing criteria under Article 230. They are concerned with issues that would be heard by the CFI in a direct action under Article 230. It is therefore difficult to argue that the CFI should not be able to hear such cases if they emerge indirectly via national courts as requests for preliminary rulings. There are moreover many Article 234 cases that involve no broad issue of principle at all. They are concerned with the detailed interpretation of a particular provision of a regulation or directive. These cases require judicial resolution. They do not require resolution by the ECJ.

The fact that the Nice Treaty modified Article 225 is therefore to be welcomed. Article 225(1) now provides that the CFI can hear actions covered by Articles 230, 232, 235, 236, and 238, with the exception of those cases assigned to a judicial panel and those reserved in the Statute for the ECJ itself. Article 225(3) accords the CFI power for the first time to hear preliminary rulings in specific areas laid down by the Statute of the Court of Justice. Where the CFI believes that the case requires a decision of principle likely to affect the unity or consistency of Community law it may refer the case to the ECJ. Preliminary rulings given by the CFI can, exceptionally, be subject to review by the ECJ, under the conditions laid down in the Statute, where there is a serious risk to the unity or consistency of Community law being affected.[130]

A Declaration was attached to Article 225 urging the ECJ and the Commission to give overall consideration to the division of competence between the ECJ and CFI, and to submit proposals as soon as the revised Treaty enters into force. Some changes have been made in relation to direct actions.[131] There has however been no move as yet to act on the power given by

---

[126] J.-P. Jacqué and J. Weiler, 'On the Road to European Union—A New Judicial Architecture: An Agenda for the Intergovernmental Conference' (1990) 27 *CMLRev.* 185.

[127] Report of the Court of Justice on Certain Aspects of the Application of the Treaty on European Union— Contribution of the Court of First Instance for the Purposes of the 1996 Intergovernmental Conference, May 1995.

[128] FJS, n. 107 above, 27.

[129] WP, n. 108 above, 22.

[130] Art. 62 of the Statute of the Court of Justice. Draft Council Dec. Amending the Protocol on the Statute of the Court of Justice of the European Communities specifies in greater detail this review function of the ECJ and is available at http://europa.eu.int/cj/en/plan/index.htm.

[131] Art. 51 of the Statute of the Court Justice had reserved jurisdiction to the ECJ in all actions brought by Member States, the Community institutions, and the ECB. This Art. has now been amended so as to give the CFI some increased jurisdiction over direct actions: Council Dec. 2004/407/EC, Euratom of 26 Apr. 2004 amending Arts. 51 and 54 of the Protocol of the Statute of the Court of Justice [2004] OJ L132/5.

Article 225(3) in order to assign preliminary rulings in certain areas to the CFI.[132] This is in part because it is difficult to decide on the nature of such areas, more especially so because there is no necessary correlation between subject-matter area and the importance of the point of Community law raised by the case. It might well therefore have been more desirable to give the CFI general jurisdiction over all preliminary rulings, subject to the dual mechanisms in Article 225(3) for shifting the case to the ECJ. The provisions of the Constitutional Treaty[133] replicated, with minor modifications, the schema from the Nice Treaty, and there was regrettably no broad-ranging discussion of the Community's judicial architecture.

9. CONCLUSION

i.   The ECJ is not a fully developed federal supreme court, either procedurally or institutionally. In procedural terms, individuals have no right of appeal to the ECJ. The ECJ will not actually decide the case, but rules on the point referred to it. In institutional terms, notwithstanding the creation of the CFI, the EC does not yet have the judicial hierarchy characteristic of federal systems. In countries such as the United States, there is a system of federal courts existing below the Supreme Court, which exercise jurisdiction over a particular area of the country.

ii. The original conception of the relationship between national courts and the ECJ does not however capture reality. Many of the developments have transformed this from a *horizontal* and *bilateral*, to a *vertical* and *multilateral*, relationship. These include: the assertion of Community law supremacy; the development of precedent; the *acte clair* doctrine; the sectoral devolution of responsibility to national courts; the ECJ's exercise of control over the cases that it will hear; and the blurring of the line between interpretation and application. These changes evidence the evolution of a Community judicial hierarchy in which the ECJ sits at the apex, as the ultimate Constitutional Court for the Community, assisted by national courts, which apply and interpret Community law.

iii. Reform of the Community's judicial architecture will remain on the agenda, notwithstanding the changes made by the Nice Treaty. It remains to be seen whether the CFI really will be given some power over preliminary rulings. If this does not occur then workload pressures on the ECJ will increase once again.

10. FURTHER READING

(a) Books

Andenas, M., (ed.), *Article 177 References to the European Court—Policy and Practice* (Butterworths, 1994)

Anderson, D., and Demetriou, M., *References to the European Court* (Sweet & Maxwell, 2002)

Dashwood, A., and Johnston, A. (eds.), *The Future of the Judicial System of the European Union* (Hart, 2001)

De Búrca, G., and Weiler, J.H.H. (eds.), *The European Court of Justice* (Oxford University Press, 2001)

---

[132] Jacobs, n. 103 above, 826.
[133] Treaty Establishing a Constitution for Europe [2004] OJ C310/1.

(b) Articles

Arnull, A., 'Judicial Architecture or Judicial Folly? The Challenge Facing the European Union' (1999) 24 *ELRev.* 516

Barnard, C., and Sharpston, E., 'The Changing Face of Article 177 References' (1997) 34 *CMLRev.* 1113

Craig, P., *EU Administrative Law* (Oxford University Press, 2006), ch. 9

Jacqué, J.-P., and Weiler, J., 'On the Road to European Union—A New Judicial Architecture: An Agenda for the Intergovernmental Conference' (1990) 27 *CMLRev.* 185

Komarek, J., 'Federal Elements in the Community Judicial System: Building Coherence in the Community Legal System' (2005) 42 *CMLRev.* 9.

Mancini, F., and Keeling, D., 'From *CILFIT* to *ERT*: The Constitutional Challenge Facing the European Court' (1991) 11 *YBEL* 1

Rasmussen, H., 'Remedying the Crumbling EC Judicial System' (2000) 37 *CMLRev.* 1071

Tridimas, T., 'Knocking on Heaven's Door: Fragmentation, Efficiency and Defiance in the Preliminary Ruling Procedure' (2003) 40 *CMLRev.* 9

Turner, C., and Munoz, R., 'Revising the Judicial Architecture of the European Union' (1999–2000) 19 *YBEL* 1

Van Gerven, W., 'The Role and Structure of the European Judiciary Now and in the Future' (1996) 21 *ELRev.* 211

Vesterdorf, B., 'The Community Court System Ten Years from Now and Beyond: Challenges and Possibilities' (2003) 28 *ELRev.* 303

Weiler, J., 'Epilogue: The Judicial Après Nice', in G. de Búrca and J.H.H. Weiler (eds.), *The European Court of Justice* (Oxford University Press, 2001), 215

REVIEW OF LEGALITY: ACCESS

1. INTRODUCTION

It is readily apparent from the previous chapters that the EC develops policy through regulations, directives, and decisions. Any developed legal system must have a mechanism for testing the legality of such measures. This chapter is, therefore, concerned with access to justice and review of legality by the Community courts.

There are, as will be seen, a number of ways in which Community norms can be challenged, but the principal Treaty provision is Article 230:

> The Court of Justice shall review the legality of acts adopted jointly by the European Parliament and the Council, of acts of the Council, of the Commission, and of the ECB other than recommendations and opinions, and acts of the European Parliament intended to produce legal effects *vis-à-vis* third parties.
>
> It shall for this purpose have jurisdiction in actions brought by a Member State, the European Parliament, the Council or the Commission on the grounds of lack of competence, infringement of an essential procedural requirement, infringement of this Treaty or of any rule of law relating to its application, or misuse of powers.
>
> The Court shall have jurisdiction under the same conditions in actions brought by the Court of Auditors and by the ECB for the purpose of protecting their prerogatives.
>
> Any natural or legal person may, under the same conditions, institute proceedings against a decision addressed to that person or against a decision which, although in the form of a regulation or decision addressed to another person, is of direct and individual concern to the former.
>
> The proceedings provided for in this Article shall be instituted within two months of the publication of the measure, or of its notification to the plaintiff, or, in the absence thereof, of the day on which it came to the knowledge of the latter, as the case may be.

It is evident that four broad conditions have to be satisfied before an act can successfully be challenged. The act has to be of a kind which is open to challenge at all; the institution or person making the challenge must have standing to do so; there must be illegality of a type mentioned in Article 230(1); and the challenge must be brought within the time limit indicated in Article 230(5).

2. CENTRAL ISSUES

i.   The judicial interpretation of Article 230 has been problematic, particularly the extent to which private individuals have standing to contest the legality of Community acts. It is, as will be seen, extremely difficult for individuals to challenge the legality of Community action directly before the Community courts.

ii. It is also possible for the validity of Community action to be challenged indirectly, via Article 234. The inter-relationship between direct challenge under Article 230 and indirect challenge is important. The Community Courts have defended their narrow interpretation of standing for direct actions by arguing that the Treaty provides a complete system of legal protection through a combination of Articles 230 and 234. There are however, as will be seen, real difficulties with this hypothesis.

3. REVIEWABLE ACTS

(a) THE COMMUNITY PILLAR

Article 230(1) allows the Court to review the legality of acts,[1] other than recommendations and opinions, taken by the institutions listed in Article 230(1).[2] This clearly covers regulations, decisions, and directives, which are listed in Article 249.[3] The ECJ has, however, also held that this list is not exhaustive, and that other acts which are *sui generis* can also be reviewed, provided that they have binding force or produce legal effects.[4]

Case 22/70 **Commission v. Council**
[1971] ECR 263

[Note ToA renumbering: Arts. 173 and 228 are now Arts. 230 and 300]

The Member States acting through the Council adopted a Resolution on 20 March 1970 to co-ordinate their approach to the negotiations for a European Road Transport Agreement (ERTA/AETR). The Commission disliked the negotiating procedure established in the Resolution, and sought to challenge it before the ECJ under Article 173.

---

[1] The Court may review acts of the Council which are intended to have legal effects irrespective of whether they have been passed pursuant to Treaty provisions: Case C–316/91 *European Parliament* v. *Council* (*Lomé Convention*) [1994] ECR I–625. However, decisions adopted by representatives of the Member States acting not as the Council, but as representatives of their governments, and thus collectively exercising the powers of the Member States, are not reviewable under Art. 230: Cases C–181 and 248/91 *European Parliament* v. *Council and Commission* (*Emergency Aid*) [1993] ECR I–3685. It will be for the Court to decide whether a measure really was an act of the institutions or whether it was an act of the Member States acting independently: *ibid.*

[2] Prior to the TEU, Art. 173 as it then was only formally applied to the Council and the Commission, but the ECJ held that the acts of the European Parliament were also susceptible to review by the ECJ: Case 294/83 *Parti Ecologiste 'Les Verts'* v. *European Parliament* [1986] ECR 1339.

[3] This includes provsions of an EC dir. which required or authorized Member States to adopt legislation in breach of, e.g., fundamental rights: Case C–540/03 *European Parliament* v. *Council (Family Reunification)* [2006] ECR I–5769 (Family Reunification Dir.).

[4] See also Case C–57/95 *France* v. *Commission (Re Pension Funds Communication)* [1997] ECR I–1627. Moreover, if a Community institution which has the power to take reviewable decisions delegates that power to another institution, the Court will not be prevented from reviewing the acts of such a delegate.

THE ECJ

48. As regards negotiating, the Council decided, in accordance with the course of action decided upon at its previous meetings, that the negotiations should be carried on and concluded by the six Member States, which would become contracting parties to the AETR.

49. Throughout the negotiations and at the conclusion of the agreement, the States would act in common and would constantly coordinate their positions according to the usual procedure in close association with the Community institutions, the delegation of the Member State currently occupying the Presidency of the Council acting as spokesman.

50. It does not appear from the minutes that the Commission raised any objections to the definition by the Council of the objective of the negotiations.

51. On the other hand, it did lodge an express reservation regarding the negotiating procedure, declaring that it considered that the position adopted by the Council was not in accordance with the Treaty, and more particularly with Article 228.

52. It follows from the foregoing that the Council's proceedings dealt with a matter falling within the power of the Community, and that the Member States could not therefore act outside the framework of the common institutions.

53. It thus seems that in so far as they concerned the objective of the negotiations as defined by the Council, the proceedings of 20 March 1970 could not have been simply the expression or the recognition of a voluntary coordination, but were designed to lay down a course of action binding on both the institutions and the Member States, and destined ultimately to be reflected in the tenor of the regulation.

54. In the part of its conclusions relating to the negotiating procedure, the Council adopted provisions which were capable of derogating in certain circumstances from the procedure laid down by the Treaty regarding negotiations with third countries and the conclusion of agreements.

55. Hence, the proceedings of 20 March 1970 had definite legal effects both on relations between the Community and the Member States and on the relationship between institutions.

Whether a particular act does produce legal effects may sometimes be controversial, as shown by the *IBM* case:

Case 60/81 **International Business Machines Corporation v. Commission**
[1981] ECR 2639

[Note ToA renumbering: Arts. 86 and 173 are now Arts. 82 and 230]

IBM sought the annulment of a Commission letter notifying it of the fact that the Commission had initiated competition proceedings against it, in order to determine whether it was in breach of Article 86. The letter was accompanied by a statement of objections, with a request that the company reply to it within a specified time. The Commission objected that the impugned letter was not an act challengeable under Article 173.

THE ECJ

9. In order to ascertain whether the measures in question are acts within the meaning of Article 173 it is necessary, therefore, to look to their substance. According to the consistent

case-law of the Court any measure the legal effects of which are binding on, and capable of affecting the legal interests of, the applicant by bringing about a distinct change in his legal position is an act or decision which may be the subject of an action under Article 173 for a declaration that it is void. However, the form in which such acts or decisions are cast is, in principle, immaterial as regards the question whether they are open to challenge under that article.

10. In the case of acts or decisions adopted by a procedure involving several stages, in particular where they are the culmination of an internal procedure, it is clear from the case-law that in principle an act is open to review only if it is a measure definitively laying down the position of the Commission or the Council on the conclusion of that procedure, and not a provisional measure intended to pave the way for the final decision.

11. It would be otherwise only if acts or decisions adopted in the course of the preparatory proceedings not only bore all the legal characteristics referred to above but in addition were themselves the culmination of a special procedure distinct from that intended to permit the Commission or the Council to take a decision on the substance of the case.

12. Furthermore, it must be noted that whilst measures of a purely preparatory character may not themselves be the subject of an application for a declaration that they are void, any legal defects therein may be relied upon in an action directed against the definitive act for which they represent a preparatory step.

The applicant failed.[5] The letter was merely the initiation of the competition procedure, a preparatory step leading to the real decision at a later stage. The statement of objections did not, in itself, alter IBM's legal position, although it might indicate, as a matter of fact, that it was in danger of being fined later.[6]

The general principle is that a reviewable act will have legal effect until it is set aside by the ECJ or the CFI,[7] and the challenge must be brought within the time limit specified in Article 230(5). The exception is where acts are tainted by particularly serious illegality and are deemed to be 'non-existent'. Three consequences flow from the ascription of this label: the normal time limits for challenge do not apply, since the act cannot be cloaked with legality by the passage of time; such acts do not have any provisional legal effects; and non-existent acts are not actually susceptible to annulment, because there is no 'act' to annul.

A judicial finding that an act is non-existent will, however, have the same effect in practice as if it had been annulled. Thus in *BASF*[8] the CFI found that a Commission decision in competition proceedings against the PVC cartel was non-existent because: the Commission could not locate an original copy of the decision duly authenticated in the manner required by the Rules of Procedure; it appeared that the Commissioners had not agreed on the precise text of

---

[5] See also Cases C–133 and 150/87 *Nashua Corporation* v. *Commission and Council* [1990] ECR I–719; Case C–282/95 P *Guérin Automobiles* v. *Commission* [1997] ECR I–503; Case T–554/93 *Saint* v. *Council* [1997] ECR II–563; Case T–81/97 *Regione Toscana* v. *Commission* [1998] ECR II–2889; Case C–159/96 *Portuguese Republic* v. *Commission* [1998] ECR I–7379; Case C–180/96 *United Kingdom* v. *Commission* [1998] ECR I–2265; Cases T–377, 379, 380/00, 260, and 272/01 *Philip Morris International Inc.* v. *Commission* [2003] ECR II–1; Case C–240/92 *Portuguese Republic* v. *Commission* [2004] ECR I–10717; Case C–131/03 P *R. J. Reynolds Tobacco Holdings Inc.* v. *Commission* [2006] ECR I–7795.

[6] Compare Case 53/85 *AKZO Chemie BV* v. *Commission* [1986] ECR 1965 and Case C–39/93 P *Syndicat Français de l'Express International (SFEI)* v. *Commission* [1994] ECR I–2681. See also Cases T–10–12 and 15/92 *SA Cimenteries CBR and others* v. *Commission* [1992] ECR II–2667; Case C–25/92 R *Miethke* v. *European Parliament* [1993] ECR I–473; Case C–480/93 *Zunis Holding SA, Finan Srl and Massinvest SA* v. *Commission* [1996] ECR I–1; Case T–120/96 *Lilly Industries Ltd* v. *Commission* [1998] ECR II–2571.

[7] Case C–137/92 P *Commission* v. *BASF AG* [1994] ECR I–2555.

[8] Cases T–79, 84–86, 89, 91–92, 94, 96, 98, 102, and 104/89 *BASF AG* v. *Commission* [1992] ECR II–315.

the decision; and it had been altered after it had been formally adopted. The non-existence of a measure should, said the CFI, be raised by the Court of its own motion at any time during the proceedings. The ECJ[9] took a different view on appeal: the defects were not so serious as to make the act non-existent, but the decision was tainted by sufficient irregularity to be annulled.

(b) THE COMMUNITY PILLAR, THE SECOND PILLAR, AND THE UNITED NATIONS

There have recently been difficult cases concerning the reviewability of acts, where the challenged Community action is designed to implement directly a Security Council resolution. This is exemplified by the *Kadi* case.[10] The applicant challenged a Community regulation, made in furtherance of a measure under the CFSP, which froze the funds of those suspected of supporting Al-Qaeda. The regulation was passed pursuant to Security Council Resolutions which established a Sanctions Committee to designate those who should be subject to such freezing orders. The applicant's name was included on the list and his assets in the EU were frozen in accord with a Community regulation. He argued that he was never involved in the provision of financial support for terrorism. The CFI held that the contested regulation could be based on Articles 60, 301, and 308 EC. The case has been considered in relation to fundamental rights[11] and supremacy.[12]

Suffice it to say for the present that the CFI declined to exercise generalized review of the contested Community regulation for compliance with fundamental rights as protected by the Community legal order, since this would entail indirect review of the Security Council Resolutions for compliance with those rights, but the CFI held that it could review the Security Council Resolutions for compliance with *jus cogens*, since this was a body of higher rules of international law binding on all, including the United Nations. This did not however avail the applicant, even though there was no right to be heard before the Sanctions Committee placed a person on its list, and even though there was no judicial remedy available to the applicant. The case highlights the pressing need for administrative law safeguards at the international level.[13]

The CFI however distinguished *Kadi* in the *Modjahedines* case.[14] In the latter case the applicant's funds were frozen pursuant to a Community regulation enacted in furtherance of a UN Security Council Resolution, but there was nothing at UN level that specifically named the applicant organization as one that supported terrorism. This decision was made by the EC pursuant to its own regulation. The CFI held that this served to distinguish the *Modjahedines* case from *Kadi*, and therefore the normal principles of judicial review, such as the obligation to state reasons, the right to effective judicial protection, and the right to a fair hearing, could, in principle, be applied to the instant case.[15]

---

[9] Case C–137/92 P, n. 7 above.

[10] Case T–315/01 *Yassin Abdullah Kadi* v. *Council and Commission* [2005] ECR II–3649. See also Case T–306/01 *Ahmed Ali Yusuf and Al Barakaat Foundation* v. *Council and Commission* [2005] ECR II–3533.

[11] See 385, 390.

[12] See 344.

[13] B. Kingsbury, N. Krisch, and R. Stewart, 'The Emergence of Global Administrative Law' (2005) 68 *LCP* 15.

[14] Case T–228/02 *Organisation des Modjahedines du peuple d'Iran* v. *Council*, 12 Dec. 2006.

[15] *Ibid.*, paras. 99–108; Case T–47/03 *Sison* v *Council*, 11 July 2007.

(c) THE THIRD PILLAR

The ECJ has, since the ToA, been given limited power under Article 35(6) TEU to review the legality of framework decisions and decisions made pursuant to the re-modelled Third Pillar dealing with Police and Judicial Co-operation in Criminal Matters (PJCC). Actions can be brought by the Commission or a Member State within two months of the publication of the measure.[16] Article 35(5) TEU however prevents the ECJ from reviewing the validity or proportionality of operations by the police or law enforcement agencies, or the exercise of responsibilities of Member States with regard to the maintenance of law and order, and the safeguarding of internal security. It is moreover clear from the *Eurojust* case[17] that there can be difficulties in ensuring review of agencies established by the Council under the Third Pillar, more especially where the measure sought to be reviewed is not a framework decision or a decision. The ECJ has however been creative in its construction of Article 35, as shown by *Gestoras*.[18]

Case C–354/04 P **Gestoras Pro Amnistia, Olano and Errasti v. Council**
27 February 2007

The Council adopted common position 2001/931 on the basis of Articles 15 and 34 TEU. The common position was passed to implement Resolution 1373 of the UN Security Council, which provided that all states should afford one another assistance relating to criminal proceedings concerning the financing or support of terrorist acts. The annex to the common position contained a list of groups in relation to which Member States should afford each other the widest cooperation in preventing and combating terrorist acts, and the list included Gestoras Pro Amnistia, which claimed compensation for the damage suffered by its inclusion in the list. The ECJ decided that Article 35 TEU conferred no jurisdiction to award damages under Title VI, Pillar three of the TEU. The applicant argued that it was therefore deprived of all judicial protection, because Article 35 TEU did not allow any direct challenge, or indirect challenge via a preliminary ruling, to a common position. The ECJ disagreed.

THE ECJ

51. As is clear from Article 6 EU, the Union is founded on the principle of the rule of law and it respects fundamental rights as general principles of Community law. It follows that the institutions are subject to review of the conformity of their acts with the treaties and the general principles of law, just like the Member States when they implement the law of the Union. [*The ECJ noted that a common postion defined the approach of the EU in relation to a particular matter, and was not intended in itself to produce legal effects in relation to third parties.*]

53. Article 35(1) EU, in that it does not enable national courts to refer a question to the Court for a preliminary ruling on a common position but only a question concerning the acts listed in that provision, treats as acts capable of being the subject of a reference for a preliminary ruling all measures adopted by the Council intended to produce legal effects in relation to third parties.

---

[16] The ECJ can also review acts made under the TEU where it is claimed that they should have been passed under the EC Pillar: Case C–170/96 *Commission* v. *Council (Airport Transit Visas)* [1998] ECR I–2763; Case C–176/03 *Commission* v. *Council (Criminal Penalties)* [2005] ECR I–7879, para. 39.

[17] Case C–160/03 *Spain* v. *Eurojust* [2005] ECR I–2077.

[18] See also Case C–355/04 P *Segi, Izaga and Galarraga* v. *Council*, 27 Feb. 2007.

Given that the procedure enabling the Court to give preliminary rulings is designed to guarantee observance of the law in the interpretation and application of the Treaty, it would run counter to that objective to interpret Article 35(1) narrowly. The right to make a reference to the Court for a preliminary ruling must therefore exist in respect of all measures adopted by the Council, whatever their nature or form, which are intended to have legal effects in relation to third parties.

54. As a result, it has to be possible to make subject to review by the Court a common position which, because of its content, has a scope beyond that assigned by the EU Treaty to that kind of act. So, a national court hearing a dispute which . . . raises serious doubts whether that common position is really intended to produce legal effects in relation to third parties, would be able, subject to the conditions fixed by Article 35, to ask the Court to give a preliminary ruling. It would then fall to the Court to find, where appropriate, that the common position is intended to produce legal effects in relation to third parties, to accord it its true classification and to give a preliminary ruling.

55. The Court would also have jurisdiction to review the lawfulness of such acts when an action has been brought by a Member State or the Commission on the conditions fixed by Article 35(6).

The broader implications of the limits on review under the Second and Third Pillars for the issue of how far there is a complete system of legal protection will be considered below.[19]

4. ARTICLE 230(2): STANDING FOR PRIVILEGED APPLICANTS

Article 230(2) states that the action may be brought by a Member State, the European Parliament, the Council, or the Commission. It appears from this that these applicants are always allowed to bring an action, even where the decision is addressed to some other person or body. EC law does not oblige a Member State to bring an action under Article 230 or 232 for the benefit of one of its citizens, although EC law does not preclude national law from containing such an obligation.[20]

The status accorded to the European Parliament in review proceedings altered over time. Prior to the TEU it was not accorded any formal privileged status. In the 'Comitology' case[21] the ECJ rejected the Parliament's argument that it should have the same unlimited standing as other privileged applicants. The issue was considered again in the 'Chernobyl' case,[22] where the ECJ took a different view and held that the EP could have a quasi-privileged status so as to protect its own prerogatives. Article 173(3), as it then was, was re-drafted in the TEU so as to reflect the legal position in the Chernobyl judgment: the Parliament had standing to defend its own prerogatives.[23] The Nice Treaty has now added the European Parliament to the list of

---

[19] See below, 525–527.

[20] Case C–511/03 Netherlands v. Ten Kate Holding Musselkanaal BV [2005] ECR I–8979.

[21] Case 302/87 European Parliament v. Council (Comitology) [1988] ECR 5615.

[22] Case C–70/88 European Parliament v. Council (Chernobyl) [1990] ECR I–2041. See also Case C–156/93 European Parliament v. Commission (Organic Production) [1995] ECR I–2019; Case C–187/93 European Parliament v. Council (Shipment of Waste) [1994] ECR I–2855; Case C–360/93 European Parliament v. Council (Common Commercial Policy) [1996] ECR I–1195.

[23] For discussion of this phrase, see K. St J. Bradley, 'Sense and Sensibility: Parliament v Council Continued' (1991) 16 ELRev. 245; J. Weiler, 'Pride and Prejudice—Parliament v Council' (1989) 14 ELRev. 334; G. Bebr, 'The Standing of the European Parliament in the Community System of Legal Remedies: A Thorny Jurisprudential Development' (1990) 10 YBEL 171.

privileged applicants. The Court of Auditors and the European Central Bank (ECB) remain covered by Article 230(3), so that they only have standing to defend their own prerogatives.[24]

5. ARTICLE 230(4): STANDING FOR NON-PRIVILEGED APPLICANTS

In many of the cases considered below the Court refers to Article 173(2) EC, which was the provision on standing for non-privileged applicants prior to the TEU, or Article 173(4), which was the relevant provision after the TEU. The matter is now governed by Article 230(4), but there has been no change in wording. Article 230(4) allows non-privileged applicants to seek review in three types of case.

The first is straightforward: the addressee of a decision can challenge it before the ECJ or CFI. The second is where there is a decision addressed to another person, and the applicant claims that it is of direct and individual concern to him or her. The third type of case is where there is a decision in the form of a regulation, and the applicant claims that it is of direct and individual concern to him or her. Litigation has, not surprisingly, been primarily concerned with categories two and three.

Article 230 does not on its face allow any challenge by non-privileged applicants to directives. It has nonetheless been held that the mere fact that the measure is a directive will not in itself render the action inadmissible, since the Community institutions cannot, by their choice of legal instrument, deprive the applicant of judicial protection. An applicant will however have an uphill struggle to convince the Community courts that it is individually concerned.[25]

(a) DIRECT CONCERN

An applicant must show that the decision was of direct concern if it is to be accorded standing. The general principle is that a measure will be of direct concern where it directly affects the legal situation of the applicant and leaves no discretion to the addressees of the measure, who are entrusted with its implementation. This implementation must be automatic and result from Community rules without the application of other intermediate rules.[26] It can be difficult to determine whether there is some autonomous exercise of will interposed between the original decision and its implementation.[27]

---

[24] For discussion in the context of the ECB see P. Craig, 'EMU, the European Central Bank and Judicial Review', in P. Beaumont and N. Walker (eds.), *Legal Framework of the Single European Currency* (Hart, 1999), 112–115.

[25] Case C–298/89 *Gibraltar* v. *Council* [1993] ECR I–3605; Case T–99/94 *Asociacion Espanalo de Empresas de la Carne (ASOCARNE)* v. *Council* [1994] ECR II–871; upheld on appeal, Case C–10/95 P [1995] ECR I–4149; Case T–135/96 *UEAPME* v. *Council* [1998] ECR II–2335, para. 63; Cases T–172, 175, and 177/98 *Salamander AG* v. *Parliament and Council* [2000] ECR II–2487; Case T–94/04 *EEB* v. *Commission* [2005] ECR II–4919.

[26] Case C–386/96 *Société Louis Dreyfus & Cie.* v. *Commission* [1998] ECR I–2309; Case T–54/96 *Oleifici Italiana SpA and Fratelli Rubino Industrie Olearie SpA* v. *Commission* [1998] ECR II–3377; Case T–69/99 *Danish Satellite TV (DSTV) A/S (Eurotica Rendez-vous Television)* v. *Commission* [2000] ECR II–4039; Case C–486/01 P *National Front* v. *European Parliament* [2004] ECR I–6289, para. 34; Case C–15/06 P *Regione Siciliana* v. *Commission*, 22 Mar. 2007, para. 31.

[27] See, e.g., Case T–12/93 *Comité Central d'Entreprise de la Société Anonyme Vittel* v. *Commission* [1995] ECR II–1247; Case T–96/92 *Comité Central d'Entreprise de la Société Générale des Grands Sources* v. *Commission* [1995] ECR II–1213; Case T–509/93, *Richco Commodities Ltd.* v. *Commission* [1996] ECR II–1181; Cases T–172, 175, and 177/98 *Salamander*, n. 25 above.

Cases 41–44/70 **NV International Fruit Company v. Commission**
[1971] ECR 411

The Community adopted a regulation which limited the import of apples from third countries from 1 April 1970 to 30 June 1970. The regulation provided for a system of import licences, which were granted to the extent to which the Community market allowed. Under this system, a Member State notified the Commission, at the end of each week, of the quantities for which import licences were requested during the preceding week. The Commission then decided on the issue of licences in the light of this information. The challenge was to a regulation applying this scheme to a particular week. The ECJ found individual concern and then considered whether the applicant was directly concerned.

THE ECJ

23. Moreover, it is clear from the system introduced by Regulation No 459/70, and particularly from Article 2(2) thereof, that the decision on the grant of import licences is a matter for the Commission.

24. According to this provision, the Commission alone is competent to assess the economic situation in the light of which the grant of import licences must be justified.

25. Article 1(2) of Regulation No 459/70, by providing that the 'Member States shall in accordance with the conditions laid down in Article 2, issue the licence to any interested party applying for it', makes it clear that the national authorities do not enjoy any discretion in the matter of the issue of licences and the conditions on which applications by the parties concerned should be granted.

26. The duty of such authorities is merely to collect the data necessary in order that the Commission may take its decision in accordance with Article 2(2) of that regulation, and subsequently adopt the national measures needed to give effect to that decision.

27. In these circumstances as far as the interested parties are concerned, the issue of or refusal to issue the import licences must be bound up with this decision.

28. The measure whereby the Commission decides on the issues of the import licences thus directly affects the legal position of the parties concerned.

29. The applications thus fulfil the requirements of the second paragraph of Article 173 of the Treaty, and are therefore admissible.

The decision in the *International Fruit* case[28] can be compared with the following judgment by the Court.[29]

Case 222/83 **Municipality of Differdange v. Commission**
[1984] ECR 2889

The Commission authorized Luxembourg to grant aid to steel firms, on the condition that they undertook reductions in capacity. The applicant municipality argued that it was directly and individually concerned by this decision, *inter alia*, on the ground that the reduction in production capacity and closure of factories would lead to a reduction in local taxes.

[28] See also Case 207/86 *Apesco* v. *Commission* [1988] ECR 2151, para. 12; Cases T–132 and 143/96 *Freistaat Sachsen and others* v. *Commission* [1999] ECR II–3663, paras. 89–90; Cases T–366/03 and 235/04 *Land Oberösterreich and Austria* v. *Commission* [2005] ECR II–4005, para. 29.

[29] See also, e.g., Case 69/69 *Alcan Alumininium Raeren* v. *Commission* [1970] ECR 385; Case 62/70 *Bock* v. *Commission* [1971] ECR 897.

THE ECJ

10. In this case the contested measure, which is addressed to the Grand Duchy of Luxembourg, authorizes it to grant certain aids to the undertakings named therein provided that they reduce their production capacity by a specified amount. However, it neither identifies the establishments in which the production must be reduced or terminated nor the factories which must be closed as a result of the termination of production. In addition, the Decision states that the Commission was to be notified of the closure dates only by 31 January 1984 so that the undertakings affected were free until that date to fix, where necessary with the agreement of the Luxembourg government, the detailed rules for the restructuring necessary to comply with the conditions laid down in the Decision.

11. That conclusion is, moreover, confirmed by Article 2 of the Decision according to which the capacity reductions may also be carried out by other undertakings.

12. It follows that the contested Decision left to the national authorities and undertakings concerned such a margin of discretion with regard to the manner of its implementation and in particular with regard to the choice of factories to be closed, that the Decision cannot be regarded as being of direct and individual concern to the municipalities with which the undertakings affected, by virtue of the location of their factories, are connected.

While applicants must therefore show direct concern, they have encountered greater difficulties in proving individual concern. It is to this issue that we now turn.

(b) INDIVIDUAL CONCERN: CHALLENGE TO DECISIONS ADDRESSED TO ANOTHER PERSON

Case 25/62 **Plaumann & Co. v. Commission**
[1963] ECR 95

In 1961 the German Government requested the Commission to authorize it to suspend the collection of duties on clementines imported from non-member countries. The Commission refused the request, and addressed its answer to the German Government. The applicant was an importer of clementines, who contested the legality of the Commission's decision. The ECJ stated that the right of interested parties to bring an action should not be interpreted restrictively. It then set out the following test for individual concern.

THE ECJ

Persons other than those to whom a decision is addressed may only claim to be individually concerned if that decision affects them by reason of certain attributes which are peculiar to them or by reason of circumstances in which they are differentiated from all other persons and by virtue of these factors distinguishes them individually just as in the case of the person addressed. In the present case the applicant is affected by the disputed Decision as an importer of clementines, that is to say, by reason of a commercial activity which may at any time be practised by any person and is not therefore such as to distinguish the applicant in relation to the contested Decision as in the case of the addressee.

For these reasons the present action for annulment must be declared inadmissible.

The *Plaumann* test is still the leading authority. It is therefore important to dwell on the test, and its application, so as to understand why private applicants have found it so difficult to succeed.

(i) *The* Plaumann *Test: Pragmatic and Conceptual Difficulties*

The *test itself* is encompassed in the first sentence in the paragraph. This emphasizes that applicants who claim to be individually concerned by a decision addressed to another can do so only if they are in some way differentiated from all other persons, and by reason of these distinguishing features singled out in the same way as the initial addressee. The test nonetheless recognizes that it is possible for there to be more than one applicant who is individually concerned. The *application of the test* to the facts is contained in the second sentence of the extract: the applicant failed because it practised a commercial activity that could be carried on by any person at any time. This reasoning can be criticized on both pragmatic and conceptual grounds.

In *pragmatic terms* the application of the test is economically unrealistic. If there are, for example, only a very limited number of firms pursuing a certain trade this is not fortuitous, but is the result of the ordinary principles of supply and demand. Even if there should be a sudden surge of desire for clementines, the result will normally be that the existing firms will import more of the produce. The argument that the activity of importing clementines can be undertaken by any person, that the number might alter significantly, and that therefore the applicant is not individually concerned is thus unconvincing. Moreover, even if there were incentives for other traders to enter the relevant industry, this might still take some considerable time, and might well not occur during the period of application of the contested decision.[30]

The ECJ's reasoning is also open to criticism in *conceptual terms*, since it renders it literally impossible for an applicant *ever* to succeed, except in a very limited category of retrospective cases. The *Plaumann* test has to be applied at some point in time. There are only three choices. The relevant question could be asked when the contested determination was made, when the application for review was lodged, or at some future, undefined date. It has been held that the test for standing must be judged when the application for review was lodged.[31] This is indeed sensible. However it is scant comfort to the applicant in a *Plaumann*-type case to be told that standing will be judged at the time the application is lodged, but then to be told the application fails because the activity of clementine-importing could be carried out by anyone at any time. On this reasoning no applicant could ever succeed, subject to the caveat considered below, since it could *always* be argued that others might engage in the trade at some juncture. This serves, in reality, to shift the focus to choice three: some future, ill-defined date. The 'possibility' of *locus standi* is like a mirage in the desert, ever receding and never capable of being grasped.

(ii) *Open and Closed Categories: Pragmatic and Conceptual Difficulties*

The preceding argument might be opposed by contending that the applicant in *Plaumann* was properly rejected, since he was a member of an open rather than closed category of applicants, and hence was not individually concerned. Open categories are regarded as those in which the

---

[30] A point made by the applicants in Case 11/82 *A.E. Piraiki-Patraiki* v. *Commission* [1985] ECR 207, although ignored by the ECJ.

[31] Case T–16/96 *Cityflyer Express Ltd.* v. *Commission* [1998] ECR II–757, para. 30.

membership is not fixed at the time of the decision; a closed category is one in which it is thus fixed. There are however practical and conceptual problems with this reasoning.

In *practical terms*, the language of open categories is used to rule out standing for any applicant, even if there is only a very limited number presently engaged in that trade, on the ground that others might undertake the trade thereafter. If the presence of such notional, future traders renders the category open, this ignores the practical economics that determine the number of those who supply a product.

In *conceptual terms*, to regard any category as open merely because others might notionally undertake the trade leads to bizarre results, since any decision with a future impact would be unchallengeable because the category would be regarded as open. The *Plaumann* test is based on the assumption that some people have attributes which distinguish them from others, and that they possess these attributes when the contested decision is made. The fact that others might acquire these attributes *later*, by joining that trade, does not mean that they are presently part of that category. The matter can be put quite simply. The fact that I may wish to become striker for England, a great pianist, or a clementine importer does not mean that I currently have the attributes associated with any of these roles in life.

(iii) *The Restrictive Impact of the* Plaumann *Test*

The *Plaumann* test has effectively prevented virtually all direct actions brought by private parties to challenge decisions addressed to others,[32] except where the challenged decision had a retrospective impact.[33] The ECJ and CFI have reiterated the *Plaumann* test for individual concern and applied it in the same manner as in *Plaumann* itself. Many of the cases concerned challenges to decisions made under the Common Agricultural Policy. The Community Courts however applied the test in other areas, as exemplified by the *Greenpeace* case.

Case T–585/93 **Stichting Greenpeace Council**
(Greenpeace International) v. Commission
[1995] ECR II–2205[34]

The applicants sought the annulment of a Commission decision granting financial assistance from the European Regional Development Fund for the construction of two power stations in the Canary Islands. The applicants were individual fishermen, farmers, and residents, and also environmental interest groups, concerned by the impact of the development on tourism and the environment. The applicants argued that the CFI should interpret *Plaumann* more liberally and accord standing because loss or detriment would be suffered from the harmful

---

[32] Case 1/64 *Glucoseries Réunies* v. *Commission* [1964] ECR 413; Case 38/64 *Getreide-Import Gesellschaft* v. *Commission* [1965] ECR 203; Case 11/82 *Piraiki-Patraiki*, n. 30 above; Case 97/85 *Union Deutsche Lebensmittelswerke GmbH* v. *Commission* [1987] ECR 2265; Case 34/88 *CEVAP* v. *Council* [1988] ECR 6265; Case 191/88 *Co-Frutta Sàrl* v. *Commission* [1989] ECR 793; Case 206/87 *Lefebvre Frère et Sœur SA* v. *Commission* [1989] ECR 275; Case T–398/94 *Kahn Scheepvaart* v. *Commission* [1996] ECR II–477; Case T–86/96 *Arbeitsgemeinschaft Deutscher Luftfahrt-Unternehmen and Hapag-Lloyd Fluggesellschaft mbH* v. *Commission* [1999] ECR II–179.

[33] Cases 106 and 107/63 *Alfred Toepfer and Getreide-Import Gesellschaft* v. *Commission* [1965] ECR 405; Case 62/70 *Bock* v. *Commission* [1971] ECR 897; Case 11/82 *Piraiki-Patraiki*, n. 30 above.

[34] Upheld on appeal: Case C–321/95 P *Stichting Greenpeace Council (Greenpeace International)* v. *Commission* [1998] ECR I–1651. See also Case T–117/94 *Associazione Agricoltori della Provincia di Rovigo* v. *Commission* [1995] ECR II–455; Case T–60/96 *Merck & Co. Inc.* v. *Commission* [1997] ECR II–849; Case T–192/95 R *Danielsson* v. *Commission* [1995] ECR II–3051.

environmental effects of the Commission's unlawful conduct. The CFI held that the *Plaumann* test was applicable irrespective of the nature, economic or otherwise, of the applicant's interest which was affected. It then continued as follows.

THE CFI

51. Consequently, the criterion which the applicants seek to have applied, restricted merely to the existence of harm suffered or to be suffered, cannot alone suffice to confer *locus standi* on an applicant, since such harm may affect, generally and in the abstract, a large number of persons who cannot be determined in advance in a way which distinguishes them individually in the same way as the addressee of a decision, in accordance with the case-law cited above [*Plaumann* etc.]. That conclusion cannot be affected by the fact, put forward by the applicants, that in the practice of national courts in matters relating to environmental protection *locus standi* may depend merely on their having a 'sufficient interest', since *locus standi* under the fourth paragraph of Article 173 of the Treaty depends on meeting the conditions relating to the applicants's being directly and individually affected by the contested decision.

[*The CFI then considered whether the applicants had standing judged by the* Plaumann *test.*]

54. The applicants are 16 private individuals who rely either on their objective status as 'local resident', 'fishermen' or 'farmer' or on their position as persons concerned by the consequences which the building of the two power stations might have on local tourism, on the health of Canary Island residents and on the environment. They do not, therefore, rely on any attribute substantially distinct from those of all the people who live or pursue an activity in the areas concerned and so for them the contested decision, in so far as it grants financial assistance for the construction of two power stations..., is a measure whose effects are likely to impinge on, objectively, generally and in the abstract, various categories of person and in fact any person residing or staying temporarily in the areas concerned.

...

[*The CFI then considered whether the applicant associations such as Greenpeace could have standing.*]

59. It has consistently been held that an association formed for the protection of the collective interests of a category of persons cannot be considered to be directly and individually concerned ... by a measure affecting the general interests of that category, and is therefore not entitled to bring an action for annulment where its members may not do so individually ... Furthermore, special circumstances such as the role played by an association in a procedure which led to the adoption of an act within the meaning of Article 173 ... may justify holding admissible an action brought by an association whose members are not directly and individually concerned by the contested measure....

60. The three applicant associations, Greenpeace, TEA and CIC, claim that they represent the general interest, in the matter of environmental protection, of people residing on Gran Canaria and Tenerife and that their members are affected by the contested decision; they do not, however, adduce any special circumstances to demonstrate the individual interest of their members as opposed to any other person residing in those areas. The possible effect on the legal position of the members of the applicant associations cannot, therefore, be any different from that alleged by the applicants who are private individuals. Consequently, in so far as the applicants ... who are private individuals cannot ... be considered to be individually concerned ... nor can the members of the applicant associations....

[*The CFI examined whether the associations could come within the exception mentioned in the second part of paragraph 59 and decided on the facts that they could not.*]

(c) INDIVIDUAL CONCERN:
CHALLENGES TO REGULATIONS

The other problematic case is where an individual asserts that, although the challenged measure is in the form of a regulation, it is in reality a decision which is of direct and individual concern to him or her.

(i) *The Abstract Terminology Test*

There were initially two tests in the case law: the closed category test[35] and the abstract terminology test. The latter was stricter than the former, and became the general test applied by the Court. It is exemplified by *Calpak* and many other judgments:[36]

Cases 789 and 790/79 **Calpak SpA and Società Emiliana
Lavorazione Frutta SpA v. Commission**
[1980] ECR 1949

[Note ToA renumbering: Arts. 173 and 189 are now Arts. 230 and 249]

The applicants were producers of William pears, and they complained that the calculation of production aid granted to them was void. Under the terms of an earlier regulation, production aid was to be calculated on the basis of the average production over the previous three years, in order to avoid the risk of over-production. The applicants alleged that the Commission had abandoned this method of assessing aid, and had based its aid calculation on one marketing year, in which production was atypically low. The applicants also claimed that they were a closed and definable group, the members of which were known to, or identifiable by, the Commission.

THE ECJ

7. The second paragraph of Article 173 empowers individuals to contest, *inter alia*, any decision which, although in the form of a regulation, is of direct and individual concern to them. The objective of that provision is in particular to prevent the Community institutions from being in a position, merely by choosing the form of a regulation, to exclude an application by an individual against a decision which concerns him directly and individually; it therefore stipulates that the choice of form cannot change the nature of the measure.

8. By virtue of the second paragraph of Article 189 of the Treaty the criterion for distinguishing between a regulation and a decision is whether the measure is of general application or not. . . .

---

[35] The ECJ adopted a closed-category approach in cases that dealt with a completed set of past events: Cases 41–44/70 *International Fruit Company BV* v. *Commission* [1971] ECR 411; Case 100/74 *Société CAM SA* v. *Commission* [1975] ECR 1393; Case C–354/87 *Weddel* v. *Commission* [1990] ECR I–3487.

[36] Cases 103–109/78 *Beauport* v. *Council and Commission* [1979] ECR 17; Case 162/78 *Wagner* v. *Commission* [1979] ECR 3467; Case 45/81 *Alexander Moksel Import-Export GmbH & Co. Handels KG* v. *Commission* [1982] ECR 1129; Cases 97, 99, 193, and 215/86 *Asteris AE and Greece* v. *Commission* [1988] ECR 2181; Case 160/88 R *Fédération Européenne de la Santé Animale* v. *Council* [1988] ECR 4121; Case C–298/89 *Gibraltar* v. *Council* [1993] ECR I–3605; Case C–309/89 *Codorniu SA* v. *Council* [1994] ECR I–1853.

9. A provision which limits the granting of production aid for all producers in respect of a particular product to a uniform percentage of the quantity produced by them during a uniform period is by nature a measure of general application within the meaning of Article 189 of the Treaty. In fact the measure applies to objectively determined situations and produces legal effects with regard to categories of persons described in a generalized and abstract manner. The nature of the measure as a regulation is not called in question by the mere fact that it is possible to determine the number or even identity of the producers to be granted the aid which is limited thereby.

The abstract terminology test placed those who challenged an act in the form of a regulation in a difficult position. The purpose of allowing such challenge is, as the ECJ recognized in *Calpak*, to prevent the Community institutions from immunizing matters from attack by the form of their classification. Article 230(4) prevented this by permitting a challenge when the regulation was in reality a decision, which was of direct and individual concern to the applicant. This required, as acknowledged in *Calpak*, the Court to look behind the *form* of the measure in order to determine whether in *substance* it really was a regulation or not.

The problem with the abstract terminology test was that, rather than looking behind form to substance, it came perilously close to looking behind form to form. A regulation would be accepted as a true regulation if, as stated in *Calpak*, it applied to 'objectively determined situations and produces legal effects with regard to categories of persons described in a generalized and abstract manner'. However, it is always possible to draft norms in this manner, and thus to immunize them from attack, more especially as the Court makes it clear that knowledge of the number or identity of those affected will not prevent the norm from being regarded as a true regulation. It was, moreover, clear that many measures regarded as 'true' regulations, and thus characterized as 'legislative' in nature, were short-lived in terms of time and applied only to a very limited group. They did not differ from many measures which in domestic legal systems would be classified as administrative in nature.

(ii) *The Promise of* Codorniu

If a regulation was found to be a 'true regulation' on the basis of the abstract terminology test then traditionally the case would stop at that point and the Court would simply conclude that the applicant was not individually concerned. It is now clear that the Community Courts are willing in principle to admit that a regulation might be a 'true' regulation as judged by the abstract terminology test, but to accept that nonetheless it might be of individual concern to an applicant.

Case C–309/89 **Codorniu SA v. Council**
[1994] ECR I–1853

The applicant challenged a regulation which stipulated that the term *crémant* should be reserved for sparkling wines of a particular quality coming from France or Luxembourg. The applicant made sparkling wine in Spain and held a trade mark which contained the word *crémant*. However, other Spanish producers also used this term. The Council argued that the measure was a regulation within the *Calpak* test, and that it could not be challenged, irrespective of whether it was possible to identify the number or identity of those affected by it.

THE ECJ

18. As the Court has already held, the general applicability, and thus the legislative nature, of a measure is not called in question by the fact that it is possible to determine more or less exactly the number or even identity of the persons to whom it applies at any given time, so long as it is established that it applies to them by virtue of objective legal or factual situation defined by the measure in question in relation to its purpose. . . .

19. Although it is true that according to the criteria in the second paragraph of Article 173 of the Treaty the contested provision is, by nature and by virtue of its sphere of application, of a legislative nature in that it applies to the traders concerned in general, that does not prevent it from being of individual concern to some of them.

20. Natural or legal persons may claim that a contested provision is of individual concern to them only if it affects them by reason of certain attributes which are peculiar to them or by reason of circumstances in which they are differentiated from all other persons (. . . *Plaumann* . . .).

21. Codorniu registered the graphic trade mark 'Gran Cremant de Codorniu' in Spain in 1924. . . . By reserving the right to use the term 'crémant' to French and Luxembourg producers, the contested provision prevents Codorniu from using its graphic trade mark.

22. It follows that Codorniu has established the existence of a situation which from the point of view of the contested provision differentiates it from all other traders.

(iii) *The Limits of* Codorniu

The willingness to accept that a norm could be a true regulation as judged by the abstract terminology test, and yet that it could be of individual concern, was certainly a liberalizing move. An applicant however must still show individual concern in accordance with the *Plaumann* test, paragraph 20 of *Codorniu*, and we have already seen the difficulties with this test. The crucial issue was therefore whether the Community Courts would interpret *Plaumann* more liberally than hitherto. Judicial practice in this respect differed.

There were some cases where the ECJ was willing to find individual concern because the applicant possessed a right that had been infringed, as in *Codorniu*,[37] or because the Community measure was held to create a duty owed to the applicant, as in *Antillean Rice*.[38] There were exceptional cases where the ECJ was willing to consider the 'degree of factual injury' in determining whether the applicant was individually concerned, as exemplified by *Extramet*,[39] or where, as in *Les Verts*,[40] the ECJ sought to reinforce the democratic nature of the Community by allowing standing to a political party to challenge a decision of the EP concerning funding that favoured parties already represented in the EP.

The dominant approach post-*Codorniu* was nonetheless 'pure *Plaumann*'. Applicants were denied standing because the Community Courts applied the *Plaumann* test *in the same manner* as in *Plaumann* itself. The fact that the applicant operated a trade which could, *in the sense considered above*, be engaged in by any other person served to deny individual concern. Thus

---

[37] See also Case T–33/01 *Infront WM AG* v. *Commission* [2005] ECR II–5897.

[38] Cases T–480 and 483/93 *Antillean Rice Mills NV* v. *Commission* [1995] ECR II–2305, paras. 70, 76; Cases T–32 and 41/98 *Government of the Netherlands Antilles* v. *Commission* [2000] ECR II–20.

[39] Case C–358/89 *Extramet Industrie SA* v. *Council* [1991] ECR I–2501, para. 17; Case T–164/94 *Ferchimex SA* v. *Council* [1995] ECR II–2681.

[40] Case 294/83 *Parti Ecologiste 'Les Verts'* v. *Parliament* [1986] ECR 1339.

in *Buralux*[41] the applicants were linked companies which challenged a regulation concerning shipment of waste. The ECJ held that the mere fact that it was possible to determine the number or even identity of those affected did not mean that the regulation was of individual concern to them, so long as the measure was abstractly formulated.[42] Individual concern was determined by the *Plaumann* test.[43] The applicants failed to satisfy this test since they were affected only as 'economic operators in the business of waste transfer between Member States, in the same way as any other operator in that business'.[44] The fact that the applicants were the only companies engaged in shipment of waste between France and Germany was not relevant, since the regulation applied to all waste shipments in the EC.[45] The laudable hope[46] that *Codorniu* might lead to a test for standing based on adverse impact, judged on the facts of the case, was not therefore realized.[47]

(d) INDIVIDUAL CONCERN: ANTI-DUMPING, COMPETITION, AND STATE AIDS

The ECJ was nonetheless more liberal in according standing in certain areas, those concerning anti-dumping, competition, and state aids. The relevant Treaty Articles and regulations had a marked impact on judicial decisions, since the procedure in these areas explicitly or implicitly envisages a role for the individual complainant, who can alert the Commission to the breach of EC law and may play a role in the measure subsequently adopted. The Community interest in these areas was moreover relatively clear, and the Community Courts were therefore likely to be receptive to arguments that, for example, a State had infringed EC law by providing illegal state aid.

We can begin by considering *anti-dumping*. The Community passes anti-dumping regulations to prevent those outside the Community from selling goods within the Community at too low a price, to the detriment of traders within the EC. Whether a firm is in fact dumping is often very controversial. Three types of applicant might wish to challenge an anti-dumping duty: the firm which initiated the complaint about dumping, the producers of the product which is subject to the anti-dumping duty, and the importers of the product on which the duty is imposed.[48] In deciding whether to accord standing to such applicants the Court was in a difficult position, since anti-dumping duties had to be imposed by regulation, as opposed to decision. If, therefore, the Court held that the regulation was not in fact a regulation at all, then it was arguable that the Commission had no power to impose the measure.

---

[41] Case C–209/94 P *Buralux SA v. Council* [1996] ECR I–615. See also Case T–472/93 *Campo Ebro Industrial SA v. Council* [1995] ECR II–421; Case T–489/93 *Unifruit Hellas EPE v. Commission* [1994] ECR II–1201; Case T–116/94 *Cassa Nazionale di Previdenza a Favore degli Avvocati e Procuratori v. Council* [1995] ECR II–1; Case T–138/98 *Armement Coopératif Artisanal Vendéen (ACAV) v. Council* [2000] ECR II–341; Cases T–38–50/99 *Sociedade Agricola dos Arinhos, Ld v. Commission* [2001] ECR II–585; Case T–155/02 *VVG International Handelsgesellschaft mbH and others v. Commission* [2003] ECR II–1949; Case T–139/01 *Comafrica SpA and Dole Fresh Fruit Europe Ltd. and Co. v. Commission* [2005] ECR II–409, paras. 100, 107–116.

[42] Case C–209/94 P *Buralux*, n. 41 above, para. 24.

[43] *Ibid.*, para. 25.

[44] *Ibid.*, para. 28.

[45] *Ibid.*, para. 29.

[46] A. Arnull, 'Private Applicants and the Action for Annulment under Article 173 of the EC Treaty' (1995) 32 *CMLRev.* 7.

[47] A. Arnull, 'Private Applicants and the Action for Annulment since *Codorniu*' (2001) 38 *CMLRev.* 7, 51–52.

[48] A. Arnull, 'Challenging EC Anti-Dumping Regulations: The Problem of Admissibility' [1992] *ECLR* 73.

The *Timex* case[49] concerned the first category of applicant, a company which initiated the complaint, but was unhappy with the resultant regulation because it felt that the anti-dumping duty was too low. The ECJ held that as the principal complainant and a leading watchmaker in the EC it had standing to contest the level of duty imposed. In the *Allied Corporation* case[50] the ECJ confirmed that the producers and exporters who were charged with dumping could also be regarded as individually concerned, at least in so far as they were identified in the measure adopted by the Commission or involved in the preliminary investigation. The third category of applicant who might wish to contest the legality of an anti-dumping regulation is the importer of the product against which the anti-dumping duty has been imposed. Some such applications were rejected on the ground that the importer could challenge the measure indirectly under Article 234 in an action against the national agency which collected the duty. The *Extramet* case indicated when an importer would be held to have standing.[51]

Case C–358/89 **Extramet Industrie SA v. Council**
[1991] ECR I–2501

Extramet (E) imported calcium from outside the EC, which it then processed itself. There was only one Community producer of calcium, P, which refused to supply the raw material to E. P also claimed that E's supplies from outside the EC were being dumped in the EC and a dumping duty was imposed. It was this duty which E then sought to have annulled. The ECJ held that an anti-dumping regulation could still be of individual concern to certain traders, who satisfied the *Plaumann* test. E satisfied that test for the following reasons.

THE ECJ

17. The applicant has established the existence of factors constituting such a situation ... The applicant is the largest importer of the product forming the subject-matter of the anti-dumping measure and, at the same time, the end-user of the product. In addition, its business activities depend to a very large extent on those imports and are seriously affected by the contested regulation in view of the limited number of manufacturers of the product concerned and of the difficulties which it encounters in obtaining supplies from the sole Community producer, which, moreover, is its main competitor for the processed product.

A second area in which the ECJ has been more liberal in according standing is *competition policy*, regulated by Articles 81 and 82 EC. Under what was Article 3(2) of Regulation 17,[52] a Member State, or any natural or legal person who claimed to have a legitimate interest, could make an application to the Commission, putting forward evidence of a breach of Articles 81 and 82.

---

[49] Case 264/82 *Timex Corporation* v. *Council and Commission* [1985] ECR 849. It seems however that participation in the procedure leading to the Anti-Dumping Reg., and being named therein, will not in itself secure standing: Case T–598/97 *British Shoe Corporation Footwear Supplies Ltd.* v. *Council* [2002] ECR II–1155.

[50] Cases 239 and 275/82 *Allied Corporation* v. *Commission* [1984] ECR 1005; Case T–155/94 *Climax Paper Converters Ltd.* v. *Council* [1996] ECR II–873; Case T–147/97 *Champion Stationery Mfg Co. Ltd.* v. *Council* [1998] ECR II–4137.

[51] Case T–161/94 *Sinochem Heilongjiang* v. *Commission* [1996] ECR II–695; Case T–2/95 *Industrie des Poudres Sphériques* v. *Council* [1998] ECR II–3939.

[52] The regime for the enforcement of competition policy has now changed: see below, Ch. 25.

Case 26/76 **Metro-SB-Großmärkte GmbH & Co. KG v. Commission**[53]
[1977] ECR 1875

[Note ToA renumbering: Arts. 85, 86, and 173 are now Arts. 81, 82, and 230]

Metro argued that the distribution system operated by SABA was in breach of Article 85 of the Treaty. It initiated a complaint under Article 3(2) of Regulation 17. The Commission decided that certain aspects of the distribution system were not in breach of Article 85, and it was this decision, addressed to SABA, that Metro sought to annul. The question arose whether Metro could claim to be individually concerned by a decision addressed to another.

THE ECJ

The contested decision was adopted in particular as the result of a complaint submitted by Metro and it relates to the provisions of SABA's distribution system, on which SABA relied and continues to rely as against Metro in order to justify its refusal to sell to the latter or to appoint it as a wholesaler, and which the applicant had for this reason impugned in its complaint.

It is in the interests of a satisfactory administration of justice and of the proper application of Articles 85 and 86 that natural or legal persons who are entitled, pursuant to Article 3(2)(b) of Regulation No 17, to request the Commission to find an infringement of Articles 85 and 86 should be able, if their request is not complied with wholly or in part, to institute proceedings in order to protect their legitimate interests.

In those circumstances the applicant must be considered to be directly and individually concerned, within the meaning of the second paragraph of Article 173, by the contested decision and the application is accordingly admissible.

Similar considerations are apparent in the case law on *state aids*. The provision of such aid is regulated by Articles 87–89 EC to prevent the conditions of competition from being distorted by a firm receiving assistance from its government, thereby giving it an unfair advantage as against other companies operating in the same area.[54] The Commission decides whether the aid is compatible with the Treaty, and addresses a decision to the State, which can challenge it under Article 230. The Treaty was less clear whether complainants could also do so. There was nothing directly comparable in state aids to the complaints procedure that operated in competition law. Notwithstanding this, the ECJ in *COFAZ*[55] reasoned by analogy from the *Metro* case in competition law and the *Timex* case in anti-dumping. The applicants in *COFAZ* had, said the ECJ, played a comparable role in the procedure under what is now Article 88 EC, more especially because Article 88(2) recognized in general terms that the undertakings concerned were entitled to submit their comments to the Commission.

---

[53] See also Case T–37/92 *Bureau Européen des Unions des Consommateurs* v. *Commission* [1994] ECR II–285, although the result was different if the applicant had not taken part in the complaints procedure: Case C–70/97 *Kruidvart BVBA* v. *Commission* [1998] ECR I–7183. See also in relation to mergers Case T–12/93 *Vittel*, n. 27 above; Case T–96/92 *Comité Central d'Entreprise de la Société Générale des Grands Sources* v. *Commission* [1995] ECR II–1213; Cases T–528, 542, 543, and 546/93 *Métropole Télévision SA* v. *Commission* [1996] ECR II–649; Case T–158/00 *ARD* v. *Commission* [2003] ECR II–3825.

[54] See Ch. 28.

[55] Case 169/84 *Compagnie Française de l'Azote (COFAZ) SA* v. *Commission* [1986] ECR 391; Case T–435/93 *ASPEC* v. *Commission* [1995] ECR II–1281; Case T–380/94 *AIUFFASS* v. *Commission* [1996] ECR II–2169; Case T–88/01 *Sniace, SA* v. *Commission* [2005] ECR II–1165, paras. 56–57.

They were therefore granted standing subject to the further condition that their position on the market was significantly affected by the aid that was the subject of the contested decision.[56]

(e) INDIVIDUAL CONCERN: THE AG, THE ECJ, AND THE *UPA* CASE

The very fact that the case law on dumping, competition, and state aids was more liberal cast into sharp relief the restrictive approach that continued to dominate the majority of cases on standing, even after *Codorniu*. It is therefore not surprising that the generality of the Courts' jurisprudence on standing for non-privileged applicants has been consistently criticized by academics as being too restrictive. The Community Courts sought to defend their case law on the ground, *inter alia*, that the Treaty provides a comprehensive mechanism for legal protection: applicants who did not have standing for a direct action under Article 230 could nonetheless test the legality of the Community measure indirectly through Article 234. Advocate General Jacobs questioned this reasoning in the *Extramet* case.[57] In the *UPA* case he subjected the hypothesis to even more searching scrutiny, found it to be unconvincing, and suggested that standing should be accorded where the contested measure had a substantial adverse effect on the applicant.

Case C–50/00 P **Unión de Pequeños Agricultores v. Council**
[2002] ECR I–6677

An association of farmers, UPA, sought the annulment of Regulation 1638/98, which amended the common organization of the olive oil market. The CFI dismissed the application because the members of the association were not individually concerned by the Regulation under Article 230(4). The UPA argued, *inter alia*, that it was denied effective judicial protection because it could not readily attack the measure via Article 234. The following extract contains the Advocate General's summary of his Opinion.

ADVOCATE GENERAL JACOBS

102. ...

(1) The Court's fundamental assumption that the possibility for an individual applicant to trigger a reference for a preliminary ruling provides full and effective judicial protection against general measures is open to serious objections:
— under the preliminary ruling procedure the applicant has no right to decide whether a reference is made, which measures are referred for review or what grounds of invalidity are raised and thus no right of access to the Court of Justice; on the other hand, the national court cannot itself grant the desired remedy to declare the general measure in issue invalid;
— there may be a denial of justice in cases where it is difficult or impossible for an applicant to challenge a general measure indirectly (e.g. where there are no challengeable

---

[56] The case law on standing in relation to state aids is complex. For more detail, see Ch. 28, and U. Soltesz and H. Bielesz, 'Judicial Review of State Aid Decisions—Recent Developments' [2004] *ECLR* 133.

[57] Case C–358/89 *Extramet Industrie SA v. Council* [1991] ECR I–2501, Jacobs AG, paras. 70–74.

implementing measures or where the applicant would have to break the law in order to be able to challenge ensuing sanctions);

— legal certainty pleads in favour of allowing a general measure to be reviewed as soon as possible and not only after implementing measures have been adopted;

— indirect challenges to general measures through references on validity under Article 234 present a number of procedural disadvantages in comparison to direct challenges under Article 230 before the Court of First Instance as regards for example the participation of the institution(s) which adopted the measure, the delays and costs involved, the award of interim measures or the possibility of third party intervention.

(2) Those objections cannot be overcome by granting standing by way of exception in those cases where an applicant has under national law no way of triggering a reference for a preliminary ruling on the validity of the contested measure. Such an approach

— has no basis in the wording of the Treaty;

— would inevitably oblige the Community Courts to interpret and apply rules of national law, a task for which they are neither well prepared nor even competent;

— would lead to inequality between operators from different Member States and to a further loss of legal certainty.

(3) Nor can those objections be overcome by postulating an obligation for the legal orders of the Member States to ensure that references on the validity of general Community measures are available in their legal systems. Such an approach would

— leave unresolved most of the problems of the current situation such as the absence of remedy as a matter of right, unnecessary delays and costs for the applicant or the award of interim measures;

— be difficult to monitor and enforce; and

— require far-reaching interference with national procedural autonomy.

(4) The only satisfactory solution is therefore to recognise that an applicant is individually concerned by a Community measure where the measure has, or is liable to have, a substantial adverse effect on his interests. That solution has the following advantages:

— it resolves all the problems set out above: applicants are granted a true right of direct access to a court which can grant a remedy, cases of possible denial of justice are avoided, and judicial protection is improved in various ways;

— it also removes the anomaly under the current case-law that the greater the number of persons affected the less likely it is that effective judicial review is available;

— the increasingly complex and unpredictable rules on standing are replaced by a much simpler test which would shift the emphasis in cases before the Community Courts from purely formal questions of admissibility to questions of substance;

— such a re-interpretation is in line with the general tendency of the case-law to extend the scope of judicial protection in response to the growth of powers of the Community institutions (*ERTA*, *Les Verts*, *Chernobyl*).

(5) The objections to enlarging standing are unconvincing. In particular:

— the wording of Article 230 does not preclude it;

— to insulate potentially unlawful measures from judicial scrutiny cannot be justified on grounds of administrative or legislative efficiency: protection of the legislative process must be achieved through appropriate substantive standards of review;

— the fears of over-loading the Court of First Instance seem exaggerated since the time-limit in Article 230(5) and the requirement of direct concern will prevent an insuperable increase of the case-load; there are procedural means to deal with a more limited increase of cases.

(6) The chief objection may be that the case-law has stood for many years. There are however a number of reasons why the time is now ripe for change. In particular:

— the case-law in many borderline cases is not stable, and has been in any event relaxed in recent years, with the result that decisions on admissibility have become increasingly complex and unpredictable;

— the case-law is increasingly out of line with more liberal developments in the laws of the Member States;

— the establishment of the Court of First Instance, and the progressive transfer to that Court of all actions brought by individuals, make it increasingly appropriate to enlarge the standing of individuals to challenge general measures;

— the Court's case-law on the principle of effective judicial protection in the national courts makes it increasingly difficult to justify narrow restrictions on standing before the Community Courts.

The hope that standing rules might be liberalized proved short-lived, since the ECJ declined to follow the lead of Advocate General Jacobs.

Case C–50/00 P **Unión de Pequeños Agricultores v. Council**
[2002] ECR I–6677

The ECJ accepted the principle from *Codorniu* that a true regulation could be challenged, provided the applicant could show individual concern in accord with the *Plaumann* test. It continued as follows.

THE ECJ

37. If that condition is not fulfilled, a natural or legal person does not, under any circumstances, have standing to bring an action for the annulment of a regulation.

38. The European Community is, however, a Community based on the rule of law in which its institutions are subject to judicial review of the compatibility of their acts with the Treaty and with the general principles of law which include fundamental rights.

39. Individuals are therefore entitled to effective judicial protection of the rights they derive from the Community legal order, and the right to such protection is one of the general principles of law stemming from the constitutional traditions common to the Member States....

40. [T]he Treaty has established a complete system of legal remedies and procedures designed to ensure judicial review of the legality of acts of the institutions.... Under that system, where natural or legal persons cannot, by reason of the conditions for admissibility laid down in the fourth paragraph of Article 173 of the Treaty, directly challenge Community measures of general application, they are able, depending on the case, either indirectly to plead the invalidity of such acts before the Community courts under Article 184 of the Treaty or to do so before the national courts and ask them, since they have no jurisdiction themselves to declare those measures invalid..., to make a reference to the Court of Justice for a preliminary ruling on validity.

41. Thus it is for the Member States to establish a system of legal remedies and procedures which ensure respect for the right to effective judicial protection.

42. In that context, in accordance with ... Article 5 of the Treaty, the national courts are required, so far as possible, to interpret and apply national procedural rules governing the

exercise of rights of action in a way that enables natural and legal persons to challenge before the courts the legality of any decision or other national measure relative to the application to them of a Community act of general application, by pleading the invalidity of such an act.

43. [I]t is not acceptable to adopt an interpretation of the system of remedies ... to the effect that a direct action for annulment before the Community courts will be available if it can be shown, following examination by that Court of the particular national procedural rules, that those rules do not allow the individual to bring proceedings to contest the validity of the Community measure at issue. Such an interpretation would require the Community court, in each individual case, to examine and interpret national procedural law. That would go beyond its jurisdiction when reviewing the legality of Community measures.

44. Finally, it should be added that, according to the system for judicial review of legality established by the Treaty, a natural or legal person can bring an action challenging a regulation only if it is concerned both directly and individually. Although this last condition must be interpreted in the light of the principle of effective judicial protection by taking account of the various circumstances that may distinguish an applicant individually ... such an interpretation cannot have the effect of setting aside the condition in question, expressly laid down in the Treaty, without going beyond the jurisdiction conferred by the Treaty on the Community Courts.

45. While it is, admittedly, possible to envisage a system of judicial review of the legality of Community measures different from established by the founding Treaty and never amended as to its principles, it is for the Member States, if necessary, in accordance with Article 48 EU, to reform the system currently in force.

The ECJ in *Jégo-Quéré* followed its reasoning and decision in *UPA*.[58] It acknowledged the right to effective judicial protection, but held once again that the Treaty established a complete system of legal protection through the combination of Articles 230 and 234. It was for the Member States to ensure that individuals should be able to challenge Community measures at national level, even where no implementing measures were involved. The criteria for standing under Article 230(4) would not be relaxed even where it was apparent that the national rules did not allow the individual to contest the validity of the measure without having contravened it. The right to effective judicial protection could not, said the ECJ, have the effect of setting aside a condition expressly laid down by the Treaty. The ECJ rejected the alternative test proposed by the CFI,[59] which the latter had given after the Opinion of Advocate General Jacobs in *UPA* but before the Court's decision.

It is clear nonetheless that although the ECJ regards reform as a matter for Treaty amendment, there is indirect pressure from the European Court of Human Rights, since there were indications, particularly in a concurring opinion, that the restrictive Community law standing rules might be inconsistent with Article 6 ECHR.[60] It is not therefore fortuitous that this

---

[58] Case C–263/02 P *Commission v. Jégo-Quéré & Cie. SA* [2004] ECR I–3425. paras. 29–39. See also Case C–258/02 P *Bactria Industriehygiene-Service Verwaltungs GmbH v. Commission* [2003] ECR I–15105; Case T–213/02 *SNF SA v. Commission* [2004] ECR II–3047; Case T–231/02 *Gonnelli and AIFO v. Commission* [2004] ECR II–1051; Case T–229/02 *PKK and KNK v. Council* [2005] ECR II–539, para. 52, reversed in part on appeal, Case C–229/05 P *Osman Ocalan, on behalf of the PKK and Serif Vanly, on behalf of the KNK v. Council*, 18 Jan. 2007; Case T–139/01 *Comafrica*, n. 41 above; Cases T–236 and 241/04 *EEB and Stichting Natuur en Milieu v. Commission* [2005] ECR II–4945.

[59] Case T–177/01 *Jégo-Quéré et Cie. SA v. Commission* [2002] ECR II–2365, where the CFI held that a person should be regarded as individually concerned by a Community measure of general application if the measure affected his legal position in a manner which was both definite and immediate, by restricting his rights or by imposing obligations.

[60] App. no. 45036/98 *Bosphorus Hava Yollari Turizm Ve Ticaret Anonim Sirketi v. Ireland* (2006) 42 EHRR 1.

issue has been raised in a number of Community cases.[61] Thus in the *Ocalan* case[62] the applicant claimed that the EC's restrictive standing rules violated Article 6 ECHR, and the ECJ self-consciously 'checked' whether the applicants would be regarded as victims under the ECHR.

(f) A COMPLETE SYSTEM OF LEGAL PROTECTION?

The premise underlying the ECJ's decisions in *UPA* and *Jégo-Quéré* is that the Treaty provided for a complete regime of legal protection in terms of access to court, via Articles 234 and 230. There are however real difficulties with this hypothesis.[63]

(1) The ECJ largely ignored the Advocate General's analysis of the difficulties faced by individuals who seek to use Article 234. They are in part procedural: proceeding via the national court can have implications for the participation of the institutions that adopted the contested measure, delays, costs, the award of interim measures, and the possibility of third party intervention. They are in part inherent in the very nature of Article 234: it is a reference system; the applicant must therefore convince the national court that a reference is required; and may have to fight through more than one national court. The difficulties with Article 234 are also substantive: the national court is precluded from invalidating the measure, and hence the applicant has to proceed to the ECJ; and an individual may not be able to challenge the illegality of the measure in the national court without placing itself in contravention of it.

(2) The ECJ exhorted national courts, in accordance with Article 10 EC, to interpret national rules procedural rules so as to enable applicants to challenge Community norms of general application before the national courts. This strategy is however of limited utility. It cannot resolve the procedural difficulties adverted to above. It cannot overcome, although it may alleviate, the difficulties flowing from the discretionary nature of the Article 234 system. It provides no answer to the critique that it is wrong for an applicant to have to place itself in breach of a Community norm in order to challenge its validity.

(3) The Article 234 mode of indirect challenge has undesirable consequences for the division of competence between the ECJ and the CFI. Preliminary rulings are the preserve of the ECJ.[64] Challenges to the validity of Community norms via Article 234 therefore go to the ECJ, where the same issues would be heard by the CFI if they were admissible as a direct challenge under Article 230. This increases the ECJ's workload and means that its scarce resources are diverted to answering such preliminary rulings, which will often not involve any point of general importance for Community law.

(4) The ECJ's reasoning in *UPA* concerning Article 230 is equally problematic. It held that the boundaries of legitimate Treaty interpretation constrained any modification to the traditional case law on direct challenge. The right to effective judicial protection could influence the application of individual concern, but could not, said the ECJ, set aside that condition, which could only be done via a Treaty amendment. This is with respect unconvincing. The Treaty has always required proof of individual concern. It is the meaning to be given to that phrase that is the question in issue. The crucial issue is not whether the Treaty imposes limits

---

[61] See above, 422–424 for a discussion in the context of fundamental rights.
[62] Case C–229/05 P, n. 58 above, paras. 75–83.
[63] The argument in this Section is developed in greater detail in P. Craig, *EU Administrative Law* (Oxford University Press, 2006), 340–344.
[64] The Nice Treaty qualified this monopoly, but the power to accord the CFI power over preliminary rulings has not been acted on: see 499–500.

on standing, but whether the interpretation of those limits has been overly restrictive. The *Plaumann* test is, as seen above, open to criticism, even given the language of Article 230(4). The ECJ has often interpreted Treaty Articles and Community legislation teleologically. It is moreover not readily apparent why Advocate General Jacobs's interpretation of individual concern would involve any transgression of the bounds of normal Treaty interpretation, let alone that it would be akin to Treaty amendment through judicial fiat. The ECJ gave no explanation of why it felt that the Advocate General's test would be incompatible with the wording of Article 230. There is in reality no reason why a test framed in terms of substantial adverse impact could not be a legitimate reading of individual concern.

(5) A legal system may have impressive principles of judicial review, but these will be of scant comfort to those who cannot access the system because the standing rules are unduly narrow. It is right and proper in normative terms that those who have suffered some substantial adverse impact should have access to judicial review. This test is no more liberal than that which prevails in most domestic legal orders and is fitting for a legal system based on the rule of law. The idea that the more people are affected by a provision, the less chance there is for any challenge is contrary to principle.

(6) The ECJ in *UPA* said nothing about the practical consequences of a more liberal test under Article 230, but one is left nonetheless with the feeling that it was concerned with possible workload problems. There is however no reason why there should necessarily be any significant net increase in the number of challenges. At present, the very fact that Article 230 is so restrictive forces applicants to use Article 234. The ECJ has however little control over the range of applicants that can challenge via Article 234, or the type of norm that can be challenged. The consequence of a more liberal interpretation of Article 230 would be to shift some of these cases back to direct challenge, and give the Community Courts scope for control through the determination of whether there was a substantial adverse impact. Moreover, the implicit assumption seems to be that there would be numerous challenges to a regulation by applicants, each of whom would claim to have suffered substantial adverse impact. This does not accord with legal or practical reality. Some cases would be joined in a single action. In any event once the ECJ or CFI pronounced on the legality of the regulation in relation to one action, that would be the end of the matter. The decision would resolve the issue in relation to any other possible claimant, unless he or she could raise some new legal argument that had not been addressed in the earlier case.

(7) There may well be valid reasons why the Community Courts are wary of intervening too far in the complex discretionary choices made by the Community institutions, and many of the standing cases involve such choices made pursuant to the Common Agricultural Policy.[65] The Community Courts can however influence the number of actions that are brought through the standards of review that are applied.[66] This will impact on the number of actions brought, since applicants will calculate their chances of success before embarking on the expense of litigation. It is of course true that a very strict test for standing may be less demanding on the Court's time. This however comes dangerously close to reductionism, since it says no more than that if a court declines to hear a case it will save more judicial resources than if the case had been heard.

(8) The difficulties with the argument that the Treaty provides a complete system of legal protection are of course compounded in relation to the Second and Third Pillars. The ECJ has

---

[65] See 509–518.
[66] See Ch. 15.

indeed admitted that the regime of legal protection is far from perfect.[67] It is largely excluded from the Second Pillar, and even in relation to the Third Pillar its preliminary ruling jurisdiction is dependent on acceptance by the Member State. Individuals have no direct action to challenge the legality of Third Pillar measures and there is no damages action.

(g) THE CONSTITUTIONAL TREATY AND THE CHARTER OF RIGHTS

The Constitutional Treaty[68] reformulated Article 230(4). The CT is unlikely to become law, but it is nonetheless worth dwelling on the proposed amendment, which was incorporated in Article III–365(4) of the CT.

> Any natural or legal person may, under the same conditions, institute proceedings against an act addressed to that person or which is of direct and individual concern to him or her, and against a regulatory act which is of direct concern to him or her and does not entail implementing measures.

The novelty of the provision was that individual concern would not have to be shown for regulatory acts which were of direct concern to a person and which did not entail implementing measures. Such liberalization would be welcome, and go some way to meet the difficulties in the existing case law. The reform was nonetheless limited. The liberalization only applied in the case of regulatory acts, which were in effect secondary norms as defined in the hierarchy of norms.[69] It would not have applied in relation to EU laws, framework laws, decisions, or implementing acts.[70] There was moreover nothing to suggest any alteration of the *Plaumann* test on individual concern. Thus if an applicant challenged an act in the form of a decision addressed to a third party, but which the applicant claimed was of individual concern to her, she would still have to satisfy the *Plaumann* test with all its difficulties. Nor did the reform address the more general difficulties with indirect challenge articulated by Advocate General Jacobs in the *UPA* case.

It is doubtful whether the Community Charter of Fundamental Rights[71] would impact on this area, even if it were accorded binding legal status. Article 41 enshrines a right to good administration. Article 41(2) sets out certain more specific rights that are included in this right. Article 47 provides that everyone whose rights and freedoms guaranteed by EU law are violated has the right to an effective remedy before a tribunal in compliance with the conditions laid down in this Article. Standing rules are not explicitly mentioned in either Article. It would be open to the Community Courts, if they wished to do so, to regard these provisions as the basis for expanding the existing standing rules. They are however unlikely to do so, given their approach to standing hitherto. This is especially so given that the explanatory memorandum stated in relation to Article 47 that there was no intent for this provision to make any change to the rules on standing other than those embodied in the revised Article

---

[67] Case C–354/04 P *Gestoras Pro Amnistia, Olano and Errasti* v. *Council*, 27 Feb. 2007, para. 50.

[68] Treaty Establishing a Constitution for Europe [2004] OJ C310/1.

[69] Art. I–33(1) CT.

[70] The only way to avoid this conclusion would have been to read the phrase 'regulatory act' to mean something broader than the term European Reg. within Art. I–33(1). This might have been possible, but it would have been difficult both textually and historically.

[71] [2000] OJ C364/01.

III–365(4) CT.[72] There is however an uneasy tension between the Charter rights and the standing rules for direct actions. The Charter accords individual rights, yet the application of the standing rules means that a person who claims that his rights have been infringed by Community law would normally not be able to meet the requirements of individual concern.[73] There is something decidedly odd about the infringement of an individual right not counting as a matter of individual concern.

(h) SUMMARY

i. The central issue is whether the applicant can show that he or she is individually concerned. This is so whether the challenged measure is a decision addressed to a third party, or a regulation which the applicant claims is in reality a decision, since a regulation can be a true regulation in substance as well as form, as judged by the abstract terminology test, but it can still be of individual concern to a particular applicant.

ii. *Plaumann* remains the test for individual concern. The applicant must show that she has attributes or characteristics which distinguish her from all other persons and mark her out in the same manner as the addressee. This will normally be interpreted in the same manner as in *Plaumann* itself. The fact that the applicant operates a trade which could be engaged in by any other person will serve to deny individual concern. It is this interpretation of the *Plaumann* test which makes it almost impossible for most applicants to succeed. The existence of particular factual injury to the applicant will not usually be relevant. Interest groups will not, in general, be in any better position than a private individual.

iii. *Plaumann* can, exceptionally, be interpreted more favourably to the applicant. This will be so where it can be shown that the challenged measure either infringed the applicant's right or was in breach of a duty owed to the applicant. It will be rare for the CFI or ECJ to allow a claim merely because of the factual injury suffered by the applicant.

iv. It is clear from *UPA*, *Jégo-Quéré*, and subsequent cases that the Community Courts are not willing to shift to the kind of more liberal test for standing proposed by Advocate General Jacobs. The rationale for adherence to the *status quo* is that the Treaty provides a complete system of legal protection for individuals through Articles 230 and 234. There are however, as seen above, real difficulties with this view.

6. ARTICLE 234: INDIRECT CHALLENGE TO THE LEGALITY OF COMMUNITY ACTS

(a) THE RATIONALE FOR USING ARTICLE 234

Article 234(1)(b) EC allows national courts to refer to the ECJ questions concerning the 'validity and interpretation of acts of the institutions of the Community'. This provision assumed increased importance for private applicants because of the Court's narrow construction of the standing criteria under Article 230.[74] Article 234 is often the only mechanism

---

[72] Charte 4473/00, Convent 49, 11 Oct. 2000, at 41; CONV 828/03, Updated Explanations Relating to the Text of the Charter of Fundamental Rights, 9 July 2003, 41.

[73] Case C–258/02 P *Bactria*, n. 58 above, paras. 48–51.

[74] H. Rasmussen, 'Why is Article 173 Interpreted against Private Plaintiffs?' (1980) 5 *ELRev.* 112, 122–127.

whereby such parties can contest the legality of Community norms, more especially so after the judgments in *UPA* and *Jégo-Quéré* reaffirmed the restrictive approach to direct challenge under Article 230. The limitations and difficulties of indirect challenge have been considered above. The present discussion will focus on the rationale for using Article 234 and the types of Community act that can be challenged in this manner.

An individual will often be affected by Community measures through their application at national level by national agencies.[75] Thus the 'standard' scenario[76] is a Common Agricultural Policy (CAP) regulation, which cannot be contested under Article 230, either because the applicant lacks standing or because of the time limit. These regulations will normally be applied by a national intervention agency. The regulation may, for example, require the forfeiture of a deposit given by a trader who believes that this forfeiture is illegal because it is disproportionate or discriminatory. If the security is forfeited the trader may seek judicial review in the national court, claiming that the regulation is invalid. It will be for the national court to decide whether to refer the matter to the ECJ under Article 234(1)(b). An alternative scenario is where a regulation demands a levy which the trader believes to be in breach of Community law. The trader's strategy might be to resist payment, be sued by the national agency, and then raise the alleged invalidity of the regulation by way of defence. Once again, it would be for the national court to decide whether to refer the matter to the ECJ.

(b) THE ACTS THAT CAN BE CHALLENGED UNDER ARTICLE 234

Article 234(1)(b) allows a challenge to be made to the validity of acts of the Community institutions. This enables challenges to be made to regulations via the national courts.

The situation with respect to individual decisions is more complex. A person who is *not* the addressee of an individual decision may, it seems, contest this decision through the national courts, in much the same way as with a regulation. Thus, if a decision is addressed to a Member State or state agency which requires that certain action should be taken, then an individual affected by this can contest the validity of the decision on which the action is based through the national courts.[77]

This is exemplified by the *Universität Hamburg* case.[78] The Commission issued a decision to all Member States refusing to allow exemption from customs duty in relation to scientific equipment imported from the United States.[79] The German authorities applied this decision, and the applicant contested this before the national court. The ECJ held that the case could be brought via Article 234. It was influenced by the fact that the Commission decision did not have to be published, and that it did not have to be notified to the person applying for the tax exemption, which would have rendered challenge within the time limit under Article 230 virtually impossible.

The Court pronounced more generally on the point in *Rau*.[80] It held that the applicants, who were margarine producers, could contest in the national courts the legality of a scheme

[75] C. Harding, 'The Impact of Article 177 of the EEC Treaty on the Review of Community Action' (1981) 1 *YBEL* 93, 96; C. Harding, 'Who Goes to Court in Europe? An Analysis of Litigation against the European Community' (1992) 17 *ELRev*. 105.

[76] See, e.g., Case 181/84 *R.* v. *Intervention Board for Agricultural Produce, ex p. E. D. & F. Man (Sugar) Ltd.* [1985] ECR 2889; Case C–66/80 *ICC* [1981] ECR 1191.

[77] Case C–188/92 *TWD Textilwerke Deggendorf GmbH* v. *Germany* [1994] ECR I–833.

[78] Case 216/82 *Universität Hamburg* v. *Hauptzollamt Hamburg-Kehrwieder* [1983] ECR 2771.

[79] The rationale being that the Commission claimed that equipment of equivalent scientific value was being manufactured in the Community itself.

[80] Cases 133–136/85 *Walter Rau Lebensmittelwerke* v. *Bundesanstalt für Landwirtschaftliche Marktordnung* [1987] ECR 2289.

whereby the Community sold cheap butter on the German market to test consumer reaction. There was no need to ascertain whether or not the applicants had the possibility of challenging the Community decision directly before the ECJ.

This ruling must, however, be seen in the light of the *TWD* case.[81] The Commission declared aid that Germany had granted to a firm to be incompatible with the common market. The aid had, therefore, to be repaid. The German Government informed the company, and told it also that the Commission's decision could be challenged under Article 230. The company did not do so, but instead sought to raise the legality of the Commission's decision in an action in the German courts. The ECJ held that no indirect challenge was possible in this instance, given that the company had been informed of its right to challenge under Article 230, and given also that it would 'without any doubt'[82] have had standing to do so.[83] A challenge under Article 234 will not therefore be possible if the matter could have been raised by a person who had standing under Article 230, and who knew of the matter within the time limits for a direct action. This same principle has been held to preclude reliance by a Member State on Article 234 to challenge a measure addressed to it that it could have challenged under Article 230, but had not done so within the time limits under Article 230(5).[84]

Where it is unclear whether the applicant would have had standing under Article 230 the ECJ is more willing to admit the indirect action. Thus in *Accrington Beef*[85] the ECJ distinguished *TWD*, and held that the failure to challenge a regulation under Article 230 was no bar to an Article 234 action, since it was not obvious that the Article 230 action would have been admissible. In *Eurotunnel* the ECJ held that a private party could challenge the validity of provisions of a directive in a national court, since the directive was addressed to Member States and it was not obvious that an action would have been possible under Article 230.[86] The ECJ is also likely to be more receptive to actions under Article 234 where the applicant would not have known of the relevant measure in time to challenge it under Article 230.[87]

7. ARTICLE 232: FAILURE TO ACT

An action for a wrongful failure to act is provided in Article 232 EC:

> Should the European Parliament, the Council or the Commission, in infringement of this Treaty, fail to act, the Member States and the other institutions of the Community may bring an action before the Court of Justice to have the infringement established.

---

[81] Case C–188/92 *TWD*, n. 77 above; Case C–178/95 *Wiljo NV* v. *Belgium* [1997] ECR I–585; Case C–239/99 *Nachi Europe GmbH* v. *Hauptzollamt Krefeld* [2001] ECR I–1197.

[82] *Ibid.*, para. 24.

[83] The ECJ distinguished *Rau* on the ground that the applicants in that case had in fact brought an annulment action before the ECJ, and that therefore the issue of the time bar under Art. 230 and the effect of this on a possible Art. 234 action did not arise.

[84] Case C–241/01 *National Farmers' Union* v. *Secretariat General du Gouvernement* [2002] ECR I–9079, para. 36.

[85] Case C–241/95 *R.* v. *Intervention Board for Agricultural Produce, ex p. Accrington Beef Co. Ltd.* [1996] ECR I–6691. See also Case C–222/04 *Ministero dell'Economia e delle Finanze* v. *Cassa di Risparmio di Firenze SpA and others* [2006] ECR I–289, paras. 72–74; Cases C–346 and 529/03 *Atzeni and others* v. *Regione Autonoma della Sardegna* [2006] ECR I–1975, paras. 30–34.

[86] Case C–408/95 *Eurotunnel SA* v. *Sea France* [1997] ECR I–6315.

[87] See the ground on which the Court distinguished the *Universität Hamburg* case in *TWD*, n. 77 above, para. 23.

The action shall be admissible only if the institution concerned has first been called upon to act. If, within two months of being so called upon, the institution concerned has not defined its position the action may be brought within a further period of two months.

Any natural or legal person may, under the conditions laid down in the preceding paragraphs, complain to the Court of Justice that an institution of the Community has failed to address to that person any act other than a recommendation or an opinion.[88]

The Court of Justice shall have jurisdiction, under the same conditions, in actions or proceedings brought by the ECB in the areas falling within the latter's field of competence and in actions or proceedings brought against the latter.

(a) REVIEWABLE OMISSIONS

There is clearly a close relationship between Articles 230 and 232 EC. This should be reflected in the omissions which are reviewable under Article 232. It seems, in principle, that the only failures to act which should come within Article 232 are failures to adopt a reviewable act, in the sense of an act which has legal effects. Article 232 refers, however, simply to failure to act. An argument could, therefore, be made that this allows the action to be used in relation to the failure to adopt a non-binding act, such as a recommendation or an opinion. There are, however, conceptual and practical objections to this view, which would create an odd distinction between the action for annulment and that for failure to act.[89] Notwithstanding this the Court stated in *Comitology*[90] that the Parliament could bring an Article 232 action for failure to adopt a measure that was not itself a reviewable act. If this is indeed so it will apply only in the context of Article 232(1), since Article 232(3) makes it clear that the action cannot be brought by private individuals with respect to recommendations or opinions.

Article 232 will be available only if the applicant can show that there was an obligation to act. The existence of wide discretionary powers in the Commission will, therefore, normally preclude such a finding.[91] Article 232 has moreover been held to refer to a failure to act in the sense of a failure to take a decision or to define a position. It does not refer to the adoption of a measure different from that desired by the applicant.[92]

The interrelationship between Articles 230 and 232 and the scope of reviewable omissions are evident in the *Eridania* case.

Cases 10 and 18/68 **Società 'Eridania' Zuccherifici Nazionali v. Commission**
[1969] ECR 459

[Note ToA renumbering: Arts. 173, 175, and 176 are now Arts. 230, 232, and 233]

The applicants sought the annulment of Commission decisions granting aid to certain sugar refineries in Italy. They claimed that their competitive position on the sugar market would be

---

[88] A.G. Toth, 'The Law as it Stands on the Appeal for Failure to Act' (1975) 2 *LIEI* 65, 79–80.

[89] T. Hartley, *The Foundations of European Community Law* (5th edn., Oxford University Press, 2003), 390–392.

[90] Case 302/87, n. 21 above.

[91] Case 247/87 *Star Fruit Company* v. *Commission* [1989] ECR 291; Case C–301/87 *France* v. *Commission* [1990] ECR I–307; Case T–277/94 *Associazone Italiana Tecnico Economica del Cemento (AITEC)* v. *Commission* [1996] ECR II–351.

[92] Cases 166 and 220/86 *Irish Cement* v. *Commission* [1988] ECR 6473; Case T–387/94 *Asia Motor France SA* v. *Commission* [1996] ECR II–961.

deleteriously affected by the grant of such aid. The Court rejected this action on the ground that the applicants were not individually concerned by the decision in question. The same applicants brought an action under Article 175, arguing that there had been a failure to act, this being the failure to revoke the decisions in question.

THE ECJ

15. This application concerns the annulment of the implied decision of rejection resulting from the silence maintained by the Commission in respect of the request addressed to it by the applicants seeking the annulment or revocation of the three disputed decisions for illegality or otherwise because they are inappropriate.

16. The action provided for in Article 175 is intended to establish an illegal omission as appears from that Article, which refers to a failure to act 'in infringement of this Treaty' and from Article 176 which refers to a failure to act declared to be 'contrary to this Treaty'.

Without stating under which provision of Community law the Commission was required to annul or revoke the said decisions, the applicants have confined themselves to alleging that those decisions were adopted in infringement of the Treaty and that this fact alone would thus suffice to make the Commission's failure to act subject to the provisions of Article 175.

17. The Treaty provides, however, particularly in Article 173, other methods of recourse by which an allegedly illegal Community measure may be disputed and if necessary annulled on the application of a duly qualified party.

To admit, as the applicants wish to do, that the parties concerned could ask the institution from which the measure came to revoke it and, in the event of the Commission's failing to act, refer such failure to the Court as an illegal omission to deal with the matter would amount to providing them with a method of recourse parallel to that of Article 173, which would not be subject to the conditions laid down by the Treaty.

18. This application does not therefore satisfy the requirements of Article 175 of the Treaty and must thus be held to be inadmissible.

The ECJ's reference to the use of what is now Article 232 to evade limits placed on Article 230, includes, *inter alia*, the ability to bypass the time limits for contesting an action under Article 230.[93]

(b) PROCEDURE

Article 232 requires the applicant to call upon the institution to act, since it may not be easy, in the context of an omission, to say when it came into existence and its content. Thus the omission is deemed to have taken place at the end of the first two-month period and its content is defined by the terms of the request.

The Treaties do not specify any time limit within which the procedure for failure to act should be initiated. The Court has, however, specified that this procedure must be initiated within a reasonable time.[94] Once the request to act has been made, the institution has a period of two months within which to define its position. If it has not done this, the applicant has a further two months within which to bring the action under Article 232.[95]

---

[93] See also Cases 21–26/61 *Meroni* v. *High Authority* [1962] ECR 73, 78.

[94] Case 59/70 *Netherlands* v. *Commission* [1971] ECR 639.

[95] The construction of these provisions is contestable. Contrast the views of Toth, n. 88 above, 81–82, with those of Hartley, n. 89 above, 397–398.

(c) STANDING

Article 232 EC, like Article 230, draws a distinction between privileged and non-privileged applicants. The former are identified in Article 232(1): the Member States and other institutions of the Community. This has been held to cover the European Parliament.[96] The latter are covered by Article 232(3), which allows a natural or legal person to complain of a failure to address an act, other than a recommendation or an opinion, to that person.[97] Some argued that standing might only be accorded for a failure to act where the act would by its very nature be addressed to the applicant. This view has not prevailed. The ECJ held in the *ENU* case[98] that standing under Article 148 of the Euratom Treaty, the equivalent of Article 232, would be available to an applicant provided that it would be directly and individually concerned: it was not necessary for the applicant to be the actual addressee of the decision.[99] This test, is, however, applied in the same restrictive manner as under Article 230.[100]

8. ARTICLE 241: THE PLEA OF ILLEGALITY

Article 241 provides:

> Notwithstanding the expiry of the period laid down in the fifth paragraph of Article 230, any party may, in proceedings in which a regulation adopted jointly by the European Parliament and the Council, or a regulation of the Council, of the Commission or of the ECB is at issue, plead the grounds specified in the second paragraph of Article 230, in order to invoke before the Court of Justice the inapplicability of that regulation.

(a) THE ACTS THAT CAN BE CHALLENGED

The essence of Article 241 is as follows.[101] An individual may wish in the course of proceedings initiated for a different principal reason to call into question the legality of some other measure. Thus, for example, the applicant may challenge a decision which is of direct and individual concern, in the course of which it wishes to raise the legality of a regulation on which the decision is based. Article 241 does not therefore constitute an independent cause of action.[102] Article 241 cannot moreover be used in proceedings before a national court. A declaration of the inapplicability of a regulation pursuant to Article 241 was only contemplated

---

[96] Case 13/83 *European Parliament* v. *Council* [1985] ECR 1513.

[97] Toth, n. 88 above, 85–86.

[98] Case C–107/91 *ENU* v. *Commission* [1993] ECR I–599; Case T–95/96 *Gestevision Telecinco SA* v. *Commission* [1998] ECR II–3407, para 58; Cases T–79/96, 260/97, and 117/98 *Camar Srl and Tico Srl* v. *Commission* [2000] ECR II–2193, para. 79; Case T–395/04 *Air One SpA* v. *Commission* [2006] ECR II–1343, para. 25. See however Case T–277/94, *AITEC*, n. 91 above, para. 58.

[99] In order to use Art. 232(3) to challenge a failure to act where the act in question was a reg. or a dir., the individual would have to show that the act which was omitted, although it might have taken the form of a reg., would have been of individual concern to him; or would have been a decision which directly and individually concerned him: Cases T–79/96 etc. *Camar*, n. 98 above, paras. 72–84.

[100] See, e.g., Case T–398/94 *Kahn Scheepvart BV* v. *Commission* [1996] ECR II–477.

[101] M. Vogt, 'Indirect Judicial Protection in EC Law: The Case of the Plea of Illegality' (2006) 31 *ELRev.* 364.

[102] Case 33/80 *Albini* v. *Council* [1981] ECR 2141; Case T–154/94 *Comité des Salines de France* v. *Commission* [1996] ECR II–1377; Case C–239/99 *Nachi Europe*, n. 81 above.

in proceedings brought before the Court of Justice itself under some other provision of the Treaty, and then only incidentally and with limited effect.[103]

Moreover the applicant must still meet the time limit for the principal action. Thus while Article 241 allows the applicant incidentally to raise the illegality of a regulation outside the time limits in Article 230, the applicant must still be within those time limits in relation to the primary challenge to the decision that is of direct and individual concern to it.

Only the legality of regulations can be contested in this way. There must, moreover, be some real connection between the individual decision which is the subject-matter of the action and the general measure the legality of which is being contested.[104] However it is the substance of the measure, and not its form, which is decisive: if the Court decides that the measure is in substance in the nature of a regulation Article 241 can be used. This is demonstrated by the *Simmenthal* case:

Case 92/78 **Simmenthal SpA v. Commission**
[1979] ECR 777

[Note ToA renumbering: Arts. 173 and 184 are now Arts. 230 and 241]

The applicant sought to annul a Commission Decision concerning the minimum selling prices for frozen beef. In support of its claim, the applicant wished to use Article 184 to challenge the legality of certain regulations and notices which formed the legal basis of the contested decision. The ECJ held that the applicant was directly and individually concerned by the primary decision, even though it was actually addressed to the Member State. The Court then considered the arguments concerning Article 184.

THE ECJ

34. While the applicant formally challenges Commission Decision No 78/258 it has at the same time criticized, in reliance on Article 184 of the EEC Treaty, certain aspects of the 'linking' system in the form in which it has been implemented pursuant to the new Article 14 of Regulation No 805/68, by Regulation No 2900/77 and No 2901/77 and also by the notices of invitations to tender of 13 January 1978.

. . .

36. There is no doubt that this provision (Article 184) enables the applicant to challenge indirectly during the proceedings, with a view to obtaining the annulment of the contested decision, the validity of the measures laid down by Regulation which form the legal basis of the latter.

37. On the other hand there are grounds for questioning whether Article 184 applies to the notices of invitations to tender of 13 January 1978 when according to its wording it only provides for the calling in question of 'regulations'.

38. These notices are general acts which determine in advance and objectively the rights and obligations of the traders who wish to participate in the invitations to tender which these notices make public.

---

103 Cases 31 and 33/62 *Milchwerke Heinz Wohrmann & Sohn KG and Alfons Lütticke GmbH* v. *Commission* [1962] ECR 501.

104 Cases T–93/00 and 46/01 *Alessandrini Srl and others* v. *Commission* [2003] ECR II–1635, paras. 76–81; A. Barav, 'The Exception of Illegality in Community Law: A Critical Analysis' (1974) 11 *CMLRev.* 366, 373–374.

39. As the Court in its judgment ... in Case 15/57, *Compagnie des Hauts Fourneaux de Chasse.* . ., and in its judgment ... in Case 9/56, *Meroni.* . ., has already held in connexion with Article 36 of the ECSC Treaty, Article 184 of the EEC Treaty gives expression to a general principle conferring upon any party to proceedings the right to challenge, for the purpose of obtaining the annulment of a decision of direct and individual concern to that party, the validity of previous acts of the institutions which form the legal basis of the decision which is being attacked, if that party was not entitled under Article 173 of the Treaty to bring a direct action challenging those acts by which it was thus affected without having been in a position to ask that they be declared void.

40. The field of application of the said article must therefore include acts of the institutions which, although they are not in the form of a Regulation, nevertheless produce similar effects and on those grounds may not be challenged under Article 173 by natural or legal persons other than Community institutions and Member States.

41. This wide interpretation of Article 184 derives from the need to provide those persons who are precluded by the second paragraph of Article 173 from instituting proceedings directly in respect of general acts with the benefit of judicial review of them at the time when they are affected by implementing decisions which are of direct and individual concern to them.

42. The notices of invitations to tender of 13 January 1978 in respect of which the applicant was unable to initiate proceedings are a case in point, seeing that only the decision taken in consequence of the tender which it had submitted in answer to a specific invitation to tender could be of direct and individual concern to it.

43. There are therefore good grounds for declaring that the applicant's challenge during the proceedings under Article 184, which relates not only to the above-mentioned regulations but also to the notices of invitations to tender of 13 January 1978, is admissible, although the latter are not in the strict sense measures laid down by Regulation.

The ECJ's reasoning in the *Simmenthal* case could also lead to the conclusion that individuals should be able to use Article 241 to challenge individual acts which would not be challengeable under Article 230, because the individual could not show direct and individual concern. Conversely where it is clear that the individual would be able to bring a direct challenge under Article 230, then an indirect action seeking to use Article 241 may not be possible.[105]

(b) THE PROCEEDINGS IN WHICH ARTICLE 241 CAN BE RAISED[106]

The most common usage of Article 241 is an additional, incidental challenge in an annulment action brought under Article 230, as exemplified by the *Simmenthal* case. It is less clear whether Article 241 can be used as an incident to enforcement proceedings brought under Article 226 against a Member State. This will not be possible where the Member State has not challenged the measure within the time limits allowed for annulment.[107] To allow the State to rely on Article 241 in such circumstances would mean that it could circumvent the time limits laid down under Article 230.[108]

---

[105] See above, 529–530; Case C–188/92 *TWD*, n. 77 above; Case C–310/97 P *Commission* v. *AssiDomän Kraft Products AB* [1999] ECR I–5363, para. 60; Case C–241/01 *National Farmers' Union*, n. 84 above.

[106] Barav, n. 104 above, 375–381.

[107] Case C–310/97 P *Kraft Products*, n. 105 above.

[108] Barav, n. 104 above, 378–379.

(c) THE PARTIES WHO CAN USE ARTICLE 241

It is clear that private parties can use Article 241. It is more contentious whether it can be used by privileged applicants, the Community institutions, and the Member States. Bebr is against privileged applicants being able to use Article 241 on the ground, *inter alia*, that such applicants can challenge any binding act of Community law under Article 230 within the time limit.[109] However, as Barav has noted,[110] the irregularities in a general act may appear only after the relevant implementation measures have been adopted, and hence the State may not have realized the necessity for challenging the general act until the time limit under Article 230 has passed. Advocate General Roemer suggested that Article 230 should be available to Member States,[111] both for the reason advanced by Barav, and because the wording of the Article refers to 'any party'. The ECJ did not deal with the point, deciding the case on other grounds.

9. CONCLUSION

i. The rules concerning standing are of considerable importance in any legal system. They constitute the main gateway through which individuals gain access to the principles of judicial review in order to render public decision-making accountable. If therefore the standing rules are drawn too narrowly then it will necessarily be difficult for individuals to take advantage of these administrative law principles.

ii. The standing rules on direct actions under Article 230 have generated significant case law since the very inception of the EC, and continue to do so even after the decisions in *UPA* and *Jégo-Quéré*. In the great majority of these cases the applicants have failed to secure standing, even though they would have done so in many such cases in national legal systems. The primary reason for this 'failure rate' has been the requirement of individual concern as interpreted in the *Plaumann* case, which renders it exceedingly difficult for non-privilged applicants to succeed, even where they have been significantly affected by the contested measure. There are empirical and conceptual problems with this interpretation of individual concern, and it would be desirable to shift to a test of the kind elaborated by Advocate General Jacobs in the *UPA* case.

iii. The ECJ's seeks to justify the *status quo* by arguing that the Treaty provides a complete system of legal protection, with indirect challenge through Article 234 supplementing direct actions under Article 230. There are however, as we have seen, real difficulties with accepting this hypothesis and the case law since *UPA* attests to the problems that applicants continue to have in securing indirect access to the ECJ.

---

[109] G. Bebr, 'Judicial Remedy of Private Parties against Normative Acts of the European Communities: The Role of the Exception of Illegality' (1966) 4 *CMLRev.* 7.

[110] N. 104 above, 371.

[111] Case 32/65 *Italy* v. *Commission* [1966] ECR 389, 414.

10. FURTHER READING

Albors Llorens, A., 'The Standing of Private Parties to Challenge Community Measures: Has the European Court Missed the Boat?' (2003) 62 *CLJ* 72.

Arnull, A., 'Private Applicants and the Action for Annulment under Article 173 of the EC Treaty' (1995) 32 *CMLRev.* 7

—— 'Private Applicants and the Action for Annulment since *Codorniu*' (2001) 38 *CMLRev.* 7

Craig, P., 'Standing, Rights and the Structure of Legal Argument' (2003) 9 *EPL* 493

—— *EU Administrative Law* (Oxford University Press, 2006), ch. 10

Harlow, C., 'Towards a Theory of Access for the European Court of Justice' (1992) 12 *YBEL* 213

Vogt, M., 'Indirect Judicial Protection in EC Law: The Case of the Plea of Illegality' (2006) 31 *ELRev.* 364

Ward, A., *Judicial Review and the Rights of Private Parties in EU Law* (2nd edn., Oxford University Press, 2007)

Wyatt, D., 'The Relationship between Actions for Annulment and References on Validity after *TWD Deggendorf*', in J. Lombay and A. Biondi (eds.), *Remedies for Breach of EC Law* (Wiley, 1996), ch. 6

REVIEW OF LEGALITY:
GROUNDS OF REVIEW

1. INTRODUCTION: THE GROUNDS OF REVIEW

The previous chapter considered standing to seek judicial review. If the applicant has standing, and is within the time limits for bringing an action, it will still have to show why the Community act should be annulled or declared invalid. Four grounds are specified in Article 230: lack of competence; infringement of an essential procedural requirement; infringement of the Treaty or any rule of law relating to its application; and misuse of power. The same grounds are relevant for indirect actions under Article 234.

2. CENTRAL ISSUES

i.   Judicial review, whether direct through Article 230 or indirect through Article 234, is designed to ensure that decision-making is legally accountable.

ii. The Community Courts have used the heads of review in Article 230 as the framework through which to develop principles of administrative legality, drawing on concepts found within national legal systems. These include fundamental rights, proportionality, legitimate expectations, non-discrimination, transparency, and more recently the precautionary principle. The dividing line between these principles is far from absolute: there are certain principles, such as the right to a fair hearing or legal and professional privilege, which some might classify as fundamental rights, while others would characterize them as principles of administrative legality. Moreover, when reading this chapter the earlier discussion of subsidiarity should not be forgotten.[1] This is in certain respects a general principle of Community law, albeit one which goes principally to the initial legality of Community conduct.

iii. Some of the principles, such as non-discrimination, have a textual foundation in the Treaty, while others have been developed in Community legislation. However, the ECJ has played a key role in developing these general principles.

iv. The principles serve as an interpretative guide, and also form part of the principles of judicial review. They can be used when evaluating Community norms, and national norms in the areas covered by Community law.

[1] See Ch. 3.

3. LACK OF COMPETENCE

The general issue of competence has been considered above.[2] The Community institutions must be able to point to a power within the Treaty which authorizes their action. If they cannot do so then the act will be declared void for lack of competence. This ground of review has been used relatively rarely. The ECJ has interpreted the Community's powers broadly and purposively, in order to achieve the Treaty objectives.

This approach has been complemented by the implied-powers doctrine, under which the Commission has been held impliedly to have the powers necessary to enable it to carry out the tasks expressly conferred on it by the Treaty.[3] There are moreover Treaty provisions that confer broad legislative power, notably Articles 95 and 308 EC,[4] which render challenge on grounds of competence more difficult. The *Tobacco* case[5] signalled the ECJ's willingness to exercise control over claims to legislative competence under Article 95, but subsequent case law reveals the continuing difficulties that applicants face in convincing the Community Courts that the act should be annulled for lack of competence,[6] although there are instances where the ECJ has enforced clear limits to Community power laid down in Community legislation.[7]

This ground of challenge may be used where the claimant alleges that there has been an unlawful delegation of power. This is exemplified by the *Meroni* case,[8] in which the High Authority had delegated certain powers to outside agencies in connection with the administration of a scrap equalization scheme. The Court held that it was legitimate to delegate clearly defined executive powers which were subject to objective criteria set by the delegating authority. It was not, however, permissible to delegate broad, discretionary powers which entailed the exercise of considerable freedom of judgement for the delegee.

It might also be argued that the Community lacked competence because of subsidiarity. A claim that Community legislation had infringed subsidiarity could be framed in terms of the Community's lack of competence to adopt the measure. However, as we have seen,[9] the case law thus far does not hold out much hope for claims of this nature.

4. INFRINGEMENT OF AN ESSENTIAL PROCEDURAL REQUIREMENT

(a) RIGHT TO BE HEARD AND RELATED RIGHTS

It is for the Community Courts to decide what constitutes an essential procedural requirement. They have read into the Treaty many of the requirements commonly associated with procedural due process, in so far as this relates to individualized decisions.[10]

---

[2] See Ch. 3.

[3] Cases 281, 283–285, 287/85 *Germany* v. *Commission* [1987] ECR 3203.

[4] See Ch. 3.

[5] Case C–376/98 *Germany* v. *European Parliament and Council* [2000] ECR I–8419.

[6] See Ch. 17. See however Cases C–317 and 318/04 *European Parliament* v. *Council and Commission (Air Passenger Records)* [2006] ECR I–4721, paras. 67–70.

[7] *Ibid.*

[8] Case 9/56 *Meroni and Co. Industrie Metallurgiche SpA* v. *ECSC* [1957–8] ECR 133.

[9] See Ch. 3.

[10] P. Craig, *EU Administrative Law* (Oxford University Press, 2006), chs. 10–11.

The Community Courts have imposed a right to be heard as a general rule of Community law, irrespective of whether this was specified in the relevant Treaty article, regulation, directive, or decision. A hearing is normally required even where no sanction is imposed, provided that there is some adverse impact or some significant affect on the applicant's interests.[11] The right to be heard has been held to be part of the fundamental rights jurisprudence.[12] It cannot be excluded or restricted by any legislative provision, and the principle must be protected both where there is no specific Community legislation and also where legislation exists, but does not take sufficient account of the principle.[13] The right to be heard before an individual measure is taken that would affect a person adversely is included within the Charter of Fundamental Rights.[14]

The Community Courts have also imposed other more particular procedural requirements. They have insisted that notice should be given of the nature of the case and that the individual should have a right to respond.[15] The individual is accorded access to the file in an increasing range of cases.[16] The Community Courts have moreover imposed an obligation to take care when making discretionary determinations in individual cases, which applies even where the individual is not accorded a hearing.[17]

(b) CONSULTATION AND PARTICIPATION

Where a duty to consult is provided by the Treaty or Community legislation it will be enforced though the courts.[18] The Community Courts have however consistently resisted claims to procedural rights, such as a right to participate or be consulted, in the making of Community legislation, unless they are expressly provided by a Treaty article or another Community norm.[19] They have also been generally unwilling to accept that the fact of participation in the making of the legislative measure accords the applicant any enhanced prospects of being given standing to challenge it.[20]

---

[11] Case 17/74 *Transocean Marine Paint* v. *Commission* [1974] ECR 1063; Case T–450/93 *Lisrestal* v. *Commission* [1994] ECR II–1177; Case C–32/95 P *Commission* v. *Lisrestal* [1996] ECR I–5373; Case T–50/96 *Primex Produkte Import-Export GmbH & Co. KG* v. *Commission* [1998] ECR II–3773, para. 59; Case C–462/98 P *MedioCurso-Etabelecimento de Ensino Particular Ld* v. *Commission* [2000] ECR I–7183, para. 36; Case T–102/00 *Vlaams Fonds voor de Sociale Integratie van Personen met een Handicap* v. *Commission* [2003] ECR II–2433, para. 59.

[12] Case C–49/88 *Al-Jubail Fertilizer* v. *Council* [1991] ECR I–3187, para. 15; Cases T–33–34/98 *Petrotub and Republica SA* v. *Council* [1999] ECR II–3837; Case C–458/98 P *Industrie des Poudres Sphériques* v. *Council and Commission* [2000] ECR I–8147, para. 99.

[13] Case T–260/94 *Air Inter SA* v. *Commission* [1997] ECR II–997, para. 60.

[14] Charter of Fundamental Rights of the European Union [2000] OJ C364/1, Art. 41(2).

[15] Cases C–48 and 66/90 *Netherlands and Koninklijke PTT Nederland NV and PTT Post* v. *Commission* [1992] ECR I–565.

[16] Case T–7/89 *SA Hercules Chemicals NV* v. *Commission* [1991] ECR II–1711, paras. 53–54; Case T–65/89 *BPB Industries plc and British Gypsum Ltd.* v. *Commission* [1993] ECR II–389; Case T–42/96 *Eyckeler & Malt AG* v. *Commission* [1998] ECR II–401; Case T–346/94 *France-Aviation* v. *Commission* [1995] ECR II–2841.

[17] Case 16/90 *Nolle* v. *Hauptzollamt Bremen-Freihafen* [1991] ECR I–5163; Case C–269/90 *Hauptzollamt München-Mitte* v. *Technische Universität München* [1991] ECR I–5469; Case C–367/95 P *Commission* v. *Sytraval and Brink's France Sàrl* [1998] ECR I–1719.

[18] Case 138/79 *Roquette Frères SA* v. *Council* [1980] ECR 3333.

[19] Case C–104/97 P *Atlanta AG* v. *Commission* [1999] ECR I–6983; Case C–258/02 P *Bactria Industriehygiene-Service Verwaltungs GmbH* v. *Commission* [2003] ECR I–15105, para. 43.

[20] Case C–10/95 P *Asociasion Española de Empresas de la Carne (Asocarne)* v. *Council* [1995] ECR I–4149, para. 39; Case T–583/93 *Stichting Greenpeace Council (Greenpeace International)* v. *Commission* [1995] ECR II–2205, para. 56; Case C–263/02 P *Commission* v. *Jégo-Quéré & Cie. SA* [2004] ECR I–3425, para. 48.

This is regrettable. Participation is one way of imbuing decisions with greater legitimacy. It renders decision-making more accessible to those affected, and enables them to have direct participatory input into the decision reached. The European Council's 1993 Inter-institutional Declaration on Democracy, Transparency, and Subsidiarity proposed the creation of a notification procedure, in which the Commission would publish a brief summary of the draft measure in the Official Journal, and there would be a deadline by which interested parties could submit their comments. There is a clear analogy between this formulation and the United States' Administrative Procedure Act 1946, which established a notice and comment procedure for rules made by agencies.

The Commission's response to this idea was, however, limited.[21] It did not bring forward any general measure for the EC akin to the APA, and the discussion of participation rights in its report for the 1996 IGC was exiguous to say the least.[22] The Commission has broadened consultation through increasing use of Green and White Papers when important areas of EC policy are being developed.[23] It has also created Interactive Policy Making, IPM, a principal component of 'Your Voice in Europe',[24] which consists of two internet-based instruments to collect feedback from citizens, consumers, and business, although the number of initiatives subjected to this process is limited. The Commission nonetheless continues to resist the creation of legally enforceable participatory rights as against itself,[25] while at the same time pressing for such rights as against the Member States.[26]

(c) DUTY TO GIVE REASONS

Article 253 imposes a duty to provide reasons,[27] breach of which constitutes violation of an essential procedural requirement for the purposes of review.[28] The duty applies to regulations, decisions, and directives, adopted either by the Council, Commission, and Parliament, or by the Council and Commission alone. Thus Article 253 imposes a duty to give reasons not only for administrative decisions, but also for legislative norms, such as regulations or directives. This is noteworthy, since many national legal systems do not impose an obligation to furnish reasons for legislative acts, or do so only in limited circumstances.

There are a number of *policy rationales* for the duty to provide reasons. From the perspective of affected parties, it renders the decision-making process more transparent, so that they can know why a measure has been adopted. From the perspective of the decision-maker, an obligation to give reasons helps to ensure that the rationale for the action has been thought through. From the perspective of the ECJ, the existence of reasons facilitates judicial review

---

[21] Craig, n. 10 above, ch. 10.

[22] P. Craig, 'Democracy and Rule-making within the EC: An Empirical and Normative Assessment' (1997) 3 *ELJ* 105.

[23] Communication from the Commission, Towards a Reinforced Culture of Consultation and Dialogue—General Principles and Minimum Standards for Consultation of Interested Parties by the Commission, COM(2002)704 final.

[24] Available at http://europa.eu.int/yourvoice/consultations/index_en.htm.

[25] Communication from the Commission, n. 23 above, 10.

[26] See, e.g., Council Dir. 96/61/EC of 24 Sept. concerning integrated pollution prevention and control [1996] OJ L257/26, Art. 4(4).

[27] Case 24/62 *Germany* v. *Commission* [1963] ECR 63; Case 5/67 *Beus GmbH & Co.* v. *Hauptzollamt München* [1968] ECR 83; Case C–143/95 P *Commission* v. *Sociedade de Curtumes a Sul do Tejo Ld (Socurte)* [1997] ECR I–1; Case T–83/96 *Gerard van der Wal* v. *Commission* [1998] ECR II–545.

[28] Case C–378/00 *Commission* v. *European Parliament and Council* [2003] ECR I–937, para. 34.

by, for example, enabling the Court to determine whether a decision was disproportionate. In the words of the ECJ:[29]

> In imposing upon the Commission the obligation to state reasons for its decisions, Article 190 is not taking mere formal considerations into account but seeks to give an opportunity to the parties defending their rights, to the court of exercising its supervisory functions and to Member States and to all interested nationals of ascertaining the circumstances in which the Commission has applied the Treaty.

The *content* of the obligation to give reasons will vary depending on the nature of the measure.[30] Where it is of a general legislative nature it will be necessary for the Community authority to show the reasoning which led to its adoption, but it will not be necessary for it to go into every point of fact and law. Where the essential objective of the measure has been clearly disclosed there is no need for a specific statement of the reasons for each of the technical choices that have been made.[31] The Court may well demand greater particularity where the measure being challenged is of an individual, rather than legislative, nature. Thus in *Germany v. Commission*,[32] the Commission made a decision restricting the amount of wine that Germany could import at a lower rate of duty, on the ground that there was ample production of wine in the EC, and because the grant of the requested quota would lead to serious disturbances on the relevant product market. The ECJ annulled the decision. It held that the Commission's reasoning was insufficiently specific concerning the size of any Community surplus, and that it was unclear from the Commission's decision why there would be serious disturbances in the market.

The content of the duty to provide reasons will also be affected by the extent to which the Court requires the Community institutions to respond to arguments advanced by the parties, which has been termed the dialogue dimension.[33] The ECJ has been cautious in this respect. In the *Sigarettenindustrie* case[34] the Court held that, although Article 253 required the Commission to state its reasons, it was not required to discuss all the issues of fact and law raised by every party during the administrative proceedings. It therefore dismissed the claim that the Commission had ignored the applicants' arguments, none of which had featured in the decision.[35] Shapiro explains why the ECJ has been reluctant to move in this direction, and also why, nonetheless, it might be pushed to do so. The references to Article 190 should now be read as referring to Article 253.

M. Shapiro, The Giving Reasons Requirement[36]

The basic reason that the parties push and the ECJ resists dialogue lies in the difference between transparency and participation. Courts are likely to be initially hostile to demands for

---

[29] Case 24/62, n. 27 above, 69. See also Case T–47/03 *Sison* v. Council, 11 July 2007, paras. 218–227.

[30] Case 5/67 *Beus* [1968] ECR 83, 95; Case C–205/94 *Binder GmbH* v. *Hauptzollamt Stuttgart-West* [1996] ECR I–2871.

[31] Case C–122/94 *Commission v. Council* [1996] ECR I–881, para. 29; Case C–84/94 *United Kingdom* v. *Council* [1996] ECR I–5755, paras. 74, 79.

[32] Case 24/62, n. 27 above; Case T–5/93 *Tremblay* v. *Commission* [1995] ECR II–185.

[33] M. Shapiro, 'The Giving Reasons Requirement' [1992] *U Chic. Legal Forum* 179, 203–204.

[34] Cases 240–242, 261–262, and 268–269/82 *Stichting Sigarettenindustrie* v. *Commission* [1985] ECR 3831, para. 88.

[35] See also Case 42/84 *Remia BV and Nutricia BV* v. *Commission* [1985] ECR 2545.

[36] N. 33 above, 204–205.

dialogue. Such requests are the last resort of regulated parties who have no substantive arguments left. Moreover, if dialogue claims are judicially accepted, they lead to a more and more cumbersome administrative process because the regulated parties will be encouraged to raise more and more arguments to which the agency will have to respond. If the only instrumental value for giving reasons is transparency, the courts will resist dialogue demands. One can discover an agency's actions and purposes without the agency rebutting every opposing argument.

. . .

If the ECJ sticks closely to transparency as the sole goal of Article 190, the ECJ is unlikely to move towards a dialogue requirement. Yet participation in government by interests affected by government decisions presents an increasingly compelling value in contemporary society, particularly where environmental matters are involved. The ECJ has already, however unintentionally, opened one avenue for linking participation to Article 190 by stating that the Council need not give full reasons to the Member States where they have participated in the decisions. To be sure, these ECJ opinions are transparency-based. They require that those Member States already know what was going on because they were there. Nevertheless they create an opening for counter-arguments from complainants who were not present and claim that, therefore, they need the Commission to be responsive. In short, full transparency can only be achieved through participation or through dialogue as a form of participation.

There has been some indication of movement in this direction. The CFI deals, *inter alia*, with cases within specialized fields, such as competition, where the facts are often complex. While it has affirmed that the Commission is under no obligation to respond to all the parties' arguments, it has also emphasized that the reasons given must be sufficient to enable it to exercise its judicial review function, *and* it will scrutinize the Commission's reasoning, annulling the decision if it does not withstand examination.[37] The limits to which the Community Courts and the Community political institutions will foster dialogue and participation have however been noted above.[38]

5. INFRINGEMENT OF THE TREATY OR ANY RULE OF LAW RELATING TO ITS APPLICATION

(a) THE SCOPE OF THIS HEAD OF REVIEW

This ground of review has provided the foundation for the development of the principles of judicial review. Infringement of the Treaty includes all provisions of the constitutive treaties as amended. The absence of the *travaux préparatoires* means that we do not know what 'any rule of law relating to its application' was meant to connote.

The intent might have been simply to ensure that decision-making should have to comply not only with the primary Treaty articles, but also regulations, directives, etc., passed pursuant thereto. If this had been the intent it could however have been expressed more simply. The intent might alternatively have been to capture compliance not only with secondary legislation, but also with other 'rules of law relating to the application' of the Treaty that might be

---

[37] See, e.g., Case T–44/90 *La Cinq SA* v. *Commission* [1992] ECR II–1; Case T–7/92 *Asia Motor France SA* v. *Commission* [1993] ECR II–669.
[38] See above, 540–541.

developed by the courts. The ambiguity in the phrase provided the ECJ with a window through which to justify the imposition of administrative law principles as grounds of review.

This strategy was reinforced by Article 220 EC, which charged the ECJ with the duty of ensuring that in the interpretation and application of the Treaty the law should be observed. The judicial task of elaborating principles of judicial review was further facilitated by more specific Treaty Articles, which made reference to, for example, non-discrimination. The ECJ then read these articles as indicative of a more general principle of non-discrimination that underpinned the entire Community legal order.[39] Moreover Article 6(1) TEU as amended by the Treaty of Amsterdam provided that the Union was founded on the principles of liberty, democracy, respect for human rights and fundamental freedoms, and the rule of law, principles which are common to the Member States.

The ECJ has therefore developed a rich body of jurisprudence on general principles of law, covering topics such as process rights, fundamental rights, equal treatment and non-discrimination, proportionality, and legal certainty and legitimate expectations.[40] In developing these concepts the ECJ drew on national administrative law doctrine. German law was perhaps the most influential in this regard, providing the inspiration for the introduction of, for example, proportionality and legitimate expectations into the Community legal order.

The general principles are used in a number of different ways. They function as interpretive guides in relation to primary Treaty Articles and other Community acts. The general principles also operate as grounds of review. The Community Courts cannot invalidate primary Treaty Articles. They can however annul other Community acts, and breach of a general principle will be a ground for annulment. The principles can also be used against national measures that fall within the scope of EU law, although the range of measures caught in this manner is not free from doubt. Breach of a general principle may also form the basis for a damages action. Judicial review for violation of fundamental rights has been considered in a previous chapter.[41] The discussion in this chapter will consider other important general principles of law.

(b) GENERAL PRINCIPLES OF LAW: PROPORTIONALITY

(i) *Meaning*

The concept of proportionality is most fully developed within German law. It appeared initially in the context of policing as a ground for challenging measures that were excessive or unnecessary in relation to the objective being pursued.[42] Some notion of proportionality also features within the legal systems of other Member States such as France, although one should be cautious about ascribing the same meaning to the concept whenever the word 'proportionality' is to be found in any guise within differing legal systems.[43]

Proportionality is now well established as a general principle of Community law. A version of the principle is enshrined in Article 5 EC, which provides that action by the Community shall not go beyond what is necessary to achieve the objectives of the Treaty, and its requirements are further fleshed out in a protocol to the Treaty. Proportionality can thus be used to

---

[39] Cases 117/76 and 16/77 *Ruckdeschel* v. *Hauptzollamt Hambourg–St. Annen* [1977] ECR 1753, para. 7.

[40] K. Lenaerts and T. Corthaut, 'Judicial Review as a Contribution to the Development of European Constitutionalism' (2002) 22 *YBEL* 1.

[41] See above Ch. 11.

[42] J. Schwarze, *European Administrative Law* (Sweet & Maxwell, 1992), 685–686.

[43] *Ibid.*, 680–685.

challenge Community action, and also to challenge the legality of state action which falls within the sphere of application of Community law.

In any proportionality inquiry the relevant interests must be identified, and there will be some ascription of weight or value to those interests, since this is a necessary condition precedent to any balancing operation. There will normally be three stages in a proportionality inquiry.

i.   whether the measure was suitable to achieve the desired end;

ii. whether it was necessary to achieve the desired end;

iii. whether the measure imposed a burden on the individual that was excessive in relation to the objective sought to be achieved (proportionality *stricto sensu*).

There has been some doubt whether stage three is part of the proportionality inquiry undertaken by the ECJ.[44] The reality is that the ECJ will consider stage three when an applicant addresses an argument concerning this stage of the inquiry. It may not do so where no such specific argument has been raised, more especially where the case can be resolved at one of the earlier stages. Moreover, in some cases the ECJ may distinguish stages two and three of the inquiry; in others it may in effect 'fold' stage three of the inquiry back into stage two. The Court will moreover have to decide how intensively it is going to apply the proportionality test. The relative intensity of judicial review is just as much a live question in relation to proportionality as it is in relation to any other tool of judicial oversight, as the following extract reveals.

G. de Búrca, The Principle of Proportionality and its Application in EC Law[45]

It becomes apparent that in reaching decisions, the Court of Justice is influenced not only by what it considers to be the nature and the importance of the interest or right claimed by the applicant, and the nature and importance of the objective alleged to be served by the measure, but by the relative expertise, position and overall competence of the Court as against the decision-making authority in assessing those factors. It becomes apparent that the way the proportionality principle is applied by the Court of Justice covers a spectrum ranging from a very deferential approach, to quite a rigorous and searching examination of the justification for a measure which has been challenged.

... Courts are generally prepared to adjudicate on issues involving traditionally categorized individual rights, where interference with a discretionary policy decision can be explained not on the ground that it is not the most sensible or effective measure, but on the ground that it unjustifiably restricts an important legally recognized right, the protection of which is entrusted to the court. Courts are accepted as having a legitimate role in deciding on civil liberties and personal rights even in controversial contexts such as euthanasia, abortion and freedom of speech. But in certain specific political contexts, in the case of measures involving, for example, national security, economic policy or national expenditure concerns, courts tend to be considerably more deferential in their review. They are more reluctant to adjudicate if the interest affected is seen as a collective or general public interest rather than an individual right, and if the interest of the State is a mixed and complex one, e.g. in an area involving national economic and social policy choices ... The ways in which a court may defer in such

---

[44] Craig, n. 10 above, ch. 17.
[45] (1993) 13 *YBEL* 105, 111–112.

circumstances range from deeming the measure to be non-justiciable, to refusing to look closely at the justification for the restrictive effects of the measure, to placing the onus of proof on the challenger who is claiming that the measure is disproportionate. Courts tend to be deferential in their review in cases which highlight the non-representative nature of the judiciary, the limited evidentiary and procedural processes of adjudication, and the difficulty of providing a defined individual remedy in contexts which involve complex political and economic policies.

(ii) *Challenge to Community Action: Proportionality and Rights*

We can distinguish three broad types of case that may be subject to challenge on grounds of proportionality, and the intensity of review may differ in each.[46]

The first category is where an individual argues that her rights have been unduly restricted by Community action. The courts are likely to engage in vigorous scrutiny. Society may well accept that these rights cannot be regarded as absolute, but the very denomination of certain interests as Community rights means that any interference should be kept to a minimum. In this sense proportionality is a natural and necessary adjunct to the recognition of such rights. Moreover, courts regard it as a natural and proper part of their legitimate function to adjudicate on the boundary lines between state action and individual rights, even though this line may be controversial.

This is exemplified by the *Hautala* case.[47] The applicant was an MEP, who sought access to a Council document concerning arms exports. The Council refused to grant access on the ground that this could be harmful to the EU's relations with third countries, and sought to justify this under Article 4(1) of Decision 93/731,[48] governing access to Council documentation. The ECJ held that the right of access to documents was to be broadly construed so as to include access to information contained in the document, not just the document itself. Proportionality required the Council to consider partial access to a document that contained information the disclosure of which could endanger one of the interests protected by Article 4(1). Proportionality also required that derogation from the right of access be limited to what was appropriate and necessary for achieving the aim in view.

Many cases concerning rights and proportionality are however more complex, because the argument arises as one of the grounds of challenge to a discretionary policy choice made by the Community. The applicant will allege that the discretionary policy infringed her property rights or the right to pursue a profession, trade, or occupation. The Community Courts acknowledge such rights within the Community legal order, but make it clear that they are not absolute and must be viewed in relation to their social function. The ECJ and CFI will therefore consider whether the restrictions imposed by the measure correspond to objectives of general interest pursued by the Community, and whether they constitute a disproportionate and intolerable interference which impairs the very substance of the rights guaranteed.[49]

---

[46] Craig, n. 10 above, ch. 17; T. Tridimas, *The General Principles of EC Law* (2nd edn., Oxford University Press, 2006), ch. 3.

[47] Case C–353/99 P *Council* v. *Hautala* [2001] ECR I–9565. See also Case C–353/01 P *Olli Mattila* v. *Council and Commission* [2004] ECR I–1073; Case T–2/03 *Verein für Konsumenteninformation* v. *Commission* [2005] ECR II–1121.

[48] [1993] OJ L340/43.

[49] Case 265/87 *Schräder HS Kraftfutter GmbH & Co. KG* v. *Hauptzollamt Gronau* [1989] ECR 2237, para. 15; Case C–280/93 *Germany* v. *Council* [1994] ECR I–4973, para. 78; Case C–200/96 *Musik Metronome GmbH* v. *Music Point Hokamp GmbH* [1998] ECR I–1953, para. 21; Case C–293/97 *R.* v. *Secretary of State for the Environment and Ministry of Agriculture, Fisheries and Food, ex p. Standley* [1999] ECR I–2603, para. 54.

Thus in *Hauer*[50] the applicant challenged a Community regulation limiting the planting of new vines. The Court found that this did not, in itself, constitute an invalid restriction on property rights. It then considered whether the planting restrictions were disproportionate, 'impinging upon the very substance of the right to property'.[51] The Court found that they were not, but in reaching this conclusion it carefully examined the purpose of the general scheme within which the contested regulation fell. The objects of this scheme were to attain a balanced wine market, with fair prices for consumers and a fair return for producers; the eradication of surpluses; and improvement in the quality of wine. The disputed regulation, which prohibited new plantings, was part of this overall plan. It was not disproportionate in the light of the legitimate, general Community policy for this area. This policy was designed to deal with an immediate problem of surpluses, while at the same time laying the foundation for more permanent measures to facilitate a balanced wine market.[52]

(iii) *Challenge to Community Action: Proportionality and Penalties*

A second type of case is where the attack is on the penalty imposed, the claim being that it is excessive. Courts are likely to be reasonably searching in this type of case. This is in part because penalties can impinge on personal liberties. It is in part also because a court can normally strike down a particular penalty, without thereby undermining the relevant administrative policy. There has been a regular stream of such cases.

In *Man (Sugar)*[53] the applicant was required to give a security deposit to the Board when seeking a licence to export sugar outside the Community. The applicant was four hours late in completing the relevant paperwork. The Board, acting pursuant to a Community regulation, declared the entire deposit of £1,670,370 to be forfeit. The Court held that the automatic forfeiture of the entire deposit because of any failure to fulfill the time requirement was too drastic, given the function performed by the system of export licences.[54]

In addition to cases dealing with penalties *stricto sensu* the Court has applied proportionality to scrutinize the charges imposed by the Community institutions. Thus in *Bela-Mühle*[55] the Court held that a scheme whereby producers of animal feed were forced to use skimmed milk, rather than soya, in their product in order to reduce a milk surplus was unlawful. Skimmed milk was three times more expensive than soya: the obligation to purchase the milk, therefore, imposed a disproportionate burden on the animal-feed producers. In *Portugal v. Commission*[56] Portugal argued that an export ban on meat products, imposed in response to mad cow disease, was disproportionate. This was because Portugal was not a significant meat exporter, and it was therefore easier to regulate low-volume exports as compared to the large-volume exports from the UK. The ECJ rejected the argument. Beef exports from the UK had not been allowed until the UK had put in place export arrangements of a kind advocated by a certain health code. This had not been done at the time when the ban was imposed on Portugal.

[50] Case 44/79 *Hauer* v. *Land Rheinland-Pfalz* [1979] ECR 3727.
[51] *Ibid.*, para. 23.
[52] See also Case C–491/01 *R.* v. *Secretary of State for Health, ex p. British American Tobacco (Investments) Ltd. and Imperial Tobacco Ltd.* [2002] ECR I–11453; Cases C–20 and 64/00 *Booker Aquacultur Ltd. and Hydro Seafood GSP Ltd.* v. *Scottish Ministers* [2003] ECR I–7411; Cases C–184 and 223/02 *Spain and Finland* v. *European Parliament and Council* [2004] ECR I–7789.
[53] Case 181/84 *R.* v. *Intervention Board, ex p. E. D. & F. Man (Sugar) Ltd.* [1985] ECR 2889.
[54] *Ibid.*, para. 29; Case 240/78 *Atalanta Amsterdam BV* v. *Produktschap voor Vee en Vlees* [1979] ECR 2137; Case 122/78 *Buitoni SA* v. *Fonds d'Orientation et de Régularisation des Marchés Agricoles* [1979] ECR 677.
[55] Case 114/76 *Bela-Mühle Josef Bergman KG* v. *Grows-Farm GmbH & Co. KG* [1977] ECR 1211.
[56] Case C–365/99 [2001] ECR I–5645.

(iv) *Challenge to Community Action: Proportionality and Discretionary Policy Choices*

A third type of case is where the individual argues that the very policy choice made by the administration is disproportionate. The judiciary is likely to be more circumspect in this type of case. The reasons are not hard to find. The administrative/political arm of government makes policy choices, and it is generally recognized that the courts should not overturn these merely because they believe that a different way of doing things would have been better. They should not substitute their judgement for that of the administration. This does not mean that proportionality is ruled out in such instances. It does mean that the courts are likely to apply the concept less intensively than in the previous categories, and will overturn the policy choice only if it is clearly or manifestly disproportionate.

Many of these cases arise from the Common Agricultural Policy (CAP), the objectives of which are set out at a high level of generality in Article 33 EC. These objectives can clash *inter se*, with the result that the Commission and Council will have to make difficult discretionary choices, often under fairly extreme time constraints, in order to decide how to balance these aims. The *Fedesa* case provides a good example of a challenge to a more general Community policy choice made under the CAP. The Court has frequently emphasized that the Community institutions possess a wide discretion in the operation of the CAP, and that review will not therefore be intensive.[57] This more deferential approach applies equally to challenges based on proportionality.

Case C–331/88 **R. v. Minister for Agriculture, Fisheries and Food, ex parte Fedesa**
[1990] ECR I–4023

Council Directive 81/602 provided that the Council would take a decision as soon as possible on the prohibition of certain hormone substances for administration to animals, but that in the meantime any arrangements made by Member States in relation to such substances would continue to apply. In 1988 Council Directive 88/146 was adopted as an approximating measure, prohibiting the use in livestock farming of certain of these hormonal substances. An earlier identical directive adopted in 1985 had been declared void by the ECJ on grounds of an infringement by the Council of an essential procedural requirement. The applicants were manufacturers and distributors of veterinary medicine who challenged the validity of the national legislative measure implementing the 1988 Directive, on the ground that the Directive itself was invalid. They argued that the Directive infringed the principles of legal certainty, proportionality, equality, and non-retrospectivity. The following extract considers the ECJ's reasoning on proportionality.

THE ECJ

12. It was argued that the Directive infringes the principle of proportionality in three respects. In the first place, the outright prohibition on the administration of the five hormones in question is inappropriate in order to attain the declared objectives, since it is impossible to apply in practice and leads to the creation of a dangerous black market. In the second place,

---

[57] See, e.g., Case 138/78 *Stolting* v. *Hauptzollamt Hamburg-Jonas* [1979] ECR 713; Case 265/87 *Schräder* v. *Hauptzollamt Gronau* [1989] ECR 2237.

outright prohibition is not necessary because consumer anxieties can be allayed simply by the dissemination of information and advice. Finally, the prohibition in question entails excessive disadvantages, in particular considerable financial losses on the part of the traders concerned, in relation to the alleged benefits accruing to the general interest.

13. The Court has consistently held that the principle of proportionality is one of the general principles of Community law. By virtue of that principle, the lawfulness of the prohibition of an economic activity is subject to the condition that the prohibitory measures are appropriate and necessary in order to achieve the objectives legitimately pursued by the legislation in question; when there is a choice between several appropriate measures recourse must be had to the least onerous, and the disadvantages caused must not be disproportionate to the aims pursued.

14. However, with regard to judicial review of compliance with those conditions it must be stated that in matters concerning the common agricultural policy the Community legislature has a discretionary power which corresponds to the political responsibilities given to it by … the Treaty. Consequently, the legality of a measure adopted in that sphere can be affected only if the measure is manifestly inappropriate having regard to the objective which the competent institution is seeking to pursue. (See in particular the judgment in Case 265/87, *Schräder* [1989] ECR 2237, paras. 21 and 22).

The applicants had therefore to show that the measure was manifestly inappropriate, and the Court concluded that they had not discharged this burden.[58] The prohibition, even though it might have caused financial loss to some traders, could not be regarded as manifestly inappropriate.

It is now clear from cases such as *British American Tobacco*[59] that this measure of review will be deemed appropriate whenever the Community legislature exercises a broad discretion involving political, economic, or social choices requiring it to make complex assessments.

It would nonetheless be wrong to assume that proportionality when interpreted in this manner necessarily has the same meaning as *Wednesbury* irrationality in UK law. The reality is that the former is still generally more exacting than the latter. The ECJ will look closely at the reasoning used when reaching the contested decision and the evidentiary foundation for it, even for cases coming within this third category.[60]

(v) *Challenge to Member State Action*

There have been many cases dealing with proportionality in the context of Community rights and Member State action that seeks to restrict the ambit of those rights.[61]

Thus the ECJ has insisted that derogation from the principle of free movement of workers can be sanctioned only in cases which pose a genuine and serious threat to public policy, and even then the measure must be the least restrictive possible in the circumstances.[62]

---

[58] See also, e.g., Case C–8/89 *Zardi* v. *Consorzio Agrario Provinciale di Ferrara* [1990] ECR I–2515; Cases C–133, 300, and 362/93 *Crispoltoni* v. *Fattoria Autonoma Tabacchi* [1994] ECR I–4863; Case C–4/96 *Northern Ireland Fish Producers' Federation and Northern Ireland Fishermen's Federation* v. *Department of Agriculture for Northern Ireland* [1998] ECR I–681; Case C–434/02 *Arnold André GmbH & Co. KG* v. *Landrat des Kreises Herford* [2004] ECR I–11825, paras. 46–56; Case C–41/03 P *Rica Foods (Free Zone) NV* v. *Commission* [2005] ECR I–6875, paras. 85–86; Case T–158/03 *Industrias Quimicas del Valles, SA* v. *Commission* [2005] ECR II–2425, para. 136.

[59] Case C–491/01 *British American Tobacco*, n. 52 above, para. 123; Case C–210/03 *The Queen, on the application of Swedish Match AB and Swedish Match UK Ltd.* v. *Secretary of State for Health* [2004] ECR I–11893, para. 48.

[60] Craig, n. 10 above, ch. 17.

[61] *Ibid.*, ch. 18; Tridimas, n. 46 above, ch. 4.

[62] Case 36/75 *Rutili* v. *Ministre de l'Intérieur* [1975] ECR 1219; Case 30/77 *R.* v. *Bouchereau* [1977] ECR 1999.

The same principle is evident in cases on freedom to provide services. In *Van Binsbergen*[63] the Court held that residence requirements limiting this freedom might be justified, but only where they were strictly necessary to prevent the evasion by those outside the territory of professional rules applicable to the activity in question. In *Canal Digital*[64] the ECJ considered the legality of national legislation requiring operators of certain television services to register details of their equipment in a national register. It held that such a measure could not satisfy the necessity requirement of the proportionality test if the registration requirement duplicated controls already carried out, either in the same State or in another Member State.

We can see the same approach at work in cases concerned with the free movement of goods. Thus in the famous *Cassis de Dijon* case[65] the Court decided that a German rule which prescribed the minimum alcohol content for a certain beverage could restrict the free movement of goods. The Court then considered whether the rule was necessary to protect consumers from being misled. It rejected the defence, because the interests of consumers could be safeguarded in other, less restrictive ways, by displaying the alcohol content on the packaging of the drinks.[66]

Proportionality will also often be of relevance in equality cases. Thus in *Kreil*[67] it was held that a German rule requiring that all armed units in the Bundeswehr be male contravened the principle of proportionality.

The Court tends to engage in fairly intensive review to determine whether the restriction which the Member State imposed on an important right granted by the Treaties really is necessary or warranted. The rationale for this is readily explicable. The paradigm application of proportionality in relation to the four freedoms entails the case where a *prima facie* breach of one of the four freedoms has been found to exist, and the Member State then seeks to raise a defence based on the relevant Treaty article. The four freedoms are central to the very idea of market integration that lies at the economic heart of the EU. They also embody non-economic values. It is therefore unsurprising that the ECJ has closely monitored defences to free movement, including in this respect proportionality. Four more particular variables affect the intensity of the Court's review in this type of case.

First, other things being equal, the Court has tended to be more intensive in its review over time. Cases which have come before the Court involving similar facts or raising similar principles have tended to be subject to more rigorous scrutiny, with the result that Member State action which was regarded as lawful in the earlier case has been held not to be so in a later action.[68]

Secondly, the intensity of the Court's review will also be a function of how seriously it takes the Member State's argument that measures really were necessary in order to protect, for example, public health. If the Court feels that these measures were really a 'front' for a national

---

[63] Case 33/74 *Van Binsbergen v. Bestuur van de Bedrijfsvereniging Metaalnijverheid* [1974] ECR 1299; Case 39/75 *Coenen v. Sociaal Economische Raad* [1975] ECR 1547; Case C–140/03 *Commission v. Greece* [2005] ECR I–3177.

[64] Case C–390/99 *Canal Satelite Digital SL v. Aministiacion General del Estado and Distribuidora de Television Gigital SA (DTS)* [2002] ECR I–607.

[65] Case 120/78 *Rewe-Zentrale AG v. Bundesmonopolverwaltung für Branntwein* [1979] ECR 649.

[66] Recent examples of the same principle are Case C–217/99 *Commission v. Belgium* [2000] ECR I–10251; Case C–473/98 *Kemikalieinspektionen v. Toolex Alpha AB* [2000] ECR I–5681; Case 270/02 *Commission v. Italy* [2004] ECR I–1559; Case C–41/02 *Commission v. Netherlands* [2004] ECR I–11375.

[67] Case C–285/98 *Kreil v. Bundesrepublik Deutschland* [2000] ECR I–69.

[68] Compare, e.g., Case 41/74 *Van Duyn v. Home Office* [1974] ECR 1337 with Cases 115 and 116/81 *Adoui and Cornuaille v. Belgian State* [1982] ECR 1665. Compare Case 34/79 *R. v. Henn and Darby* [1979] ECR 3795 with Case 121/85 *Conegate v. Customs and Excise Commissioners* [1986] ECR 1007.

protective policy designed to insulate its own producers from foreign competition, then it will be inclined to subject the Member State's argument to close scrutiny. This is exemplified by *Commission* v. *United Kingdom*.[69] The ECJ rejected a claim by the UK Government that a ban on the import of poultry could be justified on grounds of public health, because it felt that the measures were, in reality, aimed at protecting UK poultry producers from the effects of French imports before Christmas. The Court accordingly rejected the UK's defence.

A third factor is the nature of the subject-matter. Where a Member State raises genuine concerns relating to public health[70] and there is scientific uncertainty about the effects of certain foodstuffs, the Court has been more willing to accept that limitations on free movement are warranted.[71] However, one should be cautious about characterizing such cases as involving less intensive review. They may equally well be regarded as instances where the Court, *having surveyed the evidence*, believed that the Member State's action was warranted. There are, moreover, examples of public-health claims where the Court, while accepting that there was some scientific uncertainty, nonetheless concluded that there was a less restrictive way of achieving the Member State's aim.[72]

The final variable affecting the intensity of the proportionality inquiry is rather different from those considered above. In some instances the Court has passed the application of proportionality back to the national courts. This should not, however, be taken to mean that the Court is necessarily being more deferential in the application of proportionality. This can only be determined by considering the conditions, or guidelines, which the ECJ lays down for national courts on how the proportionality inquiry should be decided in a particular area.[73] There is, moreover, justifiable concern about the complexity of the issues that are sent back to national courts to be resolved through a proportionality inquiry.[74]

(c) GENERAL PRINCIPLES OF LAW: LEGAL CERTAINTY AND LEGITIMATE EXPECTATIONS

The connected concepts of legal certainty and legitimate expectations are found in many legal systems, although their precise legal content may vary.[75] These concepts are applied in a number of different ways.[76]

(i) *Actual Retroactivity*

The most obvious application of legal certainty is in the context of rules with an actual retroactive effect. Following Schwarze,[77] 'actual retroactivity' covers the situation where a rule

---

[69] Case 40/82 [1982] ECR 2793.

[70] See 701–703, 709–711 below.

[71] Case 174/82 *Officier van Justitie* v. *Sandoz BV* [1983] ECR 2445; Case 97/83 *Melkunie* v. *Commission* [1984] ECR 2367.

[72] Case 178/84 *Commission* v. *Germany* [1987] ECR 1227.

[73] G. de Búrca, 'The Principle of Proportionality and its Application in EC Law' (1993) 13 *YBEL* 105.

[74] W. van Gerven, 'The Effect of Proportionality on the Actions of Member States of the European Community: National Viewpoints from Continental Europe', in E. Ellis (ed.), *The Principle of Proportionality in the Laws of Europe* (Hart, 1999), 37.

[75] S. Schonberg, *Legitimate Expectations in Administrative Law* (Oxford University Press, 2000); Craig, n. 10 above, ch. 16; Schwarze, n. 42 above, ch. 6; Tridimas, n. 46 above, ch. 6.

[76] Thus, as we have seen, 472–473, the concept of legal certainty can have implications on how far an administrative decision that has become final should be re-opened in the light of a subsequent ruling by the Community Courts.

[77] Schwarze, n. 42 above, 1120.

is introduced and applied to events which have already been concluded. Retroactivity of this nature may occur either where the date of entry into force precedes the date of publication, or where the regulation applies to circumstances which have actually been concluded before the entry into force of the measure.

The arguments against allowing such measures to have legal effect are compelling. A basic tenet of the rule of law is that people ought to be able to plan their lives secure in the knowledge of the legal consequences of their actions. This fundamental aspect of the rule of law is violated by the application of measures that were not in force when the actual events took place. These concerns about retrospective norms are particularly marked in the context of criminal penalties, where the effect may be to criminalize activity that was lawful when it was undertaken. The application of retrospective rules may also be extremely damaging in commercial circumstances, upsetting the presuppositions on which important transactions have been based. It is therefore unsurprising that national legal systems take a very dim view of retroactive rules.

The Community is no different in this respect. The basic principle was enunciated in *Racke*.[78] The Commission had introduced monetary compensatory amounts for a certain product by a regulation, and then in two further regulations altered the amounts. Each of the relevant regulations provided that it would apply fourteen days before it was published. The Court held that it was a fundamental principle of the Community legal order that a measure should not be applicable to those concerned before they had the opportunity to make themselves acquainted with it.[79] The Court then drew out the implications for retroactive measures, stating that:[80]

> Although in general the principle of legal certainty precludes a Community measure from taking effect from a point in time before its publication, it may exceptionally be otherwise where the purpose to be achieved so demands and where the legitimate expectations of those concerned are duly respected.

The Court has, in accordance with this proviso, upheld the validity of retroactive measures, particularly in the agricultural sphere, where they were necessary to ensure market stability or where the retroactivity placed the individual in a more favourable position.[81] The normal presumption is, however, against the validity of retroactive measures. This manifests itself in both procedural and substantive terms.

In procedural terms, the Court has made it clear that it will interpret norms as having retroactive effect only if this clearly follows from their terms, or from the objectives of the general scheme of which they are a part. The general principle of construction is, therefore, against giving rules any retroactive impact.[82]

In substantive terms, the Court will strike down measures that have a retroactive effect where there is no pressing Community objective which demands this temporal dimension, or

---

[78] Case 98/78 *Firma A. Racke* v. *Hauptzollamt Mainz* [1979] ECR 69. See also Case 99/78 *Weingut Gustav Decker KG* v. *Hauptzollamt Landau* [1979] ECR 101; Case T–115/94 *Opel Austria GmbH* v. *Council* [1997] ECR II–2739.

[79] *Ibid.*, para. 84.

[80] *Ibid.*, para. 86.

[81] Case T–7/99 *Medici Grimm KG* v. *Council* [2000] ECR II–2671.

[82] Cases 212–217/80 *Salumi* [1981] ECR 2735; Case C–110/03 *Belgium* v. *Commission* [2005] ECR I–2801, para. 73.

where the legitimate expectations of those affected by the measure cannot be duly respected,[83] as the following case shows.

Case 63/83 **Regina v. Kent Kirk**
[1984] ECR 2689

Criminal proceedings were brought in the United Kingdom for infringement of fisheries legislation. During the course of these proceedings the question arose whether Council Regulation 170/83 of 25 January 1983, by which, with retroactive effect from 1 January 1983, national measures contravening Community law prohibitions on discrimination were approved by way of transitional arrangements, could also retroactively validate national penal provisions. The ECJ said no, firmly.

THE ECJ

20. The Commission ... contends that the Member States were empowered to adopt measures such as the Sea Fish Order 1982 by Article 6(1) of Regulation 170/83 of 25 January 1983 which authorises retroactively, as from 1 January 1983, the retention of the derogation regime defined in Article 100 of the 1972 Act of Accession for a further ten years, and which extends the coastal zones from six to twelve nautical miles. . . .

21. Without embarking upon an examination of the general legality of the retroactivity of Article 6(1) of that Regulation, it is sufficient to point out that such retroactivity may not, in any event, have the effect of validating ex post facto national measures of a penal nature which impose penalties for an act which, in fact, was not punishable at the time at which it was committed. That would be the case where at the time of the act entailing a criminal penalty, the national measure was invalid because it was incompatible with Community law.

22. The principle that penal provisions may not have retroactive effect is one which is common to all the legal orders of the Member States and is enshrined in Article 7 of the European Convention for the Protection of Human Rights and Fundamental Freedoms as a fundamental right; it takes its place among the general principles of law whose observance is ensured by the Court of Justice.

23. Consequently the retroactivity provided for in Article 6(1) of Regulation 170/83 cannot be regarded as validating ex post facto national measures which imposed criminal penalties, at the time of the conduct at issue, if those measures were not valid.

Where there is a pressing Community objective and where the legitimate expectations of those concerned are duly respected, then retroactivity may, *exceptionally*, be accepted by the Court in the non-criminal context. This is exemplified by *Fedesa*.[84] The applicants argued that a Directive was in breach of the principle of non-retroactivity, on the ground that it was adopted on 7 March 1988 and stipulated that it was to be implemented by 1 January 1988 at the latest. The Court drew a distinction between the retroactive effect of penal provisions and retroactive effect outside the criminal sphere. As to the former, the Court affirmed *Kent Kirk*,

---

[83] Case 224/82 *Meiko-Konservenfabrik* v. *Federal Republic of Germany* [1983] ECR 2539; Case C–459/02 *Willy Gerekens and Association agricole pour la promotion de la commercialisation laitière Procola* v. *Etat du grand-duc de Luxembourg* [2004] ECR I–7315, paras. 21–27; Cases C–189, 202, 205, 208, and 213/02 P *Dansk Rorindustri A/S and others* v. *Commission* [2005] ECR I–5425, para. 202.

[84] Case C–331/88 [1990] ECR I–4023.

but held that the Directive in the *Fedesa* case did not impose any criminal liability as such. As to the latter, the Court ruled that the Directive did not contravene the principle of non-retroactivity. It had been adopted to replace an earlier directive which had been annulled. The time frame of the challenged Directive was necessary in order to avoid a temporary legal vacuum where there would be no Community legislation to back up the Member States' existing implementing provisions. It was for this reason that the Council had maintained the date of the earlier Directive when it passed the later Directive.[85]

(ii) *Legal Certainty, Legitimate Expectations, and Apparent Retroactivity*

Apparent retroactivity covers the situation where legislative acts are applied to events which occurred in the past, but which have not yet been definitively concluded.[86] These cases can be particularly difficult.[87] The moral arguments against allowing laws to have actual retroactive effect are powerful. Cases involving apparent retroactivity are more problematic, because the administration must obviously have the power to alter its policy for the future, even though this may have implications for the conduct of private parties which was planned on the basis of the pre-existing legal regime.[88] The law in this area is complex and only an outline can be provided here.[89] The key elements in the ECJ's approach can be described as follows.

First, the protection of legitimate expectations developed initially in relation to revocation of administrative decisions. The general principle is that favourable decisions bind the administration,[90] although this principle is subject to a number of exceptions.[91]

Secondly, the protection of legitimate expectations also applies to representations.[92] The general principle is that protection of legitimate expectations extends to any individual who is in a situation from which it is clear that, in giving precise and specific assurances,[93] the Community institutions caused that person to entertain justified hopes.[94] Whether a guideline or notice has generated an expectation will depend upon its nature and wording,[95] as exemplified by case law on state aids. In *CIRFS*[96] the ECJ was willing to accept that the Commission was bound by the terms of its policy framework, and in *Ijssel-Vliet*[97] it held that Commission guidelines which had been built into a Dutch aid scheme were binding upon the

---

[85] The Court held that there was no infringement of legitimate expectations, because the earlier dir. was only annulled because of a procedural defect, and those affected by the national implementing legislation could not expect the Council to change its attitude on the substance of the matter in the dir. during the short time between the annulment of the first dir. and the notification of the second dir.: *ibid.*, para. 47.

[86] It may sometimes be difficult to decide whether the case, in legal terms, concerns actual or apparent retroactivity: Case C–162/00 *Land Nordrhein-Westfalen* v. *Beata Pokrzeptowicz-Meyer* [2002] ECR I–1049.

[87] Schwarze, n. 42 above, 1121.

[88] For a valuable analysis of the justifications for protecting legitimate expectations see Schonberg, n. 75 above, ch. 1.

[89] See material in n. 75 above.

[90] Cases 7/56 and 3–7/57 *Algera* v. *Common Assembly* [1957] ECR 39; Case T–251/00 *Lagardere SCA and Canal SA* v. *Commission* [2002] ECR II–4825.

[91] Craig, n. 10 above, ch. 16.

[92] Case 54/65 *Chatillon* v. *High Authority* [1966] ECR 185, 196; Case 81/72 *Commission* v. *Council (Staff Salaries)* [1973] ECR 575, 584–585; Case 148/73 *Louwage* v. *Commission* [1974] ECR 81, para. 12.

[93] Case T–72/99 *Meyer* v. *Commission* [2000] ECR II–2521; Case T–290/97 *Mehibas Dordtselaan BV* v. *Commission* [2000] ECR II–15.

[94] Case T–489/93 *Unifruit Hellas EPE* v. *Commission* [1994] ECR II–1201; Case T–534/93 *Grynberg and Hall* v. *Commission* [1994] ECR II–595; Case T–456/93 *Consorzio Gruppo di Azioni Locale Murgia Messapica* v. *Commission* [1994] ECR II–361.

[95] Cases C–189, 202, 205, 208, and 213/02 P *Dansk Rorindustri*, n. 83 above, paras. 209–232.

[96] Case C–313/90 *CIRFS* v. *Commission* [1993] ECR I–1125, paras. 34–36.

[97] Case C–311/94 *Ijssel-Vliet Combinatie BV* v. *Minister van Economische Zaken* [1996] ECR I–5023.

Dutch government. Moreover, in *Vlaams Gewest*[98] the CFI held that the guidelines adopted by the Commission had to be applied in accordance with the principle of equal treatment, with the implication that like cases, as defined in the guidelines, had to be treated alike.

Thirdly, the claim will fail where the Court adjudges that the applicant's expectations were not legitimate. This will be so where, for example, the challenged Community activity was designed to close a legal gap in order to prevent traders from making a speculative profit;[99] or where the expectations were not reasonable because the contested measure should have been foreseen;[100] or where the applicant has not met the conditions attached to a grant of funding;[101] or because the Court simply disagreed with the reason the applicants claimed that their expectations had been disappointed. Thus in the *Fedesa* case, the Court felt that the traders could not have had a reasonable expectation that the substances in question would not be banned in the absence of conclusive scientific findings as to their dangers.[102]

Fourthly, the mere fact that a trader is disadvantaged by a change in the law will not, in and of itself, give cause for complaint based upon disappointment of legitimate expectations. A trader will not be held to have a legitimate expectation that an existing situation, which is capable of being altered by decisions taken by the institutions within the limits of their discretionary powers, will be maintained.[103] This is particularly so in the context of the CAP, where constant adjustments to meet new market circumstances are required.[104] It may also be so in other areas, such as competition policy, where the CFI emphasized that the Commission has discretion to alter the level of fines.[105]

Fifthly, the individual must be able to point either to a bargain of some form between the individual and the authorities, or to a course of conduct or assurance on the part of the authorities which can be said to generate the legitimate expectation. The *Mulder* case illustrates the first of these situations.

Case 120/86 **Mulder v. Minister van Landbouw en Visserij**
[1988] ECR 2321

The Community had an excess of milk. In order to reduce this excess it passed Regulation 1078/77, under which producers could cease milk production for a certain period in exchange

---

[98] Case T–214/95 *Vlaams Gewest* v. *Commission* [1998] ECR II–717.

[99] Case 2/75 *Einfuhr und Vorratsstelle für Getreide und Futtermittel* v. *Firma C. Mackprang* [1975] ECR 607; Case C–179/00 *Weidacher* v. *Bundesminister für Land- und Forstwirtschaft* [2002] ECR I–501.

[100] Case 265/85 *Van den Bergh en Jurgens and Van Dijk Food Products* v. *Commission* [1987] ECR 1155; Case C–350/88 *Delacre* v. *Commission* [1990] ECR I–395; Case T–489/93 *Unifruit Hellas EPE* v. *Commission* [1994] ECR II–1201; Cases T–466, 469, 473, 474, and 477/93 *O'Dwyer* v. *Council* [1996] ECR II–2071; Cases T–142 and 283/01 *Organizacion de Productores de Tunidos Congelados (OPTUC)* v. *Commission* [2004] ECR II–329; Case C–342/03 *Spain* v. *Council* [2005] ECR I–1975, para. 48; E. Sharpston, 'Legitimate Expectations and Economic Reality' (1990) 15 *ELRev.* 103.

[101] Case T–126/97 *Sonasa—Sociedade Nacional de Seguranca Ld* v. *Commission* [1999] ECR II–2793.

[102] Case C–331/88, n. 46 above, para. 10.

[103] Case C–110/97 *Netherlands* v. *Council* [2001] ECR I–8763; Case C–402/98 *ATB* v. *Ministero per le Politiche Agricole* [2000] ECR I–5501; Cases T–64–65/01 *Afrikanische Frucht-Compagnie GmbH and another* v. *Commission* [2004] ECR II–521, paras. 83–84; Case C–17/03 *Vereniging voor Energie, Milieu en Water and others* v. *Directeur van de Dienst uitvoering en toezicht energie* [2005] ECR I–4983, paras. 73–87.

[104] See, e.g., Case C–63/93 *Duff* v. *Minister for Agriculture and Food Ireland and the Attorney General* [1996] ECR I–569; Case C–22/94 *Irish Farmers' Association* v. *Minister for Agriculture, Food and Forestry (Ireland) and the Attorney General* [1997] ECR I–1809.

[105] Case T–31/99 *ABB Asea Brown Boveri Ltd.* v. *Commission* [2002] ECR II–1881.

for a premium for non-marketing of the milk. The applicant made such an arrangement in 1979 for five years. In 1984 he began to plan a resumption of his production and applied to the relevant Dutch authorities for a reference quantity of milk which he would be allowed to produce without incurring the payment of any additional levy. He was refused on the ground that he could not prove milk production during the relevant reference year, which was 1983. This was of course impossible for Mulder since he did not produce at all during that period, because of the bargain struck in 1979. He challenged Regulation 857/84, which was the basis of the Dutch authorities' denial of his quota, arguing, *inter alia*, that it infringed his legitimate expectations.

THE ECJ

23. It must be conceded . . . that a producer who has voluntarily ceased production for a certain period cannot legitimately expect to be able to resume production under the same conditions as those which previously applied and not to be subject to any rules of market or structural policy adopted in the meantime.

24. The fact remains that where such a producer, as in the present case, has been encouraged by a Community measure to suspend marketing for a limited period in the general interest and against payment of a premium he may legitimately expect not to be subject, upon the expiry of his undertaking, to restrictions which specifically affect him precisely because he availed himself of the possibilities offered by the Community provisions.

25. However, the regulations on the additional levy on milk give rise to such restrictions for producers who, pursuant to an undertaking entered into under Regulation 1078/77, did not deliver milk during the reference year. . . . Those producers may in fact be denied a reference quantity under the new system precisely because of that undertaking if they do not fulfil the specific conditions laid down in Regulation 857/84 or if the Member States have no reference quantity available.

26. . . . There is nothing in the provisions of Regulation 1078/77 or in its Preamble to show that the non-marketing undertaking entered into under that Regulation might, upon its expiry, entail a bar to resumption of the activity in question. Such an effect therefore frustrates those producers' legitimate expectations that the effect of the system to which they had rendered themselves would be limited.

The following cases illustrate the second type of situation, where the legitimacy of the applicant's expectation is based upon some course of conduct by the administration or an assurance it has given. In *Embassy Limousines*[106] it was held that there was a breach of legitimate expectations where a company submitting a tender was encouraged to make irreversible investments in advance of the contract being awarded, and thereby to go beyond the risks inherent in making a bid.

In *CEMR*[107] it was held that the Commission could not, without infringing the principle of legitimate expectations, reduce the budgetary allocation for a project where the relevant work had been included in the original bid that had been accepted by the Commission.

In *Sofrimport*[108] the applicant sought to import apples from Chile into the Community. A licence was required in accordance with Regulation 346/88. By a later Regulation, 962/88, the Commission took protective measures and suspended all such licences for Chilean apples. The parent Regulation, 2707/72, which gave the Commission power to adopt protective

---

[106] Case T–203/96 *Embassy Limousines & Services* v. *European Parliament* [1998] ECR II–4239.
[107] Cases T–46 and 151/98 *Council of European Municipalities and Regions* v. *Commission* [2000] ECR II–167.
[108] Case C–152/88 *Sofrimport Sàrl* v. *Commission* [1990] ECR I–2477.

measures, specifically stated in Article 3 that account should be taken of the special position of goods in transit, since such measures could be particularly harmful to traders. The applicant's goods were already in transit when Regulation 962/88 was introduced, but they were refused entry to the Community. The Court held that the Commission's failure to make special provision for goods in transit as required by the parent Regulation infringed the applicant's legitimate expectations.[109]

A similar theme is apparent in the *CNTA* case.[110] The case concerned monetary compensation amounts (mcas), which were payments designed to compensate for fluctuations in exchange rates. The applicant had made export contracts on the supposition that mcas would be payable. After these contracts were made, but before they were to be performed, the Commission passed a regulation abolishing mcas in that sector. The Court held that while mcas could not be said to insulate exporters from all fluctuations in exchange rates, they did shield them from such risks, such that even a prudent exporter might choose not to cover himself against them:[111]

> In these circumstances, a trader might legitimately expect that for transactions irrevocably undertaken by him because he has obtained, subject to a deposit, export licences fixing the amount of the refund in advance, no unforeseeable alteration will occur which could have the effect of causing him inevitable loss, by re-exposing him to the exchange risk.

Sixthly, even if the applicant is able to prove a *prima facie* legitimate expectation this may be defeated if there is an overriding public interest that trumps the expectation.[112] It is for the defendant to show the overriding public interest. The Community Courts will inquire whether the public interest was overriding,[113] but this does not however tell us precisely what legal test is being used. The ECJ and CFI have been rather reluctant to assign a discrete legal label to this exercise. Schonberg has argued that the Community Courts 'will restrict the application of a policy change if there is a *significant imbalance* between the interests of those affected and the policy considerations in favour of the change'.[114] There is force in this view, which coheres with the reasoning used by the Community Courts. It nonetheless leaves open the precise difference between a test of significant imbalance and a test of proportionality, more especially because the former entails consideration of similar issues to the latter. Given that proportionality is used to test whether the infringement of a right can be justified, it is not clear why it should not also be used to determine whether the trumping of an expectation is warranted.[115]

Irrespective of whether the test is cast in terms of significant imbalance or proportionality, the application of the test is likely to depend on the nature of the case. The courts will be more reluctant to interfere with general changes of policy than with cases where a specific representation is made to a discrete group. The courts should however be very reluctant to admit that

---

[109] Cf. Case C–110/97, n. 103 above, and Case T–336/94 *Efisol SA* v. *Commission* [1997] ECR II–1343.

[110] Case 74/74 *CNTA SA* v. *Commission* [1975] ECR 533.

[111] *Ibid.*, para. 42.

[112] Craig, n. 10 above, ch. 16.

[113] See, e.g., Case 74/74 *CNTA*, n. 110 above, para. 43; Case C–189/89 *Spagl* v. *Hauptzollamt Rosenheim* [1990] ECR I–4539; Case C–183/95 *Affish BV* v. *Rijksdienst voor de Keuring van Vee en Vlees* [1997] ECR I–4315; Case T–155/99 *Dieckmann & Hansen GmbH* v. *Commission* [2001] ECR II–3143.

[114] Schonberg, n. 75 above, 150, italics in the original.

[115] The UK courts have recently developed a test for review when the public body seeks to resile from a legitimate expectation that is framed in terms of proportionality: *Nadarajah* v. *Secretary of State for the Home Department* [2005] EWCA Civ 1363, para. 68.

departure from an existing policy in relation to a particular individual was warranted by some overriding public interest, irrespective of whether there has been any detrimental reliance leading to cognizable loss, since the very departure will offend the principle of equality that like cases should be treated alike.

Finally, the mere fact that a Community decision is unlawful will not necessarily prevent the individual from claiming a legitimate expectation.[116] Unreasonable delay by the administration can operate as a bar to the revocation of an unlawful administrative act.[117] In deciding whether to allow retroactive revocation the Community Courts will balance the public interest in legality and the private interest in legal certainty. The former does not always trump the latter.[118] The position is however different in relation to unlawful representations, as opposed to unlawful decisions. The former have been held not to generate any legitimate expectations.[119] The Community Courts have however provided no explanation for their differential treatment of unlawful decisions and unlawful representations.

(d) GENERAL PRINCIPLES OF LAW: NON-DISCRIMINATION

Although equality and non-discrimination are universally recognized principles,[120] the legal concept of discrimination is not unproblematic. It is necessary to decide whether people are similarly situated such that a difference in treatment is *prima facie* discriminatory, and whether that apparent difference in treatment can be justified. These difficulties will be explored in later chapters dealing with the free movement of persons, services, and goods, as well as with sex discrimination.[121]

(i) *Treaty Foundations*

The principle of non-discrimination, although a general principle and therefore binding on both the Community and the Member States within the scope of application of EC law, is expressly mentioned in a number of distinct contexts in the Treaty:

i. Non-discrimination on grounds of nationality as expressed in Article 12, and in the free movement context as expressed in Articles 39, 43, and 49–50 EC.

ii. Equal treatment of men and women as set out now in the amended Articles 2 and 3, and in Articles 137 and 141 EC.[122]

---

116 Schwarze, n. 42 above, 991–1025; Craig, n. 10 above, 621–627.

117 Case 15/85 *Consorzio Cooperative d'Abruzzo v. Commission* [1987] ECR 1005.

118 Cases 42 and 49/59 *SNUPAT v. High Authority* [1961] ECR 53; Case 14/61 *Hoogovens v. High Authority* [1962] ECR 253.

119 Case 188/82 *Thyssen AG v. Commission* [1983] ECR 3721, para. 11; Case T–2/93 *Air France v. Commission* [1994] ECR II–323, paras. 101–102.

120 G. More, 'The Principle of Equal Treatment: from Market Unifier to Fundamental Right', in P. Craig and G. de Búrca (eds.), *The Evolution of EU Law* (Oxford University Press, 1999), ch. 14.

121 See Chs. 21, 22, and 24. See, e.g., Case C–132/92 *Roberts v. Birds Eye Walls Ltd.* [1993] ECR I–5579, and on goods see Case 2/90 *Commission v. Belgium (Walloon Waste)* [1992] ECR I–4431, later criticized by Jacobs AG in Case C–379/98 *PreussenElektra AG v. Schleswag AG* [2001] ECR I–2099 for the ECJ's reasoning on discrimination.

122 In Case C–50/99 *Deutsche Telekom v. Schröder* [2000] ECR I–743, the ECJ ruled that the economic aims of the sex equality principle in Art. 141 EC were secondary to its social aims as a fundamental human right.

iii. Non-discrimination as between producers or consumers in the field of agriculture, in accordance with Article 34(2).

iv. There are also specific provisions such as Article 90, prohibiting discriminatory taxation.

v. Article 13 EC was added by the Amsterdam Treaty.[123] It empowers the Council, acting unanimously on a proposal from the Commission and after consulting the EP, without prejudice to the other provisions of this Treaty and within the limits of the powers conferred by it upon the Community, to take appropriate action to combat discrimination based on sex, racial or ethnic origin, religion or belief, disability, age, or sexual orientation. Article 13 is not a direct prohibition against discrimination, but rather empowers the Community to take action against the forms of discrimination listed.[124] The Nice Treaty added a second paragraph to Article 13, providing for a power to adopt non-harmonizing 'incentive measures' by co-decision. Directives prohibiting discrimination on grounds of race or ethnic origin,[125] and on grounds of religion, belief, disability, age, or sexual orientation in the field of employment,[126] were adopted in 2000. In the same year, an action programme to combat discrimination on all the grounds listed in Article 13 (other than sex) was adopted,[127] and the Commission announced a policy of 'mainstreaming' so as to integrate anti-discrimination considerations such as race and disability in particular into other areas of EC policy formation.[128]

vi. Article 21(1) of the Charter of Fundamental Rights provides that any discrimination based on any ground such as sex, race, colour, ethnic or social origin, genetic features, language, religion or belief, political or any other opinion, membership of a national minority, property, birth, disability, age, or sexual orientation shall be prohibited. This provision establishes a broad general principle of non-discrimination with an open-ended list of prohibited grounds. Further, as we have seen in an earlier chapter, even though the Charter is not at present formally binding, it nonetheless has some legal effects through the practice of various institutional actors.

(ii) *Non-discrimination as a 'General' Principle of EC Law*

While the principle of equality and the prohibition of discrimination are therefore found expressly within a number of Treaty Articles,[129] the ECJ held at an early stage that these were merely specific enunciations of the general principle of equality as one of the fundamental principles of Community law,[130] which must be observed by any court.[131] The principle has

---

[123] M. Bell, 'The New Article 13 EC Treaty: A Sound Basis for European Anti-discrimination Law?' (1999) 6 *MJ* 5; L. Waddington, 'Testing the Limits of the EC Treaty Article on Non-Discrimination' (1999) 28 *ILJ* 133.

[124] For history of EC anti-discrimination policy in the fields of race and sexual orientation see M. Bell, *Anti-Discrimination Law and the EU* (Oxford University Press, 2002).

[125] Council Dir. 2000/43/EC of 29 June 2000 implementing the principle of equal treatment between persons irrespective of racial or ethnic origin [2000] OJ L180/22.

[126] Council Dir. 2000/78/EC of 27 Nov. 2000 establishing a general framework for equal treatment in employment and occupation [2000] OJ L303/16.

[127] Council Dec. 2000/750/EC of 27 Nov. 2000 establishing a Community action programme to combat discrimination (2001 to 2006) [2000] OJ L303/23.

[128] M. Bell, 'Mainstreaming Equality Norms into EU Asylum Law' (2001) 26 *ELRev.* 20.

[129] K. Lenaerts, 'L'Egalité de Traitement en Droit Communautaire' (1991) 27 *CDE* 3.

[130] Cases 117/76 and 16/77 *Ruckdeschel* v. *Hauptzollamt Hamburg–St. Annen* [1977] ECR 1753, para. 7.

[131] Case 8/78 *Milac GmbH* v. *Hauptzollamt Freiburg* [1978] ECR 1721, para.18; Case C–442/00 *Caballero* v. *Fondo de Garantia Salarial (Fogasa)* [2002] ECR I–11915, paras. 30–32.

been applied by the ECJ where there has been arbitrary or unjustifiably unequal treatment of two persons within an area of Community competence,[132] such as in the context of Community staff policy.[133]

The reach of this general principle can nonetheless be contentious,[134] as exemplified by the case law on discrimination and sexual orientation.[135] The Advocates General in *P* v. *S*[136] and *Grant*[137] argued that, prior to the enactment of Article 13 EC, the general principles of Community law imposed a requirement on the EC institutions and the Member States not to discriminate within the areas covered by Community law on arbitrary grounds, such as sexual orientation or gender reassignment. The Court in *P* v. *S* held that Directive 76/207 on equal treatment of men and women in employment was 'simply the expression, in the relevant field, of the principle of equality, which is one of the fundamental principles of Community law'.[138]

The ECJ was however more conservative in *Grant* concerning travel benefits for the same-sex partners of employees. It retreated from this broad principle of equality and decided that discrimination on grounds of sex in EC law did *not* cover discrimination on grounds of sexual orientation.[139] The Court ruled that ensuring respect for fundamental rights could not extend the scope of the Treaty provisions, which at the time required Member States only to ensure *sex* equality in employment, beyond the competences of the Community.

The ruling in *D* v. *Council*[140] appeared to reinforce the cautious approach taken in *Grant*. In *D* there was no possible doubt about Community competence, since the case concerned the EU's treatment of its own employees. The case concerned the EU's refusal to pay a staff household allowance which would have been payable to a married employee to a homosexual employee who was in a stable partnership registered under Swedish law. The Court denied that there had been any discrimination on grounds of sex, and then held, somewhat obscurely, in relation to the claim that there had been discrimination on grounds of sexual orientation, and that it was not the sex of the partner that determined whether the household allowance was granted, but the legal nature of the ties between the official and the partner. Thus, while ruling that there had been no unequal treatment on grounds of sexual orientation the Court did not actually deny the possible existence of a general principle of EC law prohibiting discrimination on grounds of sexual orientation within its field of application.

(iii) *Justifying Discrimination*

To discriminate means to differentiate or to treat differently. In Community law it is however impermissible when done without adequate justification on the basis of one of the prohibited grounds, or when there is no relevant difference between two persons or situations which would justify a difference in their treatment. These are not easy criteria to apply, since it is not

---

[132] Case C–144/04 *Mangold* v. *Helm* [2005] ECR I–9981: the general principle of equal treatment in EC law prohibited a national measure from discriminating arbitrarily on the basis of age, even though the period for transposing the Framework Employment Dir. into national law had not yet expired.

[133] Cases 75 and 117/82 *Razzouk and Beydoun* v. *Commission* [1984] ECR 1509, paras. 16–17; Case 20/71 *Sabbatini* [1972] ECR 345, para. 3; and Case 149/77 *Defrenne* v. *Sabena* [1978] ECR 1365, paras. 26–27.

[134] See, in relation to disability and sickness, Case C–13/05 *Chacon Nava* v. *Eurest Colectividades SA* [2006] ECR I–6467.

[135] For more detailed treatment in the context of fundamental rights, see above, 408–409.

[136] Case C–13/94 *P* v. *S and Cornwall County Council* [1996] ECR I–2143, Tesauro AG.

[137] Case C–249/96 *Grant* v. *South-West Trains Ltd* [1998] ECR I–621, Elmer AG.

[138] See also Case C–117/01 *KB* v. *National Health Service Pensions Agency and Secretary of State for Health* [2004] ECR I–541.

[139] *Ibid.*, para. 42.

[140] Case C–125/99 P *D* v. *Council* [2001] ECR I–4319.

always clear which factors may be taken into account in determining whether two persons are 'similarly situated'. Nor is it clear whether, if differences in situation are taken into account to justify discriminatory treatment, this should be seen as a form of justified 'positive discrimination', or should in fact be seen as not discriminatory at all.[141]

A straightforward example of discrimination on grounds of sex would be where a woman was paid a lower wage than a man for doing exactly the same job, and a simple example of discrimination on grounds of nationality would be where a UK employer refused to hire any employee who was not British. The more difficult situations arise where the discrimination is neither clear nor direct, but is indirect and disguised, or is unintentional but nonetheless discriminatory in its impact. Indirect and disguised discrimination would occur if, for example, a UK employer claimed to hire workers of any nationality so long as they had received their education in the UK, since in practice this requirement would not be fulfilled by most non-UK nationals.[142] A form of unintentional and indirect sex discrimination may occur where an employer pays part-time workers less per hour than full-time workers, where the overwhelming majority of part-time workers are women.[143]

In Community law, direct or deliberate disguised discrimination on grounds of sex or nationality is prohibited, subject to fairly limited exceptions,[144] whereas indirect and unintentional discrimination may be justified on a variety of non-exhaustive grounds.[145] Thus in the context of nationality discrimination, a language requirement which is indirectly discriminatory may be justified if it is proportionate and genuinely required for the job to be undertaken.[146] Similarly in the context of sex discrimination, the payment of a higher hourly wage to full-time than to part-time workers may, even where it indirectly discriminates against women, be 'objectively justified' on grounds relating to the needs of the employer.[147] Discrimination on grounds of nationality and sex will be discussed more fully below.[148] Indirect discrimination was expressly defined for the first time (in the context of sex discrimination) in the Burden of Proof Directive in 1997,[149] and differently again in the anti-discrimination directives adopted under Article 13 EC.[150] In addition to the 'objective justification' requirements, these directives permit other specific exceptions to the general non-discrimination principle.

---

[141] See, e.g., Case C–132/92 *Roberts*, n. 121 above; Case C–450/93 *Kalanke* v. *Freie Hansestadt Bremen* [1995] ECR I–3051; Case C–409/95 *Hellmut Marschall* v. *Land Nordrhein-Westfalen* [1997] ECR I–6363 discussed in Ch. 24.

[142] For an example of indirect discrimination see Case 152/73 *Sotgiu* v. *Deutsche Bundespost* [1974] ECR 153, where the pay differential was based on the country or place of recruitment, rather than the nationality of the worker.

[143] See further Ch. 24.

[144] See Chs. 21 and 22 on justifications for direct discrimination in the context of free movement of persons and services. See Ch. 24 on direct sex discrimination, for which limited grounds of exception are provided in some of the secondary legislation.

[145] See Chs. 21, 22, and 24.

[146] See Ch. 21 and Art. 3(1) of Reg. 1612/68 [1968] JO L257/2, [1968] OJ Spec. Ed. 475, on freedom of movement for workers.

[147] E.g. Case 96/80 *Jenkins* v. *Kingsgate (Clothing Productions) Ltd.* [1981] ECR 911. See further Ch. 24.

[148] See Chs. 23 and 24.

[149] Council Dir. 97/80/EC of 15 Dec. 1997 on the burden of proof in cases of discrimination based on sex [1998] OJ L14/6.

[150] For discussions of the various provisions of the Race Dir., n. 125 above, see the chs. by S. Fredman, D. Chalmers, and C. McCrudden in S. Fredman (ed.), *Discrimination and Human Rights: The Case of Racism* (Oxford University Press, 2001), chs. 2, 7, and 8.

(e) GENERAL PRINCIPLES OF LAW: TRANSPARENCY

(i) *Introduction*

Whether or not transparency can be counted as a general principle of EC law has been debated for some years. We shall return to this issue at the conclusion of this discussion. The notion of transparency encompasses a number of features, such as the holding of meetings in public, the provision of information, and the right of access to documents.[151]

The European Council agreed an overall policy on transparency in June 2006.[152] All Council deliberations on legislative acts to be adopted by co-decision are, in principle, to be open to the public, as are the votes and explanations of votes by Council members; so too are the initial deliberations on legislative acts other than those adopted by co-decision presented orally by the Commission, with the possibility of subsequent deliberations also being open to the public. The Council is to hold regular public debates on important issues affecting the Union and its citizens, the deliberations of Council formations on their priorities are to be public, and so too is the presentation and debate on the Commission's annual work programme.

(ii) *Treaty Provisions*

The discussion will focus on the right of access to documents, which is the most developed aspect of transparency in the EU. Transparency is a value that has become of increased importance in EU law since the Maastricht Treaty.[153] The early years of the EEC were weak in terms of democracy, accountability, and accessibility to public scrutiny. There was a greater focus on transparency in the 1990s, not least as a result of the near failure to have the TEU ratified in Denmark and France. This was particularly apparent during the IGC preceding the Amsterdam Treaty.[154] Moreover, a number of Member States, such as the Netherlands, Denmark, and Sweden, increasingly objected to the secrecy surrounding the Council of Ministers, and were dissatisfied with the steps which the Council had taken.[155]

The Council and Commission adopted a joint Code of Conduct in 1993,[156] and each implemented it into its rules of procedure by decision.[157] The 1993 Inter-institutional Declaration on Democracy, Transparency, and Subsidiarity provided further impetus for reform.[158]

---

[151] The Commission announced a Transparency Initiative, the details of which are to be set out in a Green Paper, designed to improve transparency in relation to matters such as the use of Community funds, the role played by lobby groups and consultation with civil society: available at http://europa.eu.int/comm/commission_barroso/kallas/transparency_en.htm.

[152] Brussels European Council, 15–16 June 2006.

[153] S. Peers, 'From Maastricht to Laeken: The Political Agenda of Openness and Transparency in the EU', in V. Deckmyn (ed.), *Increasing Transparency in the European Union* (Maastricht EIPA, 2002); A. Tomkins, 'Transparency and the Emergence of a European Administrative Law' (1999–2000) 19 *YBEL* 217.

[154] J. Lodge, 'Transparency and Democratic Legitimacy' (1994) 32 *JCMS* 343; G. de Búrca, 'The Quest for Legitimacy in the European Union' (1996) 59 *MLR* 359.

[155] D. Curtin, 'Betwixt and Between: Democracy and Transparency in the Governance of the European Union', in J. Winter *et al.* (eds.), *Reforming the Treaty on European Union: The Legal Debate* (Kluwer, 1996), 95; D. Curtin, 'Citizens' Fundamental Right of Access to EU Information: An Evolving Digital Passepartout?' (2000) 37 *CMLRev.* 7.

[156] Code of Conduct Concerning Access to Council and Commission Documents [1993] OJ L340/41.

[157] Council Dec. 93/731/EC of 20 Dec. on public access to Council documents [1993] OJ L340/43; Commission Dec. 94/90/ECSC, EC, Euratom of 8 Feb. 1994 on public access to Commission documents [1994] OJ L46/58.

[158] It was adopted by the Commission, Council, and EP on the margins of the 1993 Brussels European Council: M. Westlake, *The Commission and the Parliament, Partners and Rivals in the European Policy-Making Process* (Butterworths, 1994), 159–161.

The Treaty of Amsterdam enshrined access to documents as a Treaty right. Article 1 of the TEU, as amended by the Treaty of Amsterdam, states that decisions shall be taken as openly and as closely as possible to the citizen, and Article 255(1) EC provides:[159]

> Any citizen of the Union, and any natural or legal person residing or having their registered office in a Member State, shall have a right of access to European Parliament, Council and Commission documents, subject to the principles and the conditions to be defined in accordance with paragraphs 2 and 3.

Article 255(2) stipulated that the general principles concerning such access and the limits thereto should be determined by the Council, acting in accordance with the Article 251 EC procedure, within two years of entry into force of the Treaty of Amsterdam. Article 255(3) instructed each institution to adopt Rules of Procedure regarding access to documents. This was reinforced in relation to the Council by Article 207(3), specifying that access to documents, explanations and results of votes, and statements of minutes is particularly important when the Council is acting in its legislative capacity.

The legislation required by Article 255 EC was adopted in the form of a regulation in 2001,[160] following a number of earlier more specific decisions. Regulation 1049/2001 improved the position governing access to documents in several respects, by for example softening the nature of some of the exceptions and requiring a register of documents to be kept.[161] The new legislation was implemented by the three EU institutions into their own rules of procedure,[162] and has been applied to EU agencies.[163] The right of access to documents is moreover now enshrined in Article 42 of the Charter of Fundamental Rights of the European Union.[164]

The European Ombudsman has been central to the development of openness and transparency as broader principles of law. He undertook an own-initiative inquiry into public access to documents addressed to fifteen Community institutions other than the Council and Commission.[165] The Ombudsman concluded that failure to adopt rules governing public access to documents and to make those rules easily available to the public constituted maladministration. The consequence was that most other important EU bodies including the Court of Auditors, ECB, and agencies adopted rules governing access to documents.

(iii) *Transparency and the Community Courts*

The Community Courts were generally supportive of transparency, even before the reforms brought in by the Treaty of Amsterdam, but they refrained from far-reaching

---

[159] Art. 255 EC was held to lack direct effect in Case T–191/99 *Petrie* v. *Commission* [2001] ECR II–3677.

[160] Reg. (EC) 1049/2001 of the European Parliament and of the Council of 30 May 2001 regarding public access to European Parliament, Council and Commission Documents [2001] OJ L145/43.

[161] S. Peers, 'The New Regulation on Access to Documents: A Critical Analysis' (2002) 21 *YBEL* 385; M. Broberg, 'Access to Documents: A General Principle of Community Law' (2002) 27 *ELRev*. 194; M. de Leeuw, 'The Regulation on Public Access to European Parliament, Council and Commission Documents in the European Union: Are Citizens Better Off?' (2003) 28 *ELRev*. 324.

[162] Council Dec. 2002/682/EC, Euratom of 22 July 2002 adopting the Council's Rules of Procedure [2002] OJ L230/7; Commission Dec. 2001/937/EC, ECSC, Euratom of 5 Dec. 2001 amending its Rules of Procedure [2001] OJ L345/94.

[163] K. Lenaerts, ' "In the Union we Trust": Trust Enhancing Principles of Community Law' (2004) 41 *CMLRev*. 317, 321.

[164] [2000] OJ C364/19.

[165] (616/PUBAC/F/IJH), [1998] OJ C44/9.

statements of principle that would enshrine a general right of transparency or access to information.

The CFI stressed in *Carvel*[166] that when the Council exercises its discretion whether to release documents it had genuinely to balance the interests of citizens in gaining access to documents with the need to maintain confidentiality of its deliberations. It could not simply adopt a general blanket denial of access to a class of documents.

In *Netherlands* v. *Council*[167] the Dutch government argued that the principle of openness of the legislative process was an essential requirement of democracy, and that the right of access to information was an internationally recognized fundamental human right. The ECJ confirmed the importance of the right of public access to information and its relationship to the democratic nature of the institutions, but rejected the argument that such a fundamental right should not be dealt with purely as a matter of the Council's internal Rules of Procedure.

In *Hautala*, the ECJ upheld the CFI's decision to annul the Council's refusal to consider granting partial access to politically sensitive documents, but the ECJ declared that it was not necessary for it to pronounce on whether or not EC law recognized a general 'principle of the right to information'.[168]

Nonetheless, despite the failure to articulate a general principle of transparency or a general right of access to information, the Community Courts played a significant role in elaborating the nature and content of the right of access to information contained in the procedural rules and legislative decisions of the institutions. Thus the CFI and the ECJ annulled a number of decisions of the Council and Commission refusing access to their documents, not on the ground that the institutions had breached a 'general principle of transparency', but on other grounds such as the automatic application of non-mandatory exceptions, the inappropriate use of the authorship rule, the refusal to consider partial access, or the inadequacy of the reasons given for refusal.[169]

(iv) *Transparency, Regulation 1049/2001, and the Community Courts*

The detailed regime for access to documentation is governed by Regulation 1049/2001.[170] Any such regime will contain provisions defining the institutions covered, the meaning of the term document, the beneficiaries of the scheme, and the exceptions that limit access. Regulation 1049/2001 follows this general pattern.

The Community Courts have been willing to protect the reality of access, as exemplified by *Hautala*.[171] This was evident once again in *Verein für Konsumenteninformation*.[172] The

---

[166] Case T–194/94 *Carvel and Guardian Newspapers Ltd.* v. *Council* [1995] ECR II–2765; Case T–105/95 *WWF UK (World Wide Fund for Nature)* v. *Commission* [1997] ECR II–313.

[167] Case C–58/94 [1996] ECR I–2169, paras. 31–36.

[168] Case C–353/99 P *Hautala* v. *Council* [2001] ECR I–9565, para. 31.

[169] See, e.g., Case T–105/95 *WWF*, n. 166 above; Case T–188/97 *Rothmans International* v. *Commission* [1999] ECR II–2463; Case T–174/95 *Svenska Journalistforbundet* v. *Council* [1998] ECR II–2289; Case C–353/99 P *Kuijer* v. *Council* [2000] ECR II–1959; Case T–211/00 *Kuijer* v. *Council* [2002] ECR II–485.

[170] For an overview of the practical impact of the Reg., see On the Implementation of the Principles in EC Regulation 1049/2001 Regarding Public Access to European Parliament, Council and Commission Documents COM(2004)45 final. For detailed analysis of the judicial decisions made under Reg. 1049/2001, n. 160 above, see J. Heliskoski and P. Leino, 'Darkness at the Break of Noon: The Case Law on Regulation No. 1049/2001 on Access to Documents' (2006) 43 CMLRev. 735.

[171] Case C–353/99 P *Hautala*, n. 168 above. See also Case C–41/00 P *Interporc Im- und Export GmbH* v. *Commission* [2003] ECR I–2125, paras. 42–44; Case C–353/01 P *Mattila* v. *Commission* [2004] ECR I–1073, paras. 30–32.

[172] Case T–2/03 *Verein für Konsumenteninformation* v. *Commission* [2005] ECR II–1121.

applicant sought access to documents held by the Commission concerning a cartel in the banking sector, in order to pursue legal actions in Austria for customers that might have been charged excessive rates of interest. The file was large and the Commission denied the request, stating *inter alia* that partial access was not possible since detailed examination of each document would entail excessive work. The CFI held that the Regulation required the Commission in principle to carry out an individual assessment of the documents requested, except where it was manifestly clear that access should be refused or granted. The refusal to undertake any concrete assessment was therefore in principle manifestly disproportionate.[173] The CFI acknowledged that the relevant file was large, but nonetheless annulled the Commission's decision.

The effectiveness of any regime for access to information will be crucially affected by the exceptions contained in the legislation and the way they are interpreted by the courts. The exceptions in Regulation 1049/2001 are listed in Article 4. Most are qualified by provisions allowing access even if the document relates to a protected interest, provided that there is an overriding public interest in disclosure.[174] There are, however, some exceptions that are mandatory: access is prohibited where disclosure would undermine the relevant interest, with no provision allowing access on grounds of public interest.[175]

The Community Courts can exercise control in a number of ways. They can review the facts to determine whether an exception was properly invoked; they can decide on the legal meaning of an exception; and they can adjudicate on whether the public interest warranted disclosure. The Community Courts state repeatedly that the exceptions should be interpreted narrowly. There are however contestable decisions, where the ECJ and CFI have used the juridical techniques at their disposal sparingly to say the least.

The *Sison* case[176] concerned the determination of whether an exception was properly invoked. The applicant's assets were frozen pursuant to a Community regulation to combat terrorism and he sought access to documentation that had placed him on the relevant list. The CFI reiterated the principle that exceptions to access should be construed narrowly,[177] and that it was for the institution to show that the documents to which access was sought fell within one of the listed exceptions.[178] The CFI however also held that the Council had a wide discretion in deciding whether access should be refused on the ground that it might harm the public interest, and hence judicial review was limited to deciding whether procedural rules including the duty to give reasons had been complied with, and whether there had been a manifest error or misuse of power.[179] The scope of review was further qualified because the CFI held that it might be impossible to give reasons justifying the need for confidentiality in respect of individual documents without disclosing the documents and thereby depriving the exception of its purpose.[180] This argument can however be met, since the Court could

---

[173] *Ibid.*, para. 100. The CFI accepted that there could be cases where because of the number of documents requested the Commission had to retain the right to balance the interest in public access against the burden of work in order to safeguard the interests of good administration. This possibility was however applicable only in exceptional cases. The right of access, coupled with concrete individual examination, was the norm. See also Case T–237/02 *Technische Glaswerke Ilmenau GmbH* v. *Commission*, 14 Dec. 2006.

[174] Reg. 1049/2001, n. 160 above, Art. 4(2)–(3).

[175] *Ibid.*, Art. 4(1).

[176] Cases T–110, 150, and 405/03 *Sison* v. *Council* [2005] ECR II–1429. See also, in relation to other exceptions, Cases T–391/03 and 70/04 *Franchet and Byk* v. *Commission*, 6 July 2006; Case T–264/04 *WWF European Policy Programme* v. *Council*, 25 Apr. 2007.

[177] *Ibid.*, para. 45.

[178] *Ibid.*, para. 60.

[179] *Ibid.*, paras. 46–47.

[180] *Ibid.*, paras. 60, 63.

consider such reasons in private, which would enable it to take an informed view as to whether invocation of the exception really was warranted in relation to the relevant documents. The judgment rendered it virtually impossible for the applicant to challenge his inclusion on the list. The judgment was upheld on appeal to the ECJ, which endorsed the CFI's reasoning.[181]

In *IFAW*[182] it was the legal meaning of an exception to Regulation 1049/2001 that came before the CFI. It held that Article 4(5) of Regulation 1049/2001, which provides that a Member State may request the Community institution not to disclose a document originating from that Member State without its prior agreement, constituted an instruction from the Member State to the Community institution not to disclose the relevant document. This was so notwithstanding the wording of Article 4(5), which was not framed in mandatory terms. If the Community legislature had intended the Member States to have a veto power this could have been clearly expressed in terms comparable to Article 9(3) of the Regulation, which states that sensitive documents shall be released only with the consent of the originator.

The *Turco* case[183] reveals the judicial approach to the balancing test. The case concerned the exception for legal advice contained in Regulation 1049/2001.[184] The CFI held that the exception could in principle apply to advice given during the legislative as well as the judicial process, but that the mere fact that the document was a legal opinion did not in itself justify invocation of the exception.[185] The Council argued that disclosure could give rise to uncertainty as regards the legality of legislative acts adopted following such advice. The CFI acknowledged that these arguments could apply to all legal advice relating to legislative acts. It nonetheless held that the Council's reasoning was justified, since if any further information were given it would deprive the exception of its effect[186] and could give rise to 'lingering doubts as to the lawfulness of the legislative act in question'.[187] This reasoning can be criticized since the rationale proffered is unconvincing, and the effect of the judgment is that such advice relating to legislative acts will generally be *prima facie* immune from disclosure.[188]

The CFI then considered whether the exception for legal advice could be overridden on the ground that disclosure would be in the public interest. The applicant argued that this was so, because of principles of transparency, openness, and participation of the citizen in the decision-making process. The CFI rejected the argument. It held that those principles were implemented through Regulation 1049/2001 and that therefore the applicant must present arguments for an overriding public interest that were distinct from these principles, or at the very least show why those principles were especially pressing in the particular case.[189] While the CFI is surely right to point out that principles of openness, transparency, and the like permeate Regulation 1049/2001, it is for this very reason that they are likely to inform the applicant's argument that the exception should be overridden because of the public interest in disclosure. The applicant is moreover required to proffer convincing reasons why the public interest necessitates overriding the exception where the information that might sustain this argument is contained in documents that are protected and hence unseen.

---

181 Case C–266/05 P *Sison* v. *Council*, 1 Feb. 2007.

182 Case 168/02 *IFAW Internationaler Tierschultz-Fonds GmbH* v. *Commission* [2004] ECR II–4135. See also Case T–187/03 *Scippacercola* v. *Commission* [2005] ECR II–1029.

183 Case T–84/03 *Turco* v. *Council* [2004] ECR II–4061.

184 Reg. 1049/2001, n. 160 above, Art. 4(2).

185 Case T–84/03 *Turco*, n. 183 above, paras. 56, 71.

186 *Ibid.*, para. 74.

187 *Ibid.*, para. 78.

188 Craig, n. 10 above, 357–358.

189 Case T–84/03 *Turco*, n. 183 above, paras. 82–83.

(v) Conclusion

Developments such as Article 255 EC, Regulation 1049/2001, and Article 42 of the Charter of Fundamental Rights led Judge Lenaerts, writing extra-judicially, to conclude that 'it can at present hardly be denied that the principle of transparency has evolved into a general principle of Community law'.[190] This view is reinforced by the ECJ's greater willingness to read Community legislation as subject to transparency, even where there is no explicit mention of this principle in the relevant articles of the legislation.[191]

Even if transparency is regarded as a general principle of Community law, the impact of this on citizens will be crucially dependent on the meaning accorded to the principle in specific cases. The Courts' jurisprudence when interpreting Regulation 1049/2001 is a timely reminder that we should look beyond general judicial statements of the need to afford real protection for the right of access to documents, in order to consider how the judiciary interprets and applies the detailed provisions of the legislation in concrete cases.

(f) GENERAL PRINCIPLES OF LAW: PRECAUTIONARY PRINCIPLE

Risk regulation is now an important part of the EC's activities, and this regulation often has to be undertaken under conditions of scientific uncertainty. Article 174 EC makes specific mention of the precautionary principle in relation to environmental decision-making. The Community Courts have however elevated the precautionary principle into a new general principle of EC law. The foundations were laid by the ECJ. In the *BSE* case[192] the UK challenged the legality of a Commission decision banning export of beef from the UK in the wake of mad cow disease. The ECJ stated that when the contested decision was adopted there was great uncertainty as to the risks posed by such produce, and held that 'where there is uncertainty as to the existence or extent of risks to human health, the institutions may take protective measures without having to wait until the reality and seriousness of those risks become apparent'.[193]

It was however the CFI that elevated the precautionary principle to the status of a new general principle of EU law. *Pfizer*[194] and *Artegodan*[195] were the seminal judgments in this respect. The CFI began with the express mention of the precautionary principle in Article 174(2) EC concerning environmental policy. It then relied on Article 6 EC, which stipulates that environmental protection must be integrated into the implementation of other Community policies listed in Article 3 EC. It followed, said the CFI, that the precautionary principle, being a part of environmental protection, should also be a factor in other Community policies.[196] This conclusion was reinforced through interpretation of other more specific Treaty articles as requiring a high level of protection for health and consumer protection, with the precautionary principle being the means to ensure this requisite level of protection.[197]

---

[190] Lenaerts, n. 163 above, 321.

[191] Cases C–154 and 155/04 *The Queen, on the application of Alliance for Natural Health and Nutri-Link Ltd. v. Secretary of State for Health* [2005] ECR I–6451, paras. 81–82.

[192] Case C–180/96 *United Kingdom* v. *Commission* [1998] ECR I–2265.

[193] *Ibid.*, para. 99.

[194] Case T–13/99 *Pfizer Animal Health SA* v. *Council* [2002] ECR II–3305.

[195] Cases T–74, 76, 83–85, 132, 137, and 141/00 *Artegodan GmbH* v. *Commission* [2002] ECR II–4945.

[196] Case T–13/99 *Pfizer*, n. 194 above, para. 114; Cases T–74, 76, 83–85, 132, 137, and 141/00 *Artegodan*, n. 195 above, para. 183.

[197] *Ibid.*, para. 183.

The CFI buttressed the argument from the Treaty by drawing on prior case law from the ECJ, such as the *BSE* case, where the existence of the precautionary principle 'has in essence and at the very least implicitly been recognized by the Court of Justice'.[198] The Treaty articles combined with prior case law provided the foundations for the recognition of a new general principle of Community law.[199]

> It follows that the precautionary principle can be defined as a general principle of Community law requiring the competent authorities to take appropriate measures to prevent specific potential risks to public health, safety and the environment, by giving precedence to the requirements related to the protection of those interests over economic interests. Since the Community institutions are responsible, in all their spheres of activity, for the protection of public health, safety and the environment, the precautionary principle can be regarded as an autonomous principle stemming from the abovementioned Treaty provisions.

The precautionary principle is used to review the legality of Community action and also that of Member State action when it falls within the sphere of EC law.[200] It should nonetheless be recognized that the meaning and application of the principle are controversial.[201]

6. MISUSE OF POWER

Misuse of power is the final ground of review mentioned in Article 230. The concept of misuse of powers covers adoption by a Community institution of a measure with the exclusive or main purpose of achieving an end other than that stated, or evading a procedure specifically prescribed by the Treaty for dealing with the circumstances of the case.[202] There is a close connection between claims based on misuse of powers and those based on proportionality. The distinguishing feature, in principle, is that in the former instance the object or purpose which is sought to be achieved will itself be improper, whereas in the latter instance the objective will be legitimate and the issue will be whether it was achieved in a disproportionate manner.

There are, however, successful claims for misuse of power, as exemplified by *Franco Giuffrida* v. *Council*.[203] The applicant sought the annulment of a decision appointing Martino to a higher grade in the Community service, pursuant to a competition in which he and Martino were the two contestants for the post. He claimed that the competition was in reality an exercise to appoint Martino to the job, the rationale being that Martino had already been

---

[198] Case T–13/99 *Pfizer*, n. 194 above, para. 115.

[199] Cases T–74, 76, 83–85, 132, 137, and 141/00 *Artegodan*, n. 195 above, para. 184; Case T–147/00 *Les Laboratoires Servier* v. *Commission* [2003] ECR II–85, para. 52.

[200] Craig, n. 10 above, ch. 19.

[201] See, e.g., J. Scott and E. Vos, 'The Juridification of Uncertainty: Observations on the Ambivalence of the Precautionary Principle within the EU and the WTO', in C. Joerges and R. Dehousse (eds.), *Good Governance in Europe's Integrated Market* (Oxford University Press, 2002), ch. 9; E. Fisher, 'Precaution, Precaution Everywhere: Developing a "Common Understanding" of the Precautionary Principle in the European Community' (2002) 9 *MJ* 7; G. Majone, 'What Price Safety? The Precautionary Principle and its Policy Implications' (2002) 40 *JCMS* 89; C. Sunstein, 'Beyond the Precautionary Principle' (2003) 151 *Univ. Pennsylvania LR* 1003; Jose Luis da Cruz Vilaca, 'The Precautionary Principle in EC Law' (2004) 10 *EPL* 369.

[202] Case C–84/94 *United Kingdom* v. *Council (Re Working Time Directive)* [1996] ECR I–5755; Case T–72/97 *Proderec-Formacao e Desinvolvimento de Recursos Humanos, ACE* v. *Commission* [1998] ECR II–2847; Case C–48/96 P *Windpark Groosthusen GmbH & Co. Betriebs KG* v. *Commission* [1998] ECR I–2873; Case C–452/00 *Netherlands* v. *Commission* [2005] ECR I–6645, para. 114.

[203] Case 105/75 [1976] ECR 1395.

performing the duties associated with the higher grade. The Court quashed the appointment, stating that the pursuit of such a specific objective was contrary to the aims of the recruitment procedure and was, therefore, a misuse of power. Internal promotions should be based on selecting the best person for the job, rather than pre-selecting a particular candidate to whom the job would be given.

7. THE INTENSITY OF REVIEW

The discussion thus far has concentrated on the heads of review under the Treaty. Those familiar with public law will be aware of another issue which is relevant to the enquiry. This concerns the intensity of judicial review. The issue is how far the ECJ will go in reassessing decisions, particularly those involving discretion, made by the Commission and Council. The ECSC Treaty contained explicit dictates on the matter.[204] There is no directly analogous provision in the EC Treaty, but the intensity of review has, nonetheless always been an issue under the EC Treaty.

Judicial review will entail challenge to law, fact, and discretion.[205] A paradigm question of law concerns the meaning to be ascribed to a term in the enabling Treaty provisions, regulations, directives, or decisions. The Community Courts will normally treat the meaning of terms such as state aid, worker, services, goods, capital, agreement, and other such provisions as questions of law. Their general approach is simply to substitute judgment on these questions of law for that of the initial decision-maker. The ECJ or CFI will lay down the meaning of the disputed term, and if the Commission interpretation is at variance with this then it will be annulled.

The standard of judicial review for fact and discretion is different. The standard formula used by the Courts is that review should be confined to examining whether the exercise of the discretion was vitiated by a manifest error, misuse of power, or clear excess in the bounds of discretion. It is however clear that the intensity with which this standard of review has been deployed has varied over time and in relation to different subject-matter.

The Courts' early approach was to apply this test with a very light touch, more especially when the provision being reviewed concerned the exercise of discretion in relation to the Common Agricultural Policy. The foundational provisions of the CAP, Articles 33, 34, and 37, contain a number of objectives which are set out at a relatively high level of generality. This necessitates the making of discretionary choices by the Commission and the Council. In evaluating the chosen option the Court held that the Community institutions had wide discretionary power concerning, *inter alia*, the definition of the objectives to be pursued and the choice of the appropriate means of action.[206] The ECJ did not wish to second-guess evaluations made by the Community institutions, more especially where they were adopted under severe time constraints, or in situations where there was an urgent need to combat a temporary problem in the market.[207] The choice thus made would be annulled only if the applicant could show manifest error or misuse of power. The ECJ tended to apply this test

---

[204] Art. 33 ECSC.

[205] Craig, n. 10 above, ch. 13.

[206] Case 57/72 *Westzucker GmbH v. Einfuhr- und Vorratsstelle für Zucker* [1973] ECR 321; Case 78/74 *Deuka, Deutsche Kraftfutter GmbH, B.J. Stolp v. Einfuhr- und Vorratsstelle für Getreide und Futtermittel* [1975] ECR 421; Case 98/78 *Firma A. Racke v. Hauptzollamt Mainz* [1979] ECR 69; Case 59/83 *SA Biovilac NV v. European Economic Community* [1984] ECR 4057.

[207] Lord Mackenzie Stuart, *The European Communities and the Rule of Law* (Stevens, 1977), 91, 96.

with a light touch, in the sense that it would commonly devote only one or two paragraphs of its judgment to the issue before concluding that the applicant had not been able to show the requisite error.[208]

The Community Courts continue to deploy the same test for the review of fact and discretion in the more modern case law. It is still necessary for the applicant to show manifest error, misuse of power, or clear excess in the bounds of discretion. It is nonetheless clear that in some areas this test is now applied with considerably more rigour than hitherto. This is especially so in relation to judicial review of risk regulation and competition decisions.

Thus in *Pfizer*[209] the applicant challenged a regulation that withdrew authorization for an additive to animal feedingstuffs. The additive was an antibiotic that was added in very small quantities to animal feed in order to promote growth. The rationale for the withdrawal of the authorization was the fear that such additives could reduce the animals' resistance to antibiotics, and that this lessening of resistance could be transmitted to humans. This would then reduce the effectiveness not only of that particular antibiotic, but might also limit the efficacy of antibiotics of the same class. Pfizer argued that it could not be proven in the light of the scientific evidence. The CFI held that judicial review should be confined to examining whether the exercise of the discretion was vitiated by a manifest error, misuse of power, or clear excess in the bounds of discretion,[210] and that where a Community authority was required to make complex assessments in the performance of its duties, its discretion also applied to some extent to the establishment of the factual basis of its action.[211] It was not for the CFI to substitute its assessment of the facts for that of the Community institution, but should confine its review once again to manifest error, misuse of power, or clear excess in the bounds of discretion.[212] Notwithstanding this reiteration of orthodoxy, the CFI devoted nearly seventy pages of its judgment to a close assessment of the applicant's arguments concerning fact and discretion in a judgment that spanned nearly 200 pages overall. It is true that the CFI ultimately found against the applicants, but it nonetheless applied the test of manifest error, etc., far more closely than hitherto.

This is also evident in the judicial review of competition decisions, more especially those concerning mergers. The CFI annulled a number of Commission merger decisions, concluding, after close and exacting scrutiny, that they were tainted by manifest error.[213] The Commission appealed one such case, *Tetra Laval*, to the ECJ and argued that the CFI had interpreted the test of manifest error in such a way as to be tantamount to substitution of judgment. The ECJ in *Tetra Laval*[214] upheld the CFI's decision. The ECJ's reasoning is contained in the following paragraph.[215]

> Whilst the Court recognises that the Commission has a margin of discretion with regard to economic matters, that does not mean that the Community courts must refrain from reviewing the Commission's interpretation of information of an economic nature. Not only

---

208 Craig, n. 10 above, 439–446.

209 Case T–13/99 *Pfizer*, n. 194 above. See also Case T–70/99 *Alpharma Inc.* v. *Council* [2002] ECR II–3495.

210 *Ibid.*, para. 166.

211 *Ibid.*, para. 168.

212 *Ibid.*, para. 169.

213 Case T–342/99 *Airtours plc* v. *Commission* [2002] ECR II–2585; Case T–5/02 *Tetra Laval BV* v. *Commission* [2002] ECR II–4381.

214 Case C–12/03 P [2005] ECR I–987.

215 *Ibid.*, para. 39. See also Case T–464/04 *Impala* v. *Commission*, 13 July 2006; Case T–210/01 *General Electric Company* v. *Commission* [2005] ECR II–5575.

must the Community courts, *inter alia*, establish whether the evidence relied on is factually accurate, reliable and consistent but also whether that evidence contains all the information which must be taken into account in order to assess a complex situation and whether it is capable of substantiating the conclusions drawn from it. Such a review is all the more necessary in the case of a prospective analysis required when examining a planned merger with conglomerate effect.

Space precludes detailed assessment of the broader implications of this judgment. This can be found elsewhere.[216] Suffice it to say for the present that this interpretation of manifest error is a very long way from that found in the earlier case law, or from that which continues to be applied in the modern case law concerning common policies, state aids, and the like. There may well be justification for more intensive review in areas such as risk regulation and competition,[217] although this modern jurisprudence still leaves a number of questions unanswered.[218]

The varying intensity of judicial review is also evident in relation to, for example, the application of general principles of law, such as proportionality and non-discrimination. We have already seen that the application of proportionality differs depending upon the type of Community action that is being reviewed.[219] The same holds true for the way in which the Community Courts apply the principle of non-discrimination. This principle is applied far more intensively in the context of Article 12 EC, especially when this is used in conjunction with citizenship in Articles 17–18 EC, than it is when the Community Courts review claims for discrimination in the agricultural sphere pursuant to Articles 33–34 EC.[220]

8. THE CONSEQUENCES OF ILLEGALITY AND INVALIDITY

We now turn to consider the consequences of finding illegality or invalidity. Where the addressee has not challenged[221] a decision within the time limits in Article 230, it is then definitive as against that person.[222] Where there has been a successful challenge,[223] the Treaty has two principal provisions which determine the consequences of illegality.[224] Article 231

---

[216] Craig, n. 10 above, 464–481.

[217] Judge B. Vesterdorf, 'Certain Reflections on Recent Judgments Reviewing Commission Merger Control Decisions', in M. Hoskins and W. Robinson (eds.), *A True European, Essays for Judge David Edward* (Hart, 2003), ch. 10.

[218] Craig, n. 10 above, 464–481.

[219] See above, 544–546; C. Vajda, 'Some Aspects of Judicial Review within the Common Agricultural Policy—Part II' (1979) 4 *ELRev.* 341, 347–348.

[220] Craig, n. 10 above, ch. 15.

[221] Normally an act will have to be challenged for its invalidity to be established. There are, however, limited instances in which the act will be treated as absolutely void or non-existent, where the act may be treated as if it were never adopted. In general, however, proceedings will be required to establish the illegality of the act: 505 above.

[222] Case C–310/97 P *Commission* v. *AssiDomän Kraft Products AB* [1999] ECR I–5363, para. 57.

[223] The Commission cannot avoid a challenge by withdrawing the contested measure when it is challenged before the ECJ, while seeking to preserve its effects: Case C–89/96 *Portuguese Republic* v. *Commission* [1999] ECR I–8377.

[224] The ECJ has power to prescribe interim measures under Art. 243: see Case C–149/95 P(R) *Commission* v. *Atlantic Container Line AB* [1995] ECR I–2165, and it also has power to order the suspension of the contested act: Art. 242.

provides that if the action under Article 230 is well founded, the Court shall declare the act void. This is modified by Article 231(2) which states that, in the case of a regulation, the Court shall, if it considers it necessary, state which of the effects of the regulation declared void shall be considered as definitive. Article 233 complements this by stating that the institution whose act has been declared void, or whose failure to act has been declared contrary to the Treaty, shall be required to take the necessary measures to comply with the ECJ's judgment. This may involve, for example, eradicating the effects of the measure declared void, and/or refraining from adopting an identical measure.[225] It does not however require the Commission at the request of interested parties to re-examine identical or similar decisions allegedly affected by the same irregularity, addressed to persons other than the applicant.[226]

The general principle of Community law is that nullity is retroactive: once the act is annulled under Article 230 it is void *ab initio*.[227] Such a ruling has an effect *erga omnes*. In general terms, it is only the annulment of law-making measures that can produce genuine *erga omnes* effects, affecting the public at large.[228] The meaning of the phrase can be more limited, particularly where decisions are in issue, as is clear from the *Kraft Products* case.[229] The ECJ held that the scope of any annulment could not go further than that sought by the applicants. The *erga omnes* authority of its annulment ruling attached to both the operative part and the ratio decidendi of its judgment.[230] It did not however entail annulment of an act not challenged before the ECJ, even where it was alleged to be vitiated by the same illegality.

The principle of retroactive nullity can cause hardship, particularly in those instances where the measure is a regulation, which has been relied on by many and which may be the basis of other measures adopted later. This is the rationale for Article 231(2), which allows the Court to qualify the extent of the nullity.[231] This Article has been used to limit the temporal effect of the Court's ruling. Thus, in *Commission* v. *Council*[232] the Court annulled part of a regulation concerning staff salaries. However, if the regulation had been annulled retroactively then the staff would not have been entitled to any salary increases until a new regulation had been adopted. The Court, therefore, used Article 231(2), ruling that the regulation should continue to have effect until a new regulation, in accord with the Court's judgment, had been promulgated. In addition to the power to limit the temporal effect of its rulings, the Court may also find that the illegality affects only part of the measure in question.

A finding of invalidity pursuant to Article 234 EC is, in theory, different from a decision made pursuant to Article 230. The former is addressed only to the national court which

---

[225] Cases 97, 99, 193, and 215/86 *Asteris AE and Hellenic Republic* v. *Commission* [1988] ECR 2181; Cases T–480 and 483/93 *Antillean Rice Mills NV* v. *Commission* [1995] ECR II–2305; Case C–41/00 P *Interporc Im- und Export GmbH* v. *Commission* [2003] ECR I–2125, paras. 29–30. Where the applicant is dissatisfied with the measures taken pursuant to an act being found to be void there may be a further Art. 230 or 232 action: Case T–387/94 *Asia Motor France SA* v. *Commission* [1996] ECR II–961.

[226] Case C–310/97 P, n. 222 above, para. 56.

[227] Case C–228/92 *Roquette Frères SA* v. *Hauptzollamt Geldern* [1994] ECR I–1445, para. 17; Cases T–481 and 484/93 *Vereniging van Exporteurs in Levende Varkens* v. *Commission* [1995] ECR II–2941, para. 46; Case T–171/99 *Corus UK Ltd.* v. *Commission* [2001] ECR II–2967, para. 50.

[228] A.G. Toth, 'The Authority of Judgments of the European Court of Justice: Binding Force and Legal Effects' (1984) 4 *YBEL* 1, 49.

[229] Case 310/97 P, n. 222 above, paras. 52–54.

[230] Case 3/54 *ASSIDER* v. *High Authority* [1955] ECR 63; Case 2/54 *Italy* v. *High Authority* [1954–6] ECR 37, 55.

[231] The ECJ has extended the principle of Art. 231(2) to dirs.: Case C–295/90 *European Parliament* v. *Council* [1992] ECR I–4193, and to decs.: Case C–22/96 *European Parliament* v. *Council (Telematic Networks)* [1998] ECR I–3231.

[232] Case 81/72 [1973] ECR 575. See also Case C–41/95 *European Parliament* v. *Council* [1995] ECR I–4411, paras. 43–45.

requested the ruling. However, as we have seen,[233] the Court has held that its rulings on Article 234 references concerning validity have an *erga omnes* effect, and provide a sufficient reason for any other national court to treat that act as void.[234] Moreover, the Court has applied the principles of Articles 231 and 233, which technically operate only in the context of Articles 230 and 232, by analogy to cases arising under Article 234. This is exemplified by the following case.[235]

Case 112/83 **Société de Produits de Maïs v. Administration des Douanes**
[1985] ECR 719

[Note ToA renumbering: Arts. 173, 174, 176, and 177 are now Arts. 230, 231, 233, and 234]

The case concerned the effects of a ruling by the ECJ on the validity of a regulation, following a reference from the French courts under Article 177.

THE ECJ

16. It should in the first place be recalled that the Court has already held in its judgment . . . (Case 66/80, *International Chemical Corporation* . . .) that although a judgment of the Court given under Article 177 of the Treaty declaring an act of an institution, in particular a Council or Commission Regulation, to be void is directly addressed only to the national court which brought the matter before the Court, it is sufficient reason for any other national court to regard that act as void for the purposes of a judgment which it has to give.

17. Secondly, it must be emphasised that the Court's power to impose temporal limits on the effects of a declaration that a legislative act is invalid, in the context of preliminary rulings under indent (b) of the first paragraph of Article 177, is justified by the interpretation of Article 174 of the Treaty having regard to the necessary consistency between the preliminary ruling procedure and the action for annulment provided for in Articles 173, 174 and 176 of the Treaty, which are two mechanisms provided by the Treaty for reviewing the legality of acts of the Community institutions. The possibility of imposing temporal limits on the effects of the invalidity of a Community Regulation, whether under Article 173 or Article 177, is a power conferred on the Court by the Treaty in the interest of the uniform application of Community law throughout the Community. . . .

18. It must be pointed out that where it is justified by overriding considerations the second paragraph of Article 174 gives the Court discretion to decide, in each particular case, which specific effects of a Regulation which has been declared void must be maintained. It is therefore for the Court, where it makes use of the possibility of limiting the effect of past events of a declaration in proceedings under Article 177 that a measure is void, to decide whether an exception to that temporal limitation of the effect of its judgment may be made in favour of the party which brought the action before the national court or of any other trader which took similar steps before the declaration of invalidity or whether, conversely, a declaration of invalidity applicable only to the future constitutes an adequate remedy even for traders who took action at the appropriate time with a view to protecting their rights.

---

[233] See 469–471 above.
[234] Case 66/80 *International Chemical Corporation* v. *Amministrazione delle Finanze dello Stato* [1981] ECR 1191. The national court may make a reference on the same point if it is unclear about the scope, grounds, or consequences of the original ruling.
[235] See also Cases C–38 and 151/90 *R.* v. *Lomas* [1992] ECR I–1781.

In addition to the discretion to limit the temporal effects of a ruling given under Article 234, the Court has held that the principle underlying Article 233 is also applicable in the context of Article 234.[236]

It is also necessary to consider the effect of a preliminary ruling concerning the interpretation of EC law which calls into question the compatibility of national law with EC law. The general principle is that the ruling defines the legal position as it must have been understood from the time when the relevant EC norm came into force.[237] The Community norm must, therefore, be applied by national courts to situations which occurred before the actual ruling of the ECJ was given, provided that the conditions enabling an action relating to that rule to be brought before the courts having jurisdiction are satisfied. This proposition will only be qualified in exceptional circumstances.[238]

9. CONCLUSION

i.   The Community Courts have played the major role in fashioning principles of judicial review to render accountable decision-making by Community institutions and Member States when the latter act in the sphere of EU law. The ECJ and CFI have to this end developed principles of procedural and substantive judicial review within the framework of the heads of review listed in Article 230 EC.

ii. The Community Courts have developed a broad set of general principles of EC law, which continues to develop, as exemplified by the recent case law on the precautionary principle. The most familiar have been drawn from national constitutional and administrative traditions and have been adapted by the ECJ to the EC context.

iii. A key characteristic of the general principles of EC law is that they function both as aids to interpretation and as grounds for judicial review.

iv. Some principles which have not always been fully recognized in EC law, such as the emergent transparency principle, and the principle of non-discrimination on grounds such as sexual orientation, race, and age, have been implemented and concretized in detailed secondary legislation, and their legal status has been gradually enhanced in this way.

v.   While the Charter of Fundamental Rights articulates rights such as access to documents and freedom from discrimination in reasonably strong terms, their contribution to the creation and strengthening of justiciable general principles of EC law remains speculative as long as the Charter's legal status is not settled.

vi. The Community Courts have considerable discretion concerning the standard and intensity of review adopted. The case law reveals continuing developments in this regard, as the

---

[236] Cases 4, 109, and 145/79 *Société Co-opérative 'Providence Agricole de la Champagne' v. ONIC* [1980] ECR 2823.

[237] Cases 66, 127, and 128/79 *Salumi v. Amministrazione delle Finanze* [1980] ECR 1237, paras. 9–10; Case C–50/96 *Deutsche Telekom AG v. Schröder* [2000] ECR I–743, para. 43.

[238] E.g., where there is a risk of serious economic repercussions owing to the large number of legal relationships entered into in good faith on the basis of the rules considered to be validly in force, and where the individuals and national authorities have adopted practices which do not comply with EC law because of uncertainty about what EC law requires, to which the conduct of the Commission may even have contributed: Cases C–197 and 252/94 *Société Bautiaa v. Directeur des Services Fiscaux des Landes* [1996] ECR I–505; Case 61/79 *Denkavit Italiana* [1980] ECR 1205; Case C–137/94 *R. v. Secretary of State for Health, ex p. Richardson* [1995] ECR I–3407.

Community Courts re-evaluate the intensity with which they wish to apply the principles of judicial review which they have created.

10. FURTHER READING

Arnull, A., *General Principles of EEC Law and the Individual* (Leicester University Press/Pinter, 1990)

Bell, M., *Anti-Discrimination Law and the European Union* (Oxford University Press, 2002)

Bernitz, U., and Nergelius, J., *General Principles of European Community Law* (Kluwer, 2000)

Bunyan, T., *Secrecy and Openness in the EU* (Kogan Page, 1999)

Craig, P., *EU Administrative Law* (Oxford University Press, 2006)

Dashwood, A., and O'Leary, S. (eds.), *The Principle of Equal Treatment in EC Law* (Sweet & Maxwell, 1997)

Deckmyn, V. (ed.), *Increasing Transparency in the European Union* (Maastricht EIPA, 2002)

Ellis, E. (ed.), *The Principle of Proportionality in the Laws of Europe* (Hart, 1999)

Emiliou, N., *The Principle of Proportionality in European Law* (Kluwer, 1996)

Gerapetritis, G., *Proportionality in Administrative Law* (Sakkoulas, 1997)

Nehl, N., *Principles of Administrative Procedure in EC Law* (Hart, 1999)

Schonberg, S., *Legitimate Expectations in Administrative Law* (Oxford University Press, 2000)

Schwarze, J., *European Administrative Law* (Office for Official Publications of the European Communities/Sweet & Maxwell, 1992)

Tridimas, T., *The General Principles of EC Law* (2nd edn., Oxford University Press, 2006)

Usher, J., *General Principles of EC Law* (Longman, 1998)

DAMAGES ACTIONS AND
MONEY CLAIMS

1. INTRODUCTION

In any developed legal system there must be a mechanism whereby losses caused by governmental action may be recovered in an action brought by an individual. Compensation within the EC is governed by Article 288(2) (ex Article 215(2)):

> In the case of non-contractual liability, the Community shall, in accordance with the general principles common to the laws of the Member States, make good any damage caused by its institutions or by its servants in the performance of their duties.

The Article leaves the ECJ with considerable room for interpretation,[1] and directs it to consider the general principles common to the laws of the Member States.

2. CENTRAL ISSUES

i.   The key issue is as to the test for liability where losses are caused by Community acts that are illegal.

ii. It will be seen that the ECJ has fashioned different tests for cases where the challenged act is of a discretionary nature, and for those where it is not.

iii. In doing so it has drawn on its jurisprudence on state liability in damages.

iv. There is no provision for damages liability in relation to the Second and Third Pillars,[2] and this is regrettable given the importance and volume of EU action that is now enacted in this way.

---

[1] Liability under Art. 288 cannot be founded on the primary Treaty Arts., since these do not constitute 'acts of the institutions' but are international agreements: Case T–113/96 *Edouard Dubois et Fils* v. *Council and Commission* [1998] ECR II–125.

[2] Case C–354/04 *Gestoras Pro Amnistia, Olano and Errasti* v. *Council*, 27 Feb. 2007, paras. 44–48; Case C–355/04 *Segi and others* v. *Council*, 27 Feb. 2007, paras. 44–48.

3. LIABILITY FOR LEGISLATIVE AND NON-LEGISLATIVE DISCRETIONARY ACTS

(a) THE GENERAL TEST

The cases considered here are those where the decision-maker has a significant element of discretion. The norms challenged will normally be legislative in nature. An individualized norm, which contains a significant element of discretion, will however also be subject to the legal test discussed in this Section.

The norm may not have been annulled, because of the restrictive interpretation of *locus standi*. The ECJ's early approach did not augur well for individuals, for it was held in *Plaumann*[3] that annulment of the norm was a necessary condition precedent to using Article 288 EC. If this requirement had been retained Article 288 would have been of little use, given the difficulty for an individual to prove *locus standi* for annulment. The necessity for annulment was, however, generally discarded in later cases, and the action for damages came to be regarded as an independent, autonomous cause of action.[4] This is clear from *Schöppenstedt*.

Case 5/71 **Aktien-Zuckerfabrik Schöppenstedt v. Council**
[1971] ECR 975

[Note ToA renumbering: Arts. 40 and 215 are now Arts. 34 and 288]

The applicant claimed that Regulation 769/68, concerning the sugar market, was in breach of Article 40(3) EC, because it was discriminatory in the way in which it established the pricing policy for the product.

THE ECJ

11. In the present case the non-contractual liability of the Community presupposes at the very least the unlawful nature of the act alleged to be the cause of the damage. Where legislative action involving measures of economic policy is concerned, the Community does not incur non-contractual liability for damage suffered by individuals as a consequence of that action, by virtue of the provisions contained in Article 215, second paragraph, of the Treaty, unless a sufficiently flagrant violation of a superior rule of law for the protection of the individual has occurred. For that reason the Court, in the present case, must first consider whether such a violation has occurred.

---

[3] Case 25/62 *Plaumann* v. *Commission* [1963] ECR 95.

[4] Case 5/71 *Aktien-Zuckerfabrik Schöppenstedt* v. *Council* [1971] ECR 975; Cases 9 and 11/71 *Compagnie d'Approvisionnement de Transport et de Crédit SA et Grands Moulins de Paris SA* v. *Commission* [1972] ECR 391; Case T–178/98 *Fresh Marine Company SA* v. *Commission* [2000] ECR II–3331, paras. 45–50. There may, however, be instances where the failure to proceed with an Art. 230 action will have consequences for an Art. 288(2) action where the individual was directly and individually concerned by the offending norm and could have successfully challenged it under Art. 230, but either failed to do so entirely or failed to do so within the period for challenge laid down in Art. 230: Cases C–199 and 200/94 *Pesqueria Vasco-Montanesa SA (Pevasa) and Compania Internacional de Pesca y Derivados SA (Inpesca)* v. *Commission* [1995] ECR I–3709; Case T–93/95 *Laga* v. *Commission* [1998] ECR II–195; Case C–310/97 P *Commission* v. *AssiDomän Kraft Products AB* [1999] ECR I–5363, para. 59. See, generally, P. Mead, 'The Relationship between an Action for Damages and an Action for Annulment: The Return of *Plaumann*', in T. Heukels and A. McDonnell (eds.), *The Action for Damages in Community Law* (Kluwer, 1997), ch. 13.

The ECJ decided that no breach of a superior rule of law could be proven on the facts. The test laid down has been taken to establish the general conditions for liability in this area.

(b) LEGISLATIVE AND NON-LEGISLATIVE DISCRETIONARY ACTS

The ECJ held in *Bergaderm*[5] and *Antillean Rice*[6] that the crucial factor in determining the applicability of the *Schöppenstedt* test was the degree of discretion possessed by the institution in relation to the challenged measure. The general or individual nature of the measure was not a decisive criterion for identifying the limits of the discretion enjoyed by the institution in question.[7] This must be correct in principle. Many administrative measures involve discretionary choices which are just as difficult as those which have to be made in the context of legislative action. The very line between the two can be difficult to draw in substantive terms. This means that the *Schöppenstedt* test can apply to individualized acts which entail a significant element of discretion. It will also apply to legislative acts which involve an element of discretionary choice on the part of the Community authorities. Many legislative acts will have this feature, but there is no logical reason why this should be so for all acts of a legislative nature.

It is clear both in principle and on authority that whether an act is legislative for the purposes of the *Schöppenstedt* test will be dependent upon the substance of the measure, and not the legal form in which it is expressed.[8] This means that it is always open to an applicant in an Article 288(2) action to claim that the measure, although called a regulation, was in reality an administrative decision.[9] The converse is also true: it is possible for a measure to be a decision for some purposes but to be a legislative act for the purposes of Article 288(2).[10] Moreover, the mere fact that an applicant has a sufficient interest for a challenge under Article 230 will not necessarily mean that the measure is not legislative for the purposes of the Article 288(2) action.[11]

(c) THE MEANING OF SUPERIOR RULE OF LAW

The case law shows that three differing types of norms can, in principle, qualify as superior rules of law for the protection of the individual.

First, it is clear that many Treaty provisions fall within this category. One of the most commonly cited grounds in cases under Article 288(2) is the ban on discrimination contained in Article 34(3), in the context of the Common Agricultural Policy (CAP). This is not surprising, given that many of the damages actions are brought pursuant to regulations made under the CAP.[12]

---

[5] Case C–352/98 P *Laboratoires Pharmaceutiques Bergaderm SA and Goupil* v. *Commission* [2000] ECR I–5291, para. 46.

[6] Case C–390/95 P *Antillean Rice Mills NV* v. *Commission* [1999] ECR I–769, paras. 56–62.

[7] See also Case C–472/00 P *Commission* v. *Fresh Marine A/S* [2003] ECR I–7541, para. 27; Case C–312/00 P *Commission* v. *Camar Srl and Tico Srl* [2002] ECR I–11355, para. 55; Case C–282/05 P *Holcim (Deutschland) AG* v. *Commission*, 19 Apr. 2007, paras. 47–49.

[8] Case C–390/95 P *Antillean Rice Mills*, n. 6 above, para. 60; A. Arnull, 'Liability for Legislative Acts under Article 215(2) EC', in Heukels and McDonnell (eds.), n. 4 above, 131–136.

[9] Case C–119/88 *Aerpo and Others* v. *Commission* [1990] ECR I–2189; Case T–472/93 *Campo Ebro and others* v. *Commission* [1995] ECR II–421.

[10] Cases T–481/93 and 484/93 *Vereniging van Exporteurs in Levende Varkens* v. *Commission (Live Pigs)* [1995] ECR II–2941; Case C–390/95 P *Antillean Rice*, n. 6 above, para. 62.

[11] Cases T–480 and 483/93 *Antillean Rice Mills* v. *Commission* [1995] ECR II–2305; Case C–390/95 P *Antillean Rice*, n. 6 above, para. 62.

[12] See, e.g., Case 43/72 *Merkur-Aussenhandels-GmbH* v. *Commission* [1973] ECR 1055; Case 153/73 *Holtz und Willemsen GmbH* v. *Commission* [1974] ECR 675.

A second ground of claim is that a regulation is in breach of a hierarchically superior regulation.[13] The regulations made pursuant to, for example, the CAP may be 'one-off' provisions, but they may also relate to a prior network of regulations on the same topic. There may therefore be regulations enacted pursuant to more general regulations on the same topic.

A third ground that can sustain an action in damages is where the Community legislation is held to infringe certain general principles of law such as proportionality, legal certainty, or legitimate expectations.[14]

The ECJ does not articulate *why* the above might constitute superior rules of law, nor *what* other matters might be added to the list. The rules of the World Trade Organization (WTO) cannot, subject to limited exceptions, be relied on in this context.[15] It is often left to the Advocate General to question the wisdom of adding to the list of such rules.[16] Superior sometimes seems to be equated with 'important', and sometimes with a more formalistic conception of one rule being higher than another, as in the case of the regulation being in breach of a parent regulation. These various possible grounds of claim can be exemplified by considering the *CNTA* case.

Case 74/74 **Comptoir National Technique Agricole (CNTA) SA v. Commission**
[1975] ECR 533

The applicant claimed that it had suffered loss by the withdrawal of monetary compensatory amounts (MCAs) by Regulation 189/72. The system of MCAs was designed to compensate traders for fluctuations in exchange rates. Regulation 189/72, which entered into force on 1 February 1972, abolished these MCAs in so far as they had been applicable to colza and rape seeds, because the Commission decided that the market situation had altered, thereby rendering the MCAs unnecessary. The applicant had, however, entered into contracts before the Regulation was passed, even though these contracts were to be performed after the ending of the scheme. It argued that it had made these contracts on the assumption that the MCAs would still be payable, and that it had set the price on that hypothesis. The sudden termination of the system in this area, without warning, was said by the applicant, to have caused it loss. The ECJ began by citing the general principle from the *Schöppenstedt* case and then continued in the following vein.

THE ECJ

17. In this connection the applicant contends in the first place that by abolishing the compensatory amounts by Regulation 189/72 the Commission has infringed basic Regulation 974/71 of the Council.

18. That Regulation, it contends, while conferring on the Commission the power to ascertain that the conditions for the application of the compensatory amounts are met, does not

---

[13] Case 74/74 *Comptoir National Technique Agricole (CNTA) SA v. Commission* [1975] ECR 533.

[14] The duty to give reasons does not appear to qualify as a superior rule of law for these purposes: Case 106/81 *Julius Kind KG v. EEC* [1982] ECR 2885; Case C–119/88, n. 9 above; Cases T–466, 469, 473, 474, and 477/93 *O'Dwyer v. Council* [1996] ECR II–207.

[15] Case C–149/96 *Portugal v. Council* [1999] ECR I–8395; Case T–18/99 *Cordis Obst und Gemüse Grosshandel GmbH v. Commission* [2001] ECR II–913; Case T–383/00 *Beamglow Ltd. v. EP, Council, and Commission* [2005] ECR II–5459.

[16] See, e.g., Trabbuchi AG in the *CNTA* case, n. 13 above, 560–561.

allow it to take a decision withdrawing compensatory amounts once instituted and it requires in any event that the Commission's decision be taken on the basis of an assessment of solely monetary factors to the exclusion of economic factors which in this case the Commission has taken into consideration.

19. It follows from the last sentence of Article 1(2) of Regulation No 974/71 that the option for Member States to apply compensatory amounts may only be exercised where the monetary measures in question would lead to disturbances to trade in agricultural products.

20. As the application of compensatory amounts is a measure of an exceptional nature, this provision must be understood as enunciating a condition not only of the introduction but also of the maintenance of compensatory amounts for a specific product.

21. The Commission has a large measure of discretion for judging whether the monetary measure concerned might lead to disturbances to trade in the product in question.

22. In order to judge the risk of such disturbances, it is permissible for the Commission to take into account market conditions as well as monetary factors.

23. It has not been established that the Commission exceeded the limits of its power thus defined when it considered towards the end of January 1972 that the situation on the market in colza and rape seeds was such that the application of compensatory amounts for those products was no longer necessary.

[*The ECJ then considered whether the withdrawal of the compensatory amounts violated certain general principles of law. It held that Regulation 189/72 was not retroactive, as had been claimed by the applicants. The Court then considered whether this withdrawal had violated the principle of legitimate expectations. It held that the object of the regime for the fixing of refunds in advance on export orders could not be regarded as tantamount to a guarantee for traders against the risk of movements in exchange rates. It continued as follows.*]

41. Nevertheless the application of the compensatory amounts in practice avoids the exchange risk, so that a trader, even a prudent one, might be induced to omit to cover himself against such a risk.

42. In these circumstances, a trader may legitimately expect that for transactions irrevocably undertaken by him because he has obtained, subject to a deposit, export licences fixing the amount of the refund in advance, no unforeseeable alteration will occur which could have the effect of causing him inevitable loss, by re-exposing him to the exchange risk.

43. The Community is therefore liable if, in the absence of an overriding matter of public interest, the Commission abolished with immediate effect and without warning the application of compensatory amounts in a specific sector without adopting transitional measures which would at least permit traders either to avoid the loss which would have been suffered in the performance of export contracts, the existence and irrevocability of which are established by the advance fixing of the refunds, or to be compensated for such loss.

44. In the absence of an overriding matter of public interest, the Commission has violated a superior rule of law, thus rendering the Community liable, by failing to include in Regulation 189/72 transitional measures for the protection of the confidence which a trader might legitimately have had in the Community rules.

The ECJ stated, however, that the Community was not liable to pay the full cost of the mcas that would have applied to the transactions, but rather that the extent of the applicant's legitimate expectation was merely that of not suffering loss by reason of the withdrawal of the mcas. In later proceedings it was held that the applicant had not in fact suffered such losses.[17]

---

[17] Case 74/74 [1976] ECR 797.

(d) THE MEANING OF FLAGRANT VIOLATION: THE EARLY CASE LAW

It is evident from *Schöppenstedt* that the individual must prove not only breach of a superior rule of law for the protection of the individual, but also that the breach was flagrant. This term was restrictively construed in the early case law.

Cases 83, 94/76, 4, 15, and 40/77 Bayerische HNL Vermehrungsbetriebe GmbH & Co KG v. Council and Commission
[1978] ECR 1209

[Note ToA renumbering: Arts. 40 and 215 are now Arts. 34 and 288]

The Community had a surplus of milk in the form of large stocks of skimmed-milk powder. In order to reduce these stocks a Regulation was passed, which imposed an obligation to purchase skimmed-milk powder for use in certain feedingstuffs. The applicant claimed that this had rendered the costs of feeding its animals more expensive. In earlier cases the ECJ had held that the Regulation was null and void, because it was disproportionate and discriminatory.[18] The applicants then sought damages. The ECJ held that the legislature could not be hindered in making its decisions by the prospect of applications for damages whenever it adopted legislative measures in the public interest which might adversely affect the interests of individuals, and that therefore where there was a wide discretion it would be for the applicant to show that the EC had manifestly and gravely disregarded the limits on its powers.

THE ECJ

6. This is not so in the case of a measure of economic policy such as that in the present case, in view of its special features. In this connection it is necessary to observe first that this measure affected very wide categories of traders, in other words all buyers of compound feeding-stuffs, so that its effects on individual undertakings were considerably lessened. Moreover, the effects of the Regulation on the price of feeding-stuffs as a factor in the production costs of those buyers were only limited since that price rose by little more than 2 per cent. This price increase was particularly small in comparison with the price increases resulting, during the period of application of the Regulation, from the variations in the world market prices of feeding-stuffs containing protein, which were three or four times higher than the increase resulting from the obligation to purchase skimmed-milk powder introduced by the Regulation. The effects of the Regulation on the profit-earning capacity of the undertakings did not ultimately exceed the bounds of economic risks inherent in the activities of the agricultural sectors concerned.

It is apparent that the breach was held not to be manifest and grave because its *effects* were not regarded as serious enough to warrant recovery. In the *Amylum* case this condition was read in a rather different way.

---

[18] See, e.g., Case 116/76 *Granaria BV v. Hoofdproduktschap voor Akkerbouwprodukten* [1977] ECR 1247.

Cases 116 and 124/77 **Amylum NV and Tunnel Refineries Ltd. v. Council and Commission**
[1979] ECR 3497

[Note ToA renumbering: Arts. 39, 40, and 177 are now Arts. 33, 34, and 234]

The applicants manufactured isoglucose, a sweetener made from starch, which in liquid form competed with sugar. There was a surplus of sugar, which was subject to production constraints. The producers of isoglucose were therefore perceived as having an economic advantage, and it was decided that they too should be subject to a production levy. The system for levies was introduced by Council Regulation 1111/77 and Commission Regulation 1468/77. In an earlier case the ECJ held that Regulation 1111/77 was invalid because the particular production levy imposed was in breach of Article 40(3), but it also stated that the Council could nonetheless devise appropriate measures to ensure that the market in sweeteners functioned properly.[19] The applicants sought compensation for losses suffered. The Court quoted the principle from the *Bayerische* case, and then continued as follows.

THE ECJ

17. In this respect it must be recalled that the Court did not declare invalid any isoglucose production levy, but only the method of calculation adopted and the fact that the levy applied to the whole of the isoglucose production. Having regard to the fact that the production of isoglucose was playing a part in increasing sugar surpluses, it was permissible for the Council to impose restrictive measures on such production.

...

19. In fact, even though the fixing of the isoglucose production levy at 5 units of account per 100 kg. of dry matter was vitiated by errors, it must nevertheless be pointed out that, having regard to the fact that an appropriate levy was fully justified, these errors were not of such gravity that it may be said that the conduct of the institutions in this respect was verging on the arbitrary and was thus of such a kind as to involve the Community in non-contractual liability.

In the *Amylum* case the applicants did not lose because the *effects* of the breach were insufficiently serious: the losses were severe. The ECJ focused rather upon the *manner* of the breach. This was said not to be arbitrary, for the following reason. The general aim of stabilizing the market in sweeteners was a legitimate one for the Community to pursue. Mistakes had occurred in the *particular way* in which this was achieved, namely in the calculation of the levy. This was not, however, enough to render the decision arbitrary, especially given the fact that this was an emergency situation.

The result of *Bayerische* and *Amylum* was that an applicant would have to show both that the *effects* of the breach were serious, in terms of the quantum of loss suffered, and also that the *manner* of the breach was arbitrary. These hurdles were not easy to surmount, particularly the second. It was rare for the Community institutions to promulgate a regulation which was wholly unrelated to the general ends they were entitled to advance under their powers in, for example, the agricultural sphere. The mistakes were likely to be made precisely in the carrying out of general, legitimate policies in an erroneous manner. Claimants did however occasionally win.[20]

---

[19] Cases 103 and 145/77 *Royal Scholten-Honig (Holdings) Ltd. v. Intervention Board for Agricultural Produce, Tunnel Refineries Ltd. v. Intervention Board for Agricultural Produce* [1978] ECR 2037.

[20] Cases 64, 113/76, 167, 239/78, 27, 28, and 45/79 *Dumortier Frères SA v. Council* [1979] ECR 3091.

(e) THE MEANING OF FLAGRANT VIOLATION/ SERIOUS BREACH: THE CURRENT LAW

More recent cases have evinced a less restrictive interpretation of the term flagrant violation. They have done so in two ways.

First, the ECJ has modified its position in relation to the *manner of the breach*. In *Stahlwerke*[21] it was held that fault in the nature of arbitrariness was not required for liability. This modification fitted neatly with that in *Bergaderm*, which is the leading modern authority. In *Brasserie du Pêcheur*,[22] the ECJ stated that the test for state liability in damages should not be different from that of the Community itself under Article 288(2).[23] The ECJ's interpretation of the term 'serious breach' in *Brasserie du Pêcheur* will therefore be of importance in the Article 288(2) jurisprudence. This has been confirmed by *Bergaderm*, where the ECJ completed the circle by explicitly drawing on the factors mentioned in *Brasserie du Pêcheur* to determine the meaning of flagrant violation for the purposes of liability under Article 288(2).[24] This means that under Article 288(2) the seriousness of the breach will be dependent upon factors such as: the relative clarity of the rule which has been breached; the measure of discretion left to the relevant authorities; whether the error of law was excusable or not; and whether the breach was intentional or voluntary.

Case C–352/98 P **Laboratoires Pharmaceutiques Bergaderm SA and Goupil v. Commission** [2000] ECR I–5291

[Note ToA renumbering: Art. 215 is now Art. 288]

This was an appeal from the CFI to the ECJ. The applicant sought damages for losses suffered by the passage of a directive, which prohibited the use of certain substances in cosmetics. It claimed, *inter alia*, that the directive should be regarded as an administrative act, since it only concerned the applicant, the consequence being that illegality *per se* would suffice for liability, rather than having to prove a sufficiently serious breach.

THE ECJ

40. The system of rules which the Court has worked out with regard to [Article 215] takes into account, *inter alia*, the complexity of situations to be regulated, difficulties in the application or interpretation of the texts and, more particularly, the margin of discretion available to the author of the act in question (*Brasserie du Pêcheur*, para. 43).

41. The Court has stated that the conditions under which the State may incur liability for damage caused to individuals by a breach of Community law cannot, in the absence of particular justification, differ from those governing the liability of the Community in like circumstances. The

---

[21] Case C–220/91 P *Stahlwerke Peine-Salzgitter AG* v. *Commission* [1993] ECR I–2393. See also Case T–120/89 *Stahlwerke Peine-Salzgitter* v. *Commission* [1991] ECR II–279; Case C–282/90 *Industrie- en Handelsonderneming Vreugdenhil BV* v. *Commission* [1992] ECR I–1937, paras. 17–19.

[22] Cases C–46 and 48/93 *Brasserie du Pêcheur SA* v. *Germany; R.* v. *Secretary of State for Transport, ex p. Factortame Ltd.* [1996] ECR I–1029.

[23] See Ch. 9.

[24] T. Tridimas, 'Liability for Breach of Community Law: Growing Up and Mellowing Down?' (2001) 38 *CMLRev.* 301.

protection of the rights which individuals derive from Community law cannot vary depending on whether a national authority or a Community authority is responsible for the damage (*Brasserie du Pêcheur*, para. 42).

42. As regards Member State liability for damage caused to individuals, the Court has held that Community law confers a right to reparation where three conditions are met: the rule of law infringed must be intended to confer rights on individuals; the breach must be sufficiently serious; and there must be a direct causal link between the breach of the obligation resting on the State and the damage sustained by the injured parties (*Brasserie du Pêcheur*, para. 51).

43. As to the second condition, as regards both Community liability under Article 215 . . . and Member State liability for breaches of Community law, the decisive test for finding that a breach of Community law is sufficiently serious is whether the Member State or the Community institution concerned manifestly and gravely disregarded the limits on its discretion (*Brasserie du Pêcheur*, para. 55 . . .).

44. Where the Member State or the institution in question has only considerably reduced, or even no discretion, the mere infringement of Community law may be sufficient to establish the existence of a sufficiently serious breach (*Hedley Lomas*, para. 28).

45. It is therefore necessary to examine whether . . . the Court of First Instance erred in law in its examination of the way in which the Commission exercised its discretion when it adopted the Adaptation Directive.

46. In that regard, the Court finds that the general or individual nature of a measure taken by an institution is not a decisive criterion for identifying the limits of the discretion enjoyed by the institution in question.

47. It follows that the first ground of the appeal, which is based exclusively on the categorisation of the Adaptation Directive as an individual measure, has in any event no bearing on the issue and must be rejected.

The second way in which the ECJ has become more liberal relates to the *effects of the breach*. The possibility of a large number of claimants will not, in itself, rule out an Article 288(2) action. This is evident from the *Mulder* case.[25] This was a sequel to the earlier *Mulder* case,[26] where the ECJ held that a Community regulation which precluded Mulder and many others from qualifying for a milk quota violated their legitimate expectations and was invalid. The ECJ held that a damages action could lie in relation to a regulation that totally denied the farmers any quota at all. This regulation constituted a breach of the farmers' legitimate expectations, and there was no countervailing, higher public interest justifying this action.[27] The ECJ reached the opposite conclusion in relation to the illegality of a later regulation imposing a 60 per cent quota. The Court accepted that this, too, infringed the legitimate expectations of the applicants, but this illegality was not sufficiently serious, *because* there was a higher public interest at stake. The 60 per cent quota was a choice of economic policy made by the Council, seeking to balance the need to avoid excess production with the interest of the farmers who had entered the earlier scheme.

(f) THE PRESENT LAW: SUMMARY

i. For an applicant to succeed it is necessary to show that there has been a violation of a superior rule of law for the protection of individuals, that it was manifest and grave, or sufficiently serious, and that it caused the damage.

[25] Cases C–104/89 and 37/90 *Mulder* v. *Council and Commission* [1992] ECR I–3061.
[26] Case 120/86 *Mulder* v. *Minister van Landbouw en Visserij* [1988] ECR 2321.
[27] See also Case C–152/88 *Sofrimport Sàrl* v. *Commission* [1990] ECR I–2477.

ii. The key criterion as to whether it is necessary to show that the breach was sufficiently serious is the margin of discretion accorded to the author of the act. Where such discretion exists it will be necessary for the applicant to prove such a breach. This is so irrespective of whether the measure is general/legislative or individual/administrative in nature.

iii. The factors mentioned in *Brasserie du Pêcheur* and *Bergaderm*, which go to the issue of whether the breach was sufficiently serious, will be determinative in the Article 288(2) case law.

iv. The applicant should not have to show that the loss suffered was serious. It is not part of the *Brasserie du Pêcheur* test, and should not, as a matter of principle be required.

v. It is no longer fatal to a claim that there is a large number of potential applicants.

(g) THE PRESENT LAW: AN ASSESSMENT

The initial question is whether there are valid reasons for limiting liability under Article 288(2). Views on this will undoubtedly differ, but we believe that there are good arguments for doing so. Most of the major cases arise out of the CAP, under which the Community institutions have to make difficult discretionary choices of a legislative nature. This will often entail a complex process designed to balance the conflicting variables identified in Article 33. A finding of illegality *per se* should not suffice as the basis for a damages action. Such a strict standard of liability would render the decision-makers susceptible to a potentially wide liability, and would run the risk that the Court might be 'second-guessing' the decisions made by the Council and Commission on how the variables within Article 33 should be balanced.[28] Analogous considerations have influenced UK courts in similar types of case.[29] It would be feasible to regard illegality *per se* as the appropriate test under Article 288(2) if such illegality were to be taken as proven only where the conduct of the Community institutions was particularly flagrant. Such a test would however incorporate an element of serious breach into the definition of illegality.[30]

Secondly, if this is accepted the crucial issue is how to interpret the phrase 'flagrant violation' or 'serious breach'. In the past this was interpreted too restrictively to require something akin to arbitrary action. The approach in *Brasserie du Pêcheur* and *Bergaderm* is more nuanced, and is to be welcomed. The existence of such a serious breach requires attention to the very factors identified in those cases. The mere fact that the general aim being pursued by the EC was legitimate should not serve to shield it from liability, if it can be shown that there was a serious breach in the manner of attaining this end, when judged by the *Brasserie du Pêcheur* criteria.

Thirdly, where loss has been caused by sufficiently serious illegal action the applicant should not have to prove that the loss was particularly serious. The applicant will have to show that the illegality *caused* the loss, but there should be no requirement over and above this.[31] The ordinary 'economics of litigation' should ensure that claims are, in general, only pursued when it is economically worthwhile to do so.

---

[28] Cf. Capotorti AG in Cases 83 and 94/76, 4, 15, and 40/77 *Bayersiche HNL Vermehrungsbetriebe GmbH & Co. KG* v. *Council and Commission* [1978] ECR 1209, 1223–1224.

[29] P. Craig, 'Once More Unto the Breach: The Community, the State and Damages Liability' (1997) 113 *LQR* 67.

[30] Cf. Capotorti AG, n. 28 above, 1233.

[31] *Ibid.*, 1233–1234.

4. LIABILITY FOR NON-DISCRETIONARY ACTS

(a) THE GENERAL PRINCIPLE: ILLEGALITY, CAUSATION, DAMAGE

The discussion thus far has focused upon liability in damages for legislative and non-legislative acts which involve an element of discretion. The nature of the test that applies to liability for non-discretionary acts has been subtly altered.

The traditional approach was that where an act did not entail any meaningful discretionary choice then it would normally suffice to show the existence of illegality, causation, and damage.[32] Successful claims were relatively rare.

The more recent case law continues to distinguish between discretionary and non-discretionary acts, but does so within the framework of the sufficiently serious breach test. The modern formulation, set out in *Bergaderm* and subsequent cases, is that the applicant must prove that the rule of law infringed was intended to confer rights on individuals, there must be a sufficiently serious breach and a causal link between the breach and the resultant harm. Where however the Community institution has considerably reduced or no discretion, the mere infringement of Community law *may* be sufficient to establish the existence of the sufficiently serious breach.[33]

(b) APPLICATION OF THE GENERAL PRINCIPLE

The Court will inevitably have to decide whether there is discretion, with the consequence that the applicant must satisfy the sufficiently serious breach test, or whether in the absence of discretion the mere infringement of Community law may suffice for liability.[34]

Case C–390/95 P **Antillean Rice Mills NV v. Commission**
[1999] ECR I–769

The applicants challenged, *inter alia*, aspects of the basic Council Decision which governed the relationship between the overseas countries and territories (OCTs) and the EC. They also challenged a Commission Decision, which introduced safeguard measures for rice originating in the Dutch Antilles, for breach of the Council Decision. The CFI dismissed most of the claim. On appeal to the ECJ the applicants argued, *inter alia*, the CFI was wrong to have required proof of a sufficiently serious breach, since the contested measures were decisions.

---

[32] Cases 44–51/77 *Union Malt* v. *Commission* [1978] ECR 57; Cases T–481 and 484/93 *Live Pigs*, n. 10 above; Case 26/81 *Oleifici Mediterranei* v. *EEC* [1982] ECR 3057, para. 16; Case C–146/91 *KYDEP* v. *Council and Commission* [1994] ECR I–4199; Cases C–258 and 259/90 *Pesquerias de Bermeo SA and Naviera Laida SA* v. *Commission* [1992] ECR I–2901; Case T–175/94 *International Procurement Services* v. *Commission* [1996] ECR II–729, para. 44; Case T–178/98 *Fresh Marine*, n. 4 above, para. 54; Cases T–79/96, 260/97, and 117/98 *Camar Srl and Tico Srl* v. *Commission* [2000] ECR II–2193, paras. 204–205; Case T–333/03 *Masdar (UK) Ltd.* v. *Commission*, 16 Nov. 2006, paras. 59–62.

[33] Case C–352/98 P *Laboratoires Pharmaceutiques Bergaderm*, n. 5 above, paras. 42–44; Case C–472/00 P *Fresh Marine A/S*, n. 7 above, paras. 26–27; Case C–312/00 P *Camar*, n. 7 above, paras. 54–55; Cases T–198/95, 171/96, 230/97, 174/98, and 225/98 *Comafrica SpA and Dole Fresh Fruit Europa & Co. Ltd.* v. *Commission* [2001] ECR II–1975, paras. 134–136; Case T–283/02 *EnBW Kernkraft GmbH* v. *Commission* [2005] ECR II–913, para. 87; Case T–139/01 *Comafrica SpA and Dole Fresh Fruit Europe & Co. Ltd.* v. *Commission* [2005] ECR II–409, para. 142.

[34] Case T–390/94 *Aloys Schröder* v. *Commission* [1997] ECR II–501; Cases T–458 and 523/93 *ENU* v. *Commission* [1995] ECR II–2459; Case T–178/98 *Fresh Marine*, n. 4 above, para. 57; Case 79/96 *Camar Srl*, n. 32 above, para. 206; Case C–64/98 *Petrides Co. Inc.* v. *Commission* [1999] ECR I–5187, paras. 26–28.

THE ECJ

57. It must be noted, first, that it is settled case-law that in a legislative context involving the exercise of a wide discretion, the Community cannot incur liability unless the institution concerned has manifestly and gravely disregarded the limits on the exercise of its powers. . . .

58. Second, . . . the CFI proceeded on the basis that the Commission enjoyed a wide discretion in the field of economic policy, which means that the stricter criterion of liability must be applied, namely the requirements of a sufficiently serious breach of a superior rule of law for the protection of the individual.

59. It follows that the CFI correctly applied the stricter criterion of liability.

60. The fact that the contested measure is in the form of a decision, and hence in principle capable of being the subject of an action for annulment, is not sufficient to preclude its being legislative in character. In the context of an action for damages, that character depends on the nature of the measure in question, not its form.

. . .

62. . . . [I]t must be stated that the fact they are individually concerned has no effect on the character of the measure in the context of an action for damages, since that action is an independent remedy. . . .

(c) THE MEANING OF ILLEGALITY

It is also important to address the meaning attributed to 'illegality' in this context. In one sense any infringement of law can constitute illegality.[35] It is therefore possible to list types of error which *might* lead to liability, including: failure to gather the facts before reaching a decision, taking a decision based on irrelevant factors, failure to accord appropriate procedural rights, and inadequate supervision of bodies to whom power has been delegated. The mere proof of such an error will not however always ensure success in a damages action. It is always open to a court to construe illegality narrowly or to define it so as to preclude liability unless there has been some error, or something equivalent thereto.[36] The point is exemplified by the following cases.

Cases 19, 20, 25, and 30/69 **Denise Richez-Parise and Others v. Commission**
[1970] ECR 325

The applicants were Community officials who had been given incorrect information concerning their pensions. This information was supplied as a consequence of a request by the Commission to the officials concerned that they should contact the relevant department in order to obtain information concerning their financial provisions on termination of employment. The information which was given was based on an interpretation of the relevant regulation, which was believed to be correct at the time at which it was given. The department which gave the information later had reason to believe that its interpretation of the regulation was incorrect, but no immediate steps were taken to inform the applicants of this. This was done only at a later stage, by which time the applicants had already committed themselves as to the

---

[35] Case T–79/96 *Camar Srl*, n. 32 above, para. 205.

[36] Many of those who argue that a different test from that in *Bayerische* should be applied outside the discretionary, economic sphere also make it clear that they are not advocating liability being based on illegality alone: see, e.g., Darmon AG in *Vreugdenhil*, n. 20 above, 821–822.

way in which they would take their pension entitlements. The applicants sought, *inter alia*, to obtain compensation for losses which they had suffered.

THE ECJ

36. Apart from the exceptional instance, the adoption of an incorrect interpretation does not constitute in itself a wrongful act.

37. Even the fact that the authorities request those concerned to obtain information from the competent departments does not necessarily involve those authorities in an obligation to guarantee the correctness of the information supplied and does not therefore make them liable for any injury which may be occasioned by incorrect information.

38. However, whilst it may be possible to doubt the existence of a wrongful act concerning the supply of incorrect information, the same cannot be said of the department's delay in rectifying the information.

39. Although such rectification was possible as early as April 1968 it was deferred without any justification until the end of 1968.

. . .

41. A correction made shortly before or after 16 April, that is to say, before the time when those concerned had to make their decision, would have certainly enabled the defendant to avoid all liability for the consequences of the wrong information. The failure to make such a correction is, on the other hand, a matter of such a nature as to render the Communities liable.

Thus in *Richez-Parise* the ECJ construed the requisite illegality for the purposes of damages liability so as to exclude a mere incorrect interpretation of a regulation. Such regulations are often complex, and are open to more than one construction. To render the Communities liable in damages whenever such a construction proved to be incorrect would be harsh. It would, in effect, open the Community to a form of strict liability, where the only condition for recovery would be proof that the interpretation adopted was incorrect, even if that interpretation was plausible, and even if the decision-maker had taken due care in reaching it.[37]

The ability to mould or shape illegality for the purposes of damages liability is also apparent in other cases. Thus in *Adams*[38] the applicant informed the Commission that his company was engaged in anti-competitive practices, but making it clear that the Commission must conceal his identity, in order to avoid repercussions from his employer. It was clear from the facts that the Commission officials had been negligent in allowing his name to become known, with tragic consequences for him and his family. He was awarded damages, subject to reduction for contributory negligence. In *Fresh Marine*[39] the applicant sought damages because the Commission had erroneously decided that the company was in breach of an undertaking it had given in relation to the dumping of salmon. The CFI held that it was not necessary for the applicant to prove a sufficiently serious breach, since the alleged error did not involve complex discretionary choices. A mere infringement of EC law would suffice. However it then defined the relevant error leading to illegality to be lack of ordinary

---

[37] See the similar reasoning in relation to state liability in Case C–392/93 *R. v. HM Treasury, ex p. British Telecommunications plc* [1996] ECR I–1631. The same type of problem can occur in domestic law, where an agency construes a statute incorrectly and losses are caused to individuals: see P. Craig, *Administrative Law* (5th edn., Sweet & Maxwell, 2003), ch. 26.

[38] Case 145/83 *Stanley George Adams* v. *Commission* [1985] ECR 3539.

[39] Case T–178/98, n. 4 above, para. 61.

care and diligence by the Commission, and took account of the applicant's contributory negligence.[40]

(d) PRESENT LAW: SUMMARY

i.   The traditional test for liability for non-discretionary acts was proof of illegality, causation, and damage. The more modern case law continues to distinguish between liability for discretionary and non-discretionary acts, but does so from within the framework of the sufficiently serious breach test: where the Community institution has considerably reduced or no discretion, the mere infringement of Community law *may* be sufficient to establish the existence of the sufficiently serious breach.

ii. The CFI and ECJ will necessarily have to make a judgment as to whether an act, general or individual, falls to be judged by this test, rather than the test discussed in the previous Section.

iii. The CFI and ECJ will also have to decide what constitutes illegality for the purposes of liability for non-discretionary acts.

5. LIABILITY FOR OFFICIAL ACTS OF COMMUNITY SERVANTS

Article 288 allows for loss to be claimed where it has been caused either by the Community institutions or by the acts of its servants 'in the performance of their duties'. It is clear that not every act performed by a servant will be deemed to be an act in the performance of his or her duties. The matter is rendered more complex by the fact that Article 12 of the Protocol on the Privileges and Immunities of the European Communities states that: 'officials and other servants of the Community shall ... be immune from legal proceedings in respect of acts performed by them in their official capacity'.

Case 9/69 **Sayag v. Leduc**
[1969] ECR 329

Sayag was an engineer employed by Euratom. He was instructed to take Leduc, a representative of a private firm, on a visit to certain installations. He drove him there in his own car, and obtained a travel order which enabled him to claim the expenses for the trip from the Community. An accident occurred and Leduc claimed in the Belgian courts damages against Sayag for the injuries which he had suffered. It was argued that Sayag was driving the car in the performance of his duties, and that therefore the action should have been brought against the Community. Article 188(2) of the Euratom Treaty is equivalent to 288(2) EC.

THE ECJ

By referring at one and the same time to damage caused by the institutions and to that caused by the servants of the Community, Article 188 indicates that the Community is only liable for

---

[40] *Ibid.*, paras. 57–61.

those acts of its servants which, by virtue of an internal and direct relationship, are the necessary extension of the tasks entrusted to the institutions.

In the light of the special nature of this legal system, it would not therefore be lawful to extend it to categories of acts other than those referred to above.

A servant's use of his private car for transport during the course of his duties does not satisfy the conditions set out above.

A reference to a servant's private car in a travel order does not bring the driving of such car within the performance of his duties, but is basically intended to enable any necessary reimbursement of the travel expenses involved in this means of transport to be made in accordance with the standards laid down for this purpose.

Only in the rare case of *force majeure* or in exceptional circumstances of such overriding importance that without the servant's using private means of transport the Community would have been unable to carry out the tasks entrusted to it, could such use be considered to form part of the servant's performance of his duties, within the meaning of the second paragraph of Article 188 of the Treaty.

It follows from the above that the driving of a private car by a servant cannot in principle constitute the performance of his duties within the meaning of the second paragraph of Article 188 of the EAEC Treaty.

The range of acts done by its servants for which the Community will accept responsibility is therefore narrow, and more limited than that which exists in the laws of most of the Member States. No real justification for the limited nature of this liability is provided by the ECJ.

If the Community is not liable then an action can be brought against the servant in his or her personal capacity, and any such action is brought in national courts and is governed by national law. However, the Protocol on the Privileges and Immunities of the European Communities provides that servants have immunity from suit in national courts in relation to 'acts performed in their official capacity'. The language of this provision differs from that of Article 288(2), which speaks in terms of servants acting in 'performance of their duties'. Normally one would expect that where the Community is liable under Article 288(2), because the servant was acting in the performance of his or her duties, then it would also follow that the servant would not be personally liable, since he or she would be deemed to be acting in an official capacity. The interrelationship between these two provisions may, nonetheless, be more problematic, and the ECJ has held that the servant's personal immunity and the scope of the Community's liability for the acts of the servant are separate issues.[41] There is however much to be said for the view proffered by Schermers and Swaak that acts of servants 'in the performance of their duties (leading to the Communities' liability) include but are not limited to acts performed by them in their official capacity (leading to the servants' immunity)'.[42]

It has been assumed thus far that the Community will be liable for the acts of its institutions, and for the acts of its servants, subject to the limitations of the *Sayag* case. Where the EC establishes agencies it is common for the regulation establishing the agency to contain a provision equivalent to Article 288(2).[43] The Community may well be responsible even in the absence of such an express provision where it has delegated certain functions to a Community body, since the acts of that body, at least those of a governmental nature, will be imputed to the EC.[44]

---

[41] Case 5/68 *Sayag* v. *Leduc* [1968] ECR 395, 408.

[42] H.G. Schermers and R.A. Swaak, 'Official Acts of Community Servants and Article 215(4)', in Heukels and McDonnell (eds.), n. 4 above, 177.

[43] P. Craig, *EU Administrative Law* (Oxford University Press, 2006), ch. 5.

[44] Case 18/60 *Worms* v. *High Authority* [1962] ECR 195.

6. LIABILITY FOR VALID LEGISLATIVE ACTS

(a) THE NATURE OF THE PROBLEM

Individuals may well suffer loss flowing from lawful acts of the Community, as well as from acts which are tainted with some form of illegality. This problem can occur in any legal system, but the potential for its occurrence in the Community is particularly marked.

H.J. Bronkhorst, The Valid Legislative Act as a Cause of Liability of the Communities[45]

There are many reasons why private individuals may have a particular interest in the existence of a clearly defined principle concerning Community liability for legal acts which result in damage for them.... Does a fisherman, who, on very short notice, has to make very important changes to his vessel, thus incurring substantial financial costs, have an action for compensation even if the Community measures as such cannot be challenged on the ground of illegality?

[P]rivate individuals, operating in the field of the Common Agricultural Policy, may easily suffer financial injury because of the fact that competing producers are favoured by Community measures. Producers of vegetable fats may very well undergo the effects of (uneven) competition if producers of butter or milk powder are able to dispose of large quantities of their products on the European markets with the help of Community subsidies.

The problem of loss being caused by lawful governmental action is not peculiar to the Community. Thus, French law recognizes a principle of *égalité devant les charges publiques*, and German law has the concept of *Sonderöpfer*. Under these principles loss caused by lawful governmental action can be recovered, albeit in limited circumstances.[46] While there is hardship for individuals in the situations postulated by Bronkhorst, the difficulties of deciding when to grant such compensation should not be underestimated.

P. Craig, Compensation in Public Law[47]

Legislation is constantly being passed which is explicitly or implicitly aimed at benefiting one section of the population at the expense of another. It is a matter of conscious legislative policy. This may be in the form of tax changes or in a decision to grant selective assistance to one particular type of industry rather than another. Any incorporation of state liability arising out of legislation as part of a risk theory would necessitate the drawing of a difficult line. It would be between cases where the deleterious effect on a firm or group was the aim of the legislation or a necessary correlative of it, and where legislation is passed which incidentally affects a particular firm in a serious manner, but where there is no legislative objection to compensating the firm for the loss suffered.

---

[45] In Heukels and McDonnell (eds.), n. 4 above, 153–154.
[46] *Ibid.*, 155–159.
[47] (1980) 96 *LQR* 413, 450. See also Case T–113/96, n. 1 above, for a good example of this in the Community context.

The drawing of such a line in the context of the EC is particularly problematic, given that within, for example, the Common Agricultural Policy (CAP) there will often be 'winners and losers' as the result of the institutions' attempts to give effect to the often conflicting objectives which lie at the heart of that policy.

(b) THE CASE LAW

Claims to recover for lawfully caused loss have been advanced before the Community Courts on a number of occasions, and have been rejected.[48] The leading case is now *Dorsch Consult*.[49]

Case T–184/95 **Dorsch Consult Ingenieurgesellschaft mbH v. Council**
[1998] ECR II–667[50]

The case arose out of the Gulf war. The EC, acting pursuant to a resolution of the United Nations Security Council, passed a regulation banning trade with Iraq. The Iraqi government retaliated with a law which froze all assets and rights of companies doing business in Iraq, where those companies were based in countries which had imposed the embargo. The applicant was such a company. It argued, *inter alia*, that it should be compensated by the EC for the loss it had incurred, even if the EC had acted lawfully.

THE CFI

59. At the outset, the Court would point out that if the Community is to incur non-contractual liability as the result of a lawful or unlawful act, it is necessary in any event to prove that the alleged damage is real and the existence of a causal link between that act and the alleged damage.

. . .

80. It is clear from the . . . case law of the Court of Justice that, in the event of the principle of Community liability for a lawful act being recognised in Community law, such liability can be incurred only if the damage alleged, if deemed to constitute a 'still subsisting injury', affects a particular circle of economic operators in a disproportionate manner in comparison with others (unusual damage) and exceeds the economic risks inherent in operating in the sector concerned (special damage), without the legislative measure that gave rise to the alleged damage being justified by a general economic interest (*De Boer Buizen, Compagnie d'Approvisionnement, Biovilac*).

81. As regards the unusual nature of the alleged damage . . . [N]ot only the applicant's claims . . . were affected but also those of all Community undertakings which . . . had not yet been paid. . . .

82. . . . It cannot therefore claim to have suffered special damage or to have made exceptional sacrifice. . . .

---

[48] Cases 9 and 11/71 *Compagnie d'Approvisionnement de Transport et de Crédit SA and Grands Moulins de Paris SA* v. *Commission* [1972] ECR 391, para. 45; Cases 54–60/76 *Compagnie Industrielle et Agricole du Comté de Loheac* v. *Council and Commission* [1977] ECR 645, para. 19; Case 59/83 *SA Biovilac NV* v. *EEC* [1984] ECR 4057, 4080–4081; Case 265/85 *Van den Bergh & Jürgens BV and Van Dijk Food Products (Lopik) BV* v. *EEC* [1987] ECR 1155; Case 81/86 *De Boer Buizen* v. *Council and Commission* [1987] ECR 3677.

[49] See also Case T–383/00 *Beamglow*, n. 15 above.

[50] The decision was upheld on appeal: Case C–237/98 P *Dorsch Consult Ingenieurgesellschaft mbH* v. *Council* [2000] ECR I–4549.

83. ... It is common ground that Iraq ... was already regarded ... as a 'high risk country'. In those circumstances, the economic and commercial risks deriving from the possible involvement of Iraq in renewed warfare ... and the suspension of payment of its debts ... constituted foreseeable risks inherent in any provision of services in Iraq. ...

...

85. It follows that the risks involved in the applicant's providing services in Iraq formed part of the risks inherent in operating in the sector concerned.

7. CAUSATION AND DAMAGE

(a) CAUSATION

A.G. Toth, The Concepts of Damage and Causality as Elements of Non-Contractual Liability[51]

[T]he establishment of the necessary causality may give rise to difficult problems in practice. This is particularly so in the field of economic and commercial relations where the cause of an event can usually be traced back to a number of factors, objective as well as subjective, operating simultaneously or successively and producing direct as well as indirect effects. Broadly speaking, it may be said that there is no causality involving liability where the same result would have occurred in the same way even in the absence of the wrongful Community act or omission in question. The converse proposition, i.e., that the requisite causality exists whenever it can be shown that the damage would not have occurred without the Community action, is, however not always correct. Although in theory it is true that any circumstance, near or remote, without which an injury would not have been produced may be considered to be its cause, the fact that a Community act or omission is one only of several such circumstances may not in itself be sufficient to establish a causal connection entailing non-contractual liability. For that purpose, the causality must be 'direct, immediate and exclusive' which it can be only if the damage arises directly from the conduct of the institutions and does not depend on the intervention of other causes, whether positive or negative.

The difficulties of proving that it was the Community's action which caused the loss can be exemplified by the *Dumortier* case.[52]

Cases 64, 113/76, 167, 239/78, 27, 28, and 45/79
Dumortier Frères SA v. Council
[1979] ECR 3091

Council regulations provided that production refunds should be payable for maize starch, but that they should be abolished in the case of maize groats and meal (gritz), which were used in the production of beer. This differential treatment had been held to be in breach of what are

---

[51] In Heukels and McDonnell (eds.), n. 4 above, 192.
[52] See also Case T–193/04 *Tillack* v. *Commission*, 4 Oct. 2006; Case T–304/01 *Perez and others* v. *Council*, 13 Dec. 2006.

now Articles 33 and 34 EC,[53] and the applicants now claimed damages. The subsidies had been restored in the light of the ECJ's decision, but only for the future, and therefore losses had still been suffered in the intervening period. The Court found that there had been a manifest and grave breach by the Community. Some of the applicants claimed that they should be compensated because they were forced to close their factories.

THE ECJ

21. [T]he Council argued that the origin of the difficulties experienced by those undertakings is to be found in the circumstances peculiar to each of them, such as the obsolescence of their plant and managerial or financial problems. The data supplied by the parties in the course of the proceedings are not such as to establish the true cause of the further damage alleged. However, it is sufficient to state that even if it were assumed that the abolition of the refunds exacerbated the difficulties encountered by those applicants, those difficulties would not be a sufficiently direct consequence of the unlawful conduct of the Council to render the Community liable to make good the damage.

It will be necessary for an applicant to show not only that the Community action caused the loss, but also that the chain of causation has not been broken by the Member State or the applicant. The ECJ has held that where the loss arises from an independent/autonomous act by the Member State, the Community is no longer liable.[54] If, however, this conduct has been made possible by an illegal failure of the Commission to exercise its supervisory powers, then it will be this failure which will be considered to be the cause of the damage.[55] There may be instances where both the Community and the Member State are responsible. This complex issue will be considered below.

It is not entirely clear what type of conduct by the individual will serve to break the chain of causation. Negligence or contributory negligence will suffice either to defeat the claim or to reduce the award of damages.[56] It has also been held that if the individual ought to have foreseen the possibility of certain events which might cause loss, then the possibility of claiming damages will be diminished or lost.[57] Moreover, an individual who believes that a wrongful act of the Community has caused loss has been encouraged by the Court to challenge the measure through Article 234. Thus, in *Amylum* the ECJ stated that this was open to an individual, particularly where implementation was in the hands of national authorities.[58]

(b) DAMAGE

The general objective when awarding compensation for loss in the context of non-contractual liability is to provide restitution for the victim, in the sense of placing the victim in the situation

---

[53] Cases 124/76 and 20/77 *SA Moulins et Huileries de Pont-à-Mousson and Société Coopérative 'Providence Agricole de la Champagne'* v. *Office National Interprofessionnel des Céréales* [1977] ECR 1795.

[54] Case 132/77 *Société pour l'Exportation des Sucres SA* v. *Commission* [1978] ECR 1061, 1072–1073.

[55] Cases 9 and 12/60 *Vloeberghs* v. *High Authority* [1961] ECR 197, 240; Case 4/69 *Alfons Lütticke GmbH* v. *Commission* [1971] ECR 325, 336–338.

[56] Case 145/83 *Adams* v. *Commission* [1985] ECR 3539, 3592; Case T–178/98, *Fresh Marine*, n. 4 above.

[57] Case 59/83 *Biovilac*, n. 48 above; Case T–514/93 *Cobrecaf* v. *Commission* [1995] ECR II–621, 643; Case T–572/93 *Odigitria* v. *Council and Commission* [1995] ECR II–2025, 2051–2052; Case T–184/95 *Dorsch Consult* [1998] ECR II–667.

[58] Cases 116 and 124/77 *Amylum NV and Tunnel Refineries Ltd.* v. *Council and Commission* [1979] ECR 3497.

that would have pertained if the wrong had not been committed.[59] Although Article 288(2) speaks of the duty of the Community to make good 'any damage', it is clear that losses will only be recoverable if they are certain and specific, proven, and quantifiable.[60]

While the damage claimed must in general be *certain*, the Court held in *Kampffmeyer* that it is possible to maintain an action 'for imminent damage foreseeable with sufficient certainty even if the damage cannot yet be precisely assessed'.[61] The rationale was that it might be necessary to pursue an action immediately in order to prevent even greater damage.

The idea that the damage suffered must be *specific*, in the sense that it affects the applicant's interests in a special and individual way, is to be found in various guises in ECJ decisions. Thus, in the *Bayerische* case, considered above, the Court emphasized that the effects of the regulation did not exceed the bounds of economic risk inherent in the activity in question.[62] Similar themes concerning the special nature of the burden imposed on a particular trader can be found in the case law concerning the possible recovery for lawful governmental action.[63] The question whether an applicant should have to prove abnormal or special damage in a case concerning unlawful Community action has already been discussed.

The injured party will have the onus of *proving* that the damage occurred. In general the individual will have to show that the injury was actually sustained.[64] This may not be easy, and it is not uncommon for cases to fail for this reason.[65]

The damage must also be *quantifiable* if the applicant is to succeed. In order to decide whether the loss is quantifiable, one needs to know what *types* of damage are recoverable. Advocate General Capotorti put the matter in the following way:[66]

> It is well known that the legal concept of 'damage' covers both a material loss *stricto sensu*, that is to say, a reduction in a person's assets, and also the loss of an increase in those assets which would have occurred if the harmful act had not taken place (these two alternatives are known respectively as *damnum emergens* and *lucrum cessans*).... The object of compensation is to restore the assets of the victim to the condition in which they would have been apart from the unlawful act, or at least to the condition closest to that which would have been produced if the unlawful nature of the act had not taken place: the hypothetical nature of that restoration often entails a certain degree of approximation.... These general remarks are not limited to the field of private law, but apply also to the liability of public authorities, and more especially to the non-contractual liability of the Community.

The ECJ will grant damages for losses actually sustained and will exceptionally award for non-material damage.[67] It is willing in principle also to give damages for lost profits, but is

---

[59] Case C–308/87 *Grifoni* v. *EAEC* [1994] ECR I–341, para. 40; Cases C–104/89 and 37/90 *Mulder*, n. 25 above, paras. 51, 63; Case T–260/97 *Camar Srl* v. *Council* [2005] ECR II–2741, para. 97.

[60] Toth, n. 51 above, 180–191.

[61] Cases 56–60/74 *Kampffmeyer* v. *Commission and Council* [1976] ECR 711, 741; Case T–79/96 *Camar Srl*, n. 32 above, para. 207.

[62] See 581 above.

[63] See 592–593 above.

[64] Case 26/74 *Roquette Frères* v. *Commission* [1976] ECR 677, 694, Trabucchi AG.

[65] See, e.g., Case 26/68 *Fux* v. *Commission* [1969] ECR 145, 156; Case T–1/99 *T. Port GmbH & Co. KG* v. *Commission* [2001] ECR II–465.

[66] Case 238/78 *Ireks-Arkady* v. *Council and Commission* [1979] ECR 2955, 2998–2999.

[67] Case T–84/98 *C* v. *Council* [2000] ECR IA–113, paras. 98–103; Case T–307/01 *Jean-Paul François* v. *Commission* [2004] ECR II–1669, paras. 107–111; Case T–48/01 *François Vainker and Brenda Vainker* v. *European Parliament* [2004] ECR II–197, para. 180; Case T–309/03 *Grau* v. *Commission* [2006] ECR II–1173.

reluctant to do so. Thus, in *Kampffmeyer*, while the Court admitted that lost profit was recoverable, it did not grant such damages to traders who had abandoned their intended transactions because of the unlawful act of the Community, even though these transactions would have produced profits.[68] In *CNTA* it was held that lost profits were not recoverable where the claim was based on the concept of legitimate expectations, since that concept only served to ensure that losses were not suffered owing to an unexpected change in the legal position; it did not serve to ensure that profits would be made.[69] However, in *Mulder*[70] the ECJ was prepared to compensate for lost profit, although it held that any such sum must take into account the income which could have been earned from alternative activities, applying the principle that there is a duty to mitigate loss.

In quantifying the applicant's loss the Community institutions have argued that damages should not be recoverable if the loss has been passed on to the consumers. This was accepted in principle by the ECJ in the *Quellmehl and Gritz* litigation.[71] Toth has justly criticized this reasoning. He points out that whether a firm could pass on a cost increase to consumers would depend upon many variables, which might operate differently for different firms and which would be difficult to assess. He argues, moreover, that such an idea is wrong in principle, since it would mean that losses would be borne by consumers, rather than by the institutions which had committed the wrongful act.[72]

8. JOINT LIABILITY OF THE COMMUNITY AND MEMBER STATES

The joint liability of the Community and the Member States gives rise to complex problems which can be dealt with only in outline.[73] The approach of Oliver, which distinguishes between procedural and substantive issues, will be adopted here.[74]

(a) PROCEDURAL ISSUES

In procedural terms it is not possible for Community non-contractual liability to be decided by national courts. Article 235 EC confers this jurisdiction on the ECJ and, while it does not state that this jurisdiction is exclusive, this is implied by Article 240 EC.[75] Conversely, it is not possible for an individual to bring a direct action against a Member State before the ECJ, since there is no provision for this in the Treaty.

---

[68] Cases 5, 7, and 13–24/66 *Kampffmeyer* v. *Commission* [1967] ECR 245, 266–267. See also Case T–160/03 *AFCon Management Consultants* v. *Commission* [2005] ECR II–981, paras. 112–114.

[69] Case 74/74 *CNTA*, n. 13 above, 550.

[70] Cases C–104/89 and 37/90 [1992] ECR I–3061.

[71] See Case 238/78 *Ireks-Arkady*, n. 66 above, 2974.

[72] See n. 51 above, 189–190.

[73] A. Durand, 'Restitution or Damages: National Court or European Court?' (1975–6) 1 *ELRev.* 431; T.C. Hartley, 'Concurrent Liability in EEC Law: A Critical Review of the Cases' (1977) 2 *ELRev.* 249; W. Wils, 'Concurrent Liability of the Community and a Member State' (1992) 17 *ELRev.* 191.

[74] P. Oliver, 'Joint Liability of the Community and the Member States', in Heukels and McDonnell (eds.), n. 4 above, ch. 16.

[75] Art. 240: 'save where jurisdiction is conferred on the Court of Justice by this Treaty, disputes to which the Community is a party shall not on that ground be excluded from the jurisdiction of the courts or tribunals of the Member States': Cases 106–120/87 *Asteris* v. *Greece and EEC* [1988] ECR 5515; Case T–18/99 *Cordis*, n. 15 above, para. 27.

When an action is brought before the ECJ under Article 288(2), it is clear that Community law is applied. An action brought against a Member State in the national court will be governed by national law. This will, however, include Community law. The national courts are under an obligation to provide an effective remedy for the enforcement of directly effective Community provisions; and the rights against the State in such actions must be no less favourable than those which exist in domestic matters.[76]

(b) SUBSTANTIVE ISSUES

Joint liability of the Community and the Member States can arise in different situations. Two will be explored here.

The *first is where the Community has taken inadequate steps to prevent a breach of Community law by national authorities.* This issue arose in the *Lütticke* case where the Court appeared to accept that, in principle, such an action was possible.[77] However, there are considerable obstacles in the path of any such action. It is, for example, doubtful whether the Commission has a duty to bring an action under Article 226 EC against a Member State which is in breach of Community law.[78] The position may well be different where the Commission has adopted a more formal measure which approves of the illegal national action, as in *Kampffmeyer*.

Cases 5, 7, and 13–24/66 **Kampffmeyer v. Commission**
[1967] ECR 245

The case arose from the gradual establishment of a common market in cereals. On 1 October 1963 the German intervention board issued a notice stating that the levy for the import of such products would be zero. On that same day, the applicants applied for import licences for the import of maize from France, with the levy having been set at zero for January 1964. Some of the applicants had actually bought maize from France. The German Government on the same day, 1 October 1963, then suspended the zero-rated import licences for maize. Under Article 22 of Regulation 19 the German Government could refuse such applications only if there was a threat of a serious disturbance to the market in question. Such a decision had to be confirmed by the Commission, and the Commission on 3 October duly authorized this to remain in force until 4 October. This decision was annulled by the ECJ.[79] The applicants then sought compensation from the Commission under Article 215. Some of them had paid the duties imposed by the German authorities and imported the maize on these terms; others had repudiated their contracts to buy the maize, after the German Government had refused to issue the zero-rated licences. These are the two categories of applicants referred to by the ECJ in the following extract. Referring to the Commission decision authorizing the protective measures, the ECJ reasoned as follows.

THE ECJ

As is clear, moreover, from the judgment of the Court of 1 July, 1965, this decision constituted an improper application of Article 22 of Regulation No 19 ... On October 3 1963 the

---

[76] See Oliver, n. 74 above, 289.
[77] Case 4/69 *Alfons Lütticke GmbH* v. *Commission* [1971] ECR 325.
[78] See Ch. 12.
[79] Cases 106 and 107/63 *Toepfer* v. *Commission* [1965] ECR 405.

Commission applied Article 22(2) of Regulation No 19 in circumstances which did not justify protective measures in order to restore the situation resulting from the fixing by it of a zero levy. As it was aware of the existence of applications for licences, it caused damage to the interests of importers who had acted in reliance on the information provided in accordance with Community rules. The Commission's conduct constituted a wrongful act or omission capable of giving rise to liability on the part of the Community.

. . .

[*The ECJ then considered the appropriate forum in which the issue of compensation should be decided.*]

However, with regard to any injury suffered by the applicants belonging to the first and second categories above-mentioned, those applicants have informed the Court that the injury alleged is the subject of two actions for damages, one against the Federal Republic of Germany before a German court and the other against the Community before the Court of Justice. It is necessary to avoid the applicants' being insufficiently or excessively compensated for the same damage by the different assessment of two different courts applying different rules of law. Before determining the damage for which the Community should be held liable, it is necessary for the national court to have the opportunity to give judgment on any liability on the part of the Federal Republic of Germany. This being the case, final judgment cannot be given before the applicants have produced the decision of the national court on this matter, which may be done independently of the evidence asked of the applicant in the first category to the effect that they have exhausted all possible methods of recovery of the amounts improperly paid by way of levy. Furthermore, if it were established that such recovery was possible, this fact might have consequences bearing upon the calculation of the damages concerning the second category. However, the decisive nature of the said evidence required does not prevent the applicants from producing the other evidence previously indicated in the meantime.

It is clear from the *Kampffmeyer* case that the Community can, therefore, be liable when it has wrongfully authorized a measure taken by a national body. The procedural aspect of the case has, however, been criticized. It has been argued that there was no reason to require the applicants to proceed initially in the German courts, and that the ECJ's rationale for doing so was based implicitly on the assumption that the German authorities were primarily liable, with the Community bearing only a residual liability.[80]

This criticism may be overstated, and it may be necessary to distinguish the claim for the return of the levies paid from the more general tort action. As regards the former, the idea that the primary liability rested with Germany may well have substance, given that it was Germany which imposed the levy and it was Germany to which the funds were paid. As regards the latter, there is no particular reason why the liability of the Community should be seen as somehow secondary to that of the Member State.

The *second situation in which the issue of joint liability may arise is where the Member State applies unlawful Community legislation.* This can arise, for example, in the context of the CAP, where Community regulations will often be applied by national intervention boards. The general rule is that it is the national intervention boards, and not the Commission, which are responsible for the application of the CAP, and that an action must normally be commenced in the national courts.

---

[80] See Oliver, n. 74 above.

Case 96/71 R. and V. Haegeman Sprl v. Commission
[1972] ECR 1005

[Note ToA renumbering: Art. 177 is now Art. 234]

Haegeman was a Belgian company which imported wine from Greece which was at the time outside the Community. It alleged that it suffered loss because of a countervailing charge imposed on the import of wine from Greece to Belgium. This charge was imposed by a Council regulation and was levied by the Belgian authorities.

THE ECJ

7. Disputes concerning the levying on individuals of the charges and levies referred to by this provision must be resolved, applying Community law, by the national authorities and following the practices laid down by the law of the Member States.

8. Issues, therefore, which are raised during a procedure as to the interpretation and validity of regulations establishing the Communities' own resources must be brought before the national courts which have at their disposal the procedure under Article 177 of the Treaty in order to ensure the uniform application of Community law.

. . .

14. The applicant maintains further that by reason of the defendant's behaviour it has suffered exceptional damage as a result of loss of profit, unforeseen financial outlay and losses on existing contracts.

15. The question of the possible liability of the Community is in the first place linked with that of the legality of the levying of the charge in question.

16. It has just been found that, in the context of the relationship between individuals and the taxation authority which has levied the charge in dispute, the latter question comes under the jurisdiction of the national courts.

17. Accordingly, at the present stage the claim for compensation for possible damage must be dismissed.

The decision in *Haegeman* can be criticized since the money levied went into the Community's funds. The mere fact that the sums were collected by national authorities should make no difference, given that these sums were imposed by the Community and were collected on behalf of the Community by the Member State.[81] It does, however, appear to be the case that an action to recover such a charge must be commenced in the national courts and that this is also so where a trader is seeking payment of a sum to which he believes himself to be entitled under Community law.[82] It has also been held that this principle applies even where the Commission has sent telexes to the national board setting out its interpretation of the relevant regulations.[83] The authorities of a Member State may, however, be able to recover from Community funds where they have paid for losses which are the responsibility of the Community.[84]

[81] See T.C. Hartley, *The Foundations of European Community Law* (3rd edn., Oxford University Press, 2003), 480.

[82] Case 99/74 *Société des Grands Moulins des Antilles* v. *Commission* [1975] ECR 1531.

[83] Case 133/79 *Sucrimex SA and Westzucker GmbH* v. *Commission* [1980] ECR 1299; Case 217/81 *Compagnie Interagra SA* v. *Commission* [1982] ECR 2233.

[84] This may be possible in the context of the CAP. The basis for shifting the loss to the Community was Council Reg. 729/70 [1970] OJ 94/13, and was bound up with the operation of the EAGGF. For discussion see Oliver, n. 74 above, 306–308; J.A. Usher, *Legal Aspects of Agriculture in the European Community* (Oxford University Press, 1988), 104–106, 150–152.

There are, however, a number of situations in which it is possible to proceed against the Community directly. First, if the Commission sends a telex which is interpreted, in the context of the relevant legislation, as an instruction to the national agency to act in a particular manner, then an action may be brought against the Commission for damages.[85] Secondly, it is possible to proceed against the Community where no action could conceivably be brought against any national authority, and hence there would be no remedy available in the national courts. Thus, in *Unifrex* an applicant sought damages before the ECJ by reason of the failure of the Commission to pass a regulation which would have granted the applicant a subsidy for exports to Italy when the Italian lira was devalued. It was held that the action could proceed before the ECJ, since proceedings in the national court would not have helped the applicant: even if the relevant Community rules had been declared illegal pursuant to Article 234, 'that annulment could not have required the national authorities to pay higher monetary compensatory amounts to the applicant, without the prior intervention of the Community legislature'.[86] Thirdly, it is possible to bring a claim in the ECJ where the substance of the claim is that the Community has committed a tortious wrong to the applicant. Thus in *Dietz*[87] the essence of the claim was that the Community authorities had introduced a levy without transitional provisions and had thereby caused loss to the applicant in breach of its legitimate expectations. This claim could be pursued in the ECJ since the wrong alleged was entirely directed towards the Community's behaviour, and not that of the Member State.

9. LIABILITY IN CONTRACT

The discussion thus far has focused on the EC's non-contractual liability under Article 288(2). The Community will obviously also make contracts,[88] and Article 288(1) provides that contractual liability shall be governed by the law applicable to the contract in question.

The meaning of this phrase requires explanation. Contracts are often made between parties in different countries, and therefore it is necessary to determine which law should govern the contract. The answer will often be of considerable importance, since the contractual rules in different countries may differ significantly as regards matters such as the place of formation of the contract and the types of damages which are recoverable. The body of law dealing with this issue is known as the conflict of laws or private international law. Contracts often have choice-of-law clauses, specifying the law to be applied. The Commission always inserts such a clause in its contracts. It has been held that this clause prevails, and cannot be displaced by arguments that the contract was more closely connected with a different country from that specified in the choice-of-law clause.[89]

It would of course be possible in principle for a choice-of-law clause to specify Community law as that applicable to the contract. Article 288(1), in contrast to Article 288(2), does not state that the Community is to develop a system of law by drawing on the relevant general

---

[85] Case 175/84 *Krohn & Co. Import-Export GmbH & Co. KG v. Commission* [1986] ECR 753.

[86] Case 281/82 *Unifrex v. Commission and Council* [1984] ECR 1969; Case T–167/94 *Nolle v. Council and Commission* [1995] ECR II–2589; Case T–18/99 *Cordis*, n. 15 above, para. 28.

[87] Case 126/76 *Dietz v. Commission* [1977] ECR 2431; Case T–18/99 *Cordis*, n. 15 above, para. 26. The principle in the *Dietz* case, which allows the action to proceed in the ECJ, may not operate if the national authorities themselves were partially to blame for the loss caused to the individual: see, e.g., Cases 5, 7, and 13–24/66 *Kampffmeyer*, n. 68 above.

[88] T. Heukels, 'The Contractual Liability of the European Community Revisited', in Heukels and McDonnell (eds.), n. 4 above, ch. 5.

[89] Case 318/81 *Commission v. CODEMI* [1985] ECR 3693.

principles common to the laws of the Member States. The implication of this may be that the Community is not to develop its own Community contract law. However, such a development may well be necessary in the future, as an adjunct of the expansion of Community competence into novel areas.

Such a development can be seen, albeit indirectly, in staff cases. The Court has characterized contracts of employment of certain Community officials as public-law contracts, emphasizing that the work performed was of a governmental nature, with the consequence that the contracts were governed by administrative law. The Court did not state that any system of national administrative law was to be applied.[90]

Even if the parties to a contract choose a particular legal system to govern the substance of their contractual obligations, this still leaves open the issue of which court will have jurisdiction to try the dispute. The ECJ is empowered by Article 238 EC, which states that the Court of Justice shall have jurisdiction to give judgment pursuant to any arbitration clause contained in a contract concluded by or on behalf of the Community, whether that contract be governed by public or private law.

10. LIABILITY TO MAKE RESTITUTION

Most legal systems recognize some species of liability in restitution or quasi-contract, in addition to that based on contract or tort. The precise nature of this liability continues to divide academics, but the better view is that it is distinct from both contract and tort. Restitution is not based upon a promise, but rather on unjust enrichment by the defendant, hence its difference from contractual liability. Restitution does not normally require a wrongful act by the defendant, in the sense of fault, and the measure of recovery is normally determined by the extent of the defendant's unjust enrichment rather than the extent of the loss to the plaintiff, hence its difference from most forms of tort liability. A common restitutionary claim arises from payments made to public bodies when they have no right to the money. This is of considerable importance in the EC.[91] It can arise in two types of situation.

On the one hand, there can be cases where a Member State has, for example, imposed a levy which is illegal under EC law, as exemplified by *Van Gend en Loos*. The matter will be remitted to the national court, once the ECJ has found that the levy was in breach of Community law. It will be for the national court to devise a remedy to effectuate the Community right, and this will often take the form of the return of the sum which has been paid over to the national authority.[92]

On the other hand, there may be instances under, for example, the CAP in which money is paid into Community funds, pursuant to a Community law obligation, where there may be no legal obligation to pay the sum. The Community Courts have held that unjust enrichment is a general principle of Community law,[93] and that proof of some independent unlawful act by the defendant is not required.[94] Thus where a fine imposed for breach of the competition rules

---

[90] Case 1/55 *Kergall v. Common Assembly* [1955] ECR 151; Cases 43, 45, and 48/59 *Von Lachmüller v. Commission* [1960] ECR 463.

[91] A. Jones, *Restitution and European Community Law* (Mansfield Press, 2000); R. Williams, *Unjust Enrichment and Public Law, A Comparative Study of England, France and the EU* (Hart, forthcoming), chs. 6–7.

[92] See Ch. 9.

[93] Case C–259/87 *Greece v. Commission* [1990] ECR I–2845, para. 26; Case T–171/99 *Corus UK Ltd. v. Commission* [2001] ECR II–2967, para. 55; Case T–7/99 *Medici Grimm KG v. Council* [2000] ECR II–2671, para. 89; Case T–28/03 *Holcim (Deutschland) AG v. Commission* [2005] ECR II–1357, paras. 127–130.

[94] Case T–333/03 *Masdar*, n. 32 above, paras. 91–93.

is annulled there is an obligation to return the money plus interest.[95] The ECJ has applied restitutionary principles in cases where there has been unjust enrichment by an individual against the Community.[96] It is clearly correct in principle that a remedy should be available in favour of an individual, where the Community has been unjustly enriched at his or her expense, as where the EC has imposed an unlawful charge. If a levy imposed by a Member State which is unlawful because it is in breach of the Treaty is recoverable, so too should be an illegal charge levied by the Community. The matter is, however, complicated in two different ways.

First, there is case law of the ECJ, outlined above, which has insisted that, in many such instances, the action should be commenced in the national court against the national collecting agency, even where the funds are treated as Community funds.[97]

Secondly, there is the difficulty of locating restitutionary claims within the Treaty. While the wording of Article 288(2), which requires the Community to 'make good any damage caused' by its institutions, does not fit perfectly with the idea of a restitutionary action, it is however, framed in terms of 'non-contractual liability', and this is clearly wide enough to cover restitutionary relief. Moreover, if the ECJ were to find that it had no jurisdiction over such actions, then Article 240 would mean that relief could be sought in an action against the Community in national courts. It is doubtful whether the ECJ would wish to be in a position where it had 'no control' over the development of appropriate restitutionary principles involving Community liability.

11. CONCLUSION

i.   The ECJ's jurisprudence under Article 288 has, in the past, been criticized for being overly restrictive. The case law was, until recently, unclear about the precise criterion for the application of the *Schöppenstedt* test.

ii. It is now clear that the crucial issue is the discretionary or non-discretionary nature of the act. Discretionary acts will be subject to the *Schöppenstedt* test. This requires proof of a breach of a superior rule of law for the protection of the individual, the breach must be sufficiently serious, there must be causation and damage. It is clear also that the factors laid down in the case law on state liability in damages will be directly relevant when deciding whether there has been a sufficiently serious breach under Article 288.

iii. Where the challenged act is not discretionary the traditional test for liability was proof of illegality, causation, and damage. The more modern case law continues to distinguish between liability for discretionary and non-discretionary acts, but does so from within the framework of the sufficiently serious breach test: where the Community institution has considerably reduced or no discretion, the mere infringement of Community law *may* be sufficient to establish the existence of the sufficiently serious breach. It would be regrettable if this shift rendered it more difficult to recover than hitherto.

iv. The absence of any damages action in relation to Third Pillar measures is regrettable, more especially because of the increased volume of legislation and the like that is now being enacted under this Pillar.

---

[95] Case T–171/99 *Corus*, n. 93 above, paras. 53–55.

[96] See, e.g., Case 18/63 *Wollast* v. *EEC* [1964] ECR 85; Case 110/63 *Willame* v. *Commission* [1965] ECR 649.

[97] See 597–600.

12. FURTHER READING

(a) Books

Heukels, T., and McDonnell, A. (eds.), *The Action for Damages in Community Law* (Kluwer, 1997)

Schermers, H.G., Heukels, T., and Mead, P. (eds.), *The Non-Contractual Liability of the European Communities* (Martinus Nijhoff, 1988)

(b) Articles

Harding, C., 'The Choice of Court Problem in Cases of Non-Contractual Liability under EEC Law' (1979) 16 *CMLRev.* 389

Hartley, T.C., 'Concurrent Liability in EEC Law: A Critical Review of the Cases' (1977) 2 *ELRev.* 249

Hilson, C., 'The Role of Discretion in EC law on Non-Contractual Liability' (2005) 42 *CMLRev.* 677

Oliver, P., 'Enforcing Community Rights in the English Courts' (1987) 50 *MLR* 881

Tridimas, T., 'Liability for Breach of Community Law: Growing Up and Mellowing Down?' (2001) 38 *CMLRev.* 301

Wils, W., 'Concurrent Liability of the Community and a Member State' (1992) 17 *ELRev.* 191

17

THE SINGLE MARKET

1. CENTRAL ISSUES

i.   The single market is central to the EC and is still its principal economic rationale.

ii. This chapter considers the forms and techniques of economic integration, the limits of integration prior to 1986, and the subsequent steps taken to complete the single market. There is both a substantive and an institutional dimension to this story.

iii. In substantive terms, it is important to understand the economic dimension to the single market. It is equally important to understand that the realization of the single market in economic terms necessarily raises issues about the interrelationship of the economic and social dimensions of EC policy. This has now come to the forefront of Community policy. The single market has been reconceptualized to take account of broader social, consumer, and environmental issues. There are nonetheless continuing tensions between the economic and social dimensions of the single market.

iv. In institutional terms, a subtle mix of legislative, administrative, and judicial initiatives has furthered the evolution of the single market. The legislative procedures were changed to facilitate the passage of harmonization legislation. The focus of this legislation altered, through the new approach to harmonization. These developments were facilitated by judicial doctrine, based on the principle of mutual recognition, which framed the legislative and administrative initiatives.

2. FORMS AND TECHNIQUES OF ECONOMIC INTEGRATION

(a) FORMS OF ECONOMIC INTEGRATION

The discussion in the previous chapters focused on the institutional law of the EC. The remainder of the book is concerned with EC substantive law, although we shall stress the links between the two. It is important at the outset to understand the nature of a common market and how it differs from other forms of economic integration.

D. Swann, The Economics of the Common Market[1]

Economic integration can take various forms and these can be ranged in a spectrum in which the degree of involvement of participating economies, one with another, becomes greater and greater. The *free trade area* is the least onerous in terms of involvement. It consists in an arrangement between states in which they agree to remove all customs duties (and quotas) on trade passing between them. Each party is free, however, to determine unilaterally the level of customs duty on imports coming from outside the area. The next stage is the *customs union*. Here tariffs and quotas on trade between members are also removed but members agree to apply a *common* level of tariff on goods entering the union from without. The latter is called the common customs, or common external, tariff. Next comes the *common market* and this technical term implies that to the free movement of *goods* within the customs union is added the free movement of the *factors of production*—labour, capital and enterprise. Finally there is the *economic union*. This is a common market in which there is also a complete unification of monetary and fiscal policy. There would be a common currency which would be controlled by a central authority and in effect the member states would become regions within the union.

Part Three of the EC Treaty contains many of the fundamental principles for the establishment of a customs union and common market. It sets out, *inter alia*, the 'four freedoms': free movement of goods, workers, establishment and the provision of services, and capital. These Articles have, as will be seen, social as well as economic objectives. The basic economic aim is the optimal allocation of resources for the Community as a whole. This is facilitated by allowing the factors of production, the elements that are used to make a product, to move to the area where they are most valued.

Thus the provisions on the free movement of goods are designed to establish the principles of a customs union. The object is to ensure that goods can move freely, with the consequence that those most favoured by consumers will be most successful, irrespective of the country of origin. This will also serve to maximize wealth-creation in the Community as a whole.

The same point can be exemplified in relation to free movement of workers. Labour is one of the factors of production and may be valued more highly in some areas than in others. This is so if, for example, there is an excess of supply over demand for labour in southern Italy, and an excess of demand over supply in certain parts of Germany. In this situation labour is worth more in Germany than it is in Italy. The value of labour within the Community as a whole is, therefore, maximized if workers can move to the area where they are most valued.

The same idea is applicable to freedom of establishment. If a firm established in Holland believes that it could capture part of the French market if it were allowed to set up in business there, then it should not be prevented from so doing by rules of French law which discriminate on grounds of nationality.

(b) TECHNIQUES OF ECONOMIC INTEGRATION

There are two principal techniques that can be used to attain a single market. Community law can prohibit national rules that hinder cross-border trade, either because they discriminate against goods or labour, etc., from other Member States, or because they render it more

---

[1] (7th edn., Penguin, 1992), 11–12, italics in the original.

difficult for them to secure access to the market of the other State. This is the classic way in which the Treaty articles concerning the four freedoms operate. The approach is essentially negative and deregulatory, in the sense that EC law prohibits national rules that hinder cross-border trade. This approach is reinforced through what is known as mutual recognition, which requires a Member State to accept, subject to certain exceptions, goods that have been made in accordance with the rules of another Member State.

The creation of a single market also requires positive integration. Barriers to integration may flow from diversity in national rules, on matters such as health, safety, technical specification, consumer protection, and the like. Some of these barriers can be overcome through mutual recognition. In other instances the barriers to trade may only truly be overcome through the harmonization of diverse national laws by means of a Community directive. This is known as positive integration, which is attained principally through Articles 94 and 95 EC, and other more sector-specific Treaty Articles.

3. LIMITS OF INTEGRATION PRIOR TO 1986

Prior to 1986 the process of single-market integration had been advanced both by legislative and judicial means.

The most important *legislative contribution* was the harmonization of laws. The existence of divergences in national provisions can, as seen, create barriers to trade. Article 94 EC was the original Treaty provision through which this problem was addressed:

> The Council shall, acting unanimously on a proposal from the Commission, issue directives for the approximation of such laws, regulations or administrative provisions of the Member States as directly affect the establishment of the common market.

There were, however, difficulties with this legislative mechanism. Article 94 requires unanimity, which was increasingly difficult to secure in an expanding Community. This difficulty was exacerbated in the 1970s and early 1980s because harmonization directives were drafted in great detail, thereby rendering agreement more problematic. Technical developments meant, moreover, that the Commission was, in a sense, fighting a losing battle: as fast as it secured the passage of a directive to cover one technical problem, so ten more would emerge on the horizon, resulting from technical innovation and the emergence of new types of market.

The *judicial contribution* to market integration will be considered in detail in subsequent chapters dealing with goods, persons, services, competition policy, and the like. Suffice it to say for the present that the ECJ, through Article 226 and direct effect, interpreted the Treaty Articles in the manner best designed to promote the single market. Judicial doctrines, such as *Cassis de Dijon*,[2] were of particular importance in breaking down barriers to intra-Community trade by invalidating trade barriers, even if they were not discriminatory, unless they could be justified on certain limited grounds. The decision was of seminal importance, but it was nonetheless essentially negative and deregulatory.

There was therefore still much to be done by the early 1980s, notwithstanding the efforts of the Commission and the Court. The fact that the Community was falling behind its agenda

---

2 Case 120/78 *Rewe-Zentrale AG v. Bundesmonopolverwaltung für Branntwein* [1979] ECR 649.

generated a feeling of pessimism in the late 1970s and early 1980s, and the reality of single-market integration appeared to be no closer. This problem was not lost on the European Council, which, in the early 1980s, considered various techniques for expediting the passage of Community initiatives. It was in one of these meetings that the seeds of the Single European Act (SEA) were sown. In 1985 the European Council called on the Commission to draw up a detailed programme with a specific timetable for achieving a single market by 1992. The Commission, under the leadership of Jacques Delors, was not slow to respond.

4. THE SINGLE EUROPEAN ACT 1986: THE ECONOMICS AND POLITICS OF INTEGRATION

(a) THE ECONOMIC DIMENSION: THE COMMISSION'S WHITE PAPER

The Commission's White Paper, from which the extracts below are taken, addressed the problem in strident tones. It set out to establish the 'essential and logical consequences'[3] of accepting the commitment to a single market. The Commission noted that the Community had lost momentum 'partly through recession, partly through a lack of confidence and vision',[4] but it said that the mood had now changed. The Commission was ready to take up the challenge: the 'time for talk has now passed. The time for action has come. That is what this White Paper is about'.[5]

Completing the Internal Market, COM(85)310, 14 June 1985[6]

10. For convenience the measures that need to be taken have been classified in this Paper under three headings:

— Part One: the removal of physical barriers
— Part Two: the removal of technical barriers
— Part Three: the removal of fiscal barriers

11. The most obvious example of the first category are customs posts at frontiers. Indeed most of our citizens would regard the frontier posts as the most visible example of the continued division of the Community and their removal as the clearest sign of the integration of the Community into a single market. Yet they continue to exist mainly because of the technical and fiscal divisions between Member States. Once we have removed those barriers, and found alternative ways of dealing with other relevant problems such as public security, immigration and drug controls, the reasons for the existence of the physical barriers will have been eliminated.

12. The reason for getting rid entirely of physical and other controls between Member States is not one of theology or appearance, but the hard practical fact that the maintenance of any internal frontier controls will perpetuate the costs and disadvantages of a divided market. . . .

---

[3] COM(85)310, para. 3.
[4] *Ibid.*, para. 5.
[5] *Ibid.*, para. 7.
[6] References to Arts. 30–36 and 100 should now be read as to Arts. 28–30 and 94.

13. While the elimination of physical barriers provides benefits for traders ... it is through the elimination of technical barriers that the Community will give the large market its economic and industrial dimension by enabling industries to make economies of scale and therefore to become more competitive. An example of this second category—technical barriers—are the different standards for individual products adopted in different Member States for health and safety reasons, or for environmental or consumer protection.... The general thrust of the Commission's approach in this area will be to move away from the concept of harmonization towards that of mutual recognition and equivalence. But there will be a continuing role for the approximation of Member States' laws and regulations as laid down in Article 100 of the Treaty. Clearly, action under this Article would be quicker and more effective if the Council were to agree not to allow the unanimity requirement to obstruct progress where it could otherwise be made.

14. The removal of fiscal barriers may well be contentious and this despite the fact that the goals laid down in the Treaty are quite explicit and that important steps have already been taken along the road of approximation. This being so, the reasons why approximation of fiscal legislation is an essential element in any programme for completing the internal market are explained in detail in Part Three.

[*The Commission then explained that the White Paper was not intended to cover every possible issue of relevance to the integration of the Member States' economies. Matters such as the co-ordination of economic polices and competition policy were relevant in this respect; while other important areas of Community action, such as transport, the environment, and consumer protection, interacted with, and would benefit from, the completion of the internal market. The next extract looks more closely at the Commission's reasoning in relation to the second type of barrier, that which arises from differing technical rules.*]

58. [S]ubject to certain important constraints (see paragraph 65), the general principle should be approved that, if a product is lawfully manufactured and marketed in one Member State, there is no reason why it should not be sold freely throughout the Community....

60. Whilst the physical barriers dealt with in Part One impede trade flows and add unacceptable administrative costs (ultimately paid by the consumer), barriers created by different national product regulations and standards have a double-edged effect: they not only add extra costs, but they also distort production patterns; increase unit costs; increase stock holding costs; discourage business cooperation; and fundamentally frustrate the creation of a common market for industrial products. Until such barriers are removed, Community manufacturers are forced to focus on national rather than continental markets and are unable to benefit from the economies of scale which a truly unified market offers....

The Need for a New Strategy

61. The harmonization approach has been the cornerstone of Community action in the first 25 years and has produced unprecedented progress in the creation of common rules on a Community-wide basis. However, over the years, a number of shortcomings have been identified and it is clear that a genuine common market cannot be realised by 1992 if the Community relies exclusively on Article 100 of the EEC Treaty. There will certainly be a continuing need for action under Article 100; but its role will be reduced as new approaches, resulting in quicker and less troublesome progress, are agreed.... Where Article 100 is still considered the only appropriate instrument, ways of making it operate more flexibly will need to be found. Clearly, action under this Article would be quicker and more effective if the Council were to agree not to allow the unanimity requirement to obstruct progress where it could otherwise be made.

63. In principle, therefore ... mutual recognition could be an effective strategy for bringing about a common market in a trading sense. This strategy is supported in particular by Articles 30 to 36 of the EEC Treaty, which prohibit national measures which would have excessively and unjustifiably restrictive effects on free movement.

64. But while a strategy based on mutual recognition would remove barriers to trade and lead to the creation of a genuine common trading market, it might well prove inadequate for the purposes of the building-up of an expanding market based on the competitiveness which a continental-scale uniform market can generate. On the other hand experience has shown that the alternative of relying on a strategy based totally on harmonization would be over-regulatory, would take a long time to implement, would be inflexible and could stifle innovation. What is needed is a strategy that combines the best of both approaches but, that above all, allows for progress to be made more quickly than in the past.

The Chosen Strategy

65. The Commission takes into account the underlying reasons for the existence of barriers to trade, and recognises the essential equivalence of Member States' legislative objectives in the protection of health and safety, and of the environment. Its harmonization approach is based on the following principles:

— a clear distinction needs to be drawn in future internal market initiatives between what it is essential to harmonize, and what may be left to mutual recognition of national regulations and standards; this implies that, on the occasion of each harmonization initiative, the Commission will determine whether national regulations are excessive in relation to the mandatory requirements pursued and, thus, constitute unjustified barriers to trade according to Articles 30 to 36 of the EEC Treaty;

— legislative harmonization (Council Directives based on Article 100) will in future be restricted to laying down essential health and safety requirements which will be obligatory in all Member States. Conformity with this will entitle a product to free movement;

— harmonization of industrial standards by the elaboration of European standards will be promoted to the maximum extent, but the absence of European standards should not be allowed to be used as a barrier to free movement. During the waiting period while European Standards are being developed, the mutual acceptance of national standards, with agreed procedures, should be the guiding principle.

The Commission's White Paper did not rest content with the enunciation of general strategies. The Annex to the Paper listed 279 legislative measures, together with a timetable for the promulgation of each measure. The object was to complete this process by 31 December 1992. The momentum behind the proposals gathered further force with economic studies, which estimated that cost savings for the Community of twelve Member States could be somewhere between 70 billion ECU, 2.5 per cent of Gross Domestic Product, GDP, based on a relatively narrow conception of the benefits of removing the remaining internal market barriers, to around 125 to 190 billion ECU, 4.25 per cent to 6.5 per cent of GDP, on the hypothesis of a much more competitive, integrated market.[7]

(b) THE POLITICAL DIMENSION: THE POLITICS OF INTEGRATION

The compelling economic case for reform does not explain why the Commission's initiative succeeded, given that other reforms posited in the late 1970s and early 1980s failed. There are

[7] M. Emerson, M. Aujean, M. Catinat, P. Goybet, and A. Jacquemin, *The Economics of 1992, The EC Commission's Assessment of the Economic Effects of Completing the Internal Market* (Oxford University Press, 1988), 1–10. See also P. Cecchini, *The European Challenge 1992, The Benefits of a Single Market* (Gower, 1988).

differing views on who were the key players and why they were willing to accept reform at this juncture.[8]

Sandholtz and Zysman offered one thesis.[9] They rejected explanations based on neofunctionalist integration theories and on the domestic politics of the Member States, although they admitted that elements of these theories were relevant even under their own preferred explanation.[10] They argued that the success of the 1992 initiative should instead be viewed in 'terms of elite bargains formulated in response to international structural change and the Commission's policy entrepreneurship'.[11] There were three crucial factors in this regard: the domestic political context, the Commission's initiative, and the role of the business elite.

W. Sandholtz and J. Zysman, 1992: Recasting the European Bargain[12]

The question is why national government policies and perspectives have altered. Why, in the decade between the mid-1970s and the mid-1980s, did the European governments become open to European-level, market-oriented solutions? The answer has two parts: the failure of national strategies for economic growth and the transformation of the left in European politics. First, the traditional models of growth and economic management broke down. The old political strategies for the economy seemed to have run out. After the growth of the 1960s, the world economy entered a period of stagflation in the 1970s. . . .

. . . the second aspect of the changed political context was the shift in government coalitions in a number of EC Member States. Certainly the weakening of the left in some countries and a shift from the communist to the market-socialist left in others helped to make possible a debate about market solutions (including unified European markets) to Europe's dilemma. . . .

. . .

In an era when deregulation—the freeing of the market—became the fad, it made intuitive sense to extend the European market as a response to all ailments. . . .

This was the domestic political soil into which the Commission's initiatives fell. Traditional models of economic growth appeared to have played themselves out, and the left had been transformed in such a way that socialist parties began to seek market-oriented solutions to economic ills. In this setting, the European Community provided more than the mechanisms of intergovernmental negotiation. The Eurocracy was a standing constituency and a permanent advocate of European solutions and greater unity. Proposals from the European Commission transformed this new orientation into policy, and more importantly, into a policy perspective and direction. The Commission perceived the international structural changes and the failure of existing national strategies and seized the initiative.

. . .

The third actor in the story, besides the governments and the Commission, is the leadership of the European multinational corporations. The White Paper and the Single European Act gave the appearance that changes in the EC market were irreversible and politically unstoppable. Businesses have been acting on that belief. Politically, they have taken up the banner of 1992, collaborating with the Commission and exerting substantial influence on their governments.

---

[8] For a more general overview of this literature see P. Craig, 'Integration Theory and Democratic Theory: Two Discourses Passing in the Night', in P. Craig and G. de Búrca (eds.), *The Evolution of EU Law* (Oxford University Press, 1999), ch. 1.

[9] '1992: Recasting the European Bargain' (1989) 42 *World Politics* 95.

[10] *Ibid.*, 97–100.

[11] *Ibid.*, 97.

[12] *Ibid.*, 108–109, 111–112, 113, 116.

The significance of the role of business, and of its collaboration with the Commission, must not be underestimated. . . .

Moravcsik told a different tale. He contested the thesis that the SEA was the result of an elite alliance between the Commission, Parliament, and supranational business groups, and argued that the success of the reforms was principally due to inter-state bargains between Britain, France, and Germany. This was made possible by the convergence of European economic-policy preferences in the early 1980s, combined with the bargaining leverage which France and Germany used against Britain by threatening a two-track Europe, or a Europe *à deux vitesses*, with Britain in the slow lane. For Moravcsik it was regime theory, which stressed traditional ideas of national interest and power politics, which best explained the SEA.

A. Moravcsik, Negotiating the Single European Act: National Interests and Conventional Statecraft in the European Community[13]

An alternative approach to explaining the success of the 1992 initiative focuses on inter-state bargains between heads of government in the three larger Member States of the EC. This approach, which can be called 'intergovernmental institutionalism', stresses the central importance of power and interests, with the latter not simply dictated by position in the intergovernmental system. . . . Intergovernmental institutionalism is based on three principles: intergovernmentalism, lowest common denominator bargaining, and strict limits on future transfers of sovereignty.

Intergovernmentalism. From its inception, the EC has been based on inter-state bargains between its leading Member States. Heads of government, backed by a small group of ministers and advisers, initiate and negotiate major initiatives in the Council of Ministers or the European Council. Each government views the EC through the lens of its own policy preferences; EC politics is the continuation of domestic politics by other means. . . .

Lowest-common-denominator bargaining. Without a 'European hegemony' capable of providing universal incentives or threats to promote regime formation and without the widespread use of linkages and logrolling, the bargains struck in the EC reflect the relative power positions of the Member States. Small states can be bought off with side-payments, but larger states exercise a de facto veto over fundamental changes in the scope or rules of the core element of the EC, which remains economic liberalization. Thus, bargaining tends to converge toward the lowest common denominator of large state interests. The bargains initially consisted of bilateral agreements between France and Germany; now they consist of trilateral agreements including Britain.

The only tool that can impel a state to accept an outcome on a major issue that it does not prefer to the status quo is the threat of exclusion. . . . If two major states can isolate the third and credibly threaten it with exclusion and if such exclusion undermines the substantive interests of the excluded state, the coercive threat may bring about an agreement at a level of integration above the lowest common denominator.

Protection of sovereignty. The decision to join a regime involves some sacrifice of national sovereignty in exchange for certain advantages. Policymakers safeguard their countries against the future erosion of sovereignty by demanding the unanimous consent of regime members to sovereignty-related reforms. They also avoid granting open-ended authority to

[13] (1991) 45 *International Organization* 19, 25–27, italics in the original.

central institutions that might infringe on their sovereignty, preferring instead to work through intergovernmental institutions such as the Council of Ministers, rather than through supra-national bodies such as the Commission and Parliament.

There is no need to decide unequivocally between these two theories. Most would agree that there were two connected conditions for the success of the new initiatives. There had to be *legislative reform* to facilitate the passage of measures designed to complete the internal market. There had also to be a *new approach to harmonization* which would expedite the process of breaking down the technical barriers to intra-Community trade. These will be considered in turn.

5. THE INTERNAL MARKET: LEGISLATIVE REFORM AND THE SEA

The European Council endorsed the Commission's White Paper in June 1985. The SEA was signed on 17 February 1986 and entered into force after ratification by Member States on 1 July 1987. The Act contained new procedures designed to facilitate the passage of legislation for completion of the internal market. It should not, however, be thought that the SEA was uncontroversial, or that there was complete agreement between the major political players on the content of the new legislative norms. There was not. The Commission pressed for more far-reaching changes than the Member States were willing to accept. The importance of the political background should not therefore be 'left behind'.

The SEA introduced two major legislative innovations of prime importance for the single market project: Article 14[14] and Article 95.

(a) ARTICLE 14: THE OBLIGATION STATED

1. The Community shall adopt measures with the aim of progressively establishing the internal market over a period expiring on 31 December 1992, in accordance with the provisions of this Article and of Articles 15, 26, 47(2), 49, 80, 93 and 95[15] and without prejudice to the other provisions of this Treaty.

2. The internal market shall comprise an area without internal frontiers in which the free movement of goods, persons, services and capital is ensured in accordance with the provisions of the Treaty.

3. The Council, acting by a qualified majority on a proposal from the Commission, shall determine the guidelines and conditions necessary to ensure balanced progress in all the sectors concerned.

We can begin by considering the *content of the obligation* contained in Article 14(1). The Community was obliged to attain the internal market by the specified date. This obligation

---

[14] Prior to the passage of the TEU this was Art. 8a. What was Art. 7 stated that the common market should be progressively established during a transitional period of 12 years. This was repealed by the ToA, since it was otiose.

[15] Ex Arts. 7c, 28, 57(2), 59, 84, 99, and 100a respectively.

was imposed on the Community institutions, but the Member States had a duty to co-operate pursuant to Article 10. Article 14(1) indicated the specific Treaty provisions to achieve the internal market. These were either introduced or amended by the SEA, but it was clear from Article 14(1) that this list was without prejudice to other provisions of the Treaty.

Article 14(2) contained the *definition of the internal market*. Article 14(2) provides a two-part formulation: it was to be an area without internal frontiers, in which there could be free movement of goods, persons, etc. The first of these is more precise than the second. The attainment of an area without internal frontiers can be judged by whether border controls still exist on the free movement of goods or persons, etc. It is more difficult to determine how freely goods, persons, and capital can move within the Community, *even when* border controls have been removed. It would be mistaken to assume that attaining the internal market is an once-and-for-all, static objective. It is not. Continuing technological developments pose new challenges for the single market ideal, and this is so notwithstanding the fact that the Commission programme from its White Paper has been largely realized.

We must now consider the *legal effect* of Article 14. The Commission, in an early working paper for the Intergovernmental Conference leading to the SEA, intended what is now Article 14 to have direct effect. This was reinforced by the Commission proposal that if national rules on free movement were not removed by the agreed date, then they would automatically be recognized as equivalent. These suggestions 'stunned the participants at the Intergovernmental Conference'.[16] The Commission was forced to modify its suggestions.[17] The Member States were still concerned that the Article might have legal consequences and therefore they attached a Declaration to the Article:

> The Conference wishes by means of the provisions in Article 7a[18] to express its firm political will to take before January 1, 1993 the decisions necessary to complete the internal market defined in those provisions, and more particularly the decisions necessary to implement the Commission's programme described in the White Paper on the Internal Market.
> Setting the date of December 31, 1992 does not create an automatic legal effect.

The possibility that Article 14 might have *legal effects against the Community itself*[19] cannot however be discounted, given its mandatory wording. The possibility of using Article 232 in the event of Commission or Council inaction would depend on whether the criteria for such actions were met.[20] It is necessary that the measures which it is claimed should have been enacted are defined with sufficient specificity for them to be identified individually, and adopted pursuant to Article 233.[21] This will not be so where the relevant institutions possess discretionary power, with consequential policy options, the content of which cannot be identified with precision. It would therefore be difficult to argue via Article 232 that the Commission had failed to promote measures designed to ensure the free movement of goods, persons, services, or capital. There may be a greater possibility for such an action where the allegation is that the Council had failed to adopt a specific Commission proposal, although

---

[16] C.-D. Ehlermann, 'The Internal Market Following the Single European Act' (1987) 24 *CMLRev.* 361, 371.

[17] *Ibid.*, 371–372.

[18] Now Art. 14.

[19] Ehlermann, n. 16 above, 372. See also H.J. Glaesner, 'The Single European Act: Attempt at an Appraisal' (1987) 10 *Fordham Intl. LJ* 446.

[20] On Art. 232 see Ch. 14.

[21] Case 13/83 *European Parliament* v. *Council* [1985] ECR 1513.

even here much would depend upon the nature of the proposal. A damages claim will be even more difficult to prove.[22]

There is also the possibility that Article 14 might have *legal consequences for the Member States*. This could mean that, even if the relevant Community measures had not been enacted, it would be open to an individual to argue that Member States' rules which constituted a barrier to the completion of the internal market should not be applied if they were incompatible with Article 14. Toth[23] has argued that the Declaration set out above does not, in and of itself, prevent the Article from having direct effect, since it is merely interpretive without binding force. It would still have to be shown that Article 14 fulfilled the conditions for direct effect,[24] the most problematic of which is that there must be no further action required before the norm can have direct effect. The ECJ has been willing to accord direct effect to certain Treaty Articles, notwithstanding the fact that further action is required to flesh out Article 14.[25] It would, however, be bold for the Court to hold that Article 14 is directly effective, given that the Declaration clearly signals Member State intent in this respect.[26] It is, moreover, clear that the Court has been reluctant to accord direct effect to Article 14. In *Wijsenbeek*[27] the applicant claimed that a Dutch penalty for failure to produce a passport when entering the country was invalid, *inter alia*, for breach of Article 14. He argued that the Article had direct effect from the end of December 1992, with the consequence that the Member States no longer had competence in this field. They could not therefore impose border controls, at least in relation to internal frontiers. The ECJ rejected the argument. It held that in the absence of Community measures requiring Member States to abolish controls of persons at the internal frontiers, Article 14 could not have direct effect notwithstanding the expiry of the December 1992 deadline. Any such obligation presupposed harmonization of the laws of the Member States governing the crossing of the external borders, immigration, the grant of visas, and asylum.[28]

The question until now has been of the possibility of direct effect where relevant Community measures to implement the internal market have not been passed. Where, however, they have been promulgated matters are different. The Community measure adopted might itself have direct effect, and so, too, might Article 14.

(b) ARTICLE 15: THE OBLIGATION QUALIFIED

Article 15 qualifies Article 14. It requires the Commission, when drawing up proposals pursuant to Article 14, to take into account the extent of the effort that certain economies showing differences in developments will have to sustain during the period of establishment of the internal market, and it may propose appropriate provisions. If the provisions take the form of derogations, they must be temporary and cause the least possible disturbance to the

---

[22] Case T–113/96 *Edouard Dubois et Fils SA v. Council and Commission* [1998] ECR II–125.

[23] A.G. Toth, 'The Legal Status of the Declarations Annexed to the Single European Act' (1986) 23 *CMLRev.* 803.

[24] Ch. 8.

[25] *Ibid.*

[26] In Case C–378/97 *Criminal Proceedings against Wijsenbeek* [1999] ECR I–6207, para. 9 the ECJ referred to the Declaration attached to Art. 14 but did not comment on its legal effect.

[27] *Ibid.*

[28] *Ibid.*, para. 40. Moreover, even if Art. 14 were to be regarded as according Community nationals an unconditional right to move freely, Member States would still be able to impose passport controls at internal frontiers in order to be able to check whether a person was in fact a Community national: para. 43. A similar reluctance to accord direct effect to Art. 14 is evident in Case C–9/99 *Echirolles Distribution SA v. Association du Dauphiné* [2000] ECR I–8207.

functioning of the common market.[29] Ehlermann captures the purpose of Article 15:[30]

> It makes allowance for the fact that the Community has become more heterogeneous through the accession of new Member States. If the objective laid down in Article 8A[31] appears rather ambitious for the original Member States, it is far more so for most of the new Member States, given their relative economic weakness compared with the old established members and the considerable risks which the complete opening up of their domestic markets would therefore entail.

(c) ARTICLE 95(1): FACILITATING THE PASSAGE OF HARMONIZATION MEASURES

We have seen that a principal difficulty in ensuring the passage of harmonization measures was the requirement of unanimity under Article 100 (now Article 94), which gives a general power to pass directives for the approximation of laws of the Member States that affect the establishment or functioning of the common market. The SEA therefore provided in Article 100a (now Article 95) a general legislative power akin to Article 100, without the unanimity requirement. Article 95(1) reads as follows:

> By way of derogation from Article 94 and save where otherwise provided in this Treaty, the following provisions shall apply for the achievement of the objectives set out in Article 14. The Council shall, acting in accordance with the procedure referred to in Article 251 and after consulting the Economic and Social Committee, adopt the measures for the approximation of the provisions laid down by law, regulation or administrative action in Member States which have as their object the establishing and functioning of the internal market.

It should be noted that whereas Article 94 authorizes only the passage of directives, Article 95 empowers the Council to pass measures, which includes directives but also covers regulations.[32] It is also noteworthy that whereas Article 94 merely requires that the European Parliament be consulted, Article 95(1) accords the Parliament a greater say by making the measures subject to the co-decision procedure of Article 251. Two more general features of Article 95 should be appreciated.

(i) *Article 95: A Residual Provision*

Article 95 is a residual provision. It operates only 'save where otherwise provided in this Treaty'. This means that other, more specific Treaty provisions, such as Articles 37, 44, 47, and 71, should be used for measures designed to attain the internal market where they fall within

---

[29] In a study from 2000 de Búrca found 41 directives that provided some degree of differentiation. In some instances there were objective reasons for this; in others the reasons were not readily apparent: G. de Búrca, 'Differentiation within the Core: The Case of the Common Market', in G. de Búrca and J. Scott (eds.), *Constitutional Change in the EU: From Uniformity to Flexibility?* (Hart, 2000), 143–145.

[30] Ehlermann, n. 16 above, 374.

[31] For which now read Art. 14.

[32] For an expansive interpretation of 'measures' see Case C–359/92 *Germany* v. *Council* [1994] ECR I–3681.

the subject-matter areas of those Articles.[33] This can generate boundary-dispute problems about the correct legal basis for Community legislation. Such disputes arose in the past normally because the European Parliament wished to ensure that its legislative rights under Article 95 were not by-passed by legislation enacted on a different Treaty Article, which gave it less extensive rights in the legislative process.[34]

The general test propounded by the ECJ for the resolution of such boundary disputes was that regard should be had to the nature, aim, and content of the act in question.[35] Where these factors indicated that the measure was concerned with more than one area of the Treaty, then it might be necessary to satisfy the legal requirements of two Treaty Articles.[36] The ECJ also made it clear that this would not be insisted upon where the relevant legal bases under the two Articles prescribed procedures which were incompatible.[37] Boundary disputes are less likely to occur now, since the legislative procedure applicable for many Treaty Articles is co-decision.

(ii) *Article 95: The Limits*

Article 95 is broadly framed, but the ECJ confirmed in *Tobacco Advertising* that there are limits to this Article.[38] The ECJ struck down a directive[39] designed to harmonize the law relating to the advertising and sponsorship of tobacco products. It read Article 95 in the light of Articles 3(1)(c) and 14 and concluded that the measures must be intended to improve the conditions for the establishment and functioning of the internal market.

Article 95 did not, as argued by the Commission, Council, and EP,[40] give any general power of market regulation. This would, said the ECJ, be contrary to Articles 3(1)(c) and 14, and be incompatible with the principle in Article 5 that the Community's powers were limited to those specifically conferred on it.[41] The ECJ held that a measure enacted pursuant to Article 95 must genuinely have as its object the improvement of the conditions for the establishment and functioning of the internal market. If mere disparities between national rules, and the abstract risk of obstacles to the exercise of fundamental freedoms, or distortions of competition, could justify the use of Article 95, then judicial review of compliance with the proper legal basis would be rendered 'nugatory'.[42] Any distortion of competition must, moreover, be appreciable, since otherwise 'the powers of the Community legislature would be practically unlimited'.[43]

This was because national laws often imposed different regulatory conditions on activities which could impact indirectly on competition between undertakings. If the EC could rely on the smallest distortions of competition to justify using Article 95 this would contradict the

---

[33] Case C–338/01 *Commission* v. *Council* [2004] ECR I–4829, paras. 54–60; Case C–533/03 *Commission* v. *Council* [2006] ECR I–1025, paras. 43–48.

[34] See, e.g., Case 68/86 *United Kingdom* v. *Council* [1988] ECR 855; Case 11/88 *Commission* v. *Council* [1989] ECR 3799; Case C–151/91 *Commission* v. *Council* [1993] ECR I–939; Case C–187/93 *European Parliament* v. *Council* [1994] ECR I–2857.

[35] Case C–300/89 *Commission* v. *Council* [1991] ECR I–2867; Case C–426/93 *Germany* v. *Council* [1995] ECR I–3723; Case C–271/94 *European Parliament* v. *Council* [1996] ECR I–1689.

[36] Case 165/87 *Commission* v. *Council* [1988] ECR 5545.

[37] Case C–338/01, n. 33 above.

[38] Case C–376/98 *Germany* v. *European Parliament and Council* [2000] ECR I–8419; T. Hervey, 'Up in Smoke? Community (Anti)-Tobacco Law and Policy' (2001) 26 *ELRev.* 101.

[39] [1998] OJ L213/9.

[40] Case C–376/98, n. 38 above, para. 45.

[41] *Ibid.*, para. 83.

[42] *Ibid.*, para. 84.

[43] *Ibid.*, para. 107.

principle in Article 5 that the Community has only the powers specifically conferred on it.[44] It followed that the ECJ must verify whether a measure enacted under Article 95 pursued the objectives stated by the Community legislature,[45] and whether the distortion of competition which the measure purported to eliminate was appreciable.[46] When viewed in this way the directive had not been validly made under Article 95.

While there are therefore limits to the use of Article 95, subsequent case law on related subject-matter has shown that the ECJ is willing to accept the use of Article 95 as the legal basis for the enacted measure.[47] This is evident especially in the 2006 *Tobacco Advertising* case,[48] where the ECJ upheld the validity of a revised directive on tobacco advertising, which included prohibitions on advertising in the press and radio. The Court concluded that this measure could be validly adopted under Article 95 EC, since there were disparities between the relevant national laws on advertising and sponsorship of tobacco products, and these disparities could affect competition and inter-state trade. The ECJ also stated more generally the circumstances in which Article 95 could be used. The 'criterion' is broad.[49]

> It follows ... that when there are obstacles to trade, or it is likely that such obstacles will emerge in the future, because the Member States have taken, or are about to take, divergent measures with respect to a product or a class of products, which bring about different levels of protection and thereby prevent the product or products concerned moving freely within the Community, Article 95 EC authorises the Community legislature to intervene by adopting appropriate measures, in compliance with Article 95(3) EC and with the legal principles mentioned in the EC Treaty or identified in the case law, in particular the principle of proportionality.

(d) ARTICLE 95(2)–(10): QUALIFICATIONS TO ARTICLE 95(1)

The remainder of Article 95 qualifies the powers given by Article 95(1). These qualifications differ in nature, and are the result of political negotiation.

Article 95(2) encapsulates a straightforward exception to Article 95(1), by providing that the latter shall not apply to fiscal provisions, to those relating to the free movement of persons, or to those relating to the rights and interests of employed persons. These areas were felt by the Member States to be particularly sensitive, hence their exclusion from Article 95(1). Legislation for these areas will therefore have to be passed under either Article 94 or a more specific Treaty provision.[50]

Article 95(3) instructs the Commission, when passing measures under Article 95(1) relating to health, safety, environmental protection, and consumer protection, to take as a base a

---

[44] *Ibid.*, para. 107.

[45] *Ibid.*, para. 85.

[46] *Ibid.*, para. 106.

[47] Case C–377/98 *Netherlands* v. *Parliament and Council* [2001] ECR I–7079; Case C–491/01 *The Queen* v. *Secretary of State for Health, ex p. British American Tobacco (Investments) Ltd. and Imperial Tobacco Ltd.* [2002] ECR I–11453; Case C–210/03 *R.* v. *Secretary of State for Health, ex p. Swedish Match* [2004] ECR I–11893.

[48] Case C–380/03 *Germany* v. *European Parliament and Council*, 12 Dec. 2006.

[49] *Ibid.*, para. 41.

[50] For fiscal provisions see Art. 93, which requires unanimity in the Council and consultation with the EP; for free movement of persons see Art. 18(2), which now imposes the Art. 251 procedure, but stipulates that unanimity is nonetheless required by the Council when using this procedure; for the rights of employed persons see Arts. 44 and 47.

high level of protection, taking into account in particular any new development based on scientific facts. The European Parliament and the Council are also to use their respective powers to achieve this objective. Article 95(3) was included to placate countries such as Germany and Denmark, which were concerned that the harmonization measures might not be stringent enough. The wording of Article 95(3) does not, however, compel the Commission to enact a measure in accordance with the standards pertaining in the countries with high levels of protection. It merely requires that a high level of protection should be taken as the base.

Article 95(4)–(9) has received most critical attention. The provisions are complex and therefore should be set out in full:

> 4. If, after the adoption by the Council or by the Commission of a harmonization measure, a Member State deems it necessary to maintain national provisions on grounds of major needs referred to in Article 30, or relating to protection of the environment or the working environment, it shall notify the Commission of these provisions as well as the grounds for maintaining them.
>
> 5. Moreover, without prejudice to paragraph 4, if, after the adoption by the Council or the Commission of a harmonization measure, a Member State deems it necessary to introduce national provisions based on new scientific evidence relating to the protection of the environment or the working environment on grounds of a problem specific to that Member State arising after the adoption of the harmonization measure, it shall notify the Commission of the envisaged provisions as well as the grounds for introducing them.
>
> 6. The Commission shall, within six months of the notifications as referred to in paragraphs 4 and 5, approve or reject the national provisions involved after having verified whether or not they are a means of arbitrary discrimination or a disguised restriction on trade between Member States and whether or not they shall constitute an obstacle to the functioning of the internal market.
>
> In the absence of a decision by the Commission within this period the national provisions referred to in paragraphs 4 and 5 shall be deemed to have been approved. When justified by the complexity of the matter and in the absence of danger for human health, the Commission may notify the Member State concerned that the period referred to in this paragraph may be extended for a further period of up to six months.
>
> 7. When, pursuant to paragraph 6, a Member State is authorised to maintain or introduce a national provision derogating from a harmonization measure, the Commission shall immediately examine whether to propose an adaptation to that measure.
>
> 8. When a Member State raises a specific problem on public health in a field which has been the subject of prior harmonization measures, it shall bring it to the attention of the Commission which shall immediately examine whether to propose appropriate measures to the Council.
>
> 9. By way of derogation from the procedure laid down in Articles 226 and 227, the Commission and any Member State may bring the matter directly before the Court of Justice if it considers that another Member State is making improper use of the powers provided for in this Article.

It should be noted that Article 95(5), (7), and (8) were new provisions introduced by the ToA, whereas the remainder of the paragraphs are modifications of pre-existing provisions. The inclusion of Article 95(4) gave rise to much critical comment.[51] The genesis of this Article and its exceptional character are evident in the following extract.

---

51 P. Pescatore, 'Some Critical Remarks on the "Single European Act" ' (1987) 24 *CMLRev.* 9.

C.-D. Ehlermann, The Internal Market Following the Single European Act[52]

Whereas paragraph 1[53] is the most significant provision of the Single European Act, paragraph 4 is the most problematic. Its purpose is the same as that of the preceding paragraph, namely to protect any Member State in a minority position from being forced to accept the majority line. However, the method devised is completely different. Whereas paragraph 3 is in keeping with the approach followed by the Community in the past, paragraph 4 represents a radical new departure.

It goes back to the fact that the United Kingdom, and later Ireland, wished to safeguard certain special measures connected with their island status against the threat of majority voting. Neither country was satisfied with the safeguard offered by paragraph 3. But they both accepted that retention of the unanimity requirement would have emasculated Article 100a.

The way out of this dilemma was paragraph 4, which was drafted by the European Council itself. . . .

Any assessment of Article 95(4)–(9) must take into account political and legal issues. In *political terms* many of the more dramatic fears about the impact of Article 95(4) have not been borne out. Concerns that Member States would routinely seek to invoke the Article to prevent the application of harmonization measures have proven unfounded.

In *legal terms* the Member State concerns which can trigger Article 95(4) are finite: the matters covered by Article 30, plus the environment and working environment. The ToA has, moreover, modified Article 95(4). Whereas it had previously spoken of a State 'applying' national provisions on one of the specified grounds, Article 95(4) is now framed in terms of 'maintaining' such provisions. A Member State cannot therefore invoke the Article to justify *new* national provisions that derogate from the harmonization measure, but only to justify the *retention* of existing provisions.[54] Article 95(5) by way of contrast deals with the situation where the Member State seeks to *introduce a new national measure* after the adoption of the harmonization directive. The Member State concerns which can trigger Article 95(5) are more limited: there must be new scientific evidence relating to the environment, etc., and there must be a problem which is specific to that State.[55]

Article 95(4) and (5) is an exception that derogates from the principles of the Treaty and will therefore be restrictively construed by the Commission and the ECJ. The Member State seeking to rely on this Article has the burden of proving that the conditions for their application exist.[56] The Commission's powers of scrutiny have been reinforced by Article 95(6). Prior to the ToA, Article 100a(4) spoke in terms of the Commission 'confirming' the national provisions. Article 95(6) now speaks of the Commission 'approving or rejecting' them. This shift in emphasis has been reinforced by changes to Article 95(4) by the ToA, requiring the State to explain the reasons for maintaining the national provisions.[57] The ECJ has, moreover, confirmed that it can judicially review invocation of Article 95(4).[58] The process under Article 95

---

[52] N. 16 above, 389.

[53] Of Art. 100a as it then was, now Art. 95.

[54] Case C–3/00 *Commission* v. *Denmark* [2003] ECR I–2643, paras. 57–58.

[55] *Ibid.*, paras. 57–59.

[56] Cases T–366/03 and 235/04 *Land Oberösterreich and Austria* v. *Commission* [2005] ECR II–4005, para. 63.

[57] Art. 95(5) contains a similar reasoning requirement.

[58] Case C–41/93 *France* v. *Commission* [1994] ECR I–1829, Case C–3/00 *Commission* v. *Denmark*, n. 54 above.

should not, however, be thought of in overly adversarial terms. Article 95(7) and (8), introduced by the ToA, are both designed to facilitate a negotiated solution to the problem.

Article 95(10) is the final qualification to Article 95(1). It provides that harmonization measures may include safeguard clauses authorizing Member States to take, for one of the non-economic reasons in Article 30, provisional measures subject to Community control procedures. Recourse to Article 30 is normally precluded when Community harmonization measures have been enacted. The purpose of Article 95(10) is to allow a Member State, subject to a Community control procedure, to adopt temporary measures in the event of a sudden and unforeseen danger to health, life, etc.

6. THE INTERNAL MARKET: THE NEW APPROACH TO HARMONIZATION

(a) THE RATIONALE FOR THE NEW APPROACH

We noted earlier that the completion of the single market was dependent upon two conditions. There had to be reform of the legislative procedure to facilitate the passage of measures to complete the internal market. There also had to be a new approach to harmonization to make it easier to secure the passage of these measures.

Reforms in the legislative process would not have been sufficient to secure the internal market, even though harmonization measures could now be passed more easily. This was because traditional Community harmonization techniques had a number of disadvantages.[59] They were slow, and generated excessive uniformity. There was a failure to develop links between harmonization and standardization, thereby leading to inconsistencies and wastage of time. Problems of certification and testing were not sufficiently addressed, and implementation within Member States was imperfect.

The Commission recognized these shortcomings in its White Paper.[60] Thus in its proposals to the Council and Parliament for a New Approach to Technical Harmonization and Standards,[61] the Commission acknowledged that experience had shown the difficulties with the existing approach, which was predicated on attempts to harmonize through detailed technical specification. The Commission admitted that the results of harmonization had been negligible in certain fields, given the multiplicity of national technical regulations and the speed of technological change.

(b) THE NEW APPROACH TO HARMONIZATION

The general direction of the new approach to harmonization is apparent in the extract from the Commission's White Paper on Completing the Internal Market. There was to be mutual recognition through the *Cassis de Dijon* principle.[62] National rules which did not come within one of the mandatory requirements would be invalid; legislative harmonization was to be restricted to laying down health and safety standards; and there would be promotion of

---

[59] J. Pelkmans, 'The New Approach to Technical Harmonization and Standardization' (1987) 25 *JCMS* 249, 252–253; M. Egan, *Constructing a European Market* (Oxford University Press, 2001), 78–81.

[60] COM(85)310, para. 64.

[61] Bull. EC 1–1985.

[62] Case 120/78 *Cassis de Dijon*, n. 2 above.

European standardization. A number of elements can be identified in the Community's new strategy.[63]

One building block concerns the provision of information, introduced by Directive 83/189,[64] now overtaken by Directive 98/34.[65] This measure, known as the Mutual Information or Transparency Directive, imposes an obligation on a State to inform the Commission before it adopts any legally binding regulation setting a technical specification, except where it transposes a European or international standard. The Commission then notifies the other States, and adoption of the national measure is delayed for a minimum of three months, in order that possible amendments can be considered. A year's delay can result if the Commission decides to press ahead with a harmonization directive on the issue. The Directive was given added force by the ECJ's decision in the *CIA* case[66] that a national measure that had not been notified in accordance with the Directive could not be relied on. Decision 3052/95[67] also imposes an obligation on a Member State to notify the Commission where it takes steps to prevent goods lawfully produced in another Member State from being placed on its market. This duty to notify is however subject to a number of exceptions[68] and has been interpreted narrowly by the ECJ.[69] A further obligation to furnish information is found in Regulation 2679/98, which requires Member States that have relevant information concerning obstacles to the free movement of goods that can lead to serious trade disruption and loss to individuals to notify the Commission.[70]

A *second facet* of the new approach was the willing acceptance of the *Cassis* jurisprudence.[71] A product lawfully manufactured in a Member State should be capable of being sold in any other Member State. Mutual recognition should be the norm. No harmonization measures were required with respect to those national measures that would be condemned under the *Cassis* reasoning.[72] Harmonization efforts should therefore be concentrated on those measures that would still be lawful under the *Cassis* exceptions or under Article 30.

This leads naturally on to the *third aspect* of the new approach. Legislative harmonization was to be limited to laying down essential health and safety requirements. Thus far twenty-five such directives have been enacted. Each measure deals however with a general product area, such as personal protective equipment, toys, construction products, explosives, medical devices, and the like. Each directive can therefore apply to hundreds or thousands of products that fall within the relevant generic category. The trading volume of products covered by the major sectors where the new approach has been applied has been estimated to be 1,500 billion euros *per annum*. The essence of this approach is brought out by Pelkmans.

---

[63] Enhancing the Implementation of New Approach Directives, COM(2003)240.

[64] [1983] OJ L109/8; S. Weatherill, 'Compulsory Notification of Draft Technical Regulations: The Contribution of Directive 83/189 to the Management of the Internal Market' (1996) 16 *YBEL* 129.

[65] Dir. 98/34/EC of the European Parliament and of the Council laying down a procedure for the provision of information in the field of technical standards and regulations [1998] OJ L204/37. The regime was extended to information services by Dir. 98/48/EC [1998] OJ L217/18.

[66] Case C–194/94 *CIA Security International SA* v. *Signalson SA and Securitel Sprl* [1996] ECR I–2201; Case C–443/98 *Unilever* v. *Central Food* [2000] ECR I–7535.

[67] Dec. 3052/95/EC of the European Parliament and of the Council establishing a procedure for the exchange of information on national measures derogating from the principle of the free movement of goods within the Community [1995] OJ L321/1.

[68] *Ibid.*, Art. 3.

[69] Cases C–388 and 429/00 *Radiosistemi* v. *Prefetto di Genova* [2002] ECR I–5845.

[70] Council Reg. 2679/98/EC on the functioning of the internal market in relation to the free movement of goods among the Member States [1998] OJ L337/8.

[71] Case 120/78 *Cassis de Dijon*, n. 2 above.

[72] See below, 677–679 for detailed consideration of this reasoning.

J. Pelkmans, The New Approach to Technical Harmonization and Standardization[73]

— harmonization of legislation is limited to the adoption ... of the essential safety requirements ... with which the products brought on the market must comply in order to qualify for free movement in the Community;

— it is the task of the competent (private) standardization organs, given technical progress, to formulate the technical specifications, on the basis of which industry needs to manufacture and market products complying with the fundamental requirements of the directives;

— these technical specifications are not binding and retain their character of voluntary (European) standards;

— but, at the same time, the governments are *obliged to presume* that the products manufactured in accordance with the European standards comply with the 'fundamental requirements' stipulated in the directive. It is this presumption that guarantees business free market access.

When a standard has been approved by the Commission and published in the Official Journal all Member States must accept goods which conform to it. If a Member State disputes whether the standard conforms to the safety objectives set out in the directive, the burden of proof will be on the State to substantiate its contentions. An analogous reversal of the burden of proof operates in the case of producers in the following sense. It is open to producers to manufacture according to specifications other than those laid down. The burden of proof will, however, then be on the producer to show that the goods meet the essential requirements specified in the directive.

The *final element* of the new approach is the promotion of European standardization. Standardization is important both because it reduces barriers to intra-Community trade and because it increases the competitiveness of European industry:[74]

Standards can have a market-creating effect or, in other words, the lack of a standard between adjoining countries can make the Euromarket (i. e. trade between Member States) impossible, as is for instance the case with car telephones. Standards can also have an anticipatory effect. For instance, sufficient investment in product development, process technology and further innovations takes place in some products only when compatibility is secured first.

The principal bodies are the European Committee for Standardization (CEN), the European Committee for Electrotechnical Standardization (CENELEC), and the European Telecommunications Standards Institute (ETSI). They 'ensure that standardization processes take place in parallel with harmonization at Council level and are based on "essential requirements".'[75] Provided that standardization complies with these 'essential requirements' then it is very likely to be approved. Standardization initiatives will also be undertaken in newly emerging

---

[73] N. 59 above, italics in the original.

[74] *Ibid.*, 260; On the Role of European Standardization in the Framework of European Policies and Legislation, COM(2004)674, para. 2.2.

[75] Pelkmans, n. 59 above, 256.

fields, or where there is rapid technological change, in order to facilitate creation of a more European market. The Community standardization bodies have moved to qualified-majority voting to expedite decision-making. The standard will be drafted by a Technical Committee of the standardization body. Standards may be mandated or unmandated. The former are created when the Commission calls for the standardization bodies to draw up a standard; the latter where the initiative comes from the standardization body itself. Compliance with a mandated standard means that the product is presumed to be safe under the General Product Liability Directive,[76] and that it can, subject to certain qualifications, circulate freely within the EU.

It is important to be clear about the relationship between Community harmonization of essential requirements and the standardization process. A directive passed pursuant to the new approach will lay down in general terms the health and safety requirements that the goods must meet. The setting of standards is designed to help manufacturers prove conformity to these essential requirements, and to allow inspection to test for conformity with them. Promoting Community-wide standards in the manner described above is designed to foster this process by encouraging the development of consensus on what the relevant standards in a particular area should be. Allowing a manufacturer to show that its goods comply with the essential safety requirements, even if they do not comply with the Community standard, provides flexibility.

The advantages of the new approach to harmonization are considerable. Directives can be drafted more easily since they are less detailed. The excessive 'Euro-uniformity' of the traditional approach is avoided by combining stipulated safety objectives with flexibility as to the standards through which this compliance can be achieved. The need for unanimity is obviated through Article 95. Harmonization and standardization are related. More Community directives can be made, and hence the gap between Community harmonization and the volume of national technical regulations can be reduced. Finally, incentives for proper implementation of directives by the Member States have been increased through judicial doctrine such as state liability in damages.[77]

This is not to say that the new approach has been problem-free. The efficiency of the standardization bodies, the sufficiency of the bodies able to undertake the certification process, and the representation of consumer interests have all been causes for concern.[78] The Commission has recognized the need for improvements in these areas.[79]

---

[76] Dir. 2001/95/EC of the European Parliament and of the Council on general product safety [2002] OJ L11/4, Art. 3(2).

[77] See Ch. 9.

[78] Pelkmans, n. 59 above, 263–265; B. Farquhar, 'Consumer Representation in Standardisation' (1995) 3 *Consumer Law Journal* 56; K. Armstrong and S. Bulmer, *The Governance of the Single European Market* (Manchester University Press, 1998), 157–163; E. Vos, *Institutional Frameworks of Community Health and Safety Regulation: Committees, Agencies and Private Bodies* (Hart, 1999); C. Joerges, H. Schepel, and E. Vos, *The Law's Problems with the Involvement of Non-Governmental Actors in Europe's Legislation Processes: The Case of Standardisation*, EUI Working Paper 99/9; European Association for the Co-ordination of Consumer Representation, ANEC, *Consumer Participation in Standardisation* (ANEC, 2000); H. Schepel, *The Constitution of Private Governance* (Hart, 2005), ch. 2.

[79] The Development of Standardization: Action for Faster Technical Integration in Europe, COM(90)456 final; The Broader Use of Standardization in Community Policy, COM(95)412 final; General Guidelines for the Co-operation between CEN, CENELEC and ETSI and the European Commission and EFTA [2003] OJ C91/04.

(c) THE NEW APPROACH TO HARMONIZATION: LEGISLATIVE FORMAT

The new approach to harmonization will be clearer by way of an example, such as Council Directive 89/392 on the approximation of the laws of the Member States relating to machinery.[80]

This Directive does not stipulate detailed requirements for how to build machinery. It concentrates on the health and safety risks from use of machinery, and states explicitly that the Directive was passed within the framework of the new approach to harmonization. The recitals to the Directive note that the Member States have different systems of accident prevention; that the disparities in the national rules constitute barriers to trade; that approximation of these national laws is therefore necessary to ensure free movement of goods without prejudicing protection of health and safety; that the Directive is designed to define the essential health and safety requirements; and that standards (generated in the manner described above) will enable manufacturers to prove conformity with the essential requirements and allow inspection to ensure conformity with these requirements. The recitals also locate this Directive within the broader Treaty framework, including the *Cassis* jurisprudence: national technical rules which impede trade, even if not discriminatory, are contrary to Community law unless saved by one of the mandatory requirements or Article 30. It is therefore only those national rules which survive the *Cassis* test which have to be harmonized:

> *Whereas* Community law, in its present form, provides—by way of derogation from one of the fundamental rules of the Community, namely the free movement of goods—that obstacles to movement within the Community resulting from disparities in national legislation relating to the marketing of products must be accepted in so far as the provisions concerned can be recognized as being necessary to satisfy imperative requirements; *whereas*, therefore, the harmonization of laws in this case must be limited only to those requirements necessary to satisfy the imperative and essential health and safety requirements relating to machinery; *whereas* these requirements must replace the relevant national provisions because they are essential.

Article 1 of the Directive defines its scope: it is to apply to machinery, which is further specified both inclusively and exclusively. The essential health and safety requirements for machinery are set out in Annex 1 at a relatively high level of generality. Article 2(1) imposes a duty on Member States to ensure that machinery is marketed only when it complies with the essential requirements. Article 3 states that the machinery covered by the Directive shall satisfy the essential requirements set out in Annex 1. Under Article 4, Member States are not to restrict the placing on the market of machinery that complies with the Directive. Article 5 refers to standards. If machinery bears the 'EC mark' and is accompanied by a declaration that it conforms to the essential health and safety requirements, the Member States are to accept this.[81] If there are no harmonized standards Member States are to apply existing national standards relevant to the proper implementation of the essential health and safety requirements. Where a national standard transposes a harmonized standard, then machinery constructed in accordance with this standard is to be presumed to comply with the essential requirements. Article 6 contains safeguards in the event that machinery bearing the EC mark is perceived to

---

[80] See also, e.g., Dir. 88/378 on toy safety; Dir. 89/106 on construction products; Dir. 89/336 on electromagnetic compatibility.

[81] See more generally Dir. 93/68 [1993] OJ L220/1.

be dangerous. The provisions of Article 8 describe the procedure whereby a manufacturer can obtain a certificate that its goods conform to the Directive; an EC mark can then be affixed to the goods.

The Safety of Machinery Directive provides a good example of the legislative format used by the Community under the new approach to harmonization. It should not, however, be thought that the Community has only one legislative strategy for trade barriers which are lawful under the Treaty. The following extract distinguishes three such strategies open to the Community.

A. McGee and S. Weatherill, The Evolution of the Single Market-Harmonisation or Liberalisation[82]

1. It may pass legislation which covers the entire field in question, albeit in a very general way. This approach is referred to here as 'Exhaustive Regulation' because it involves Community rule-making which excludes Member States' competence to regulate the area. A good example of this is provided by product safety.

2. It may pass legislation which deals with some issues in the area under consideration, but leaves others to national law. This approach is referred to here as 'Partial Regulation'. Two good examples of this are provided by the Product Liability Directive and the Regulation creating the European Economic Interest Grouping. . . .

3. It may not act at all; there are numerous possible reasons for this. One is simply lack of resources, since there is much to be done in the pursuit of the Single Market, and some matters inevitably have higher priority than others. Another possibility is political difficulty in reaching an agreed position. This may in turn take either of two forms. There may be agreement that regulation is required, but no consensus about the form of the regulation, or there may be disagreement as to whether any form of regulation is called for. . . . Such failure to act, for whatever reason, is referred to here as 'No Regulation'.

If a Community harmonization measure is exhaustive in the above sense then it will preempt inconsistent national rules. Whether the harmonization measure is intended to preclude any national measures that differ from the Community directive may be a contentious issue.

In *Ratti*[83] the ECJ had to decide whether Directive 73/173 on packaging and labelling of dangerous substances precluded a State from prescribing 'obligations and limitations which are more precise than, or at all events different from, those set out in the directive'. The Italian rules required that more information should be attached to the packaging than was specified in the Directive. The Court held that the Directive was intended to prevent the State from laying down any specific, stricter rules of its own. It may, by way of contrast, be apparent that the Directive only partially regulates the area. In *Grunert*[84] a French producer of food preservative containing lactic and citric acid was prosecuted for selling the preservative for use in the making of certain pork meats. French law prohibited the use of preservatives unless authorized by the national authorities, and the acids used were not on the national list. Community

---

[82] (1990) 53 *MLR* 578, 582.

[83] Case 148/78 *Pubblico Ministero* v. *Ratti* [1979] ECR 1629.

[84] Case 88/79 *Ministère Public* v. *Grunert* [1980] ECR 1827. See also Case C–11/92 *R.* v. *Secretary of State for Health, ex p. Gallaher Ltd.* [1993] ECR I–3545; Cases C–54 and 74/94 *Cacchiarelli* [1995] ECR I–391; Cases C–320, 328–329, and 337–339/94 *RTI* v. *Ministero delle Poste e Telecomunicazione* [1996] ECR I–6471.

Directives 64/54 and 70/357 did, however, list the two acids as among those that could be used to protect food against deterioration. This was Grunert's defence. The Directives, however, went on to provide that, subject to certain conditions, they were not to affect provisions of national law specifying the foodstuffs to which the preservatives listed could be added. The ECJ decided therefore that the Member States had discretion as to the foodstuffs to which listed preservatives could be added.

It is questionable how far the current Community approach is indicative of minimum or maximum harmonization.[85] The latter entails exhaustive regulation of the given field, with the Community rules setting both the floor and the ceiling of regulatory protection, the corollary being the pre-emption of national action. Minimum harmonization enables Member States to maintain more stringent regulatory standards than those prescribed by Community standards, provided that these are compatible with the Treaty. The Community legislation sets a floor, and the Treaty a ceiling, with Member States free to pursue their own policies within these boundaries. There is evidence that the Commission now favours maximum harmonization, at least in areas such as consumer policy.[86]

(d) THE NEW APPROACH TO HARMONIZATION: REFORM INITIATIVES

The new approach has been valuable in furthering the single market ideal, but there have, as noted above, been problems with the strategy. The Commission has set in motion certain reform initiatives designed to improve the system, two of which are of particular interest.

It has, on the one hand, engaged in a wide-ranging consultation exercise to review and extend the New Approach in order to make it more effective.[87] The essence of the proposal is that there should be an admixture of horizontal and sectoral legislation in this area. The former would contain as much as possible of all elements that are common to sectoral legislation, in order to reduce the need for the latter to repeat or copy these elements. The horizontal measure would therefore attempt to set, *inter alia*, the overall framework for safety legislation, provide the legal basis for matters such as accreditation and market surveillance, specify common definitions, the requirements for the development of European standards, and those for conformity assessment bodies and accreditation bodies, as well as common safeguard mechanisms. The sectoral legislation would then be limited to matters such as the essential health and safety requirements for the relevant product area, and the mechanism by which conformity assessment would be tested in that area.

The Commission, on the other hand, published an Action Plan for European Standardisation in 2006, developing ideas canvassed in its 2004 Communication. The Action Plan is designed to enhance the use of standardization in different policy areas, and improve

---

85 S. Weatherill, 'Beyond Preemption? Shared Competence and Constitutional Change in the European Community', in D. O' Keefe and P. Twomey (eds.), *Legal Issues of the Maastricht Treaty* (Chancery Law Publishing, 1994), ch. 2; M. Dougan, 'Minimum Harmonization and the Internal Market' (2000) 37 *CMLRev.* 853; S. Weatherill, 'Pre-emption, Harmonization and the Distribution of Competence to Regulate the Internal Market', in C. Barnard and J. Scott (eds.), *The Law of the Single European Market* (Hart, 2002), ch. 2; S. Weatherill, 'Supply of and Demand for Internal Market Regulation: Strategies, Preferences and Interpretation', in N. Nic Shuibhne (ed.), *Regulating the Internal Market* (Edward Elgar, 2006), 42–49.

86 S. Weatherill, *EU Consumer Law and Policy* (2nd edn., Edward Elgar, 2005), ch. 1.

87 Commission, Elements for a Horizontal Legislative Approach to Technical Harmonisation (2006), available at http://ec.europa.eu/enterprise/newapproach/.

its efficiency and coherence, including in this respect strategies to promote the effective participation of interested parties.[88]

7. THE INTERNAL MARKET: TENSIONS AND CONCERNS

The analysis thus far has shown the advantages of the new approach to harmonization. It would, however, be wrong to imagine that the single-market strategy has been problem-free. Commentators have perceived a number of tensions.

(a) CONSUMER INTERESTS AND COMMERCIAL POWER

One concern is whether consumer interests are sufficiently protected in the process of attaining a single market. We should remember that many national rules that impede intra-Community trade are designed to protect consumers. This has been recognized in the Treaty, through provisions such as Article 30. It has been acknowledged in the ECJ's jurisprudence through the *Cassis* mandatory requirements. It has been accepted by the Commission, since harmonization under the new approach will be necessary where Member States have legitimate health and safety interests. So far so good. No conflict between the realization of the single market and consumer protection. The latter will, where necessary, be addressed through Community measures that remove disparities between national rules, thereby easing barriers to trade, and ensure the continued protection of the consumer through Community directives or regulations. The problem is, however, whether such Community directives adequately balance consumer and manufacturing interests.

A. McGee and S. Weatherill, The Evolution of the Single Market—Harmonisation or Liberalisation[89]

It is submitted that there are structural reasons why the New Approach might serve the European consumer ill. The difficulty lies in the privatisation of the standards making process which supports the New Approach. For financial reasons it is likely that business will capture the standardisation process within CEN. Consumer organisations lack resources to participate fully in CEN committee work; in any event, consumer representation is ill-organized and haphazard in several Member States. . . . If standards making becomes the province of business alone, the balance between consumer protection and free trade will be distorted, prejudicing overall public confidence in the Community.

[*The authors return to the theme in their conclusion:*]

Not surprisingly, national governments appear to be the most effective at controlling developments. . . . Business and commercial interests have proved less successful in blocking developments, but have been highly effective in getting control of the standard-setting

---

[88] On the Role of Standardization, n. 74 above. The 2006 Action Plan is available at http://ec.europa.eu/enterprise/newapproach/standardization/harmstds/index_en.html.

[89] N. 82 above, 585, 595. See also N. Reich, 'Protection of Diffuse Interests in the EEC and the Perspective of Progressively Establishing an Internal Market' (1988) 11 *Cons. Policy* 395.

process, as in the case of Toy Safety, and in ensuring that other provisions take the form which they want. Thus, the EEIG Regulation[90] excluded worker participation, the Product Liability Directive allowed for the inclusion of the development risks defence and the Merger Regulation ignores all considerations of social policy. Again, it is not surprising to find that the highly motivated, well organised and generously resourced interests at work here have proved effective. Far less successful have been the consumer and employee interests, whose concerns seem largely to have been overridden. This too need not be a cause for surprise, but it is important to ask the fundamental question, what sort of Single Market is being created here? The answer seems to be that it is a Market in which business flourishes, relatively free from protective regulation, but the legitimate interests of other social groups are at risk of being ignored.

These concerns should be taken seriously. They were addressed in part by the establishment in 1992 of ANEC, the European Association for the Co-ordination of Consumer Representation in Standardization, a body which is independent of the European standards agencies themselves. This has served to alleviate the concerns expressed above, but not to dispel them. Problems still remain concerning access of ANEC to the CEN technical board, and also to the Commission's own standing committee.[91] As Amstrong and Bulmer note:[92]

> [T]he representation of consumer interests provides the third and linking part of the triangle between public legislative institutions on the one side and private standards-setters on the other. Whether that side of the triangle will serve to legitimate the actions of the other two sides will depend not only on its ability to harness technical resources, but also on its ability to increase its human and financial resources to enable it effectively to represent the consumer interest.

We should at the same time recognize that these concerns also exist when regulations about product safety and the like are made at national level. Tensions which result from the imbalance in power between consumer and commercial interests are not *created* because harmonization measures are passed at Community rather than national level. They are endemic in most Western-style market economies. Whether consumer interests fare better in the regulatory process at national or Community level will therefore depend, *inter alia*, on the relative capacities of commercial and consumer interests to influence the legislative process within the Community and the nation State, and the relative costs involved in operating within these differing polities.

(b) THE SINGLE MARKET, MARKET FREEDOM, AND STRUCTURAL BALANCE

A second tension inherent in the single-market project is that between a Community-wide free market and its impact on the weaker economies of the Community. We have already seen that the SEA addressed this problem to some extent through Article 15.[93] Whether this sufficed to meet the difficulty is more contestable.

---

90 European Economic Interest Grouping.
91 N. 78 above.
92 N. 78 above, 165.
93 See 614–615 above.

R. Dehousse, Completing the Internal Market: Institutional Constraints and Challenges[94]

At some point . . . a major challenge will have to be faced, for the objective of market integration itself remains unacceptable, politically speaking, for some Member States if it is not accompanied by specific effort to improve the social and economic cohesion within the Community. It is worth recalling in this respect that economically weaker countries have been reluctant to accept majority voting, precisely because they are those who might suffer most in the short term from the creation of a single market. Of the many problems linked to the completion of the internal market, this one is perhaps the most difficult: unlike the concerns for a high level of health, consumer safety or the environment, this kind of fear cannot be allayed by derogatory measures alone. A parallel in the Community's allocative and redistributive policies has been strongly advocated by recent studies, both from a theoretical and from a practical viewpoint. The Single Act pledges the Community to reinforce its action in favour of backward areas; it even explicitly states that the completion of the internal market should be pursued taking into account the existence of different levels of development within the Community. . . .

However, it fails to give the Community additional means to reach that end. The crucial point is that, at a given stage, progress towards the single European market might be conditioned by the capacity to tackle the problem of structural imbalances: if the Community does not find a way to offer some compensation to those countries which feel they have more to lose, market integration could be severely hampered. More than institutional pragmatism will be needed in order to cut this Gordian knot.

Fulfillment of the single-market project can generate macro-economic and social tensions between rich, poor, and middle-class economies within the Community. This should come as no surprise. Reflect on experience within nation States. A market-driven national economic policy will often create regional problems within a particular country, with areas of high unemployment and relative poverty. It is not therefore surprising that a vigorous EC policy of increased competitiveness and breaking down trade barriers will produce similar tensions, albeit on a larger scale. Some countries will be concerned about their ability to survive and prosper within this barrier-free, competitive environment. Dehousse is therefore quite right to point to the connections between the single-market project and the need to tackle structural imbalances within the Community. Articles 158–162 provide the foundation for structural policies to address this problem. The balance between the single market and structural intervention will, however, always be problematic.

(c) THE CHALLENGE TO POSITIVE INTEGRATION

The assumption in the earlier part of this chapter was that the single-market project required both negative and positive integration, and that in so far as the SEA and subsequent reforms facilitated the latter by rendering it easier to enact harmonization measures, this was a 'good thing'. Majone has however challenged this assumption. He argues that the real costs of such regulations are borne by those who have to comply with them and not by those who make them, and hence that budgetary constraints have limited impact on the regulators, with the consequence that the 'volume, detail and complexity of Community regulations are often out

---

[94] R. Bieber, R. Dehousse, J. Pinder, and J. Weiler (eds.), *1992: One European Market?* (Nomos, 1988), 336.

of proportion with the benefits that they may reasonably be expected to produce'.[95] He argues moreover that Member States often enjoy a comparative advantage in devising regulations in areas such as telecommunications, consumer protection, and environmental protection because they are not tied to the lowest common denominator approach that often limits Community regulatory provisions, and because Member States have superior implementation mechanisms as compared to the EU.[96]

Space precludes detailed analysis of this thesis. Suffice it to say for the present that while we should be mindful of the scope and application of EU regulatory competence, Majone's argument in this respect is but part of a broader and controversial thesis concerning the interpretation of EU competence, which is itself premised on distinctions between positive and negative rights, and between economic and social regulation.[97]

(d) POLITICS, ECONOMICS, AND THE SINGLE MARKET ENTERPRISE

Conceptions of market freedom are not value-free. The meaning of this phrase and the appropriate limits to free markets are contestable. These are key issues that divide political parties. There is, as we have seen, sound economic evidence that removing barriers to intra-Community trade will bring economic benefits. There is nonetheless still room for considerable diversity of opinion about the desirable scope of protective Community measures, even among those of differing political persuasions who are committed to the European ideal. The politicization which accompanies market integration has been noted by commentators, such as Pelkmans, who states that an internal-market strategy that cuts deeply into the regulatory environment, severely limiting the options available to Member States, cannot pretend to be entirely apolitical.[98] Weiler develops the same theme.

J. Weiler, The Transformation of Europe[99]

It is an article of faith for European integration that the Commission is not meant to be a mere secretariat, but an autonomous force shaping the agenda and brokering the decisionmaking of the Community. And yet at the same time, the Commission, as broker, must be ideologically neutral, not favouring Christian Democrats, Social Democrats or others.

This neutralization of ideology has fostered the belief that an agenda could be set for the Community, and the Community could be led towards an ever closer union among its peoples, without having to face the normal political cleavages present in the Member States. In conclusion, the Community political culture which developed in the 1960s and 1970s led … to an habituation of all political forces to thinking of European integration as ideologically neutral in, or transcendent over, the normal debates on the left–right spectrum. It is easy to understand how this will have served the process of integration, allowing a nonpartisan coalition to emerge around its overall objectives.

[95] G. Majone, *Dilemmas of European Integration, The Ambiguities and Pitfalls of Integration by Stealth* (Oxford University Press, 2005), 145.
[96] *Ibid.*, 149–150.
[97] See, e.g., *ibid.*, 107–136, 157–158.
[98] J. Pelkmans, 'A Grand Design by the Piece? An Appraisal of the Internal Market Strategy', in Bieber *et al.* (eds.), n. 94 above, 371.
[99] (1991) 100 *Yale LJ* 2403, 2476–2478.

1992 changes this in two ways. The first is a direct derivation from the turn to majority voting. Policies can be adopted now within the Council that run counter not simply to the perceived interests of a Member State, but more specifically to the ideology of the government in power. The debates about the European Social Charter and the shrill cries of 'Socialism through the backdoor', as well as the emerging debate about Community adherence to the European Convention on Human Rights and abortion rights are harbingers of things to come. . . .

The second impact of *1992* on ideological neutrality is subtler. The entire program rests on two pivots: the single market plan encapsulated in the White Paper, and its operation through the instrumentalities of the Single European Act. . . . It is not simply a technocratic program to remove the remaining obstacles to the free movement of all factors of production. It is at the same time a highly politicized choice of ethos, ideology and political culture: the culture of 'the market'. It is also a philosophy, at least one version of which—the predominant version—seeks to remove barriers to the free movement of factors of production, and to remove distortion to competition as a means to maximize utility. The above is premised on the assumption of formal equality of individuals. It is an ideology the contours of which have been the subject of intense debate within the Member States in terms of their own political choices. . . . A successful single market requires widespread harmonization of standards and environmental protection, as well as the social package of employees. This need for a successful market not only accentuates the pressure for uniformity, but also manifests a social (and hence ideological) choice which prizes market efficiency and European-wide neutrality of competition above other competing values.

The continuing relevance of this issue was starkly exemplified by the French negative vote in the referendum on the Constitutional Treaty, a result, in part, of the perception that the EU was too dominated by market considerations, thereby endangering traditional French social values. The same theme is apparent in the passage of the Services Directive,[100] which was radically revised because of pressure from the EP, which felt, *inter alia*, that it jeopardized provision of traditional public services by giving undue weight to market competition.

8. THE RECONCEPTUALIZATION OF THE INTERNAL MARKET

The single-market project did not magically come to an end in December 1992. There was a continuing flow of internal market legislation post-1992. This was matched by a number of reports that addressed various aspects of the Community regulatory process.[101] These can be broadly divided into groups.

There have been *many reports focusing on attainment of the internal market in the economic sense of the term.* In 1993 the Commission produced its strategic programme on *Making the Most of the Internal Market,*[102] in which it reviewed issues such as the completion of the legal framework and the management of the single market. In 1996 the Commission undertook a wide-ranging study on *The Impact and Effectiveness of the Single Market.*[103] The study measured the economic gains from the internal market, and highlighted areas where further action

---

[100] See below, 634, 841–845.
[101] P. Craig, 'The Evolution of the Single Market', in Barnard and Scott, n. 85 above, ch. 1.
[102] COM(93)632 final.
[103] COM(96)520 final.

was required, such as public procurement, tax harmonization, company law, and the transposition of directives. The Commission developed these themes in its *Single Market-Action Plan*,[104] in which it identified four principal goals for the development of the single market: making the rules more effective, dealing with market distortions, removing sectoral obstacles to market integration, and delivering a single market for the benefit of all citizens. The Amsterdam European Council officially endorsed these goals in 1997. The 1997 *Action Plan* led to further reports that focused on matters such as making mutual recognition more effective.[105] Single-market reform has, more recently, been focused heavily on the services sector. This is exemplified by initiatives relating to financial services,[106] mutual recognition of professional qualifications,[107] and the more general market for services.[108]

A broader conception of the internal market is however also to be found in a number of the papers from the Commission and the European Council. The internal market is conceptualized in more holistic terms, to include not only economic integration, but also consumer safety, social rights, labour policy, and the environment. This material is therefore of relevance for the concerns voiced in the previous section. This shift did not occur at any single moment. It developed across time. Certain important steps can nonetheless be identified.

The *1997 Action Plan* was significant in this respect. The fourth strategic target was to deliver a single market for the benefit of all citizens. The Commission's introduction to the *Action Plan* consciously stressed that 'the single market was not simply an economic structure', but included basic standards of health and safety, equal opportunities, and labour law measures.[109] This theme was carried over in the *1997 Action Plan* itself. The strategic target of delivering a single market for the benefit of all citizens was particularized through action directed towards, *inter alia*, the protection of social rights, consumer rights, health and the environment, and the right of residence.[110]

The Lisbon European Council constituted another important stage in the reconfiguration of the internal market agenda. The meeting, held in March 2000, focused on employment, economic reform, and social cohesion. It set a 'new' strategic goal: the Union was to become 'the most competitive and dynamic knowledge-based economy in the world, capable of sustainable economic growth with more and better jobs and greater social cohesion'.[111] Completion of the internal market was to be one way of achieving this strategy.[112] The modernization of the European social model through the building of an active welfare state was to be another. This was crucial to ensure that 'the emergence of this new economy does not compound the existing social problems of unemployment, social exclusion, and poverty'.[113] This objective was further particularized in terms of better education, an active employment

---

[104] Action Plan for the Single Market, SEC(97)1 final.

[105] Communication from the Commission to the European Parliament and the Council, Mutual Recognition in the Context of the follow-up to the Action Plan for the Single Market, 16 June 1999.

[106] Financial Services—Implementing the Framework for Financial Markets: Action Plan, COM(1999)232; Financial Services Priorities and Progress, Third Report, COM(2000)692/2 final; White Paper, Financial Services Policy 2005–2010 (Dec. 2005).

[107] Dir. 2005/36/EC of the European Parliament and of the Council of 7 Sept. 2005 on the recognition of professional qualifications [2005] OJ L255/22.

[108] An Internal Market Strategy for Services, COM(2000)888; Dir. 2006/123/EC of the European Parliament and of the Council of 12 Dec. 2006 on services in the internal market [2006] OJ L376/36.

[109] Single Market Action Plan sets Agenda, 18 June 1997, 2.

[110] *Action Plan*, n. 104 above, 9–11.

[111] Lisbon European Council, 23–24 Mar. 2000, para. 5.

[112] *Ibid.*, paras. 5, 16–21.

[113] *Ibid.*, para. 24.

policy, modernizing social protection, and promoting social inclusion.[114] These commitments were reiterated at the Feira European Council.[115] The same theme permeated the Nice European Council.[116] It considered a 'New Impetus for an Economic and Social Europe'. It approved the European Social Agenda developed by the Commission, which was characterized by the 'indissoluble link between economic performance and social progress'.[117] This link had been forged by the Commission and endorsed by the European Parliament.[118] Economic growth and social cohesion were seen as mutually reinforcing.[119] The Stockholm European Council echoed the same idea. There was 'full agreement that economic reform, employment and social policies were mutually reinforcing';[120] a 'dynamic Union should consist of active welfare states'.[121]

The principal Commission reports concerning the internal market in 2000 developed the ideas articulated by the European Council. Thus the *2000 Review of the Internal Market Strategy*[122] took the strategic remit of the Lisbon European Council as its starting point. The internal market should be made economically effective, but it should also foster job creation, social cohesion, and safety.[123] The interconnection between the economic and social aspects of the internal market is also apparent in the later report on the *Functioning of Community Product and Capital Markets*.[124] In economic terms, a properly functioning internal market was the key to prosperity for Community citizens. In social terms, the internal market was seen as the guarantee of rights to safe, high-quality products.[125] The Commission accepted the conclusions of the Internal Market Council of March 2000 that high levels of consumer protection were needed for a well-functioning internal market,[126] and acknowledged that environmental concerns required a 'reinforced, symbiotic integration of environmental policy and economic reforms inside the Internal Market'.[127] The revised Commission Communication on *Services of General Interest*[128] consciously drew on the conclusions of the Lisbon and Feira European Councils, and stressed the economic and social aspects of such services.

The willingness to consider the internal market in more holistic terms is to be welcomed. The EC Treaty does not moreover preclude the taking account of non-market values, such as health and safety, even within internal market legislation, provided that the initial economic hurdle is met.

---

[114] *Ibid.*, paras. 25–34.

[115] Feira European Council, 19–20 June 2000, paras. 19–39, 44–49.

[116] Nice European Council, 7–9 Dec. 2000.

[117] *Ibid.*, para. 15.

[118] *Ibid.*, Annex 1, paras. 8–9.

[119] *Ibid.*, Annex 1, paras. 9, 11.

[120] Stockholm European Council, 23–24 Mar. 2001, para. 2.

[121] *Ibid.*, para. 25.

[122] COM(2000)257 final.

[123] *Ibid.*, 15–17.

[124] Economic Reform: Report on the Functioning of Community Capital and Product Markets, COM(2000)881 final.

[125] *Ibid.*, 3–4.

[126] *Ibid.*, 5.

[127] *Ibid.*, 5.

[128] Services of General Interest in Europe, COM(2000)580 final. These are services that public authorities decide should be provided even though ordinary market forces may not do so: para. 14.

B. de Witte, Non-market Values in Internal Market Legislation[129]

> The conclusion is . . . that internal market legislation, to be constitutionally valid, *must* satisfy a specific internal market test, in the sense that the authors of the act must make a plausible case that the act either helps to remove disparities between national provisions that hinder the free movement of goods, services or persons, or helps to remove disparities that cause distorted conditions of competition. However these need not be, and cannot logically be, the only purposes of internal market legislation. Such legislation also invariably and legitimately pursues other public policy objectives. . . . Internal market legislation is always *also* about 'something else', and that something else may, in fact, be the main reason why the internal market measure was adopted. The multifaceted nature of internal market legislation is one of the inherent characteristics of that legislation and not a perverse ploy of European actors to extend the range of their competences.

There are nonetheless continuing tensions between the economic and social dimensions of the internal market. Thus the priorities in the *Internal Market Strategy* for 2003–2006 were heavily economic in nature.[130] The passage of the Services Directive is a further timely reminder of the tensions that exist between the economic and social dimensions of the internal market.[131] The Commission's proposal[132] was strongly criticized by the EP,[133] on the ground, *inter alia*, that it was too economic in its orientation and jeopardized the provision of public services. The Commission was forced to revise its proposals significantly,[134] and this is reflected in the final version of the Services Directive.[135] It is also the case that the balance between the economic and social dimensions of the Lisbon Strategy has altered over time. While both remain part of the Strategy,[136] the economic focus has often predominated, although the French rejection of the Constitutional Treaty on the ground, *inter alia*, that it was too economic in its orientation has led to some renewed emphasis on the social dimension, albeit still within a 'tight' economic frame.[137]

9. CONCLUSION

i. The most significant contribution of the SEA and the single market project to the process of European integration might, in the long term, be that it jolted the Community out of the Euro-pessimism of the 1970s and early 1980s. If there had been no SEA, the new approach

---

[129] Nic Shuibhne (ed.), n. 85 above, 75, emphasis in the original.

[130] Internal Market Strategy—Priorities 2003–2006, COM(2003)238; B. de Witte, 'Non-market Values in Internal Market Legislation', in Nic Shuibhne, n. 85 above, 78–79.

[131] See below, 841–845.

[132] Proposal for a Dir. of the European Parliament and of the Council, on services in the internal market, COM(2004)2 final/3.

[133] EP Committee on the Internal Market and Consumer Protection, Report on the Proposal for a Dir. of the European Parliament and of the Council, on Services in the Internal Market, A6-0409/2005, Rapporteur Evelyne Gebhardt.

[134] Amended Proposal for a Dir. of the European Parliament and of the Council, on services in the internal market, COM(2006)160 final.

[135] Dir. 2006/123/EC, n. 108 above.

[136] Brussels European Council, 8–9 Mar. 2007, paras. 1–20.

[137] See, e.g., J. Barroso, 'Alive and Kicking: The Renewed Lisbon Strategy', Brussels, 5 Mar. 2007, available at http://ec.europa.eu/commission_barroso/president/index_en.htm.

to harmonization might never have taken hold. The SEA laid the foundations for the institutional and substantive changes which have occurred since then. Causality in international affairs is difficult to determine. But it is doubtful whether the TEU would ever have been negotiated had the SEA not preceded it.

ii.   The focus in the 1980s and early 1990s was, not unnaturally, on the economic dimensions of the single market. Legislative, administrative, and judicial initiatives contributed towards the breaking down of the economic barriers to the single market. This is still a central aspect of single-market policy.

iii. The focus from the mid-1990s onwards has shifted. The internal market is now felt to embrace broader concerns relating to social, environmental, and consumer policy. This has been a conscious shift by the EC, anxious to avoid the critique that pursuit of the single market has undercut social, etc., protections within the Member States. There are nonetheless continuing tensions between the economic and social dimensions of the internal market.

10. FURTHER READING

(a) Books

Armstrong, K., *Regulation, Deregulation, Re-regulation* (Kogan Page, 2000)

—— and Bulmer, S., *The Governance of the Single European Market* (Manchester University Press, 1998)

Barnard, C., and Scott, J. (eds.), *The Law of the Single European Market* (Hart, 2002)

Bieber, R., Dehousse, R., Pinder, J., Weiler, J. (eds.), *1992: One European Market?* (Nomos, 1988)

Egan, M., *Constructing a European Market* (Oxford University Press, 2001)

Joerges, C., and Dehousse, R. (eds.), *Good Governance in Europe's Integrated Market* (Oxford University Press, 2002)

Majone, G., *Regulating Europe* (Routledge, 1996)

—— *Dilemmas of European Integration, The Ambiguities and Pitfalls of Integration by Stealth* (Oxford University Press, 2005)

Nic Shuibhne, N. (ed.), *Regulating the Internal Market* (Edward Elgar, 2006)

Schepel, H., *The Constitution of Private Governance* (Hart, 2005)

Snyder, F. (ed.), *Constitutional Dimensions of European Economic Integration* (Kluwer, 1996)

(b) Articles

Armstrong, K., 'Governance and the Single European Market', in P. Craig and G. de Búrca (eds.), *The Evolution of EU Law* (Oxford University Press, 1999), ch. 21

Craig, P., 'The Evolution of the Single Market', in C. Barnard and J. Scott (eds.), *The Law of the Single European Market* (Hart, 2002), ch.1

de Witte, B., 'Non-market Values in Internal Market Legislation', in N. Nic Shuibhne (ed.), *Regulating the Internal Market* (Edward Elgar, 2006), ch. 3

Dougan, M., 'Minimum Harmonization and the Internal Market' (2000) 37 *CMLRev.* 853

Ehlermann, C.-D., 'The Internal Market Following the Single European Act' (1987) 24 *CMLRev.* 361

McGee, A., and Weatherill, S., 'The Evolution of the Single Market—Harmonisation or Liberalisation' (1990) 53 *MLR* 578

Moravcsik, A., 'Negotiating the Single European Act: National Interests and Conventional Statecraft in the European Community' (1991) 45 *International Organization* 19

Pelkmans, J., 'The New Approach to Technical Harmonization and Standardization' (1987) 25 *JCMS* 249

Sandholtz, W., and Zysman, J., '1992: Recasting the European Bargain' (1989) 42 *World Politics* 95

Streit, M., and Mussler, W., 'The Economic Constitution of the European Community: From "Rome" to "Maastricht" ' (1995) 1 *ELJ* 5

Sun, J.-M., and Pelkmans, J., 'Regulatory Competition and the Single Market' (1995) 33 *JCMS* 67

Weatherill, S., 'Pre-emption, Harmonization and the Distribution of Competence to Regulate the Internal Market', in C. Barnard and J. Scott (eds.), *The Law of the Single European Market* (Hart, 2002), ch. 2

—— 'New Strategies for Managing the EC's Internal Market' (2000) 53 *CLP* 595

18

FREE MOVEMENT OF GOODS: DUTIES, CHARGES, AND TAXES

1. THE STRUCTURE OF THE PROVISIONS CONCERNING FREE MOVEMENT OF GOODS

In this and the following chapter we shall consider the ECJ's case law on the free movement of goods. This can be impeded in a number of different ways.

The most obvious form of protectionism will occur through customs duties or charges which have an equivalent effect, with the object of rendering foreign goods more expensive than their domestic counterparts. This is dealt with by Articles 23–25 (ex Articles 9–12). A State may also attempt to benefit domestic goods by taxes that discriminate against imports. This is covered by Articles 90–93 (ex Articles 95–99). These issues will be considered within this chapter.

A State may, however, seek to preserve advantages for its own goods by imposing quotas or measures which have an equivalent effect on imports, thereby reducing the quantum of imported products. This aspect of free movement is dealt with in Articles 28–31 (ex Articles 30–37), and is addressed in the next chapter.

This and the following chapters are concerned with state action that creates barriers to trade. Such action can also result from aid granted by a Member State to a specific industry. This will obviously disadvantage competing products from other Member States, and Community law therefore closely regulates the granting of such aid through Articles 87–89 (ex Articles 92–94).[1]

Private parties may also take action that partitions the market along national lines, and hence impedes the realization of the Single Market. This can occur when private parties use industrial property rights to divide the Community on the basis of national divisions, or when firms agree among themselves not to compete in each other's markets. Community law has to address both of these issues in order to prevent private action from recreating barriers to trade analogous in their effect to duties or quotas.[2]

---

[1] See Ch. 28.
[2] See Chs. 24–27.

2. CENTRAL ISSUES

i.   The abolition of customs duties and charges having an equivalent effect is central to the idea of a customs union and a single market. As the Commission has stated, the Customs Union is a foundation of the EU and essential to the functioning of the single market, with the implication that the 'twenty five Customs administrations of the EU must act as though they were one'.[3]

ii. The ECJ has therefore interpreted Articles 23–25 strictly in order to ensure that this fundamental aim is fulfilled. It has made it clear that it will look to the effect of a duty, and not its purpose, and has given a broad reading to 'charges having equivalent effect' to a customs duty. It has allowed only very limited exceptions to these Articles, and any breach will be unlawful *per se*.

iii. The prohibition of taxes that discriminate against imports is equally central to the single market ideal. Customs duties apply when goods cross the border, and are caught by Articles 23–25. A State may however discriminate against imports through differential taxes once the goods are in its country. Articles 90–93 proscribe such conduct.

iv. The case law concerning Articles 90–93 can be controversial. This is in part because the Treaty language requires the ECJ to make decisions about difficult matters, such as whether goods are similar to each other or whether a differential tax regime is protective of home State products. It is also in part because tax rules may be used to foster national preferences in relation to matters such as the environment. The ECJ has to adjudicate on whether such rules are compatible with Articles 90–93.

v.   It is essential when reading the materials in this chapter to have some idea of the broader context into which they fit. The discussion of the legal materials will therefore be placed within the context of the more general issues concerning the customs union and taxation respectively.

3. ARTICLES 23–25: DUTIES AND CHARGES

Article 23(1)[4] (ex Article 9(1)) is the foundational provision of this part of the Treaty:

> The Community shall be based upon a customs union which shall cover all trade in goods and which shall involve the prohibition between Member States[5] of customs duties on imports and exports and of all charges having an equivalent effect, and the adoption of a common customs tariff in their relation with third countries.[6]

---

[3] See http://ec.europa.eu/taxation_customs/customs/policy_issues/customs_strategy/index_en.htm.

[4] Art. 23 will almost always be used in conjunction with one of the other Treaty Arts. in this area. When it is employed in this manner it will have direct effect: see, e.g., Case 18/71 *Eunomia di Porro & Co.* v. *Italian Ministry of Education* [1971] ECR 811.

[5] The ECJ has interpreted Art. 9 (now Art. 23) to prohibit customs duties, etc., even when they are applied within a Member State and are imposed on goods which enter or leave one particular region of that State: Cases C–363, 407, 409, and 411/93 *René Lancry SA* v. *Direction Générale des Douanes* [1994] ECR I–3957; Case C–72/03 *Carbonati Apuani Srl* v. *Commune di Carrara* [2004] ECR I–8027.

[6] The goods which benefit from the provisions on free movement contained in Arts. 23–25 and 28–31 are those which originate in a Member State and those which come from outside the Community, but are in free

It is important to understand the structure of the other provisions in this part of the Treaty. The old Article 12 prohibited the imposition of *new* customs duties and charges equivalent thereto,[7] while the old Article 13 obliged Member States to abolish *existing* duties within the transitional period, in accordance with Articles 13–15; the old Article 16 concerned the abolition of duties on exports. The passage of time has rendered redundant the distinction between new and existing duties. The previous Articles 12–17 have thus been repealed. Article 25 (ex Article 12) now relates to any customs duties and charges equivalent thereto, whether concerning imports or exports, with no distinction being drawn as to when such duties were imposed:

> Customs duties on imports and exports and charges having equivalent effect shall be prohibited between Member States. This prohibition shall also apply to customs duties of a fiscal nature.

(a) DUTIES AND CHARGES: EFFECT, NOT PURPOSE

In its early case law the Court made it clear that whether the old Article 12 would bite would depend upon the effect of the duty or charge, and not on its purpose. This comes out clearly from the *Italian Art* case. There is no doubt that this approach is equally applicable to Article 25.

Case 7/68 **Commission v. Italy**
[1968] ECR 423

[Note ToA renumbering: Art. 169 is now Art. 226; Art. 16 has been repealed, but the substance of this Art. is now covered by the amended Art. 25]

Italy imposed a tax on the export of artistic, historical, and archæological items. The Commission brought an action under Article 169 alleging that this was in breach of Article 16 which prohibited duties and charges on exports. Italy argued that the items should not be regarded as goods for the purpose of the rules on the customs union and that the purpose of the tax in question was not to raise revenue, but to protect the artistic etc. heritage of the country. The Court rejected these arguments.

THE ECJ

1. The Scope of the Disputed Tax

. . .

Under Article 9 of the Treaty the Community is based on a customs union 'which shall cover all trade in goods'. By goods, within the meaning of that provision, there must be understood

circulation within the Member States: Art. 23(2). The criteria for goods which come from outside the Community to be in free circulation within the Community are contained in Art. 24: the goods must have complied with import formalities, and any customs duties and charges must have been paid by the trader and not have been reimbursed.

[7] It was Art. 12 (now Art. 25) which was in issue in the famous *Van Gend* case which laid the foundations for the concept of direct effect within Community law. See Ch. 8.

products which can be valued in money and which are capable, as such, of forming the subject of commercial transactions.

The articles covered by the Italian law, whatever may be the characteristics which distinguish them from other types of merchandise, nevertheless resemble the latter, inasmuch as they can be valued in money and so be the subject of commercial transactions. That view corresponds with the scheme of the Italian law itself, which fixes the tax in question in proportion to the value of the articles concerned.

It follows from the above that the rules of the Common Market apply to these goods subject only to the exceptions expressly provided by the Treaty.

2. The Classification of the Disputed Tax Having Regard to Article 16 of the Treaty

In the opinion of the Commission the tax in dispute constitutes a tax having an effect equivalent to a customs duty on exports and therefore the tax should have been abolished, under Article 16 of the Treaty, no later than the end of the first stage of the common market, that is to say, from 1 January 1962. The defendant argues that the disputed tax does not come within the category, as it has its own particular purpose which is to ensure the protection and safety of the artistic, historic and archaeological heritage which exists in the national territory. Consequently, the tax does not in any respect have a fiscal nature, and its contribution to the budget is insignificant.

Article 16 of the Treaty prohibits the collection in dealings between Member States of any customs duty on exports and of any charge having an equivalent effect, that is to say, any charge which, by altering the price of an article exported, has the same restrictive effect on the free circulation of that article as a customs duty. That provision makes no distinction based on the purpose of the duties and charges the abolition of which it requires.

It is not necessary to analyse the concept of the nature of the fiscal system on which the defendant bases its argument upon this point, for the provisions of the section of the Treaty concerning the elimination of customs duties between the Member States exclude the retention of customs duties and charges having an equivalent effect without distinguishing in that respect between those which are and those which are not of a fiscal nature.

The disputed tax falls within Article 16 by reason of the fact that export trade in the goods in question is hindered by the pecuniary burden which it imposes on the price of the exported articles.

When a tax is caught by Article 25 as a duty or charge that is of equivalent effect then it is in effect *per se* unlawful. Thus, attempts by Italy to argue that its tax could be defended on the basis of Article 36 (now Article 30) were rejected by the Court. Article 36 can only be used as a defence in relation to quantitative restrictions which are caught by Article 30 (now 28). It cannot validate fiscal measures that are prohibited by Articles 9–12 (now Articles 23–25).

The emphasis in the *Italian Art* case on effect as opposed to purpose is clearly justifiable. The peremptory force of what is now Article 25 would be significantly weakened if it were open to a State to argue that a duty or charge should not be prohibited because its purpose was in some sense non-fiscal in nature. Had the Court proved receptive to this argument it would, moreover, have meant that the judiciary would have had to adjudicate on which types of social policy should be regarded as possessing a legitimate purpose sufficient to take them outside the Treaty.

The ECJ has reaffirmed its emphasis on effect rather than purpose in other cases. It has also made it clear that the Treaty provisions can be applicable even if the state measure was not designed with protectionism in mind. Thus in *Diamantarbeiders*[8] the Court considered the legality of a Belgian law requiring 0.33 per cent of the value of imported diamonds to be paid into a social fund for workers in the industry. The fact that the purpose of the fund was neither to raise money for the exchequer nor to protect domestic industry[9] did not save the charge in question. It was sufficient that the charge was imposed on goods by reason of the fact that they had crossed a border.

(b) CHARGES HAVING AN EQUIVALENT EFFECT: GENERAL PRINCIPLES

Article 25 prohibits not only customs duties, but also charges having an equivalent effect (CEE).[10] The reason is obvious. It is designed to catch protectionist measures that create a similar barrier to trade to customs duties *stricto sensu*. It is therefore unsurprising that the ECJ should have interpreted the term expansively.

Case 24/68 **Commission v. Italy**
[1969] ECR 193

[Note ToA renumbering: Arts. 9 and 12 are now Arts. 23 and 25.
Arts. 13 and 16 have been repealed]

Italy imposed a levy on goods which were exported to other Member States with the ostensible purpose of collecting statistical material for use in discerning trade patterns. The Court reiterated its holding that customs duties were prohibited irrespective of the purpose for which the duties were imposed, and irrespective of the destination of the revenues which were collected. It then continued as follows.

THE ECJ

8. The extension of the prohibition of customs duties to charges having an equivalent effect is intended to supplement the prohibition against obstacles to trade created by such duties by increasing its efficiency.

The use of these two complementary concepts thus tends, in trade between Member States, to avoid the imposition of any pecuniary charge on goods circulating within the Community by virtue of the fact that they cross a national border.

9. Thus, in order to ascribe to a charge an effect equivalent to a customs duty, it is important to consider this effect in the light of the objectives of the Treaty, in the Parts, Titles and Chapters in which Articles 9, 12, 13 and 16 are to be found, particularly in relation to the free movement of goods.

---

[8] Cases 2 and 3/69 *Sociaal Fonds voor de Diamantarbeiders* v. *SA Ch. Brachfeld & Sons* [1969] ECR 211. See also Cases 485 and 486/93 *Maria Simitzi* v. *Municipality of Kos* [1995] ECR I–2655; Cases C–441 and 442/98 *Michailidis AE* v. *IKA* [2000] ECR I–7145; Case C–293/02 *Jersey Produce Marketing Association Ltd.* v. *States of Jersey and Jersey Potato Marketing Board* [2005] ECR I–9543, paras. 55–56; Case C–72/03 *Carbonati Apuani*, n. 5 above, paras. 30–31.

[9] Belgium did not produce diamonds.

[10] R. Barents, 'Charges Having an Equivalent Effect to Customs Duties' (1978) 15 *CMLRev.* 415.

> Consequently, any pecuniary charge, however small and whatever its designation and mode of application, which is imposed unilaterally on domestic or foreign goods by reason of the fact that they cross a frontier, and which is not a customs duty in the strict sense, constitutes a charge having equivalent effect within the meaning of Articles 9, 12, 13 and 16 of the Treaty, even if it is not imposed for the benefit of the State, is not discriminatory or protective in effect and if the product on which the charge is imposed is not in competition with any domestic product.
>
> 10. It follows ... that the prohibition of new customs duties or charges having equivalent effect, linked to the principle of the free movement of goods, constitutes a fundamental rule which, without prejudice to the other provisions of the Treaty, does not permit of any exceptions.

This clear message was repeated in *Diamantarbeiders*.[11] The ECJ reiterated the broad definition of a CEE. It made it clear that this would bite whether those affected by the charge were all Community citizens, those from the importing State, or only the nationals from the State that was responsible for passing the measure under scrutiny.

These decisions signalled the Court's intent that the Articles of the Treaty concerned with customs duties and CEEs were to be taken seriously.[12] They were not to be circumvented by the form in which the charge was imposed. They were applicable whether the duty/charge discriminated or not. They had an impact irrespective of whether the product on which the charge was imposed was in competition with domestic goods, and they admitted of no exceptions.

This strident approach by the ECJ was unsurprising and warranted, given the centrality of abolishing customs duties and CEEs to the very notion of a single Community market. The abolition of such measures goes to the very heart of this Community ideal. It was a necessary first step in the attainment of market integration. Eradicating customs duties and the like was vital if the broader aims of the common market were to be fulfilled.

(c) CHARGES HAVING AN EQUIVALENT EFFECT: INSPECTIONS AND THE 'EXCHANGE EXCEPTION'

A common defence is that the charge imposed on imported goods is justified because it is merely payment for a service which the State has rendered to the importer, and that therefore it should not be regarded as a CEE. The Court has been willing to accept this argument in principle. It has however been equally alert to the fact that a State might present a charge in this way when in reality it was seeking to impede imports or in circumstances where there was no commercial exchange at all. The Court has therefore closely scrutinized such claims from States and has not readily accepted them.

Thus in *Commission* v. *Italy*,[13] considered above, the Italian Government argued that the charge should be seen as the consideration for the statistical information which it collected.

---

[11] Cases 2 and 3/69 *Diamantarbeiders*, n. 8 above.

[12] See also Case 29/72 *Marimex SpA* v. *Italian Finance Administration* [1972] ECR 1309; Case 39/73 *Rewe-Zentralfinanz* v. *Direktor der Landwirtschaftskammer Westfalen-Lippe* [1973] ECR 1039; Case C–130/93 *Lamaire NV* v. *Nationale Dienst voor Afzet van Land- en Tuinbouwprodukten* [1994] ECR I–3215; Case C–16/94 *Edouard Dubois et Fils SA* v. *Garonor Exploitation SA* [1995] ECR I–2421; Case C–72/03 *Carbonati Apuani*, n. 25 above, para. 20; Case C–234/99 *Niels Nygard* v. *Svineafgiftsfonden* [2002] ECR I–3657, para. 19.

[13] Case 24/68 [1969] ECR 193, paras. 15–16.

The Government contended that this information 'affords importers a better competitive position in the Italian market whilst exporters enjoy a similar advantage abroad';[14] and that therefore the charge should be viewed as consideration for a service rendered, as a *quid pro quo*, and not as a CEE. The Court was unconvinced. It held that the statistical information was beneficial to the whole economy and to the administrative authorities. It then continued in the following vein:[15]

> Even if the competitive position of importers and exporters were to be particularly improved as a result, the statistics still constitute an advantage so general, and so difficult to assess, that the disputed charge cannot be regarded as the consideration for a specific benefit actually conferred.

The same theme is to be found in other ECJ decisions.[16] Even when the charge *is* more directly related to some action taken by the State with respect to specific imported goods, the Court has still been reluctant to accept that the charge can be characterized as consideration for a service rendered. This is apparent from the *Bresciani* case.

Case 87/75 **Bresciani v. Amministrazione Italiana delle Finanze**
[1976] ECR 129

The Italian authorities imposed a charge for the compulsory veterinary and public-health inspections which were carried out on imported raw cowhides. Was this to be regarded as a CEE or not?

THE ECJ

6. The national court requests that the three following considerations be taken into account:
First, the fact that the charge is proportionate to the quantity of the goods and not to their value distinguishes a duty of the type at issue from charges which fall within the prohibition under Article 13 of the EEC Treaty. Second, a pecuniary charge of the type at issue is no more than the consideration required from individuals who, through their own action in importing products of animal origin, cause a service to be rendered. In the third place, although there may be differences in the method and time of its application, the duty at issue is also levied on similar products of domestic origin.

. . .

8. The justification for the obligation progressively to abolish customs duties is based on the fact that any pecuniary charge, however small, imposed on goods by reason of the fact that they cross a frontier constitutes an obstacle to the free movement of such goods.
The obligation progressively to abolish customs duties is supplemented by the obligation to abolish charges having equivalent effect in order to prevent the fundamental principle of the free movement of goods within the common market from being circumvented by the imposition of pecuniary charges of various kinds by a Member State.

---

[14] *Ibid.*, para. 15.
[15] *Ibid.*, para. 16.
[16] Case 63/74 *W. Cadsky SpA v. Istituto Nazionale per il Commercio Estero* [1975] ECR 281.

The use of these two complementary concepts thus tends, in trade between Member States, to avoid the imposition of any pecuniary charge on goods circulating within the Community by virtue of the fact that they cross a national frontier.

9. Consequently, any pecuniary charge, whatever its designation and mode of application, which is unilaterally imposed on goods imported from another Member State by reason of the fact that they cross a frontier, constitutes a charge having an effect equivalent to a customs duty. In appraising a duty of the type at issue it is, consequently, of no importance that it is proportionate to the quantity of the imported goods and not to their value.

10. Nor, in determining the effects of the duty on the free movement of goods, is it of any importance that a duty of the type at issue is proportionate to the costs of a compulsory public health inspection carried out on entry of the goods. The activity of the administration of the State intended to maintain a public health inspection system imposed in the general interest cannot be regarded as a service rendered to the importer such as to justify the imposition of a pecuniary charge. If, accordingly, public health inspections are still justified at the end of the transitional period, the costs which they occasion must be met by the general public which, as a whole benefits from the free movement of Community goods.

11. The fact that the domestic production is, through other charges, subjected to a similar burden matters little unless those charges and the duty in question are applied according to the same criteria and at the same stage of production, thus making it possible for them to be regarded as falling within a general system of internal taxation applying systematically and in the same way to domestic and imported products.

The ECJ's judgment in *Bresciani* indicates clearly its reluctance to accede to arguments that will take pecuniary charges outside the Treaty. In paragraph 9 it rejected the *first* of the Italian arguments: the fact that the charge was proportionate to the quantity of imported goods made no difference, since Article 12 (now Article 25 as amended) prohibited *any* charge imposed by reason of the fact that goods crossed a frontier.[17] The rejection of the *second* argument in paragraph 10 was equally significant. The State's argument had some plausibility: if you wish to import a product that requires health inspection, then you, the importer, should bear the cost. The Court's response was, however, unequivocal: the cost of inspections to maintain public health should be borne by the general public. It is doubtful whether this makes sense in micro-economic terms.[18] The ECJ's conclusion was, however, designed to limit the ambit of any exceptions to Articles 9–12 (now Articles 23–25). This is equally apparent in the way in which the Court disposed of the State's *third* contention. The ECJ's response is to be found in paragraph 11 of its judgment and required a strict equivalence between the charges levied on domestic and imported goods. Other attempts to employ the exchange argument have not generally proven successful.[19]

[17] A charge will be deemed to be a CEE if it is a flat-rate charge which is based on the value of the goods: Case 170/88 *Ford España* v. *Spain* [1989] ECR 2305.

[18] By placing the cost on the general public it means that the importer of the product will not have to bear what is in reality one of the costs of making that product.

[19] See, e.g., Case 43/71 *Politi SAS* v. *Italian Ministry of Finance* [1971] ECR 1039; Case 132/82 *Commission* v. *Belgium* [1983] ECR 1649; Case 340/87 *Commission* v. *Italy* [1989] ECR 1483; Case C–209/89 *Commission* v. *Italy* [1991] ECR I–3533; Case C–272/95 *Bundesantalt für Landwirtschaft und Ernährung* v. *Deutsches Milch-Kontor GmbH* [1997] ECR I–1905.

(d) CHARGES HAVING AN EQUIVALENT EFFECT: INSPECTIONS AND FULFILMENT OF MANDATORY LEGAL REQUIREMENTS

Where Community legislation *permits* an inspection to be undertaken by a State, the national authorities cannot recover any fees charged from the traders.[20] The Court has, however, accepted that a charge imposed by a State will escape the prohibition contained in Articles 9–12 (now Articles 23–25) when it is levied to cover the cost of a *mandatory* inspection required by Community law.[21]

Case 18/87 **Commission v. Germany**
[1988] ECR 5427

[Note ToA renumbering: Arts. 9–12, 36, are now Arts. 23–25, 30]

German regional authorities charged certain fees on live animals imported into the country. These charges were to cover the cost of inspections undertaken pursuant to Directive 81/389. The question arose whether they should be regarded as CEEs. The ECJ began by stating the now orthodox proposition that any pecuniary charge imposed as a result of goods crossing a frontier was caught by the Treaty, either as a customs duty or as a CEE. It then recognized an exception to this basic principle.

THE ECJ

6. However, the Court has held that such a charge escapes that classification if it relates to a general system of internal dues applied systematically and in accordance with the same criteria to domestic products and imported products alike (... Case 132/78 *Denkavit* v *France* ...), if it constitutes payment for a service in fact rendered to the economic operator of a sum in proportion to the service (... Case 158/82 *Commission* v *Denmark* ...), or again, subject to certain conditions, if it attaches to inspections carried out to fulfil obligations imposed by Community law (... Case 46/76 *Bauhuis* v *Netherlands* ...).

7. The contested fee, which is payable on importation and transit, cannot be regarded as relating to a general system of internal dues. Nor does it constitute payment for a service rendered to the operator, because this condition is satisfied only if the operator in question obtains a definite specific benefit ..., which is not the case if the inspection serves to guarantee, in the public interest, the health and life of animals in international transport. ...

8. Since the contested fee was charged in connection with inspections carried out pursuant to a Community provision, it should be noted that according to the case law of the Court ... such fees may not be classified as charges having an effect equivalent to a customs duty if the following conditions are satisfied:

(a) they do not exceed the actual costs of the inspections in connection with which they are charged;

---

[20] Case 314/82 *Commission* v. *Belgium* [1984] ECR 1543.

[21] Case 46/76 *Bauhuis* v. *Netherlands* [1977] ECR 5; Case 1/83 *IFG* v. *Freistaat Bayern* [1984] ECR 349; Case 389/00 *Commission* v. *Germany* [2003] ECR I–2001. The costs of checks carried out pursuant to mandatory obligations imposed by international conventions to which all the Member States are party are treated in the same way: Case 89/76 *Commission* v. *Netherlands* [1977] ECR 1355.

(b) the inspections in question are obligatory and uniform for all the products concerned in the Community;

(c) they are prescribed by Community law in the general interest of the Community;

(d) they promote the free movement of goods, in particular by neutralizing obstacles which could arise from unilateral measures of inspection adopted in accordance with Article 36 of the Treaty.

9. In this instance these conditions are satisfied by the contested fee. In the first place it has not been contested that it does not exceed the real cost of the inspections in connection with which it is charged.

10. Moreover, all the Member States of transit and destination are required, under, *inter alia*, Article 2(1) of Directive 81/389/EEC . . . to carry out the veterinary inspections in question when the animals are brought into their territories, and therefore the inspections are obligatory and uniform for all the animals concerned in the Community.

11. Those inspections are prescribed by Directive 81/389/EEC, which establishes the measures necessary . . . for the protection of live animals during international transport, with a view to the protection of live animals, an objective which is pursued in the general interest of the Community and not a specific interest of individual states.

12. Finally, it appears in the preambles to the . . . directives that they are intended to harmonize the laws of the Member States regarding the protection of animals in international transport in order to eliminate technical barriers resulting from disparities in the national laws. . . . In addition, failing such harmonization, each Member State was entitled to maintain or introduce, under the conditions laid down in Article 36 of the Treaty, measures restricting trade which were justified on grounds of the protection of the health and life of animals. It follows that the standardization of the inspections in question is such as to promote the free movement of goods.

13. The Commission has claimed, however, that the contested fee is to be regarded as a charge having equivalent effect to a customs duty because, in so far as fees of this type have not been harmonized, such harmonization, moreover, being unattainable in practice—their negative effect on the free movement of goods could not be compensated or, consequently, justified by the positive effects of the Community standardization of inspections.

14. In this respect, it should be noted that since the fee in question is intended solely as the financially and economically justified compensation for an obligation imposed in equal measure on all the Member States by Community law, it cannot be regarded as equivalent to a customs duty; nor, consequently, can it fall within the ambit of the prohibition laid down in Articles 9 and 12 of the Treaty.

15. The negative effects which such a fee may have on the free movement of goods in the Community can be eliminated only by virtue of Community provisions providing for the harmonization of fees, or imposing the obligation on the Member States to bear the costs entailed in the inspections or, finally, establishing that the costs in question are to be paid out of the Community budget.

(e) RECOVERY OF UNLAWFUL CHARGES

The general principle[22] is that a Member State must repay charges that have been unlawfully levied.[23] The procedural conditions for such repayment may be less favourable than those

---

[22] For more general discussion of remedies see Ch. 9.

[23] Case 199/82 *Amministrazione delle Finanze dello Stato* v. *San Giorgio* [1983] ECR 3595.

applying in actions between private individuals, provided that they apply in the same way to actions based on Community law and national law, and provided also that they do not make recovery impossible or excessively difficult.[24] There is, however, an exception to this general rule for circumstances in which the trader has passed on the loss to customers, since reimbursement could lead to the trader being unjustly enriched. This very exception may itself be qualified where the trader can, nonetheless, show that it has suffered loss.[25] The burden of proving that the duties have not been passed on to others cannot however be placed on the taxpayer.[26]

(f) THE CUSTOMS UNION: THE BROADER PERSPECTIVE

The discussion thus far has focused on the important legal issues surrounding Articles 23–25, and the limits placed on the capacity of Member States to impose duties or charges when goods cross a frontier. It would, however, be mistaken to believe that this constitutes the entirety of EC law in this area.

The *substantive importance of* customs law is far greater than this.[27] The consequence of the breaking down of customs barriers between Member States is that once goods are in the EC they move freely. The corollary is that 'the ring fence around the single market is only as strong as its weakest link', and that there is no 'second chance' to impose limits on goods coming from a third country.[28] The maintenance of effective customs control for goods coming from outside the Community is important for a number of reasons. Such goods will be subject to a tariff which is a significant part of the Community's own resources. The EC has, therefore, a strong interest in combating fraud. The fact that there is in effect only ever one customs barrier for goods to enter the EC also has implications for the battle against organized crime, counterfeit goods, and the like. It is clear moreover that customs has a role to play in the fight against terrorism.

This has led to a number of *organizational initiatives* designed to meet these new challenges. There is no Community customs service. The EC works through and with the customs authorities in the Member States. Much time has been spent on implementing the Customs 2002 Programme,[29] the object of which is that the customs administrations of the Member States should operate as efficiently and as effectively as would a single administration.[30] This is especially important in the light of enlargement. Commission initiatives from 2003,[31] endorsed by the Council,[32] have been designed to expedite customs checks through increased use of electronic communication that can be applied by the customs authorities of

[24] Case C–343/96 *Dilexport Srl* v. *Amministrazione delle Finanze dello Stato* [1999] ECR I–579.

[25] Cases C–192–218/95 *Société Comateb* v. *Directeur Général des Douanes et Droits Indirects* [1997] ECR I–165.

[26] Case C–343/96 *Dilexport*, n. 24 above, para. 52; Cases C–441 and 442/98 *Michailidis*, n. 8 above, para. 38.

[27] Communication from the Commission to the Council, the European Parliament, and the Economic and Social Committee, Concerning a Strategy for the Customs Union, COM(2001)51 final.

[28] The Changing Role of Customs (EC Commission, 2000), 1.

[29] Dec. 210/97 [1996] OJ L33/24.

[30] Commission Report to the European Parliament and the Council, On the Implementation of the Customs 2000 Programme, Doc. XXI/1065/98 EN, para. 2.1.

[31] A Simple and Paperless Environment for Customs and Trade; On the Role of Customs in the Integrated Management of External Borders, COM(2003)452 final.

[32] Council Resolution of 5 Dec. 2003, On Creating a Simple and Paperless Environment for Customs and Trade [2003] OJ C305/1.

all Member States. These have been combined with initiatives designed to use customs in order to combat crime, fraud, and terrorism and the creation of a Customs Security Programme.[33]

4. ARTICLES 90–93: DISCRIMINATORY TAX PROVISIONS

The preceding discussion has focused on Articles 23–25. It is necessary now to shift our focus to the provisions on discriminatory taxes to understand the importance of these Articles and the way in which they relate to those concerning customs duties and charges having an equivalent effect.

Article 90 (ex Article 95) is the central provision in this area. It has been directly effective since 1 January 1962.[34]

> No Member State shall impose, directly or indirectly, on the products of other Member States any internal taxation of any kind in excess of that imposed directly or indirectly on similar domestic products.
>
> Furthermore, no Member State shall impose on the products of other Member States any internal taxation of such a nature as to afford indirect protection to other products.

(a) THE PURPOSE OF ARTICLE 90

The aim of Article 90 can be stated quite simply: it is to prevent the objectives of Articles 23–25 from being undermined by discriminatory internal taxation. We have already seen that Articles 23–25 are designed to prevent customs duties, or charges equivalent thereto, from impeding the free flow of goods. The Treaty outlaws such measures, whatever legal form they assume, when they are imposed as a result of a product *crossing a frontier*. These provisions would, however, be to little avail if it were open to a State to prejudice foreign products once they were *inside* its own territory by levying discriminatory taxes, thereby disadvantaging those imported products in competition with domestic goods. Article 90 is designed to prevent this from happening, and this has been recognized by the ECJ, which demands complete neutrality of internal taxation as regards domestic and imported products.[35]

---

[33] Available at http://ec.europa.eu/taxation_customs/customs/policy_issues/customs_security/index_en.htm; Reg. (EC) 648/2005 of the European Parliament and of the Council of 13 Apr. 2005, Amending Council Reg. 2913/92 Establishing the Community Customs Code [2005] OJ L117/13.

[34] Case 57/65 *Alfons Lütticke GmbH v. Hauptzollamt Saarlouis* [1966] ECR 205; Case 28/67 *Mölkerei-Zentrale Westfalen/Lippe GmbH v. Hauptzollamt Paderborn* [1968] ECR 143; Case 74/76 *Ianelli & Volpi v. Meroni* [1977] ECR 557.

[35] Cases 2 and 3/62 *Commission v. Belgium and Luxembourg* [1962] ECR 425, 431; Case 252/86 *Gabriel Bergandi v. Directeur Général des Impôts* [1988] ECR 1343, 1374; Case C–101/00 *Tulliasiamies and Antti Siilin* [2002] ECR I–7487, para. 52; Case C–387/01 *Weigel and Weigel v. Finanzlandirektion für Vorarlberg* [2004] ECR I–4981, para. 66; Cases C–393/04 and 41/05 *Air Liquide Industries Belgium SA v. Ville de Seraing and Province de Liege* [2006] ECR I–5293, paras. 55–57.

(b) ARTICLE 90(1): DIRECT DISCRIMINATION

Article 90(1) (ex Article 95(1)) does not stipulate that a Member State must adopt any particular regime of internal taxation. It requires only that whatever system is chosen should be applied without discrimination to similar imported products.

Thus in *Commission v. Italy*[36] the Italian Government charged lower taxes on regenerated oil than on ordinary oil. The policy was motivated by ecological considerations, but imported regenerated oil did not benefit from the same advantage. In its defence Italy argued that it was not possible to determine whether imported oil was regenerated or not. This argument was rejected by the ECJ, which held that it was for the importers to show that their oil came within the relevant category, subject to reasonable standards of proof, and that a certificate from the State of export could be employed to identify the nature of the oil. Similarly in the *Hansen* case[37] the ECJ insisted that a German rule making tax relief available to spirits made from fruit by small businesses and collective farms must be equally applicable to spirits in the same category coming from elsewhere in the Community.[38]

The rules relating to non-discrimination with respect to the payment of taxes will also be broken if the procedure for collection of the tax treats domestic goods and those which come from another Member State unequally.[39] This is demonstrated by *Commission v. Ireland*.[40] In this case, although the tax applied to all goods irrespective of origin, domestic producers were treated more leniently as regards payment, being allowed a number of weeks before payment was actually demanded, whereas importers had to pay the duty directly on importation.

(c) ARTICLE 90(1): INDIRECT DISCRIMINATION

The discussion thus far has focused on cases of direct discrimination under Article 90(1), where the contested measure explicitly treated domestic goods and imports differently to the detriment of the latter. It is, however, clear that indirect discrimination may be caught by this Article. There may well be tax rules that do not on their face differentiate between the tax liability of goods based on country of origin, but which nonetheless do place a greater burden on commodities coming from another Member State. The ECJ has emphasized that a tax system will be compatible with Article 90 only if it excludes 'any possibility' of imported products being taxed more heavily than similar domestic goods.[41]

---

[36] Case 21/79 [1980] ECR 1.

[37] Case 148/77 *H. Hansen* v. *Hauptzollamt Flensburg* [1978] ECR 1787.

[38] See also Case 196/85 *Commission* v. *France* [1987] ECR 1597; Case C–327/90 *Commission* v. *Greece* [1992] ECR I–3033; Case C–375/95 *Commission* v. *Greece* [1997] ECR I–5981.

[39] See, e.g., Cases C–290 and 333/05 *Nadasdi* v. *Vam-es Penzugyorseg Eszak-Alfoldi Regionalis Parancnoksaga* [2006] ECR I–10115.

[40] Case 55/79 [1980] ECR 481; Case C–68/96 *Grundig Italiana SpA* v. *Ministero delle Finanze* [1998] ECR I–3775.

[41] Case C–228/98 *Dounias* v. *Oikonomikon* [2000] ECR I–577, para. 41; Case C–265/99 *Commission* v. *French Republic* [2001] ECR I–2305, para. 40; Case C–101/00 *Tulliasiamies*, n. 35 above, para. 52.

Case 112/84 **Humblot v. Directeur des Services Fiscaux**
[1985] ECR 1367

[Note ToA renumbering: Art. 95 is now Art. 90]

French law imposed an annual car tax. The criterion for the amount of tax to be paid was the power rating of the car. Below a 16CV rating the tax increased gradually to a maximum of 1,100 francs. For cars above 16CV in power there was a flat rate of 5,000 francs. There was no French car which was rated above 16CV, and therefore the higher charge was borne only by those who had imported cars. Humblot was charged the 5,000 francs on a 36CV imported vehicle, and argued that this tax violated Article 95 (now Article 90).

THE ECJ

12. It is appropriate in the first place to stress that as Community law stands at present the Member States are at liberty to subject products such as cars to a system of road tax which increases progressively in amount depending on an objective criterion, such as the power rating for tax purposes, which may be determined in various ways.

13. Such a system of domestic taxation is, however, compatible with Article 95 only in so far as it is free from any discriminatory or protective effect.

14. That is not true of a system like the one at issue in the main proceedings. Under that system there are two distinct taxes: a differential tax which increases progressively and is charged on cars not exceeding a given power rating for tax purposes and a fixed tax on cars exceeding that rating which is almost five times as high as the highest rate of the differential tax. Although the system embodies no formal distinction based on the origin of the products it manifestly exhibits discriminatory or protective features contrary to Article 95, since the power rating determining liability to the special tax has been fixed at a level such that only imported cars, in particular from other Member States, are subject to the special tax whereas all cars of domestic manufacture are liable to the distinctly more advantageous differential tax.

15. In the absence of considerations relating to the amount of the special tax, consumers seeking comparable cars as regards such matters as size, comfort, actual power, maintenance costs, durability, fuel consumption and price would naturally choose from among cars above and below the critical power rating laid down by French law. However, liability to the special tax entails a much larger increase in taxation than passing from one category of car to another in a system of progressive taxation embodying balanced differentials like the system on which the differential tax is based. The resultant additional taxation is liable to cancel out the advantages which certain cars imported from other Member States might have in consumers' eyes over comparable cars of domestic manufacture, particularly since the special tax continues to be payable for several years. In that respect the special tax reduces the amount of competition to which cars of domestic manufacture are subject and hence is contrary to the principle of neutrality with which domestic taxation must comply.

The *Humblot* case provides a good example of the ECJ's determination to catch indirect as well as direct discrimination. Its reasoning is cogent, demonstrating as it does the way in which such tax provisions can distort the competitive process in the car market. The French authorities duly revised the tax rules in the light of the Court's decision, but the new scheme was challenged and found to be in breach of Community law. Under this new regime the French authorities replaced the 5,000 franc tax for cars above 16CV with nine more specific tax bands, the application of which was dependent on the power of the car. Although this scheme was less obviously discriminatory than that condemned in *Humblot*, it was still the case that the tax rate increased sharply above 16CV. This new tax system was therefore condemned in *Feldain*.[42]

(d) ARTICLE 90: NATIONAL AUTONOMY AND FISCAL CHOICES

While the Treaty prohibits indirect as well as direct discrimination under Article 90(1), it may be necessary to determine which is in issue in any particular case, because while direct discrimination on grounds of nationality cannot be justified, tax rules of a Member State that tend nonetheless to favour the national producers may be saved if there is some *objective justification*. This idea of objective justification is one which recurs in relation to other Articles concerning, for example, free movement of goods, free movement of workers, and competition policy.[43] The essential idea is that the Court will allow the defence to plead that there was some objective policy reason, which is acceptable to the Community, to justify the State's action. In this way such Treaty Articles are prevented from becoming too harsh or draconian in their application. The *Chemial* case exemplifies this judicial approach.

Case 140/79 **Chemial Farmaceutici v. DAF SpA**
[1981] ECR 1[44]

Italy taxed synthetic ethyl alcohol more highly than ethyl alcohol obtained from fermentation. This was so even though the products could be used interchangeably. Italy was not a major producer of the synthetic product. The object was to favour the manufacture of ethyl alcohol from agricultural products, and to restrain the processing into alcohol of ethylene, a petroleum derivative, in order to reserve that raw material for more important economic uses. The Court made the following observations on this policy choice.

THE ECJ

13. ... It accordingly constitutes a legitimate choice of economic policy to which effect is given by fiscal means. The implementation of that policy does not lead to any discrimination since although it results in discouraging imports of synthetic alcohol into Italy, it also has the consequence of hampering the development in Italy itself of production of alcohol from ethylene, that production being technically perfectly feasible.

14. As the Court has stated on many occasions ... in its present stage of development Community law does not restrict the freedom of each Member State to lay down tax arrangements which differentiate between certain products on the basis of objective criteria, such as the nature of the raw materials used or the production process employed. Such differentiation is compatible with Community law if it pursues economic policy objectives which are themselves compatible with the requirements of the Treaty and its secondary law and if the detailed

---

42 Case 433/85 *Feldain* v. *Directeur des Services Fiscaux* [1987] ECR 3536; Case 76/87 *Seguela* v. *Administration des Impôts* [1988] ECR 2397; Case C–265/99, n. 41 above.

43 See Chs. 19, 21, and 27.

44 See also Case 46/80 *Vinal SpA* v. *Orbat SpA* [1981] ECR 77.

rules are such as to avoid any form of discrimination, direct or indirect, in regard to imports from other Member States or any form of protection of competing domestic products.

15. Differential taxation such as that which exists in Italy for denatured synthetic alcohol on the one hand and denatured alcohol obtained by fermentation on the other satisfies these requirements. It appears in fact that that system of taxation pursues an objective of legitimate industrial policy in that it is such as to promote the distillation of agricultural products as against the manufacture of alcohol from petroleum derivatives. That choice does not conflict with the rules of Community law or the requirements of a policy decided within the framework of the Community.

16. The detailed provisions of the legislation at issue before the national court cannot be considered as discriminatory since, on the one hand, it is not disputed that imports from other Member States of alcohol by fermentation qualify for the same tax treatment as Italian alcohol produced by fermentation and, on the other hand, although the rate of tax prescribed for synthetic alcohol results in restraining the importation of synthetic alcohol originating in other Member States, it has an equivalent economic effect in the national territory in that it also hampers the establishment of profitable production of the same product in Italian industry.

It is true that the Court predicates its acceptance of the Italian policy on the basis that it does not result in any discrimination, whether direct or indirect. Notwithstanding this, the ECJ's reasoning bears testimony to its willingness to accept objective justifications where the national policy is acceptable from the Community's perspective, even if this benefits domestic traders more than importers. It is clear, as the Court points out, that the Italian policy would hamper an Italian producer that wished to make synthetic ethylene alcohol. However, there was little domestic production of that product, and therefore the Italian tax hit importers harder than firms based in Italy. The same reasoning can be seen in other decisions.

Thus in *Commission* v. *France* the Commission[45] alleged that a French rule which taxed sweet wines produced in a traditional manner at a lower rate than liqueur wines was contrary to what is now Article 90. The Court disagreed. It found that there was no direct discrimination on grounds of origin or nationality. Sweet wines made in the natural manner tended to be produced in areas where the growing conditions were less than optimal; there would often be poor soil and low rainfall. The rationale for the French policy was to provide some fiscal incentives for production in these areas. The Court was willing to accept that this could constitute an objective justification. In *Outokumpu Oy*[46] the ECJ held that it was legitimate for a Member State to tax the same or similar product differentially, provided that this was done on the basis of objective criteria, such as the nature of the raw materials used or the production process employed. Article 90 did not preclude differential tax rates on electricity where they were based on environmental considerations, provided that there was no discrimination against imports.[47]

It is, moreover, possible for differential tax rates on cars, the *Humblot* case notwithstanding, to escape the prohibition of Article 90. This could be so if the differential rates were to encourage the use of more environmentally friendly models, provided that they did not discriminate against imports. This is exemplified by *Commission* v. *Greece*.[48] The ECJ was once again faced with a national fiscal measure that imposed a progressively higher tax based on the cylinder capacity of the car. It held that this would not constitute a breach of what is now Article 90

---

[45] Case 196/85 [1987] ECR 1597.

[46] Case C–213/96 [1998] ECR I–1777.

[47] A. Easson, 'Fiscal Discrimination: New Perspectives on Article 95 of the EEC Treaty' (1981) 18 *CMLRev.* 521.

[48] Case C–132/88 [1990] ECR I–1567; Case C–421/97 *Tarantik* v. *Direction des Services Fiscaux de Seine-et-Marne* [1999] ECR I–3633.

unless it was discriminatory, and this would not be the case unless it both discouraged customers from buying highly taxed imported cars and encouraged them to buy domestic cars instead. The mere fact that all cars in the highest tax bracket were imported was not sufficient to establish a violation of Article 90. EC law did not prohibit the use of tax policy to attain social ends, provided that the tax was based on an objective criterion, was not discriminatory, and did not have a protective effect.

(e) THE RELATIONSHIP BETWEEN ARTICLE 90(1) AND 90(2)

Article 90(1) prohibits the imposition of internal taxes on products from other Member States in excess of those levied on *similar* domestic products. Thus once the two relevant products are judged to be similar then Article 90(1) bites, with the consequence that excessive taxes levied on the imported goods are banned. The dividing line between Article 90(1) and 90(2) may be problematic, since it will obviously be a contestable issue whether goods are deemed to be similar or not. This issue will be addressed below.

Article 90(2) is designed to catch national tax provisions that apply unequal tax ratings to goods that may not be strictly similar, but which may nonetheless be in competition with each other. The object is to prevent these differential tax ratings from affording indirect protection to the domestic goods. Thus, wine and beer may not be similar goods as such, but there may, notwithstanding this, be some competition between them. Economists term this relationship cross-elasticity of demand: as the price of one product rises in relation to another, so consumers switch to the lower-priced product. The extent to which they switch will depend on factors such as the price difference between the products, and the degree to which consumers perceive them to be interchangeable. If a State that produces little wine but much beer taxes the former considerably higher than the latter, then wine sellers will be relatively disadvantaged and beer producers afforded indirect protection. The relationship between Article 90(1) and (2) is brought out in the following case.

Case 168/78 **Commission v. France**
[1980] ECR 347

[Note ToA renumbering: Arts. 9 to 17 have been replaced by Arts. 23 to 25;
Art. 95 is now 90; Art. 169 is now Art. 226]

France had higher tax rates for spirits based on grain, such as whisky, rum, gin, and vodka, than those based on wine or fruit, such as cognac, calvados, and armagnac. France produced very little of the former category of drinks, but was a major producer of fruit-based spirits. The Commission brought an Article 169 action alleging that the French tax regime violated Article 95. The ECJ emphasized the connection between Article 95 and Articles 9 to 17 as they then were: Article 95 was to supplement the provisions on customs duties and charges by prohibiting internal taxation which discriminated against imported products. It continued as follows.

THE ECJ

5. The first paragraph of Article 95, which is based on a comparison of the tax burdens imposed on domestic products and on imported products which may be classified as 'similar',

is the basic rule in this respect. This provision, as the Court has had occasion to emphasize in its judgment . . . in Case 148/77, *H. Hansen* v. *Haupzollamt Flensburg* [1978] ECR 1787, must be interpreted widely so as to cover all taxation procedures which conflict with the principle of the equality of treatment of domestic products and imported products; it is therefore necessary to interpret the concept of 'similar products' with sufficient flexibility. The Court specified in the judgment . . . in the *Rewe* case (Case 45/75 [1976] ECR 181) that it is necessary to consider as similar products those which 'have similar characteristics and meet the same needs from the point of view of consumers'. It is therefore necessary to determine the scope of the first paragraph of Article 95 on the basis not of the criterion of the strictly identical nature of the products but on that of their similar and comparable use.

6. The function of the second paragraph of Article 95 is to cover, in addition, all forms of indirect tax protection in the case of products which, without being similar within the meaning of the first paragraph, are nevertheless in competition, even partial, indirect or potential, with certain products of the importing country. The Court has already emphasized certain aspects of that provision in . . . Case 27/77, *Firma Fink-Frucht GmbH* . . . [1978] ECR 223, in which it stated that for the purposes of the application of the first paragraph of Article 95 it is sufficient for the imported product to be in competition with the protected domestic production by reason of one of several economic uses to which it may be put, even though the condition of similarity for the purposes of the first paragraph of Article 95 is not fulfilled.

7. Whilst the criterion indicated in the first paragraph of Article 95 consists in the comparison of tax burdens, whether in terms of the rate, the mode of assessment or other detailed rules for the application thereof, in view of the difficulty of making sufficiently precise comparisons between the products in question, the second paragraph of that Article is based upon a more general criterion, in other words the protective nature of the system of internal taxation.

(f) ARTICLE 90(1) AND (2): THE DETERMINATION OF SIMILARITY

It is clear from the preceding discussion that the first step is therefore to determine whether the products are similar. If they are then Article 90(1) applies; if they are not then the tax rules may still be caught by Article 90(2). This issue has arisen in a number of cases. In an early judgment the ECJ held that products would be regarded as similar if they came within the same tax classification.[49] However, in some cases the ECJ condemned the tax without too detailed an analysis of whether this was because of Article 90(1) or (2). This approach is particularly apparent in the early 'spirits cases', in which the Commission brought a number of Article 169 (now Article 226) actions against Member States, alleging that their tax rules on spirits infringed what is now Article 90.[50] The reason the ECJ did not trouble unduly whether the condemnation should be based on Article 90(1) or (2) is

---

[49] Case 27/67 *Fink-Frucht GmbH* v. *Hauptzollamt München-Landsbergerstrasse* [1968] ECR 327.

[50] See also Case 169/78 *Commission* v. *Italy* [1980] ECR 385; Case 171/78 *Commission* v. *Denmark* [1980] ECR 447.

apparent in the following extract:

Case 168/78 **Commission v. France**
[1980] ECR 347

[Note ToA renumbering: Art. 95 is now Art. 90]

The facts have been set out above. The Commission argued that all spirits constituted a single market. France responded by contending that they should be broken down into a number of more specific markets, depending on their composition, physical characteristics and consumer usages. The ECJ, having considered the characteristics of the spirits, decided, on the one hand, that they possessed certain generic features (such as high alcohol content); and on the other hand, that they were made from differing materials, and were consumed in different ways.

THE ECJ

12. Two conclusions follow from this analysis of the market in spirits. First, there is, in the case of spirits considered as a whole, an indeterminate number of beverages which must be classified as 'similar products' within the meaning of the first paragraph of Article 95, although it may be difficult to decide this in specific cases, in view of the nature of the factors implied by distinguishing criteria such as flavour and consumer habits. Secondly, even in cases in which it is impossible to recognize a sufficient degree of similarity between the products concerned, there are nevertheless, in the case of all spirits, common characteristics which are sufficiently pronounced to accept that in all cases there is at least partial or potential competition. It follows that the application of the second paragraph of Article 95 may come into consideration in cases in which the relationship of similarity between the specific varieties of spirits remains doubtful or contested.

13. It appears from the foregoing that Article 95, taken as a whole, may apply without distinction to all the products concerned. It is sufficient therefore to examine whether the application of a given national tax system is discriminatory or, as the case may be, protective, in other words whether there is a difference in the rate or the detailed rules for levying the tax and whether that difference is likely to favour a given national production.

[*The Court then considered various arguments adduced by the French authorities designed to show that the spirits differed in terms of taste, use, and the like.*]

39. After considering all these factors the Court deems it unnecessary for the purposes of solving this dispute to give a ruling on the question whether or not the spiritous beverages concerned are wholly or partially similar products within the meaning of the first paragraph of Article 95 when it is impossible reasonably to contest that without exception they are in at least partial competition with the domestic products to which the application refers and that it is impossible to deny the protective nature of the French tax system within the second paragraph of Article 95.

40. In fact, as indicated above, spirits obtained from cereals have, as products obtained from distillation, sufficient characteristics in common with other spirits to constitute at least in certain circumstances an alternative choice for consumers. . . .

41. As the competitive and substitution relationships between the beverages in question are such, the protective nature of the tax system criticized by the Commission is clear. A characteristic of that system is in fact that an essential part of domestic production, . . . spirits

obtained from wine and fruit, come within the most favourable tax category whereas at least two types of product, almost all of which are imported from other Member States, are subject to higher taxation under the 'manufacturing tax'.

These early 'spirits' cases demonstrate that the Court will not be overly concerned whether a case is characterized as relating to Article 90(1) or (2) if the nature of the products renders such classification difficult (paragraph 12 above); and if the Court feels that the tax should be condemned because the goods are in competition and the tax is protective (paragraph 39 above).

This approach can however be problematic. The consequence of 'globalizing'[51] Article 90(1) and (2) in this manner is that it obscures the appropriate response of the infringing State. A breach of Article 90(1) means that the offending State has to equalize the taxes on domestic and imported goods. Breach of Article 90(2) requires the State to remove the protective effect, but this may not entail equalization of the tax burdens on the respective goods.

Later courts have been more careful to determine whether the analysis should proceed under Article 90(1) or (2), as exemplified by *John Walker* v. *Ministeriet for Skatter*.[52] The issue was whether liqueur fruit wine was similar to whisky for the purposes of what is now Article 90(1). The ECJ analysed the objective characteristics of the products, their alcohol content and method of manufacture, and consumer perceptions of the product. It decided that the goods were not similar, since they did not possess the same alcohol content, nor was the process of manufacture the same. Further scrutiny of the tax would therefore have to be pursuant to Article 90(2).[53] The same approach can be perceived in *Commission* v. *Italy*.[54] The Commission brought an action against Italy claiming that its consumption tax on fruit was discriminatory under what is now Article 90. Italy produced large amounts of fruit, such as apples, pears, peaches, plums, and oranges, but almost no bananas, which were imported from France. Italy imposed a consumption tax on bananas that was almost half the import price; other fruit was not subject to the tax. The Court considered whether bananas and other fruit were similar for the purposes of Article 90(1). It found that they were not, taking account of the objective characteristics of the products, including their organoleptic properties and the extent to which they could satisfy the same consumer need.[55] Further examination of the Italian tax would have to be under what is now Article 90(2).

(g) ARTICLE 90(2): THE DETERMINATION OF PROTECTIVE EFFECT

One of the original 'spirits' cases was against the UK for discriminatory taxation of wine with respect to beer. This was more difficult than the other cases within this category, since there is undoubtedly a greater difference between wine and beer than between two spirits. It is for this reason that the ECJ initially declined to rule that the UK provisions were in breach of Article 95 (now Article 90), and required further information on the nature of the competitive relationship between the two products. Its judgment was finally delivered some years later, and

---

51 Easson, n. 47 above, 521, 535.
52 Case 243/84 [1986] ECR 875.
53 Cf. Case 106/84 *Commission* v. *Denmark* [1986] ECR 833.
54 Case 184/85 [1987] ECR 2013.
55 Bananas do not have the same water content as other fruit, and therefore their thirst-quenching qualities are not the same; and bananas were perceived to have a nutritional value in excess of other fruit: *ibid.*, para. 10.

provides insights in to the way in which the Court approaches the difficult adjudicatory problems presented by this Article.

Case 170/78 **Commission v. United Kingdom**
[1983] ECR 2265

[Note ToA renumbering: Arts. 95 and 169 are now Arts. 90 and 226 respectively]

The UK levied an excise tax on certain wines that was roughly five times that levied on beer. The tax on wine represented about 38 per cent of the sale price of the product, as compared to the tax on beer which was 25 per cent of the product's price. The UK produces considerable amounts of beer, but very little wine. The Commission brought an Article 169 action, claiming that the differential excise tax was in breach of Article 95.

THE ECJ

8. As regards the question of competition between wine and beer, the Court considered that, to a certain extent at least, the two beverages in question were capable of meeting identical needs, so that it had to be acknowledged that there was a degree of substitution for one another. It pointed out that, for the purpose of measuring the possible degree of substitution, attention should not be confined to consumer habits in a Member State or in a given region. Those habits, which were essentially variable in time and space, could not be considered to be immutable; the tax policy of a Member State must not therefore crystallize given consumer habits so as to consolidate an advantage acquired by national industries concerned to respond to them.

9. The Court nonetheless recognized that, in view of the substantial differences between wine and beer, it was difficult to compare the manufacturing processes and the natural properties of those beverages, as the Government of the United Kingdom had rightly observed. For that reason, the Court requested the parties to provide additional information with a view to dispelling the doubts which existed concerning the nature of the competitive relationship between the two products.

. . .

11. The Italian Government contended in that connection that it was inappropriate to compare beer with wines of average alcoholic strength or, *a fortiori*, with wines of greater alcoholic strength. In its opinion, it was the lightest wines with an alcoholic strength in the region of 9, that is to say the most popular and cheapest wines, which were genuinely in competition with beer. . . .

12. The Court considers that observation by the Italian Government to be pertinent. In view of the substantial differences in the quality and, therefore, in the price of wines, the decisive competitive relationship between beer, a popular and widely consumed beverage, and wine must be established by reference to those wines which are the most accessible to the public at large, that is to say, generally speaking the lightest and cheapest varieties. Accordingly, that is the appropriate basis for making fiscal comparisons by reference to the alcoholic strength or to the price of the two beverages in question.

[*The Commission, Italy, and the UK differed as regards the criteria which should be used to determine whether the tax on the two products was discriminatory. The Commission argued that assessment of the tax burden should be based on volume plus alcohol content; Italy contended that volume alone should be determinative; while the UK argued that the true basis of comparison was product price net of tax. The ECJ held that none of these tests was sufficient in itself, but that all three could provide 'significant information for the assessment of the contested tax system'.]*

26. After considering the information provided by the parties, the Court has come to the conclusion that, if a comparison is made on the basis of those wines which are cheaper than the types of wine selected by the United Kingdom and of which several varieties are sold in significant quantities on the United Kingdom market, it becomes apparent that precisely those wines which, in view of their price, are most directly in competition with domestic beer production are subject to a considerably higher tax burden.

27. It is clear, therefore, . . .—whatever criterion for comparison is used, there being no need to express a preference for one or the other—that the United Kingdom's tax system has the effect of subjecting wine imported from other Member States to an additional burden so as to afford protection to domestic beer production . . . Since such protection is most marked in the case of the most popular wines, the effect of the United Kingdom tax system is to stamp wine with the hallmarks of a luxury product which, in view of the tax burden which it bears, can scarcely constitute in the eyes of the consumer a genuine alternative to the typically produced domestic beverage.

28. It follows . . . that, by levying excise duty on still light wines made from fresh grapes at a higher rate, in relative terms, than on beer, the United Kingdom has failed to fulfil its obligations under the second paragraph of Article 95 of the EEC Treaty.

The decision in the UK *Wine/Beer* case throws interesting light on the Court's methodology when adjudicating on Article 90(2). Its judgment proceeds in two stages.[56]

At the first stage the ECJ is concerned to establish that there is some competitive relationship between the two products in order to render Article 90(2) applicable at all (paragraphs 8–12). The ECJ rightly accepted that the meaningful comparison was between beer and the cheaper end of the wine market. Product substitutability is central in this respect. However, the degree to which consumers currently perceive the two products to be substitutable will not be regarded as fixed for all time (paragraph 8). Consumer preferences are not immutable, and are affected by, *inter alia*, the relative tax rates of the two products. If the varying taxes levied on the commodities serve to place them artificially within separate categories in consumers' eyes, this will correspondingly reduce the extent to which the buying public perceives the products to be substitutable. It is this which the Court has in mind when castigating the UK tax policy for stamping wine with the hallmark of being a luxury product which is in a different category from beer (paragraph 27).

At the second stage, the Court then considered whether the tax system was protective of beer. It was willing to apply varying criteria suggested by the parties to decide whether a protective effect had been established or not. It was difficult on the facts to contest the conclusion that the UK tax was discriminatory. Where the disparity in tax rates between the two products is less dramatic than that between wine and beer, more finely tuned analysis may be required to determine whether there is any protective effect.[57] Thus it may, for example, be necessary to determine the degree of cross-elasticity between the two products. If this is low, then only a

---

[56] The same two stages can be perceived in other decisions concerning Art. 90(2): Case 184/85, n. 54 above, paras. 11–15.

[57] The existence of a tax differential between a domestic and an imported product will not, however, always suffice to establish protectionism for the purposes of Art. 90(2). Thus, where the tax differential was small and the cost of the two products was substantially different, no breach of Art. 90(2) was found: Case 356/85 *Commission v. Belgium* [1987] ECR 3299.

'large difference in tax burdens will have a protective tendency'.[58] Similarly, if the level of tax is low with respect to the final selling price of the goods, then it will take a very significant tax differential to have any protective impact.[59]

The existence of Community harmonization will not preclude the application of Article 90 where it is only minimum harmonization. Thus in *Socridis*[60] Community legislation was held to require only that Member States imposed a minimum duty on beer. It did not preclude the application of Article 90 to determine whether a State was being protectionist in its treatment of beer as opposed to wine.

(h) TAXATION: THE BROADER LEGAL PERSPECTIVE

The discussion thus far has been concerned with taxation and Article 90. It is however important to realize that tax issues can be judged for compliance with other Treaty provisions concerning free movement.[61] This is significant because, while the approach under Article 90 is discrimination-based, the case law on free movement has moved beyond this to catch national rules that impede trade even if they are not discriminatory. This has placed the ECJ in something of a dilemma, having to choose whether to preserve coherence in its case law on free movement, even when concerned with fiscal or tax measures; or whether to follow the disparate impact approach in accordance with Article 90 when dealing with analogous situations that arise relating to, for example, capital or services.[62] The case law is not entirely clear, but the ECJ has been cautious about applying the full force of its case law on free movement to national fiscal rules.[63]

(i) TAXATION: THE BROADER POLITICAL PERSPECTIVE

The discussion thus far has concentrated on the legal constraints imposed by the Treaty on the taxation policies of the Member States, in order to prevent discrimination against imports. It is important, as in the case of the customs union, to place this material in a broader perspective.

Taxation can be direct or indirect. The paradigm of direct taxation is income tax; the paradigm of indirect taxation is a tax on sales. The EC does not exercise any general control over direct taxation. This is regarded as central to sovereignty. EC law will be of relevance only to prevent cross-border discrimination, interference with free movement, and the like, although some tax matters have been dealt with through Articles 94 and 95, where the conditions liad down therein have been satisfied.[64] The sensitivity of tax matters is reflected in the requirement

---

[58] Easson, n. 47 above, 539.

[59] *Ibid.*

[60] Case C–166/98 *Société Critouridienne de Distribution (Socridis)* v. *Receveur Principal des Douanes* [1999] ECR I–3791.

[61] See, e.g., Case C–391/97 *Gschwind* [1999] ECR I–5451, free movement of workers; Case C–376/03 *D* v. *Inspecteur van de Belastingdienst/Particulieren/Ondernerningen/ buitenland te Heerlen* [2005] ECR I–5821, free movement of capital; Case C–290/95 *Futura Participations SA* v. *Administration des Contributions* [1997] ECR I–2471, freedom of establishment.

[62] See, e.g., Case C–134/03 *Viacom Outdoor Srl* v. *Giotto Immobilier SARL* [2005] ECR I–1167; Cases C–544 and 545/03 *Mobistar SA* v. *Commune de Fleron* [2005] ECR I–7723.

[63] J. Snell, 'Non-discriminatory Tax Obstacles in Community Law' (2007) 56 *ICLQ* 339.

[64] See http://ec.europa.eu/taxation_customs/taxation/gen_info/tax_policy/index_en.htm.

of unanimity that still prevails even after the Nice Treaty. EC law has a much greater impact on indirect taxation. Value Added Tax (VAT) was the first such tax to be harmonized in 1977. This was because the 'proper functioning of the internal market requires VAT and excise systems that are efficient and fully reflect the needs of EU businesses and consumers'.[65]

The Community is now striving for a more coherent tax policy.[66] In the context of indirect taxation, this is manifest in proposed improvements to the existing regimes governing VAT, excise duty, and the like. In the context of indirect and direct taxation, there is the growing realization of the extent to which national tax policy can impact on other policies, over which the Community does have competence. These include employment, the environment, economic and monetary union, health, and consumer protection.[67]

The tension this produces is readily apparent in the Commission's language. It recognized that there is no need for 'across the board harmonization of Member States' tax systems', that Member States are free to choose the 'tax systems they consider most appropriate and according to their preferences'.[68] It cautioned, however, that the level of public expenditure was a matter for national preference, so long as the budget remained in balance. It emphasized that Member States' choices did not take place in isolation and that international aspects should be taken into account. It reaffirmed the need for a high degree of harmonization in relation to indirect taxation. It admitted also that some harmonization of the tax treatment accorded to pay might be necessary[69] in order to remove obstacles to free movement, as in the case of occupational pensions.

The Commission was candid about the difficulties of securing the passage of Community legislation, given the obstacle of unanimity. It is unsurprising that the Commission has always advocated a shift to qualified-majority voting,[70] all the more so in the light of enlargement. What is particularly interesting is the Commission's willingness to talk openly about other mechanisms for achieving its objectives, given the difficulties of securing agreement in the Council.[71] The Commission considered in detail a range of options including greater use of Article 226, resort to soft law, and use of the enhanced co-operation procedure.[72]

5. THE BOUNDARY BETWEEN ARTICLES 23–25 AND 90–93

The relationship between Articles 23–25 and Articles 90–93 has been touched on in the preceding analysis. It is now time to consider this in more detail.

The general principle is that the two sets of Articles are mutually exclusive.[73] They both concern the imposition of fiscal charges by the State. Articles 23–25 bite on those duties or

[65] Tax Policy in the European Union—Priorities for the Years Ahead, COM(2001)260 final, para. 3.1.

[66] *Ibid.*, para. 1.

[67] Commission, Tax Policy in the European Union (2000), 8–9; Commission, The Key, Taxation and Customs Union, No. 15, Mar. 2001.

[68] Tax Policy in the European Union, n. 65 above, para. 2.4.

[69] *Ibid.*, para. 2.4.

[70] See http://ec.europa.eu/taxation_customs/taxation/gen_info/tax_law/conference/index_en.htm.

[71] Tax Policy in the European Union, n. 65 above, paras. 4.1–4.4.

[72] For more recent initiatives see Tackling the corporation tax obstacles of small and medium-sized enterprises in the Internal Market—outline of a possible Home State Taxation Pilot Scheme, COM(2005)702; Implementing the Community Lisbon Programme: Progress to date and next steps towards a Common Consolidated Corporate Tax Base (CCCTB), COM(2006)157.

[73] Case 10/65 *Deutschmann v. Federal Republic of Germany* [1965] ECR 469; Case 57/65 *Lütticke*, n. 34 above; Case 105/76 *Interzuccheri SpA v. Ditta Rezzano e Cavassa* [1977] ECR 1029.

charges levied as a result of goods crossing a border. The duty or charge is exacted at the time of, or on account of, the importation, and is borne specifically by the imported product to the exclusion of similar domestic products.[74] Articles 90–93, by way of contrast, are designed to catch fiscal policy which is internal to the State: they prevent discrimination against goods once they have entered a particular Member State. The Court has construed both sets of provisions so as to ensure that there is no gap between them.

Which set of Treaty Articles is applicable is however of importance, since the result can be significant for the legal test that is applied.[75] If a State fiscal measure is caught by Article 25 then it will be unlawful. This reflects the importance of breaking down trade barriers. Customs duties or charges are the quintessential barriers to the establishment of a customs union, and hence the Treaty's insistence that they should be removed. If, by way of contrast, a fiscal measure falls within Article 90 then the obligation on the State is different. The taxation levels set by the State are not unlawful under the Treaty, and thus the inquiry will be whether the tax discriminates against the importer under Article 90(1), or has a protective effect under Article 90(2). In most circumstances there will be little difficulty in determining whether the case should fall under Article 25 or under Article 90. Certain situations are however more difficult. Three are worthy of mention here.

The *first type of case* which can be problematic is that in which a State imposes a levy on an importer. Such a case would normally be decided on the basis of Article 25, and the levy would be deemed to be a CEE. The State would be condemned unless it could show that the levy was consideration for a service given to the importer, or that it was imposed pursuant to mandatory requirements of Community law.[76] Attempts to argue that the levy should instead be considered under Article 90, because domestic producers also had to pay, have not been notably successful, as the *Bresciani* case demonstrates.[77] In exceptional circumstances the Court may, however, decide that although the charge or levy is taken at the border it is not to be characterized as a CEE within Article 25, but as a tax the legality of which will be tested under Article 90. In *Denkavit*[78] the applicant was an importer of feedingstuffs from Holland into Denmark. Danish law required, *inter alia*, that the importer obtain an authorization from the Ministry of Agriculture, *and* it charged an annual levy to meet the costs of checking samples of the goods. The ECJ held that the requirement of an authorization was caught by what is now Article 28,[79] but that it could be justified under what is now Article 30.[80] The Court then considered whether the levy was itself lawful. This levy was imposed on all those engaged in the feedingstuffs trade, whether importers or domestic producers. The ECJ held that it related to a general system of internal dues applied systematically and in accordance with the same criteria to domestic products and imported products alike, and therefore came within Article 90.[81] The ECJ has however made it clear in *Michailidis*[82] that a charge levied at the border will

[74] Case 193/85 *Cooperative Co-Frutta Srl* v. *Amministrazione delle Finanze dello Stato* [1987] ECR 2085, para. 8; Cases C–290 and 333/05 *Nadasdi*, n. 39 above, paras. 39–42.

[75] Case 105/76, *Interzuccheri*, n. 73 above, para. 9.

[76] See 645–646 above.

[77] See 643–644 above.

[78] Case 29/87 *Dansk Denkavit ApS* v. *Danish Ministry of Agriculture* [1988] ECR 2965.

[79] As a measure having equivalent effect to a quantitative restriction, on which see Ch. 19.

[80] On the basis that although there was a Community dir. relevant to the case, which would normally render recourse to Art. 36 (now Art. 30) impossible, the dir. did not extend to the situation in the instant case.

[81] Case 29/87 *Denkavit*, n. 78 above, para. 33. See also Case C–130/93 *Lamaire*, n. 12 above; Case C–90/94 *Haahr Petroleum Ltd.* v. *Abenra Havn* [1997] ECR I–4085; Case C–72/03 *Carbonati Apuani*, n. 5 above, paras. 17–18; Case C–387/01 *Weigel*, n. 35 above, para. 64.

[82] Cases C–441 and 442/98 *Michailidis*, n. 8 above, para. 24.

be regarded as an internal tax, rather than a CEE, only where the comparable charge levied on national products is applied at the same rate, at the same marketing stage, and on the basis of an identical chargeable event.

The *second type of case* in which there can be boundary-line problems between Articles 25 and 90 is that in which the importing State does not make the imported product, but imposes a tax on it nonetheless. Should this be considered to be a charge within Article 25 or a tax within Article 90? One might have thought that the ECJ would choose the former characterization, since there are no similar domestic goods. This will not always be so, as demonstrated by *Co-Frutta*.

Case 193/85 **Cooperative Co-Frutta Srl v. Amministrazione delle Finanze dello Stato**
[1987] ECR 2085

[Note ToA renumbering: Arts. 12, 95, and 177 are now Arts. 25, 90, and 234 respectively]

This was another case which arose from the imposition by Italy of a consumption tax on bananas, even though no such tax was levied on other fruit produced in Italy. It will be remembered from the earlier discussion that Italy produced only a negligible number of bananas. This action was brought by a banana importer via Article 177 to test the legality of the tax. The Court considered whether the tax should be viewed as a CEE within Article 12, or as a tax to be assessed under Article 95.

THE ECJ

8. According to established case law of the Court, the prohibition laid down by Articles 9 and 12 of the Treaty in regard to charges having an equivalent effect covers any charge exacted at the time of or on account of importation which, being borne specifically by an imported product to the exclusion of the similar domestic product, has the result of altering the cost price of the imported product, thereby producing the same restrictive effect on the free movement of goods as a customs duty.

9. The essential feature of a charge having an effect equivalent to a customs duty which distinguishes it from an internal tax therefore resides in the fact that the former is borne solely by an imported product as such whilst the latter is borne both by imported and domestic products.

10. The Court has however recognized that even a charge which is borne by a product imported from another Member State, when there is no identical or similar domestic product, does not constitute a charge having equivalent effect but internal taxation within the meaning of Article 95 of the Treaty if it relates to a general system of internal dues applied systematically to categories of products in accordance with objective criteria irrespective of the origin of the products.

11. Those considerations demonstrate that even if it were necessary in some cases, for the purpose of classifying a charge borne by imported products, to equate extremely low domestic production with its non-existence, that would not mean that the levy in question would necessarily have to be regarded as a charge having an effect equivalent to a customs duty. In particular, that will not be so if the levy is part of a general system of internal dues applying systematically to categories of products according to the criteria indicated above.

12. A tax on consumption of the type at issue in the main proceedings does form part of a general system of internal dues. The 19 taxes on consumption are governed by common tax rules and are charged on categories of products irrespective of their origin in accordance with an objective criterion, namely the fact that the product falls into a specific category of goods. Some of those taxes are charged on products intended for human consumption, including the tax on the consumption of bananas. Whether those goods are produced at home or abroad does not seem to have a bearing on the rate, the basis of assessment or the manner in which the tax is levied. The revenue from those taxes is not earmarked for a specific purpose; it constitutes tax revenue identical to other tax revenue and, like it, helps to finance State expenditure generally in all sectors.

13. Consequently, the tax at issue must be regarded as being an integral part of a general system of internal dues within the meaning of Article 95 of the Treaty and its compatibility with Community law must be assessed on the basis of that Article rather than Articles 9 and 12 of the Treaty.

The ECJ's reasoning makes good sense. If any charge imposed by a State on a product which it did not make at all, or only in negligible quantities, were to be classified as a CEE under Article 25 then two consequences would follow. The charge would be automatically unlawful,[83] and the importing State could not tax goods which it did not produce itself, since any such tax would be condemned under Article 25. This draconian conclusion would make little social, economic, or political sense, and it is not therefore surprising that the Court avoided this result.[84] There may be good reasons why a State should choose to tax, for example, a luxury product even if there is no domestic production. The criterion adopted by the ECJ provides a sensible resolution of this problem. If the test propounded by the ECJ is met the charge will not necessarily be regarded as lawful; it will still fall to be assessed under Article 90 of the Treaty. In the instant case the tax was in fact held to be in breach of what is now Article 90(2), for the same reasons as given in the action brought against Italy by the Commission.[85]

The *third type of case* arises when a State chooses to make a selective refund of a tax, or if it uses the money to benefit a particular group. The position appears to be as follows. If the money from a tax flows into the national exchequer and is then used for the benefit of a particular domestic industry, this could be challenged as a state aid: Articles 87–89.[86]

Classification problems as between Articles 25 and 90 arise when the money that has been refunded can be linked to that which has been levied pursuant to a specific tax. The correct classification will then depend upon whether the refund or other benefit to the national producers wholly or partially offsets the tax. If the former, then the tax will be treated under Article 25, the rationale being that what in effect exists is a charge levied only on the imported or exported product.[87] If, however, the refund or benefit is only partial the matter will fall to be assessed under Article 90, the rationale being that the partial refund in effect means that

---

[83] Assuming of course that it could not be saved on the ground that it represented consideration for a service, etc.

[84] See also Case 90/79 *Commission* v. *France* [1981] ECR 283; Case C–383/01 *De Danske Bilimportører* v. *Skatteministeriet* [2003] ECR I–6065, paras. 35–42.

[85] See 656 above.

[86] Cases C–78–83/90 *Compagnie Commerciale de l'Ouest* v. *Receveur Principal des Douanes de la Pallice Port* [1992] ECR I–1847.

[87] Note in this respect that Art. 25 expressly includes customs duties of a fiscal nature.

there could be a discriminatory tax.[88] Barents, summarizing the early case law,[89] identifies three conditions for a charge to be considered under Article 25 rather than Article 90:[90]

> Firstly, the charge must be destined exclusively for financing activities which very largely benefit the taxed domestic product; secondly, there must exist identity between the taxed product and the domestic product benefiting from the charge; and thirdly, the charges imposed on the domestic product must be completely compensated.

This approach is exemplified by the decision in *Scharbatke*.[91] There was a challenge to mandatory contributions levied in Germany when slaughtered animals were presented for inspection. The contribution was applied under the same conditions to national and imported products, and the money was assigned to a marketing fund for agricultural, forestry, and food products. The ECJ held that the mandatory contribution constituted a parafiscal charge.[92] Where the resulting revenue benefited solely national products, so that the advantages accruing *wholly* offset the charge imposed on the products, then the charge would be regarded as a CEE within Article 25.[93] If the advantages which accrued only *partially* offset the charges imposed on national products, then the charge might constitute discriminatory internal taxation under Article 90.[94]

6. CONCLUSION

i. There is little doubt that the ECJ's decisions in relation to duties and taxation have made a significant contribution to the realization of a single market. The Court's jurisprudence has consistently looked behind the form of a disputed measure to its substance, and the ECJ has interpreted the relevant Articles in the manner best designed to ensure that the Treaty objectives are achieved.

ii. In relation to the customs union, the main challenges in the years ahead are concerned with the need to forge an efficient and effective customs force from the twenty-seven Member State authorities so as to be able to fight fraud, the import of illegal goods, terrorism, and the like.

iii. In relation to taxation, the issues are more complex. The original Rome Treaty left a considerable degree of autonomy to Member States in the fiscal field, albeit subject to the

---

[88] Where the benefits from the activities financed by the charge accrue to both domestic producers and importers, but the former obtain proportionately greater benefits, the charge will fall under Art. 25 or Art. 90, depending on whether the advantage accruing to domestic producers fully or partially offsets their burdens: Case C–28/96 *Fazenda Publica* v. *Fricarnes SA* [1997] ECR I–4939.

[89] Case 77/76 *Fratelli Cuchi* v. *Avez* [1977] ECR 987; Case 94/74 *Industria Gomma Articoli Vari* v. *Ente Nazionale per la Cellulosa e per la Carta* [1975] ECR 699; Case 105/76 *Interzuccheri*, n. 73 above.

[90] N. 10 above, 430.

[91] Case C–72/92 *H. Scharbatke GmbH* v. *Federal Republic of Germany* [1993] ECR I–5509. See also Cases C–78–83/90 *Compagnie Commerciale*, n. 86 above; Case C–234/99 *Niels Nygard*, n. 12 above, para. 23; Case C–517/04 *Visserijbedrijf* v. *Productschap Vis* [2006] ECR I–5015, paras. 18–20.

[92] The ECJ held that the charge which was levied might also constitute state aid under Art. 87.

[93] It is not entirely clear whether *Scharbatke* is intended to modify earlier cases, which had held that in order for the charge to be regarded as a CEE within Art. 25 there must, *inter alia*, be a strict coincidence between the product which was being taxed and that which was receiving the benefit: Case 105/76 *Interzuccheri*, n. 73 above.

[94] See also Case 73/79 *Commission* v. *Italy* [1980] ECR 1533; Case C–347/95 *Fazenda Publica* v. *Uniao das Cooperativas Abastecedoras de Leite de Lisboa, URCL (UCAL)* [1997] ECR I–4911.

constraints imposed by Articles 23–25 and 90. Many of the problems concerning divergences between national taxation systems could only ever be fully resolved if legislative harmonization occurred. Taxation is however regarded as central to national sovereignty, and hence any extension of Community competence over tax is a hotly contested issue.

iv. It should, however, be noted that in this area, as in many others, there is often a link between judicial doctrine and legislative initiatives. The very fact that a challenged national tax policy will, according to the ECJ's decisions in *Chemial* and the *French Sweet Wines* case,[95] be upheld only if the Court deems it to be compatible with the Treaty can lead to paradoxical results. It has been noted[96] that the absence of harmonization has led to the ironical result that the Commission, abetted by the European Court, has managed to wield perhaps more influence over Member State tax policies, and thus their economic and social policies, than would be the case if the Council had agreed on a uniform tax regime.

v. The Commission has more recently emphasized the contribution of taxation and customs policy to implementation of the Lisbon Strategy.[97]

7. FURTHER READING

Barents, R., 'Charges of Equivalent Effect to Customs Duties' (1978) 15 *CMLRev.* 415

—— 'Recent Case Law on the Prohibition of Fiscal Discrimination Under Article 95' (1986) 23 *CMLRev.* 641

Danusso, M., and Denton, R., 'Does the European Court of Justice Look for a Protectionist Motive Under Article 95?' (1990) 1 *LIEI* 67

Easson, A., 'The Spirits, Wine and Beer Judgments: A Legal Mickey Finn?' (1980) 5 *ELRev.* 318

—— 'Fiscal Discrimination: New Perspectives on Article 95 of the EEC Treaty' (1981) 18 *CMLRev.* 521

Grabitz, E., and Zacker, C., 'Scope for Action by the EC Member States for the Improvement of Environmental Protection under EEC Law: The Example of Environmental Taxes and Subsidies' (1989) 26 *CMLRev.* 423

Schwarze, J., 'The Member States' Discretionary Powers under the Tax Provisions of the EEC Treaty', in J. Schwarze (ed.), *Discretionary Powers of the Member States in the Field of Economic Policies and their Limits under the EEC Treaty* (Nomos, 1988)

Snell, J., 'Non-Discriminatory Tax Obstacles in Community Law' (2007) 56 *ICLQ* 339

---

[95] See 651–653 above.

[96] J. Lonbay, 'A Review of Recent Tax Cases' (1989) 14 *ELRev.* 48, 50.

[97] The Contribution of Taxation and Customs Policies to the Lisbon Strategy, COM(2005)532 final. See above, 632–633, for discussion of this strategy.

FREE MOVEMENT OF GOODS: QUANTITATIVE RESTRICTIONS

1. CENTRAL ISSUES

i.   It is necessary to understand the way in which Articles 28–31 fit into the more general strategy concerning the free movement of goods. Articles 23–27 lay the foundations for a customs union by providing for the elimination of customs duties between Member States and by establishing a Common Customs Tariff. If matters rested there free movement would be only imperfectly attained. It would still be open to States to place quotas on the amount of goods that could be imported, and to restrict the flow of goods by measures that have an equivalent effect to quotas. The object of Articles 28–31 is to prevent Member States from engaging in these strategies.

ii. The ECJ's interpretation of Articles 28–31 has been very important in achieving single-market integration. It has given a broad interpretation to the phrase 'measures having equivalent effect' to a quantitative restriction (MEQR), and has construed the idea of discrimination broadly to capture both direct and indirect discrimination.

iii. The ECJ has also held that Article 28 can apply even where there is no discrimination. The famous *Cassis de Dijon* case[1] decided that Article 28 can bite, subject to certain exceptions, when the same rule applies to both domestic goods and imports, where the rule inhibits the free flow of goods within the Community. Discrimination is therefore a sufficient, but not necessary, condition for the invocation of Article 28. There are, however, three central problems to be aware of in this area.

iv. First, the ECJ's jurisprudence has led to difficult issues about where this branch of EC law 'stops'. The ECJ's decision that Article 28 is applicable to trade rules even where they do not discriminate has led to difficulties about the outer boundaries of Community law. The law in this respect is still evolving.

v.   Secondly, there is a problem concerning the relationship between negative and positive integration. The ECJ's approach in *Cassis de Dijon* leads to 'negative integration': indistinctly applicable rules will be rendered unenforceable when they hinder cross-border trade unless they come within one of the exceptions. Integration is essentially negative and deregulatory, in the sense that the national rules are held not to apply. This can be contrasted with 'positive integration', which results from Community legislative measures,

---

[1] Case 120/78 *Rewe-Zentrale AG* v. *Bundesmonopolverwaltung für Branntwein* [1979] ECR 649.

stipulating which rules should apply across the Community. There are, as will be seen, important consequences that flow from developing Community policy by these differing strategies.

vi. Thirdly, there is a tension between Community integration and national regulatory autonomy. The impact of Article 28 will often be to render national regulatory measures inapplicable. Article 28 therefore is a tool for policing the borderline between legitimate and illegitimate national regulation, and the nature of this border may well be contestable.[2]

vii. This topic exemplifies the interconnection between judicial and legislative initiatives for attaining the Community's objectives, a theme stressed throughout this book. One way of dealing with trade rules that differ between Member States is through legislative harmonization. The process of such harmonization was, however, slow, a difficulty exacerbated by the requirement of unanimity in the Council.[3] The ECJ's jurisprudence constituted an alternative means for ensuring the free flow of goods even in the absence of legislation which harmonized the relevant rules. The message was clear: attainment of this central part of Community policy was not to be held up indefinitely by the absence of harmonization legislation. The Court's approach to Article 28 was welcomed by the Commission, which made it clear that its own scarce resources should be best directed towards achieving harmonization in respect of those rules which were still lawful under the *Cassis de Dijon* formula, on the grounds that, for example, they were necessary to protect consumers or safeguard public health. The judicial approach, therefore, caused the Commission to reorient its own legislative programme.

viii. The Community Courts have also maintained tight control over the application of Article 30, which is concerned with defences against a *prima facie* breach of Article 28. The ECJ has interpreted Article 30 strictly in order to ensure that discriminatory restrictions on the free movement of goods are not easily justified. There are however difficulties concerning the relationship between defences to discrimination and defences to indistinctly applicable rules.

2. INTRODUCTION

The discussion in the previous chapter focused on duties, taxes, and the like. This is, however, only part of the strategy for an integrated single market. The free movement of goods is dealt with in Articles 28–31 (ex Articles 30–36). The renumbering of the Treaty provisions pursuant to the ToA has meant that the old Article 30 is now Article 28, and the old Article 36 is now Article 30. Particular care is therefore required when reading case law based on the old numbering.[4] Article 28 is the central provision within this Chapter of the Treaty. It states that:

Quantitative restrictions on imports and all measures having equivalent effect shall be prohibited between Member States.

---

[2] W.P.J. Wils, 'The Search for the Rule in Article 30 EEC: Much Ado About Nothing?' (1993) 18 *ELRev.* 475, 478; M. Maduro, *We the Court, the European Court of Justice and the European Economic Constitution* (Hart, 1998), 54–58.

[3] See Ch. 17.

[4] The old Arts. 31 to 33 which concerned transitional measures were repealed by the ToA.

Article 29 contains similar provisions relating to exports, while Article 30 (ex Article 36) provides an exception for certain cases in which a State is allowed to place restrictions on the movement of goods.

3. DIRECTIVE 70/50 AND *DASSONVILLE*

Article 28 will catch quantitative restrictions and all measures which have an equivalent effect (MEQR). It can apply to Community measures,[5] as well as those adopted by Member States. The notion of a quantitative restriction was defined broadly in the *Geddo* case[6] to mean 'measures which amount to a total or partial restraint of, according to the circumstances, imports, exports or goods in transit'. MEQRs are more difficult to define. The Commission and the Court have taken a broad view of such measures.

Guidance on the Commission's view can be found in Directive 70/50. This Directive was only formally applicable during the Community's transitional period, but it continues to furnish some idea of the scope of MEQRs. The list of matters which can constitute an MEQR are specified in Article 2 and include:[7] minimum or maximum prices for imported products; less favourable prices for imported products; lowering the value of the imported product by reducing its intrinsic value or increasing its costs; payment conditions for imported products which differ from those for domestic products; conditions in respect of packaging, composition, identification, size, weight, etc., which apply only to imported goods or which are different and more difficult to satisfy than in the case of domestic goods; the giving of a preference to the purchase of domestic goods as opposed to imports, or otherwise hindering the purchase of imports; limiting publicity in respect of imported goods as compared with domestic products; prescribing stocking requirements which are different from and more difficult to satisfy than those which apply to domestic goods; and making it mandatory for importers of goods to have an agent in the territory of the importing State.

Article 2, therefore, lists a number of ways in which the importing State can discriminate against goods. It should be noted that, even as early as 1970, the Commission was thinking of the potential reach of Article 28 to indistinctly applicable rules, since Article 3 of the Directive, which will be considered below, regulates such rules to some degree.

The seminal early judicial decision on the interpretation of MEQRs is *Dassonville*.

Case 8/74 **Procureur du Roi v. Dassonville**
[1974] ECR 837

[Note ToA renumbering: Art. 36 is now Art. 30]

Belgian law provided that goods bearing a designation of origin could only be imported if they were accompanied by a certificate from the government of the exporting country certifying their right to such a designation. Dassonville imported Scotch whisky into Belgium from France without being in possession of the certificate from the British authorities. The certificate would have been very difficult to obtain in respect of goods which were already in free circulation in

---

[5] Case C–114/96 *Criminal Proceedings against Kieffer and Thill* [1997] ECR I–3629.
[6] Case 2/73 *Geddo v. Ente Nazionale Risi* [1973] ECR 865.
[7] Dir. 70/50 [1970] OJ L13/29, Art. 2(3).

a third country, as in this case. Dassonville was prosecuted in Belgium and argued by way of defence that the Belgian rule constituted a MEQR.

THE ECJ

5. All trading rules enacted by Member States which are capable of hindering, directly or indirectly, actually or potentially, intra-Community trade are to be considered as measures having an effect equivalent to quantitative restrictions.

6. In the absence of a Community system guaranteeing for consumers the authenticity of a product's designation of origin, if a Member State takes measures to prevent unfair practices in this connection, it is however subject to the condition that these measures should be reasonable and that the means of proof required should not act as a hindrance to trade between Member States and should, in consequence, be accessible to all Community nationals.

7. Even without having to examine whether such measures are covered by Article 36, they must not, in any case, by virtue of the principle expressed in the second sentence of that Article, constitute a means of arbitrary discrimination or a disguised restriction on trade between Member States.

8. That may be the case with formalities, required by a Member State for the purpose of proving the origin of a product, which only direct importers are really in a position to satisfy without facing serious difficulties.

9. Consequently, the requirement by a Member State of a certificate of authenticity which is less easily obtainable by importers of an authentic product which has been put into free circulation in a regular manner in another Member State than by importers of the same product coming directly from the country of origin constitutes a measure equivalent to a quantitative restriction as prohibited by the Treaty.

Two aspects of the ECJ's reasoning should be noted. First, it is clear from paragraph 5 that the crucial element in proving a MEQR is its *effect*: a discriminatory intent is not required. The ECJ takes a broad view of measures that hinder the free flow of goods within the EC, and the definition does not even require that the rules actually discriminate between domestic and imported goods. *Dassonville* thus sowed the seeds which bore fruit in *Cassis de Dijon*,[8] where the ECJ decided that Article 28 could apply to rules which were not discriminatory. Secondly, the ECJ indicates, in paragraph 6, that reasonable restraints may not be caught by Article 28. This is the origin of what became known as the 'rule of reason', the meaning of which will be examined below.

We can now consider the application of Article 28 to cases involving discrimination, both direct and indirect.

4. DISCRIMINATORY BARRIERS TO TRADE

Article 28 can bite if the national rule favours domestic goods over imports, even if the case, on its facts, is confined to products and parties from one Member State.[9] Article 28 can also apply to a national measure preventing import from one to another part of a Member State.[10]

---

[8] Case 120/78 *Rewe-Zentrale AG*, n. 1 above.

[9] Cases C–321–4/94 *Criminal Proceedings against Pistre* [1997] ECR I–2343; Case C–448/98 *Criminal Proceedings against Guimont* [2000] ECR I–10663.

[10] Case C–67/97 *Criminal Proceedings against Bluhme* [1998] ECR I–8033.

There are numerous types of case involving direct or indirect discrimination between domestic and imported goods.

(a) IMPORT AND EXPORT RESTRICTIONS

The ECJ has always been particularly harsh on discriminatory import or export restrictions. Thus import or export licences are caught by Article 28.[11] So, too, are provisions which subject imported goods to requirements that are not imposed on domestic products. This is exemplified by *Commission* v. *Italy*,[12] in which the ECJ held that procedures and data requirements for the registration of imported cars, making their registration longer, more complicated, and more costly than that of domestic vehicles, were prohibited by Article 28.[13] The same approach is apparent with respect to discriminatory export rules. Thus in *Bouhelier*[14] a French rule which imposed quality checks on watches for export, but not on those intended for the domestic market, was in breach of what is now Article 29.

(b) PROMOTION OR FAVOURING OF DOMESTIC PRODUCTS

Article 28 prohibits action by a State that promotes or favours domestic products to the detriment of competing imports. This can occur in a number of different ways.

The most obvious is where a *State engages in a campaign to promote the purchase of domestic as opposed to imported goods.*

Case 249/81 **Commission v. Ireland**
[1982] ECR 4005

[Note ToA renumbering: Arts. 30, 92, 93, and 169 are now
Arts. 28, 87, 88, and 226 respectively]

The Irish Government sought to promote sales of Irish goods, the object being to achieve a switch of 3 per cent in consumer spending from imports to domestic products. It adopted a number of measures including: an information service indicating to consumers which products were made in Ireland and where they could be obtained (the Shoplink Service); exhibition facilities for Irish goods; the encouragement of the use of the 'Buy Irish' symbol for goods made in Ireland; and the organization of a publicity campaign by the Irish Goods Council in favour of Irish products, designed to encourage consumers to buy Irish products. The first two of these activities were subsequently abandoned by the Irish Government, but the latter two strategies continued to be employed. The Commission brought Article 169 proceedings, alleging that the campaign was an MEQR. Ireland argued that it had never adopted 'measures'

---

[11] Cases 51–54/71 *International Fruit Company* v. *Produktschap voor Groenten en Fruit (No. 2)* [1971] ECR 1107; Case 68/76 *Commission* v. *French Republic* [1977] ECR 515; Case C–54/05 *Commission* v. *Finland*, 25 Mar. 2007.

[12] Case 154/85 [1987] ECR 2717.

[13] See also Case 4/75 *Rewe-Zentralfinanz* v. *Landwirtschaftskammer* [1975] ECR 843.

[14] Case 53/76 *Procureur de la République Besançon* v. *Bouhelier* [1977] ECR 197.

for the purpose of Article 30, and that any financial aid given to the Irish Goods Council should be judged in the light of Articles 92 to 93, and not Article 30. The members of the Irish Goods Council were appointed by an Irish Government minister and its activities were funded in proportions of about six to one by the Irish Government and private industry respectively. The ECJ held that the Irish government was responsible under the Treaty for the activities of the Council even though the campaign was run by a private company, and then continued as follows.

THE ECJ

21. The Irish government maintains that the prohibition against measures having an effect equivalent to quantitative restrictions in Article 30 is concerned only with 'measures', that is to say, binding provisions emanating from a public authority. However, no such provision has been adopted by the Irish government, which has confined itself to giving moral support and financial aid to the activities pursued by the Irish industries.

22. The Irish government goes on to emphasise that the campaign has had no restrictive effect on imports since the proportion of Irish goods to all goods sold on the Irish market fell from 49.2% in 1977 to 43.4% in 1980.

23. The first observation to be made is that the campaign cannot be likened to advertising by private or public undertakings ... to encourage people to buy goods produced by those undertakings. Regardless of the means used to implement it, the campaign is a reflection of the Irish government's considered intention to substitute domestic products for imported products on the Irish market and thereby to check the flow of imports from other Member States.

. . .

25. Whilst it may be true that the two elements of the programme which have continued in effect, namely the advertising campaign and the use of the 'Guaranteed Irish' symbol, have not had any significant success in winning over the Irish market to domestic products, it is not possible to overlook the fact that, regardless of their efficacy, those two activities form part of a government programme which is designed to achieve the substitution of domestic products for imported products and is liable to affect the volume of trade between Member States.

. . .

27. In the circumstances the two activities in question amount to the establishment of a national practice, introduced by the Irish government and prosecuted with its assistance, the potential effect of which on imports from other Member States is comparable to that resulting from government measures of a binding nature.

28. Such a practice cannot escape the prohibition laid down by Article 30 of the Treaty solely because it is not based on decisions which are binding upon undertakings. Even measures adopted by the government of a Member State which do not have binding effect may be capable of influencing the conduct of traders and consumers in that State and thus of frustrating the aims of the Community as set out in Article 2 and enlarged upon in Article 3 of the Treaty.

29. That is the case where, as in this instance, such a restrictive practice represents the implementation of a programme defined by the government which affects the national economy as a whole and which is intended to check the flow of trade between Member States by encouraging the purchase of domestic products, by means of an advertising campaign on a national scale and the organization of special procedures applicable solely to domestic products, and where those activities are attributable as a whole to the government and are pursued in an organized fashion throughout the national territory.

30. Ireland has therefore failed to fulfil its obligations under the Treaty by organizing a campaign to promote the sale and purchase of Irish goods within its territory.

The ECJ's reasoning provides an excellent example of its general strategy under Article 28. It looks to substance, not form. This is manifested in the way in which it rebuts the Irish argument that only formally binding measures are caught by the Article, (paragraphs 21 and 28); and in its rejection of the argument that, as the campaign appeared to have failed, therefore EC law should be unconcerned with it (paragraph 25).[15]

A second type of case caught by Article 28 is where *a State has rules on the origin-marking of certain goods.*

Case 207/83 Commission v. United Kingdom
[1985] ECR 1201

[Note ToA renumbering: Arts. 30 and 169 are now Arts. 28 and 226]

The Commission brought an Article 169 action, arguing that UK legislation which required that certain goods should not be sold in retail markets unless they were marked with their country of origin was in breach of Article 30, as an MEQR. The UK argued that the legislation applied equally to imported and national products, and that this information was of importance to consumers since they regarded origin as an indication of the quality of the goods. The extract relates to the first of these arguments.

THE ECJ

17. [I]t has to be recognized that the purpose of indications of origin or origin-marking is to enable consumers to distinguish between domestic and imported products and that this enables them to assert any prejudices which they may have against foreign products. As the Court has had occasion to emphasise in various contexts, the Treaty, by establishing a common market . . . seeks to unite national markets in a single market having the characteristics of a domestic market. Within such a market, the origin-marking requirement not only makes the marketing in a Member State of goods produced in other Member States in the sectors in question more difficult; it also has the effect of slowing down economic interpenetration in the Community by handicapping the sale of goods produced as the result of a division of labour between Member States.

18. It follows from those considerations that the United Kingdom provisions in question are liable to have the effect of increasing the production costs of imported goods and making it more difficult to sell them on the United Kingdom market.[16]

Member State legislation which contains rules on origin-marking will normally be acceptable only if the origin implies a certain quality in the goods, that they were made from certain materials or by a particular form of manufacturing, or where the origin is indicative of a special place in the folklore or tradition of the region in question.[17]

---

[15] The campaign may have had some impact, since the diminution in sales of Irish goods might have been greater had the campaign not existed. Not all measures which promote domestic goods will, however, be caught by the Treaty: Case 222/82 *Apple and Pear Development Council* v. *K.J. Lewis Ltd.* [1983] ECR 4083.

[16] The ECJ also rejected the UK's argument that origin-marking was related to consumer protection. The Court held that the origin-marking rules were only equally applicable to domestic and imported products as a matter of form: in reality they were intended to enable consumers to give preference to national goods: *ibid.*, para. 20.

[17] Case 12/74 *Commission* v. *Germany* [1975] ECR 181; Case 113/80 *Commission* v. *Ireland* [1981] ECR 1625.

The Court's clear intent to stamp firmly on national measures that favour domestic over imported products is equally apparent in a third type of case: *public procurement* cannot be structured so as to favour domestic producers.[18]

Case 45/87 **Commission v. Ireland**
[1988] ECR 4929

[Note ToA renumbering: Arts. 30 and 169 are now Arts. 28 and 226]

Dundalk Council put out to tender a contract for water supply. One of the contract clauses (4.29) was that tenderers had to submit bids based on the use of certain pipes which complied with a particular Irish standard (IS 188: 1975). One of the bids was based on the use of a piping which had not been certified by the Irish authorities, but which complied with international standards. The Council refused to consider it for this reason. The Commission brought an Article 169 action claiming a breach of Article 30.

THE ECJ

19. [I]t must first be pointed out that the inclusion of such a clause (as 4.29) in an invitation to tender may cause economic operators who produce or utilize pipes equivalent to pipes certified with Irish standards to refrain from tendering.

20. It further appears . . . that only one undertaking has been certified by the IIRS[19] to IS 188: 1975 to apply the Irish Standard Mark to pipes of the type required for the purposes of the public works contract at issue. That undertaking is located in Ireland. Consequently, the inclusion of Clause 4.29 had the effect of restricting the supply of the pipes needed for the Dundalk scheme to Irish manufacturers alone.

21. The Irish government maintains that it is necessary to specify the standards to which materials must be manufactured, particularly in a case such as this where the pipes utilized must suit the existing network. Compliance with another standard, even an international standard such as ISO 160: 1980, would not suffice to eliminate technical difficulties.

22. That technical argument cannot be accepted. The Commission's complaint does not relate to compliance with technical requirements but to the refusal of the Irish authorities to verify whether those requirements are satisfied where the manufacturer of the materials has not been certified by the IIRS to IS 188. By incorporating in the notice in question the words 'or equivalent' after the reference to the Irish standard, as provided for by Directive 71/305 where it is applicable, the Irish authorities could have verified compliance with the technical conditions without from the outset restricting the contract to tenderers proposing to utilize Irish materials.

A fourth type of case is where *the discrimination in favour of domestic goods is evident in administrative practice*, as exemplified by *Commission v. France*.[20] French law discriminated against imported postal franking machines. The law was changed, but a British company claimed that, notwithstanding this, the French authorities repeatedly refused to approve its machines. The ECJ held that consistent and general administrative discrimination against

---

[18] Case C–21/88 *Du Pont de Nemours Italiana SpA v. Unità Sanitaria Locale No. 2 di Carrara* [1990] ECR I–889; Case 72/83 *Campus Oil Ltd. v. Minister for Industry and Energy* [1984] ECR 2727.

[19] Institute for Industrial Research and Standards.

[20] Case 21/84 *Commission v. France* [1985] ECR 1356.

imports could be caught by Article 28. The discrimination could, for example, take the form of delay in replying to applications for approval, or refusing approval on the grounds of various alleged technical faults that were inaccurate.

(c) PRICE FIXING

A State can treat imported goods less favourably than domestic products through price-fixing regulations which render it more difficult for importers to market their goods.

If the price fixing is discriminatory it is clearly caught by Article 28.[21] However, Article 28 can catch pricing rules even where they are not, on their face, discriminatory.

Case 82/77 **Openbaar Ministerie v. Van Tiggele**
[1978] ECR 25[22]

Dutch legislation laid down minimum selling prices for certain spirits. A seller was accused in criminal proceedings of selling them below the stipulated price. The question before the ECJ was whether the minimum selling prices were a MEQR within Article 30 (28).

THE ECJ

12. For the purposes of this prohibition it is sufficient that the measures in question are likely to hinder, directly or indirectly, actually or potentially, imports between Member States.

13. Whilst national price-control rules applicable without distinction to domestic products and imported products cannot in general produce such an effect they may do so in certain specific cases.

14. Thus imports may be impeded in particular when a national authority fixes prices or profit margins at such a level that imported products are placed at a disadvantage in relation to identical domestic products either because they cannot profitably be marketed in the conditions laid down or because the competitive advantage conferred by lower cost prices is cancelled out.

The ECJ found that the Dutch rule contravened what is now Article 28. It seems that rules that fix prices by reference to a maximum percentage profit will, by way of contrast, be found to be more readily compatible with this Article. Such rules may take account of differences in production cost between domestic goods and imports.[23]

(d) MEASURES WHICH MAKE IMPORTS
MORE DIFFICULT OR COSTLY

There are numerous ways in which a Member State can render it more difficult for importers to break into that market, as exemplified by the *Schloh* case.

---

[21] Case 181/82 *Roussel Labaratoria BV* v. *The State of The Netherlands* [1983] ECR 3849; Case 56/87 *Commission* v. *Italy* [1988] ECR 2919.

[22] See also Case 65/75 *Riccardo Tasca* [1976] ECR 291.

[23] Case 78/82 *Commission* v. *Italy* [1983] ECR 1955.

Case 50/85 **Schloh v. Auto Contrôle Technique**
[1986] ECR 1855

[Note ToA renumbering: Arts. 30 and 36 are now Arts. 28 and 30]

Schloh bought a car in Germany and obtained from a Ford dealer in Belgium a certificate of conformity with vehicle types in Belgium. Under Belgian law he was required to submit his car to two roadworthiness tests, for which fees were charged. He challenged the tests, arguing that they were an MEQR. The extract concerns the first roadworthiness test.

THE ECJ

12. ... Roadworthiness testing is a formality which makes the registration of imported vehicles more difficult and more onerous and consequently is in the nature of a measure having an effect equivalent to a quantitative restriction.

13. Nevertheless, Article 36 may justify such a formality on grounds of the protection of human life and health, provided that it is established, first, that the test at issue is necessary for the attainment of that objective and, secondly, that it does not constitute a means of arbitrary discrimination or a disguised restriction on trade between Member States.

14. As far as the first condition is concerned, it must be acknowledged that roadworthiness testing required prior to the registration of an imported vehicle may ... be regarded as necessary for the protection of human health and life where the vehicle in question has already been put on the road. In such cases roadworthiness testing performs a useful function inasmuch as it makes it possible to check that the vehicle has not been damaged and is in a good state of repair. However such testing cannot be justified on those grounds where it relates to an imported vehicle carrying a certificate of conformity which has not been placed on the road before being registered in the importing Member State.

15. As far as the second condition is concerned, it must be stated that the roadworthiness testing of imported vehicles cannot, however, be justified under the second sentence of Article 36 of the Treaty if it is established that such testing is not required in the case of vehicles of national origin presented for registration in the same circumstances. If that were the case it would become apparent that the measure in question was not in fact inspired by a concern for the protection of human health and life but in reality constituted a means of arbitrary discrimination in trade between Member States. It is for the national court to verify that such non-discriminatory treatment is in fact ensured.

The ECJ held that the Belgian rule was contrary to Article 28, save in relation to cars which were already on the road, provided that in this type of case the rules were applied in a non-discriminatory fashion.

(e) NATIONAL MEASURES VERSUS PRIVATE ACTION

It seems clear that Article 28 applies to measures taken by the State,[24] as opposed to those taken by private parties.[25] Other Treaty provisions, notably Articles 81 and 82, will apply

---

[24] S. Van den Bogaert, 'Horizontality: The Court Attacks?', in C. Barnard and J. Scott (eds.), *The Law of the Single European Market, Unpacking the Premises* (Hart, 2002), ch. 5.

[25] Case 311/85 *Vereniging van Vlaamse Reisebureau's* v. *Sociale Dienst de Plaatselijke en Gewestelijke Overheidsdiensten* [1987] ECR 3821, para. 30; Case C–159/00 *Sapod-Audic* v. *Eco-Emballages SA* [2002] ECR I–5031, para. 74.

to actions by private parties that restrict competition and have an impact on inter-state trade.[26]

This means that the issue of what is a state entity has to be addressed. Thus in the '*Buy Irish*'[27] case we have already seen that the ECJ rejected the argument that the Irish Goods Council was a private body and therefore immune from the application of Article 28. The Irish Government's involvement with the funding of the organization and the appointment of its members was sufficient to render it public for these purposes, while in the *Apple and Pear Development Council* case[28] the existence of a statutory obligation on fruit growers to pay certain levies to the Council sufficed to render the body public for these purposes. It is clear that institutions such as those concerned with trade regulation may come within the definition of the State for these purposes, even if they are nominally private, provided that they receive a measure of state support or 'underpinning'.[29]

This Article can also apply against the State even though private parties have taken the main role in restricting the free movement of goods, as exemplified by *Commission* v. *France*.[30] The Commission brought an Article 226 action against the French government for breach of what is now Article 28 combined with Article 10, because the government had taken insufficient measures to prevent French farmers from disrupting imports of agricultural produce from other EC countries. The ECJ held that it was incumbent on a government to take all necessary and appropriate measures to ensure that free movement was respected in its territory, even where the obstacles were created by private parties.[31]

(f) SUMMARY

i.   If a polity decides to embrace a single market, then discriminatory or protectionist measures will be at the top of the list of those to be caught, since they are directly opposed to the single market ideal.

ii. The court entrusted with policing such a regime must be mindful of the many different ways in which a State can seek to discriminate against imported goods.

iii. The ECJ has been aware of this, and has made sure that indirect as well as direct discrimination is caught by Article 28.

---

[26] See Chs. 25–26.

[27] Case 249/81 *Commission* v. *Ireland* [1982] ECR 4005. See also Case 325/00 *Commission* v. *Germany* [2002] ECR I–9977.

[28] Case 222/82 *Apple and Pear Development Council*, n. 15 above.

[29] Cases 266 and 267/87 *R.* v. *The Pharmaceutical Society, ex p. API* [1989] ECR 1295.

[30] Case C–265/95 [1997] ECR I–6959; Case C–112/00 *Schmidberger, Internationale Transporte und Planzuge* v. *Austria* [2003] ECR I–5659, paras. 57–59.

[31] See also Reg. 2679/98 of 7 Dec. 1998 on the functioning of the internal market in relation to the free movement of goods among the Member States [1998] OJ L337/8, but for the weakness of this Reg. see Report from the Commission to the Council and European Parliament on the application of Regulation 2679/98, COM(2001)160 final.

5. INDISTINCTLY APPLICABLE RULES: *CASSIS DE DIJON*

(a) FOUNDATIONS: *CASSIS DE DIJON*

The removal of discriminatory trade barriers is undoubtedly a necessary condition for the attainment of single-market integration. It is not, however, sufficient. There are many rules that do not discriminate between goods dependent upon the country of origin, but which nevertheless create real barriers to the passage of products between Member States.

The Commission appreciated this when framing Directive 70/50.[32] Article 2 was concerned with discriminatory measures. Article 3 provided that the Directive also covered measures governing the marketing of products which deal, *inter alia*, with shape, size, weight, composition, presentation, and identification, where the measures were equally applicable to domestic and imported products, and where the restrictive effect of such measures on the free movement of goods exceeded the effects intrinsic to such rules.

The possibility that Article 28 could be applied to indistinctly applicable rules was also apparent in *Dassonville*.[33] The definition of an MEQR in paragraph 5 did not require a measure to be discriminatory. The seeds that were sown in Directive 70/50 and *Dassonville* came to fruition in the seminal *Cassis de Dijon* case.

Case 120/78 **Rewe-Zentrale AG v. Bundesmonopolverwaltung für Branntwein**
[1979] ECR 649

[Note ToA renumbering: Art. 30 is now Art. 28]

The applicant intended to import the liqueur 'Cassis de Dijon' into Germany from France. The German authorities refused to allow the importation because the French drink was not of sufficient alcoholic strength to be marketed in Germany. Under German law such liqueurs had to have an alcohol content of 25 per cent, whereas the French drink had an alcohol content of between 15 and 20 per cent. The applicant argued that the German rule was an MEQR, since it prevented the French version of the drink from being lawfully marketed in Germany.

THE ECJ

8. In the absence of common rules relating to the production and marketing of alcohol ... it is for the Member States to regulate all matters relating to the production and marketing of alcohol and alcoholic beverages on their own territory.

Obstacles to movement within the Community resulting from disparities between the national laws relating to the marketing of the products in question must be accepted in so far as those provisions may be recognized as being necessary in order to satisfy mandatory requirements relating in particular to the effectiveness of fiscal supervision, the protection of public health, the fairness of commercial transactions and the defence of the consumer.

9. The Government of the Federal Republic of Germany ... put forward various arguments which, in its view, justify the application of provisions relating to the minimum alcohol content of

---

[32] Dir. 70/50 [1970] OJ L13/29, Art. 2(3).
[33] Case 8/74 *Procureur du Roi* v. *Dassonville* [1974] ECR 837.

alcoholic beverages, adducing considerations relating on the one hand to the protection of public health and on the other to the protection of the consumer against unfair commercial practices.

10. As regards the protection of public health the German Government states that the purpose of the fixing of minimum alcohol contents by national legislation is to avoid the proliferation of alcoholic beverages on the national market, in particular alcoholic beverages with a low alcohol content, since, in its view, such products may more easily induce a tolerance towards alcohol than more highly alcoholic beverages.

11. Such considerations are not decisive since the consumer can obtain on the market an extremely wide range of weakly or moderately alcoholic products and furthermore a large proportion of alcoholic beverages with a high alcohol content freely sold on the German market is generally consumed in a diluted form.

12. The German Government also claims that the fixing of a lower limit for the alcohol content of certain liqueurs is designed to protect the consumer against unfair practices on the part of producers and distributors of alcoholic beverages.

This argument is based on the consideration that the lowering of the alcohol content secures a competitive advantage in relation to beverages with a higher alcohol content, since alcohol constitutes by far the most expensive constituent of beverages by reason of the high rate of tax to which it is subject.

Furthermore, according to the German Government, to allow alcoholic products into free circulation wherever, as regards their alcohol content, they comply with the rules laid down in the country of production would have the effect of imposing as a common standard within the Community the lowest alcohol content permitted in any of the Member States, and even of rendering any requirements in this field inoperative since a lower limit of this nature is foreign to the rules of several Member States.

13. As the Commission rightly observed, the fixing of limits to the alcohol content of beverages may lead to the standardization of products placed on the market and of their designations, in the interests of a greater transparency of commercial transactions and offers for sale to the public.

However, this line of argument cannot be taken so far as to regard the mandatory fixing of minimum alcohol contents as being an essential guarantee of the fairness of commercial transactions, since it is a simple matter to ensure that suitable information is conveyed to the purchaser by requiring the display of an indication of origin and of the alcohol content on the packaging of products.

14. It is clear from the foregoing that the requirements relating to the minimum alcohol content of alcoholic beverages do not serve a purpose which is in the general interest and such as to take precedence over the requirements of the free movement of goods, which constitutes one of the fundamental rules of the Community.

In practice, the principal effect of requirements of this nature is to promote alcoholic beverages having a high alcohol content by excluding from the national market products of other Member States which do not answer that description.

It therefore appears that the unilateral requirement imposed by the rules of a Member State of a minimum alcohol content for the purposes of the sale of alcoholic beverages constitutes an obstacle to trade which is incompatible with the provisions of Article 30 of the Treaty.

There is therefore no valid reason why, provided that they have been lawfully produced and marketed in one of the Member States, alcoholic beverages should not be introduced into any other Member State; the sale of such products may not be subject to a legal prohibition on the marketing of beverages with an alcohol content lower than the limits set by the national rules.

The significance of *Cassis de Dijon* can hardly be overstated, and it is therefore worth dwelling upon the result and the reasoning.

In terms of *result* the Court's ruling in *Cassis* affirmed and developed the *Dassonville* judgment. It *affirmed* paragraph 5 of *Dassonville*: what is now Article 28 could apply to national rules that did not discriminate against imported products, but which inhibited trade because they were different from the trade rules applicable in the country of origin. The fundamental assumption was that, once goods had been lawfully marketed in one Member State, they should be admitted into any other State without restriction, unless the State of import could successfully invoke one of the mandatory requirements. The *Cassis* judgment encapsulated therefore a principle of *mutual recognition*: paragraph 14(4). The *Cassis* ruling also *built* upon paragraph 6 of *Dassonville*, in which the ECJ introduced the rule of reason: in the absence of Community harmonization, reasonable measures could be taken by a State to prevent unfair trade practices. Paragraph 8 of *Cassis* developed this idea. Four matters (fiscal supervision, etc.) were listed that could prevent a trade rule which inhibited the free movement of goods from being caught by what is now Article 28. This list is not, as will be seen below, exhaustive. The mandatory requirements that constitute the rule of reason are taken into account within the fabric of Article 28, and are separate from what is now Article 30.

The *reasoning* in *Cassis* is as significant as the result. The core of the reasoning is to be found in paragraph 8 of the judgment. This is a paragraph to be savoured, and we can learn a lot about the Court's style of adjudication by focusing upon it. The ECJ began by affirming the right of the States to regulate all matters that had not yet been the subject of Community harmonization. Yet within half a dozen lines the whole balance shifted. State regulation of such areas must be accepted, together with any obstacles to trade which might follow from disparities in national laws, *but* only in so far as these trade rules could be justified by one of the mandatory requirements listed in paragraph 8. What began as an assertion of States' rights was transformed into a legal conclusion that required the State to justify the indistinctly applicable rules under the rule of reason.

The ECJ scrutinized closely assertions that the mandatory requirements applied. Now to be sure the German government's claim in paragraph 10 was risible, and the Court was more polite in its response than the argument warranted. The substance of the main claim in paragraph 12 was little better, and was countered in paragraph 13. The one point of real substance raised by the German government was to be found in paragraph 12(3), and it elicited no direct response from the Court. The effect of *Cassis* was deregulatory: it rendered inapplicable trade rules that prevented goods lawfully marketed in one State from being imported into another State. The result might be a common standard based on the country with the least demanding rules, what is often referred to as the 'regulatory race to the bottom'.[34] The implications of this will be considered below.[35]

(b) APPLICATION: THE POST-*CASSIS* JURISPRUDENCE

There were numerous cases applying *Cassis* to various trade rules.[36] In *Déserbais*[37] an importer of Edam cheese from Germany into France was prosecuted for unlawful use of a trade name.

---

[34] This will not always be so: see 711–712.

[35] See below, 717–720.

[36] Case 298/87 *Smanor* [1988] ECR 4489; Case 407/85 *Drei Glocken* v. *USL Centro-Sud* [1988] ECR 4233; Case C–362/88 *GB-INNO-BM* v. *Confédération du Commerce Luxembourgeois Asbl* [1990] ECR I–667; Case C–30/99 *Commission* v. *Ireland* [2001] ECR I–4619; Case C–123/00 *Criminal Proceedings against Bellamy and English Shop Wholesale SA* [2001] ECR I–2795; Case C–14/02 *ATRAL SA* v. *Belgium* [2003] ECR I–4431.

[37] Case 286/86 *Ministère Public* v. *Déserbais* [1988] ECR 4907.

In Germany such cheese could be lawfully produced with a fat content of only 34.3 per cent, whereas in France the name Edam was restricted to cheese with a fat content of 40 per cent. The importer relied on Article 28 by way of defence to the criminal prosecution. The ECJ held, in accord with *Cassis*, that the French rule was incompatible with this Article, and could not be saved by the mandatory requirements.[38]

The same result was reached in *Gilli and Andres*,[39] where importers of apple vinegar from Germany into Italy were prosecuted for fraud because they had sold vinegar in Italy which was not made from the fermentation of wine. The rule hampered Community trade and did not benefit from the mandatory requirements, since proper labelling could alert consumers to the nature of the product, thereby avoiding consumer confusion.

The same approach was apparent in *Rau*,[40] which was concerned with national rules on packaging rather than content. Belgian law required all margarine to be marketed in cube-shaped packages, irrespective of where it had been made, but it was clearly more difficult for non-Belgian manufacturers to comply without incurring cost increases. The ECJ held Article 28 was applicable, and that the Belgian rule could not be justified on the basis of consumer protection, since any consumer confusion could be avoided by clear labelling.

(c) INDISTINCTLY APPLICABLE RULES: ARTICLE 29

Article 29 prohibits quantitative restrictions and MEQRs in relation to exports in the same manner as does Article 28 in relation to imports. The ECJ has, however, held that there is a difference in the scope of the two provisions. Whereas Article 28 will apply to discriminatory provisions and also to indistinctly applicable measures, Article 29 will, it seems, apply only if there is discrimination.[41] An exporter faced with a national rule on, for example, quality standards for a product to be marketed in that State cannot use Article 29 to argue that such a rule renders it more difficult for that exporter to penetrate other Community markets.

This was established in *Groenveld*.[42] Dutch legislation prohibited all manufacturers of meat products from having in stock or processing horsemeat. The purpose was to safeguard the export of meat products to countries which prohibited the marketing of horseflesh. It was impossible to detect the presence of horsemeat within other meat products, and therefore the ban was designed to prevent its use by preventing meat processors from having such horse-meat in stock at all. The sale of horsemeat was not actually forbidden in the Netherlands. Nonetheless the Court held that the Dutch rule did not infringe what is now Article 29. The Article was aimed at national measures which had as their specific object or effect the restriction of exports, so as to provide a particular advantage for national production at the expense of the trade of other Member States. This was not the case here, said the Court, since the

---

[38] The ECJ acknowledged that there might be cases where a product presented under a particular name was so different in terms of its content from products generally known by that name that it could not be regarded as falling within the same category. This was not so on the facts of the instant case.

[39] Case 788/79 *Italian State* v. *Gilli and Andres* [1980] ECR 2071. See also Case C–17/93 *Openbaar Ministerie* v. *Van der Veldt* [1994] ECR I–3537.

[40] Case 261/81 *Walter Rau Lebensmittelwerke* v. *de Smedt Pvba* [1982] ECR 3961. See also Case C–317/92 *Commission* v. *Germany* [1994] ECR I–2039; Case C–369/89 *Groupement des Producteurs, Importeurs et Agents Généraux d'Eaux Minérales Etrangères (Piagème) Asbl* v. *Peeters Pvba* [1991] ECR I–2971.

[41] Case C–12/02 *Criminal Proceedings against Marco Grilli* [2003] ECR I–11585, paras. 41–42.

[42] Case 15/79 *P.B. Groenveld BV* v. *Produktschap voor Vee en Vlees* [1979] ECR 3409. See also Case 237/82 *Jongeneel Kaas* v. *The State (Netherlands) and Stichting Centraal Organ Zuivelcontrole* [1984] ECR 483; Case 98/86 *Ministère Public* v. *Mathot* [1987] ECR 809; Case C–293/02 *Jersey Produce Marketing Organisation* v. *States of Jersey* [2005] ECR I–9543.

prohibition applied to the production of goods of a certain kind without drawing a distinction depending on whether such goods were intended for the national market or for export.[43]

The rationale for making Article 28 applicable to measures which do not discriminate is that they impose a dual burden on the importer who will have to satisfy the relevant rules in his or her own State and also the State of import. This will not normally be so in relation to Article 29. Thus, in a case such as *Groenveld* the rule applied to all goods, those for both the domestic and the export market, and the goods were subject to no further rule at that stage of production or sale.[44] One could, however, imagine instances where a dual burden might exist. There are, moreover, indications from the ECJ's jurisprudence under what is now Article 49 that rules which apply to exporters will be caught even if they are not discriminatory.[45] We shall discuss this issue further below.[46]

(d) INDISTINCTLY APPLICABLE RULES: THE LIMITS OF ARTICLE 28

Cassis signalled the ECJ's willingness to extend Article 28 to catch indistinctly applicable rules. The difficulty is that all rules that concern trade, directly or indirectly, could be said to affect the free movement of goods in various ways. Thus, as Weatherill and Beaumont note, it could be said that rules requiring the owner of a firearm to have a licence, or spending limits imposed on government departments, reduce the sales opportunities for imported products.[47] It would, as they say, seem absurd to bring such rules within Article 28, yet they could be caught by the *Dassonville* formula.[48]

A distinction can however be drawn, as Weatherill and Beaumont note,[49] between what may be termed dual-burden rules and equal-burden rules. *Cassis* is concerned with dual-burden rules. State A imposes rules on the content of goods. These are applied to goods imported from State B, even though such goods will already have complied with the trade rules in State B. *Cassis* prevents State A from imposing its rules in such instances, unless they can be saved by the mandatory requirements. Equal-burden rules are those applying to all goods, irrespective of origin, which regulate trade in some manner. They are not designed to be protectionist. These rules may have an impact on the overall volume of trade, but this will be no greater impact for imports than for domestic products.

A key issue is whether rules of this latter nature should be held to fall within Article 28, subject to a possible justification, or whether they should be deemed to be outside Article 28 altogether. The result might be the same, in that the rule might be held lawful. The choice is nonetheless important. If these rules are within Article 28 they are *prima facie* unlawful, and the burden is on those seeking to uphold the rule to show objective justification. Both strategies were evident in the ECJ's jurisprudence prior to *Keck.*[50]

---

[43] N. 42 above, para. 7.

[44] R. Barents, 'New Developments in Measures Having Equivalent Effect' (1981) 18 *CMLRev.* 271.

[45] Case C–384/93 *Alpine Investments BV* v. *Minister van Financiën* [1995] ECR I–1141. Jacobs AG doubted whether *Groenveld*, n. 42 above, would apply to rules of the exporting State which concerned the marketing of goods: [1995] ECR I–1141, para. 55.

[46] See Ch. 22.

[47] S. Weatherill and P. Beaumont, *EU Law* (3rd edn., Penguin, 1999), 608.

[48] Case 8/74 [1974] ECR 837, para. 5.

[49] N. 47 above, 608–609.

[50] Cases C–267 and 268/91 *Criminal Proceedings against Keck and Mithouard* [1993] ECR I–6097.

In some cases it held that rules which did not relate to the *characteristics* of the goods and did not impose a dual burden on the importer, but concerned only the conditions on which all goods were *sold*, were outside Article 28. Thus in *Oebel*[51] the Court held that a rule which prohibited the delivery of bakery products to consumers and retailers, but not wholesalers, at night was not caught, since it applied in the same way to all producers wherever they were established.[52]

In other cases the Court held, however, that Article 28 could apply to rules which were not dissimilar to those in the preceding paragraph. Thus in *Cinéthèque*[53] the ECJ held that a French law banning the sale or hire of videos of films during the first year in which the film was released, the objective being to encourage people to go to the cinema and hence protect the profitability of cinematographic production, was caught by Article 28, even though it did not favour domestic production and did not seek to regulate trade. The ECJ held that the French law could however be justified, since it sought to encourage the creation of films irrespective of their origin.[54] The same approach is apparent in the *Sunday Trading* cases.

Case 145/88 **Torfaen BC v. B & Q plc**
[1989] ECR 3851

B & Q was prosecuted for violation of the Sunday trading laws which prohibited retail shops from selling on Sundays, subject to exceptions for certain types of products. B & Q claimed that these laws constituted an MEQR within Article 30. The effect of the laws was to reduce total turnover by about 10 per cent, with a corresponding diminution of imports from other Member States. But imported goods were, in this respect, in no worse a position than domestic goods: the reduction in total turnover affected all goods equally.

THE ECJ

11. The first point which must be made is that national rules prohibiting retailers from opening their premises on Sunday apply to imported and domestic products alike. In principle, the marketing of products imported from other Member States is not therefore made more difficult than the marketing of domestic products.

12. Next, it must be recalled that in its judgment . . . in Joined Cases 60 and 61/84 (*Cinéthèque*) the Court held, with regard to a prohibition of the hiring of video-cassettes applicable to domestic and imported products alike, that such a prohibition was not compatible with the principle of the free movement of goods provided for in the Treaty unless any obstacle to Community trade thereby created did not exceed what was necessary in order to ensure the attainment of the objective in view and unless that objective was justified with regard to Community law.

13. In those circumstances it is therefore necessary in a case such as this to consider first of all whether rules such as those at issue pursue an aim which is justified with regard to

---

[51] Case 155/80 [1981] ECR 1993, para. 20.

[52] See also Case 148/85 *Direction Générale des Impôts and Procureur de la République v. Forest* [1986] ECR 3449, para. 11; Case 75/81 *Belgian State v. Blesgen* [1982] ECR 1211; Case C–23/89 *Quietlynn Ltd. v. Southend-on-Sea BC* [1990] ECR I–3059.

[53] Cases 60 and 61/84 *Cinéthèque SA v. Fédération Nationale des Cinémas Français* [1985] ECR 2605.

[54] The ECJ's approach can be contrasted with that taken by Slynn AG, who argued that the French law should fall outside Art. 28, since it did not impose any additional requirement on importers: *ibid.*, 2611.

Community law. As far as this question is concerned the Court has already stated in its judgment ... in Case 155/80 (*Oebel* [1981] ECR 1993) that national rules governing the hours of work, delivery and sale in the bread and confectionery industry constitute a legitimate part of economic and social policy, consistent with the objectives of public interest pursued by the Treaty.

14. The same consideration must apply as regards national rules governing the opening hours of retail premises. Such rules reflect certain political and economic choices in so far as their purpose is to ensure that working and non-working hours are so arranged as to accord with national or regional socio-cultural characteristics, and that, in the present state of Community law, is a matter for Member States. Furthermore such rules are not designed to govern the patterns of trade between Member States.

15. Secondly, it is necessary to ascertain whether the effects of such national rules exceed what is necessary to achieve the aim in view. As is indicated in Article 3 of Commission Directive 70/50 ... the prohibition laid down in Article 30 covers national measures governing the marketing of products where the restrictive effect of such measures on the free movement of goods exceeds the effects intrinsic to trade rules.

16. The question whether the effects of specific national rules do in fact remain within that limit is a question to be determined by the national court.

17. The reply to the first question must therefore be that Article 30 of the Treaty must be interpreted as meaning that the prohibition which it lays down does not apply to national rules prohibiting retailers from opening their premises on Sunday where the restrictive effects on Community trade which may result therefrom do not exceed the effects intrinsic to rules of that kind.

The approach in *Torfaen* was conceptually identical to that in *Cinéthèque*. The rule was *prima facie* caught by what is now Article 28, but it could escape prohibition provided that there was some objective justification, and that the effects of the rule were proportionate, the latter issue to be determined by national courts. Subsequent case law within the United Kingdom attested to the difficulty in applying the ECJ's test.[55] The ECJ sought to resolve these difficulties by making it clear that Sunday trading rules were proportionate.[56] The fundamental approach nonetheless remained the same: such rules were *prima facie* within Article 28. The post-*Torfaen* case law simply made things easier for national courts by providing guidance on proportionality.

The ECJ's case law provided academics with much material concerning the proper boundaries of Article 28. Some saw little wrong with the ECJ's approach in *Cinéthèque* and *Torfaen*. Others were less happy with the Court's approach.[57] White distinguished between the characteristics of the goods and selling arrangements, a theme picked up by the ECJ in *Keck*.

---

[55] *Stoke City Council* v. *B & Q plc* [1990] 3 CMLR 31; *Wellingborough BC* v. *Payless* [1990] 1 CMLR 773; *B & Q plc* v. *Shrewsbury BC* [1990] 3 CMLR 535; *Payless* v. *Peterborough CC* [1990] 2 CMLR 577; A. Arnull, 'What Shall We Do On Sunday?' (1991) 16 *ELRev.* 112.

[56] Case C–312/89 *Union Département des Syndicats CGT de l'Aisne* v. *SIDEF Conforama* [1991] ECR I–997; Case C–332/89 *Ministère Public* v. *Marchandise* [1991] ECR I–1027; Cases C–306/88, 304/90, and 169/91 *Stoke-on-Trent CC* v. *B & Q plc* [1992] ECR I–6457, 6493, 6635; Cases C–418–421, 460–462, and 464/93, 9–11, 14–15, 23–24, and 332/94 *Semeraro Casa Uno Srl* v. *Sindaco del Commune di Erbusco* [1996] ECR I–2975.

[57] J. Steiner, 'Drawing the Line: Uses and Abuses of Art. 30 EEC' (1992) 29 *CMLRev.* 749.

E. White, In Search of the Limits to Article 30 of the EEC Treaty[58]

[A]s the judgment of the Court in *Cassis de Dijon* clearly shows, Member States are not entitled to require that imported products have the same characteristics as are required of, or are traditional in, domestic products unless this is strictly necessary for the protection of some legitimate interest. There is not, however, the same need to require the rules relating to the circumstances in which certain goods may be sold or used in the importing Member State to be overridden for this purpose as long as imported products enjoy equal access to the market of the importing Member State compared with national goods. In such a case the imported product is not deprived of any advantage it derives from the different legal and economic environment prevailing in the place of production. In fact, any reduction of total sales (and therefore imports) which may result from restrictions on the circumstances in which they may be sold does not arise from disparities between national rules but rather out of the existence of the rules in the importing Member State.

6. INDISTINCTLY AND DISTINCTLY APPLICABLE RULES: *KECK* AND SELLING ARRANGEMENTS

(a) *KECK*: SELLING ARRANGEMENTS

Cases C–267 and 268/91 **Criminal Proceedings against Keck and Mithouard**
[1993] ECR I–6097

[Note ToA renumbering: Arts. 30 and 177 are now Arts. 28 and 234]

Keck and Mithouard (K & M) were prosecuted in the French courts for selling goods at a price which was lower than their actual purchase price (resale at a loss), contrary to a French law of 1963 as amended in 1986. The law did not ban sales at a loss by the manufacturer. K & M claimed that the French law was contrary to Community law concerning, *inter alia*, free movement of goods.

THE ECJ

12. It is not the purpose of national legislation imposing a general prohibition on resale at a loss to regulate trade in goods between Member States.

13. Such legislation may, admittedly, restrict the volume of sales, and hence the volume of sales of products from other Member States, in so far as it deprives traders of a method of sales promotion. But the question remains whether such a possibility is sufficient to characterize the legislation in question as a measure having equivalent effect to a quantitative restriction on imports.

---

[58] (1989) 26 *CMLRev.* 235, 246–247, italics in the original. See also K. Mortelmans, 'Article 30 of the EEC Treaty and Legislation Relating to Market Circumstances: Time to Consider a New Definition' (1991) 28 *CMLRev.* 115, 130.

14. In view of the increasing tendency of traders to invoke Article 30 of the Treaty as a means of challenging any rules whose effect is to limit their commercial freedom even where such rules are not aimed at products from other Member States, the Court considers it necessary to re-examine and clarify its case law on this matter.

15. In 'Cassis de Dijon' ... it was held that, in the absence of harmonization of legislation, measures of equivalent effect prohibited by Article 30 include obstacles to the free movement of goods where they are the consequence of applying rules that lay down requirements to be met by such goods (such as requirements as to designation, form, size, weight, composition, presentation, labelling, packaging) to goods from other Member States where they are lawfully manufactured and marketed, even if those rules apply without distinction to all products unless their application can be justified by a public-interest objective taking precedence over the free movement of goods.

16. However, contrary to what has previously been decided, the application to products from other Member States of national provisions restricting or prohibiting certain selling arrangements is not such as to hinder directly or indirectly, actually or potentially, trade between Member States within the meaning of the *Dassonville* judgment ... provided that those provisions apply to all affected traders operating within the national territory and provided that they affect in the same manner, in law and fact, the marketing of domestic products and of those from other Member States.

17. Where those conditions are fulfilled, the application of such rules to the sale of products from another Member State is not by nature such as to prevent their access to the market or to impede access any more than it impedes the access of domestic products. Such rules therefore fall outside the scope of Article 30 of the Treaty.

18. Accordingly, the reply to be given to the national court is that Article 30 of the EEC Treaty is to be interpreted as not applying to legislation of a Member State imposing a general prohibition on resale at a loss.

It is clear that the rationale for the decision was based in part upon the distinction between dual-burden rules and equal-burden rules: paragraphs 15 to 17.

Cassis-type *rules relating to the goods themselves* were within Article 28, in part because these rules would have to be satisfied by the importer *in addition* to any such provisions existing within his or her own State (paragraph 15). Such rules were by their very nature[59] likely to impede access to the market for imported goods.

Rules concerning selling arrangements, by way of contrast, imposed an equal burden on all those seeking to market goods in a particular territory (paragraph 17). They did not impose extra costs on the importer,[60] their purpose was not to regulate trade (paragraph 12), and they did not prevent access to the market. They were therefore not within Article 28, *provided* that they affected in the same manner in law or fact domestic and imported goods: the second part of paragraph 16.

The reference to the earlier case law that was being reassessed (paragraph 16) was unclear, because the Court did not name specific cases. It appeared to encompass decisions such as *Torfaen* and probably *Cinéthèque*,[61] since the challenged rules concerned selling arrangements which affected importers no more than domestic producers and the effect on intra-Community trade was a reduction in the volume of sales.

---

[59] Cases C–401 and 402/92 *Criminal Proceedings against Tankstation 't Heuskte vof and J.B.E. Boermans* [1994] ECR I–2199, 2220.

[60] *Ibid.*

[61] In Cases C–401 and 402/92 *Tankstation*, n. 59 above, Van Gerven AG felt that *Cinéthèque* would be decided differently now in the light of *Keck*.

The ECJ's desire to exclude selling arrangements from the ambit of Article 28 is apparent from later case law. In *Tankstation*[62] the Court held that national rules which provided for the compulsory closing of petrol stations were not caught by Article 28. The ECJ repeated its ruling in *Keck*, and concluded that the rules related to selling arrangements that applied equally to all traders without distinguishing the origin of the goods. In *Punto Casa*[63] and *Semeraro*[64] the Court reached the same conclusion in relation to Italian legislation on the closure of retail outlets on Sundays. The rule applied equally to domestic and imported products, and therefore was outside the scope of Article 28. The same theme is apparent in *Hunermund*,[65] where the ECJ held that a rule prohibiting pharmacists from advertising para-pharmaceutical products that they were allowed to sell was not caught by Article 28. The Court observed that the rule was not directed towards intra-Community trade, that it did not preclude traders other than pharmacists from advertising such goods, and that it applied evenly as between all traders. Although the rule might have some impact on the overall volume of sales, this was not enough to render it an MEQR for the purpose of Article 28. The ECJ also held that national provisions restricting the number of outlets for a given product, or imposing a licensing requirement, were outside Article 28. This was either because the rule related to selling arrangements, or because the impact was too indirect and uncertain.[66]

(b) *KECK*: STATIC AND DYNAMIC SELLING ARRANGEMENTS

While one can appreciate the ECJ's desire to limit Article 28, the distinction drawn in *Keck* between rules that go to the nature of the product itself and those which relate to the selling arrangements for that product is problematic. The problem resides in ambiguity about the meaning of the term 'selling arrangements'.

This could connote only what may be termed *static selling arrangements*: rules relating to the hours at which shops may be open, the length of time for which people may work, or the type of premises in which certain goods may be sold. *Non-static or dynamic selling arrangements* include the ways in which a manufacturer chooses *to market this specific product*, through a certain form of advertising, free offers, and the like.

The objection to taking the latter out of Article 28 is that they may relate more closely to the definition of the product itself. Legislation that restricted certain forms of advertising or sales-promotion might limit intra-Community trade, even if the rules were indistinctly applicable. It might force a producer to adopt sales-promotion or advertising schemes which differed as between States, or to discontinue a scheme which was thought to be particularly effective.[67] Non-static selling arrangements can therefore form an integral aspect of the goods, in much the same way as do rules relating to composition, labelling, or presentation.

Yet it is clear from *Keck* that the Court regarded some such rules as selling arrangements and hence outside Article 28. Thus in paragraph 13 of its judgment it admitted that a rule

---

62 *Ibid.*
63 Cases C–69 and 258/93 *Punto Casa SpA* v. *Sindaco del Commune di Capena* [1994] ECR I–2355.
64 N. 56 above.
65 Case C–292/92 *R. Hunermund* v. *Landesapothekerkammer Baden-Württemberg* [1993] ECR I–6787.
66 Case C–387/93 *Banchero* [1995] ECR I–4663; Case C–379/92 *Peralta* [1994] ECR I–3453; Cases C–140–142/94 *Dip SpA* v. *Commune di Bassano del Grappa* [1995] ECR I–3257.
67 Case 286/81 *Oosthoek's Uitgeversmaatschappij BV* [1982] ECR 4575. See also Case 382/87 *Buet* v. *Minstère Public* [1989] ECR 1235; Cases C–34–36/95 *Konsumentombudsmannen (KO)* v. *De Agostini (Svenska) Forlag AB and TV-Shop i Sverige AB* [1997] ECR I–3843.

prohibiting sales at a loss deprived traders of a method of sales-promotion, and hence reduced the volume of sales, and yet treated this rule as a selling arrangement which was outside Article 28. While in *Hunermund*[68] and *Leclerc-Siplec*[69] a limited ban on advertising was characterized as a method of sales-promotion and held to be outside Article 28, and in *Schmidt*[70] a prohibition on doorstep sales of silver jewellery was held *prima facie* to fall outside Article 28.

(c) *KECK* AND SELLING ARRANGMENTS: TWO JUDICIAL QUALIFICATIONS

It is clear that if the challenged national rule requires the alteration of packaging or labelling of the imported products this generally precludes it from being a selling arrangement within *Keck*.[71] The exclusion of selling arrangements from the ambit of Article 28 is moreover subject to two important qualifications.

First, *it is open to the ECJ to characterize rules which affect selling as part of the product itself, and hence within the ambit of Article 28.* This is exemplified by *Familiapress*.[72]

Case C–368/95 **Vereinigte Familiapress Zeitungsverlags- und Vertreibs GmbH v. Heinrich Bauer Verlag**
[1997] ECR I–3689

[Note ToA renumbering: Art. 30 is now Art. 28]

Familiapress, an Austrian newspaper publisher, sought to restrain HBV, a German publisher, from publishing in Austria a magazine containing crossword puzzles for which the winning readers would receive prizes. Austrian legislation prohibited publishers from including such prize competitions in their papers. Austria argued that its legislation was not caught by Article 30, since the national law related to a method of sales promotion, and was therefore, according to *Keck*, outside Article 30.

THE ECJ

11. The Court finds that, even though the relevant national legislation is directed against a method of sales promotion, in this case it bears on the actual content of the products, in so far as the competitions in question form an integral part of the magazine in which they appear. As a result, the national legislation in question as applied to the facts of the case is not concerned with a selling arrangement within the meaning of the judgment in *Keck and Mithouard*.

12. Moreover, since it requires traders established in other Member States to alter the contents of the periodical, the prohibition at issue impairs access of the products concerned to the market of the Member State of importation and consequently hinders free movement of

---

[68] Case C–292/92 *Hunermund*, n. 65 above.

[69] Case C–412/93 *Société d'Importation Edouard Leclerc-Siplec* v. *TFI Publicité SA* [1995] ECR I–179.

[70] Case C–441/04 *A-Punkt Schmuckhandels GmbH* v. *Schmidt* [2006] ECR I–2093.

[71] Case C–12/00 *Commission* v. *Spain* [2003] ECR I–459, para. 76; Case C–416/00 *Morellato* v. *Commune di Padova* [2003] ECR I–9343, paras. 29–30. Compare Case C–159/00 *Sapud Audic*, n. 25 above, paras. 72–75.

[72] See also Case C–67/97 *Criminal Proceedings against Bluhme* [1998] ECR I–8033, para. 21; Cases C–158 and 159/04 *Alfa Vita Vassilopoulos AE and Carrefour Marinopoulos AE* v. *Elliniko Dimosio and Nomarchiaki Aftodioikisi Ioanninon* [2006] ECR I–8135.

goods. It therefore constitutes in principle a measure having equivalent effect within the meaning of Article 30 of the Treaty.

The very distinction drawn between selling arrangements and product characteristics nonetheless generates further questions as to how, for example, cases concerned with the *use* of products should be regarded. In *Mickelsson*,[73] Advocate General Kokott proposed that restrictions on use should be treated analogously with selling arrangements. They should therefore be regarded as falling outside Article 28, provided that they were not product-related, applied to all relevant traders in the national territory, and affected in the same manner, in law and fact, domestic and imported goods.

Secondly, *even if a rule is categorized as being about selling, it will still be within Article 28 if the rule has a differential impact, in law or fact, for domestic traders and importers.*[74] This is made clear in paragraph 16 of *Keck* and is exemplified by the following cases.[75]

Cases C–34–36/95 **Konsumentombudsmannen (KO) v. De Agostini (Svenska) Forlag AB and TV-Shop i Sverige AB**
[1997] ECR I–3843

[Note ToA renumbering: Arts. 30 and 36 are now Arts. 28 and 30]

The case concerned a Swedish ban on television advertising directed at children under 12 and a ban on commercials for skincare products. It was argued that this was in breach of Article 30, and hence could not be applied in relation to advertising broadcast from another Member State. The ECJ, following *Leclerc-Siplec*, characterized the Swedish law as one concerning selling arrangements. It then continued as follows.

THE ECJ

40. In ... *Keck* ... at paragraph 16, the Court held that national measures restricting or prohibiting certain selling arrangements are not covered by Article 30 ... so long as they apply to all traders operating within the national territory and as long as they affect in the same manner, in law and fact, the marketing of domestic products and of those from other Member States.

41. The first condition is clearly fulfilled in the cases before the national court.

42. As regards the second condition, it cannot be excluded that an outright ban, applying in one Member State, of a type of promotion for a product which is lawfully sold there might have a greater impact on products from other Member States.

43. Although the efficacy of the various types of promotion is a question of fact to be determined in principle by the referring court, it is to be noted that ... de Agostini stated that television advertising was the only effective form of promotion enabling it to penetrate the Swedish market since it had no other advertising methods for reaching children and their parents.

---

[73] Case C–142/05 *Åklagaren v. Mickelsson and Roos*, 14 Dec. 2006. At the time of writing the ECJ's decision is awaited. Compare Case C–110/05 *Commission v. Italy*, 5 Oct. 2006, Leger AG.

[74] The determination of this possible differential impact will often be left to the national court: see, e.g., Case C–20/03 *Burmanjer* [2005] ECR I–4133; Case C–441/04 *Schmidt*, n. 70 above.

[75] P. Koutrakos, 'On Groceries, Alcohol and Olive Oil: More on Free Movement of Goods after *Keck*' (2001) 26 *ELRev.* 391.

44. Consequently, an outright ban on advertising aimed at children less than 12 years of age and of misleading advertising ... is not covered by Article 30 ... , unless it can be shown that the ban does not affect in the same way, in fact and in law, the marketing of national products and of products from other Member States.

45. In the latter case, it is for the national court to determine whether the ban is necessary to satisfy overriding requirements of general public importance or one of the aims listed in Article 36 of the Treaty, if it is proportionate to that purpose and if those aims or requirements could not have been attained or fulfilled by measures less restrictive of intra-Community trade.

Case C–405/98 **Konsumentombudsmannen (KO) v. Gourmet International Products AB (GIP)**
[2001] ECR I–1795

[Note ToA renumbering: Art. 30 is now Art. 28]

The Swedish Consumer Ombudsman sought an injunction restraining GIP from placing advertisements for alcohol in magazines. Swedish law prohibited advertising of alcohol on radio and television, and prohibited advertising of spirits, wines, and strong beer in periodicals other than those distributed at the point of sale. The prohibition on advertising did not apply to periodicals aimed at traders such as restaurateurs. GIP published a magazine containing advertisements for alcohol. 90 per cent of the subscribers were traders, and 10 per cent were private individuals. GIP argued that the advertising ban was contrary to, *inter alia*, Article 30. It contended that the advertising ban had a greater effect on imported goods than on those produced in Sweden.

THE ECJ

18. It should be pointed out that, according to paragraph 17 of its judgment in *Keck and Mithouard*, if national provisions restricting or prohibiting selling arrangements are to avoid being caught by Article 30 of the Treaty, they must not be of such a kind to prevent access to the market by products from another state or to impede access any more than they impede the access of domestic products.

19. The Court has also held, in paragraph 42 of ... *De Agostini* ... that it cannot be excluded that an outright prohibition, applying in one Member State, of a type of product which is lawfully sold there might have a greater impact on products from other Member States.

20. It is apparent that a prohibition on advertising ... not only prohibits a form of marketing a product but in reality prohibits producers and importers from directing any advertising messages at consumers, with a few insignificant exceptions.

21. Even without its being necessary to carry out a precise analysis of the facts characteristic of the Swedish situation, which it is for the national court to do, the Court is able to conclude that, in the case of products like alcoholic beverages, the consumption of which is linked to traditional social practices and to local habits and customs, a prohibition of all advertisements in the press, on the radio and on television, the direct mailing of unsolicited material or the placing of posters on the public highway is liable to impede access to the market by products from other Member States more than it impedes access by domestic products, with which consumers are instantly more familiar.

...

> 25. A prohibition on advertising such as that in issue ... must therefore be regarded as affecting the marketing of products from other Member States more heavily than the marketing of domestic products and as therefore constituting an obstacle to trade between Member States caught by Article 30 of the Treaty.

In *de Agostini* and *Gourmet* the relevant advertising ban was total. However the ECJ has also brought cases which impeded market access within Article 28. In *Franzen* Swedish law required a licence for those, including importers, engaged in the making of alcohol or in wholesaling it. This was held to infringe Article 28, since it imposed additional costs on importers, and because most licences had been issued to Swedish traders.[76] In *Heimdienst* the ECJ showed that it was willing to consider the proviso to paragraph 16 of *Keck* in relation to a selling arrangement that impeded, rather than prevented, access to the market.[77]

Case C–254/98 **Schutzverband gegen unlauteren Wettbewerb v. TK-Heimdienst Sass GmbH**
[2000] ECR I–151

The case concerned an Austrian rule relating to bakers, butchers, and grocers. They could make sales on rounds in a given administrative district only if they also traded from a permanent establishment in that district or an adjacent municipality, where they offered for sale the same goods as they did on their rounds. The ECJ classified the rule as one relating to selling arrangements, since it specified the geographical areas in which such operators could sell their goods in this manner. The ECJ found that the legislation did have a differential impact on domestic traders and others. Local economic operators would be more likely to have a permanent establishment in the administrative district or an adjacent municipality, whereas others would have to set up such an establishment, thereby incurring additional costs.

THE ECJ

29. It follows that the application to all operators trading in the national territory of national legislation such as that in point in the main proceedings in fact impedes access to the market of the Member State of importation for products from other Member States more than it impedes access for domestic products (see to this effect ... *Alpine Investments* ...).

(d) JUDICIAL AND ACADEMIC OPINION CONCERNING *KECK*: EQUALITY AND MARKET ACCESS

Reaction to the *Keck* decision was not generally favourable.[78] It was argued that *Keck* placed too much emphasis on factual and legal equality at the expense of market access. The

---

[76] Case C–189/95 *Criminal Proceedings against Franzen* [1997] ECR I–5909.

[77] See also Case C–322/01 *Deutscher Apothekerverband v. 0800 Doc Morris NV and Jacques Waterval* [2003] ECR I–14887, paras. 68–75; Case C–20/03 *Burmanjer*, n. 74 above.

[78] See, e.g., N. Reich, 'The "November Revolution" of the European Court of Justice: *Keck*, *Meng* and *Audi* Revisited' (1994) 31 *CMLRev.* 459; D. Chalmers, 'Repackaging the Internal Market—The Ramifications of the *Keck* Judgment' (1994) 19 *ELRev.* 385; L. Gormley, 'Reasoning Renounced? The Remarkable Judgment in *Keck*

approach in *Keck* was, as we have seen, to deny that rules relating to selling arrangements came within Article 28, provided that such rules did not discriminate in law or fact between traders from different Member States. It was argued that this ignored the importance of market access: trading rules could be formally equal in the preceding sense, and still operate so as to inhibit market access. In so far as this might be so, it would, therefore, be misguided to exclude them from Article 28. This line of argument has been advanced judicially and in the academic literature. They will be considered in turn.

(i) *Judicial Concern*

The concern was voiced judicially by Advocate General Jacobs in *Leclerc-Siplec*.[79] The case concerned a prohibition on television advertising imposed by French law on the distribution sector, the purpose being to protect the regional press by forcing the sector to advertise through that medium. He felt that advertising could play a very important part in breaking down barriers to inter-state trade, and was therefore unhappy that it should always be outside Article 28.[80] His preferred approach represented a subtle modification of the *Keck* formula.

Advocate General Jacobs' starting point was that all undertakings engaged in legitimate economic activity should have unfettered access to the market. If there was a *substantial* restriction on that access then it should be caught by Article 28. When the measure affected the goods themselves, as in *Cassis*-type cases, then it would be *presumed to have this substantial impact.* If, however, the contested measure affected selling arrangements and was not discriminatory, the substantiality of the impact would depend, *inter alia*, on: the range of goods affected, the nature of the restriction, whether the impact was direct or indirect, and the extent to which other selling arrangements were available. If there was no substantial impact, or the effect on trade was *de minimis*, then such measures would not be within Article 28. The ECJ however declined to follow the suggestions of the Advocate General and applied *Keck* to the case.

The approach suggested by Advocate General Jacobs has nonetheless influenced the ECJ in its more recent jurisprudence. The ECJ has, as seen from *de Agostini* and *Heimdienst*, been willing to consider market access more seriously, and this has also been emphasized in other recent cases.[81] It has done so through consideration of whether the proviso to paragraph 16 of *Keck* should be applicable. It has considered in particular whether the selling rule could have the same factual impact for the importer. It was not fortuitous that Advocate General Jacobs wrote the Opinions in *de Agostini*[82] and *Gourmet International*,[83] and that the ECJ adopted much of his reasoning.

& Mithouard' [1994] *EBLRev.* 63; S. Weatherill, 'After *Keck*: Some Thoughts on how to Clarify the Clarification' (1996) 33 *CMLRev.* 885; Maduro, n. 2 above, 83–87; C. Barnard, 'Fitting the Remaining Pieces into the Goods and Persons Jigsaw?' (2001) 26 *ELRev.* 35.

[79] N. 69 above, paras. 38–45. There is an interesting analogy here with competition law which in effect treats certain types of cartel behaviour as unlawful in and of themselves, while other types of activity are subjected to a market analysis to determine whether they do impede competition: see Ch. 25.

[80] See also Jacobs AG in Case C–384/93 *Alpine Investments*, n. 45 above; Lenz AG in Case C–391/92 *Commission* v. *Greece* [1995] ECR I–1621, 1628–1629.

[81] Case C–416/00 *Morellato*, n. 71 above, para. 31; Case C–98/01 *Commission* v. *United Kingdom and Northern Ireland* [2003] ECR I–4641, para. 46.

[82] Cases C–34–36/95 *de Agostini*, n. 67 above, paras. 95–105.

[83] Case C–405/98 *Konsumentombudsmannen (KO)* v. *Gourmet International Products AB (GIP)* [2001] ECR I–1795.

Judicial concern has been voiced more recently by Advocate General Maduro in *Alfa Vita*.[84] He noted that while *Keck* was intended to clarify the ambit of Article 28 it had 'proved to be a source of uncertainty for economic operators'[85] because of difficulties in distinguishing between rules relating to selling arrangements and product characteristics. It had also led to difficulty since this distinction did not apply in other areas of free movement, which could be especially problematic when the same facts raised issues concerning, for example, goods and services.[86]

Advocate General Maduro therefore proposed three criteria to guide the resolution of cases.[87] First, discriminatory provisions, whether direct or indirect, were prohibited. Secondly, the imposition of supplementary costs on cross-border activity had to be justified. This served to explain classic *Cassis de Dijon*-type cases, where the imported products already had to comply with product rules and the attendant costs of the State of origin. The exclusion of selling arrangements from Article 28 was, said Maduro, explicable because they normally did not impose such costs, but where they did so they should be caught by Article 28. Thirdly, 'any measure which impedes to a greater extent the access to the market and the putting into circulation of products from other Member States is considered to be a measure having equivalent effect within the meaning of Article 28 EC'.[88]

(ii) *Academic Concern*

The academic argument for an approach based on market access was put forcefully by Weatherill.[89] He drew upon the reasoning of Advocate General Jacobs considered above, and on jurisprudence concerned with Articles 49 and 39.[90] Weatherill argued that the correct approach to Article 28, and the other Treaty Articles was to focus upon market access, and not just factual and legal equality. The reason the applicants failed in *Keck* was that 'they were measures applying equally in law and in fact and exercising no direct impediment to the access to markets of a Member State'.[91] He proposed the following test.

S. Weatherill, After Keck: Some Thoughts on How to Clarify the Clarification[92]

Only issue.

Measures introduced by authorities in a Member State which apply equally in law and in fact to all goods and services without reference to origin and which impose no direct or substantial hindrance to the access of imported goods or services to the market of that Member State escape the prohibition of Articles 30 and 59.[93]

---

84 Cases C–158 and 159/04 *Alfa Vita*, n. 72 above.
85 *Ibid.*, para. 31, Maduro AG.
86 *Ibid.*, paras. 33, 51.
87 *Ibid.*, paras. 43–45.
88 *Ibid.*, para. 45.
89 (1996) 33 *CMLRev.* 885.
90 Case C–384/93 *Alpine Investments*, n. 45 above; Case C–415/93 *Union Royale Belge des Sociétés de Football Association ASBL* v. *Jean-Marc Bosman* [1995] ECR I–4921.
91 N. 89 above, 895.
92 *Ibid.*, at 885, 896–897, 904–906, italics in the original.
93 Now Arts. 28 and 49.

[*Weatherill summarizes the argument in the following way*:]

Pre-*Keck*, the Court had lost sight of the link between Article 30 and internal market building by pushing it too far in the direction of general review of national market regulation disassociated from a need to show a hindrance to trading activities aimed at the realization of the internal market. The most notorious example was the 'Sunday Trading' saga. The subjection of *all* measures of national market regulation to supervision under Community law was beginning to damage the image and legitimacy of the European Court. *Keck* exploded the notion that there might be an individual 'right to trade' capable of vindication *via* EC internal market law, but *Keck* itself created a risk of toppling too far in the opposite direction, thereby imperilling the internal market, by focusing on factual and legal equality of application to the exclusion of questions of market access and obstruction to the construction of the cross-border commercial strategies. The principal significance of the post-*Keck* adjustment is the welcome confirmation that internal market law is not confined to supervision of measures that are legally or factually unequal in application. . . .

In *Keck*, *Leclerc-Siplec* and other similar cases, the limit on commercial freedom could not be directly connected to any cross-border aspect of the activity. In *Alpine Investments*, by contrast, the cross-border aspect was of direct significance; so too in *Bosman*, whose access to employment in another state was directly affected by the rules.

. . . The injection of an adequate cross-border element enables a claim not simply to an equality right, but instead to the dynamic protection of Community law on free movement, subject only to the capacity of the regulator to show justification for the restrictions. . . .

The academic argument in favour of market access was reinforced by Barnard who, like Weatherill, drew on case law from persons and services, as well as goods.

C. Barnard, Fitting the Remaining Pieces into the Goods and Persons Jigsaw?[94]

[A]n approach based on the access to the market provides us with a more sophisticated framework for analysing the goods and persons case law. . . . [T]his is the approach advocated by Advocate General Jacobs in *Leclerc*. Non-discriminatory measures which directly and substantially impede access to the market (including the extreme case of preventing access to the market altogether) breach the Treaty provision unless they can be justified under one of the public interest grounds or the express derogations and are proportionate (*Schindler*, *Alpine* and *Bosman*). In the case of non-discriminatory measures which do not substantially hinder access to the market the Court will say either that the impediment is too uncertain and remote and so does not breach the Treaty provision at all (*Graf*, *Krantz*), or that the measure has no effect whatsoever on inter-state trade and so is not caught by EC law at all—the outcome is the same. This means that national restrictions on, for example, planning or the green belt, which were introduced for a variety of environmental and social reasons not directly concerned with inter-state trade, can be dealt with adequately. They are not 'certain selling arrangements' in the formal sense, but they are not discriminatory and they do not substantially hinder access to the market. Similarly, national restrictions on the opening hours of shops do not substantially hinder access to the market but merely curtail the exercise of that freedom. However extreme limits on opening hours may well substantially hinder access to the market and so should breach Article 28 and need to be justified.

[94] (2001) 26 *ELRev*. 35, 52.

(e) *KECK*, ARTICLE 28, AND MARKET ACCESS:
MEANING AND APPLICATION

Market access may well be the idea underlying the jurisprudence on free movement. It is, however, necessary to clarify the meaning and application of this concept.

First, it is important to be clear about the *meaning accorded to market access in the ECJ's case law on goods*. In *Keck* prevention or impediment to market access appeared to be simply the consequence of a national rule that applied differentially as between domestic traders and importers: paragraphs 16 and 17. The focus in the post-*Keck* case law was on the existence of such factual or legal differentiation. The ECJ has more recently subtly shifted its position, according greater status to market access in its own right. In *Gourmet International*[95] the ECJ stated that selling arrangements would be outside Article 28 only if they did not prevent access to the market by imported products *or* impede access by imports more than they impeded access by domestic products.

Secondly, it is equally important to understand the *general meaning of market access*. Market access can be viewed from the perspective of both producer and consumer. For the producer, free movement facilitates sales of goods into different national markets, with the primary objective of challenging existing producers in the country of import and the secondary objective of allowing economies of scale to be reaped. Market access is a means to an end, the end being to maximize sales/profits for the individual producer, and to enhance the optimal allocation of resources for the Community as a whole. From the perspective of the consumer, free movement increases choice. If Germans are given the option of drinking Dutch beer then some may prefer it to the domestic product.

Thirdly, *it is doubtful whether a rigid distinction can be drawn between dynamic and static selling arrangements so far as market access is concerned*. The market-access approach is normally thought to apply to dynamic selling arrangements. There is, however, a reluctance to apply the reasoning to static selling arrangements, in the sense of shop hours, locations, and the like. If, however, *limitations* on the mode of marketing/advertising are to be regarded as going to market access, then why should this not also be so in terms of *limitations* on points of sale? The success of the producer in penetrating new markets may be affected by limitations on where and when goods can be sold as by constraints on marketing.[96] It may be argued that restrictions on where and when goods can be sold would not have a direct and substantial impact on market access. This is, however, contingent on the factual circumstances of the particular case. It cannot be regarded as an *a priori* proposition. It is similarly difficult to maintain a rigid distinction between rules going to access and those that merely affect the volume of sales. A producer perceives rules that limit advertising as detrimental *because* they will lead to a reduction in sales. There is no difference between a rule prohibiting certain forms of marketing or advertising leading to a diminution in sales of 30 per cent, and a rule which limits the number or operating hours of shops, leading to the same sales reduction. Both rules can affect the volume of sales and penetration of the new market. Non-discriminatory static selling arrangements may therefore, as Barnard rightly notes, substantially hinder market access.[97]

Finally, *we must be cognizant of the difficulties of applying a test based on direct and substantial impact of access to the market*. Proponents of the test recognize that this can be difficult to

---

[95] Case C–405/98 *Gourmet International*, n. 83 above, para. 18.

[96] This was the argument made, unsuccessfully, in Cases C–418–421, 460–462, and 464/93, 9–11, 14–15, 23–24, and 332/94 *Semeraro*, n. 56 above.

[97] Barnard, n. 94 above, 52; C. Barnard, *The Substantive Law of the EU: The Four Freedoms* (Oxford University Press, 2004), 144–148.

estimate.[98] A court may have to take into account the range of goods affected, the existence or not of alternative selling arrangements, and the nature of the restriction itself. This will not be an easy task for the ECJ. It will be even more difficult for national courts.[99] However, the ECJ may provide guidance to the national court, as in *de Agostini*,[100] or it may go further and state there has been an impediment to market access, as in *Gourmet International*.[101] It is true that the ECJ, CFI, and national courts have to face not dissimilar tasks in the context of competition law, when deciding whether an agreement has an effect on competition. There are, however, real differences between the two areas. In competition law the backdrop to the inquiry is a developed micro-economic theory about cartels which deviate from perfect or imperfect competition; in free movement of goods there is no ready consensus on what does or does not come within the meaning of market access. In competition law private agreements are at stake; in free movement it is national regulations.

(f) SUMMARY AND CHOICES

i.   The case law prior to *Keck* exemplified the difficulties in defining the outer boundaries of Article 28. The ECJ in its pre-*Keck* jurisprudence was being asked to apply this Article to an ever-wider range of rules, the effect of which on trade was marginal. We have seen, however, that *Keck* itself was criticized for being overly formalistic, by drawing a distinction between rules relating to the characteristics of the product and those concerning selling arrangements, which is unsatisfactory. This dissatisfaction led to the call to focus on market access. There are in essence three choices concerning the approach to Article 28.

ii. The first choice is to *use prevention, or direct and substantial hindrance, of access to the market as the criterion for the applicability of Article 28*. This would be beneficial in focusing attention on a key policy reason underlying free movement of goods, services, and persons. The need to consider whether there has been some substantial restriction of market access does, however, inevitably entail costs, both for courts applying the test and for private parties who may be uncertain about the legality of their planned conduct.

iii. The second choice is *for a test based on substantial hindrance to market access, subject to presumptions based on the type of case*. This was the approach of Advocate General Jacobs in *Leclerc-Siplec*.[102] When the measure affected the goods themselves, as in *Cassis*-type cases, then it would be presumed to have this substantial impact. If, however, the contested measure affected selling arrangements and was not discriminatory, the substantiality of the impact would depend on factors such as the range of goods affected, the nature of the restriction, whether the impact was direct or indirect, and the extent to which other selling arrangements were available. It would on this view still be necessary to distinguish between cases concerning product characteristics and those concerning selling arrangements.

iv. The third choice *would be to persist with the test in Keck as developed by later case law*. Selling arrangements are presumptively outside Article 28, but can be caught either by

---

[98]   Weatherill, n. 89 above, 898–901; Barnard, n. 94 above, 55–56.

[99]   National courts are intended to apply Art. 28 and hence to disapply conflicting national law of their own initiative, subject always to the possibility of an Art. 234 reference: Case C–358/95 *Tommaso Morellato* v. *Unità Sanitairia Locale (USL) No. 11 di Pordenone* [1997] ECR I–1431.

[100] Cases C–34–36/95 *de Agostini*, n. 67 above.

[101] Case C–405/98 *Gourmet International*, n. 83 above.

[102] N. 69 above.

being reclassified as concerned with product characteristics, or because they have a differential application in law or fact. The ECJ in *Keck* intended to draw a more formal line as to the types of rule caught by Article 28. It was hoped that public and private costs would thereby be reduced, and that there would be clearer guidance on the limits of legitimate trading activity. However the more the ECJ reclassifies cases, the more closely it inquires into whether a selling arrangement has a differential impact, and the more it places direct emphasis on market access, the less certain is the outcome in any particular case. The reduction in public and private costs thereby diminishes, and the guidance on the legitimate limits of trading activity becomes less clear.

v.   The indications are that the ECJ is in reality moving away from the third test, and towards the second.

7. DEFENCES TO DISCRIMINATORY MEASURES: ARTICLE 30

If trade rules are found to be discriminatory[103] they can be saved through Article 30 (ex Article 36):

> The provisions of Articles 28 and 29 shall not preclude prohibitions or restrictions on imports, exports or goods in transit justified on grounds of public morality, public policy or public security; the protection of health and life of humans, animals or plants; the protection of national treasures possessing artistic, historic or archaeological value; or the protection of industrial and commercial property. Such prohibitions or restrictions shall not, however, constitute a means of arbitrary discrimination or a disguised restriction on trade between Member States.

It will come as no surprise to learn that the Court has construed Article 30 strictly. Discriminatory rules will be closely scrutinized to ensure that the defence pleaded is warranted on the facts of the case, and they must also pass a test of proportionality: the discriminatory measure must be the least restrictive possible to attain the end in view. The burden of proof under Article 30 rests with the Member State.[104]

(a) PUBLIC MORALITY

Two of the main precedents concerned challenges to laws dealing with pornography. In *Henn and Darby*[105] the ECJ was willing to accept that a UK ban on the import of pornography could be justified under what is now Article 30, notwithstanding the fact that domestic law did not ban absolutely the possession of such material. The ECJ concluded that the overall purpose of UK law was to restrain the manufacture and marketing of pornography, and that there was no lawful trade in such goods within the UK. However, a different result was reached in *Conegate*.

---

[103]   It may of course be debatable whether a rule really is discriminatory, and therefore whether it is caught by Art. 28, and requires justification under Art. 30. A good example is Case C–2/90 *Commission* v. *Belgium* [1992] ECR I–4431, noted by L. Hancher and H. Sevenster (1993) 30 *CMLRev.* 351, and D. Geradin (1993) 18 *ELRev.* 144.

[104]   Case C–17/93 *Openbaar Ministerie* v. *Van der Veldt* [1994] ECR I–3537.

[105]   Case 34/79 *R.* v. *Henn and Darby* [1979] ECR 3795.

Case 121/85 **Conegate Ltd. v. Commissioners of Customs and Excise**
[1986] ECR 1007

[Note ToA renumbering: Arts. 30, 36, and 177 are now Arts. 28, 30, and 234]

Conegate imported life-size inflatable dolls from Germany into the UK. The invoice for the dolls claimed that they were for window displays, but the Customs officials were unconvinced, particularly when they found items described as 'love love dolls'. They seized the goods, and magistrates ordered them to be forfeit. Conegate argued that the seizure and forfeiture were in breach of Article 30. The national court asked whether a prohibition on imports could be justified even though the State did not ban the manufacture or marketing of the same goods within the national territory. The ECJ repeated its reasoning from *Henn and Darby* that it was for each Member State to decide upon the nature of public morality for its own territory. It continued as follows.

THE ECJ

15. However, although Community law leaves the Member States free to make their own assessments of the indecent or obscene character of certain articles, it must be pointed out that the fact that goods cause offence cannot be regarded as sufficiently serious to justify restrictions on the free movement of goods where the Member State concerned does not adopt, with respect to the same goods manufactured or marketed within its territory, penal measures or other serious and effective measures intended to prevent the distribution of such goods in its territory.

16. It follows that a Member State may not rely on grounds of public morality to prohibit the importation of goods from other Member States when its legislation contains no prohibition on the manufacture or marketing of the same goods on its territory.

17. It is not for the Court, within the framework of the powers conferred on it by Article 177 ... to consider whether, and to what extent, the United Kingdom legislation contains such a prohibition. However, the question whether or not such a prohibition exists in a State comprised of different constituent parts which have their own internal legislation can be resolved only by taking into consideration all the relevant legislation. Although it is not necessary, for the purposes of the application of the above-mentioned rule, that the manufacture and marketing of the products whose importation has been prohibited should be prohibited in the territory of all the constituent parts, it must at least be possible to conclude from the applicable rules, taken as a whole, that their purpose is, in substance, to prohibit the manufacture and marketing of those products.

18. In this instance ... the High Court took care to define the substance of the national legislation the compatibility of which with Community law is a question which it proposes to determine. Thus it refers to rules in the importing Member State under which the goods in question may be manufactured freely and marketed subject only to certain restrictions ... namely an absolute prohibition on the transmission of such goods by post, a restriction on their public display and, in certain areas of the Member States concerned, a system of licensing of premises for the sale of those goods to customers aged 18 years and over. Such restrictions cannot however be regarded as equivalent in substance to a prohibition on manufacture and marketing.

The UK defence based on what is now Article 30 failed. The distinction between *Conegate* and *Henn and Darby* lies in the ECJ's evaluation of whether the banned imported goods were being treated more harshly than similar domestic goods. In *Henn and Darby* the ECJ was willing to find that UK law restrained the manufacture and marketing of pornography sufficiently to enable it to conclude that there was no lawful trade in such goods within the UK. In *Conegate*, by way of contrast, the ECJ reached the opposite conclusion.

It is clear, then, that while Member States are free to determine the sense of public morality applicable within their territory, they cannot place markedly stricter burdens on goods coming from outside than those that are applied to equivalent domestic goods.

(b) PUBLIC POLICY

Public policy constitutes a separate head of justification within Article 30. The phrase is potentially broad, but the ECJ has resisted attempts to interpret it too broadly. The Court has, for example, rejected arguments that the term 'public policy' can embrace consumer protection. The ECJ has reasoned that since Article 30 derogates from a fundamental rule of the Treaty enshrined in Article 28, it must be interpreted strictly, and cannot be extended to objectives not expressly mentioned therein.[106] A public policy justification must, therefore, be made in its own terms, and cannot be used as a means to advance what amounts to a separate ground for defence. It is for this reason that relatively few cases contain detailed examination of the public policy argument. The issue was considered in *Centre Leclerc*:

Case 231/83 **Cullet v. Centre Leclerc**
[1985] ECR 305

[Note ToA renumbering: Arts. 30 and 36 are now Arts. 28 and 30]

French legislation imposed minimum retail prices for fuel fixed primarily on the basis of French refinery prices and costs. The Court found that this constituted an MEQR within Article 30, since imports could not benefit fully from lower cost prices in the country of origin. The French Government sought to justify its action on the basis, *inter alia*, of public policy within Article 36. It argued that, in the absence of the pricing rules, there would be civil disturbances, blockades, and violence. Both the Advocate General and the ECJ rejected this argument, but for different reasons.

ADVOCATE GENERAL VERLOREN VAN THEMAAT[107]

However, I would add that the acceptance of civil disturbances as justification for encroachments upon the free movement of goods would, as is apparent from experiences of last year (and before, during the Franco–Italian 'wine war') have unacceptably drastic consequences. If roadblocks and other effective weapons of interest groups which feel threatened by the importation and sale at competitive prices of certain cheap products or services, or by immigrant workers or foreign businesses, were accepted as justification, the existence of the four fundamental freedoms of the Treaty could no longer be relied upon. Private interest groups would then, in the place of the Treaty and Community (and, within the limits laid down by the

---

106 Case 113/80 *Commission* v. *Ireland* [1981] ECR 1625; Case 177/83 *Kohl* v. *Ringelhan* [1984] ECR 3651; Case 229/83 *Leclerc* v. *Au Blé Vert* [1985] ECR 1.
107 [1985] 2 CMLR 524, 534.

Treaty, national) institutions, determine the scope of those freedoms. In such cases, the concept of public policy requires, rather, effective action on the part of the authorities to deal with such disturbances.

THE ECJ

32. For the purpose of applying Article 36, the French Government has invoked the disturbances to law and order (*ordre public*) and public security caused by violent reactions which should be expected from retailers affected by unrestricted competition.

33. On this point it is sufficient to observe that the French Government has not shown that an amendment of the regulations in question in conformity with the principles set out above would have consequences for law and order (*ordre public*) and public security which the French Government would be unable to meet with the resources available to it.

Thus, while the Advocate General rejected the French argument on principle, the ECJ appeared to accept that it could be pleaded under what is now Article 30, while rejecting it on the facts. The ECJ's approach might well have been simply a more diplomatic way of disposing of the point, but the Advocate General is more convincing as a matter of principle. If interest-group pressure leading to potential violence could constitute justification under Article 30 then fundamental Community freedoms would be placed in jeopardy.[108]

(c) PUBLIC SECURITY

Case 72/83 **Campus Oil Ltd. v. Minister for Industry and Energy**
[1984] ECR 2727

[Note ToA renumbering: Arts. 30 and 36 are now Arts. 28 and 30]

Irish law required importers of petrol into Ireland to buy 35 per cent of their requirements from a state-owned oil refinery at prices fixed by the Irish Government. This rule was held to constitute a MEQR within Article 30. In defence Ireland relied on public policy and security within Article 36. It argued that it was vital for Ireland to maintain its own oil refining capacity. The challenged rule was the means of ensuring that its refinery products could be marketed.[109] The ECJ held that recourse to Article 36 would not be possible if there were Community rules providing the necessary protection for oil supplies. Certain Community measures existed, but they were not comprehensive. The Court continued as follows.

---

[108] In Case C–265/95 *Commission v. France* [1997] ECR I–6959, the ECJ accepted that serious disruption to public order could justify non-intervention by the police in relation to a specific incident, but that it could not justify any general policy of this nature. See also *R. v. Chief Constable of Sussex, ex p. International Traders' Ferry Ltd.* [1997] 2 CMLR 164.

[109] The applicants who challenged the Irish system argued that the real issue was not whether Ireland should maintain an independent refining capacity, but whether such a refinery should operate at a profit or loss. They claimed that this was an economic issue which could not come within public policy or security.

THE ECJ

31. Consequently, the existing Community rules give a Member State whose supplies of petroleum products depend totally or almost totally on deliveries from other countries certain guarantees that deliveries from other Member States will be maintained in the event of a serious shortfall in proportions which match those of supplies to the market of the supplying State. However, this does not mean that the Member State concerned has an unconditional assurance that supplies will in any event be maintained at least at a level sufficient to meet its minimum needs. In those circumstances, the possibility for a Member State to rely on Article 36 to justify appropriate complementary measures at national level cannot be excluded, even where there exist Community rules on the matter.

[*The Court then considered whether the term 'public security' could cover this situation.*]

34. It should be stated in this connection that petroleum products, because of their exceptional importance as an energy source in the modern economy, are of fundamental importance for a country's existence since not only its economy but above all its institutions, its essential public services and even the survival of the inhabitants depend upon them. An interruption of supplies of petroleum products, with the resultant dangers for the country's existence, could therefore seriously affect the public security that Article 36 allows States to protect.

35. It is true that, as the Court has held on a number of occasions, most recently in ... (Case 95/81, *Commission v Italy*), Article 36 refers to matters of a non-economic nature. A Member State cannot be allowed to avoid the effects of measures provided for in the Treaty by pleading the economic difficulties caused by elimination of barriers to intra-Community trade. However, in the light of the seriousness of the consequences that an interruption in supplies of petroleum products may have for a country's existence, the aim of ensuring a minimum supply of petroleum products at all times is to be regarded as transcending purely economic considerations and thus as capable of constituting an objective covered by the concept of public security.

36. It should be added that to come within the ambit of Article 36 the rules in question must be justified by objective circumstances corresponding to the needs of public security. ...

37. As the Court has previously stated ... Article 36, as an exception to a fundamental principle of the Treaty, must be interpreted in such a way that its scope is not extended any further than is necessary for the protection of the interests which it is intended to secure and the measures taken pursuant to that Article must not create obstacles to imports which are disproportionate to those objectives. Measures adopted on the basis of Article 36 can therefore be justified only if they are such as to serve the interest which that Article protects and if they do not restrict intra-Community trade more than is absolutely necessary.

While the ECJ, therefore, accepted the public-security argument in *Campus Oil*, the circumstances to which it will be applicable are likely to be factually limited.[110] There is little enthusiasm for extending the reasoning, and in *Centre Leclerc* Advocate General VerLoren van Themaat distinguished *Campus Oil* from the situation in *Centre Leclerc*.[111]

It should not, however, be forgotten in this respect that Member States can take certain measures relating to national security pursuant to what are now Articles 296 to 298 EC.

---

110 Case C–367/89 *Richardt* [1991] ECR I–4621; Case C–398/98 *Commission* v. *Greece* [2001] ECR I–7915, paras. 29–30; but compare Case C–503/99 *Commission* v. *Belgium* [2002] ECR I–4809, para. 46.
111 [1985] 2 CMLR 524, 535–536.

(d) PROTECTION OF HEALTH AND LIFE OF HUMANS, ANIMALS, OR PLANTS

There have been numerous cases in which States have attempted to defend measures on this ground. The ECJ will closely scrutinize such claims.

First, *the Court will determine whether the protection of public health is the real purpose behind the Member States' action, or whether it was designed to protect domestic producers.* This is exemplified by *Commission* v. *United Kingdom*.[112] The UK in effect banned poultry meat imports from most other Member States, justifying this on the ground that it was necessary to protect public health, by preventing the spread of Newcastle disease which affected poultry. The ECJ held that the import ban was in fact motivated more by commercial reasons, to block French poultry, than by considerations of public health.[113] The ECJ will also closely examine the cogency of arguments concerning public health to determine whether they make sense on the facts.[114]

Secondly, the *ECJ may have to decide whether a public-health claim is sustainable where there is no perfect consensus on the scientific or medical impact of particular substances.* The ECJ's approach is exemplified by the *Sandoz* decision.

Case 174/82 Officier van Justitie v. Sandoz BV
[1983] ECR 2445

Authorities in Holland refused to allow the sale of muesli bars that contained added vitamins, on the ground that the vitamins were dangerous to public health. The muesli bars were readily available in Germany and Belgium. It was accepted that vitamins could be beneficial to health, but it was also acknowledged that excessive consumption could be harmful to health. Scientific evidence was not, however, certain as regards the point at which consumption of vitamins became excessive, particularly because vitamins consumed in one source of food might be added to those eaten from a different food source. There had been some Community legislation which touched on the general issue of food additives.

THE ECJ

15. The above mentioned Community measures clearly show that the Community legislature accepts the principle that it is necessary to restrict the use of food additives to the substances specified, whilst leaving the Member States a certain discretion to adopt stricter rules....

16. As the Court found in its judgment ... in Case 272/80 (*Frans-Nederlandse Maatschappij voor Biologische Producten* [1981] ECR 3277), in so far as there are uncertainties at the present state of scientific research it is for the Member States, in the absence of harmonization, to decide what degree of protection of the health and life of humans they intend to assure, having regard however for the requirements of the free movement of goods within the Community.

---

[112] Case 40/82 [1982] ECR 2793.

[113] The ECJ also noted that less stringent measures could have been taken to reach the same end as that desired by the UK government: *ibid.*, para. 41. See also Case 42/82 *Commission* v. *France* [1983] ECR 1013.

[114] Case 124/81 *Commission* v. *United Kingdom* [1983] ECR 203.

17. Those principles also apply to substances such as vitamins which are not as a general rule harmful in themselves but may have special harmful effects solely if taken to excess as part of the general nutrition, the composition of which is unforeseeable and cannot be monitored. In view of the uncertainties inherent in the scientific assessment, national rules prohibiting, without prior authorization, the marketing of foodstuffs to which vitamins have been added are justified on principle within the meaning of Article 36 of the Treaty on the grounds of the protection of human health.

18. Nevertheless the principle of proportionality which underlies the last sentence of Article 36 of the Treaty requires that the power of the Member States to prohibit imports of the products in question from other Member States should be restricted to what is necessary to attain the legitimate aim of protecting public health. . . .

19. Such an assessment is, however, difficult to make in relation to additives such as vitamins the above mentioned characteristics of which exclude the possibility of foreseeing or monitoring the quantities consumed as part of the general nutrition and the degree of harmfulness of which cannot be determined with sufficient certainty. Nevertheless, although in view of the present stage of harmonization of national laws at the Community level a wide discretion must be left to the Member States, they must, in order to observe the principle of proportionality, authorize marketing when the addition of vitamins to foodstuffs meets a real need, especially a technical or nutritional one.

20. The first question must therefore be answered to the effect that Community law permits national rules prohibiting without prior authorization the marketing of foodstuffs marketed in another Member State to which vitamins have been added, provided that the marketing is authorized when the addition of the vitamins meets a real need, especially a technical or nutritional one.

The ECJ's approach in *Sandoz* is finely tuned. It will decide whether the public-health claim is sustainable in principle. If there is uncertainty about the medical implications of some substance it will,[115] in the absence of Community harmonization measures, be for the Member State to decide upon the appropriate degree of protection for its citizens. This will, however, be subject to the principle of proportionality: paragraph 18.[116] When assessing proportionality the Community Courts will pay special attention to the factual basis of the defence. It is not enough for a Member State simply to assert that a measure is warranted on grounds of public health. It will also need to produce evidence or data to substantiate this claim.[117] This is so even where there may be some scientific uncertainty about the matter in issue.[118]

Thirdly, a Member State might not ban imports, but *it might subject them to checks that rendered import more difficult, and it might do so even though the goods were checked in the State of origin.* This problem of double-checking has arisen frequently, and the ECJ has become stricter over time.

---

115 See, however, Case 178/84 *Commission* v. *Germany* [1987] ECR 1227.

116 See also Case 53/80 *Officier van Justitie* v. *Koniklijke Kaasfabriek Eyssen BV* [1981] ECR 409; Case 94/83 *Albert Heijin BV* [1984] ECR 3263; Case 304/84 *Ministère Public* v. *Muller* [1986] ECR 1511; Case C–62/90 *Commission* v. *Germany* [1992] ECR I–2575; Case C–192/01 *Commission* v. *Denmark* [2003] ECR I–9693, para. 42; Case C–24/00 *Commission* v. *France* [2004] ECR I–1277, para. 49; Case C–95/01 *Criminal Proceedings against John Greenham and Leonard Abel* [2004] ECR I–1333; Case C–366/04 *Schwarz* v. *Burgermeister der Landeshauptstadt Salzburg* [2005] ECR I–10139, paras. 30–38.

117 Case 270/02 *Commission* v. *Italy* [2004] ECR I–1559.

118 Case C–41/02 *Commission* v. *Netherlands* [2004] ECR I–11375; Case C–192/01 *Commission* v. *Denmark*, n. 116 above; Case C–24/00 *Commission* v. *France*, n. 116 above.

The early approach in *Denkavit*[119] was to urge national authorities to co-operate to avoid dual burdens. National authorities had a duty to ascertain whether the documents from the State of export raised a presumption that the goods complied with the demands of the importing State. The Court admitted, however, that a second set of checks in the State of import might be lawful, provided that the requirements were necessary and proportionate.

The Court's more recent case law exhibits a healthy scepticism regarding whether a second set of controls is really required. This is evident from *Commission v. United Kingdom*[120] concerning UHT milk. The ECJ held that the UK's concerns about the product could be met by less restrictive means than the import ban and marketing system which it had instituted. The UK could, said the Court, lay down requirements that imported milk had to meet, and could demand certificates from the authorities of the exporting State.[121] If such certificates were produced then it would be for the authorities within the importing State to ascertain whether these certificates raised a presumption that the imported goods complied with the demands of domestic legislation. The ECJ concluded that the conditions for such a presumption existed in this case.[122] A similar unwillingness to subject goods to a second set of checks can be seen in the *Biologische Producten* case.[123] Dual checks would not be lawful where they unnecessarily imposed technical tests that had already been done in the State of origin, nor where the practical effect of the tests in the exporting State met the demands of the importing State.[124]

(e) OTHER GROUNDS FOR VALIDATING DISCRIMINATORY MEASURES?

The nature of this problem will be explored here and then considered in more detail below.[125] The list of defences for discriminatory rules caught by Article 28 is contained in Article 30. The ECJ has extended Article 28 to indistinctly applicable rules, and created defences that overlap with, but are not identical to, those found in Article 30. The salient issue is therefore whether justification for discriminatory rules is limited to the specific matters listed in Article 30, or whether a rule that is discriminatory might also be defended on one of the grounds listed in *Cassis*,[126] as developed by subsequent case law. The traditional view was that a Member State could not justify a discriminatory measure on grounds other than those listed in Article 30. This was so, even if the justification was in the list that could be invoked for indistinctly applicable measures.[127]

It was questionable whether *Commission v. Belgium*[128] was an exception to this proposition. The Commission challenged a Belgian regional decree, the effect of which was to ban the

---

[119] Case 251/78 *Denkavit Futtermittel* v. *Minister für Ernährung, Landwirtschaft und Forsten des Landes* [1979] ECR 3369.

[120] Case 124/81 *Commission* v. *United Kingdom* [1983] ECR 203.

[121] *Ibid.*, paras. 27–28.

[122] *Ibid.*, para. 30.

[123] Case 272/80 *Frans-Nederlandse Maatschappij voor Biologische Producten* [1981] ECR 3277.

[124] *Ibid.*, paras. 14–15; Case C–400/96 *Criminal Proceedings against Jean Harpegnies* [1998] ECR I–5121; Case C–432/03 *Commission* v. *Portugal* [2005] ECR I–9665, para. 46.

[125] See below, 706–707; P. Oliver, 'Some Further Reflections on the Scope of Articles 28–30 (ex 30–36)' (1999) 36 *CMLRev.* 738; J. Scott, 'Mandatory or Imperative Requirements in the EU and WTO', in Barnard and Scott (eds.), n. 24 above, ch. 10; P. Oliver and W.-H. Roth, 'The Internal Market and the Four Freedoms' (2004) 41 *CMLRev.* 407, 434–436.

[126] Case 120/78 *Cassis de Dijon*, n. 1 above.

[127] See 706–707 below.

[128] Case C–2/90 [1992] ECR I–4431.

importation of waste into that area. The decree could be seen as discriminatory, since it did not cover disposal of locally produced waste. Notwithstanding this, the Court allowed environmental protection to be taken into account when considering the legality of the regional decree. The case could, therefore, be seen as allowing justifications to be pleaded which are not found in Article 30. However, the ECJ in effect held that the decree was not discriminatory, notwithstanding appearances to the contrary in the challenged instrument. This was because of the special nature of the subject-matter, waste. There were strong arguments, the Court said, for disposing of such material locally, and each area had the responsibility for disposing of its own waste. Thus, although the decree applied only to imports it was not discriminatory.[129]

The relationship between Article 30 and the exceptions in *Cassis* is complicated by the fact that the dividing line between cases involving indirect discrimination and indistinctly applicable rules can be a fine one. This is exemplified by *Commission* v. *Austria*,[130] which concerned an Austrian rule banning lorries in excess of a certain weight from using certain roads in order to protect the environment and air quality. Advocate General Geelhoed acknowledged that it was open to question whether the rule should be regarded as indirectly discriminatory or indistinctly applicable, and accepted that this could have implications for whether protection of the environment could be pleaded by way of defence. The ECJ implicitly assumed that the Austrian rule was indistinctly applicable and that therefore protection of the environment could constitute an objective justification.

Advocate General Jacobs in *PreussenElektra*[131] has, however, questioned whether the list in Article 30 really is exhaustive. He argued that the approach in the *Walloon Waste* case was flawed, in the sense that whether a measure was discriminatory was logically distinct from whether it could be justified. He suggested moreover that there could be good reasons for allowing environmental protection to be pleaded as a justification, even in cases where there was direct discrimination. He argued more generally for a relaxation in the distinction between the justifications that could be pleaded under Article 30, and the rule of reason exceptions to *Cassis*. The ECJ did not, as Advocate General Jacobs suggested, give general guidance on the relationship between Article 30 and the exceptions to *Cassis*. It did however allow the national measure to be justified on environmental grounds.[132]

It will be argued below that the same justifications should be applicable, irrespective of whether the measure is discriminatory or not, although the application of the justification could be affected by this factor.[133]

(f) THE RELATIONSHIP BETWEEN HARMONIZATION AND ARTICLE 30

Community harmonization measures may make recourse to Article 30 inadmissible. This will be so where the Community measure is intended to harmonize the area totally. Member State action is thereby pre-empted. Thus in *Moormann*[134] the ECJ held that the existence of

---

[129] For indications that protection of the environment can however be raised in discrimination cases see, e.g., Case C–203/96 *Chemische Afvalstoffen Dusseldorp BV* v. *Minister van Volkshuisvesting, Ruimtelijke Ordening en Milieubeheer* [1998] ECR I–4075, para. 50.

[130] Case C–320/03 [2005] ECR I–9871.

[131] Case C–379/98 *PreussenElektra AG* v. *Schleswag AG* [2001] ECR I–2099, paras. 225–238. See also Case C–320/03 *Commission* v. *Austria* [2005] ECR I–9871, paras. 96–108, Geelhoed AG.

[132] See also Case C–389/98 *Aher-Waggon GmbH* v. *Bundesrepublik Deutschland* [1998] ECR I–4473.

[133] See below, 711–712.

[134] Case 190/87 *Oberkreisdirektor* v. *Moormann BV* [1988] ECR 4689. See also Case 5/77 *Tedeschi* v. *Denkavit* [1977] ECR 1555; Cases C–277, 318, and 319/91 *Ligur Carni Srl* v. *Unità Sanitaria Locale No. XV di Genova*

harmonization measures for poultry health inspections meant that a State could no longer use Article 30 to legitimate national rules on the matter. In *Commission v. Germany*[135] it was held that Community directives had harmonized the measures that could be taken 'for the detection of a pronounced sexual odour in uncastrated male pigs', thereby preventing Germany from applying different measures.

Many Community measures are however not intended to harmonize an area totally. The objective will be minimum harmonization. It will be for the ECJ to decide, in the case of doubt, whether the harmonization measure covers the whole field or whether it leaves room for national regulatory initiatives.[136] In the case of minimum harmonization, Member States are permitted to 'maintain and often to introduce more stringent regulatory standards than those prescribed by Community legislation, for the purposes of advancing a particular social or welfare interest, and provided that such additional requirements are compatible with the Treaty'.[137] Thus in *de Agostini* it was held that Community directives on 'Television without Frontiers' only partially harmonized the relevant law. They did not preclude national rules to control television advertising designed to protect consumers.[138] In the case of exhaustive harmonization, any national measure relating thereto must be assessed in the light of the harmonizing measure rather than the Treaty provisions.[139]

The ECJ will ensure that such national regulations are proportionate and do not constitute a means of arbitrary discrimination.[140] Difficult issues can however arise, even in the context of minimum harmonization, as to whether a Member State can impose more stringent welfare standards on goods entering its territory than those prescribed by the directive.[141]

8. DEFENCES TO INDISTINCTLY APPLICABLE RULES: THE MANDATORY REQUIREMENTS

(a) THE RATIONALE FOR THE MANDATORY REQUIREMENTS

It is necessary in the present state of the law to consider separately defences to indistinctly applicable rules, although, as we shall see below, it is questionable whether there should be a separate set of defences for discriminatory and non-discriminatory rules.

The rationale for the mandatory requirements is that many rules which regulate trade are also capable of restricting trade, yet some serve objectively justifiable purposes. The 'list' of

---

[1993] ECR I–6621; Case C–294/92 *Commission v. Italy* [1994] ECR I–4311; Case C–5/94 *R. v. Ministry of Agriculture, Fisheries and Food, ex p. Hedley Lomas (Ireland) Ltd.* [1996] ECR I–2553; Case C–1/96 *R. v. Minister of Agriculture, Fisheries, and Food, ex p. Compassion in World Farming Ltd.* [1998] ECR I–1251; Case C–443/02 *Nicolas Schreiber* [2004] ECR I–7275; Case C–309/02 *Radberger Getränkegesellschaft mbH and Co. and Spitz KG v. Land Baden-Württemberg* [2004] ECR I–11763.

[135] Case C–102/96 [1998] ECR I–6871.

[136] See, e.g., Case C–1/96 *Compassion in World Farming Ltd.*, n. 134 above; Case C–443/02 *Nicolas Schreiber*, n. 134 above; Case C–309/02 *Radberger*, n. 134 above.

[137] M. Dougan, 'Minimum Harmonization and the Internal Market' (2000) 37 *CMLRev.* 853, 855.

[138] Cases C–34–36/95 *De Agostini*, n. 67 above, paras. 32–35.

[139] Case C–324/99 *DaimlerChrysler AG v. Land Baden-Württemberg* [2001] ECR I–9897, para. 32; Case C–309/02 *Radberger*, n. 134 above, para. 53.

[140] Case 4/75 *Rewe-Zentralfinanz*, n. 13 above; Case C–317/92 *Commission v. Germany* [1994] ECR I–2039; Case C–17/93, *Van der Veldt*, n. 104 above.

[141] Compare Case C–1/96 *Compassion in World Farming*, n. 134 above, with Case C–389/98 *Aher-Waggon*, n. 132 above; Dougan, n. 137 above, 868–884.

mandatory requirements in *Cassis* is sometimes referred to as the rule of reason, drawing upon the earlier hint in *Dassonville* that, in the absence of Community measures, reasonable trade rules would be accepted in certain circumstances. A similar approach is evident in other areas of Community law.[142] Thus Advocate General VerLoren van Themaat[143] regarded the rule of reason as a general principle of interpretation designed to mitigate the effects of strict prohibitions laid down in the Treaty provisions on free movement.[144] The burden of proving justification rests on the State relying on the mandatory requirement.[145]

(b) THE RELATIONSHIP BETWEEN THE MANDATORY REQUIREMENTS AND ARTICLE 30

The traditional view has been that the *Cassis* mandatory requirements are separate from the justifications under Article 30. The ECJ held that the *Cassis* exceptions could be used only in respect of rules that were not discriminatory.[146] The *Cassis* list of mandatory requirements includes matters such as the protection of consumers and the fairness of commercial transactions which are not mentioned within Article 30 and the *Cassis* list is not exhaustive. The ECJ's willingness to create a broader category of justifications for indistinctly applicable rules is explicable because discriminatory rules strike at the very heart of the Community, and hence any possible justifications should be narrowly confined. The distinction between Article 30 and the mandatory requirements in *Cassis* has however come under increasing strain in recent years for three reasons.

First, there has, as we have seen, been discussion about whether the list in Article 30 should be regarded as exhaustive.[147] It has been argued that there might be instances where, for example, environmental considerations should be able to be pleaded even in cases of discrimination.

Secondly, the distinction has also become less tenable because of the difficulty of distinguishing between cases involving indirect discrimination and indistinctly applicable rules. The ECJ may well characterize a case as within the *Cassis* category because it wishes to allow the State to avail itself of one of the mandatory requirements, even though, as in *Aher-Waggon*,[148] the measure appeared to be discriminatory or distinctly applicable.

Thirdly, the reasoning in *Keck* has contributed to confusion in this respect. Selling arrangements are outside Article 28 so long as they apply to all traders in the national territory, and so long as they affect in the same manner, in law and fact, the marketing of domestic and imported products. Later cases have focused on the possible differential impact of national selling arrangements. If this is proven then Article 28 is applicable, subject to possible justifications raised by the State. In some instances it will not matter whether the justification is considered within the mandatory requirements or under Article 30, since it is covered by both, as in the case of public health.[149] In other instances it will be of relevance, since the alleged

---

[142] See Chs. 21, 22, and 24.

[143] Case 286/81 *Oosthoek*, n. 67 above.

[144] See also the discussion of the rule of reason in competition law, Ch. 25.

[145] Case C–14/02 *ATRAL*, n. 36 above, paras. 67–68.

[146] Case 788/79 *Gilli*, n. 39 above, para. 6; Case 113/80 *Commission v. Ireland* [1981] ECR 1625, paras. 5–8.

[147] See above, 703–704.

[148] See Jacobs AG in Case C–379/98 *PreussenElektra*, n. 131 above, para. 227, commenting on Case C–389/98 *Aher-Waggon*, n. 132 above.

[149] See, e.g., Case C–189/95 *Franzen*, n. 76 above; Case C–405/98 *Gourmet International*, n. 83 above; Case C–322/01 *Deutscher Apothekerverband*, n. 77 above.

justification falls only within the *Cassis* list. The ECJ has equivocated in some cases. Thus in *de Agostini*[150] the ECJ held that the advertising ban might be justified to satisfy one of the mandatory requirements *or* one of the aims listed in Article 30. Consumer protection and fair trading are in the former list, but not the latter.

There is much to be said for simplification. It would be best for the same justifications to be available in principle, irrespective of whether the measure is discriminatory or indistinctly applicable. This should only be relevant to the application of the justification in the instant case, in the sense that greater justification should be required for discriminatory measures.

It might be argued that this is not possible, given the wording of Article 30. This objection is not convincing. There is no reason why phrases within Article 30, such as protection of the health and life of humans, could not be interpreted to include matters such as consumer protection and the environment. The ECJ has construed other Treaty provisions in a far more expansive manner when it wished to do so. Moreover, if it was legitimate for the ECJ in *Cassis* to create an open-ended list of mandatory exceptions, not mentioned in the Treaty, then why would it not be legitimate for the ECJ to read Article 30 to include matters such as the environment or consumer protection?

(c) THE MANDATORY REQUIREMENTS: CONSUMER PROTECTION

Case 178/84 **Commission v. Germany**
[1987] ECR 1227

German law prohibited the marketing of beer which was lawfully manufactured in another Member State unless it complied with sections 9 and 10 of the Biersteuergesetz (Beer Duty Act 1952). Under this law only drinks which complied with the German Act could be sold as '*Bier*', and this meant that the term could be used only in relation to those drinks which were made from barley, hops, yeast, and water. The German Government argued that the reservation of the term '*Bier*' to beverages made only from these substances was necessary to protect consumers who associated the term '*Bier*' with beverages made from such ingredients. It also argued that its legislation was not protectionist in aim, in that any trader who made beer from such ingredients could market it freely in Germany. The ECJ cited the principles from *Dassonville* and *Cassis*; it found that the German rule constituted an impediment to trade and then considered whether the rule was necessary to protect consumers.

THE ECJ

31. The German Government's argument that section 10 of the Biersteuergesetz is essential in order to protect German consumers because, in their minds, the designation 'Bier' is inseparably linked to the beverage manufactured solely from the ingredients laid down in section 9 ... must be rejected.

32. Firstly, consumers' conceptions which vary from one Member State to the other are also likely to evolve in the course of time within a Member State. The establishment of the Common Market is, it should be added, one of the factors that may play a major contributory

---

[150] Cases C–34–36/95 *De Agostini*, n. 67 above, 45–47.

role in that development. Whereas rules protecting consumers against misleading practices enable such a development to be taken into account, legislation of the kind contained in section 10 . . . prevents it from taking place. As the Court has already held in another context (Case 170/78, *Commission* v *United Kingdom*), the legislation of a Member State must not 'crystallize given consumer habits so as to consolidate an advantage acquired by national industries concerned to comply with them'.

33. Secondly, in the other Member States of the Community the designations corresponding to the German designation 'Bier' are generic designations for a fermented beverage manufactured from barley, whether malted barley on its own or with the addition of rice or maize. The same approach is taken in Community law as can be seen from heading 22.03 of the Common Customs Tariff. The German legislature itself utilises the designation 'Bier' in that way in section 9(7) and (8) of the Biersteuergesetz in order to refer to beverages not complying with the manufacturing rules laid down in section 9(1) and (2).

34. The German designation 'Bier' and its equivalents in the languages of the other Member States may therefore not be restricted to beers manufactured in accordance with the rules in force in the Federal Republic of Germany.

35. It is admittedly legitimate to seek to enable consumers who attribute specific qualities to beers manufactured from particular raw materials to make their choice in the light of that consideration. However, as the Court has already emphasised (Case 193/80, *Commission* v *Italy*) that possibility may be ensured by means which do not prevent the importation of products which have been lawfully manufactured and marketed in other Member States and, in particular, 'by the compulsory affixing of suitable labels giving the nature of the product sold'. By indicating the raw materials utilised in the manufacture of beer 'such a course would enable the consumer to make his choice in full knowledge of the facts and would guarantee transparency in trading and in offers to the public'. It must be added that such a system of mandatory consumer information must not entail negative assessments for beers not complying with the requirements of section 9 of the Biersteuergesetz.

The ECJ therefore held the German law to be in breach of what is now Article 28. The way in which it dealt with the argument concerning consumer protection is instructive. The argument was closely scrutinized to determine whether it really 'worked' on the facts of the case. The ECJ then assessed whether the interests of consumers could be safeguarded by less restrictive means: paragraph 35. The same approach is apparent in other cases.[151]

The ECJ has often rejected justifications based on consumer protection by stating that adequate labelling requirements can achieve the national objective with less impact on intra-Community trade. However, even labelling requirements may not escape Article 28. Thus in *Fietje*[152] the ECJ held that the obligation to use a certain name on a label could make it more difficult to market goods coming from other Member States, and would therefore have to be justified on the ground of consumer protection. Labelling requirements which demanded that the purchaser was provided with sufficient information on the nature of the product in order to prevent confusion with similar products, could, said the Court, be justified, even if the effect was to make it necessary to alter the labels of some imported goods.[153] However,

---

151 See, e.g., Case 261/81 *Rau*, n. 40 above; Case 94/82 *De Kikvorsch Groothandel-Import-Export BV* [1983] ECR 947; Case C–293/93 *Ludomira Neeltje* v. *Barbara Houtwipper* [1994] ECR I–429; Case C–470/93 *Verein gegen Unwesen in Handel und Gewerbe Köln eV* v. *Mars GmbH* [1995] ECR I–1923; Case C–315/92 *Verband Sozialer Wettbewerb eV* v. *Clinique Laboratoires SNC* [1994] ECR I–317; Case C–14/00 *Commission* v. *Italy* [2003] ECR I–513.

152 Case 27/80 *Fietje* [1980] ECR 3839.

153 *Ibid.*, para. 11.

such protection would not be necessary or justifiable if the details given on the original labels of the goods contained the same information as required by the State of import, and that information was just as capable of being understood by consumers. Whether there was such equivalence was for the national court to determine.[154]

(d) THE MANDATORY REQUIREMENTS: FAIRNESS OF COMMERCIAL TRANSACTIONS

There is clearly an overlap between consumer protection and the fairness of commercial transactions. This particular mandatory requirement has been used to justify national rules that seek to prevent unfair marketing practices, such as the selling of imported goods that are precise imitations of familiar domestic goods. It seems, however, that in order to be justified on this ground the national rule must not prohibit the marketing of goods which have been made according to fair and traditional practices in State A merely because they are similar to goods which have been made in State B.[155]

(e) THE MANDATORY REQUIREMENTS: PUBLIC HEALTH

We have already noted that the traditional view was that only indistinctly applicable rules could take advantage of the mandatory requirements. However, the ECJ has, on occasion, not been too concerned about whether it considers a justification within Article 30, or within the list of mandatory requirements, *provided* that the justification pleaded by the State comes within both lists, more especially where it is unclear whether the impugned rule is discriminatory or indistinctly applicable. Public health finds a place both in the list of *Cassis* mandatory requirements and in Article 30. The following extract from the *German Beer* case provides an apt example of this:[156]

Case 178/84 **Commission v. Germany**
[1987] ECR 1227

[Note ToA renumbering: Arts. 36 and 169 are now Arts. 30 and 226]

A second rule of German law was challenged in the *German Beer* case. Under the German Foodstuffs Act 1974 there was an absolute ban on the marketing of beer which contained additives. In essence this Act prohibited non-natural additives on public-health grounds. The Commission challenged this rule. It was accepted that the German rule constituted a barrier to the import of beer lawfully marketed in other States which contained additives. The question before the ECJ was whether the rule could come within Article 36 on public-health grounds.

---

[154] *Ibid.*, para. 12. See also Case 76/86 *Commission v. Germany* [1989] ECR 1021.
[155] Case 58/80 *Dansk Supermarked* v. *Imerco* [1981] ECR 181; Case 16/83 *Karl Prantl* [1984] ECR 1299.
[156] See also Case 53/80 *Officier van Justitie* v. *Koniklijke Kaasfabriek Eyssen BV* [1981] ECR 409; Case 97/83 *Criminal Proceedings against Melkunie BV* [1984] ECR 2367.

THE ECJ

41. The Court has consistently held (in particular in Case 174/82, *Criminal Proceedings Against Sandoz BV*) that 'in so far as there are uncertainties at the present state of scientific research it is for the Member States, in the absence of harmonization, to decide what degree of protection of the health and life of humans they intend to assure, having regard to the requirements of the free movement of goods within the Community.'

42. As may also be seen from the decision of the Court (and especially the *Sandoz* case, cited above, in Case 247/84, *Motte*, and in Case 308/84, *Ministère Public* v *Muller*), in such circumstances Community law does not preclude the adoption by Member States of legislation whereby the use of additives is subjected to prior authorisation granted by a measure of general application for specific additives, in respect of all products, for certain products only or for certain uses. Such legislation meets a genuine need of health policy, namely that of restricting the uncontrolled consumption of food additives.

43. However, the application to imported products of prohibitions on marketing products containing additives which are authorised in the Member State of production but prohibited in the Member State of importation is permissible only in so far as it complies with the requirements of Article 36 of the Treaty as it has been interpreted by the Court.

44. It must be borne in mind, in the first place, that in its judgments in *Sandoz, Motte* and *Muller*, the Court inferred from the principle of proportionality underlying the last sentence of Article 36 of the Treaty that prohibitions on the marketing of products containing additives authorised in the Member State of production but prohibited in the Member State of importation must be restricted to what is actually necessary to secure the protection of public health. The Court also concluded that the use of a specific additive which is authorised in another Member State must be authorised in the case of a product imported from that Member State where, in view, on the one hand, of the findings of international scientific research, and in particular the work of the Community's Scientific Committee for Food, the Codex Alimentarius Committee of the Food and Agriculture Organisation of the United Nations (FAO) and the World Health Organisation, and, on the other, of the eating habits prevailing in the importing Member State, the additive in question does not present a risk to public health and meets a real need, especially a technical one.

45. Secondly, it should be remembered that, as the Court held in *Muller*, by virtue of the principle of proportionality, traders must also be able to apply, under a procedure which is easily accessible to them and can be concluded within a reasonable time, for the use of specific additives to be authorised by a measure of general application.

[*The Court then pointed out that the German rule prohibited all additives; that there was no procedure whereby traders could obtain authorization for a specific additive; and that additives were permitted by German law in beverages other than beer. The German Government argued that such additives would not be needed in the manufacture of beer if it were made in accordance with section 9 of the Biersteuergesetz. The ECJ responded as follows:*]

51. It must be emphasised that the mere reference to the fact that beer can be manufactured without additives if it is made from only the raw materials prescribed in the Federal Republic of Germany does not suffice to preclude the possibility that some additives may meet a technological need. Such an interpretation of the concept of technological need, which results in favouring national production methods, constitutes a disguised means of restricting trade between Member States.

52. The concept of technological need must be assessed in the light of the raw materials utilised and bearing in mind the assessment made by the authorities of the Member States where the product was lawfully manufactured and marketed. Account must also be taken of the findings of international scientific research and in particular the work of the Community's

Scientific Committee for Food, the Codex Alimentarius Committee of the FAO and the World Health Organisation.

53. Consequently, in so far as the German rules on additives in beer entail a general ban on additives, their application to beers imported from other Member States is contrary to the requirements of Community law as laid down in the case law of the Court, since that prohibition is contrary to the principle of proportionality and is therefore not covered by Article 36 of the EEC Treaty.

(f) OTHER MANDATORY REQUIREMENTS

The list of mandatory requirements in *Cassis* is not exhaustive, as evident from the fact that the ECJ stated that the mandatory requirements included *in particular* those mentioned in the judgment.[157] This has been confirmed by later cases. It can, in the absence of Community harmonization measures, include the protection of the environment.[158]

Case 302/86 **Commission v. Denmark**
[1988] ECR 4607

[Note ToA renumbering: Art. 30 is now Art. 28]

Danish law required that containers for beer and soft drinks should be returnable and that a certain proportion should be re-usable. A national environmental agency had to approve containers to ensure compliance with these criteria. There was also a deposit-and-return system for empty containers. The Danish Government argued that the rule was justified by a mandatory requirement related to the protection of the environment.

THE ECJ

8. The Court has already held in ... Case 240/83, *Procureur de la République* v *Association de Défense des Brûleurs d'Huiles Usagées* ... that the protection of the environment is 'one of the Community's essential objectives', which may as such justify certain limitations of the principle of free movement of goods. That view is moreover confirmed by the Single European Act.

9. In view of the foregoing, it must therefore be stated that the protection of the environment is a mandatory requirement which may limit the application of Article 30 of the Treaty. [*The Commission argued that the Danish laws were disproportionate.*]

13. First of all, as regards the obligation to establish a deposit-and-return system for empty containers, it must be observed that this requirement is an indispensable element of a system intended to ensure the re-use of containers and therefore appears necessary to achieve the aims pursued by the contested rules. That being so, the restrictions which it imposes on the free movement of goods cannot be regarded as disproportionate.

14. Next it is necessary to consider the requirement that producers and importers must use only containers approved by the National Agency for the Protection of the Environment.

---

[157] [1979] ECR 649, para. 8.
[158] See also Case C–379/98 *PreussenElektra*, n. 131 above; Case C–309/02 *Radberger Getränkegesellschaft mbH and Co. and Spitz KG* v. *Land Baden-Württemberg* [2004] ECR I–11763, para. 75.

[*The Danish Government argued that the number of approved containers had to be limited because otherwise retailers would not take part in the system. This meant that a foreign producer might have to manufacture a type of container already approved, with consequent increases in costs. To overcome this problem the Danish law was amended to allow a producer to market up to 3,000 hectolitres a year in non-approved containers, provided that a deposit-and-return system was established. The Commission argued that the limit of 3,000 hectolitres was unnecessary to achieve the objectives of the scheme.*]

20. It is undoubtedly true that the existing system for returning approved containers ensures a maximum rate of re-use and therefore a very considerable degree of protection of the environment since empty containers can be returned to any retailer of beverages. Non-approved containers, on the other hand, can be returned only to the retailer who sold the beverages, since it is impossible to set up such a comprehensive system for those containers as well.

21. Nevertheless, the system for returning non-approved containers is capable of protecting the environment and, as far as imports are concerned, affects only limited quantities of beverages compared with the quantity of beverages consumed in Denmark owing to the restrictive effect which the requirement that containers should be returnable has on imports. In those circumstances, a restriction of the quantity of products which may be marketed by importers is disproportionate to the objective pursued.

22. It must therefore be held that by restricting . . . the quantity of beer and soft drinks which may be marketed by a single producer in non-approved containers to 3,000 hectolitres a year, the Kingdom of Denmark has failed, as regards imports of those products from other Member States, to fulfil its obligations under Article 30 of the EEC Treaty.

Environmental protection is not the only new addition to this catalogue. In *Familiapress*[159] the ECJ recognized pluralism of the press as a value that could legitimate a national measure that was in breach of Article 28. The offering of prizes for games in magazines could drive out smaller papers, which could not afford to make such offers. In *Cinéthèque*[160] the ECJ was willing to recognize that the fostering of certain forms of art could constitute a justifiable objective within the context of Community law. While in *Torfaen*[161] it accepted that rules governing the opening hours of premises pursued a justifiable aim, in that such rules reflected certain social and political choices which might differ between Member States.[162] It is clear moreover from *Schmidberger* that protection of fundamental rights can be relevant as justification of an indistinctly applicable measure.

Case C–112/00 **Eugen Schmidberger, Internationale Transporte und Planzuge v. Austria** [2003] ECR I–5659

The ECJ held that a decision by Austria not to ban a demonstration by an environmental group that led to closure of the Brenner motorway was caught by Article 28 in so far as it impeded

---

[159] Case C–368/95 *Vereinigte Familiapress Zeitungsverlags- und vertriebs GmbH v. Heinrich Bauer Verlag* [1997] ECR I–368.
[160] Cases 60 and 61/84 [1985] ECR 2605.
[161] Case 145/88 [1989] ECR 3851.
[162] While *Cinéthèque* and *Torfaen* would probably now fall outside Art. 28, the recognition of these grounds of objective justification could be of relevance in cases that do fall within Art. 28 even after *Keck*.

trade for the relevant period. The ECJ then considered whether the restriction was justified, more especially because the Austrian Government in allowing the demonstration was influenced by considerations relating to freedom of expression and assembly as enshrined in the ECHR and the Austrian Constitution. The ECJ accepted that fundamental rights were part of the Community legal order, but that these rights and the principles concerning free movement of goods were not absolute.

THE ECJ

81. In those circumstances, the interests involved must be weighed having regard to all the circumstances of the case in order to determine whether a fair balance was struck between those interests.

82. The competent authorities enjoy a wide margin of discretion in that regard. Nevertheless, it is necessary to determine whether the restrictions placed upon intra-Community trade are proportionate in the light of the legitimate objectives pursued, namely . . . the protection of fundamental rights.

[*The ECJ emphasized that the demonstrators had sought permission from the Austrian Government, and that the demonstration was limited in scope and time.*]

86. [I]t is not in dispute that by the demonstration, citizens were exercising their fundamental rights by manifesting in public an opinion which they considered to be of importance in society; it is also not in dispute that the purpose of that public demonstration was not to restrict trade in goods of a particular type or from a particular source. . . .

87. [I]n the present case various administrative and supporting arrangements were taken by the competent authorities in order to limit as far as possible the disruption to road traffic. . . .

88. Moreover, it is not in dispute that the isolated incident in question did not give rise to a general climate of insecurity such as to have a dissuasive effect on intra-Community trade flows as a whole . . .

89. Finally . . . the competent national authorities were entitled to consider that an outright ban on the demonstration would have constituted unacceptable interference with the fundamental rights of the demonstrators to gather and express peacefully their opinion in public.

[*The ECJ accepted that alternative solutions would have been liable to lead to more serious disruption of trade, such as unauthorized demonstrations.*]

93. [T]he national authorities were reasonably entitled, having regard to the wide discretion which must be accorded to them in the matter, to consider that the legitimate aim of that demonstration could not be achieved in the present case by measures less restrictive of intra-Community trade.

(g) MANDATORY REQUIREMENTS AND HARMONIZATION

A Community harmonization measure may render it impossible for a State to rely on a mandatory requirement.[163] Whether it has this effect will depend upon whether the Community measure is directed at total or only a minimum harmonization. The previous discussion of this issue is applicable here.[164]

---

[163] See, e.g., Case C–383/97 *Criminal Proceedings against Van der Laan* [1999] ECR I–731.
[164] See above, 704–705.

(h) SUMMARY

i.   The ECJ was creative in *Cassis* when it set out the mandatory requirements, and it has shown similar flexibility since then, by adding new defences to the list. The Court has, not surprisingly, interpreted the requirements strictly, obliging Member States to satisfy it that a defence is really warranted in the circumstances. There are however two causes for concern.

ii. First, the dividing line between the mandatory requirements and Article 30 is problematic. It has been argued that the same public interest defences should be available irrespective of whether the measure is discriminatory or not. Whether the measure was discriminatory or not would simply be of relevance in the application of the defences to the facts of the particular case.

iii. Secondly, the decision on whether the mandatory requirements provide a defence for the Member State can involve difficult balancing exercises for the ECJ, and for the national courts, to which many such issues are delegated by the ECJ. This issue will be examined more fully in the following section.

9. FREE MOVEMENT OF GOODS AND *CASSIS*: THE BROADER PERSPECTIVE

(a) THE COMMISSION RESPONSE TO *CASSIS*

The Court's judgment in *Cassis* was, in part, a response to the difficulties faced by the Commission in securing acceptance by the Member States of harmonization measures. The judgment in *Cassis* rendered indistinctly applicable rules which impeded trade incompatible with Article 28, unless they could be saved by a mandatory requirement. This was so even in the absence of relevant harmonization provisions. *Cassis* therefore fostered single-market integration, and obviated the need for many Community harmonization provisions.

It was argued at the beginning of this Chapter that the ECJ's jurisprudence could not be viewed in isolation. It had an impact upon how the other Community institutions perceived their role. The Commission was not slow to respond to the Court's initiative. It published a Communication setting out its interpretation of the *Cassis* decision, which also provided insights into how the Commission perceived its legislative role in this area.

Commission Communication, 3 October 1980
[1980] OJ C256/2

Whereas Member States may, with respect to domestic products and in the absence of relevant Community provisions, regulate the terms on which such products are marketed, the case is different for products imported from other Member States.

Any product imported from another Member State must in principle be admitted to the territory of the importing Member State if it has been lawfully produced, that is, conforms to rules and processes of manufacture that are customarily and traditionally accepted in the exporting country, and marketed in the territory of the latter.

. . .

Only under very strict conditions does the Court accept exceptions to this principle; barriers to trade resulting from differences between commercial and technical rules are only admissible:

— if the rules are necessary, that is appropriate and not excessive, in order to satisfy mandatory requirements . . .;

— if the rules serve a purpose in the general interest which is compelling enough to justify an exception to a fundamental rule of the Treaty such as the free movement of goods;

— if the rules are essential for such a purpose to be attained, ie. are the means which are the most appropriate and at the same time least hinder trade.

[*The Commission then set out a number of guidelines in the light of the Court's judgment.*]

—The principles deduced by the Court imply that a Member State may not in principle prohibit the sale in its territory of a product lawfully produced and marketed in another Member State even if the product is produced according to technical or quality requirements which differ from those imposed on its domestic products. Where a product 'suitably and satisfactorily' fulfils the legitimate objective of a Member State's own rules (public safety, protection of the consumer or the environment, etc.), the importing country cannot justify prohibiting its sale in its territory by claiming that the way it fulfils the objective is different from that imposed on domestic products.

In such a case, an absolute prohibition of sale could not be considered 'necessary' to satisfy a 'mandatory requirement' because it would not be an 'essential guarantee' in the sense defined in the Court's judgment.

The Commission will therefore have to tackle a whole body of commercial rules which lay down that products manufactured and marketed in one Member State must fulfill technical or qualitative conditions in order to be admitted to the market of another and specifically in all cases where the trade barriers occasioned by such rules are inadmissible according to the very strict criteria set out by the Court.

The Commission is referring in particular to rules covering the composition, designation, presentation and packaging as well as rules requiring compliance with certain technical standards.

—The Commission's work of harmonization will henceforth have to be directed mainly at national laws having an impact on the functioning of the common market where barriers to trade to be removed arise from national provisions which are admissible under the criteria set out by the Court.

The Commission will be concentrating on sectors deserving priority because of their economic relevance to the creation of a single internal market.

There are two important themes in the Commission's Communication. The first is what has become known as the principle of *mutual recognition*. Goods lawfully marketed in one Member State should, in principle, be admitted to the market of any other State. This leads to competition among rules, or regulatory competition. A producer will normally only have to comply with the national rules of one State in order that its goods can move freely in the EC. Firms are then able to choose between different national regulations. Consumers can choose between the products that comply with those rules. This creates a 'competitive process among the different national rules: the choice of producers of where to produce and of consumers of what to buy will determine the "best rules"'.[165]

The second theme concerns the Commission's enforcement and legislative strategy for trade rules post-*Cassis*. This was to be double-edged. It would tackle trade rules that were

---

[165] Maduro, n. 2 above, 132.

inadmissible in the light of *Cassis* by using its powers under Article 226 against recalcitrant Member States. The harmonization process would be directed towards those trade rules which were *admissible* under the *Cassis* test. The effect of *Cassis* was thus to induce the Commission to re-orient its legislative programme, and concentrate on national rules that were still valid under the Court's case law.

This strategy was reinforced by a decision[166] establishing a procedure for the exchange of information about national measures that derogate from the free movement of goods. A Member State which seeks to prevent free movement of goods that have been lawfully produced or marketed in another Member State must notify the Commission. This information will enable the Commission to decide whether this should be the subject of an Article 226 action, or whether harmonization measures will be necessary to obviate the concerns of the State that is impeding free movement. The ECJ has taken a broad view of 'national measures' that trigger the obligation to notify.[167]

This Decision should be viewed in tandem with Directive 98/34[168] on the provision of information on technical standards and regulations. This measure, known as the Mutual Information or Transparency Directive, imposes an obligation on a State to inform the Commission before it adopts any legally binding regulation setting a technical specification. The Commission notifies the other States, and may require that the adoption of the national measure be delayed by up to six months, in order that possible amendments can be considered. A further delay can result if the Commission decides to push ahead with a harmonization directive on the issue.

(b) PROBLEMS WITH REALIZING THE *CASSIS* STRATEGY

Mutual recognition is the core of the ECJ's and Commission's strategy.[169] The general assumption is that this works just fine. Matters are not so simple. The Commission's paper on Mutual Recognition[170] emphasized that it did not always operate effectively, and made a number of proposals to improve it.[171] There is to be increased monitoring of mutual recognition by the Commission, to be complemented by measures designed to improve awareness of mutual recognition by producers of goods and services. Member States should deal with requests concerning mutual recognition within a reasonable time, and should include mutual recognition clauses in national legislation.

We see here once again the inter-relationship of judicial and legislative strategies. The obligation to insert such clauses derives from the *Foie Gras* case.[172] The French imposed requirements on the composition of *foie gras*. The Commission argued that the French decree

---

166 Dec. 3052/95/EC of the European Parliament and of the Council of 13 Dec. 1995 establishing a procedure for the exchange of information on national measures derogating from the principle of free movement of goods within the Community [1995] OJ L321/1.

167 Cases C–388 and 429/00 *Radiosistemi Srl* v. *Prefetto di Genova* [2002] ECR I–5845, para. 73; Case C–432/03 *Commission* v. *Portugal*, n. 124 above, paras. 56–60.

168 Dir. 98/34/EC of the European Parliament and of the Council of 22 June 1998 laying down a procedure for the provision of information in the field of technical standards and regulations [1998] OJ L204/37; Case C–194/94 *CIA Security International SA* v. *Signalson SA and Securitel Sprl* [1996] ECR I–2201; Barnard, n. 97 above, 119–127.

169 K. Armstrong, 'Mutual Recognition', in Barnard and Scott (eds.), n. 24 above, ch. 9.

170 Commission Communication to the European Parliament and the Council, Mutual Recognition in the Context of the Follow-up to the Action Plan for the Single Market, 16 June 1999.

171 *Ibid.,* 7–12.

172 Case C–184/96 *Commission* v. *France* [1998] ECR I–6197.

containing the requirements for *foie gras* must also contain a mutual recognition clause in the legislation itself, permitting preparations for *foie gras* which had been lawfully marketed in another Member State to be marketed in France. The ECJ agreed.[173] Henceforth any State which imposes requirements as to product characteristics and the like must also include a mutual-recognition clause in the enabling legal instrument. The Commission acknowledged their importance: 'it is through such clauses that not only individuals, but also the competent national authorities and the heads of inspection and control bodies become aware of how mutual recognition has to be applied in a given area'.[174] Such clauses are especially important, given the difficulties that persist with mutual recognition of complex technical products, foodstuffs, and the like.[175]

(c) PROBLEMS FLOWING FROM THE *CASSIS* STRATEGY

The effect of *Cassis* was that Community policy would be developed through a mixture of adjudication and rule-making. *Adjudication* by the ECJ pursuant to *Cassis* resulted in negative integration: trade rules would be incompatible with Article 28 unless they could be saved by a mandatory requirement. *Rule-making* would be used for national rules that survived because of the mandatory requirements, and therefore still posed a problem for market integration. This resulted in positive integration, in the sense that there would be Community rules which would bind all States. There are, however, four problems with this general strategy.

The *first problem* is that it is dependent upon agreement with the outcome of the adjudicative process. If the challenged rule failed the *Cassis* test then it would have to be removed from national law. This conclusion was fine, provided that one agreed with it. The result was less satisfactory if one felt that the trade rule should have been saved by a mandatory requirement. Thus the ECJ has, for example, generally held that national rules on food standards are not saved by the mandatory requirements, because the policy of the importing State can be met by less restrictive rules on product labelling.[176] Weatherill has argued forcefully that the ECJ often takes a robust view of consumers, and has given relatively little attention to the prospects of consumer confusion.[177] Lasa has also argued that labelling requirements, as opposed to food standards, may not adequately protect the consumer.

H.-C. von Heydebrand u. d. Lasa, Free Movement of Foodstuffs, Consumer Protection and Food Standards in the European Community: Has the Court of Justice Got it Wrong?[178]

First of all, the Court might simply not be right that consumers are adequately informed through labels. After all, the majority of the consumers apparently do not pay much attention to the information given on the label. . . .

---

[173] *Ibid.*, para. 28.

[174] Mutual Recognition Communication, n. 170 above, 11. See also Council Resolution of 28 Oct. 1999 on Mutual Recognition [2000] OJ C141/5.

[175] Report from the Commission to the Council, European Parliament, and ECOSOC, Second Biannual Report on the Application of the Principle of Mutual Recognition in the Single Market, COM(2002)419 final.

[176] See above 707–709.

[177] S. Weatherill, 'Recent Case Law Concerning the Free Movement of Goods: Mapping the Frontiers of Market Deregulation' (1999) 36 *CMLRev.* 51.

[178] (1991) 16 *ELRev.* 391, 409–413. See also O. Brouwers, 'Free Movement of Foodstuffs and Quality Requirements: Has the Commission Got it Wrong?' (1988) 25 *CMLRev.* 237.

Secondly, the Court's approach can confer an unfair competitive advantage on the importer ...The consumer associates with the name or presentation of the product a familiar domestic product of a certain quality which is not met by the imported product, and will therefore perhaps be misled. ...

Fourthly, the Court's case law, if implemented strictly in the long run, may well result in a 'labelling jungle' which even judges would find difficult to penetrate. ...

Fifthly, while administrative resources are saved by foregoing harmonization, authorities of the Member States have to struggle with the food standards of the various Member States, since the imported product must still be 'lawfully produced and marketed' in the Member States of export. Mutual recognition of official inspections has its difficulties too, especially where the product designated for export is not at all or less carefully examined than the product which is sold on the home market.

Sixthly, depending on the market of the foodstuff in question, mutual recognition can lead to discrimination against manufacturers situated in the importing Member State, if that Member State does not timely adjust the food standard. ...

More important ... the Member State of export can by way of the economic damage caused by inverse discrimination impose de facto its food standard or standard free food law on the Member State of import. Relocation of production to the exporting Member State in an effort to secure market share at home has already occurred in practice. ...

Seventhly, the preference of the Court for labelling is not sufficiently responsive to the local needs of the people of the importing Member State to define and classify the food they eat according to their conceptions, expectations and habits. ...

...The attitude of the Court of Justice towards food standards makes it de facto impossible for the people of a Member State to enforce requirements about the quality, composition, designation and presentation of their food when their views are not shared by the people in the Member State of export. ...

The *second problem* relates to the balancing exercise performed pursuant to Article 30 and the mandatory requirements. The ECJ has to adjudicate on the balance between market integration and the attainment of other societal goals, when deciding on the legitimacy of such defences. This can also be problematic for national courts, as is readily apparent from the *Sunday Trading* cases and more recent jurisprudence. Thus in *de Agostini*[179] the national court had to decide whether the advertising ban affected imported goods differentially from domestic goods, whether the ban might satisfy a mandatory requirement, and whether it was proportionate. In *Familiapress*[180] the task given to the national court was even more problematic. The ban on the import of newspapers offering prizes was held to breach Article 28. It was for the national court to decide whether the ban could be saved on the ground that it was a proportionate method of preserving press diversity, and whether that objective could be achieved by less restrictive means. The national court was, moreover, required to decide on the degree of competition between papers offering prizes and those small newspapers that could not afford to do so, and to estimate the extent to which sales of the latter would decline if the former could be offered for sale.

The *third problem* concerns the balance between market integration and the protective function played by national rules. Community legislative initiatives may be required to ensure that the protective function of certain trade rules is not lost sight of in the desire to enhance

---

[179] Cases C–34–36/95 *de Agostini*, n. 67 above.
[180] Case C–368/95 *Vereinigte Familiapress*, n. 159 above.

single-market integration.[181] Thus consumer groups were worried that trade liberalization could have negative consequences on consumer safety.[182] It is true that safety and the like can be taken into account under the *Cassis* mandatory requirements. There is, however, as Weatherill and Beaumont note, a risk inherent in the *Cassis* line of authority. The risk is 'that the Court has introduced a legal test that tends to tip the balance away from legitimate social protection towards a deregulated (perhaps unregulated) free market economy in which standards of, *inter alia*, consumer protection will be depressed'.[183] Positive harmonization through Community rules may be required to ensure the appropriate level of protection in the relevant area.

The *final problem* concerns the allocation of regulatory competence between the Community and the Member States. The interpretation of Article 28 serves to define the sphere of regulatory competence left to the Member States, and the extent to which Community harmonization is required. This entails important choices.

M. Maduro, We the Court: the European Court of Justice and the European Economic Constitution[184]

[Art. 30 should be read as Art. 28]

The institutional choices, regarding the allocation of regulatory powers, that can be detected in different interpretations of Article 30 [28] and its co-ordination with Treaty rules on harmonisation may be represented in three ideal constitutional models of the European Economic Constitution: the centralised constitutional model, the competitive constitutional model and the decentralised constitutional model. The centralised model reacts to the erosion of national regulatory powers through Article 30 by favouring a process of market integration by means of the replacement of national laws with Community legislation. The competitive model promotes 'competition among national rules', notably through the principle of mutual recognition of national legislation. In the decentralised model, States will retain regulatory powers, but are, at the same time, prevented from developing protectionist policies. These models are heuristic devices. They are all present—and compete with each other—in the European Union.... These, in turn, can be linked with three different visions of the European Economic Constitution and its legitimation.

The first argues that negative integration, deriving from the application of market integration rules, must be followed by positive integration which is legitimised through the development of traditional democratic mechanisms in the European Union.

The second argues for the constitutionalisation of negative integration. No traditional democratic developments are required for the European Union institutions since powers are left to the market.... This vision protects market freedom and individual rights against public power.

The third vision still sees the highest source of legitimacy in national democratic legitimacy. The legitimacy of the European Economic Constitution derives therefrom and is thus conditioned....

---

[181] See, however, Case C–320/93 *Lucien Ortscheit GmbH* v. *Eurim-Pharm Arzneimittel GmbH* [1994] ECR I–5243, for judicial recognition of this problem.

[182] K.J. Alter and S. Meunier-Aitsahalia, 'Judicial Politics in the European Community: European Integration and the Pathbreaking Cassis de Dijon Decision' (1994) 26 *Comparative Political Studies* 535, 544.

[183] N. 47 above, 600.

[184] (Hart, 1998), 108–109.

The disputes over Article 30 and European regulation are basically disputes over these different economic constitutional models and the different legitimacy they presuppose.

10. CONCLUSION

i. The ECJ had certain fundamental choices open to it when interpreting Article 28. It could have limited the remit of this Article to measures that were discriminatory or protectionist. It chose not to do so, and extended Article 28 to cover indistinctly applicable rules. Consequences flow from any choice, and this applies as much to those made by courts as other decision-makers.

ii. The *legislative consequence* of *Cassis* was far-reaching. The decision facilitated the creation of a single market. The Commission re-oriented its legislative strategy to concentrate on trade rules that were still lawful in the light of *Cassis* and could be justified by the mandatory requirements. There would be harmonization pursuant to Article 95, albeit often only minimum harmonization.

iii. The *judicial consequence* of *Cassis* was equally significant. The ECJ 'reaped the burden of its own success'. Litigants sought to challenge all manner of national trade rules claiming that they constituted an impediment, direct or indirect, actual or potential, to Community trade. It was this that led the ECJ to re-think its own jurisprudence in *Keck* in an attempt to stem the tide. The distinction between rules going to the characteristics of the goods and those pertaining to selling arrangements has proven fragile. The ECJ has increasingly brought selling arrangements within Article 28 either by treating them as going to the character of the goods, or because they apply unevenly, in fact or law, to imports. Market access has come closer to centre stage in the ECJ's reasoning.

iv. *Cassis* also had a *second-order judicial consequence*. The ECJ had to decide whether a Member State could legitimately plead a mandatory requirement as a defence. It was forced to make difficult decisions between the imperatives of market integration and the pursuit of other social goals. National courts are often faced with complex empirical and normative issues, having to decide whether a mandatory requirement is proportionate, whether another less restrictive measure would be possible and balance matters such as press diversity against market integration.

v. *Cassis* had significant *regulatory consequences*. Member States lost regulatory competence. They could no longer apply their trade rules to imported goods. These had to be admitted because of mutual recognition, unless they could be saved by a mandatory requirement. The EC acquired regulatory competence, since the existence of a proven mandatory requirement brought Article 95 into play. Difficult choices had to be made about the balance between the imperatives of market integration, and the pursuit of other social objectives.

11. FURTHER READING

(a) Books

Barnard, C., *The Substantive Law of the EU: The Four Freedoms* (Oxford University Press, 2004)

——and Scott, J. (eds.), *The Law of the Single European Market, Unpacking the Premises* (Hart, 2002)

Jarvis, M., *The Application of EC Law by National Courts: The Free Movement of Goods* (Oxford University Press, 1998)

Maduro, M.P., *We the Court: The European Court of Justice and the European Economic Constitution* (Hart, 1998)

Nic Shuibhne, N., *Regulating the Internal Market* (Edward Elgar, 2006)

Oliver, P., assisted by Jarvis, M., *Free Movement of Goods in the European Community: Under Articles 28 to 30 of the EC Treaty* (4th edn., Sweet & Maxwell, 2003)

Woods, L., *Free Movement of Goods and Services within the European Community* (Ashgate, 2004)

(b) Articles

Armstrong, K., 'Mutual Recognition', in C. Barnard and J. Scott (eds.), *The Law of the Single European Market, Unpacking the Premises* (Hart, 2002), ch. 9

Barnard, C., 'Fitting the Remaining Pieces into the Goods and Persons Jigsaw' (2001) 26 *ELRev.* 35

——and Deakin, S., 'Market Access and Regulatory Competition', in C. Barnard and J. Scott (eds.), *The Law of the Single European Market, Unpacking the Premises* (Hart, 2002), ch. 8

Bernard, N., 'Discrimination and Free Movement in EC Law' (1996) 45 *ICLQ* 82

Biondi, A., 'Free Trade, a Mountain Road and the Right to Protest: European Economic Freedoms and Fundamental Individual Rights' [2004] *EHRLRev.* 51

Chalmers, D., 'Repackaging the Internal Market—The Ramifications of the *Keck* Judgment' (1994) 19 *ELRev.* 385

Connor, T., 'Accentuating the Positive: the "Selling Arrangement", the First Decade and Beyond' (2005) 54 *ICLQ* 127

De Búrca, G., 'Unpacking the Concept of Discrimination in EC and International Trade Law', in C. Barnard and J. Scott (eds.), *The Law of the Single European Market, Unpacking the Premises* (Hart, 2002), ch. 7

Dougan, M., 'Minimum Harmonization and the Internal Market' (2000) 37 *CMLRev.* 853

Enchelmaier, S., 'The Awkward Selling of a Good Idea, or a Traditionalist Interpretation of *Keck*' (2003) 22 *YBEL* 249

Gormley, L.W., 'Reasoning Renounced? The Remarkable Judgment in *Keck & Mithouard*' [1994] *European Business L Rev.* 63

Greaves, R., 'Advertising Restrictions and the Free Movement of Goods and Services' (1998) 23 *ELRev.* 305

Hilson, C., 'Discrimination in Community Free Movement Law' (1999) 24 *ELRev.* 445

Koutrakos, P., 'On Groceries, Alcohol and Olive Oil: More on Free Movement of Goods after *Keck*' (2001) 26 *ELRev.* 391

Maduro, M.P., 'Reforming the Market or the State? Article 30 and the European Constitution: Economic Freedoms and Political Rights' (1997) 3 *ELJ* 55

Mortelmans, K., 'The Common Market, the Internal Market and the Single Market, What's in a Market' (1998) 35 *CMLRev.* 101

Nic Shuibhne, N., 'The Free Movement of Goods and Article 28: An Evolving Framework' (2002) 27 *ELRev.* 408

Oliver, P., 'Some Further Reflections on the Scope of Articles 28–30 (ex 30–36)' (1999) 36 *CMLRev.* 738

—— and Roth, W.-H., 'The Internal Market and the Four Freedoms' (2004) 41 *CMLRev.* 407

Reich, N., 'The "November Revolution" of the European Court of Justice: *Keck, Meng* and *Audi* Revisited' (1994) 31 *CMLRev.* 459

Scott, J., 'Mandatory or Imperative Requirements in the EU and the WTO', in C. Barnard and J. Scott (eds.), *The Law of the Single European Market, Unpacking the Premises* (Hart, 2002), ch. 10

Weatherill, S., 'After *Keck*: Some Thoughts on how to Clarify the Clarification' (1996) 33 *CMLRev.* 885

—— 'Recent Case Law Concerning the Free Movement of Goods: Mapping the Frontiers of Market Deregulation' (1999) 36 *CMLRev.* 51

—— 'Pre-emption, Harmonisation and the Distribution of Competence to Regulate the Internal Market', in C. Barnard and J. Scott (eds.), *The Law of the Single European Market, Unpacking the Premises* (Hart, 2002), ch. 2

Weiler, J.H.H, 'From *Dassonville* to *Keck* and Beyond: An Evolutionary Reflection on the Text and Context of the Free Movement of Goods', in P. Craig and G. de Búrca (eds.), *The Evolution of EU Law* (Oxford University Press, 1999), ch. 10

White, E., 'In Search of the Limits to Article 30 of the EEC Treaty' (1989) 26 *CMLRev.* 235

Wils, W.P.J., 'The Search for the Rule in Article 30 EEC: Much Ado About Nothing?' (1993) 18 *ELRev.* 475

FREE MOVEMENT OF CAPITAL AND ECONOMIC AND MONETARY UNION

1. CENTRAL ISSUES

i. This chapter is concerned with free movement of capital and economic and monetary union (EMU).

ii. The initial discussion will focus on the free movement of capital. This is one of the four freedoms enshrined in the original Rome Treaty. The Treaty Articles were altered radically by the TEU. There is now a growing body of case law testing the scope of these provisions. This jurisprudence raises similar issues to those encountered in the context of goods, persons, establishment, and services.

iii. The remainder of the discussion will be devoted to EMU. There will be an analysis of the movement towards EMU, and the Treaty provisions in the TEU that set the legal framework for EMU. There will be consideration of the arguments for and against EMU. The position of the European Central Bank (ECB) will be analysed. The discussion will conclude with an overview of the stresses and strains of EMU.

2. FREE MOVEMENT OF CAPITAL

(a) THE ORIGINAL TREATY PROVISIONS

While Articles 67–73 of the Rome Treaty contained provisions on the free movement of capital,[1] they were less peremptory than those applicable to the free movement of goods, workers, services, and establishment. Thus while Article 67(1) imposed an obligation to abolish progressively restrictions on capital movements during the transitional period, this was only to the extent necessary to ensure the proper functioning of the common market. This same theme was carried over to, for example, Article 71, which required Member States to endeavour to

---

[1] J. Usher, *The Law of Money and Financial Services in the European Community* (Oxford University Press, 1994), 14–16.

avoid the introduction of new exchange restrictions on capital movements. The wording of these Treaty Articles necessarily had an impact on the ECJ's approach to this area.[2] The Council enacted various directives pursuant to these Treaty provisions, the most important being Council Directive 88/361.[3]

(b) THE CURRENT PROVISIONS: THE BASIC PRINCIPLE

The TEU completely revised the provisions on free movement of capital with effect from 1 January 1994.[4] Article 56 now provides:

> 1. Within the framework of the provisions set out in this Chapter, all restrictions on the movement of capital between Member States and between Member States and third countries shall be prohibited.
>
> 2. Within the framework of the provisions set out in this Chapter, all restrictions on payments between Member States and between Member States and third countries shall be prohibited.[5]

What is now Article 56 was held to have direct effect in *Sanz de Lera*.[6] The ECJ held that it laid down a clear and unconditional prohibition for which no implementing measure was required. The existence of Member State discretion to take all measures necessary to prevent infringement of national law and regulations contained within what is now Article 58(1)(b) did not prevent Article 56 from having direct effect, because the exercise of such discretion was subject to judicial review. This ruling concerned an action against the State. Treaty articles normally have vertical and horizontal direct effect, and thus can be used against the State and private individuals, and there is nothing in *Sanz de Lera* to indicate the contrary. It would not be difficult, as Usher states,[7] to envisage a situation in which the unilateral conduct of a financial institution could restrict payments between States. This interpretation is reinforced by the fact that Article 56 does not, on its face, refer only to the State.[8] The argument to the contrary would be derived by way of analogy with Article 28 on the free movement of goods, which has been largely confined to actions against the State itself.[9]

---

[2] Case 203/80 *Casati* [1981] ECR 2595.

[3] [1988] OJ L178/5.

[4] S. Peers, 'Free Movement of Capital: Learning Lessons or Slipping on Spilt Milk?', in C. Barnard and J. Scott (eds.), *The Law of the Single European Market* (Hart, 2002), ch. 13; L. Flynn, 'Coming of Age: The Free Movement of Capital Case-Law 1993–2002' (2002) 39 *CMLRev.* 773.

[5] This does not cover national procedural rules governing actions by a creditor seeking payment from a recalcitrant debtor: Case C–412/97 *ED Srl* v. *Italo Fenocchio* [1999] ECR I–3845.

[6] Cases C–163, 165, and 250/94 *Criminal Proceedings against Lucas Emilio Sanz de Lera* [1995] ECR I–4821, paras. 41–47.

[7] N. 1 above, 27.

[8] In Case C–464/98 *Westdeutsche Landesbank Girozentrale* v. *Stefan and Republik Österreich* [2001] ECR I–173 a private defendant relied on Art. 56. and in Case C–213/04 *Burtscher* v. *Stauderer* [2005] ECR I–10309, the defendant was a private individual, although the case was concerned with a State measure.

[9] The rationale for this limitation on Art. 28 is, however, based in large part on the overlap which would otherwise occur between Art. 28 and Arts. 81 and 82.

The Treaty provisions do not define movement of capital, but the ECJ held that reference can be made to the non-exhaustive list in Directive 88/361.[10] It will be for the ECJ to decide, with the aid of the Directive, whether a measure constitutes a restriction on the movement of capital. Thus a national prohibition on the creation of a mortgage in a foreign currency was prohibited by Article 56.[11] Restrictions on the acquisition and disposal of property,[12] such as requirements of prior administrative authorization, are proscribed.[13] Measures taken by a Member State that are liable to dissuade its residents from obtaining loans or making investments in other Member States constitute restrictions on the movement of capital.[14] While direct taxation remains within Member States' competence, they must exercise that competence consistently with EC law and avoid discrimination on the grounds of nationality.[15] It is clear moreover that Article 56 covers not only measures that discriminate on grounds of nationality, but also measures that may impede capital movements, even though they are not discriminatory.[16]

The ECJ has, by way of contrast, held that a Member State can apply a tax to income notwithstanding the fact that it has already been taxed in another Member State,[17] with the consequence that double taxation is not contrary to free movement of capital.[18]

Article 56 gives the impression that capital movements within the EC, and between Member States and non-member countries, are to be treated the same. This is not so, since other Treaty Articles qualify the application of Article 56 to non-member countries. Article 57(1) in effect allows lawful restrictions on capital movements which existed on 31 December 1993 to remain in being, and Article 57(2) requires the Council only to endeavour to achieve free movement with non-member countries to the greatest extent possible. The Council is also empowered under Article 59 to take safeguard measures in exceptional circumstances where capital movements to or from non-member countries cause, or threaten to cause, serious difficulties for the operation of economic and monetary union. Such measures cannot last longer than six months, and can be taken only where strictly necessary.[19]

---

[10] Case C–222/97 *Proceedings brought by Trummer and Mayer* [1999] ECR I–1661, para. 21; Case C–452/01 *Ospelt v. Schlossle Weissenberg Familienstiftung* [2003] ECR I–9743.

[11] Case C–464/98 *Westdeutsche Landesbank*, n. 8 above.

[12] Case C–376/03 *D v. Inspecteur van de Belastingdienst/Particulieren/Ondernerningen/buitenland te Heerlen* [2005] ECR I–5821.

[13] Case C–302/97 *Konle v. Austrian Republic* [1999] ECR I–3099; Case C–423/98 *Albore* [2000] ECR I–5965; Cases C–515, and 527–540/99 *Reisch v. Bürgemeister der Landeshauptstadt Salzburg* [2002] ECR I–2157; Case C–300/01 *Salzmann* [2003] ECR I–4899; Case C–213/04 *Burtscher*, n. 8 above.

[14] Case C–439/97 *Sandoz GmbH v. Finanzlandesdirektion für Wien, Niederösterreich und Burgenland* [1999] ECR I–7041, para. 19; Case C–478/98 *Commission v. Belgium* [2000] ECR I–7587, para. 18; Case C–513/03 *Heirs of van Hiltern-van der Heijden* [2006] ECR I–1957, para. 44.

[15] Case C–80/94 *Wielockx v. Inspecteur der Directe Belastingen* [1995] ECR I–2493, para. 16; Case C–251/98 *Baars v. Inspecteur der Belastingen Particulieren/Ondernemingen Gorinchem* [2000] ECR I–2787, para. 17; Cases C–397 and 410/98 *Metallgesellschaft Ltd., Hoechst AG and Hoechst (UK) Ltd. v. Commissioners of the Inland Revenue and HM Attorney General* [2001] ECR I–1727, para. 37; Case C–242/03 *Ministre des Finances v. Weidert and Paulus* [2004] ECR I–7379, para. 12; Case C–346/04 *Conjin v. Finanzamt Hamburg-Nord* [2006] ECR I–6137, paras. 14–15.

[16] Case C–367/98 *Commission v. Portugal* [2002] ECR I–4731, paras. 44–45; Case C–174/04 *Commission v. Italy* [2005] ECR I–4933, para. 12.

[17] Case C–513/04 *Kerckhaert and Morres v. Belgium* [2006] ECR I–10967. See also Case C–374/04 *Test Claimants in Class IV of the ACT Group Litigation v. Commissioners of Inland Revenue*, 12 Dec. 2006. Compare in the context of Arts. 43 and 48 EC Case C–446/03 *Marks & Spencer plc v. Halsey (Her Majesty Inspector of Taxes)* [2005] ECR I–10837.

[18] For difficulties with this reasoning see J. Snell, 'Non-Discriminatory Tax Obstacles in Community Law' (2007) 56 *ICLQ* 339, 358–366.

[19] See also Art. 60.

(c) THE CURRENT PROVISIONS: THE EXCEPTIONS

Article 58(1)(a) concerns taxation and constitutes one of the main exceptions to Article 56. It provides that the provisions of Article 56 shall be without prejudice to the right of Member States:

> to apply the relevant provisions of their tax law which distinguish between tax-payers who are not in the same situation with regard to their place of residence or with regard to the place where their capital is invested.

Article 58(1)(a) is expressly made subject to Article 58(3), which stipulates that the measures taken must not constitute a means of arbitrary discrimination or a disguised restriction on the free movement of capital and payments. The ECJ will decide whether, for example, residents and non-residents are in a comparable position, and whether there has been discrimination.[20] For a difference in treatment not to be regarded as arbitrary for the purposes of Article 58(3) it must be objectively justified.[21] This will require the Member State to show, for example, that the differential treatment was intended to protect the integrity of the tax system and was necessary to achieve this end. The ECJ interprets this requirement strictly. Thus in *Verkooijen*[22] it was held that a national provision making the grant of exemption from income tax on dividends paid to shareholders conditional on the company having its seat in the Netherlands was contrary to EC law. The ECJ rejected the defence that the rule was justified to encourage investment in the Netherlands: such purely economic objectives could not justify a limit placed on a fundamental freedom. The ECJ also rejected arguments that the contested rule was justified on the ground that it was necessary to preserve the cohesion of the Netherlands' tax system.[23]

Article 58(1)(b) provides that the provisions of Article 56 shall be without prejudice to the right of Member States:

> to take all requisite measures to prevent infringements of national law and regulations, in particular in the field of taxation and the prudential supervision of financial institutions, or to lay down procedures for the declaration of capital movements for purposes of administrative or statistical information, or to take measures which are justified on grounds of public policy or public security.

Article 58(1)(b) is also made subject to Article 58(3): the restrictions cannot constitute a means of arbitrary discrimination, etc. Article 58(1)(b) effectively divides into two parts.

The first part covers the whole of the Article apart from the reference to public policy and public security. It has been convincingly argued[24] that this 'relates to the effective administration

---

20 Case C–279/93 *Schumacker* [1995] ECR I–225; Case C–376/03 *D*, n. 12 above; Case C–374/04 *ACT Group Litigation*, n. 17 above, para. 46; Case C–446/04 *Test Claimants in the FII Group Litigation* v. *Commissioners of Inland Revenue*, 12 Dec. 2006.

21 Usher, n. 1 above, 34.

22 Case C–35/98 *Staatssecretaris van Financiën* v. *Verkooijen* [2000] ECR I–4071; Case C–512/03 *Blanckaert* [2005] ECR I–7685, para. 42.

23 See also Case C–251/98, *Baars*, n. 15 above; Case C–319/02 *Manninen* [2004] ECR I–7477; Case C–265/04 *Bouanich* v. *Skatteverket* [2006] ECR I–923; Case C–386/04 *Centro di Musicologia* v. *Finanzamt München für Körperschaften* [2006] ECR I–8203; Case C–292/04 *Meilicke, Wiede, Stoffler* v. *Finanzamt Bonn-Innenstedt*, 6 Mar. 2007.

24 Usher, n. 1 above, 36.

and enforcement of the tax system and the effective supervision of, for example, banks and insurance companies, rather than to matters of underlying economic policy', the latter being dealt with under Articles 119 and 120. The ECJ will inquire closely before accepting this defence. In *Commission v. Belgium*[25] the ECJ held that a national rule forbidding Belgian residents from subscribing to securities of a loan on the Eurobond market was caught by Article 56. The Belgian Government argued that the measure was justified under Article 58(1)(b) because it preserved fiscal coherence. This argument was rejected because there was no direct link between any fiscal advantage and disadvantage which should be preserved in order to ensure such coherence. The Belgian Government argued moreover that the contested measure prevented tax evasion by Belgian residents, and ensured effective fiscal supervision. The ECJ disagreed, and held that the national rule was disproportionate: a general presumption of tax evasion could not justify a measure that compromised a Treaty Article.

The second part of Article 58(1)(b) covers public policy and public security. The ECJ draws on its jurisprudence from other freedoms when interpreting these terms. This exception will be interpreted narrowly and the Member State has the burden of proof. The restriction must be justified in terms of national public interest of a kind referred to in Article 58(1) or by grounds of overriding public interest.[26] The restriction must also be proportionate, and will be struck down if a less restrictive measure could have achieved the desired end. In *Scientology International*[27] the ECJ held that a national law requiring prior authorization for capital investments that threatened public policy or security could, in principle, come within Article 58(1)(b). However, the particular French rule, which did not specify further details about the threat to public security, was regarded as too imprecise, and hence could not come within this Article.[28] However in *Commission v. Belgium*[29] a national rule vesting the Government with a 'golden share' in gas and electricity companies that had been privatized, enabling it to control certain subsequent dispositions of strategic assets, was held to fall within Article 58(1)(b) because it guaranteed energy supplies in the event of a crisis, and hence fell within public security.[30]

Article 58(2) states that the provisions of this Chapter of the Treaty shall be without prejudice to the applicability of restrictions on the right of establishment which are compatible with the Treaty. This Article is once again made subject to Article 58(3). These restrictions therefore include the exception in the case of official activities contained in Article 45.

Articles 119 and 120 contain a different type of qualification to Article 56. These Articles cease to operate from the third stage of EMU, except for States with a derogation, and deal with balance-of-payments crises. The 'strategy' is to look initially to a Community-sponsored solution via Article 119, and then to authorize unilateral action by the State if this is not forthcoming via Article 120.

---

[25] Case C–478/98, n. 14 above. See also Case C–315/02 *Lenz* v. *Finanzlandesdirektion für Tirol* [2004] ECR I–7063, paras. 45–49; Case C–334/02 *Commission* v. *France* [2004] ECR I–2229, paras. 27–34.

[26] Cases C–515, and 527–540/99 *Reisch*, n. 13 above, para. 33; Case C–213/04 *Burtscher*, n. 8 above, para. 44; Case C–174/04 *Commission* v. *Italy*, n. 16 above, para. 35.

[27] Case C–54/99 *Association Eglise de Scientologie de Paris and Scientology International Reserves Trust* v. *The Prime Minister* [2000] ECR I–1355.

[28] Case C–423/98 *Albore*, n. 13 above, paras. 17–24.

[29] Case C–503/99 [2002] ECR I–4809.

[30] Compare however the different results in Case C–367/98 *Commission* v. *Portugal*, n. 16 above; Case C–483/99 *Commission* v. *France* [2002] ECR I–4781; Cases C–282–283/04 *Commission* v. *Netherlands* [2006] ECR I–9141.

3. EARLY ATTEMPTS AT EMU AND
THE EUROPEAN MONETARY SYSTEM

Discussion of Economic and Monetary Union (EMU) must be seen in historical context. In 1969 the Heads of State resolved that a plan should be drawn up in relation to EMU.[31] A committee was established under the chairmanship of Werner, the Luxembourg Prime Minister. It concluded[32] that EMU would entail either the total convertibility of the Community currencies, free from fluctuations in exchange rates, or that preferably such currencies would be replaced by a single Community currency. The report recognized that EMU would entail the centralization of monetary policy, and that there would have to be some Community system for national central banks. The report was followed by a Council Resolution on the attainment of EMU by stages.[33] Progress was, however, halted as a result of changed economic circumstance. The Werner Report was premised on the assumption of fixed exchange rates, and this was undermined by developments in the early 1970s.[34] Largely as a result of problems with the US economy,[35] European currencies began to float, and there was an urgent need to prevent them from floating too far apart. This was the catalyst for the initiation of the 'snake', which established the principle that the difference between the exchange rates of two Member States should not be greater than 2.25 per cent. Economic pressures on particular Member States resulted in departures from the 'snake', such that by 1977 only half of the ten Member States remained within it. This early attempt to forge some form of EMU was further hampered by lack of progress towards the co-ordination of national economic policies, a step seen as vital to the success of the enterprise.[36]

A more general attempt to engender monetary stability took shape in 1978 through the establishment, by a Resolution of the European Council,[37] of the European Monetary System (EMS).[38] There was growing dissatisfaction with floating exchange rates, which were perceived to have a detrimental impact on cross-border investment. Foreign currency movements were, moreover, having a destabilizing effect on European currencies.[39] The EMS instituted the Exchange Rate Mechanism (ERM) and the European Currency Unit (ECU). The ECU rate was determined against a basket of currencies of the Member States. The ERM operated by setting for each participating State a currency rate against the ECU. These values, once determined collectively, could only be altered in the same manner. Once the value of each currency was specified against the ECU it was then possible to determine the worth of any particular national currency against all other national currencies. These relative values were known as the bilateral central rates. Any participant country would not allow its exchange rate to fluctuate by more than 2.25 per cent above or below these bilateral central rates, with an exceptional band of 6 per cent. When a currency reached its bilateral limits

---

[31] For earlier developments see F. Snyder, 'EMU Revisited: Are We Making a Constitution? What Constitution Are We Making', in P. Craig and G. de Búrca (eds.), *The Evolution of EU Law* (Oxford University Press, 1999), 421–424.

[32] Bull. EC Supp. 11–1970.

[33] [1971] OJ C28/1.

[34] Usher, n. 1 above, 138.

[35] D. Swann, *The Economics of Europe, From Common Market to European Union* (9th edn., Penguin, 2000), 204–205.

[36] *Ibid.*, 208.

[37] Bull. EC 12–1978. This Resolution was reinforced by an Agreement between the national central banks.

[38] Snyder, n. 31 above, 428–433.

[39] Swann, n. 35 above, 209–210.

against another currency intervention was required by the relevant central banks to redress the matter. The normal workings of the ERM were, however, thrown into disarray by the currency crises of 1992–1993. Currency dealers speculated that certain weaker currencies could not be sustained within the relatively narrow bands of the ERM. Central banks sought to preserve the integrity of the ERM, but could not ultimately resist market pressures. The lira and the pound were suspended from the ERM. Further market pressures led to the widening of the bilateral bands to 15 per cent,[40] and to the devaluation of certain currencies which stayed within the ERM. These measures preserved the ERM in formal terms, but undermined its primary rationale, since they significantly weakened the search for exchange rate stability.

4. ECONOMIC AND MONETARY UNION: THE THREE STAGES[41]

(a) STAGE ONE AND THE DELORS REPORT

While the SEA contained no commitment to EMU, it stated in a preamble that in 1972 the Heads of State had approved the objective of progressing towards EMU. This was the catalyst for bringing the issue back onto the political agenda at the Hanover Summit of 1988. A committee chaired by Jacques Delors, the President of the Commission, was established to assist the European Council, and reported to the Madrid Summit in 1989.[42] It recommended that EMU should be approached in three stages.[43]

Stage One was the completion of the internal market, closer economic convergence, and the membership of all States in the ERM. This did not require new Treaty powers. In Stage Two a European System of Central Banks (ESCB) would be created, with the tasks of co-ordinating national monetary policies and formulating a common monetary policy for the Community. Stage Three would see the locking of exchange rates and the emergence of a single currency managed by the ESCB. The ESCB was to be independent and have price stability as a primary goal. The Delors Report also recognized that there would have to be central control over national fiscal policy, since otherwise the action of a particular State could have deleterious consequences for inflation or interest rates in all States.

(b) STAGE TWO AND THE TREATY ON EUROPEAN UNION

It was the Treaty on European Union which laid the Treaty foundations for progress towards EMU, and stipulated that the second stage should begin on 1 January 1994.[44] The provisions on EMU are complex. The best way to understand the maze of relevant Treaty Articles is to divide them in the following manner.

---

[40] Subject to a special agreement between Germany and the Netherlands to retain the 2.25% fluctuation band.

[41] K. Dyson and K. Featherstone, *The Road to Maastricht: Negotiating Economic and Monetary Union* (Oxford University Press, 1999).

[42] Report on Economic and Monetary Union in the European Community (EC Commission, 1988).

[43] Snyder, n. 31 above, 432–435.

[44] Art. 116(1).

First, and foremost, the TEU added a new Article 3a to Part 1 concerned with Principles underlying the Treaty. Since the ToA this is now Article 4 EC. Article 4(1) stipulates that the activities of the Member States and the Community shall include the adoption of an economic policy based on the close co-ordination of Member States' economic policies, on the internal market, and on the definition of the common objectives, conducted in accordance with the principle of an open market economy with free competition. Article 4(2) provides that the activities of the States and the Community shall include the irrevocable fixing of exchange rates leading to the introduction of a single currency, the ECU, and the definition of a single monetary and exchange-rate policy. The primary objective is the maintenance of price stability and support of the Community's general economic policies, in accordance with the principle of an open market and free competition. Article 4(3) states that the preceding activities should comply with the following guidelines: stable prices, sound public finances and monetary conditions, and a sustainable balance of payments.

Secondly, there are provisions dealing with economic policy. We have seen from the previous discussion the intimate connection between monetary union in terms of a single currency and broader issues of macro-economic policy. This connection was perceived by both the Werner and Delors Reports, and is supported by sound economic logic. Monetary union is not plausible without some measure of centralized control over fiscal policy, and in particular over budgetary matters. This is the rationale for the inclusion of Articles 98–104.[45] Article 99 provides that the States are to regard their economic policies as a matter of common concern and shall co-ordinate them within the Council. To this end, it is intended that the Council, on the basis of reports from the Commission, shall monitor economic developments in each of the States and make recommendations where necessary. Articles 101 and 102 prohibit overdraft and related facilities by government and public bodies with national central banks. Article 104 is of particular importance: Member States are under an obligation in the second stage to endeavour to avoid excessive budget deficits.[46] The Commission is to monitor the development of the national budgetary situation with a view to identifying gross errors, and there are criteria to determine whether an actual or predicted national deficit exceeds a certain reference value.[47] It is open to the Commission to make a report to the Council, and the Council may then issue recommendations to the State concerned.[48]

Thirdly, there are Treaty Articles dealing with monetary policy. A European Monetary Institute (EMI) was established.[49] This was the forerunner to the European Central Bank (ECB), which came into being at Stage Three of EMU. The EMI helped to pave the way to Stage Three of EMU. The EMI had, by 31 December 1996, to specify the regulatory, organizational, and logistical framework necessary for the European System of Central Banks (ESCB) to perform its tasks in the third stage. This framework had to be submitted to the ECB when it was established.[50] Member States had to ensure that their central banks were independent,[51] and were instructed to treat their exchange rate policies as a matter of common interest.[52]

---

[45] Some of the provisions contained within these Arts. apply only at the third stage of EMU. This will become clear from the subsequent discussion.

[46] Art. 116(4).

[47] Art. 104(2).

[48] At the third stage of EMU the Council is empowered to take tougher measures: see 733 below.

[49] Art. 117.

[50] Art. 117(3).

[51] Arts. 109 and 116(5).

[52] Art. 124.

(c) STAGE THREE: THE BASIC LEGAL FRAMEWORK

The third stage of EMU had, according to the Treaty,[53] to start no later than 1 January 1999. The TEU contained detailed criteria concerning the shift from Stage Two to Stage Three, which are contained in Article 121. The Commission and the EMI had to report to the Council on the progress made by the States towards EMU. These reports would examine, *inter alia*, the extent to which the States had made their central banks independent, and, most importantly, whether the convergence criteria had been met. Meeting these criteria is a condition precedent for a State to adopt the single currency.[54] The four criteria were set out in Article 121(1), and were fleshed out by a Protocol attached to the TEU. Member States that do not fulfil the criteria are referred to as 'Member States with a derogation'.[55] Their position is reassessed at least once every two years to determine whether they now meet the conditions.[56] While they remain outside the single currency certain Treaty Articles do not apply to them.[57]

i. The achievement of a high degree of price stability. This is to be judged by an average rate of inflation, over a one year period prior to the examination, which does not exceed by more than 1.5 per cent the average of the three best-performing States.

ii. The sustainability of the government's financial position. This is defined as the avoidance of an excessive government budgetary deficit: an annual budget deficit of less than 3 per cent of Gross Domestic Product (GDP), and an overall public debt ratio of not more than 60 per cent of GDP.

iii. The observance of the normal fluctuation margins provided by the ERM for at least two years without severe tensions and without devaluation against the currency of any other Member State.

iv. The durability of convergence achieved by the Member State as reflected in long-term interest rates. This is defined as meaning that over a period of one year prior to the examination, the Member State has had an average nominal long-term interest rate that does not exceed by more than 2 per cent that of the three best performing Member States in terms of price stability.

It was on the basis of these reports that the Council under Article 121(2), acting by qualified majority on a recommendation of the Commission, assessed whether each Member State fulfilled the conditions for adoption of a single currency. It also had to assess whether a majority of the Member States fulfilled these conditions. The Council then recommended its findings to the Council meeting in the composition of the Heads of State or Government,[58] the rationale being that only the formal heads of state should make decisions of this magnitude. The Council, meeting as the Heads of State or Government, had to decide by qualified majority, in the light of this Council recommendation, not later than 31 December 1996, whether a majority of the Member States fulfilled the conditions for the adoption of a single currency. It also had to decide whether it was appropriate for the Community to enter the third stage and, if so, to set a date for the beginning of the third stage.[59]

[53] Art. 121(4).
[54] Art. 121(2).
[55] Art. 122(1).
[56] Art. 122(2).
[57] Art. 122(3).
[58] The European Parliament must be consulted and forward its view to the Council meeting as the Heads of State, etc.
[59] Art. 121(3).

If the date for the beginning of the third stage had not been set by the end of 1997 then the third stage was deemed to start on 1 January 1999.[60] Prior to 1 July 1998 the Council, meeting as the Heads of State or Government, had to repeat the exercise contained in Article 121(1) and (2) of deciding whether individual States met the convergence criteria, but it no longer had to decide whether a majority of the States fulfilled these conditions. The Council, meeting in this form, had then to confirm which States met the conditions for the adoption of a single currency.

(d) LEGAL CONSEQUENCES OF MOVING TO STAGE THREE

The move to the third stage of EMU has important consequences concerning institutional structure, monetary policy, and economic policy.

In *institutional terms*, immediately after the decision was taken on the starting date for Stage Three the ECB was brought into being,[61] and the EMI went into liquidation.[62] The ECB has legal personality.[63] It has an Executive Board and a Governing Council. The Executive Board is composed of a President, Vice-President, and four other members, who must be recognized experts in monetary or banking matters. They serve for eight years and the posts are non-renewable.[64] The Governing Council consists of the Executive Board plus the governors of the national central banks.[65] The independence of the ECB is enshrined in Article 108, which stipulates that the ECB shall not take any instruction from Community institutions, Member States, or any other body. This independence is reflected in the ECB's decision-making structure: the President of the Council and a member of the Commission may participate in meetings of the ECB's Governing Council, but they do not have the right to vote.[66] The ECB is given the power to make regulations and take decisions. It is also empowered to make recommendations and deliver opinions.[67] These terms have the same meaning as in Article 249. The ECB is entitled, subject to certain conditions, to impose fines or periodic penalty payments on undertakings for failure to comply with obligations contained in its regulations and decisions.[68] The ECB is part of the European System of Central Banks (ESCB), the other members being the national central banks.[69] The start of the third stage of EMU also saw the establishment of the Economic and Financial Committee, composed of no more than two members drawn from the Member States, the Commission, and the ECB. This Committee has a number of tasks, including:[70] delivering opinions to the Council or Commission; keeping under review the economic and financial situation of the Member States and the Community; examining the situation regarding free movement of capital; and contributing to the preparation of Council work.

---

[60] Art. 121(4).
[61] Art. 123(1).
[62] Art. 123(2).
[63] Art. 107(2).
[64] Art. 112(2).
[65] Art. 112(1).
[66] Art. 113(1).
[67] Art. 110.
[68] Art. 110(3).
[69] Art. 107(1).
[70] Art. 114(2).

The most important consequence in terms of *monetary policy* was of course the establishment of a single currency. At the start of the third stage the Council fixed the conversion rates for the Member States entering the single currency.[71] The ECU was then substituted for these currencies at this rate, and became a currency in its own right. The objectives of EC monetary policy are set out in Article 105. The primary objective of the ESCB is to maintain price stability. Without prejudice to this objective, the ESCB must support the general economic policies of the Community with a view to attaining the objectives set out in Article 2. The ESCB is to act in accordance with the principle of an open market economy with free competition, and in compliance with the principles in Article 4. The basic tasks of the ESCB are:[72] to define and implement the Community's monetary policy; to conduct foreign-exchange operations; to hold and manage the official foreign reserves of the Member States; and to promote the smooth operation of the payment system. The ECB, in its fields of competence, must be consulted on any Community act and, subject to certain conditions, by national authorities regarding any draft legislative provision.[73] The ECB has the exclusive right to issue banknotes within the EC.[74] The ESCB is to 'contribute' to the smooth conduct of policies pursued by other competent authorities relating to the prudential supervision of credit institutions and the stability of the financial system.[75]

The shift to Stage Three also signalled *the application of more peremptory Treaty provisions concerning economic policy*, particularly in relation to fiscal and budgetary matters. Member States have the obligation to avoid excessive government deficits and not just to endeavour to avoid them.[76] The Council's powers to deal with States that do not adhere to its recommendations on excessive budgetary deficits are reinforced in the third stage of EMU.[77]

(e) THE TRANSITION TO EMU

The formal decision of the Council, meeting as the Heads of State or Governments, that the applicant States apart from Greece had met the convergence criteria was made on 2 May 1998. The third stage of EMU duly began on 1 January 1999. The exchange rates of the participating countries were irrevocably set, and the Euro became a currency in its own right, notwithstanding those who doubted whether some States really would meet the convergence criteria,[78] given the high debt levels in Italy and Belgium. The UK negotiated an opt-out Protocol, which was appended to the TEU, the import of which is that it is not bound to move to the third stage of EMU even if it meets the convergence criteria. On 1 January 2002 the new banknotes and coins were introduced, and national currencies were withdrawn from circulation towards the end of February 2002. There are currently thirteen Member States that have adopted the Euro: Austria, Belgium, Finland, France, Germany, Greece, Ireland, Italy, Luxembourg, Netherlands, Portugal, Slovenia, and Spain.

---

[71] This decision is made unanimously by those States which do not have a derogation, on a proposal from the Commission and after consulting the ECB: Art. 123(4).

[72] Art. 105(2).

[73] Art. 105(4).

[74] Art. 106. The ECB and the national banks can actually issue the banknotes.

[75] Art. 105(5).

[76] Art. 104(1).

[77] Arts. 104(9) and (11). These Treaty obligations have been given added force by the Stability and Growth Pact [1997] OJ C236/1, Reg. 1466/97 [1997] OJ L209/1, and Reg. 1467/97 [1997] OJ L209/6.

[78] For discussion of the interpretative leeway in these criteria see Snyder, n. 31 above, 457–463.

5. ECONOMIC GOVERNANCE:
CO-ORDINATION OF ECONOMIC POLICY

The co-ordination of economic policy has been especially important in the light of monetary union.[79] It is clear that the economic health of individual Member State economies can have a marked impact on the valuation of the Euro,[80] and this is the broad rationale for co-ordination. The Treaty embodies two forms of co-ordination.

The *softer version is the multilateral surveillance procedure.* Member States are to regard their economic policies as a matter of common concern, and are to co-ordinate them in the Council.[81] The Council, acting by qualified majority on a recommendation from the Commission, formulates a draft for the broad guidelines[82] of the economic policies of the Member States and the Community, and reports this to the European Council. The guidelines are discussed by the European Council, and its conclusion forms the basis for a Council recommendation setting out the broad guidelines.[83] It is then for the Council, on the basis of reports from the Commission, to monitor economic developments in the Member States. This constitutes the multilateral surveillance.[84] If it becomes apparent that the economic policies of the Member States are not consistent with the broad economic guidelines, the Council may, acting by qualified majority on a recommendation from the Commission, make the necessary recommendations to the Member State concerned.[85] The Treaty provisions have been complemented by the Stability and Growth Pact, SGP. The Regulation[86] provides rules covering the content, submission, examination, and monitoring of the stability and convergence programmes so as to prevent at an early stage the occurrence of excessive government deficit, and to promote the surveillance and co-ordination of economic policies.[87]

The *harder version of co-ordination is embodied in the excessive deficit procedure.* Member States are under an obligation to avoid excessive deficits.[88] The Commission monitors the budgetary situation and government debt in the Member States to identify whether the ratio of the planned or actual government deficit to gross domestic product exceeds a reference value, this being 3 per cent, or whether the ratio of government debt to gross domestic product exceeds such a reference value, this being 60 per cent.[89] These reference values are specified in the Protocol on the Excessive Deficit Procedure.[90] The Commission reports where a

---

[79] D. Hodson and I. Maher, 'The Open Method as a New Mode of Governance: The Case of Soft Economic Policy Co-ordination' (2001) 39 *JCMS* 719; F. Amtenbrink and J. de Haan, 'Economic Governance in the European Union' (2003) 40 *CMLRev.* 1075; D. Hodson and I. Maher, 'Soft Law and Sanctions: Economic Policy Coordination and Reform of the Stability and Growth Pact' (2004) 11 *JEPP* 798; J.-V. Louis, 'The Economic and Monetary Union: Law and Institutions' (2004) 41 *CMLRev.* 575.

[80] Council Reg. (EC) 1467/97 of 7 July 1997 on speeding up and clarifying the implementation of the excessive deficit procedure [1997] OJ L209/6, rec. 8.

[81] Art. 99(1) EC.

[82] Council Recommendation 95/326/EC of 10 July 1995 on the broad guidelines of the economic policies of the Member States and of the Community [1995] OJ L191/24.

[83] Art. 99(2) EC.

[84] Art. 99(3) EC.

[85] Art. 99(4) EC.

[86] Council Reg. (EC) 1466/97 of 7 July 1997 on the strengthening of the surveillance of budgetary positions and the surveillance and coordination of economic policies [1997] OJ L209/1.

[87] *Ibid.*, Art. 1.

[88] Art. 104(1) EC.

[89] Art. 104(2) EC.

[90] Protocol No. 20 (1992), Art. 1.

Member State does not fulfil these criteria, and may do so if it believes that there is a risk of an excessive deficit in a Member State.[91] The Economic and Financial Committee, ECOFIN, gives an opinion on this report.[92] Where the Commission considers that there is an excessive deficit, or that it may occur, the Commission must address an opinion to the Council.[93] It is then for the Council, acting by qualified majority on the Commission's recommendation and having considered the views of the Member State, to decide whether the excessive deficit exists.[94] If the Council decides that it exists it must make recommendations to the Member State to bring the situation to an end.[95] Where the Member State fails to act on these recommendations the Council may decide to give notice to the Member State that it should take certain measures within a specified time to remedy the situation.[96] Where the Member State fails to comply with these measures, the Council may decide to take further measures, such as the imposition of fines, until the excessive deficit has been corrected.[97] The Treaty provisions on excessive deficit have, like those on surveillance, been complemented by a regulation concerning excessive deficit,[98] this being the other limb of the Stability and Growth Pact.

The frailty of the deficit procedure was however revealed in relation to the deficits run by France, Germany, Portugal, and Italy in 2002–2003. They undertook to balance their budgets over the medium term, but departed from their corrective programmes. This led to the Commission having recourse to legal action when ECOFIN placed the excessive deficit procedure in abeyance for France and Germany.[99] The ECJ's judgment is complex and cannot be examined in detail here.[100] Suffice it to say that the Court held that the Council's decision to place the excessive deficit procedure in abeyance was unlawful, since there was no authority for this in the Treaty. The ECJ however rejected the other Commission claim, that the Council's failure to adopt the Commission's recommendations pursuant to Article 104(8) and (9) EC was a decision that should be annulled. It held that where the requisite majority for the Commission recommendations was not secured in the Council there was no decision that could be reviewed under Article 230 EC.

The flouting of the system by France and Germany brought the Stability and Growth Pact into disrepute. The Commission was in a dilemma. If reforms were not made then resistance to the SGP was likely to continue. If however any reform significantly weakened the pre-existing regime then its practical effectiveness for the future would correspondingly diminish. Changes were made to the Stability and Growth Pact Regulations,[101] the net effect being to soften and render more discretionary the multilateral surveillance and excessive deficit procedures, thereby rendering it more unlikely that soft or hard sanctions will be imposed.

---

[91] Art. 104(3) EC.

[92] Art. 104(4) EC.

[93] Art. 104(5) EC.

[94] Art. 104(6) EC.

[95] Art. 104(7) EC.

[96] Art. 104(9) EC.

[97] Art. 104(11) EC.

[98] Reg. 1467/97, n. 80 above.

[99] 2546th Meeting of the Council of the European Union (Economic and Financial Affairs), Brussels, 25 Nov. 2003.

[100] Case C–27/04 *Commission* v. *Council* (*Excessive Deficits*) [2004] ECR I–6649; I. Maher, 'Economic Policy Co-ordination and the European Court: Excessive Deficits and ECOFIN Discretion' (2004) 29 *ELRev.* 831.

[101] Council Reg. (EC) 1055/2005 of 27 June 2005 amending Reg. 1466/97 [2005] OJ L174/1; Council Reg. (EC) 1056/2005 of 27 June 2005 amending Reg. 1467/97 [2005] OJ L174/5; J.-V. Louis, 'The Review of the Stability and Growth Pact (2006) 43 *CMLRev.* 85.

6. UNDERSTANDING EMU:
THE ECONOMIC FOUNDATIONS

The economic arguments for and against a single currency are hotly debated. They are also complex.[102] What follows is an outline of some of the main themes in this debate.

(a) THE CASE FOR EMU

The case for EMU rests essentially on two connected foundations. It is argued that EMU will foster economic growth and engender greater price stability through low inflation. These will be considered in turn.

The argument that EMU will enhance *economic growth* is based on a number of factors, the most important of which are as follows. The most obvious factor is the *saving of transaction costs*. A single currency removes the cost of exchange-rate conversions when money moves within the EC. The Commission calculated that the total savings would be approximately 25 billion Euros.[103]

An equally important, albeit contested, factor is the *link between the single market and a single currency*. This was captured most vividly in the Commission's slogan of 'one market, one money'. While it is possible to have a single market without a single currency, it is argued that the single market will work better with a single currency than without. The link between the completion of a single market and a single currency was explicitly drawn in Commission publications.[104] By having a single currency businesses save on 'menu costs', and do not have to maintain different sets of prices for each market. From the manufacturer's perspective, this facilitates the development of marketing strategies for the Community as a whole. From the consumer's perspective, it enables direct price comparisons to be made of products in different countries.

The existence of a single currency also protects against the *costs associated with large exchange-rate changes and competitive devaluation*, which can 'distort the single market by unpredictable shifts of advantage between countries unrelated to fundamentals'.[105] In this sense 'the single market needs a single currency not just to push it forwards, but to stop it sliding backwards'.[106] Such currency fluctuations can slow economic growth by creating uncertainty for business which is not conducive to investment.[107] The very existence of wide price differentials fuelled in part by different currencies serves moreover to fuel attempts by Member States to prevent parallel imports and impede intra-Community trade.

It is argued that a single currency will in addition foster growth by *lowering interest rates and stimulating investment*. Countries will no longer have to raise their interest rates above German levels in order to stop their currencies from falling in relation to the D-mark.[108] Investment projects 'will become economic which were not so when they had to earn higher

---

102 P. de Grauwe, *Economics of Monetary Union* (6th edn., Oxford University Press, 2005).
103 *One Market, One Money* (European Commission, 1990), ch. 3.
104 See, e.g., *Commission's Work Programme for 1998* (EC Commission, 1997).
105 C. Johnson, *In with the Euro, Out with the Pound* (Penguin, 1996), 47.
106 *Ibid.*
107 The Impact of Currency Fluctuations on the Internal Market, COM(95)503 final.
108 Johnson, n. 105 above.

returns to repay expensive borrowed money, compensate for exchange rate uncertainty, and hand out high dividends to share-holders'.[109]

The case for EMU is also, as seen, based on the argument that it fosters *stable prices and low inflation*. Savers tend to gain from low inflation, since their money retains its purchasing power for longer.[110] Inflation makes it more difficult to maintain long-term business plans, and redistributes income in an arbitrary manner. Businesses incur 'menu costs' when inflation rates are high or constantly changing. The ERM exerted some discipline over inflation rates by the very fact that countries, in effect, linked their exchange rates to the D-mark, and limited their use of devaluation. There was, however, a tendency for some countries to have overvalued exchange rates, and this was in part the rationale for the currency crises in 1992 and 1993. It is argued then that EMU offers a better, cheaper, and more stable way of reducing inflation, particularly when monetary policy is run by an independent central bank which is not subject to short-term political pressures.

(b) THE CASE AGAINST EMU

There are a number of differing types of argument made against EMU. These can for the sake of analysis be divided into 'contingent disapproval' and 'outright rejection'.

The essence of the *contingent disapproval argument* was that the Member States were not ready for EMU, since they could not meet the convergence criteria, except by creative accounting that threw the whole enterprise into disrepute. This was exemplified by the letter signed by 155 German university professors, arguing that the time was not yet ripe for EMU.[111] It is moreover reasonably clear that EMU may well suit some States more than others.[112]

The *outright rejection argument* was more complex, and was part political, part symbolic, and part economic.

In political terms, it was argued by some that a single currency was a major step towards a European super State.[113] Important facets of economic policy were shifted from the domestic to the Community arena. National governments no longer had the ultimate option of devaluation. There would no longer be any point in having parliamentary debates on matters such as inflation, interest rates, and unemployment, since power over such matters would be taken from national polities and given to the ECB. This would, so it was said, exacerbate problems of democratic deficit within the EC, given that the demise of national parliamentary power over such matters would not be offset by any meaningful control through the European Parliament.[114]

In symbolic terms, a national currency was felt by some to be part of the very idea of nationhood. This point is captured well by Johnson:[115]

> Advocates of monetary and exchange rate autonomy argue that it may not be perfect, but it is preferable to the alternative. The dishonour of a national currency may seem better than its

---

[109] *Ibid.*, 55.

[110] This is so notwithstanding the fact that price rises are often accompanied by higher interest rates, since such high rates do not normally fully compensate for price rises.

[111] *Financial Times*, 9 Feb. 1998.

[112] De Grauwe, n. 102 above, 115–6.

[113] J. Redwood, *The Single European Currency* (Tecla, 1995), 11–12.

[114] *Ibid.*, 19–20.

[115] N. 105 above, 87.

death. Monetary sovereignty is sometimes felt to be part of a national sovereignty, so that giving it up involves a loss of political independence, and ultimately political union. It is almost a case of 'my country, right or wrong'.

In economic terms, it was argued that a single currency would lead to a variety of undesirable consequences. Prices would increase, since businesses would take advantage of the change from national currencies to the Euro to raise prices before consumers were accustomed to the new money.[116] A single currency could moreover create tensions because economic conditions in Member States followed different cycles, and hence removing the possibility of exchange rate fluctuation eliminated a significant mechanism for economic adjustment between States.

(c) EMU: ECONOMICS, POLITICS, AND LAW

It is readily apparent that the debates about EMU are only in part economic. The economic dimension shades into the political, and these often manifest themselves in legal form.

F. Snyder, EMU Revisited[117]

The legal aspects of EMU are sometimes extremely controversial, either in public or behind the closed doors of diplomatic and monetary negotiations. Legal and other technical debates often act as a kind of shorthand for political disagreement. Competing economic theories frequently play the same role. This was the case long before EMU was set as a priority European Union objective. This does not mean, of course, that all legal aspects of EMU have been or are politically controversial. But, in the future also, political conflicts about EMU are likely often to appear in legal camouflage. This dialectical relationship between politics and law, political discourse and monetary discourse, and political discourse and legal discourse should not be surprising. The driving force in EMU, including its main legal aspects, has always been politics.

---

7. UNDERSTANDING EMU: CENTRAL BANK INDEPENDENCE

We have seen that the Treaty places particular emphasis upon the independence of the ECB.[118] The degree of independence possessed by national central banks varies.[119] Gormley and de Haan[120] identified five criteria that shape the division of responsibilities between national governments and their central banks.[121]

---

116 Redwood, n. 113 above, 22.

117 Snyder, n. 31 above, 468.

118 C. Zilioli and M. Selmayr, *The Law of the European Central Bank* (Hart, 2001).

119 F. Amtenbrink, *The Democratic Accountability of Central Banks* (Hart, 1999), ch. 4.

120 L. Gormley and J. de Haan, 'The Democratic Deficit of the European Central Bank' (1996) 21 *ELRev.* 95, 97–99; Amtenbrink, n. 119 above, 17–22.

121 See also R. Lastra, 'European Monetary Union and Central Bank Independence', in M. Andenas, L. Gormley, C. Hadjiemmanuil, and I. Harden (eds.), *European Economic and Monetary Union: The Institutional Framework* (Kluwer, 1997), ch. 15; T. Daintith, 'Between Domestic Democracy and an Alien Rule of Law? Some Thoughts on the "Independence" of the Bank of England', in *ibid.*, ch. 17.

The first is the ultimate objective of monetary policy, which in many countries is price stability. The second feature is the specification of inflation targets. In some countries such as New Zealand this is agreed by the central bank with the government; in others, such as Germany, there is no obligation as such on the Bundesbank to announce or agree to any such targets. The third criterion is the degree of independence possessed by the bank and the juridical basis on which this rests. There will, for example, often be a statute dealing with such matters, which stipulates the extent to which the government can or cannot give any instructions to its central bank. The fourth criterion is the extent to which the government can override the central bank's view. The final factor is the appointment of bank officials, and the extent to which the government has any real discretion over this matter.

When judged by these criteria the ECB has a high degree of independence. Its independence is enshrined in Article 108. It is further reinforced by the fact that the Statute of the ESCB was attached as a Protocol to the TEU, and most of its provisions can be altered only by Treaty amendment. The Treaty has therefore constitutionalized the position of the ESCB: the organic law governing its operation cannot be altered by the ordinary legislative process, but only by revising the very provisions of the Treaty themselves.[122] The Treaty establishes the primary and secondary objectives of the ESCB. There is no formal requirement for the ECB to agree with the other Community institutions on the specification of price stability in particular economic circumstances, or on inflation targets. Nor is there is any formal provision allowing the other Community institutions to override the choices made by the ECB.[123]

There is little doubt that this degree of independence was influenced by German desires to have an ECB which mirrored closely the powers and status of the Bundesbank. This sentiment was further strengthened because the ECB would be considering price stability, etc., for the Community as a whole. It was therefore important that the short-term interests of certain Member States, or even the Community institutions, could not sway the ECB. While political considerations, therefore, played a role in shaping the ESCB, there are also sound economic arguments for central bank independence.

L. Gormley and J. de Haan, The Democratic Deficit of the European Central Bank[124]

It is widely believed that the success of monetary policy in achieving a stable and low rate of inflation depends very much on the credibility of the monetary authorities. It makes quite a difference whether economic agents believe policy announcements and behave accordingly, or not. If a central bank with a high level of credibility indicates, for instance, that inflation is too high and that it will strive for a reduction, trade unions will take this announcement seriously in bargaining about wage levels. If the credibility of the central bank is low, trade unions may not believe that inflation will come down and demand higher wages, thereby fuelling the inflationary process.

By delegating monetary policy to an independent Central Bank with a clear mandate for price stability the credibility of the monetary authorities can be enhanced. A Central Bank which is independent will not be exposed to the same incentives to create unexpected inflation.

---

[122] Gormley and de Haan, n. 120 above, 101.

[123] The ECB's independence does not however render it immune from anti-fraud investigations via OLAF: Case C–11/00 *Commission* v. *ECB* [2003] ECR I–7147.

[124] Gormley and de Haan, n. 120 above, 110.

The public can assume that the Central Bank will strive for a low level of inflation. Trade unions will lower their wage demands and investors will ask for lower interest rates as their inflationary expectations are reduced. Due to lower inflationary expectations, actual inflation will also decline.

There is not, however, only one way to structure a central bank, even given acceptance of independence as an ideal. Numerous factors can influence the precise degree of independence accorded to such an institution. In economic terms, it has been argued, for example, that the relationship between a central bank and government should be conceived in terms of an agent/principal contract, whereby the principal, the government, would establish inflation targets and make the agent, the central bank, responsible for attaining them.[125] In political terms, a fully independent central bank with little provision for policy override by the government may well attain price stability, but at the expense of any real measure of democratic control. Monetary policy is, in this sense, taken off the normal political agenda, with a corresponding diminution in democratic control.[126]

L. Gormley and J. de Haan, The Democratic Deficit of the European Central Bank[127]

By now it is well-known that Central Bank independence may improve upon monetary policy. In that sense, the independence of the ESCB and its mandate to strive for price stability are to be applauded, given the virtues of a low and stable rate of inflation. An important problem is how Central Bank independence is related to democratic accountability. Some authors argue that monetary policy should be treated like other instruments of economic policy, like fiscal policy, and should be fully decided upon by democratically elected representatives. Such an approach implies, however, too much a direct involvement of politicians with monetary policy.... Nevertheless, it is respectfully submitted that monetary policy ultimately must be controlled by democratically elected politicians.... Some way or another, the Central bank has to be accountable, and in relation to the ECB, the European Parliament is undoubtedly the appropriate body. National parliaments are, of course, responsible for Central Bank legislation; so too, logically, should the European Parliament be responsible for the legislative framework of the ECB, at least by way of co-decision. In other words, the 'rules of the game' (i. e. the objective of monetary policy) are decided upon according to normal democratic procedures, but the 'game' (monetary policy) is delegated to the Central Bank.

8. CONCLUSION

i.   In terms of *free movement of capital*, there has been a growing body of case law testing the provisions introduced by the TEU. This case law should be viewed alongside that dealing with goods, persons, establishment, and services.

---

[125] *Ibid.*, 111–112.

[126] See the exchange between W. Buiter, 'Alice in Euroland' (1999) 37 *JCMS* 181 and O. Issing, 'The Eurosystem Transparent and Accountable or "Willem in Euroland"' (1999) 37 *JCMS* 503.

[127] Gormley and de Haan, n. 120 above, 112. See Amtenbrink, n. 119 above, ch. 5 for suggestions on how democratic accountability could be improved.

ii.   There are a number of stresses and strains on EMU.

iii. In *monetary terms*, the Euro had a rocky introduction to the world of currency markets and fell considerably in relation to other currencies such as the pound and the dollar.[128] It has however more recently recovered relative to the strength of other currencies.

iv.   In *institutional terms*, there has been some criticism of the ECB for its general management of the Euro, and for individual decisions such as whether to cut interest rates, and by how much. There also continues to be debate about the optimum degree of control over the issues dealt with by the ECB.

v.   The relationship between *monetary policy and broader economic policy* remains problematic. The EC has far greater control over monetary policy, as encapsulated in the Euro and the attendant ECB, than it does over broader economic policy. This is so notwithstanding the stability and growth pact.[129] The EC is nonetheless caught in a conundrum in this respect. It is generally recognized that there is an intimate relationship between monetary policy and economic policy: if countries run long-term budgetary deficits then this will cause the currency markets to take a poor view of the value of the Euro. There are however political difficulties for the EC in extending control over national economic policy, or even in making full use of the existing regime, lest it be accused of excessive centralization of economic decision-making.

vi.   In more practical terms the switch to the Euro *has implications for a range of Community policies*, such as the budget, agriculture, and the internal market, all of which are particularly affected by the introduction of the new currency.[130]

9. FURTHER READING

(a) Books

Amtenbrink, F., *The Democratic Accountability of Central Banks* (Hart, 1999)

Andenas, M., Gormley, L., Hadjiemmanuil, C., and Harden, I. (eds.), *European Economic and Monetary Union: The Institutional Framework* (Kluwer, 1997)

Beaumont, P., and Walker, N. (eds.), *The Legal Framework of the Single European Currency* (Hart, 1999)

Dahlberg, M., *Direct Taxation in Relation to the Freedom of Establishment and the Free Movement of Capital* (Kluwer Law International, 2005)

De Grauwe, P., *Economics of Monetary Union* (6th edn., Oxford University Press, 2005)

Dyson, K., *Elusive Union, The Process of Economic and Monetary Union in Europe* (Longman, 1994)

—— *The Politics of the Euro-Zone: Stability or Breakdown* (Oxford University Press, 2000)

---

[128] K. Dyson, *The Politics of the Euro-Zone: Stability or Breakdown* (Oxford University Press, 2000).

[129] Snyder, n. 31 above, 448–462; I. Harden, 'The Fiscal Constitution of EMU', in P. Beaumont and N. Walker (eds.), *Legal Framework of the Single European Currency* (Hart, 1999), ch. 5; I. Harden, J. von Hagen, and R. Brookes, 'The European Constitutional Framework for Member States' Public Finances', in M. Andenas *et al.*, n. 121 above, ch. 9.

[130] The Impact of the Changeover to the Euro on Community Policies, Institutions and Legislation, COM(97)560.

Dyson, K., and Featherstone, K., *The Road to Maastricht: Negotiating Economic and Monetary Union* (Oxford University Press, 1999)

Johnson, C., *In with the Euro, Out with the Pound* (Penguin, 1996)

—— and Collingnon, S. (eds.), *The Monetary Economics of Europe* (Pinter, 1994)

Swann, D., *The Economics of Europe, From Common Market to European Union* (9th edn., Penguin, 2000)

Usher, J., *The Law of Money and Financial Services in the European Community* (Oxford University Press, 1994)

Zilioli, C., and Selmayr, M., *The Law of the European Central Bank* (Hart, 2001)

(b) Articles

Amtenbrink, F., and De Haan, J., 'Economic Governance in the European Union: Fiscal Policy Discipline versus Flexibility' (2003) 40 *CMLRev.* 1075

Craig, P., 'EMU, the ECB and Judicial Review', in P. Beaumont and N. Walker (eds.), *The Legal Framework of the Single European Currency* (Hart, 1999), ch. 4

Flynn, L., 'Coming of Age: The Free Movement of Capital Case-Law 1993–2002' (2002) 39 *CMLRev.* 773

Harden, I., 'The Fiscal Constitution of EMU', in P. Beaumont and N. Walker (eds.), *Legal Framework of the Single European Currency* (Hart, 1999), ch. 5

Hodson, D., and Maher, I., 'Soft Law and Sanctions: Economic Policy Coordination and Reform of the Stability and Growth Pact' (2004) 11 *JEPP* 798

Louis, J.V., 'The Economic and Monetary Union: Law and Institutions' (2004) 41 *CMLRev.* 575

—— 'The Review of the Stability and Growth Pact' (2006) 43 *CMLRev.* 85

Peers, S., 'Free Movement of Capital: Learning Lessons or Slipping on Spilt Milk?', in C. Barnard and J. Scott (eds.), *The Legal Foundations of the Single Market* (Hart, 2000), ch. 13

Snyder, F., 'EMU Revisited: Are We Making a Constitution? What Constitution Are We Making', in P. Craig and G. de Búrca (eds.), *The Evolution of EU Law* (Oxford University Press, 1999), ch. 12

FREE MOVEMENT OF WORKERS

1. CENTRAL ISSUES

i. The free movement of persons is one of the four fundamental freedoms of Community law, along with the free movement of goods, services, and capital. This chapter deals primarily with the free movement of employed persons (workers), the next chapter with the free movement of the self-employed and of companies (establishment and services), and the following chapter with the more recent category of European citizens.

ii. There are several central legal issues that arise in the context of the free movement of workers. These include the scope of Article 39; the meaning accorded to 'worker', the rights of intermediate categories such as 'job-seeker', the kinds of restrictions which States may justifiably impose on workers and their families; and the rights which family members enjoy under Community law.

iii. Tensions are frequently evident in the relationship between the economic and the social dimensions of the free movement of workers. The image of EU workers as mobile units of production contributing to the economic prosperity of Europe's single market contrasts with that of EU workers as human beings, exercising a personal right to live in another State and to enjoy equality of treatment for themselves and their families. The policy of furthering the free movement of workers has been linked with a broader notion of European solidarity, with the underlying aspiration of integration of the peoples of Europe.

iv. The creation of the status of EU citizenship, which is dealt with in Chapter 23, has had some influence on the development of the law governing the free movement of workers, affecting issues such as the rights of job-seekers. Further, the overlap between the two categories—workers and citizens—is reflected in the consolidation of the secondary legislation governing the free movement of persons in Directive 2004/38 on the rights of movement and residence of EU citizens. This Directive includes workers and self-employed persons, and their families, as well as students and all other kinds of non-economically active EU nationals.

v. Two recent trends may be noted in the law on free movement of workers. The first is an increase in the number of cases arising from enforcement actions brought by the Commission against Member States.[1] The second is a significant increase in the number

---

[1] This is more likely to reflect the new strategy of the Commission in prioritizing certain types of infringement for the purposes of the enforcement procedure, rather than a sudden increase in Member State non-compliance in this field.

of cases involving challenges to non-discriminatory national regulations. In this way, the case law on free movement of workers after the *Bosman* case is, albeit many decades later, following a similar path to that which the case law on free movement of goods took after *Dassonville*.[2]

2. THE EFFECT OF ARTICLE 39

The basic provision is set out in Article 39 EC, which provides as follows:[3]

1. Freedom of movement of workers shall be secured within the Community.
2. Such freedom of movement shall entail the abolition of any discrimination based on nationality between workers of the Member States as regards employment, remuneration and other conditions of work and employment.
3. It shall entail the right, subject to limitations justified on grounds of public policy, public security or public health:

 (a) to accept offers of employment actually made;
 (b) to move freely within the territory of Member States for this purpose;
 (c) to stay in a Member State for the purpose of employment in accordance with the provisions governing the employment of nationals of that State laid down by law, regulation or administrative action;
 (d) to remain in the territory of a Member State after having been employed in that State, subject to conditions which shall be embodied in implementing regulations to be drawn up by the Commission.

4. The provisions of this Article shall not apply to employment in the public service.

The Court has repeatedly emphasized the central importance of the twin principles of freedom of movement and non-discrimination on grounds of nationality. Article 39 is said to represent an application, in the specific context of workers, of the general principle in Article 12 EC that 'within the scope of application of this Treaty . . . any discrimination on grounds of nationality shall be prohibited'. However, as we shall see below, just as in the context of the other 'freedoms' under the Treaty, the ECJ has interpreted Article 39 to go beyond merely prohibiting direct or indirect discrimination and has ruled that it applies to any obstacles which impede the free movement of workers.

The ECJ in *Walrave and Koch*[4] held that Article 39 (ex Article 48) would apply even where the work was done outside the Community, so long as the legal relationship of employment was entered into within the Community. This was extended further in *Boukhalfa*, in which the Court ruled that the Article applied also to the employment relationship of a Member State national which was entered into and primarily performed in a non-member country in which the national resided, at least as regards all aspects of the employment relationship which were governed by the legislation of the employing Member State.[5]

---

2 See Ch. 19 on measures of equivalent effect to a quantitative restriction.
3 The ToA amended para. (1) so as to delete the words 'by the end of the transitional period at the latest'.
4 Case 36/74 *Walrave and Koch* v. *Association Union Cycliste Internationale* [1974] ECR 1405.
5 Case C–214/95 *Boukhalfa* v. *BRD* [1996] ECR I–2253.

The Court also ruled in *Walrave and Koch*[6] and in *Bosman*[7] that the provisions of Article 39 are not just of 'vertical' direct effect. The rules challenged in these cases were made by international sporting associations, concerning cycling and football respectively, which were neither public nor state bodies. However, the Court ruled that this did not exempt them from the application of Article 39:

> Prohibition of such discrimination does not only apply to the action of public authorities but extends likewise to rules of any other nature aimed at regulating in a collective manner gainful employment and the provision of services....
>
> Since, moreover, working conditions in the various Member States are governed sometimes by means of provisions laid down by law or regulations and sometimes by agreements and other acts concluded or adopted by private persons, to limit the prohibitions in question to acts of a public authority would risk creating inequality in their application.[8]

The *Angonese* case subsequently went further still and indicated that Article 39 is also horizontally applicable to the actions of individuals who—unlike the associations in *Walrave and Koch* and *Bosman*—do not have the power to make rules regulating gainful employment, e.g. a single employer who refuses to employ someone on the ground of their nationality.[9] In this way, *Angonese* introduces a distinction between the law on free movement of workers and that governing the free movement of goods, since the ECJ has made clear that Article 28 applies only to *state* measures, and not to those adopted by private actors.[10]

Case C–281/98 **Angonese v. Cassa di Riparmio di Bolzano SpA**
[2000] ECR I–4139

[Note ToA renumbering: Arts. 48 and 119 are now Arts. 39 and 141]

Angonese was an Italian national whose mother tongue was German. He applied to take part in a competition for a post with the Cassa di Riparmio bank in Bolzano, Italy. A condition for entry to the competition imposed by the bank was a certificate of bilingualism (in Italian and German). The certificate was to be issued by the public authorities in Bolzano after an examination held *only* in that province. The national court found as a fact that Angonese was bilingual, and that non-residents of Bolzano could face difficulties obtaining the certificate in good time. Since Angonese did not obtain the certificate the bank refused to admit him to the competition for the post, and he argued that the requirement to have the certificate was contrary to Article 48.

THE ECJ

30. It should be noted at the outset that the principle of non-discrimination set out in Article 48 is drafted in general terms and is not specifically addressed to the Member States.

---

[6] Case 36/74, *Walrave* n. 4 above.

[7] Case C–415/93 *Union Royale Belge des Sociétés de Football Association and others* v. *Bosman* [1995] ECR I–4921, paras. 82–84; Case C–411/98, *Ferlini* v. *Centre Hospitalier de Luxembourg* [2000] ECR I–8081, para. 50.

[8] *Walrave*, n. 4 above, paras. 17–19.

[9] Art. 7(4) of Reg. 1612/68 also supports this reasoning by stipulating that clauses in individual contracts of employment will be void in so far as they discriminate on grounds of nationality. For a note on *Angonese* see R. Lane and N. Nic Shuibhne (2000) 37 *CMLRev.* 1237.

[10] See Ch. 19.

31. Thus, the Court has held that the prohibition of discrimination based on nationality applies not only to the actions of public authorities but also to rules of any other nature aimed at regulating in a collective manner gainful employment and the provision of services (see ... *Walrave* ...).

32. The Court has held that the abolition, as between Member States, of obstacles to freedom of movement would be compromised if the abolition of State barriers could be neutralised by obstacles resulting from the exercise of their legal autonomy by associations or organizations not governed by public law (see *Walrave*, paragraph 18 ... and ... *Bosman* ... paragraph 83).

33. Since working conditions in the different Member States are governed sometimes by provisions laid down by law or regulation and sometimes by agreements and other acts concluded or adopted by private persons, limiting application of the prohibition of discrimination based on nationality to acts of a public authority risks creating inequality in its application (see *Walrave*, paragraph 19, and *Bosman*, paragraph 84).

34. The Court has also ruled that the fact that certain provisions of the Treaty are formally addressed to the Member States does not prevent rights from being conferred at the same time on any individual who has an interest in compliance with the obligations thus laid down (see ... *Defrenne* ...). The Court accordingly held ... that the prohibition of discrimination applied equally to all agreements intended to regulate paid labour collectively, as well as to contracts between individuals. ...

35. Such considerations must, *a fortiori*, be applicable to Article 48 ..., which lays down a fundamental freedom and which constitutes a specific application of the general prohibition of discrimination contained in Article 6 (now ... Article 12 EC). In that respect, like Article 119 ... it is designed to ensure that there is no discrimination on the labour market.

36. Consequently, the prohibition of discrimination on grounds of nationality laid down in Article 48 ... must be regarded as applying to private persons as well.

3. WHO IS PROTECTED BY ARTICLE 39?

Article 40 of the Treaty provides for the Council to adopt secondary legislation to bring about the freedoms set out in Article 39. A range of directives and regulations were adopted under this provision to govern the conditions of entry, residence, and treatment of EC workers and their families. Many of these have recently been consolidated by Directive 2004/38 on the free movement and residence of EU citizens and their families.[11]

The 2004 Directive has replaced Directive 64/221, which governed the main derogations from the rules on free movement, and has further tightened up the extent to which Member States may derogate from free movement requirements. It has also replaced Directive 68/360, which regulated the formalities and conditions of entry and residence of workers and self-employed persons, and has sought to reduce and simplify further the bureaucratic hurdles which migrant workers and 'mobile' EU citizens face. The 2004 Directive amended Regulation 1612/68, which fleshes out the equal-treatment principle and specifies many of the substantive rights and entitlements of workers and their families. The Directive also replaced Regulation 1251/70 governing the conditions under which the worker and family may remain

---

11 Dir. 2004/38/EC of the European Parliament and of the Council of 29 Apr. 2004 on the right of citizens of the Union and their family members to move and reside freely within the territory of the Member States [2004] OJ L158/77.

in the territory of a Member State following the worker's retirement, permanent incapacity to work, or death.[12] Apart from these amendments and extensions, one of the main innovations of the 2004 Directive was to introduce the right of permanent residence for EU nationals and their families after five years of continuous legal residence in another Member State.

A fundamental issue which was not immediately apparent from Article 39 was whether 'workers of the Member States' in paragraph (2) covered only nationals of the Member States, or whether it included non-EU nationals resident and working within the Community.[13] However, the secondary legislation which was passed to implement Article 39, in particular Regulation 1612/68, specifically restricted its application to workers who are nationals of the Member States, and that has been the interpretation adopted by the ECJ.

(a) DEFINITION OF 'WORKER': A COMMUNITY CONCEPT

Despite the array of secondary legislation which existed, many of the basic terms were not defined either in the Treaty or in the legislation itself, but have been shaped by the ECJ, including the meaning of the core term 'worker'. The Court has insisted from the outset that the definition of a 'worker' was a matter for Community law, not national law.[14] The issue arose early in the case of *Hoekstra*, in the context of the interpretation of a Council social security regulation, where the ECJ declared that:

> If the definition of this term were a matter for the competence of national law, it would therefore be possible for each Member State to modify the meaning of the concept of 'migrant worker' and to eliminate at will the protection afforded by the Treaty to certain categories of person ... Articles 48 to 51 [now 39–42] would therefore be deprived of all effect and the above-mentioned objectives of the Treaty would be frustrated if the meaning of such a term could be unilaterally fixed and modified by national law.

In requiring the term worker to be a Community concept, the Court was also claiming ultimate authority to define its meaning and scope. In the words of the late Federico Mancini, formerly Advocate General and Judge of the Court, the ECJ conferred on itself a 'hermeneutic monopoly' to counteract possible unilateral restrictions of the application of the rules on freedom of movement by the different Member States.[15] Thus the Court has held that a spouse can be employed by the other spouse as a worker,[16] and that Article 39 can be relied on by the employer,[17] or by a relevant third party,[18] rather than only by the employee. Further, as we shall see, the Court has consistently construed the term broadly, and has presented this freedom as part of the foundations of the Community.

---

[12] For a recent case on the 'continuous residence' condition set by Reg. 1251/70 see Case C–257/00 *Givane* v. *Home Secretary* [2003] ECR I–345.

[13] See F. Burrows, *Free Movement in European Community Law* (Clarendon Press, 1987), 124. For an argument that the Treaty drafters intended all Community workers to be covered, regardless of nationality, see R. Plender, 'Competence, European Community Law and Nationals of Non-Member States' (1990) 39 *ICLQ* 599.

[14] Case 75/63 *Hoekstra* v. *Bestuur der Bedrijfsvereniging voor Detailhandel en Ambachten* [1964] ECR 177, 184.

[15] G.F. Mancini, 'The Free Movement of Workers in the Case-Law of the European Court of Justice', in D. Curtin and D. O'Keeffe (eds.), *Constitutional Adjudication in European Community and National Law* (Butterworths, 1992), 67.

[16] Case C–337/97 *C.P.M. Meeusen* v. *Hoofddirectie van de Informatie Beheer Groep* [1999] ECR I–3289.

[17] Case C–350/96 *Clean Car Autoservice GmbH* v. *Landeshauptmann von Wien* [1998] ECR I–2521.

[18] Case C–208/05 *ITC Innovative Technology Center GmbH* v. *Bundesagentur für Arbeit*, 11 Jan. 2007.

To summarize the position: any person who pursues employment activities which are effective and genuine, to the exclusion of activities on such a small scale as to be regarded as purely marginal and ancillary, is treated as a worker.[19] For an economic activity to qualify as employment under Article 39 rather than self-employment under Article 43, there must be a relationship of subordination.[20] However, we shall also see that there is no 'single Community concept of worker', and that it varies according to the EU law context in which it arises.[21]

(b) DEFINITION OF 'WORKER': ARE THERE MINIMUM-INCOME AND WORKING-TIME REQUIREMENTS?

A number of cases have been concerned with the interplay between the economic aspect of free movement, as determined by the level of remuneration, and the social aspect underlying free-movement policy. This issue arose in *Levin*, in the context of part-time workers.

Case 53/81 **Levin v. Staatssecretaris van Justitie**
[1982] ECR 1035

The appellant was a British citizen married to a non-EC national and living in the Netherlands, but whose application for a residence permit had been refused. She argued that she had sufficient income for her own and her husband's maintenance, and that she had taken up part-time employment as a chambermaid. The Staatssecretaris van Justitie argued that she was not an EC worker within the meaning of Article 39 because her employment did not provide sufficient means for her support, not being equal at least to the minimum legal wage prevailing in The Netherlands. When the case was referred to the ECJ, the Court alluded to its argument in *Hoekstra* that Member States could not unilaterally restrict the scope and meaning of the term worker.

THE ECJ

12. Such would, in particular, be the case if the enjoyment of the rights conferred by the principle of freedom of movement for workers could be made subject to the criterion of what the legislation of the host State declares to be a minimum wage, so that the field of application *ratione personae* of the Community rules on this subject might vary from one Member State to another. The meaning and the scope of the terms 'worker' and 'activity as an employed person' should thus be clarified in the light of the principles of the legal order of the Community.

13. In this respect it must be stressed that these concepts define the field of application of one of the fundamental freedoms guaranteed by the Treaty and, as such, may not be interpreted restrictively.

---

[19] Case C–337/97 *Meeusen*, n. 16 above.

[20] Case C–268/99 *Jany* v. *Staatssecretaris van Justitie* [2001] ECR I–8615, para. 34; Cases C–151–152/04 *Nadin and Durre* [2005] ECR I–11203.

[21] See recently Case C–256/01 *Allonby* v. *Accrington and Rossendale College* [2004] ECR I–873, para. 63. Indeed, the meaning of 'worker' varies even within a single piece of legislation (Reg. 1612/68)—see below Case C–138/02 *Collins* v. *Secretary of State for Work and Pensions* [2004] ECR I–2703.

14. In conformity with this view the recitals to Regulation No 1612/68 contain a general affirmation of the right of all workers in the Member States to pursue the activity of their choice within the Community, irrespective of whether they are permanent, seasonal or frontier workers or workers who pursue their activities for the purpose of providing services. Furthermore, although Article 4 of Directive 68/360 grants the right of residence to workers upon the mere production of the document on the basis of which they entered the territory and of a confirmation of engagement from the employer or a certificate of employment, it does not subject this right to any condition relating to the kind of employment or to the amount of income derived from it.

15. An interpretation which reflects the full scope of these concepts is also in conformity with the objectives of the Treaty which include, according to Articles 2 and 3, the abolition, as between Member States, of obstacles to freedom of movement for persons, with the purpose *inter alia* of promoting throughout the Community a harmonious development of economic activities and a raising of the standard of living. Since part-time employment, although it may provide an income lower than what is considered to be the minimum required for subsistence, constitutes for a large number of persons an effective means of improving their living conditions, the effectiveness of Community law would be impaired and the achievement of the objectives of the Treaty would be jeopardized if the enjoyment of rights conferred by the principle of freedom of movement for workers were reserved solely to persons engaged in full-time employment and earning, as a result, a wage at least equivalent to the guaranteed minimum wage in the sector under consideration.

...

17. It should however be stated that whilst part-time employment is not excluded from the field of application of the rules on freedom of movement for workers, those rules cover only the pursuit of effective and genuine activities, to the exclusion of activities on such a small scale as to be regarded as purely marginal and ancillary. It follows both from the Statement of the principle of freedom of movement for workers and from the place occupied by the rules relating to that principle in the system of the Treaty as a whole that those rules guarantee only the free movement of persons who pursue or are desirous of pursuing a genuine economic activity.

There are a number of important aspects to this judgment. The ECJ begins by reaffirming that the rules on free movement of persons are fundamental to the Community, and must therefore be broadly and inclusively interpreted (paragraphs 13 and 14). The freedom to take up employment is important not only as a means towards the creation of a single market for the benefit of the Member State economies, but as a right for the worker to raise her or his standard of living. This is so even if the worker does not reach the minimum level of subsistence in a particular State (paragraph 15). Moreover, in response to the suggestion that Levin may only have sought work in order to obtain a residence permit to remain in the country, the Court ruled that the purpose or motive of the worker is immaterial, once he or she is pursuing or wishing to pursue a genuine and effective economic activity (paragraph 17).

We shall subsequently see that the ECJ has consistently adopted this kind of response to allegations of 'abuse of rights' in the area of free movement, even while the Council insisted on the inclusion of a new 'abuse of rights' exception in Article 35 of the consolidating Free Movement Directive 2004/38. The articulated requirement in *Levin* that work be undertaken as a genuine economic activity was probably a response to Member State concerns that their social security schemes would become overburdened. This might be so as a result of migrants entering from other countries whose systems of social benefits are less generous, and who do not really intend to engage in effective work. Advocate General Slynn acknowledged this concern.

However, he noted the increasing dependence on part-time work, especially in times of unemployment. He emphasized that the exclusion of part-time work from the protection of Article 39 would exclude not only women, the elderly, and disabled who, for personal reasons, might wish only to work part-time, but also women and men who would prefer to work full-time but are obliged to accept part-time work. *Levin* thus clarified that part-time workers were covered by the Treaty provisions on free movement, and that it did not matter if workers chose to supplement their income from other private sources.

In *Kempf*,[22] the issue was taken a step further. A German national who was living and working in the Netherlands as a music teacher, giving approximately twelve lessons a week, was refused a residence permit. The Dutch and Danish governments argued that work providing an income below the minimum means of subsistence in the host State could not be regarded as genuine and effective work if the person doing the work claimed social assistance from *public* funds. The Court disagreed, ruling that when a genuine part-time worker sought to supplement earnings below the subsistence level, it was:

> [I]rrelevant whether those supplementary means of subsistence are derived from property or from the employment of a member of his family, as was the case in *Levin,* or whether, as in this instance, they are obtained from financial assistance drawn from the public funds of the Member State in which he resides.[23]

Member State concerns about possible abuse of the Treaty provisions by those who were simply seeking a Member State with better social provision in which to reside did not, said Advocate General Slynn, justify the exclusion of part-time workers in Kempf's position from the scope of the Treaty.[24] The State could address these concerns in the criteria it set for access to certain kinds of social assistance, but it could not exclude the part-time employee from the status of 'worker' under EC law.

A similarly inclusive reading of the term 'worker' is evident in many cases where the economic dimension of the activity concerned was in question. Thus the Court has ruled that the practice of sport falls within Community law in so far as it constitutes an economic activity, although the composition of national teams could be a question of purely sporting and not of economic interest.[25] It has also ruled that fishermen who are paid a share of the proceeds of sale of their catches can be considered to be 'workers', despite the irregular nature of their remuneration.[26] Yet the guidelines laid down by the Court on the need for 'genuine and effective work', the importance of 'remuneration' of some kind, and the exclusion of 'marginal and ancillary activities' have not reduced the steady flow of cases arising concerning the concrete application of these terms in specific contexts.

In *Lawrie-Blum*,[27] the Court was asked to rule on the compatibility of German measures restricting access for non-nationals to the preparatory service stage which was necessary for qualification as a secondary school teacher. Addressing the question whether a trainee teacher

---

22 Case 139/85 *Kempf* v. *Staatsecretaris van Justitie* [1986] ECR 1741.

23 *Ibid.*, para. 14.

24 [1986] ECR 1741, 1744.

25 Case 36/74 *Walrave*, n. 4 above; Case C–415/93 *Bosman*, n. 7 above; Case 13/76 *Donà* v. *Mantero* [1976] ECR 1333. Compare *Bosman*, paras. 120–129 and Case C–438/00 *Deutscher Handballbund eV* v. *Maros Kolpak* [2003] ECR I–4135.

26 Case 3/87 *R.* v. *Ministry of Agriculture, Fisheries and Food, ex p. Agegate Ltd.* [1989] ECR 4459, paras. 33–36.

27 Case 66/85 *Lawrie-Blum* v. *Land Baden-Württemberg* [1986] ECR 2121, emphasis added.

at this stage would qualify as a 'worker' for the purposes of the relevant Treaty provisions, the Court provided a more elaborate three-part definition of the term:

> That concept must be defined in accordance with objective criteria which distinguish the employment relationship by reference to the rights and duties of the persons concerned. The essential feature of an employment relationship, however, is that *for a certain period of time a person performs services for and under the direction of another person in return for which he receives remuneration.*[28]

The Court ruled that a trainee teacher did qualify as a worker since, during the period of preparatory service, these three conditions would be fulfilled: she would perform services of economic value, under the direction of the school in question, and would receive a measure of remuneration in return.[29] The fact that the pay was less than a full teacher's salary was immaterial, for the same sorts of reasons given in *Levin* and *Kempf:* what mattered was the genuinely economic nature of the work and the receipt of some remuneration, and not the amount of the pay. In *Steymann*, the ECJ pushed the concept of remuneration, and hence of economic activity, a little further.

Case 196/87 Steymann v. Staatsecretaris van Justitie
[1988] ECR 6159

Steymann was a German national living in the Netherlands, where he had worked for a short time as a plumber. He then joined the Bhagwan Community, a religious community which provided for the material needs of its members. He participated in the life of the community by performing plumbing work, general household duties, and other commercial activity on the community's premises. His application for a residence permit to pursue an activity as an employed person was refused and, on his application for review of this, a reference was made to the Court.

THE ECJ

9. It must be observed *in limine* that, in view of the objectives of the European Economic Community, participation in a community based on religion or another form of philosophy falls within the field of application of Community law only in so far as it can be regarded as an economic activity within the meaning of Article 2 of the Treaty.

. . .

11. As regards the activities in question in this case, it appears from the documents before the Court that they consist of work carried out within and on behalf of the Bhagwan Community in connection with the Bhagwan Community's commercial activities. It appears that such work plays a relatively important role in the way of life of the Bhagwan Community and that only in special circumstances can the members of the community avoid taking part

---

[28] *Ibid.*, para. 17. See also Case C–3/90 *Bernini* v. *Minister van Onderwijs en Wetenschappen* [1992] ECR I–1071.

[29] See also Case C–10/05 *Mattern and Cikotic* [2006] ECR I–3145. On trainee lawyers as workers see Case C–109/04 *Kranemann* v. *Land-Rheinland Westfalen* [2005] ECR I–2421.

therein. In turn, the Bhagwan Community provides for the material needs of its members, including pocket-money, irrespective of the nature and the extent of the work which they do.

12. In a case such as the one before the national court it is impossible to rule out *a priori* the possibility that work carried out by members of the community in question constitutes an economic activity within the meaning of Article 2 of the Treaty. In so far as the work, which aims to ensure a measure of self-sufficiency for the Bhagwan Community, constitutes an essential part of participation in that community, the services which the latter provides to its members may be regarded as being an indirect *quid pro quo* for their work.

The fact that the work might be seen in conventional terms as being unpaid did not mean that it was not effective economic activity. He provided services of value to the religious community which would otherwise have to be performed by someone else, and in return for which his material needs were satisfied.

An expansive approach is also evident in *Raulin*.[30] The case concerned a French national, employed in the Netherlands as a waitress under an on-call contract which gave no guarantee of the hours to be worked, but under which she had worked for sixty hours in all over an eight-month period. The ECJ held that she was not precluded, by virtue of the conditions of the on-call contract, from being considered a worker within Article 39. The question whether she would qualify as a worker was, with certain guidance offered, ultimately left to the national court to determine as a matter of fact:

The national court may, however, when assessing the effective and genuine nature of the activity in question, take account of the irregular nature and limited duration of the services actually performed under a contract for occasional employment. The fact that the person concerned worked only a very limited number of hours in a labour relationship may be an indication that the activities exercised are purely marginal and ancillary. The national court may also take account, if appropriate, of the fact that the person must remain available to work if called upon to do so by the employer.[31]

(c) DEFINITION OF 'WORKER': IS THE PURPOSE OF THE EMPLOYMENT RELEVANT?

The general rule is that the purpose for which the employment is undertaken will not be relevant in determining whether a person is a worker. Provided that the employment is genuine and not marginal it will benefit from Article 39. There are, however, cases where some account has been taken of the purpose of the employment.

In *Bettray* the ECJ ruled on the application of Article 39 to someone who was undertaking therapeutic work as part of a drug-rehabilitation programme under Dutch social employment law.[32] The aim of the programme was to reintegrate people who were temporarily incapacitated into the workforce. They would be paid a certain amount, and treated, in so far as possible, in accordance with normal conditions of paid employment. The ECJ began by noting that a job was being carried out under supervision and in return for remuneration, and that the low pay from public funds and the low productivity of the worker would not in

---

30 Case C–357/89 *Raulin v. Minister van Onderwijs en Wetenschappen* [1992] ECR I–1027.
31 [1992] ECR I–1027, para. 14.
32 Case 344/87 *Bettray v. Staatssecretaris van Justitie* [1989] ECR 1621.

themselves prevent the application of Article 48. However, unlike in its judgment in *Levin* where the reason for undertaking work was said not to be relevant to its genuineness, the ECJ went on to examine the purpose of the work performed:

> However, work under the Social Employment Law cannot be regarded as an effective and genuine economic activity if it constitutes merely a means of rehabilitation or reintegration for the persons concerned and the purpose of the paid employment, which is adapted to the physical and mental possibilities of each person, is to enable those persons sooner or later to recover their capacity to take up ordinary employment or to lead as normal as possible a life.
>
> It also appears from the order for reference that persons employed under the Social Employment Law are not selected on the basis of their capacity to perform a certain activity; on the contrary, it is the activities which are chosen in the light of the capabilities of the persons who are going to perform them in order to maintain, re-establish or develop their capacity for work. Finally, the activities involved are pursued in the framework of undertakings or work associations created solely for that purpose by local authorities.[33]

Clearly the purpose for undertaking the work was crucial to the decision which was reached by the Court here. The fact that the main or sole purpose of the work was to rehabilitate the person, and to find work suited to his or her capabilities rather than to meet a genuine economic need (as was the case in *Steymann*), resulted in a ruling against Bettray. The case is open to criticism, partly because ensuring the mobility of a well-trained workforce would seem to be an important part of the Treaty's aims, and the reintegration of people back into the workforce through sheltered employment is a part of this. Further, if the *Bettray* ruling were to be applied to the case of sheltered employment for disabled people, this could have the effect of excluding many categories of disabled persons from being considered as workers under EC law.

In *Trojani*, however, where a French national worked in Belgium in a reintegration programme run by the Salvation Army, the ECJ seemed to distinguish *Bettray* on the ground that the applicant in that case had apparently been unable for an indefinite period, on account of his drug addiction, to work under normal conditions.

Case C–456/02 **Trojani v. CPAS**
[2004] ECR I–7573

18. In this respect, the Court has held that activities cannot be regarded as a real and genuine economic activity if they constitute merely a means of rehabilitation or reintegration for the persons concerned (*Bettray*, paragraph 17).

19. However, that conclusion can be explained only by the particular characteristics of the case in question, which concerned the situation of a person who, by reason of his addiction to drugs, had been recruited on the basis of a national law intended to provide work for persons who, for an indefinite period, are unable, by reason of circumstances related to their situation, to work under normal conditions (see, to that effect, Case C–1/97 *Birden* [1998] ECR I–7747, paragraphs 30 and 31).

20. In the present case, as is apparent from the decision making the reference, Mr Trojani performs, for the Salvation Army and under its direction, various jobs for approximately

---

[33] *Ibid.*, paras. 17–19.

30 hours a week, as part of a personal reintegration programme, in return for which he receives benefits in kind and some pocket money.

21. Under the relevant provisions of the decree of the *Commission communautaire française* of 27 May 1999 on the grant of authorisation and subsidies to hostels (*Moniteur belge*, 18 June 1999, p. 23101), the Salvation Army has the task of receiving, accommodating and providing psycho-social assistance appropriate to the recipients in order to promote their autonomy, physical well-being and reintegration in society. For that purpose it must agree with each person concerned a personal reintegration programme setting out the objectives to be attained and the means to be employed to attain them.

22. Having established that the benefits in kind and money provided by the Salvation Army to Mr Trojani constitute the consideration for the services performed by him for and under the direction of the hostel, the national court has thereby established the existence of the constituent elements of any paid employment relationship, namely subordination and the payment of remuneration.

23. For the claimant in the main proceedings to have the status of worker, however, the national court, in the assessment of the facts which is within its exclusive jurisdiction, would have to establish that the paid activity in question is real and genuine.

24. The national court must in particular ascertain whether the services actually performed by Mr Trojani are capable of being regarded as forming part of the normal labour market. For that purpose, account may be taken of the status and practices of the hostel, the content of the social reintegration programme, and the nature and details of performance of the services.

Thus although the ECJ left it ultimately to the national court to decide whether his employment was real and genuine, it made clear that the fact that social reintegration was the main purpose of the employment would not itself disqualify the employment from being considered as such. Instead, the crucial factor was whether the services 'are capable of being regarded as forming part of the normal labour market'.

In a somewhat different context in *Brown*, the ECJ took into account the purpose behind the employment.[34] The Court in that case indicated that, although someone who has engaged in genuine and effective work before leaving to begin a course of study will be considered to be a 'worker' within Article 48 (now Article 39), the fact that the work was undertaken purely in order to prepare for the course of study, rather than to prepare for an occupation or employment, would mean that not all of the advantages provided for workers within Community law may be claimed.

In other words, although he could be considered a worker for certain purposes under Article 39, he was not entitled to all of the rights and advantages which would normally flow to workers because, although he was engaged in genuine and effective work, this was done purely in order to become a student rather than to prepare for an occupation. Brown was a dual national relying on his French nationality in the UK, who had worked for nine months for a company in Scotland as a form of 'pre-university industrial training', before beginning an electrical engineering degree at Cambridge University. The Court ruled that although he was to be regarded as a 'worker' (since he had clearly engaged in eight months of effective, full-time economic activity, satisfying the three criteria of *Lawrie-Blum*), he was not entitled to all of the social advantages (in this case, a maintenance grant) which would normally be open to workers. This was because his employment was merely 'ancillary' to the course of study he wished to undertake. Thus the purpose of the work, to gain pre-University experience, was

---

[34] Case 197/86 *Brown* v. *Secretary of State for Scotland* [1988] ECR 3205.

taken into account not to disqualify him as a worker, but to limit the rights that he could enjoy based on that status. The conclusion can be seen as a response by the ECJ to concerns voiced by the Member States about the 'abuse' of the provisions on free movement of workers by those who merely wished to avail themselves of the generous educational provision in a particular Member State.

We shall see in the later chapter on EU citizenship that the ECJ in *Bidar* has changed its position on the specific question of the entitlement of a national who moves to study in another Member State to apply there for a maintenance grant.[35] However, the *Brown* case remains an authority for the proposition that an EU national who undertakes work for a temporary period purely as a means to qualify for an educational course will not be entitled to all of the same social advantages and rights as a fully-fledged 'worker' under EU law.

In *Ninni-Oraschi*, the ECJ again reiterated the importance of 'objective' factors such as hours worked and remuneration over other more subjective factors such as motive and conduct, and dismissed as irrelevant the argument that the applicant had 'abused' EC rights in order to gain the status of worker.

Case C–413/01 **Ninni-Orasche v. Bundesminister für Wissenschaft, Verkehr und Kunst** [2003] ECR I–13187

[Note ToA renumbering: Art. 48 is now Art. 39]

28. It should be stated that, with respect to the assessment whether employment is capable of conferring the status of worker within the meaning of Article 48 of the Treaty, factors relating to the conduct of the person concerned before and after the period of employment are not relevant in establishing the status of worker within the meaning of that article. Such factors are not in any way related to the objective criteria referred to in the case-law cited in paragraphs 23 and 24 of this judgment.

29. In particular, the three factors referred to by the national court, namely the fact that the person concerned took up employment as a waitress only several years after her entry into the host Member State, that, shortly after the end of her short term of employment, she obtained a diploma entitling her to enrol at university in that State and that, after that employment had come to an end, she attempted to find a new job, are not linked either to the possibility that the activity pursued by the appellant in the main proceedings was ancillary or to the nature of that activity or of the employment relationship.

30. For the same reasons, nor can the Court accept the argument put forward by the Danish Government that, in order to assess whether activities pursued as an employed person are effective and genuine, it is necessary to take account of the short term of the employment in relation to the total duration of residence by the person concerned in the host Member State, which, in the main proceedings, was two and a half years.

31. Finally, as regards the argument that the national court is under an obligation to examine, on the basis of the circumstances of the case, whether the appellant in the main proceedings has sought abusively to create a situation enabling her to claim the status of a worker within the meaning of Article 48 of the Treaty with the aim of acquiring advantages linked to that status, it is sufficient to state that any abusive use of the rights granted by the Community

---

[35] Case C–209/03 *Bidar* v. *London Borough of Ealing* [2005] ECR I–2119.

legal order under the provisions relating to freedom of movement for workers presupposes that the person concerned falls within the scope ratione personae of that Treaty because he satisfies the conditions for classification as a worker within the meaning of that article. It follows that the issue of abuse of rights can have no bearing on the answer to the first question.

While the ECJ agreed, as we shall see below, that the national court was entitled to investigate, for the purposes of deciding whether to grant or refuse educational assistance, whether the applicant had taken up (and subsequently left) employment purely in order to gain access to education in the host Member State, this was not relevant to the question whether or not she was a worker under Article 39 as a consequence of the period of employment.

(d) DEFINITION OF 'WORKER': WHERE DOES THE JOB-SEEKER FIT?

The discussion thus far has been concerned with those who have a job of some kind. An important issue is how far those seeking work can benefit from Article 39. In *Royer*, the ECJ had referred to the right 'to look for or pursue an occupation'.[36] The issue was addressed more directly in *Antonissen*, where the Court held that those who are actively seeking work do not have the full status of a worker, but are nonetheless covered by Article 39.

Case C–292/89 R. v. Immigration Appeal Tribunal, ex parte Antonissen
[1991] ECR I–745

[Note ToA renumbering: Art. 48 is now Art. 39]

Antonissen was a Belgian national who had arrived in the UK in 1984, and had attempted unsuccessfully to find work. Following his imprisonment for a drug-related offence, the Secretary of State decided to deport him. Following his appeal, the case was referred to the ECJ where it was argued that only Community nationals in possession of a confirmation of engagement of employment were entitled to a right of residence in another Member State.

THE ECJ

9. In that connection it has been argued that, according to the strict wording of Article 48 of the Treaty, Community nationals are given the right to move freely within the territory of the Member States for the purpose only of accepting offers of employment actually made (Article 48(3)(a) and (b)) whilst the right to stay in the territory of a Member State is stated to be for the purpose of employment (Article 48(3)(c)).

10. Such an interpretation would exclude the right of a national of a Member State to move freely and to stay in the territory of the other Member States in order to seek employment there, and cannot be upheld.

. . .

12. Moreover, a strict interpretation of Article 48(3) would jeopardize the actual chances that a national of a Member State who is seeking employment will find it in another Member State, and would, as a result, make that provision ineffective.

---

[36] Case 48/75 *Royer* [1976] ECR 497, para. 31.

13. It follows that Article 48(3) must be interpreted as enumerating, in a non-exhaustive way, certain rights benefiting nationals of Member States in the context of the free movement of workers and that that freedom also entails the right for nationals of Member States to move freely within the territory of the other Member States and to stay there for the purposes of seeking employment.

Antonissen provides a clear example of the Court's purposive or teleological approach, in suggesting a wider scope for Article 39 than the words of the Article convey. The ECJ examined the Article and identified its purpose: in this case, to ensure the free movement of workers. It then concluded that a literal interpretation of its terms would hinder that purpose. If nationals could move to another Member State only when they already held an offer of employment, the number of people who could move would be small, and many workers who could readily seek and find employment on arrival in a Member State would be prevented from so doing. A particularly interesting feature of *Antonissen* was the ECJ's statement that the rights expressly enumerated in Article 39 are not exhaustive. This open-ended approach leaves the Court with the power to adapt the scope of the Article through interpretation, in accordance with the changing social, economic, and political climate in the Community.

However, the ECJ was also clear that the status of an EC national searching for work was not the same as that of an EC national who was actually employed. Member States retain the power to expel a job-seeker who does not have prospects of finding work after a reasonable period of time, without needing to invoke one of the grounds of exception set out in Article 39(3). Moreover, there may be provisions, such as unemployment insurance, that cannot be used by someone who has never participated in the employment market.

This was seen in the earlier case of *Commission* v. *Belgium*,[37] and also in *Lebon*, where the ECJ ruled that the social and tax advantages guaranteed to workers under EC law (in particular by Article 7(2) of Regulation 1612/68) were not available to those moving in search of work.[38] In the more recent *Collins* case, the ECJ confirmed the distinction between fully-fledged workers who can benefit from all of the provisions of Regulation 1612/68 concerning social advantages and equality of treatment with national workers, and job-seekers who, although covered by Article 39, can benefit only from the provisions of Regulation 1612/68 governing *access* to employment.[39] Nonetheless, the ECJ also departed from the strict implications of its earlier judgment in *Lebon* by ruling that (when interpreted in the light of EU citizenship) equal treatment in access to employment under Article 39(2) should include the right to apply for a job-seekers' allowance under the same conditions as nationals of the host State, if they are genuinely linked to the employment market of that State.[40]

The *Collins* ruling was confirmed in *Ioannidis*, in which the ECJ ruled that a Greek national seeking his first employment in Belgium was entitled in principle to a tideover allowance intended specifically to facilitate the transition from education to the employment market,

---

[37] Case C–278/94 *Commission* v. *Belgium* [1996] ECR I–4307.

[38] Case 316/85 *Lebon* [1987] ECR 281. Compare Case C–57/96 *Meints* v. *Minister van Landbouw* [1997] ECR I–6689, on a one-off payment to agricultural workers who had been made redundant.

[39] Case C–138/02 *Collins*, n. 21 above, paras. 30–33. We shall see in Ch. 23, however, that by interpreting the rights of the job-seeker in the light of the provisions of the EC Treaty on citizenship, the ECJ decided that a job-seeker under Art. 39 should be entitled to apply for a jobseeker's allowance under the same conditions as nationals of the host Member State.

[40] *Ibid.*, paras. 54–73. The aspects of the judgment which deal with EU citizenship will be considered in more detail in Ch. 23.

and that a national eligibility condition requiring applicants to have completed their secondary education in Belgium was contrary to Article 39.[41]

4. DISCRIMINATION, MARKET ACCESS, AND JUSTIFICATION

It is clear that rules which directly discriminate on the grounds of nationality will be caught by Article 39.[42] It is equally clear that indirect discrimination, and even impediments to market access which do not depend on a showing of unequal impact,[43] can also lead to infringement of Article 39.[44] Discrimination, whether direct or indirect, will, however, be found only where two groups which are comparable in relevant ways are treated differently, or where groups which are not comparable are treated in the same way.[45]

(a) DIRECT DISCRIMINATION

In proceedings brought by the Commission against France for failing to repeal provisions of the French Maritime Code, which had required a certain proportion of the crew of a ship to be of French nationality, the Court ruled that Article 39 was 'directly applicable in the legal system of every Member State' and would render inapplicable all contrary national law.[46] Further, a State can be held in breach of Article 39 where the discrimination is practised by any public body, including public universities. Thus Italy was responsible for the discriminatory practice of certain public universities which did not recognize the acquired rights of former foreign-language assistants.[47] While cases involving direct discrimination on grounds of nationality are much less common, such cases do still arise but they raise a strong burden of justification.[48]

(b) INDIRECT DISCRIMINATION

Indirect as well as direct discrimination on grounds of nationality is prohibited by Article 39, so that a condition of eligibility for a benefit which is more easily satisfied by national than by non-national workers is likely to fall foul of the Treaty.

---

[41] Case C–258/04 *Office national de l'emploi* v. *Ioannidis* [2005] ECR I–8275.

[42] See, e.g., Case C–55/00 *Gottardo* v. *INPS* [2002] ECR I–413.

[43] *Bosman*, n. 7 above.

[44] A. Castro Oliveira, 'Workers and Other Persons: Step-by-Step from Movement to Citizenship' (2002) 39 *CMLRev.* 77.

[45] Case C–391/97 *Frans Gschwind* v. *Finanzamt Aachen-Aussenstadt* [1999] ECR I–5451, para. 21; Case C–356/98 *Arben Kaba* v. *Home Secretary* [2000] ECR I–2623. See, for criticism of the Kaba case, S. Peers, 'Dazed and Confused: Family Members' Residence Rights and the Court of Justice' (2001) 26 *ELRev.* 76.

[46] Case 167/73 *Commission* v. *French Republic* [1974] ECR 359; Case C–185/96 *Commission* v. *Hellenic Republic* [1998] ECR I–6601.

[47] Case C–212/99 *Commission* v. *Italy* [2001] ECR I–4923. On Italy's sluggishness in complying with the latter judgment see Case C–119/04 *Commission* v. *Italy* [2006] ECR I–6885. Although the ECJ refused in the latter case to impose a penalty payment on Italy, this appeared to be because the Commission had not proven its case properly, rather than that Italy had properly complied with the earlier judgment.

[48] On the use of nationality restrictions when fielding players in sport see Case C–415/93 *Bosman*, n. 7 above; Case C–438/00 *Kolpak*, n. 25 above; Case C–265/03 *Simutenkov* v. *Ministerio de Educación y Cultura* [2005] ECR I–2579. Compare Case 13/76 *Donà*, n. 25 above.

A common species of indirect discrimination is where benefits are made conditional, in law or fact, on residence or place-of-origin requirements (or place-of-education requirements, as in *Ioannidis*[49]) that can more easily be satisfied by nationals as opposed to non-nationals.[50] In *Ugliola*, an Italian worker in Germany challenged a German law under which a worker's security of employment was protected by having periods of military service taken into account in calculating the length of employment.[51] The law in question applied only to those who had done their military service in the Bundeswehr, although the nationality of the worker was irrelevant. The Court stressed that Article 48 allowed for no restrictions on the principle of equal treatment other than as provided for in paragraph 3. It concluded that the German law had created an unjustifiable restriction by 'indirectly introducing discrimination in favour of their own nationals alone', since the requirement that the service be done in the Bundeswehr would clearly be satisfied by a far greater number of nationals than non-nationals.[52]

In *Sotgiu* the German Post Office increased the separation allowance paid to workers employed away from their place of residence within Germany, but did not pay the increase to workers (whatever their nationality) whose residence at the time of their initial employment was situated abroad, and this was held by the ECJ to be contrary to the Treaty.[53] In *Commission v. Belgium*[54] the ECJ held that a system of retirement pension points that could be more easily satisfied by workers possessing the nationality of that Member State than by workers from other Member States was indirectly discriminatory, and hence caught by Article 39. In *Zurstrassen*,[55] one of a growing number of cases concerning the discriminatory effect of taxation rules which are based on residence,[56] the Court held that national rules under which the joint assessment to tax of spouses was conditional on their both being resident on the national territory were incompatible with Article 48.

Another obvious form of indirect discrimination is the imposition of a *language requirement* for certain posts, since it is likely that a far higher proportion of non-nationals than nationals will be affected by it.[57] However, since such a requirement may well be legitimate, Article 3(1) of Regulation 1612/68 allows for the imposition of 'conditions relating to linguistic knowledge required by reason of the nature of the post to be filled'. The Court considered the scope of this exception in *Groener*, where a Dutch national working in Ireland as a part-time art teacher was rejected for the full-time art-teaching post for which she was otherwise selected, because she did not pass an oral examination in the Irish language.[58] The ECJ ruled

---

[49] N. 41 above. See also Case C–109/04 *Kranemann*, n. 29 above.

[50] Case C–355/98 *Commission v. Belgium* [2000] ECR I–1221; Case C–350/96 *Clean Car*, n. 17 above.

[51] Case 15/69 *Württembergische Milchverwertung-Südmilch-AG v. Salvatore Ugliola* [1970] ECR 363.

[52] Case C–419/92 *Scholz v. Universitaria di Cagliari* [1994] ECR I–505; Case C–15/96 *Kalliope Schöning-Kougebetopoulou v. Freie und Hansestadt Hamburg* [1998] ECR I–47; Case C–187/96 *Commission v. Hellenic Republic* [1998] ECR I–1095; Case C–278/03 *Commission v. Italy* [2005] ECR I–3747.

[53] Case 152/73 *Sotgiu v. Deutsche Bundespost* [1974] ECR 153.

[54] Case 35/97 *Commission v. Belgium* [1998] ECR I–5325.

[55] Case C–87/99 *Zurstrassen v. Administration des Contributions Directes* [2000] ECR I–3337.

[56] See, e.g., Case C–169/03 *Wallentin v. Riksskatteverket* [2004] ECR I–6443; Case C–400/02 *Merida v. Bundesrepublik Deutschland* [2004] ECR I–8471; Case C–152/03 *Ritter-Coulais v. Finanzamt Germersheim* [2006] ECR I–1711.

[57] For an example of unjustifiable indirect discrimination see Cases C–259 and 331–332/91 *Allué and Coonan* [1993] ECR I–4309, in which the Member State had imposed restrictions on the contracts of foreign-language teaching assistants. For a similar case involving direct discrimination see Case C–124/94 *Commission v. Greece* [1995] ECR I–1457. For a case in which the exclusion of foreign-language assistants from eligibility for temporary university teaching vacancies was held not to violate Art. 39 see Case C–90/96 *Petrie v. Università degli Studi di Verona and Camilla Bettoni* [1997] ECR I–6527.

[58] Case 379/87 *Groener v. Minister for Education* [1989] ECR 3967.

that even though the teaching was likely to be exclusively in English, the language requirement could, so long as it was not imposed in a disproportionate way,[59] fall within Article 3(1) on account of the policy of the Irish Government to maintain and promote the use of Irish as a means of expressing national identity and culture.

Another form of indirect discrimination frequently encountered in the law on free movement of goods and services, but which is equally relevant to the context of the free movement of workers, is the imposition of a *'double-burden' regulatory requirement*, which does not recognize appropriate qualifications or certifications already received in the home State. Such a regulation was held to be contrary to Article 39 in *Commission* v. *Portugal*.[60]

Finally, as has been done in other fields of EU anti-discrimination law, the ECJ has also relaxed the requirements for proof of indirect discrimination, ruling in *O'Flynn* that in order for indirect discrimination to be established, it was not necessary to prove that a national measure in practice affected a higher proportion of foreign workers, but merely that the measure was 'intrinsically liable' to affect migrant workers more than nationals.[61]

(c) OBSTACLES TO ACCESS TO THE EMPLOYMENT MARKET

It was for some time unclear whether Article 39 applied to national measures which restricted the freedom of movement of EC workers, but which were neither directly nor indirectly discriminatory on grounds of nationality. This is a central issue that has arisen in relation to all of the 'freedoms', but perhaps with greatest frequency in the field of free movement of goods. In the context of each of the freedoms, the ECJ has ruled that even non-discriminatory restrictions may breach the Treaty if they constitute an excessive obstacle to freedom of movement. While it is sometimes difficult to distinguish between cases of indirect discrimination and those where the ECJ intervenes to protect access to the employment market, there are nonetheless cases that fall clearly within the latter category.

The issue was first addressed directly in the context of free movement of workers in the famous *Bosman* ruling, in which the transfer system developed by national and transnational football associations was found to be in breach of Article 39.[62] In short, that system required a football club, which sought to engage a player whose contract with another club had come to an end, to pay a sum of money (often substantial) to the latter club. In the case of Bosman himself, who had been employed by a Belgian football club, this rule effectively prevented him from securing employment with a French club. The fact that the transfer system applied equally to players moving from one club to another within a Member State as to players moving between States, and that a player's nationality was entirely irrelevant, did not prevent the system, according to the ECJ, from falling foul of Article 39. This was so notwithstanding the reliance placed by the football associations on the *Keck* ruling,[63] which had narrowed

---

[59] It would, e.g., be disproportionate to require the knowledge of Irish to be acquired or certified only within the state: see Case C–281/98 *Angonese* [2000] ECR I–4139.

[60] Case C–171/02 *Commission* v. *Portugal* [2004] ECR I–5645.

[61] Case C–237/94 *O'Flynn* v. *Adjudication Officer* [1996] ECR I–2617; Case C–278/94 *Commission* v. *Belgium* [1996] ECR I–4307 on tideover allowances for young people who had completed their secondary education in a Belgian establishment.

[62] Case C–415/93 *Bosman*, n. 7 above, paras. 98–103 (although see the earlier suggestion in Case 321/87 *Commission* v. *Belgium* [1989] ECR 997, para. 15); Case C–176/96 *Lehtonen* v. *FRBSB* [2000] ECR I–2681.

[63] See Cases C–267 and 268/91 *Keck and Mithouard* [1993] ECR I–6097, discussed in Ch. 19.

the scope of the Treaty provisions on free movement of goods. According to the Court in *Bosman*:

> 103. It is sufficient to note that, although the rules in issue in the main proceedings apply also to transfers between clubs belonging to different national associations within the same Member State and are similar to those governing transfers between clubs belonging to the same national association, they still directly affect players' access to the employment market in other Member States and are thus capable of impeding freedom of movement for workers. They cannot, thus, be deemed comparable to the rules on selling arrangements for goods which in *Keck and Mithouard* were held to fall outside the ambit of Article 30 of the Treaty (see also, with regard to the freedom to provide services, Case C–384/93 *Alpine Investments* v. *Minister van Financiën* [1995] ECR I–1141, paras. 36–38).

In the absence of any sufficiently convincing public-interest justification for the rule, it was found by the ECJ to be contrary to Article 39. The fact that there was no discrimination was irrelevant: the existence of an obstacle to the access of workers from one Member State to employment in another Member State was enough to attract the application of Article 39.[64]

The principle established in *Bosman*—that non-discriminatory rules which nonetheless impede access of workers to the employment market of another State (whether imposed by the State of origin or destination) are caught by Article 39—has been repeatedly applied in a steady stream of subsequent cases, including *De Groot*,[65] *Schilling*,[66] *Rockler*,[67] *Commission* v. *Portugal*,[68] and *Lyyski*.[69] In *Terhoeve*, the ECJ ruled that provisions, such as a national law concerning the payment of social contributions, which could preclude or deter a national of a Member State from leaving his country of origin in order to exercise his free-movement rights constituted an obstacle to that freedom even if they applied without regard to the nationality of the workers concerned.[70] In *Commission* v. *Denmark*[71] and *Van Lent*,[72] the Court condemned national rules which prohibited workers domiciled in one particular State from using a vehicle registered in another Member State (normally a vehicle owned by an employer established in the latter State), on the basis that these rules might preclude workers from exercising their right to free movement or might impede access to employment between States.

The fact that non-discriminatory provisions which impede market access can be caught does, nonetheless, raise concerns about the outer boundaries of Article 39, just as we saw in the case law concerning free movement of goods under Article 28. The issue was thrown into sharp relief by *Graf*.[73] The applicant claimed that rules providing that compensation on termination of employment did not apply when the worker voluntarily ended the employment to take up employment elsewhere were in breach of Article 39. Advocate General Fennelly

---

[64] For criticism see L. Daniele, 'Non-Discriminatory Restrictions to the Free Movement of Persons' (1997) 22 *ELRev*. 191.

[65] Case C–385/00 *De Groot* v. *Staatssecretaris van Financiën* [2002] ECR I–11819.

[66] Case C–209/01 *Schilling and Fleck-Schilling* v. *Finanzamt Nürnberg-Süd* [2003] ECR I–13389.

[67] Case C–137/04 *Rockler* v. *Försäkringskassan* [2006] ECR I–1441.

[68] Case C–345/05 *Commission* v. *Portugal* [2006] ECR I–10633.

[69] Case C–40/05 *Lyyski* v. *Umeå Universitet*, 11 Jan. 2007.

[70] Case C–18/95 *F.C. Terhoeve* v. *Inspecteur van de Belastingdienst Particulieren/Ondernemingen Buitenland* [1999] ECR I–345, para. 39.

[71] Case C–464/02 *Commission* v. *Denmark* [2005] ECR I–7929.

[72] Case C–232/01 *Van Lent* [2003] ECR I–11525; Cases C–151–152/04 *Nadin and Durre* [2005] ECR I–11203, on self-employed workers.

[73] Case C–190/98 *Volker Graf* v. *Filzmoser Mashinenbau* GmbH [2000] ECR I–493.

adverted to the dangers of regarding such rules as constituting a breach of Article 39. He argued that neutral national rules could be regarded as material barriers to market access only if it were established that they had actual effects on market actors akin to exclusion from the market.[74]

The ECJ shared these concerns. It reiterated the principle from *Bosman* concerning market access. It held however on the facts that the impugned legislation did not offend this principle. The entitlement to compensation was not dependent on the worker's choosing whether or not to stay with his current employer. It was, rather, dependent on a future and hypothetical event, namely the subsequent termination of the contract without this being at his initiative. This was too uncertain and indirect a possibility for the legislation to be regarded as being in breach of Article 39.[75]

Similarly in *Weigel*, the ECJ ruled that the negative tax consequences for an individual who moves to work from one Member State to another will not necessarily be contrary to Article 39—even if it is likely to deter the worker from exercising rights of free movement—if it does not place that individual under any greater disadvantage than those already resident and subject to the same tax.[76]

(d) INTERNAL SITUATIONS

Article 39 does not prohibit discrimination in a so-called 'wholly internal' situation. This is sometimes referred to as a situation of 'reverse discrimination', since its effect is frequently that national workers cannot claim rights in their own Member States, which workers who are nationals of other Member States could claim there. In *Saunders* the ECJ held that since there was 'no factor connecting' the defendant 'to any of the situations envisaged by Community law', she could not rely on Article 39 to challenge an order which effectively excluded her from part of her own national territory.[77]

Attempts have since been made to circumvent the 'internal situation' barrier by relying on the right to freedom of movement conferred by Article 18 on European citizens, as something over and above the rights of movement of EC workers, but these have not so far succeeded before the ECJ.[78] It will be seen below that this 'internal situation' approach by the Court has given rise to some particularly invidious results in the context of the rights of workers and their families.[79]

It is nonetheless clear, as exemplified by cases such as *Terhoeve*[80] and *De Groot*,[81] that a worker will be able to use Article 39 against his or her own State where the worker has been

---

[74] *Ibid.*, para. 32 of the AG's Opinion

[75] *Ibid.*, paras. 24–25 of the ECJ's judgment.

[76] Case C–387/01 *Weigel v. Finanzlandesdirektion für Vorarlberg* [2004] ECR I–4981, paras. 50–55.

[77] Case 175/78 *R. v. Saunders* [1979] ECR 1129. See also Case 298/84 *Pavlo Iorio v. Azienda Autonomo delle Ferrovie dello Stato* [1986] ECR 247; Cases C–225–227/95 *Kapasakalis, Skiathis and Kougiagkas v. Greece* [1998] ECR I–4329.

[78] Cases C–64 and 65/96 *Uecker* and *Jacquet v. Land Nordrhein-Westfalen* [1997] ECR I–3171; Case C–299/95 *Kremzow v. Austria* [1997] ECR I–2629, following Case 180/83 *Moser v. Land Baden-Württemberg* [1984] ECR 2539, where the prospect of being disadvantaged in a possible future search for employment abroad was deemed insufficient as a 'connecting factor' to attract the application of Art. 39. Compare, however, Case C–148/02 *Garcia Avello* [2003] ECR I–11613, discussed further in Ch. 23, and see the Draft Recommendation of the European Ombudsman to the Commission in Complaint, 3317/2004/GG.

[79] See, e.g., Cases 35 and 36/82 *Morson and Jhanjan v. Netherlands* [1982] ECR 3723.

[80] Case C–18/95 *Terhoeve*, n. 70 above.

[81] Case C–385/00 *De Groot*, n. 65 above.

employed and resided in another Member State. Such a worker may then claim that he or she has been discriminated against in relation to, for example, social security contributions or taxation, when returning to work in his or her own Member State.

(e) OBJECTIVE JUSTIFICATION

The possible grounds for justifying indirect discrimination are broad, and not confined to the exceptions set out in the Treaty or in secondary legislation. This is exemplified in *Sotgiu*,[82] *O'Flynn*,[83] *Lehtonen*,[84] and in a range of decisions concerning taxation provisions. In *Schumacker*, the Court ruled that indirect discrimination based on the residence of a worker, whereby an EC national employed but not resident in a particular Member State could not benefit from personal tax allowances, could in certain circumstances be justified.[85] This was because of the likely difference in position between workers from other Member States and resident workers, but such indirect discrimination could not be justified where, for example, the non-resident worker could not benefit from personal allowances in the Member State of residence either.

In *Commission* v. *Belgium*[86] and *Bachmann*,[87] the Court held that although national rules which allowed the deductibility from income tax of various insurance and pension contributions only if those contributions were paid in Belgium were indirectly discriminatory contrary to Article 39, they could be justified. The rationale was the need to ensure the cohesion of the Belgian tax system. The ECJ accepted that contributions paid in Belgium were permitted to be deducted under the law because these deductions were offset by the tax imposed on sums paid out by insurers in Belgium. There could be no such certainty that the sums paid out by insurers not based in Belgium had been taxed.[88] These discriminatory measures were held by the Court to be justified, without the need for the State to invoke the special grounds of exception in Article 39(3), which are discussed in more detail below. However, in a number of other cases involving taxation measures which were found to be obstacles to the free movement of workers, the ECJ ultimately ruled that arguments based on the cohesion of the tax system or the need to supervise taxation or to prevent tax avoidance were not justified on the facts.[89]

---

[82] Case 152/73 *Sotgiu*, n. 53 above. The ECJ held that such indirect discrimination might be justified on the basis of objective differences, e.g. if the payment of the allowance to those resident in Germany was coupled with an obligation to transfer residence to the new place of work, whereas those resident outside Germany were not subject to such an obligation.

[83] Case C–237/94 *O'Flynn*, n. 61 above.

[84] Case C–176/96 *Lehtonen*, n. 62 above, paras. 51–60. The ECJ held that rules establishing transfer deadlines in basketball could in principle be justified, since late transfers could change the sporting strength of a team in the course of the championship. The Court left open the question, however, whether a different and later deadline date for transfers of players outside the European zone than for those within that zone went beyond what was necessary for the aim pursued.

[85] Case C–279/93 *Finanzamt Köln-Altstadt v. Roland Schumacker* [1995] ECR I–225. See F. Vanistendael, 'The Consequences of Schumacker and Wielockx: Two Steps Forward in the Tax Procession of Echternach' (1996) 33 *CMLRev.* 255.

[86] Case C–300/90 *Commission* v. *Belgium* [1992] ECR I–305.

[87] Case C–204/90 *Bachmann* v. *Belgium* [1992] ECR I–249.

[88] Contrast the Opinion of Mischo AG, *ibid.*, 260, who concluded that the Belgian legislation was disproportionately restrictive, since there were other means available to obviate the risk of tax evasion. See also Case C–175/88 *Biehl* v. *Luxembourg* [1990] ECR I–1779; Case C–151/94 *Commission* v. *Luxembourg* [1995] ECR I–3685.

[89] Case C–385/00 *De Groot*, n. 65 above; Case C–169/03 *Wallentin* v. *Riksskatteverket* [2004] ECR I–6443; Case C–152/03 *Ritter-Coulais*, n. 56 above; Case C–150/04 *Commission* v. *Denmark*, 30 Jan. 2007.

The ECJ in general undertakes close scrutiny of claims that restrictions are justified.[90] Thus in *Terhoeve*[91] the ECJ considered whether heavier social security contributions levied on a worker who transferred his residence from one Member State to another to take up work during the course of a year could be justified. The ECJ rejected justifications based on the need to simplify and co-ordinate the levying of such contributions and technical difficulties preventing other methods of collection. In *Rockler*, the ECJ rejected arguments based on the supposed financial burden on the national social security scheme, ruling—as in the case of the other freedoms under the Treaty—that justifications based on purely economic grounds could not be accepted, and that the justification put forward in any case was not proportionate.[92] Arguments based on the cohesion of the national tax system have also often failed, despite the *Bachmann* and *Belgium* taxation cases discussed above.[93]

5. THE PUBLIC SERVICE EXCEPTION

We have seen that the ECJ's approach to the definition of worker has been a relatively expansive one. Conversely, its approach to the limiting clause in Article 39(4), which provides that Article 39 shall not apply to 'employment in the public service', has been restrictive. The ECJ has endeavoured to ensure that the scope of the exception does not go further than is necessary to fulfil the purpose for which it was included in the Treaty. This requires an analysis of why the exception was created. The case law provides a good example of the contrast between a kind of 'original intent' interpretation argued for by the Member States, and the less historically rooted 'purposive' interpretation employed by the Court. The ECJ does not confine its 'hermeneutic monopoly' to the right-conferring terms such as 'worker', but extends it also to the public service derogation: it is for the Court and not the Member State to decide what constitutes 'employment in the public service'. The battle over the scope of the public service exception has been hard fought, perhaps even more strongly than that over the scope of the term worker. An explanation for this was offered by Mancini, who attributed it to 'the widespread view that the functioning of the public service is an exercise of full-State sovereignty'.[94] Certain fundamentals concerning the interpretation of Article 39(4) emerge from the case law.

(a) THE MEANING OF THE PUBLIC SERVICE EXCEPTION IS DETERMINED BY THE COURT, NOT THE MEMBER STATES

In *Sotgiu* the ECJ made it clear that it, and not the respective Member States, would define the scope of the exception:[95]

> It is necessary to establish further whether the extent of the exception provided for by Article 48(4) [now Art 39(4)] can be determined in terms of the designation of the legal relationship between the employee and the employing administration.

---

[90] See the cases listed in n. 89 above. See also Case C–464/02 *Commission* v. *Denmark*, n. 71 above, where the ECJ rejected arguments that the obligation for employees to have a company car registered in Denmark was justified to avoid abuse of the 'company car' system or to prevent fiscal erosion and tax avoidance.

[91] Case C–18/95 *Terhoeve*, n. 70 above, paras. 43–47.

[92] Case C–137/04 *Rockler*, n. 67 above.

[93] See, e.g., Case C–209/01 *Schilling*, n. 66 above; Case C–345/05 *Commission* v. *Portugal*, n. 68 above; and the cases cited at n. 89 above.

[94] Mancini, n. 15 above, 77.

[95] Case 152/73 *Sotgiu*, n. 53 above, para. 5.

In the absence of any distinction in the provision referred to, it is of no interest whether a worker is engaged as a workman (*ouvrier*), a clerk (*employé*), or an official (*fonctionnaire*) or even whether the terms on which he is employed come under public or private law.

These legal designations can be varied at the whim of national legislatures and cannot therefore provide a criterion for interpretation appropriate to the requirements of Community law.

Thus the Member States cannot deem a particular post to be 'in the public service' by the name or designation they give to that post, or by the mere fact that the terms of the post are regulated by public law. Further, it is irrelevant, according to the ECJ, whether the State's rules governing nationality as a necessary condition for entry to any post in the public service have constitutional status, in view of the need for the 'unity and efficacy' of Community law.[96]

(b) THE ECJ'S TEST FOR PUBLIC SERVICE

In the case extracted below, the Belgian Government (supported by the UK, German, and French governments) argued that Article 39(4) differed from Article 45 (ex Article 55). The latter provides a somewhat similar derogation in the context of freedom of establishment and freedom to provide services, when an activity involves the 'exercise of official authority'. This difference, according to the Belgian Government, was deliberately reflected in the respective wording of each. Article 55 specifically mentions the exercise of official authority, which implies a *functional* concept, whereas Article 48(4) refers to 'employment in the public service', which is an *institutional* concept. On the latter definition, what is important is the institution within which the worker is employed, rather than the nature of the work itself. The ECJ did not accept this argument.

Case 149/79 **Commission v. Belgium**
[1980] ECR 3881

[Note ToA renumbering: Art. 48 is now Art. 39]

Possession of Belgian nationality was required as a condition of entry for posts with Belgian local authorities and public undertakings, regardless of the nature of the duties to be performed. Examples of such posts were those of unskilled railway workers, hospital nurses, and night-watchmen. The Belgian Government argued that, when the Treaties were drafted, there was no Community concept of the objectives and scope of public authorities and that the Member States' governments had wished the conditions of entry to public office to remain their preserve.

THE ECJ

10. That provision [Article 48(4)] removes from the ambit of Article 48(1) to (3) a series of posts which involve direct or indirect participation in the exercise of powers conferred by public law and duties designed to safeguard the general interests of the State or of other public authorities. Such posts in fact presume on the part of those occupying them the existence of

---

[96] [1980] ECR 3881, paras. 18–19; Case C–473/93 *Commission* v. *Luxembourg* [1996] ECR I–3207, para. 38.

a special relationship of allegiance to the State and reciprocity of rights and duties which form the foundation of the bond of nationality.

11. The scope of the derogation made by Article 48(4) to the principles of freedom of movement and equality of treatment laid down in the first three paragraphs of the article should therefore be determined on the basis of the aim pursued by that article. However, determining the sphere of application of Article 48(4) raises special difficulties since in the various Member States authorities acting under powers conferred by public law have assumed responsibilities of an economic and social nature or are involved in activities which are not identifiable with the functions which are typical of the public service yet which by their nature still come under the sphere of application of the Treaty. In these circumstances the effect of extending the exception contained in Article 48(4) to posts which, whilst coming under the States or other organizations governed by public law, still do not involve any association with tasks belonging to the public service properly so called, would be to remove a considerable number of posts from the ambit of the principles set out in the Treaty and to create inequalities between Member States according to the different ways in which the State and certain sectors of economic life are organized.

Thus a State cannot bring certain activities, e.g. of an economic or social kind, within the Treaty derogation simply by including them in the scope of the public law of the State, and taking responsibility for their performance.[97] The ECJ took the view that the aim of the Treaty provision was to permit Member States, should they so wish, to reserve for nationals those posts which would require a *specific bond of allegiance and mutuality of rights and duties between State and employee.*

The Court's description of the posts that could be said to require such allegiance and to depend upon the bond of nationality was twofold. They must involve (i) participation in the exercise of powers conferred by public law, and (ii) they must entail duties designed to safeguard the general interests of the State. The notion of 'powers conferred by public law' is rather a vague one, given the difficulties inherent in defining the scope of public law, but the idea of 'safeguarding the general interests of the State' is somewhat more concrete. Different views have been expressed on this point, but it seems that the two requirements are cumulative rather than alternative. A post will benefit from the derogation in Article 39(4) only if it involves *both* the exercise of power conferred by public law *and* the safeguarding of the general interests of the state.[98]

(c) APPLICATION OF THE ECJ'S TEST

In the *Belgium* case[99] the ECJ ruled that it did not have enough information to be able to identify which of the specified posts fell outside the Treaty derogation. It invited Belgium and the Commission to re-examine and resolve the issue in the light of its judgment, and to report any solution to the ECJ. When they failed to agree on certain of the posts, the case came back to the

---

[97] The converse, however, is also true. In other words, the application of the Art. 39(4) exception is not excluded simply because the employer in question is a private party rather than a public body: Case C–405/01 *Colegio de Oficiales de la Marina Mercante Española* v. *Administracion del Estado* [2003] ECR I–10391.

[98] Case 66/85 *Lawrie-Blum*, n. 27 above, para. 27; Case C–473/93 *Commission* v. *Luxembourg* [1996] ECR I–3207, para. 18, Léger AG. See also D. O'Keeffe, 'Judicial Interpretation of the Public Service Exception to the Free Movement of Workers', in Curtin and O'Keeffe (eds.), n. 15 above, 89, 96.

[99] Case 149/79 *Commission* v. *Belgium* [1980] ECR 3881.

ECJ two years later. The Court ruled that, with the exception of a limited number of posts, including certain supervisory posts, night watchman, and architect with the municipality of Brussels, none of the other posts satisfied the criteria for the application of the public service exception.[100]

A further argument made by the four governments represented in the *Belgium* cases was that certain posts which may not at the outset involve participation in the powers conferred by public law require a certain flexibility of character. They argued that the duties and responsibilities of the post may change, or the holders of such initial posts may subsequently become eligible for careers at a higher grade with duties involving the exercise of public powers. This, too, was rejected as a reason for treating the initial post as being within the public service exception, since that exception 'allows Member States to reserve to their nationals, by appropriate rules, entry to posts involving the exercise of such powers and such responsibilities within the same grade, the same branch, or the same class'.[101]

The point was made again by the ECJ in enforcement proceedings brought by the Commission against Italy, concerning laws protecting the security and tenure of researchers at the National Research Council (CNR) which were not applied to non-nationals.[102] Italy argued, first, that the work undertaken by the CNR involved satisfying the general interests of the State and was financed out of public funds. It argued, secondly, that if researchers became established members of staff, they could be promoted to higher managerial positions, which would entail participation in the exercise of public power. The ECJ rejected the first argument:[103]

> Simply referring to the general tasks of the CNR and listing the duties of all its researchers is not sufficient to establish that the researchers are responsible for exercising powers conferred by public law or for safeguarding the general interests of the State. Only the duties of management or of advising the State on scientific and technical questions could be described as employment in the public service within the meaning of Article 48(4).

The second argument was equally summarily dismissed, with reference being made to the Court's ruling in the *Belgium* cases:[104]

> It is sufficient to point out that Community law does not prohibit a Member State from reserving for its own nationals those posts within a career bracket which involve participation in the exercise of powers conferred by public law or the safeguarding of the general interests of the State.

However, the Court also emphasized in a later case concerning posts as master and chief mate of merchant ships flying the Spanish flag that the Article 39(4) exception could only be validly used if the rights under powers conferred by public law (e.g., the exercise of police powers in the event of danger on board) are in fact exercised on a regular basis by those holders and do not represent a very minor part of their activities.[105]

---

[100] Case 149/79 *Commission* v. *Belgium II* [1982] ECR 1845.
[101] *Ibid.*, para. 21.
[102] Case 225/85 *Commission* v. *Italy* [1987] ECR 2625.
[103] *Ibid.*, para. 9.
[104] *Ibid.*, para. 10.
[105] Case C–405/01 *Colegio de Oficiales de la Marina Mercante Española*, n. 97 above.

Member States have attempted to use the exception in numerous other cases.[106] There is no secondary legislation which attempts to clarify the concept. The Commission once proposed to draft legislation to clarify the derogation, but its proposal was opposed by those who thought that the Member States might take advantage of detailed legislation to undermine the established case law, and also that such legislation could ossify the process of creating a 'citizens' Europe'.[107] The Commission instead, in 1988, published a document in the Official Journal on the scope of Article 39(4), providing some guidance on the sorts of state functions which it considered would or would not fall within that provision.[108] Those which probably would be covered included the armed forces, police, judiciary, tax authorities, and certain public bodies engaged in preparing or monitoring legal acts, and those which probably would not included nursing, teaching, and non-military research in public establishments.

The issue is still one which is fraught with ideological tensions, the underlying debate being about the relevance of nationality, and specifically about when it is legitimate for the Member States to require nationality as a condition for employment. The efforts of the Member States to define the public service derogation in institutional terms by reference to the 'public sector' have repeatedly failed.[109] The Court has adhered to a rather more difficult but narrower 'functional' approach, which examines closely the character of posts which might be said to require the reciprocal bond of allegiance which is said to be characteristic of nationality. The debate provides a clear example of the federal tensions, which emerge in many areas of Community law, over the proper scope of national as opposed to Community jurisdiction and competence, and in particular where the sensitive issue of nationality is concerned. Member State resistance to the ECJ's approach, and the judicial response thereto, is evident in Advocate General Mancini's critical and trenchant opinion in infringement proceedings involving public nursing posts in France:[110]

The decisions to which I have referred gave rise to severe criticisms from academic lawyers and, what is more important, they have not been 'taken in' by numerous governments. Such resistance is not surprising if it is borne in mind how deep-rooted is the conviction that the public service is an area in which the State should exercise full sovereignty and how wide-spread is the tendency, in times of high unemployment, to see the public service as a convenient reservoir of posts. Such resistance is a matter for concern and should be tackled head-on before cases similar to the present one multiply. . . .

. . . In short, in order to be made inaccessible to nationals of another State, it is not sufficient for the duties inherent in the post at issue to be directed specifically towards public objectives which influence the conduct and action of private individuals. Those who occupy the post must don full battle dress: in non-metaphorical terms, the duties must involve acts of will which affect private individuals by requiring their obedience or, in the event of disobedience, by

106 Case 66/85 *Lawrie-Blum*, n. 27 above, para. 28; Case 33/88 *Allué and Coonan* v. *Università degli Studi di Venezia* [1989] ECR 1591; Case C–213/90 *ASTI* v. *Chambre des Employés Privés* [1991] ECR I–3507; Case C–4/91 *Bleis* v. *Ministère de l'Education Nationale* [1991] ECR I–5627.

107 Mancini, n. 15 above.

108 [1988] OJ C72/2.

109 Case C–473/93 *Commission* v. *Luxembourg* [1996] ECR I–3207; Case C–173/94 *Commission* v. *Belgium* [1996] ECR I–3265; Case C–290/94 *Commission* v. *Greece* [1996] ECR I–3285, where the ECJ was asked once again to depart entirely from its previous case law.

110 Case 307/84 *Commission* v. *France* [1986] ECR 1725, 1727–1733. For criticism of the Court's ruling in this case see O'Keeffe, n. 98 above, 89, 101–103.

compelling them to comply. To make a list ... is practically impossible; but certainly the first examples which come to mind are posts relating to policing, defence of the State, the administration of justice and assessments to tax.

... It is a fact that an extremist disciple of Hegel might truly think that access to posts like the ones at issue here [nursing] should be denied to foreigners. But anyone who does not regard the State as 'the march of God in the world' must of necessity take the contrary view.

It was suggested soon after the TEU was adopted that the new provisions in the EC Treaty on citizenship might undermine the thinking behind, and reduce the importance of, the public service exception, given the emphasis of the latter on a traditional notion of loyalty between the State and its own nationals, to the exclusion of foreigners.[111] However, the Commission has continued to bring a variety of infringement proceedings concerning misuse of the public service exception, which have often been vigorously defended by the Member States.[112] In proceedings brought against Luxembourg the ECJ was confronted with the argument that the public service derogation was an important means for the Member States to preserve their national identities. But although it accepted that the preservation of such identities was a legitimate aim, and one which was acknowledged in Article 6(1) TEU, the ECJ ruled that that interest could be safeguarded through other means than by generally excluding nationals of other Member States, for example by the imposition of language, experience, and training conditions.[113]

(d) DISCRIMINATORY CONDITIONS OF EMPLOYMENT WITHIN THE PUBLIC SERVICE ARE PROHIBITED

It is clear from *Sotgiu* that Article 39(4) cannot be used to justify discriminatory conditions for employment within the public service. Germany had invoked Article 39(4) in an attempt to justify its provisions on separation allowances for post office workers, which worked to the disadvantage of non-nationals, and the ECJ responded as follows:[114]

The interests which this derogation [Article 39(4)] allows Member States to protect are satisfied by the opportunity of restricting admission of foreign nationals to certain activities in the public service.

On the other hand this provision cannot justify discriminatory measures with regard to remuneration or other conditions of employment against workers once they have been admitted to the public service.

The very fact that they have been admitted shows indeed that those interests which justify the exceptions to the principle of non-discrimination permitted by [Article 39(4)] are not at issue.

Thus the Treaty derogation must be confined to restricting the *admission* of non-nationals into the public service, and does permit discrimination in conditions once they are admitted.

---

[111] D. O'Keeffe, 'Judicial Interpretation of the Public Service Exception to the Free Movement of Workers', in Curtin and O'Keeffe (eds.), n. 15 above.

[112] See the cases listed at n. 109 above.

[113] Case C–473/93 *Commission* v. *Luxembourg*, n. 96 above, para. 35.

[114] Case 152/73 *Sotgiu*, n. 53 above, para. 4; Case C–195/98 *Österreicher Gewerkschaftsbund, Gewerkschaft Öffentlicher Dienst* v. *Republik Österreich* [2000] ECR I–10497, para. 37.

If they are deemed sufficiently loyal to the State to be admitted to such employment, there can be no grounds for paying them less on account of their nationality.

6. THE RIGHT OF ENTRY AND RESIDENCE OF WORKERS AND THEIR FAMILIES: DIRECTIVE 2004/38

(a) FORMAL REQUIREMENTS FOR WORKERS

Directive 68/360 was initially adopted under Article 40, with a view to facilitating freedom of movement and the abolition of restrictions on employed persons, in part by clarifying the formal requirements relating to the right of entry and residence of non-nationals.[115] This Directive has now been repealed and replaced by the relevant provisions of Directive 2004/38[116] on the movement and residence of EU citizens and their families, with 'family members' defined in Articles 2 and 3 thereof. Article 6 of the 2004 Directive gives an initial right of entry and residence for up to three months to all EU citizens and their families without any conditions other than presentation of an identity card *or* passport. The interim status of job-seeker is also recognized in the preamble to the Directive, which implicitly confirms the ECJ case law on this subject.[117] Article 8 of the Directive provides that workers and their families may be required to register with the host state authorities, and, upon presentation of a valid passport or identity card and confirmation of employment (and, in the case of family members, a document attesting to the existence of the relevant family relationship, dependency etc.), to receive a certification of registration as evidence of their underlying right of residence.[118] Thus the previous system of residence permits under Directive 68/360 has been replaced with a simpler registration procedure for workers and their families. However, family members who are not EU nationals are to be issued a residence card under Articles 9 and 10.

Member States are required by Article 4 to grant citizens and their families the right to leave their territory to go and work in other Member States, simply on producing an identity card or passport (of at least five years' validity) which their Member State must provide for them and which will be valid throughout the Community and any necessary transit countries between Member States. No exit visa requirement may be imposed. Article 5 sets out similar conditions for the right to enter another Member State: all that is required is a valid identity card or passport and a visa requirement is impermissible,[119] except for certain third-country nationals. The conditions under which a visa can be imposed for family members who are third-country nationals have been tightened up by Article 5(2);[120] they are to be issued free of

---

115 Dir. 68/360 [1968] II OJ Spec. Ed. 485; Dir. 64/221 [1963–4] OJ Spec. Ed. 117.

116 N. 11 above.

117 Case C–292/89 *R.* v. *Immigration Appeal Tribunal ex p. Antonissen* [1991] ECR I–745.

118 This provision was apparently intended to respond to the ECJ ruling in Case 48/75 *Royer*, n. 36 above, which indicated that the residence permit did not grant any rights, but was merely evidence of a pre-existing right under the Treaty.

119 For a case interpreting the same requirement under the earlier Dir. 68/360 strictly, so that a passport stamp could not be required, see Case 157/79 *R.* v. *Pieck* [1980] ECR 2171.

120 The only third-country-national family members of an EU citizen who can be subject to a visa requirement are those referred to in Reg. 539/2001 which lists the third countries whose nationals must be in possession of visas when crossing the external borders, and—in the case of the UK and Ireland which do not participate in the common EU visa policy—those provided for by national law.

charge and as soon as possible, and those holding a valid residence card issued by a Member State under Article 9 are exempt from the requirement.

It is made clear in the Directive, as it was under the previous legislation and as the ECJ repeatedly emphasized in its case law, that the rights to reside and to work are not conditional upon initial satisfaction of the formalities for which the Directive provides.[121] Various provisions of Directive 2004/38, including Articles 5(5), 8(2), and 9(3), follow this line of case law by referring to the right of States to impose proportionate and non-discriminatory penalties for non-satisfaction of the formal requirements.[122] It is clear that deportation, refusal of entry, or revocation of the right of residence constitutes a disproportionate penalty for failure to fulfil administrative formalities.[123] Even with respect to the right to enter, Article 5(4) of the Directive—following the ECJ ruling on the relevant provisions of the predecessor Directive 68/360 in *MRAX*[124]—provides that where the EU national or family member does not have the requisite documents or visas, the Member State shall give them every reasonable opportunity to obtain the documents, to have them brought to them, or to prove their right to movement and residence by other means.

Some confusion was introduced by the ECJ's ruling in *Akrich* that a non-EU national spouse who was not lawfully resident in a Member State—e.g. who had entered unlawfully—could not avail of rights of movement and residence under EU law.[125] Even assuming that this ruling—which was softened by the Court's final statement that any decision to deport the spouse would have to take account of the right to family life under the European Convention on Human Rights[126]—were applicable also to the newer provisions of Directive 2004/38, it seems difficult to reconcile with the judgment one year earlier in *MRAX*.[127]

In *MRAX*, the ECJ ruled that although a Member State could impose proportionate sanctions for violation of entry requirements on a third-country national who was the spouse of an EU worker, the State could not 'refuse issue of a residence permit and issue an expulsion order against a third country national who is able to furnish proof of his identity and of his marriage to a national of a Member State on the sole ground that he has entered the territory of the Member State concerned unlawfully'.[128] Thus while *MRAX* indicated that the right of residence of a non-EU national spouse is not lost by virtue of having entered the State unlawfully, *Akrich* seemed to indicate that a spouse who is not lawfully resident in a Member State cannot benefit from rights under Article 10 of Regulation 1612/68.

In the subsequent case of *Jia*,[129] the ECJ did not—unlike the Advocate General—explicitly acknowledge the conflict between the *MRAX* and *Akrich* cases, but seemed to confine *Akrich* to its own facts. The Court in *Jia* described *Akrich* as having indicated the 'measures the

---

[121] See in particular Case 48/75 *Royer*, n. 36 above.

[122] Case 321/87 *Commission v. Belgium*, n. 62 above; Case C–24/97 *Commission v. Germany* [1998] ECR I–2133; Case C–215/03 *Oulane v. Minister voor Vreemdelingenzaken en Integratie* [2005] ECR I–1215, on minimizing the differences in treatment between nationals and non-nationals as far as checking compliance with the formal ID or residence requirements is concerned.

[123] Case 118/75 *Watson and Belmann* [1976] ECR 1185; Case C–363/89 *Roux* [1991] ECR I–273; Case C–459/99 *MRAX v. Belgium* [2002] ECR I–6591; Case C–215/03 *Oulane*, n. 122 above, where the ECJ nonetheless agreed that where an EU national could not provide proof of entitlement to residence, the Member State would ultimately be justified in deporting him or her.

[124] Case C–459/99 *MRAX*, n. 123 above; see also Case C–157/03 *Commission v. Spain* [2005] ECR I–2911.

[125] Case C–109/01 *Secretary of State for the Home Department v. Akrich* [2003] ECR I–9607, paras. 49–53.

[126] *Ibid.*, paras. 58–59.

[127] Case C–459/99 *MRAX*, n. 123 above.

[128] Case C–109/01 *Akrich*, n. 125 above, paras. 78–80.

[129] Case C–1/05 *Jia v. Migrationsverket*, 9 Jan. 2007.

Member States were entitled to take in order to combat steps taken by members of the family of a Community national who did not meet the conditions laid down by national law for entry and residence in a Member State', and did not repeat the statement in *Akrich* that a non-EU spouse who had entered a Member State illegally could not derive any rights of residence or movement under EU law. Further, the ECJ went on to distinguish the facts of *Jia*, and to rule that 'having regard to the judgment in ... *Akrich* ..., Community law does not require Member States to make the grant of a residence permit to nationals of a non-Member State, who are members of the family of a Community national who has exercised his or her right of free movement, subject to the condition that those family members have previously been residing lawfully in another Member State'.[130]

It may be that the ECJ in *Jia* was adopting a retrospective reading of *Akrich* which was closer to the opinion of the Advocate General in *Akrich*,[131] which would permit (but not require) a Member State to rely on national immigration rules to restrict the rights of a non-EU national spouse under Regulation 1612/68 where, for example, there had been a deliberate evasion of immigration law by that person.

(b) JOB-SEEKERS AND THE UNEMPLOYED

Article 7(3) of Directive 2004/38 governs the position of former workers who, although they have ceased working, nevertheless retain some of the rights of workers for themselves and their families. This provision replaces the pertinent parts of Directive 68/380, and supplements them with the relevant case law of the ECJ on voluntary and involuntary unemployment.

It provides that EU citizens who are no longer workers shall retain the status of worker where they are temporarily unable to work as the result of an illness or accident; or where they are involuntarily unemployed after having been employed for more than one year and having registered with the employment office as job-seekers. Where involuntary unemployment follows employment of less than one year, the Directive provides that the status of worker is to be retained for at least six months, if the person registers as a job-seeker. Article 7 also provides, following ECJ case law,[132] that a worker who embarks on vocational training may retain the status of worker, but that in cases where the worker has voluntarily given up employment, retention of this status is conditional upon the training being related to the previous employment.

The Directive does not otherwise deal with voluntary unemployment, and so the assumption may reasonably be made that persons will not retain the status of worker if they become voluntarily unemployed unless they are pursuing related vocational training.[133] However, as we have seen from the *Antonissen* and *Collins* cases,[134] a person who is seeking work enjoys certain

---

130 *Ibid.*, para 33. Another case which tends to reinforce the reasoning in *MRAX* and *Jia* that the rights of non-EU national spouses do not depend on the particular immigration conditions imposed by each Member State but rather on the underlying conditions set by EU law is Case C–157/03 *Commission* v. *Spain* [2005] ECR I–2911.

131 Ironically, the same Advocate General, Gelhoed AG, who had proposed a more liberal approach than the Court took in *Akrich*, later adopted a more restrictive approach in *Jia* than the Court ultimately did in the latter case.

132 Case C–3/90 *Bernini*, n. 28 above; Case C–357/89 *Raulin*, n. 30 above.

133 In Case C–413/01 *Ninni-Orasche* v. *Bundesminister für Wissenschaft, Verkehr und Kunst* [2003] ECR I–13187, the ECJ ruled that a worker would not necessarily be considered to be *voluntarily* unemployed upon the expiry of a fixed-term contract, since it may well be the case that an employee has little or no control over the nature or duration of the contract s/he is offered.

134 Case C–292/89 *Antonissen*, n. 117 above; Case C–138/02 *Collins*, n. 21 above.

rights under Article 39. By comparison with the category of persons in Article 7(3) who have become involuntarily employed in the host Member State, these job-seekers do not enjoy the status of 'worker' in the full sense of the term, although they enjoy a right of residence during the period they are seeking work, and they enjoy access to certain benefits which are specifically intended to facilitate access to employment.[135]

As far as the length of this period is concerned, the ECJ in *Antonissen* left it somewhat flexible, ruling that while the period of six months allowed by the UK seemed reasonable, the right to remain in search of work must continue even after that period so long as the person concerned 'provides evidence that he is continuing to seek employment and that he has genuine chances of being engaged'.[136] Although this is not explicitly governed by the provisions of the Directive, recital 9, concerning the three-month right of residence for all EU citizens, declares that it is without prejudice to the 'more favourable treatment applicable to job-seekers as recognized by the case-law of the Court of Justice'.

It should also be noted that the ECJ also indicated in *Collins* that although rights linked to the status of worker may be retained even when someone is no longer in an employment relationship, the relevant links with the status of worker will not continue for an excessively lengthy period of time.[137] In *Collins* itself, the applicant job-seeker could not rely on the fact that he had been employed as a worker seventeen years earlier to claim current entitlement to rights as a worker.

(c) THE RIGHT OF PERMANENT RESIDENCE

One of the innovations of Directive 2004/38, as we have seen, was the introduction of the right of permanent residence for EU citizens and their families (including non-nationals) who have resided lawfully for a continuous period of five years in the host State. These provisions replace and build on the previously existing legislation allowing workers or their families under specific conditions to acquire a right of permanent residence in less than three years in the event of retirement, injury, or death.[138]

Articles 16–18 indicate the conditions under which EU citizens may enjoy this right, which clearly covers EU workers and their families. Article 16(3) makes provision for temporary absences, and 16(4) provides that the right of permanent residence may only be lost through absences of more than two consecutive years. Article 17 details the shorter qualifying period for workers and their families in the event of retirement, incapacity, or death, and Article 18 concerns the right of permanent residence of family members of EU nationals, including workers, who have satisfied the five-year legal residence requirement.

The administrative formalities are regulated by Articles 19–21. A document certifying permanent residence is to be issued as soon as possible to EU nationals who have verified their duration of residence. Non-EU-national family members of workers who enjoy a derivative right of permanent residence are to be given a 'permanent residence card', which is to be automatically renewed every ten years, and the validity of the card will not be affected by absences of less than two consecutive years. Continuity of residence, for any person with the right of permanent residence, will be broken by an expulsion decision which has been enforced against the person.

---

[135] Case C–138/02, *Collins*, n. 21 above; Case C–258/04 *Ioannidis*, n. 41 above.
[136] Case C–292/89, *Antonissen*, n. 117 above, para. 21.
[137] Case C–138/02 *Collins*, n. 21 above.
[138] See n. 12 above.

(d) CONDITIONS UNDER WHICH THE RIGHT OF RESIDENCE FOR WORKERS AND THEIR FAMILIES IS ENJOYED

Articles 22–26 regulate conditions under which the right of residence—including the right of permanent residence—is to be enjoyed. It is to cover the whole of the territory, and includes the right of equal treatment with nationals of the host State within the scope of the Treaty, subject to such exceptions as are provided for by the Treaty or in secondary law.[139] Article 23 guarantees the right to take up employment for EU- and non-EU-national family members alike, replacing the relevant provisions of Regulation 1612/68, which is discussed below.

7. SUBSTANTIVE RIGHTS AND SOCIAL ADVANTAGES: REGULATION 1612/68

(a) REGULATION 1612/68

The main focus thus far has been on the negative effects of Article 39 and the associated legislation: the prohibition of discrimination and of barriers to freedom of movement, and the prohibition of entry visas or similar restrictions. The other side of the coin is that this Treaty Article confers positive, substantive rights of freedom of movement and equality of treatment on EU workers. These rights are, to some extent, given flesh by the secondary legislation, and in particular by Regulation 1612/68,[140] which has been amended by Directive 2004/38.

The ECJ's approach to Regulation 1612/68 has been similar to its approach to the other free movement legislation, in ruling that the legislation protects and facilitates the exercise of the primary rights conferred by the Treaty, rather than of itself creating rights. However, although the principle of equal treatment (which is now also expressly contained in Article 24 of Directive 2004/38) forms the backbone of the legislation, its degree of detail and specificity goes beyond what is express in the Treaty, and requires the Member States to ensure that Community workers enjoy a wide range of the substantive benefits available to nationals. In particular, the Regulation covers the families of EU workers, which are not mentioned in the Treaty chapter.

There are three titles within Part I of the Regulation, Title I (Articles 1–6) on eligibility for employment, Title II (Articles 7–9) on equality of treatment within employment, and Title III (formerly Articles 10–12, but Articles 10–11 have been repealed and replaced by Directive 2000/34) on workers' families. Part II of the Regulation contains detailed provisions which require co-operation amongst the relevant employment agencies of the Member States, and between the Member State agencies, the Commission, and the European Co-ordination Office, on applications for employment and the clearance of vacancies. Part III of the Regulation established an Advisory Committee and a Technical Committee made up of Member State representatives, to ensure close co-operation on matters concerning free movement of workers and employment. Parts II and III of the Regulation, which were amended several times over the years, have attracted comparatively little legal attention. Yet they may be

---

[139] This would include exceptions such as 'employment in the public service', benefits such as rewards for war-time loyalty on which the ECJ has ruled, and the right to vote in national elections, which are discussed below.

[140] [1968] OJ L257/2, [1968] OJ Spec. Ed. 475.

very significant for a worker who is seeking to move to another Member State to find employment. The Member State authorities are required to provide detailed information on vacancies, working conditions, and the state of the national labour market, and to co-operate with the Commission in conducting studies on various matters.

However, it is Part I of the Regulation which has been the subject of most comment and analysis, and its provisions have generated a large amount of litigation. Article 1 sets out the right of Member State nationals to take up employment in another Member State under the same conditions as its nationals, and Article 2 prohibits discrimination against such workers or employees in concluding and performing contracts of employment. Articles 3 and 4 prohibit certain directly or indirectly discriminatory administrative practices, such as reserving a quota of posts for national workers, restricting advertising or applications, or setting special recruitment or registration procedures for other Member State nationals, but with an exception for genuine linguistic requirements.[141] Article 5 guarantees the same assistance from employment offices to non-nationals as well as to nationals, and Article 6 prohibits discriminatory vocational, or medical criteria for recruitment and appointment. Article 7 fleshes out Article 39(2) of the Treaty by providing for the same social and tax advantages for nationals and non-nationals, for equal access to vocational training, and declares void any discriminatory provisions of collective or individual employment agreements. Article 8 provides for equality of trade-union rights with nationals,[142] and Article 9 for the same access to all rights and benefits in matters of housing.

Prior to the adoption of Directive 2004/38, Article 10 of the Regulation set out the family members who had the right to install themselves with a worker who was employed in another Member State. These were the spouse and their descendants, who were either under 21 or dependent,[143] and dependent relatives in the ascending line of the worker and spouse.[144] This group has now been extended by Article 2(2) of Directive 2004/38 to include, along with spouses, a partner with whom an EU citizen has a registered partnership under the national legislation of a Member State, if the host Member State treats registered partnerships as equivalent to marriage. Similarly, the under-21 or dependent children of a registered partner and the dependent direct relatives in the ascending line of the registered partner are also now included by Article 2(2).

Article 3 of Directive 2004/38, extending the previous provision in Article 10(2) of Regulation 1612/68, requires Member States to 'facilitate entry and residence' for other family members (whatever their nationality), who in the State of origin were dependants or members of the household of the EU citizen (in this case, the worker). The two innovations introduced by Directive 2004/38 to this provision are that Member States must also facilitate the admission of (i) any family member where serious health grounds strictly require the personal care of that family member by the EU citizen, and (ii) the partner with whom the Union citizen has a durable relationship, duly attested. Article 3 provides that the obligation of the host State is to 'undertake an extensive examination of the personal circumstances' and to provide a justification for any denial of entry or residence to such persons. The provisions of Directive 2004/38 governing registered partners and this second-tier category of partners in a 'durable

---

[141] On linguistic requirements see *Groener* and *Angonese*, nn. 58–59 above.

[142] Case C–213/90 *ASTI*, n. 106 above; Case C–118/92 *Commission* v. *Luxembourg* [1994] ECR I–1891; Case C–465/01 *Commission* v. *Austria* [2004] ECR I–8291.

[143] The notion of dependency in Art. 10 is, according to the ECJ in Case 316/85 *Lebon*, n. 38 above, a matter of fact, in that it includes a member of the family who is in fact supported by the worker, whatever the reason for the support.

[144] Case C–1/05 *Jia*, n. 129 above, on what dependency in fact means, and how it can be proven.

relationship' represent the cautious outcome of a heated legislative debate concerning the definition of family and the need to move beyond traditional definitions by conferring rights also on same-sex and non-marital partners.

Article 11 of Regulation 1612/68, which provided that the spouse and children mentioned in Article 10 had the right to take up activity as employed persons in the host Member State, has been superseded by Article 23 of Directive 2004/38, discussed above, which grants this right to *all* family members covered by the Directive, whatever their nationality.[145] And we have seen that Article 24 of the Directive provides a new explicit equal treatment guarantee for all EU nationals and their family members who enjoy the right of residence, which clearly includes workers and their families. Article 12 of Regulation 1612/68, which has been updated by Directive 2004/38, in part to reflect ECJ case law on the subject, provides for equal access for the children of a resident worker to the State's educational courses.

Regulation 1612/68 has provoked a good deal of litigation.[146] Indeed, Article 7 has probably been the most fruitful provision for workers and their families, raising interesting questions about when, if at all, Member States are entitled to treat their own nationals more favourably than other EC nationals. Clearly, there are some advantages enjoyed by citizens of a State which are not available to others, for example political rights such as the right to vote in national elections.[147] The evolving interpretation by the ECJ of this Article and its related provisions illustrates how the initial conferral of limited rights on economic actors has evolved into something more substantial, and this is reflected in the new Article 24 of Directive 2004/38, which expressly extends the general equal treatment principle (subject to the exceptions provided for in the treaty and secondary legislation) to all lawfully resident EU nationals and their families.

(b) ARTICLE 7(2) OF REGULATION 1612/68

Initially in *Michel S*, the Court read Article 7(2) in a limited way, ruling that it concerned only benefits connected with employment.[148] Shortly afterwards, however, the ECJ departed from this restrictive interpretation and ruled that Article 7(2) should be read so as to include all social and tax advantages, whether or not attached to the contract of employment,[149] that it applied not just to workers but also to surviving family members of a deceased worker, and that although Article 7 refers only to advantages for workers, it covers any advantage to a family member which provides an indirect advantage to the worker.[150]

The limits to the rights which may be claimed by a worker under Article 7(2) were addressed in the case of *Even*, concerning preferential retirement-pension treatment given in Belgium to nationals who were in receipt of a Second World War service invalidity pension granted by an Allied nation.

---

[145] Art. 11 of Reg 1612/68 was interpreted by the ECJ to mean that the non-EU-national spouse of an EU national migrant worker in a Member State had the right to work only in the Member State in which the spouse was employed: Case C–10/05 *Mattern*, n. 29 above.

[146] Many of the cases, in particular those concerning the meaning of 'social advantages' in Art. 7(2), are concerned also with distinguishing a social advantage under this Reg. from a social security benefit under Reg. 1408/71, since the latter is more restrictive than the concept of a social advantage in Art. 7(2).

[147] See, however, the Commission's reference to the ECtHR decision in *Piermont v. France*, Series A no. 314 (1994), in its second report on citizenship of the Union, COM(97)230, which suggested that nationals of EU Member States should not be treated as 'aliens' for the purposes of restricting their political activities.

[148] Case 76/72 *Michel S v. Fonds National de Reclassement Handicapés* [1973] ECR 457.

[149] Case 32/75 *Cristini v. SNCF* [1975] ECR 1085, para 13.

[150] Case 63/76 *Inzirillo* [1976] ECR 2057; Case 94/84 *Deak* [1985] ECR 1873; Case 152/82 *Forcheri v. Belgium* [1983] ECR 2323.

Case 207/78 **Ministère Public v. Even and ONPTS**
[1979] ECR 2019

THE ECJ

22. It follows from all its provisions and from the objective pursued that the advantages which this regulation extends to workers who are nationals of other Member States are all those which, whether or not linked to a contract of employment, are generally granted to national workers primarily because of their objective status as workers or by virtue of the mere fact of their residence on the national territory and the extension of which to workers who are nationals of other Member States therefore seems suitable to facilitate their mobility within the Community.

23. ...The main reason for a benefit such as that granted by the Belgian national legislation in question to certain categories of national workers is the services which those in receipt of the benefit have rendered in wartime to their own country and its essential objective is to give those nationals an advantage by reason of the hardships suffered for that country.

24. Such a benefit, which is based on a scheme of national recognition, cannot therefore be considered as an advantage granted to a national worker by reason primarily of his status of worker or resident on the national territory and for that reason does not fulfil the essential characteristics of the 'social advantages' referred to in Article 7(2) of Regulation No 1612/68.

Similarly in *de Vos* the ECJ ruled that the statutory obligation on an employer to continue paying pension insurance contributions on behalf of workers who were absent on military service was not a 'social advantage' to the worker within Article 7(2) of the Regulation, since it was an advantage provided by the State as partial compensation for the obligation to perform military service, rather than merely an advantage granted to workers by virtue of the fact of their residence in the Member State.[151]

By comparison in *Ugliola*,[152] which concerned the taking into account of military service in calculating seniority at work, the Court found that there was impermissible discrimination under Article 7(2). The difference between the benefit which the employer was required to provide in *Ugliola* and that in *de Vos* is rather difficult to discern, since each was concerned with ensuring that workers who were away on military service would not be disadvantaged as a result. However, the ECJ seemed to treat the obligation to protect a worker's seniority and security of tenure as a condition of employment imposed by the State on employers in *Ugliola*, whereas the obligation on employers to continue paying pension contributions was treated as part of the State's mechanism for compensating those undergoing military service rather than as being linked to the employment contract.

Similarly in *Baldinger*, the ECJ ruled in relation to an allowance for former prisoners of war which was paid only to nationals of the Member State that because 'compensatory allowances which are linked to service rendered in wartime by citizens to their own country and whose essential aim is to provide those citizens with a benefit because of the hardships they endured for that country ... does not fall within the category of advantages granted to national workers

---

[151] Case C–315/94 *De Vos* v. *Bielefeld* [1996] ECR I–1417, paras. 17–22. Contrast Case C–131/96 *Romero* v. *Landesversicherungsanstalt* [1997] ECR I–3659 dealing with Reg. 1408/71 on social security rather than Reg. 1612/68.

[152] Case 15/69 *Ugliola*, n. 51 above.

principally because of their status as workers or national residents' and it therefore did not fall within Article 7(2).[153]

In *Reina*, an interest-free 'childbirth loan' granted under German law to German nationals in order to stimulate the birth-rate of the population was held to be a social advantage within Article 7(2).[154] Thus an Italian couple in Germany, one of whom was a worker, was also required to be eligible for the loan, despite the argument made by the defendant bank that, being principally a matter of demographic policy, such a discretionary loan fell within the area of political rights linked to nationality. The Court however ruled that the loan was a social advantage since its main aim was to alleviate the financial burden on low-income families, even if was also a part of national demographic policy.[155]

(c) ARTICLE 7(3) OF REGULATION 1612/68 AND EDUCATIONAL RIGHTS FOR WORKERS

Article 7(3) provides that EC workers shall 'by virtue of the same right and under the same conditions as national workers, have access to training in vocational schools and retraining centres'. The Article has been held to confer equal rights of access for non-national workers to all the advantages, grants, and facilities available to nationals.

It was somewhat restrictively interpreted by the ECJ in *Lair*, ruling that universities were not 'vocational schools' since the concept of a vocational school referred 'exclusively to institutions which provide only instruction either alternating with or closely linked to an occupational activity, particularly during apprenticeship'.[156] The ECJ however went on to hold that workers could also invoke the 'social advantages' provision of Article 7(2) to claim entitlement to any advantage available to improve their professional qualifications and social advancement, such as a maintenance grant in an educational institution not covered by Article 7(3).[157] Nonetheless, the Court imposed other limits on the ability of workers to invoke Article 7(2) in this way by ruling that, although they did not have to be in the employment relationship just before or during the course of study, and although a fixed minimum period of employment could not be required by a State,[158] there must be some continuity or link between the previous work and the purpose of the studies in question.[159] The one exception permitted was where a worker *involuntarily* became unemployed and was 'obliged by conditions on the job market to undertake occupational retraining in another field of activity'.[160] This case law is confirmed by Article 7(3)(d) of Directive 2004/38.

The likely reason for the limitations imposed by the ECJ on Article 7(2) and (3) is that the status of worker carries with it a substantial range of social and other benefits, and the Member States wish to restrict those claiming such benefits to 'genuine' workers. If someone gives up

---

153 Case C–386/02 *Baldinger* v. *Pensionsversicherungsanstalt der Arbeiter* [2004] ECR I–8411.

154 Case 65/81 *Reina* v. *Landeskreditbank Baden-Württemberg* [1982] ECR 33. See also Case C–111/91, *Commission* v. *Luxembourg* [1993] ECR I–817.

155 See also Case C–237/94 *O'Flynn*, n. 61 above, that a state payment to cover funeral expenses falls within Art. 7(2).

156 Case 39/86, *Lair* [1988] ECR 3161.

157 Case 235/87 *Matteucci* v. *Communauté Français de Belgique* [1988] ECR 5589; Case C–337/97 *Meeusen*, n. 16 above.

158 See Case 157/84 *Frascogna* v. *Caisse des Dépôts et Consignations* [1985] ECR 1739 on the requirement of a fixed period of residence; Case C–3/90 *Bernini*, n. 28 above; Case C–357/89 *Raulin*, n. 30 above.

159 Case 39/86 *Lair*, n. 156 above, para. 37.

160 *Ibid.*

work to pursue education or training, ceasing to be economically active, the States clearly fear that this could enable migrants to gain generous educational benefits after a short and purely instrumental period of employment. The Court also made clear in *Brown*, above, that not only must there be a link between the previous employment and the subsequent studies, but the employment must not be 'ancillary' to the main purpose of pursuing a course of study.[161]

In *Ninni-Orasche*, however, the ECJ ruled that the conduct of a person who took up a short term of employment as a waitress only several years after entering the host Member State, and who shortly after finishing that term of employment obtained a diploma entitling her to enrol at university in that State, was irrelevant to her status as worker or to the question whether the work was 'ancillary'.[162] The ECJ similarly—echoing its rulings in *Akrich*[163] and *Chen*[164] in which it dismissed the allegations of abuse of rights—ruled that there was no such thing as 'abusively creating' the situation where she became a worker for the purposes of EC law.[165] However, the Court also ruled that, while the fact that the fixed-term contract she had accepted had come to an end did not necessarily make her 'voluntarily unemployed', factors such as the short term of the job and the fact that she obtained the diploma entitling her to enrol at university immediately afterwards, might be relevant to the question whether she took up employment with the sole aim of benefiting from the system of student assistance in the host State.

Finally, there is now in Article 35 of Directive 2004/38 a novel exception permitting Member States to refuse or withdraw rights under the Directive 'in the case of abuse of rights or fraud'. However, we have seen that the Court's case law so far has not confirmed any example of abuse or fraud, other than the case of a sham marriage entered for the purpose of gaining EU rights.

(d) ARTICLE 12 OF REGULATION 1612/68: EDUCATIONAL RIGHTS FOR CHILDREN

Article 12 provides that 'the children of a national of a Member State, who is or has been employed in the territory of another Member State, shall be admitted to courses of general education, apprenticeship and vocational training under the same conditions as the nationals of that State, if those children reside in its territory'. Member States are to encourage 'steps allowing such children to follow the above mentioned courses under the best conditions'.[166]

We saw in *Michel S*[167] that the ECJ interpreted Article 7(2) narrowly, but in the same case it interpreted Article 12 broadly, so that a benefit for disabled nationals was included in Article 12 on access to education for the children of workers.[168] This expansive reading was continued in *Casagrande*,[169] where the ECJ ruled—controversially, at the time[170]—that Article 12 applied

---

[161] Case 197/86 *Brown*, n. 34 above.

[162] Case C–413/01 *Ninni-Orasche*, n. 133 above.

[163] Case C–109/01 *Akrich*, n. 125 above.

[164] Case C–200/02 *Zhu and Chen* v. *Secretary of State for the Home Department* [2004] ECR I–9925. See the discussion in Ch. 23.

[165] Case C–413/01 *Ninni-Orasche*, n. 133 above.

[166] See also the provisions of Dir. 77/486 on language teaching for the children of migrant workers: [1977] OJ L199/32.

[167] N.148 above.

[168] For a later ruling in which the ECJ gave a broader interpretation to the personal scope of Art. 12 than that of Art. 7 of the Dir. see Case C–7/94 *Landesamt für Ausbildungsförderung Nordrhein-Westfalen* v. *Lubor Gaal* [1996] ECR I–1031.

[169] Case 9/74 *Casagrande* v. *Landeshauptstadt München* [1974] ECR 773.

[170] Strong submissions were made that the areas of educational and cultural policy in Germany were specifically reserved to the *Länder*, and that this interpretation would constitute an encroachment on those powers by Community law. See Warner AG, *ibid.*, 783–784.

not just to admission to courses but also to any 'general measures intended to facilitate educational attendance', including an educational grant. Essentially, Article 12 places the children of EC workers residing in a Member State in the same position as the children of nationals of that State in so far as any education is concerned, which means that they have considerably more generous educational rights than their EC-worker parents.

It has been held to require that, where grants are available to the children of nationals to study abroad, these must also be made available to the children of migrant EC workers, even if the studies abroad are to be in the Member State of the child's nationality.[171]

In *Gaal*, the ECJ ruled that the term children in Article 12 was wider than that in Article 10, so that Article 12 conferred educational rights on children who were over 21 and non-dependent, even though they were not covered by Article 10.[172] The ECJ held that the principle in Article 12 required the children of a migrant worker to be able to continue their studies in order to complete their education successfully, so long as the children had lived with a parent in the Member State at a time when that parent resided there as a worker and, presumably, although the ECJ does not actually say this, at a time when the child was either dependent or under 21.

In *Echternach and Moritz*, the ECJ ruled that Article 12 covers the child's right to educational assistance even where the working parents have returned to their State of nationality.[173] While the rationale given in *Echternach* was that the child in question was obliged by reason of the non-compatibility of educational systems to remain and to complete the education in the host State, the ECJ moved beyond this in *Baumbast and R.*, ruling that it would offend against both the letter and the spirit of Article 12 to limit the rights of children to remain in the host State to complete their education only to situations where they could not complete it in their Member State of origin.[174] The Court continued its expansive ruling in *Baumbast* by declaring that the fact that the parents of the children concerned had meanwhile divorced, the fact that only one parent was a citizen of the Union and that parent had since ceased to be a migrant worker in the host Member State, and the fact that the children were not themselves citizens of the Union were all irrelevant to the enjoyment of the rights under Article 12.[175]

This case law is now confirmed by Article 12(3) of Directive 2004/38, which also confirms the right of the children (and the right of residence of the carer-parent) to remain and complete their education after the death of the worker parent. However, in a situation where the worker has left the host State and returned to the Member State of origin in which her children also live, EC law does not confer any right to have her children's studies financed by the former host State under the same conditions as those applying to nationals.[176]

(e) RIGHTS OF FAMILIES AS PARASITIC ON THE WORKER'S RIGHTS

Although the interpretation of 'social advantages' in Article 7 is broad, it is only workers and the family members covered by Directive 2004/38 (formerly by Article 10 of Regulation 1612/68) who may avail of them. In *Lebon*, the ECJ ruled that once the child of a worker

---

[171] Case C–308/89 *Di Leo* v. *Land Berlin* [1990] ECR I–4185.
[172] Case C–7/94 *Gaal*, n. 168 above.
[173] Cases 389 and 390/87 *Echternach and Moritz* [1989] ECR 723.
[174] Case C–413/99 *Baumbast and R.* v. *Secretary of State for the Home Department* [2002] ECR I–7091.
[175] *Ibid.*, paras. 56–63.
[176] Case C–33/99 *Fahmi and Cerdeiro-Pinedo Amado* [2001] ECR I–2415.

reached 21, and was no longer dependent on the worker,[177] benefits to that child could not be construed as an advantage to the worker.[178] And we have seen how lawfully resident job-seekers are entitled under EC law only to those advantages which are specifically made available for job-seekers nationally.[179]

The creative interpretation given by the ECJ to Article 7(2) is evident also in *Reed*, where the ECJ ruled that the possibility for a migrant worker to have his unmarried companion reside with him could constitute a social advantage under Article 7(2), where the host Member State treated stable companions as akin to spouses.[180] This was so even though Reed's companion would not have been covered by Article 10 of the Regulation at the time, since it covered only marital spouses. Since the case was decided, as we have seen, Directive 2004/38 has included registered partners (in States which recognize the status of registered partnerships) within the protected family, and also requires Member States generally to facilitate the admission of companions in a 'durable relationship'.

The 2004 Directive also clarifies a question which arose in *Diatta*[181] and *Singh*[182] concerning the status of a spouse—and in particular a spouse who lacks EU nationality—under Regulation 1612/68. The ECJ in those cases had indicated that, even where the spouses were separated or where a decree *nisi* of divorce had been granted, the non-working spouse did not lose the right of residence while the marriage was still formally in existence and had not actually been dissolved. The Court in *Baumbast* had also ruled that a non-EU national spouse could, even after divorce, continue residing in the host Member State under EC law where the children (whether or not they had EU nationality) were exercising their educational rights under Article 12 of the Regulation and the divorced spouse was their primary carer.[183]

Article 13(1) of Directive 2004/38 now provides that even after divorce, annulment of marriage, or termination of a registered partnership, the right of residence of the family members who are EU nationals will not be affected. In the case of non-EU national family members, Article 13(2) provides that the right of residence will not be lost where (a) the marriage or registered partnership had lasted at least three years including one year in the host Member State, or (b) where the spouse who is not an EU national retains custody of the EU citizen's children, or (c) where it is warranted by particularly difficult circumstances such as having been a victim of domestic violence during the marriage/partnership, or (d) where the non-EU national spouse or partner has the right of access to a minor child and where the court has ruled that such access must be in the host Member State, for as long as required.

Article 13 provides that such family members will retain the right of residence on an exclusively personal basis, and that if they are to go on to qualify for the right of permanent residence, they must show that they are themselves workers or self-employed or have sufficient resources to avoid becoming a burden on the host State. The case of *Akrich*—and, since then, Article 35 of Directive 2004/38—make clear, however, that a spouse will not gain any rights of residence or social advantages if the marriage is merely a marriage of convenience or a 'sham'.[184]

---

[177] For a recent interpretation of dependency see Case C–1/05 *Jia*, n. 129 above.

[178] Case 316/85, n. 38 above. See also Case C–243/91 *Belgium* v. *Taghavi* [1992] ECR I–4401; Case C–33/99 *Fahmi*, n. 176 above.

[179] Case C–138/02 *Collins*, n. 21 above; Case C–258/04 *Ioannidis*, n. 41 above.

[180] Case 59/85 *Netherlands* v. *Reed* [1986] ECR 1283.

[181] Case 267/83 *Diatta* v. *Land Berlin* [1985] ECR 567.

[182] Case C–370/90 *R.* v. *Immigration Appeal Tribunal, ex p. Secretary of State for the Home Department* [1992] ECR I–4265.

[183] Case C–413/99 *Baumbast*, n. 174 above.

[184] Case C–109/01 *Akrich*, n. 125 above, paras. 57–58.

(f) FAMILY MEMBERS IN AN INTERNAL SITUATION

The *Akrich* case also highlights some of the curious distinctions which arise as a result of the ECJ's approach to the so-called 'wholly internal situation', which has been the subject of considerable academic criticism.[185]

In *Saunders*[186] the ECJ ruled that a national could not rely on Article 39 in his or her own Member State to challenge a restriction on freedom of movement, since there was no factor connecting the situation with Community law.[187] This was rather more harshly illustrated in *Morson and Jhanjan*, where it was held that two Dutch nationals working in the Netherlands had no right under Community law to bring their parents, of Surinamese nationality, into the country to reside with them.[188] Had they been nationals of any other Member State working in the Netherlands, they would have been entitled under Article 10 of Regulation 1612/68 (now Article 2 of Directive 2004/38). However, because they were nationals working in their own Member State 'who had never exercised the right to freedom of movement within the Community', they had no rights under Community law.[189]

This was confirmed in *Uecker and Jacquet*, despite the referring German court's obvious invitation to the ECJ to depart from its previous position.[190] The case concerned two non-EC nationals who came to Germany to live with their spouses, both of whom were German nationals residing and working in Germany. They invoked Article 7 of Regulation 1612/68 to claim equal treatment with German nationals in their employment, but the ECJ reiterated its stance on wholly internal situations, despite the national court's suggestion that the sort of reverse discrimination brought about by that stance was in conflict with 'the fundamental principle of a Community moving towards European Union'.[191]

In *Singh*, however, the situation was somewhat different. An Indian national had married a British national, and had travelled with her to Germany where they had both worked for some years before returning to the UK. The UK argued that the British spouse's right to re-enter the UK derived from national law and not from Community law. However, the ECJ clearly considered that the period of working activity in another Member State made all the difference, and enabled Singh now to claim rights as the spouse of a Community worker.

Case C–370/90 **R. v. Immigration Appeal Tribunal and Surinder Singh, ex parte Secretary of State for the Home Department**
[1992] ECR I–4265

119. A national of a Member State might be deterred from leaving his country of origin in order to pursue an activity as an employed or self-employed person as envisaged by the Treaty

---

185 N. Nic Shuibhne, 'Free Movement of Persons and the Wholly Internal Rule: Time to Move on?' (2002) 39 *CMLRev.* 731. Compare C. Ritter, 'Purely Internal Situations, Reverse Discrimination, Guimont, Dzodzi and Article 234' (2006) 31 *ELRev.* 690.

186 Case 175/78 *Saunders*, n. 77 above.

187 Compare however the recent Draft Recommendation of the European Ombudsman to the Commission concerning a future intention to travel abroad, in Complaint 3317/2004/GG, available at www.ombudsman.europa.eu.

188 Cases 35 and 36/82 *Morson*, n. 79 above.

189 *Ibid.*, para. 17.

190 Cases C–64 and 65/96 *Uecker* and *Jacquet*, n. 78 above.

191 *Ibid.*, para. 22.

in the territory of another Member State if, on returning to the Member State of which he is a national in order to pursue an activity there as an employed or self-employed person, the conditions of his entry and residence were not at least equivalent to those which he would enjoy under the Treaty or secondary law in the territory of another Member State.

20. He would in particular be deterred from so doing if his spouse and children were not also permitted to enter and reside in the territory of his Member State of origin under conditions at least equivalent to those granted them by Community law in the territory of another Member State.

The Court subsequently confirmed this stance in *Akrich*, in which it rejected the suggestion that there was any 'abuse of rights' involved where a couple moved on a temporary basis to work in another Member State in order to avoid the 'internal situation' problem and to acquire rights for a non-EU national in the spouse's Member State of origin.[192]

We saw that some confusion was introduced by the ECJ's ruling in *Akrich* that a non-EU national spouse who was not lawfully resident in a Member State—e.g., who had entered unlawfully—could not avail of rights under Article 10 of Regulation 1612/68, and could not 'cure' the illegality by moving to work in another Member State and returning to the original Member State where s/he had been residing unlawfully.[193] It seems from the cases of *MRAX*[194] and *Jia*[195] however that the ECJ subsequently limited the scope of *Akrich*, and distinguished it on its facts from other cases where a non-EU-national family member entered without satisfying national immigration requirements, but nonetheless was entitled to enjoy rights of movement and residence under EU law.[196]

8. PUBLIC POLICY, SECURITY, AND HEALTH RESTRICTIONS ON THE RIGHT OF ENTRY AND RESIDENCE: DIRECTIVE 2004/38

Articles 27–33 of Directive 2004/38 govern the restrictions on the right of entry and residence which Member States may impose on grounds of public policy, security, or health. These provisions repeal and replace the previous Directive 64/221, and incorporate much of the relevant jurisprudence of the Court of Justice.

One of the innovations of Directive 2004/38 is to introduce three different levels of protection against expulsion on these grounds: (i) a general level of protection for all individuals covered by EU law; (ii) an enhanced level of protection for individuals who have already gained the right of permanent residence on the territory of a Member State; and (iii) a super-enhanced level of protection for minors or for those who have resided for ten years in a host State. The Directive also simplifies the previous requirements of Directive 64/221 by making access to judicial and administrative redress procedures compulsory, and by eliminating references to comparability with national procedures.

---

[192] Case C–109/01 *Akrich*, n. 125 above, paras. 55–56.
[193] *Ibid.*, paras. 49–53.
[194] Case C–459/99 *MRAX*, n. 123 above.
[195] Case C–1/05 *Jia*, n. 129 above.
[196] See also Case C–503/03 *Commission* v. *Spain* [2006] ECR I–1097.

Article 27 begins by setting out the general principles governing the exercise of the exceptions, specifying that all measures adopted on grounds of public policy or security shall comply with the principle of proportionality[197] and shall be based exclusively on the personal conduct of the individual concerned. The Directive makes clear, as did its predecessor, that the public policy, security, and health exceptions cannot be invoked to serve economic ends. Article 27(1) provides that past criminal convictions are not in themselves grounds for taking such measures. This provision was earlier interpreted in *Santillo* to mean that such convictions may be relied on as a basis for expulsion only where the past conviction in some way provides evidence of a *present* threat,[198] and that the threat must be assessed by the Member State at the time of the decision ordering expulsion.[199] Article 27(2) goes on to incorporate the case law of the ECJ in *Bouchereau*,[200] providing that the personal conduct of the individual must represent a 'genuine, present, and sufficiently serious threat affecting one of the fundamental interests of society', and stipulates—drawing on *Bonsignore, Bouchereau, Adoui and Cornuaille*, and a steady stream of subsequent case law—that general preventative measures or justifications isolated from the particular facts of the case are unacceptable.[201] The *Calfa* judgment in particular indicates that automatic expulsion for commission of a particular offence, without any consideration of whether any specific threat was posed by the individual in question, is prohibited.[202] Article 27(3) sets a time limit after entry into the host Member State for the latter to seek, and for the Member State of origin to provide, information on an EU national's police record, and stipulates that such information shall not be sought on a routine basis. Subparagraph (4) provides that upon expulsion the Member State of origin must re-admit the person in question.

Despite the substantive and procedural conditions imposed on the exercise of the exceptions in the Directive, the ECJ has nevertheless always made clear that States retain a certain discretion as regards the public policy exception (and, though perhaps to a lesser extent, the public security exception) since 'the particular circumstances justifying recourse to the concept of public policy may vary from one country to another and from one period to another'.[203] Or, as the ECJ phrased it more recently, no 'uniform code of values' is imposed by EC law.[204]

There is however a significant body of case law concerning the circumstances in which a Member State may expel EU nationals or their family members on public policy or security grounds. In *Van Duyn*, the ECJ ruled that a Member State need not criminalize an organization whose activities it considers to be socially harmful—in this case, the Church of Scientology—in order to justify taking restrictive action against non-national members of the

---

[197] The proportionality requirement, based on ECJ case law, has been added by the 2004 legislation to the original provision of Dir. 68/360.

[198] The ECJ in Case 30/77 *Bouchereau* [1977] ECR 1999 also suggested that past conduct alone, rather than the likelihood of future conduct, might be sufficient to indicate that someone is a *present* threat to public policy, but it is not easy to imagine what this might be.

[199] Case 131/79 *Santillo* [1980] ECR 1585; Case C–441/02 *Commission* v. *Germany* [2006] ECR I–3449.

[200] Case 30/77 *Bouchereau*, n. 198 above.

[201] Case 67/74 *Bonsignore* [1975] ECR 297; Cases 115 and 116/81 *Adoui and Cornuaille* [1982] ECR 1665. See also Case C–340/97 *Nazli* v. *Stadt Nürnberg* [2000] ECR I–957 (concerning workers covered by the EEC–Turkey Assocation Agreement); Cases C–482 and 493/01 *Orfanopoulos and others* v. *Land Baden-Württemberg* [2004] ECR I–5257; Case C–441/02 *Commission* v. *Germany*, n. 199 above; Case C–383/03 *Dogan* v. *Sicherheitsdirektion für das Bundesland Vorarlberg* [2005] ECR I–6237. See also Case C–503/03 *Commission* v. *Spain*, n. 196 above, ruling that the same requirements apply to the circumstances in which a Member State can issue a 'Schengen alert' against a third-country-national spouse of an EU worker.

[202] Case C–348/96 *Calfa* [1999] ECR I–11.

[203] Case 41/74 *Van Duyn* v. *Home Office* [1974] ECR 1337, para. 18.

[204] Case C–268/99 *Jany*, n. 20 above.

organization on grounds of public policy and security.[205] The case was controversial because it appeared to enable a State to take repressive measures—specifically, a refusal to permit entry—against an EU migrant for conduct (employment in the organization) which did not give rise to any kind of restriction against nationals of the host State.

Later cases however emphasized the need for some kind of comparability, if not exactly equality, in the treatment of nationals and non-nationals as far as such alleged threats to public policy and security were concerned. In *Adoui and Cornuaille*,[206] for instance, the ECJ ruled that Member States may not expel a national of another Member State from its territory or refuse entry by reason of conduct—in this case, suspected prostitution—which, when attributable to its own nationals, does not give rise to genuine and effective or repressive measures intended to combat such conduct.

Similarly in *Rutili*, the ECJ ruled that partial measures of territorial restriction, short of expulsion, could be imposed on EU nationals for reasons of public policy or security only to the same extent that such measures could be imposed against nationals.[207] However, the more recent case of *Olazabal* took a different stance from the earlier *Rutili* case on the issue of an internal territorial limitation, in a somewhat different set of circumstances. In *Olazabal* the ECJ ruled it was not necessary for identical measures to be taken against nationals and non-nationals,[208] and that a territorial restriction could be imposed on an EU migrant worker in circumstances in which it could not be imposed on a national, subject to one proviso:

Case C–100/01 **Ministre de l'Interieur v. Olazabal**
[2002] ECR I–10981

40. The Court has held many times that the reservations contained in Article 48 (now, after amendment, Article 39 EC) of the Treaty and Article 56 of the EC Treaty (now, after amendment, Article 46 EC) permit Member States to adopt, with respect to nationals of other Member States, and in particular on the grounds of public policy, measures which they cannot apply to their own nationals, inasmuch as they have no authority to expel the latter from the territory or to deny them access thereto. . . .

41. In situations where nationals of other Member States are liable to banishment or prohibition of residence, they are also capable of being subject to less severe measures consisting of partial restrictions on their right of residence, justified on grounds of public policy, without it being necessary that identical measures be capable of being applied by the Member State in question to its own nationals. . . .

42. It should, however, be remembered that a Member State cannot, by virtue of the public policy reservation contained in Articles 48 and 56 of the Treaty, adopt measures against a national of another Member State by reason of conduct which, when engaged in by nationals of the first Member State, does not give rise to punitive measures or other genuine and effective measures intended to combat that conduct

---

[205] Case 41/74 *Van Duyn*, n. 203 above.

[206] Cases 115 and 116/81, *Adoui and Cornuaille* n. 201. See also Case C–268/99 *Jany*, n. 20 above.

[207] Case 36/75 *Rutili* [1975] ECR 1219.

[208] See also Cases C–65 and 111/95 *Shingara and Radiom* [1997] ECR I–3341, in which the ECJ ruled that it was permissible for a Member State to provide only a remedy by way of judicial review to an EC national who was refused entry on grounds of public policy, even where there was a more substantial remedy by way of appeal for nationals whose immigration status was in question, because it considered that the two situations were not comparable.

Interestingly, Article 22 of Dir 2004/38 reiterates the language of *Rutili* by providing that 'Member States may impose territorial restrictions on the right of residence and the right of permanent residence only where the same restrictions apply to their own nationals'. It is not entirely clear whether Article 22 was intended as a deliberate reversal of the ruling in *Olazabal* and to confirm the Court's stance in *Rutili* as the general rule, or whether it also leaves room for the specific circumstances in *Olazabal*, in which, had it not been for the possibility of restricting his residence within France, the individual in question would in all probability have been deported on public policy grounds.

Article 28 of Directive 2004/38 sets out a range of substantive and procedural protections for individuals who are subject to an expulsion order. Paragraph 1 builds in part on existing ECJ case law such as *Orphanopoulos*[209] and also, although without expressly referring to it, on European Court of Human Rights case law,[210] to provide that Member States must, before taking an expulsion decision on public policy or security grounds, 'take account of considerations such as how long the individual concerned has resided on its territory, his/her age, state of health, family and economic situation, social and cultural integration into the host Member State and the extent of his/her links with the country of origin'.

Article 28(2) then sets out the enhanced level of protection for EU citizens and their families who have gained the right of permanent residence, by providing that they may only be expelled for 'serious grounds' of public policy or security. This requirement of 'serious grounds' seems to be additional to the general requirement for all persons established in Article 27(2) that the personal conduct of an individual subject to expulsion must constitute a 'sufficiently serious threat affecting one of the fundamental interests of society'. Article 28(3) provides for an even more stringent level of protection for minors[211] or EU citizens and their families who have resided in the host State for the previous ten years, stipulating that an expulsion decision can only be taken 'on imperative grounds of public security'.

Article 29(1) governs the public health requirement, and tightens up the provisions of the earlier Directive 64/221 slightly by specifying that the only diseases justifying measures restricting freedom of movement are diseases with epidemic potential as defined by the relevant instruments of the WTO and other infectious diseases or contagious parasitic diseases if they are the subject of protection provisions applying to nationals of the host Member State. Article 29(2) sets a three-month period following arrival in the host State after which diseases occurring cannot constitute grounds for expulsion. Article 29(3) introduces a new provision, apparently in order to combat the practice in some Member States of carrying out medical examinations on beneficiaries of the right to residence, which stipulates that in cases where there are 'serious indications that it is necessary, Member States may, within 3 months of the date of arrival, require persons entitled to the right of residence to undergo, free of charge, a medical examination to certify that they are not suffering from any of the conditions referred to in paragraph 1'. Like the provision in Article 27 prohibiting routine inquiries into the police records of EU nationals and their families who enter the State, Article 29(3) stipulates that such medical examinations may not be required as a matter of routine.

---

[209] Case C–493/01, n. 201 above. See also Case 36/75 *Rutili*, n. 207 above; Case C–459/99 *MRAX*, n. 123 above, which—like many other cases on the subject—refer expressly to the ECHR.

[210] See, e.g., App. no. 54273/00 *Boultif* v. *Switzerland*, judgment of the ECtHR of 2 Aug. 2001, which has been cited by the ECJ in Cases C–482 and 493/01 *Orfanopoulos*, n. 201 above. See also App. no. 47160/99 *Ezzouhdi* v. *France*, judgment of the ECtHR of 13 Feb. 2001.

[211] Except if the expulsion is necessary for the best interests of the child as provided under the 1989 UN Convention on the Rights of the Child.

Article 30 deals with the notification of decisions to the persons concerned, and paragraph 1 incorporates the ruling in *Adoui and Cornuaille*[212] to provide that they must be notified in such a way that the people addressed can comprehend its content and implications. Building on the ECJ ruling in *Rutili*,[213] Article 30(2) provides that the persons concerned are entitled to full and precise information about the grounds on which their case is based, unless it is contrary to public security to do so, and Article 30(3) requires the notification to provide the person with certain information on how to make an appeal. The latter includes specifying the relevant administrative authority or court to which they may appeal, the time limit for appeal, and—where relevant—the time limit allowed for the person to leave the territory of the State. It specifies that, save in cases of urgency, the time allowed is not to be less than one month from the date of notification. This minimum period is intended to allow the person to fulfil the necessary formalities for making an appeal.

Article 31 builds on Article 30 by providing for procedural safeguards, and it simplifies the provisions of the predecessor Directive 64/221 and the somewhat complicated case law on the latter.[214] Article 31(1) provides for 'access to judicial and, where appropriate, administrative redress procedures in the host Member State to appeal against or seek review of' an adverse decision. Paragraph 2 is a new section which provides—subject to three specific exceptions—for the automatic suspension of enforcement of an adverse measure, until such time as a decision is taken on a person's application for an interim order to suspend the measure's enforcement. Paragraph 3 incorporates the ruling of the ECJ in *Adoui and Cornuaille*[215] that the judicial or administrative redress procedures must review not only the legality of the decision but also the facts and circumstances on which it is based, with a view to ensuring its proportionality in light of considerations including the human-rights criteria listed in Article 28(1). Paragraph 4, which is apparently based on the *Pecastaing* case,[216] provides that Member States may exclude an individual from their territory pending the redress procedure, but that they may not prevent such individual from submitting his or her defence in person, except where such appearance may cause serious public policy or security difficulties or where the appeal concerns denial of entry to the territory.

Article 32 deals with the duration of exclusion orders and reflects various aspects of the rulings in *Adoui and Cornuaille*,[217] as well as *Calfa*,[218] providing that where someone has been validly excluded on public policy or security grounds, he or she may apply to have the exclusion order lifted after a reasonable period, and no later than three years from the enforcement of the final exclusion order, by arguing that there has been a material change in the circumstances justifying their exclusion. States must decide on such applications for re-admission within six months, but the applicants have no right of entry to the territory while the application is being considered. Article 33(1) contains an interesting new provision which directly governs Member States' penal policies and criminal law powers, stipulating that expulsion

---

[212] Cases 115 and 116/81 *Adoui and Cornuaille*, n. 201 above.

[213] Case 36/75 *Rutili*, n. 207 above.

[214] Arts. 8 and 9 of Dir. 64/221 had generated a significant case law in particular concerning the circumstances in which there was no right of appeal to a court, or where the appeal could not have suspensory effect, in which case a 'competent authority' was required to provide an opinion before expulsion could take place. See, e.g., Case 48/75 *Royer*, n. 36 above; Case C–175/94 *Gallagher* [1995] ECR I–4253; Case 131/79 *Santillo*, n. 199 above; Case C–357/98 *R. v. Secretary of State for the Home Department, ex p. Yiadom* [2000] ECR I–9265; Case C–136/03 *Dorr v. Sicherheitsdirektion für das Bundesland Kärnten* [2005] ECR I–4759.

[215] Cases 115 and 116/81 *Adoui and Cornuaille*, n. 201 above.

[216] Case 98/79 *Pecastaing v. Belgium* [1980] ECR 691.

[217] Cases 115 and 116/81, n. 201 above, concerning lifelong exclusion orders.

[218] Case C–348/96 *Calfa*, n. 202 above.

orders may not be issued by the host State as a penalty (or as a legal consequence of a custodial sentence) other than in circumstances which fulfil the conditions set out in Articles 27–29 (viz., that the person's conduct constitutes a sufficiently serious threat, etc.).[219] Finally, Article 33(2) provides that if an expulsion order is enforced more than two years after it was issued, the State must check that the person concerned is still a genuine threat to public policy or security and must assess whether there has been any material change in circumstances since the original order was issued.[220]

As with other parts of the law governing the free movement of workers,[221] the ECJ has tended to interpret provisions of the EC–Turkey Agreement—as well as those of other association agreements which provide for the free movement of labour—in the light of the principles established under Directive 64/221 concerning deportation of EU nationals on public policy, security, and health grounds. This will, no doubt, continue to be the case with the provisions of Directive 2004/38.[222]

9. THE TRANSITIONAL REGIME ON FREE MOVEMENT OF WORKERS AFTER THE 2004 AND 2007 ENLARGEMENTS

At the time of the 'big bang' enlargement of 2004 when ten Central and Eastern European States joined, the EU took the unprecedented step of admitting new Members while denying them the immediate right to benefit from one of the four fundamental freedoms. A transitional regime for the free movement of workers from the new States was introduced, delaying the full implementation of their rights of free movement for up to seven years. While this arrangement was made in order to allay the fears of existing Member States that their labour markets would be flooded with new migrant workers, the effective creation of a 'second-class' membership, however temporary, gave rise to an understandably critical reaction from the new Member States and from other commentators.

The transitional period is for seven years from the date of accession in 2004, and is itself divided into three stages. During the first two years, the fifteen existing Member States were permitted to restrict the access of workers from the ten new Member States—with the exception of Cyprus and Malta,[223] due to their size—to their markets. After that, the restrictive measures could be extended for a further period of three years. Finally, the restrictive national measures could be authorized for a further and final two years if the Member State in question experienced serious disturbance in its labour market. During the transitional period, workers from the new Member States must be given priority over workers from third countries. To the extent that workers from the new Member States are admitted they must be accorded equal treatment. Any new Member States whose nationals faced restrictions from the pre-existing EU–15 could impose equivalent restrictions on workers from the restricting Member State.

---

[219] For a discussion of whether German law and practice provided for mandatory expulsion of non-nationals pursuant to certain criminal convictions see Case C–441/02 *Commission v. Germany*, n. 199 above.

[220] This reflects part of the ruling in Case 131/79 *Santillo*, n. 199 above, under the earlier provisions of Dir. 64/221.

[221] See, e.g., Case C–1/97 *Birden* [1998] ECR I–7747; Case C–188/00 *Kurz* [2002] ECR I–10691; Case C–317 and 369/01 *Abatay* [2003] ECR I–12301.

[222] See, e.g., Case C–340/97 *Nazli*, n. 201 above; Case C–383/03 *Dogan*, n. 201 above.

[223] In the case of Malta, a safeguard clause was included in the Accession Treaty to permit Malta to adopt restrictive measures if its labour market was threatened.

Of the fifteen 'old' Member States, twelve chose to impose various kinds of restriction, and only three—the UK (albeit with registration requirements), Ireland, and Sweden—opened their labour markets to workers from the new States. Three of the new Member States—Poland, Slovenia, and Hungary—applied reciprocity restrictions to the EU–15. By the time of the second phase of the transitional period, at the end of two years, eight of the EU–15 had opened their labour markets completely; others maintained some restrictions albeit with simplified procedures; and a number—Germany and Austria in particular—continued to maintain restrictive national measures. The second transitional regime, which was a similar regime of seven years divided into three phases, was introduced in 2007 when Bulgaria and Romania joined the EU. Ten of the existing twenty-five Member States chose to open their labour markets immediately (albeit some with registration and monitoring requirements), while fifteen others maintained work-permit systems of various kinds.

Interestingly, at the end of the first phase of the first transitional regime, the Commission issued a report which suggested that there was a positive correlation between the States which had chosen to liberalize movement of labour immediately and their strong economic performance.[224] Nevertheless it is also notable that the UK and Ireland, which had chosen to open their labour markets to the ten new Member States in 2004, did not do so when Bulgaria and Romania joined in 2007.

10. CONCLUSION

i. The free movement of workers is of central importance to the EU, in both economic and social terms. This is reflected in the legislation which fleshes out the basic rights contained in Article 39 and in the ECJ's consistently purposive interpretation of the Treaty Articles and secondary legislation to achieve the Community's objectives in this area.

ii. The rights of workers and their families under EC law are very substantial, adding up to a right of equal treatment with nationals of the host Member State in almost every respect, apart from a few core areas (e.g., employment in the public service, rewards for loyalty during wartime, the right to vote in national elections) which reflect the special nature of the relationship between the State and its citizens.

iii. Directive 2004/38 (which covers all EU citizens, and not only workers and their families) has consolidated, simplified, and replaced most of the prior legislation on the subject. The Directive reflects the general approach of the ECJ in that it strengthens the substantive rights and procedural protections for migrant workers, expands slightly on the category of protected family members, and tightens up the circumstances in which States may derogate from or restrict free movement rights. It has also introduced a number of novel provisions, such as the right of permanent residence, and a provision allowing Member States to restrict rights in the case of abuse or fraud. Finally, the Directive also incorporates many of the ECJ's rulings concerning the relevant provisions of the prior legislation.

iv. The transitional period for free movement of labour which was introduced at the time of the 2004 and 2007 accessions has been controversial. However, it is strictly limited in time, and by 2011 and 2014 respectively, there should be complete freedom of movement of workers within the enlarged EU.

---

[224] COM(2006)48 final.

11. FURTHER READING

(a) Books

Barnard, C., *The Substantive Law of the EU: The Four Freedoms* (Oxford University Press, 2004)

Carlier, J.-Y., and Guild, E. (eds.), *The Future of Free Movement of Persons in the EU* (Bruylant, 2006)

Toner, H., *Partnership Rights, Free Movement, and EU Law* (Hart, 2004)

Rogers, N., and Scannell, R., *Free Movement of Persons in the Enlarged European Union* (Sweet & Maxwell, 2004)

Weiss, F., and Wooldridge, F., *Free Movement of Persons within the European Community* (Kluwer, 2002)

White, R., *Workers, Establishment and Services in the European Union* (Oxford University Press, 2004)

(b) Articles

Adinolfi, A., 'Free Movement and Access to Work of Citizens of the New Member States: The Transitional Measures' (2005) 42 *CMLRev.* 469

Carrera, S., 'What Does Free Movement Mean in Theory and in Practice in an Enlarged EU?' (2005) 11 *ELJ* 699

Castro Oliveira, A., 'Workers and Other Persons: Step-by-Step from Movement to Citizenship' (2002) 39 *CMLRev.* 77

Giubboni, S., 'Free Movement of Persons and European Solidarity' (2007) 13 *ELJ* 360

O'Keeffe, D., 'Judicial Interpretation of the Public Service Exception to the Free Movement of Workers', in D. Curtin and D. O'Keeffe (eds.), *Constitutional Adjudication in European Community Law and National Law* (Butterworths Ireland, 1992)

O'Leary, S., 'The Free Movement of Persons and Services', in P. Craig and G. de Búrca (eds.), *The Evolution of EU Law* (Oxford University Press, 1999), ch. 11

FREEDOM OF ESTABLISHMENT
AND TO PROVIDE SERVICES

1. CENTRAL ISSUES

i. In addition to the category of workers, the EC Treaty has two separate chapters on self-employed persons who move on a permanent or temporary basis between Member States. These are the chapters on freedom of establishment and freedom to provide services.

ii. The central principles governing establishment and services are laid down in the EC Treaty and have been developed through case law. Important developments have also been brought about through secondary legislation in sectors such as insurance, broadcasting, financial services, electronic commerce, telecommunications, and other 'services of general economic interest'. However, with the exception of the two general directives mentioned in (iii), this chapter focuses on the broad constitutional principles applicable to every sector and not on the particularities of the secondary legislation in specific sectors.

iii. Two important general pieces of secondary legislation dealing with services and establishment were adopted in 2005 and 2006 respectively. In 2005, a consolidating Directive on the recognition of professional qualifications replaced most of the previous general and sectoral legislation on this issue.[1] And in 2006, after a lengthy and politically controversial debate, a general Directive on services in the internal market was adopted.[2]

iv. Articles 43–48 (ex Articles 52–58) EC on freedom of establishment require the removal of restrictions on the right of individuals and companies to maintain a permanent or settled place of business in a Member State. Establishment is defined as 'the actual pursuit of an economic activity through a fixed establishment in another Member State for an indefinite period'.[3]

v. Articles 49–55 (ex Articles 59–66) EC on the free movement of services require the removal of restrictions on the provision of services between Member States, whenever a cross-border element is present. This element can result from the fact that the provider

---

[1] Dir. 2005/36/EC of the European Parliament and of the Council of 7 Sept. 2005 on the recognition of professional qualifications [2005] OJ L255/22.

[2] Dir. 2006/123/EC of the European Parliament and of the Council of 12 Dec. 2006 on services in the internal market [2006] OJ L376/36.

[3] Case C–221/89 *R.* v. *Secretary of State for Transport, ex p. Factortame* [1991] ECR I–3905, para. 20.

is not established in the State where the services are supplied, or that the recipient has travelled to receive services in a Member State other than that in which he or she is established. A movement of services within the scope of Articles 49–50 (ex Articles 59–60) may also occur without the provider or the recipient moving, e.g., where the provision of the service takes place by telecommunication.[4]

vi. The Treaty provisions governing the free movement of services are residual, in that they apply only in so far as the provisions concerning capital,[5] persons, or goods do not apply. Nonetheless it is often difficult, in contexts such as broadcasting or telecommunications, to separate the issues concerning goods from those concerning services,[6] and several of the Treaty freedoms are often affected by a single national measure.[7]

vii. Although the principle of non-discrimination in Article 12 (ex Article 6) EC is an important aspect of these two Treaty chapters,[8] the ECJ has ruled, just as in the case of the other internal market freedoms, that non-discriminatory obstacles are also *prima facie* caught by the relevant Treaty provisions. However, the concept of 'discriminatory measures' is not sharply defined, and the distinction between discriminatory and non-discriminatory measures is often unclear.

viii. In addition to the Treaty-based exceptions to freedom of movement on grounds of public policy, security, and health, the ECJ has ruled—just as in the cases of goods and workers—that a range of other public-interest justifications may be invoked by Member States to restrict the free movement of services and freedom of establishment.

2. DIFFERENCES AND COMMONALITIES BETWEEN THE FREE MOVEMENT OF PERSONS, SERVICES, AND ESTABLISHMENT

(a) COMPARING THE TREATY CHAPTERS

There are several points of similarity between the various chapters on the free movement of persons and services, including also now the Treaty provisions on EU citizenship. Advocate General Mayras in *Van Binsbergen* pointed out that the principle of equal treatment on grounds of nationality underpinned workers, services, and establishment alike.[9] Articles 39 (ex Article 48) on workers and 43 (ex Article 52) on establishment are comparable, in that each requires equal treatment for persons who are *settled* in a Member State, having exercised

---

[4] See, e.g., Case C–384/93 *Alpine Investments BV* v. *Minister van Financiën* [1995] ECR I–1141; Case C–36/02 *Omega Spielhallen- und Automatenaufstellungs-GmbH* v. *Oberbürgermeisterin der Bundesstadt Bonn* [2004] ECR I–9609.

[5] See, e.g., Case C–423/98 *Albore* [2000] ECR I–5965.

[6] See, e.g., Case C–390/99 *Canal Satélite Digital* v. *Administracion General del Estado* [2002] ECR I–607, paras. 31–33. For a case in which the ECJ treated the goods and services dimensions of a restriction on alcohol advertising separately, but reached the same conclusion in each case, see Case C–405/98 *Konsumentombudsmannen* v. *Gourmet International Products* [2001] ECR I–1795. For fishing permits as services rather than goods see Case C–97/98 *Jägerskiöld* v. *Gustafsson* [1999] ECR I–7319. For an early case on the relationship between goods and services see Case 155/73 *Sacchi* [1974] ECR 409.

[7] See, e.g., Case C–150/04 *Commission* v. *Denmark* 30 Jan. 2007; Case C–522/04 *Commission* v. *Belgium* 3 Oct. 2006, Stix-Hackl AG, concerning taxation of pension benefits and insurance.

[8] Case 2/74 *Reyners* v. *Belgium* [1974] ECR 631, paras. 15–16.

[9] Case 33/74 *Van Binsbergen* v. *Bestuur van de Bedrijfsvereniging voor de Metaalnijverheid* [1974] ECR 1299.

their freedom of movement,[10] the essential difference being whether they are working in an employed or a self-employed capacity.[11] The overlap between workers (Article 39) and temporary service providers (Article 49) can be seen in a series of cases concerning posted workers in which the ECJ distinguished the two by ruling that 'workers employed by a business established in one Member State who are temporarily sent to another Member State to provide services do not, in any way, seek access to the labour market in that second State if they return to their country of origin or residence after completion of their work'.[12]

The similarities between establishment and services are evident when considering at what stage a self-employed person providing regular services into or within a Member State may be considered to be sufficiently connected with that State to be established, rather than merely providing services there.[13] The factors which go to distinguish the temporary provision of services from the exercise of the right of establishment in a Member State were addressed by the ECJ in *Gebhard*:[14]

> 25. The concept of establishment within the meaning of the Treaty is therefore a very broad one, allowing a Community national to participate, on a stable and continuous basis, in the economic life of Member State other than his state of origin and to profit therefrom, so contributing to economic and social interpenetration within the Community in the sphere of activities as self-employed persons (see *Reyners* para. 21).
>
> 26. In contrast, where the provider of services moves to another Member State, the provision of the chapter on services, in particular the third paragraph of Article 60, envisage that he is to pursue his activity there on a temporary basis.
>
> 27. As the Advocate General has pointed out, the temporary nature of the activities in question has to be determined in the light, not only of the duration of the provision of the service, but also of its regularity, periodicity or continuity. The fact that the provision of services is temporary does not mean that the provider of services within the meaning of the Treaty may not equip himself with some form of infrastructure in the host Member State (including an office, chambers or consulting rooms) in so far as such infrastructure is necessary for the purposes of performing the services in question.

The crucial features of establishment are the 'stable and continuous basis' on which the economic or professional activity is carried on, and the fact that there is an established professional base within the host Member State.[15] For the provision of services, the temporary nature of the activity is to be determined by reference to its 'periodicity, continuity and regularity', and providers of services will not be deemed to be 'established' simply by virtue of the

---

[10] See, e.g., Case C–345/05 *Commission v. Portugal* [2006] ECR I–10633; Case C–104/06 *Commission v. Sweden*, 18 Jan. 2007, dealing simultaneously with Arts. 39 and 43 on workers and establishment, and Art. 18 on citizenship.

[11] See Mayras AG in Case 2/74 *Reyners*, n. 8 above, and the ECJ in Case C–107/94 *Asscher* v. *Staatsecretaris van Financiën* [1996] ECR I–3089. See also Case C–268/99 *Jany* v. *Staatssecretaris van Justitie* [2001] ECR I–8615, paras. 68–70, in the context of the EU–Poland Association Agreement.

[12] See, e.g., Case C–49/98 *Finalarte Sociedade Construçao Civil* v. *Urlaubs- und Lohnausgleichskasse der Bauwirtschaft* [2001] ECR I–7831, paras. 22–23.

[13] See Case 205/84 *Commission v. Germany* [1986] ECR 3755, para. 22; Case 33/74 *Van Binsbergen*, n. 9 above, para. 13. See also the Opinion of Jacobs AG in Case C–76/90 *Säger* v. *Dennemeyer & Co. Ltd.* [1991] ECR I–4221.

[14] Case C–55/94 *Gebhard* v. *Consiglio dell'Ordine degli Avvocati e Procuratori di Milano* [1995] ECR I–4165.

[15] Where a person or company establishes in a Member State to provide services to recipients there for an *indefinite* period, this does not fall within the Treaty provisions on freedom to provide services: Case C–70/95 *Sodemare* v. *Regione Lombardia* [1997] ECR I–3395.

fact that they equip themselves with some form of infrastructure in the host Member State.[16] The ECJ's graduated distinction between establishment and temporary service-provision has been adopted by the consolidating Directive on the recognition of professional qualifications in 2005. [17]

In the past, it was suggested that Article 49 was more concerned with liberalizing the mobility of services and setting up a single market,[18] and had more in common with the Treaty provisions on free movement of goods[19] than with the Treaty provisions on workers and establishment, which were based primarily on the principle of non-discrimination. In recent years, however, a robust approach has been adopted to the rights of establishment too, placing as much emphasis on liberalization as on equal treatment, and thus bringing the law on establishment and services closer together.[20] It will be evident from the discussion in this chapter that the gradual extension of EC rules to cover genuinely non-discriminatory restrictions on establishment and services has reached into sensitive areas of national policy, often with a deregulatory emphasis, and that many controversies have arisen as a result.

(b) ARE THE FREEDOMS HORIZONTALLY APPLICABLE?

We saw in Chapter 21 that the ECJ ruled that, unlike Article 28 on the free movement of goods, the provisions of Article 39 are binding not only on the State but also on private bodies.[21] In the field of services, the ECJ ruled in the early case of *Walrave and Koch* that the Treaty rules applied not only 'to the action of public authorities but extends likewise to rules of any other nature aimed at regulating in a collective manner gainful employment and the provision of services'.[22] It remains unclear however, even after the case of *Angonese* in the field of free movement of workers,[23] whether the Treaty provisions on establishment and services are fully horizontally applicable, in the sense of imposing legal obligations on all individuals and not only on powerful, self-regulating collective actors such as sporting organizations, which possess powers akin to public law. In *Wouters* the ECJ applied the *Walrave* ruling to a regulatory measure adopted by the Netherlands Bar Council concerning partnerships between barristers and accountants, but gave no further guidance on the applicability of the Treaty rules to purely individual private conduct.[24]

---

16 Case C–215/01 *Schnitzer* [2003] ECR I–14847. Further, providers of services cannot be made subject to a particular type of mandatory 'employment' relationship, since that would deprive them of their self-employed status: see Case C–398/95 *SETTG v. Ypourgos Ergasias* [1997] ECR I–3091; Case C–255/04 *Commission v. France* [2006] ECR I–5251.

17 See Art. 5(2) of Dir. 2005/36 [2005] OJ L255/22, discussed below.

18 See Warner AG in Case 52/79 *Procureur du Roi v. Debauve* [1980] ECR 833, 872.

19 See Jacobs AG in Case C–76/90 *Säger*, n. 13 above, 4234–4235, and Gulmann AG in Case C–275/92 *HM Customs and Excise v. Schindler* [1994] ECR I–1039, 1059; J. Snell, *Goods and Services in EC Law* (Oxford University Press, 2002).

20 See, e.g., Case C–212/97 *Centros Ltd. v. Erhvervs- og Selskabsstyrelsen* [1999] ECR I–1459; Case C–55/94 *Gebhard*, n. 14 above.

21 Case C–415/93 *Union royale belge des sociétés de football association ASBL v. Jean-Marc Bosman* [1995] ECR I–4921, paras. 83 and 84; Case C–281/98 *Angonese v. Cassa di Risparmio di Bolzano SpA* [2000] ECR I–4139, para. 32.

22 Case 36/74 *Walrave and Koch* [1974] ECR 1405.

23 Case C–281/98 *Angonese*, n. 21 above.

24 Case C–309/99 *Wouters and others v. Algemene Raad van de Nederlandse Orde van Advocaten* [2002] ECR I–1577, para. 120. See also Case C–411/98 *Ferlini v. CHL* [2000] ECR I–8081, para. 50.

(c) THE 'OFFICIAL AUTHORITY' EXCEPTION

Article 45 EC, which is extended by Article 55 to cover the chapter on services, states that the provisions of the chapter on freedom of establishment shall not apply 'so far as any given Member State is concerned, to activities which in that State are connected, even occasionally, with the exercise of official authority'. This provision has a similar role to that of the public-service derogation for workers in Article 39(4). Advocate General Mayras defined it as follows:

> Official authority is that which arises from the sovereignty and majesty of the State; for him who exercises it, it implies the power of enjoying the prerogatives outside the general law, privileges of official power and powers of coercion over citizens.[25]

The wording of Article 45 refers to those 'activities' which are connected with the use of official power, rather than to professions or vocations within which official authority might, under certain circumstances, be exercised. In *Reyners*, the ECJ was asked whether the whole of the legal profession of *avocat* was exempt from the Treaty rules, by reason of the fact that it comprised activities connected with the exercise of such authority. According to the Luxembourg Government, the whole profession should be excepted because it was 'connected organically' with the public service of the administration of justice.

Case 2/74 **Reyners v. Belgium**
[1974] ECR 63

[Note ToA renumbering: Arts. 52 and 55 are now Arts. 43 and 45 respectively]

THE ECJ

43. Having regard to the fundamental character of freedom of establishment and the rule on equal treatment with nationals in the system of the Treaty, the exceptions allowed by the first paragraph of Article 55 cannot be given a scope which would exceed the objective for which this exemption clause was inserted.

44. The first paragraph of Article 55 must enable Member States to exclude non-nationals from taking up functions involving the exercise of official authority which are connected with one of the activities of self-employed persons provided for in Article 52.

45. This need is fully satisfied when the exclusion of nationals is limited to those activities which, taken on their own, constitute a direct and specific connection with the exercise of official authority.

46. An extension of the exception allowed by Article 55 to a whole profession would be possible only in cases where such activities were linked with that profession in such a way that freedom of establishment would result in imposing on the Member State concerned the obligation to allow the exercise, even occasionally, by non-nationals of functions appertaining to official authority.

47. This extension is on the other hand not possible when, within the framework of an independent profession, the activities connected with the exercise of official authority are separable from the professional activity in question taken as a whole.

---

[25] Case 2/74 *Reyners*, n. 8 above, 664.

Ultimately the Court ruled that the professional activities of an *avocat*, involving regular and official contact and even compulsory co-operation with the courts, did not amount to the necessary connection with the exercise of official authority since it left the discretion of judicial authority and the free exercise of judicial power intact.

The ECJ has continued to interpret the official-authority exception narrowly in response to attempts by Member States to invoke it for a range of somewhat unlikely professions.[26] In *Thijssen*, the Court ruled that the post of commissioner of insurance companies and undertakings was not covered by the exception, since although the post involved monitoring companies and reporting on possible infringements of the penal code, the power to prevent insurance companies from implementing certain decisions was not a definitive or final one.[27]

(d) THE PUBLIC POLICY, SECURITY, AND HEALTH EXCEPTIONS

Article 46 in the chapter on establishment and Article 55 in the chapter on services provide that the provisions of those chapters 'shall not prejudice the applicability of provisions laid down by law, regulation or administrative action providing for special treatment for foreign nationals on grounds of public policy, public security or public health'. In their application to natural persons these derogations are regulated, together with their application to workers, by the provisions of Directive 2004/38.[28] In their application to companies the derogations are governed by the Treaty and by the general principles of Community law,[29] and more recently by the relevant provisions of the Services Directive.[30] The general principles of Community law articulated by the ECJ include the principles of non-discrimination and of proportionality, which are also part of the test for justifying public-interest restrictions on freedom of movement which have been judicially developed alongside the Treaty derogations.[31] Further, the ECJ has ruled that Article 46 does not permit a Member State to exclude an entire economic sector from the application of the principles on freedom of establishment and services.[32]

(e) LEGISLATION GOVERNING ENTRY, RESIDENCE, AND EXPULSION

As seen in Chapter 21, Directive 2004/38 governs the terms and conditions of entry of all EU citizens and their families into a host Member State, as well as their right to remain there after

---

[26] Case C–306/89 *Commission* v. *Greece* [1991] ECR I–5863 on traffic accident experts; Case C–272/91 *Commission* v. *Italy* [1994] ECR I–1409 on operating a computerization system for a national lottery; Case C–263/99 *Commission* v. *Italy* [2001] ECR I–4195 on transport consultants; Case C–114/97 *Commission* v. *Spain* [1998] ECR I–6717, Case C–355/98 *Commission* v. *Belgium* [2000] ECR I–1221, and Case C–283/99 *Commission* v. *Italy* [2001] ECR I–4363, on private security activities.

[27] Case C–42/92 *Thijssen* v. *Controledienst voor de Verzekeringen* [1993] ECR I–4047.

[28] See Ch. 21, sect. 8.

[29] For examples of the application of Arts. 46 and 55 to companies see Case 3/88 *Commission* v. *Italy* [1989] ECR 4035; Case 352/85 *Bond van Adverteerders* v. *Netherlands* [1988] ECR 2085; Case C–114/97 *Commission* v. *Spain* [1998] ECR I–6717; Case C–355/98 *Commission* v. *Belgium* [2000] ECR I–1221. For a failed attempt see Case C–171/02 *Commission* v. *Portugal* [2004] ECR I–5645.

[30] For further discussion see sect. 6(b) below.

[31] See more generally on the role of EC law in a situation which was not covered by the Treaty's free-movement provisions, given the special geographical status of the British Channel islands, Case C–171/96 *Pereira Roque* v. *Governor of Jersey* [1998] ECR I–4607.

[32] Case C–496/01 *Commission* v. *France* [2004] ECR I–2351.

having pursued an economic activity, and the conditions under which their rights may be restricted or revoked.[33] This includes self-employed persons and service providers, so that the discussion of Directive 2004/38 in sections 6 and 8 of Chapter 21 is equally relevant here.

The provisions of the earlier legislation governing self-employed persons, Directive 73/148, which regulated rights of 'abode' and rights of temporary residence for the duration of the services, have been replaced with the simple right of residence for self-employed persons in Article 7(a) of Directive 2004/38. Further, as we shall see in greater detail in Chapter 23 on citizenship, even where a self-employed person is no longer engaged in economic activity, the right of residence as an EU citizen continues unless that person has, through lack of sufficient resources, become an unreasonable burden on the host State.

3. THE RIGHT OF ESTABLISHMENT

Article 43 EC provides:

> Within the framework of the provisions set out below, restrictions on the freedom of establishment of nationals of a Member State in the territory of another Member State shall be prohibited. Such prohibition shall also apply to restrictions on the setting up of agencies, branches, or subsidiaries by nationals of any Member State established in the territory of any Member State.
> Freedom of establishment shall include the right to take up and pursue activities as self-employed persons and to set up and manage undertakings, in particular companies or firms within the meaning of the second paragraph of Article 48, under the conditions laid down for its own nationals by the law of the country where such establishment is effected, subject to the provisions of the chapter relating to capital.

Paragraph one requires the *abolition of restrictions* on freedom of primary and secondary establishment, whereas paragraph two provides for the right to pursue self-employed activities *on an equal footing* with the nationals of the Member State of establishment. The reference to capital acknowledges that there is a separate chapter on the free movement of capital, which has been subject to a different and more gradual regime of liberalization.[34]

Article 43 on its face appears to give rights only to persons in a Member State other than their Member State of nationality. Secondly, it appears to prohibit discrimination, and to imply that its requirements are satisfied if the person exercising the right of establishment is treated in the same way as a national. However, we shall see that Article 43 has been given a broader reading on these two points. First, nationals may in appropriate circumstances rely on Article 43 against their own State, and secondly Article 43 prohibits not merely unequal treatment but also unnecessary obstacles to freedom of establishment.

Article 44 originally required the Council to draw up a General Programme for the abolition of restrictions on establishment (which it did in 1961[35]) and to issue directives to attain freedom for particular activities. Article 47 contains the requirement for the Council to issue directives—by qualified majority other than where the existing principles governing

---

[33] Dir. 2004/38 [2004] OJ L158/77, replaces the previously existing Dir. 73/148 [1973] OJ L172/14, in this respect.
[34] See Ch. 20.
[35] OJ Spec. Ed., Second Ser., IX.

professional training and access are being amended[36]—for the mutual recognition of diplomas and other qualifications, and Article 48 places companies in the same position as natural persons for the purpose of the application of this chapter of the Treaty.

(a) THE EFFECT OF ARTICLE 43

In 1974 in *Reyners*, the ECJ ruled that Article 43 EC was directly effective, despite the fact that the conditions for direct effect set out in *Van Gend en Loos* were arguably not met,[37] and despite the Council's failure to adopt the necessary implementing legislation envisaged by the Treaty provisions. Such legislation had not yet been adopted at the time of *Reyners*, partly on account of the slow progress of legislation in the Council in the aftermath of the Luxembourg Accords, and partly on account of the opposition within Member States to the process of opening the professions, and in particular the legal profession, to non-nationals.[38]

Reyners was a Dutch national who had obtained his legal education in Belgium, and who was refused admission to the Belgian Bar solely because he lacked Belgian nationality. The ECJ ruled that, despite the Treaty requirement that directives should be adopted, Article 43 laid down a precise result which was to be achieved by the end of the transitional period, namely the requirement of non-discrimination on grounds of nationality. The fulfillment of this result had to be made easier by, but was not made dependent on, the implementation of a programme of progressive measures.[39] Thus he could invoke Article 43 directly. The ECJ acknowledged, however, that the directives had 'not lost all interest since they preserve an important scope in the field of measures intended to make easier the effective exercise of the right of freedom of establishment'.[40]

However, even before the relevant secondary legislation had begun to be adopted, it was argued to the ECJ that where a national restriction was based not on nationality but on the adequacy of qualifications, Article 43 could be relied on by an EC national seeking to practise a profession in another Member State. In *Thieffry*, a Belgian national, who obtained a doctorate in law in Belgium and practised as an advocate in Brussels, subsequently obtained French university recognition of his qualifications as equivalent to a degree in French law, and obtained a certificate of aptitude for the profession of *avocat*.[41] He was refused admission to the training stage as an advocate at the Paris Bar on the ground that he lacked a degree in French law. According to the ECJ, the responsible professional bodies had a duty to ensure that their practices were in accordance with Treaty objectives:

> Consequently, if the freedom of establishment provided for by Article 52 can be ensured in a Member State either under the provisions of the laws and regulations in force, or by virtue of the practices of the public service or of professional bodies, a person subject to Community law cannot be denied the practical benefit of that freedom solely by virtue of the fact that, for

---

36 For discussion of the different voting procedures see the challenge brought to Dir. 98/5 on establishment for lawyers [1998] OJ L77/36 in Case C–168/98 *Luxembourg* v. *Parliament and Council* [2000] ECR I–9131. For commentary see P. Cabral (2002) 39 *CMLRev.* 129.

37 Case 2/74 *Reyners*, n. 8 above; see Ch. 8 on direct effect.

38 *Ibid.*, Mayras AG, 658.

39 *Ibid.*, para. 26.

40 *Ibid.*, para. 31.

41 Case 71/76 *Thieffry* v. *Conseil de l'Ordre des Avocats à la Cour de Paris* [1977] ECR 765.

a particular profession, the directives provided for by Article 57 of the Treaty have not yet been adopted.[42]

Since Thieffry had already obtained what was recognized in France, for both professional and academic purposes, to be an equivalent qualification, and had satisfied the necessary practical training requirements, the state authorities were not justified in refusing to admit him to the Bar solely on the ground that he did not possess a French qualification, despite the absence of EC directives in the field.[43]

In subsequent cases the ECJ went further still and ruled that Article 43 precluded the competent national authorities from simply refusing, without further explanation, to allow nationals of another Member State to practise their trade or profession on the ground that their qualification was not equivalent to the corresponding national qualification. Instead, the Treaty provisions imposed specific, positive obligations on national authorities and professional bodies to take steps to secure the free movement of workers and freedom of establishment, even in the absence of Community or national legislation providing for equivalence or for the recognition of qualifications.

In *Heylens* the ECJ ruled, in the case of a Belgian football trainer working in France whose application for recognition of the equivalence of his Belgian diploma was refused by the French Ministry of Sport, that Member States were entitled, in the absence of harmonizing directives, to regulate the knowledge and qualifications necessary to pursue a particular occupation. However:

[T]he procedure for the recognition of equivalence must enable the national authorities to assure themselves, on an objective basis, that the foreign diploma certifies that its holder has knowledge and qualifications which are, if not identical, at least equivalent to those certified by the national diploma. That assessment of the equivalence of the foreign diploma must be effected exclusively in the light of the level of knowledge and qualifications which its holder can be assumed to possess in the light of that diploma, having regard to the nature and duration of the studies and practical training which the diploma certifies that he has carried out.[44]

Further, where employment was dependent on possession of a diploma, it must be possible for a national of a Member State to obtain judicial review of a decision of the authorities of another Member State, and to ascertain the reasons for refusing to recognize the equivalence of a diploma.

In *Vlassopoulou,* a Greek national who had obtained a Greek law degree and had practised German law for several years in Germany applied for admission to the Bar there. Her authorization to practise was rejected on the ground that she lacked the necessary qualifications because she had not passed the relevant German examinations. The ECJ began by ruling that even the non-discriminatory application of national qualification requirements could hinder the exercise of freedom of establishment.

---

[42] *Ibid.,* para. 17.
[43] See also Case 11/77 *Patrick v. Ministre des Affairs Culturelles* [1977] ECR 1199.
[44] Case 222/86 *UNECTEF v. Heylens* [1987] ECR 4097, para. 13.

Case 340/89 **Vlassopoulou v. Ministerium für Justiz, Bundes und Europaangelegenheiten Baden-Württemberg**
[1991] ECR 2357

[Note ToA renumbering: Art. 52 is now Art. 43]

THE ECJ

16. Consequently, a Member State which receives a request to admit a person to a profession to which access, under national law, depends upon the possession of a diploma or a professional qualification must take into consideration the diplomas, certificates and other evidence of qualifications which the person concerned has acquired in order to exercise the same profession in another Member State by making a comparison between the specialized knowledge and abilities certified by those diplomas and the knowledge and qualifications required by the national rules.

Thus the national authorities must consider any education and training received by the holder of the diploma or certificate, and must compare the knowledge and skills acquired with those required by the domestic qualification.[45] If they are found to be equivalent, the State must recognize the qualification, and if they are not so found, the State must assess whether any knowledge or practical training the person may have acquired in the host Member State is sufficient to make up for what was lacking in the qualification.

Vlassopoulou highlights the extent to which the effectiveness of Article 43 was bolstered by the ECJ in the years following *Reyners*, which had held that in the absence of legislation only the non-discrimination 'core' of the Article was directly effective. By the time of *Vlassopoulou* it had been held that, despite the diversity of national educational and training systems and despite the lack of EU co-ordinating legislation, Article 43 imposed a precise obligation on national authorities to examine thoroughly the basis for the qualification held by a Community national, to inform the person concerned of the reasons if the qualification is deemed not to be equivalent, and to respect their rights in the process. The effect was that a Member State could no longer simply refuse someone entry to a profession or to practise a trade solely on the ground that he or she lacked the domestic qualification, even where there was as yet no domestic recognition of the equivalence of the foreign qualification.[46]

The approach adopted by the ECJ in *Vlassopoulou* closely reflected the provisions of Council Directive 89/48 on the mutual recognition of higher-education diplomas which had been adopted around that time,[47] but not in time to be applicable in the case of *Vlassopoulou*. Directive 89/48 has since been replaced by the consolidating Directive 2005/35, which embodies the same approach and the same principles. Further, as we shall see, the principles articulated in the *Vlassopoulou* and *Heylens* cases continue to be applicable to situations which are not covered by the secondary legislation.

---

[45] See also Case C–104/91 *Borrell* [1992] ECR I–3001.

[46] See also Case C–164/94 *Arantis* v. *Land Berlin* [1996] ECR I–135.

[47] See n. 222 and text below. For proceedings brought against Italy concerning inadequate implementation of Dir. 89/48 in relation to lawyers see Case C–145/99 *Commission* v. *Italy* [2002] ECR I–2235.

(b) THE SCOPE OF ARTICLE 43

(i) *Non-discriminatory Restrictions*

It was noted above that the wording of Article 43 emphasizes the requirement of equal treatment of nationals and non-nationals. In some of its earlier case law, such as *Commission v. Belgium*[48] and *Fearon*,[49] the ECJ appeared to suggest that in the absence of discrimination, rules which restricted the right of establishment would not violate Article 43. However, in keeping with the pattern of its case law on the free movement of goods, services, and workers, the ECJ moved away from the emphasis on unequal treatment.

In *Klopp*, a German lawyer who was refused admission to the Paris Bar on the sole ground that he already maintained an office as a lawyer in another Member State successfully challenged the rule under Article 43, even though the rule applied equally to nationals and non-nationals alike.[50] The ECJ ruled that Article 43 specifically guarantees the freedom to set up more than one place of work in the Community, and there were less restrictive ways, given modern transport and telecommunications, of ensuring that lawyers maintain sufficient contact with their clients and the judicial authorities, and obey the rules of the profession.

Klopp was not of itself authority for a general proposition that even non-discriminatory rules may breach Article 43, given that Article 43 expressly guarantees the right to secondary establishment which was being denied in that case,[51] but it demonstrated that freedom of establishment requires more than equal treatment in certain circumstances. In *Wolf*,[52] *Stanton*,[53] and *Kemmler*,[54] the ECJ ruled that certain indistinctly applicable national rules on social-security exemptions for the self-employed were impermissible, because they constituted an unjustified and excessive impediment to the pursuit of occupational activities in more than one Member State, even though the rules contained no direct or indirect discrimination on grounds of nationality.[55] Similarly in cases concerning non-discriminatory registration requirements, the ECJ found a violation of Article 43 in the absence of objective justification.[56]

The *Gebhard* ruling gave the clearest indication of the Court's broad interpretation of Article 43, where it indicated that the same principles underpin all of the Treaty provisions on freedom of movement, and stated that the provisions on goods,[57]

---

[48] Case 221/85 *Commission v. Belgium* [1987] ECR 719 on clinical biology services.

[49] Case 182/83 *Fearon* v. *Irish Land Commission* [1984] ECR 3677, on a residence requirement for exemption from compulsory purchase of land. For other cases concerning nationality and residence restrictions on land use see Case 305/87 *Commission* v. *Greece* [1989] ECR 1461; Case C–302/97 *Konle* v. *Austria* [1999] ECR I–2651.

[50] Case 107/83 *Ordre des Avocats* v. *Klopp* [1984] ECR 2971.

[51] See also Case 96/85 *Commission* v. *France* [1986] ECR 1475; Case C–351/90 *Commission* v. *Luxembourg* [1992] ECR I–3945, condemning other similar single-practice rules for doctors, dentists, and vets. See also Case C–106/91 *Ramrath* v. *Ministre de la Justice* [1992] ECR I–3351; Case C–162/99 *Commission* v. *Italy* [2001] ECR I–541.

[52] Cases 154–155/87 *RSVZ* v. *Wolf* [1988] ECR 3897.

[53] Case 143/87 *Stanton* v. *INASTI* [1988] ECR 3877.

[54] Case C–53/95 *INASTI* v. *Kemmler* [1996] ECR I–704. See also Case C–68/99 *Commission* v. *Germany* [2001] ECR I–1865, concerning social insurance law affecting artists. Compare however Case C–249/04 *Allard* v. *INASTI* [2005] ECR I–4535, where the rules were not an impediment to freedom of establishment.

[55] Case 143/87 *Stanton*, n. 53 above, para. 9.

[56] Case 292/86 *Gullung* v. *Conseil de l'Ordre des Avocats* [1988] ECR 111; Case 271/82 *Auer* v. *Ministère Public* [1983] ECR 2727, para. 18.

[57] Case 8/74 *Procureur du Roi* v. *Dassonville* [1974] ECR 837, Case 120/78 *Rewe-Zentrale* v. *Bundesmonopolverwaltung für Branntwein* (*Cassis de Dijon*) [1979] ECR 649; Cases C–267 and 268/91 *Keck and Mithouard* [1993] ECR I–6097; Cases C–34–36/95 *de Agostini* [1997] ECR I–3843; Case C–254/98

services,[58] workers,[59] and establishment should be similarly construed.[60] *Gebhard* concerned a German national against whom disciplinary proceedings were brought by the Milan Bar Council for pursuing a professional activity as a lawyer in Italy on a permanent basis. He had set up his chambers using the title *avvocato*, although he had not been admitted as a member of the Milan Bar and although his training, qualifications, and experience had not formally been recognized in Italy. Having established that in the absence of Community rules, Member States may justifiably subject the pursuit of self-employed activities to *bona fide* rules relating to organization, ethics, qualifications, titles, etc., the ECJ continued:[61]

> It follows, however, from the Court's case law that national measures liable to hinder or make less attractive the exercise of fundamental freedoms guaranteed by the Treaty must fulfil four conditions: they must be applied in a non-discriminatory manner; they must be justified by imperative requirements in the general interest; they must be suitable for securing the attainment of the objective which they pursue; and they must not go beyond what is necessary in order to attain it (*Kraus*, paragraph 32).

There is no mention in this paragraph of a requirement of discrimination, whether direct or indirect. Instead, any national rule which is liable to hinder or make less attractive the exercise of the 'fundamental' freedom of establishment (or any of the other fundamental freedoms) may violate the Treaty unless it is justified by an imperative requirement and applied in a proportionate and non-discriminatory manner.[62] Moreover while rules which create 'equally applicable' obstacles to freedom of establishment often impose a heavier burden in practice on non-nationals than on nationals,[63] not all equally applicable rules are indirectly discriminatory in this way. The essence of *Gebhard*, adopting an obstacle approach rather than a discrimination approach, has been affirmed by the Court on many occasions since.[64]

It should be noted, however, that the discriminatory nature of a restriction is not irrelevant, for several reasons. First, if a restriction on establishment discriminates directly on grounds of nationality, it will, without further question, fall within the scope of the Treaty prohibition (whereas not every non-discriminatory restriction is likely to constitute a sufficient hindrance, by analogy with the case law on goods[65] and on workers, as in *Graf*[66]). Secondly, it seems that, at least in certain contexts, if a restriction is directly or deliberately discriminatory, the Member State may rely for justification only on the express derogations on grounds of

---

Schutzverband gegen unlauteren Wettbewerb v. *TK-Heimdienst Sass GmbH* [2000] ECR I–151. See more generally the discussion in Ch. 19.

58 See, e.g., Case C–384/93 *Alpine Investments*, n. 4 above; Cases C–369 and 376/96 *Arblade* [1999] ECR I–8453.

59 Case C–415/93 *Bosman*, n. 21 above, paras. 82–84.

60 Case C–55/94 *Gebhard*, n. 14 above.

61 *Ibid.*, para. 37.

62 See also Case C–108/96 *MacQuen* [2001] ECR I–837, paras. 26–27.

63 G. Marenco, 'The Notion of a Restriction on the Freedom of Establishment and the Provisions of Services in the Case Law of the ECJ' (1991) 11 *YBEL* 111.

64 See, e.g., Case C–108/96 *MacQuen*, n. 62 above; Case C–212/97 *Centros*, n. 20 above, para. 34; Case C–289/02 *AMOK Verlags GmbH* v. *A. & R. Gastronomie GmbH* [2003] ECR I–15059, para. 36; Case C–8/02 *Leichtle* v. *Bundesanstalt für Arbeit* [2004] ECR I–2641, para. 32; Case C–346/04 *Conijn* v. *Finanzamt Hamburg-Nord* [2006] ECR I–6137; Case C–433/04 *Commission* v. *Belgium* [2006] ECR I–10653. See also Case C–19/92 *Kraus* v. *Land Baden-Württemberg* [1993] ECR I–1663 and the comment by P. Stanley (1996) 33 *CMLRev.* 713.

65 See Cases 267 and 268/91 *Keck*, n. 57 above, and the discussion in Ch. 19.

66 Case C–190/98 *Graf* v. *Filzmoser Maschinenbau* [2000] ECR I–493.

public policy, security, and health in Article 46 EC.[67] On the other hand, when the obstacle stems from an equally applicable rule which does not constitute deliberate discrimination, it seems that a wider and open-ended range of public-interest grounds (which are referred to *inter alia* as mandatory requirements, imperative requirements, objective justifications) may be relied upon to justify the restrictive measure. It should be noted, however, that the internal-market case law on what constitutes discrimination, whether direct or indirect, and on what kinds of justification are available, is highly confused.[68] This problem has been discussed in more detail in Chapter 19 in the context of the free movement of goods.[69]

(ii) *Reverse Discrimination and Wholly Internal Situations: When can Nationals Rely on Article 43 in their own Member State?*

We noted above that the wording of the first sentence of Article 43 refers to the situation of nationals of a Member State wishing to establish themselves 'in the territory of another Member State'. A first reading of this sentence suggests that nationals setting up in a self-employed capacity in their own Member State cannot complain under Article 43 about the domestic regulation of those activities. The situation is somewhat more complex, however.

In the first place, a Member State is clearly obliged under both Article 43 and Directive 2004/38 not to restrict its own nationals who wish to *leave* the territory in order to set up an establishment in another Member State.

Secondly, it is obvious that nationals who wish to establish themselves within their own Member State may be disadvantaged if the qualifications they have obtained in another Member State are not recognized by their own State. In *Knoors* where a Dutch national sought to practise as a plumber in the Netherlands, having obtained training and experience in Belgium, the Dutch government argued that a national could not rely on his own Member State under Article 43 to gain recognition for qualifications obtained since he might be seeking to evade the application of legitimate national provisions. The ECJ firmly rejected this argument:[70]

> 20. In fact these liberties, which are fundamental in the Community system, could not be fully realized if the Member States were in a position to refuse to grant the benefit of the provisions of Community law to those of their nationals who have taken advantage of the facilities existing in the matter of freedom of movement and establishment and who have acquired, by

---

[67] Case 352/85 *Bond van Adverteerders* v. *Netherlands* [1988] ECR 2085, paras. 32–33. See also Cases C–17/92 *Federación de Distribuidores Cinematográficos* v. *Estado Español et Unión de Productores de Cine y Televisión* [1993] ECR I–2239, para. 16; Case C–484/93 *Svensson and Gustavsson* v. *Ministre du Logement et de l'Urbanisme* [1995] ECR I–3955, para. 15.

[68] See, e.g., Case C–204/90 *Bachmann* v. *Belgium* [1992] ECR I–249 in the context of free movement of workers, where the ECJ seemed to say that restrictions which appeared to be discriminatory could be justified without recourse to the specific Treaty exceptions. See also the range of justifications considered by the ECJ for the (arguably directly discriminatory) nationality restrictions in Case C–415/93 *Bosman*, n. 21 above. For a more general discussion of this confusion see J. Scott, 'Mandatory Requirements', in C. Barnard and J. Scott (eds.), *Law of the Single European Market* (Hart, 2002), ch. 10.

[69] See Ch. 19.

[70] Case 115/78 *Knoors* v. *Secretary of State for Economic Affairs* [1979] ECR 399. See also Case 246/80 *Broekmeulen* v. *Huisarts Registratie Commissie* [1981] ECR 2311. Compare however the restrictive approach of the ECJ in the first *Auer* case, Case 136/78 *Ministère Public* v. *Auer* [1979] ECR 437, especially paras. 20–21, and see the later Case 271/82 *Auer*, n. 56 above.

virtue of such facilities, the trade qualifications referred to by the Directive in a Member State other than that whose nationality they possess.

...

24. Although it is true that the provisions of the Treaty relating to establishment and the provision of services cannot be applied to situations which are purely internal to a Member State, the position nevertheless remains that the reference in Article 52 to 'nationals of a Member State' who wish to establish themselves 'in the territory of another Member State' cannot be interpreted in such a way as to exclude from the benefit of Community law a given Member State's own nationals when the latter, owing to the fact that they have lawfully resided on the territory of another Member State and have there acquired a trade qualification which is recognized by the provisions of Community law, are, with regard to their State of origin, in a situation which may be assimilated to that of any other persons enjoying the rights and liberties guaranteed by the Treaty.

In *Bouchoucha*, however, where a French national sought to practise osteopathy in France by relying on a diploma he had obtained in the UK, the ECJ ruled that France was entitled in the absence of Community-level regulation (since this was before the adoption of the mutual-recognition directives) to prohibit him from practising without being fully qualified as a medical doctor in France.[71] The Court's approach in *Bouchoucha* was markedly different from that in *Heylens* and *Vlassopoulou*, above, in which nationals of other Member States were permitted to rely in a host Member State on Article 43 in order to require the host State to consider the equivalence of their particular qualifications, despite the fact that there was no EC legislation governing the recognition of those qualifications at the time.[72] The main difference between *Bouchoucha* and those cases seems to have been the fact that the applicant was a national of the host Member State, and the ECJ may have been responding to France's concern about a possible 'abuse'.[73]

Now, however, the situation in *Bouchoucha* is unlikely to arise, since a national who has obtained a qualification in another Member State and has returned to practise in his or her Member State of origin will in all probability be covered by the terms of Directive 2005/36 on the recognition of professional qualifications. Further, even where the 2005 Directive does not cover the facts of the situation, the cases of *Kraus* and *Fernández de Bobadilla* indicate that the principles in *Heylens* and *Vlassopoulou* will apply, despite the fact that the applicant is a national of the host State.[74] Whenever a national of a Member State has obtained a qualification in another Member State and has returned to practise in the home State, it is no longer a purely internal situation and the right of establishment in Article 43 applies.[75]

Thus, so long as some 'Community element' is present and the situation is not wholly internal, individuals can rely on Article 43 in their own State.[76] In *Werner*, for example, the ECJ

---

[71] Case C–61/89 *Bouchoucha* [1990] ECR I–3551, especially para. 12.

[72] See also Case C–108/96 *MacQuen*, n. 62 above.

[73] See also Cases C–330–331/90 *Ministero Fiscal* v. *Lopez Brea* [1992] ECR I–323.

[74] See Case C–19/92 *Kraus*, n. 64 above; Case C–234/97 *Fernández de Bobadilla* v. *Museo Nacional del Prado* [1999] ECR I–4773.

[75] Ibid., paras. 30–34.

[76] For cases involving a wholly internal situation, see Cases 54 and 91/88 and 14/89 *Niño and others* [1990] ECR 3537; Case 204/87 *Bekaert* [1988] ECR 2029; Case C–152/94 *Openbaar Ministerie* v. *Geert van Buydner* [1995] ECR I–3981; Case C–134/94 *Esso Española SA* v. *Comunidad Autónoma de Canarias* [1995] ECR I–4223; Case C–17/94 *Gervais* [1995] ECR I–4353; Case C–134/95 *Unità Socio-Sanitaria Locale no. 47 de Biella* v. *INAIL* [1997] ECR I–195, Cases C–225–227/95 *Kapasakalis* v. *Greece* [1998] ECR I–4329. See for discussion E. Cannizzaro, 'Producing "Reverse Discrimination" through the Exercise of Competences' (1997) 17 *YBEL* 29;

indicated that even if a national was resident in a Member State other than that of his nationality, so long as he maintained his place of establishment and professional practice in his own
Member State, he could not rely on Article 43 to challenge tax provisions of his own State
which favoured residents over non-residents.[77] By way of contrast, in *Asscher*, a Dutch
national residing in Belgium who was a director of companies *both* in Belgium and in the
Netherlands, and who, on account of his non-resident status and the level of his earnings outside the Netherlands, was subject within the Netherlands to a considerably higher rate of tax
than residents of that State, was entitled to invoke Article 43 against his own Member State.[78]
The ECJ ruled this was not an 'internal' situation because his exercise of his Treaty rights of
establishment and his dual economic activities in Belgium and the Netherlands had resulted
in this unfavourable tax situation. Although differential treatment of resident and non-
resident taxpayers which constitutes *prima facie* discrimination under Article 43 could be justified by the State, given the possible objective differences between them, there can be no
justification where such differences do not actually exist.[79]

Cases such as *Kraus* and *Asscher* indicate clearly that EU law on freedom of establishment is
not only about the elimination of unequal treatment of non-nationals or the elimination of
protectionism, but also entails a robust attempt to liberalize the 'single market' such that,
whatever their nationality, self-employed individuals and companies can set up business in
various locations within that market without encountering unnecessary obstacles.

(iii) *Are Restrictions on Social Benefits Contrary to Article 43?*

We have seen that many different national rules and provisions may constitute impermissible
obstacles to freedom of establishment under the Treaty. On the other hand, there is no equivalent, within the law on freedom of establishment, to Regulation 1612/68 governing the rights of
workers and their families. In particular there is no provision like Article 7(2) of that
Regulation guaranteeing the same social and tax advantages to non-nationals as are available to
nationals, nor any mention of housing or educational rights for children. However, apart from
the general non-discrimination clause in Article 12 EC and the specific non-discrimination
requirement in Article 43 which had already been interpreted by the Court in the context of
establishment,[80] Article 24 of Directive 2004/38 on the rights of movement and residence of
EU citizens now contains an umbrella equal treatment clause.

We shall see below that the denial of tax advantages to companies whose primary establishment or registered office is not within the State may also infringe Article 43 (ex Article 52).[81]

C. Ritter, 'Purely Internal Situations, Reverse Discrimination, Guimont, Dzodzi and Article 234' (2006) 31
ELRev. 690.

[77] Case C–112/91 *Werner* v. *Finanzamt Aachen-Innenstadt* [1993] ECR I–429.

[78] Case C–107/94 *Asscher*, n. 11 above.

[79] See also Case C–80/94 *Wielockx* [1995] ECR I–2493; Case C–279/93 *Finanzamt Köln-Altstadt* v.
Schumacker [1995] ECR I–225; Case C–324/00 *Lankhorst-Hohorst GmbH* v. *Finanzamt Steinfurt* [2002] ECR
I–11779; Case C–383/05 *Talotta* v. *Belgium*, 22 Mar. 2007; Case C–470/04 *N* v. *Inspecteur van de Belastingdienst
Oost/kantoor Almelo* [2006] ECR I–7409. In the context of services see Case C–484/93 *Svensson and Gustavsson*,
n. 67 above; Case C–294/97 *Eurowings Luftverkehrs AG* v. *Finanzamt Dortmund-Unna* [1999] ECR I–7447, and
see the series of cases on corporate taxation at n. 103 below.

[80] For some examples of cases requiring equality of treatment for persons exercising the right of establishment see, e.g., Case 63/86 *Commission* v. *Italy* [1988] ECR 29; Case C–337/97 *Meeusen* v. *Hofddirectie van de
Informatie Beheer Groep* [1999] ECR I–3289; Case 197/84 *Steinhauser* v. *City of Biarritz* [1985] ECR 1819; Case
143/87 *Stanton*, n. 53 above; Case 79/85 *Segers* [1986] ECR 2375; Case C–334/94 *Commission* v. *France* [1996]
ECR I–1307, para. 21; Case C–151/96 *Commission* v. *Ireland* [1997] ECR I–3327.

[81] Case 270/83 *Commission* v. *France* [1986] ECR 273. On indirect disadvantages to non-established credit
institutions, due to the conditions imposed on subsidies for borrowers, see Case C–484/93 *Svensson and*

Such measures, although they may not directly regulate or curb the right of establishment, nevertheless constitute disadvantages for those exercising such Treaty rights.

(c) ESTABLISHMENT OF COMPANIES

Article 48 EC provides:

> Companies or firms formed in accordance with the law of a Member State and having their registered office, central administration or principal place of business within the Community shall, for the purposes of this Chapter, be treated in the same way as natural persons who are nationals of Member States.
>
> 'Companies or firms' means companies or firms constituted under civil or commercial law, including co-operative societies, and other legal persons governed by public or private law, save for those which are non-profit making.

Although this Article requires companies to be treated in the same way as nationals for the purposes of the Treaty provisions on freedom of establishment, this is not strictly possible, given the differences between natural and legal persons. It may be easier, for example, to recognize what is a primary as opposed to a secondary establishment in the case of the registered office of a company and one of its subsidiaries or branches, than it is in the case of a professional who has two places of practice in different Member States.[82] Further, despite the many company law directives which have been adopted, considerable differences in the way the various Member States regulate companies and their activities remain.

The definition of a company in Article 48 is wide, referring to 'legal persons governed by private or public law'. However, it excludes non-profit-making companies even though non-profit-making economic activities may be covered by Article 43.[83] The exclusion of non-profit-making companies can be compared with the exclusion from the scope of the Treaty of workers who are not remunerated, and services which are not provided for remuneration. These exclusions reflect what is still the predominantly commercial focus of these provisions, despite the changes made in other areas by the TEU and the despite the increasing focus on 'citizenship' as a category to cover most of the free movement chapters of the Treaty.[84]

(i) *When is a Company 'Established' in a Member State?*

It is clear that, so long as a company is formed in accordance with the law of a Member State and has its registered office there and its principal place of business *somewhere* in the Community, it will be established in the first Member State within the meaning of the Treaty. The ECJ made it clear in *Segers* that this would hold true even if the company conducted no business of any kind in that Member State, but instead conducted its business through one of

---

Gustavsson, n. 67 above. See also Case C–410/96 *André Ambry* [1998] ECR I–7875 concerning restrictions imposed on travel agencies arranging security with a financial institution in another Member State to ensure a guarantee agreement is concluded with a credit institution situated in the host Member State.

[82] V. Edwards, 'Secondary Establishment of Companies—The Case Law of the Court of Justice' (1998) 18 *YBEL* 221.

[83] Case C–70/95 *Sodemare*, n. 15 above.

[84] The fact that a company is non-profit-making does not however mean that it is not engaged in economic activity. For an illustration of this point in a different context see Case C–382/92 *Commission* v. *United Kingdom* [1994] ECR I–2435, para. 45, and see the cases on cross-border access to health care in the context of services, n. 183 below.

the various forms of secondary establishment—such as a subsidiary, branch, or agency—in another Member State.[85]

This was affirmed in *Centros*, where the ECJ ruled that a company was lawfully established in the UK even though it had never traded there, and that the Danish authorities were not justified in restricting its right to a secondary establishment in the form of a branch in Denmark.[86]

In the *Insurance Services* case, the Court held that even an office managed for a company by an independent person on a permanent basis would amount to establishment in that Member State.[87] This latter form of establishment would amount to a secondary establishment, since the registered office or seat of the company and its principal place of business would presumably be elsewhere in the Community. A company has a right of secondary establishment only if it already has its principal place of business or central or registered office within the Community.

(ii) *Court-led Liberalization in the Absence of EU Harmonization*

While companies are not covered by Directive 2004/38 on citizens (nor were they by its predecessor Directive 73/148), governing the right of natural persons to leave their Member State, the ECJ ruled in the *Daily Mail* case that companies enjoy similar rights under the Treaty.[88] However, *Daily Mail* also ruled that the Treaty provisions on freedom of establishment did not give companies an unfettered right to move their registered offices or their central management and control to another Member State, whilst retaining an establishment in the first Member State. On the contrary, the Court ruled that the Member State from which the company wishes to move its registered offices or central place of administration is entitled to subject the company to certain conditions. In this particular case, the UK could legitimately require a company which wished to transfer its central management and control to the Netherlands first to settle its taxes and even to wind up the company in the UK. The reason given by the Court for this was that the laws of the Member States on what constitutes the place of incorporation or the 'real seat' of the company are not harmonized, and that different Member States may legitimately have different views and different ways of regulating how a transfer of head office may be effected.[89]

The general question underlying *Daily Mail*, i.e. to what extent a company can rely on Article 43 when it seeks to set up various forms of establishment in more than one Member State which have different systems of corporate regulation, given the continued absence of EU harmonization, was revisited just over ten years later in *Centros*. This time the restriction was imposed not by the State in which the company had its primary establishment (which was

---

[85] Case 79/85 *Segers*, n. 80 above, para. 16.

[86] Case C–212/97 *Centros*, n. 20 above. For commentaries see W.-H. Roth (2000) 37 *CMLRev.* 147 and P. Cabral and P. Cunha (2000) 25 *ELRev.* 157.

[87] Case 205/84 *Commission* v. *Germany*, n. 13 above, para. 21. Compare Case C–386/04 *Centro di Musicologia Walter Stauffer* v. *Finanzamt München für Körperschaften* [2006] ECR I–8203, paras. 18–20.

[88] Case 81/87 *R.* v. *HM Treasury and Commissioners of Inland Revenue, ex p. Daily Mail and General Trust plc* [1988] ECR 5483.

[89] Art. 220 EC recognized the need for the adoption of agreements for the mutual recognition of companies and the retention of legal personality in the event of transfer of their seats from one country to another, but the Convention on the Mutual Recognition of Companies, which was adopted pursuant to this Art. in 1968, did not come into force. For a recent discussion of this and related matters see J. Wouters, 'European Company Law: Quo Vadis?' (2000) 37 *CMLRev.* 257.

again the UK), but by the State in which the company sought to conduct business through a secondary establishment, which in this case was Denmark.

Case C–212/97 **Centros Ltd. v. Erhvervs- og Selskabsstyrelsen**
[1999] ECR I–1459

[Note ToA renumbering: Arts. 52, 54, and 58 are now Arts. 43, 44, and 48 EC]

The facts concerned a company which was registered (and therefore had its primary establishment) in the UK, but which had never traded there. It had chosen the UK in which to register because UK law imposed no requirements on limited liability companies as to the provision for, or the paying-up of, a minimum share capital. The main purpose of establishing in the UK was to conduct business in Denmark, whose minimum capital requirement laws were considerably stricter, through a branch. The Danish Board of Trade and Companies refused to register the branch on the ground that Centros was not in fact seeking to establish a branch in Denmark, but rather a principal establishment, while circumventing legitimate national rules including those on the paying-up of minimum capital. The Board claimed that, had the establishment in the UK been genuine, in the sense that the company was actually trading there, it would not have refused to register a branch in Denmark. The initial question for the ECJ was therefore whether the company could rely on Article 43 to plead infringement of the right to secondary establishment. Two possible arguments against such a right were raised in the case. First, the Danish government argued that Centros was seeking to abuse EC rights of establishment; and, secondly, following the reasoning in *Daily Mail*, the absence of harmonization of national corporate laws seemed to militate against permitting Centros to rely on Article 43.

THE ECJ

21. Where it is the practice of a Member State, in certain circumstances, to refuse to register a branch of a company having its registered office in another Member State, the result is that companies formed in accordance with the law of that other Member State are prevented from exercising the freedom of establishment conferred on them by Articles 52 and 58 of the Treaty.

22. Consequently, that practice constitutes an obstacle to the exercise of the freedoms guaranteed by those provisions.

23. According to the Danish authorities, however, Mr and Mrs Bryde cannot rely on those provisions, since the sole purpose of the company formation which they have in mind is to circumvent the application of the national law governing formation of private limited companies and therefore constitutes abuse of the freedom of establishment. In their submission, the Kingdom of Denmark is therefore entitled to take steps to prevent such abuse by refusing to register the branch.

24. It is true that according to the case-law of the Court a Member State is entitled to take measures designed to prevent certain of its nationals from attempting, undercover of the rights created by the Treaty, improperly to circumvent their national legislation or to prevent individuals from improperly or fraudulently taking advantage of provisions of Community law. . . .

25. However, although, in such circumstances, the national courts may, case by case, take account—on the basis of objective evidence—of abuse or fraudulent conduct on the part of

the persons concerned in order, where appropriate, to deny them the benefit of the provisions of Community law on which they seek to rely, they must nevertheless assess such conduct in the light of the objectives pursued by those provisions. . . .

26. In the present case, the provisions of national law, application of which the parties concerned have sought to avoid, are rules governing the formation of companies and not rules concerning the carrying on of certain trades, professions or businesses. The provisions of the Treaty on freedom of establishment are intended specifically to enable companies formed in accordance with the law of a Member State and having their registered office, central administration or principal place of business within the Community to pursue activities in other Member States through an agency, branch or subsidiary.

27. That being so, the fact that a national of a Member State who wishes to set up a company chooses to form it in the Member State whose rules of company law seem to him the least restrictive and to set up branches in other Member States cannot, in itself, constitute an abuse of the right of establishment. The right to form a company in accordance with the law of a Member State and to set up branches in other Member States is inherent in the exercise, in a single market, of the freedom of establishment guaranteed by the Treaty.

28. In this connection, the fact that company law is not completely harmonised in the Community is of little consequence. Moreover, it is always open to the Council, on the basis of the powers conferred upon it by Article 54(3)(g) of the EC Treaty, to achieve complete harmonisation.

29. In addition, it is clear from paragraph 16 of *Segers* that the fact that a company does not conduct any business in the Member State in which it has its registered office and pursues its activities only in the Member State where its branch is established is not sufficient to prove the existence of abuse or fraudulent conduct which would entitle the latter Member State to deny that company the benefit of the provisions of Community law relating to the right of establishment.

30. Accordingly, the refusal of a Member State to register a branch of a company formed in accordance with the law of another Member State in which it has its registered office on the grounds that the branch is intended to enable the company to carry on all its economic activity in the host State, with the result that the secondary establishment escapes national rules on the provision for and the paying-up of a minimum capital, is incompatible with Articles 52 and 58 of the Treaty, in so far as it prevents any exercise of the right freely to set up a secondary establishment which Articles 52 and 58 are specifically intended to guarantee.

While the principles of law expressed in *Centros* were familiar principles long articulated by the ECJ in the context of freedom of establishment, their application to this factual situation and with this outcome caused considerable surprise, in particular amongst company lawyers, generating a vast commentary from practitioners and scholars alike. The fact that the particular manoeuvre engaged in by the company to choose its preferred regulatory environment within the EU internal market (the UK), even while conducting its business on a different geographic part of the market (Denmark), was not caught by the 'avoidance' or 'abuse' exception was unexpected.

Far from constituting an *abuse* of Article 43, the ECJ ruled that deliberate choice of a Member State with lenient legislative requirements concerning incorporation in order to enjoy the right of secondary establishment more freely in a Member State with stricter incorporation requirements was simply an exercise of the rights inherent in the notion of freedom of establishment.[90] Further, the absence of legislative harmonization, which had been used by

---

[90] For discussion of the ECJ's similar approach to allegations of abuse in the context of the rights of citizenship and the rights of free movement of workers see Ch. 21, 749, 755–756, 779, and Ch. 23, 855.

the ECJ in *Daily Mail* as a reason for declaring Article 43 to be inapplicable to the facts of that case, was deemed in paragraph 28 of *Centros* to be irrelevant, and indeed gave the Court occasion to point to the availability to Member States of the option of adopting EC harmonizing legislation in this area of company law.[91]

There were other options (including by virtue of the existence of EC legislation governing corporate accounting and disclosure) open to Member States seeking to protect creditors, or to counter fraud or to prevent unjustified corporate evasion of *legitimate* regulatory requirements, which would be less restrictive than imposing the full range of its company law requirements on a branch whose primary establishment was lawfully in another Member State. However, apart from mentioning the possibility of measures to enable public creditors to secure sufficient guarantees, the ECJ did not indicate what other sorts of restrictions would be acceptable and proportionate.

The case has been described as reflecting a judicial 'willingness to break down the remaining constraints to the free movement of companies in the Community' and as 'opening the door to competition among national rules as an alternative approach to ensure the completion of the internal market',[92] while others have noted that it nonetheless left the ruling in *Daily Mail* for the moment untouched.[93]

Centros was followed by the *Überseering*[94] and *Inspire Art*[95] rulings which confirmed and extended the *Centros* approach. Überseering was a company incorporated in the Netherlands under Dutch law, where it had its registered office. It then sought to transfer its centre of administration to Germany, and its entire share capital was bought by German shareholders. Unlike the position of the UK in the *Daily Mail* case, this did not create any problem for the Netherlands, which did not seek to prevent the company from transferring its administration, nor to deny the validity of its continued incorporation under Dutch law. German law, however, would not recognize the legal capacity of a company incorporated in the Netherlands and therefore would not permit it to appear before the German courts. German law followed the 'company seat principle' rather than the 'incorporation principle' as the relevant factor of connection for a company, and since Überseering had moved its real seat from the Netherlands to Germany, German law would not recognize the company's legal capacity unless it re-incorporated under German law. Put more simply, in the absence of EU harmonization of national laws regarding the connecting factor for the purposes of incorporation, Germany did not recognize Überseering's incorporation in the Netherlands.

Although the ECJ distinguished the *Daily Mail* case on its facts (where the restriction on the company's right to retain legal personality in the event of a transfer of registered office or centre of administration was imposed by the Member State of incorporation), the reality is that the reasoning in *Überseering* clearly moves away from the underlying broad rationale in *Daily Mail*. *Überseering* establishes that, despite the lack of harmonization of the laws governing the connecting factor for incorporation, a company which is legitimately incorporated in one Member State and which moves its centre of administration to another State cannot be

---

[91] For a similar dismissal of the relevance, for the freedom of establishment of companies, of the fact that EU law in the field of cross-border mergers had not been harmonized see Case C–411/03 *Sevic Systems* [2005] ECR I–10805, para. 26. For comment see P. Behrens (2006) 43 *CMLRev.* 1669.

[92] P. Cabral and P. Cunha, ' "Presumed Innocent": Companies and the Exercise of the Right of Establishment under Community Law' (2000) 25 *ELRev.* 157; S. Deakin, 'Two Types of Regulatory Competition: Competitive Federalism versus Reflexive Harmonisation. A Law and Econmoics Perspective on *Centros*' (1999) 2 *CYELS* 231.

[93] W. Roth (2000) 37 *CMLRev.* 147, 153–155.

[94] Case C–208/00 *Überseering* v. *NCC* [2002] ECR I–9919.

[95] Case C–167/01 *Kamer van Koophandel en Fabrieken voor Amsterdam* v. *Inspire Art Ltd.* [2003] ECR I–10155.

denied recognition of its legal personality by the latter. While the Court accepted that the enhancement of legal certainty, protection of creditors and minority investors, and legitimate fiscal requirements could in principle provide grounds to justify rules restricting the freedom of establishment, the German rule in question which denied the legal capacity of *Überseering* amounted to an outright denial of freedom of establishment and was disproportionate.

The case of *Inspire Art* tested another of the questions which was left open by *Überseering*, i.e. whether a restriction on a company's secondary establishment which is less drastic than an outright denial of the right of establishment might be compatible with Article 43.[96] In this case, Dutch legislation sought to impose regulatory requirements on a company which was incorporated in the UK, including minimum share capital requirements and directors' liability requirements. Once again, while the ECJ accepted in principle the argument that restrictive regulations could be justified in the interests of protecting creditors and investors, or ensuring an effective tax inspection system, the rules at issue in the case were found to be disproportionate and unnecessary.

Underlying this important series of cases on the right of establishment of companies is the familiar mutual-recognition rationale which we have seen in many areas of EU internal market law. In the context of Articles 43 and 48, it implies that a Member State should recognize the legitimacy of a company's incorporation (and primary establishment) under the laws of another Member State and should not impose unnecessary restrictions on the right of secondary establishment within its territory.

(iii) *Direct Taxation Rules as Restrictions on the Freedom of Establishment of Companies*

While many of the cases before the ECJ have concerned restrictions or disadvantages imposed by Member States on companies—or on the employees of companies[97]—whose registered offices were in another Member State, there have also been many cases involving restrictions—and in particular tax restrictions—imposed by States on companies whose registered office is within that State, but which have subsidiaries or branches in other Member States.

In *Commission* v. *France*, the Court drew an analogy between the location of the registered office of a company and the place of residence of a natural person.[98] It ruled that discrimination in tax laws against branches or agencies in a Member State by taxing them on the same basis as companies whose registered office is in that State yet not giving them the same tax advantages as such companies was an infringement of Article 43. Neither the lack of harmonization of the tax laws of the different Member States nor the risk of tax avoidance by companies could justify the restriction. According to the ECJ, Article 43 'expressly leaves traders free to choose the appropriate legal form in which to pursue their activities in another Member State and that freedom of choice must not be limited by discriminatory tax provisions'.[99] According to the

---

[96] *Ibid.*

[97] Case 79/85 *Segers*, n. 80 above. See also Case 93/89 *Commission* v. *Ireland* [1991] ECR I–4569, Art. 43 requiring nationals of other Member States who owned a vessel registered in Ireland to establish a company in Ireland. For similar vessel registration cases see Case C–221/89 *Factortame*, n. 3 above; Case C–246/89 *Commission* v. *United Kingdom* [1991] ECR I–4585; Case C–334/94 *Commission* v. *France*, n. 80 above; Case C–151/96 *Commission* v. *Ireland*, n. 80 above, Case C–299/02 *Commission* v. *Netherlands* [2004] ECR I–9761. For a controversial pending case see Case C–438/05 *International Transport Workers Federation* v. *Viking Line* [2006] OJ C60/16.

[98] Case 270/83 *Commission* v. *France*, n. 81 above, para. 18.

[99] *Ibid.*, para. 22. See also Case C–330/91 *R.* v. *Inland Revenue Commissioners, ex p. Commerzbank AG* [1993] ECR I–4017; Case C–1/93 *Halliburton Services BV* v. *Staatssecretaris van Financiën* [1994] ECR I–1137; Case C–253/03 *CLT-UFA SA* v. *Finanzamt Köln-West* [2006] ECR I–1831.

Court, 'it is their corporate seat . . . that serves as the connecting factor with the legal system of a Member State, like nationality in the case of natural persons'.[100]

Nevertheless, the ECJ has accepted that a distinction based on the location of the registered office of a company or the place of residence of a natural person may, under certain conditions, be justified in an area such as tax law.[101] In *Futura*, it was permissible for a Member State to impose conditions as regards the keeping of accounts and the location where losses were incurred on a non-resident company (which had a branch but not a main establishment in the state) for the purposes of assessing liability to tax and allowable losses, although the specific restrictions imposed by Luxembourg in the case were closely scrutinized for proportionality, and the accounting requirement—even in the absence of harmonized Community rules in this area—was found to be excessively restrictive.[102]

In recent years there has been a significant amount of important litigation, including the high-profile *Marks & Spencer* case and a series of other test cases, to clarify the applicability and scope of Article 43 to a range of corporate taxation laws directed at cross-border situations—governing matters such as tax credits, deductibility of losses (group relief), and taxation of dividends—as they are applied to companies which are established in more than one Member State.[103] The Court has ruled that while States may in appropriate circumstances treat resident companies differently from non-resident companies, and resident companies with non-resident subsidiaries differently from resident companies with resident subsidiaries, and foreign-sourced dividends differently from domestic-sourced dividends, as far as direct taxation rules are concerned, this is always subject to the requirement of demonstrating reasonable and proportionate justification. While the Court has accepted that goals such as preventing tax avoidance or preventing companies from benefiting twice from rules governing tax relief may be legitimate objectives, it has continued to apply strict scrutiny to the national laws which claim to be necessitated by such objectives.

(d) SUMMARY

i.   Despite restrictive early case law on the point, Article 43 may be invoked by a national in his or her Member State of establishment so long as there is a Community element present. This element often consists of the fact that the individual has obtained a qualification or professional training in another Member State, so long as the situation involves no attempted 'abuse' of Community rights. The notion of abuse or evasion of legitimate control remains hypothetical and largely unspecified.

---

[100]   Case C–330/91 *Commerzbank*, n. 99 above, para. 18. See also Case C–264/96 *ICI* v. *Colmer* [1998] ECR I–4695, para. 20; Case C–307/97 *Compagnie de Saint-Gobain* v. *Finanzamt Aachen-Innenstadt* [1999] ECR I–6161, para. 35; Cases C–397 and 410/98 *Metallgesellschaft Ltd.* v. *Internal Revenue* [2001] ECR I–4727, para. 42.

[101]   Case 270/83 *Commission* v. *France*, n. 81 above, para. 19. See also Case C–279/93 *Schumacker*, n. 79 above; Case C–80/94 *Wielockx*, n. 79 above; Case C–107/94 *Asscher*, n. 11 above; Case C–311/97 *Royal Bank of Scotland* v. *Greece* [1999] ECR I–2651. Compare Case C–264/96 *ICI*, n. 100 above; Case C–200/98 *X and Y* v. *Riksskatteverket* [1999] ECR I–8261; Case C–9/02 *de Lasteyrie du Saillant* [2004] ECR I–2409.

[102]   Case C–250/95 *Futura Participations SA Singer* v. *Administration des Contributions* [1997] ECR I–2471. For indirect tax discrimination against companies having their principal place of business in other Member States see, e.g., Case C–254/97 *Société Baxter* v. *Premier Ministre* [1999] ECR I–4809; Case C–436/00 *X and Y* v. *Riksskatteverket* [2002] ECR I–10829; Case C–334/02 *Commission* v. *France* [2004] ECR I–2229.

[103]   See, e.g., Case C–446/03 *Marks & Spencer* v. *Hasley* [2005] ECR I–10837; Case C–253/03 *CLT-UFA*, n. 99 above; Case C–347/04 *Rewe-Zentralfinanz* v. *Finanzamt Köln-Mitte*, 29 Mar. 2007; Case C–374/04 *Test Claimants in Class IV of the ACT Group Litigation* v. *Inland Revenue*, 12 Dec. 2006; Case C–196/04 *Cadbury Schweppes plc* v. *Inland Revenue* [2006] ECR I–7995; Case C–446/04 *Test Claimants in the FII Group Litigation*, 12 Dec. 2006, Case C–524/04 *Test Claimants in the Thin Cap Group Litigation* v. *Inland Revenue*, 13 Mar. 2007.

ii. Despite the importance of equal treatment and non-discrimination in the field of establishment, the ECJ adopts broadly the same approach to freedom of establishment as it does in other areas of free movement. In other words, any obstacle to the right of establishment in a Member State, whether or not it has a differential impact on nationals and non-nationals, is caught by Article 43 unless it can be justified.

iii. The law governing establishment of companies is more complex than that governing natural persons, mainly due to the differences between national company laws. Rather than await legislative harmonization at EU level, the ECJ has required host States to permit companies validly incorporated in another State, even under a very different corporate law regime, to exercise rights of secondary establishment in a host State without imposing undue regulatory restrictions.

iv. Tax restrictions on companies established in more than one Member State, which seek to combine the advantages and minimize the disadvantages of different tax regimes within the different States in which they are established, have been regularly and successfully challenged in recent years.

4. FREE MOVEMENT OF SERVICES

We have seen that the right of establishment entails the pursuit of an economic activity from a fixed base in a Member State for an indefinite period. Freedom to provide services under EU law, on the other hand, entails the carrying out of an economic activity for a temporary period in a Member State in which either the provider or the recipient of the service is not established.

According to the *Insurance Services* case, if a person or an undertaking maintains a *permanent* base in a Member State, even if only an office, it cannot avail itself of the right to provide services in that State but will be governed by the law on freedom of establishment.[104] In *Gebhard*, however, we saw that the ECJ acknowledged that the provision of services did not necessarily cease to be *temporary* simply because the provider might need to equip herself with the necessary infrastructure—e.g., an office or chambers—to perform those services.[105] Thus what is relevant in order to determine whether a self-employed person is covered by the Treaty provisions on establishment or services is not the mere existence of an office in a Member State, but rather the temporary or permanent nature of the economic activities carried on there.

Further, the Court has ruled that if someone directs most or all of his or her services at the territory of a particular Member State, but maintains his or her place of establishment outside that State in order to evade its professional rules (the abuse/evasion theory), that person may in certain circumstances be treated as being established within the Member State, and thus covered not by Article 49 but by Article 43 instead.[106] In such a case the professional rules

---

[104] Case 205/84 *Commission* v. *Germany*, n. 13 above, para. 21. The earlier decision in Case 39/75 *Coenen* v. *Sociaal-Economische Raad* [1975] ECR 1547, was somewhat contradictory on this point.

[105] Case C–55/94 *Gebhard*, n. 14 above, para. 27.

[106] Case 33/74 *Van Binsbergen*, n. 9 above, para. 13. See also Case 205/84 *Commission* v. *Germany*, n. 13 above, para. 22. For an example of a justified state restriction to prevent an abuse where a provider of services was established outside the Netherlands in order to evade broadcasting regulations, yet was directing its services at the Netherlands, see Case C–148/91 *Vereniging Veronica Omroep Organisatie* v. *Commissariaat voor de Media* [1993] ECR I–487; Case C–23/93 *TV10 SA* v. *Commissariaat voor de Media* [1994] ECR I–4795. Contrast Cases C–369 and 376/96 *Arblade*, n. 58 above, para. 32.

which that person was attempting to evade by maintaining an establishment in a different Member State could be applied as though they were established in the regulating State.

However, in a statement which anticipated a similar ruling of the ECJ in the context of establishment in *Centros*,[107] Advocate General Léger in *Gebhard* declared that the fact that someone opened an office or chambers in order to provide occasional services within a Member State, while having their permanent establishment in another Member State, could not of itself give rise to an irrebuttable presumption of fraud or evasion of national requirements by that person: instead, the onus was on the State in each case to prove the existence of such fraud.[108]

Article 49 provides:

> Within the framework of the provisions set out below, restrictions on freedom to provide services within the Community shall be prohibited in respect of nationals of Member States who are established in a State of the Community other than that of the person for whom the services are intended.
>
> The Council may, acting by a qualified majority on a proposal from the Commission, extend the provisions of the Chapter to nationals of a third country who provide services and who are established within the Community.

In order to benefit from the right to provide services, this provision indicates that the person in question (natural or legal) must already have a place of establishment within the Community and, if a natural person, must possess the nationality of a Member State.[109] The General Programme on freedom to provide services specified in more detail that the right to provide services was available only to nationals established in the Community, or to companies formed under the laws of a Member State and having their seats, centres of administration, or main establishments within the Community.[110] If only the seat of a company is situated within the Community, then its activity must have a 'real and continuous link' with the economy of a Member State, other than a link of nationality.

Without that economic foothold within the Community, there is no right under EC law for a company or a Community national established *outside* the Community to provide temporary services *within* the Community.[111] A permanent economic base must first be established within a Member State, and from that base the person may provide temporary services in other Member States.

Article 50 provides:

> Services shall be considered to be 'services' within the meaning of this Treaty where they are normally provided for remuneration, insofar as they are not governed by the provisions relating to freedom of movement for goods, capital and persons.
>
> 'Services' shall in particular include
>
> (a) activities of an industrial character;
> (b) activities of a commercial character;

---

[107] Case C–212/97 *Centros*, n. 20 above, para. 29.

[108] Case C–55/94 *Gebhard*, n. 14 above, para. 84 of his Opinion.

[109] Case C–290/04 *FKP Scorpio Konzertproduktionen GmbH* v. *Finanzamt Hamburg-Eimsbüttel* [2006] ECR I–9461.

[110] See the 1961 General Programme, n. 35 above.

[111] Case C–452/04 *Fidium Finanz* v. *Bundesanstalt für Finanzdienstleistungsaufsicht* [2006] ECR I–9521.

(c) activities of craftsmen;

(d) activities of the professions.

Without prejudice to the provisions of the Chapter relating to the right of establishment, the person providing a service may, in order to do so, temporarily pursue his activity in the State where the service is to be provided, under the same conditions as are imposed by that State on its own nationals.

Article 50 specifies that the provisions on free movement of services will apply only in so far as a particular restriction is not covered by the provisions on free movement of goods, persons, or capital. Article 51 also excludes transport services from the chapter on services since transport is dealt with elsewhere in the Treaty,[112] and provides that banking and insurance services connected with capital movements are to be dealt with in line with the Treaty provisions on movement of capital.[113]

As in the chapter on establishment, Article 52 provided for a General Programme to be drawn up, and for directives to be issued by the Council so as to liberalize specific services. The General Programme which was drawn up was similar in many respects to that adopted on establishment, with an emphasis on the abolition of discrimination.

(a) THE EFFECT OF ARTICLE 49

The chapter on the free movement of services is very similar to that on establishment, except that the activity in question is pursued on a temporary rather than a permanent basis in a Member State. Shortly after the *Reyners* ruling first established that Article 43 was directly effective, the *Van Binsbergen* case on the direct effect of Article 49 came before the Court.[114] The UK and Irish Governments intervened to argue that, despite the ECJ's ruling in *Reyners*, the area of provision of services was subject to even greater problems of control and discipline than that of establishment, that Articles 49 and 50 should not be found to have direct effect, and that the only satisfactory solution was the adoption of directives as provided for by the Treaty.

Case 33/74 **Van Binsbergen v. Bestuur van de Bedrijfsvereniging voor de Metaalnijverheid**
[1974] ECR 1299

[Note ToA renumbering: Arts. 59, 60, 63, and 66 are now Arts. 49, 50, 52, and 55 respectively]

A Dutch national acting as legal adviser to Van Binsbergen in respect of proceedings before a Dutch social security court transferred his place of residence from the Netherlands to Belgium during the course of the proceedings. He was told that he could no longer represent his client since, under Dutch law, only persons established in the Netherlands could act as legal

---

[112] See Arts. 70–80 EC.

[113] See Ch. 20.

[114] Case 33/74 *Van Binsbergen*, n. 9 above.

advisers. A reference was made to the ECJ to determine whether Article 59 had direct effect, and whether the Dutch rule was compatible with it.

THE ECJ

20. With a view to the progressive abolition during the transitional period of the restrictions referred to in Article 59, Article 63 has provided for the drawing up of a 'general programme'—laid down by Council Decision of 18 December 1961—to be implemented by a series of directives.

21. Within the scheme of the chapter relating to the provision of services, these directives are intended to accomplish different functions, the first being to abolish, during the transitional period, restrictions on freedom to provide services, the second being to introduce into the law of Member States a set of provisions intended to facilitate the effective exercise of this freedom, in particular by the mutual recognition of qualifications and the coordination of laws with regard to the pursuit of activities as self-employed persons.

22. These directives also have the task of resolving the specific problems resulting from the fact that where the person providing the service is not established, on a habitual basis, in the State where the service is performed he may not be fully subject to the professional rules of conduct in force in that State.

. . .

24. The provisions of Article 59, the application of which was to be prepared by directives issued during the transitional period, therefore became unconditional on the expiry of that period.

25. The provisions of that article abolish all discrimination against the person providing the service by reason of his nationality or the fact that he is established in a Member State other than that in which the service is to be provided.

26. Therefore, at least as regards the specific requirement of nationality or of residence, Articles 59 and 60 impose a well-defined obligation, the fulfilment of which by the Member States cannot be delayed or jeopardized by the absence of provisions which were to be adopted in pursuance of powers conferred under Articles 63 and 66.

The Court here identified two reasons for the Treaty provisions on the adoption of directives: first, to abolish restrictions and, secondly, to facilitate the freedom to provide services. An example of the latter would be the adoption of directives to harmonize or provide for mutual recognition of qualifications. In so far as the first was concerned, where the restriction was a straightforward restriction on the ground of nationality or place of establishment, the ECJ considered that no directive was necessary and the provisions of Article 49 could be relied on directly by the end of the transitional period. The residence requirement in issue in the case was a particularly straightforward infringement of that Treaty provision, given that the precise aim of the provision was to abolish state restrictions on the freedom to provide services which were imposed on non-resident providers.

It should be noted too that the lawyer in *Van Binsbergen* was a national relying on Article 49 in the Member State of his own nationality. This did not pose any problem because the relevant factor for the application of Article 49 is simply that the provider must be established in a Member State other than that of the person for whom the service is to be provided. The provider may rely on Article 49 as against the State in which he or she is established, so long as the services are provided for persons established in another Member State.[115] The ECJ has

---

115 See, e.g., Case C–18/93 *Corsica Ferries* [1994] ECR I–1783, para. 30; Case C–379/92 *Peralta* [1994] ECR I–3453, para. 40. For a 'wholly internal situation' in the services context see Case C–108/98 *RI.SAN* v. *Comune di Ischia* [1999] ECR I–5219.

ruled on several occasions since *Van Binsbergen* that restrictions imposed on the basis of residence are liable to operate mainly to the detriment of nationals of other Member States, since non-residents are in the majority of cases foreigners.[116]

(b) THE SCOPE OF ARTICLE 49

(i) *The Need for an Inter-state Element*

As in the context of workers and establishment, the 'wholly internal situation' restriction also applies to the chapter on services. In *Debauve*, criminal proceedings were brought against Belgian cable television companies for infringing a prohibition on the transmission of broadcasts of commercial advertisements in Belgium,[117] and the ECJ held that 'the provisions of the Treaty on freedom to provide services cannot be applied to activities whose relevant elements are confined within a single Member State'.[118] A different outcome was reached in *Koestler*, which concerned a bank in France carrying out certain stock-exchange orders and account transactions for a customer established in France.[119] Despite the fact that both the provider and the recipient of services were established in the same Member State, the ECJ ruled that there was a provision of services within the meaning of Article 50 because the customer moved, before the contractual relationship with the bank was terminated, to establish himself in Germany.

In *Coditel*[120] and *Bond van Adverteerders*,[121] which, like *Debauve*, concerned the provision of broadcasting services, the ECJ was asked whether there could be a provision of services within the meaning of the Treaty where the providers and recipients were firmly established within the same Member State. It will be remembered that Article 49 refers to a provider who is established 'in a State of the Community other than that of the person for whom the services are intended'. This requirement did not appear to be fulfilled on the facts as presented in these two cases, but there was a certain inter-state element, in that the substance of the services, the cable television broadcasts, originated in a different Member State. The ECJ did not answer the question in *Coditel*, because it held that, even if the Treaty provisions did apply, the restriction could be justified by reference to the legitimate protection of industrial property rights.[122] In *Deliège*, in which a Belgian sportswoman had challenged the selection rules of the Belgian Judo Federation, the ECJ rejected the argument that this was a wholly internal situation, relying on the fact that 'a degree of extraneity may derive in particular from the fact that an athlete participates in a competition in a Member State other than that in which he is established'.[123] Arguably, the ECJ—just as in the context of free movement of goods—is focusing

---

[116] Case C–350/96 *Clean Car Autoservice* v. *Landeshauptmann von Wien* [1998] ECR I–2521; Case C–224/97 *Ciola* v. *Land Vorarlberg* [1999] ECR I–2517.

[117] Case 52/79 *Debouve*, n. 18 above.

[118] *Ibid.*, para. 9.

[119] Case 15/78 *Société Générale Alsacienne de Banque SA* v. *Koestler* [1978] ECR 1971.

[120] Case 62/79 *Compagnie Générale pour la Diffusion de la Télévision, Coditel* v. *SA Ciné Vog Films* [1980] ECR 881.

[121] Case 352/85 *Bond van Adverteerders*, n. 67 above.

[122] Case 62/79 *Coditel*, n. 120 above, paras. 10 and 15. See also Case 352/85 *Bond van Adverteerders*, n. 67 above, paras. 14–15, where the ECJ again avoided the question by identifying a provider and recipient of services established in two different Member States. See the subsequent 'TV without frontiers' Broadcasting Dir. 89/552 [1989] OJ L298/23.

[123] Cases C–51/96 and 191/97 *Deliège* v. *Ligue Francophone de Judo et Disciplines Associées ASBL* [2000] ECR I–2549, para. 59. See S. van den Bogaert (2000) 25 *ELRev.* 554.

increasingly on the mobility and availability of the service in question rather than emphasizing the *person*, i.e., the provider or the recipient, who is involved.[124]

It also seems to be the case in certain sectors such as public procurement, where harmonizing legislation has been adopted, that the legislation is made applicable even to wholly internal situations.[125]

(ii) *The Freedom to Receive Services*

Article 49 expressly refers to the freedom to *provide* services, and Article 50 to the rights of the *provider* of services, and does not mention the recipient of the services. In *Luisi and Carbone*, however, the ECJ confirmed that the Treaty Articles cover the situation of recipients as well as providers of services, and ruled that the freedom for the recipient to move was the necessary corollary of the freedom for the provider:

> It follows that the freedom to provide services includes the freedom, for the recipients of services, to go to another Member State in order to receive a service there, without being obstructed by restrictions, even in relation to payments, and that tourists, persons receiving medical treatment and persons travelling for the purposes of education or business are to be regarded as recipients of services.[126]

This holding was confirmed in several later judgments,[127] most notably in *Cowan*, in which the ECJ held that the refusal, under the French criminal compensation scheme, to compensate a British tourist who had been attacked while in Paris was a restriction within the meaning of Article 49, without specifying exactly what service he had received.[128]

(iii) *The Commercial Nature of the Services*

Whether a provision of services falls within Articles 49–50 of the Treaty depends not just on the inter-state element, but also on the services being commercial in nature, in that they must be provided for remuneration. The ECJ has ruled that remunerated services do not lose their economic nature either because the provider is a non-profit-making enterprise,[129] or because of an 'element of chance' inherent in the return, or because of the recreational or sporting nature of the services.[130]

In *Deliège* the ECJ ruled further that 'that the mere fact that a sports association or federation unilaterally classifies its members as amateur athletes does not in itself mean that those

---

124 See the discussion on the cases concerning cross-border access to health-care, below. For more general discussion see V. Hatzopoulos, 'Recent Developments of the Case Law of the ECJ in the Field of Services' (2000) 37 *CMLRev.* 43, and Snell, n. 19 above.

125 V. Hatzopoulos and T. Do, 'The Case Law of the ECJ Concerning the Free Provision of Services: 2000–2005' (2006) 43 *CMLRev.* 923.

126 Cases 286/82 and 26/83 *Luisi and Carbone* v. *Ministero del Tesoro* [1984] ECR 377, para. 16.

127 See, e.g., Case C–17/00 *De Coster* v. *Collège des Bourgmestre et échevins de Watermael-Boitsford* [2001] ECR I–9445; Case C–294/97 *Eurowings Luftverkehrs*, n. 79 above; Case C–158/96 *Kohll* v. *Union des Caisses de Maladie* [1998] ECR I–1931.

128 Case 186/87 *Cowan* v. *Le Trésor Public* [1989] ECR 195.

129 Case C–70/95 *Sodemare*, n. 15 above.

130 Case C–275/92 *Schindler*, n. 19 above, paras. 33–34. See the similar rulings on the concept of an economic activity under Art. 39 in Case 36/74 *Walrave*, n. 22 above; Case C–415/93 *Bosman*, n. 21 above; Cases C–51/96 and 191/97, *Deliège*, n. 123 above; Case C–176/96 *Lehtonen* v. *FRBSB* [2000] ECR I–2681.

members do not engage in economic activities'[131] and in *Bond van Adverteerders* the Court specified that the remuneration did not have to come from the recipient of the services, so long as there was remuneration from some party.[132] This was elaborated upon further in *Deliège* where the ECJ drew on its case law in the field of free movement of workers concerning economic activity which was not 'marginal or ancillary' and ruled:

56. In that connection, it must be stated that sporting activities and, in particular, a high-ranking athlete's participation in an international competition are capable of involving the provision of a number of separate, but closely related, services which may fall within the scope of Article 59 of the Treaty even if some of those services are not paid for by those for whom they are performed . . .

57. For example, an organiser of such a competition may offer athletes an opportunity of engaging in their sporting activity in competition with others and, at the same time, the athletes, by participating in the competition, enable the organiser to put on a sports event which the public may attend, which television broadcasters may retransmit and which may be of interest to advertisers and sponsors. Moreover, the athletes provide their sponsors with publicity the basis for which is the sporting activity itself.[133]

What is the legal position where the remuneration for the service is provided by the State? This issue has been highlighted recently in a series of cases concerning cross-border access to medical and health-care services, which have threatened to disrupt the operation of national welfare systems.[134] The question arose in the context of a course taught under the national educational system in *Humbel*, and here the ECJ ruled that it did not fall within the scope of the Treaty rules on services:

Case 263/86 **Belgium v. Humbel**
[1988] ECR 5365

17. The essential characteristic of remuneration thus lies in the fact that it constitutes consideration for the service in question, and is normally agreed upon between the provider and the recipient of the service.

18. That characteristic is, however, absent in the case of courses provided under the national education system. First of all, the State, in establishing and maintaining such a system, is not seeking to engage in gainful activity but is fulfilling its duties towards its own population in the social, cultural and educational fields. Secondly, the system in question is, as a general rule, funded from the public purse and not by pupils or their parents.

19. The nature of the activity is not affected by the fact that pupils or their parents must sometimes pay teaching or enrolment fees in order to make a certain contribution to the operating expenses of the system.

---

[131] Cases C–51/96 and 191/97 *Deliège*, n. 123 above.

[132] Case 352/85, *Bond van Adverteerders*, n. 67 above. See also Case C–159/90 *SPUC* v. *Grogan* [1991] ECR I–4685 where student distributors of information in Ireland concerning abortion services in the UK received no payment or other remuneration from the providers of the actual service in the second Member State, and, in the absence of such an economic link between the information ban and the freedom to provide the service, the connection between them was 'too tenuous' to attract the application of Art. 49 EC.

[133] N. 123 above.

[134] Case C–120/95 *Decker* [1998] ECR I–1831 (albeit dealing with goods rather than services); Case C–158/96 *Kohll*, n. 127 above; Case C–368/98 *Vanbraekel* v. *ANMC* [2001] ECR I–5363; Case C–157/99

Following the logic of this decision, the ECJ in *Wirth* ruled that, although most institutions of higher education were financed from public funds, those which sought to make a profit and were financed mainly out of private funds, for example by students or their parents, could constitute providers of services within Articles 49 and 50.[135] The distinction between publicly and privately remunerated services on which these cases are based is however a difficult one, as a series of subsequent cases concerning access to cross-border health-care demonstrate.

The *Humbel* case has not been overruled, but the applicability of its reasoning has certainly been restricted by later case law, in particular by the cases on access to cross-border health care. In *Kohll*,[136] which was decided on the same day as the parallel *Decker*[137] case concerning free movement of goods, the ECJ took the view that treatment provided by an orthodontist established in a different Member State from the applicant amounted to a service provided for remuneration, and that the requirement to obtain prior authorization from the competent social-security institution in the applicant's home State before the cost would be reimbursed constituted an unjustified restriction on the freedom to receive cross-border services. Because the individual concerned in *Kohll* had actually paid in another Member State for the service received, there was no real argument about the commercial nature of the service nor about whether Article 49 was applicable.

The subsequent cases of *Geraets-Smits/Peerbooms*,[138] *Inizan*,[139] and *Vanbraekel*,[140] however involved a more complex situation in which the financial balance of the national social-insurance systems would certainly have been affected. The cases therefore demonstrate more vividly the potentially disruptive effects on national welfare systems of the decision to bring essential and publicly organized services within the scope of the Treaty's free movement provisions.

In *Geraets-Smits/Peerbooms*, the two applicants were insured for their medical costs under a Dutch social-insurance scheme for persons whose income is below a certain level. Some of the funding in this scheme was derived from individual premiums, some from the State, and some from subsidization by other private insurance funds. Each of the applicants received medical treatment outside the Netherlands without having obtained prior authorization from the fund, apparently because of the restrictive conditions under which such authorization would be granted. The first condition was that the treatment must be regarded as 'normal in the professional circles concerned' and the second that the treatment must be 'necessary' for the person in question, in the sense that adequate care could not be provided without undue delay by a care provider which had entered into an agreement with the sickness-insurance

---

Geraets-Smits and *Peerbooms* [2001] ECR I–5473, Case C–385/99 *Müller-Fauré* [2003] ECR I–4509; Case C–372/04 *Watts* v. *Bedford Primary Care Trust* [2006] ECR I–4325; Case C–444/05 *Stamatelaki* v. *OAEE*, 19 Apr. 2007.

[135] Case C–109/92 *Wirth* v. *Landeshauptstadt Hannover* [1993] ECR I–6447. See also Cases C–159/90 *Grogan*, n. 132 above, and the comment by S. O'Leary (1992) 17 *ELRev.* 138; Case C–70/95 *Sodemare*, n. 15 above, in which the ECJ considered the applicability of Art. 49 to Italian conditions on the involvement of economic operators in the provision of the State's social-welfare services, such as the running of old people's homes.

[136] Case C–158/96 *Kohll*, n. 127 above. For a note on *Decker* and *Kohll* see P. Cabral (1999) 24 *ELRev.* 387. For a case concerning non-discriminatory access to medical care under Art. 6 EC see Case C–411/98 *Ferlini*, n. 24 above.

[137] Case C–120/95 *Decker*, n. 134 above, which concerned a prior authorization requirement from the competent social-security institution before reimbursement of spectacles purchased in another Member State could be made.

[138] N. 134 above; for commentaries see E. Steyger (2002) 29 *LIEI* 97, and G. Davies (2002) 29 *LIEI* 27.

[139] Case C–56/01 *Inizan* v. *Caisse primaire d'assurance maladie des Hauts-de-Seine* [2003] ECR I–12403.

[140] Case C–368/98 *Vanbraekel*, n. 134 above.

fund in the home State. The question referred to the ECJ was whether this particular kind of prior authorization requirement was prohibited by Articles 49 and 50.[141]

The Court began by reaffirming that Member States retain the power to organize their social-security systems, subject to compliance with the rules of EC law, and went on to consider the argument made by several governments, in reliance on the *Humbel* case, that hospital services did not constitute an economic activity when provided free of charge under a sickness-insurance scheme.

Case C–157/99 **Geraets-Smits v. Stichting Ziekenfonds,**
Peerbooms v. Stichting CZ Groep Zorgverzekeringen
[2001] ECR I–5473

[Note ToA renumbering: Art. 60 is now Art. 50 EC]

53. It is settled case-law that medical activities fall within the scope of Article 60 of the Treaty, there being no need to distinguish in that regard between care provided in a hospital environment and care provided outside such an environment. . . .

54. It is also settled case-law that the special nature of certain services does not remove them from the ambit of the fundamental principle of freedom of movement (Case 279/80 *Webb* [1981] ECR 3305, paragraph 10, and *Kohll*, paragraph 20), so that the fact that the national rules at issue in the main proceedings are social security rules cannot exclude application of Articles 59 and 60 of the Treaty (*Kohll*, paragraph 21).

55. With regard more particularly to the argument that hospital services provided in the context of a sickness insurance scheme providing benefits in kind, such as that governed by the ZFW, should not be classified as services within the meaning of Article 60 of the Treaty, it should be noted that, far from falling under such a scheme, the medical treatment at issue in the main proceedings, which was provided in Member States other than those in which the persons concerned were insured, did lead to the establishments providing the treatment being paid directly by the patients. It must be accepted that a medical service provided in one Member State and paid for by the patient should not cease to fall within the scope of the freedom to provide services guaranteed by the Treaty merely because reimbursement of the costs of the treatment involved is applied for under another Member State's sickness insurance legislation which is essentially of the type which provides for benefits in kind.

56. Furthermore, the fact that hospital medical treatment is financed directly by the sickness insurance funds on the basis of agreements and pre-set scales of fees is not in any event such as to remove such treatment from the sphere of services within the meaning of Article 60 of the Treaty.

57. First, it should be borne in mind that Article 60 of the Treaty does not require that the service be paid for by those for whom it is performed . . .

58. Second, Article 60 of the Treaty states that it applies to services normally provided for remuneration and it has been held that, for the purposes of that provision, the essential characteristic of remuneration lies in the fact that it constitutes consideration for the service in question (*Humbel*, paragraph 17). In the present cases, the payments made by the sickness insurance funds under the contractual arrangements provided for by the ZFW, albeit set at a flat rate, are indeed the consideration for the hospital services and unquestionably represent

---

[141] Several of the health-care cases involve an interpretation of Reg. 1408/71 on the cross-border co-ordination of social security, and particularly of Art. 22 thereof, but for the purposes of this ch. the focus will be only on the ECJ's conclusions about the applicability of Art. 49 EC on the free movement of services.

remuneration for the hospital which receives them and which is engaged in an activity of an economic character.

Geraets-Smits was followed by the cases of *Müller-Fauré*[142] and *Watts*,[143] which confirmed and extended its reasoning. Both cases dealt with a national requirement for prior authorization before travelling to receive medical care in another State. *Watts*, however, concerned the UK's tax-funded National Health Service (NHS) and not the kind of insurance-based health-care systems at issue in the previous cases. The referring court asked the ECJ whether Article 49 EC was applicable to the situation in which the applicant had travelled to another State for medical care and was now seeking reimbursement, despite the fact that the NHS had no fund out of which to pay for health-care received in another State, and despite the fact that it had no obligation to pay for private health care obtained *within* the UK.

The ECJ's answer was that Article 49 was applicable to the facts of the case despite these features of the NHS. However, the Court refused to be drawn on the question (which was arguably parallel to the question in the *Humbel* case concerning state-funded education[144]) whether the provision of health-care services by the NHS within the UK amounted to the provision of a commercial service:

Case C–372/04 **Watts v. Bedford Primary Care Trust**
[2006] ECR I–4325

88 It should be noted as regards the main proceedings that the establishment in another Member State in which Mrs Watts received treatment was paid by her directly.

89 The fact that reimbursement of the hospital treatment in question is subsequently sought from a national health service such as that in question in the main proceedings does not mean that the rules on the freedom to provide services guaranteed by the Treaty do not apply (see to that effect *Smits and Peerbooms*, paragraph 55, and *Müller-Fauré and van Riet*, paragraph 39) . . .

90 It must therefore be found that Article 49 EC applies where a patient such as Mrs Watts receives medical services in a hospital environment for consideration in a Member State other than her State of residence, regardless of the way in which the national system with which that person is registered and from which reimbursement of the cost of those services is subsequently sought operates.

91 It must therefore be found that a situation such as that which gave rise to the dispute in the main proceedings, in which a person whose state of health necessitates hospital treatment goes to another Member State and there receives the treatment in question for consideration, falls within the scope of the Treaty provisions on the freedom to provide services, there being no need in the present case to determine whether the provision of hospital treatment in the context of a national health service such as the NHS is in itself a service within the meaning of those provisions.

While the outcomes on the facts of these cases may not in themselves be alarming, since the Court in each case acknowledged the importance of the stable financing of national

---

142 Case C–385/99 *Müller-Fauré*, n. 134 above.
143 Case C–372/04 *Watts*, n. 134 above.
144 Case 263/86 *Belgium* v. *Humbel* [1988] ECR 5365.

social-insurance systems and the justifiability of measures which seek to maintain a balanced and manageable national health-care system, they have undoubtedly opened up to the rigours of the Treaty rules to cross-border economic activity, some of the core aspects of national welfare systems. In the case of *Watts*, for example, the Court engaged in a detailed review of the way in which the NHS treated waiting lists for the purposes of managing health-care provision.[145]

The upshot of the Court's rulings is that Articles 49–50 apply to any service, however essential a public service it may be, which is 'provided for remuneration', and the line between publicly and privately remunerated services remains uncertain. Health-care services, however funded, fall within the scope of the Treaty where a patient who has travelled to another State and paid for health-care there seeks remuneration from their national system. There is no exception from the Treaty rules for state-provided welfare services.

Despite the *Humbel* ruling that state-funded education falls outside the scope of Article 49, and despite the possibility that this may also be true for the provision of health-care *within* the UK by the NHS, it seems that once there is a cross-border dimension which enables a patient to act as a 'consumer' of health-care services in another State and to seek reimbursement for the cost of those from their own system, the Treaty provisions on the free movement of commercial services will apply.[146]

(iv) *Can Illegal Activities Constitute Services within Articles 49–50?*

Several cases have raised the question of illegal or 'immoral' services, concerning activities which are lawful in certain States but not in others. Clearly if a person established in a Member State in which a particular activity is lawful wishes to provide services in another Member State in which it is not lawful, the second State may have good reasons for restricting the provision of that service. An initial question is whether such activities, on the legality of which the Member States cannot agree, can constitute 'services' at all within Community law.

In *Koestler*, the ECJ ruled that Germany's refusal to allow a French bank which had provided services for a German national, including a stock-exchange transaction which was treated as an illegal wagering contract in Germany but not in France, to recover from that client was not contrary to Article 49 if the same refusal would apply to banks established in Germany.[147] Despite the fact that the services were considered illegal in Germany, the ECJ ruled that the conclusion of the wagering contract could constitute a service, although the Member State was justified in restricting that service by refusing to allow the bank to sue for recovery.

In *Grogan*, the Court considered whether the provision of abortion was a service within the meaning of the Treaty, in order to determine whether the restriction in one Member State on information about the provision of abortion in another State was contrary to Article 49.[148] In response to the argument that abortion could not be categorized as a service on the ground that it was immoral, the ECJ ruled that it was not for the Court 'to substitute its assessment for that of the legislature in those Member States where the activities are practiced legally'.[149] The fact that abortion constitutes a service within Article 49 does not mean that a Member State in which that activity is illegal may not prohibit or restrict the provision of such services in its territory from providers who are established in another Member State, as was made clear in

---

[145] Case C–372/04 *Watts*, n. 134 above.
[146] For discussion of some of the cases see G. Davies, 'Welfare as a Service' (2002) 29 *LIEI* 27.
[147] Case 15/78 Koestler, n. 119 above.
[148] Case C–159/90 *SPUC* v. *Grogan*, n.132 above.
[149] *Ibid.*, para. 20.

Koestler. Less clear, even after *Grogan,* is whether a Member State can restrict the access of its citizens to services in another Member State, where those services are prohibited or restricted within the regulating State.[150]

In *Schindler,* the defendants were acting as agents on behalf of a German public lottery, seeking to promote that lottery by post and otherwise within the UK, and they were charged with an offence under the UK lotteries legislation. When the case was referred to the ECJ, several Member States argued that lotteries were not an 'economic activity' within the meaning of the Treaty, since they were traditionally prohibited or operated by public authorities in the public interest. The Court rejected the argument, ruling that lotteries were services provided for remuneration (the price of the lottery ticket), and that, although they were closely regulated in some Member States, they were not totally prohibited in any:[151]

> In these circumstances, lotteries cannot be regarded as activities whose harmful nature causes them to be prohibited in all the Member States and whose position under Community law may be likened to that of activities involving illegal products (see, in relation to drugs, the judgment in Case 294/82, *Einberger* v. *Hauptzollamt Freiburg* [1984] ECR 1177) even though, as the Belgian and Luxembourg Governments point out, the law of certain Member States treats gaming contracts as void. Even if the morality of lotteries is at least questionable, it is not for the Court to substitute its assessment for that of the legislatures of the Member States where the activity is practised legally.

Similarly in a recent series of cases concerning gambling, the Court stated that although 'moral, religious or cultural factors, as well as the morally and financially harmful consequences for the individual and for society associated with betting and gaming, may serve to justify a margin of discretion for the national authorities', the regulation of such services must be done in a genuine, non-discriminatory, proportionate, and consistent manner.[152]

In *Jany,* the ECJ ruled that the relevant provisions of the EU's Association Agreement with Poland on freedom of establishment and services were to have the same meaning and scope as those under the EC Treaty, so that 'the activitiy of prostitution pursued in a self-employed capacity can be regarded as a service provided for remuneration'.[153] In response to arguments based on the immoral nature of the services, the Court cited its rulings in *Grogan* and *Schindler,* and declared that 'far from being prohibited in all Member States, prostitution is tolerated, even regulated, by most of those States'.[154]

The result of these rulings appears to be that provided it is lawful in some Member States (*quaere* whether one Member State would be sufficient), a remunerated activity constitutes a service within the meaning of Articles 49–50 EC, although other Member States remain free

---

150 The AG in *Grogan,* n. 132 above, took the view that the restriction on information in the case in question was disproportionate. For an interesting example of an indirect restriction on access to artificial insemination services in another Member State which arose in the UK but was not referred to the ECJ see *R.* v. *Human Fertilisation and Embryology Authority, ex p. Diane Blood* [1997] 2 CMLR 591. For a recent revival of the 'Irish problem' concerning whether a woman seeking access to abortion in another Member State may be restricted by the State from travelling for that purpose see *D* v. *Health Service Executive,* judgment of the Irish High Court, 9 May 2007.

151 Case C–275/92 *Schindler,* n. 19 above, para. 32.

152 Case C–67/98 *Zenatti* [1999] ECR I–7289; Case C–42/02 *Lindman* [2003] ECR I–13519; Case C–6/01 *Anomar* [2003] ECR I–8621; Case C–243/01 *Gambelli* [2003] ECR I–13031; Cases C–338, 359, and 360/04 *Placanica,Palazzese and Sorricchio,* 6 Mar. 2007.

153 Case C–268/99 *Jany,* n. 11 above.

154 *Ibid.,* para. 57.

to regulate and restrict it,[155] as long as they do so proportionately and without arbitrary discrimination on grounds of nationality or place of establishment.[156]

(v) Are Restrictions on Social Benefits Contrary to Article 49?

We saw in the context of establishment that, despite the absence of secondary legislation such as Regulation 1612/68 for workers, restrictions on certain social advantages and benefits which are linked to the exercise of the self-employed activity may fall within the prohibition in the Treaty. The same is true of the free movement of services. In the *Italian Housing* case, discussed also in the establishment context above, the ECJ ruled that a nationality requirement for access to reduced-rate mortgage loans and to social housing was contrary to Article 43 on freedom of establishment, but the Italian Government argued that access to publicly built housing could not possibly be relevant to the exercise of the right to provide services, which was precisely the right to provide services without having to have a place of residence in that State.

Case 63/86 **Commission v. Italy**
[1988] ECR 29

18. It is true, as the Italian Government has contended, that in practice not all instances of establishment give rise to the same need to find permanent housing and that as a rule that need is not felt in the case of the provision of services. It is also true that in most cases the provider of services will not satisfy the conditions, of a non-discriminatory nature, bound up with the objectives of the legislation on social housing.

19. However, it cannot be held to be *a priori* out of the question that a person, whilst retaining his principal place of establishment in one Member State, may be led to pursue his occupational activities in another Member State for such an extended period that he needs to have permanent housing there and that he may satisfy the conditions of a non-discriminatory nature for access to social housing. It follows that no distinction can be drawn between different forms of establishment and that providers of services cannot be excluded from the benefit of the fundamental principle of national treatment.

Thus, even if temporary providers of services would be unlikely to satisfy the eligibility criteria for social housing, the ECJ ruled that they must in principle be given the benefit of access to such on the same terms as nationals.

In *Cowan*, a British tourist in France was refused state compensation for victims of violent crime which was available to nationals and to residents.[157] The ECJ cited the general prohibition on discrimination 'within the scope of application of this Treaty' in Article 12,[158] and

---

[155] See, e.g., Case C–36/02 *Omega*, n. 4 above.

[156] The ECJ's conclusion in *Schindler* that the UK legislation was justified on public-policy grounds had been criticized for ignoring the discrimination practised in favour of national small-scale lotteries, and for applying the proportionality test excessively loosely: see the comment by G. Straetmans (2000) 37 *CMLRev.* 991 on the subsequent gaming cases, Case C–124/97 *Läärä* [1999] ECR I–6067; Case C–67/98 *Zenatti*, n. 152 above.

[157] Case 186/87 *Cowan*, n. 128 above.

[158] For cases in which the ECJ ruled that Art. 12 EC could be the sole basis for a claim of discrimination in treatment, without being linked to another specific Treaty provision see Cases C–92 and 326/92 *Phil Collins* v. *Imtrat Handelsgesellschaft* [1993] ECR I–5145; Case C–274/96 *Bickel and Franz* [1998] ECR I–7637; Case C–411/98 *Ferlini*, n. 24 above. That Art. will not however apply where another specific Treaty provision such as Art. 43 applies: see Case C–1/93 *Halliburton*, n. 99 above.

referred to its ruling in *Luisi and Carbone* to the effect that tourists were covered by Article 49 as recipients of services:

> When Community law guarantees a natural person the freedom to go to another Member State, the protection of that person from harm in the Member State in question, on the same basis as that of nationals and persons residing there, is a corollary of that freedom of movement. It follows that the prohibition of discrimination is applicable to recipients of services within the meaning of the Treaty as regards protection against the risk of assault and the right to obtain financial compensation provided for by national law when that risk materialises. The fact that the compensation at issue is financed by the Public Treasury cannot alter the rules regarding the protection of the rights guaranteed by the Treaty.[159]

Thus, although the state compensation is publicly funded, it is not (following *Humbel*[160]) the compensation which constitutes the commercial service being provided. Instead the relevant services in these cases, although not specifically identified by the ECJ, must be other services (such as hotels, restaurants, etc.) for which, as tourists, the recipients provide remuneration. If, whilst in the course of a temporary stay in a Member State in order to avail themselves of remunerated services of this nature, such tourists are denied equal treatment with nationals in matters such as compensation for assault and entry fees to museums, they may be able to invoke Article 49 EC.[161]

Article 24 of Directive 2004/38 also now articulates a general rule of equal treatment for EU citizens who are resident in a host Member State. In the case of a person who is temporarily resident in order to provide or receive services, however, it seems likely that there will have to be some general link between the nature and purpose of the temporary residence and the nature of the social benefit sought.

(c) JUSTIFYING RESTRICTIONS ON THE FREE MOVEMENT OF SERVICES

As in the case of workers and establishment, once a potential restriction on the free movement of services is found to exist, it is open to the Member States to try to justify it either under the Treaty exceptions or under a broader category of Court-developed exceptions.

Alongside the express exceptions for public policy, security, and health contained in Article 46 EC, which are made applicable to the field of services by Article 55,[162] the ECJ has developed a justificatory test for workers, services, and establishment alike which is similar to the *Cassis de Dijon* 'rule of reason' in the free movement of goods context.[163] Although in the area of goods, these open-ended exceptions have generally been referred to as 'mandatory

---

[159] [1989] ECR 195, para. 17. See also Case C–45/93 *Commission* v. *Spain* [1994] ECR I–911, concerning free admission to national museums.

[160] N. 144 above.

[161] For cases which did not concern tourists, but others who may be seeking or providing inter-State services, see Case C–43/95 *Data Delecta and Forsberg* v. *MSL Dynamics* [1996] ECR I–4661; Case C–323/95 *Hayes* v. *Kronenberger* [1997] ECR I–1171; Case C–122/96 *Saldanha and MTS Securities Corporation* v. *Hiross Holdings* [1997] ECR I–5325 on national procedures requiring non-residents to provide security for costs in litigation, which the ECJ held to be capable of having an effect, even though indirect, on trade in goods and services between Member States. Compare Case C–177/94 *Perfili* [1996] ECR I–161.

[162] See sect. 2(d) above.

[163] See Ch. 19.

requirements', we see that in the field of services the term 'imperative requirements' or the generic term 'objective justification' is more often used. The origins of this approach in the services context can be found in the case of *Van Binsbergen*.[164]

We saw in that case how various Member States had argued that there were greater dangers in the area of freedom to provide services than in the area of establishment, since the evasion of national regulation and control would be easier where the providers of services were not resident, or only temporarily rather than permanently present, within the State where the service was provided.[165] These concerns about temporary service-provision are to some extent reflected in the distinction between establishment and services in the 2005 Directive on recognition of professional qualifications.[166] The ECJ in Van *Binsbergen* addressed the issue by indicating that, although the imposition of a residence requirement would probably be excessive in this case, it might not always be so:[167]

> 12. However, taking into account the particular nature of the services to be provided, specific requirements imposed on the person providing the service cannot be considered incompatible with the Treaty where they have as their purpose the application of professional rules justified by the general good—in particular rules relating to the organization, qualifications, professional ethics, supervision and liability—which are binding upon any person established in the State in which the service is provided, where the person providing the service would escape from the ambit of those rules being established in another Member State.
>
> ...
>
> 14. In accordance with those principles, the requirement that persons whose functions are to assist the administration of justice must be permanently established for professional purposes within the jurisdiction of certain courts or tribunals cannot be considered incompatible with the provisions of Article 59 and 60, where such requirement is objectively justified by the need to ensure observance of professional rules of conduct connected, in particular, with the administration of justice and with respect for professional ethics.[168]

The test for justification initially laid down by the Court in *Van Binsbergen* contains several conditions which must be satisfied if a restriction on the freedom to provide services is to be compatible with Article 49.

First, the restriction must be adopted in pursuit of a *legitimate public interest* which is not incompatible with Community aims. And in keeping with the scope of permissible exceptions to other Treaty freedoms, the ECJ has ruled that an *economic* aim is not a legitimate aim. Thus the aim of protecting a particular economic sector within the Member State is not legitimate,[169] whereas the maintenance of the financial balance of the social-security system with

---

[164] Case 33/74 *Van Binsbergen*, n. 9 above. See also Cases 110–111/78 *Ministère Public* v. *Van Wesemael* [1979] ECR 5; Case 279/80 *Webb* [1981] ECR 3305.

[165] See Mayras AG in *Van Binsbergen*, n. 9 above, 1317.

[166] Dir 2005/36, Arts. 7–9 in particular, and recital 6.

[167] See also Case 39/75 *Coenen*, n. 104 above, para. 9; Case C–131/01 *Commission* v. *Italy* [2003] ECR I–1659.

[168] Case 33/74 *Van Binsbergen*, n. 9 above. For a case in which the protection of creditors (and the 'sound administration of justice') was held to be an important objective justifying the imposition of restrictions on the practice of debt-collection see Case C–3/95 *Reisebüro Broede* v. *Sandker* [1996] ECR I–6511. See more recently, on restrictions preventing legal advocates from practising in partnership with accountants, Case C–309/99 *Wouters*, n. 24 above, paras. 97–99, 122.

[169] Case C–398/95 *SETTG* v. *Ypourgos Ergasias* [1997] ECR I–3091, paras. 22–23. See also Case C–49/98 *Finalarte*, n. 12 above, para. 39.

a view to protecting public health is legitimate.[170] In *Finalarte* the ECJ ruled that that the aim of a measure is something to be determined 'objectively' by the national court,[171] although the ECJ retains the ultimate role of pronouncing on the legitimacy of the aim.

Secondly, the restriction must be one which is *equally applicable* to persons established within the State, and which must be applied *without discrimination*.[172] In a series of cases concerning broadcasting restrictions, for example, the Court held that, although the promotion of cultural policy through ensuring a balance of programmes and restricting the content and frequency of advertisements was a legitimate aim, it must not be pursued in a discriminatory or protectionist manner.[173]

Thirdly, the restriction imposed on the provider of services must be *proportionate* to the need to observe the legitimate rules in question.[174] The proportionality test entails examining whether the rule is 'suitable' or 'appropriate' in achieving its (legitimate) aim, and—although the ECJ has not consistently applied this part of the proportionality test in all cases—whether that aim could be satisfied by other, less restrictive means.[175] In *Van Binsbergen* itself, the Court ruled that the public interest in the proper administration of justice could be ensured by requiring an address for service to be maintained within the State, rather than a residence there. A crucial factor in appraising the proportionality and necessity of any restriction is whether the provider is subject to similar regulation in the Member State in which that person is established.[176] If the requirement duplicates a condition already satisfied, it imposes a double or 'dual burden' on the provider of a service, and it therefore cannot be justified.[177] Although the proportionality test in principle is for the national court to apply to the restriction on the facts of the case, the ECJ frequently indicates which requirements or restrictions may be unnecessary/disproportionate in the context of the preliminary reference procedure,[178] or more directly in the context of infringement proceedings under Article 226,[179] such as the series of insurance services cases.[180]

---

[170] See the health-care cases in n. 134 above. In these cases, the States could not rely on aims of a purely economic nature, and in order to plead the 'risk to the financial balance of the social security system' as a justification, they had to frame the argument as a risk to public health rather than to the economic interests of the State.

[171] Case C–49/98 *Finalarte*, n. 12 above, paras. 40–41.

[172] For an example of a discriminatory and inappropriate way of protecting the confidentiality of data by imposing a requirement of state ownership of shares see Case 3/88 *Commission v. Italy* [1989] ECR 4035. See also Case C–272/91 *Commission v. Italy*, n. 26 above; Case C–101/94 *Commission v. Italy* [1996] ECR I–2691.

[173] See Case 352/85 *Bond van Adverteerders*, n. 67 above; Case C–288/89 *Stichting Collectiëve Antennevoorsiening Gouda v. Commissariaat voor de Media* [1991] ECR I–4007; Case C–353/89 *Commission v. Netherlands* [1991] ECR I–4069. The subsequent adoption of the Broadcasting Dir. 89/552 [1989] OJ L298/23, which was enacted with the aim of ensuring services and freedom to provide services and freedom of establishment in the sphere of television, generated a further spate of litigation: e.g., Case C–222/94 *Commission v. United Kingdom* [1996] ECR I–4025; Case C–11/95 *Commission v. Belgium* [1996] ECR I–4115; Case C–14/96 *Denuit* [1997] ECR I–2785.

[174] See, e.g., the tourist-guide cases, Case C–180/89 *Commission v. Italy* [1991] ECR I–709; Case C–154/89 *Commission v. France* [1991] ECR I–659; Case C–198/89 *Commission v. Greece* [1991] ECR I–727; Case C–375/92 *Commission v. Spain* [1994] ECR I–923.

[175] For an interesting case concerning alcohol advertising in France, in which the ECJ did not apply a strict proportionality test, see Case C–262/02 *Commission v. France* [2004] ECR I–6569.

[176] See Case C–272/95 *Guiot and Climatec* [1996] ECR I–1905; Cases C–369 and 376/96 *Arblade*, n. 58 above.

[177] See Ch. 19, in relation to the free movement of goods.

[178] See, e.g., Cases 16/78 *Choquet* [1978] ECR 2293; Case C–193/94 *Skanavi and Chyssanthakopoulos* [1996] ECR I–929 on driving-licence requirements. In Case C–49/98 *Finalarte*, n. 12 above, paras. 49–52, the Court gave a very directional set of guidelines on how the national court should assess whether the rules are a proportionate restriction. See also Case C–390/99 *Canal Satélite*, n. 6 above, paras. 34–42.

[179] See, e.g., the Lawyers' Services case, Case 427/85 *Commission v. Germany* [1988] ECR 1123, para. 26.

[180] Case 205/84 *Commission v. Germany*, n. 13 above; Case 206/84 *Commission v. Ireland* [1986] ECR 3817; Case 220/83 *Commission v. France* [1986] ECR 3663; Case 252/83 *Commission v. Denmark* [1986] ECR 3713.

A *fourth* condition of the test for justification, which was not mentioned in *Van Binsbergen* and has less frequently been highlighted by the ECJ, but which was clearly enunciated in the *Carpenter* case,[181] is the requirement that the restrictive measure should also *respect fundamental rights*.[182]

The question whether specific restrictions on free movement can be justified is one of the most regularly litigated before the Court. For present purposes, we will briefly mention three lines of case law to exemplify the way in which the Court has dealt with claims that a restriction on the free movement of services was justified. The first is a series of cases on the subject of 'posted workers', the second is the series of cases on cross-border access to health-care discussed above,[183] and the third is a series of cases on direct taxation rules.

In a line of cases on the issue of *posted workers*,[184] concerning the provision of manpower on a temporary basis by a service provider from a different Member State, the ECJ has ruled that the aims of preserving the interests of the workforce and of ensuring good relations on the labour market are, in principle, legitimate aims. As a result, the imposition of a licence requirement could be justified so long as it did not duplicate the requirements imposed by the Member State of establishment and so long as it took account of the relevant evidence and guarantees already furnished by the service provider in the State of establishment.[185] Further, while it was permissible in principle for a host Member State to apply its own labour legislation to non-EU national staff members of a company providing temporary services, a requirement that they must obtain work permits was unjustified, and in all cases the claim that the legislative restriction was intended for the protection of the posted workers must be carefully scrutinized.[186] A case which is currently pending before the ECJ and which has generated considerable controversy in Sweden and elsewhere raises the justifiability under Article 49 of permitting industrial action in the form of a blockade by Swedish labour unions against a Latvian company which—largely due to its considerably lower labour costs—won a construction contract to carry out temporary work in Sweden, where the industrial action was aimed at forcing the company to sign a collective agreement containing wage conditions and other terms of employment.[187]

The second example *is the line of cases governing access to cross-border health-care* which were discussed above.[188] In both *Decker* and *Kohll*, the Court rejected the argument that the financial balance of the social security scheme would be upset, given that the expenses

---

[181] Case C–60/00 *Carpenter* v. *Home Secretary* [2002] ECR I–6279.

[182] See also Case C–260/89 *ERT* v. *DEP* [1991] ECR 2925, para. 42 on establishment; Case C–368/95 *Vereinigte Familiapress Zeitungsverlags* [1997] ECR I–3689 in the context of goods.

[183] Nn. 136–145 above and text.

[184] There is a dir. on posted workers, Dir. 96/71 [1997] OJ L18/1, but much of the litigation has concerned situations which are not covered by the Dir., so that the Treaty provisions have been directly applied instead. The Commission recently issued a communication with a view to providing guidance on the consequences of the case law: COM(2006)159.

[185] Case 279/80 *Webb*, n. 164 above.

[186] Case C–113/89 *Rush Portuguesa* v. *Office National d'Immigration* [1990] ECR I–1417; Case C–43/93 *Vander Elst* v. *Office des Migrations Internationales* [1994] ECR I–3803. For a range of other cases dealing with a variety of national restrictions on posted workers see Cases C–369 and 376/96 *Arblade*, n. 58 above; Case C–493/99 *Commission* v. *Germany* [2001] ECR I–8163; Case C–165/98 *Mazzoleni, Guillame and others* [2001] ECR I–2189; Case C–164/99 *Portugaia Construções* [2002] ECR I–787; Case C–445/03 *Commission* v. *Luxembourg* [2004] ECR I–10191; Case C–244/04 *Commission* v. *Germany* [2006] ECR I–885; Case C–168/04 *Commission* v. *Austria* [2006] ECR I–9041.

[187] Case C–341/05 *Laval* [2005] OJ C281/10. For a parallel pending case on freedom of establishment see Case C–438/05 *Viking Line*, n. 97 above.

[188] N. 134 above.

incurred were to be reimbursed at exactly the same rate as that applicable in the home State.[189] In *Leichtle*, the ECJ ruled that the conditions imposed for reimbursement of accommodation and other expenses associated with obtaining a spa health-cure in another Member State were excessive and thus unjustified.[190]

In *Geraets-Smits*,[191] the Court concluded that the requirement of prior authorization (subject to the conditions of the necessity and 'normality' of the treatment obtained) was in principle capable of being justified in the interests of maintaining a balanced medical and hospital service open to all, or of preventing the risk of the social-security system's financial balance being seriously undermined, or for essential public-health reasons under Article 46 EC.[192] However, the Court clearly indicated that the two conditions must be applied fairly in a non-discriminatory manner, so that the condition that the treatment sought should be 'normal' must, for example, take into account the findings of international medical science, and the condition concerning the 'necessity' should be applied to refuse authorization only if the same or equally effective treatment cannot be obtained without undue delay from an establishment with which the insured person's sickness insurance fund has contractual arrangements.

In *Müller-Fauré*,[193] the ECJ held that the objective of maintaining a high-quality, balanced medical and hospital service open to all fell potentially within the derogations provided by Article 46 EC, so long as the restrictive measure (in this case the refusal to reimburse the cost of health-care received in another Member State without prior authorization, unless the providing institution had entered a contractual arrangement with the insurance fund) satisfied the proportionality and necessity requirements. The Court distinguished between hospital and non-hospital services, holding that the restrictive measures were more readily justified in the case of the former than the latter. Similarly in *Watts*, the Court ruled that 'ensuring sufficient and permanent access to a balanced range of high-quality hospital treatment in the State' was indeed a legitimate aim, if applied in a proportionate way.[194]

Thirdly, just as in the context of freedom of establishment, there has been an increase in recent years in challenges to *national taxation rules* on the ground that they constitute unjustifiable restrictions on the freedom to provide services. In cases such as *Danner*,[195] *Gerritse*,[196] *FKP*,[197] *Centro Equestre da Lezíria*,[198] and *Commission v. Belgium*,[199] the ECJ has accepted in principle that restrictive tax rules may be justified on grounds such as prevention of fraud or tax avoidance, effective fiscal supervision, and the effective collection of taxes, or on social grounds, but has regularly rejected the argument on the facts of the case. Further, the Court has indicated clearly that objectives such as the prevention of erosion of the tax revenue base, or compensation for the low level of tax paid in the company's State of establishment do not constitute legitimate aims.[200]

---

189 Case C–120/95 *Decker*, n. 134 above; Case C–158/96 *Kohll*, n. 134 above.

190 Case C–8/02 *Leichtle* [2004] ECR I–2641.

191 Case C–157/99 *Geraets-Smits*, n. 134 above.

192 See also Case C–368/98 *Vanbraekel*, n. 134 above, where a refusal to make an equivalent payment for hospital treatment received in another Member State with prior authorization was held to be unjustified under the Treaty and under Reg. 1408/71.

193 Case C–385/99 *Müller-Fauré*, n. 134 above.

194 Case C–372/05 *Watts*, n. 134 above.

195 Case C–136/00 *Danner* [2002] ECR I–8147.

196 Case C–234/01 *Gerritse* [2003] ECR I–5933 above.

197 Case C–290/04 *FKP Scorpio*, n. 109 above.

198 Case C–345/04 *Centro Equestre da Lezíria Grande Lda v. Bundesamt für Finanzen*, 15 Feb. 2007.

199 Case C–433/04 *Commission v. Belgium*, n. 64 above.

200 See, e.g., Case C–294/97 *Eurowings Luftverkehrs*, n. 79 above; Case C–422/01 *Försäkringsaktiebolaget Skandia v. Riksskatteverket* [2003] ECR I–6817.

Finally, it should be noted that the ECJ has rejected attempts to justify national restrictions where the goals allegedly pursued by such restrictive measures are already satisfied by the existence of EC legislation.[201] Conversely, the ECJ has also indicated that in the absence of co-ordination of Member State regulations on a given issue, a national rule will not be deemed to be disproportionate simply because it is stricter than rules which apply in other Member States.[202] Further, EU secondary legislation which implements the provisions on free movement of services in particular sectors or for particular activities must also be interpreted in the light of the fundamental principles laid down in the Treaty and in the case law, including the principles relating to the scope of permissible exceptions and imperative requirements.[203] It will be interesting to see how the derogation provisions contained in Article 16(1)(b) and 16(3) of the new Services Directive, discussed below,[204] will be interpreted in this respect, and in particular whether they will be held by the ECJ to be exhaustive or not.

(d) ARE NON-DISCRIMINATORY RESTRICTIONS COVERED BY ARTICLE 49?

It has been increasingly clear in recent years that, in the field of free movement of services, even genuinely non-discriminatory restrictions (as opposed to indirectly discriminatory restrictions) are likely to fall within the scope of Article 49 and to be subjected to the 'objective justification' test. While many of the early cases on their facts appeared to involve a heavier burden or a dual burden, and thus could have been described as indirectly discriminatory,[205] there were also a number of cases involving rules which could not be said to have burdened established providers of services any less than non-established providers, and yet which were found to be incompatible with Article 49. In more recent years, the Court has explicitly declared that it is not necessary for any kind of direct or indirect discrimination to be established, but simply an impediment to free movement or a restriction on access to the market of another Member State. At the same time, the ECJ has emphasized the commonality of the principles underpinning all of the internal market freedoms in this respect.[206]

In the *Lawyers' Services* case, concerning the implementation by Germany of Directive 77/249 on the exercise by lawyers of freedom to provide services, one of the complaints of the Commission concerned a rule of territorial exclusivity which provided that, in order to practise before certain of the higher German courts, a lawyer must first be admitted to practise before that judicial authority.[207] The Commission argued that this rule could not be applied to lawyers established in other Member States who were merely providing temporary services in Germany, and the ECJ agreed. The Advocate General drew attention to the fact that the territoriality rule had an equal impact on lawyers established within and outside Germany,

---

[201] See, e.g., C–158/96 *Kohll*, n. 127 above, paras. 45–49.

[202] See Case C–108/96 *MacQuen*, n. 62 above; Case C–67/98 *Zenatti*, n. 152 above.

[203] See, e.g., Case C–205/99 *Analir v. Administración General de l'Estado* [2001] ECR I–1271.

[204] See the extract from de Witte, n. 245 below.

[205] Marenco, n. 63 above; see Case C–379/92 *Peralta*, n. 115 above, para. 51, where, in the absence of any direct or indirect discrimination or any advantage for domestic interests, Art. 49 was held not to apply to a prohibition on discharging harmful chemicals at sea.

[206] See Case C–55/94 *Gebhard*, n. 14 above, para. 37; Case C–390/99 *Canal Satélite*, n. 6 above, in which the case law on goods and services was treated as being the same. On the convergence of the freedoms see C. Barnard, 'Fitting the Remaining Pieces into the Goods and Persons Jigsaw' (2001) 26 *ELRev.* 35.

[207] [1977] OJ L78/17. Case 427/85 *Commission v. Germany* [1988] ECR 1123. For other cases on this dir. see Case 292/86 *Gullung*, n. 56 above; Case C–294/89 *Commission v. France* [1991] ECR I–3591; Case C–289/02 *AMOK*, n. 64 above.

although the Court appeared to base its reasoning on the premise that a lawyer established in another State was potentially in a less favourable position. However, the judgment in *Säger* addressed the issue of non-discrimination directly. The case concerned German legislation which reserved activities relating to the maintenance of industrial property rights to patent agents.[208] The UK government, intervening in the case, referred to the decision in *Koestler*[209] to argue that in the absence of discrimination or unequal application, a restriction on the provision of services would not breach Article 49. Advocate General Jacobs responded as follows:

> It does not seem unreasonable that a person establishing himself in a Member State should as a general rule be required to comply with the law of that State in all respects. In contrast, it is less easy to see why a person who is established in one Member State and who provides services in other Member States should be required to comply with all the detailed regulations in force in each of those States. To accept such a proposition would be to render the notion of a single market unattainable in the field of services.
>
> For this reason, it may be thought that services should rather be treated by analogy with goods, and that non-discriminatory restrictions on the free movement of services should be approached in the same way as non-discriminatory restrictions on the free movement of goods under the '*Cassis de Dijon*' line of case-law. That analogy seems particularly appropriate where, as in the present case, the nature of the service is such as not to involve the provider of the service in moving physically between Member States but where instead it is transmitted by post or telecommunications. . . .
>
> [I] do not think that it can be right to state as a general rule that a measure lies wholly outside the scope of Article 59 simply because it does not in any way discriminate between domestic undertakings and those established in other Member States. Nor is such a view supported by the terms of Article 59: its expressed scope is much broader. If such a view were accepted, it would mean that restrictions on the freedom to provide services would have to be tolerated, even if they lacked any objective justification, on condition that they did not lead to discrimination against foreign undertakings. There might be a variety of restrictions in different Member States, none of them intrinsically justified, which collectively might wholly frustrate the aims of Article 59 and render impossible the attainment of a single market in services. The principle should, I think, be that if an undertaking complies with the legislation of the Member State in which it is established it may provide services in another Member State, even though the provision of such services would not normally be lawful under the laws of the second Member State. Restrictions imposed by those laws can only be applied against the foreign undertaking if they are justified by some requirement that is compatible with the aims of the Community.[210]

The Advocate General's approach is a strongly liberalizing one, since almost any national law which regulates the domestic market even in pursuance of important national policies is potentially subject to rigorous scrutiny by the ECJ for justification. However, this approach has been confirmed by the ECJ in several judgments, beginning with *Alpine Investments*.[211] The case concerned a Dutch prohibition on cold-calling, i.e., on the making of unsolicited

---

[208] Case C–76/90 *Säger*, n. 13 above.

[209] Case 15/78 Koestler, n. 119 above. See also the discussion in the Opinion of Gulman AG in Case C–275/92 *Schindler*, n. 19 above.

[210] Case C–76/90 *Säger*, n. 13 above, 4234–4235.

[211] Case C–384/93 *Alpine Investments*, n. 4 above. For criticism see L. Daniele, 'Non-discriminatory Restrictions on the Free Movement of Persons' (1997) 22 *ELRev.* 191 and C. Hilson, 'Discrimination in Community Free Movement Law' (1999) 24 *ELRev.* 445.

telephone calls without the prior written consent of the individuals concerned in order to offer financial services, and the prohibition applied both to calls made within the Netherlands and to calls made to other Member States. According to the ECJ:

> 28. However, such a prohibition deprives the operators concerned of a rapid and direct technique for marketing and for contacting potential clients in other Member States. It can therefore constitute a restriction on the freedom to provide cross border services.
>
> ...
>
> 35. Although a prohibition such as the one at issue in the main proceedings is general and non-discriminatory and neither its object nor its effect is to put the national market at an advantage over providers of services from other Member States, it can, none the less, as has been held (paragraph 28) constitute a restriction on the freedom to provide services.
>
> 36. Such a prohibition is not analogous to the legislation concerning selling arrangements held in *Keck and Mithouard* to fall outside the scope of Article 30 of the Treaty.
>
> 37. According to that judgment, the application to products from other Member States of national provisions restricting or prohibiting, within the Member State of importation, certain selling arrangements is not such as to hinder trade between Member States so long as, first, those provisions apply to all relevant traders operating within the national territory and, secondly, they affect in the same manner, in law and in fact, the marketing of domestic products and of those from other Member States. The reason is that the application of such provisions is not such as to prevent access by the latter to the market of the Member State of importation or to impede such access more than it impedes access by domestic products.
>
> 38. A prohibition such as that at issue is imposed by the Member State in which the provider of services is established and affects not only offers made by him to addressees who are established in that State or move there in order to receive services but also offers made to potential recipients in another Member State. It therefore directly affects access to the market in services in the other Member States and is thus capable of hindering intra-Community trade in services.

Although the reasoning is not altogether clear, the effect of paragraphs 37 and 38 is that a restrictive regulation will not fall outside the scope of Article 49 or Article 28 simply because it is genuinely non-discriminatory in law and in fact, unless it is *also* a restriction which does not in any way affect the access of the person in question to the market in goods or services of another Member State. If an effect on an individual's access to the market of another Member State can be shown, then, regardless of the equally restrictive effect on situations wholly internal to a Member State, the measure in question will fall within the scope of Community law and require objective justification.[212]

Further, the ruling in *Gebhard* in the context of freedom of establishment, which suggested that the same rules were applicable to all four freedoms, and that discrimination is not necessary for a national rule to constitute an impediment to freedom of movement under the Treaty, has since been repeated in several cases concerning the free movement of services. In a

---

[212] It should however be noted that not every restrictive measure has been held by the Court to fall within the scope of Art. 49. Just as in the case of goods, workers, and establishment, there are restrictions which are insufficiently direct or significant to be considered liable to have an effect on access to the market: see, e.g., Cases C–51/96 and 191/97 *Deliège*, n. 123 above, for example, in which the Judo Federation selection rules for competitions were held not to determine access to the labour market, but instead were 'inherent in the conduct of a high-level international sports event'; therefore they did not amount to a restriction under Art. 49 and did not require justification. See also Case C–190/98 *Graf*, n. 66 above.

paragraph in *Arblade*, which has been repeated in a number of other rulings,[213] the ECJ declared:

> It is settled case-law that Article 59 [now Art 49] of the Treaty requires not only the elimination of all discrimination on grounds of nationality against providers of services who are established in another Member State but also the abolition of any restriction, even if it applies without distinction to national providers of services and to those of other Member States, which is liable to prohibit, impede or render less advantageous the activities of a provider of services established in another Member State where he lawfully provides similar services.[214]

Thus there appears to be an emergent harmony of rules relating to freedom of movement and the internal market, which is rather different from the earlier emphasis on discrimination and protectionism in these areas of EC law. The emphasis instead is on the creation of a genuinely 'single' Community market, so that any national rules, whether discriminatory or not, which may impede inter-state trade and movement by affecting the access of goods, persons (whether employed, self-employed or economically inactive), or services from one national market to another is in principle caught by Community law and must be justified by the regulating State.

5. GENERAL LEGISLATION TO FACILITATE ESTABLISHMENT AND SERVICES: RECOGNITION OF PROFESSIONAL QUALIFICATIONS

The recognition of qualifications is a matter of considerable importance for the free movement of services, freedom of establishment, and free movement of workers alike. We have seen that there has been a great deal of litigation before the ECJ on this issue. However, in tandem with the developing case law of the ECJ, there has also been an active legislative programme on recognition of qualifications for many years. The discussion below examines the EU's gradual move towards a comprehensive mutual-recognition approach, culminating in the adoption of an umbrella directive consolidating the prior legislation on the recognition of professional qualifications in 2005.[215]

(a) THE INITIAL SECTORAL HARMONIZATION/ CO-ORDINATION APPROACH

Initially, the EU legislature pursued a harmonization or co-ordination approach which focused on specific sectors of economic or professional life, with a view to reaching agreement between all Member States on the minimum standard[216] of training and education needed for

---

213 Case C–165/98 *Mazzoleni and ISA* [2001] ECR I–2189, para. 22; Case C–49/98 *Finalarte*, n. 12 above, para. 28.

214 Cases C–369 and 376/96 *Arblade*, n. 58 above, para. 33.

215 Dir. 2005/36 on the Recognition of Professional Qualifications [2005] OJ L 255/22.

216 For a case in which Austria was found to violate the sectoral Dirs. on dentists' qualifications by recognizing persons as qualified to practise who had not met the minimum training criteria laid down see Case C–437/03 *Commission* v. *Austria* [2005] ECR I–9373.

a qualification in that field.[217] These directives mainly covered activities in the medical and health-related sphere—general practitioners, nurses, pharmacists, veterinary surgeons—and also architects, and there was a range of transitional and other directives on various activities and industries such as small craft, food and beverage, wholesale, intermediary, retail, and coal-trade industries.[218] A directive on lawyers' services was also adopted in 1977,[219] and a directive on the right of establishment for lawyers in 1998.[220]

(b) INTRODUCTION OF THE MUTUAL RECOGNITION APPROACH

It was far from easy, however, to gain agreement on the content of such 'harmonizing' sectoral directives, and to get them adopted through the cumbersome Community legislative process. In 1974, the Council passed a resolution on the mutual recognition of formal qualifications, expressing the wish that future work on mutual recognition be based on 'flexible and qualitative criteria', and that directives 'should resort as little as possible to the prescription of detailed training requirements'.[221]

The 1984 summit of the European Council at Fontainebleu marked the beginning of a move away from the harmonization approach, and the first mutual recognition Directive 89/48 was adopted five years later, providing for 'a general system for the recognition of higher-education diplomas awarded on completion of professional education and training of at least three years' duration'.[222] The Directive differed from previous sectoral directives in several ways.[223]

First, it was intended to apply to all regulated professions for which university-level training of at least three years was required and which were not covered by a specific directive. Secondly, recognition was to be based on the principle of mutual trust, without prior co-ordination of the preparatory educational and training courses for the various professions in question. The basic principle was that a host Member State may not refuse entry to a regulated profession to a national of a Member State who holds the qualifications necessary for exercise of that profession in another Member State.[224] Thirdly, recognition was granted to the 'end

---

[217] This has been referred to as 'passive' recognition, since the active recognition work is done by the sectoral legislation and Member States need only passively recognize qualifications which comply with the standards set in that legislation: see K. Armstrong, 'Mutual Recognition', in C. Barnard and J. Scott (eds.), *The Legal Foundations of the Single Market: Unpacking the Premises* (Hart, 2002), ch. 9.

[218] For a case concerning one of the transitional dirs. see Case C–58/98 *Corsten* [2000] ECR I–7919, and on pharmacists see Case C–221/05 *McCauley* v. *Pharmaceutical Society of Ireland* [2006] ECR I–6869.

[219] Dir. 77/249 [1977] OJ L78/17. On the interpretation of the Dir. see Case C–289/02 *AMOK*, n. 64 above.

[220] For a challenge to the Lawyers' Establishment Dir. see Case C–168/98 *Luxembourg* v. *Parliament and Council*, n. 36 above, analysed by P. Cabral in (2002) 39 *CMLRev.* 129; Case C–351/01 *Commission* v. *France* [2002] ECR I–8101; Case C–506/04 *Wilson* v. *Ordre des avocats du barreau de Luxembourg* [2006] ECR I–8613; Case C–193/05 *Commission* v. *Luxembourg* [2006] ECR I–8673. Proceedings against 15 Member States were initiated in relation to this Dir.

[221] [1974] OJ C98/1.

[222] [1989] OJ L19/16. For cases involving non-implementation by Member States of Dir. 89/48 see, e.g., Case C–216/94 *Commission* v. *Belgium* [1995] ECR I–2155; Case C–365/93 *Commission* v. *Greece* [1995] ECR I–499; Case C–285/00 *Commission* v. *France* [2001] ECR I–3801.

[223] For a summary see Bull. EC 6–1988, 11.

[224] For an interesting case challenging the French requirement that applicants seeking employment in the hospital public service must pass the entrance examination for the Ecole Nationale de Santé Publique, despite the fact that they have obtained an equivalent diploma in another Member State see Case C–285/01 *Burbaud* v. *Ministère de l'Emploi et de la Solidarité* [2003] ECR I–8219. For a similar case involving a selection examination

product', i.e. to fully qualified professionals including any professional training required in addition to their university diplomas. Fourthly, where there were major differences in education and training, or in the structure of a profession, in different States, the Directive provided for compensation mechanisms in the form of either an adaptation period or an aptitude test.

While the mutual recognition approach[225] has clear advantages over the time-consuming sectoral harmonization approach, there are also some obvious disadvantages. It does not provide an automatic guarantee to persons holding specified qualifications that they will be accepted to practise in any Member State, but merely provides them with a starting point. Their qualification may still be subject to scrutiny and control by the authorities of the host Member State. States remain free, where either the content of the education or training received is inadequate or the structure of the profession it represents is different, to impose the additional requirements of an aptitude test or an adaptation period.[226] By allowing Member States to control and to supervise the process of recognition at each step, the mutual recognition approach is heavily reliant on mutual trust and on the adoption of a non-protectionist attitude by national competent authorities.[227] Nevertheless, the mutual recognition approach has become the dominant approach, and even the sectors in which harmonization-type directives were adopted have been affected by this approach, most recently under the terms of Directive 2005/36.

(c) THE MUTUAL RECOGNITION APPROACH AND ITS EXPANSION

The basic thrust of Directive 89/48 was that, if a Community national wished to pursue a regulated profession in any Member State, the competent authorities in the Member State could not refuse permission on the ground of inadequate qualifications if the person satisfied certain conditions. The conditions were that the person had pursued the equivalent of a three-year higher-education course in the Community, and had completed the necessary professional training in order to be qualified to take up the 'regulated profession' in question.[228]

Satisfaction of these conditions did not mean that the person had to be given permission to pursue that profession, but it meant that the competent national authorities could not refuse permission solely on the ground of inadequate qualifications. If the qualifications were considered adequate, then permission to practise should be given. If the duration of the person's training and education was however at least one year less than that required in the host State, the Directive permitted Member States to require certain evidence of professional experience.

imposed in relation to Dir. 93/16 on doctors' qualifications see Case C–232/99 *Commission* v. *Spain* [2002] ECR I–4235; Cases C–10–11/02 *Fascicolo et al.* [2004] ECR I–11107.

[225] This approach has been referred to as active rather than passive recognition, by comparison with the sectoral harmonization approach: see Armstrong, n. 217 above.

[226] For a dispute concerning the scope of the professional qualifications of an Italian national seeking recognition as a hydraulic engineer in Spain under the provisions of Dir. 89/48 see Case C–330/03 *Colegio de Ingenieros de Caminos, Canales y Puertos* v. *Administracion del Estado* [2005] ECR I–801.

[227] J. Pertek, 'Free Movement of Professionals and Recognition of Higher Education Diplomas' (1992) 12 *YBEL* 320–321.

[228] For an 'unregulated' profession see Case C–164/94 *Arantis*, n. 46 above, on geologists, and more recently on a profession which is unregulated in the State in which the qualification was obtained see Case C–149/05 *Price* v. *Conseil des ventes volontaires de meubles aux enchères publiques* [2006] ECR I–7691. For the Community definition of a 'regulated profession' in Dirs. 89/48 [1989] OJ L19/16 and 92/51 [1992] OJ L208/25, which includes being governed by the terms of a collective agreement: see Case C–234/97 *de Bobadilla*, n. 74 above, paras. 14–21.

If, on the other hand, the matters covered by the person's education and training differed substantially from those covered by the host-State qualification, or if the host-state profession comprised specific regulated activities which were not within the profession regulated in the Member State where the qualification was obtained, the Member State was permitted to require the completion of an adaptation period or that an aptitude test be taken.[229]

Directive 89/48 was followed by Directive 92/51, which supplemented it and adopted the same approach.[230] The 1992 Directive covered education and training other than the three-year higher-education requirement of Directive 89/48. It covered diplomas awarded after a post-secondary course of at least one year in length, and which qualified the holder to take up a regulated profession. It also covered certificates awarded after educational or training courses other than these post-secondary courses of one year's duration, or after a probationary or professional practice period, or after vocational training, which qualify the holder to take up a regulated profession. The third general directive was Directive 99/42, which replaced the series of earlier transitional and other sectoral directives in a range of industrial and professional fields (discussed at (i) above), using a mutual recognition approach based on periods of consecutive experience and possession of skills, rather than the possession of formal qualifications or diplomas.[231]

Directives 89/48 and 92/51 were amended in 2001 along with most of the sectoral directives by a general (so-called SLIM) Directive 2001/19/EC.[232] The SLIM Directive simplified the co-ordination procedure under the general directives and introduced a range of other changes, including extension to the general system of the concept of 'regulated education and training', requiring host States to examine professional experience gained, incorporating some of the ECJ's case law on third-country diplomas, and specifying procedural rights.

(d) DIRECTIVE 2005/36 ON THE RECOGNITION OF PROFESSIONAL QUALIFICATIONS

In 2005, virtually all of the previous legislation—most importantly the three mutual recognition Directives of 1989, 1992, and 1999 and twelve of the sectoral directives (dealing with nurses, dentists, vets, midwives, architects, pharmacists, and doctors, but not including the two Lawyers' Directives[233])—was consolidated and replaced by a single Directive 2005/36 on the recognition of professional qualifications. The new Directive maintains the same approach and principles as the earlier mutual recognition legislation.[234]

Apart from consolidation, the aim of the 2005 Directive was to maintain the guarantees afforded by each of the prior recognition systems, and at the same time 'to create a single, consistent legal framework based on further liberalization of the provision of services, more automatic recognition of qualifications, and greater flexibility in the procedures for updating

---

[229] On the circumstances in which a Member State must permit the partial taking-up of a profession see Case C–330/03 *Colegio de Ingenieros de Caminos*, n. 226 above.

[230] For a case involving recognition of a teacher's qualifications under both Dirs. 89/48 and 92/51 see Case C–102/02 *Beuttenbuller v. Land Baden-Württemberg* [2004] ECR I–5405.

[231] See [1999] OJ L201/77.

[232] [2001] OJ L206/1.

[233] These two lawyers' dirs. govern the recognition of the authorization of lawyers to practise, rather than recognition of their qualifications. Dir. 2005/36 thus applies to the recognition of lawyers' qualifications. Dir. 2005/35 however leaves unaffected other 'specific legal provisions regarding the recognition of professional qualifications, such as those existing in the field of transport, insurance intermediaries and statutory auditors'.

[234] Dir. 2005/36/EC, n. 1 above.

the Directive'. Like the Services Directive, which is discussed below, the original proposal for the Directive on Recognition of Professional Qualifications was amended and diluted in various ways in response to the concerns of Member States, in particular in relation to controls over the temporary provision of services.

The Directive contains six titles: Title I containing General Provisions, Title II on the Provision of Temporary Services, Title III on Establishment, Title IV on Knowledge of Languages and Use of Titles, Title V on Administrative Co-operation and Responsibility for Implementation, and Title VI containing the final 'Other Provisions'. Title III on Establishment is by far the longest, and effectively comprises the three prior regimes under the two mutual recognition Directives and the sectoral Directives.

Apart from integrating and streamlining the existing legislation, the Directive contains some significant innovations. Three in particular should be mentioned. First, Title II establishes a more liberalized regime containing detailed procedures and stricter deadlines for decision-making, and for the temporary provision of services under the provider's original professional title. Secondly, the part of Title III on establishment dealing with the former general mutual recognition regime introduces the notion of 'common platforms'. Common platforms are defined in Article 15 as a set of criteria which make it possible to compensate for the widest range of substantial differences which have been identified as between the training requirements in at least two thirds of the Member States including all the Member States which regulate that profession. Thirdly, Title V provides for close collaboration between the competent administrative authorities of home and host States, involving confidential exchanges of information including in relation to disciplinary action taken or criminal sanctions imposed.

An extract from EU's official website which provides a helpful summary of the key provisions of Directive 2005/36, which is a lengthy and detailed instrument, is set out below:[235]

Reform of the System for the Recognition of Professional Qualifications

Facilitating *temporary and occasional provision* of cross-border services

Any nationals of a Community Member State legally established in a given Member State may provide services on a temporary and occasional basis in another Member State under their original professional title without having to apply for recognition of their qualifications. However, if service providers relocate outside of their Member State of establishment in order to provide services, they must also provide evidence of two years' professional experience if the profession in question is not regulated in that Member State.

The host Member State may require the service provider to make a declaration prior to providing any services on its territory and to renew it annually, including the details of any insurance cover or other means of personal or collective protection with regard to professional liability. The host Member State may also require that the first application be accompanied by certain documents listed in the Directive, such as proof of the nationality of the service provider, of their legal establishment, and of their professional qualifications.

If the host Member State requires *pro forma* registration with the competent professional association, this must occur automatically upon the competent authority which received the prior declaration forwarding the applicant's file to the professional organisation or body. For

---

235 See http://europa.eu/scadplus/leg/en/cha/c11065.htm.

professions which have public health or safety implications and do not benefit from automatic recognition, the host Member State may carry out a prior check of the service provider's professional qualifications within the limits of the principle of proportionality.

In cases where the service is provided under the professional title of the Member State of establishment or under the formal qualification of the service provider [i.e. the original professional title], the competent authorities of the host Member State may require service providers to furnish the recipient of the service with certain information, particularly with regard to insurance coverage against the financial risks connected with any challenge to their professional liability.

The competent authorities shall ensure the exchange of all information necessary for complaints by a recipient of a service against a service provider to be correctly pursued. The host Member State may also ask the Member State of establishment for information regarding the service provider's legal establishment, good conduct, and the absence of any penalties for professional misconduct. With regard to both the temporary provision of services and permanent establishment in another Member State, the Directive provides for the proactive exchange of information relating to any serious circumstances which arose when the individual in question was established on their territory and which are liable to have consequences for the pursuit of the professional activities concerned. This exchange of information must, at any rate, be carried out in compliance with existing legislation on data protection.

Improving the existing systems of recognition for the purpose of *permanent establishment* in another Member State

On the other hand, 'freedom of establishment' is the framework which applies when a professional enjoys the effective freedom to become established in another Member State in order to conduct a professional activity there on a stable basis. With respect to establishment, the Directive comprises the three existing systems of recognition:

- **General system for the recognition of professional qualifications (Chapter I of the Directive)**. This system applies as a fallback to all the professions not covered by specific rules of recognition and to certain situations where the migrant professional does not meet the conditions set out in other recognition schemes. This general system is based on the principle of mutual recognition, without prejudice to the application of compensatory measures if there are substantial differences between the training acquired by the migrant and the training required in the host Member State. The compensatory measure may take the form of an adaptation period or an aptitude test. The choice between one or other of these tests is up to the migrant unless specific derogations exist;

- **System of automatic recognition of qualifications attested by professional experience (Chapter II of the Directive)**. The industrial, craft and commercial activities listed in the Directive are subject, under the conditions stated, to the automatic recognition of qualifications attested by professional experience;

- **System of automatic recognition of qualifications for specific professions (Chapter III of the Directive)**. The automatic recognition of training qualifications on the basis of coordination of the minimum training conditions covers the following professions: doctors, nurses responsible for general care, dental practitioners, specialised dental practitioners, veterinary surgeons, midwives, pharmacists and architects.

. . .

Procedure for the mutual recognition of professional qualifications
An individual application must be submitted to the competent authority in the host Member State, accompanied by certain documents and certificates. The competent authorities will in

future have one month to acknowledge receipt of an application and to draw attention to any missing documents. A decision will have to be taken within three months of the date on which the application was received in full. Reasons will have to be given for any rejection and it must be possible for a rejection, or a failure to take a decision by the deadline, to be appealed under national law.

Member State nationals shall be able to use the title conferred on them, and possibly an abbreviated form thereof, as well as the professional title of the corresponding host Member State. If a profession is regulated in the host Member State by an association or organisation (see Annex I), Member State nationals must be able to become members of that organisation or association in order to be able to use the title.

Knowledge of languages

Member States may require migrants to have the knowledge of languages necessary for practising the profession. . . .

Administrative cooperation and other provisions

In order to facilitate the application of the above provisions, this proposal seeks close collaboration between the competent authorities in the host Member State and the home Member State, and the introduction of the following provisions:

each Member State shall designate a coordinator to facilitate the uniform application of this directive;

each Member State shall designate contact points by no later than 20 October 2007. These will have the task of providing citizens with such information as is necessary concerning the recognition of professional qualifications and to assist them in enforcing their rights, particularly through contact with the competent authorities to rule on requests for recognition;

the nomination of Member States' representatives to the Committee on the recognition of professional qualifications. This comitology committee, which is chaired by the Commission representative, is to assist the Commission within the limits of the enforcement powers conferred on it by the Directive.

The Commission shall consult with experts from the professional groups in an appropriate manner

Apart from Directive 2005/36 two other relevant developments in the field of recognition of qualifications are Decision 2241/2004, which introduced a set of European instruments to be used by individuals to describe their qualifications and competences,[236] and the European Qualifications Framework (EQF) which is intended to act as 'a translation device and neutral reference point for comparing qualifications across different education and training systems and to strengthen co-operation and mutual trust between the relevant stakeholder'.[237] Unlike Directive 2005/36/EC, the EQF does not grant any right of recognition to employed or self-employed persons of the qualifications which they have acquired in one Member State with a view to exercising a regulated profession in another Member State.

(e) SITUATIONS NOT COVERED BY THE LEGISLATION

Despite the comprehensive scope of Directive 2005/36 and the other remaining legislation dealing with mutual recognition of qualifications, there are still likely to be cases and

---

[236] Dec. 2241/2004 of the European Parliament and Council on a single Community framework for the transparency of qualifications and competences (Europass) [2004] OJ L390/6.

[237] See COM(2006)479.

circumstances in which the legislation does not provide a decisive answer. Examples may include the situation of a person seeking to pursue a profession which is unregulated in the host State[238] and other cases which are not covered by the secondary legislation.[239] In such situations, the basic principles outlined by the ECJ in *Vlassopoulou*[240] and *Heylens*[241] apply— i.e., Article 43 EC imposes a requirement on Member State authorities to examine the knowledge and qualifications already recognized or acquired by the person concerned in another Member State, and to give adequate reasons for the non-recognition of any qualification held, as well as access to a judicial remedy.

Qualifications obtained by EU nationals outside the EU are covered by Directive 2005/36 to the extent that the holder has at least three years' certified professional experience in the territory of a Member State which has chosen to give due recognition to the third-country qualification.[242] However, apart from EEA and Swiss nationals, nationals of non-member countries who are established in the Community have no general rights of mutual recognition or permission to practise in a self-employed capacity under Community law, even when they have undergone precisely the same education and training as Community nationals within a Member State. Thus non-EU nationals are protected neither by the Treaty nor by the legislation. In a weak gesture towards recognizing this gap, recital 10 of Directive 2005/36 states that it does not impose any 'obstacle' to the right of Member States to recognize professional qualifications acquired outside the territory of the EU by third-country nationals, but stipulates that all recognition should respect the minimum training conditions for certain professions.

Finally, it should be noted that 'wholly internal situations' are not covered by the Directive, in the sense that the applicant must be seeking to practise in a host State other than the State in which that person's qualification was obtained. [243]

6. GENERAL LEGISLATION TO FACILITATE ESTABLISHMENT AND SERVICES: THE SERVICES DIRECTIVE

Late in 2006, following a long and heated political process, Directive 2006/123 on services in the internal market was adopted.[244] Although called the 'Services Directive', in fact the legislation— just like Directive 2005/36 on recognition of qualifications—covers both temporary-service provision as well as freedom of establishment. Initially known as the Bolkenstein Directive after the Commissioner who first introduced the proposal, this has been a controversial legislative

---

[238] Case C–164/94 *Aranitis*, n. 46 above; Case C–234/97 *de Bobadilla*, n. 74 above.

[239] See also Case C–31/00 *Conseil National de l'Ordre des Architectes v. Dreessen* [2002] ECR I–663; Case C–313/01 *Morgenbesser v. Consiglio dell'Ordine degli avvocati di Genova* [2003] ECR I–13467.

[240] Case 340/89 *Vlassopoulou* [1991] ECR 2357.

[241] Case 222/86 *Heylens*, n. 44 above.

[242] Art. 3(3) of Dir. 2005/36 [2005] OJ L255/22. This reflects the general approach which had been taken by the ECJ in relation to earlier dirs. in Case C–238/98 *Hocsman v. Ministre de l'Emploi* [2000] ECR I–6623, and Case C–110/01 *Tennah-Durez v. Conseil national de l'ordre des médecins* [2003] ECR I–6239 to the effect that national competent authorities must consider all diplomas or evidence of formal qualifications, and all relevant training and experience of an EU national seeking to exercise the right of establishment, whether or not they were obtained within the EU. See also the earlier Case C–319/92 *Haim v. Kassenzahnärtzliche Vereinigung Nordrhein* [1994] ECR I–425 on recognition of periods of professional experience in other Member States.

[243] Art. 2(1) of Dir. 2005/36. See Cases C–225–227/95 *Kapasakalis v. Greece* [1998] ECR I–4329 for a 'purely internal situation' under Dir. 89/48.

[244] Dir. 2006/123/EC, n. 2 above. The deadline for implementation of the Dir. is 28 Dec. 2009.

initiative which was seen by some of its opponents (who dubbed it the Frankenstein Directive) as a threat to the social systems and public-service ethic of many Member States. Some believe that opposition to the Directive played a part in the debate in France which led to a negative outcome in the referendum on the Constitutional Treaty in 2005.

Apart from the many objections which were voiced during the legislative process, several questions remain after its adoption. Three in particular will be addressed here. In the first place, why was a *general* directive on the liberalization of service-provision in the EU considered to be necessary so long after the General Programme of the 1960s, and more than a decade after the single market programme of the 1990s? Secondly, why was the 'country-of-origin' principle which was central to the original proposal for the Directive so controversial? And thirdly, what are the main significant features of the Services Directive following the removal of the country-of-origin principle by the European Parliament's amendments? These questions are addressed in the extract below.

B. de Witte, Setting the Scene—How did Services get to *Bolkestein* and Why?[245]

There was . . . in the early 1990s, a clear double-track approach to the establishment and functioning of the internal market for services: on the one hand, the most 'obstructed' and economically important sectors had been the subject of sector-specific internal market legislation as part of the 1992 programme, and on the other hand, the European Court of Justice had put in place a 'catch-all' legal regime, which allowed the Commission (in its other capacity of guardian of the Treaty) and interested firms or individuals to tackle national impediments to the services market that had been left in place by the EC legislative programme.

In addition, both elements of this legal strategy were elastic and therefore able to cope, in principle, with future challenges. The *judicial* approach was inherently open-ended, and therefore fit to identify new forms of trade in services as well as newly emerging impediments to such trade; it also covered gaps left even where internal market legislation had been adopted. The *legislative* approach was not exhausted by the deadline set for the 1992 programme, but could be used also later to deal with newly emerging problem sectors. . . .

. . .

Why and when did the Commission start considering that this double-track approach was not sufficient for the establishment of a 'true' single market of services? One explanation could be the inherent weakness of the judicial limb of the double-track approach. There was a strong suspicion that the European Court of Justice, in its case-law, only dealt with the proverbial tip of the iceberg and that most impediments to trade in services remained hidden under the surface because the Commission failed to identify them in its infringement investigations, because the individual persons or firms suffering from those restrictions failed to take legal action, and because national courts, when confronted with such cases, failed to enforce the Treaty and/or to refer preliminary questions to the European Court of Justice. This suspicion—that many humanly and economically obnoxious impediments to the cross-border provision of services continue to exist in the post-1992 European Community—would seem to be confirmed by the marked increase of services cases before the ECJ in recent years. . . . Whatever the reasons, the growing amount of ECJ cases—assuming that they still only constitute the tip of the iceberg, though perhaps a slightly bigger tip than before—seems to indicate that there are serious problems with the effective application of the internal market rules on services.

---

[245] European University Institute Working Paper of the Law Department (2007).

[*The author goes on to discuss the most controversial parts of the legislation as it was initially proposed, i.e., the parts dealing with temporary-service-provision and specifically with the country-of-origin principle, rather than the more acceptable part on freedom of establishment which deals mainly with administrative simplification.*]

As far as provision of services without establishment was concerned, the main emphasis was not on getting rid of administrative formalities but on the much more radical idea that these service providers should in principle be *regulated by the state of origin* and not by the host state. . . .

This element was less obviously necessary, its implications were less clearly spelled out, and it created the virulent opposition which led to a painful retreat in the revised version of 2006.

This 'regulatory competition' part of the Bolkestein draft was more problematic because, unlike the administrative simplification part, it represented a substantive shift compared to the ECJ's case law, and compared to the Commission's own approach in drafting internal market legislation. The case law of the European Court of Justice does not challenge, as a matter of principle, the application of the host country's laws and regulations. The principle of mutual recognition, as adopted by the Court, simply meant that the host state must take into account the laws and regulations to which the service provider is subject in its home state, so as not to create unjustified double burdens. This is not the same thing as imposing, as a matter of principle, the application of the laws of the country of origin.

[*De Witte further points out that the previous, carefully-targeted sector-specific approach of the Commission to the liberalization of services contrasts sharply with the general approach of the Services Directive, and was part of the reason for diluting the original draft. He argues that the final version of the Services Directive adopts instead the 'targeted cross-sector harmonization' approach seen above in the 2005 Directive on recognition of professional qualifications.*]

This time, with the Bolkestein draft, the Commission proposed a regulatory programme applying to the whole range of services (rather than a single one), without an attempt at listing those services. . . . Moreover, the regulatory balance was decidedly tilted away towards deregulation with only a little amount of re-regulation. The basic principle was that the laws of the host country would not apply to the service provision, but instead the laws of the home country in which the service provider was established.

. . .

The idea of adopting the country of origin approach to regulation without identifying the sectors to which it would apply was the core innovation of the Bolkestein draft, compared to the Commission's earlier internal market policy, but it was also the cause of its troubles. This idea was abandoned in the final version of the Directive. The main innovative content left after the revision of the draft is its programme for 'smooth administration' (chapters II and III of the Directive), which fits better in the tradition of targeted cross-sector harmonisation that had been initiated by the diploma and public procurement directives.

. . .

As far as the regulation of services is concerned, the country-of-origin clause has been removed, but the price for the removal was the enactment of a highly complex and very confusing Article 16, which, taken as a whole, is reminiscent of the existing case-law of the ECJ on restrictions of services, but with some major differences which are not well explained in the rambling preamble of the Directive. Although the second sentence of Article 16(1) states that the 'Member State in which the service is provided shall ensure free access to and free exercise of a service activity within its territory', this promise of sweeping liberalisation is immediately tempered by the next sentence which makes clear that the host states may continue to apply their laws and regulations, as long as these are non-discriminatory, necessary and pro-portional—as the Court of Justice has consistently held in its case law on services. So far, Article 16 is only a restatement of existing court-made law. Paragraph 2 of Article 16 adds a number of prohibited requirements which, again, probably correspond to the Court's views of what is permissible, but the specification adds to legal clarity.

However, paragraph 3 of Article 16 attempts (whether deliberately or not) to modify existing services law by specifying which are the acceptable justifications for host country require-ments, namely: reasons of public policy, public security, public health, the protection of the environment, and rules on employment conditions. This list is much shorter than the list of mandatory requirements that the Court of Justice has come to recognize in the course of the years. Neither the text of the Directive nor its preamble explain why the Directive attempts to modify the Court's case law on this point. . . .

So, although the 'revolution' proposed in the Bolkestein draft was turned back by the Council and Parliament, the laborious compromise reached during the codecision procedure seems nevertheless to have produced (whether intentionally or not) a deregulatory shift compared to existing EC services law. This is only one of the many uncertainties raised by the text of the Directive.

In its final form, therefore, the Services Directive accomplishes a certain amount of useful administrative simplification and co-operation with a view to reducing obstacles to the free movement of services and establishment. In this sense, it follows the pattern set by Directive 2005/36 (which deals with one particular obstacle, viz. the non-recognition of qualifications) and is in the tradition of previous sectoral legislation.

Articles 5–8 of the Services Directive deal with procedural simplification, the setting-up of 'points of single contact', the right to information and electronic procedures. Articles 9–15 deal with freedom of establishment, covering authorization procedures and indicating which requirements are prohibited and which are subject to evaluation. Many of these are based directly on ECJ case law, in some cases with more specific detail.

When it comes to temporary-service provision, however, we have seen that the retreat from the country-of-origin principle in the Services Directive has resulted in a complicated but arguably weakly deregulatory set of provisions in Articles 16–18. It remains to be seen whether the ECJ will continue to permit Member States to invoke a longer list of grounds for objective justification than the five specific grounds set out in Article 16(3) of the Directive, in keeping with its long-standing interpretation of the Treaty provisions on the free movement of ser-vices in this respect.[246] Articles 19–21 then govern the rights of recipients of services

Lastly, Articles 22–27 cover a range of detailed provisions on the 'quality of services' (covering issues such as availability of information, commercial communications, liability insurance, and dispute-settlement), Articles 28–36 deal with administrative co-operation (covering issues such as supervision, safety alerts, reputational information, and mutual assistance) and Articles 37–43 contain a range of provisions (including a code of conduct, mutual evaluation and review mechanisms, and a comitology procedure) intended to further the aims of the Directive.

Finally, while the Directive is a general one applicable in principle to all kinds of services, its scope is not comprehensive. Rather it is negatively defined by a series of exclusions of

---

[246] One of several arguments in favour of adherence by the ECJ to its wider, non-exhaustive list of potential justifications is that otherwise the field of services will differ in an apparently arbitrary way from those of goods and workers, where restrictions on free movement can, as long as they are proportionate, be justified on an open-ended public interest ground. Recital 40 to the Dir. arguably also supports the broader reading.

particular kinds of services from its coverage, many of which were again a consequence of parliamentary amendments to the initial draft legislation. Apart from the exclusion of sectors already covered by legislation such as financial services, e-communication, and transport, Articles 1–3 contain a range of exclusions (e.g., non-economic services of general interest, social services, health-care, private security services) explanations of the areas which the Directive 'does not affect' or 'does not concern', and indications of how it should interact with overlapping legislation such as that on mutual recognition of qualifications. These are in addition to the series of derogations provided for in Articles 17–18. Many of these provisions, which were politically crucial to the adoption process and which were often animated by concerns about the impact of the Directive on the different social protection systems of Member States,[247] are rather convoluted and unpredictable in their legal effect. To give one example, the declaration in Article 1 that the Directive 'does not affect labour law … which Member States apply in accordance with national law which respects Community law' is circular and confusing.

In all, even if not exactly a Frankenstein, the Directive is at best a patchy, complicated, and legally rather unsatisfactory outcome to a fraught and lengthy legislative process.

7. CONCLUSIONS

i. The ECJ increasingly adopts a similar approach to the various Treaty freedoms, including the free movement of services and establishment, such that any national rule which constitutes an inter-state impediment to market access falls within the scope of the free movement rules and requires justification.

ii. Relevant differences remain between temporary-service provision on the one hand and establishment on the other. These differences are reflected partly in the more extensive case law on objective justification in the field of services, and partly in the distinction drawn between services and establishment in the two recent Directives on recognition of professional qualifications and services in the internal market, with an emphasis on greater liberalization in the case of temporary-service provision.

iii. It is unclear whether the Treaty provisions on establishment and services are fully horizontally applicable, although they have been applied to private professional organizations which adopt their own collective rules or which are largely responsible for the organization of a particular economic sector.

iv. After years of pursuing a slow sectoral strategy of legislative harmonization (passive recognition) of professional qualifications, there was a change of approach in the late 1980s to one of general (active) mutual recognition. In 2005, three general mutual recognition directives and a dozen sectoral directives were consolidated into a single directive on the recognition of professional qualifications. This Directive retains the main elements of the previous legislation, but seeks to simplify and liberalize further the recognition of entitlement to practise in the case of temporary service providers, and to strengthen the system of recognition for those exercising rights of establishment .

v. Together with Directive 2004/38 on the free movement and residence of EU citizens discussed in Chapters 21 and 23, these Directives signify a general move towards legislative consolidation in the field of free movement.

---

[247] For similar concerns arising in recent litigation before the ECJ see Case C–341/05 *Laval*, n. 187 above; Case C–438/05 *Viking Line*, n. 187 above

vi. Although EC law on establishment and services applies only to economic activity, recent developments have indicated that important or 'special' public services such as health, welfare, and education will not escape the Treaty rules if they are organized and provided through a system which lends itself to market behaviour, and where some kind of remuneration is provided. The key example in recent years has been access to cross-border health-care.

8. FURTHER READING

(a) Books

Barnard, C., *The Substantive Law of the EU: The Four Freedoms* (Oxford University Press, 2004)

Mei, A.P., van der, *Free Movement of Persons within the EC: Cross-Border Access to Public Benefits* (Hart, 2002)

Snell, J., *Goods and Services in EC Law* (Oxford University Press, 2002)

White, R., *Workers, Establishment and Services in the European Union* (Oxford University Press, 2004)

Woods, L., *Free Movement of Goods and Services within the European Community* (Ashgate, 2004)

(b) Articles

Daniele, L. 'Non-discriminatory Restrictions on the Free Movement of Persons' (1997) 22 *ELRev.* 191

Davies, G., 'Welfare as a Service' (2002) 29 *LIEI* 27

Dyrberg, P., 'Full Free Movement of Companies in the European Community at Last?' (2003) 28 *ELRev.* 528

Hatzopoulos, V., and Do, T., 'The Case Law of the ECJ Concerning the Free Provision of Services 2000–2005' (2006) 43 *CMLRev.* 923

Martinsen, D.S., 'Towards an Internal Health Market with the European Court of Justice' (2005) 28 *West European Politics* 1035

Newdick, C., 'Citizenship, Free Movement and Health Care: Cementing Individual Rights by Corroding Social Solidarity' (2006) 43 *CMLRev.* 1645

Roth, W.-H., 'From Centros to Überseering: Free Movement of Companies, Private International Law and Community Law' (2003) 52 *ICLQ* 177

Sørensen, J.E., 'Abuse of Rights in Community Law: A Principle of Substance or Merely Rhetoric?' (2006) 43 *CMLRev.* 423

Spaventa, E., 'From Gebhard to Carpenter: Towards a (Non)-Economic European Constitution' (2004) 41 *CMLRev.* 743

Van Nuffel, P., 'Patients' Free Movement Rights and Cross-border Access to Health-Care' (2005) 12 *MJ* 253

CITIZENSHIP OF
THE EUROPEAN UNION

1. CENTRAL ISSUES

i. The TEU introduced the legal concept of EU citizenship as part of an effort to move from a mainly economic community to a political union. In addition to affirming rights of movement and residence, and gathering some existing entitlements together under the umbrella of citizenship, Articles 17–22 created a number of new political-electoral rights.

ii. To judge by the reports of the Commission and the litigation brought before the ECJ, these political rights have so far not been extensively availed of by EU citizens, nor have they been implemented with particular rigour or enthusiasm by the Member States.

iii. Directive 2004/38 consolidates, updates, and replaces most of the legislation governing the rights of movement and residence of all previous categories of persons enjoying such rights under EU law, including workers, the self-employed, students, etc., under the title of 'citizens'.

iv. The most significant judicial development of the legal concept of citizenship so far has involved interpreting Articles 12 and 18 of the Treaty in a way which has extended incrementally the entitlement of EU nationals in host Member States to equal treatment in access to various social benefits.

2. INTRODUCTION

The Treaty on European Union first introduced the legal concept of citizenship into European Union law. This was a key part of the symbolic move made by the Maastricht Treaty from the European *Economic* Community to the European Community, and from the Community to the Union.[1] Although this represented the first formal 'constitutionalization' of European Union citizenship, the idea of Community citizenship and the rhetoric of a 'People's Europe' had been in circulation for a long time.[2] It is fair to say, however, that the introduction of the

---

[1] C. Closa, 'The Concept of Citizenship in the Treaty on European Union' (1992) 29 *CMLRev.* 1137; S. O'Leary, 'Nationality Law and Community Citizenship: A Tale of Two Uneasy Bedfellows' (1992) 12 *YBEL* 353.

[2] See, e.g., 'Towards a Citizens' Europe', Bull. EC, Supp. 7–1975, 11, and the Report on 'A People's Europe' following the Fontainebleau summit of the European Council, COM(84)446 final. See also D. O'Keeffe, 'Union Citizenship', in D. O'Keeffe and P. Twomey (eds.), *Legal Issues of the Maastricht Treaty* (Wiley, 1994), 87; A. Wiener, 'Assessing the Constructive Potential of Union Citizenship? A Socio-Historical Perspective', European Integration Online Papers, Vol. 1 (1997) No. 17.

legal concept of EU citizenship was greeted with scepticism and critical comment by many scholars.[3] Amongst other things, critics focused on the absence of reciprocal duties which might give rise to a more active or participatory citizenship,[4] the subjection of the right of residence to the limiting conditions laid down in earlier directives, and the continued discrimination against resident third-country nationals.[5]

In terms of its legal implications, one of the recurrent questions has been whether the introduction of EU citizenship has made any significant changes in practice, or whether it remains primarily a matter of symbolism. While the ECJ in its early case law such as *Skanavi* appeared to treat the rights of movement of EU citizens as residual and apparently secondary to other more specific Treaty rights,[6] it has since then given more substance to the provision, and has occasionally included Article 18 in its analysis when the case could have been decided on other Treaty grounds alone.[7] Further, it has continued to include the following delphic phrase, first uttered in the *Grzelczyk* case, in virtually all of its rulings on EU citizenship: 'Union citizenship is destined to be the fundamental status of nationals of the Member States'.[8]

The citizenship provisions are contained in Articles 17–22 EC. Article 17 provides:

> 1. Citizenship of the Union is hereby established. Every person holding the nationality of a Member State shall be a citizen of the Union. Citizenship of the Union shall complement and not replace national citizenship.
> 2. Citizens of the Union shall enjoy the rights conferred by this Treaty and shall be subject to the duties imposed thereby.

Three preliminary points may briefly be noted here. The first is that EU citizenship is expressly made 'complementary' to national citizenship.[9] It remains, as we shall see, a somewhat thin concept which, although not insignificant in practice, does not seriously challenge the centrality of national citizenship. Secondly, EU citizenship is contingent upon—or, to put it more

---

[3] See, e.g., on the narrow and exclusionary nature of EU citizenship M. Everson, 'The Legacy of the Market Citizen', in J. Shaw and G. More (eds.), *New Legal Dynamics of European Union* (Oxford University Press, 1995), 73; C. Lyons, 'Citizenship in the Constitution of the European Union: Rhetoric or Reality?', in R. Bellamy (ed.), *Constitutionalism, Democracy, and Sovereignty: American and European Perspectives* (Avebury, 1996), 96; H. D'Oliveira, 'European Citizenship: Its Meaning, Its Potential', in R. Dehousse (ed.), *Europe after Maastricht* (Munich, 1994).

[4] J. Weiler, 'Citizenship and Human Rights', in J. Winter *et al.* (eds.), *Reforming the TEU: The Legal Debate* (Kluwer, 1996).

[5] See now Dir. 2003/109/EC of 25 Nov. 2003 concerning the status of third-country nationals who are long-term residents [2004] OJ L16/44, and the various proposals of the Commission for developing best practices amongst Member States on conditions of integration, conditions for naturalization, and 'civic citizenship', A Common Agenda for Integration, Framework for the Integration of Third-Country Nationals in the European Union, COM(2005)389.

[6] Case C–193/94 *Skanavi and Chyssanthakopoulos* [1996] ECR I–929. See also Case C–92/01 *Stylianakis* v. *Greece* [2003] ECR I–1291. In Case C–258/04 *Office National de l'Emploi* v. *Ioannidis* [2005] ECR I–8275, the ECJ ruled that it was not necessary to consider the arguments based on citizenship, since the facts of the case clearly demonstrated that the individual enjoyed rights as an EU job-seeker under Art. 39. However, there was no indication that the ECJ considered the status of citizenship to be secondary to that of worker or job-seeker.

[7] See, e.g., Case C–135/99 *Ursula Elsen* v. *Bundesversicherungsanstalt* [2000] ECR I–10409, para. 34; Case C–104/06 *Commission* v. *Sweden*, 18 Jan. 2007.

[8] Case C–184/99 *Grzelczyk* v. *Centre public d'aide sociale d'Ottignies-Louvain-la-Neuve* [2001] ECR I–6193, para. 31.

[9] This provision was not in the original version introduced by the Maastricht Treaty on European Union, but was added by the Amsterdam Treaty—suggesting the concerns that the EU citizenship provisions raised for certain Member States.

crudely, piggybacks upon—possession of the nationality of a Member State. EU law does not purport to regulate the conditions under which Member States confer nationality,[10] other than by requiring them to recognize the nationality duly granted by another Member State.[11] Thirdly, the provision which mentions the *duties* imposed on EU citizens seems largely rhetorical, since there are no obvious duties or obligations imposed by the Treaty on individuals.[12]

3. THE RIGHTS OF FREE MOVEMENT AND RESIDENCE OF EU CITIZENS

Article 18 provides:

1. Every citizen of the Union shall have the right to move and reside freely within the territory of the Member States, subject to the limitations and conditions laid down in this Treaty and by the measures adopted to give it effect.

2. If action by the Community should prove necessary to attain this objective and this Treaty has not provided the necessary powers, the Council may adopt provisions with a view to facilitating the exercise of the rights referred to in paragraph 1. The Council shall act in accordance with the procedure referred to in Article 251.

3. Paragraph 2 shall not apply to provisions on passports, identity cards, residence permits or any other such document or to provisions on social security or social protection.

One of the central questions raised by Articles 17 and 18 has been whether they introduced any innovation, other than the title of citizenship and its symbolic dimension, into existing EU law on the free movement of persons. Have they simply given a new name to the existing EU status-categories of entitlement to movement and residence, which include workers, the self-employed, job-seekers, service-recipients, students, and those with sufficient means to support themselves? This general question about the added value of Articles 17–18 can be broken down into a series of more specific queries, which will be addressed in turn below.

(a) Do the new provisions introduce an autonomous and directly effective right to move and reside in a Member State, regardless of whether the person falls within any previously existing EU law status-category?

(b) Do Articles 17 and 18 change the law as it relates to 'wholly internal situations'?[13] In particular, do they allow individuals to challenge restrictions on their right to move and reside within their own Member State, where they have not otherwise exercised EU rights of free movement?

---

[10] Declaration No. 2 on Nationality of a Member State appended to the Maastricht Treaty confirms that the question whether an individual possesses the nationality of a Member State is determined by reference to the national law of the Member State concerned. This includes the conditions for naturalization, although see Immigration, Integration and Employment, COM(2003)33.

[11] Case C–369/90 *Micheletti* v. *Delegación del Gobierno en Cantabria* [1992] ECR I–4239; Case C–192/99 *R.* v. *Secretary of State for the Home Department, ex p. Kaur* [2001] ECR I–1237; Case C–200/02 *Chen* v. *Home Secretary* [2004] ECR I–9925. See S. O'Leary, *The Evolving Concept of Community Citizenship* (Kluwer, 1996), ch. 2; S. Hall, 'Determining the Scope *Ratione Personae* of European Citizenship: Customary International Law Prevails for Now' (2001) 28 *LIEI* 355.

[12] J. Weiler, 'Citizenship and Human Rights', in Winter *et al.* (eds.), n. 4 above.

[13] See the discussion in Ch. 22, sects. 4(d) and 7(f).

(c) Have Articles 17 and 18 contributed to the creation of new substantive rights for EU nationals who do not fall within any prior status-category? In particular, may EU citizens who are neither economically active nor economically self-sufficient claim entitlement, in any circumstances, to substantive equality of treatment with nationals of a host Member State?

(a) DOES ARTICLE 18 CREATE A NEW AND DIRECTLY EFFECTIVE RIGHT?

The question whether Article 18 introduces an autonomous and directly effective right to move and reside in a Member State, regardless of whether the person falls within any other status-category of EU law, requires a brief preliminary discussion of those other status-categories.

Chapter 21 discussed the categories of worker, former worker, job-seeker, and protected family member, and Chapter 22 discussed the categories of self-employed person and service-recipient. Three other particularly relevant categories are those persons covered by the 1990 Residence Directives, which have now been repealed and replaced by the relevant provisions of Directive 2004/38.[14] These were students exercising the right to vocational training under EC law,[15] persons who had ceased to work or had retired,[16] and a catch-all covering all those persons who did not already enjoy a right of residence under EC law.[17] These Directives required Member States to grant the right of residence to those persons and certain of their family members, subject to the proviso that they had adequate resources not to become a burden on the social assistance schemes of the Member States and were covered by sickness insurance.[18]

The right of EU citizens to move and to reside which was introduced by Article 18(1) EC is expressly made *subject to the limitations and conditions laid down in the EC Treaty and by the measures adopted to give it effect*. While this clearly includes limitations such as those listed in the Treaty enabling Member States to adopt restrictive measures on grounds of public policy, security, and health, it also seemed probable that Article 18 intended to refer to the financial and health-insurance conditions which were imposed by the three Residence Directives—and now by Article 7(1)(b) and (c) of Directive 2004/38—on students and other non-economically active persons. This therefore raised the question whether Article 18(1) actually added anything to the existing law, or whether it simply renamed the existing rights (and their limits) as the rights of EU citizenship.

In the *Baumbast* case, the ECJ was asked whether Article 18 conferred a directly effective right of residence on an EU national who had been found by the relevant national tribunal to be neither a worker nor a person covered by one of the Residence Directives.

---

[14] Dir. 2004/38/EC of the European Parliament and of the Council of 29 Apr. 2004 on the right of citizens of the Union and their family members to move and reside freely within the territory of the Member States [2004] OJ L158/77.

[15] Dir. 90/366 (replaced later by Dir. 93/96) [1993] OJ L317/59.

[16] See Dir. 90/365 [1990] OJ L180/28. This covered persons who had not necessarily ever worked in a Member State other than that of their nationality, but who moved after retirement or ceasing to work.

[17] Dir. 90/364 [1990] OJ L180/26.

[18] For the most recent report by the Commission on the application of these Dirs., which continues to indicate the lack of enthusiasm on the part of Member States in their implementation and interpretation of the requirements of the legislation: COM(2006)156. For some of the enforcement actions brought by the Commission pursuant to the residence Dirs. see Case C–157/03 *Commission* v. *Spain* [2005] ECR I–2911 (followed by a letter of formal notice under Art. 228 EC); Case C–424/98 *Commission* v. *Italy* [2000] ECR I–4001; Case C–408/03 *Commission* v. *Belgium* [2006] ECR I–2647. A range of other reasoned opinions and formal letters which had to be issued by the Commission against other States are also documented in this report.

Case C–413/99 **Baumbast and R. v. Secretary of State**
for the Home Department
[2002] ECR I–7091

Baumbast was a German national married to a Colombian national with two children. They resided in the UK from 1990 on, during which time Baumbast worked as an employed person and then as head of his own company. After the company failed he obtained employment in 1993 from German companies based in China and Lesotho. Mrs Baumbast and the two children lived in the UK. They received no social benefits and enjoyed comprehensive medical insurance in Germany where they travelled occasionally for treatment. In 1995 the Home Secretary refused to renew Mr Baumbast's and the family's residence permit and documents. When the case was appealed and came before the ECJ, the Court was asked whether an EU citizen who no longer enjoys a right of residence as a migrant worker in the host Member State can, as a citizen of the EU, enjoy there a right of residence by direct application of Article 18(1) EC.

THE ECJ

81. Although, before the Treaty on European Union entered into force, the Court had held that that right of residence, conferred directly by the EC Treaty, was subject to the condition that the person concerned was carrying on an economic activity within the meaning of Articles 48, 52 or 59 of the EC Treaty (now, after amendment, Articles 39 EC, 43 EC and 49 EC) (see Case C–363/89 *Roux* [1991] ECR I–273, paragraph 9), it is none the less the case that, since then, Union citizenship has been introduced into the EC Treaty and Article 18(1) EC has conferred a right, for every citizen, to move and reside freely within the territory of the Member States.

82. Under Article 17(1) EC, every person holding the nationality of a Member State is to be a citizen of the Union. Union citizenship is destined to be the fundamental status of nationals of the Member States. . . .

83. Moreover, the Treaty on European Union does not require that citizens of the Union pursue a professional or trade activity, whether as an employed or self-employed person, in order to enjoy the rights provided in Part Two of the EC Treaty, on citizenship of the Union. Furthermore, there is nothing in the text of that Treaty to permit the conclusion that citizens of the Union who have established themselves in another Member State in order to carry on an activity as an employed person there are deprived, where that activity comes to an end, of the rights which are conferred on them by the EC Treaty by virtue of that citizenship.

84. As regards, in particular, the right to reside within the territory of the Member States under Article 18(1) EC, that right is conferred directly on every citizen of the Union by a clear and precise provision of the EC Treaty. Purely as a national of a Member State, and consequently a citizen of the Union, Mr Baumbast therefore has the right to rely on Article 18(1) EC.

85. Admittedly, that right for citizens of the Union to reside within the territory of another Member State is conferred subject to the limitations and conditions laid down by the EC Treaty and by the measures adopted to give it effect.

86. However, the application of the limitations and conditions acknowledged in Article 18(1) EC in respect of the exercise of that right of residence is subject to judicial review. Consequently, any limitations and conditions imposed on that right do not prevent the provisions of Article 18(1) EC from conferring on individuals rights which are enforceable by them and which the national courts must protect. . . .

87. As regards the limitations and conditions resulting from the provisions of secondary legislation, Article 1(1) of Directive 90/364 provides that Member States can require of the nationals of a Member State who wish to enjoy the right to reside within their territory that they themselves and the members of their families be covered by sickness insurance in respect of all risks in the host Member State and have sufficient resources to avoid becoming a burden on the social assistance system of the host Member State during their period of residence.

. . .

[*The ECJ then found that while Mr Baumbast satisfied the condition requiring adequate resources in the 1990 Directive, the adjudicator in the UK had taken the view that he did not satisfy the requirement of having fully adequate sickness insurance.*]

90. In any event, the limitations and conditions which are referred to in Article 18 EC and laid down by Directive 90/364 are based on the idea that the exercise of the right of residence of citizens of the Union can be subordinated to the legitimate interests of the Member States. In that regard, according to the fourth recital in the preamble to Directive 90/364 beneficiaries of the right of residence must not become an unreasonable burden on the public finances of the host Member State.

91. However, those limitations and conditions must be applied in compliance with the limits imposed by Community law and in accordance with the general principles of that law, in particular the principle of proportionality. That means that national measures adopted on that subject must be necessary and appropriate to attain the objective. . . .

92. In respect of the application of the principle of proportionality to the facts of the Baumbast case, it must be recalled, first, that it has not been denied that Mr Baumbast has sufficient resources within the meaning of Directive 90/364; second, that he worked and therefore lawfully resided in the host Member State for several years, initially as an employed person and subsequently as a self-employed person; third, that during that period his family also resided in the host Member State and remained there even after his activities as an employed and self-employed person in that State came to an end; fourth, that neither Mr Baumbast nor the members of his family have become burdens on the public finances of the host Member State and, fifth, that both Mr Baumbast and his family have comprehensive sickness insurance in another Member State of the Union.

93. Under those circumstances, to refuse to allow Mr Baumbast to exercise the right of residence which is conferred on him by Article 18(1) EC by virtue of the application of the provisions of Directive 90/364 on the ground that his sickness insurance does not cover the emergency treatment given in the host Member State would amount to a disproportionate interference with the exercise of that right.

94. The answer to the first part of the third question must therefore be that a citizen of the European Union who no longer enjoys a right of residence as a migrant worker in the host Member State can, as a citizen of the Union, enjoy there a right of residence by direct application of Article 18(1) EC. The exercise of that right is subject to the limitations and conditions referred to in that provision, but the competent authorities and, where necessary, the national courts must ensure that those limitations and conditions are applied in compliance with the general principles of Community law and, in particular, the principle of proportionality.

The first notable aspect of the case is that it establishes clearly that Article 18(1) of the Treaty confers a directly effective right on EU citizens to reside in a host Member State, regardless of whether they are employed or self-employed. The question posed above nonetheless remains to be answered: does this involve anything new, or does it merely place on a Treaty footing the rights that existed under the prior Residence Directives? The answer is a nuanced one. While the main overall impact of Article 18(1) is to move the rights of residence of citizens from a legislative to a Treaty footing, this move has some significant legal consequences. This can be seen in *Baumbast*, where the ECJ ruled that the 'limitations and conditions' accepted by the Treaty on the rights of movement and residence must be interpreted and applied in a proportionate way. On the facts of the case, this meant that to read the requirement of 'sickness insurance' in the Residence Directive restrictively would undermine the right of residence conferred directly by the Treaty.

Thus, the new Treaty status of the rights of movement and residence may require a change in the interpretation of the secondary legislation to avoid any disproportionate interference with the Treaty rights. This means that the conditions and limitations set by the State and by EU secondary legislation are to be read in the light of the fundamental rights of movement and residence established by the Treaty, and that they must be adjusted where they are disproportionately restricted. We shall see that this reasoning recurs often in the ECJ's case law, and in particular in those cases concerning access to social benefits for EU citizens.

In the subsequent case of *Chen*, the ECJ confirmed that Article 18(1) does indeed confer a directly effective right of residence on an EU citizen who falls within no other existing EU law status-category, in particular since in this case the citizen in question was a new-born baby. The key questions raised by the case were (i) whether the child enjoyed a directly effective right to movement and residence based solely on EU citizenship derived from her Irish nationality; (ii) whether the circumstances amounted to an abuse of rights; and (iii) whether the resources of the mother could be taken into account in determining whether the child had sufficient resources not to become a burden on the social assistance scheme of the state.

Case C–200/02 **Zhu and Chen v. Secretary of State for the Home Department**
[2004] ECR I–9925

Mrs Chen was a woman of Chinese nationality who came to the UK, and moved temporarily to Northern Ireland in order to give birth to her child, Catherine, there, with a view to the child obtaining Irish birthright citizenship. Catherine's mother and father were both employed by a company established in China, and the mother now lived with Catherine in Wales, UK. Their applications for long-term residence permits were rejected by the Home Secretary who took the view that, although the child was fully dependent on her mother and together they had health insurance as well as sufficient resources to avoid becoming a burden on the State's resources, Catherine was not exercising any EU law rights, and that her mother was not covered by EU law. The Court began by ruling that this was not a wholly internal situation since, even though the child had been born in the UK and had never left the territory, she held the nationality of another State (Ireland). Secondly the Court rejected the argument that a very young child cannot take advantage of the rights of movement and residence. It then moved on to consider whether she enjoyed rights under Article 18(1).

THE ECJ

26. As regards the right to reside in the territory of the Member States provided for in Article 18(1) EC, it must be observed that that right is granted directly to every citizen of the Union by a clear and precise provision of the Treaty. Purely as a national of a Member State, and therefore as a citizen of the Union, Catherine is entitled to rely on Article 18(1) EC. That right of citizens of the Union to reside in another Member State is recognised subject to the limitations and conditions imposed by the Treaty and by the measures adopted to give it effect. . . .

27. With regard to those limitations and conditions, Article 1(1) of Directive 90/364 provides that the Member States may require that the nationals of a Member State who wish to benefit from the right to reside in their territory and the members of their families be covered by sickness insurance in respect of all risks in the host Member State and have sufficient resources to avoid becoming a burden on the social assistance system of the host Member State during their period of residence.

28. It is clear from the order for reference that Catherine has both sickness insurance and sufficient resources, provided by her mother, for her not to become a burden on the social assistance system of the host Member State.

29. The objection raised by the Irish and United Kingdom Governments that the condition concerning the availability of sufficient resources means that the person concerned must, in contrast to Catherine's case, possess those resources personally and may not use for that purpose those of an accompanying family member, such as Mrs Chen, is unfounded.

30. According to the very terms of Article 1(1) of Directive 90/364, it is sufficient for the nationals of Member States to 'have' the necessary resources, and that provision lays down no requirement whatsoever as to their origin.

31. The correctness of that interpretation is reinforced by the fact that provisions laying down a fundamental principle such as that of the free movement of persons must be interpreted broadly.

[*The ECJ then reiterated paragraphs 91–92 of its ruling in* Baumbast *to the effect that limitations on the exercise of the Treaty rights must be compatible with the principle of proportionality.*]

33. An interpretation of the condition concerning the sufficiency of resources within the meaning of Directive 90/364, in the terms suggested by the Irish and United Kingdom Governments, would add to that condition, as formulated in that directive, a requirement as to the origin of the resources which, not being necessary for the attainment of the objective pursued, namely the protection of the public finances of the Member States, would constitute a disproportionate interference with the exercise of the fundamental right of freedom of movement and of residence upheld by Article 18 EC.

. . .

[*The ECJ then addressed the argument that Mrs Chen could not rely on EU law because she had abused EU rights by moving to Northern Ireland with the aim of having her child acquire the nationality of another Member State.*]

35. That argument must also be rejected.

36. It is true that Mrs Chen admits that the purpose of her stay in the United Kingdom was to create a situation in which the child she was expecting would be able to acquire the nationality of another Member State in order thereafter to secure for her child and for herself a long-term right to reside in the United Kingdom.

37. Nevertheless, under international law, it is for each Member State, having due regard to Community law, to lay down the conditions for the acquisition and loss of nationality.

38. None of the parties that submitted observations to the Court has questioned either the legality, or the fact, of Catherine's acquisition of Irish nationality.

39. Moreover, it is not permissible for a Member State to restrict the effects of the grant of the nationality of another Member State by imposing an additional condition for recognition of that nationality with a view to the exercise of the fundamental freedoms provided for in the Treaty.

40. However, that would be precisely what would happen if the United Kingdom were entitled to refuse nationals of other Member States, such as Catherine, the benefit of a fundamental freedom upheld by Community law merely because their nationality of a Member State was in fact acquired solely in order to secure a right of residence under Community law for a national of a non-member country.

Finally, the ECJ ruled that the child's mother, Mrs Chen, could not be considered a 'dependent relative'[19] for the purposes of deriving a right of residence through her child's EU citizenship, since the reality was that the child was dependent on the mother rather than vice versa. However, the Court ruled that a refusal to grant a right of residence to the parent (whether an EU national or not) who is the carer of the child possessing EU citizenship, and enjoying sufficient resources and health insurance, 'would deprive the child's right of residence of any useful effect'.[20]

Chen thus confirms the ruling in *Baumbast* that the rights of movement and residence deriving from EU citizenship under Article 18(1) are autonomous and directly effective, and that the conditions and limitations which a State may impose on these rights must be interpreted and applied in a proportionate manner which does not unduly restrict their exercise. It further confirms the robust approach adopted by the ECJ in *Akrich*,[21] *Centros*,[22] *Ninni-Orasche*,[23] and *Commission* v. *Austria*,[24] below, to allegations that EU rights have been 'abusively' acquired.

Finally, in *Commission* v. *Belgium* the ECJ underscored again the fundamental Treaty status of the rights of movement and residence of EU citizens under Article 18.[25] The Court condemned Belgium's excessively restrictive interpretation of how the 'sufficient resources' condition of the Residence Directive could be satisfied,[26] as well as the disproportionate penalty (automatic deportation) imposed by Belgian law for failure to produce the relevant documents needed to obtain a residence permit within the prescribed time limit.

Ultimately, therefore, the answer to the question posed at (a) above is that Article 18 does create a new and directly effective right, and that while the most obvious novel element is the conferral of fundamental Treaty status on the right of non-economically active persons to move and reside, this is not a purely symbolic change. The case law indicates that the limits which States may legitimately impose on the rights of movement and residence of non-economically active persons must be interpreted in the light of their status as citizens, and in particular must be proportionate.

(b) DO ARTICLES 17 AND 18 CHANGE WHAT CAN BE CONSIDERED AS A 'WHOLLY INTERNAL SITUATION'?

We saw in Chapter 21 that the ECJ has repeatedly held that EU law rights of movement and residence cannot be invoked in a 'wholly internal situation'. The issue generally arose either where a national sought to challenge an internal restriction on his or her freedom of movement within a Member State, as in *Saunders*,[27] or where a national of a Member State who had

---

[19] This was regulated by Dir. 90/364 [1990] OJ L180/26, at the time, and now by Arts. 2(2)(d) and 7(2) of Dir. 2004/38 [2004] OJ L158/77.

[20] Para. 45. See Ch. 21, sect. 7(d) for a similar ruling in Case C–413/99 *Baumbast and R.* v. *Secretary of State for the Home Department* [2002] ECR I–7091 concerning the carer parent of children enjoying educational rights in a Member State after the worker parent has left the State or has divorced the other.

[21] Case C–109/01 *Secretary of State for the Home Department* v. *Akrich* [2003] ECR I–9607, paras. 55–56, discussed in Ch. 21 at n. 196 and text.

[22] Case C–212/97 *Centros Ltd.* v. *Erhvervs- og Selskabsstyrelsen* [1999] ECR I–1459, discussed in Ch. 22.

[23] Case C–413/01 *Ninni-Orasche* v. *Bundesminister für Wissenschaft, Verkehr und Kunst* [2003] ECR I–13187, discussed in Ch. 21, sect. 3(c), and n. 163.

[24] Case C–147/03 *Commission* v. *Austria* [2005] ECR I–5969.

[25] Case C–408/03 *Commission* v. *Belgium* [2006] ECR I–2647.

[26] Belgian law excluded the income of a partner in the absence of an agreement concluded before a notary, and containing an assistance clause.

[27] Case 175/78 *R.* v. *Saunders* [1979] ECR 1129.

not previously exercised rights of movement outside that State sought to rely on EU law to bring a non-EU-national family member to reside with him or her, as in *Morson and Jhanjan*.[28]

After the provisions on EU citizenship were introduced, attempts were made to challenge the 'wholly internal situation' approach in reliance on the new EC Treaty rights of residence and movement. In *Uecker*,[29] however, the ECJ ruled, in a factual context similar to that of *Morson and Jhanjan* involving non-EU-national family members, that the provisions on citizenship did not extend the scope of the Treaty to cover these internal situations 'which otherwise had no link with Community law'. Moreover in *Kremzow*, in a factual context akin to that in *Saunders* involving an internal restriction (in this case, imprisonment) imposed by a State on one of its own nationals, the ECJ was equally dismissive of the argument that the provisions on EU citizenship brought the circumstances within the scope of Community law.[30]

However, in *Schempp*, the ECJ ruled that the legal situation of a national in a Member State who had not himself made use of the right to freedom of movement could not be treated as a wholly internal situation, because his former spouse, to whom he continued to pay maintenance, had exercised her right as an EU citizen to move to another Member State, and this affected his tax position within Germany.[31]

Further, in *Garcia Avello*[32] and *Chen*,[33] the ECJ also found that the EC Treaty provisions on citizenship conferred rights on the applicants in a situation where they had never left the territory of the Member State in which they were born, and were not presently intending to move. However, in each case the person claiming rights as an EU citizen also possessed the nationality of a Member State other than that of the host State. Chen was an Irish national resident in the UK, and Garcia Avello was a dual Belgian-Spanish national resident in Belgium.

The *Chen* case, as we saw, concerned the right of residence in a host State, whereas *Garcia Avello* concerned a challenge to a Belgian rule prohibiting any change in a registered surname, where Belgian law required the father's surname to be registered but the children wished—given their Spanish nationality—to add the surname of their mother. The children relied on Article 12 EC, together with Article 17, to claim that they were being discriminated against by comparison with other Belgian nationals. The ECJ ruled in their favour on both the 'internal situation' point as well as on the claim of discrimination:

Case C–148/02 **Garcia Avello v. Belgium**
[2003] ECR I–11613

26. Citizenship of the Union, established by Article 17 EC, is not, however, intended to extend the scope *ratione materiae* of the Treaty also to internal situations which have no link with Community law (Joined Cases C–64/96 and C–65/96 *Uecker and Jacquet* [1997] ECR I–3171, paragraph 23).

27. Such a link with Community law does, however, exist in regard to persons in a situation such as that of the children of Mr Garcia Avello, who are nationals of one Member State lawfully resident in the territory of another Member State.

---

28 Cases 35 and 36/82 *Morson and Jhanjan v. Netherlands* [1982] ECR 3723.
29 Cases C–64/96 and 65/96 *Uecker* and *Jacquet v. Land Nordrhein-Westfalen* [1997] ECR I–3171.
30 Case C–299/95 *Kremzow v. Austria* [1997] ECR I–2629.
31 Case C–403/03 *Schempp v. Finanzamt München* [2005] ECR I–6421, paras. 22–25.
32 Case C–148/02 *Garcia Avello v. Belgium* [2003] ECR I–11613.
33 Case C–200/02 *Chen*, n. 11 above, para. 19.

28. That conclusion cannot be invalidated by the fact that the children involved in the main proceedings also have the nationality of the Member State in which they have been resident since their birth and which, according to the authorities of that State, is by virtue of that fact the only nationality recognised by the latter. It is not permissible for a Member State to restrict the effects of the grant of the nationality of another Member State by imposing an additional condition for recognition of that nationality with a view to the exercise of the fundamental freedoms provided for in the Treaty (see in particular, to that effect, Case C–369/90 *Micheletti and Others* [1992] ECR I–4239, paragraph 10). Furthermore, Article 3 of the Hague Convention, on which the Kingdom of Belgium relies in recognising only the nationality of the forum where there are several nationalities, one of which is Belgian, does not impose an obligation but simply provides an option for the contracting parties to give priority to that nationality over any other.

29. That being so, the children of the applicant in the main proceedings may rely on the right set out in Article 12 EC not to suffer discrimination on grounds of nationality in regard to the rules governing their surname.

. . .

35. In contrast to persons having only Belgian nationality, Belgian nationals who also hold Spanish nationality have different surnames under the two legal systems concerned. More specifically, in a situation such as that in issue in the main proceedings, the children concerned are refused the right to bear the surname which results from application of the legislation of the Member State which determined the surname of their father.

36. As the Advocate General has pointed out in paragraph 56 of his Opinion, it is common ground that such a discrepancy in surnames is liable to cause serious inconvenience for those concerned at both professional and private levels resulting from, *inter alia*, difficulties in benefiting, in one Member State of which they are nationals, from the legal effects of diplomas or documents drawn up in the surname recognised in another Member State of which they are also nationals. As has been established in paragraph 33 of the present judgment, the solution proposed by the administrative authorities of allowing children to take only the first surname of their father does not resolve the situation of divergent surnames which those here involved are seeking to avoid.

37. In those circumstances, Belgian nationals who have divergent surnames by reason of the different laws to which they are attached by nationality may plead difficulties specific to their situation which distinguish them from persons holding only Belgian nationality, who are identified by one surname alone.

The ECJ therefore rejected the various arguments put forward by Belgium to justify the refusal to allow a change of surname in these circumstances, and ruled that the refusal was in violation of Articles 12 and 17 of the EC Treaty.

Further, in a recent complaint to the Ombudsman by a German businessman who had been ordered by the German authorities to hand in his passport on the ground that he was likely to go abroad in order to avoid having to pay taxes, the Ombudsman took the view—contrary to the Commission's conclusion that it appeared to be a wholly internal situation[34]—that such circumstances should be considered to fall within Article 18.[35]

---

[34] The Commission had cited *Uecker* and *Morson*, nn. 28–29 above, arguing that a purely hypothetical prospect of working in another Member State did not establish a link that would be sufficiently close to justify the application of the rules on free movement.

[35] See Draft Recommendation of the European Ombudsman to the Commission in Complaint 3317/2004/GG: '[g]iven the broad wording of Article 18, the Ombudsman takes the view that this provision also protects the right of EU nationals to go to other Member States with a view to spending a holiday there'.

The answer to the question posed at (b) therefore is that Articles 17 and 18 have modified the 'wholly internal situation' problem somewhat, in that certain factual situations such as those in *Schempp*, *Garcia Avello*, and *Chen*, which would probably otherwise have been considered as a wholly internal situation, now have a sufficient connection with EU law due to the status of EU citizenship.

(c) DO ARTICLES 17 AND 18 CREATE NEW SUBSTANTIVE RIGHTS FOR EU NATIONALS, IN PARTICULAR FOR THOSE WHO ARE NEITHER ECONOMICALLY ACTIVE NOR ECONOMICALLY SELF-SUFFICIENT?

We have seen that the rights of movement and residence of EU citizens arising from Articles 17 and 18 are subject to the limits and conditions laid down in the Treaty and in secondary legislation. We also saw that the 1990 Residence Directives, now replaced by Directive 2004/38, imposed two conditions on the freedom of movement and residence of EU nationals who were not workers or self-employed (i.e., not economically active): first that such persons have sufficient resources to avoid becoming a burden on the social assistance scheme of the State, and secondly that they have comprehensive sickness insurance.

Below we will examine three groups of cases, the first concerning access to social assistance for *non-workers*, the second concerning access to social or educational assistance for *students*, and the third concerning access to various kinds of job-seeker's allowance for *persons seeking work*. In all three, the ECJ has ruled that the provisions on citizenship have expanded the circumstances in which an EU national may be entitled to specific social benefits in a host Member State. Finally, we will look at a fourth category of case in which other kinds of disproportionate restrictions, not involving access to social benefits, have been found to be in breach of Article 18 in circumstances which would probably not otherwise have violated any Treaty provision.

(i) *Non-workers*

Given the conditions concerning adequate resources and health insurance in the Residence Directives, the argument made on behalf of the applicant in *Martinez Sala*, which was the first major case dealing with this aspect of EU citizenship, did not initially appear promising. She was a Spanish national resident in Germany who had not been working for some time, and who was in receipt of social assistance. In other words, she could probably not be considered to have been economically active or economically self-sufficient.[36]

Case C–85/96 **Maria Martinez Sala v. Freistaat Bayern**
[1998] ECR I–2691

[Note ToA renumbering: Arts. 6, 8(2), and 8a are now Arts. 12, 17(2), and 18 respectively]

Martinez Sala was a Spanish national resident in Germany for twenty-five years, who had previously worked in Germany but was not presently working and was receiving social assistance

---

[36] However, the ECJ left open the possibility that the national court could, depending on the facts, consider her to be a worker.

there. She applied for a child-raising allowance but was refused on the basis that she did not have German nationality, a residence entitlement, or a residence permit in Germany. The ECJ found that the requirement of a residence permit for receipt of a benefit was discriminatory where a Member State's own nationals were not subject to the same condition. The German government argued that even if this was so, the facts of the case did not come within the scope of the Treaty, and therefore the applicant could not rely on Article 6 of the EC Treaty, which prohibits discrimination on grounds of nationality only within the scope of application of the Treaty. The ECJ held that a child-raising allowance was within the scope *ratione materiae* of the Treaty, and went on to consider the argument concerning EU citizenship.

THE ECJ

60. It should, however, be pointed out that, in a case such as the present, it is not necessary to examine whether the person concerned can rely on Article 8a . . . in order to obtain recognition of a new right to reside in the territory of the Member State concerned, since it is common ground that she has already been authorised to reside there, although she has been refused a residence permit.

61. As a national of a Member State lawfully residing in the territory of another Member State, the appellant . . . comes within the scope *ratione personae* of the provisions of the Treaty on European citizenship.

62. Article 8(2) . . . attaches to the status of citizen of the Union the rights and duties laid down by the Treaty, including the right, laid down in Article 6 . . . not to suffer discrimination on grounds of nationality within the scope *ratione materiae* of the Treaty.

63. It follows that a citizen of the European Union . . . lawfully resident in the territory of the host Member State, can rely on Article 6 . . . in all situations which fall within the scope *ratione materiae* of Community law, including the situation where that member State delays or refuses to grant to that claimant a benefit that is provided to all persons lawfully resident in the territory of that State on the ground that the claimant is not in possession of a document which nationals of that same State are not required to have and the issue of which may be delayed or refused by the authorities of that State.

Sala established that so long as an EU national is lawfully resident within another Member State, he or she is entitled, on a combined reading of Articles 12 and 17(2) of the Treaty, to equal treatment with Member State nationals in relation to benefits which fall within the scope of the Treaty. The ECJ applied the general principle of non-discrimination on grounds of nationality to Martinez Sala, on the basis of her EU citizenship.[37] It has been said that the ECJ in this case was willing to 'explode the linkages'[38] which had previously been required in order for the principle of non-discrimination to apply. It was not necessary for there to be involvement in any economic activity as a worker or service provider, nor was it necessary to show preparation for a future economic activity as a student, etc.

The fact that the ECJ did not base the applicant's right to residence on Article 18 EC, having found that Germany had authorized her residence (under the terms of a Council of

---

[37] *Martinez Sala* thus builds on the earlier Case C–411/98 *Angelo Ferlini* v. *Centre hospitalier de Luxembourg* [2000] ECR I–8081, which did not involve EU citizenship, but which applied Art. 12 and the principle of non-discrimination on grounds of nationality to a lawfully resident EU national.

[38] S. O'Leary, 'Putting Flesh on the Bones of European Union Citizenship' (1999) 24 *ELRev.* 68, 77–78. See also H. Toner, 'Judicial Interpretation of European Union Citizenship? Consolidation or Transformation' (2000) 7 *MJ* 158.

Europe Convention on social and medical assistance), meant that the Court did not have to confront the limiting conditions within that Article, and especially the requirement that she should have sufficient resources to avoid becoming a burden on the social assistance scheme of the State. The ECJ instead based itself simply on Articles 12 and 17(2) of the Treaty.

In *Trojani*, however, the ECJ directly confronted the limiting conditions of Article 18, since the question whether Trojani had a right of residence under that provision was specifically raised by the national court. *Trojani* was a French national taking part in a reintegration programme with the Salvation Army in Belgium,[39] who applied for social assistance in the form of a minimum subsistence allowance ('minimex') there.

Case C–456/02 **Trojani v. CPAS**
[2004] ECR I–7573

THE ECJ

31. It must be recalled that the right to reside in the territory of the Member States is conferred directly on every citizen of the Union by Article 18(1) EC (see Case C–413/99 *Baumbast and R* [2002] ECR I–7091, paragraph 84). Mr Trojani therefore has the right to rely on that provision of the Treaty simply as a citizen of the Union.

32. That right is not unconditional, however. It is conferred subject to the limitations and conditions laid down by the Treaty and by the measures adopted to give it effect.

33. Among those limitations and conditions, it follows from Article 1 of Directive 90/364 that Member States can require of the nationals of a Member State who wish to enjoy the right to reside within their territory that they themselves and the members of their families be covered by sickness insurance in respect of all risks in the host Member State and have sufficient resources to avoid becoming a burden on the social assistance system of that State during their period of residence.

34. As the Court has previously held, those limitations and conditions must be applied in compliance with the limits imposed by Community law and in accordance with the general principles of that law, in particular the principle of proportionality (*Baumbast and R*, paragraph 91).

35. It follows from the judgment making the reference that a lack of resources was precisely the reason why Mr Trojani sought to receive a benefit such as the minimex.

36. In those circumstances, a citizen of the Union in a situation such as that of the claimant in the main proceedings does not derive from Article 18 EC the right to reside in the territory of a Member State of which he is not a national, for want of sufficient resources within the meaning of Directive 90/364. Contrary to the circumstances of the case of *Baumbast and R* (paragraph 92), there is no indication that, in a situation such as that at issue in the main proceedings, the failure to recognise that right would go beyond what is necessary to achieve the objective pursued by that directive.

It would appear therefore that the ECJ ruled against Trojani on the basis that, given his lack of adequate resources, he could not rely on a right of residence under Article 18. The implications would therefore seem to be that he could be refused a minimex and, if necessary, deported from Belgium. However, the Court went on to qualify the first part of the ruling, following the line of its reasoning in *Martinez Sala*.

---

[39] A longer excerpt from the case dealing with his possible status as a worker is set out in Ch. 21, sect. 3(c).

37. However, it must be observed that, according to information put before the Court, Mr Trojani is lawfully resident in Belgium, as is attested by the residence permit which has in the meantime been issued to him by the municipal authorities of Brussels.

. . .

39. In the context of the present case, it should be examined more particularly whether, despite the conclusion in paragraph 36 above, a citizen of the Union in a situation such as that of the claimant in the main proceedings may rely on Article 12 EC, under which, within the scope of application of the Treaty and without prejudice to any special provisions contained therein, all discrimination on grounds of nationality is prohibited.

40. In the present case, it must be stated that, while the Member States may make residence of a citizen of the Union who is not economically active conditional on his having sufficient resources, that does not mean that such a person cannot, during his lawful residence in the host Member State, benefit from the fundamental principle of equal treatment as laid down in Article 12 EC.

41. In that connection three points should be made.

42. First, as the Court has held, a social assistance benefit such as the minimex falls within the scope of the Treaty (see Case C–184/99 *Grzelczyk* [2001] ECR I–6193, in particular paragraph 46).

43. Second, with regard to such benefits, a citizen of the Union who is not economically active may rely on Article 12 EC where he has been lawfully resident in the host Member State for a certain time or possesses a residence permit.

44. Third, national legislation such as that at issue in the main proceedings, in so far as it does not grant the social assistance benefit to citizens of the European Union, non-nationals of the Member State, who reside there lawfully even though they satisfy the conditions required of nationals of that Member State, constitutes discrimination on grounds of nationality prohibited by Article 12 EC.

45. It should be added that it remains open to the host Member State to take the view that a national of another Member State who has recourse to social assistance no longer fulfils the conditions of his right of residence. In such a case the host Member State may, within the limits imposed by Community law, take a measure to remove him. However, recourse to the social assistance system by a citizen of the Union may not automatically entail such a measure . . .

Ultimately, therefore, the ECJ ruled that although EU citizens cannot derive a right of residence from Article 18 where they lack sufficient resources within the meaning of the Residence Directive, they are nonetheless entitled, so long as they are lawfully resident (on some other basis) within a Member State, to have access to social assistance on the same conditions as nationals under Articles 12 and 17 EC. If Member States wish to deny an EU citizen access to social benefits under such circumstances, they must move to revoke that person's residence on the ground that they lack sufficient resources. The final protection offered by the ECJ to the EU citizen in such a situation is that recourse to the social assistance system cannot *automatically* lead to revocation of residence permission or deportation. In other words, Member States are not entitled to equate 'recourse to social assistance' with 'lack of sufficient resources'. They must—as recital 16 to the Directive suggests—apply the limiting condition in a proportionate manner, and they must presumably make a proper inquiry into the sufficiency of an EU citizen's resources before moving to revoke his or her residence.

Sala and *Trojani* thus both concerned the circumstances of persons whose status in the host State was uncertain, and whose rights as EU citizens might have seemed precarious since they did not seem to satisfy the sufficient-resources and sickness-insurance conditions of the

Residence Directives (now contained in Article 7(b) of Directive 2004/38). Yet in both cases the ECJ ruled that, by virtue of the fact that they were EU citizens lawfully resident within a host Member State, they were in principle entitled to equal access to those social benefits which were available to nationals purely on the basis of their nationality or residence.

(ii) *Students*

In the case of students, too, the introduction of EU citizenship has been used by the ECJ to extend the circumstances under which EU nationals pursuing educational courses in States other than that of their nationality are entitled to claim certain social advantages. This requires a brief discussion of the law relating to students prior to the introduction of EU citizenship.

In *Gravier*, a French national who was studying for a course in strip-cartoon art in Belgium had challenged the requirement of an enrolment fee for non-Belgians.[40] The ECJ ruled that, since Article 150 EC specified that the EU should lay down principles for developing a common vocational training policy, Belgium was prohibited from discriminating against her under Article 12 EC on the ground of her nationality, in access to vocational training. The Court held that, since access to vocational training was likely to promote the free movement of persons, the 'conditions of access to vocational training' fell within the scope of the Treaty, and the enrolment fee (*minerval*) for non-nationals was contrary to the requirement of non-discrimination in Article 12.[41]

Given the financial consequences for the Member States if they were required to treat all students of EC nationality on an equal footing with national students in conditions of access to vocational training, the *Gravier* ruling clearly had far-reaching potential. However, the ECJ interpreted 'vocational training' expansively in this context,[42] ruling that any form of education which prepared for a profession, trade, or employment was included, even if it included 'an element of general education'.[43] In *Blaizot*, the ECJ ruled that vocational training could include university education, unless the course was one intended for people to improve their general knowledge rather than to prepare themselves for an occupation.[44] The Court however chose to limit the financial consequences of *Gravier* for Member States in a different way, by restricting the interpretation of what non-discrimination in the 'conditions of access' to vocational training meant. In the cases of *Lair* and *Brown* the Court ruled that only grants intended to cover charges relating specifically to *access* to vocational training, such as registration and tuition fees, were covered by the prohibition on discrimination, whereas a maintenance and training grant provided by the State to pursue university study was not covered.[45]

Subsequently in *Raulin*, the Court held that the principle of non-discrimination deriving from Articles 12 and 150 meant that an EC national admitted to a vocational training course

---

[40] Case 293/83 *Gravier* v. *City of Liège* [1985] ECR 593.

[41] For subsequent litigation over continuing forms of discrimination in the Belgian higher education system see Case 42/87 *Commission* v. *Belgium* [1988] ECR 5445; Case C–47/93 *Commission* v. *Belgium* [1994] ECR I–1593.

[42] In particular, the interpretation was much broader than the Court's interpretation of the term 'vocational schools' for workers in Art. 7(3) of Reg. 1612/68: Case 39/86 *Lair* [1988] ECR 3161. See Ch. 21, sect. 7(c).

[43] Case 293/83 *Gravier*, n. 40 above, para. 30; Case 263/86 *Belgium* v. *Humbel* [1988] ECR 5365; Case 242/87 *Commission* v. *Council* [1989] ECR 1425.

[44] Case 24/86 *Blaizot* v. *University of Liège* [1988] ECR 379, para. 20. The ECJ drew for support on Art. 10 of the Council of Europe's European Social Charter, which treats university education as a form of vocational training. However, the ECJ limited the retroactivity of its ruling in *Blaizot*, because of Belgium's fear that it would throw the financing of university education into chaos.

[45] Case 39/86 *Lair*, n. 42 above, para. 15; Case 197/86 *Brown* [1988] ECR 3205.

in another Member State must have a right of residence in that State for the duration of the course, but that the State could legitimately impose conditions on the right of residence, such as the covering of maintenance costs and health insurance.[46] We have seen above that the substance of the *Raulin* ruling was embodied in the Students' Residence Directive 93/96[47] (later replaced by Article 7(c) of Directive 2004/38). Further, the TEU had also added Article 149 EC on education, and amended Article 150 EC on vocational training,[48] but the provisions were carefully worded in such a way as to recognize the primary responsibility of the Member States for their own educational systems, and to indicate that the Community's role is to be supplementary and co-operative. Article 149 EC expressly provides that no attempt is to be made to harmonize or to jeopardize the diversity of the Member States in these areas, and provides that the Council is to adopt 'incentive measures' under the co-decision procedure, listing a range of projects at which Community action should be aimed. Similarly, Article 150 on vocational training contains its own list of objectives for Community action.

Given this background, the argument of *Grzelczyk*, a French national studying in Belgium, that he was entitled under Article 12 EC to apply for state social assistance may have seemed unlikely to succeed. However, the influence of EU citizenship on the outcome of the case was once against crucial.

Case C–184/99 **Rudy Grzelczyk v. CPAS**
[2001] ECR I–6193

[Note ToA renumbering: Arts. 6 and 8a are now Arts. 12 and 18]

Grzelczyk (G) was a French national studying in Belgium. In his fourth year of study he applied to the CPAS for payment of the minimex, a non-contributory minimum subsistence allowance. The CPAS initially granted this, but withdrew it after the Belgian minister decided that Grzelczyk was not entitled to it since he was not a Belgian national.

THE ECJ

29. It is clear ... that a student of Belgian nationality, though not a worker ..., who found himself in exactly the same circumstances as Mr Grzelczyk would satisfy the conditions for obtaining the minimex. The fact that Mr Grzelczyk is not of Belgian nationality is the only bar to its being granted to him. It is not therefore in dispute that the case is one of discrimination solely on the ground of nationality.

30. Within the sphere of application of the Treaty, such discrimination is, in principle, prohibited by Article 6. In the present case, Article 6 must be read in conjunction with the provisions of the Treaty concerning citizenship of the Union in order to determine its sphere of application.

31. Union citizenship is destined to be the fundamental status of nationals of the Member States, enabling those who find themselves in the same situation to enjoy the same treatment in law irrespective of their nationality, subject to such exceptions as are expressly provided for.

---

[46] Case C–357/89 *Raulin v. Minister van Onderwijs en Wetenschappen.*[1992] ECR I–1027.

[47] The original students' residence directive, Dir. 90/366 [1990] OJ L180/30 was annulled by the ECJ on procedural grounds in Case C–295/90 *European Parliament* v. *Council* [1992] ECR I–4193, but replaced in 1993 by a virtually identical measure, Dir. 93/96 [1993] OJ L317/59. See also Case C–424/98 *Commission* v. *Italy* [2000] ECR I–4001.

[48] K. Lenaerts, 'Education in European Community Law after "Maastricht"' (1994) 31 *CMLRev.* 7.

32. As the Court held in paragraph 63 . . . in *Martinez Sala* . . . a citizen of the European Union, lawfully resident in the territory of a host Member State, can rely on Article 6 . . . in all situations which fall within the scope *ratione materiae* of Community law.

33. Those situations include those involving the exercise of the fundamental freedoms guaranteed by the Treaty and those involving the exercise of the right to move and reside freely in another Member State, as conferred by Article 8a . . . (see . . . *Bickel & Franz* . . . paragraphs 15 and 16).

34. It is true that, in paragraph 18 of its judgment in Case 197/86 *Brown* [1988] ECR 3205, the Court held that, at that stage in the development of Community law, assistance given to students for maintenance and training fell in principle outside the scope of the EEC Treaty for the purposes of Article 7 thereof (later Article 6 of the EC Treaty).

35. However, since *Brown*, the Treaty on European Union has introduced citizenship of the European Union into the EC Treaty and added to Title VIII of Part Three a new chapter 3 devoted to education and vocational training. There is nothing in the amended text of the Treaty to suggest that students who are citizens of the Union, when they move to another Member State to study there, lose the rights which the Treaty confers on citizens of the Union. Furthermore, since *Brown*, the Council has also adopted Directive 93/96, which provides that the Member States must grant right of residence to student nationals of a Member State who satisfy certain requirements.

36. The fact that a Union citizen pursues university studies in a Member State other than the State of which he is a national cannot, of itself, deprive him of the possibility of relying on the prohibition of all discrimination on grounds of nationality laid down in Article 6 of the Treaty.

37. As pointed out in paragraph 30 above, in the present case that prohibition must be read in conjunction with Article 8a(1) of the Treaty, which proclaims the right to move and reside freely within the territory of the Member States, subject to the limitations and conditions laid down in this Treaty and by the measures adopted to give it effect.

38. As regards those limitations and conditions, it is clear from Article 1 of Directive 93/96 that Member States may require of students who are nationals of a different Member State and who wish to exercise the right of residence on their territory, first, that they satisfy the relevant national authority that they have sufficient resources to avoid becoming a burden on the social assistance system of the host Member State during their period of residence, next, that they be enrolled in a recognised educational establishment for the principal purpose of following a vocational training course there and, lastly, that they be covered by sickness insurance in respect of all risks in the host Member State.

39. Article 3 of Directive 93/96 makes clear that the directive does not establish any right to payment of maintenance grants by the host Member State for students who benefit from the right of residence. On the other hand, there are no provisions in the directive that preclude those to whom it applies from receiving social security benefits.

The Court's reasoning thus far is similar to that in *Martinez Sala* and *Trojani*, except that in *Grzelczyk* the student's right of movement and residence is based directly by the Court on Article 18 EC, rather than on national or international law. And as a lawfully resident EU citizen, Grzelczyk was entitled to equal treatment on grounds of nationality under Article 12 EC, in relation to benefits which fall within the scope of application of the Treaty.

Here the ECJ made its novel move, declaring in paragraphs 34–36 that although it had previously ruled that assistance for students fell outside the scope of the EC Treaty, the combination of a new EC Treaty title on education and the new provisions on EU citizenship had introduced relevant changes. Despite the fact that the rights in Article 18 EC are subject to limitations and conditions, and that the Students' Residence Directive had imposed relevant conditions of sufficient resources and sickness insurance, there was no provision expressly precluding students from entitlement to social security benefits.

The Court went on to rule that the requirement for students to possess 'sufficient resources' under the Directive did not specify any particular amount, but merely required the student to make a declaration to that effect, and that the truthfulness of that declaration could only be assessed at the time it was made.[49] Finally, the ECJ ruled, just as in paragraph 45 of *Trojani* above, that while Member States were free to conclude that a student who had recourse to social assistance no longer fulfilled the conditions for a right of residence, and to withdraw the residence permit, this conclusion could not be the automatic consequence of an application for social assistance. Interestingly too, the Court read the preamble to the various residence directives, which provided (as does the preamble to Directive 2004/38 on citizenship) that the person must not become an 'unreasonable burden' on the public finances of the host State, as an indication that host States could nevertheless be expected to carry a reasonable burden. More specifically, the Court ruled that the legislation 'thus accepts a certain degree of financial solidarity between nationals of a host Member State and nationals of other Member States, particularly if the difficulties which a beneficiary of the right of residence encounters are temporary'.[50]

Grzelczyk dealt with the issue of access to social security for EU nationals pursuing studies in another Member State, and the ECJ in paragraph 39 of that judgment (above) drew attention to the fact that the Students' Residence Directive did not establish any right to payment of a maintenance grant. In *Bidar*, however, the ECJ was confronted with precisely this latter situation—i.e., a student of French nationality applying in the UK for a student maintenance loan or grant to finance the cost of his studies there.[51] The question was whether such maintenance assistance, despite the limiting conditions in the Residence Directive and the earlier case law in *Brown* and *Lair*,[52] fell within the scope of the Treaty for the purposes of discrimination under Article 12. The Court, following a very similar line of reasoning to that in *Grzelczyk*, relied on the introduction of EU citizenship and the changes in educational and vocational training competence under the EC Treaty to depart from its earlier conclusions in *Brown* and *Lair*, and to rule that maintenance grants for students did indeed now fall within the scope of Article 12.[53]

The ECJ went on to emphasize that its ruling was given support by the recently adopted provisions of Directive 2004/38, which provides for equal treatment within the scope of the Treaty for all EU citizens residing in the territory of another Member States, and which provides that Member States may, if they wish, restrict eligibility for maintenance grants for students to those who have acquired permanent residence. Thus, while students could not rely on the earlier Students' Residence Directive (nor on the later 2004 Directive) to obtain a right to a maintenance grant, they could rely on Article 18 together with Article 12 EC to claim a right of equal access to maintenance grants with national students, on the basis that a maintenance grant is henceforth to be considered a benefit falling within the scope of the Treaty.

The Court ultimately accepted in *Bidar* that the host State was entitled to grant access to student maintenance grants only to students who had demonstrated a certain degree of integration into the society of that State, but it ruled that a requirement to show a link with the State's employment market would not be acceptable, and that the particular conditions of the

---

[49] Note that Art. 8(3) of Dir. 2004/38 now stipulates that Member States may not require this declaration to refer to any specific amount of resources.

[50] Para. 46.

[51] Case C–209/03 *Bidar* v. *London Borough of Ealing* [2005] ECR I–2119.

[52] N. 45 above.

[53] Case C–209/03, *Bidar*, n. 51 above, paras. 31–42.

UK's requirement that the student be 'settled' in the UK was also excessively restrictive and unjustified.[54]

To conclude, *Grzelczyk* and *Bidar* thus clearly indicate that the advent of EU citizenship has changed the earlier restriction on the entitlement of students to social welfare and to maintenance grants in a host Member State.[55] More recently the case of *Commission v. Austria* confirmed the bolstering effect of EU citizenship on the rights of students in a host Member State, although in this case the restriction on the students' rights did not concern access to financial benefits, but rather the imposition of additional conditions of access to university education on students whose secondary education diplomas were obtained in another Member State.[56] The Court, following earlier cases such as *Commission v. Belgium*[57] and *Gravier* ruled that this constituted indirect discrimination which could not be justified on any of the various grounds put forward by the Austrian government.

(iii) *Job-seekers*

The cases of *D'Hoop*, *Collins*, and *Ioannidis* involved the situation of job-seekers covered by Article 39 EC who wished to apply for a form of job-seeker's allowance. In *D'Hoop*, the ECJ ruled that a Belgian national who was refused a 'tideover' allowance when seeking her first job on the Belgian job market, purely on the grounds that she had completed her secondary school education in France, had suffered discrimination on the basis of her EU citizenship, and in particular on account of her exercise of the EC right to move and avail of educational opportunities in France.[58] The Court ruled that while it might in theory be possible to justify a refusal to grant a tideover allowance to an EU citizen on the basis that there must be a sufficient link between the job-seeker and the host State, the condition which Belgium actually imposed was based on the place where the diploma of completion of secondary education was obtained. This was a disproportionate condition since it did not represent the real and effective degree of connection between the applicant and the Belgian job market. The *D'Hoop* ruling was further developed in *Collins*.

Case C–138/02 **Collins v. Secretary of State for Work and Pensions** [2004] ECR I–2703

[Note ToA renumbering: Arts. 6, 8, and 48 EC are now Arts. 12, 17, and 39 respectively]

An Irish national was seeking employment in the UK and had applied for a job-seeker's allowance. Unlike D'Hoop in Belgium, Collins was neither a national nor a resident of the UK, but had moved there in order to seek work. UK legislation however made entitlement to a job-seeker's allowance conditional on a residence requirement, and Collins sought to challenge this condition as a violation of EU law. The ECJ began by reflecting on its past case law holding

---

54 *Ibid.*, paras. 52–63.

55 See also pending Cases C–11–12/06 *Morgan and Bucher*, concerning German restrictions on the availability of study finance abroad for students who had not already completed one year of study in Germany, or who had moved to border towns outside Germany: AG's Opinion, 20 Mar. 2007.

56 Case C–147/03 *Commission v. Austria*, n. 24 above.

57 Case C–65/03 *Commission v. Belgium* [2004] ECR I–6427.

58 Case C–224/98 *D'Hoop v. Office Nationale de l'Emploi* [2002] ECR I–6191.

that job-seekers did not enjoy rights of equal access to social benefits under Article 39 EC governing the free movement of workers, or under the secondary legislation governing workers.

THE ECJ

56. Among the rights which Article 48 of the Treaty confers on nationals of the Member States is the right to move freely within the territory of the other Member States and to stay there for the purposes of seeking employment (*Antonissen*, cited above, paragraph 13).

57. Nationals of a Member State seeking employment in another Member State thus fall within the scope of Article 48 of the Treaty and, therefore, enjoy the right laid down in Article 48(2) to equal treatment.

58. As regards the question whether the right to equal treatment enjoyed by nationals of a Member State seeking employment in another Member State also encompasses benefits of a financial nature such as the benefit at issue in the main proceedings, the Court has held that Member State nationals who move in search of employment qualify for equal treatment only as regards access to employment in accordance with Article 48 of the Treaty and Articles 2 and 5 of Regulation No 1612/68, but not with regard to social and tax advantages within the meaning of Article 7(2) of that regulation (*Lebon*, paragraph 26, and Case C–278/94 *Commission* v *Belgium*, cited above, paragraphs 39 and 40).

59. Article 2 of Regulation No 1612/68 concerns the exchange of applications for and offers of employment and the conclusion and performance of contracts of employment, while Article 5 of the regulation relates to the assistance afforded by employment offices.

60. It is true that those articles do not expressly refer to benefits of a financial nature. However, in order to determine the scope of the right to equal treatment for persons seeking employment, this principle should be interpreted in the light of other provisions of Community law, in particular Article 6 of the Treaty.

61. As the Court has held on a number of occasions, citizens of the Union lawfully resident in the territory of a host Member State can rely on Article 6 of the Treaty in all situations which fall within the scope *ratione materiae* of Community law. Citizenship of the Union is destined to be the fundamental status of nationals of the Member States, enabling those who find themselves in the same situation to enjoy the same treatment in law irrespective of their nationality, subject to such exceptions as are expressly provided. . . .

62. It is to be noted that the Court has held, in relation to a student who is a citizen of the Union, that entitlement to a non-contributory social benefit, such as the Belgian minimum subsistence allowance ('minimex'), falls within the scope of the prohibition of discrimination on grounds of nationality and that, therefore, Articles 6 and 8 of the Treaty preclude eligibility for that benefit from being subject to conditions which are liable to constitute discrimination on grounds of nationality (*Grzelczyk*, paragraph 46).

63. In view of the establishment of citizenship of the Union and the interpretation in the case-law of the right to equal treatment enjoyed by citizens of the Union, it is no longer possible to exclude from the scope of Article 48(2) of the Treaty—which expresses the fundamental principle of equal treatment, guaranteed by Article 6 of the Treaty—a benefit of a financial nature intended to facilitate access to employment in the labour market of a Member State.

64. The interpretation of the scope of the principle of equal treatment in relation to access to employment must reflect this development, as compared with the interpretation followed in *Lebon* and in Case C–278/94 *Commission* v *Belgium*.

Here we see the Court revisiting its prior case law, in which it had ruled that job-seekers, although covered by Article 39 as far as access to employment was concerned, were not entitled to social advantages under Article 39. It is precisely the introduction of EU citizenship in the Treaty which provided the Court with reason to depart from this earlier case law, and to rule that the rights of job-seekers under Article 39 should be interpreted in the light of the more general right to equal treatment of EU citizens. Given this new interpretive framework, the Court ruled, contrary to its prior ruling in *Lebon*, that a job-seeker was henceforth entitled under Article 39 to a 'benefit of a financial nature intended to facilitate access to employment in the labour market of a Member State'.

As far as the compatibility with EC law of the residence condition was concerned, the Court, following the reasoning in *D'Hoop*, ruled that although it was legitimate for a State to require that a job-seeker has a genuine link with the employment market of the State, (e.g., by requiring that the person has for a reasonable period genuinely sought work in that State) a residence condition would have to be applied in a proportionate and non-discriminatory way. *Collins* was confirmed and applied in the subsequent case of *Ioannidis*.[59]

(iv) *Freedom from Other Discriminatory or Restrictive National Measures*

A variety of other cases exemplify some of the new rights which have been developed or enhanced by the introduction of EU citizenship. These cases involve different kinds of discriminatory or restrictive national measures, and in each case the ECJ has emphasized that, whether or not the person concerned was a worker/service-provider, etc., such measures potentially violate the Treaty provisions on citizenship.

Thus in *Bickel and Franz*[60] the ECJ emphasized that German and Austrian nationals who were subject to criminal proceedings in Italy and who requested the use of German in the proceedings were exercising their right to free movement as European citizens based on Article 18 and were entitled not to be discriminated against on grounds of nationality.

Similarly in *Turpeinen*,[61] *Pusa*,[62] and *N*,[63] the Court ruled that a range of restrictive tax measures imposed by Member States were potentially in violation of Article 18 regardless of the status of the applicant as a worker.[64] Moreover in *De Cuyper*[65] and *Tas-Hagen*,[66] concerning unemployment benefit and wartime benefits respectively, the Court ruled that national residence restrictions were *prima facie* in breach of Article 18.

Overall, therefore, what we see is that the answer to each of the three questions posed at the outset, concerning whether the introduction of EU citizenship has changed the existing law, is 'yes', albeit a qualified yes in certain respects. In a cautious but persistent line of case law, the ECJ has interpreted Articles 17 and 18 in a way that has brought about symbolic as well as practical changes in the status and entitlements of EU citizens.

---

[59] Case C–258/04 *Ioannidis*, n. 6 above, in which it was held that a Greek national seeking his first employment in Belgium could not be refused entitlement to a job-seeker's allowance under Belgian law purely on the ground that he had completed his secondary education outside Belgium.

[60] Case C–274/96 [1998] ECR I–7637, para. 15.

[61] Case C–520/04 *Turpeinen* [2006] ECR I–10685.

[62] Case C–224/02 *Pusa* v. *Osuuspankkien Keskinäinen Vakuutusyhtiö* [2004] ECR I–5763.

[63] Case C–470/04 *N* v. *Inspecteur van de Belastingdienst* [2006] ECR I–7409.

[64] See also Case C–403/03 *Schempp*, n. 31 above, another tax case, and Case C–148/02 *Garcia Avello*, concerning restrictions on the right to change surnames, which are discussed at nn. 31–32 and text.

[65] Case C–406/04 *De Cuyper* v. *ONEM* [2006] ECR I–6947. Here however the restrictive residence condition was ultimately found to be justifiable on the ground of the need to monitor the circumstances of those in receipt of unemployment benefit.

[66] Case C–192/05 *Tas-Hagen* v. *Raadskamer WUBO van de Pensioen- en Uitkeringsraad* [2006] ECR I–10451.

4. POLITICAL RIGHTS OF CITIZENSHIP

Thus far we have examined Articles 17–18 of the Treaty in some detail. Articles 19–22 also confer a number of rights which, although limited in their range, are of both practical and symbolic importance.

The most important of these are the rights of 'alien suffrage'—the passive and active electoral rights created for EU citizens in host Member States.[67] Article 19 provides that citizens of the Union[68] shall have the right in a Member State other than that of their nationality to vote and to stand as a candidate both in municipal and in European Parliament elections.[69] This Article was controversial because of its incompatibility with constitutional provisions in some Member States, and Article 19 therefore allows for the possibility of derogations.[70] Article 20 provides that Union citizens have the right, in a third country where their own Member State is not represented, to the protection of the diplomatic authorities of any Member State.[71] Article 21 confirms two rights which already existed under EC law, providing that EU citizens have the right to petition the European Parliament and apply to the Ombudsman.[72] EU citizens who write to any of the Community institutions in one of the official languages are granted the right to an answer in that language. Article 22 requires the Commission to report every three years on the application of these provisions on citizenship, and thus far it has adopted four reports.[73] The Council is also empowered 'to adopt provisions to strengthen or to add to the rights laid down' in this part of the Treaty. However, the Council must act unanimously and Article 22 envisages that such action may require constitutional amendment at the national level.[74]

While the most recent report of the Commission on EU citizenship suggests that most of the problems with giving effect to the rights of EU citizens identified are 'due to bad application and incorrect practices rather than to failure of national legislation to comply with Community legislation', it is clear that significant problems of the former kind remain.[75] Further, the take-up and impact of the electoral rights have so far not been substantial. In its 2002 Report on the right to

---

[67] For a comprehensive analysis see J. Shaw, *The Transformation of Citizenship in the European Union* (Cambridge University Press, 2007).

[68] In Case C–145/04 *Spain* v. *United Kingdom* [2006] ECR I–7917, especially paras. 78–80, the ECJ ruled the EC Treaty provisions on citizenship did not prevent Member States from granting rights to vote and stand in European Parliament elections to persons other than EU citizens—in this case, residents of Gibraltar. The action by the UK had been necessitated by the judgment of the ECtHR in App. no. 24833/94, *Matthews* v. *United Kingdom*, judgment of 18 Feb. 1999.

[69] See Council Dir. 93/109 on exercising the right to vote in European Parliament elections: [1993] OJ L329/34. See also the resolution of the European Parliament on the implementation of this Dir.: [1994] OJ C44/159. On the right to vote and stand in municipal elections see Dir. 94/80 [1994] OJ L368, modified by Dir. 96/30 [1996] OJ L122/12. See COM(2000)843 on the 1999 European Parliament elections. Also Council Dec. 2002/772 amending the Act concerning the election of the representatives of the European Parliament by direct universal suffrage [2002] OJ L283/1.

[70] See the Commission's Reports on granting derogations under Art. 19(2) of the EC Treaty, COM(2003)31 and COM(2005)382.

[71] Dec. 95/553 regarding protection for citizens of the Union by diplomatic and consular representations of the Member States in non-member countries [1995] OJ L314/73, which eventually entered into force in May 2002.

[72] Non-citizens resident in the EU can also do so: Arts. 194 and 195.

[73] COM(93)702, COM(97)230, COM(2001)506, and COM(2004)695.

[74] Denmark entered various reservations about the concept of Union citizenship in a 'Unilateral Declaration' at the 1992 Edinburgh summit, after the initial rejection by referendum in that Member State of the TEU.

[75] COM(2004)695.

vote and stand as a candidate in municipal elections, the Commission indicated that there were very low levels of voter registration.[76] Similarly in a working paper on the 2004 European Parliament elections, the Commission reported that while between 342 and 343 million EU nationals exercised their right to vote within their own State, only approximately six and a half million EU citizens exercised their right to vote in a host State.[77]

In other words, of all those voting in the European Parliament elections, approximately 2 per cent were EU citizens exercising their rights of alien suffrage. Given the low turnout overall for the European Parliament elections, this again suggests the limited practical impact, at least so far, of the political rights of EU citizenship.[78] Nonetheless, the Commission continues to press, most recently in its 2004 report on Citizenship of the Union, for consideration to be given to extending to EU citizens the right to vote also in national and regional elections, rather than only in municipal and European elections.

5. DIRECTIVE 2004/38 ON THE RIGHTS OF FREE MOVEMENT AND RESIDENCE FOR EU CITIZENS AND THEIR FAMILIES

We saw in Chapter 21 that Directive 2004/38[79] consolidated virtually all of the existing legislation on the free movement of persons into a single instrument, repealing and replacing most of the pre-existing laws including the three Residence Directives. It created, according to the Commission 'a single legal regime for free movement and residence within the context of citizenship of the Union while maintaining the acquired rights of workers'. While in substance Directive 2004/38 does not significantly change the conditions and terms which were laid down in the previous Residence Directives, the Directive now implements a fundamental Treaty-based right of residence for citizens, rather than creating such a right by legislation, as was the case with the 1990 Residence Directives.

A full discussion of the main provisions of Directive 2004/38 is contained in sections 6 and 8 of Chapter 21 dealing with the free movement of workers. All of the main provisions discussed in that context—the initial three-month period of residence, the general right of residence, and the right of permanent residence, the reduction in formalities required for entry and residence, the category of family members included, the enhanced procedural and substantive protections in the event of restrictive measures being taken, a general right to equal treatment—apply to all EU citizens and not just to those who are employed or self-employed. The main provisions of the Directive which are specific to EU citizens who are not economically active, or who are students are set out below.

Article 7(1)(b) and (c) set out the preconditions for the right of residence of EU citizens who are neither workers nor self-employed persons. Article 7(1)(b) essentially incorporates the conditions relating to sufficient resources and comprehensive sickness-insurance conditions from the previous Residence Directives. Article 7(1)(b) governs students and provides in substance that an EU citizen shall enjoy a right of residence where he or she is enrolled at a

---

76 COM/2002/260.

77 Available at http://ec.europa.eu/justice_home/doc_centre/citizenship/doc/eu_voters_working_paper_230304.pdf.

78 For the Commission's efforts to stimulate the Member States to take all measures necessary to ensure the participation of all EU citizens prior to the 2004 European Parliamentary elections see COM(2003)174.

79 N. 14 above.

recognized educational establishment for the purposes of study, has comprehensive sickness insurance, and can provide an assurance (whether by declaration or otherwise[80]) that he or she has sufficient resources to avoid becoming a burden on the social assistance scheme.[81]

We have seen from the case law discussed above—including *Grzelczyk*, *Martinez Sala*, *D'Hoop*, *Trojani*, *Collins*, *Bidar*, and *Commission* v. *Belgium*—that the ECJ has required these conditions (at least when they were contained in the Residence Directives, and presumably all the more so now that they are contained in Directive 2004/38), to be interpreted and applied in a proportionate manner, recognizing that a degree of solidarity between citizens of different Member States had been created by the status of EU citizenship.

Article 8(4) of the Directive elaborates further on the requirement of sufficient resources, providing that no fixed amount may be laid down by Member States, that in any case the amount must not be higher than the eligibility threshold for social assistance or the minimum state social security pension, and that the personal situation of the person concerned must be taken into account.[82]

Article 12 concerns acquisition of the right of permanent residence by the family members of an EU citizen who is deceased or departs from the Member State. Article 12(2) provides that before acquiring the right of permanent residence, the persons in question (if they are not workers or self-employed) remain subject to the requirements of sufficient resources and adequate sickness insurance. The right of residence of such family members is said to be retained 'exclusively on a personal basis'. Article 13 similarly governs the right of family members to remain, and again to gain permanent residence in the event of divorce, annulment, or termination of registered partnership, and it contains similar conditions to those in Article 12. Article 14 governs the general initial three-month right of residence for all EU citizens,[83] and subjects it to one condition only: i.e., that they do not become an unreasonable burden on the social assistance scheme of the host State. Article 14(4) codifies the case law in *Grzelczyk* and *Trojani* to the effect that expulsion cannot be an automatic consequence of a person's recourse to the social assistance scheme of the host State.

Finally, and importantly, Article 24 governs the right to equal treatment of all EU citizens in a host Member State. Article 24, having set out the right to equal treatment in paragraph 1, paragraph 2 provides by way of derogation that host States are not obliged to confer entitlement to social assistance during the first three months of residence, nor (in the case of job-seekers) during the longer period in which a job-seeker is entitled to reside in search of work.

We have seen from *D'Hoop* and *Collins*, above,[84] that job-seekers are entitled under the Treaty to equal treatment in access to social assistance which is specifically designed to facilitate access to employment, but Article 24(2) governs social assistance more generally. Article 24(2) further provides that, prior to acquiring the right of permanent residence (after which

---

[80] Art. 8(3) of the Dir. specifies that the Member States cannot require the declaration of sufficient resources to refer to any specific amount: n. 49 above.

[81] Art. 7(4) also limits slightly the category of protected family members of a student who can enjoy rights of residence: only the spouse, registered partner, and dependent children of a student are covered, and dependent direct relatives in the ascending line are not included. Instead, Member States are merely required to facilitate the admission of such other relatives under Art. 3(2) of Dir. 2004/38.

[82] See also Case C–408/03 *Commission* v. *Belgium* [2006] ECR I–2647 concerning Belgium's excessively restrictive definition of the sufficient resources condition of the 1990 Residence Dir., which did not take into account the resources of a partner in particular circumstances.

[83] Art. 39 of the Dir. provides that in its report on the application of the legislation after 4 years, the Commission may submit a proposal on the possibility for extending this initial period of (almost) unconditional residence for all EU citizens.

[84] Nn. 58–59, and text.

an EU citizen can only be deported on public policy, security, and health grounds, and not on the ground of having become an unreasonable burden on the host State), Member States shall not be obliged to grant maintenance aid to those whose status in the host State is as a student.

The obvious question raised by this provision is how it fits with the rulings of the ECJ in cases like *Trojani*[85] and *Bidar*.[86] In *Trojani*, as we have seen, the ECJ ruled that EU citizens who were lawfully resident in a host State were entitled to equality of treatment in access to social advantages, unless the Member State independently reached the conclusion that they had become an unreasonable burden on the social assistance scheme of the State and was prepared to deport them. And in *Bidar* the ECJ ruled that students who were engaged in a course of study in a host Member State and were otherwise lawfully resident were entitled to equality of treatment in access to maintenance grants, subject to reasonable prior-integration conditions.

Although Article 24 on first reading seems to contradict these two rulings, the ECJ in *Bidar* made it clear that even though no right to maintenance assistance for students (nor, presumably, to social assistance for economically inactive EU citizens) could be derived from Directive 2004/38, such a right could be derived directly from Articles 12 and 18 of the EC Treaty so long as the person in question was lawfully resident in the host State.[87] In other words, the ECJ's reading of Article 24 seems to be that while the Directive cannot be relied on for a right to maintenance assistance for students (nor, presumably to social assistance for non-economically active citizens), it does not prevent such persons from relying directly on Articles 12 and 18 EC for these rights. And to the extent that a Member State wishes to deny social assistance or maintenance grants to such persons, it must independently show reason—presumably to demonstrate that they have become an unreasonable burden on the social assistance scheme of the State—to revoke their lawful residence within that State.

6. CONCLUSIONS

i. The limits of EU citizenship as it has been formalized in the Treaty—and even despite the relatively progressive interpretation of some of the rights of citizenship by the ECJ—have been the subject of much adverse comment. There has been objection to the symbolism of super-statehood, criticism of the paucity of the rights created and the conditions imposed on their enjoyment, concern over the Member States' reluctance to enforce the rights which have been created, and disappointment at the limited take-up of the newly created electoral rights.

ii. A broader dimension of the critique of citizenship is that any meaningful idea of European citizenship would require not merely concrete legal and practical measures on the matters examined in this chapter (i.e., rights of residence, travel, voting, etc.), but that it is also inextricably connected with the need for deeper political, institutional, and democratic change within the EU.

iii. However, it is possible to consider other aspects of EU law as potentially significant dimensions of citizenship. These include the non-discrimination clause in Article 13 EC, the embryonic principle of transparency seen in the right of access to documents of the European institutions in Article 255 EC, and the right to good administration in Article

---

[85] Case C–456/02 *Trojani* v. *CPAS* [2004] ECR I–7573.
[86] Case C–209/03 *Bidar*, n. 51 above.
[87] *Ibid.*, paras. 43–47.

41 of the EU Charter of Fundamental Rights. More generally, the Charter of Fundamental Rights (which would have been incorporated into Part II of the Constitutional Treaty) contains a chapter devoted to Citizens' Rights.

iv. Furthermore, European citizenship can also be viewed more positively in terms of both its potential and also its wider current meaning. In this sense, not only the narrowly defined Treaty provisions on citizenship, but other aspects of transnational civic engagement within the EU should be part of the picture. In other words, it is important to look beyond the formal provisions on citizenship to see how and to what extent EU citizens are constituted as members having a stake in the European Union as a political entity.[88]

7. FURTHER READING

(a) Books

Guild, E., *Legal Elements of European Identity: EU Citizenship and Migration Law* (Kluwer, 2005)

Shaw, J., *The Transformation of Citizenship in the European Union* (Cambridge University Press, 2007)

(b) Articles

Dougan, M., 'The Constitutional Dimension to the Case Law on Union Citizenship' (2006) 31 *ELRev.* 613

Golynker, O., ' "Jobseekers Rights in the EU": Challenges of Changing the Paradigm of Social Solidarity' (2005) 30 *ELRev.* 111

—— 'Student Loans: The European Concept of Social Justice according to Bidar' (2006) 31 *ELRev.* 390

Hailbronner, K., 'Union Citizenship and Access to Social Benefits' (2005) 42 *CMLRev.* 1245

Mather, J., 'The Court of Justice and the Union Citizen' (2005) 11 *ELJ* 722

White, R., 'The Citizen's Right to Free Movement' (2005) 16 *EBLR* 547

---

[88] J. Shaw, 'European Union Citizenship: The IGC and Beyond' (1997) 3 *EPL* 413, 417.

EQUAL TREATMENT OF WOMEN AND MEN

1. CENTRAL ISSUES

i.   This chapter focuses primarily on Article 141 (ex Article 119), which first established the principle of equal pay between the sexes. Various other Treaty provisions have since been added which address the issue of equal treatment. Article 141 has been amended to incorporate equal treatment of men and women at work going beyond the field of pay, and to permit forms of 'positive action'. Article 13 EC, introduced in 1997, provides that the EC may take action to combat discrimination based on sex, racial or ethnic origin, religion or belief, disability, age or sexual orientation.[1] And Article 137 (ex Article 118) makes equal treatment of men and women in the labour market an area for 'supportive' Community action, giving the Council power to adopt directives.

ii. Although express competence to do so was included in Article 141 only in 1997, the EC many years earlier had adopted broader legislation in the field of sex equality going beyond pay. The principle of equal treatment on grounds of sex has been strengthened and expanded over the years through legislation, judicial action, Treaty amendment, and by means of other policy developments. It is an area of law which illustrates clearly the competing priorities of the economic and the social objectives of the Community.

iii. The sex equality principle remained for a long time limited in scope and confined largely to employment-related sex discrimination. However, the last decade appears to have brought a more serious institutional commitment to 'mainstream gender equality' across all EU policies and activities.[2] This commitment was enshrined by the Amsterdam Treaty in Article 3 of the EC Treaty.[3] The Charter on Fundamental Rights also contains a number of provisions relating to gender equality (Articles 21, 23, and 33(2)). Gender equality law has more recently been influenced by the newer anti-discrimination law adopted under Article 13 EC, in particular by the Race Directive.

---

[1] Developments concerning these other grounds of discrimination apart from sex are discussed in Ch. 11, sect. 7(d)(iii).

[2] See most recently the Commission's 'Roadmap' on gender equality COM(2006)92, which discusses the state of mainstreaming policy and its latest communication on mainstreaming in the field of development policy, COM(2007)100. See F. Beveridge, 'Building against the Past: The Impact of Mainstreaming on EU Gender Law and Policy' (2007) 32 *ELRev.* 193.

[3] Art. 3 EC declares that in all of the activities listed 'the Community shall aim to eliminate inequalities, and to promote equality, between men and women'.

iv. While equal treatment on grounds of sex—now referred to in official EU documents as gender equality—has been interpreted by the ECJ as prohibiting discrimination on grounds of gender reassignment, the Court has not been willing to include discrimination on grounds of sexual orientation within the concept. Sexual orientation discrimination is however now included in Article 13 EC, and in Directive 2000/78 on equal treatment in employment.

v. EC sex-discrimination law was originally divided principally into three parts: equal pay, equal treatment in access to and conditions of employment, and social security. The basic principle of non-discrimination on grounds of sex was common to all three, but they were governed by different bodies of secondary legislation, based on different Treaty articles. Now, with the exception of state social security and sex equality for self-employed persons (which is covered by a separate measure, Directive 86/613), these are dealt with together in a single consolidating measure, Directive 2006/54. This consolidating Directive replaces the prior directives on equal pay, equal treatment, occupational social security, and the burden of proof. Apart from the consolidating Directive, there is specific gender equality legislation on state social security (Directive 79/7), on access to and supply of goods and services (Directive 2004/113), and on pregnancy and parental leave (Directives 96/34 and 92/85 respectively).

vi. There has also been a considerable amount of soft law in the area of equal treatment, with the adoption of memoranda, resolutions, and recommendations on a range of equal-opportunities issues. Soft measures are sometimes a form of precursor to further, harder law, sometimes an alternative to legislation, and sometimes a hybrid of the two. The Commission also adopted a range of action programmes over the years, and more recently a 'Roadmap for Equality between Men and Women 2006–2010',[4] while the European Council in 2006 announced a 'European Pact for Gender Equality'. Finally, in 2006 a European Institute for Gender Equality was established 'to ensure the best implementation of Community policy in the field of gender equality'.[5]

2. THE LEGAL FRAMEWORK FOR EU GENDER EQUALITY

(a) THE REMIT OF EU SOCIAL POLICY

EU social policy is a large field, and this chapter focuses on only one very specific issue, that of gender equality. EU 'social policy' is a loose term which lacks an agreed definition within EU law, being for some synonymous with labour and employment law, while for others implying a much wider field. The main EC Treaty provisions grouped under this heading are those in Articles 136–148 (ex Articles 117–125) EC. These Articles contain the basis for Community legislative action concerning improvement of working conditions and the living standard of workers, and equality between men and women with regard to the labour market and treatment at work. These are followed by other provisions on what could broadly be called Community social policy, i.e., the Treaty Articles governing education, culture, and

---

[4] COM(2006)92.
[5] Reg. 1922/2006 [2006] OJ L403/9. See further http://ec.europa.eu/employment_social/gender_equality/gender_institute/index_en.html.

public health, as well as a later chapter dealing with economic and social cohesion. An important chapter on employment policy, focusing on the promotion of high employment, was added by the ToA to Articles 125–130 of the EC Treaty, and this area has remained prominent on the political agenda as a result of the EU's overarching Lisbon Strategy which was initiated in 2000.[6] Articles 146–148 (ex Articles 123–125) concern the European Social Fund, which was established to provide financial assistance for some of the Community's social-policy objectives.

(b) THE LEGAL BASIS FOR EU GENDER EQUALITY LEGISLATION

Gender equality, on which this chapter concentrates, is a prominent issue in legal and in policy terms, which now takes its place as part of a broader emerging body of EU anti-discrimination law.[7] While it is a long-established EC policy, having its origins in the equal pay provisions of the 1957 Treaty, we have seen above that the available legal basis for EU gender equality legislation has changed over the years as specific Treaty Articles have been amended or added. Thus the recent consolidating Directive 2006/54 is based on Article 141, the Social Security Directive 79/7 on Article 308, the Pregnancy Directive on Article 138 and the recent action programmes and framework strategy on gender equality, as well as Directive 2004/113 on access to and supply of goods and services on Article 13 EC. For the Parental Leave and Part-Time Workers Directives the so-called Social Policy Protocol (now repealed) was used, and the relevant legal basis is now Article 137 EC.

The relevance of this plethora of different legal bases is that the type of legal basis used will have a significant influence, in many cases, on the nature and content of the measure adopted. Both the legislative process followed—e.g., whether one of the consultation, co-operation, or co-decision procedures, or pursuant to an agreement of the social partners—and possibly also the form of the legal instrument used are likely to shape the substantive nature of the measure which emerges.

(c) SOFT LAW AND SUPPLEMENTARY MEASURES PROMOTING GENDER EQUALITY

Supporting and interacting with these legislative measures has been a range of softer measures including the Commission's five action programmes to promote equality in the workplace (the last from 2001 to 2005), and its more recent 'framework strategy' on gender equality (2000–2005), and its 'Roadmap' for equality (2006–2010). An action programme to promote organizations active in the field of gender equality was adopted in 2004,[8] and since 1996 the Commission has adopted an Annual Report on Equal Opportunities for Women and Men in the EU. The framework strategy on gender equality introduced in 2000 was a comprehensive programme going beyond the compartmentalized approach of earlier action plans, and

---

[6] A useful summary of the Lisbon Agenda and its progress is available on the EU's official Scadplus website, at http://europa.eu/scadplus/leg/en/cha/c11325.htm.

[7] See Ch. 11 for discussion of the range of EC anti-discrimination policies and laws emerging under Art. 13 EC.

[8] Dec. 848/2004/EC establishing a Community action programme to promote organisations active at European level in the field of equality between men and women [2004] OJ L195/7.

intended to 'embrace all Community policies in its efforts to promote gender equality',[9] and the 'Roadmap' continues this integrated approach. Most of these measures—including the European Council's recent 'Gender Equality Pact'—acknowledge that, despite the EU's wide range of hard and soft instruments to combat gender discrimination, there are persistent problems of lower pay for women, reduced participation of women in the workforce, child-care shortages, sex stereotyping, a work/life 'imbalance', and overall, clear gender gaps in employment and social protection.

(d) THE 'GENERAL PRINCIPLE' OF EQUAL TREATMENT ON GROUNDS OF SEX

Apart from the various regimes of sex equality law outlined above, the ECJ has frequently stated that the *general principle* of equal treatment between men and women is a fundamental one in the Community legal order.[10] The Court ruled, originally in *Defrenne III*[11] and later in the cases of *P* v. *S*[12] and *Schröder*,[13] that the elimination of sex discrimination was one of the fundamental personal human rights which had to be protected within Community law. However, at the time of *Defrenne III* in 1978, this principle was held not to be directly applicable against Member States, since the Community had not yet assumed competence in the area of equal treatment at work.[14] Indeed it remains the case, despite the frequent judicial rulings on the fundamental status of the principle of equal treatment on grounds of sex, that this principle is not directly effective *per se* and requires the existence of further legislative implementation to be fully effective in challenging national law or employer practice.[15]

(e) THE LIMITS OF GENDER EQUALITY

Further, it appeared for a time after the *P* v. *S* ruling concerning discrimination against trans-gendered persons under Directive 76/207[16] that the notion of 'sex equality' in EC law would be given a broad interpretation. Having ruled in that case that sex discrimination under the Directive included discrimination arising from the gender-reassignment of the employee,[17] the ECJ backtracked in the equal-pay case of *Grant*. There the Court ruled, against the Opinion of the Advocate General, that the prohibition against discrimination on grounds of sex within Article 141 did not cover discrimination on grounds of sexual orientation.[18] The Court confirmed this stance in *D* v. *Council*,[19] and in both *D* and *Grant* it retreated from the

---

[9] COM(2000)335. See also Dec. 1672/2006/EC establishing a Community Programme for Employment and Social Solidarity (Progress) [2006] OJ L315/1.

[10] In Case 20/71 *Sabbatini* [1972] ECR 345; Case 21/74 *Airola* [1972] ECR 221; Cases 75 and 117/82 *Razzouk and Beydoun* v. *Commission* [1984] ECR 1509, the Court held that the *Community* institutions were bound by the principle of non-discrimination on grounds of sex in the treatment of their staff.

[11] Case 149/77 *Defrenne* v. *Sabena* [1978] ECR 1365, paras. 26–27.

[12] Case C–13/94 *P* v. *S and Cornwall County Council* [1996] ECR I–2143, para. 19.

[13] Case C–50/96 *Deutsche Telekom* v. *Schröder* [2000] ECR I–743, para. 56.

[14] Case 149/77 *Defrenne*, n. 11 above, para. 30.

[15] See more recently on the principle of equal treatment in relation to disability Case C–13/05 *Chacón Navas* judgment of 11 July 2006. In relation to age discrimination see Case C–144/04 *Mangold* v. *Rüdiger Helm* [2005] ECR I–9981.

[16] Case C–13/94 *P* v. *S*, n. 12 above. See also Case C–117/01 *K.B.* v. *NHS* [2004] ECR I–541.

[17] *Ibid.*, para. 20.

[18] Case C–249/96 *Grant* v. *South-West Trains* [1998] ECR I–621. For commentaries see M. Bell (1999) 5 *ELJ* 63, C. Barnard (1998) 57 *CLJ* 352.

[19] Case C–125/99P *D* v. *Council* [2001] ECR I–4319. For further discussion see Ch. 11.

judicial expansiveness of *P* v. *S* by pointing to the new legislative powers in the field of equal treatment, and passing responsibility for the protection of fundamental personal rights within the sphere of employment discrimination back to the political institutions.[20]

Nevertheless, the Court has continued to apply the reasoning in *P* v. *S* to other kinds of discrimination against transgendered persons. In *K.B.*, the applicant sought to nominate her domestic partner as the recipient of a widower's pension in the event of her death.[21] Her domestic partner was a female-to-male transsexual, and K.B. was informed by the NHS pensions agency that she could not nominate him for a widower's pension because they were not lawfully married. Under British law at the time, it was not possible for transgendered persons to change their birth certificate to recognize their new gender, and consequently it was not possible to marry a person of the opposite sex. The ECJ, in a somewhat convoluted judgment, ruled that benefits granted under a pension scheme, including a surviving spouse's pension, constituted pay within Article 141 EC, and that under the British legislation there was unequal treatment affecting one of the conditions of access to that pay. Since the legal obstacle to K.B. securing entitlement to a widower's pension for her partner was a violation of the European Convention of Human Rights, her situation fell in principle within the scope of Article 141:

> Legislation, such as that at issue in the main proceedings, which, in breach of the ECHR, prevents a couple such as K.B. and R. from fulfilling the marriage requirement which must be met for one of them to be able to benefit from part of the pay of the other must be regarded as being, in principle, incompatible with the requirements of Article 141 EC.

The reasoning in *P* v. *S* was also applied in the case of *Richards* to the social security context, where the ECJ ruled that Directive 79/7 on state social security prohibited national legislation which denied a person who had undergone male-to-female gender-reassignment surgery from enjoying a pension at the age of 60, at which women were entitled under national law to a pension, but permitted it only at the age of 65, which was the age of eligibility for men.[22]

(f) ARTICLE 141: THE SOCIAL AND ECONOMIC UNDERPINNINGS OF GENDER EQUALITY

The EEC Treaty from the outset included the principle of equal pay for equal work within the scope of Community competence and made it applicable to the Member States. Later rulings of the ECJ, secondary legislation, and ultimately the ToA amendments to Article 141 indicated that not only equal work, but also work of equal value, was covered. The ToA also added paragraphs 3 and 4. Article 141 now provides:

> 1. Each Member State shall ensure that the principle of equal pay for male and female workers for equal work or work of equal value is applied.
> 2. For the purpose of this Article, 'pay' means the ordinary basic or minimum wage or salary and any other consideration, whether in cash or in kind, which the worker receives directly or indirectly, in respect of his employment from his employer.

---

[20] Case C–249/96 *Grant*, n. 18 above, paras. 47–48.
[21] Case C–117/01 *K.B.*, n. 16 above.
[22] Case C–423/04 *Richards* v. *Secretary of State for Work and Pensions* [2006] ECR I–3585.

Equal pay without discrimination based on sex means:

(a) that pay for the same work at piece rates shall be calculated on the basis of the same unit of measurement;

(b) that pay for work at time rates shall be the same for the same job.

3. The Council, acting in accordance with the procedure referred to in Article 251, and after consulting the Economic and Social Committee, shall adopt measures to ensure the application of the principle of equal opportunities and equal treatment of men and women in matters of employment and occupation, including the principle of equal pay for equal work or work of equal value.

4. With a view to ensuring full equality in practice between men and women in working life, the principle of equal treatment shall not prevent any Member State from maintaining or adopting measures providing for specific advantages in order to make it easier for the underrepresented sex to pursue a vocational activity or to prevent or compensate for disadvantages in professional careers.

The historical explanation for the original Article 141, given the absence of any mention in the Treaty of equal treatment other than in the context of pay, appears to have been France's concern that it would be placed at a competitive disadvantage in observing the principle of equal pay for equal work more thoroughly than it was observed in other Member States.[23] In other words, concern over unfair treatment of women in the labour market was not the primary factor motivating the drafters of this Article. Nevertheless, it can be said that Article 141 and the other provisions of Community sex-discrimination law are now viewed and interpreted not only as an instrument of economic policy, but also as an important part of Community social policy.[24]

While undoubtedly the equal-pay rule was intended to 'level the playing field' by ensuring that employers in no one Member State would have this competitive advantage over those in another Member State, the ECJ declared, even in its early case law, that Article 141 had a social, and not just an economic, aim. In the first *Defrenne* case, Belgium had argued that the aim of this provision was economic only, namely 'to avoid discrepancies in cost prices due to the employment of female labour less well paid for the same work than male labour'.[25] The Court rejected this view in *Defrenne II*.

Case 43/75 **Defrenne v. Sabena**
[1976] ECR 455

[Note ToA renumbering: Art. 119 is now Art. 141]

THE ECJ

8. Article 119 pursues a double aim.

9. First, in the light of the different stages of the development of social legislation in the various Member States, the aim of Article 119 is to avoid a situation in which undertakings

---

[23] C. Barnard, 'The Economic Objectives of Article 119', in D. O'Keeffe and T. Hervey (eds.), *Sex Equality Law in the European Union* (Wiley, 1996).

[24] Case C–50/96 *Schröder*, n. 13 above.

[25] Case 80/70 *Defrenne v. Belgium (Defrenne I)* [1971] ECR 445.

established in States which have actually implemented the principle of equal pay suffer a competitive disadvantage in intra-Community competition as compared with undertakings established in States which have not yet eliminated discrimination against women workers as regards pay.

10. Secondly, this provision forms part of the social objectives of the Community, which is not merely an economic union, but is at the same time intended, by common action, to ensure social progress and seek the constant improvement of the living and working conditions of their peoples, as is emphasized by the Preamble to the Treaty.

. . .

12. This double aim, which is at once economic and social, shows that the principle of equal pay forms part of the foundations of the Community.

We saw in Chapter 8 that various Member States had avoided the implementation of the equal-pay principle for years, eventually arguing unsuccessfully to the ECJ in *Defrenne* that Article 141 lacked direct effect. The Court ruled that it had been directly effective since the end of the first stage of the transitional period. Nevertheless, the ECJ was swayed by the arguments of the Member States on the serious financial consequences of such a ruling for them, and it declared that in view of the incorrect understanding of the Member States of the effects of Article 141, due in part to the fact that the Commission had not brought infringement proceedings against them earlier, its ruling should have effect only prospectively. This meant that only those who had already brought legal proceedings or made a claim could rely on the Article in respect of pay claims for periods prior to the date of judgment. Prospective overruling of this kind by the Court has not been frequent, and the cases tend to be those in which there are considerable financial implications for the Member States or their industries.[26]

More recently in *Schröder*, the ECJ was confronted with an apparent conflict between the social aim (ensuring fairness to individual women and men) and the economic aim (ensuring equal conditions for competing employers) of Article 141.[27] If the social aim were to take priority, German law could apply the equal-pay principle retroactively so as to permit part-time workers access to an occupational pension scheme, whereas if the economic aim were to take priority, Germany—in order to ensure that its firms were not operating under less favourable conditions than those of Member State competitors—should not do so. The ECJ began by repeating the 'double aim' ruling in paragraphs 8–11 of *Defrenne II* (above) and continued:

56. However, in later decisions the Court has repeatedly held that the right not to be discriminated against on grounds of sex is one of the fundamental human rights whose observance the Court has a duty to ensure (see, to that effect, Case 149/77 *Defrenne III* [1978] ECR 1365, paragraphs 26 and 27, Joined Cases 75/82 and 117/82 *Razzouk and Beydoun* v. *Commission* [1984] ECR 1509, paragraph 16, and Case C–13/94 *P.* v. *S. and Cornwall County Council* [1996] ECR I–2143, paragraph 19).

57. In view of that case-law, it must be concluded that the economic aim pursued by Article 119 of the Treaty, namely the elimination of distortions of competition between undertakings established in different Member States, is secondary to the social aim pursued by the same provision, which constitutes the expression of a fundamental human right.

---

[26] See e.g. below Case 262/88 *Barber* v. *Guardian Royal Exchange Assurance Group* [1990] ECR 1889; N. Hyland, 'Temporal Limitation of the Effects of the Judgments of the Court of Justice' (1995) 4 *IJEL* 208.

[27] N. 13 above. For comments see L. Besselink (2001) 38 *CMLRev.* 437; E. Ellis (2000) 25 *ELRev.* 564.

According to the Court, therefore, the social aim of Article 141, read in the light of its case law on fundamental human rights, has come to take precedence over its economic rationale. Moreover, while *Schröder* is an equal-pay case, the Court's ruling seems to refer to Article 141 and the equal treatment principle more generally.

The emphasis on human rights rather than on economic competitiveness as the primary rationale for EU equal treatment law is evident also in the preambles to the more recent legislation, including Directive 2006/54[28] and the Equal Treatment Amendment Directive of 2002,[29] as well as in the Article 13 Anti-Discrimination Directives adopted in 2000.[30]

(g) THE 'RECAST' EQUAL TREATMENT DIRECTIVE 2006/54

As part of the EU's general programme of legislative consolidation, and with a view to tidying up and recasting the existing legislation on equal pay, equal treatment, occupational social security, and the burden of proof, Directive 2006/54 was adopted.[31] Apart from systematizing and tidying up the existing legislation and incorporating relevant rulings of the ECJ, the Directive does not introduce any substantially new amendments. Matters of equal treatment in state social security are dealt with separately by Directive 79/7, and matters of equal treatment in access to and supply of goods and services by Directive 2004/113. Directive 2006/54 also leaves unamended the Pregnancy and the Parental Leave Directives, and Directive 86/613 on equal treatment for self-employed persons. While the partial and relatively unambitious nature of this consolidation has been criticized, it appears that the reason for the selective approach was so that the recast Directive could be adopted on the basis of Article 141 EC, without needing to use a legal basis such as Article 137, which is more onerous in both procedural and substantive terms.[32]

Directive 2006/54 therefore now governs equal treatment in access to employment and promotion, vocational training, working conditions including pay, and occupational social security. Title I sets out the purpose and scope of the Directive, defines its key terms, and makes reference to the positive action provision in Article 141(4) EC. Title II contains the main substantive sections. Chapter 1 of Title II deals with pay, Chapter 2 with occupational social security, and Chapter 3 with access to employment and promotion, vocational training, and working conditions. Title III contains the 'horizontal provisions', with a chapter on remedies and enforcement (including adequate compensation, recourse to judicial and conciliation procedures, and the burden of proof); a chapter on the promotion of equal treatment through dialogue (including provision for the establishment of national equality bodies, the promotion of dialogue and adoption of agreements by the social partners, the imposition of positive obligations on the Member States, and dialogue with NGOs); and a final chapter dealing broadly with Member State compliance (including the requirement of adoption of appropriate penalties, prevention of discrimination, protection against victimization, gender mainstreaming, and dissemination of information). Article 27 of the Directive indicates that

---

[28] N. 31 above.

[29] N. 62 above.

[30] N. 36 above.

[31] Dir. 2006/54/EC of the European Parliament and of the Council of 5 July 2006 on the implementation of the principle of equal opportunities and equal treatment of men and women in matters of employment and occupation (recast) [2006] OJ L204/23.

[32] N. Burrows and M. Robison, 'An Assessment of the Recast of Community Equality Laws' (2006) 13 *ELJ* 186.

it sets minimum conditions only, so that States may adopt more extensive protection, and it contains a qualified non-regression clause.

The core provision of the Directive which applies across the three fields of pay, occupational social security, and employment conditions more generally, is the prohibition on direct or indirect discrimination on grounds of sex in the public and private sectors.[33] Discrimination, according to the Directive, includes harassment and sexual harassment,[34] instruction to discriminate, and any less favourable treatment of a woman related to pregnancy or maternity leave. All of the relevant terms, including direct and indirect discrimination and harassment, are defined in Article 2. The reference to discrimination on the basis of 'marital and family status', which had not been the subject of dispute, has however been omitted from the Directive.[35]

In terms of tidying up, some of the significant contributions made by the new Directive are the adoption of a definition of indirect discrimination which is consistent with other EU equality legislation and the application of the horizontal general provisions on remedies, equality bodies, compliance, information, dialogue, etc., to all three fields. These changes bring the EU's sex equality legislation (and not only that dealing with employment conditions, which had already been amended in 2002) into line with the other newer EU anti-discrimination Directives covering racial and ethnic origin, disability, age, sexual orientation, and religion.[36]

(h) DIRECTIVE 2004/113 ON EQUAL TREATMENT IN ACCESS TO AND SUPPLY OF GOODS AND SERVICES

Apart from the general move towards gender mainstreaming across all areas of EU law and policy, one of the first targeted pieces of 'hard law' on gender equality going beyond the labour market context is Directive 2004/113,[37] which was intended to combat sex discrimination in the access to and supply of goods and services.

The Directive was particularly intended to apply to the field of insurance, and it specifically excludes education and the content of media and advertising from its scope. These exclusions reflect a lively debate which took place when the measure was first proposed, including whether it should apply to ban sex-stereotyping in advertising. It also does not apply to the fields of employment or self-employment.

Like the broad anti-discrimination directives adopted in 2000[38] under Article 13 EC (covering race, disability, age, religion, and sexual orientation), the prohibition of discrimination as between women and men in Directive 2004/113 applies to both the public and private sectors. However, unlike the Race Directive in particular, Directive 2004/113 does not have any broader application beyond the fields of access to and supply of goods and services. In keeping with the provisions of the EC Treaty on the free movement of services, the term 'services' in the Directive refers to commercial services provided for payment. The Directive applies to goods and services available to the public, irrespective of the individual situation of the consumer,

---

[33] Art. 14.

[34] These also include 'any less favourable treatment based on a person's rejection of or submission to such conduct'.

[35] For criticism see S. Koukoulis-Spiliotopoulos, 'The Amended Equal Treatment Directive 2002/73: An Expression of Constitutional Principles/Fundamental Rights' (2005) 12 *MJ* 327.

[36] Council Dir. 2000/78/EC of 27 Nov. 2000 establishing a general framework for equal treatment in employment and occupation [2000] OJ L303/16; Council Dir. 2000/43/EC of 29 June 2000 implementing the principle of equal treatment between persons irrespective of racial or ethnic origin [2000] OJ L180/22.

[37] Council Dir. 2004/113/EC of 13 Dec. 2004 implementing the principle of equal treatment between men and women in the access to and supply of goods and services [2004] OJ L373/37.

[38] N. 36 above.

'which are offered outside the area of private and family life'.[39] Article 3(2) provides that 'this Directive does not prejudice the individual's freedom to choose a contractual partner as long as an individual's choice of contractual partner is not based on that person's sex'.

The Goods and Services Directive has much in common with Directive 2006/54,[40] and with the two broader anti-discrimination directives adopted in 2000.[41] Thus it prohibits direct and indirect sex discrimination, including harassment and sexual harassment, as well as adverse treatment on grounds of pregnancy or maternity,[42] and the various directives contain the same definitions of these terms. There is a positive action provision like that contained in the 2000 Directives,[43] and there are also similar provisions on remedies, the burden of proof, compliance, the role of equality bodies, dialogue, and the dissemination of information.[44] Article 7 introduces a non-regression clause and indicates that it is a minimum-harmonization directive only. Article 4(5) of the Directive contains an interesting provision introducing the familiar concept of objective justification, but not limiting it to cases of indirect discrimination:

> This Directive shall not preclude differences in treatment, if the provision of the goods and services exclusively or primarily to members of one sex is justified by a legitimate aim and the means of achieving that aim are appropriate and necessary.

The examples given in the preamble to the Directive include single-sex shelters, which can be justified on grounds of protection of victims of violence, and single-sex private clubs, on the grounds of freedom of association.

In substantive terms, the Directive was intended in particular to apply to the insurance sector, and it prohibits the use of sex as a factor in the calculation of premiums and benefits for the purposes of insurance and related financial services in all new contracts concluded after 21 December 2007, in so far as that results in differences in individuals' premiums and benefits.[45] Prior to 21 December 2007, however, Member States are allowed to permit 'proportionate differences in individuals' premiums and benefits where sex is a determining factor in the assessment of the risk, based on relevant and accurate actuarial and statistical data'. States are required to inform the Commission of this and to ensure that their data are accurate and relevant, as well as being regularly published and updated. They are also required to review their decision to avail of this provision after five years. Article 5(3) provides that costs related to pregnancy and maternity shall not result in differences to individuals' premiums and benefits.

The Commission is to report on the practices of Member States in this regard by December 2010.

3. EQUAL PAY

(a) THE LEGISLATIVE FRAMEWORK

Equal pay was originally governed by Directive 75/117, which has now been repealed and replaced essentially without amendment, other than to update it in the light of relevant case

---

[39] N. 37 above, Art. 3(1).
[40] N. 31 above.
[41] N. 36 above.
[42] N. 37 above, Art. 4.
[43] *Ibid.*, Art. 6.
[44] *Ibid.*, Arts. 8–15.
[45] *Ibid.*, Art. 5.

law, by Directive 2006/54.[46] The basic thrust is to require the elimination of sex discrimination in pay in cases involving the same work or work to which equal value is attributed, and to require job-classification schemes to be similarly free from discrimination.[47] Member States are required to abolish any such discrimination in legislative or administrative provisions and to ensure that any breaches of the equal-pay principle in collective agreements or contracts are rendered void or amended. There is, as we have seen, a chapter in the consolidating legislation on 'promotion of equal treatment' (*inter alia* through dialogue with social partners and NGOs and through the establishment of equality bodies), which replaces the previous and more cursory positive obligation to take appropriate measures to ensure that the equal-pay principle is observed.[48] The consolidating Directive also now contains more extensive provisions than the earlier Directive on remedies, enforcement, and compliance.[49] These provisions incorporate various aspects of the ECJ's case law such as the rule that there can be no prior ceiling on damages,[50] that the burden of proof shifts to the defendant where the plaintiff can establish facts which raise a presumption of direct or indirect discrimination,[51] and that penalties must be 'effective, proportionate and dissuasive'.

Although the original Equal Pay Directive fleshed out the provisions of Article 141, the right to equal pay has always been said by the Court to stem directly from the Treaty, so that the terms of the legislation are to be given the same meaning as those in the Treaty.[52] Further, the Treaty could be directly invoked in 'horizontal' cases against an employer, thus avoiding problems concerning the horizontal effect of the Directive. The Equal Pay Directive was intended to address the problem of how to apply the equal-pay principle when the work performed by two employees is quite different, but is alleged to be of equal value, and its aim was to place the onus on the states of putting the principle into practice.

For example, in a case brought against the UK for failure to ensure an adequate job-classification system, the ECJ ruled that where there was disagreement on the application of the equal-pay principle, a worker had to have at least a right of access to an appropriate authority for a binding ruling on whether or not his or her work has the same value as other work.[53]

In *Brunnhofer*, the Court indicated that the personal qualities of the employee and the manner in which the work was performed could not simply be conflated and used retrospectively by an employer to argue that the employee was not carrying out similar work or work of equal value to other employees, for the purposes of explaining a pay differential which existed from the outset.[54] Individual work capacity could however be taken into account in other

---

[46] Dir. 2006/54, n. 31 above.

[47] See Case 237/85 *Rummler* [1986] ECR 2101 where the Court ruled that the use of criteria such as muscle-demand for the purpose of determining rates of pay was permitted. See S. Fredman, 'EC Discrimination Law: A Critique' (1992) 21 *ILJ* 119, 123. See also Case C–400/93 *Royal Copenhagen, Specialarbejderforbundet i Danmark* v. *Dansk Industri* [1995] ECR I–1275; Case C–236/98 *Jämställdhetsombudsmannen* v. *Örebro läns landsting* [2000] ECR I–2189, para. 48.

[48] See Title III, chap. 2 of Dir 2006/54, and previously see Art. 6 of Dir. 75/117.

[49] Dir. 2006/54, n. 31 above, Title II, chaps. 1 and 3.

[50] Case C–271/91 *Marshall* v. *Southampton and South-West Hampshire Area Health Authority (No. 2)* [1993] ECR I–4367; Case C–180/95 *Draehmpaehl* v. *Urania Immobilienservice* [1997] ECR I–2195.

[51] See, e.g., Case 109/88 *Handels- og Kontorfunktionærernes Forbund I Danmark* v. *Dansk Arbejdsgiverforening, acting on behalf of Danfoss* [1989] ECR 3199.

[52] See e.g. Case C–381/99 *Brunnhofer* v. *Bank der österreichischen Postsparkasse AG* [2001] ECR I–4961, para. 29; Case C–309/97 *Angestelltenbetriebsrat der Wiener Gebietskrankenkasse* v. *Wiener Gebietskrankenkasse* [1999] ECR I–2865 on the 'same work'.

[53] Case 61/81 *Commission* v. *United Kingdom* [1982] ECR 2601, para. 9.

[54] Case C–381/99 *Brunnhofer*, n. 52 above.

ways, e.g., in relation to an employee's career development as compared with that of a more effective colleague, and therefore in *subsequent* postings and pay. The ECJ has been criticized, however, for stating that professional training could be a valid criterion for ascertaining whether or not employees were engaged in the 'same work'.[55] While a person's higher qualifications or training may provide grounds for *justifying* a higher level of pay for work done, it does not render such work qualitatively different from the same task carried out by other employees with lower qualifications.[56]

The difficulties of assessment and proof which frequently confront employees wishing to make an equal-pay claim are illustrated by *Danfoss*, in which the ECJ ruled that employers were not entitled to maintain 'opaque' pay practices:

Case 109/88 Handels- og Kontorfunktionærernes Forbund i Danmark v. Dansk Arbejdsgiverforening, acting on behalf of Danfoss
[1989] ECR 3199

Danfoss, an employer, paid the same basic wage to employees in the same wage group, but it also awarded individual pay supplements which were calculated on the basis of mobility, training, and seniority. A complaint was brought before the industrial arbitration board on behalf of two female employees, each of whom worked within a different wage group, and within these two wage groups it was shown that a man's average wage was higher than that of a woman. Several questions were referred to the ECJ.

THE ECJ

10. It is apparent from the documents before the Court that the issue between the parties to the main proceedings has its origin in the fact that the system of individual supplements applied to basic pay is implemented in such a way that a woman is unable to identify the reasons for a difference between her pay and that of a man doing the same work. Employees do not know what criteria in the matter of supplements are applied to them and how they are applied. They know only the amount of their supplemented pay without being able to determine the effect of the individual criteria. Those who are in a particular wage group are thus unable to compare the various components of their pay with those of the pay of their colleagues who are in the same wage group.

11. In those circumstances the questions put by the national court must be understood as asking whether the Equal Pay Directive must be interpreted as meaning that where an undertaking applies a system of pay which is totally lacking in transparency, it is for the employer to prove that his practice in the matter of wages is not discriminatory, if a female worker establishes, in relation to a relatively large number of employees, that the average pay for women is less than for men.

12. In that respect, it must first be borne in mind that in its judgment of 20 June 1988 in Case 318/86 *Commission* v. *France* [1988] ECR 3559, paragraph 27, the Court condemned a system of recruitment, characterized by a lack of transparency, as being contrary to the principle of equal access to employment on the ground that the lack of transparency prevented any form of supervision by the national courts.

---

[55] *Ibid.*, para. 78; Case C–309/97 *Angestelltenbetriebsrat*, n. 52 above, para. 19.
[56] E. Ellis, 'The Recent Jurisprudence of the Court of Justice in the Field of Sex Equality' (2000) 37 *CMLRev.* 1403.

13. It should next be pointed out that in a situation where a system of individual pay supplements which is completely lacking in transparency is at issue, female employees can establish differences only in so far as average pay is concerned. They would be deprived of any effective means of enforcing the principle of equal pay before the national courts if the effect of adducing such evidence was not to impose upon the employer the burden of proving that his practice in the matter of wages is not in fact discriminatory.

...

15. To show that his practice in the matter of wages does not systematically work to the disadvantage of female employees the employer will have to indicate how he has applied the criteria concerning supplements and will thus be forced to make his system of pay transparent.

Here the ECJ decided that the requirement of effectiveness imposed on the employer, in a reversal of the normal onus of proof, an obligation to show that a non-transparent pay policy did not discriminate on grounds of sex. If the normal burden of proof were to apply in such a situation, it would be excessively difficult or impossible for an affected employee to show that pay discrimination had actually occurred.

Prior to *Danfoss*, the Commission had proposed a directive on reversing the burden of proof in sex-discrimination cases, but this was blocked in the Council.[57] Yet the ECJ, implicitly overriding the Member States' objections reflected in the blocking of this proposal, achieved a similar result at least in the field of pay. Such an assertion by the Court of its authority in the face of opposition on the part of the States and within the Community legislative process in the field of sex discrimination is not uncommon, as we shall see in the occupational pensions context below. In this particular context, the *Danfoss* case arguably had some influence in unblocking the legislative process, and in 1997 the Council adopted a Directive on the Burden of Proof,[58] which, as we saw above, has now been incorporated into the consolidated Directive 2006/54.[59] All Member States now accept that the employer/respondent bears the burden of proof, once the employee/plaintiff has established facts from which it may be presumed that there has been direct or indirect discrimination.

(b) INDIRECT DISCRIMINATION IN PAY AND OBJECTIVE JUSTIFICATION

(i) *Indirect Discrimination*

Indirect discrimination is a concept which has been discussed in Chapters 19, 21, and 22 in the context of discriminatory restrictions on freedom of movement. In the context of gender equality, indirect discrimination is a concept well known in many jurisdictions as a means of confronting and redressing systemic discrimination.

Where a rule or a practice, although not framed in terms which apply only to one sex, has the effect of disadvantaging members of one sex that rule or practice will be considered indirectly discriminatory. The concept was initially defined in the case law, then subsequently in

---

[57] [1988] OJ C176/5. For comment on this aspect of *Danfoss* see J. Shaw, 'The Burden of Proof and the Legality of Supplementary Payments in Equal Pay Cases' (1990) 15 *ELRev.* 260, 263–264.

[58] Council Dir. 97/80 [1997] OJ L14/6. See also Council Dir. 98/52 on the extension of Dir. 97/80 to the UK [1998] OJ L205/66.

[59] N. 31 above.

the Directive on the Burden of Proof,[60] and later in the new Anti-discrimination Directives under Article 13 EC,[61] as well as in the 2002 amended version of the Sex Equality Directive 76/207.[62] Confusingly, however, the legislative definitions were not uniform. Now, consolidating Directive 2006/54 adopts the definition from the Anti-discrimination Directives and makes it generally applicable, abandoning the more complicated definition incorporating reference to statistics which had been used in the Burden of Proof Directive.[63]

Initially in *Defrenne III*, the ECJ seemed to take the position that Article 141 would not have direct effect in the case of indirect or disguised discrimination,[64] e.g., where the workers being compared were not within the same establishment or were hypothetical,[65] and that further legislation would be required in such cases. However, it soon became clear that Article 141 does apply to cases of indirect discrimination, and that cases such as *Defrenne III* and *Macarthys* established other limits to the scope of Article 141.

For more controversial recent examples of this, the ECJ ruled in the cases of *Lawrence* and *Allonby* that where employees had been dismissed and re-employed by sub-contractors on a different basis, Article 141 would not be applicable because the differences between the pay of employees doing the same work or work of equal value could not be attributable to the same 'source'.[66] And in *Wippel*, the ECJ ruled that no discrimination, direct or indirect, arose for the purposes of Article 141 where there was no comparable category of worker against whom the complainant's case could be measured.[67] Here the claimed comparison was not between part-time and full-time workers, but between a casual female worker employed on a work-on-demand contract and full-time workers. Further, Article 141 does not of itself require proportionate pay, so that, although a woman is entitled to at least the same pay as a man doing work of lower value, she cannot necessarily rely directly on the Treaty for payment of a higher wage to reflect the value of her work.

The first major ruling on the application of Article 141 to indirect discrimination however was *Jenkins*.[68] In this case the ECJ effectively ruled that, although the fact that part-time work was paid at a lower hourly rate than full-time work did not *per se* amount to discrimination, a presumption of discrimination in breach of the Treaty would arise 'if it is established that a considerably smaller percentage of women than of men perform the minimum number of weekly working hours required in order to be able to claim the full-time hourly rate of pay', and no other objective justification existed for the pay differential.[69] The Court also suggested that an employer's policy of encouraging a greater number of full-time workers might be an example of legitimate justification.[70] Ultimately, the ECJ ruled that the issue of objective

[60] N. 58 above.

[61] N. 36 above.

[62] Dir. 2002/73 [2002] OJ L269/15.

[63] See n. 58 above.

[64] Case 149/77 *Defrenne*, n. 11 above, para. 18.

[65] See Case 129/79 *Macarthys Ltd.* v. *Smith* [1980] ECR 1275, paras. 14–15, Case C–400/93 *Royal Copenhagen*, n. 47 above, paras. 29–38; Case C–200/91 *Coloroll Pension Trustees Ltd.* v. *James Richard Russell* [1994] ECR I–4389, paras. 103–104 on the difficulties of comparisons between employees who are and who are not within the same establishment, for the purposes of showing discrimination. See also Case 157/86 *Murphy* v. *Bord Telecom Eireann* [1988] ECR 673 on discrimination where a man was paid the same for doing the work of lower value.

[66] Case C–320/00 *Lawrence* v. *Regent Office Care Ltd.* [2002] ECR I–7325; Case C–256/01 *Allonby* v. *Accrington & Rossendale College* [2004] ECR I–873. See Burrows and Robison, n. 32 above, for discussion of the decision to omit a specific provision on the *Allonby* ruling in the recast Dir. 2006/54, n. 31 above.

[67] Case C–313/02 *Wippel* v. *Peek & Cloppenburg GmbH* [2004] ECR I–9483.

[68] Case 96/80 *Jenkins* v. *Kingsgate (Clothing Productions) Ltd.* [1981] ECR 911.

[69] Warner AG in the case noted that women constituted 90% of part-time workers in the Community.

[70] *Ibid.*, para. 12.

justification was for the national court to weigh, with the onus being on the employer to demonstrate that it was based on something legitimate other than the sex of the worker.

The broadening of the formal criterion of direct sex-based discrimination in *Jenkins* to include the less obvious but equally, or even more, pervasive forms of pay discrimination affecting women was an important development. However, the parallel development of an equally broad concept of objective justification reduced its impact.[71] The definition of indirect discrimination in Directive 2006/54, Article 2(1)(b), now integrates the notion of 'objective justification' into the definition itself:

> [W]here an apparently neutral provision, criterion or practice would put persons of one sex at a particular disadvantage compared with persons of the other sex, unless that provision, criterion or practice is objectively justified by a legitimate aim, and the means of achieving that aim are appropriate and necessary.

Exactly what can constitute objective justification remains unclear. The ECJ often leaves the matter for the national court to decide, raising the likelihood of differences amongst the various Member State tribunals as to whether an indirectly discriminatory pay policy is justified. The Court however has given some guidance by declaring certain grounds of justification to be too general and indicating that others may be sufficient. Problems of inconsistency and uncertainty nonetheless remain, contributing to the volume of expensive and possibly duplicated litigation in different Member States.

In *Bilka*, concerning eligibility of part-time workers for an occupational pension scheme, the ECJ formulated a test for objective justification very similar to the three-part proportionality test developed when examining state justifications for restrictions on the free movement of goods and services.[72]

Case 170/84 **Bilka-Kaufhaus GmbH v. Karin Weber von Hartz**
[1986] ECR 1607

33. In its observations Bilka argues that the exclusion of part-time workers from the occupational pension scheme is intended solely to discourage part-time work, since in general part-time workers refuse to work in the late afternoon and on Saturdays. In order to ensure the presence of an adequate workforce during those periods it was therefore necessary to make full-time work more attractive than part-time work, by making the occupational pension scheme open only to full-time workers. Bilka concludes that on the basis of the judgment of 31 March 1981 it cannot be accused of having infringed Article 119.

. . .

36. It is for the national court, which has sole jurisdiction to make findings of fact, to determine whether and to what extent the grounds put forward by an employer to explain the adoption of a pay practice which applies independently of a worker's sex but in fact affects far more women than men may be regarded as objectively justified economic grounds. If the national court finds that the measures chosen by the employer correspond to a real need on the part of the undertaking, are appropriate with a view to achieving the objectives pursued and are

---

[71] See also cl. 4(1) and (4) of the Framework Agreement of the social partners on part-time work, subsequently included in Council Dir. 97/81 [1997] OJ L14/9.

[72] See in particular Chs. 19 and 22.

necessary to that end, the fact that the measures affect a far greater number of women than men is not sufficient to show that they constitute an infringement of Article 119.

Thus it seems that an indirectly discriminatory measure of this kind may be justified if, first, the measure answers a 'real need' of the employer; secondly, the measures are 'appropriate' to achieve the objectives they pursue; and, finally, the measures are 'necessary' to achieve those objectives. Phrased in slightly different language, this test corresponds broadly to the proportionality test in the context of restrictions on the free movement of goods and services. However, the ECJ in *Bilka*, while it appeared to accept that the encouragement of full-time workers was an acceptable policy, did not rule on whether this policy justified the pay disadvantage to women, and ultimately left the proportionality test for the national court to apply.

Some years later in *Rinner-Kühn*, the Court was faced with a similar case involving the exclusion of part-time workers from sick-pay provision.[73] On this occasion the indirectly discriminatory provisions were contained in national legislation, rather than in the act of an employer. The ECJ ruled that although the legislative provision was in principle contrary to the aim of Article 141, it was capable of objective justification. However, the justification offered by the government was inadequate:

> 13. In the course of the procedure, the German Government stated, in response to a question put by the Court, that workers whose period of work amounted to less than 10 hours a week or 45 hours a month were not as integrated in, or as dependent on, the undertaking employing them as other workers.
>
> 14. It should, however, be stated that those considerations, in so far as they are only generalizations about certain categories of workers, do not enable criteria which are both objective and unrelated to any discrimination on grounds of sex to be identified. However, if the Member State can show that the means chosen meet a necessary aim of social policy and that they are suitable and requisite for attaining that aim, the mere fact that the provision affects a much greater number of female workers than male workers cannot be regarded as constituting an infringement of Article 119.

Despite the Advocate General's argument that no presumption of indirect discrimination should arise in the case of national legislative provisions (on the ground that they could be presumed to take into account many social, economic, and political circumstances other than the adverse effects on women) as compared with employer agreements, the ECJ disagreed and applied the same analysis as it had done in *Bilka*.[74] The onus was on the employee—save in a case like *Danfoss*, where the employer's system was insufficiently transparent—to show in the first instance that those receiving lower payments were predominantly or disproportionately women. The onus then shifts to the employer to justify such indirect discrimination, without the employee having to impute a discriminatory intent or to prove that the pay policy was in some way based on sex.[75]

Now, Article 19(1) of the consolidating Directive 2006/54[76] imposes a requirement on Member States to ensure that, where an employee establishes 'facts from which it may be

---

[73] Case 171/88 *Rinner-Kühn* v. *FWW Spezial-Gebäudereinigung GmbH* [1989] ECR 2743.

[74] See, however, below 943, that in the context of *social security* legislation, the Court normally applies the proportionality test loosely, leaving a considerable 'margin of discretion' to the Member States.

[75] See J. Shaw, 'Sick Pay for Cleaners' (1989) 14 *ELRev.* 428, for criticism of the AG's argument and the difficulties it would pose for employees.

[76] N. 31 above.

presumed that there has been direct or indirect discrimination', it is for the respondent to prove that there has been no breach of the principle of equal treatment. In *Elsner-Lakeberg* the ECJ accepted that, although requiring part-time and full-time workers to exceed their monthly working time by three hours in order to be eligible for excess pay appeared on the surface to be equal treatment, it was in fact indirectly discriminatory against part-time workers in that it imposed a greater burden on them by requiring them to work a higher percentage of their normal monthly hours.[77] It was then for the national court to determine whether this discrimination could be objectively justified.

Although phrased in slightly different terms in *Bilka* and *Rinner-Kühn*, the thrust of the 'objective justification' test is the same in each, namely to require the responsible authority to demonstrate that any discrimination which does occur is effective in achieving a legitimate purpose and goes no further than is necessary to achieve that purpose. And although the ECJ declared that generalized considerations about the tendency of full-time as opposed to part-time workers to integrate more in the workplace could not constitute good grounds for indirect discrimination, it suggested that 'social policy' aims might do so.[78]

In *Bötel*,[79] *Lewark*,[80] and *Freers*,[81] the ECJ acknowledged that while the payment of compensation for attending training courses to full-time workers on a more favourable basis than that paid to part-time workers[82] was likely to discriminate indirectly against women, and to deter them from performing staff committee functions for which the training courses provided preparation, it was nonetheless possible that such discrimination was justified by reference to social-policy aims unrelated to sex. The government's apparent desire to ensure the honorary nature and independence of staff committees in their promotion of harmonious labour relations, and ensure that there would be no financial incentive to stand for election to a staff committee, was accepted in principle by the ECJ as a legitimate aim.[83]

In *Danfoss*, the ECJ considered what kinds of justification for indirect discrimination in the criteria for supplementary pay might be acceptable.[84] The pay criteria included factors such as mobility, training, and length of service of employees. 'Mobility'—a term used, somewhat oddly, apparently to describe characteristics such as enthusiasm and initiative—was, in the ECJ's view, a neutral criterion which should not disadvantage women unless the employer misapplied it. However, if mobility meant adaptability to hours and places of work, the ECJ considered that it could disadvantage women because of family and household duties for which they so often bear responsibility. The criteria of training and length of service, too, although apparently 'neutral', could disadvantage women, but the ECJ concluded that they might be objectively justified if the employer could show, for example, that it was of importance for the performance of specific tasks that the employee could be adaptable and mobile, or had valuable experience. In the case of a length-of-service criterion, the ECJ indicated that

---

77 Case C–285/02 *Elsner-Lakeberg* v. *Land Nordrhein-Westfalen* [2004] ECR I–5861.

78 In the UK, the House of Lords in *EOC* v. *Secretary of State for Employment* [1994] 1 WLR 409 concluded that, although the aim of increasing the availability of part-time work was a proper social-policy aim, discrimination against part-time workers in pay or in the requirement of qualifying periods for statutory protection was neither a suitable nor a requisite means of achieving that aim. Contrast the decision of the ECJ in Case C–189/91 *Kirsammer-Hack* v. *Nurhan Sidal* [1993] ECR I–6185.

79 Case C–360/90 *Arbeiterwohlfahrt der Stadt Berlin* v. *Bötel* [1992] ECR I–3589.

80 Case C–457/93 *Kuratorium für Dialyse und Nierentransplantation* v. *Lewark* [1996] ECR I–243.

81 Case C–278/93 *Freers and Speckmann* v. *Deutsche Bundespost* [1996] ECR I–1165.

82 Whether the basis for payment did in fact give preferential treatment to full-time workers was perhaps open to question: Case C–457/93 *Lewark*, n. 80 above, Jacobs AG; J. Shaw (1997) 22 *ELRev.* 256, 259.

83 Contrast the view of Darmon AG in Case C–278/93 *Freers*, n. 81 above, 1179–1180, who concluded that the national rules were not in the circumstances objectively justifiable.

84 Case 109/88 *Danfoss*, n. 51 above.

this did not normally need specific justification, unless there were specific reasons shown to suggest that it was not an appropriate way of rewarding experience which enabled an employee to perform better.[85]

In *Kowalska*,[86] indirect discrimination stemming from a provision in a collective-bargaining agreement was said to breach the Treaty unless objectively justified.[87] In *Nimz*, the ECJ considered whether an indirectly discriminatory term in a collective agreement, whereby only half of the period of service of certain part-time workers was taken into account in calculating their salary grade, could be justified on general grounds.

Case C–184/89 **Nimz v. Freie und Hansestadt Hamburg**
[1991] ECR I–297

13. In this regard, the City of Hamburg claimed during the procedure that full-time employees or those who work for three-quarters of normal working time acquire more quickly than others the abilities and skills relating to their particular job. The German Government also relied on their more extensive experience.

14. It should however, be stated that such considerations, in so far as they are no more than generalizations about certain categories of workers, do not make it possible to identify criteria which are both objective and unrelated to any discrimination on grounds of sex. ... Although experience goes hand in hand with length of service, and experience enables the worker in principle to improve performance of the tasks allotted to him, the objectivity of such a criterion depends on all the circumstances in a particular case, and in particular on the relationship between the nature of the work performed and the experience gained from the performance of that work upon completion of a certain number of working hours. However, it is a matter for the national court, which alone is competent to evaluate the facts, to determine in the light of all the circumstances whether and to what extent a provision in a collective agreement such as that here at issue is based on objectively justified factors unrelated to any discrimination on grounds of sex.

This ruling underscores the point made in *Rinner-Kühn*:[88] general assumptions or assertions about the attributes of part-time workers are unlikely to constitute adequate grounds for justifying a measure which has a disproportionately adverse impact on one sex. Even the argument relating to the greater experience of full-time workers was not treated here as being sufficient as a justification, since the ECJ considered that it depended very much on the nature of the work performed. In the later *Cadman* case, however, the ECJ appears to treat the criteria of seniority and length of service as presumptively justifiable reasons for indirect discrimination, unless particular reasons can be shown why they do not satisfy the aim of rewarding employees who have learned to perform their tasks better.[89]

---

[85] See also Case C–17/05 *Cadman* v. *Health & Safety Executive* [2006] ECR I–9583, paras. 33–39.

[86] Case C–33/89 *Kowalska* v. *Freie und Hansestadt Hamburg* [1990] ECR I–2591.

[87] In Cases C–3/99, 409, and 425/92, 34, 50, and 78/93 *Stadt Lengerich* v. *Helmig* [1994] ECR I–5727, the ECJ ruled that there was no indirect discrimination where collective agreements restricted payment of overtime supplements to cases where the normal working hours fixed for full-time workers were exceeded. Compare Case C–285/02 *Elsner-Lakeberg*, n. 77 above. See also Case C–236/98 *JämO*, n. 47 above, on an 'inconvenient hours' supplement.

[88] Case 171/88 *Rinner-Kühn*, n. 73 above.

[89] Case C–17/05 *Cadman*, n. 85 above.

Apart from discrimination as between part-time versus full-time workers, indirect sex discrimination also potentially arises in other situations. One further example is where certain professions are predominantly female while others—which are more highly paid—are predominantly male.

Case C–127/92 **Enderby v. Frenchay Health Authority and the Secretary of State for Health**
[1993] ECR I–5535

Enderby, who was employed as a speech therapist by the defendant authority, complained of sex discrimination. She argued that members of her profession, which was overwhelmingly a female profession, were paid appreciably less well than members of comparable professions whose jobs were of equal value to hers. She cited the higher pay received by clinical psychologists and pharmacists, since these were professions in which, at an equivalent professional level, there were more men than women. The Court of Appeal referred a number of questions under Article 234 (ex Article 177) and, having cited its rulings on the burden of proof in *Bilka*, *Kowalska*, and *Danfoss* (discussed above), the ECJ continued:

THE ECJ

15. In this case, as both the FHA and the United Kingdom observe, the circumstances are not exactly the same as in the cases just mentioned. First, it is not a question of *de facto* discrimination arising from a particular sort of arrangement such as may apply, for example, in the case of part-time workers. Secondly, there can be no complaint that the employer has applied a system of pay wholly lacking in transparency since the rates of pay of NHS speech therapists and pharmacists are decided by regular collective bargaining processes in which there is no evidence of discrimination as regards either of those two professions.

16. However, if the pay of speech therapists is significantly lower than that of pharmacists and if the former are almost exclusively women while the latter are predominantly men, there is a *prima facie* case of sex discrimination, at least where the two jobs in question are of equal value and the statistics describing that situation are valid.

17. It is for the national court to assess whether it may take into account those statistics, that is to say, whether they cover enough individuals, whether they illustrate purely fortuitous or short-term phenomena, and whether, in general, they appear to be significant.

18. Where there is a *prima facie* case of discrimination, it is for the employer to show that there are objective reasons for the difference in pay. Workers would be unable to enforce the principle of equal pay before national courts if evidence of a *prima facie* case of discrimination did not shift to the employer the onus of showing that the pay differential is not in fact discriminatory.

Although the reference had been made from the national court on the assumption that the two jobs were of equal value, *Enderby* illustrates the problem of establishing indirect discrimination in the sense of showing that work which is performed predominantly by women is undervalued in comparison to work which is performed predominantly by men.[90] In the case of part-time and full-time workers, it is clear that the actual tasks being done are the same,

---

[90] See Case C–236/98 *JämO*, n. 47 above, where a comparison of the pay of midwives and clinical technicians was in issue.

whereas in the case of two distinct types of work, and in the absence of a job-classification scheme, it is considerably more difficult to establish this.

The situation is more complex still where the average pay of several groups is compared, and where, although the highest-paid group consists principally of women, so also does the lowest-paid group. This arose in the *Royal Copenhagen* case, in which it was argued that the system of piece-work pay schemes, in which pay depends largely on the individual output of each worker, led to indirect discrimination against women.[91] The ECJ ruled that the mere finding that the average pay, within such a pay scheme, of a group of workers consisting predominantly of women was appreciably lower than the average pay of a group of predominantly male workers carrying out work of equal value would not be sufficient to establish indirect pay discrimination. This was because, so long as the same unit of measurement was used for the two groups—a matter which was for the national court to assess—the difference in pay received could be due to their different individual output.

However, the Court went on to cite its reasoning in *Enderby* and *Danfoss* concerning the situations in which the burden of proof would shift to the employer to establish that there was no discrimination or that it was justified. On the facts of the *Royal Copenhagen* case, the burden of proof might indeed shift if the pay consisted in part of a variable element, depending on each worker's output, and it was not possible to identify the factors determining the unit of measurement used to calculate this variable element.[92]

In *Seymour-Smith*, the question was what kind of statistical evidence would be necessary to establish 'unfavourable impact' such that indirect discrimination could be inferred.[93] The case concerned the two-years-employment requirement for eligibility for compensation for unfair dismissal, and the ECJ gave some guidelines for the national court to follow in determining whether the statistics were adequate and whether they established that 'a considerably smaller percentage of women than men' could meet the requirement imposed.[94] In *Schnorbus*, by contrast, the ECJ ruled that it was not necessary to rely on statistics to prove indirect discrimination in the case of preferential admission to practical legal training being given to those who had completed compulsory military or civilian service, since under the relevant German legislation women were not required to do military or civilian service.[95] Now too, we have seen, Article 19(1) of Directive 2006/54[96] on the burden of proof no longer makes reference to any requirement to produce statistical evidence in order to establish a *prima facie* case of indirect discrimination.

In *Gruber* the ECJ rejected the argument that there was indirect discrimination against women in the context of national legislation which granted a lower termination payment to workers who ended their employment relationship prematurely in order to take care of their children owing to a lack of child-care facilities than it did to workers who resigned for an important reason related to working conditions or to the employer's conduct.[97] These two situations, according to the ECJ, were relevantly different, so that there was no inequality of treatment and no indirect discrimination.

---

[91] Case C–400/93 *Royal Copenhagen*, n. 47 above.

[92] *Ibid.*, paras. 24–27. The ECJ acknowledged that the employer could deny discrimination by showing that the pay differentials were due, e.g., to differences in the worker's choice concerning the rate of work.

[93] Case C–167/97 *R. v. Secretary of State for Employment, ex p. Seymour-Smith and Perez* [1999] ECR I–623.

[94] *Ibid.*, paras. 54–65. See Case C–243/95 *Hill and Stapleton v. Revenue Commissioners* [1998] ECR I–3739, where statistical evidence showed that 99.2% of clerical assistants who job-shared and 98% of all civil servants who job-shared were women.

[95] Case C–79/99 *Schnorbus v. Land Hessen* [2000] ECR I–10997.

[96] N. 31 above.

[97] Case C–249/97 *Gruber v. Silhouette International Schmied* [1999] ECR I–5295.

However, although workers who had taken parenting leave were held to be in a different situation from actively employed workers, so that the payment to the latter of a voluntary exceptional Christmas bonus would not in itself breach Article 141, the ECJ in *Lewen* ruled that there *would* on the other hand be unlawful indirect discrimination if the bonus was in fact a retrospective payment for work done during the year, since female workers were 'likely … to be on parenting leave when the bonus is awarded far more often than male workers'.[98]

Finally, the ECJ has ruled that while sex-segregation—the restriction of a particular category of work to one sex only—does not *per se* amount to discrimination, the subsequent introduction of unfavourable treatment by reference to that category, whether relating to equal pay or other kinds of equal treatment, could amount to such discrimination unless objectively justified.[99]

(ii) *Objective Justification*

Once indirect discrimination is established to have occurred, of course, the next difficulty is in showing that the justification offered for the pay differential between two different but equally valuable sorts of work is not adequate. The onus is on the employer to show justification, but it is often difficult for an employee to counter the justifications offered in particular when broad economic grounds are pleaded.

Two grounds were offered by the employer in *Enderby*, and while the Court ruled that the separate bargaining processes could not of themselves justify the discrimination, since otherwise the employer could 'easily circumvent the principle of equal pay by using separate bargaining processes',[100] it stated that the needs of the market might constitute adequate justification, depending on whether the proportion of the increase in pay was in fact attributable to the need to attract suitable candidates to the less popular job. The case shows some of the weaknesses of the concept of indirect sex discrimination, and indeed of law, in addressing inequality within the labour market. The fact that women traditionally tend to pursue certain careers and professions which allow for flexibility, even if they offer less competitive salary rates than other professions which attract a greater number of men, means that women's pay is likely remain at lower levels than other work which may be objectively equal in value.

Just as the cases of *Nimz*[101] and *Kowalska*,[102] *Enderby* also shows that there may be a conflict between the principle of non-discrimination on grounds of sex and the collective-bargaining process, which was described by the Health Authority in its defence as 'a process of industrial democracy in which those affected by the terms and conditions of employment can participate', sometimes after many years of negotiation and comprehensive studies. The ECJ, however, made clear in these and other cases[103] that the prohibition on sex discrimination, direct or indirect, must take priority over the autonomy of the industrial-bargaining process. On the other hand, in *Royal Copenhagen*, the ECJ stated that the fact that rates of pay had been determined by collective bargaining or negotiation at local level could be taken into account by the national court as a factor in assessing whether differences between the average pay of two groups of workers were due to objective factors unrelated to sex.[104]

98 Case C–333/97 *Lewen* v. *Denda* [1999] ECR I–7243, para. 40.
99 Case C–196/02 *Nikoloudi* v. *Organizmos Tilepikoinonion Ellados* [2005] ECR I–1789.
100 Case 127/ 92 *Enderby* [1993] ECR I–5535, para. 22.
101 Case C–184/89 *Nimz* v. *Freie und Hansestadt Hamburg* [1991] ECR I–297.
102 Case C–33/89 *Kowalska*, n. 86 above.
103 See, e.g., Case C–281/97 *Krüger* v. *Kreiskrankenhaus Ebersberg* [1999] ECR I–5127.
104 Case C–400/93 *Royal Copenhagen*, n. 47 above. Compare Case C–381/99 *Brunnhofer*, n. 52 above, paras. 44–47.

In *Schnorbus*, the ECJ considered that indirect discrimination against women in access to practical legal training could be objectively justified in order to compensate for the delay occasioned to the careers of men who had undergone compulsory military or civilian service, and the preferential treatment was not disproportionate since it was limited to twelve months maximum.[105] In *JämO*, differences in working hours could constitute objective justification, although the employer would have to demonstrate that this was in fact the case.[106]

In *Hill and Stapleton*, however, the Court gave a clear indication that discrimination against job-sharers (who were overwhelmingly women) in the method of determining pay progression could not be justified on a range of dubious grounds offered by the Revenue Commissioners,[107] which rather bizarrely included 'established practice', and an unsubstantiated assertion that this practice maintained staff morale and motivation. An economic justification based solely on the avoidance of increased costs was also held to be unacceptable. This ruling is particularly interesting for the fact that the ECJ drew attention to the specific type of indirect discrimination involved—i.e., against job-sharers—by noting that job-sharing was overwhelmingly chosen by women seeking to combine work and family responsibilities, and that the protection of women within family life and at work 'in the same way as for men' was a principle recognized by EC law as a 'natural corollary' of the equal-treatment principle. The implication in the context of this case seems to be that an even stronger onus to justify such indirect discrimination would therefore lie on the defendant whose practices undermined such a principle.

The shortcomings of the indirect discrimination/objective justification tests in the endeavour to promote equality in employment for women have been critically noted by many,[108] given the male norm on which the concept of discrimination used is generally based, and given the relative ease with which the commercial objectives of the undertaking or employer can defeat a claim of indirect discrimination.[109] On the other hand, rulings such as *Hill and Stapleton*, *Seymour-Smith*, and *Kutz-Bauer*[110] arguably show the ECJ adopting a less deferential and more robust approach to scrutinizing the 'objective justifications' offered by States (rather than private employers) for indirectly discriminatory legislative measures. In *Seymour-Smith*, in which the UK had argued that legislation on protection against unfair dismissal which discriminated indirectly against women was designed to stimulate recruitment by employers, the ECJ accepted that this was a legitimate social-policy aim, and that the Member States in that respect had a margin of discretion.[111] But it went on to rule:

> 75. However, although social policy is essentially a matter for the Member States under Community law as it stands, the fact remains that the broad margin of discretion available to

---

[105] Case C–79/99 *Schnorbus*, n. 95 above.

[106] Case C–236/98 *JämO*, n. 47 above, paras. 61–62.

[107] Case C–243/95 *Hill*, n. 94 above. See also Case C–77/02 *Steinicke* v. *Bundesanstalt für Arbeit* [2003] ECR I–9027; Case C–187/00 *Kutz-Bauer* v. *Freie und Hansestadt Hamburg* [2003] ECR I–2741, although the ECJ decided this case under the Equal Treatment Dir. 76/207 rather than as an equal pay case. For comment on *Hill* see C. McGlynn and C. Farrelly, 'Equal Pay and the "Protection of Women within Family Life"' (1999) 24 *ELRev.* 202.

[108] S. Fredman, 'European Community Discrimination Law: A Critique' (1992) 21 *ILJ* 119, 125; G. More, 'Equal Treatment of the Sexes: What does "Equal" Mean?' (1993) 1 *Feminist Legal Studies* 45, 70; E. Szyszczak, 'L'Espace Social Européenne: Reality, Dreams or Nightmares?' [1990] *German Yearbook of International Law* 284, 296.

[109] See, e.g., Case C–189/91 *Kirsammer-Hack*, n. 78 above; Case C–297/93 *Grau-Hupka* v. *Stadtgemeinde Bremen* [1994] ECR I–5535; T. Hervey, 'Small Business Exclusion in German Dismissal Law' [1994] *ILJ* 267.

[110] Case C–243/95 *Hill*, n. 94 above; Case C–187/00 *Kutz-Bauer*, n. 107 above, paras. 54–60.

[111] Case C–167/97 *Seymour-Smith*, n. 93 above, paras. 71–73.

the Member States in that connection cannot have the effect of frustrating the implementation of a fundamental principle of Community law such as that of equal pay for men and
women.

76. Mere generalisations concerning the capacity of a specific measure to encourage
recruitment are not enough to show that the aim of the disputed rule is unrelated to any discrimination based on sex nor to provide evidence on the basis of which it could reasonably be
considered that the means chosen were suitable for achieving that aim.

(c) CAN DIRECT PAY DISCRIMINATION BE JUSTIFIED?

While the ECJ has never actually declared that direct rather than indirect pay discrimination
can be 'objectively justified', it has nonetheless in a number of cases considered whether men
and women who appear *prima facie* to be paid differently for performing similar work or work
of equal value may actually be 'differently situated' such that the unequal pay does not in fact
amount to discrimination.

In an unusual judgment in *Birds Eye Walls*, especially given its earlier ruling in
Worringham[112] to the effect that a difference in the actual gross sum paid by an employer to
men as opposed to women was discriminatory even though their situations were slightly different in certain respects, the ECJ ruled that the payment of different bridging pensions to
men and women did not constitute discrimination since they were not similarly situated in
relevant respects.[113] This has more recently been confirmed in the case of *Hlozek*.[114]

In *Abdoulaye*, the ECJ ruled that the situation of a male worker was not comparable to that
of a female worker where the advantage granted specifically to the female is designed to offset
the occupational disadvantages, inherent in maternity leave, which arise for female workers as
a result of being away from work.[115]

Moreover in *Griesmar*, the ECJ considered the argument that differential service credits for
the calculation of retirement pensions for female (and not male) workers who had had children did not constitute discrimination, since the positions of male and female workers were
not comparable in this respect.[116] Ultimately, the ECJ rejected the argument on the basis that
their situations could indeed be comparable if the male worker had assumed the task of bringing up his children. However, the *Griesmar* ruling also drew attention to another possible basis
for justifying apparently discriminatory pay practices, namely the 'positive action' provisions
which appeared first in the Social Policy Agreement and are now contained in Article 141(4)
EC. Article 3 of the recast Equal Treatment Directive 2006/54, which governs pay as well as
conditions of work, also provides that the States may maintain or adopt measures within the
meaning of Article 141(4), 'with a view to ensuring full equality in practice between men and
women in working life'.

---

112 Case 69/80 *Worringham* v. *Lloyds Bank* [1981] ECR 767.
113 Case C–132/92 *Roberts* v. *Birds Eye Walls Ltd.* [1993] ECR I–5579. For criticism see B. Fitzpatrick,
'Equality in Occupational Pension Schemes' (1994) 23 *ILJ* 155.
114 Case C–19/02 *Hlozek* v. *Roche Austria Gesellschaft* [2004] ECR I–11491.
115 Case C–218/98 *Abdoulaye and others* v. *Régie nationale des usines Renault SA* [1999] ECR I–5723, paras.
18–20. See C. McGlynn (1999) 24 *ELRev.* 202.
116 Case C–366/99 *Griesmar* v. *Ministre de l'Economie* [2001] ECR I–9383.

(d) THE BREADTH OF ARTICLE 141: WHAT CAN CONSTITUTE PAY?

This relatively simple question has not given rise to simple answers, despite the guidance given in the Article itself on the meaning of the term 'pay'. The ECJ has given the term a very wide scope, which caused some confusion in relation to the borderline between pay and social security. While some of the Court's rulings appeared to undermine measures adopted by the Community legislative institutions—and thus the bargains struck by the Member States in the Council when adopting those measures—at other times its rulings appeared responsive to the political context by retreating from earlier expansive positions in the face of obvious dissatisfaction from the Member States or the other institutions.

(i) Social Security Benefits are Not Pay

In *Defrenne I*, which was brought against Belgium, the ECJ gave an early ruling on what subsequently became a very tangled relationship between pay and pensions.

Case 80/70 **Defrenne v. Belgium**
[1971] ECR 445

[Note ToA renumbering: Art. 119 is now Art. 141]

The ECJ was asked whether a Belgian law concerning retirement pensions which excluded air hostesses from its scope fell within the ambit of Article 119. The retirement pension was granted under the terms of a social security scheme financed by contributions from workers, employers, and state subsidy. Defrenne argued that there was a direct and necessary link between the retirement pension and salary, since certain conditions of the employment directly influenced the amount of the pension. The Commission argued that social security benefits in general and pensions in particular were excluded from the scope of Article 119.

THE ECJ

6. The provision in the second paragraph of the article extends the concept of pay to any other consideration, whether in cash or in kind, whether immediate or future, provided that the worker receives it, albeit indirectly, in respect of his employment from his employer.

7. Although consideration in the nature of social security benefits is not therefore in principle alien to the concept of pay, there cannot be brought within this concept, as defined in Article 119, social security schemes or benefits, in particular retirement pensions, directly governed by legislation without any element of agreement within the undertaking or the occupational branch concerned, which are obligatorily applicable to general categories of workers.

8. These schemes assure for the workers the benefit of a legal scheme, the financing of which workers, employers and possibly the public authorities contribute in a measure determined less by the employment relationship between the employer and the worker than by considerations of social policy.

9. Accordingly, the part due from the employers in the financing of such schemes does not constitute a direct or indirect payment to the worker.

10. Moreover the worker will normally receive the benefits legally prescribed not by reason of the employer's contribution but solely because the worker fulfils the legal conditions for the grant of benefits.

Although the ECJ stressed that 'consideration in the nature of social security benefits' was not in itself excluded from the concept of pay, the factors which went to exclude the employer's contributions to the retirement pension in this case from the scope of Article 119 (now Article 141) were threefold: first, the pension scheme was directly governed by legislation; secondly, there was no agreement on the scheme within the particular company or occupational branch concerned; and, thirdly, the retirement scheme was *obligatorily* applicable to *general* categories of workers. The determining role of the State and the lack of involvement of the particular employer are crucial: in sum, the pension scheme was set up essentially as a matter of social policy and not as a part of the employment relationship in question. The Court's definition of the difference between pay and social security is important, since equal treatment in social security is not covered by Article 141 but primarily by Directive 79/7, whereas occupational social security is covered in part by this Article and in part by Directive 2006/54.

(ii) *Widening the Definition of Pay*

The wide interpretation of pay under Article 141 was already evident in cases such as *Garland*,[117] where the ECJ ruled that the fact that female employees could on retirement no longer enjoy *travel facilities* for their spouses and dependent children, whilst male employees continued to do so, constituted discrimination contrary to the Treaty.[118] Since these were benefits conferred in respect of employment, even if after retirement and irrespective of any specific contractual obligation, they were held to constitute pay.[119] Similarly in *Kowalska*, a severance grant was covered by Article 141 since it was compensation to which a worker was entitled by reason of her employment, even though it was not paid in the course of employment, but rather on termination of the employment relationship.[120] In *Seymour-Smith*, *compensation for unfair dismissal* was held to constitute pay, since it was designed to replace pay to which the employee would have been entitled had she not been unfairly dismissed.[121] And in the famous case of *Barber* the ECJ ruled that *severance benefits*, including statutory redundancy payments, would constitute pay under Article 141, even though it was required by statute, since the worker was entitled to the payment upon termination of the employment 'by reason of the existence of the employment relationship'.[122] In *Nimz*, the complainant was not challenging pay rates in themselves, but rather the *rules governing the system of salary-classification into grades*, and the Court confirmed that such rules fell within the concept of pay in Article 141 since they directly governed changes in employees' salaries.[123]

In contrast, rules governing the calculation of the length of service of public servants for the purposes of determining eligibility for promotion, and thus indirectly determining the possibility of access to a higher level of remuneration, were a matter of equal treatment rather than

---

117 Case 12/81 *Garland* v. *British Rail Engineering Ltd.* [1982] ECR 359.
118 See also Case C–249/96 *Grant*, n. 18 above.
119 On voluntary Christmas bonuses as pay see Case C–333/97 *Lewen*, n. 98 above.
120 Case C–33/89 *Kowalska*, n. 86 above, para. 10.
121 Case C–167/97 *Seymour-Smith*, n. 93 above.
122 Case 262/88 *Barber*, n. 26 above, paras. 13–18.
123 Case C–184/89 *Nimz*, n. 101 above.

equal pay.[124] Indeed, as early as *Defrenne II* the ECJ had ruled that the fact that the fixing of certain working conditions could have pecuniary consequences was not sufficient to bring such conditions within the scope of Article 141, and this point was confirmed again in *JämO*[125] and *Seymour-Smith*,[126] *Steinicke*,[127] and *Lommers*.[128] Such conditions fell to be dealt with instead under Directive 76/207 on Equal Treatment.

In *Rinner-Kühn*, the Court ruled that *statutory sick pay*, i.e., wages which an employer is required by law to continue to pay an employee in the event of illness, fell within the meaning of pay in Article 141.[129] It is difficult to distinguish this kind of pay from a social-security benefit, since although the wages were to be paid by the employer, 80 per cent of such payment, in the case of employees who worked a certain number of hours for a particular period of time, was thereafter to be reimbursed by the State. Obviously however it is in the employee's interests that such sick pay is classified as pay rather than social security, given that Article 141, unlike Directive 79/7, is directly effective both against the State and against private employers.

In *Gillespie*, the ECJ ruled that since *maternity benefit* paid by an employer under legislation or collective agreements was based on the employment relationship, it constituted pay within Article 141.[130] Although this did not mean that women were required to receive full pay during maternity leave, they had to receive pay which was not so low as to undermine the purpose of such leave, and they must, like any other worker still linked to the employer by the contract of employment, benefit from any pay rise which is awarded during the period of maternity leave.[131] Although the facts of *Gillespie* arose prior to the adoption of the Pregnancy Directive 92/85, the case has been confirmed in several other cases arising subsequent to the Directive.[132]

In *Bötel*,[133] *Lewark*,[134] and *Freers*,[135] the ECJ ruled that *statutorily required compensation* payments to workers attending training courses which gave them the knowledge required for working on staff councils would constitute pay, since, even though it did not derive from the contract of employment, it was nevertheless paid by the employer by virtue of legislative provisions and under a contract of employment.

In *Worringham*, two female employees of Lloyds Bank challenged the payment to male staff under 25 years of a higher gross salary than to female staff of the same age engaged in the same work.[136] The reason for the higher salary was that contributions to a retirement scheme were compulsory for men under 25 but not for women under 25, and so, in order to cover their contribution, the bank added a sum equal to that amount to the gross salary for men. But since the calculation of various other benefits was linked to gross salary, the ECJ ruled that there was a breach of the equal-pay principle.[137]

---

[124] Case C–1/95 *Gerster* v. *Freistaat Bayern* [1997] ECR I–5253.

[125] Case C–236/98 *JämO*, n. 47 above, paras. 59–60.

[126] Case C–167/97 *Seymour-Smith*, n. 93 above, paras. 36–37.

[127] Case C–77/02 *Steinicke*, n. 107 above.

[128] Case C–476/99 *Lommers* v. *Minister van Landbouw, Natuurbeheer en Visserij* [2002] ECR I 2891.

[129] Case 171/88 *Rinner-Kühn*, n. 73 above, para. 7.

[130] Case C–342/93 *Gillespie* v. *Northern Health and Social Services Boards* [1996] ECR I–475.

[131] *Ibid.*, paras. 20–22.

[132] Case C–411/96 *Boyle* v. *EOC* [1998] ECR I–6401; Case C–147/02 *Alabaster* v. *Woolwich plc and Secretary of State for Social Security* [2004] ECR I–3101.

[133] Case C–360/90 *Bötel*, n. 79 above.

[134] Case C–457/93 *Lewark*, n. 80 above.

[135] Case C–278/93 *Freers*, n. 81 above.

[136] Case 69/80 *Worringham*, n. 112 above. See also Case 23/83 *Liefting* v. *Directie van het Academisch Ziekenhuis bij de Universiteit van Amsterdam* [1984] ECR 5225.

[137] *Ibid.*, para. 25.

(iii) Bilka *and* Barber: *Occupational Pensions May Constitute Pay*

Some of the most significant developments in relation to the uncertain zone between pay and social security were the rulings on *occupational pensions* in both *Bilka-Kaufhaus* and *Barber*,[138] along with the flood of litigation which followed *Barber*. The ECJ first addressed the issue of occupational pension schemes directly in *Bilka-Kaufhaus*. At the time judgment was given, the Council was considering adopting legislation on occupational social security (which subsequently became Directive 86/378[139]) to supplement Directive 79/7 on statutory social security.

The terms of the 1986 Directive clearly showed that the institutions considered occupational pensions to be a matter of social security rather than pay, so that they were dealt with in a more gradual manner similar to matters covered by Directive 79/7, rather than under the strictures of Article 141. However, the ECJ in *Bilka* took a different view, in the context of a supplementary occupational pension scheme entirely financed by the employer, and ruled that although the scheme was adopted in accordance with conditions laid down by German law, it was based on an agreement between the employer and the employee staff committee:

> 21. The contractual rather than the statutory nature of the scheme in question is confirmed by the fact that, as has been pointed out above, the scheme and the rules governing it are regarded as an integral part of the contracts of employment between Bilka and its employers.
> 22. It must therefore be concluded that the scheme does not constitute a social security scheme governed directly by statute and thus does not fall outside the scope of Article 119. Benefits paid to employees under the scheme therefore constitute consideration received by the worker from the employer in respect of his employment, as referred to in the second paragraph of Article 119.

By contrast with the statutory pension scheme in *Defrenne I*, the ECJ in this case highlighted three factors: (1) the contractual nature of the pension scheme, (2) the fact that it was not directly governed by statute but by an agreement between employer and employee, and (3) that it was not financed in part by the public authorities but entirely by the employer. The fact that the employer chose to arrange the scheme in a way which corresponded to the statutory social-security scheme was irrelevant, and the benefits paid to employees under the occupational scheme thus constituted 'pay' under Article 141.[140] The fact that employee affiliation to an occupational pension scheme is made compulsory by legislation was also held by the ECJ to be irrelevant to the application of Article 141.[141] Although the ruling in *Bilka* should have warned the EU institutions that occupational pensions were viewed by the ECJ as pay rather than social security, Directive 86/387 was nonetheless adopted shortly after the case.

The *Barber* judgment which followed, however, rendered much of Directive 86/378 redundant, by ruling that even if an occupational pension scheme was contracted out,

---

[138] Case 262/88 *Barber*, n. 26 above; Case 170/84 *Bilka-Kaufhaus GmbH* v. *Karin Weber von Hartz* [1986] ECR 1607.

[139] Council Dir. 86/378/EEC of 24 July 1986 on the implementation of the principle of equal treatment for men and women in occupational social security schemes [1986] OJ L225/40.

[140] The later Case 192/85 *Newstead* v. *Department of Transport* [1987] ECR 4735 concerning employee contributions to a contracted-out occupational pension scheme took a different view, but it was later implicitly overruled by Case 262/88 *Barber*, n. 26 above, and Case C–152/91 *Neath* v. *Hugh Steeper Ltd.* [1993] ECR I–6935, para. 31; D. Curtin, 'Scalping the Community Legislator: Occupational Pensions and "Barber"' (1990) 27 *CMLRev.* 475.

[141] Case C–435/93 *Dietz* v. *Stichting Thuiszorg Rotterdam* [1996] ECR I–5223.

i.e., where it was set up by an employer in direct substitution for and in fulfilment of the obligations of the statutory scheme, payments of benefits to employees would constitute pay rather than social security.

Case C–262/88 **Barber v. Guardian Royal Exchange Assurance Group**
[1990] ECR I–1889

[Note ToA renumbering: Art. 119 is now Art. 141]

Barber was an employee of Guardian and was made redundant at the age of 52. He belonged to an occupational pension scheme set up and wholly financed by Guardian, which was a 'contracted-out' scheme under social-security legislation as a substitute for the earnings-related part of the state pension scheme. This meant that members of the contracted-out scheme would contractually waive that part of the state pension scheme. Barber claimed that the terms of redundancy relating to his entitlement to an early retirement pension were in breach of Article 119, since a woman would be entitled to an immediate pension on reaching 50, whereas for a man the relevant age was 55. The ECJ was asked whether redundancy-related benefits, including a private occupational pension, constituted pay within Article 119.

THE ECJ

22. It must be pointed out in that regard that, in its judgment of 25 May 1971 in Case 80/70 *Defrenne* v. *Belgium* [1971] ECR 445, paragraphs 7 and 8, the Court stated that consideration in the nature of social security benefits is not in principle alien to the concept of pay. However, the Court pointed out that this concept, as defined in Article 119, cannot encompass social security schemes or benefits, in particular retirement pensions, directly governed by legislation without any element of agreement within the undertaking or the occupational branch concerned, which are compulsorily applicable to general categories of workers.

23. The Court noted that those schemes afford the workers the benefit of a statutory scheme, to the financing of which workers, employers and possibly the public authorities contribute in a measure determined less by the employment relationship than by considerations of social policy.

24. In order to answer the second question, therefore, it is necessary to ascertain whether those considerations also apply to contracted-out private occupational schemes such as that referred to in this case.

25. In that regard it must be pointed out first of all that the schemes in question are the result either of an agreement between workers and employers or of a unilateral decision taken by the employer. They are wholly financed by the employer or by both the employer and the workers without any contribution being made by the public authorities in any circumstances. Accordingly, such schemes form part of the consideration offered to workers by the employer.

26. Secondly, such schemes are not compulsorily applicable to general categories of workers. On the contrary, they apply only to workers employed by certain undertakings, with the result that affiliation to those schemes derives of necessity from the employment relationship with a given employer. Furthermore, even if the schemes in question are established in conformity with national legislation and consequently satisfy the conditions laid down by it for recognition as contracted-out schemes, they are governed by their own rules.

27. Thirdly, it must be pointed out that, even if the contributions paid to those schemes and the benefits which they provide are in part a substitute for those of the general statutory

scheme, that fact cannot preclude the application of Article 119. It is apparent from the documents before the Court that occupational schemes such as that referred to in this case may grant to their members benefits greater than those which would be paid by the statutory scheme, with the result that their economic function is similar to that of the supplementary schemes which exist in certain Member States, where affiliation and contribution to the statutory scheme is compulsory and no derogation is allowed. In its judgment of 13 May 1986 in Case 170/84 *Bilka-Kaufhaus* v. *Weber von Hartz* [1986] ECR 1607, the Court held that the benefits awarded under a supplementary pension scheme fell within the concept of pay, within the meaning of Article 119.

28. It must therefore be concluded that, unlike the benefits awarded by national statutory social security schemes, a pension paid under a contracted-out scheme constitutes consideration paid by the employer to the worker in respect of his employment and consequently falls within the scope of Article 119 of the Treaty.

29. That interpretation of Article 119 is not affected by the fact that the private occupational scheme in question has been set up in the form of a trust and is administered by trustees who are technically independent of the employer, since Article 119 also applies to consideration received indirectly from the employer.

The distinction between social security and pay at issue in the case was particularly important in relation to pensions, because of the exceptions to the equal-treatment principle which are allowed under Social Security Directive 79/7 in relation to pensionable age and related benefits.[142] No such exception exists under Article 141, and companies which had operated contracted-out occupational pension schemes had, prior to *Barber*, proceeded on the assumption that they could maintain discriminatory pensionable ages as between men and women.

The question was, in essence, whether contracted-out occupational pension schemes were governed by the principle set out in *Defrenne I*,[143] in which case they were social security, or that in *Bilka*,[144] in which case they were pay. Mirroring its reasoning in *Bilka*, the ECJ focused on three features of the contracted-out scheme: first, it was agreed and entirely financed by the employer, not imposed directly by statute;[145] secondly, unlike most social-security benefits the scheme was not compulsorily applicable to general categories of employees and, although in conformity with national legislation, was governed by its own rules; and finally, although it was in substitution for the statutory scheme, its provisions could also go further and provide additional benefits, thereby making it indistinguishable from supplementary schemes such as those in *Bilka*. The fact that the fund was administered by trustees did not prevent the benefits paid from constituting pay, and this point was underlined later in *Coloroll*[146] and again in *Menauer*,[147] where the Court held that Article 141 could be relied upon directly as against the trustees, who were bound in their duties by the equal treatment principle.

---

[142] See further below, sect. 4(a)(iv).

[143] Case 80/70 *Defrenne I*, n. 25 above.

[144] Case 170/84 *Bilka-Kaufhaus*, n. 138 above.

[145] The ECJ made it clear subsequently in Case C–200/91 *Coloroll*, n. 65 above, para. 88, that all benefits payable to an employee under an occupational pension scheme, whether the scheme was contributory or non-contributory, constituted pay within Art. 141 EC.

[146] *Ibid.*, para. 24.

[147] Case C–379/99 *Pensionskasse für die Angestellten der Barmer Ersatzkasse* v. *Menauer* [2001] ECR I–7275, where neither the legal independence of the funds, nor their status as insurers, was a relevant argument against this.

Having established that private 'contracted out' occupational pension schemes were covered by the equal-pay principle, the ECJ in *Barber* went on to consider whether the different pension entitlements on redundancy for men and women were in breach thereof, and whether equal pay had to be ensured with respect to each element of pay:[148]

32. In the case of the first of those two questions thus formulated, it is sufficient to point out that Article 119 prohibits any discrimination with regard to pay as between men and women, whatever the system which gives rise to such inequality. Accordingly, it is contrary to Article 119 to impose an age condition which differs according to sex in respect of pensions paid under a contracted-out scheme, even if the difference between the pensionable age for men and that for women is based on the one provided for by the national statutory scheme.

. . .

34. With regard to the means of verifying compliance with the principle of equal pay, it must be stated that if the national courts were under an obligation to make an assessment and a comparison of all the various types of consideration granted, according to the circumstances, to men and women, judicial review would be difficult and the effectiveness of Article 119 would be diminished as a result. It follows that genuine transparency, permitting an effective review, is assured only if the principle of equal pay applies to each of the elements of remuneration granted to men or women.

The *Barber* case had serious repercussions throughout the Community, and fundamentally changed the way pension schemes would henceforth have to be organized.

D. Curtin, Scalping the Community Legislator: Occupational Pensions and Barber[149]

One of the major points to emerge from the Court's decision in *Barber* is that the limitation originally imposed by the Court as to the scope of the direct effect of Article 119 is, to all intents and purposes, redundant. It has been consistently argued over the years that highly complex problems such as the different life expectancies of men and women, different retirement ages, putative pensionable service during maternity leave etc. all militated against direct effect being ascribed to Article 119 in the pensions sphere in the absence of implementing legislation. The view was that since pension benefits were not tangible and calculable in money terms, detailed criteria determining how equality had to be achieved would have to be established through appropriate measures at either Community level or national level. However the Court's judgment in *Barber* adopts the approach that once the question of deciding that occupational benefits fall within the scope of 'pay' in Article 119 has been answered, the national court will *ipso facto* be in a position to decide whether the litigant receives less pay than a member of the opposite sex engaged in the same work. What is radical about this approach is that it confirms that equal treatment in the pension context does not require that the total amount of a particular benefit be mathematically equal since neither the costs nor the value of total pension benefits received will ever be known in advance. What seems to be required is rather that the rate at which the benefit is enjoyed be equal.

---

[148] See, more recently, Case C–381/99 *Brunnhofer*, n. 52 above; Case C–236/98 *JämO*, n. 47 above.
[149] N. 140 above, 484.

The radical nature of *Barber*, unsurprisingly, met with criticism from Member States, who had argued strongly against the Court's conclusion in their submissions during the case, and from employers alike. It was felt that the judgment did not take sufficient account of the social policy requirements underlying many occupational pension schemes, that it ignored the close link between statutory and occupational pension schemes, and that it involved deliberate judicial bypassing of a legitimate piece of EU legislation, the Occupational Pension Directive of 1986.[150]

The ECJ however made one major concession to the concerns of the Member States,[151] and to those of employers who would henceforth have to organize occupational pensions differently, by limiting the retroactivity of its ruling. While the ECJ has regularly insisted that financial consequences alone do not justify limiting the temporal effect of a ruling,[152] it took the view in *Barber* that the Member States and others had reasonably been entitled, in light of the authorization in the two Social Security Directives to defer implementation of the equal-treatment principle in relation to pensionable ages, to consider that Article 141 did not apply to pensions paid under contracted-out schemes.[153] However, the relevant paragraphs of the judgment in which it purported to limit the effects of its ruling were ambiguous as to whether Article 141 could be relied on in relation to *periods of service* completed before the date of the judgment when no pension payments in respect of those periods had yet been received, or whether it could only be relied on in relation to periods of service completed after the date of the judgment. Clearly the latter interpretation would have the least serious financial consequences for employers.

However, before the ECJ itself had the opportunity to clarify its meaning in later case law, the concern aroused by *Barber* in the Member States had prompted the annexation of a Protocol to the EC Treaty by the Maastricht TEU, purporting to limit the retroactive effect of the judgment by adopting this latter more limited interpretation. The ECJ itself, when called upon in the case of *Ten Oever* to clarify the meaning of the relevant paragraphs in *Barber*, pragmatically agreed with the version chosen by the States in the Protocol.[154]

(iv) *The Post-*Barber *Case Law*

However, despite this clear attempt by the States to rein in the interpretative autonomy of the ECJ, the Court in subsequent case law reasserted its independence by limiting the potential scope of the Protocol, ruling in *Fisscher* and *Vroege* that it had to be read 'in conjunction with the *Barber* judgment and cannot have a scope wider than the limitation of its effects in time'.[155] This meant that the Protocol related only to *benefits* and not to the *right to join or belong* to an occupational pension scheme. Thus discriminatory conditions governing *membership* of an occupational scheme, such as a full-time requirement or the exclusion of married women, were governed by the ECJ's earlier ruling in *Bilka* on this issue,[156] rather than by the Protocol.

---

150 N. 139 above.

151 The UK in particular argued that, unless the retroactive effect of the judgment was limited, the increase in cost would run to between £33 and £45 billion, with disastrous effects for the UK economy as a whole.

152 See e.g. Case C–184/99 *Grzelczyk* v. *CPAS* [2001] ECR I–6193, paras. 50–54; Case C–366/99 *Griesmar*, n. 116 above, paras. 73–78.

153 Case 262/88 *Barber*, n. 26 above, paras. 44–45.

154 Case C–109/91 *Ten Oever* v. *Stichting Bedrijfspensioenfonds voor het Glazenwassers- en Schoonmaakbedrijf* [1993] ECR I–4879, paras. 16–19. See Case C–166/99 *Defreyn* v. *Sabena* [2000] ECR I–6155 for a case in which the ECJ actually applied the Protocol.

155 Case C–128/93 *Fisscher* v. *Voorhuis Hengelo BV and Stichting Bedrijfspensioenfonds voor de Detailhandel* [1994] ECR I–4583; Case C–57/93 *Vroege* v. *NCIV Institut voor Volkshuisvesting BV and Stichting Pensioenfonds NCIV* [1994] ECR I–4541; Case C–7/93 *Bestuur van het Algemeen Burgerlijk Pensioenfonds* v. *Beune* [1994] ECR I–4471.

156 Case 170/84 *Bilka-Kaufhaus*, n. 138 above.

The ECJ found that the reasons for limiting the retroactivity of the *Barber* ruling—i.e., the fact that the discrimination in pension schemes could reasonably have been considered to be permissible under Directive 86/378—did not apply to the issue of discrimination in access to membership of a pension scheme in *Bilka*, which was decided before the Directive had been adopted. The same was true of the entitlement to receive a retirement pension in *Dietz*,[157] or entitlement to additional special benefits in *Magorrian*,[158] which were indissolubly linked to the right to join or the right fully to participate in an occupational scheme, and the same was equally true of indirect discrimination in access to an occupational pension scheme in *Schröder*.[159] Thus, subject to the application of national time limits for bringing an action,[160] Article 141 could be relied on to challenge a discriminatory exclusion from a pension scheme as from the date of the *Defrenne II* judgment, in which Article 141 had been held to be directly effective. However, the ECJ also ruled that the right retroactively to join a pension scheme did not mean that such workers could avoid paying the value of the past contributions.[161]

In *Ten Oever* the ECJ also ruled that Article 141 covered pension benefits payable not just to an employee, but also to the employee's survivor, in this case a widow's pension, since the crucial factor was that the pension was paid by reason of the employment relationship between the employee and employer.[162] Following from this, the ECJ ruled in *Coloroll*[163] and later in *Menauer*[164] that Article 141 could be invoked against the employer or the trustees of the pension scheme, not just by an employee under the scheme, but also by the employee's dependants.[165] The *Moroni* ruling also confirmed that *Barber* applied in the same way to supplementary pension schemes as to contracted-out schemes,[166] thus extending the reasoning in *Bilka* (which concerned the exclusion of part-time workers from a supplementary pension scheme) to the existence of discriminatory pensionable ages *within* such a scheme.[167]

(v) *Other Kinds of Pension*

In the case of *Beune*,[168] concerning civil service pensions, the ECJ reviewed the criteria it had developed in its case law from *Defrenne I* to *Ten Oever* for determining whether a pension scheme constituted pay under Article 141 or social security under Directive 79/7. Ultimately,

---

[157] Case C–435/93 *Dietz* v. *Stichting Thuiszorg Rotterdam* [1996] ECR I–5223, paras. 23–25.

[158] Case C–246/96 *Magorrian and Cunningham* v. *Eastern Health and Social Services Board and Department of Health and Social Services* [1997] ECR I–7153.

[159] Case C–50/96 *Schröder*, n. 13 above; Cases C–270 and 271/97 *Deutsche Post* v. *Sievers and Schrage* [2000] ECR I–929.

[160] As in the Court's general case law on remedies, the rules relating to national time limits must be no less favourable than for similar actions of a domestic nature and must not render impossible the exercise of the right. See, however, Case C–147/95 *DEI* v. *Efthimios Evrenopoulos* [1997] ECR I–2057.

[161] Case C–128/93 *Fisccher*, n. 155 above, para. 37.

[162] See also Case C–147/95 *DEI*, n. 160 above; Case C–50/99 *Podesta* v. *CRICA* [2000] ECR I–4039.

[163] Case C–200/91 *Coloroll*, n. 65 above, paras. 17–19.

[164] Case C–379/99 *Menauer*, n. 147 above.

[165] This was sharply criticized by the German Government in the case, which argued that a survivor's pension benefit should be not regarded as pay, since it did not represent consideration for work performed, but reflected social-policy concerns connected to the traditional allocation of men's and women's roles: see Case C–109/91 *Ten Oever* [1993] ECR I–4879.

[166] Case C–110/91 *Moroni* v. *Collo GmbH* [1993] ECR I–6591.

[167] See also Case C–173/91 *Commission* v. *Belgium* [1993] ECR I–673, in which redundancy supplements were held to constitute pay within Art. 141, and Case C–166/99 *Defreyn*, n. 154 above, where the *Barber* protocol was applied.

[168] Case C–7/93 *Bestuur van het Algemeen Burgerlijk Pensioenfonds* v. *Beune* [1994] ECR I–4471. See also Case C–50/99 *Podesta*, n. 162 above.

having considered the criteria of (a) agreement between employer and employee rather than statutory origin, (b) the absence of public funding of a scheme, and (c) the provision of benefits supplementary to state social security benefits, the ECJ concluded that the 'decisive' though not the 'exclusive' criterion was (d) that set out in Article 141 itself: i.e., that the pension is paid to the worker by reason of the employment relationship between the worker and the former employer.[169] Consequently, even if the civil service pension scheme was affected by 'considerations of social policy, of State organisation, or of ethics or even budgetary preoccupations'—i.e., factors which would normally point to its classification as a state social-security scheme rather than pay—these could not prevail if three other factors were also present: if the pension paid by a public employer (1) concerned only a particular category of workers rather than general categories, (2) was directly related to the period of service, and (3) was calculated, in its amount, by reference to the civil servant's last salary, then it was comparable to a pension paid by a private employer and would constitute pay.[170]

These principles were applied by the ECJ in *Griesmar*[171] and *Mouflin*[172] where French retirement pensions for civil servants were held to be pay rather than social security, and similarly to German and Finnish pension schemes in *Schönheit*[173] and *Niemi*[174] respectively. In these cases the ECJ ruled that, whenever the legal criteria of pay and equal work could be identified, an employee could rely directly on Article 141, thus effectively overriding the relevant provision of the Occupational Pension Directive 86/378, which had purported to allow the postponement until 1993 of the establishment of equal pensionable ages in occupational schemes. However, the limitation on the retroactive effect of *Barber* was held to be applicable to discriminatory age conditions in both non-contracted-out and contracted-out occupational pension schemes.[175]

(vi) *A Limited Retreat from* Barber

Among the various other issues raised in post-*Barber* case law was the question whether payments by an employer to a contracted-out occupational pension scheme (rather than payments to an *employee*, as in *Barber*) were covered by Article 141.[176] This question arose because actuarial calculations of the different life expectancies of men and women were used in determining the sums payable by an employer into the scheme.

In both *Coloroll* and *Neath*, a 'defined-benefit' pension scheme was in issue, under which employees would receive a pension the criteria for which were fixed in advance, e.g., by reference to a fraction of their final year's salary for each year of service.[177] It was held that contributions of *employees* to the scheme must consist of an identical amount for men and women, since, according to *Worringham*,[178] employee contributions were pay within Article 141. However, in such defined-benefit schemes, *employers'* contributions varied over time and were

---

[169] *Ibid.*, paras. 43–44.

[170] *Ibid.*, para. 45.

[171] Case C–366/99 *Griesmar*, n. 116 above.

[172] Case C–206/00 *Mouflin* v. *Recteur de l'académie de Reims* [2001] ECR I–10201.

[173] Cases C–4–5/02 *Schönheit and Becker* [2003] ECR I–12575.

[174] Case C–351/00 *Niemi* [2002] ECR I–7007.

[175] Case C–200/91 *Coloroll*, n. 65 above, para. 71. It had been argued that it was clear, since the ruling in Case 170/84 *Bilka-Kaufhaus*, n. 138 above, in 1986, that supplementary occupational pension schemes were covered by Art. 141, but neither the AG nor the Court accepted this.

[176] Case C–200/91 *Coloroll*, n. 65 above; Case C–152/91 *Neath*, n. 140 above.

[177] *Ibid.*

[178] Case 69/80 *Worringham*, n. 112 above.

adjusted to take account of the pensions which would have to be paid. As a consequence of using the sex-based actuarial factors in calculating such employers' contributions, the amount which a male employee would receive on redundancy either in the form of a capital sum, transfer benefits, or a deferred pension would be less than that which a woman would receive. Contrary to the arguments of the Commission and the Advocate General that the use of sex-based actuarial factors to ascertain the funding needed for pension schemes would violate Article 141, the ECJ ruled that although the pension which was promised according to fixed criteria constituted pay, neither were the employer contributions paid in order to ensure the adequacy of the funds to cover the cost of that promised pension, nor would the value of those contributions as represented by a lump sum or transfer benefits fall within Article 141.[179]

Thus, having gradually broadened the concept of pay, eroding the distinction between pay and occupational social security, and creating a distinction between the latter and state social security, the ECJ drew back somewhat in *Neath* and *Coloroll*.[180] The outcome of these and the other cases decided after *Barber* were subsequently enacted into legislation, which is now contained in the consolidating Directive 2006/54.[181] The Directive also contains another 'exception' to the scope of the equal treatment principle in occupational pensions which was established by the ECJ in *Coloroll*, i.e., that certain pension benefits purchased by voluntary *employee's* contributions to an occupational scheme do not fall within Article 141 thus do not constitute pay.[182] Other exceptions to the scope of the Directive include individual contracts for self-employed workers, schemes for the self-employed having only one member, insurance contracts of salaried workers to which the employer is not a party, and individual optional additional benefits within an occupational scheme.[183] It also incorporates the outcome of the somewhat surprising judgment in *Birds Eye Walls*,[184] which permits Member States to introduce differential treatment between men and women in a bridging pension scheme in order to counterbalance the effects of the state system, which maintains different retirement ages for men and women.[185]

(vii) *Remedying Discrimination in Occupational Pensions*

A major question following *Barber* was how the discrimination identified was to be remedied. In *Coloroll*, the ECJ ruled that, between the date of the *Barber* ruling and the date of entry into force of measures designed to eliminate discrimination, 'correct implementation of the principle of equal pay requires that the disadvantaged employees should be granted the same advantages as those previous enjoyed by other employees'.[186] In other words, until amending measures were adopted, pension schemes could only 'level up', by giving men the same advantages as women enjoyed.

This principle was first enunciated in *Defrenne II*,[187] in which the ECJ ruled that compliance with the equal pay principle could not be achieved other than by raising the lowest salaries,

---

[179] Case C–152/91 *Neath*, n. 140 above, paras. 31–32; Case C–200/91 *Coloroll*, n. 65 above, paras. 80–81.

[180] Following these cases, Dir. 96/97 [1997] OJ L46/20, amended Dir. 86/378 largely by enacting the case law of the Court, including *Neath* and *Coloroll*, since *Barber*. Dirs. 86/378 and 96/97 have now been replaced by Dir. 2006/54, n. 31 above.

[181] Dir. 2006/54, n. 31 above, Art. 9 now provides that Art. 141 EC also applies to so-called 'money-purchase' or 'defined-contribution' schemes as opposed to 'defined-benefit' schemes.

[182] Case C–200/91 *Coloroll*, n. 65 above, paras. 90–93. See Dir. 2006/54, n. 31 above, Art. 8(1)(e).

[183] Dir. 2006/54, n. 31 above, Art. 8(1).

[184] Case C–132/92 *Birds Eye Walls*, n. 113 above.

[185] Dir. 2006/54, n. 31 above, Art. 8(2).

[186] Case C–200/91 *Coloroll*, n. 65 above.

[187] Case 43/75 *Defrenne* v. *Sabena* [1976] ECR 455, para. 15.

since Article 141 appeared in the context of the harmonization of working conditions while maintaining an improvement in those conditions.

However, the Court in *Coloroll* took a more limited approach than that in *Defrenne II*, and applied the 'levelling up' or improvement in conditions of pay only to the transitional stage between the date of the *Barber* ruling and the date on which measures were adopted to comply with it.[188] The ECJ further ruled in *Smith* that, during this transitional stage, it was not open to the pension scheme or the employer to plead that a levelling-down approach was objectively justified by reason of the financial difficulties for the pension scheme, since 'the space of time involved is relatively short and attributable in any event to the conduct of the scheme administrators themselves'.[189] However, once equalizing measures were adopted, 'Article 119 does not then preclude measures to achieve equal treatment by reducing the advantages of the persons previously favoured.'[190] With regard to the period before the date of the *Barber* ruling, however, during which the pensionable age for women under these occupational schemes was lower than that for men, the ECJ made clear that, since it had limited the retroactivity of its ruling in this respect, EC law gave the States no reason at all for 'equalizing' the positions of men and women by retroactively reducing the advantages enjoyed by women during that period. In other words, EC law had nothing to say about age discrimination between men and women in occupational pension schemes prior to the date of *Barber*. The Court also ruled in *Smith* that once an employer took steps for the future to comply with Article 141, the achievement of equality could not be made partial or progressive.[191]

It is noticeable that the Court uses the language of 'advantage' in the occupational pensions case law to describe the position of women, since the retirement age for women was generally, being linked to that of state pension schemes, lower than that for men. However, it has been pointed out that the language of 'advantage' or 'favoured group' is hardly appropriate to apply to women in this context, since 'unquestionably, the less favoured group is in reality composed of women, who have worked and contributed to the scheme but receive very low pensions because of the level of pay which they earned during their working life, itself frequently shorter than the men's'.[192]

Finally, it should be said that Directive 2006/54, which replaced the 1986 and 1996 Directives on occupational social security, now incorporates the outcome of the stream of case law from *Barber* onwards, with all of its details and anomalies, virtually without amendment.[193]

4. EQUAL TREATMENT

(a) EQUAL TREATMENT AS A GENERAL PRINCIPLE

The original terms of Article 141 clearly established the principle of equal pay, but until the amendments made by the ToA in 1997 they did not expressly refer to the equal treatment of men and women other than in terms of pay. This was arguably consistent with the historical

---

[188] Case C–200/91 *Coloroll*, n. 65 above.

[189] Case C–408/92 *Smith* v. *Advel Systems Ltd.* [1994] ECR I–4435, para. 30.

[190] *Coloroll*, n. 65 above, para. 33.

[191] Case C–408/92 *Smith*, n. 189 above, para. 27. See also Case C–28/93 *Van den Akker* v. *Stichting Shell Pensioenfonds* [1994] ECR I–4527, as regards the impermissibility of any advantages for women once a uniform retirement age for men and women is introduced.

[192] D. de Vos, 'Pensionable Age and Equal Treatment from Charybdis to Scylla' (1994) 23 *ILJ* 175, 179.

[193] For criticism of the 'purely declaratory' approach of the initial Dir. 96/97 and its failure to address certain deficiencies in this field see E. Cassell, 'The Revised Directive on Equal Treatment for Men and Women in

explanation for Article 141 suggested above, which was to ensure equal conditions of competition for businesses operating in the different Member States as regards the cost of labour. On the other hand, the social rather than the economic objectives of the Treaty would evidently be better achieved in the context of a general commitment to employment equality between women and men.

In *Defrenne III*, it was argued to the ECJ that the principle of equal treatment of men and women was a fundamental principle of Community law.[194] More specifically, it was argued, following the successful equal-pay claim in *Defrenne II*, that the discriminatory compulsory termination of the plaintiff's employment contract at age 40 was contrary to Article 141. The ECJ however ruled that it was not possible at that stage to extend the scope of Article 141 to elements of the employment relationship other than pay. Nonetheless the Court went on to say that the elimination of sex discrimination more generally was a fundamental personal human right, and thus part of the general principles of Community law the observance of which it must ensure. In its previous rulings in *Sabbatini*[195] and *Airola*,[196] the Court had ruled that the *Community* had to ensure equality of working conditions as between men and women in respect of its own staff, but it held in *Defrenne III* that, as far as the Member States' employment law was concerned, the Community had not yet assumed any responsibility 'for supervising and guaranteeing the observance of the principle of equality between men and women in working conditions other than remuneration'.[197] Subsequently however, Directive 76/207 on equal treatment in conditions of employment, based on Article 308 EC, was adopted.[198]

In *Rinke*, the ECJ ruled that the principle of equal treatment of men and women was a condition for the lawfulness of EU action, so that any EU legislative measure which violated the principle would be illegal.[199] Although it ruled ultimately that they were justified on objective grounds, the Court found that the terms of two EU directives on the recognition of qualifications for general medical practice did indeed place women at a disadvantage as compared with men.[200]

(b) EQUAL TREATMENT UNDER DIRECTIVE 2006/54

(i) *General Schema*

Directive 76/207 as originally adopted was intended to secure equal treatment between men and women in three broad, employment-related areas: access to employment and promotion, vocational training, and working conditions.[201] The Directive was amended in 2002, which amongst other things made clear that its protection extended also to retaliatory measures

Occupational Social Security Schemes—The Dog that Didn't Bark' (1997) 26 *ILJ* 269, and more recently for criticism of the 'recast' Equal Treatment Dir. 2006/54 incorporating much of this legislation see Burrows and Robison, n. 32 above.

[194] Case 149/77 *Defrenne III*, n. 11 above.
[195] Case 20/71 *Sabbatini*, n. 10 above.
[196] Case 21/74 *Airola*, n. 10 above.
[197] Case 149/77 *Defrenne III*, n. 11 above, para. 30.
[198] [1976] OJ L39/40.
[199] Case C–25/02 *Rinke* v. *Ärztekammer Hamburg* [2003] ECR I–8349.
[200] *Ibid.*, paras. 32–35.
[201] Council Dir. 76/207/EEC of 9 Feb. 1976 on the implementation of the principle of equal treatment for men and women as regards access to employment, vocational training and promotion, and working conditions [1976] OJ L39/40.

adopted by an employer after the end of the employment relationship.[202] Not long after its amendment in 2002, Directive 76/207 was repealed and replaced by the recast Directive 2006/54, which has been introduced above.[203]

The general rule, as we have seen, is the prohibition of direct and indirect discrimination on grounds of sex. The original Equal Treatment Directive contained three 'exceptions' to this prohibition—an occupational qualification provision, a 'pregnancy and maternity' provision, and a positive action provision. Under the recast Directive, only the occupational qualification provision could still be said to be phrased as an exception, while the other two provisions are more affirmatively expressed.

The positive action provision now appears in Article 3, covering all matters which fall within the scope of the Directive, and declares that 'Member States may maintain or adopt measures within the meaning of Article 141(4) of the Treaty with a view to ensuring full equality in practice between men and women in working life'.

The provision on protection of women in the event of pregnancy or maternity has disappeared and has been replaced by Article 15 which essentially provides that women returning from maternity leave shall be entitled to return to conditions which are equally favourable to those they enjoyed before. A new Article 16 also now provides that the Directive is 'without prejudice to the right of Member States to recognise distinct rights to paternity and/or adoption leave'.

(ii) *The Occupational Qualification Provision*

Article 14(2) of Directive 2006/54 maintains the essence of the occupational qualification requirement[204] which was previously contained in Directive 76/207:

> Member States may provide, as regards access to employment including the training leading thereto, that a difference of treatment which is based on a characteristic related to sex shall not constitute discrimination where, by reason of the nature of the particular occupational activities concerned or of the context in which they are carried out, such a characteristic constitutes a genuine and determining occupational requirement, provided that its objective is legitimate and the requirement is proportionate.

The goal of the EU seems to be to encourage States to scrutinize and eradicate sexual stereotyping in the employment sphere, while at the same time permitting 'genuine' occupational requirements.

The scope of this 'occupational requirement' was considered in the *Male Midwives* case in the UK.[205] The Court found that legislation which limited access for men to the profession of

---

[202] Dir. 2002/73/EC of the European Parliament and of the Council of 23 Sept. 2002 amending Council Dir. 76/207/EEC on the implementation of the principle of equal treatment for men and women as regards access to employment, vocational training and promotion, and working conditions (Text with EEA relevance) [2002] OJ L269/15. This embodied the result of the ECJ's ruling in Case C–185/97 *Coote* v. *Granada Hospitality Ltd.* [1998] ECR I–5199.

[203] N. 31 above. See above, 881–882.

[204] See recently Case C–196/02 *Nikoloudi*, n. 99 above, to the effect that the creation of a category of exclusively female workers is in principle permitted by the Dir. (although the introduction of unfavourable treatment by reference to that category could amount to sex discrimination). The rather curious example in this case was the creation of a category of part-time cleaners which was exclusively female, ostensibly in order to cater to the particular needs of women.

[205] Case 165/82 *Commission* v. *United Kingdom* [1983] ECR 3431.

midwife was in conformity with the exception in Article 2(2) of Directive 76/207, in view of the fact that 'personal sensitivities' could play an important role in the relationship between midwife and patient. The arguments of the Commission and the Advocate General that this could be adequately catered for by giving the patient the choice of a male or female midwife were not addressed by the Court (nor indeed the fact that other presumably equally 'sensitive' relationships such as between gynaecologist and patient did not seem to necessitate such limited access), which ruled that the UK had not violated the Directive.[206]

The provision was also considered in *Johnston* in which the Royal Ulster Constabulary, RUC, sought to justify its decision not to employ women as full-time members of the RUC Reserve.[207] It was argued that if women were permitted to carry and use firearms, they would be at greater risk of becoming targets for assassination. The Commission, however, argued that the occupational activity of an armed police officer could not be considered an activity for which the sex of the officer was a determining factor, and that if an exception were to be made in relation to specific duties, the principle of proportionality would have to be observed. The Court accepted the UK's argument that the carrying of firearms by policewomen might create additional risks of assassination, without requiring any evidence to support the implication that women could not be trained to use firearms just as safely and effectively as men.[208] Hence the Court accepted that the sex of police officers could constitute a 'determining factor' for carrying out certain policing activities.[209] The assessment of the proportionality of the decision was left to the national court, e.g., to consider 'whether the refusal to renew Mrs Johnston's contract could not have been avoided by allocating to women duties which, without jeopardizing the aims pursued, can be performed without firearms'.[210]

Similar questions came before the Court in the cases of *Sirdar* and *Kreil*.[211] In *Sirdar*, a woman who was refused employment as a chef with the UK Royal Marines challenged their policy of excluding women from service on the ground that their presence was incompatible with the requirement of 'interoperability', i.e., 'the need for every Marine, irrespective of his specialisation, to be capable of fighting in a commando unit'. The ECJ ruled that this could be justified as an occupational requirement on the basis that the Marine corps was an exceptional and small force intended to be in the first line of attack.

In *Kreil*, on the other hand, the applicant was challenging a more general prohibition under German law which barred women from military posts involving the use of arms, and allowed them access only to the medical and military-music services. Here the ECJ ruled that, since the Article 2(2) derogation in Directive 76/207 was intended to apply only to specific activities, the scope and breadth of this prohibition exceeded even the discretion given to Member States when adopting measures they consider necessary to guarantee public security. Its disproportionate nature was also evident from the fact that basic training in the use of arms was already provided to women in the services of the Bundeswehr which remained accessible to them.

The *Kreil* judgment was a high-profile one, not least because of the fact that the German Federal Constitution at the time barred women from service involving the use of arms.[212] The relevant constitutional provision was subsequently amended to provide that women could not be forced to render armed service.

---

[206] *Ibid.*, para. 20.

[207] Case 222/84 *Johnston* v. *Chief Constable of the RUC* [1986] ECR 1651.

[208] See Fredman, n. 108 above, 128; More, n. 108 above, 52–53.

[209] See also Case 318/86 *Commission* v. *France* [1988] ECR 3559, para. 27.

[210] Case 222/84 *Johnston*, n. 207 above, para. 39.

[211] Case C–273/97 *Sirdar* v. *Army Board* [1999] ECR I–7403; Case C–285/98 *Kreil* v. *Bundesrepublik Deutschland* [2000] ECR I–69. For comment on both cases see P. Koutrakos (2000) 25 *ELRev.* 433.

[212] M. Trybus, 'Sisters in Arms: EC Law and Sex Equality in the Armed Forces' (2003) 9 *ELJ* 631.

This in turn gave rise to the case of *Dory*, in which a German man challenged the fact that compulsory military service was applicable only to men and not to women. According to Dory, this constituted discrimination as between men and women as regards access to employment, since the need to complete compulsory military service delayed his entry onto the labour market and imposed a disadvantage on him as compared with a similarly situated woman. Interestingly, the ECJ in this case accepted an argument which it had rejected in *Kreil* and earlier cases, i.e., that the case fell outside the scope of application of EC law.

Case C–186/01 **Dory v. Bundesrepublik Deutschland**
[2003] ECR I–2479

39. The decision of the Federal Republic of Germany to ensure its defence in part by compulsory military service is the expression of such a choice of military organisation to which Community law is consequently not applicable.

40. It is true that limitation of compulsory military service to men will generally entail a delay in the progress of the careers of those concerned, even if military service allows some of them to acquire further vocational training or subsequently to take up a military career.

41. Nevertheless, the delay in the careers of persons called up for military service is an inevitable consequence of the choice made by the Member State regarding military organisation and does not mean that that choice comes within the scope of Community law. The existence of adverse consequences for access to employment cannot, without encroaching on the competences of the Member States, have the effect of compelling the Member State in question either to extend the obligation of military service to women, thus imposing on them the same disadvantages with regard to access to employment, or to abolish compulsory military service.

42. In the light of all the foregoing, the answer to the national court's question must be that Community law does not preclude compulsory military service being reserved to men

While clearly the reasoning in *Dory* could just as easily have been applied to the 'choice of military organization' adopted by Germany in *Kreil*, the ECJ was obviously motivated in *Dory* by pragmatic concerns. If it had followed the logic of its previous judgments and held that compulsory military service for men only constituted sex discrimination, it would have left Germany with the choice of abolishing compulsory military service altogether or extending compulsory service also to women. The first would clearly have been seen as a major encroachment by EC law into national military matters, whereas the second would involve taking a controversial option in social terms.[213]

It should be noted that Member States are required by Article 31(3) of Directive 2006/54 to keep any sex-based 'occupational requirements' which it maintains under periodic review, and to notify the Commission at least every eight years whether 'in the light of social developments, . . . there is justification for maintaining the exclusions'.

(iii) *Protection for Maternity*

Under Article 2(3) of Directive 76/207, the legislation was said to be without prejudice to 'provisions concerning the protection of women, particularly as regards pregnancy and

---

[213] *Ibid.*, and Trybus (2003) 40 *CMLRev.* 1269; G. Anagnostaras (2003) 28 *ELRev.* 713.

maternity'. The ECJ on the whole read this provision narrowly,[214] limiting it essentially to measures aimed at 'protecting a woman's biological condition during and after pregnancy and, second, of protecting the special relationship between a woman and her child over the period which follows pregnancy and childbirth'.[215]

In *Stoeckel*, 'protective' treatment in the form of a prohibition on night-work for women but not for men was ruled impermissible by the ECJ.[216] The case was confirmed and extended in *Minne*, where the ECJ ruled that even if legislation prohibited night-work for men and women alike, it was nevertheless contrary to the Directive for such legislation to provide different derogations from the prohibition for men and for women.[217] Only in the context of pregnancy and maternity would a ban on night-work for women be acceptable.[218] Similarly, a general prohibition in Austrian legislation on the employment of women in work in a high-pressure atmosphere and in diving work was incompatible with the Directive.[219]

The 'exception' for maternity protection in Article 2(3) of the earlier Directive has been dropped from Directive 2006/54, and instead Article 15 specifies that 'a woman on maternity leave shall be entitled, after the end of her period of maternity leave, to return to her job or to an equivalent post on terms and conditions which are no less favourable to her and to benefit from any improvement in working conditions to which she would have been entitled during her absence'.[220] We shall see below that the 1992 Pregnancy Directive also supplies further detail by imposing a requirement to provide a minimum of employment protection for women who are pregnant, breast-feeding, or who have recently given birth.[221]

(iv) *The Positive Action Provision*

Under the earlier Equal Treatment Directive, 76/207, Article 2(4) included a 'positive-action' provision permitting measures designed to redress inequality between men and women and to 'promote equal opportunity for men and women, in particular by removing existing inequalities which affect women's opportunities'. This provision was amended in 2002, and again in Article 3 of the 2006 recast Directive, so as to align it with Article 141(4) EC. Article 3 of Directive 2006/54 now reads 'Member States may maintain or adopt measures within the meaning of Article 141(4) of the Treaty with a view to ensuring full equality in practice between men and women in working life'. Although the wording is now slightly different from, and simpler than, the original wording of the Article 2(4) provision, it seems likely that the ECJ will continue to interpret it in much the same way that it interpreted Article 2(4).

That earlier provision was initially read narrowly by the Court, so that a provision of French law which permitted collective agreements to provide special rights for women—including shorter working hours for older women, the obtaining of leave when a child was ill, the granting of extra days of leave in respect of children—was held to be unjustified.[222] France had not

---

[214] Case 222/84 *Johnston*, n. 207 above; Case C–285/98 *Kreil*, n. 211 above, para. 30.

[215] Case C–394/96 *Brown* v. *Rentokil Ltd.* [1998] ECR I–4185, para. 17.

[216] Case C–345/89 *Ministère Public* v. *Stoeckel* [1991] ECR I–4047. See also Case C–197/96 *Commission* v. *France* [1997] ECR I–1489.

[217] Case C–13/93 *Office Nationale de l'Emploi* v. *Minne* [1994] ECR I–371.

[218] Case C–421/92 *Habermann-Beltermann* v. *Arbeiterwohlfahrt, Bezirksverband* [1994] ECR I–1657.

[219] Case C–203/03 *Commission* v. *Austria* [2005] ECR I–935.

[220] For a case in which a collective agreement disadvantaging a woman whose employer would not include her extended maternity leave as part of her qualifying period for calculating her salary grade was held to be contrary to the previous Equal Treatment Dir. 76/207, see Case C–284/02 *Land Brandenburg* v. *Sass* [2004] ECR I–11143.

[221] Dir. 92/85 [1992] OJ L348/1.

[222] Case 312/86 *Commission* v. *France* [1988] ECR 6315.

adequately shown that 'the generalized preservation of special rights for women' would reduce actual instances of inequality in social life.[223] The Court's and the Advocate General's assumption seemed to be that there was no inequality faced by women which required these advantages, whereas the Commission's ground for condemning the French law was that 'the evolution of society is such that in many cases working men, if they are fathers, must share the tasks previously performed by the wife as regards the care and organisation of the family'.[224]

It has been pointed out, however, that there are difficulties with arguments like the Commission's which claim that positive action for women reinforces traditional assumptions, such as that the female is always the primary carer and the male the main breadwinner. Although positive action measures may risk perpetuating stereotypes, this does not necessarily mean that the law should ignore disadvantage broadly shared by members of a group.[225]

In the more recent case of *Lommers*,[226] however, the ECJ upheld the compatibility with Article 2(4) of a scheme set up within a national ministry to tackle the extensive under-representation of women, in a situation 'characterised by a proven insufficiency of proper, affordable child-care facilities'. Under the scheme, the ministry made available a limited number of subsidized nursery places to its staff, and reserved those for female staff alone, while permitting male officials access only in individual cases of emergency. The ECJ ruled that this scheme would be acceptable on condition that the emergency exception was construed as allowing any male officials who took care of their children by themselves to have access to the nursery places on the same conditions as female officials.

Obviously the *Lommers* situation was very different from the *France* case, in that it did not involve the generalized preservation of rights for women, but was quite a specific advantage granted in an attempt to tackle the under-representation of women in a particular employment context. It nonetheless shows the willingness of the ECJ to accept positive action measures even where they are premised on the assumption that women are the primary child-carers in two-parent families.

Positive action by Member States took something of a knock in the mid-1990s with the ruling in *Kalanke*.[227] In this case the ECJ took the view that Article 2(4) was a derogation from the right to equal treatment which must be strictly interpreted. Consequently, a German regional law which provided, where candidates of different sexes who had been shortlisted for promotion were equally qualified, that priority must to be given to women in sectors where they were under-represented (i.e., made up less than half of the staff) would breach the Directive. The fact that the Bremen system involved a 'soft' rather than a 'rigid' quota, and was intended to overcome the disadvantages faced by women and the perpetuation of past inequalities, as a result of which few women held senior posts, was insufficient to bring it within Article 2(4):

> 22. National rules which guarantee women absolute and unconditional priority for appointment or promotion go beyond promoting equal opportunities and overstep the limits of the exception in Article 2(4) of the Directive.
>
> 23. Furthermore, in so far as it seeks to achieve equal representation of men and women in all grades and levels within a department, such a system substitutes for equality of

---

223 *Ibid.*, para. 15.

224 *Ibid.*, 6322. See the similar argument of Jacobs AG at para. 14 of his Opinion in Case 373/89 *Integrity* v. *Rouvroy* [1990] ECR 4243 concerning 'positive discrimination' in national social-security benefits in favour of women, where the Court found a breach of the equal-treatment principle in Dir. 79/7.

225 Fredman, n. 108 above, 129.

226 Case C–476/99 *Lommers*, n. 128 above.

227 Case C–450/93 *Kalanke* v. *Freie Hansestadt Bremen* [1995] ECR I–3051.

opportunity as envisaged in Article 2(4) the result which is only to be arrived at by providing such equality of opportunity.

The *Kalanke* ruling prompted a flood of criticism and comment, not only from women's interest groups and from academic and practising lawyers,[228] but also from the European Commission itself, which issued a communication on the interpretation of the judgment.[229] The Commission took the view that not all quotas would be unlawful, and listed a range of positive-action measures which would, in its view, be acceptable despite the ruling. It proposed also an amendment/clarification of the terms of Article 2(4) to provide that a soft quota such as that in issue in *Kalanke* would not be contrary to the Directive, so long as it did not automatically give preference to the under-represented sex, but permitted the assessment of an individual's specific circumstances in a given case.[230]

In the subsequent case of *Marschall*, Advocate General Jacobs suggested that even if individual candidates' circumstances had to be taken into account, a national measure which gave priority to women over men in underrepresented sectors where the candidates were equally qualified would still breach the Equal Treatment Directive.[231] He criticized the Commission's proposed clarificatory amendment to Article 2(4) and deemed criticisms of *Kalanke* to be 'misconceived'.[232] However, the ECJ did not follow his Opinion and it narrowed the scope of the *Kalanke* ruling along the lines of the Commission's proposal, by confirming that, while a rule guaranteeing 'absolute and unconditional priority' for women was impermissible, a softer quota which allowed for individual consideration of circumstances would fall within the existing terms of Article 2(4).

Marschall concerned a German regional law which provided that where there were fewer men than women in a higher grade post in a career bracket, women were to be given priority for promotion in the event of equal suitability, competence, and professional performance unless reasons specific to an individual male candidate tilted the balance in his favour. In contrast with the *Kalanke* proceedings, in which the only intervening Member State was the UK, which supported the applicant against the German law, five governments intervened in *Marschall* to support the compatibility of the positive-action legislation with EC law. Only the UK and France opposed it. The ECJ distinguished the rule in *Kalanke* from the *Marschall* rule by reference to its 'saving clause',[233] but also adopted a more nuanced view of the 'equal' chances of men and women on the labour market.

Case C–409/95 **Hellmut Marschall v. Land Nordrhein Westfalen**
[1997] ECR I–6363

29. As the Land and several governments have pointed out, it appears that even where male and female candidates are equally qualified, male candidates tend to be promoted in

---

[228] For some of the commentaries see L. Charpentier [1996] *RTDE* 281; S. Dagmar (1996) 25 *ILJ* 239; S. Moore (1996) 21 *ELRev.* 156; A. Peters (1996) 2 *ELJ* 177; S. Prechal (1996) 33 *CMLRev.* 45; D. Schiek (1996) 25 *ILJ* 239; L. Senden (1996) 3 *MJ* 146; E. Szyszczak (1996) 59 *MLR* 876; S. Fredman (1997) 113 *LQR* 575.

[229] COM(96)88.

[230] [1996] OJ C179/8.

[231] Case C–409/95 *Hellmut Marschall* v. *Land Nordrhein Westfalen* [1997] ECR I–6363.

[232] *Ibid.*, para. 47 of his Opinion.

[233] See also the significant role of the 'exceptional clause' in Case C–476/99 *Lommers*, n. 128 above. See also Case C–380/01 *Schneider* v. *Bundesminister für Justiz* [2004] ECR I–1389, in which the national court had

preference to female candidates particularly because of prejudices and stereotypes concerning the role and capacities of women in working life and the fear, for example, that women will
interrupt their careers more frequently, that owing to household and family duties they will be
less flexible in their working hours, or that they will be absent from work more frequently
because of pregnancy, childbirth and breastfeeding.

30. For these reasons, the mere fact that a male candidate and a female candidate are
equally qualified does not mean that they have the same chances.

31. It follows that a national rule in terms of which, subject to the application of the saving
clause, female candidates for promotion who are equally as qualified as the male candidates
are to be treated preferentially in sectors where they are underrepresented may fall within the
scope of Article 2(4) if such a rule may counteract the prejudicial effects on female candidates
of the attitudes and behaviour described above and thus reduce actual instances of inequality
which may exist in the real world.

32. However, since Article 2(4) constitutes a derogation from an individual right laid down by
the Directive, such a national measure specifically favouring female candidates cannot guarantee absolute and unconditional priority for women in the event of a promotion without going
beyond the limits of the exception laid down in that provision. (*Kalanke* paras 21 and 22)

33. Unlike the rules at issue in *Kalanke*, a national rule which, as in the case in point in the
main proceedings, contains a saving clause does not exceed those limits, if, in each individual
case, it provides for male candidates who are equally as qualified as the female candidates a
guarantee that the candidatures will be the subject of an objective assessment which will take
account of all criteria specific to the individual candidates and will override the priority accorded
to female candidates where one or more of those criteria tilts the balance in favour of the male
candidate. In this respect, however, it should be remembered that those criteria must not be
such as to discriminate against female candidates.

Shortly after *Marschall*, Article 141(4) EC was amended to include a provision permitting
Member States to adopt positive action 'with a view to ensuring full equality in practice
between men and women in working life'. Article 141(4) refers now in formally neutral terms
to the permissibility of providing specific advantages for the 'under-represented sex' to pursue
vocational training or to compensate for career disadvantages [234] rather than referring, as previously, to women only.[235] Although the terms of Article 141(4)—on which Article 3 of
Directive 2006/54 is now based, replacing Article 2(4) of Directive 76/207—are not exactly the
same as those of the earlier Directive, the ECJ in *Abrahamsson* below reached the same conclusion under both the Directive and Article 141(4).

In *Badeck*,[236] the ECJ followed its more permissive post-*Kalanke* approach in finding that a
whole series of German public-service rules designed to give priority to women in promotion,
access to training, and recruitment were compatible with Article 2(4), since they contained
sufficient flexibility and non-rigidity to comply with the criteria it had articulated in

applied the *Kalanke* and *Marschall* rulings to deem an Austrian law which did not contain a savings clause to be
incompatible with EC law.

[234] In Case C–366/99 *Griesmar*, n. 116 above, the ECJ ruled that the predecessor to Art. 141(4) EC (which
was Art. 6(3) of the Maastricht Social Policy Agreement) could not be used to justify pay discrimination which
consisted of service credits for the calculation of retirement pensions only for female workers who had had
children, since this discrimination would not itself offset the disadvantages to which the careers of female civil
servants were exposed.

[235] A declaration appended to the Amsterdam Treaty, however, stated that in adopting measures referred to
in para. 4, the Member States should 'aim at improving the situation of women in working life'.

[236] Case C–158/97 *Badeck* v. *Landesanwalt beim Staatsgerichtshof des Landes Hessen* [1999] ECR I–1875.

Marschall. Some of the provisions in question in *Badeck* seemed quite strong and even rather strict forms of positive action—for example the quota for training places and the rule on calling women to interview—but the ECJ did not hesitate in exempting them under Article 2(4), finding none to be 'automatic or unconditional' priority rules.

In *Briheche*, however, a French rule which exempted widows who had not remarried and were obliged to work from a rule setting an age limit for entry to competitive civil service examinations was found to constitute discrimination against widowers who had not remarried and were in the same situation.[237] According to the ECJ, such a rule automatically and unconditionally gave priority to women over men, and was not saved by Article 2(4).

In the Swedish case of *Abrahamsson*, the ECJ was asked to consider a practice which, unlike the various German provisions in *Kalanke, Marschall,* and *Badeck,* enabled preference to be given to a candidate of the under-represented sex who, although sufficiently qualified, did not possess qualifications equal to those of other candidates of the opposite sex.[238] The question framed by the ECJ was whether the Equal Treatment Directive would permit legislation 'under which a candidate for a public post who belongs to the under-represented sex and possesses sufficient qualifications for that post must be chosen in preference to a candidate of the opposite sex who would otherwise have been appointed, where this is necessary to secure the appointment of a candidate of the under-represented sex and the difference between the respective merits of the candidates is not so great as to give rise to a breach of the requirement of objectivity in making appointments'.

Case C–407/98 **Abrahamsson v. Fogelqvist**
[2000] ECR I–5539

46. As a rule, a procedure for the selection of candidates for a post involves assessment of their qualifications by reference to the requirements of the vacant post or of the duties to be performed.

47. In paragraphs 31 and 32 of *Badeck*, cited above, the Court held that it is legitimate for the purposes of that assessment for certain positive and negative criteria to be taken into account which, although formulated in terms which are neutral as regards sex and thus capable of benefiting men too, in general favour women. Thus, it may be decided that seniority, age and the date of last promotion are to be taken into account only in so far as they are of importance for the suitability, qualifications and professional capability of candidates. Similarly, it may be prescribed that the family status or income of the partner is immaterial and that part-time work, leave and delays in completing training as a result of looking after children or dependants in need of care must not have a negative effect.

48. The clear aim of such criteria is to achieve substantive, rather than formal, equality by reducing *de facto* inequalities which may arise in society and, thus, in accordance with Article 141(4) EC, to prevent or compensate for disadvantages in the professional career of persons belonging to the under-represented sex.

49. It is important to emphasise in that connection that the application of criteria such as those mentioned in paragraph 47 above must be transparent and amenable to review in order to obviate any arbitrary assessment of the qualifications of candidates.

---

[237] Case C–319/03 *Briheche v. Ministre de l'Intérieur, Ministre de l'Education nationale and Ministre de la Justice* [2004] ECR I–8807.
[238] Case C–407/98 *Abrahamsson v. Fogelqvist* [2000] ECR I–5539.

50. As regards the selection procedure at issue in the main proceedings, it does not appear from the relevant Swedish legislation that assessment of the qualifications of candidates by reference to the requirements of the vacant post is based on clear and unambiguous criteria such as to prevent or compensate for disadvantages in the professional career of members of the under-represented sex.

51. On the contrary, under that legislation, a candidate for a public post belonging to the under-represented sex and possessing sufficient qualifications for that post must be chosen in preference to a candidate of the opposite sex who would otherwise have been appointed, where that measure is necessary for a candidate belonging to the under-represented sex to be appointed.

52. It follows that the legislation at issue in the main proceedings automatically grants preference to candidates belonging to the under-represented sex, provided that they are sufficiently qualified, subject only to the proviso that the difference between the merits of the candidates of each sex is not so great as to result in a breach of the requirement of objectivity in making appointments.

53. The scope and effect of that condition cannot be precisely determined, with the result that the selection of a candidate from among those who are sufficiently qualified is ultimately based on the mere fact of belonging to the under-represented sex, and that this is so even if the merits of the candidate so selected are inferior to those of a candidate of the opposite sex. Moreover, candidatures are not subjected to an objective assessment taking account of the specific personal situations of all the candidates. It follows that such a method of selection is not such as to be permitted by Article 2(4) of the Directive.

54. In those circumstances, it is necessary to determine whether legislation such as that at issue in the main proceedings is justified by Article 141(4) EC.

55. In that connection, it is enough to point out that, even though Article 141(4) EC allows the Member States to maintain or adopt measures providing for special advantages intended to prevent or compensate for disadvantages in professional careers in order to ensure full equality between men and women in professional life, it cannot be inferred from this that it allows a selection method of the kind at issue in the main proceedings which appears, on any view, to be disproportionate to the aim pursued.

Thus in order for acceptable positive-action measures such as job-qualification criteria which indirectly favour the underrepresented sex to be compatible with EC law, (i) they must genuinely be designed to reduce *de facto* inequalities and compensate for career disadvantages, and (ii) they must be based on transparent and objective criteria which can be reviewed.

The ruling does not give a great deal of guidance on the scope of Article 141(4) for the future, other than to indicate that the particular job-selection method at issue would be a clearly disproportionate way of attempting to compensate for past disadvantages and to ensure full equality in professional life between women and men. However, it seems unlikely that the *Marschall* and *Briheche* cases would be any differently decided under Article 141(4) or Article 3 of Directive 2006/54 either, and that the existence of a savings clause of some kind will remain important for the compatibility with EC law of national positive action measures.

(v) *Other Exceptions*

The ECJ has also addressed the question whether there are any other possible exceptions to the equal treatment principle. In *Gerster*, the Court ruled that a Member State could not exclude public-service employment from the scope of Article 141.[239] Moreover in *Johnston* it rejected

---

[239] Case C–1/95 *Gerster v. Freistaat Bayern* [1997] ECR I–5253.

the argument that the Directive was subject to a general public-safety proviso which was applicable across the whole of the Treaty, similar to the specific derogations expressly provided in the context of free movement of persons, services, goods, and in serious military situations.[240] However, we saw in *Dory* that the ECJ, while not creating a new exception to the sex equality provisions, accepted that there could be areas of national law and policy—such as compulsory military service—which lay entirely outside the reach of EC law.

In *Levy*[241] and *Minne*,[242] the Court acknowledged that the Member States were entitled to maintain a provision which was in breach of the Equal Treatment Directive if its adoption had been necessary to ensure performance by the Member State, under Article 307 EC, of obligations arising from agreements concluded with non-member countries before the entry into force of the EC Treaty. Those cases concerned Convention No. 89 of the International Labour Organization, which involved night-work of women employed in industry. However, the ECJ limited the scope of the Article 307 exception by requiring the national court to ascertain the extent to which the Convention actually constituted an obstacle to the Directive's application, as well as the extent to which the national provisions breaching the Equal Treatment Directive were designed to implement the Convention.[243]

(c) THE DISTINCTION BETWEEN CONDITIONS OF WORK, PAY, AND SOCIAL SECURITY

We have seen above how the distinction between pay and social security gave rise to considerable confusion. Similarly, the distinction between equal pay and equal treatment in conditions of work,[244] as well as between the latter and equal treatment in social security, has not always been clear. Following the adoption of Directive 2006/54,[245] however, which seeks to unify the legal principles governing equal pay, occupational social security, and equal treatment in other employment conditions, the most relevant distinction for the future is between these three on the one hand, and state social security on the other. The Social Security Directive 79/7,[246] as we shall see below, allows the Member States to maintain certain exceptions to the principle of equal treatment, and permits a more progressive move towards equality than the legislation on pay and conditions of employment.

---

[240] Case 222/84 *Johnston*, n. 207 above. The specific derogations mentioned by the Court were those in Arts. 30, 39, 46, 296, and 297 EC. See also Case C–273/97 *Sirdar*, n. 211 above; Case C–285/98 *Kreil*, n. 211 above.

[241] Case C–158/91 *Ministère Public and Direction du Travail et de l'Emploi* v. *Levy* [1993] ECR I–4287. Contrast the earlier Case C–345/89 *Stoeckel*, n. 216 above; and the later Case C–197/96 *Commission* v. *France*, n. 216 above.

[242] Case C–13/93 *Minne*, n. 217 above; Case C–203/03 *Commission* v. *Austria*, n. 219 above.

[243] The issue of this ILO Convention was addressed in COM(87)105, in which the Commission indicated that a ban on night-work for women was incompatible with the Equal Treatment Dir. Thus the Member States were required to denounce Convention No. 89 in 1992 when the opportunity to do so in accordance with the terms of ILO Conventions arose. See N. Wuiame, 'Night Work for Women—*Stoeckel* Revisited' (1994) 23 *ILJ* 95 and Case C–197/96 *Commission* v. *France*, n. 216 above.

[244] See Case C–1/95 *Gerster*, n. 124 above in which the ECJ ruled that provisions governing the calculation of the length of service of employees, for the purpose of determining possible access to promotion and to higher remuneration, was a not a matter of equal pay but of equal treatment under Dir. 76/207. See also Case C–476/99 *Lommers*, n. 128 above, and contrast Case C–342/93 *Gillespie*, n. 130 above, para. 24; Case C–166/99 *Defreyn*, n. 154 above, para. 35.

[245] N. 31 above.

[246] Council Dir. 79/7/EEC of 19 Dec. 1978 on the progressive implementation of the principle of equal treatment for men and women in matters of social security [1979] OJ L6/24.

In *Bilka*, in which the ECJ had ruled that the exclusion of part-time workers from a sup-plementary occupational pension scheme constituted indirect pay discrimination,[247] the Court rejected the argument that Article 141 imposed an obligation on employers to organ-ize their occupational pension schemes in a way which took into account the fact that women's family responsibilities prevented them from fulfilling the pension requirements. And even now, although Article 141 provides for the adoption of measures to ensure equal treatment beyond the sphere of pay, this merely gives an express Treaty basis for legislation in the area, but does not create any directly effective obligation on the States or on employ-ers to facilitate or promote equal treatment of men and women in employment, other than in relation to pay. Similarly, although Directive 2006/54 now contains an entire chapter devoted to 'promotion' of equal treatment, most of the provisions impose obligations on Member States to encourage employers to do so, rather than imposing positive obligations directly on employers.

The complex relationship between equal treatment in working conditions, pay, and state social security is evident in a series of cases beginning with *Burton*.[248] The ECJ ruled that the maintenance of different age conditions in access to voluntary redundancy was compatible with the Equal Treatment Directive, because the terms of the redundancy scheme had been tied by the employer to the national statutory retirement scheme. The national scheme, which maintained different pensionable ages for men and women, was covered by the exception in Social Security Directive 79/7, and the employer was permitted to arrange a redundancy scheme to correspond with this without breaching the Equal Treatment Directive.

Subsequently in *Roberts*, however, the complainant belonged to an occupational pension scheme providing for compulsory retirement with a pension at age 65 for men and 60 for women.[249] At the time, the pension scheme was not thought to be pay within Article 141. Under its compulsory redundancy terms, the company provided that both men and women could receive an immediate early pension at age 55. Since Roberts was 53 when she was made redundant, she did not receive a pension. She argued that the scheme was in breach of the equal-treatment principle, since men could receive an early pension ten years before their normal retirement age, whereas women could receive one only five years before. This time, the Court decided the case on the basis of the Equal Treatment Directive, thus apparently nar-rowing the scope of the exception in the Social Security Directive. The imposition of an age limit for compulsory redundancy was not about the terms on which an early pension was *granted* (i.e., it was not about social security)—even if it involved the grant of a pension—but about the terms of *dismissal* (i.e., about equal treatment).

---

247 Case 170/84 *Bilka-Kaufhaus*, n. 138 above. In Case C–256/01 *Allonby*, n. 66 above, the ECJ also ruled that the legislative exclusion of workers employed on a contracted-out basis from membership of an occupational pension scheme constituted indirect discrimination in violation of Art. 141, even where the workers in question were unsuccessful in their equal pay claim for the reason that they were not paid from the same 'source' as work-ers employed directly by the organization in question.

248 Case 19/81 *Burton* v. *British Railways Board* [1982] ECR 555.

249 Case 151/84 *Roberts* v. *Tate & Lyle Industries* [1986] ECR 703. See also Case 262/84 *Beets-Proper* v. *Van Lanschot Bankiers* [1986] ECR 773.

Case 151/84 **Roberts v. Tate & Lyle Industries**
[1986] ECR 703

THE ECJ

34. As the Court emphasized in its judgment in the *Burton* case, Article 7 of Directive No 79/7 expressly provides that the Directive does not prejudice the right of Member States to exclude from its scope the determination of pensionable age for the purposes of granting old-age and retirement pensions and the possible consequences thereof for other benefits falling within the statutory social security schemes. The Court thus acknowledged that benefits linked to a national scheme which lays down a different minimum pensionable age for men and women may lie outside the ambit of the aforementioned obligation.

35. However, in view of the fundamental importance of the principle of equality of treatment, which the Court has reaffirmed on numerous occasions, [the Equal Treatment Directive], which excludes social security matters from the scope of that directive, must be interpreted strictly. Consequently, whereas the exception to the prohibition of discrimination on grounds of sex provided for in Article 7(1) (a) of Directive No 79/7 concerns the consequences which pensionable age has for social security benefits, this case is concerned with dismissal within the meaning of [the Equal Treatment Directive]. In those circumstances the grant of a pension to persons of the same age who are made redundant amounts merely to a collective measure adopted irrespective of the sex of those persons in order to guarantee them all the same rights.

Thus if Roberts' employer had done as Burton's had done, and had tied the age for receipt of an immediate pension on compulsory redundancy to the statutory social-security scheme, it would not have been able to gain the benefit of the exception in Directive 79/7 for pensionable ages in statutory social-security schemes. Since the redundancy was classified by the ECJ as dismissal (rather than *voluntary* redundancy as in *Burton*), the receipt of a pension on redundancy was a condition of dismissal within the scope of the Equal Treatment Directive.[250]

The narrowing of the social security exception continued in *Marshall I*.[251] In this case, the Court was dealing, not with voluntary or compulsory *redundancy*, but with a compulsory *retirement* provision which mirrored the different statutory pensionable ages for men and women. Marshall was required to retire some time after reaching the age of 60, which was the statutory pensionable age and the compulsory retirement age which the company had set for women. The ECJ followed *Roberts* and treated the compulsory retirement as dismissal within the terms of the Equal Treatment Directive, rather than as a consequence of the different statutory pensionable ages falling within the exception in Directive 79/7. More recently in *Hlozek*, the ECJ implicitly overruled *Burton* in so far as it stood as authority for the proposition that benefits paid after termination of the employment relationship, such as voluntary redundancy, does not constitute pay.[252]

The distinction between conditions of work under the Equal Treatment Directive and social security under Directive 79/7 arose also in *Jackson and Cresswell*, where the ECJ held

---

[250] See also Case C–207/04 *Vergani* v. *Agenzia delle Entrate* [2005] ECR I–7453, concerning tax benefits on the taking of voluntary redundancy, which was held to violate the Equal Treatment Dir. and was not saved by Dir. 79/7.

[251] Case 152/84 *Marshall* v. *Southampton and South-West Hampshire Area Health Authority (Teaching)* [1986] ECR 723.

[252] Case C–19/02 *Hlozek*, n. 114 above, paras. 36–40.

that a scheme of benefits would not be excluded from the scope of the Equal Treatment Directive solely because it was formally part of a national social-security system.[253] However, the subject-matter of any scheme falling within the Equal Treatment Directive must concern access to employment,[254] access to promotions, vocational training, or conditions of work. Consequently an income-support scheme the purpose of which was to supplement the income of those with inadequate means of subsistence would not be brought within the scope of the Directive solely by virtue of the fact that the method for calculating eligibility could affect a single mother's ability to take up vocational training or employment.[255]

In *Meyers*, however, the ECJ ruled that family credit, which was an income-related benefit awarded under UK social-security legislation, would fall within the scope of the Equal Treatment Directive.[256] This was because one of the conditions for its award was that the claimant should be engaged in remunerative work, and because its function was to encourage unemployed workers to accept low-paid work and to keep poorly paid workers in employment, thus concerning access to employment. Since the benefit was 'necessarily linked to a contract of employment' it did not matter that it was not a condition set out in the contract of employment, nor that entitlement to the benefit would not be affected by loss of employment or a salary increase for a certain period.[257]

In sum, the disparities between the EC legal regimes governing pay and conditions of work on the one hand (now Directive 2006/54), and social security on the other (Directive 79/7), and the fact that matters of social assistance are left to be regulated by the Member States, mean that the categorizations within EC sex-discrimination law are important, and have regularly given rise to complex litigation of this kind.

(d) THE EQUAL TREATMENT DIRECTIVE AND PREGNANCY

We have seen above that the previous Equal Treatment Directive 76/207 contained a provision in Article 2(3) stipulating that the Directive was without prejudice to provisions concerning the protection of women, particularly as regards pregnancy and maternity. This was designed to prevent any EC equality-based challenge to national employment provisions granting leave or other special conditions to women who are pregnant or have given birth, rather than to impose any obligation on States or employers to adopt such provisions.

This has now been replaced by the more positive requirement in Article 15 of Directive 2006/54, which provides that a woman on maternity leave is to be entitled to return to equivalent employment on no less favourable terms and to benefit from any improvement in working conditions to which she would have been entitled during her absence, and Article 16 contains a similar provision for men returning from paternity leave, or for men and women returning from adoption leave.

An early challenge was made to provisions of German law under the previous Equal Treatment Directive in *Hofmann*, in which it was argued that where maternity leave provisions went beyond what was necessary to protect women before and after childbirth, e.g., by giving

---

253 Cases C–63–64/91 *Jackson* v. *Chief Adjudication Officer* [1992] ECR I–4737, para. 27.

254 See, e.g., Case C–100/95 *Kording* v. *Senator für Finanzen* [1997] ECR I–5289.

255 Cases C–63–64/91 *Jackson*, n. 253 above, paras. 29–30.

256 Case C–116/94 *Meyers* v. *Adjudication Officer* [1995] ECR I–2131, paras. 19–22.

257 *Ibid.*, para. 23. Contrast the Opinion of Jacobs AG in Cases C–245 and 312/94 *Hoever and Zachow* v. *Land Nordrhein Westfalen* [1996] ECR I–4895.

a longer period of leave in order to care for a child, they would breach the Directive unless the leave period was made available to men and women alike.[258] The case concerned a man who wished to take leave to care for his newborn child, but who was not eligible for the longer six-month period of paid maternity leave which German law provided for mothers. The ECJ rejected the argument, however, ruling that the provision of a period of extended maternity leave was intended to protect women in connection with the effects of pregnancy and mother-hood, and that such leave could legitimately be reserved to the mother 'in view of the fact that it is only the mother who may find herself subject to undesirable pressures to return to work prematurely'.[259] The Court also said that the Equal Treatment Directive was not intended 'to alter the division of responsibility between parents', and that Member States had a measure of discretion as to the social measures they adopted to protect women in the event of pregnancy and maternity.

It is however arguable that the Court's ruling in fact supported the continuation by the Member States of the traditional division of responsibility which entrenches the role of the mother as primary carer, and which, by protecting 'the special relationship between a woman and her child', deprives the father of the opportunity to develop such a relationship in the period after birth by refusing to give the parents a choice of who shall take leave. On the other hand, if the Court had ruled that the Equal Treatment Directive prohibited Member States from providing special protection for women other than when this was strictly necessary to protect women's biological condition during and after pregnancy and childbirth, the Member States would have been free to 'level down' as well as to 'level up', in other words to abolish the more extended maternity leave for women rather than providing it for men.

A clear example of the reinforcement of the view that only the mother should develop a special relationship with a child after birth is in the case of *Commission* v. *Italy*, concerning national laws giving compulsory maternity leave to the mother of an adopted child under 6 years of age, but not to the father.[260] The ECJ accepted Italy's 'legitimate concern to assimilate as far as possible the conditions of entry of the child into the adoptive family to those of the arrival of a newborn child in the family during the very delicate initial period',[261] although it is not obvious why the initial three-month period is not equally delicate for an adoptive father as for an adoptive mother, especially when the child is not newborn.

Although the *Hofmann* and *Italy* cases involved an interpretation of a provision of the earlier Equal Treatment Directive which no longer exists, it seems likely that the same kind of challenges could be brought on the basis of general prohibition on discrimination in the recast Equal Treatment Directive 2006. Legislation actually requiring Member States to provide a period of maternity leave for women was not adopted until the 1992 Pregnancy Directive,[262] and a Framework Agreement and Directive on parental leave providing for a minimum-level individual right to three months' parental leave was finally adopted in 1996.[263] Directive 2006/54 now provides that it is without prejudice to the Pregnancy and Parental Leave Directives, and it supplements the other legislation by its provision in Articles 15 and 16

---

[258] Case 184/83 *Hofmann* v. *Barmer Ersatzkasse* [1984] ECR 3047.

[259] *Ibid.*, para. 26.

[260] Case 163/82 *Commission* v. *Italy* [1983] ECR 3273.

[261] *Ibid.*, para. 16.

[262] Council Dir. 92/85/EEC of 19 Oct. 1992 on the introduction of measures to encourage improvements in the safety and health at work of pregnant workers and workers who have recently given birth or are breastfeeding [1992] OJ L348/1.

[263] Council Dir. 96/34 on the framework agreement on parental leave concluded by UNICE, CEEP, and the ETUC [1996] OJ L145/4.

concerning favourable treatment of women on their return from maternity leave, of men on their return from paternity leave, and of men and women returning from adoption leave.

While it was clear that the original Equal Treatment Directive permitted Member States to maintain protective provisions favouring women in relation to pregnancy and maternity, it was not clear for some years whether it also *prohibited* measures which discriminated against women on grounds of pregnancy. In a steady line of case law which followed, the ECJ ruled that discrimination on grounds of pregnancy constitutes sex discrimination under Directive 76/207, and this case law remains equally applicable to the 2006 recast Equal Treatment Directive.

In *Dekker*, a pregnant woman who was chosen by an appointments committee as the most suitable candidate for the job she had applied for was informed that she would not be appointed because the employer would not be able to obtain reimbursement of the maternity benefits it would have to pay her.[264] The ECJ ruled:

> 12. In that regard it should be noted that only women can be refused employment on grounds of pregnancy and such a refusal therefore constitutes direct discrimination on grounds of sex. A refusal of employment on account of the financial consequences of absence due to pregnancy must be regarded as based, essentially, on the fact of pregnancy. Such discrimination cannot be justified on grounds relating to the financial loss which an employer who employed a pregnant woman would suffer for the duration of her maternity leave.
>
> ...
>
> 17. It should be stressed that the reply to the question whether the refusal to employ a woman constitutes direct or indirect discrimination depends on the reason for that refusal. If that reason is to be found in the fact that the person concerned is pregnant, then the decision is directly linked to the sex of the candidate. In those circumstances the absence of male candidates cannot affect the answer to the first question.

The reason given by the Court in *Dekker* for why refusal of employment on grounds of pregnancy is direct sex discrimination is that pregnancy is a condition which applies to women only. Did this mean that if certain physical or medical conditions applied only to men, such refusal or dismissal on grounds of absence due to such a condition would be considered sex discrimination in breach of Directive 76/207? In *Hertz*, the ECJ ruled that dismissal on grounds of sickness to which one sex only is susceptible would not constitute sex discrimination, since both sexes were equally exposed to illness.[265] Yet the reason given by the Court for why dismissal on grounds of pregnancy constitutes sex discrimination seems formal and inadequate, since its only basis is that, since pregnancy is a condition affecting women alone, such dismissal must constitute sex discrimination. A more plausible reason why pregnancy-related dismissal is seen as impermissible is not just that pregnancy affects women only, but that it is a unique condition which is also of social value, and that the role women play in reproduction and childbirth is an important one in which employers, men, and society as a whole have an interest.[266] Indeed, this was acknowledged by Advocate General Tesauro in his Opinion.[267]

---

[264] Case C–177/88 *Dekker* v. *Stichting Vormingscentrum voor Jong Volwassenen (VJV-Centrum) Plus* [1990] ECR I–3941.

[265] Case C–179/88 *Handels- og Kontorfuntionærernes Forbund i Danmark* v. *Dansk Arbejdsgiverforening* [1990] ECR I–3979.

[266] S. Fredman, 'A Difference with Distinction: Pregnancy and Parenthood Reassessed' (1994) 110 *LQR* 106.

[267] See his Opinion in Case C–421/92 *Habermann-Beltermann*, n. 218 above, 1664. See also Case C–207/98 *Mahlburg* v. *Land Mecklenburg-Vorpommern* [2000] ECR I–549; Case C–136/95 *Caisse nationale d'assurance vieillesse des travailleurs salariés (CNAVTS)* v. *Thibault* [1998] ECR I–2011.

Dekker established that the refusal to employ a worker for financial reasons consequent upon pregnancy constitutes sex discrimination. Subsequent cases then addressed related questions concerning refusal of employment due to an illness arising from pregnancy, or because of a legislative prohibition on women performing certain work during pregnancy, or because of unavailability for essential work while absent during pregnancy.

In *Hertz*, where a woman was dismissed on account of absence owing to sickness originating in pregnancy, ECJ rejected the argument that the protection provided by the Directive against dismissal owing to illness caused by pregnancy was unlimited in time. [268]

Case C–179/88 Handels- og Kontorfunktionærernes Forbund i Danmark v. Dansk Arbejdsgiverforening
[1990] ECR I–3979

14. On the other hand, the dismissal of a female worker on account of repeated periods of sick leave which are not attributable to pregnancy or confinement does not constitute direct discrimination on grounds of sex, inasmuch as such periods of sick leave would lead to the dismissal of a male worker in the same circumstances.

15. The Directive does not envisage the case of an illness attributable to pregnancy or confinement. It does, however, admit of national provisions guaranteeing women specific rights on account of pregnancy and maternity, such as maternity leave. During the maternity leave accorded to her pursuant to national law, a woman is accordingly protected against dismissal due to absence. It is for every Member State to fix periods of maternity leave in such a way as to enable female workers to absent themselves during the period in which the disorders inherent in pregnancy and confinement occur.

16. In the case of an illness manifesting itself after the maternity leave, there is no reason to distinguish an illness attributable to pregnancy or confinement from any other illness. Such a pathological condition is therefore covered by the general rules applicable in the event of illness.

17. Male and female workers are equally exposed to illness. Although certain disorders are, it is true, specific to one or other sex, the only question is whether a woman is dismissed on account of absence due to illness in the same circumstances as a man; if that is the case, then there is no direct discrimination on grounds of sex.

Advocate General Darmon admitted that he was 'tempted to propose a solution whereby medical conditions which were directly, definitely and preponderantly due to pregnancy or confinement would enjoy a sort of 'immunity' in the sense that the principle of equality of treatment would restrain the employer from dismissing his employee for a reasonable period after the event in question',[269] but he decided ultimately that such a solution was a matter for legislation. The ECJ followed his compromise, making the extent of protection against dismissal for pregnant women depend on the varying periods of maternity leave granted by the national legislation of different States.

In *Larsson*, the Court ruled that the equal-treatment principle did not prevent a woman being dismissed due to absence caused by continuing illness which began *during* the

---

[268] Case C–179/88 *Handels- og Kontorfunktionærernes Forbund i Danmark*, n. 265 above.

[269] *Ibid.*, para. 43 of his Opinion. For criticism of the *Hertz* case for imposing a model of equality where women must be compared with men, save for the 'exceptional' case of pregnancy, see G. More, 'Reflections on Pregnancy Discrimination under European Community Law' [1992] *JSWFL* 48.

pregnancy, nor did it prevent account being taken of absences from work during the period of pregnancy and maternity leave when calculating the period providing grounds for dismissal.[270]

However in one of its rare moves of this kind, the ECJ later in *Brown* expressly departed from this second part of its ruling in *Larsson* and ruled that where a woman was absent owing to illness resulting from pregnancy or childbirth, where the illness arose during pregnancy and persisted during and after maternity leave, her absence during maternity leave and during the period extending from the start of her pregnancy to the start of her maternity leave should not be taken into account for computation of the period justifying her dismissal under national law.[271] One of the factors which the Court in *Brown* took into account was the recent adoption of the Pregnancy Directive 92/85 which, although not in issue in the case, was in the Court's view part of the general context which had to be taken into consideration.

In *Habermann-Beltermann*, the ECJ was asked whether it was compatible with the Equal Treatment Directive for an employee who had chosen to work nights only to be dismissed on becoming pregnant, because of national legislation prohibiting the assignment of night-work to women who were pregnant or breast-feeding; and also whether it was compatible with the Directive for her contract of employment to be declared void for mistake—since her employer did not know that she was pregnant when she was hired—given that the legislation provided that any term in an employment contract breaching the prohibition on night-work would be void.[272] The ECJ ruled that since it was not a fixed-term contract, and since the prohibition on night-time work by pregnant women therefore would take effect only for a limited period in relation to the total length of the contract, it would be incompatible with the Directive to invalidate the contract simply because of her temporary inability to perform night-time work. In other words (in contrast with *Levy* and *Minne* above where pregnancy was not in issue[273]), a ban on night-time work for pregnant women in itself would be compatible with the Equal Treatment Directive, but termination of a female employee's contract on this account would not be, since this was not a fixed-term contract. [274]

The case of *Webb* concerned the dismissal of a woman who discovered, shortly after being employed on a contract of indefinite duration to replace another employee on maternity leave, that she herself was pregnant.[275] In addressing the question whether this would breach the Equal Treatment Directive, the ECJ made extensive reference to the protections introduced by the Pregnancy Directive 92/85[276] (which at the time was not yet in effect), and in particular its provision that there is to be no exception to or derogation from the prohibition on the dismissal of pregnant women during the period of pregnancy and maternity leave save in exceptional cases not connected with their condition.

> 26. Furthermore, contrary to the submission of the United Kingdom, dismissal of a woman recruited for an indefinite period cannot be justified on grounds relating to her inability to fulfil

---

[270] Case C–400/95 *Handels- og Kontorfunktionærernes Forbund i Danmark, acting on behalf of Larsson* v. *Dansk Handel & Services, acting on behalf of Føtex Supermarked A/S* [1997] ECR I–2757. See also Case C–191/03 *North Western Health Board* v. *McKenna* [2005] ECR I–7631, although this was on the subject of equal pay rather than equal treatment.

[271] Case C–394/96 *Brown*, n. 215 above. For a case involving pregnancy-related sick-leave after the period of maternity leave in relation to pay see Case C–191/03 *McKenna*, n. 270 above.

[272] Case C–421/92 *Habermann-Beltermann*, n. 218 above.

[273] Case C–158/91 *Levy*, n. 241 above; Case C–13/93 *Minne*, n. 217 above.

[274] See also Case C–207/98 *Mahlburg* , n. 267 above.

[275] Case C–32/93 *Webb* v. *EMO* [1994] ECR I–3567.

[276] N. 262 above.

a fundamental condition of her employment contract. The availability of an employee is necessarily, for the employer, a precondition for the proper performance of the employment contract. However, the protection afforded by Community law to a woman during pregnancy and after childbirth cannot be dependent on whether her presence at work during maternity is essential to the proper functioning of the under-taking in which she is employed. Any contrary interpretation would render ineffective the provisions of the Directive.

27. In circumstances such as those of Mrs Webb, termination of a contract for an indefinite period on grounds of the woman's pregnancy cannot be justified by the fact that she is prevented, on a purely temporary basis, from performing the work for which she has been engaged

The case of women employed on fixed-term contracts who are dismissed owing to pregnancy arose in the later cases of *Jiménez Melgar* and *Tele Danmark*. In these cases the Court ruled that both the Equal Treatment Directive and the Pregnancy Directive 92/85 prohibited the dismissal of a woman on grounds of pregnancy also in the case of a fixed-term contract.[277] However, in *Jiménez Melgar* the ECJ accepted that where non-renewal of a fixed-term contract was concerned, this could not always be equated with dismissal, and so it was for the national court to decide whether a decision not to renew a fixed-term contract which had come to an end was motivated by the worker's pregnancy (thus being illegal) or not.[278]

In *Tele Danmark* the Court made two further observations: first, that the duration of an employment relationship was almost always uncertain, even where a worker was initially recruited for a fixed period, and secondly that the Equal Treatment and Pregnancy Directives themselves had chosen to make no distinctions based on the duration of the employment relationship, which suggested that the legislature had not intended to exclude all those on fixed-term contracts from the protective scope of their provisions.[279]

Moreover in *Busch*, the ECJ ruled, relying on both the Equal Treatment and the Pregnancy Directives, that there was no obligation on an employee who chose to return to work before the end of her parental leave to inform her employer that she was pregnant, even though her aim in terminating her parental leave and coming back to work was to make herself eligible for maternity benefit which was at a higher level than the parental leave benefit she received.[280] The Directives prohibited the employer from refusing or rescinding consent to her return to work on the ground of her non-disclosure of her pregnancy.

We can see that in most of the cases the ECJ has given an interpretation of the Equal Treatment Directive which corresponds with the relevant provisions of the Pregnancy Directive, by providing essentially that dismissal for any pregnancy-related reason *during the period of maternity leave* is impermissible, and that the imposition of other disadvantages (such as refusal of consent to return from parental leave) on grounds of pregnancy is equally prohibited.

(e) THE PREGNANCY DIRECTIVE

In a move away from the treatment of pregnancy as an issue of sex equality, Directive 92/85 was expressly based at the time on Article 138 EC concerning health and safety at work, under

---

[277] Case C–438/99 *Jiménez Melgar* v. *Ayuntamiento de Los Barrios* [2001] ECR I–6915; Case C–109/00 *Tele Danmark A/S* v. *HK* [2001] ECR I–6993.

[278] Case C–438/99 *Melgar*, n. 277 above, paras. 45–47.

[279] Case C–109/00 *Tele Danmark*, n. 277 above, paras. 32–33.

[280] Case C–320/01 *Busch* v. *Klinikum Neustadt* [2003] ECR I–2041.

which legislation could be adopted by a qualified majority.[281] The Directive was adopted after considerable negotiation and compromise, which included, at the insistence of the UK, the setting of the minimum level of pay for workers on maternity leave at the level of sick pay, despite the arguments against drawing parallels between sickness and pregnancy.

The Directive introduced a requirement of minimum protection by the Member States for three categories of female workers: pregnant workers, workers who have recently given birth, and workers who are breast-feeding. There is a non-regression clause which states that the Directive cannot be used to justify any reduction in higher levels of protection already provided in Member States. In other words, this does not seek to be a fully harmonizing Directive, and it does not attempt to require uniform rights of maternity leave for women in all of the Member States, but merely to set a floor.

The Directive provides for guidelines to be drawn up by the Commission on substances and processes which are considered hazardous or stressful to those three categories of workers. It requires employers to assess the extent to which such women are exposed to specified risks and, under Article 5, to take any appropriate action such as adjusting their working hours or conditions, moving them to another job, or granting leave. Article 7 provides that they cannot be obliged to perform night-work for a period to be set by national law, and the option of day-work or extended maternity leave must be possible. Article 6 provides that pregnant or breast-feeding workers cannot be required to carry out duties involving the risk of exposure to specified substances, and Article 9 stipulates that pregnant workers must be entitled, where necessary, to time off work without loss of pay to attend ante-natal examinations.

The core provision on maternity leave is contained in Article 8, which specifies that the three categories of workers are to be given a minimum of fourteen continuous weeks' maternity leave before and/or after confinement, including at least two weeks of compulsory maternity leave. This is bolstered by Article 10, which requires Member States to prohibit the dismissal of such workers during the period of maternity leave, other than in exceptional cases unconnected with pregnancy.[282] It has however been pointed out that the Pregnancy Directive does not cover the *Dekker* situation, i.e., refusal to employ a woman on grounds of pregnancy, and that in this situation it will still be necessary to rely on the prohibition of discrimination under the Equal Treatment Directive.[283] In *Boyle*, the ECJ ruled that it was not contrary to Article 8 of the Pregnancy Directive for an employer to specify when the obligatory fourteen-week period of maternity leave should commence, even if the employee was on sick leave at the time of giving birth.[284]

Article 12 covers the requirement of access to a judicial remedy. Under Article 11, the right to maintenance of payment and other employment rights must be protected in the case of those workers who are on leave in the circumstances provided in Articles 5, 6, and 7. Significantly, the same is not required in the case of workers who are on maternity leave, as provided in Article 8.[285] Instead, Article 11 specifies that they must be entitled to an 'adequate

---

[281] [1992] OJ L348/1, n. 262 above. For a critical analysis of the Dir. and of the various possible explanations for its adoption see V. Cromack, 'The EC Pregnancy Directive: Principle or Pragmatism?' [1993] *JSWFL* 261.

[282] For an interpretation of the requirement of Member State consent in exceptional cases under Art. 10(1) see Case C–438/99 *Melgar*, n. 277 above.

[283] For a critique see Cromack, n. 281 above.

[284] Case C–411/96 *Boyle*, n. 132 above. The employer could not, however, make the right to take sick leave during the period of maternity leave conditional on the employee first agreeing to return to work and terminate maternity leave, except in the case where the period of maternity leave in question was an additional period granted by the employer in excess of that required by statute.

[285] In Case C–342/93 *Gillespie*, n. 130 above, on facts which arose before the Dir. was applicable, the ECJ ruled that the Treaty did not require a woman on maternity leave to continue to receive full pay, although the

allowance' of not less than the amount of statutory sick pay. It should be noted that the 'special concept of pay' under the Pregnancy Directive is not the same as the concept of pay for the purposes of Article 141,[286] which has given rise to some complexity. The fact that the opportunity was not taken, when the recast Directive 2006/54 was adopted, to align the principles governing pay under Article 141 and under the Pregnancy Directive has been criticized.[287]

Eligibility for the allowance under the Pregnancy Directive can be subjected by national legislation to conditions, other than a condition which requires previous employment of more than twelve months prior to confinement. In *Boyle*, the ECJ ruled that a contractual term under which a higher level of pay than the statutory maternity payments was made conditional on the worker undertaking to return to work after the birth for at least one month was compatible with this provision and also with Article 141 EC.[288]

In other words, the Pregnancy Directive guarantees only a minimum level of maternity pay, and not any higher amount that the employer may choose to pay. Similarly in the case of the period of maternity leave granted, the employer is only required under Article 8 to grant fourteen weeks' leave and, if supplementary leave is also granted, there is nothing in the Pregnancy Directive or the Equal Treatment Directive to prevent the employer from limiting the entitlement to accrual of annual leave to the period of fourteen weeks. However, accrual of annual leave and accrual of occupation pension rights are firmly protected during the fourteen-week period, as basic rights of the employment contract,[289] by Article 11(2)(a).[290]

In a further series of cases we see how the Equal Treatment Directive and other EU equality legislation have been interpreted so as to supplement or complement the Pregnancy Directive in protecting women against suffering adverse consequences as a result of pregnancy and maternity leave. In *Woolwich*, the ECJ referred to its ruling in *Gillespie*[291] in which it held that a woman on maternity leave could not usefully rely on Article 141 to argue for the right to full pay since she was in a different and specially protected legal position, but that where a woman is still linked to her employer by a contract of employment or by an employment relationship during maternity leave she is, like any other worker, entitled under Article 141 to benefit from any pay rise awarded between the beginning of the period covered by reference pay and the end of maternity leave.[292] This was in part because, even though maternity pay is not the same as pay for the purposes of Article 141, it is nevertheless equivalent to a weekly payment calculated on the basis of the average pay received by the worker at the time when she was actually working. The thrust of much of this case law is also now reflected in Article 14 of the recast Directive 2006/54, which protects the rights of women returning from maternity leave.

The case of *McKenna* raised the additional complication of a woman who was absent on pregnancy-related sick leave after the period of her maternity, and who sought to challenge

---

amount payable could not be so low as to undermine the purpose of maternity leave in protecting women before and after birth. See also Case C–66/96 *Handels- og Kontorfunktionærernes Forbund i Danmark, acting on behalf of Berit Høj Pedersen* v. *Fællesforeningen for Danmarks Brugsforening* [1998] ECR I–7327.

[286] In Case C–333/97 *Lewen*, n. 98 above, it was held that while a voluntary Christmas bonus given to employees constituted pay within Art. 141 EC it did not fall within the special concept of pay under Art. 11(2)(b) of the Pregnancy Dir. in relation to maternity leave.

[287] Burrows and Robison, n. 32 above.

[288] Case C–411/96 *Boyle*, n. 132 above.

[289] *Ibid.*, paras. 84–87.

[290] See also Case C–333/97 *Lewen*, n. 98 above, para. 50, on the difference between periods of parenting leave and periods of leave required for the protection of mothers, in relation to the calculation of entitlement to an allowance.

[291] Case C–342/93 *Gillespie*, n. 130 above.

[292] Case C–147/02 *Woolwich*, n. 132 above.

the lower level of sick-pay (which was equivalent to that provided for non-pregnancy-related illness) she received during this additional period of sick leave.[293] Here the ECJ ruled that this was not prohibited by Article 141 or the Equal Pay Directive (the scope of which is now covered by Directive 2006/54).

In *Meroni Gómez*, the Court ruled that the Working Time Directive, read together with the Pregnancy Directive and the Equal Treatment Directive, required that a worker be allowed to take her annual leave during a period other than the period of her maternity leave, even if the period of annual leave of the entire workforce happened to coincide with when she was on maternity leave.[294] And in *Sarkatzis Herrero*, the ECJ ruled that, although the case was not covered by the Pregnancy Directive since it did not involve adverse treatment for a woman returning to an existing job from maternity leave, the Equal Treatment Directive was breached where a woman's maternity leave was not taken into account in calculating her seniority, where she had deferred taking up a new post in order to take maternity leave.[295] Finally, in *Mayer*, the ECJ ruled that the Occupational Social Security Directives (now replaced by the recast Directive 2006/54) prohibited a woman who was on maternity leave from being denied a particular insurance benefit which was part of a supplementary occupational social security scheme, on the ground that she was not in receipt of taxable pay during her maternity leave.[296]

(f) DIRECTIVE 86/613 ON THE SELF-EMPLOYED

Since the original Equal Treatment Directive dealt with equal treatment in relation to employed persons, Directive 86/613 was adopted under Articles 94 and 308 EC in order to apply the principle of equal treatment also to the self-employed.[297] Article 2 sets out the personal scope of the Directive, providing that it applies to the self-employed 'including farmers and members of the liberal professions' as well as their spouses who are not employees or partners, but who participate in the same activities. Article 3 sets out the principle of equal treatment in a similar way to that in the other Equal Treatment and Social Security Directives.[298]

Articles 4–8 then set out the 'material scope' of the scheme, which requires Member States to take action to eliminate sex discrimination in a range of matters, such as establishing a business or activity, forming a company, and providing for social-security schemes for spouses of the self-employed. Member States are also to 'examine under what conditions' the recognition of the work of spouses may be encouraged, and under what conditions female self-employed workers or wives of such workers may be protected in the event of pregnancy or motherhood—specifically, the Directive mentions access to temporary replacements or national social services and entitlement to cash benefits under public social-security or social-protection schemes. The Directive has been criticized as being weak in content and providing insufficient protection, but it was not included in the terms of the recast Directive in 2006.

---

293 Case C–191/03 *McKenna*, n. 270 above.

294 Case C–342/01 *María Paz Merino Gómez* v. *Continental Industrias del Caucho SA* [2004] ECR I–2605.

295 Case C–294/04 *Sarkatzis Herrero* v. *Imsalud* [2006] ECR I–1513.

296 Case C–356/03 *Mayer* v. *Versorgungsanstalt des Bundes und der Länder* [2005] ECR I–295.

297 Council Dir. 86/613/EEC of 11 Dec. 1986 on the application of the principle of equal treatment between men and women engaged in an activity, including agriculture, in a self-employed capacity, and on the protection of self-employed women during pregnancy and motherhood [1986] OJ L359/56 and COM(94)163.

298 For a case discussing the concept of indirect discrimination under this Dir. and Dir. 76/207 see Case C–226/98 *Jørgensen* v. *Foreningen af Speciallæger* [2000] ECR I–2447.

(g) PARENTAL LEAVE

Following a number of unsuccessful attempts by the Commission to introduce legislation on parental leave, in 1996 a Framework Agreement on parental leave was concluded by the main organizations representing confederations of European employers' and employees' representatives, and this was implemented by Council Directive 96/34, under the terms of the Social Policy Agreement which at the time was attached by a Protocol to the EC Treaty.[299]

The main provisions of the Framework Agreement grant men and women workers a minimum-level individual right to at least three months' parental leave on the grounds of the birth or adoption of a child in order to care for the child, until a given age (up to 8 years) to be specified by the Member State or the social partners. The right to parental leave is in principle to be granted on a non-transferable basis, but the specific conditions of access and rules governing the leave are left to the Member States to define, either by law or by collective agreement.

The Framework Agreement sets out a number of permissible conditions on which Member States may decide, such as whether leave is to be granted on a full- or part-time basis, whether it is to be subject to a period of work qualification, what notice periods may be required, in what circumstances employers may postpone the grant of leave, and the making of special arrangements for small undertakings.

Workers are to be protected against dismissal on grounds of applying for or taking the permitted parental leave, and they shall have the right to return to the same or an equivalent or similar job at the end of the leave period without any other of their acquired rights being affected by the leave. No provision is made in the Agreement regarding pay or any other allowance, and clause 2(8) specifies that all matters relating to social security are to be determined by the Member States in accordance with national law.[300] The Agreement also provides, in a less detailed clause, that Member States or the social partners shall take 'the necessary measures' to entitle workers to time off work 'on grounds of *force majeure* for urgent family reasons in cases of sickness or accident'.

Since the right to leave granted by the Framework Agreement is a minimum-level right, the final provisions specify that Member States may introduce more favourable provisions, and that the provisions of the Agreement will not in themselves justify reducing the general level of protection afforded to workers in this field. The interpretation of provisions of the Agreement was referred in the first instance to the signatory parties, without prejudice to the role of the Commission, national courts, and the ECJ.

In *Österreichischer Gewerkschaftsbund*, the ECJ ruled that the equal pay provisions of Article 141 EC were not violated where Austrian law took account of periods of civilian or military service, which were largely taken by men, but not periods of (nationally-granted) parental leave, which were overwhelmingly taken by women.[301] The Court distinguished maternity leave from parental leave, ruling that the latter was voluntary, and also distinguished it from military and civilian service, ruling that while parental leave served the individual interests of workers and their families, military and civilian service served the national interest.

Finally, we have seen that Article 16 of Directive 2006/54 also now makes reference to the rights of those who have taken paternity (rather than parental) or adoption leave granted by

---

[299] Council Dir. 96/34, n. 263 above. This was extended to the UK by Dir. 97/75 [1998] OJ L10/24.

[300] See, however, Case C–333/97 *Lewen*, n. 98 above, on this issue.

[301] Case C–220/02 *Österreichischer Gewerkschaftsbund, Gewerkschaft der Privatangestellten* v. *Wirtschaftskammer Österreich* [2004] ECR I–5907.

national law, to return to jobs and conditions which are equivalent and no less favourable than those they enjoyed before, and to benefit from any improvement in working conditions to which they would have been entitled during their absence.

5. SOCIAL SECURITY

The main legislative provision in the field of social security is now Directive 79/7 on statutory social security,[302] since occupational social security has been defined as pay and brought within the umbrella of the recast Equal Treatment Directive 2006/54.

(a) DIRECTIVE 79/7

Directive 79/7 was adopted on the basis of Article 308, and its purpose is said to be the progressive implementation of the principle of equal treatment for men and women in the field of social security.[303] Following the ToA amendments, directives and other social security measures may be adopted unanimously by the Council under Article 137(3) EC. Although this provision was amended again by the Nice Treaty, social security still remains firmly subject to the unanimity requirement.

The term 'progressive implementation' in the Social Security Directive is significant since, unlike equal pay and also now unlike equal treatment more generally, Directive 79/7 provided for significant exceptions to the equal-treatment principle, and allowed Member States a considerably longer period of time to adapt their laws to its requirements than under the Equal Treatment Directive.

Article 2 establishes the personal scope of the Directive, setting out two broad categories of persons to which it applies. First, it covers the 'working population', which is subdivided into three categories: (i) those who are employed or self-employed; (ii) those under (i) whose work is interrupted by illness, accident, or involuntary unemployment; and (iii) those who are seeking employment. Secondly, it covers employees and the self-employed who are retired or invalided-out. Thus, in keeping with the Equal Pay and Equal Treatment Directives, Directive 79/7 covers only *employment-related* social security.

Article 3, which sets out the material scope of the Directive, indicates that it does not cover all forms of employment-related social security. Rather, it covers those statutory schemes which provide protection against five specified risks, as well as social assistance which is intended to supplement or replace those statutory schemes. The five categories of risk are sickness, invalidity, old age, accidents at work and occupational diseases, and finally unemployment. Article 3(2) specifies that the Directive will not apply to provisions concerning survivors' benefits or family benefits, except family benefits due in respect of one of the five listed risks. Article 3(3) indicates that occupational social security is not covered.

The basic principle of equal treatment is set out in Article 4(1), providing that there is to be no discrimination on grounds of sex, either directly or indirectly, by reference in particular to marital or family status. Provisions concerning the protection of women on grounds of maternity are again specifically exempted.[304] The Member States are required, as in the other equality directives, to take the necessary measures to ensure that any provisions in breach of

---

302 Dir. 79/7 [1979] OJ L6/24, n. 246 above.
303 Dir. 79/7, n. 246 above Art. 1.
304 *Ibid.*, Art. 4(2).

the equal-treatment principle are abolished, and they are required to provide an adequate remedy for those who feel aggrieved.[305]

The permissible exceptions to the scope of the Directive are set out in Article 7(1). Five specific matters are listed which the Member States may choose to exclude from the application of the Directive. The first, which was mentioned above in relation to the cases of *Marshall* and *Roberts* on the Equal Treatment Directive, relates to the 'determination of pensionable age for the purposes of granting old-age and retirement pensions and the possible consequences thereof for other benefits'.[306] This has been the subject of much litigation. The second exception concerns advantages in respect of old-age pension schemes for persons who have brought up children and the acquisition of benefit entitlements following periods of interruption of employment due to the bringing up of children. The third concerns the granting of old-age or invalidity benefit entitlements 'by virtue of the derived entitlements of a wife', the fourth the granting of increases in long-term invalidity, old-age, accidents-at-work, and occupational-disease benefits for a dependent wife, and the fifth the consequences of the exercise of a right of option not to acquire rights or incur obligations under a statutory scheme.[307]

However, Article 7(2) requires Member States to examine periodically any areas they have excluded, to see whether the justification for exclusion has altered in the light of social developments. Further, Member States must communicate to the Commission the provisions adopted pursuant to Article 7(2) and inform it of their reasons for maintaining existing provisions under Article 7(1), as well as the possibilities for future review of such derogations.

(i) *Direct Effect of Directive 79/7*

The direct effect of the equal-treatment principle in Article 4(1) was confirmed in *FNV*, in which the ECJ was asked whether it could be relied upon after the deadline for implementation, either if the Member States failed to implement it or if they implemented it only partially.[308] The ECJ ruled that the prohibition in Article 4(1) was sufficiently precise to be relied upon in a national court, and that the exceptions contained in Article 7 did not affect the unconditionality of this prohibition, but merely excluded certainly clearly defined areas from the scope of the equal treatment principle.[309]

In *Borrie Clark*, the ECJ ruled that it was contrary to Article 4(1) for a Member State, by means of legislation passed after the coming into effect of the Directive, to extend the discriminatory effects of an old benefit to the criteria for eligibility for a new benefit.[310] The case concerned an application for a severe-disablement allowance, which had been brought in to replace the earlier invalidity allowance. The invalidity allowance had discriminated against married women by requiring them not only to be incapable of continuing to work, but also 'incapable of performing normal household duties', and the new severe-disablement allowance effectively continued the discriminatory criteria for eligibility. This was not permissible, and Article 4(1) could be directly relied on by the affected applicant.[311]

---

[305] *Ibid.*, Arts. 5 and 6.
[306] *Ibid.*, Art. 7(1)(a).
[307] *Ibid.*, Art. 7(1)(b)–(e).
[308] Case 71/85 *Netherlands* v. *FNV* [1986] ECR 3855.
[309] *Ibid.*, paras. 18–21.
[310] Case 384/85 *Borrie Clark* v. *Chief Adjudication Officer* [1987] ECR 2865.
[311] See also Case 80/87 *Dik* v. *College van Burgemeester en Wethouders* [1988] ECR 1601.

(ii) *Personal Scope*

The personal scope of the Directive was given a broad reading by the ECJ in *Drake*, in which a woman who had given up work in order to care for her disabled mother was refused an invalid care allowance under national legislation on the ground that such an allowance was not payable to a married woman who was living with her husband. No such restriction was imposed by the legislation on a married man who was living with his wife, and the question for the ECJ was whether the applicant fell within the personal scope of Directive 79/7.

Case 150/85 **Drake v. Chief Adjudication Officer**
[1986] ECR 1995

THE ECJ

21. According to Article 3(1), Directive 79/7 applies to statutory schemes which provide protection against, inter alia, the risk of invalidity . . . and social assistance in so far as it is intended to supplement or replace the invalidity scheme. . . . In order to fall within the scope of the Directive, therefore, a benefit must constitute the whole or part of a statutory scheme providing protection against one of the specified risks or a form of social assistance having the same objective.

22. Under Article 2, the term 'working population', which determines the scope of the directive, is defined broadly. . . . That provision is based on the idea that a person whose work has been interrupted by one of the risks referred to in Article 3 belongs to the working population. That is the case of Mrs. Drake, who has given up work solely because of one of the risks listed in Article 3, namely the invalidity of her mother. She must therefore be regarded as a member of the working population for the purposes of the Directive.

23. Furthermore, it is possible for the Member States to provide protection against the consequences of the risk of invalidity in various ways. For example, a Member State may, as the United Kingdom has done, provide for two separate allowances, one payable to the disabled person himself and the other payable to a person who provides care, while another Member State may arrive at the same result by paying an allowance to the disabled person at a rate equivalent to the sum of those two benefits. In order, therefore, to ensure that the progressive implementation of the principle of equal treatment referred to in Article 1 of Directive 79/7 and defined in Article 4 is carried out in a harmonious manner throughout the Community, Article 3(1) must be interpreted as including any benefit which in a broad sense forms part of one of the statutory schemes referred to or a social assistance provision intended to supplement or replace such a scheme.

24. Moreover the payment of the benefit to a person who provides care still depends on the existence of a situation of invalidity inasmuch as such a situation is a condition *sine qua non* for its payment, as the Adjudication Officer admitted during the oral procedure. It must also be emphasized that there is a clear economic link between the benefit and the disabled person, since the disabled person derives an advantage from the fact that an allowance is paid to the person caring for him.

25. It follows that the fact that a benefit which forms part of a statutory invalidity scheme is paid to a third party and not directly to the disabled person does not place it outside the scope of Directive 79/7. Otherwise, as the Commission emphasized in its observations, it would be possible, by making formal changes to existing benefits covered by the directive, to remove them from its scope.[312]

---

312 Cases 48, 106, and 107/88 *Achterberg-te Riele v. Sociale Versekeringsbank, Amsterdam* [1989] ECR 1963.

Thus the fact that Mrs Drake had given up work in order to care for someone else who had become an invalid was sufficient to bring her within the scope of the Directive. The care allowance was treated by the Court in the same way as the mother's severe-disablement allowance, being simply the legislature's way of dividing up the payment of social-security benefits consequent on invalidity.

Directive 79/7 is strictly employment-related, in that it does not cover someone who has never worked. This was established in the case of *Achterberg-te Riele*, in which the Court also ruled that persons who give up work for a reason other than one of the five listed in the Directive—e.g., to look after children—fall outside its scope. Benefits such as old-age pensions and invalidity allowances, which are referred to in Article 3, will fall within the scope of the Directive only when they are claimed by someone who is within one of the categories of people in Article 2:

> This interpretation is in conformity with the objectives of Community law and the wording of the other provisions in the same field as Directive 79/7. Article 119 . . . Directive 75/117 . . . and Directive 76/207 . . . implement equal treatment between men and women not generally but only in their capacity as workers.[313]

These conditions were tightened further in the case of *Johnson I* where the Court ruled that in order to be covered by the Directive not only must one of the risks listed in the Directive have materialized, but the person in question must either have given up employment or been obliged to give up seeking employment *at the time of materialization of the risk*.[314] Johnson had given up work for some years in order to care for her child, and in the meantime had developed a serious back condition which rendered her unable to return to work. She was refused an invalidity pension or severe-disablement allowance because she was cohabiting with her partner, and since this restriction did not apply to men and thus was discriminatory, she argued that it was in breach of Directive 79/7. Despite the Commission's argument that, since those who give up work to look after children are largely women, who would be at a considerable disadvantage if they were excluded from the Social Security Directive on account of an illness or disability *subsequently* arising, the ECJ ruled that they would not be within the personal scope of the Directive, and shifted the responsibility for removing the disadvantage faced by women who give up work to care for children onto the Community legislature.[315]

This narrower reading of the personal scope of the Directive firmly underlines its employment-related focus, by excluding someone who cannot seek employment on account of a disability or illness he or she has suffered. Where someone seeking a benefit does satisfy the conditions of the Directive, however, the Court has ruled that the right to rely on the Directive is not confined to that person. In *Verholen*, one of the applicants before the Dutch court was the husband of a woman who was claiming sex discrimination in the conditions for determining affiliation of an old-age pension scheme, and the ECJ ruled that the right to rely on Directive 79/7 was not confined to individuals coming within the personal scope of the Directive, since 'other persons may have a direct interest in ensuring that the principle of non-discrimination is respected as regards persons who are protected'.[316] Accordingly, because the

---

[313] *Ibid.*, para. 12.

[314] Case C–31/90 *Johnson* v. *Chief Adjudication Officer* [1991] ECR I–3723, paras. 18–23.

[315] *Ibid.*, paras. 25–26. See also Case C–297/93 *Grau-Hupka* v. *Stadtgemeinde Bremen* [1994] ECR I–5535, even where such disadvantage affects women's pay.

[316] Cases C–87–89/90 *Verholen* v. *Sociale Versekeringsbank* [1991] ECR I–3757, para. 22.

claimant's husband had suffered the effects of the discriminatory national legislation concerning his spouse, in that his pension would also be reduced, he could invoke the provisions of the Directive so long as his spouse came within its personal scope.[317]

However, in *Züchner*, the ECJ applied the narrower reasoning of its earlier judgments in *Achterberg-te Riele* and *Johnson*, rather than the broader approach in *Drake* and *Verholen*,[318] ruling that a woman who provided special home care and therapeutic treatment for her disabled husband would not fall within the scope of Directive 79/7, even though she had had to undergo a form of occupational training in order to provide the care which would otherwise have to be paid for, since she had not been working or seeking work when her husband's disability materialized. The ECJ strongly resisted the claim, supported by the Commission, that she should be counted as a member of the 'working population' for the purposes of Article 2, however hard the work which she now performed in caring for her husband:

Case C–77/95 Züchner v. Handelskrankenkasse (Ersatzkasse) Bremen
[1996] ECR I–5689

THE ECJ

14. It must be recognised that a person may be obliged to have recourse to the services of another when he is unable, or no longer able, to perform a particular activity himself, whether it be the education of children, housework, management of private property or mere incidents of daily life. In the main, such activities call for a degree of competence, are of a certain scope and must be provided by an outsider in return for a certain degree of remuneration if there is no-one else, whether or not a member of the family, who will do so without payment.

15. It follows that an interpretation purporting to include within the concept of working population a member of the family who, without payment, undertakes an activity for the benefit of another member of the family on the ground that such an activity calls for a degree of competence, is of a particular nature or scope or would have to be provided by an outsider in return for remuneration if the member of the family in question did not provide it would have the effect of infinitely extending the scope of the directive, whereas the purpose of Article 2 of the directive is precisely to delimit that scope.

In *Nolte* and *Megner*, on the other hand, the ECJ rejected the German Government's argument that persons who were in minor or short-term employment were excluded from the 'working population' in Article 2 of Directive 79/7.[319] Drawing on its more generous case law concerning the free movement of workers, the ECJ ruled that the fact that a worker's earnings do not cover all of her needs cannot prevent her from being a member of the working population, even if the employment yields an income lower than the minimum required for subsistence.

(iii) *Material Scope*

With regard to the material scope of the Directive, although the ECJ initially gave Article 3 quite a broad reading, this was narrowed in subsequent case law in which various social-security

---

317 See also Case C–200/91 *Coloroll*, n. 65 above, para. 19 on occupational social security.

318 For criticism of this aspect of *Züchner* see L. Waddington (1997) 22 *ELRev*. 587.

319 Case C–317/93 *Nolte* v. *Landesversicherungsanstalt Hannover* [1995] ECR I–4625; Case C–444/93 *Megner and Scheffel* v. *Innungskrankenkasse Vorderpfalz* [1995] ECR I–4741.

benefits were deemed to be outside the scope of the Directive despite being linked to the risks set out in Article 3. We have seen that in *Drake* the Court considered an invalid care allowance to be a benefit falling within the scope of the Directive because it was indirectly of benefit to the disabled person who would receive the care. Later cases however indicate that the link between one of the risks listed and the benefit paid must be quite strong for the benefit to fall within the scope of the Directive. In *Smithson* an allegedly discriminatory housing benefit was challenged under the Directive, where the criteria of eligibility for the benefit included matters such as receipt of invalidity benefit, i.e., criteria related to protection against risks covered by the Directive.

Case C–243/90 R. v. Secretary of State for Social Security, ex parte Smithson
[1992] ECR I–467

THE ECJ

15. However, Article 3(1)(a) of Directive 79/7 does not refer to statutory schemes which are intended to guarantee any person whose real income is lower than a notional scheme calculated on the basis of certain criteria a special allowance enabling that person to meet housing costs.

16. The age and invalidity of the beneficiary are only two of the criteria applied in order to determine the extent of the beneficiary's financial need for such an allowance. The fact that those criteria are decisive as regards eligibility for the higher pensioner premium is not sufficient to bring that benefit within the scope of Directive 79/7.

17. The premium is an inseparable part of the whole benefit which is intended to compensate for the fact that the beneficiary's income is insufficient to meet housing costs, and cannot be characterised as an autonomous scheme intended to provide protection against one of the risks listed in Article 3(1) of Directive 79/7.

The approach adopted here to the material scope of Directive 79/7 is narrower than that adopted in *Drake*, where the allowance was not paid to protect the recipient against invalidity, but to make up for the loss of income on the part of the recipient who has given up work to care for an invalid. Thus the benefit was indirectly linked to invalidity. The reference to methods of funding in paragraph 14 of *Smithson* may indicate that the mere fact that a benefit is non-contributory does not mean that it falls outside the scope of the Directive. However, the Court considered that housing benefit was outside the scope of the Directive even though the criteria for calculating the benefit included two of the listed risks, namely age and invalidity. This was because the link between these criteria and the purpose of the benefit—i.e., to provide for those whose income was inadequate to cover housing costs—was insufficiently strong to conclude that the housing benefit was intended to protect against the risks of old age or invalidity.

Arguably, had this approach had been taken in *Drake*, looking strictly at the intended aim of the benefit, the conclusion might have been that the aim of the invalid care allowance was to provide a source of income to someone who had given up work to care for another. The conclusion of the ECJ in *Smithson* seems to be that the housing benefit was really a form of social assistance which was not intended to supplement or replace one of the listed social security benefits, and it suggests a stricter approach to determining the scope of the equal treatment principle in the sphere of social security under EC law.

Subsequently in *Jackson and Cresswell*, the question was whether a supplementary allowance or income support could, in certain circumstances, fall within the scope of the Directive as a form of protection against the risk of unemployment.[320] The applicants argued that the reduction in their benefits breached Directive 79/7, since it was a consequence of their not being able to deduct child-minding expenses when calculating their income in order to determine the amount of benefit they should receive. The prohibition on deduction of child-minding expenses was argued to be indirectly discriminatory against women. However, despite the attempts of Advocate General van Gerven to distinguish the benefits at issue in *Smithson*, the ECJ ruled that the benefits here were not 'directly and effectively' linked to protection against the risk of unemployment. Indeed, the national income support scheme exempted the applicants from the obligation to be available for work, and the amount of the benefit was set without any consideration of the risks listed in Article 3(1) of the Directive.[321] Unlike the Advocate General's approach, the Court concentrated on the need which the scheme was 'designed' to meet, rather than on its 'effect' in meeting one of the risks listed in the Directive. One problem with an intention-oriented approach, however, is that it may enable the Member States to structure their social-security and assistance schemes so as to avoid the application of the equal-treatment principle to many benefits which do, in fact, provide protection against one or more of the risks set out in the Directive.[322]

In *Hoever and Zachow*, the ECJ was asked whether a child-raising allowance intended to secure the maintenance of the family while children were being raised fell within the material scope of the Directive.[323] Although one of the effects of the benefit could be said to be that it helped keep people in employment, the ECJ, focusing again on the intended aim, ruled that it did not provide direct and effective protection against one of the risks listed in the Directive, and noted that Article 3(2) in fact largely excludes family benefits from its scope. However, although certain benefits, such as survivors' benefits, may be excluded from the Directive's scope, if a benefit such as invalidity benefit which *did* fall within its scope were to be withdrawn on becoming entitled to a survivor's benefit, this situation would be governed by the Directive.[324]

In *Richardson*, the ECJ ruled that UK national health regulations, which exempted those who qualify for an old-age pension from prescription charges, came within the scope of Directive 79/7, since they were part of a statutory scheme affording direct and effective protection against the risk of sickness, even though they did not strictly form part of national social-security rules.[325] Similarly in *Taylor*, a winter-fuel payment was held to be directly linked to protection against the risk of old age.[326]

By way of contrast in the case of *Atkins*, also referred from a UK court, the ECJ ruled that a system of concessionary fares on public transport for those who had reached pensionable age, which was operated on an optional basis under national statutory authority by a District

---

[320] Cases C–63–64/91 *Jackson*, n. 253 above.

[321] *Ibid.*, paras. 20–21.

[322] J. Sohrab, 'Women and Social Security Law: The Limits of EEC Equality Law' [1994] *JSWFL* 5.

[323] Cases C–245 and 312/94 *Hoever and Zachow*, n. 257 above. Compare Case C–116/94 *Meyers*, n. 256 above, and text, in which family credit was held to fall within the scope of Dir. 76/207 concerning access to employment, since one of its effects was to help keep people in employment. The ECJ did not address Dir. 76/207 in its ruling in *Hoever and Zachow*.

[324] Case C–338/91 *Steenhorst-Neerings v. Bestuur van de Bedrijfsvereniging voor Detailhandel, Ambachten en Huisvrouwen* [1993] ECR I–5475.

[325] Case C–137/94 *R. v. Secretary of State for Health, ex p. Richardson* [1995] ECR I–3407.

[326] Case C–382/98 *R. v. Secretary of State for Social Security, ex p. Taylor* [1999] ECR I–8955.

Council, fell outside the material scope of the Directive.[327] This was because the purpose or aim of the benefit was to facilitate access to public transport for certain classes of persons needing such transport who were less well off financially and, as in *Smithson*, old age and invalidity were merely two of the criteria which could be applied to define the classes of beneficiaries for the concessionary scheme. The ECJ rejected the Commission's argument that Directive 79/7 could extend to measures of 'social protection' of this kind, going beyond the scope of social security proper, so long as they were granted to persons affected by one of the risks listed in the Directive, and it reaffirmed that a scheme of benefits would fall within the scope of the Directive only if it were intended to afford *direct and effective protection* against one of the risks listed in Article 3, or to supplement or replace such a scheme.

(iv) *The Exceptions in Article 7*

We have seen that the Council in adopting Directive 79/7 did not attempt to require Member States to bring about immediate equality between women and men in social security, but permitted the gradual introduction of equal treatment in areas which would require considerable financial restructuring of existing state schemes. The exact scope of these exceptions, however, has given rise to a considerable amount of litigation. The most frequently litigated point, which has briefly been considered above in relation to conditions of dismissal under the Equal Treatment Directive, is the derogation concerning the determination of pensionable age.

In the *EOC* case, the ECJ was asked whether the UK scheme, which required men to pay contributions for 44 years and women for 39 years where the pensionable age for men was 65 and for women was 60, fell within the scope of the exception in Article 7(1)(a).[328] The ECJ ruled that it did, and that discrimination with respect to the obligation to contribute fell within the scope of the exception in so far as it was necessary to achieve the objectives of the Directive:

> 15. Although the preamble to the Directive does not state the reasons for the derogations which it lays down, it can be deduced from the nature of the exceptions contained in Article 7(1) of the Directive that the Community legislature intended to allow Member States to maintain temporarily the advantages accorded to women with respect to retirement in order to enable them progressively to adapt their pension systems in this respect without disrupting the complex financial equilibrium of those systems, the importance of which could not be ignored. Those advantages include the possibility for female workers of qualifying for a pension earlier than male workers, as envisaged by Article 7(1)(a) of the directive.
>
> 16. In a system such as the one concerned in the main proceedings, whose financial equilibrium is based on men contributing for a longer period than women, a different pensionable age for men and women cannot be maintained without altering the existing financial equilibrium, unless such inequality with respect to the length of contribution periods is also maintained.
>
> Any more limited interpretation of the derogation, the ECJ ruled, would render it entirely ineffective, since the financial upheaval which the exception was intended to avoid by permitting states to readjust their financing of pension schemes over a period of years would have to

---

[327] Case C–228/94 *Atkins v. Wrekin District Council and Department of Transport* [1996] ECR I–3633.
[328] Case C–9/91 *R. v. Secretary of State for Social Security, ex p. Equal Opportunities Commission (EOC)* [1992] ECR I–4927.

be faced before the deadline for implementation of the Directive. Thus the maintenance of different pensionable ages was not the only form of discrimination permitted by Article 7(1)(a), but 'also forms of discrimination such as those described by the national court which are necessarily linked to [the difference in statutory pensionable ages]'.

We have seen above that the derogation in Article 7(1)(a) extends not just to the setting of different pensionable ages, but also, in relation to the *Burton* and *Roberts* cases,[329] to 'the possible consequences thereof for other benefits'. In *Thomas* the ECJ considered whether the scope of the derogation was exceeded where the cessation of entitlement to invalid-care and severe-disablement allowances was linked to the attainment of statutory retirement age, which was 65 for men and 60 for women.[330] Having considered its reasoning in *EOC*, the ECJ ruled that the same sort of link between the discrimination and the difference in pensionable ages would have to be shown when the complaint concerned discrimination as regards 'other benefits'. The requisite link did not exist in relation to the disablement and invalid-care allowances at issue, since that grant of benefits under non-contributory schemes had no direct influence on the financial equilibrium of the contributory pension schemes.[331]

In the case of *Graham*, the rate of invalidity pension payable to those who opted, on reaching pensionable age, to continue receiving an invalidity rather than a retirement pension was reduced by reference to the rate of retirement pension which they would have received.[332] Given the difference in pensionable ages between men and women, it was argued that such a reduction was discriminatory and in breach of Directive 79/7, but the ECJ ruled that the discrimination was objectively and necessarily linked to the setting of different pensionable ages, and so was covered by the exception in Article 7(1)(a). This was because the invalidity benefit was designed to replace income from occupational activity, and the Member State was quite entitled to cease the invalidity benefit and to replace it with a retirement pension at the time when the recipients would have ceased to work on reaching retirement age. To hold otherwise, in the Court's view, would undermine the legitimate coherence of the national retirement scheme and the invalidity benefit scheme. In *De Vriendt* and *Wolfs* the Court ruled further that discrimination in the method of *calculating* pensions was necessarily and objectively linked to the difference which had been maintained regarding the specification of pensionable age.[333]

Similarly in *Balestra*, the link between sex discrimination in an early retirement-benefit scheme and the difference in pensionable ages was necessary to preserve the coherence between the retirement-pensions scheme and the early-retirement scheme in question.[334] On the other hand, in *Richardson* the discrimination in the system of exemption from prescription charges was held not to be necessarily linked to the difference in pensionable ages, since the grant of such health-related non-contributory benefits would have no direct influence on the financial equilibrium of contributory pension schemes, so that the Article 7(1)(a) exception

---

[329] Case 19/81 *Burton*, n. 248 above; Case 151/84 *Roberts*, n. 249 above. See also Case 262/84 *Beets-Proper*, n. 249 above; Case 152/84 *Marshall*, n. 251 above; Case C–303/02 *Haackert* v. *Pensionsversicherungsanstalt der Angestellten* [2004] ECR I–2195.

[330] Case C–328/91 *Secretary of State for Social Security* v. *Thomas* [1993] ECR I–1247.

[331] *Ibid.*, para. 14. See also Case C–207/04 *Vergani*, n. 250 above, on a tax incentive linked to the taking of voluntary redundancy at different ages for men and women.

[332] Case C–92/94 *Secretary of State for Social Security* v. *Graham* [1995] ECR I–2521.

[333] Cases C–377 and 384/96 *De Vriendt* v. *Rijksdienst voor Pensioenen* [1998] ECR I–2105; Case C–154/96 *Wolfs* v. *ONC* [1998] ECR I–6173.

[334] Case C–139/95 *Balestra* v. *Istituto Nazionale della Previdenza Sociale (IPNS)* [1997] ECR I–549.

SOCIAL SECURITY | 941

did not apply.[335] Finally, in *Buchner*, the ECJ ruled that there was no necessary link and therefore no need for the preservation of coherence between the early old-age pension on account of incapacity for work on the one hand, and the old-age pension on the other, so that the Article 7(1)(a) exception was inapplicable.[336]

We have seen above that Article 7(2) encourages Member States to carry out periodical examinations of any areas exempted from the application of the Directive to see whether these are still justified in the light of social changes. Once the Member State has acted to abolish discrimination from a previously exempt area, however, it cannot rely on the derogation to continue discriminatory practices in that area. In *Van Cant*, the applicant was challenging the provisions of Belgian legislation which in 1990 had abolished discriminatory pensionable ages and had fixed entitlement to a retirement pension for both men and women at age 60.[337] However, the method for calculating the amount of the pension, which had been based on the forty most favourable years for women and forty-five for men, remained unchanged so that it now favoured women. The ECJ ruled that, once discriminatory retirement ages had been abolished, Article 7(1)(a) could no longer be relied on to justify maintaining a difference in calculating the retirement pension which was linked to that difference in retirement ages.

In *Bramhill*, however, a more progressive abolition of discrimination which was the subject of an exception in Article 7(1)(d) was found to be compatible with the Directive.[338] The case involved the scope of the derogation concerning increases in benefits for a 'dependent wife' in that provision. The applicant was refused an increase, in respect of her dependent husband, on the pension she had received when she retired at 60, on the ground that she did not satisfy the conditions in the social-security legislation. The conditions, which required her to have been in receipt of certain benefits for adult dependents prior to retirement, were clearly discriminatory since they did not apply to a married man in similar circumstances, but the UK argued that the provision was covered by the derogation in Article 7(1)(d). According to Mrs Bramhill, the derogation applied to increases in benefit for a dependent *wife* only, and did not apply to an increase in pension like that in the present case, which had been made available by legislation in 1984 in respect of dependent husbands and wives alike. She argued that, since the benefit was made available for both, whereas before the amending legislation in 1984 it had been available for dependent wives only, it fell outside the scope of the exception:

> To interpret the Directive in the way contended for by Mrs Bramhill, which would mean that in the case of benefits which a Member State has excluded from the scope of the Directive pursuant to Article 7(1)(d) it could no longer rely on the derogation provided for by that provision if it adopted a measure which, like that in question in the main proceedings, has the effect of reducing the extent of unequal treatment based on sex, would therefore be incompatible with the purpose of the Directive and would be likely to jeopardize the implementation of the aforesaid principle of equal treatment.[339]

---

[335] Case C–137/94 *Richardson*, n. 325 above, paras. 18–25. See also Case C–382/98 *R. v. Secretary of State for Social Security, ex p. Taylor* [1999] ECR I–8955, on winter fuel payments.

[336] Case C–104/98 *Buchner* v. *Sozialversicherungsanstalt der Bauern* [2000] ECR I–3625. Contrast Case C–196/98 *Hepple* v. *Adjudication Officer* [2000] ECR I–3701, in which the reduced earnings allowance was sufficiently linked, in terms of the coherence of the system, to the legislation governing old-age pensions to benefit from the derogation in Art. 7(1)(a).

[337] Case C–154/92 *Van Cant* v. *Rijksdienst voor Pensioenen* [1993] ECR I–3811.

[338] Case C–420/92 *Bramhill* v. *Chief Adjudication Officer* [1994] ECR I–3191.

[339] *Ibid.*, para. 21.

The difference between *Van Cant* and *Bramhill* seems to be that, once a Member State abolishes a discriminatory provision in an area which has previously been exempted under Article 7(1), it cannot retain other associated forms of discrimination which existed only because of the now-abolished provision. However, where the State chooses not to abolish the original discrimination, but to alleviate it progressively by means of gradually improving the position of the disadvantaged sex, this cannot be said to be outside the scope of the derogation.

Article 7(1)(c) permits the exclusion from the Directive of the granting of old-age benefits by virtue of the derived entitlements of a wife. This provision was interpreted in *Van Munster*, in which it was held that the principle of equal treatment in Directive 79/7 permitted a Member State to refuse a retired worker the higher rate of pension which its legislation provided for persons with dependent spouses, where that worker's spouse was entitled in her own right to a retirement pension in another Member State.[340]

(v) *Indirect Discrimination in Social Security*

We have seen that in the context of pay and equal treatment more generally, Article 141 (and Directive 2006/54) prohibits both direct and indirect discrimination on grounds of sex. In the social-security context, Article 4(1) of Directive 79/7 similarly prohibits both forms of discrimination, and the ECJ has interpreted them in a very similar way. In *Teuling*,[341] where a Dutch system of incapacity benefits which provided for increased benefit for beneficiaries with a dependent spouse or children was challenged as being discriminatory, the ECJ ruled:

> 13. In that regard, it should be pointed out that a system of benefits in which, as in this case, supplements are provided for which are not directly based on the sex of the beneficiaries but take account of their marital status or family situation, and in respect of which it emerges that a considerably smaller proportion of women than of men are entitled to such supplements, is contrary to Article 4(1) of the Directive if that system of benefits cannot be justified by reasons which exclude discrimination on grounds of sex.
>
> 14. It appears from the documents before the Court that according to statistics provided to the Commission by the Netherlands Government a significantly greater number of married men than married women receive a supplement linked to family responsibilities. According to the plaintiff and the Commission, that results from the fact that in the Netherlands there are at present considerably more married men than married women who carry on occupational activities, and therefore considerably fewer women who have a dependent spouse.
>
> 15. In such circumstances a supplement linked to family responsibilities is contrary to Article 4(1) of the Directive if the grant thereof cannot be justified by reasons which exclude discrimination on grounds of sex.

However, the ECJ accepted that the indirect discrimination could be justified by social policy considerations related to the heavier burdens borne by those with dependents, and left to the national court to determine whether the supplements actually corresponded to the additional burden borne by those with dependent families.[342] In subsequent proceedings

---

340 Case C–165/91 *Van Munster* v. *Rijksdienst voor Pensioenen* [1994] ECR I–4661.
341 Case 30/85 *Teuling* v. *Bedrijfsvereniging voor de Chemische Industrie* [1987] ECR 2497.
342 See also Case 102/88 *Ruzius-Wilbrink* v. *Bestuur van de Bedrijfsvereniging voor Overheidsdiensten* [1989] ECR 4311, where there was indirect discrimination against part-time workers in eligibility for invalidity benefits. The Court did not accept, as a justification, the claim that it would be unjust to grant such workers benefits which would exceed the income they had previously received.

against Belgium, the ECJ widened further the discretion left to Member States in justifying indirect discrimination in unemployment allowances in favour of those with dependent households, who were predominantly men, by upholding Belgian legislation which linked the allowances in question with previous income, rather than basing it strictly on need.[343] The Court ruled that the aims of the scheme were 'part of a social policy which in the current state of Community law is a matter for the Member States which enjoy a reasonable margin of discretion as regards both the nature of the protective measures and the detailed arrangements for their implementation'.[344]

In *De Weerd/Roks* on the other hand, the Court ruled that although an indirectly discriminatory national measure, such as a previous income requirement for eligibility for incapacity benefits, could be justified on social-policy grounds, and although budgetary considerations could influence the nature or scope of a Member State's social policy, budgetary policy and the state of the public finances could not *of themselves* constitute adequate justification for such discrimination.[345] Yet in *Posthuma-Van Damme*, the ECJ confirmed that a similar income requirement laid down in a national scheme concerning insurance against incapacity for work could be justified by reference to the social-policy aim of restricting eligibility for a given benefit to persons who lost income following materialization of the risk which the benefit was intended to cover, even if the scheme was replacing a previous scheme of pure national insurance unconnected with loss of income.[346]

The readiness with which the ECJ has permitted indirect discrimination in the grant of social security benefits to be justified by reference to national social-policy aims can be seen in the cases of *Nolte* and *Megner*,[347] which concerned the exclusion of persons in minor or short-term employment from statutory social security schemes, and in the case of *Laperre*,[348] which concerned the imposition of conditions relating to age and previous employment on the grant of certain income-support benefits. Since the excluded groups in these cases consisted predominantly of women, indirect discrimination was presumptively established, but in each case the ECJ suggested that the discrimination could be justified by reference to social-policy aims. In *Nolte* and *Megner*, it ruled that the desire to respond to the social demand for minor and short-term employment and to foster its supply was a legitimate policy aim unrelated to any discrimination on grounds of sex, and in *Laperre*, the social aim of supporting the long-term unemployed who had little chance of further employment could justify indirect discrimination in access to income support.

The criticisms of indirect discrimination and objective justification which we have seen above in relation to equal pay and equal treatment in employment are applicable with perhaps even greater force in the context of social security, given that the ECJ allows an even wider 'margin of discretion' to Member States in this respect. Further, Directive 79/7 and the whole area of equal treatment in Community social security law have been the subject of a more

---

[343] Case C–229/89 *Commission v. Belgium* [1991] ECR I–2205.

[344] *Ibid.*, para. 22. See also Case C–221/91 *Molenbroek v. Bestuur van de Soziale Verzekeringsbank* [1992] ECR I–5943 for a similarly broad margin of discretion left to the State.

[345] Case C–343/92 *De Weerd (née Roks) v. Bestuur van de Bedrijfsvereniging voor de Gezondheid, Geestelijke en Maatschappelijke Belangen* [1994] ECR I–571, paras. 35–36. See also Case C–187/00 *Kutz-Bauer*, n. 107 above, although this case was decided eventually under the Equal Treatment Dir. rather than Dir. 79/7.

[346] Case C–280/94 *Posthuma Van Damme v. Bestuur van de Bedrijfsvereniging voor Detailhande* [1996] ECR I–179.

[347] Case C–317/93 *Nolte*, n. 319 above; Case C–444/93 *Megner*, n. 319 above.

[348] Case C–8/94 *Laperre v. Bestuurscommissie beroepszaken in de provincie Zuid-Holland* [1996] ECR I–273.

wide-ranging critique on account of its narrow focus and, once again, its use of a male norm and pattern of working life against which to measure standards of treatment.[349]

(b) OCCUPATIONAL SOCIAL SECURITY

Occupational social security is currently governed by Title II, Chapter 2, of the recast Equal Treatment Directive 2006/54. We have seen above that occupational social security was originally governed by Directive 86/378, based on principles similar to those governing state social security schemes under Directive 79/7. Following *Barber* and the stream of case law which followed it however, much of Directive 86/378 was effectively overridden by the ECJ, and much of what had previously been considered as occupational social security was reclassified as 'pay'. As a consequence, Directive 96/97 was adopted in order to amend the 1986 Directive in a way which would comply with the radical implications of the case law. Now, the 1986 and 1996 Directives have been repealed and replaced by the relevant provisions of Directive 2006/54.[350]

Occupational social security schemes are defined in the 2006 Directive broadly as schemes (other than those covered by Directive 79/7), whether membership is optional or compulsory, the purpose of which is to provide workers or self-employed persons in an economic sector or undertaking with benefits intended to supplement or replace those provided by statutory social security schemes. Certain schemes are excluded by Article 8, such as individual contracts for self-employed workers, insurance contracts to which the employer is not a party, and individual options for additional benefits.

Article 6 sets out the personal scope of the Directive, covering the working population (including the self-employed) in terms very similar to those of Article 2 of Directive 79/7, except that, in addition to covering those whose work is interrupted by illness, accident, or involuntary unemployment, and to retired and disabled workers or those seeking employment, it also covers interruption by maternity and it now covers persons who are claiming under those persons specified. Article 7 sets out the material scope of the Directive, and again the risks covered are almost exactly the same—sickness, invalidity, old-age including early retirement, industrial accidents and occupational diseases, and unemployment. Article 7(1)(b) also provides that any other social benefits provided for in an occupational scheme, such as family or survivor's benefits, will fall within the scope of the Directive in so far as they constitute consideration for the worker by reason of the worker's employment. Article 5 sets out the principle of equal treatment in terms virtually identical to those of Article 4 of Directive 79/7, and Article 9 sets out a range of examples of provisions which contravene the principle of equal treatment by discriminating on the basis of sex, or marital or family status.

Article 10 provides for the implementation of the obligations of equal treatment in relation to occupational pension schemes as regards self-employed workers, and the three derogations provided for in Article 11 (concerning pensionable age, survivors' pensions, and actuarial calculations in defined-contribution schemes), which specify matters in relation to which Member States may defer the application of the principle of equal treatment, now apply only in relation to self-employed workers, since as far as employed workers are concerned it is clear since the *Barber* judgment that the equal pay principle applies.

One of the novel results of repealing the 1986 and 1996 Occupational Social Security Directives, and incorporating their provisions into Directive 2006/54 is that this area is now

---

[349] Sohrab, n. 322 above, 16. See, more generally, J. Sohrab, *Sexing the Benefit* (Dartmouth, 1996).
[350] N. 31 above.

governed by the 'horizontal' provisions of the Directive, including the positive action provision in Article 3 and the extensive provisions on remedies, promotion of equal treatment, compliance, and dialogue in Title III.

6. REMEDIES

The general subject of remedies has been discussed in Chapter 9, but it is notable how many of the cases on remedies have arisen in the specific context of sex discrimination.

In *Defrenne II*, the ECJ had appeared to reject the possibility of 'levelling down' salaries in order to comply with the equal-pay principle in Article 119 (now Article 141):

> In particular, since Article 119 appears in the context of the harmonisation of working conditions while the improvement is being maintained, the objection that the terms of this article may be observed in other ways than by raising the lowest salaries may be set aside.[351]

Subsequently, in the context of social security rather than pay in *FNV*, the Court, having ruled that Article 4(1) of Directive 79/7 was directly effective from the date on which it should have been implemented, went on to elaborate the proper 'point of reference' pending such proper implementation:

> It follows that until such time as the national government adopts the necessary implementing measures, women are entitled to be treated in the same manner, and to have the same rules applied to them, as men who are in the same situation, since, where the directive has not been implemented, those rules remain the only valid point of reference.[352]

This formula has since been repeated in many other cases concerning transitional measures where there has been discrimination on grounds of sex, in various fields including pay and social security, and both where the discrimination was contained in legislative measures as well as in collective bargaining agreements.[353]

However, once the legislature or the employer responsible for the discrimination takes measures to abolish the discriminatory provisions, there is no 'levelling-up' requirement. Although this was not clear from the original *Defrenne II* ruling, the ECJ ruled in *Coloroll* that when action is taken to eliminate sex discrimination, the benefits may be abolished altogether rather than being provided for both sexes.[354]

In *Emmott*,[355] *Cotter*,[356] and *Marshall II*,[357] the ECJ stressed the importance of ensuring the effectiveness of Community sex-discrimination law, by requiring the provision of adequate national remedies. In all three cases, as we saw in Chapter 9, the Court ruled that particular national rules—both procedural and substantive—must be set aside where they have the effect

---

[351] Case 43/75 *Defrenne II*, n. 187 above, para. 15.

[352] Case 71/85 *FNV*, n. 308 above, para. 22.

[353] See e.g. Case C–377/89 *Cotter and McDermott* v. *Minister for Social Welfare* [1991] ECR I–1155, para. 18; Case 102/88 *Ruzius Wilbrink* v. *Bestuur van de Bedrijfsvereniging voor Overheidsdiensten* [1989] ECR 4311, para. 20; Case C–184/89 *Nimz*, n. 101 above; Case C–33/89 *Kowalska*, n. 86 above.

[354] Case C–200/91 *Coloroll*, n. 65 above, para. 33. See also Case C–137/94 *Richardson*, n. 325 above, para. 24. See also Case C–280/94 *Posthuma Van Damme*, n. 346 above.

[355] Case C–208/90 *Emmott* v. *Minister for Social Welfare* [1991] ECR I–4269.

[356] Case C–377/89 *Cotter*, n. 353 above.

[357] Case C–271/91 *Marshall*, n. 50 above.

of depriving an aggrieved person of an effective remedy. In *Cotter*, the rule in question was a principle of unjust enrichment which would have barred the plaintiff's remedy; in *Marshall II* it was a ceiling on damages in a statute and a prohibition on the award of interest by certain tribunals, and in *Emmott* it was a time limit within which proceedings had to be brought.

In *Coote*, the ECJ cited Article 6 of the European Convention on Human Rights while underscoring the fundamental right of access to court, and it ruled that the principle of judicial control must extend also to retaliatory measures adopted by an employer in reaction to legal proceedings brought against it under Directive 76/207, even after the employment relationship has ended.[358] Further, the requirement to do all that is necessary to give effect to Community equal-treatment law applies not just to the national courts, in accordance with cases such as *Von Colson*,[359] but also to those authorities, such as trustees, who are responsible for the scheme in question, requiring them to use all the means available to them under domestic law.[360]

We have seen in Chapter 9 too, however, that the principle in *Emmott* was limited by subsequent rulings such as *Johnson II, Texaco A/S*, and *Steenhorst-Neerings*.[361] In these cases the ECJ ruled that national legislation which provided that benefits would not be payable retroactively for more than one year before the date on which they were claimed was compatible with EC law. The Court simply concluded, without reference to earlier cases such as *Marshall II* or to the adequacy and effectiveness of the remedy, that the national provision did not discriminate between Community-based actions and domestic actions, and did not render the exercise of the right impossible. Subsequently in *Magorrian*, however, the Court ruled that a national measure which provided that the right to be admitted to membership of an occupational pension scheme (from which the applicants had previously been excluded on indirectly discriminatory grounds) should only have effect from a date no earlier than two years before the institution of proceedings was incompatible with Community law since it would deprive the applicants of an adequate remedy.[362] The Court distinguished the rules in the various cases on the basis that, whereas those in *Steenhorst-Neerings* and *Johnson II* had merely limited the period in respect of which backdated benefits could be obtained, the rule in *Magorrian* had the effect of preventing the entire record of service of the employees in question from being taken into account for the purpose of calculating the pension benefits which would be payable even after the date of the claim. Moreover in *Levez*, in a kind of compromise between the more generous reasoning in the *Emmott* ruling and the more conservative reasoning underpinning the *Steenhorst-Neerings* ruling, the ECJ ruled that a two-year limit on arrears of damages could not be applied to the applicant's case on account of the role played by her employer's deception in the delay occasioned.[363]

Following the restriction of *Emmott* in *Steenhorst-Neerings* and *Johnson II*, the scope of the principle of adequate compensation laid down in the case of *Marshall II* was later circumscribed

---

[358] Case C–185/97 *Coote*, n. 202 above.

[359] Case 14/83 *Von Colson and Kamann* v. *Land Nordrhein-Westfalen* [1984] ECR 1891, See the discussion in Ch. 6.

[360] Case C–200/91 *Coloroll*, n. 65 above, para. 28.

[361] Case C–338/91 *Steenhorst-Neerings*, n. 324 above; Case C–410/92 *Johnson* v. *Chief Adjudication Officer (No. 2)* [1994] ECR I–5483, para. 26; Cases C–114–115/95 *Texaco A/S* v. *Havn* [1997] ECR I–4263.

[362] Case C–246/96 *Magorrian*, n. 158 above; See also Case C–78/98 *Preston* v. *Wolverhampton Healthcare NHS Trust* [2000] ECR I–3201 on the justifiability of a 6-month period following the termination of employment within which a claim for membership of an occupational pension scheme must be brought. For a thorough analysis of many of these cases see C. Kilpatrick, 'Turning Remedies Around: A Sectoral Analysis of the Court of Justice', in G. de Búrca and J.H.H. Weiler (eds.), *The European Court of Justice* (Oxford University Press, 2001).

[363] Case C–326/96 *Levez* v. *Jennings Ltd.* [1998] ECR I–7835. For comment see T. Connor (1999) 24 *ELRev.* 300.

further by the ruling in *Sutton*, where the ECJ offered an explanation of why a one-year limit on the retroactive effect of a claim for social security arrears under Directive 79/7 in *Johnson II* and *Steenhorst-Neerings* would not deprive the applicants of an effective remedy, whereas a refusal of interest or an overall limit on the amount of damages which could be awarded for loss caused by discriminatory dismissal under Directive 76/207 in *Marshall II* would do so in breach of EC law.[364] On the ECJ's reasoning, an award of damages for discriminatory dismissal was concerned with compensation for harm and the restoration of equal treatment, and thus must be commensurate with the loss suffered, whereas the award of arrears of social security benefits did not constitute reparation for damage sustained, even where those benefits had been denied in a discriminatory way, so that the sum was not 'compensatory' and could more readily be limited or restricted by the State in the interest of matters such as financial balance. In *Draehmpaehl*, however, the Court made clear that the ruling in *Marshall II* did not mean that *any* ceiling on the maximum amount of a compensatory award for discrimination contrary to Directive 76/207 would be in breach of EC law.[365]

Many of these consequences of the ECJ's remedial jurisprudence are now to be found in Directive 2006/54, including the prohibition, in certain cases, of a prior ceiling on damages for sex discrimination and the strengthening of the sanctions and preventive action provisions more generally.[366] Further, we have seen that a feature shared by all of the recent EU antidiscrimination law is an enhanced emphasis on promotion of equal treatment and prevention of discrimination, as well as a renewed emphasis on compliance, remedies, and enforcement. There has been a certain broadening out from the traditional individual-rights based legal approach to remedies to include equality bodies and other collective actors such as the social partners and NGOs in the endeavour to redress gender discrimination.

7. CONCLUSIONS

i. It is evident that EU sex-equality law is a complex field whose aims are mixed and whose impact is inevitably confined, not only by the inherent limits of the formal concept of equality which has often informed Community law-making in this field, and by the primary emphasis on employment-related or market-related discrimination, but also by the limits of law's capacity to bring about change, particularly in the face of entrenched social patterns and gender roles.

ii. Assessments of the contribution of EU equal-treatment law in this respect, and assessments of the contribution of the Court of Justice in particular, are not uniform. Some perceive EU law as having been progressive and significant in assisting social change in this field, while others note its initial attempt to block positive-action measures and, more importantly, the inconsistent and even contradictory positions taken by the Court on a range of matters relating to the reconciliation of work and family life.

iii. Broader policy developments in recent years, however, show some cause for optimism. These include (1) the move towards more systematic gender mainstreaming and a thematically prioritized overall strategy, including the apparent intent of both the

---

[364] Case C–66/95 *R. v. Secretary of State for Social Security, ex p. Eunice Sutton* [1997] ECR I–2163.

[365] Case C–180/95 *Draehmpaehl*, n. 50 above. Here a maximum compensatory award of 3 months' salary could be adequate where the candidate who had been ruled ineligible for a job on grounds of sex was less well qualified than the successful candidate and so would not have obtained the job.

[366] See sect. 2(g) above.

Commission and the European Council to focus on some of the more entrenched and intractable dimensions of gender inequity; (2) the widening and maturation of the field of EU anti-discrimination law more generally, including the classification of harassment as a form of discrimination, and the more concerted emphasis on dialogue and compliance to supplement other legal remedies, including through the involvement of equality bodies, social partners, and NGOs; (3) the reduction in the grounds of 'exception' to equal treatment requirements and the strengthening and generalization of the legal bases for 'positive action' measures in the course of the recent legislative consolidation; and (4) the appearance of some female judges and Advocates General on the Court of Justice and the Court of First Instance.

8. FURTHER READING

(a) Books

Barnard, C., *EC Employment Law* (3rd edn., Oxford University Press, 2006)

Ellis, E., *EU Anti-Discrimination Law* (Oxford University Press, 2005)

Sohrab, J., *Sexing the Benefit* (Dartmouth, 1996)

(b) Articles

Ahtela, K., 'The Revised Provisions on Sex Discrimination in European Law: A Critical Assessment' (2005) 11 *ELJ* 57

Beveridge, F., 'Building against the Past: The Impact of Mainstreaming on EU Gender Law and Policy' (2007) 32 *ELRev.* 193

Caracciolo di Torella, E., and Masselot, A., 'Pregnancy, Maternity and the Organisation of Family Life: An Attempt to Classify the Case Law of the Court of Justice' (2001) 26 *ELRev.* 239

Costello, C. and Davies, G., 'The Case Law of the Court of Justice in the Field of Sex Equality Since 2000' (2006) 43 *CMLRev.* 1567

Cromack, V., 'The EC Pregnancy Directive: Principle or Pragmatism?' [1993] *JSWFL* 261

Fredman, S., 'European Community Discrimination Law: A Critique' (1992) 21 *ILJ* 119

—— 'Affirmative Action before the Court of Justice: A Critical Analysis', in J. Shaw (ed.), *Social Law and Policy in an Evolving EU* (Hart, 2000)

—— 'Changing the Norm: Positive Duties in Equal Treatment Legislation' (2005) 12 *MJ* 369

Hervey, T., 'Thirty Years of EU Sex Equality Law: Looking Backwards, Looking Forwards' (2005) 12 *MJ* 307

Koukoulis-Spiliotopoulos, S., 'The Amended Equal Treatment Directive 2002/73: An Expression of Constitutional Principles/Fundamental Rights' (2005) 12 *MJ* 327

Masselot, A., 'The State of Gender Equality Law in the European Union' (2007) 13 *ELJ* 152

McGlynn, C., and Farrelly, C., 'Equal Pay and the Protection of Women within Family Life' (1999) 24 *ELRev.* 202

Prechal, S., 'Equality of Treatment, non-Discrimination and Social Policy: Achievements in Three Themes' (2004) 41 *CMLRev.* 533

Schiek, D., 'A New Framework on Equal Treatment of Persons in EU Law' (2002) 8 *ELJ* 290

Shaw, J., 'Gender and the Court of Justice', in G. de Búrca and J.H.H. Weiler (eds.), *The European Court of Justice* (Oxford University Press, 2001)

Trybus, M., 'Sisters in Arms: EC Law and Sex Equality in the Armed Forces' (2003) 9 *ELJ* 631

Waddington, L., 'The Development of a New Generation of Sex Equality Directives' (2004) 11 *MJ* 3

COMPETITION LAW: ARTICLE 81

1. CENTRAL ISSUES

i.   Competition law has always been of central importance for the EC. This area of Community policy covers anti-competitive agreements between firms, abuse of a dominant position, and mergers.

ii. It is important to be clear at the outset about the objectives of EC competition law. These are considered in the section that follows.

iii. Article 81 is the principal vehicle for the control of anti-competitive agreements. Such agreements can be horizontal, being made between firms at the same level of the production cycle, such as agreements between cement manufacturers. Vertical agreements are those between firms at different levels of the distribution cycle, such as an agreement between a producer of stereo equipment and a retailer.

iv. The key features of Article 81 will be examined within this chapter. These include: the meaning given to the terms 'agreement' and 'concerted practice'; the relationship between Article 81(1) and 81(3); the extent to which economic analysis does and should take place within Article 81(1); and the interpretation accorded to Article 81(3), including whether non-economic factors can be taken into account.

v.   The discussion then shifts to more detailed examination of vertical agreements, a typical example being a distribution agreement between a manufacturer of a product and a retailer. There is controversy in this area about the extent to which these agreements are economically harmful, and hence disagreement about the 'correct' approach for competition policy.

vi. The enforcement regime for Articles 81 and 82 has recently been reformed, and the chapter will conclude with an outline of these reforms.

2. COMPETITION LAW: OBJECTIVES

Competition law has always played an important part in Community law. Its precise role is, however, contestable. A number of differing objectives can be pursued by competition policy, not all of which are mutually compatible.

One objective is to *enhance efficiency*, in the sense of maximizing consumer welfare and achieving the optimal allocation of resources. Traditional economic theory indicates that goods and services will be produced most efficiently where there is perfect competition or, more realistically, workable competition.[1] It is generally agreed that certain types of agreement can have a deleterious impact on market efficiency. Thus, for example, a horizontal agreement between the major producers of cement to fix selling prices will result in higher prices for cement, and also in the production of less cement, than would otherwise be produced in conditions of ordinary competition. There is more disagreement between economists concerning the effects of vertical agreements, and hence less certainty concerning how the competition rules should apply in these instances.

Efficiency is not the only goal of competition policy. A second objective may be *to protect consumers and smaller firms* from large aggregations of economic power, whether in the form of the monopolistic dominance by a single firm or through agreements whereby rival firms co-ordinate their activity so as to act as one unit.

A third objective of EC competition law is to facilitate the *creation of a single European market*, and to prevent this from being frustrated by the activities of private undertakings. Community law prohibits tariffs, quotas, and the like which can impede the attainment of this goal. The effectiveness of such Community norms would, however, be undermined if private undertakings could partition the Community market along national lines, such as where firms agree to allow each of them exclusive control of their respective national markets.

It should not, moreover, be thought that the objectives and priorities of EC competition policy have remained static across time.[2] Wesseling identifies three phases in the development of EC competition policy.

R. Wesseling, The Modernisation of EC Antitrust Law[3]

Initially, the antitrust law provisions were inserted into the Treaty in view of their role in the process of market integration. The antitrust rules were no more than the private counterpart to the rules, enshrined in Articles 28–30 EC. . . . The framers of the Treaty wanted to preclude private undertakings replacing the prohibited public obstacles to inter-state trade. The first period . . . saw the Commission enforcing the rules with constant reference to ensuring the free flow of goods, thus promoting market integration.

Subsequently, in the second period, antitrust policy was employed to establish a broader Community industrial policy. Exemptions for the antitrust rules were granted to forms of (transnational) co-operation between undertakings which the Commission considered desirable, to promote either integration (Eurocheque) or broader Community policy aims (for example employment in crisis sectors). . . .

The momentum created by the Commission's '1992 programme' provided the occasion for expanding the scope of Community antitrust policy even further . . . the control of corporate mergers and the gradual liberalisation of public economic sectors, both highly political exercises, which commenced by the end of the 1980s, symbolise the altered character of Community antitrust law enforcement.

---

[1] F. Scherer and D. Ross, *Industrial Market Structure and Economic Performance* (3rd edn., Houghton Mifflin, 1990); R. Lipsey and K. Chrystal, *Economics* (10th edn., Oxford University Press, 2003); S. Bishop and M. Walker, *The Economics of EC Competition Law: Concepts, Application and Measurement* (2nd edn., Sweet & Maxwell, 2002).

[2] I. Maher, 'Competition Law and Intellectual Property Rights: Evolving Formalism', in P. Craig and G. de Búrca (eds.), *The Evolution of EU Law* (Oxford University Press, 1999), ch. 16.

[3] (Hart, 2000), 48–49.

Although the system was originally devised for promoting market integration, antitrust policy is now also—and mainly—directed at promoting the various other objectives of the Community enshrined in Article 2. Absent a clear hierarchy between those objectives, priorities are selected on a case by case basis....

3. ARTICLE 81: THE TREATY TEXT

Article 81 (ex Article 85) is the principal weapon to control anti-competitive behaviour by cartels:

1. The following shall be prohibited as incompatible with the common market; all agreements between undertakings, decisions by associations of undertakings and concerted practices which may affect trade between Member States and which have as their object or effect the prevention, restriction or distortion of competition within the common market, and in particular those which:
   (a) directly or indirectly fix purchase or selling prices or any other trading conditions;
   (b) limit or control production, markets, technical development, or investment;
   (c) share markets or sources of supply;
   (d) apply dissimilar conditions to equivalent transactions with other trading parties, thereby placing them at a competitive disadvantage;
   (e) make the conclusion of contracts subject to acceptance by the other parties of supplementary obligations which, by their nature or according to commercial usage, have no connection with the subject of such contracts.

2. Any agreements or decisions prohibited pursuant to this Article shall be automatically void.
3. The provisions of paragraph 1 may, however, be declared inapplicable in the case of:

   — any agreement or category of agreements between undertakings;
   — any decision or category of decisions by associations of undertakings;
   — any concerted practice or category of concerted practices;

which contributes to improving the production or distribution of goods or to promoting technical or economic progress, while allowing consumers a fair share of the resulting benefit, and which does not:
   (a) impose on the undertakings concerned restrictions which are not indispensable to the attainment of these objectives;
   (b) afford such undertakings the possibility of eliminating competition in respect of a substantial part of the products in question.

4. ARTICLE 81(1): UNDERTAKINGS

Article 81(1) catches agreements, etc., which are made by undertakings, but the Treaty does not define this term. The Community Courts and the competition authorities have, not surprisingly, taken a broad view.

In *Höfner*, the ECJ held that the term 'undertaking' covers any entity engaged in an economic activity regardless of its legal status and the way in which it is financed.[4] This has been

---

[4] Case C–41/90 *Höfner and Elser* v. *Macroton GmbH* [1991] ECR I–1979, para. 21; Case C–244/94 *Fédération Française des Sociétés d'Assurance* v. *Ministère de l'Agriculture et de la Pêche* [1995] ECR I–4013; Case T–319/99 *FENIN* v. *Commission* [2003] ECR II–351, paras. 35–41, upheld in Case C–205/03 P *FENIN* v. *Commission* [2006] ECR I–6295; Case T–155/04 *SELEX Sistemi Integrati SpA* v. *Commission*, 12 Dec. 2006.

held to include: corporations, partnerships, individuals, trade associations, the liberal professions, state-owned corporations, and co-operatives.[5]

The concept of undertaking does not however cover bodies that pursue an exclusively social objective and do not engage in economic activity, such as bodies entrusted with the management of statutory health insurance and old-age insurance schemes. Whether an undertaking operating in such a field engages in any 'economic' activity so as to bring it within Article 81 can, however, be dependant on close inquiry into the way in which the undertaking operates.[6]

While state-owned corporations can qualify as undertakings when they operate in a commercial context, this may not be so when they exercise their public-law powers.[7] Organizations representing management and labour that conclude a collective agreement are not regarded as undertakings for the purposes of Article 81.[8] This is because the social objectives of such agreements, which come within the sphere of social policy protected by the Treaty, would be undermined if such agreements were subject to Article 81. Employees are, for the duration of their employment relationship, part of the undertakings that employ them, and therefore do not themselves constitute undertakings for the purposes of Article 81.[9]

In certain circumstances firms which are legally distinct may be treated as a single unit because of the close economic link between them. This may be the case with agreements made between parent and subsidiary, where it is decided that they are, in reality, to be regarded as one economic unit. The agreement will be regarded as an internal allocation of function or role within that economic unit.[10] The key issue is whether the subsidiary has any real autonomy, or whether it merely carries out the instructions of its parent.[11] Even where Article 81 is inapplicable, it may be possible to use Article 82.[12]

Changing the legal form of an undertaking will not, however, allow the new legal entity to escape liability for acts done by its predecessor, if there is a functional and economic continuity between the original undertaking and that into which it has merged.[13]

5. ARTICLE 81(1): AGREEMENTS, DECISIONS, AND CONCERTED PRACTICES

(a) AGREEMENTS

Article 81 requires the existence of an agreement, decision, or concerted practice. The rationale for this range of terms is that if the competition rules operated only when an explicit, formal

---

[5] R. Whish, *Competition Law* (5th edn., Butterworths, 2003), 80–91.

[6] See Cases 159 and 160/91 *Poucet and Pistre* v. *Assurances Générales de France* [1993] ECR I–637; Case C–244/94 *Fédération Française*, n. 4 above; Case C–67/96 *Albany International BV* v. *Stichting Bedrijfspesnioenfonds Textielindustrie* [1999] ECR I–5751; Case T–319/99 *FENIN*, n. 4 above; Case C–218/00 *Cisal di Battistello Venanzio & C. Sas* v. *INAIL* [2002] ECR I–691; Cases C–264, 306, 354, and 355/01 *AOK Bundesverband and others* v. *Ichthyol-Gesellschaft Cordes, Hermani & Co.* [2004] ECR I–2493.

[7] Whish, n. 5 above, 84–86.

[8] Case C–67/96 *Albany*, n. 6 above.

[9] Case C–22/98 *Criminal Proceedings against Becu* [1999] ECR I–5665.

[10] See, e.g., Case 22/71 *Béguelin Import* v. *GL Import-Export* [1971] ECR 949; Dec. 89/113 *Racal Group Services* [1989] OJ L43/27, [1990] 4 CMLR 627; Dec. 91/50 *NV IGMO* v. *Ijsselcentrale* [1991] OJ L28/32, [1992] 5 CMLR 154. For counter examples see Case C–266/93 *Bundeskartellamt* v. *Volkswagen AG and VAG Leasing GmbH* [1995] ECR I–3477, para. 19; Case T–145/89 *Baustahlgewebe GmbH* v. *Commission* [1995] ECR II–987.

[11] Case C–73/95 P *Viho Europe BV* v. *Commission* [1996] ECR I–5457, para. 15.

[12] *Ibid.*

[13] Cases 29 and 30/83 *Compagnie Royale Asturienne des Mines SA and Rheinzik GmbH* v. *Commission* [1984] ECR 1679; Dec. 89/515 *Welded Steel Mesh* [1989] OJ L260/1, [1991] 4 CMLR 13.

agreement was made then they would be of little practical use, since undertakings will try to achieve their anti-competitive goals in less formal ways. All legal systems that regulate anti-competitive activity therefore have provisions to catch less formal species of agreements.[14] The *Quinine Cartel* case provides a good example of this aspect of competition law.

Cases 41, 44, and 45/69 **ACF Chemiefarma NV v. Commission**
[1970] ECR 661

[Note ToA renumbering: Art. 85 is now Art. 81]

A number of firms agreed to fix prices and divide the market in quinine. They made an agreement to this effect, which affected trade with non-Member States (the export agreement). They also made a gentlemen's agreement, which extended this to sales within the common market.

THE ECJ

107. The applicant states that the gentlemen's agreement, unlike the export agreement, did not constitute an agreement within the meaning of Article 85(1) and in any event it definitively ceased to exist from the end of October 1962.

108. The conduct of the parties to the export agreement does not in the applicant's view indicate that they continued the restrictions on competition which were originally provided for in the gentlemen's agreement.

109. The opposite conclusions reached by the contested decision are therefore alleged to be vitiated because they are based on incorrect findings.

110. The gentlemen's agreement, which the applicant admits existed until the end of October 1962, had as its object the restriction of competition within the Common Market.

111. The parties to the export agreement mutually declared themselves willing to abide by the gentlemen's agreement and concede that they did so until the end of October 1962.

112. This document thus amounted to the faithful expression of the joint intention of the parties to the agreement with regard to their conduct in the Common Market.

113. Furthermore it contained a provision to the effect that infringement of the gentlemen's agreement would ipso facto constitute an infringement of the export agreement.

114. In those circumstances account must be taken of this connection in assessing the effects of the gentlemen's agreement with regard to the categories of acts prohibited by Article 85(1).

115. The defendant bases its view that the gentlemen's agreement was continued until February 1965 on documents and declarations emanating from the parties to the agreement the tenor of which is indistinct and indeed contradictory so that it is impossible to conclude whether those undertakings intended to terminate the gentlemen's agreement at their meeting on 29 October 1962.

116. The conduct of the undertakings in the Common Market after 29 October 1962 must therefore be considered in relation to the following four points: sharing out of domestic markets, fixing of common prices, determination of sales quotas and prohibition against manufacturing synthetic quinidine.

---

[14] See, e.g., in the USA, Sherman Act 1890, s. 1.

117. The gentlemen's agreement guaranteed protection of each domestic market for the producers in the various Member States.

118. After October 1962 when significant supplies were delivered on one of those markets by producers who were not nationals, as for example in the case of sales of quinine and quinidine in France, there was a substantial alignment of prices conforming to French domestic prices which were higher than the export prices to third countries.

119. It does not appear that there were alterations in the insignificant volume of trade between the other Member States referred to by the clause relating to domestic protection in spite of considerable differences in the prices prevailing in each of those States.

120. The divergences between the domestic legislation of those States cannot by itself explain those differences in price or the substantial absence of trade.

121. Obstacles which might arise in the trade in quinine and quinidine from differences between national legislation governing pharmaceutical products under trade-mark cannot relevantly be invoked to explain those facts.

122. The correspondence exchanged in October and November 1963 between the parties to the export agreement with regard to the protection of domestic markets merely confirmed the intention of those undertakings to allow this state of affairs to remain unchanged.

123. This intention was subsequently confirmed by Nedchem during the meeting of the undertakings concerned in Brussels on 14 March 1964.

124. From those circumstances it is clear that with regard to the restriction on competition arising from the protection of the producers' domestic markets the producers continued after the meeting on 29 October 1962 to abide by the gentlemen's agreement of 1960 and confirmed their common intention to do so.

The *Quinine Cartel* case serves as a good example of the ECJ's approach. Informal agreements can be caught under Article 81, and the mere fact that the parties claim to have terminated them will not be taken to be conclusive. The Court will examine the facts with care, in order to determine whether it was economically plausible that the pricing behaviour of the parties could have been achieved in the absence of collusion.

The Commission, CFI, and ECJ have continued to take an expansive view of the meaning of 'agreement'. Thus, in *Polypropylene*[15] the Commission held that there was a single agreement between firms in the petrochemical industry which had continued over many years. This was so even though the agreement was oral, even though there were no sanctions for breach, and even though it was not legally binding. The finding of a single overall agreement facilitated a finding of guilt against the fifteen firms involved, notwithstanding the fact that not all the firms had taken part in all aspects of the cartel. An agreement existed if the parties reached a consensus on a plan which limited, or was likely to limit, their commercial freedom by determining the lines of their mutual action or abstention from action in the market. The CFI upheld the Commission in this respect,[16] holding that the firms' pattern of conduct was in pursuit of a single economic aim, the distortion of the market in question. It would therefore be artificial to split this continuous conduct into a number of separate infringements.

---

[15] Dec. 86/398 [1986] OJ L230/1, [1988] 4 CMLR 347. See also Dec. 89/190 *PVC* [1989] OJ L74/1, [1990] 4 CMLR 345, reversed on other grounds in Case C–137/92 P *Commission v. BASF AG* [1994] ECR I–2555; *LdPE* [1989] OJ L74/21, [1990] 4 CMLR 382; *Italian Flat Glass* [1989] OJ L33/44, [1990] 4 CMLR 535.

[16] Case T–7/89 *SA Hercules Chemicals NV v. Commission* [1991] ECR II–1711, paras. 262–264, upheld on appeal: Case C–51/92 P *Hercules Chemicals NV v. Commission* [1999] ECR I–4235; Case T–305/94 *NV Limburgse Vinyl Maatschappij v. Commission* [1999] ECR II–93, para. 773.

The CFI has moreover held that for there to be an agreement within Article 81 it was sufficient that the undertakings in question should have expressed their joint intention to conduct themselves on the market in a specific way. Such was the case where there were common intentions between undertakings to achieve price and sales-volume targets.[17] It sufficed for the Commission to show that an undertaking participated in meetings at which an anti-competitive agreement was concluded without opposing it.[18] If an undertaking participated[19] with others in the making of an agreement it was not open to that undertaking to argue that, because of its limited size, it could not have had a restrictive effect on competition.[20]

An agreement does, however, require the concurrence of will between at least two parties, as distinct from unilateral measures, although the precise form in which this concurrence is manifest is not important, provided that it constitutes the faithful expression of the parties' intentions.[21] Unilateral measures do not therefore suffice, but an agreement can be deduced from conduct. However for an agreement to be based on tacit acceptance it is necessary that the manifestation of the wish of one contracting party to achieve an anti-competitive goal constitutes an invitation to the other party, whether express or implied, to fulfill that goal jointly.[22]

The other way in which the Commission and CFI have tackled the problems flowing from complex cartels that extend over many years, with multiple participants, is to frame the claim in terms of 'agreement and/or concerted practice'. This strategy was upheld in *Limburgse Vinyl*.[23] The CFI stated that where there were complex infringements over many years, involving many parties, the Commission could not be expected to classify the infringements precisely for each undertaking at any given moment. The dual classification designated a complex whole, where some factual elements were relevant to an agreement, others to a concerted practice. This classification did not mean that the Commission had to prove that there was an agreement and a concerted practice throughout the whole period of the cartel.

The ECJ confirmed the preceding approach in *ANIC*.[24] This is clearly correct. Any other interpretation would have allowed parties to such agreements to escape liability through the creation of impossible evidential barriers.[25]

---

[17] Case T–9/89 *Hüls AG* v. *Commission* [1992] ECR II–499; Case T–11/89 *Shell International Chemical Company Ltd.* v. *Commission* [1992] ECR II–757; Case T–56/02 *Bayerische Hypo- und Vereinsbank AG* v. *Commission* [2004] ECR II–3495.

[18] Case C–199/92 P *Hüls* v. *Commission* [1999] ECR I–4287, para. 155; Cases C–204, 205, 211, 213, 217, and 219/00 P *Aalborg Portland AS* v. *Commission* [2004] ECR I–123, paras. 81–86; Case C–113/04 P *Technische Unie BV* v. *Commission* [2006] ECR I–8831, para. 114.

[19] The participation need not be 'active'. It is sufficient if an undertaking attends the relevant meetings and does not publicly distance itself from what occurred, thereby giving the impression that it subscribes to the results of the meeting: Case T–142/89 *Usines Gustave Boël*, n. 20 below.

[20] Case T–143/89 *Ferriere Nord SpA* v. *Commission* [1995] ECR II–917; Case T–142/89 *Usines Gustave Boël SA* v. *Commission* [1995] ECR II–867.

[21] Case T–41/96 *Bayer AG* v. *Commission* [2000] ECR II–3383; Case C–338/00 P *Volkswagen AG* v. *Commission* [2003] ECR I–9189, paras. 63–65; Cases T–49–51/02 *Brasserie Nationale SA and others* v. *Commission* [2005] ECR II–3033, para. 119; Case C–74/04 P *Commission* v. *Volkswagen AG* [2006] ECR I–6585, paras. 34–39; O. Black, 'What is an Agreement' [2003] *ECLR* 504.

[22] Cases C–2 and 3/01 P *Bundersverband der Arzneimittel-Importeure eV and Commission* v. *Bayer AG* [2004] ECR I–23, paras. 100–102.

[23] Case T–305/94 *NV Limburgse Vinyl*, n. 16 above, paras. 695–698; *Interbrew and Alken-Maes* [2003] OJ L200/1, paras. 222–227.

[24] Case C–49/92 P *Commission* v. *ANIC Partecipazioni SpA* [1999] ECR I–4125; Cases T–202, 204, and 207/98 *Tate & Lyle plc, British Sugar plc and Napier Brown & Co. Ltd.* v. *Commission* [2001] ECR II–2035.

[25] See more generally the approach taken to the massive cement cartel in Cases T–25 etc./95 *Cimenteries CBR SA and others* v. *Commission* [2000] ECR II–491.

(b) CONCERTED PRACTICE

Even if there is no agreement, undertakings will be caught by Article 81 if there is a concerted practice. Two principal factors have to be taken into account when construing this term.

On the one hand, firms can be very devious. They may well have colluded, but they may have been astute enough to destroy all paper evidence. They may never have committed anything to paper at all, relying instead on understandings and verbal exchanges. The collusion may be real nonetheless, and the construction of a term such as concerted practice must be flexible enough to capture this 'fact' of business life.

On the other hand, if the term is interpreted too broadly it may catch parallel pricing that is a rational, natural response of firms in that market. In normal competitive markets, it is unlikely that firms will price at the same level without some species of collusion, because of differences in cost structures and the like. This may be different in oligopolistic markets, which have the following characteristics: relatively few sellers, high barriers to entry, little product differentiation and price transparency, such that price changes are easily detectable by competitors. It has been argued that firms in such markets will naturally price at the same level, not because of any collusion, but because each firm independently recognizes its mutual interdependence. If any firm attempted to increase its market share by cutting prices, this would lead to a similar response from the others. There would be a downward spiral of prices, but no actual increase in market share for any of the firms involved. No firm could unilaterally increase price, because its customers would switch their trade to a competitor.[26]

The relevance of this theory for Article 81 is readily apparent. If price uniformity really is the result of rational action in an oligopoly, and there is no actual collusion, then it is not sensible or fair to penalize such parties through fines for colluding. The problem is no longer behavioural, in the sense that the parties are engaging in behaviour different from that which would exist in normal circumstances in that type of market. The problem is structural, in the sense that this type of market will naturally generate this type of response. This theory has, however, been criticized.

R. Whish, Competition Law[27]

The theory of oligopolistic interdependence has attracted criticism. Four particular problems have been pointed out. The first is that the theory overstates the interdependence of oligopolists. Even in a symmetrical three-firm oligopoly one firm might be able to steal a march on its rivals by cutting its price if, for example, there would be a delay before the others discovered what it had done: in the meantime the price-cutter may make sufficient profit to offset the cost of any subsequent price-war. . . .

A second problem is that the theory of oligopoly presents too simplistic a picture of industrial market structures. In a symmetrical oligopoly where producers produce identical goods at the same costs interdependence may be strong, but in reality market conditions are usually more complex. The oligopolists themselves will almost inevitably have different cost levels;

---

[26] Moreover, the uniformity of prices which is said to be expected in an oligopoly will, on this theory, arise even if the respective firms have differing cost structures, because the nature of the demand curve facing the industry assumes a peculiar 'kinked' form: G. Stigler, 'The Kinked Oligopoly Demand Curve' (1947) 55 *J Pol. Econ.* 431.

[27] N. 5 above, 510–511.

they may be producing differentiated goods and will usually command at least some consumer loyalty; and their market shares will not be equal. . . . Many other factors affect the competitive environment in which oligopolists operate. The concentration of the market on the buying side is also important: the more concentrated it is, the less the oligopolists might compete with one another since it will be relatively easy to detect attempts to attract the custom of particular customers. The transparency of price information is significant: the easier it is to conceal the price of goods from competitors, the less will be the interdependence or mutual awareness of the oligopolists. . . .

A third problem with the theory of interdependence is that it fails to explain why in some oligopolistic markets competition is intense. Firms quite clearly do compete with one another in some oligopolies. Such competition may take various forms. Open price competition may be limited, although price wars do break out periodically in some oligopolistic markets. . . . Where open price competition is restricted, this does not mean that secret price cutting does not occur. Non-price competition may be particularly strong in oligopolistic markets. This may manifest itself in various ways: offering better quality products and after sales service; striving for a lead in technical innovation and research and development . . .; and by making large investments in advertising to improve brand image. . . .

A fourth objection to the theory of oligopolistic interdependence is that it does not explain satisfactorily its central proposition, which is that oligopolists can earn supra-competitive profits without actually colluding. The interdependence theory says that they cannot increase price unilaterally because they will lose custom to their rivals, and yet to earn supra-competitive profits, prices must have been increased from time to time: how could this have been achieved without collusion? A possible answer to this is that a pattern of price leadership develops whereby one firm raises its price and this acts as a signal for the others to follow suit. Prices therefore remain parallel without conspiracy amongst the oligopolists, although this is not particularly convincing. . . .

Having analysed the economic problems with the term concerted practice we should now consider the leading ECJ decision.

Case 48/69 ICI v. Commission
[1972] ECR 619

[Note ToA renumbering: Art. 85 is now Art. 81]

The Court considered allegations that there had been concerted practices in the dyestuffs industry. The firms argued that any identity of price was the result of the oligopolistic nature of the market. The extract begins with the Court providing a definition of concerted practice.

THE ECJ

64. Article 85 draws a distinction between the concept of 'concerted practices' and that of 'agreements between undertakings' or of 'decisions by associations of undertakings'; the object is to bring within the prohibition of that Article a form of coordination between undertakings which, without having reached the stage where an agreement properly so-called has been concluded, knowingly substitutes practical cooperation between them for the risks of competition.

65. By its very nature, then, a concerted practice does not have all the elements of a contract but may inter alia arise out of coordination which becomes apparent from the behaviour of the participants.

66. Although parallel behaviour may not by itself be identified with a concerted practice, it may however amount to strong evidence of such practice if it leads to conditions of competition which do not correspond to the normal conditions of the market, having regard to the nature of the products, the size and number of the undertakings and the volume of the said market.

67. This is especially the case if the parallel conduct is such as to enable those concerned to attempt to stabilize prices at a level different from that to which competition would have led, and to consolidate established positions to the detriment of effective freedom of movement of the products in the Common Market and of the freedom of consumers to choose their suppliers.

68. Therefore the question whether there was concerted action in this case can only be correctly determined if the evidence upon which the contested decision is based is considered, not in isolation, but as a whole, account being taken of the specific features of the market in the products in question.

[*The Court found that 80 per cent of the dyestuffs market was supplied by ten producers; that these firms possessed differing cost structures; that there were a large number of dyes produced by each firm; that while standard dyes could be replaced by other products relatively easily, this was not the case with specialist dyes; that the market for specialist dyes tended to be oligopolistic; that the Community market in dyestuffs consisted of five separate national markets which had different price levels; and that this division along national lines was in part due to the need to supply local assistance to users of the product, and also to ensure immediate delivery of quantities which were often small. The Court then considered price increases which occurred in 1964, 1965, and 1967. It found that the increases were factually connected, and then continued as follows:*]

88. In 1964 all the undertakings in question announced their increases and immediately put them into effect, the initiative coming from Ciba-Italy which, on 7 January 1964, following instructions from Ciba-Switzerland, announced and immediately introduced an increase of 15 per cent. This initiative was followed by the other producers on the Italian market within two or three days.

89. On 9 January ICI Holland took the initiative in introducing the same increase in the Netherlands, whilst on the same day Bayer took the same initiative on the Belgo-Luxembourg market.

. . .

91. As regards the increase of 1965 certain undertakings announced in advance price increases amounting, for the German market, to an increase of 15 per cent for products whose prices had already been similarly increased on the other markets, and to 10 per cent for products whose prices had not yet been increased. These announcements were spread over the period between 14 October and 28 December 1964.

92. The first announcement was made by BASF, on 14 October 1964, followed by an announcement by Bayer on 30 October and by Casella on 5 November.

93. These increases were simultaneously applied on 1 January 1965 on all the markets except for the French market because of the price freeze in that State, and the Italian market where, as a result of the refusal by the principal Italian producer, ACNA, to increase its prices on the said market, the other producers also decided not to increase theirs.

. . .

95. Otherwise the increase was general, was simultaneously introduced by all the producers mentioned in the contested decision, and was applied without any differences concerning the range of products.

[*The Court then considered a similar pattern in relation to the 1967 price increases. It continued as follows:*]

99. Viewed as a whole, the three consecutive increases reveal progressive cooperation between the undertakings concerned.

100. In fact, after the experience of 1964, when the announcement of the increases and their application coincided, although with minor differences as regards the range of products affected, the increases of 1965 and 1967 indicate a different mode of operation. Here, the undertakings taking the initiative, BASF and Geigy respectively, announced their intentions of making an increase some time in advance, which allowed the undertakings to observe each other's reactions on the different markets, and to adapt themselves accordingly.

101. By means of these advance announcements the various undertakings eliminated all uncertainty between them as to their future conduct and, in doing so, also eliminated a large part of the risk usually inherent in any independent change of conduct on one or several markets.

102. This was all the more the case since these announcements, which led to the fixing of general and equal increases in prices for the markets in dyestuffs, rendered the market transparent as regard the percentage rates of increase.

. . .

104. The fact that this conduct was not spontaneous is corroborated by an examination of other aspects of the market.

105. In fact, from the number of producers concerned it is not possible to say that the European market in dyestuffs is, in the strict sense, an oligopoly in which price competition could no longer play a substantial role.

106. These producers are sufficiently powerful and numerous to create a considerable risk that in times of rising prices some of them might not follow the general movement but might instead try to increase their share of the market by behaving in an individual way.

107. Furthermore, the dividing-up of the Common Market into five national markets with different price levels and structures makes it improbable that a spontaneous and equal price increase would occur on all the national markets.

. . .

109. Therefore, although parallel conduct in respect of prices may well have been an attractive and risk-free objective for the undertakings concerned, it is hardly conceivable that the same action could be taken spontaneously at the same time, on the same national markets and for the same range of products.

. . .

111. As regards the increases of 1965 and 1967 concertation took place openly, since all the announcements of the intention to increase prices with effect from a certain date and for a certain range of products made it possible for producers to decide on their conduct regarding the special cases of France and Italy.

112. In proceeding in this way, the undertakings mutually eliminated in advance any uncertainties concerning their reciprocal behaviour on the different markets and thereby also eliminated a large part of the risk inherent in any independent change of conduct on those markets.

113. The general and uniform increase on those different markets can only be explained by a common intention on the part of those undertakings, first, to adjust the level of prices and the situation resulting from competition in the form of discounts, and secondly, to avoid the risk, which is inherent in any price increase, of changing the conditions of competition.

The ECJ's approach emerges clearly in the above extract.[28] It is, moreover, clear from the *Sugar Cartel* case that there can be a concerted practice even though there is no actual 'plan'

---

[28] See also Case 172/80 *Gerhard Züchner* v. *Bayerische Vereinsbank AG* [1981] ECR 2021.

operative between the parties. The key idea was that each undertaking should operate independently on the market:[29]

> Although it is correct to say that this requirement of independence does not deprive economic operators of the right to adapt themselves intelligently to the existing and anticipated conduct of their competitors, it does however strictly preclude any direct or indirect contact between such operators, the object or effect whereof is either to influence the conduct on the market of an actual or potential competitor or to disclose to such a competitor the course of conduct which they themselves have decided to adopt or contemplate adopting on the market.

Four points should be made about the concept of concerted practice and its application. First, the burden of proving an infringement of Article 81 rests with the Commission, and the mere existence of parallel conduct will not, in itself, be sufficient to prove the existence of a concerted practice. Thus, if the parties can show that, although there is parallel behaviour, there are explanations for what has taken place other than the existence of concertation then they may be exonerated.[30] The Court will investigate whether there really is 'room' for the competition rules to operate in a particular context.[31]

Secondly, the Court will not readily accept that uniformity of price is the result of oligopolistic market structure. If the facts do not indicate that the market structure will naturally lead to price uniformity, and if there are other factors indicative of collusion, then the onus may effectively shift to the firms to suggest how the identity of price came about without some concertation.

Thirdly, there can, however, be differences of opinion on which side of the line a case falls. In *Wood Pulp*[32] the Commission considered allegations of concerted practices by a large number of wood pulp producers. In reaching the conclusion that there was a concerted practice, the Commission refused to accept that the market was oligopolistic, because of the large number of firms. The fact that they charged similar prices, and altered them uniformly and simultaneously, was itself *prima facie* evidence that they were acting in concert. A significant part of the Commission's findings was annulled by the ECJ.[33] It held that parallel conduct cannot be regarded as proof of concertation unless concertation constituted the only plausible explanation for the conduct. Article 81 did not deprive firms of the ability to adapt their behaviour intelligently to that of their competitors.[34] It held, moreover, that the parallelism of the prices and the price trends could satisfactorily be explained by the oligopolistic tendencies of the market and the specific circumstances prevailing during the relevant period.[35] The ECJ

---

[29] Cases 40–48, 50, 54–56, 111, 113, and 114/73 *Cooperatiëve Vereniging 'Suiker Unie' UA v. Commission* [1975] ECR 1663, 1942; Cases T–202, 204, and 207/98 *Tate & Lyle plc*, n. 24 above; Dec. 97/84, *Commission v. P & O European Ferries Ltd.* [1997] OJ L26/23, [1997] 4 CMLR 798.

[30] Cases 29 and 30/83 *Compagnie Royale Asturienne*, n. 13 above.

[31] Cases 40–48 etc./73 '*Suiker Unie*', n. 29 above, 1916–1924, the ECJ found that the degree of state regulation of the Italian sugar market left no appreciable room in which Art. 81 could operate; in Case C–219/95 P *Ferriere Nord SpA v. Commission* [1997] ECR I–4411, and Cases T–202, 204, and 207/98 *Tate & Lyle plc*, n. 24 above, an analogous argument was rejected.

[32] Dec. 85/202 [1985] OJ L85/1, [1985] 3 CMLR 474.

[33] Cases 89, 104, 114, 116–117, and 125–129/85 *A. Ahlström Oy v. Commission* [1993] ECR I–1307. See also Case T–36/91 *Imperial Chemical Industries plc v. Commission* [1995] ECR II–1847.

[34] *Ibid.*, para. 71.

[35] *Ibid.*, paras. 126–127. It may have been no coincidence that the *juge rapporteur* in *Wood Pulp* was Joliet who had, a number of years earlier, expressed misgivings about the possible impact of the *Dyestuffs* case: R. Joliet, 'La Notion de Pratique Concertée et l'Arrêt dans une Perspective Comparative' [1974] *CDE* 251.

insisted that rigorous economic analysis is required to determine whether there is another plausible explanation for the parties' conduct. In the absence of overt communication between the parties, the Commission will have to defend its assumptions against experts who can suggest an innocent explanation for the challenged behaviour.[36]

The *Polypropylene* cases provide a good contrast to *Wood Pulp*. In a series of decisions the CFI cited the definition of concerted practice in the *Sugar Cartel* case. It held that participation in meetings concerning the fixing of price and sales-volume targets during which information was exchanged between competitors about the prices they intended to charge, their profitability thresholds, the sales volumes they judged to be necessary, or their sales figures constituted a concerted practice. This was because the participant undertakings could not fail to take account of the information thus disclosed in determining their conduct on the market.[37] The CFI took a similarly strident view in relation to cases concerned with *Welded Steel Mesh*, holding that the exchange of information between competing undertakings that might be used to establish a cartel itself constituted a concerted practice.[38] This was particularly so in relation to exchange of information by parties to a cartel concerning their respective deliveries, since such information could be used to monitor the effective operation of the cartel.[39]

Fourthly, there is the issue of whether a concerted practice must have been put into effect. This issue was addressed in *Hüls*.

Case C–199/92 P **Hüls AG v. Commission**
[1999] ECR I–4287

[Note ToA renumbering: Art. 85 is now Art. 81]

This was one of the appeals from the CFI to the ECJ resulting from the *Polypropylene* decision of the Commission. The Commission had found that there was a concerted practice of fixing prices on this market. Hüls argued that there was a lack of proof of conduct on the market corresponding to a concerted practice. The ECJ set out the definition of concerted practice, and then continued as follows.

THE ECJ

161. It follows, first, that the concept of a concerted practice . . . implies, besides undertakings' concerting with each other, subsequent conduct on the market, and a relationship of cause and effect between the two.

162. However, subject to proof to the contrary, which the economic operators concerned must adduce, the presumption must be that the undertakings taking part in the concerted action and remaining active on the market take account of the information exchanged with their competitors for the purposes of determining their conduct on that market. This is all the

---

[36] G. van Gerven and E. N. Varona, 'The *Wood Pulp* Case and the Future of Concerted Practices' (1994) 31 *CMLRev.* 575; F. Alese, 'The Economic Theory of Non-Collusive Oligopoly and the Concept of Concerted Practice under Article 81' [1999] *ECLR* 379.

[37] Case T–11/89 *Shell International*, n. 17 above. See also Cases T–202, 204, and 207/98 *Tate & Lyle plc*, n. 24 above.

[38] Case T–142/89 *Boël*, n. 20 above.

[39] Case T–148/89 *Tréfilunion SA* v. *Commission* [1995] ECR II–1063.

more true where the undertakings concert together on a regular basis over a long period, as was the case here....

163. Secondly, contrary to Hüls's argument, a concerted practice ... is caught by Article 81(1) EC, even in the absence of anti-competitive effects on the market.

164. ... it follows from the actual text of that provision that ... concerted practices are prohibited regardless of their effect, when they have an anti-competitive object.

165. ... although the very concept of a concerted practice presupposes conduct by the participating undertakings on the market, it does not necessarily mean that that conduct should produce the specific effect of restricting, preventing or distorting competition.

. . .

167. Consequently, contrary to Hüls's argument, the Court of First Instance was not in breach of the rules applying to the burden of proof when it considered that, since the Commission had established to the requisite legal standard that Hüls had taken part in polypropylene producers' concerting together for the purpose of restricting competition, it did not have to adduce evidence that their concerting together had manifested itself in conduct on the market or that it had effects restrictive of competition; on the contrary, it was for Hüls to prove that that did not have any influence whatsoever on its own conduct on the market.

6. ARTICLE 81(1): THE OBJECT OR EFFECT OF PREVENTING, RESTRICTING, OR DISTORTING COMPETITION

Article 81(1) requires that the agreement, decision, or concerted practice has the object or effect of preventing, restricting, or distorting competition in the Common Market. The interpretation of this phrase has generated a significant body of literature, with rival views on what the Court is, and what it should be, doing under this Article.

(a) THE NATURE OF THE PROBLEM

Article 81(1) captures all agreements, concerted practices, etc., which have as their object or effect the prevention, etc., of competition. However all contracts concerning trade impose restraints in some manner, 'to bind, to restrain is of their very essence',[40] yet it would be absurd if every contract were caught by competition law.

Moreover an agreement may have features that both enhance and restrict competition. Imagine that a supplier wishes to break into a new market, and decides to use Brown as its distributor for a particular area. Brown may be willing to risk marketing the new product only if given certain incentives and protection, such as that the supplier will not supply any other firm in the same area. This is a restriction of competition, but the agreement may enhance competition, since there is a new product on the market.

The appropriate response to these issues is contentious. An aspect of this debate has been the extent to which the EC should follow the approach in the United States, and distinguish between a rule of reason and *per se* rules. A glance at the US experience is, therefore, necessary in order to understand the diversity of opinion in the EC.

---

[40] *Chicago Board of Trade* v. *US*, 246 US 231 (1918).

(b) EXPERIENCE IN THE UNITED STATES

The dilemmas identified above are evident in section 1 of the Sherman Act, which states that every contract, combination, or conspiracy in restraint of trade is illegal. The courts responded by developing the rule of reason. In *Standard Oil* v. *US* White CJ stated that a standard of reason had to be applied in order to determine whether a restraint was within the Sherman Act, and that only undue or unreasonable restraints should be condemned.[41]

The precise meaning of this idea was contested, and still is today.[42] The concept appears, however, to demand a broad inquiry into whether the restrictions increase or decrease competition in the market. The pro- and anti-competitive effects of the agreement are weighed to determine whether it suppresses or promotes competition.[43]

There is, however, continuing disagreement on what the effects of particular types of agreement actually are, and therefore whether they should be prohibited or not. There has also been disagreement on the range of considerations that should be taken into account within this analysis. For some this should be restricted to economic factors. Others advocate a more wide-ranging inquiry, or are willing to ascribe economic value to social factors.[44]

Per se rules developed from a rule-of-reason analysis. The type of inquiry demanded by the rule of reason may be time-consuming and costly. With the passage of time the courts came to identify certain types of agreement that were conclusively presumed to be 'without redeeming virtue' and which had a 'pernicious effect on competition'. The courts condemned these without the need for an elaborate inquiry into whether they had an impact on the market. The cases held to fall within this category were those which were most obviously anti-competitive, such as horizontal price-fixing[45] and market division.[46] In these instances proof of the agreement was sufficient to condemn it, obviating the need for more detailed market investigation.[47]

(c) THE ACADEMIC DEBATE IN THE EC

There has been an interesting debate about whether we should adopt a rule of reason in EC law. This debate was affected by Article 81(3), whereby agreements that are held to restrict competition can be exempted following an economic analysis. No such provision exists in the United States, thereby rendering the need for some species of rule-of-reason analysis more necessary in that country. The debate was also affected by the fact that until recently national courts could apply Article 81(1), but they could not apply Article 81(3).

---

[41] 221 US 1 (1911).

[42] R. Bork, 'The Rule of Reason and the Per Se Concept: Price Fixing and Market Division' (1965) 74 *Yale LJ* 775; T. Piraino, 'Reconciling the Per Se Rule and the Rule of Reason Approaches to Antitrust Analysis' (1991) 45 *So. Cal. L. Rev.* 689 and 'Making Sense of the Rule of Reason: A New Standard for Section 1 of the Sherman Act' (1994) 48 *Vand. L. Rev.* 1770; O. Black, 'Per Se Rules and Rules of Reason: What are They?' [1997] *ECLR* 145; T. Calvani, 'Some Thoughts on the Rule of Reason' [2001] *ECLR* 201.

[43] *National Society of Professional Engineers* v. *US*, 435 US 679, 691–692 (1978).

[44] Compare R. Bork, *The Antitrust Paradox: A Policy at War with Itself* (Basic Books, 1978) with E. Fox, 'The Modernization of Antitrust: A New Equilibrium' (1981) 66 *Cornell L. Rev.* 1140 and 'The Politics of Law and Economics' (1986) 61 *NYU L Rev.* 554.

[45] *US* v. *Trenton Potteries Co.*, 273 US 392 (1927).

[46] *US* v. *Topco Associates*, 405 US 596 (1972).

[47] Because classification as a price-fixing agreement can have these serious consequences the courts will, on occasion, strive to avoid characterizing a case in this way if they believe that it has redeeming features, notwithstanding an element of price control: *National Collegiate Athletic Assn.* v. *Board of Regents of the University of Oklahoma*, 468 US 85 (1984); *Broadcast Music Inc.* v. *Columbia Broadcasting Systems Inc.*, 441 US 1 (1979).

Korah was an early advocate of adopting a rule of reason analysis in EU law.[48] References to Article 85 should now be read as to Article 81.

V. Korah, The Rise and Fall of Provisional Validity— The Need for a Rule of Reason in EEC Antitrust[49]

The Community Court and Commission have not developed the same theory of per se offences so brilliantly developed in the early cases under the Sherman Act. Naked restraints on pricing, market sharing, and some kinds of collective boycott ... are likely to be condemned with fairly short reasoning if they are found capable of restricting trade between Member States, but more market analysis is required in the case of ancillary restraints. In *Consten & Grundig*, the Court seems to have developed a per se rule against absolute territorial protection conferred by export bans..., and this has been consistently applied by the Commission, despite mounting criticism. For all other restraints, however, the Court seems to be applying a rule of reason, requiring an analysis of the actual or intended effects in the light of market conditions.

The Commission, however, habitually analyzes agreements under Article 85(1) in the formalistic way developed by the German case law ... and condemns any restriction on the conduct of the parties, or third parties, provided the restriction has, or may be expected to have, appreciable effects on the market. Only under Article 85(3) does the Commission usually try to balance any pro-and anti-competitive effects.

If national courts adopt the Commission's practice, it is feared that many desirable contracts which restrict only competition that could not take place without such an agreement, or which restrict competition less than they increase it, may not be made. The Commission grants few exemptions.... Important agreements are unlikely to be exempted unless certain clauses are altered. These alterations may help one party more than the other, and the whole contract may have to be renegotiated after the parties have been implementing it, when their relative bargaining power may have been altered as a result of the collaboration. This is a considerable disincentive to notification.

...

There is fear that European firms that may have to compete in world markets may fall behind technologically or have to merge completely, so as to reduce the risk of collaboration. Market analyses are difficult, especially for lawyers and bureaucrats. But if such analyses are not made, agreements that may have overall desirable consequences should not be controlled. This means that national courts will have to be strong in resisting claims that agreements are anti-competitive just because some competitor is harmed.

Whish and Sufrin presented the contrasting view. They argued that the ECJ's case law did not, properly understood, signify acceptance of a rule of reason in EC law; or that, at the least, differing labels expressed the essence of what the ECJ was doing better than the simple adoption

---

[48] See also R. Joliet, *The Rule of Reason in Antitrust Law: American, German and Common Market Laws in Comparative Perspective* (Faculté de Droit, Liège, 1967); M. Schecter, 'The Rule of Reason in European Competition Law' [1982] 2 *LIEI* 1; I. Forrester and C. Norall, 'The Laïcization of Community Law: Self-Help and the Rule of Reason: How Competition Law is and Could be Applied' (1984) 21 *CMLRev.* 11; V Korah, 'EEC Competition Policy—Legal Form or Economic Efficiency' (1986) 39 *CLP* 85.

[49] (1981) 3 *NW J. Int. L and Bus.* 320, 354–355.

of labels from the United States. This will be considered below.[50] They also contended that there were very real differences between the antitrust laws of the United States and the EC, which rendered any transfer of terminology of limited utility.[51]

R. Whish and B. Sufrin, Article 85 and the Rule of Reason[52]

The call for the adoption of a US-style rule of reason should be resisted and, indeed, there is much to be said for dropping this term (and the terms 'ancillary restraint' and 'per se illegality') from EEC antitrust law altogether, on the basis that they do more to confuse than to clarify. EEC competition law requires its own vocabulary, carefully honed to express its own particular tensions.

One ground for jettisoning the term 'rule of reason' from the vocabulary of EEC competition law is that it is now used in other areas of the law, for example, in the provisions on free movement of goods. . . .

A different reason for abandoning this terminology in EEC competition law is that it invites misleading comparison with antitrust law analysis in the United States. We have suggested above that the context of US antitrust law is so dissimilar from that of the EEC that comparative analysis should be undertaken with great caution.

Quite apart from the issue of terminology, the writers have other doubts about the wisdom of analysing Article 85(1) in a way that relies on an approach similar to that of the Sherman Act. It would not help the cause of certainty.

. . .

The matter of certainty is, of course, important. It is in no one's interest to retard beneficial collaboration between firms striving to compete in a competitive international market. However, the best answer to this problem is for the Commission to continue to improve its procedures, to publish block exemptions where this is possible, and to develop such notions as objective necessity and potential competition. We also expect its sophistication in dealing with economics to continue to improve, but do not consider that this goes hand in hand with rule-of-reason analysis. This would stifle the proper application of Article 85 which, precisely because of its more ample wording, does not bear the same intellectual burden that the words 'restraint of trade' do in the Sherman Act. We doubt, too, that it would be helpful to draw the national courts further into the application of Article 85 by asking them to undertake extensive economic analysis under Article 85(1). We are happy for them to enforce the competition rules against blatant cartels and abuses of a dominant position. We do not consider them to be appropriate fora for deciding upon complex economic issues.

(d) THE CASE LAW

The academic debate provides a framework within which to evaluate the case law. In reading these materials two matters should be borne in mind. How far is the Court balancing the pro- and anti-competitive effects of an agreement to determine whether it is caught within Article 81(1), and how far is the terminology of the rule of reason an apt description of this approach?

---

[50] See 966–975 below.
[51] (1987) 7 *YBEL* 12–20.
[52] *Ibid.*, 36–37.

Case 56/65 Société La Technique Minière v. Maschinenbau Ulm GmbH
[1966] ECR 235

[Note ToA renumbering: Art. 85 is now Art. 81]

The case concerned an exclusive supply contract, whereby STM had the exclusive right to sell in France certain grading equipment produced by Maschinenbau Ulm (MBU), a German undertaking. The contract did not, however, insulate the French territory: STM could sell the goods outside France, and parallel imports could be obtained from other countries. A contract dispute between STM and MBU led the former to argue that this contract was invalid under Article 85.

THE ECJ

Finally, for the agreement at issue to be caught by the prohibition contained in Article 85(1) it must have as its 'object or effect the prevention, restriction or distortion of competition within the Common Market'.

The fact that these are not cumulative but alternative requirements, indicated by the conjunction 'or', leads first to the need to consider the precise purpose of the agreement, in the economic context in which it is to be applied. This interference with competition referred to in Article 85(1) must result from all or some of the clauses of the agreement itself. Where, however, an analysis of the said clauses does not reveal the effect on competition to be sufficiently deleterious, the consequences of the agreement should then be considered and for it to be caught by the prohibition it is then necessary to find that those factors are present which show that competition has in fact been prevented or restricted or distorted to an appreciable extent.

The competition in question must be understood within the actual context in which it would occur in the absence of the agreement in dispute. In particular it may be doubted whether there is an interference with competition if the said agreement seems really necessary for the penetration of a new area by an undertaking. Therefore, in order to decide whether an agreement containing a clause 'granting an exclusive right of sale' is to be considered as prohibited by reason of its object or its effect, it is appropriate to take into account in particular the nature and quantity, limited or otherwise, of the products covered by the agreement, the position and importance of the grantor and the concessionaire on the market for the products concerned, the isolated nature of the disputed agreement or, alternatively, its position in a series of agreements, the severity of the clauses intended to protect the exclusive dealership or, alternatively, the opportunities allowed for other commercial competitors in the same products by way of parallel re-exportation and importation.

Cases 56 and 58/64 Etablissements Consten Sàrl and
Grundig-Verkaufs-GmbH v. Commission
[1966] ECR 299

[Note ToA renumbering: Art. 85 is now Art. 81]

Grundig granted to Consten a sole distributorship for its electronic products in France. Consten had an obligation to take a minimum amount of the product; it had to provide publicity and after-sales service; and it undertook not to sell the products of competing manufacturers. Moreover, the French territory was in effect insulated: there was absolute territorial protection. Consten undertook not to sell the goods outside the contract territory. A similar prohibition existed on other Grundig distributors in other countries. Grundig assigned to Consten its trade-mark, GINT, which Consten could use against any unauthorized sales in France. In 1961 a company called UNEF bought Grundig goods from sellers in Germany and sold them in France more cheaply than Consten. The latter brought an action for infringement of its trade-mark, and UNEF contended that the whole agreement between Grundig and Consten violated Article 85.

THE ECJ

The applicants and the German Government maintain that since the Commission restricted its examination solely to Grundig products the decision was based upon a false concept of competition ... contained in Article 85(1), since this concept applies particularly to competition between similar products of different makes; the Commission, before declaring Article 85(1) to be applicable, should, by basing itself upon the 'rule of reason', have considered the economic effects of the disputed contract upon competition between the different makes. There is a presumption that vertical sole distributorship agreements are not harmful to competition and in the present case there is nothing to invalidate that presumption. On the contrary, the contract in question has increased the competition between similar products of different makes.

The principle of freedom of competition concerns the various stages and manifestations of competition. Although competition between producers is generally more noticeable than that between distributors of products of the same make, it does not thereby follow that an agreement tending to restrict the latter kind of competition should escape the prohibition of Article 85(1) merely because it might increase the former.

Besides, for the purpose of applying Article 85(1), there is no need to take account of the concrete effects of an agreement once it appears that it has as its object the prevention, restriction or distortion of competition.

Therefore, the absence in the contested decision of any analysis of the effects of the agreement on competition between similar products of different makes does not, of itself, constitute a defect in the decision.

[*The Court considered the system of absolute territorial protection established by the agreement between Consten and Grundig. It then continued as follows:*]

The situation as ascertained above results in the isolation of the French market and makes it possible to charge for the products in question prices which are sheltered from all effective competition.... Since the agreement thus aims at isolating the French market for Grundig products and maintaining artificially, for products of a very-well known brand, separate national markets within the Community, it is therefore such as to distort competition in the Common Market.

It was therefore proper for the contested decision to hold that the agreement constitutes an infringement of Article 85(1). No further considerations, whether of economic data ... or of the correctness of the criteria upon which the Commission relied in its comparisons between the situations of the French and German markets, and no possible favourable effects of the agreement in other respects, can in any way lead, in the face of the above-mentioned restrictions, to a different solution under Article 85(1).

It is clear from the *STM* case that the Court, even at this early date, accepted that the words of Article 81 were to be read disjunctively: if the object or purpose of the agreement was anti-competitive then it could be condemned without pressing further.[53] Agreements which were particularly heinous, such as horizontal price-fixing, market-division, and collective boycotts,

---

[53] O. Odudu, 'Interpreting Article 81(1): Object as Subjective Intention' (2001) 26 *ELRev.* 60.

would be condemned without further analysis of market circumstances.[54] If one were using the language of the United States courts, such agreements would be *per se* illegal. This reading of Article 81 is confirmed by *Ferriere Nord*.[55] The Commission has moreover made it clear that it is unnecessary to demonstrate any actual effects on the market for such agreements. Proof of the existence of such agreements will suffice for the purpose of Article 81.[56] An agreement may moreover have a restrictive object even if restriction of competition is not its sole aim.[57]

Where the anti-competitive quality of an agreement is not evident from its object then it is necessary to consider its effects,[58] as emphasized in the *Delimitis* case.[59] The contrast between *STM* and *Consten and Grundig* is instructive. It is clear that the *STM* case countenanced some economic analysis within Article 81(1): the ECJ took into account the fact that the exclusive-supply contract may have been a necessary step in allowing the firm to penetrate the French market; and that this was something to be encouraged. The ECJ's response in *Consten and Grundig* to the argument concerning the rule of reason must be seen in the light of the facts. The parties sought to use that doctrine to legitimate a scheme that gave absolute territorial protection to the French distributor. If one were engaging in a pure economic analysis, which involved trade-offs between the pro- and anti-competitive effects of an agreement, then even absolute territorial protection might be warranted.[60] However, the EC competition rules have been influenced by the desire to create a single market.[61] Agreements that have the effect of partitioning the market along national lines will, therefore, be treated harshly. The *Consten and Grundig* case should not be perceived as rejecting economic analysis within Article 81(1), but rather as indicating that such analysis could not validate absolute territorial protection. Economic analysis is apparent in a number of other decisions,[62] such as *Nungesser*.

Case 258/78 L.C. Nungesser KG and Kurt Eisele v. Commission
[1982] ECR 2015

[Note ToA renumbering: Art. 85 is now Art. 81]

The case concerned a contract between INRA, a French research institute specializing in the development of plant seeds, and Eisele, a German supplier of seeds. The contract gave Eisele,

---

[54] See also Case 45/85 *Verband der Sachversicherer eV* v. *Commission* [1987] ECR 405, para. 39; Case T–77/92 *Parker Pen Ltd.* v. *Commission* [1994] ECR II–549; Case T–66/92 *Herlitz AG* v. *Commission* [1994] ECR II–531; Cases T–374, 375, 384, and 388/94 *European Night Services* v. *Commission* [1998] ECR II–3141, para. 136; Case T–213/00 *CMA CGM* v. *Commission* [2003] ECR II–913, paras. 100, 175–179, 210; A. Jones and B. Sufrin, *EC Competition Law: Text, Cases, and Materials* (2nd edn, Oxford University Press, 2004), 190–201.

[55] Case C–219/95 P *Ferriere Nord*, n. 31 above.

[56] Commission Guidelines on the Application of Art. 81(3) [2004] OJ C101/97, paras. 21–23.

[57] Case C–551/03 *General Motors BV* v. *Commission* [2006] ECR I–3173, para. 64.

[58] Case 23/67 *Brasserie de Haecht SA* v. *Wilkin* [1967] ECR 407; Case 5/69 *Völk* v. *Vervaecke* [1969] ECR 295; Case T–7/93 *Langnese-Iglo GmbH* v. *Commission* [1995] ECR II–1533. See O. Odudu, 'Interpreting Article 81(1): Demonstrating Restrictive Effect' (2001) 26 *ELRev.* 261.

[59] Case C–234/89 *Delimitis* v. *Henninger Bräu AG* [1991] ECR I–935.

[60] The protection might be necessary to enable the manufacturer to penetrate a new market, and any reduction in intra-brand competition (competition between distributors of the same product) would be more than offset by an increase in inter-brand competition (competition between those who distribute goods of the same kind, e.g., different brands of stereo equipment).

[61] Jones and Sufrin, n. 54 above, 197–198; G. Amato, *Antitrust and the Bounds of Power* (Hart, 1997), 48–49.

[62] See, e.g., Case 262/81 *Coditel SA* v. *Ciné-Vog Films SA* [1982] ECR 3381; Case C–234/89 *Delimitis*, n. 59 above; Cases T–374, 375, 384, and 388/94 *European Night Services*, n. 54 above; Case C–238/05 *Asnef-Equifax* v. *Ausbanc* [2006] ECR I–11125; Case T–168/01 *GlaxoSmithKline Services Unlimited* v. *Commission*, 27 Sept. 2006.

and through him Nungesser, absolute territorial protection: INRA would not sell the seed to any other undertaking in Germany, and would prevent third parties from doing so; Eisele could use the plant breeder's rights assigned to him by INRA to prevent third parties selling into Germany. The Commission found that the agreement violated Article 85(1). The applicant argued, *inter alia*, that the exclusive licence was necessary to enable INRA to enter a new market, and compete with comparable products therein, since no trader would risk launching a new product unless he were given protection from competition from the licensor and from other licensees. The Court distinguished between an open exclusive licence, whereby the owner merely undertook not to compete himself, nor to grant licences to others in the same territory; and an exclusive licence with absolute territorial protection, under which all competition from third parties was eliminated.

THE ECJ

54. That point having been clarified, it is necessary to examine whether, in the present case, the exclusive nature of the licence, in so far as it is an open licence, has the effect of preventing or distorting competition within the meaning of Article 85(1) of the Treaty.

. . .

56. The exclusive licence which forms the subject-matter of the contested decision concerns the cultivation and marketing of hybrid maize seeds which were developed by INRA after years of research and experimentation and were unknown to German farmers at the time when the cooperation between INRA and the applicants was taking shape. For that reason the concern shown by the interveners as regards the protection of new technology is justified.

57. In fact, in the case of a licence of breeders' rights over hybrid maize seeds newly developed in one Member State, an undertaking in another Member State which was not certain that it would not encounter competition from other licensees for the territory granted to it, or from the owner of the right himself, might be deterred from accepting the risk of cultivating and marketing that product; such a result would be damaging to the dissemination of a new technology and would prejudice competition in the Community between the new product and similar existing products.

58. Having regard to the specific nature of the products in question, the Court concludes that, in a case such as the present, the grant of an open exclusive licence, that is to say a licence which does not affect the position of third parties such as parallel importers and licensees for other territories, is not in itself incompatible with Article 85(1) of the Treaty.

[*In relation to those aspects of the agreement which conferred absolute territorial protection, the Court, however, continued to follow* Consten and Grundig, *and to hold that these were illegal.*]

Closely related to the material considered thus far is the case law on what are termed ancillary restraints. The case law indicates that 'restrictions on the conduct of the parties ancillary, or objectively necessary, to the operation of pro-competitive or non-restrictive agreement cannot be said to restrict competition'.[63] Thus, in *Remia*[64] it was held that non-competition clauses included in the sale of an undertaking would not come within Article 81(1). Such clauses were necessary to give effect to the sale, since otherwise the vendor, with his specialist knowledge of the transferred undertaking, could simply win back the custom from the

---

[63] Jones and Sufrin, n. 56 above, 212; Commission Guidelines, n. 56 above, paras. 28–31.

[64] Case 42/84 *Remia BV and Verenigde Bedrijven Nutricia NV v. Commission* [1985] ECR 2545; Case C–250/92 *Gottrup-Klim Grovvareforeninger v. Dansk Landburgs Grovvareselskab AmbA* [1994] ECR I–5641.

purchaser of that undertaking. Clauses of this type could, therefore, enhance competition by leading to an increase in the number of undertakings on the relevant market. This will, however, exclude only certain clauses from the operation of Article 81(1). Thus, in *Remia* the Court held that the non-competition clause must be limited in time and scope.[65] Similar reasoning is evident in *Pronuptia*.

Case 161/84 **Pronuptia de Paris GmbH v. Pronuptia de Paris Irmgard Schillgallis**
[1986] ECR 353

[Note ToA renumbering: Art. 85 is now Art. 81]

The case was concerned with franchising arrangements for wedding apparel. Under the franchise, the franchisor granted the franchisee the exclusive right to use the Pronuptia mark for a certain area; it agreed not to open another shop in that area, or aid any third party to do so; and it assisted the franchisee in setting up the store, providing know-how, etc. In return the franchisee, who remained the owner of the business, agreed to use the Pronuptia name; to pay the franchisor a royalty on turnover; to purchase 80 per cent of its requirements for wedding dresses from the franchisor; to take account of the recommended resale prices proposed by the franchisor; and not to compete with any Pronuptia business. The Court noted the diversity in types of franchise agreement: there were service, production, and distribution franchise agreements. The judgment is directed at distribution franchises.

THE ECJ

15. In a distribution system such as this, an enterprise which has established itself as a distributor in a market and which has thus been able to perfect a range of commercial methods gives independent businessmen the chance, at a price, of establishing themselves in other markets by using its mark and the commercial methods which created the franchisor's success.... At the same time this system gives businessmen who lack the necessary experience access to methods which they could otherwise only acquire after prolonged effort and research and allows them also to profit from the reputation of the mark.... Such a system, which permits the franchisor to take advantage of his success, is not by itself restrictive of competition. For it to function two conditions must be satisfied.

16. First, the franchisor must be able to communicate his know-how to the franchisees and provide them with the necessary assistance in putting his methods into effect, without running the risk that this know-how will aid his competitors, even indirectly. It thus follows that those clauses which are essential to prevent this risk do not constitute restrictions on competition in the sense of Article 85(1). These include the prohibition on the franchisee opening, for the duration of the franchise or for a reasonable period after its termination, a shop with an identical or similar purpose in an area where he could be in competition with one of the members of the network. The same applies to the obligation on the franchisee not to sell his shop without the prior approval of the franchisor: this clause serves to ensure that the benefit of the know-how and assistance provided does not go directly to a competitor.

17. Secondly, the franchisor must be able to take appropriate measures to preserve the identity and reputation of the network which is symbolised by the mark. It thus follows that

---

[65] Case 42/84, n. 64 above.

those clauses which provide a basis for such control as is indispensable for this purpose also do not constitute restrictions on competition in the sense of Article 85(1).

18. This covers then the obligation on the franchisee to apply the commercial methods developed by the franchisor and to utilise the know-how provided.

19. This is also the case with the franchisee's obligation only to sell the merchandise covered by the agreement in premises set up and decorated according to the franchisor's specifications, which have as their purpose to guarantee a uniform image corresponding to specified requirements.

...

21. Thanks to the control exercised by the franchisor over the selection of goods offered by the franchisee, the public can find at each franchisee's shop merchandise of the same quality.... A clause prescribing that the franchisee can only sell products provided by the franchisor or by suppliers selected by him must, in these circumstances, be considered necessary for the protection of the reputation of the network. It must not, however, operate to prevent the franchisee from obtaining the products from other franchisees.

However in *Pronuptia* the Court decided that certain of the clauses were not necessary for the integrity of the franchise agreement, and hence were restrictive of competition within Article 81(1).[66]

Notwithstanding the above the CFI in *Métropole Télévision* denied that there is a rule of reason as such within Article 81(1), and it has reiterated this stance in subsequent decisions.[67]

Case T–112/99 **Métropole Télévision (M6), Suez-Lyonnaise des Eaux, France Telecom, and Television Française 1 SA (TFI) v. Commission**
[2001] ECR II–2459

[Note ToA renumbering: Art. 85 is now Art. 81]

The applicant companies sought to annul a Commission decision relating to the creation of TPS, a company providing digital satellite television for payment. The agreement had an exclusivity clause, whereby the general-interest channels provided by the applicants would be broadcast exclusively by TPS. The applicants argued, based on cases such as *Nungesser*, that the Commission should have applied Article 85(1) in the light of the rule of reason to this clause. There were already strong companies on the pay TV market, into which TPS was seeking to gain entry.

THE CFI

72. According to the applicants, as a consequence of the existence of the rule of reason in Community competition law, when Article 85(1) ... is applied it is necessary to weigh the

---

66 Case 161/84 [1986] ECR 353, 382–385. This was particularly the case for those clauses which partitioned the market between franchisor and franchisee, or between franchisees themselves. Thus, the obligation on the franchisor not to allow franchisees to open shops outside their allotted territory was held to fall foul of the *Consten and Grundig* principle. The fact that such a clause might be necessary for any franchisee to make the initial investment was recognized by the Court, but was considered to be of relevance only within Art. 81(3).

67 Case T–65/98 *Van den Bergh Foods Ltd.* v. *Commission* [2003] ECR II–4653, para. 107; Case T–328/03 *O2 (Germany) GmbH & Co. OHG* v. *Commission* [2006] ECR II–1231, paras. 65–73. See however the more economic approach in Case T–168/01 *GlaxoSmithKline*, n. 62 above, paras. 148–190.

pro- and anti-competitive effects of an agreement in order to determine whether it is caught by the prohibition laid down in that article. It should, however, be observed, first of all, that contrary to the applicants' assertions the existence of such a rule has not, as such, been confirmed by the Community courts. Quite the contrary, in various judgments the Court of Justice and Court of First Instance have been at pains to indicate that the existence of a rule of reason in Community law is doubtful (see Case C–235/92, *Montecatini* . . . [1999] ECR I–4539, paragraph 133 . . . Case T–148/89, *Tréfilunion* [1995] ECR II–1063, paragraph 109).

73. Next, it must be observed that an interpretation of Article 85(1) . . ., in the form suggested by the applicants, is difficult to reconcile with the rules prescribed by that provision.

74. Article 85 . . . expressly provides, in its third paragraph, for the possibility of exempting agreements that restrict competition where they satisfy a number of conditions. . . . It is only in the precise framework of that provision that the pro- and anti-competitive effects of a restriction may be weighed (see . . . *Pronuptia* paragraph 24 . . . and *European Night Services* paragraph 136). Article 85(3) would lose much of its effectiveness if such an examination had to be carried out already under Article 85(1). . . .

75. It is true that in a number of judgments the Court of Justice and the Court of First Instance have favoured a more flexible interpretation of the prohibition laid down in Article 85(1) (see . . . *STM* . . . *Nungesser* . . . *Coditel* . . . *Pronuptia* . . . *European Night Services* . . .).

76. Those judgments cannot, however, be interpreted as establishing the existence of a rule of reason in Community competition law. They are, rather, part of a broader trend in the case law according to which it is not necessary to hold, wholly abstractly and without drawing any distinction, that any agreement restricting the freedom of action of one or more of the parties is necessarily caught by . . . Article 85(1). . . . In assessing the applicability of Article 85(1) to an agreement, account should be taken of the actual conditions in which it functions, in particular the economic context in which the undertakings operate, the products or services covered by the agreement and the actual structure of the market concerned. . . .

77. . . . It must, however, be emphasized that such an approach does not mean that it is necessary to weigh the pro- and anti-competitive effects of an agreement when determining whether . . . Article 85(1) . . . applies.

[*The CFI then considered whether the exclusivity clause could be considered as a valid ancillary restraint.*]

104. In Community competition law the concept of an ancillary restriction covers any restriction which is directly related and necessary to the implementation of a main operation. . . .

. . .

106. The condition that a restriction be necessary implies a two-fold examination. It is necessary to establish, first, whether the restriction is objectively necessary for the implementation of the main operation and, second, whether it is proportionate to it. . . .

107. As regards the objective necessity of a restriction, it must be observed that inasmuch as, as has been shown in paragraph 72 et seq above, the existence of a rule of reason in Community competition law cannot be upheld, it would be wrong, when classifying ancillary restrictions, to interpret the requirement for objective necessity as implying a need to weigh the pro and anti-competitive effects of an agreement. Such an analysis can take place only in the specific framework of Article 81(3) of the Treaty.

. . .

109. Consequently . . . examination of the objective necessity of a restriction in relation to the main operation cannot but be relatively abstract. It is not a question of analyzing whether, in the light of the competitive situation on the relevant market, the restriction is indispensable to the commercial success of the main operation, but of determining whether, in the specific

context of the main operation, the restriction is necessary to implement that operation. If, without the restriction, the main operation is difficult or even impossible to implement, the restriction may be regarded as objectively necessary for its implementation.
[*The CFI held that the claimants did not satisfy this test.*]

(e) SUMMARY

i. It is reasonably clear that the ECJ condemns certain types of agreement on the basis of their object or purpose without any extensive market analysis; in this sense it effectively proscribes these agreements as *per se* illegal. It is also clear that the ECJ has engaged in economic analysis within Article 81(1). While it has not employed the language of the rule of reason, there is evidence of a balancing of the pro- and anti-competitive effects of an agreement, subject to the caveats made above.

ii. The Community Courts may choose to undertake this analysis by considering all the clauses of the agreement as a whole, or they might distinguish between the main and ancillary clauses of the agreement. The fact that the Court chooses the latter mode should not disguise the fact that there is some weighing of the pro- and anti-competitive effects of the agreement, as exemplified by *Pronuptia*.

iii. The reasoning in *Métropole* is problematic for two reasons. First, there are problems with the CFI's rationalization of the prior case law. The Community Courts considered the entire economic context precisely because it was only by doing so that it was possible to tell whether, for example, a clause restricting conduct should nonetheless be allowed, because it enabled a party to break into the market. It is for this reason that such restrictions on freedom of action were not restrictive of competition. The Community Courts have, in this sense, balanced the pro- and anti-competitive effects of the agreement.[68] The exclusivity clause in *Métropole* was designed to give subscribers something attractive so as to enable TPS to break into a market where there was strong competition. Secondly, the reasoning assumes that a rule of reason is incompatible with the existence of Article 81(3). It is however possible to balance the pro- and anti-competitive effects of an agreement within Article 81(1), and still to preserve a role for Article 81(3).[69]

iv. The Commission has not been enthusiastic about economic analysis in the past, and has been criticized for equating a restriction on conduct with a restriction on competition. This is clearly mistaken, since restriction of competition is an economic concept, which must be assessed in relation to a market. It is unclear how far its approach has changed. In the White Paper on Modernization[70] the Commission stated that it adopted the ECJ's approach in *Nungesser*[71] and *Pronuptia*[72] and balanced the pro- and anti-competitive effects of an agreement within Article 81(1) in relation to some restrictive practices. It however went on to say that any more systematic use of such rule-of-reason analysis

---

[68] R. Nazzini, 'Article 81 EC between Time Present and Time Past: A Normative Critique of "Restriction of Competition" in EU Law' (2006) 43 *CMLRev.* 487.

[69] R. Wesseling, 'The Commission White Paper on Modernisation of EC Antitrust Law: Unspoken Consequences and Incomplete Alternative Options' [1999] *ECLR* 420.

[70] White Paper on the Modernisation of the Rules Implementing Arts. 85 and 86 of the EC Treaty, Comm. Programme 99/027, para. 57; Commission Guidelines, n. 56 above, para. 18.

[71] Case 258/78 [1982] ECR 2015.

[72] Case 161/84 [1986] ECR 353.

under Article 81(1) would mean that Article 81(3) would be 'cast aside'. The Commission said that this would be paradoxical, given that Article 81(3) contains all the elements of a rule of reason.[73] This reasoning, although it derives support from the CFI in *Métropole*, has been vigorously contested. It has been argued that a more thoroughgoing balancing of pro- and anti-competitive effects within Article 81(1) would be beneficial, and would still leave room for a distinctive role for Article 81(3).[74]

7. ARTICLE 81(1): THE EFFECT ON TRADE BETWEEN MEMBER STATES

In order for Article 81(1) to apply, the agreement, etc., must have an effect on trade between Member States,[75] otherwise the matter will remain within the jurisdiction of the relevant Member State. The hurdle has not, however, proven difficult for the Court to surmount. It has adopted a broad test and applied it in a similar fashion. The ECJ held in *STM* that the test was whether it was possible to 'foresee with a sufficient degree of probability on the basis of a set of objective factors of law or of fact that the agreement in question may have an influence, direct or indirect, actual or potential, on the pattern of trade between Member States'.[76]

The ability to focus on potential or indirect effects on trade means that it will be very rare for the Community to lack jurisdiction. Proof that the agreement had an actual impact on trade is not necessary, provided that it was capable of having that effect.[77] Moreover, the mere fact that all the parties to the agreement are from one Member State will not preclude the application of Article 81(1). It will be held to increase the compartmentalization of the Community along national lines, thereby rendering it more difficult for firms from other States to penetrate that national market.[78] Nor will the Court's jurisdiction be barred merely because the agreement relates to trade outside the EC if it might have an impact on trade within the Community.[79]

The Commission has however published guidelines indicating when it believes that an agreement is not capable of appreciably affecting trade.[80]

---

[73] White Paper, n. 70 above, para. 57.

[74] Wesseling, n. 69 above.

[75] Jones and Sufrin, n. 54 above, 168–176.

[76] Case 56/65 [1966] ECR 235, 249. Moreover, provided that the agreement has this effect, it is not necessary for each of the restrictions to do so: Case 193/83 *Windsurfing International Inc.* v. *Commission* [1986] ECR 611.

[77] Case 19/77 *Miller International Schallplatten GmbH* v. *Commission* [1978] ECR 131; Case C 219/95 P *Ferriere Nord*, n. 31 above. This extends to the situation where the relevant restriction has not been implemented, since the very existence of the restriction can still have a psychological effect which contributes to the partitioning of the market: Case T–77/92 *Parker Pen*, n. 54 above, Case T–66/92 *Herlitz*, n. 54 above.

[78] Case 8/72 *Vereeniging van Cementhandelaren* v. *Commission* [1972] ECR 977; Case 246/86 *Société Coopérative des Asphalteurs Belges (BELASCO)* v. *Commission* [1989] ECR 2117; Case T–66/89 *Publishers Association* v. *Commission (No. 2)* [1992] ECR II–1995.

[79] See, e.g., Dec. 74/634 *Franco-Japanese Ballbearings Agreement* [1974] OJ L343/19, [1975] 1 CMLR D8; Dec. 75/77 *French and Taiwanese Mushroom Packers* [1975] OJ L29/26, [1975] 1 CMLR D83.

[80] Commission Guidelines on the effect on trade concept contained in Arts. 81 and 82 of the Treaty [2004] OJ C101/81, paras. 44–57.

8. ARTICLE 81(1):
THE DE MINIMIS DOCTRINE

An agreement will not be caught by Article 81(1) if it does not have an appreciable impact on competition or on inter-state trade.[81] This principle has been imbued with greater specificity by Commission notices. The Commission will not institute proceedings in cases covered by the Notice, nor will it impose fines where the parties assume, in good faith, that the Notice covers the agreement. The current Notice dates from 2001.[82]

The criterion is that agreements between undertakings do not appreciably restrict competition where the aggregate market share held by the parties to the agreement does not exceed 10 per cent on markets where the parties are actual or potential competitors. The relevant figure is 15 per cent for cases where the parties are not competitors on the relevant markets.[83] In cases where it is difficult to classify the agreement then the 10 per cent threshold applies. Paragraph 8 of the Notice deals with vertical cases, in which competition may be restricted by the cumulative effect of agreements. In such instances, the threshold is reduced to 5 per cent for agreements between both competitors and non-competitors. The Notice further provides that individual suppliers or distributors with a market share not exceeding 5 per cent will, in general, not be considered to contribute significantly to a cumulative foreclosure effect. Moreover, such an effect will be unlikely to exist if parallel networks of agreements having similar effects cover less than 30 per cent of the relevant market. The Notice provides a further buffer, in stipulating that agreements will not be restrictive of competition where the preceding thresholds are not exceeded by more than 2 per cent in two successive years.[84]

However, the benefits of the Notice are excluded if the agreement contains hardcore restrictions listed in paragraph 11. Agreements between competitors cannot contain restrictions as to sale price, limitation of output, or allocation of markets or customers.[85] Agreements between non-competitors cannot, for example, contain restrictions on minimum resale price, or the territory into which, or the customers to whom, the buyer may sell the contract goods.[86] There are, however, exceptions for types of vertical restriction that are not regarded as hardcore. The remainder of paragraph 11 contains other limitations on the types of restriction that cause the benefits of the Notice to be lost.

9. ARTICLE 81(3): EXEMPTIONS

If an agreement is held to be within Article 81(1) it can gain exemption under Article 81(3), provided that four conditions are satisfied: it must improve the production or distribution of goods or promote technical or economic progress; consumers must receive a fair share of the resulting benefit; it must contain only restrictions which are indispensable to the attainment of the agreement's objectives; and it cannot lead to the elimination of competition in respect

---

[81] Case 5/69 *Völk*, n. 58 above; Case T–77/92 *Parker Pen*, n. 54 above; Case C–180/98 *Pavlov v. Stichting Pensioenfonds Medische Specialisten* [2000] ECR I–6451.

[82] Commission Notice on agreements of minor importance which do not appreciably restrict competition under Art. 81(1) (de minimis) [2001] OJ C368/13.

[83] *Ibid.*, para. 7.

[84] *Ibid.*, para. 9.

[85] *Ibid.*, para. 11(1).

[86] *Ibid.*, paras. 11(2)(a),(b).

of a substantial part of the products in question. These four conditions are cumulative: they must all be fulfilled before an exemption can be granted.[87] There are individual and block exemptions.

(a) INDIVIDUAL EXEMPTION

The Commission had until recently the sole power to grant exemptions under Article 81(3), subject to review by the Court. This has however now been changed as a result of the new scheme for enforcement of competition law, whereby national courts and national competition authorities can apply the entirety of Article 81.[88] The Commission has published guidelines on the application of Article 81(3) which provide a useful frame of reference.[89]

The Commission makes clear that any balancing of the pro- and anti-competitive effect of an agreement should take place within Article 81(3), rather than Article 81(1).[90] All restrictive agreements that are caught by Article 81(1) can in principle be exempted under Article 81(3), but especially heinous agreements such as horizontal price fixing are unlikely to satisfy the conditions for exemption.[91]

The *first condition* for exemption under Article 81(3) is that there must be some efficiency gains flowing from the restrictive agreement. The efficiencies may take the form of lower costs, resulting from new production methods, synergies consequent upon integration of existing assets, economies of scale, or cost savings.[92] Efficiency gains may also be qualitative in nature, generating improved products or better research and development.[93] The Commission will nonetheless require proof of such gains and of the causal link between them and the restrictive agreement.

Commission Guidelines on the Application of Article 81(3) of the Treaty[94]

50. The purpose of the first condition of Article 81(3) is to define the types of efficiency gains that can be taken into account . . . The aim of the analysis is to ascertain what are the objective benefits created by the agreement and what is the economic importance of such efficiencies. . . .

51. All efficiency claims must therefore be substantiated so that the following can be verified:

(a) The nature of the claimed efficiencies;

(b) The link between the agreement and the efficiencies;

(c) The likelihood and magnitude of each claimed efficiency; and

(d) How and when each claimed efficiency would be achieved.

The *second condition* is that consumers receive a fair share of resulting benefits. The Commission's view of this requirement emerges from the following extract.

---

[87] Case T–213/00 *CMA CGM*, n. 54 above, para. 226.

[88] Council Reg. (EC) 1/2003 of 16 Dec. 2002 on the implementation of the rules on competition laid down in Arts. 81 and 82 of the Treaty [2003] OJ L1/1.

[89] L. Kjolbye, 'The New Commission Guidelines on the Application of Article 81(3): An Economic Approach to Article 81' [2004] *ECLR* 566.

[90] Commission Guidelines, n. 56 above, para. 11.

[91] *Ibid.*, para. 46.

[92] *Ibid.*, paras. 64–68.

[93] *Ibid.*, paras. 69–72.

[94] *Ibid.*, paras. 50–51.

Commission Guidelines on the Application of Article 81(3) of the Treaty[95]

85. The concept of 'fair share' implies that the pass-on of benefits must at least compensate consumers for any actual or likely negative impact caused to them by the restriction of competition found under Article 81(1)....

86. It is not required that consumers receive a share of each and every efficiency gain identified under the first condition. It suffices that sufficient benefits are passed on to compensate for the negative effects of the restrictive agreement....

87. The decisive factor is the overall impact on consumers of the products within the relevant market and not the impact on individual members of this group of consumers. In some cases a period of time may be required before the efficiencies materialize. Until such time the agreement may have only negative effects. The fact that pass-on to the consumer occurs with a certain time lag does not in itself exclude the application of Article 81(3). However the greater the time lag, the greater must be the efficiencies to compensate also for the loss to consumers during the period preceding the pass-on.

The *third condition* under Article 81(3) concerns the indispensability of the restrictions. This implies for the Commission a twofold test: the restrictive agreement as such must be reasonably necessary in order to achieve the efficiencies; and the individual restrictions of competition that flow from the agreement must also be reasonably necessary for the attainment of those efficiencies.[96] The ECJ will also consider closely whether the restriction is indispensable, as exemplified by *Nungesser*.

Case 258/78 L.C. Nungesser KG and Kurt Eisele v. Commission
[1982] ECR 2015

The facts were set out above. It will be remembered that the Court held that the clauses in the agreement that gave absolute territorial protection were caught by Article 85(1). The Commission had also refused exemption under Article 85(3) for certain aspects of the agreement because of this territorial protection. The applicants argued that the Court should overturn this part of the Commission's decision.

THE ECJ

76. It must be remembered that under the terms of Article 85(3) ... an exemption from the prohibition contained in Article 85(1) may be granted in the case of an agreement between undertakings which contributes to improving the production or distribution of goods or to promoting technical progress, and which does not impose on the undertakings concerned restrictions which are not indispensable to the attainment of those objectives.

77. As it is a question of seeds intended to be used by a large number of farmers for the production of maize, which is an important product for human and animal foodstuffs, absolute territorial protection manifestly goes beyond what is indispensable for the improvement of production or distribution or the promotion of technical progress, as is demonstrated ... by the

---

95 *Ibid.*, paras. 85–87.
96 *Ibid.*, para. 73.

prohibition agreed to by both parties to the agreement, of any parallel imports of INRA maize seeds into Germany even if those seeds were bred by INRA itself and marketed in France.

78. It follows that the absolute territorial protection conferred on the licensee ... constituted a sufficient reason for refusing to grant an exemption under Article 85(3).... It is therefore no longer necessary to examine the other grounds set out in the decision for refusing to grant such an exemption.

The *final condition* for exemption is that the agreement should not lead to the elimination of competition in respect of a substantial part of the products in question. This reflects the fact that the 'protection of rivalry and the competitive process is given priority over potentially pro-competitive efficiency gains which could result from restrictive agreements'.[97] Whether competition is being eliminated will depend on the degree of competition existing prior to the agreement and on the impact of the restrictive agreement on competition. Thus the 'more competition is already weakened in the market concerned, the slighter the further reduction required for competition to be eliminated within the meaning of Article 81(3)'.[98]

In considering the conditions elaborated in the Commission's Notice, one should not lose sight of its overall impact.

P. Lugard and L. Hancher, Honey I Shrunk the Article! A Critical Assessment of the Commission's Notice on Article 81(3) of the EC Treaty[99]

In clarifying the analytical framework for the application of both Art. 81(1) and (3), the Notice provides useful guidance to national courts, authorities and firms. In addition to several questionable aspects of the analysis ... the main concern is that,, by significantly raising the threshold in terms of quantification and verification of efficiencies under Art. 81(3), the role of Art. 81(3) in national court proceedings may—paradoxically—be limited. It is not unlikely that national proceedings will in the future increasingly centre around the applicability of Art. 81(1) ... Indeed, once the applicability of Art. 81(1) is established, the Notice may not leave much scope to adduce convincingly the extensive evidence required under Art. 81(3). Such an outcome would be at odds with the very purpose underlying the Notice and indeed Regulation 1/2003.

(b) BLOCK EXEMPTION

Article 81(3) allows the Commission to declare the provisions of Article 81(1) inapplicable to a category of agreements. This is the foundation for block exemptions made by the Commission, acting under delegated authority from the Council. The object of such exemptions is to exclude a generic type of agreement from the ambit of Article 81(1), thereby obviating the need for separate and time-consuming individual exemptions. In some ways the technique of block exemption is conceptually similar to the evolution of *per se* rules, although the result is to exclude rather than condemn the agreement: experience with individual agreements leads to the conclusion that certain types of agreement, which contain particular terms, warrant exemption. A block exemption encapsulates this conclusion, and gives more definite guidance to firms.

---

[97] *Ibid.*, para. 105.
[98] *Ibid.*, para. 107.
[99] [2004] *ECLR* 410, 420.

Block exemptions have certain common features. They state the reasons for their enactment, set out the substance of the exemption, contain provisions limiting the size of the firms that can take advantage of them, and list the types of clauses that are and are not allowed within the relevant agreement. Such exemptions have been made for a number of areas, including: specialization agreements;[100] research and development;[101] vertical restraints;[102] technology transfer;[103] and franchising.[104] The structure and operation of block exemptions will be examined more closely in the context of vertical restraints.[105]

10. ARTICLE 81: COMPETITION AND NON-COMPETITION CONSIDERATIONS

There has been debate as to whether the Community Courts should or should not take into account non-competition considerations, in the context of either Article 81(1) and/or Article 81(3).

(a) ARTICLE 81(1)

The general academic consensus is that the Community Courts should restrict their analysis within Article 81(1) to considerations that relate to competition, and that they do limit their analysis in this manner. This follows moreover from the analysis of the rule of reason debate set out above in the following sense: if there is reluctance to consider the full pro- and anti-competitive effects of an agreement within Article 81(1), then there will be even greater opposition to the inclusion of non-competition considerations in that context.

There is relatively little evidence of such matters being taken into account by the Community Courts, although *Wouters*[106] appears to be an exception in this regard. The Netherlands Bar adopted rules that prevented members of the Bar from practising in full partnership with accountants. The ECJ found that this *prima facie* limited production within Article 81(1)(b).[107] It nonetheless concluded that the rules did not violate Article 81(1) because they were designed to ensure the independence of members of the Bar and hence the sound administration of justice. In that sense the Court appeared to weigh the anti-competitive effect of the rules against the non-economic benefits that they were designed to achieve. It has however been argued that the case can be regarded either as an instance of 'regulatory ancillarity', in the sense that restraints on competition that are ancillary to a legitimate purpose can be accepted;[108] or that the decision can be seen, by way of analogy with case law on free movement, as one in which the ECJ weighed the impact of non-discriminatory national rules that limited competition against mandatory national public policy.[109]

---

100 Reg. 2658/2000 [2000] OJ L304/3.
101 Reg. 2659/00 [2000] OJ L304/7.
102 Reg. 2790/99 [1999] OJ L336/21.
103 Reg. 772/2004 [2004] OJ L123/11.
104 Reg. 4087/88 [1988] OJ L359/46.
105 See 995–998.
106 Case C–309/99 *Wouters* v. *Algemene Raad van de Nederlandse Orde van Advocaten* [2002] ECR I–1577.
107 *Ibid.*, paras. 90, 94.
108 Whish, n. 5 above, 121–122.
109 G. Monti, 'Article 81 EC and Public Policy' (2002) 39 *CMLRev.* 1057, 1087–1089.

The ECJ has however more recently returned to the 'Wouters theme' in Meca-Medina.[110] It held that anti-doping rules adopted by the International Olympic Committee, even if they could be regarded as a decision of an association of undertakings limiting the applicants' freedom of action, did not come within Article 81, since they were justified by a legitimate objective, this being to ensure fair rivalry between athletes in sport, and were proportionate.

(b) ARTICLE 81(3)

Some authors argue that non-competition considerations can be taken into account within Article 81(3).[111] The predominant academic view is however that they should not be, more especially so now that national courts can apply the entirety of Article 81: if a broad range of non-competition considerations could be taken into account then the criteria that national courts should apply would be uncertain.[112]

R. Whish, Competition Law[113]

A narrow view of Article 81(3) is that it permits only improvements in economic efficiency to be invoked by the parties to an agreement: according to this view, the very wording of Article 81(3), which speaks of improvement to production and distribution and to technical and economic progress, is suggestive of an efficiency standard. Article 81(3), therefore, allows a balancing of the restrictive effects of an agreement under Article 81(1) against the enhancement of efficiency under Article 81(3).... The Commission's White Paper on Modernisation ... explained Article 81(1) and 81(3) in this way.

...

However, an alternative, and broader view of Article 81(3) is possible: that it allows policies other than economic efficiency to be taken into account when deciding whether to allow agreements that are restrictive of competition. There are many important policies in the Community, for example on industry, the environment, employment, the regions and culture, which go beyond the simple enhancement of efficiency. According to a broad view of Article 81(3), a benefit in terms of any of these policies may be able to 'trump' a restriction of competition under Article 81(1).

[Whish reviews a number of decisions where such factors seem to have had some impact on the Commission's reasoning. He continues as follows:]

It is clear ... that a number of factors have been influential in decisions under Article 81(3), not all of which can be considered to be 'narrow' improvements in efficiency. There are significant proponents of the view that Article 81(3) does admit broad, non-competition considerations....

...

This discussion suggests that there is uncertainty—even confusion—as to the proper application of Article 81(3). However, it is necessary to achieve a resolution of the various approaches, in particular because under the Modernization Regulation, decisions under Article

---

[110] Case C–519/04 P Meca-Medina and Majcen v. Commission [2006] ECR I–6991, paras. 40–56.

[111] Monti, n. 109 above; R. Wesseling, 'The Draft Regulation Modernising the Competition Rules: The Commission is Married to One Idea' (2001) 26 ELRev. 357.

[112] O. Odudu, The Boundaries of EC Competition Law, The Scope of Article 81 (Oxford University Press, 2006), ch. 6.

[113] N. 5 above, 152–155.

81(3) will … be made by NCAs[114] and national courts as well as by the Commission itself. These institutions must know the limits of their discretion under Article 81(3); furthermore, they seem ill-placed to balance the restriction of competition that an agreement might entail against a broad range of Community policies; they would have less difficulty, however, in applying a 'narrow' interpretation of Article 81(3), limited to a consideration of economic efficiencies.

These considerations may suggest that Article 81(3) ought to be interpreted in a narrow rather than a broad manner, according to standards and by reference to principles that can properly be regarded as justiciable in courts of law. …

11. ARTICLE 81: VERTICAL RESTRAINTS

Space precludes detailed analysis of all types of restraint that competition authorities have to deal with. However, consideration of the general principles of EC competition law takes one only so far. This section will, therefore, consider one important area of competition policy, that of vertical restraints. Vertical agreements are made between parties at differing levels of the production process, a typical example being a distribution agreement between a manufacturer of a product and a retailer.

There is controversy in this area about the extent to which these agreements are economically harmful, and hence disagreement about the 'correct' approach for competition policy. It is therefore important to understand the policy arguments, and these will be considered within the following section. There are a number of differing types of vertical restraint. It must be determined whether these are caught by Article 81(1). The criterion used by the ECJ and the Commission has not always been the same, and the Commission has been strongly criticized for taking too formalistic an approach to vertical agreements.

In terms of Article 81(3), the EC has primarily used block exemptions to deal with vertical restraints. The initial approach was to have different block exemptions for different types of vertical agreement. The law has now changed, and there is a new-style block exemption that covers the great majority of vertical agreements.

(a) THE ECONOMIC DEBATE

There is considerable diversity of opinion on whether vertical restraints are economically harmful or not.[115] Some believe that they are not harmful at all, or only where there is some real degree of market power at the production level. Others believe that vertical restraints may produce a variety of anti-competitive effects, and that therefore they should be scrutinized by competition authorities.

(i) *The First View*

The first view can be presented as follows. A manufacturer will have to decide how to market its product. It may decide to establish its own retail outlets; to establish a joint venture with a company that has expertise in the retailing area; to sell its products through any outlet that is

---

114 National Competition Authorities.

115 Whish, n. 5 above, 588–594; D. Neven, P. Papandropolous, and P. Seabright, *Trawling for Minnows: European Competition Policy and Agreements between Firms* (Centre for Economic Policy Research, 1998); J. Lever and S. Neubauer, 'Vertical Restraints, Their Motivation and Justification' [2000] *ECLR* 7.

willing to stock them; to sell through certain specialized shops, because the product requires sales expertise; or to sell through certain retail outlets, each of which will be given exclusive rights to distribute the product in a geographical area, either because retailers will only take the goods on these terms or because this will maximize total sales. This list is by no means exhaustive. The argument of those who do not see vertical restraints as harmful has four parts.

The *first* is that the manufacturer will choose the most efficient marketing option. It will, for example, only give such outlets exclusivity if this will lead to greater sales than if it had not been given. If it is wrong in its assumptions then the market will 'punish' it, through reduced sales or by the ultimate sanction of bankruptcy. In any event, it is not the function of competition authorities to play at management consultancy and devise a better marketing strategy for the manufacturer. This is not their function, and they are in a less good position than the manufacturer to make this choice.

The *second* aspect of the argument is that a manufacturer which imposes such restraints will not restrict output to any greater degree than it would otherwise do, and will not take any greater monopoly profit, if such is available, through the presence of a vertical restraint than it would otherwise be able to extract from that market.

The *third* part of the argument is that any restraints are either outweighed by the pro-competitive effects of the agreement, and/or are necessary to persuade the distributor to undertake marketing of the goods. Thus take the producer who wishes to enter a new geographical market, but does not have retailing expertise. If the product is to break into the new market it may require advertising, and also a commitment to provide both pre- and post-sales service. A retailer may not be willing to undertake this expense unless it is accorded some exclusivity because of the 'free-rider' problem: the retailer will expend money on advertising, pre-sales service, and the like, only to witness the sales being taken by a rival retailer who has not incurred these costs. The grant of exclusivity will necessarily restrict intra-brand competition between retailers of the same product, but inter-brand competition will be enhanced by having a new product on the market, and this will control retail prices. A retailer of Sony stereos who has exclusivity in a certain area will not be able to raise prices significantly, since there will be competition from other stereo brands.

The *final* part of the argument of those who contend that vertical restraints should be lawful is that they do not accept that these restraints produce anti-competitive effects. The nature of these effects will be considered in more detail below.

A prominent exponent of the preceding view is Bork, and the following extract provides a summary of the argument.

R. Bork, The Antitrust Paradox: A Policy at War with Itself[116]

We have seen that vertical price fixing (resale price maintenance), vertical market division (closed dealer territories), and, indeed, all vertical restraints are beneficial to consumers and should for that reason be completely lawful. Basic economic theory tells us that the manufacturer who imposes such restraints cannot intend to restrict and must (except in the rare case of price discrimination, which the law should regard as neutral) intend to create efficiency. The

---

[116] N. 44, 297–298. See also R. Bork, 'The Rule of Reason and the *Per Se* Concept in Price Fixing and Market Division II' (1966) 75 *Yale LJ* 373. For debate on this issue see J. R. Gould and B. S. Yamey, 'Professor Bork on Vertical Price Fixing' (1967) 76 *Yale LJ* 722; R. Bork, 'A Reply to Professors Gould and Yamey' (1967) 76 *Yale LJ* 731; J.R. Gould and B.S. Yamey, 'Professor Bork on Vertical Price Fixing: A Rejoinder' (1968) 77 *Yale LJ* 936.

most common efficiency is the inducement or purchase by the manufacturer of extra reseller sales, service or promotional effort.

The proposal to legalize all truly vertical restraints is so much at variance with conventional thought on the topic that it will doubtless strike many readers as troublesome, if not bizarre. But I have never seen any economic analysis that shows how manufacturer-imposed resale price maintenance, closed dealer territories, customer allocation clauses, or the like can have the net effect of restricting output. We have too quickly assumed something that appears untrue.

Perhaps the ambiguity of the word 'restraint' accounts for some of our confusion on this topic. When the Supreme Court speaks of a restraint it often, or even usually, refers to the manufacturer's control of certain activities of his resellers or to the elimination by the manufacturer of some forms of rivalry among his resellers. There is, of course, nothing sinister or unusual about using 'restraint' in that sense. It is merely a form of vertical integration by contract, a less complete integration than that which would obtain if the manufacturer owned his outlets and directed their activities. It is merely one instance of the coordination of economic activities which is ubiquitous in the economic world and upon which our wealth depends. The important point is that such vertical control never creates 'restraint' in that other common meaning, restriction of output. Perhaps, if we are more careful about the ambiguity of the word and make it clear in which sense we use it, our reasoning about antitrust problems, including the problem of vertical restraints, will improve.[117]

(ii) *The Second View*

There are, however, many commentators who perceive possible dangers to the competitive process from such agreements. The principal concerns are as follows.

The first is *market foreclosure*. If a producer has made exclusive contracts with certain outlets to sell only its brand of a particular product, then it may be difficult for other producers to secure outlets for their own sales. This is especially so where either the best outlets have already been taken, or the number of outlets for distributing a particular product is limited by the nature of that product or by external factors such as planning laws.

A second concern is that *consumers will be harmed* by certain types of vertical restraints, resale-price maintenance being the most commonly cited example, although this has been vigorously contested.[118] Consumer harm is said to be apparent in other ways. Thus, it is argued that systems of selective or exclusive distribution force a 'package' on consumers, which includes the basic price of the product, plus advertising costs, after-sales service, and the like, even though some consumers would prefer to take the raw product itself and worry about maintenance, etc., themselves.

A third disadvantage said to attend vertical agreements is that they can serve as a *mask for cartels between producers or distributors*. A producer may grant an exclusive distribution right where the distributor has agreed with other distributors of competing products to divide the market horizontally: the consequence will be that inter- as well as intra-brand competition is reduced. It has however been questioned whether this actually happens, and whether it is exacerbated by the existence of the vertical agreement. It has also been argued that if this

---

117 See also F. Easterbrook, 'Vertical Arrangements and the Rule of Reason' (1984) 53 *Antitrust LJ* 135; B. Bok, 'An Economist Appraises Vertical Restraints' (1985) 30 *Antitrust Bull.* 117.

118 See n. 116 above.

occurred then the horizontal agreement, which is the real problem, should be the target of the competition authorities.[119]

A final cause for concern with vertical agreements is peculiar to the EC. Community competition law is not concerned solely with efficiency. The *creation of a single European market is also of prime importance*. Agreements which either explicitly or implicitly divide the market along national or regional lines will, therefore, be treated particularly severely by the competition authorities, as exemplified by the Court's continuing opposition to agreements which attempt to provide absolute territorial protection.

Comanor expresses the concerns of this second, more cautious, school of thought. He reviews Bork's arguments, but does not believe that vertical agreements should always be regarded as legal.[120]

W. Comanor, Vertical Price-Fixing, Vertical Market Restrictions, and the New Antitrust Policy[121]

When vertical restraints are used to promote the provision of distribution services, the critical issue for antitrust purposes remains whether consumers are better served by lower prices and fewer services or by higher prices and more services. In its *Spray-Rite* brief, the Department of Justice suggested that pure vertical restraints always lead to increased consumer welfare. This position is unfounded, and a more hostile treatment of vertical restraints is appropriate.

Because vertical restraints can either enhance or diminish consumer welfare, depending upon the situation, it is tempting to apply the rule of reason on a case-by-case basis.

. . . Yet it is no easy task to determine whether particular restraints increase or decrease efficiency: the answer depends in each case largely on the relative preferences of different groups of consumers. In the interests of judicial economy, therefore, it may be more expeditious to set general policy standards, even though they will sometimes lead to improper results.

Vertical restraints that concern established products are more likely to reduce consumer welfare. Large numbers of consumers are already familiar with such products and are therefore unlikely to place much value on acquiring further information about them. In this context, stringent antitrust standards should be applied to vertical price and non-price restraints alike. This approach could take the form either of a direct *per se* prohibition, or of a modified rule of reason analysis under which the defendant would be required to demonstrate that the restraints have benefited consumers generally. By contrast, in the case of new products or products of new entrants into the market, vertical restraints are less likely to lessen consumer welfare, because their novelty should create greater demand for information. In these circumstances, the restraints should be permissible, or at the least should be treated more leniently in any modified rule of reason analysis.

(b) THE COMMISSION AND VERTICAL RESTRAINTS

(i) *The Critique of the Commission*

The approach of the Community authorities towards vertical restraints has been criticized, the main target being the Commission rather than the CFI or ECJ. References to Article 85 should now be read as to Article 81.

---

[119] See Bork, n. 44 above, ch. 14.
[120] See also G. Monti, 'Article 81 EC and Public Policy' (2002) 39 *CMLRev.* 1057.
[121] (1985) 98 *Harv. L Rev.* 983, 1001–1002.

B. Hawk, System Failure: Vertical Restraints and EC Competition Law[122]

The most fundamental, and the most trenchant, criticism is that the Commission too broadly applies Article 85(1) to agreements having little or no anticompetitive effects. This criticism rests on three pillars . . .

Inadequate economic analysis under 85(1)
The majority of Commission decisions fail adequately to consider whether the restraint at issue harms competition in the welfare sense of economics, i.e., effect on price or output. Concomitantly, market power, which should be the threshold issue, frequently is hardly examined (let alone given a central role) or is simply found to exist in a conclusory fashion under the rubric of 'appreciability'.

. . .

The Commission's rationale under 85(1) is unpersuasive
The . . . explanation for the inadequate economic analysis under 85(1) lies in the Commission's stubborn (in the face of Court judgments) adherence to the definition of a restriction on competition as a restriction on the 'economic freedom' of operators in the marketplace. The principal weaknesses of the Freiburg School notion of restriction on economic freedom are (1) its failure to generate precise operable legal rules, (i.e. its failure to provide an analytical framework); (2) its distance from and tension with (micro) economics which does provide an analytical framework; (3) its tendency to favour traders/competitors over consumers and consumer welfare (efficiency); and (4) its capture under Article 85(1) of totally innocuous contract provisions having no anti-competitive effects in an economic sense.

. . .

Commission refusal to follow Community Courts
The Court of Justice and the Court of First Instance have taken a more nuanced approach toward vertical arrangements under Article 85(1). The Courts have increasingly required an analysis of economic effects, particularly the possibility of foreclosure. This approach has been largely ignored or distinguished by the Commission, which adheres to its non-economics based application of Article 85(1), i.e. restriction on economic freedom.

(ii) *The Commission's Green Paper*

In part as a result of this criticism, the Commission re-examined its approach in 1996 in a wide-ranging Green Paper on Vertical Restraints.[123] A number of important points emerged from this document.

First, the Commission accepted that the academic consensus on the economic effects of vertical restraints is that market structure is of prime importance. The fiercer is the inter-brand competition, the more likely will it be that the pro-competitive and efficiency aspects of the agreement outweigh any anti-competitive effects. This is even more so when market power at the production level is limited and barriers to entry are low.[124]

Secondly, the report made it clear that the desire to create a single market means that vertical restraints that seek to insulate markets through the grant of absolute territorial protection will not be tolerated under either Article 81(1) or (3).[125]

---

[122] (1995) 32 *CMLRev.* 973, 974–975, 977–978, 982. See also C. Bright, 'EU Competition Policy: Rules, Objectives and Deregulation' (1996) 16 *OJLS* 535.

[123] COM(96)721 final [1997] 4 CMLR 519.

[124] *Ibid.*, paras. 82–85.

[125] *Ibid.*, para. 276.

Thirdly, the Commission accepted[126] that it did not engage in meaningful economic analysis within Article 81(1), but rather reserved such matters for consideration under Article 81(3).

Fourthly, the Commission set out a number of options on which it invited comment. Option 1 was to preserve the then present system, which seemed to mean a broad, formalistic interpretation of Article 81(1), coupled with existing block exemptions.[127] Option 2 was to widen the block exemptions by, for example, rendering them applicable to agreements involving more than two parties, and broadening the range of allowable clauses.[128] Option 3 was to develop more focused block exemptions, placing emphasis on the EC's market-integration objectives.[129] The final option was to have some economic analysis within Article 81(1), coupled with block exemptions.[130]

It is clear that the Commission faced a dilemma. It was aware that many vertical restraints do not have any net anti-competitive impact. It was probably also aware that logically they should not therefore be held to fall within Article 81(1). It was, however, mindful of the costs of engaging in extensive economic analysis within this Article.[131]

The Commission presented more concrete proposals in the Follow-up to the Green Paper on Vertical Restraints.[132] It concluded that there should be a more economics-based approach to vertical restraints, and that there should also be one broad block exemption for all vertical agreements. The new Regulation was adopted on 22 December 1999, and came fully into force on 1 June 2000.[133] It will be analysed in detail below. Before doing so, we should consider the differing kinds of vertical restraints and the extent to which they are caught by Article 81(1).

(c) EXCLUSIVE DISTRIBUTION

The essential idea behind an exclusive distribution agreement (EDA) is that the producer agrees to supply only to a particular distributor within a particular territory. This may be buttressed by attempts to prevent third parties from selling into the contract territory of the designated distributor, either through contract terms in agreements which the producer has with other distributors, and/or by assigning to the designated distributor trade mark rights, which will enable the latter to stop such infringements. This type of agreement may be necessary to persuade a distributor to market a new product, or to market an existing product in a new area. An EDA may also be beneficial to the producer by facilitating the efficient distribution of its goods, in the sense that it will not have to incur transport costs, etc., to multiple sites. The central issue is whether an EDA will be caught by Article 81(1), and whether it will be exempted under Article 81(3), either individually or pursuant to a block exemption.

The applicability of Article 81(1) to an EDA has been touched on in the earlier discussion. It is clear that such an agreement can be caught by Article 81(1), and that it must, said the ECJ, be considered in its factual, legal, and economic context in order to consider whether it is caught by Article 81(1).[134] The Commission nonetheless often adopted a more formalistic approach, eschewing the ECJ's contextual approach.

---

[126] *Ibid.*, paras. 180, 193, and 216.
[127] *Ibid.*, para. 281.
[128] *Ibid.*, paras. 282–285.
[129] *Ibid.*, paras. 286–292.
[130] *Ibid.*, paras. 293–298.
[131] See *ibid.*, para. 86 for an express statement to this effect.
[132] [1998] OJ C365/3, [1999] 4 CMLR 281.
[133] Reg. 2790/99 [1999] OJ L336/21, [2000] 4 CMLR 398.
[134] Case 56/65 *Société Technique Minière* v. *Maschinenbau Ulm GmbH* [1966] ECR 235; Case 23/67 *Brasserie de Haecht SA*, n. 58 above; Case T–25/99 *Roberts* v. *Commission* [2001] ECR II–1881; Case T–328/03 *O2 (Germany)*, n. 67 above, paras. 65–73. See 967–969.

Notwithstanding this divergence between Court and Commission, it is apparent from their combined jurisprudence that certain types of restrictions within an EDA are especially likely to fall within Article 81(1). Thus, export bans which prohibit a distributor from exporting the product outside a designated area will be judged particularly severely, as will any other attempt to establish absolute territorial protection for a distributor.[135] Indirect attempts to attain the same end will also be condemned, as in the case of customer guarantees which are available only if the product is bought from the distributor in that State.[136]

If an EDA is caught by Article 81(1) the parties may either seek individual exemption or try to come within the block exemption. The principles that govern individual exemption have been examined above.[137] There was until recently a separate block exemption for EDAs.[138] This has now been replaced by the general block exemption for vertical restraints, which will be examined below.

(d) SELECTIVE DISTRIBUTION

The approach of the Court and the Commission to selective distribution agreements (SDA) stands in marked contrast to that adopted towards EDAs. A selective distribution system is one in which the supplier chooses to distribute the goods only through certain outlets, normally those which fulfil certain criteria concerning expertise. There was, until recently, no block exemption for SDAs as such. They can now come within the new block exemption for vertical restraints, provided that the conditions therein are met. The present discussion will consider whether such agreements fall within Article 81(1).

Case 26/76 **Metro-SB-Groβmärkte GmbH & Co. KG v. Commission and SABA**
[1977] ECR 1875

[Note ToA renumbering: Art. 85 is now Art. 81]

Metro was a wholesaler of goods in Germany. It operated a system of self-service wholesaling and a cash-and-carry service, which enabled it to undercut the prices charged by other wholesalers. Metro applied to SABA to be allowed to stock the electronic equipment produced by the latter, but SABA refused to supply it, claiming that it did not fulfill the conditions that SABA required before supplying its goods. Metro complained to the Commission that SABA's policy was in breach of Article 85(1), but the Commission found in favour of SABA after the latter had amended its terms of trade in certain respects. Metro then sought to have the Commission decision annulled.

THE ECJ

20. ... In the sector covering the production of high quality and technically advanced consumer durables, where a relatively small number of large and medium-scale producers offer a

---

135 Cases 56 and 58/64 *Consten and Grundig* [1966] ECR 299; Case 258/78 *Nungesser*, n. 71 above; Case 19/77 *Miller*, n. 77 above; Case C–279/87 *Tipp-Ex GmbH & Co. KG v. Commission* [1990] ECR I–261; Case T–77/92 *Parker Pen*, n. 54 above; Case T–66/92 *Herlitz AG*, n. 54 above.
136 Case 31/85 *ETA Fabriques d'Ebauches v. DK Investments SA* [1985] ECR 3933.
137 See 977–979.
138 Reg. 1983/83 [1983] OJ L173/1.

varied range of items which, or so consumers may consider, are readily inter-changeable, the structure of the market does not preclude the existence of a variety of channels of distribution adapted to the peculiar characteristics of the various producers and to the requirements of the various categories of consumers. On this view the Commission was justified in recognising that selective distribution systems constituted, together with others, an aspect of competition which accords with Article 85(1), provided that the resellers are chosen on the basis of object-ive criteria of a qualitative nature relating to the technical qualifications of the reseller and his staff and the suitability of his trading premises and that such conditions are laid down uniformly for all potential resellers and are not applied in a discriminatory fashion.

21. It is true that in such systems of distribution price competition is not generally empha-sised either as an exclusive or indeed as a principal factor. . . . However, although price compe-tition is so important that it can never be eliminated, it does not constitute the only effective form of competition or that to which absolute priority must in all circumstances be accorded. . . . For specialist wholesalers and retailers the desire to maintain a certain price level, which corresponds to the desire to preserve, in the interests of consumers, the possi-bility of the continued existence of this channel of distribution in conjunction with new methods of distribution based on a different type of competition policy, forms one of the objectives which may be pursued without necessarily falling under the prohibition of Article 85(1), and if it does fall thereunder, either wholly or in part, coming within the framework of Article 85(3). . . .

The significance of *Metro* is that, when the conditions elaborated therein are fulfilled, the SDA is held not to be within Article 81(1).[139] There are, however, limits to the application of this principle.

(i) *First Condition: The Nature of the Product*

The product has to be of the kind in relation to which the Court and the Commission believe that it is justifiable to limit price competition and to operate the regime of selective distribu-tion with an element of non-price competition. Such products tend to be those that require specialist sales staff,[140] or goods where brand image is of particular importance.[141] Plumbing fittings are, by way of contrast, not deemed to be a technically advanced product which neces-sitates a selective distribution system.[142]

(ii) *Second Condition: Qualitative Criteria*

The *Metro* principle operates to legitimate outlets chosen on qualitative criteria. It can how-ever be difficult to determine whether a particular requirement for a distributor to be accept-able to a supplier should be classified as qualitative or not.[143] Subject to this uncertainty, the

---

[139] See also, e.g., Case 210/81 *Demo-Studio Schmidt v. Commission* [1983] ECR 3045; Case 107/82 *AEG-Telefunken AG v. Commission* [1983] ECR 3151; Case C–376/92 *Metro SB-Großmärkte GmbH & Co. KG v. Cartier SA* [1994] ECR I–15; Case T–67/01 *JCB Service v. Commission* [2004] ECR II–49, para. 131.

[140] Such as electronic equipment: *AEG*; audiovisual equipment: *Demo-Studio Schmidt*; computers: Dec. 84/233 *IBM Personal Computers* [1984] OJ L118/24, [1984] 2 CMLR 342.

[141] Such as ceramic tableware: Dec. 85/616 *Villeroy & Boch* [1985] OJ L376/15, [1988] 4 CMLR 461; jew-ellery: Dec. 83/610 *Murat* [1983] OJ L348/20, [1984] 1 CMLR 219; luxury cosmetics: Case T–19/92 *Groupement d'Achat Edouard Leclerc v. Commission* [1996] ECR II–1851.

[142] Dec. 85/44, *Grohe* [1985] OJ L19/17, [1988] 4 CMLR 612.

[143] Whish, n. 5 above, 559.

Metro principle does not allow a supplier to impose quantitative limits on those who can distribute the product, or to discriminate as between distributors.[144]

The logic of the distinction drawn between qualitative and quantitative criteria for restrictions on distribution is questionable. We have seen that producers will choose the distribution method that they believe will best maximize their sales. Whether they believe that this is best achieved by qualitative or quantitative criteria, or a mixture of both, will vary depending upon the nature of the product. The pro- and anti-competitive effects of such distribution strategies will not, however, differ radically depending on which of these criteria is chosen, as the following extract reveals.

J.S. Chard, The Economics of the Application of Article 85 to Selective Distribution Systems[145]

It should be clear from this discussion of the economic effects of qualitative and quantitative selection criteria that the Commission's attempts to distinguish between the criteria is essentially arbitrary and confusing. To be meaningful, qualitative criteria must have a quantitative effect . . . while quantitative criteria may have qualitative implications. With regard to the latter aspect for example, in *Omega*, the Commission recognised that the number of concessionaires needed to be limited otherwise no concessionaire could attain a sufficient turnover to be able to undertake service and guarantee commitments. Thus, qualitative and quantitative criteria should be subject to the same analytical procedure.

[*The author suggests that a proper economic analysis along the following lines is required:*]

First, the Commission should examine whether there is direct evidence of collusion between manufacturers and/or distributors of different brands or whether the restriction embraces so large a fraction of the market . . . as to make cartelisation a plausible motivation for the restriction. If it finds the answer is no . . . there should be a presumption that the restriction has pro-competitive effects. The parties to the agreements in question can be expected to indicate the alleged pro-competitive effects and the Commission should not query these too closely. It should not be tempted to second-guess business judgments as to what arrangements would or would not provide adequate means for achieving the pro-competitive effects and attach conditions to the granting of negative clearance or exemption under Article 85(3), as its record in this respect does not inspire confidence.

Secondly, if there is some evidence of restrictions in competition between manufacturers and/or distributors, but the evidence is not conclusive, . . . the Commission should carefully examine whether pro-competitive effects are being achieved, . . . the burden of justification being shifted firmly onto the defendant. . . .

What evidence there is seems to cast doubt on the likely importance of anti-competitive effects while pro-competitive effects seem likely to be more common . . . If anti-competitive effects are usually absent, then the greater freedom of manufacturers to choose the distribution arrangements which suit them best will tend to result in the most efficient forms of arrangements being used.

It should, however, be noted that the greater leniency accorded to SDAs as opposed to EDAs may be partially explained by the importance attached to the attainment of a single European

---

144 See Case 107/82 *AEG-Telefunken*, n. 139 above; Cases 25 and 26/84 *Ford* v. *Commission* [1985] ECR 2725; Case T–19/92 *Edouard Leclerc*, n. 141 above; Dec. 90/38 *Bayo-N-Ox* [1990] OJ L21/71, [1990] 4 CMLR 930.

145 (1982) 7 *ELRev.* 83, 97, 100–101. See also C. Vajda, 'Selective Distribution in the European Community' (1979) 13 *JWTL* 409.

market. EDAs are more likely to divide the Community along national lines than are SDAs and, as seen, the EC is particularly antagonistic towards such forms of market division.

(iii) *Third Condition: Non-elimination of Competition through Multiple SDAs*

The compatibility of a particular SDA with Article 81(1) may be affected by the existence of other such SDAs, if the overall impact is to eliminate or unduly restrict competition.

Case 75/84 **Metro-SB-Großmärkte GmbH & Co. KG v. Commission (No. 2)**
[1986] ECR 3021

[Note ToA renumbering: Art. 85 is now Art. 81]

The Commission had renewed an exemption for SABA's selective distribution system. Metro, the original objector, contested the renewal of the SDA. In the original decision the Court had intimated that its view (that SDAs were compatible with Article 85(1)), might be different if, in a particular area, the existence of a large number of SDAs similar to that operated by SABA eliminated firms such as Metro from the market. Metro argued that this had occurred, and that therefore the exemption for the SABA SDA should not be renewed.

THE ECJ

40. It must be borne in mind that, although the Court has held in previous decisions that 'simple' selective distribution systems are capable of constituting an aspect of competition compatible with Article 85(1), there may nevertheless be a restriction or elimination of competition where the existence of a certain number of such systems does not leave any room for other forms of distribution based on a different type of competition policy or results in a rigidity in price structure which is not counterbalanced by other aspects of competition between other products of the same brand and by the existence of effective competition between different brands.

41. Consequently, the existence of a large number of selective distribution systems for a particular product does not in itself permit the conclusion that competition is restricted or distorted. Nor is the existence of such systems decisive as regards the granting or refusal of exemption under Article 85(3), since the only factor to be taken into consideration in that regard is the effect which such systems actually have on the competitive situation. Therefore the coverage ratio of selective distribution systems for colour television sets, to which Metro refers, cannot in itself be regarded as a factor preventing an exemption from being granted.

42. It follows that an increase in the number of 'simple' selective distribution systems after an exemption has been granted must be taken into consideration, when application for renewal of that exemption is being considered, only in the special situation in which the relevant market was already so rigid and structured that the element of competition inherent in 'simple' systems is not sufficient to maintain workable competition. Metro has not been able to show that a special situation of that kind exists in the present case.

43. As regards the effect on the market of the existence of selective distribution systems other than 'simple' systems, the Commission in renewing the exemption based itself on the relatively small market share covered by the SABA system and on the fact that that system is distinguished from 'simple' systems only by the existence of obligations pertaining to the

promotion of sales. By so doing, it did not misdirect itself in exercising its discretion to assess, within the framework of Article 85(3), the economic context in which the SABA system is situated.

The judgment in *Metro II* clearly builds upon the cautionary remarks in the earlier *Metro* case. The situations in which a market analysis will be required to determine whether an SDA is within Article 81(1) are, however, bound to render it more difficult to predict whether a particular SDA will be caught by that Article. Moreover, it would be unfair if the creation of one further SDA brought it, but not those already existing, within Article 81(1). It would be equally odd if the creation of the most recent SDA had the effect of retrospectively bringing the previous SDAs within the ambit of Article 85(1).

(iv) *Fourth Condition: No Absolute Territorial Protection*

The ECJ will not tolerate a SDA if it operates so as to confer absolute territorial protection. This is apparent from the *BMW* case.[146]

Case C–70/93 **Bayerische Motorenwerke AG v. ALD Autoleasing D GmbH**
[1995] ECR I–3439

[Note ToA renumbering: Art. 85 is now Art. 81]

BMW sold its vehicles through a selective distribution system. There was an agreement between BMW and its dealers that the latter were not to deliver vehicles to independent leasing companies that made vehicles available to customers residing or having their seat outside the contract territory of the dealer in question. This was challenged by an independent leasing company, ALD, which had supplied BMW cars in the manner which the agreement was designed to prohibit. Was the agreement caught by Article 85(1)?

THE ECJ

6. BMW claims that the appearance of independent leasing companies ... has created an imbalance in its commercial organisation. Those independent companies concentrate on purchasing from certain BMW dealers and lease the vehicles to customers established outside the contract territory of those dealers. Those customers then turn for the customer services and maintenance to the BMW dealer in the contract territory in which they are established. Since those dealers are not involved in the original sales transaction, they do not obtain any profit margin. They therefore complained to BMW about the activities of independent leasing companies which were disturbing the network.
[*As a result of these complaints BMW instituted the agreement which was the subject-matter of this action.*]
. . .
19. As regards the requirement that competition be restricted, it should be noted that, by virtue of the agreement in question BMW dealers are able to supply vehicles of the BMW

---

146 See also Case T–67/01 *JCB Service*, n. 139 above, para. 85.

mark to independent leasing companies only if the vehicles are to be made available to lessees having their seat in the contract territory of the dealer in question. Consequently, only the dealer in whose territory the lessee has its seat is authorised by the manufacturer to supply to ALD vehicles of the BMW mark, to the exclusion of all other BMW dealers. That amounts to absolute territorial protection for the BMW dealer on whose territory the customer of ALD is established. Furthermore, the agreement reduces each dealer's freedom of commercial action in so far as each individual dealer's choice of customer is confined exclusively to those leasing companies which have concluded contracts with lessees established within that dealer's contract territory.

(e) FRANCHISING

A franchise differs from other distribution methods considered thus far. The franchisor allows the franchisee to use intellectual-property rights belonging to the former, such as trade names, logos, and the like. The premises on which the goods are sold are owned by the franchisee, who pays a royalty to the franchisor for the use of the trade name, etc. Franchises, therefore, benefit both parties: the franchisor receives a payment for the use of its intellectual-property rights; the franchisee can start an independent business with the assurance that the product has been tried and tested elsewhere.

It is of the essence of a franchise that the franchisor will require the franchisee to comply with certain standards and methods of sale. Failure to meet such standards by a particular franchisee can harm both the franchisor and other franchisees by damaging the reputation of the product and trade name. It is also central to the franchising system that the franchisor is able to impose terms to protect the intellectual-property rights assigned to the franchisee.

In the seminal *Pronuptia* case the Court held that terms which related to both of the above issues were not caught by Article 81(1). However, other restrictions in the agreement, such as those which divided the market territorially, were examined under Article 81(3).[147] In *Yves Rocher* the Commission held that a franchise agreement under which the franchisor appointed only one franchisee for a particular area, agreed not to compete with the latter in that area, and forbade franchisees from opening more than one shop resulted in a degree of market-sharing which brought the agreement within Article 81(1).[148] The Commission made other decisions that built upon the judgment in *Pronuptia*.[149]

A block exemption, Regulation 4087/88, was passed to cover certain types of franchise agreements.[150] This has now been replaced by the new general block exemption for vertical restraints.

(f) EXCLUSIVE PURCHASING

Exclusive purchasing agreements (EPAs) are those in which one party agrees to buy all it needs of a product from a particular supplier. Common examples include petrol stations which stock only one brand of petrol and public houses which carry only one general brand of beer.

---

[147] Case 161/84 *Pronuptia*, n. 66 above. The case is set out in the text, at 971–972, above. See J. Venit, '*Pronuptia*: Ancillary Restraints or Unholy Alliances' (1986) 11 *ELRev.* 213.

[148] Dec. 87/14 [1987] OJ L8/49, [1988] 4 CMLR 592, 607.

[149] See, e.g., Dec. 87/407 *Computerland* [1987] OJ L222/12, [1989] 4 CMLR 259; Dec. 88/604 *ServiceMaster Ltd.* [1988] OJ L332/38, [1989] 4 CMLR 581.

[150] [1988] OJ L359/46.

Whether EPAs are within the ambit of Article 81(1) requires a market analysis: if the agreement, considered in its legal, factual, and economic context, could have the effect of restricting, preventing, or distorting competition then it will be within Article 81(1).[151]

Case T–7/93 Langnese-Iglo GmbH v. Commission
[1995] ECR II–1533

[Note ToA renumbering: Art. 85 is now Art. 81]

The CFI considered whether a network of exclusive purchasing agreements was caught by Article 85(1). The Commission had argued that there was no need for any real market analysis to determine whether the agreements restricted competition since the market share covered by the contested agreements was more than 15 per cent of the relevant market and the turnover of the undertakings concerned was well in excess of the ceilings laid down by the Notice on Agreements of Minor Importance.

THE CFI

98. It must be borne in mind that the Notice is intended only to define those agreements which, in the Commission's view, do not have an appreciable effect on competition or trade between Member States. The Court considers that it cannot however be inferred with certainty that a network of exclusive purchasing agreements is automatically liable to prevent, restrict or distort competition appreciably merely because the ceilings laid down in it are exceeded. Moreover, it is apparent from the actual wording of paragraph 3 of that Notice that it is entirely possible, in the facts of the present case, that agreements ... which exceed the ceilings indicated affect ... competition only to an insignificant extent and consequently are not caught by Article 85(1). . . .

99. As to whether the exclusive purchasing agreements fall within ... Article 85(1) ... , it is appropriate, according to the case-law, to consider whether, taken together, all the similar agreements entered into in the relevant market and the other features of the economic and legal context of the agreements at issue show that those agreements cumulatively have the effect of denying access to that market for new domestic and foreign competitors. If ... that is found not to be the case, the individual agreements making up the bundle of agreements as a whole cannot undermine competition within the meaning of Article 85(1). . . . If, on the other hand, such examination reveals that it is difficult to gain access to the market, it is necessary to assess the extent to which the contested agreements contribute to the cumulative effect produced, on the basis that only agreements which make a significant contribution to any partitioning of the market are prohibited (*Delimitis*, paragraphs 23 and 24).

100. It must then be borne in mind, that as the Court of Justice held in ... *Brasserie de Haecht*, consideration of the effects of an exclusive agreement implied that regard must be had to the economic and legal context of the agreement, in which it might combine with others to have a cumulative effect on competition.

---

151 Case 23/67 *Brasserie de Haecht*, n. 58 above; Case C–234/89 *Delimitis*, n. 59 above; Case C–393/92 *Municipality of Almelo v. NV Energiebedrijf Ijsselmij* [1994] ECR I–1477; Case T–65/98 *Van den Bergh Foods Ltd.* v. *Commission* [2003] ECR II–4653, paras. 83–84, 91. The competition authorities will take account of clauses which, although not constituting an obligation as such on the reseller to purchase all its requirements of a product from a supplier, nonetheless constitute inducements to do so. Offering discounts to the reseller is one obvious example.

[The CFI found that the agreements were liable to affect competition appreciably and therefore came within Article 85(1).]

The parties to an EPA can seek exemption, either on an individual basis or pursuant to the block exemption. There was a specific block exemption, Regulation 1984/83, covering exclusive purchasing.[152] This has now been replaced by the new block exemption for vertical restraints.

(g) THE BLOCK EXEMPTION

(i) *The New-style Block Exemption*

We have already seen the impetus for reform of vertical restraints. Regulation 2790/99[153] is properly regarded as a new-style block exemption.[154] It differs from the previous block exemptions in this area in a number of ways. It is less formalistic than its predecessors, and is more economics-oriented. It applies to all species of vertical restraints, with the exception of distribution agreements for motor vehicles. It is less prescriptive than the earlier regulations. These had generally followed a format of having a specific list of white clauses that were allowed and black clauses that were forbidden. The new Regulation no longer contains a white list: if conduct is not prohibited it is therefore permitted. It must be read in tandem with Commission Guidelines.[155]

The recitals to Regulation 2790/99 state that it is possible to define a category of vertical agreements that will normally satisfy the conditions of Article 81(3). These agreements are said to improve economic efficiency by facilitating co-ordination and reducing distribution costs.[156]

(ii) *Article 1: Definitions*

Article 1 of Regulation 2790/99 provides definitions of matters such as exclusive supply obligation, selective distribution system, and the like. The definition of 'non-compete obligation' is worthy of note.

'Non-compete obligation' means any direct or indirect obligation causing the buyer not to manufacture, purchase, sell or resell goods or services which compete with the contract goods or services, or any direct or indirect obligation on the buyer to purchase from the supplier or from another undertaking designated by the supplier more than 80 per cent of the buyer's total purchases of the contract goods or services on the relevant market. . . .

---

[152] [1983] OJ L173/5.

[153] Commission Reg. 2790/99 of 22 Dec. 1999 on the application of Art. 81(3) of the Treaty to categories of vertical agreements and concerted practices [1999] OJ L336/21.

[154] R. Whish, 'Regulation 2790/99: The Commission's "New Style" Block Exemption for Vertical Agreements' (2000) 37 *CMLRev.* 887.

[155] Guidelines on Vertical Restraints [2000] OJ C291/1. See also European Commission, *Competition Policy in Europe, The Competition Rules for Supply and Distribution Agreements* (Office for Official Publications of the European Communities, 2002).

[156] Reg. 2790/99, n. 153 above, rec. 6.

(iii) *Article 2: The Core of the Block Exemption*

The core of the block exemption is to be found in Article 2. *Article 2(1)* provides that:

> … Article 81(1) shall not apply to agreements or concerted practices entered into between two or more undertakings each of which operates, for the purposes of the agreement, at a different level of the production or distribution chain, and relating to the conditions under which the parties may purchase, sell, or resell certain goods or services ('vertical agreements').
>
> This exemption shall apply to the extent to which such agreements contain restrictions of competition falling within the scope of Article 81(1) ('vertical restraints').

It is clear therefore that an agreement that does not fall within Article 81(1) will not need to use the block exemption. Subject to this, the block exemption applies to all types of vertical agreements, and the exempted agreement can be multilateral. Article 2(1) is framed in terms of *two or more undertakings*, whereas the old block exemptions applied only to bilateral agreements. It is, however, necessary for *each* of the undertakings to operate, for the purposes of the agreement, at a different level of the production or distribution chain. The fact that Article 2(1) includes the phrase *for the purposes of the agreement* means that it is possible, subject to the limits of Article 2(4), for two firms that are, for example, both cement manufacturers to come within the Regulation. This would be so where one supplies material to the other.

Article 2(2) applies the block exemption to vertical agreements between an association of undertakings and its members, or its suppliers. All members of the association must however be retailers, and no individual member must have an annual turnover in excess of 50 million Euros.

Article 2(3) makes the block exemption applicable where intellectual property rights are ancillary to the main purpose of the vertical agreement.[157]

Article 2(4) is designed to prevent the block exemption being used by competing undertakings to engage in market division. Competing undertakings are actual or potential suppliers in the same product market.[158] Article 2(4) provides that Article 2(1) shall not apply to vertical agreements between competing undertakings. Article 2(4) then provides that the exemption can apply where such undertakings enter into a non-reciprocal vertical agreement. There are other conditions to be met. The buyer must have a turnover not greater than 100 million Euros. Or the supplier is a manufacturer and distributor of goods, while the buyer is a distributor not manufacturing goods that compete with the contract goods. Or the supplier is a provider of services at several levels of trade, while the buyer does not provide competing services at the level of trade where it purchases the contract goods.

Article 2(5) states that the block exemption shall not apply to vertical agreements the subject-matter of which falls within the scope of any other block exemption.

(iv) *Article 3: The Market Share Cap*

The likelihood of efficiency gains from vertical agreements outweighing anti-competitive effects is said in the recitals to be dependent on the market power of the undertakings concerned, and the Regulation therefore has limits as to the market share of the participating firms.[159] Article 3(1) states that the exemption contained in Article 2 only applies on the condition

---

[157] For detailed treatment see Jones and Sufrin, n. 54 above, 661–662.
[158] Reg. 2790/99, n. 153 above, Art. 1(a); Guidelines, n. 155 above, para. 26.
[159] Reg. 2790/99, n. 153 above, recs. 7–8.

that the market share held by the supplier does not exceed 30 per cent of the relevant market on which it sells the contract goods or services. In the case of vertical agreements containing exclusive supply obligations, the condition is that the market share of the buyer must not exceed 30 per cent of the relevant market on which it purchases the contract goods or services: Article 3(2).[160] The method of calculating market share is laid down in Article 9.

(v) *Article 4: The Black List*

The recitals make it clear that certain types of clauses that are regarded as especially anti-competitive will not benefit from the block exemption. These include clauses relating to vertical price fixing and territorial protection.[161] This issue is dealt with in Article 4. It excludes the Regulation for vertical agreements which, directly or indirectly, in isolation or combination with other factors under the control of the parties, have as their object any of the following restrictions.

Resale price maintenance is excluded. Maximum selling prices and recommendations as to selling prices are allowed, subject to the caveat that they do not amount to a fixed or minimum sale price, as a result of pressure from, or incentives offered by, any of the parties.[162]

Restrictions on the territory into which, or the customers to whom, the buyer can sell the goods or services are also precluded.[163] This is subject to a number of exceptions. It is permissible to have a restriction on active sales into the exclusive territory or to an exclusive customer group reserved to the supplier, or allocated by the supplier to another buyer, where such a restriction does not limit sales by the customers to the buyer.[164] It is permissible to restrict sales to end users by a buyer operating at the wholesale level of trade, and to restrict sales to unauthorized distributors by the members of a selective distribution system. The final exception is that it is possible to restrict the buyer of components for use from selling them to a customer who would use them to make goods that would compete with those of the supplier.

The restriction of active or passive sales to end users by members of a selective distribution system operating at the retail level is not allowed. This is without prejudice to the possibility of prohibiting a member of the system from operating out of an unauthorized place of establishment.[165] It is important to note that, subject to this condition, selective and exclusive distribution can be combined within one agreement. Such an agreement could still come within the block exemption, provided that it complied with the other conditions laid down therein.[166]

It is not possible to have restrictions of cross-supplies between distributors within a selective distribution system, including between distributors operating at different levels of trade.[167] A selected distributor must therefore be able to buy from any approved distributor.

The final blacklisted provision relates to the supply of components. It is designed to allow end-users and independent service-providers to obtain spare parts.[168]

---

[160] Guidelines, n. 155 above, paras. 21–22.
[161] Reg. 2790/99, n. 153 above, rec. 10.
[162] *Ibid.*, Art. 4(a); Guidelines, n. 155 above, para. 47.
[163] Reg. 2790/99, n. 153 above, Art. 4(b).
[164] Guidelines, n. 155 above, para. 50.
[165] Reg. 2790/99, n. 153 above, Art. 4(c); Guidelines, n. 155 above, para. 53.
[166] Whish, n. 154 above, 916.
[167] Reg. 2790/99, n. 153 above, Art. 4(d).
[168] *Ibid.*, Art. 4(e).

(vi) *Article 5: Obligations that Do Not Benefit from the Exemption*

The restrictions in Article 4 prevent the entire vertical agreement from benefiting from the block exemption. Article 5 excludes the benefit of the block exemption from certain terms contained in such an agreement. The agreement itself may however still gain the benefit of the block exemption if the objectionable clause can be severed. There are three types of obligation listed in Article 5.

Non-compete obligations cannot be indefinite or last longer than five years. Obligations not to compete after the term of the agreement are also excluded. This is subject to a qualification allowing such an obligation for one year on sales of competing goods or services from the place of sale that the buyer operated from during the contract, provided that this is necessary to protect the supplier's know-how. The benefit of the block exemption is also excluded from an obligation causing the members of a selective distribution system from selling brands of particular competing suppliers.

(vii) *Articles 6–8: Withdrawing the Benefit of the Regulation*

Articles 6–8 provide certain limits to the application of the block exemption. *Article 6* allows the Commission to withdraw the benefit of the block exemption where it finds that vertical agreements to which the Regulation applies nevertheless have effects incompatible with Article 81(3). This will apply in particular where access to the relevant market or competition therein is significantly restricted by the cumulative effect of parallel networks of similar vertical restraints by competing suppliers or buyers.[169] *Article 7* allows the competent authority of a Member State, where the State has the characteristics of a distinct geographic market, to withdraw the benefit of the block exemption for that State under the same conditions as in Article 6. *Article 8* empowers the Commission to pass a regulation declaring that the block exemption is inapplicable where there are vertical restraints covering more than 50 per cent of that market.

(h) SUMMARY

i. There has been fierce debate about whether vertical agreements are harmful, and if so when.

ii. There has been criticism of the Commission for not talking with the same voice as the ECJ, and for employing a test that equates a restriction of conduct with a restriction of competition.

iii. The degree of difference between the Community Courts and the Commission has diminished more recently. It would however be premature to say that the Commission has fully adopted the ECJ's approach to Article 81(1).[170] Moreover, the very approach of the Community Courts has been thrown into some doubt as a result of the CFI's decision in *Métropole*.[171]

iv. The importance of this difference has been lessened by the passage of the new block exemption. This Regulation is undoubtedly less formalistic than its predecessors. It should not however be forgotten that the Regulation has a market share cap of 30 per cent. Some

---

[169] Guidelines, n. 155 above, paras. 71–75.

[170] Jones and Sufrin, n. 54 above, 685–686.

[171] Case T–112/99 *Métropole Télévision (M6), Suez-Lyonnaise des Eaux, France Telecom, and Télévision Française 1 SA (TFI)* v. *Commission* [2001] ECR II–2459.

commentators feel that this is warranted, since economic theory tells us that it is only when there is some degree of market power that vertical agreements are dangerous.[172] This may well be accepted, but other commentators regard the existing cap as too low, and have characterized the new Regulation as little more than an extended *de minimis* provision.[173]

12. COMPETITION LAW: ENFORCEMENT

(a) THE TRADITIONAL APPROACH AND THE MODERNIZATION WHITE PAPER

The discussion thus far has focused on the central elements of Article 81 and the way in which they have been interpreted by the Commission and the Community Courts. The enforcement regime for Articles 81 and 82 was however reformed in 2003. Space precludes detailed treatment of the new regime, but it is nonetheless important to convey the core elements of this new regime.

The traditional approach to the enforcement of EC competition law had two foundations. Agreements had, subject to certain exceptions, to be notified to the Commission, and the Commission had a monopoly over the application of Article 81(3). The system was, in this sense, centralized, although there were decentralized aspects. Articles 81 and 82 had direct effect and national courts could therefore apply Article 81(1), but could not grant an individual exemption under Article 81(3).

The traditional approach came under increasing strain. The Commission did not have the resources to deal with all the agreements notified to it, nor did it have the resources to adjudicate on anything but a handful of individual exemptions. The Commission therefore encouraged national courts to apply Articles 81 and 82. However, in the White Paper on Modernization[174] it proposed a thorough overhaul of the enforcement regime, abolishing notification and the Commission's monopoly over Article 81(3). National courts and national competition authorities (NCAs) would be empowered to apply Article 81 in its entirety and Article 82. The White Paper generated a voluminous literature, which contained all shades of opinion.[175]

(b) THE NEW REGIME

Article 1 of Regulation 1/2003, which implemented the new regime,[176] provides that agreements, etc., caught by Article 81(1) which do not satisfy the conditions of Article 81(3) shall be prohibited, no prior decision to that effect being required. The same principle is applicable

---

[172] Whish, n. 154 above.

[173] M. Griffiths, 'A Glorification of De Minimis? The Regulation on Vertical Agreements' [2000] *ECLR* 241.

[174] White Paper on Modernization of the Rules Implementing Arts. 85 and 86 of the EC Treaty, Commission Programme 99/27, 28 Apr. 1999.

[175] See, e.g., R. Wesseling, 'The Commission White Paper on Modernisation of EC Antitrust Law: Unspoken Consequences and Incomplete Treatment of Alternative Options' [1999] *ECLR* 420; C.-D. Ehlermann, 'The Modernization of EC Antitrust Policy: A Legal and Cultural Revolution' (2000) 37 *CMLRev.* 537; A. Schaub, 'Modernisation of EC Competition Law: Reform of Regulation No. 17', in B. Hawk (ed.), *Fordham Corporate Law Institute* (Fordham University, 2000), ch. 10; R. Whish and B. Sufrin, 'Community Competition Law: Notification and Exemption—Goodbye to All That', in D. Hayton (ed.), *Law's Future(s): British Legal Developments in the 21st Century* (Hart, 2000), ch. 8; M. Monti, 'European Competition Law for the 21st Century', in B. Hawk (ed.), *Fordham Corporate Law Institute* (Fordham University, 2001), ch. 15.

[176] Council Reg. (EC) 1/2003 of 16 Dec. 2002 on the implementation of the rules on competition laid down in Arts. 81 and 82 of the Treaty [2003] OJ L1/1; J. Venit, 'Brave New World: The Decentralization and Modernization of Enforcement under Articles 81 and 82 of the EC Treaty' (2003) 40 *CMLRev.* 545.

to abuse of a dominant position in Article 82. NCAs and national courts can apply the entirety of Articles 81 and 82.[177] The Regulation contains wide-ranging powers of investigation,[178] and far-reaching provisions concerning fines and penalty payments.[179]

There are provisions facilitating co-operation between an NCA and the Commission.[180] NCAs have an obligation to inform the Commission of proceedings begun in the Member States,[181] and the NCAs are also obliged to inform the Commission before they adopt a decision requiring an infringement of Article 81 or 82 to be brought to an end, before they accept commitments or withdraw the benefit of a block exemption.[182] The NCAs are 'relieved of their competence' to apply Article 81 and 82 if the Commission initiates proceedings for the adoption of a decision.[183] NCAs cannot make rulings in relation to Articles 81 and 82 that are counter to a decision already reached by the Commission on that same subject-matter.[184]

There are also provisions facilitating co-operation between NCAs in different Member States,[185] and a European Competition Network has been established for discussion and co-operation between NCAs.[186] Where two or more NCAs have received a complaint, or are acting on their own initiative, against the same agreement, etc., 'the fact that one authority is dealing with the case shall be sufficient grounds for the others to suspend proceedings before them or to reject the complaint'.[187] The Commission may also reject a complaint on the ground that an NCA is dealing with the matter. Where a case has already been dealt with by an NCA or by the Commission, any other NCA may reject it.[188]

There are separate provisions dealing with co-operation with national courts.[189] National courts may, in proceedings for the application of Articles 81 and 82, ask the Commission for information in its possession, or for its opinion on questions concerning the application of Community competition rules.[190] Member States are obliged to send the Commission copies of judgments applying Article 81 or 82.[191] NCAs may submit written observations to national courts in relation to cases concerning Articles 81 and 82, and may submit oral argument with the permission of the national court. The Commission may do likewise where the coherent application of Articles 81 and 82 so requires.[192] National courts cannot make rulings in relation to Articles 81 and 82 that are counter to a decision already reached by the Commission on the same subject-matter, and they must avoid giving decisions that would conflict with a decision contemplated by the Commission in proceedings which it has initiated.[193]

---

177 Reg. 1/2003, n. 176 above, Arts. 5 and 6.
178 *Ibid.*, Arts. 17–22.
179 *Ibid.*, Arts. 23–26; Guidelines on the method of setting fines imposed pursuant to Art. 23(2)(a) of Reg. 1/2003 [2006] OJ C210/2.
180 Reg. 1/2003, n. 176 above, Arts. 11–12.
181 *Ibid.*, Art. 11(3).
182 *Ibid.*, Art. 11(4).
183 *Ibid.*, Art. 11(6).
184 *Ibid.*, Art. 16(2).
185 Commission Notice on co-operation within the Network of Competition Authorities [2004] OJ C101/43; Joint Statement of the Council and the Commission on the Functioning of the Network of Competition Authorities, available at http://ec.europa.eu/comm/competition/ecn/more_details.html.
186 See http://ec.europa.eu/comm/competition/ecn/more_details.html.
187 Reg. 1/2003, n. 176 above, Art. 13(1).
188 *Ibid.*, Art. 13(2).
189 Commission Notice on the co-operation between the Commission and the courts of the EU Member States in the application of Arts. 81 and 82 EC [2004] OJ C101/54.
190 Reg. 1/2003, n. 176 above, Art. 15(1).
191 *Ibid.*, Art. 15(2).
192 *Ibid.*, Art. 15(3).
193 *Ibid.*, Art. 16(1).

The Commission continues to have enforcement power under the new regime. It can act on a complaint or on its own initiative and find an infringement of Article 81 or Article 82.[194] It can impose behavioural or structural remedies, although the Regulation is framed in favour of the former.[195] The Commission has power, for reasons of the Community public interest, acting on its own initiative to make a decision either that Article 81(1) is inapplicable to an agreement or that the conditions of Article 81(3) are fulfilled. The Commission has an analogous power in relation to Article 82.[196] The Commission must consult an Advisory Committee on Restrictive Practices and Dominant Positions prior to taking decisions under Article 7, 8, 9, 10, 23, 24(2), or 29(1).[197] The Committee is composed of representatives of the NCAs, and the Commission must take 'utmost account' of its opinion.[198]

(c) JUDICIAL REVIEW

Commission Decisions may be reviewed under Articles 230 and 232, and since 1989 this has been undertaken initially by the CFI. The general principles concerning these actions have been considered above.[199] There is appeal from the CFI to the ECJ, but the latter will only review the legal characterization of the facts found by the CFI and the conclusions drawn from them. The ECJ will not examine the facts or the evidence the CFI accepted in support of the facts.[200]

The applicant will have to show standing under Article 230. This hurdle is less problematic for competition matters than it is in relation to other issues. The party against whom a competition decision has been made can seek to have it annulled, and a complainant will normally be accorded standing.[201] There is nonetheless an important issue concerning the range of measures that may be annulled under Article 230. There is little difficulty with formal Commission decisions, such as findings of infringement. More difficulty has been encountered with less formal measures.[202] The grounds of review are listed in Article 230(1). Thus, for example, failure to authenticate the decision taken by the College of Commissioners in the proper manner constitutes breach of an essential procedural requirement.[203] The CFI has held that review of situations entailing complex economic assessments should be confined to verifying compliance with procedural rules, verifying the material accuracy of facts, and checking to ensure that there has been no manifest error of assessment or misuse of power.[204] Notwithstanding such statements, the intensity of review has increased since the task has been allocated to the CFI.[205]

---

[194] *Ibid.*, Art. 7.

[195] *Ibid.*, Art. 7(1)

[196] *Ibid.*, Art. 10.

[197] *Ibid.*, Art. 14(1).

[198] *Ibid.*, Art. 14(5).

[199] See Chs. 14–15.

[200] Case C–8/95 P *New Holland Ford Ltd.* v. *Commission* [1998] ECR I–3175.

[201] Case 26/76 *Metro-SB-Großmärkte GmbH & Co. KG* v. *Commission* [1977] ECR 1875; Cases 228 and 229/82 *Ford Werke AG* v. *Commission* [1984] ECR 1129; Case T–12/93 *Comité Central d'Entreprise de la Société Anonyme Vittel* v. *Commission* [1995] ECR II–1247.

[202] Case 99/79 *Lancôme* v. *Etos* [1980] ECR 2511; Case 60/81 *IBM* v. *Commission* [1981] ECR 2639; Cases T–125 and 127/97 *The Coca-Cola Company and Coca-Cola Enterprises Inc.* v. *Commission* [2000] ECR II–1733; Cases 142 and 156/84 *British American Tobacco Co. Ltd. and R. J. Reynolds Inc.* v. *Commission* [1987] ECR 4487.

[203] Case C–286/95 P *Commission* v. *Imperial Chemical Industries plc (ICI)* [2000] ECR I–2341, paras. 41–43; Cases C–287–288/95 P *Commission* v. *Solvay SA* [2000] ECR I–2391, paras. 45–46.

[204] See, e.g., Case T–44/90 *La Cinq SA* v. *Commission* [1992] ECR II–1; Case T–7/92 *Asia Motor France SA* v. *Commission (No. 2)* [1993] ECR II–669.

[205] See, e.g., Cases T–79/89 etc. *BASF* v. *Commission* [1992] ECR II–315; Cases C–89/85 etc. *A. Ahlström Oy*, n. 33 above; P. Craig, *EU Administrative Law* (Oxford University Press, 2006), ch. 13.

An action may also be brought against the Commission for failure to act under Article 232. However, the Commission is not obliged to proceed with a complaint, and it has discretion whether to use its scarce resources to proceed, taking account of the Community interest.[206]

The mode of challenging decisions of NCAs or national courts is to seek a preliminary ruling under Article 234. Such cases will be heard by the ECJ and the normal rules relating to indirect challenge under Article 234 will apply.[207]

(d) DAMAGES ACTIONS

We must also consider the availability of damages for breach of Article 81 or 82.[208] The ECJ has confirmed that state liability in damages is in principle available where a state entity is the defendant in an Article 82 action.[209] It is now also clear that damages are available as a matter of EC law where the defendant is a private party. In *Crehan*[210] the ECJ held that the full effectiveness of Article 81 would be put at risk if it were not open to any individual, even a party to the agreement, to claim damages for loss caused by a contract or by conduct liable to distort competition. There should not therefore be any absolute bar in national law to such actions, even by parties to the agreement. It was however open to national law to prevent a party from being unjustly enriched or profiting from his unlawful conduct. The national court should take into account, *inter alia*, the respective bargaining strength of the contracting parties and the extent to which a contracting party had responsibility for the breach of Article 81.[211]

The Commission is keen to develop the potential of damages actions as an effective mechanism for ensuring the enforcement of Articles 81 and 82 in national courts pursuant to Regulation 1/2003.[212]

The issue of how far benefits conferred under a contract which is illegal can be recovered is a complex topic detailed treatment of which can be found elsewhere.[213] The relevant principles of EC law have been considered above,[214] and the ECJ has confirmed that these principles apply to recovery pursuant to an Article 81 or 82 action, at least where the defendant is a public undertaking.[215]

---

[206] Case T–24/90 *Automec Srl* v. *Commission* [1992] ECR II–2223.

[207] See Ch. 13.

[208] This discussion should be read in conjunction with Ch. 9; C. Jones, *Private Enforcement of Antitrust Law in the EU, UK and USA* (Oxford University Press, 1999).

[209] Case C–242/95 *GT-Link A/S* v. *De Danske Statsbaner (DSB)* [1997] ECR I–4449.

[210] Case C–453/99 *Courage Ltd.* v. *Crehan* [2001] ECR I–6297, paras. 26–36; Cases C–295–298/04 *Manfredi* v. *Lloyd Adriatico Assicurazione SpA* [2006] ECR I–6619.

[211] A. Jones and D. Beard, 'Co-contractors, Damages and Article 81: The ECJ Finally Speaks' [2002] *ECLR* 246; O. Odudu and J. Edelman, 'Compensatory Damages for Breach of Article 81' (2002) 27 *ELRev.* 327.

[212] Green Paper—Damages Actions for Breach of the EC Antitrust Rules, COM(2005)672 final; J. Pheasant, 'Damages Actions for Breach of the EC Antitrust Rules: The European Commission's Green Paper' [2006] *ECLR* 365; C. Diemer, 'The Green Paper on Damages Actions for Breach of the EC Antitrust Rules' [2006] *ECLR* 309.

[213] A. Jones, 'Recovery of Benefits Conferred under Contractual Obligations Prohibited by Article 85 or 86 of the Treaty of Rome' (1996) 112 *LQR* 606.

[214] See Ch. 9.

[215] Case C–242/95 *GT-Link*, n. 209 above.

13. CONCLUSION

i. The Community Courts have given a broad reading to Article 81, with the objectives of enhancing efficiency and preventing the single market programme from being hindered by private actors. They have therefore read key concepts such as agreement and concerted practice expansively.

ii. The interpretation of Article 81 has also been markedly affected by the extent to which an economic analysis is mandated within Article 81(1). The ECJ has insisted that object and effect should be read disjunctively. Certain agreements will be condemned merely because of proof of their existence. They will be illegal *per se*. Horizontal market division, horizontal price fixing, and boycotts are the classic examples. In relation to many other agreements, a market analysis will be required to determine whether they are within Article 81(1). The CFI and Commission have been more reluctant to embrace a full economic analysis of the pro- and anti-competitive effects of an agreement within Article 81(1).

iii. The jury is still out on whether Article 81(3) should be interpreted according to the narrow or broad view. This issue has been thrown into sharp relief by the devolution of competence over Article 81(3) to national courts and national competition authorities. It is likely that this will tilt the balance in favour of the narrow view.

iv. The reach of Community competition law has not been the work of the courts alone. The legislature has intervened through measures such as the Merger Regulation. The Commission itself has orchestrated developments in diverse ways, through the passage of block exemptions, the control of mergers, the increased attention paid to competition in the public sector, and the reform of the enforcement mechanisms.

14. FURTHER READING[216]

Amato, G., *Antitrust and the Bounds of Power* (Hart, 1997)

Bellamy, C., and Child, G., *European Community Law of Competition* (edited by P. Roth QC and V. Rose, 6th edn., Oxford University Press, 2007)

Bishop, S., and Walker, M., *The Economics of EC Competition Law: Concepts, Application and Measurement* (2nd edn., Sweet & Maxwell, 2002)

Bork, R., *The Antitrust Paradox: A Policy at War with Itself* (Basic Books, 1978)

Faull, J., and Nikpay, A. (eds.), *The EC Law of Competition* (2nd edn., Oxford University Press, 2007)

Furse, M., *Competition Law of the UK and EC* (5th edn., Oxford University Press, 2006)

Gerber, D., *Law and Competition in Twentieth Century Europe* (Oxford University Press, 1998)

Goyder, D., *EC Competition Law* (4th edn., Oxford University Press, 2003)

Harding, C., and Joshua, J., *Regulating Cartels in Europe: A Study of Legal Control of Corporate Delinquency* (Oxford University Press, 2003)

---

[216] There is a voluminous literature on this topic. The references will therefore be confined to books.

Jones, A., and Sufrin, B., *EC Competition Law; Text, Cases, and Materials* (2nd edn., Oxford University Press, 2004)

Kerse, C., and Khan, N., *EC Antitrust Procedure* (5th edn., Sweet & Maxwell, 2005)

Korah, V., *EC Competition Law and Practice* (8th edn., Hart, 2004)

——, and O'Sullivan, D., *Distribution Agreements under the EC Competition Rules* (Hart, 2002)

Middleton, K., Rodger, B., and MacCulloch, A., *Cases and Materials on UK and EC Competition Law* (Oxford University Press, 2003)

Odudu, O., *The Boundaries of EC Competition Law: The Scope of Article 81* (Oxford University Press, 2006)

Wesseling, R., *The Modernisation of EC Antitrust Law* (Hart, 2000)

Whish, R., *Competition Law* (5th edn., LexisNexis, 2003)

26

COMPETITION LAW: ARTICLE 82

1. INTRODUCTION

In the previous chapter we considered the applicability of Article 81. We now focus on the other principal provision concerned with competition policy: Article 82 (ex Article 86):

> Any abuse by one or more undertakings of a dominant position within the common market or in a substantial part of it shall be prohibited as incompatible with the common market in so far as it may affect trade between Member States. Such abuse may, in particular, consist in:
>
> (a) directly or indirectly imposing unfair purchase or selling prices or unfair trading conditions
>
> (b) limiting production, markets or technical development to the prejudice of consumers
>
> (c) applying dissimilar conditions to equivalent transactions with other trading parties, thereby placing them at a competitive disadvantage
>
> (d) making the conclusion of contracts subject to acceptance by the other parties of supplementary obligations which, by their nature or according to commercial usage, have no connection with the subject of such contracts.

2. CENTRAL ISSUES

i. The essence of Article 82 is the control of market power, whether by a single firm or, subject to certain conditions, a number of firms. Article 82 does not however prohibit market power *per se*. It proscribes the *abuse* of market power. Firms are encouraged to compete, with the most efficient players being successful. It would therefore be odd if the winner should be legally penalized, since it may simply be more efficient than the competitors.

ii. There are a number of stages in the Article 82 analysis. It is necessary: to define the relevant market, since this is a pre-condition for deciding whether a firm is dominant; to decide whether the firm is dominant within that market; to determine whether it has abused its dominant position; and whether there are any available defences.

iii. There are difficult issues at each of these stages of analysis. There can be differences of opinion as to, for example, the nature of the product market in a particular case, whether certain behaviour by a dominant firm should always be regarded as abusive, and the very purpose to be served by Article 82, whether this is primarily to protect competitors or consumers.

iv.   The Commission has conducted a review of Article 82. This generated much comment as to the purpose served by this Article, and the extent to which it should be based on legal form or economic effect.

v.   The enforcement of Article 82 is now subject to the reformed regime discussed in the previous chapter, to which reference should be made.[1]

3. DOMINANT POSITION: DEFINING THE RELEVANT MARKET

Article 82 requires that the undertaking[2] or undertakings be in a dominant position. Dominance must be assessed in relation to three variables: the product market, the geographical market, and the temporal factor.

(a) THE PRODUCT MARKET

Any firm will only have market power in the supply of particular goods or services. Other things being equal, the narrower the definition of the product market, the easier it is to conclude that an undertaking is dominant under Article 82. It is not, therefore, surprising to find that many cases have been fought on this terrain, with the firm contesting that the Commission adopted too narrow a definition of the product.[3]

The general approach of the Commission and the Court has been to focus upon *interchangeability*: the extent to which the goods or services under scrutiny are interchangeable with other products.[4] This is addressed by looking at both the demand and supply sides of the market.

From the *demand side* interchangeability requires investigation of cross-elasticities of the product. The basic idea is simple. Cross-elasticity is high where an increase in the price of one product, for example beef, will lead buyers to switch in significant numbers to lamb or pork. The existence of high cross-elasticity indicates that the products are in reality part of the same market. It may, however, be difficult to obtain reliable data on the relative cross-elasticities of different products. In these circumstances the Commission and the Court may well look to related factors to determine whether the products really are interchangeable, including the prices of the respective products and their physical characteristics. For example, wines may vary significantly in price and quality. An increase in the price of a top-quality wine may not lead buyers to switch to 'plonk', although it may lead them to buy more of another high-grade wine. The relevance of the physical characteristics of the product is exemplified by *United Brands*, where the Court took into account the taste, seedlessness, and softness of bananas in

---

[1] See 999–1001.

[2] The definition of an undertaking is the same as in the context of Art. 85: see 952–953. It covers any entity engaged in economic activity, regardless of its legal status and the way it is financed: Case T–128/98 *Aéroports de Paris* v. *Commission* [2000] ECR II–3929, para. 107.

[3] Cases 6 and 7/73 *Istituto Chemioterapico Italiano SpA and Commercial Solvents* v. *Commission* [1974] ECR 223; Case 6/72 *Europemballage Corporation and Continental Can Co. Inc.* v. *Commission* [1973] ECR 215; Case 85/76 *Hoffmann-La Roche and Co. AG* v. *Commission* [1979] ECR 461; Case C–333/94 P *Tetra Pak International SA* v. *Commission* [1996] ECR I–5951.

[4] See, e.g., Case 27/76 *United Brands Company and United Brands Continentaal BV* v. *Commission* [1978] ECR 207.

order to determine whether they constituted a separate market from other fruits.[5] More recently in *France Télécom*[6] the CFI held that the markets for low- and high-speed internet access were distinct, since there was insufficient substitutability between them.

The degree of product interchangeability may also be affected by factors on the *supply side*. Even if firms are producing differing products it may be relatively simple for one firm to adapt its machinery to make the goods produced by a rival. In these circumstances the two products may be thought to be part of the same market.[7]

The following cases indicate how the Court defines the relevant product market, and the problems that this can entail:

Case 27/76 **United Brands Company and United Brands Continentaal BV v. Commission**
[1978] ECR 207

[Note ToA renumbering: Art. 86 is now Art. 82]

United Brands produced bananas, and was accused of a variety of abusive practices, which will be examined below. An initial issue concerned the definition of the relevant product market. UB argued that bananas were part of a larger market in fresh fruit, and produced studies designed to show that the cross-elasticity between bananas and other fruit was high. The Commission contended that cross-elasticity was low, and that bananas were a distinct market because they constituted an important part of the diet for certain consumers, and because they had specific qualities which made other fruits unacceptable as substitutes.

THE ECJ

22. For the banana to be regarded as forming a market which is sufficiently differentiated from other fruits it must be possible for it to be singled out by such special features distinguishing it from other fruits that it is only to a limited extent interchangeable with them and is only exposed to their competition in a way that is hardly perceptible.

23. The ripening of bananas takes place the whole year round without any season having to be taken into account.

. . .

27. Since the banana is a fruit which is always available in sufficient quantities the question whether it can be replaced by other fruits must be determined over the whole of the year for the purpose of ascertaining the degree of competition between it and other fresh fruit.

28. The studies of the banana market on the Court's file show that on the latter market there is no significant long term cross-elasticity any more than ... there is any seasonal substitutability in general between the banana and all the seasonal fruits, as this only exists between the banana and two fruits (peaches and table grapes) in one of the countries (West Germany) of the relevant geographical market.

29. As far as concerns the two fruits available throughout the year (oranges and apples) the first are not interchangeable and in the case of the second there is only a relative degree of substitutability.

---

[5] *Ibid.*

[6] Case T–340/03 *France Télécom SA* v. *Commission*, 30 Jan. 2007, paras. 78–91.

[7] Case 6/72 *Continental Can*, n. 3 above; Case T–65/96 *Kish Glass & Co. Ltd.* v. *Commission* [2000] ECR II–1885, para. 68.

30. This small degree of substitutability is accounted for by the specific features of the banana and all the factors which influence consumer choice.

31. The banana has certain characteristics, appearance, taste, softness, seedlessness, easy handling, a constant level of production which enable it to satisfy the constant needs of an important section of the population consisting of the very young, the old and the sick.

32. As far as prices are concerned two FAO studies show that the banana is only affected by the prices—falling prices—of other fruits (and only of peaches and table grapes) during the summer months and mainly in July and then by an amount not exceeding 20 per cent.

. . .

34. It follows from all these considerations that a very large number of consumers having a constant need for bananas are not noticeably or even appreciably enticed away from the consumption of this product by the arrival of fresh fruit on the market and that even the seasonal peak periods only affect it for a limited period of time from the point of view of substitutability.

35. Consequently the banana market is a market which is sufficiently distinct from the other fresh fruit market.

Case 322/81 Nederlandsche Banden-Industrie Michelin NV v. Commission
[1983] ECR 3461

[Note ToA renumbering: Art. 86 is now Art. 82]

The Commission brought an action against Michelin based on the practice of awarding discounts on tyre sales which were not related to objective differences in costs. The allegation was, therefore, that the discounts were granted so as to tie purchasers to Michelin. Michelin was held to have a dominant position in the market for new replacement tyres for lorries, buses, and similar vehicles. Michelin argued that this definition of the product market was arbitrary and artificial, and that regard should also be had to tyres for cars and vans, and to retreads.

THE ECJ

37. As the Court has repeatedly emphasised . . . for the purposes of investigating the possibly dominant position of an undertaking on a given market, the possibilities of competition must be judged in the context of the market comprising the totality of the products which, with respect to their characteristics, are particularly suitable for satisfying constant needs and are only to a limited extent interchangeable with other products.

However, it must be noted that the determination of the relevant market is useful in assessing whether the undertaking concerned is in a position to prevent effective competition from being maintained and behave to an appreciable extent independently of its competitors and customers and consumers. For this purpose, therefore, an examination limited to the objective characteristics only of the relevant products cannot be sufficient: the competitive conditions and the structure of supply and demand must also be taken into consideration.

38. Moreover, it was for that reason that the Commission and Michelin NV agreed that new, original-equipment tyres should not be taken into consideration in the assessment of market shares. Owing to the particular structure of demand for such tyres characterised by direct orders from car manufacturers, competition in this sphere is in fact governed by completely different factors and rules.

39. As far as replacement tyres are concerned, the first point which must be made is that at the user level there is no interchangeability between car and van tyres on the one hand and

heavy-vehicle tyres on the other. Car and van tyres therefore have no influence at all on competition on the market in heavy-vehicle tyres.

40. Furthermore, the structure of demand for each of these groups of products is different. Most buyers of heavy-vehicle tyres are trade users ... for whom ... the purchase of replacement tyres represents an item of considerable expenditure.... On the other hand, for the average buyer of car or van tyres the purchase of tyres is an occasional event....

41. The final point which must be made is that there is no elasticity of supply between tyres for heavy vehicles and car tyres owing to significant differences in production techniques and in the plant and tools needed for their manufacture. The fact that time and considerable investment are required in order to modify production plant for the manufacture of light-vehicle tyres instead of heavy-vehicle tyres or vice versa means that there is no discernible relationship between the two categories of tyre enabling production to be adapted to demand on the market.

...

45. In establishing that Michelin NV has a dominant position the Commission was therefore right to assess its market share with reference to replacement tyres for lorries, buses and similar vehicles and to exclude consideration of car and van tyres.

The product market may be particularly narrow. Thus in *Hugin*[8] the Commission held Hugin to be in breach of Article 82 by refusing to supply spare parts for its cash registers to Liptons, which competed with Hugin in servicing Hugin's machines. The Commission defined the relevant market as being spare parts for Hugin machines, which were needed by independent repairers. Hugin argued that the proper product market was cash registers in general, which was very competitive. The Court found that users of cash registers would require the services of a specialist to service the machines and upheld the product definition applied by the Commission.[9]

(b) THE GEOGRAPHIC MARKET

The geographic market is defined as the territory in which all traders operate in the same or sufficiently homogenous conditions of competition in relation to the relevant products or services, without it being necessary for those conditions to be perfectly homogenous.[10] In the absence of special factors, the relevant geographic market was held in *Hilti* to be the entire EC.[11] The *United Brands* case provides insights into this aspect of the Court's thinking:

Case 27/76 **United Brands Company and United Brands Continentaal BV v. Commission**
[1978] ECR 207

The facts were set out above. UB argued that the Commission misconstrued the geographic market. The Commission had excluded France, Italy, and the UK, because of particular trading

---

[8] Case 22/78 *Hugin Kassaregister AB and Hugin Cash Registers Limited* v. *Commission* [1979] ECR 1869. See also Case 26/75 *General Motors Continental NV* v. *Commission* [1975] ECR 1367.

[9] For criticism see E. Fox, 'Monopolization and Dominance in the US and the EC: Efficiency, Opportunity and Fairness' (1986) 61 *Notre Dame LRev.* 981, 1003–1004.

[10] Case T–83/91 *Tetra Pak* v. *Commission* [1994] ECR II–755, para. 91, confirmed on appeal in Case C–333/94 P *Tetra Pak*, n. 3 above; Case T–219/99 *British Airways plc* v. *Commission* [2003] ECR II–5917, para. 108.

[11] Dec. 88/138 [1988] OJ L65/19, upheld on appeal: Case C–53/92 P *Hilti AG* v. *Commission* [1994] ECR I–667.

conditions which existed there. The applicants accepted this, but contended that trading conditions were also different in each of the other countries that had been treated by the
Commission as the relevant geographic market.

THE ECJ

44. The conditions for the application of Article 86 to an undertaking in a dominant position
presuppose the clear delimitation of the substantial part of the Common Market in which it
may be able to engage in abuses which hinder effective competition and this is an area where
the objective conditions of competition applying to the product in question must be the same
for all traders.

45. The Community has not established a common organisation of the agricultural market
in bananas.

46. Consequently import arrangements vary considerably from one Member State to
another and reflect a specific commercial policy to the States concerned.

[*The Court then examined the special arrangements for bananas in France, Italy, and the UK.
These arrangements differed in detail, but in general entailed preferential treatment for
bananas coming from overseas territories of the three countries, or from the Commonwealth.
It continued as follows:*]

51. The effect of the national organisation of these three markets is that the applicant's
bananas do not compete on equal terms with the other bananas sold in these States which
benefit from a preferential system and the Commission was right to exclude these three
national markets from the geographic market under consideration.

52. On the other hand the six other States are markets which are completely free, although
the applicable tariff provisions and transport costs are of necessity different but not discriminatory, and in which the conditions of competition are the same for all.

53. From the standpoint of being able to engage in free competition these six States form
an area which is sufficiently homogeneous to be considered in its entirety.

In some instances the scope of the geographical market will be relatively straightforward.
This was the case in *British Telecommunications*,[12] where the issue was whether BT had abused
its dominant position with regard to message-forwarding agencies in the UK: the geographical market was the UK, within which BT had a monopoly in the provision of telecommunication services. In other instances the scope of the geographical market may be influenced by
factors such as transport costs. This was so in *Napier Brown–British Sugar*.[13] The Commission
held that in determining whether a UK company had a dominant position in the production
and sale of sugar the relevant market was Great Britain, since imports were very limited and
acted as a complement to British sugar, rather than an alternative.

(c) THE TEMPORAL FACTOR

Markets may have a temporal quality or element to them. Thus, a firm may possess market
power at a particular time of year, during which competition from other products is low
because these other products are available only seasonally. It is equally important to note that
the very definition of the product market will have a temporal dimension to it, in the sense

---

12 Dec. 82/861 [1982] OJ L360/36. On appeal see Case 41/83 *Italy* v. *Commission* [1985] ECR 873.
13 Dec. 88/518 [1988] OJ L284/41.

that technological progress and changes in consumer habits will shift boundaries between markets.[14]

(d) THE COMMISSION NOTICE ON MARKET DEFINITION

The Commission published a Notice on the Definition of the Relevant Market for the Purposes of Community Competition Law.[15] It is important in three related ways.[16]

First, the Commission makes it clear that the definition of the relevant market will be viewed differently depending upon the nature of the competition inquiry: an investigation into a proposed concentration is essentially prospective, whereas other types of investigation may be concerned primarily with an analysis of past behaviour.[17]

Secondly, the Notice signalled a shift in Commission thinking on market definition.[18] The Notice begins in orthodox fashion, by stating that the Commission will inquire into demand substitutability, supply substitutability, and potential competition.[19] The novelty stems from the Commission's detailed indication as to how these principles will be applied. In essence, the Commission adopts what is known as the SSNIP test: 'small but significant and non-transitory increase in prices'. On this test, a relevant market is the narrowest range of products such that a hypothetical monopolist in the relevant product area would find it both possible and worthwhile to institute an SSNIP. If demand substitution would be enough to make the price increase unprofitable because of the resulting loss of sales, then additional product substitutes would be included in the relevant market.[20]

Thirdly, while it is axiomatic that the Commission cannot overrule ECJ decisions, the Commission is nonetheless moving away from some of the benchmarks used by the ECJ. Thus the similarity of product characteristics and intended use, which have featured in case law,[21] are regarded as insufficient to determine whether two products are demand substitutes.[22] The same is true of functional interchangeability,[23] because the responsiveness of customers to price changes may be determined by other considerations.[24] In positive terms, the Commission states that it will consider: evidence of substitution in the recent past or where there have been shocks in the market; the views of customers and competitors; quantitative econometric tests; evidence of consumer preferences where available; barriers and costs entailed in substitution; and whether there are distinct groups of customers for the product.

---

[14] Dec. 92/163, *Elopak Italia Srl v. Tetra Pak (No. 2)* [1992] OJ L72/1.

[15] [1997] OJ C372/5, available at http://ec.europa.eu/comm/competition/antitrust/legislation/market.html.

[16] W. Bishop, 'Editorial: The Modernization of DGIV' [1997] *ECLR* 481.

[17] Commission Notice, n. 15 above, para. 12.

[18] We have benefited in this para. from a competition memo published by *Lexecon*, 4 June 1997.

[19] Commission Notice, n. 15 above, paras. 15–24.

[20] See however the reservations expressed about the SSNIP test in the more recent Commission study, DG Competition Discussion Paper on the Application of Art. 82 of the Treaty to Exclusionary Abuses (2005), paras. 11–17. Available at http://ec.europa.eu/comm/competition/antitrust/art82/index.html.

[21] See Case 27/76 *United Brands*, n. 4 above, and Cases 6 and 7/73 *Commercial Solvents*, n. 3 above.

[22] Commission Notice, n. 15 above, para. 36.

[23] Case 6/72 *Continental Can*, n. 3 above.

[24] Commission Notice, n. 15 above, para. 36.

4. DOMINANT POSITION: MARKET POWER

(a) SINGLE FIRM DOMINANCE

When the Court has defined the relevant product, geographical, and temporal elements of the market, it then has to decide whether the undertaking is dominant within that sphere. Some measurement of the firm's market power is, therefore, necessary.[25] The legal test used by the Court was laid down by the *United Brands* case:[26]

> The dominant position referred to in this Article relates to a position of economic strength enjoyed by an undertaking which enables it to prevent effective competition being maintained on the relevant market by giving it the power to behave to an appreciable extent independently of its competitors, customers and ultimately of its consumers.

This test was quoted with approval in *Hoffmann-La Roche*, and the Court then added the following rider:[27]

> Such a position does not preclude some competition, which it does where there is a monopoly or a quasi-monopoly, but enables the undertaking which profits by it, if not to determine, at least to have an appreciable influence on the conditions under which that competition will develop, and in any case to act largely in disregard of it so long as such conduct does not operate to its detriment. A dominant position must also be distinguished from parallel courses of conduct which are peculiar to oligopolies in that in an oligopoly the courses of conduct interact, while in the case of an undertaking occupying the dominant position the conduct of the undertaking which derives profits from that position is to a great extent determined unilaterally. The existence of a dominant position may derive from several factors which, taken separately, are not necessarily determinative but among these factors a highly important one is the existence of very large market shares.

Where there is no statutory monopoly, the Court will consider two types of evidence to determine whether the firm has market power: the market share possessed by the undertaking and whether other factors serve to reinforce its dominance. It should however be noted at the outset that the test of dominance has been criticized.

J. de Azevedo and M. Walker, Market Dominance: Measurement Problems and Mistakes[28]

The legal definition is based on the notion of a firm being able to act to a significant extent independently of its customers, consumers and competitors. Our criticism of the notion of acting independently of customers and consumers is largely conceptual: all firms, whether dominant or not, are constrained by the discipline of the demand curve and so do not act independently

---

[25] D. Landes and R. Posner, 'Market Power in Antitrust Cases' (1981) 94 *Harvard LR* 937; R. Schmalensee, 'Another Look at Market Power' (1982) 95 *Harvard LR* 1789.

[26] Case 27/76 [1978] ECR 207, para. 65; Case T–128/98 *Aéroports de Paris*, n. 2 above, para. 147.

[27] Case 85/76 *Hoffmann-La Roche*, n. 3 above, para. 39.

[28] [2003] *ECLR* 640, 640. See also F. Dethmers and N. Dodoo, 'The Abuse of *Hoffmann-La Roche*: The Meaning of Dominance under EC Competition Law' [2006] *ECLR* 537.

of customers or consumers. Our criticism of the notion of acting independently of competitors is largely empirical: it will only rarely be possible to measure this independence, as in general a dominant firm will exercise its market power to the point at which it is constrained from exercising it any further. For instance, a dominant firm may face little pricing constraint at the competitive price level, but for precisely this reason it will raise prices above the competitive price level until prices are high enough that competitors do impose a price constraint.

(i) *Market Share*

An undertaking with a statutory monopoly may be dominant for the purposes of Article 82. The grant of the statutory monopoly confers no immunity from EC competition law, subject to Article 86(2).[29]

The actual size of the market share possessed by the undertaking will be central to the determination of whether it has market power.[30] Few firms, other than those with a statutory monopoly, will have 100 per cent of the market. Nor is a market share of this size necessary in order for Article 82 to 'bite'.

Thus, in *United Brands* UB's 40 to 45 per cent of the market was held to be sufficient, although the Court also considered other factors indicative of its dominance.[31] However, in *Hoffmann-La Roche* the Court overturned a Commission finding that the firm was dominant in the market for B3 vitamins, in which it had only 43 per cent. It was not satisfied that there were other factors sustaining the conclusion that the undertaking had dominance in this market.[32] The Court, however, made it clear that, save in exceptional circumstances, the existence of a very large market share, which was held for some time, would in itself be indicative of dominance. It would secure for the undertaking concerned the freedom of action that was the hallmark of a dominant position.[33] In the *Akzo* case[34] the ECJ held that a market share of 50 per cent could be said to be very large, and hence indicative of a dominant position, and this finding was repeated in *Irish Sugar*.[35]

It seems moreover that there is a concept of 'super-dominance' emerging, held to be applicable to undertakings with very large market shares. The Commission and Court regard such bodies as having a particular responsibility towards the competitive process.[36]

(ii) *Other Factors Indicating Dominance: Barriers to Entry*

It can be problematic to determine which other factors indicate dominance.[37] It is clear that the Court should pay attention to factors other than market share, since, even if a firm

---

[29] Case 41/83 *Italy* v. *Commission*, n. 12 above.

[30] DG Competition Discussion Paper, n. 20 above, paras. 28–32.

[31] Case 27/76 *United Brands*, n. 4 above.

[32] Case 85/76 *Hoffmann-La Roche*, n. 3 above.

[33] *Ibid.*, para. 41; Case T–30/89 *Hilti AG* v. *Commission* [1991] ECR II–1439, para. 92; Case T–65/98 *Van den Bergh Foods Ltd.* v. *Commission* [2003] ECR II–4653, para. 154.

[34] Case C–62/86 *Akzo Chemie BV* v. *Commission* [1991] ECR I–3359, para. 60.

[35] Case T–228/97 *Irish Sugar plc* v. *Commission* [1999] ECR II–2969, para. 70, upheld on appeal: Case C–497/99 P *Irish Sugar plc* v. *Commission* [2001] ECR I–5333.

[36] Cases C–395 and 396/96 P *Compagnie Maritime Belge Transports SA* v. *Commission* [2000] ECR I–1365, Fennelly AG, para. 137; Dec. 2000/12 *1998 World Cup* [2000] OJ L5/55, para. 86; R. Whish, *Competition Law* (5th edn., LexisNexis UK, 2003), 189–190; A. Jones and B. Sufrin, *EC Competition Law: Text, Cases, and Materials* (2nd edn., Oxford University Press, 2004), 266, 372.

[37] Whish, n. 36 above, 183–188; Jones and Sufrin, n. 36 above, 355–364.

possesses a relatively large market share, this may be fragile because of the possibilities of new entrants on to the market. An essential aspect of the analysis must, therefore, be how far there are *barriers to entry* that render it difficult for other firms to penetrate this market. There is, however, considerable controversy about the meaning to be ascribed to this concept.

For some, it is a broad idea, embracing almost anything that makes it particularly difficult for a new firm to enter the market. For others, the term has a much narrower construction, since there is concern that matters will be characterized as barriers to entry when they are merely indicative of the superior efficiency of the incumbent firm. The following extract exemplifies this aspect of the argument.

R. Bork, The Antitrust Paradox: A Policy at War with Itself[38]

The concept of barriers to entry is crucial to antitrust debate. Those who advocate extensive and increasing legal intervention in market processes cite the existence of entry barriers as a reason to believe that unassisted market forces very often fail to produce adequate results. . . . The ubiquity and potency of the concept are undeniable.

Yet it is demonstrable that barriers of the sort these commentators and jurists believe they see do not exist. They are the ghosts that inhabit antitrust theory. Until the concept of barriers to entry is thoroughly revised, it will remain impossible to make antitrust law more rational or, indeed, to restrain the growth of its powerful irrational elements.

We may begin by asking what a 'barrier to entry' is. There appears to be no precise definition, and in current usage a 'barrier' often seems to be anything that makes the entry of new firms into an industry more difficult. It is at once apparent that an ambiguity lurks in the concept, and it is this ambiguity that causes the trouble. When existing firms are efficient and possess valuable plant, equipment, knowledge, skill, and reputation, potential entrants will find it correspondingly more difficult to enter the industry, since they must acquire those things. . . . But these difficulties are natural; they inhere in the nature of the tasks to be performed. There can be no objection to barriers of this sort. Their existence means only that when market power is achieved by means other than efficiency, entry will not dissipate the objectionable power instantaneously, and law may therefore have a role to play. . . .

The question for antitrust is whether there exist artificial entry barriers. These must be barriers that are not forms of superior efficiency and which yet prevent the forces of the market—entry or the growth of smaller firms already within the industry—from operating to erode market positions not based on efficiency. Care must be taken to distinguish between forms of efficiency and artificial barriers. Otherwise the law will find itself—indeed, it has found itself—attacking efficiency in the name of market freedom. Joe Bain, whose work has done much to popularize the concept, lists among entry barriers such things as economies of scale, capital requirements, and product differentiation.[39] There may be disagreement about two of these barriers, but it is clear that at least one of them, economies of scale, is a form of efficiency. Uncritical adapters of Bain's work have not sufficiently inquired whether the others may not also be efficiencies.

Before examining some claimed entry barriers to determine whether they are efficiencies or artificial clogs upon competition, it should be noted that . . . an artificial barrier is, of course, an exclusionary practice. . . . Every barrier will be either a form of efficiency deliberately created or an instance of deliberate predation. There is no 'intermediate case' of non-efficient and unintended exclusion. Failure to bear that in mind leads to serious policy mistakes.

---

38 (Basic Books, 1978), 310–311.
39 The reference is to J. Bain, *Barriers to New Competition* (Harvard University Press, 1956), ch. 1.

There may well be reservations about aspects of Bork's analysis, but similar concerns about the broad meaning accorded to barriers to entry in EC law have been expressed by a number of other writers.[40]

The Court's approach can be exemplified by *Hoffmann-La Roche*.[41] The case was concerned with alleged abusive behaviour in relation to vitamins. Having defined the relevant markets, the Court considered whether HLR was dominant. Its market share was taken into account, and the ECJ then evaluated the relevance of other factors that might be indicative of market power. The Commission had listed a number of such factors. The ECJ rejected, for example, the fact that HLR had retained its market share, since this might have resulted from effective competitive behaviour.[42] It also rejected the fact that HLR produced a wider range of vitamins than other undertakings, since the Commission itself had found that each group of the vitamins constituted a separate market.[43] The following factors were, however, deemed to be of relevance:[44]

On the other hand the relationship between the market shares of the undertaking concerned and of its competitors, especially those of the next largest, the technological lead of an undertaking over its competitors, the existence of a highly developed sales network and the absence of potential competition are relevant factors, the first because it enables the competitive strength of the undertaking in question to be assessed, the second and third because they represent in themselves technical and commercial advantages and the fourth because it is the consequence of the existence of obstacles preventing new competitors from having access to the market.

The ECJ has persisted in taking a relatively wide view of barriers to entry, as has the Commission.[45] It is questionable whether a number of these factors ought to be regarded as barriers to entry.

Thus, *economies of scale* have been considered to be relevant in assessing the market power of a particular firm,[46] as has the capital strength of the undertaking and its access to capital markets.[47] However, as seen above, the former is almost certainly indicative of efficiency. As for the latter, many commentators contend that access to capital is not a barrier to entry, since capital markets accurately reflect the cost of capital to a particular firm, and any inefficiency in this regard is best dealt with through reform of capital markets themselves.

It is equally questionable whether the existence of *vertical integration* should be regarded as a factor indicating dominance.[48] The motivation for a firm to become vertically integrated

---

[40] D. Harbord and T. Hoehn, 'Barriers to Entry and Exit in European Competition Policy' (1994) 14 *International Review of Law and Economics* 422; S. Turnbull, 'Barriers to Entry, Article 86 and the Abuse of a Dominant Position: An Economic Critique of European Community Competition Law' [1996] *ECLR* 96; O. Arowolo, 'Application of the Concept of Barriers to Entry under Article 82 of the EC Treaty: Is There a Case for Review?' [2005] *ECLR* 247; J. Heit, 'The Justifiability of the ECJ's Wide Approach to the Concept of Barriers to Entry' [2006] *ECLR* 117.

[41] Case 85/76 *Hoffmann-La Roche*, n. 3 above.

[42] *Ibid.*, para. 44. The ECJ did, however, state that if there is a dominant position then its retention may be indicative that abusive behaviour within Art. 86 has been used to maintain this dominance.

[43] *Ibid.*, paras. 45–46.

[44] *Ibid.*, para. 48; Case T–219/99 *British Airways*, n. 10 above, para. 210.

[45] DG Competition Discussion Paper, n. 20 above, paras. 38–40.

[46] Case 27/76 *United Brands*, n. 4 above.

[47] *Ibid.*

[48] *Ibid.* See also Case 85/76 *Hoffmann-La Roche*, n. 3 above.

was considered earlier,[49] where it was seen that the rational firm would normally choose to integrate vertically only if that was the most efficient method of marketing its product.[50]

It is also doubtful whether *superior technology* should be perceived as a barrier to entry, even though the Court has consistently regarded it in this manner.[51] Any new firm wishing to enter the market should expect to have to expend money on developing technology and know-how. These costs will not necessarily be any greater than for the incumbent firm.

Legal provisions within Member States which render it more difficult for new firms to break into the market have also been regarded as indicative of dominance.[52]

It is also clear that the Court will take into account, in determining dominance, the *conduct of the firm* which is alleged to be the abusive behaviour, notwithstanding the apparent circularity that this entails. Thus, in *Michelin* the Court took account of Michelin's price discrimination as an indication of its dominance, even though it noted the circularity thereby involved.[53]

It is difficult to regard the decisions in this area as satisfactory. It may be argued, by way of response, that it is perfectly legitimate for the Court to take account of the preceding factors, since it is only seeking to determine whether the firm has some dominance, not whether it has actually abused that dominance. However, a finding of dominance renders the firm liable to investigation, with attendant costs for the company. Moreover, as we shall see below, while the existence of a dominant position is not itself illegal, a firm in such a position is regarded as having a 'special responsibility' not to allow its conduct to impair genuine undistorted competition on the relevant market.

(b) JOINT DOMINANCE

The discussion thus far has proceeded on the assumption that one firm occupies a dominant position on the market. However, Article 82 speaks of an abuse of a dominant position by *one or more undertakings*. It is clear that this covers the situation, exemplified by *Continental Can* and *Commercial Solvents*, where the dominant position is held by firms that are part of the same corporate group or economic unit.

What has been less clear is whether the phrase also covers oligopolistic markets, in which a number of independent firms operate in a parallel manner. The ECJ appeared to have rejected this in *Hoffmann-La Roche*,[54] when it held that unilateral behaviour by a single firm occupying a dominant position had to be distinguished from interactive behaviour by a number of independent firms, which made up an oligopoly. It does however now appear to be the case that some species of oligopolistic behaviour can be caught by Article 82.

---

[49] See 982–985.

[50] It is, moreover, doubtful whether the existence of vertical integration enables the firm with some dominance to achieve any greater monopoly profit than it would do without the vertical integration.

[51] See, e.g., Case 27/76 *United Brands*, n. 4 above; Case 85/76 *Hoffmann-La Roche*, n. 3 above; Case 322/81 *Nederlandsche Banden-Industrie Michelin NV* v. *Commission* [1983] ECR 3461.

[52] Case 22/78 *Hugin*, n. 8 above; Case T–30/89 *Hilti*, n. 33 above, para. 93.

[53] Case 322/81 *Michelin*, n. 51 above.

[54] Case 85/76 *Hoffmann-La Roche*, n. 3 above, para. 39.

Cases T–68, 77–78/89 **Re Italian Flat Glass: Società Italiana Vetro v. Commission**
[1992] ECR I–1403

[Note ToA renumbering: Arts. 85 and 86 are now Arts. 81 and 82]

A company, Cobelli, a wholesaler of glass, alleged that three producers of flat glass were in breach of the Treaty by maintaining agreed price lists and identical conditions of sale. It also alleged that two of these companies had engaged in practices designed to achieve full control, not only of the production of glass, but also of its distribution, by excluding from the market independent wholesaler-distributors. The Commission found that there had been a breach of Article 85, by the producers of the flat glass, and also a breach of Article 86. In relation to the latter, it held that the undertakings had a collective dominant position, that they were able to pursue a commercial policy which was independent of ordinary market conditions, and that they presented themselves on the market as a single entity, rather than as individual concerns. The CFI partially annulled the findings with respect to Article 85, holding that the Commission had failed to establish the requisite agreement or concerted practice between the three producers. It then proceeded to consider Article 86.

THE CFI

358. The Court considers that there is no legal or economic reason to suppose that the term 'undertaking' in Article 86 has a different meaning from the one given to it in the context of Article 85. There is nothing, in principle, to prevent two or more independent economic entities from being, on a specific market, united by such economic links that, by virtue of that fact, together they hold a dominant position *vis-à-vis* the other operators on the same market. This could be the case, for example, where two or more undertakings jointly have, through agreements or licences, a technological lead affording them the power to behave to an appreciable extent independently of their competitors, their customers and ultimately of their consumers (*Hoffmann-La Roche*).

. . .

360. However, it should be pointed out that for the purposes of establishing an infringement of Article 86 EEC, it is not sufficient, as the Commission's agent claimed at the hearing, to 'recycle' the facts constituting an infringement of Article 85, deducing from the finding that the parties to an agreement or to an unlawful practice jointly hold a substantial share of the market, that by virtue of that fact alone they hold a collective dominant position, and that their unlawful behaviour constitutes an abuse of that collective dominant position. Amongst other considerations, a finding of a dominant position, which is in any case not in itself a matter of reproach, presupposes that the market in question has been defined (Case 6/72, *Continental Can*, Case 322/81, *Michelin*). The Court must therefore examine, first the analysis of the market made in the decision and, secondly, the circumstances relied on in support of the finding of a collective dominant position.

The CFI annulled the Commission's decision on Article 86, on the ground that there were errors in its reasoning both with respect to the definition of the relevant market and because it had not adduced the necessary proof of a collective dominant position.[55] Notwithstanding the reversal of the Commission, the CFI's decision was important for its affirmation of the

---

[55] There are difficulties with the reasoning of the CFI: see Whish, n. 36 above, 522–523.

existence of collective dominance.[56] The ECJ endorsed the idea of collective dominance,[57] and gave further guidance on its meaning in the following case.[58]

Cases C–395–396/96 P Compagnie Maritime Belge Transports SA, Compagnie Maritime Belge SA, and Dafra Lines A/S v. Commission
[2000] ECR I–1365

[Note ToA renumbering: Art. 85 is now Art. 81]

The members of the liner conference argued that it was wrong of the Commission and the CFI to have concluded that they occupied a collectively dominant position. They contended that the Commission and CFI had, in making this finding, merely 'recycled' facts relating to the existence of a concerted practice.

THE ECJ

41. In order to establish the existence of a collective entity . . . it is necessary to examine the economic links or factors which give rise to a connection between the undertakings concerned. . . .

42. In particular, it must be ascertained whether economic links exist between the undertakings concerned which enable them to act independently of their competitors, their customers and consumers (see *Michelin*).

43. The mere fact that two or more undertakings are linked by an agreement, a decision . . . or a concerted practice within the meaning of Article 85(1) . . . does not, of itself, constitute a sufficient basis for such a finding.

44. On the other hand, an agreement, decision or concerted practice (whether or not covered by an exemption under Article 85(3) . . .) may undoubtedly, where it is implemented, result in the undertakings concerned being so linked as to their conduct on a particular market that they present themselves as a collective entity vis-à-vis their competitors, their trading partners and consumers.

45. The existence of a collective dominant position may therefore flow from the nature and terms of an agreement, from the way in which it is implemented and, consequently, from the links or factors which give rise to a connection between undertakings which result from it. Nevertheless, the existence of an agreement or of other links in law is not indispensable to a finding of a collective dominant position; such a finding may be based on other connecting

---

56 M. Schodermeier, 'Collective Dominance Revisited: An Analysis of the EC Commission's New Concepts of Oligopoly Control' [1990] *ECLR* 28; R. Whish and B. Sufrin, 'Oligopolistic Markets and EC Competition Law' (1992) 12 *YBEL* 59; D. Ridyard, 'Economic Analysis of Single Firm and Oligopolistic Dominance' [1994] *ECLR* 255; B. Rodger, 'Oligopolistic Market Failure: Collective Dominance versus Complex Monopoly' [1995] *ECLR* 21; C. Caffarra and K.-U. Kuhn, 'Joint Dominance: The CFI Judgment on Gencor/Lonhro' [1999] *ECLR* 355; R. Whish, 'Collective Dominance', in D. O'Keefe and A. Bavasso (eds.), *Judicial Review in European Union Law* (Kluwer, 2000), ch. 37; G. Monti, 'The Scope of Collective Dominance under Article 82' (2001) 38 *CMLRev.* 131; G. Niels, 'Collective Dominance—More Than Just Oligopolistic Independence' [2001] *ECLR* 168; E. Kloosterhuis, 'Joint Dominance and the Interaction between Firms' [2001] *ECLR* 79; C. Withers and M. Jephcott, 'Where to Now for EC Oligopoly Control?' [2001] *ECLR* 295.

57 Case C–393/92 *Almelo*, n. 71 below; Cases C–140–142/94 *DIP SpA* v. *Commune di Bassano del Grappa* [1995] ECR I–3257, paras. 25–26.

58 Cases T–191, 212–214/98 *Atlantic Container Line AB* v. *Commission* [2003] ECR II–3275, paras. 594–602, 610.

factors and would depend on an economic assessment and, in particular, on an assessment of the structure of the market in question.

The same approach to collective dominance is apparent in the context of mergers. In *Gencor*[59] the CFI held that collective dominance within the Merger Regulation could catch oligopolistic collusion, and that the existence of structural links between the relevant firms was not a necessary condition for collective dominance to apply.

It is still necessary to find that there has been an abuse by the firms that occupy a collective dominant position. The meaning of abuse in this context is difficult.[60] If there is a concerted practice by oligopolists this will be caught by Article 81. For Article 82 to be of use collective dominance will have to embrace non-collusive behaviour. However, to condemn parallel pricing behaviour by oligopolists as an abuse under Article 82 would be tantamount to condemning oligopoly *per se*, since this is the rational behaviour of firms in such markets. There is nonetheless still room for the concept of abuse to apply. Thus, if those occupying a collective dominant position seek to drive a competitor from the market, as exemplified by *Compagnie Maritime Belge*, they should properly be caught by Article 82.

5. ABUSE: THREE PROBLEMS OF INTERPRETATION

An undertaking will be condemned only if it has abused its dominant position. The list of abusive practices in Article 82 is not exhaustive; the practices specified are merely examples of abuse.[61] There are three important interpretive issues when considering the meaning of 'abuse'.

(a) WHO IS ARTICLE 82 DESIGNED TO PROTECT?

The first issue is *who* Article 82 is intended to protect: consumers, competitors, or both? There can, as we shall see, be instances where the interests of consumers and competitors clash. Behaviour by a dominant undertaking that injures a competitor will not necessarily be injurious to consumers.[62]

It is common to subdivide the situations to which Article 82 can apply into *exploitation and anti-competitiveness*.[63] The former signifies behaviour harmful to consumers. The latter, generally, connotes conduct deleterious to competitors, actual or potential. This division should not, however, be treated too rigidly, and in any event the same conduct by the dominant firm may be both exploitative and anti-competitive. Although it is now clear that Article 82 covers both exploitation and anti-competitive behaviour, this was not so apparent at the inception of the Treaty. Some commentators argued strenuously that Article 82 should be restricted to

---

[59] Case T–102/96 *Gencor Ltd.* v. *Commission* [1999] ECR II–753, paras. 276–277.
[60] Whish, n. 36 above, 526–529.
[61] Case C–95/04 P *British Airways plc* v. *Commission*, 15 Mar. 2007, para. 57.
[62] Case C–7/97 *Oscar Bronner GmbH & Co. KG* v. *Mediaprint Zeitungs- und Zeitschriftenverlag GmbH & Co. KG* [1998] ECR I–7791, Jacobs AG, para. 58.
[63] See, e.g., Whish, n. 36 above, 194–207; J. Temple Lang, 'Monopolisation and the Definition of Abuse of a Dominant Position under Art. 86 EEC Treaty' (1979) 16 *CMLRev*. 345.

exploitative behaviour harmful to consumers, and that there should be some real link between the harm and the market power of the dominant undertaking.[64] This construction was rendered untenable by *Continental Can*, which will be considered below.

We shall see when discussing reform that the Commission now views prevention of harm to consumers as the ultimate goal of Article 82, although it argues that this may require the protection of the competitive process.[65]

(b) WHAT KINDS OF BEHAVIOUR ARE ABUSIVE?

The second issue relates to the *kinds* of behaviour held to be abusive. Such behaviour must be distinguished from normal competitive strategy. It would, therefore, be odd if the ordinary, rational pricing and output decisions of the dominant firm were abusive, since this would, in reality, mean that we were proscribing those with dominant market power *per se*. Having said this, it is also clear that Article 82 explicitly prohibits unfair pricing and limits on productive capacity, and that some meaning must, therefore, be ascribed to these terms.

It might be thought that this problem could be overcome if the concept of abuse was confined to practices such as price discrimination, predation, tying, and the like which look 'bad' or 'abnormal', even for the firm with dominance. The problem is not so easily resolved since, as will be seen, there is considerable disagreement among economists, both on whether these activities are always harmful and on how they are to be measured. The application of Article 82 can, therefore, be particularly controversial.

The tension in the preceding paragraph is thrown into sharp relief by the Court's case law, which states that while a finding of dominance does not in itself imply any reproach to the undertaking concerned, it nonetheless has a '*special responsibility*', irrespective of the cause of that position, not to allow its conduct to impair genuine and undistorted competition on the common market.[66] The consequence is that an undertaking in a dominant position may be deprived of the right to adopt a course of conduct which is not itself abusive, and which would be unobjectionable if taken by a non-dominant undertaking.[67] Thus, while it is accepted that a dominant undertaking can take steps to protect its own interests when they are attacked by competitors, it is not allowed to strengthen its dominant position, which will be held to be an abuse.[68] This divide is difficult to apply, more especially given that it has to be judged in the light of the specific circumstances of each case where competition has been weakened.[69]

(c) ABUSE OF WHICH MARKET?

It is clear that abuse of a dominant position in one market may be censured because of the effects that it produces on a different market, even where there is no dominance on the latter

---

[64] R. Joliet, *Monopolization and Abuse of a Dominant Position* (Martinus Nijhoff, 1970).

[65] See below, 1037–1038.

[66] Case 322/81 *Michelin*, n. 51 above, para. 57; Case T–228/97 *Irish Sugar*, n. 35 above, para. 112; Case T–203/01 *Michelin v. Commission* [2003] ECR II–4071, para. 55; Case T–65/98 *Van den Bergh Foods*, n. 33 above, paras. 157–158; Case C–552/03 P *Unilever Bestfoods (Ireland) v. Commission* [2006] ECR I–9091, para. 136.

[67] Case 322/81 *Michelin*, n. 51 above, para. 57; Case T–51/89 *Tetra Pak v. Commission* [1990] ECR II–309, para. 23; Case T–111/96 *ITT Promedia NV v. Commission* [1998] ECR II–2937, para. 138.

[68] Case 27/76 *United Brands*, n. 4 above, para. 189; Case T–228/97 *Irish Sugar plc*, n. 35 above, para. 112; Case T–219/99 *British Airways*, n. 10 above, paras. 241–243; Case T–203/01 *Michelin*, n. 66 above, paras. 54–55.

[69] Case C–333/94 P *Tetra Pak*, n. 3 above, para. 24; Cases C–395–396/96 P *Compagnie Maritimes Belge*, n. 36 above, para. 114.

market. This is especially so where the dominant undertaking can control access to the other market. This is exemplified by *Aéroports de Paris*.[70] The airport authority controlled access to the supply of catering services and abused its dominant position by discriminatory pricing.

6. ABUSE: PARTICULAR EXAMPLES

(a) ABUSE AND MERGERS

The Community waited a long time for a specific regulation concerning mergers. The ECJ made it clear in the *Continental Can* case that some mergers would however be caught by Article 82. The case is also of more general importance for the interpretation of the meaning of abuse.

Case 6/72 **Europemballage Corporation and Continental Can Co. Inc. v. Commission**
[1973] ECR 215

[Note ToA renumbering: Arts. 3f, 85, and 86 are now
Arts. 3(1)(g), 81, and 82]

Continental Can (CC) was a US manufacturer of metal packaging which had a presence in Europe through a German firm (SLW), which it acquired in 1969. In 1970 it sought to purchase, through its subsidiary Europemballage, a controlling interest in a Dutch company, TDV. The Commission found that CC had a dominant position in Europe for certain types of packaging through SLW, and that there had been an abuse of that position by the purchase of TDV. CC argued that there had been no abuse.

THE ECJ

20. ... The question is whether the word 'abuse' in Article 86 refers only to practices of undertakings which may directly affect the market and are detrimental to production or sales, to purchasers or consumers, or whether this word refers also to changes in the structure of an undertaking, which lead to competition being seriously disturbed in a substantial part of the Common Market.

21. The distinction between measures which concern the structure of the undertaking and practices which affect the market cannot be decisive, for any structural measure may influence market conditions, if it increases the size and the economic power of the undertaking.

22. In order to answer this question one has to go back to the spirit, general scheme and wording of Article 86, as well as to the system and objectives of the Treaty. ...

23. Article 86 is part of the chapter devoted to the common rules on the Community's policy in the field of competition. This policy is based on Article 3(f) of the Treaty according to which the Community's activity shall include the institution of a system ensuring that competition in the Common Market is not distorted. ...

24. But if Article 3(f) provides for the institution of a system ensuring that competition in the Common Market is not distorted, then it requires a fortiori that competition must not be

---

[70] Case 128/98, n. 2 above, paras. 164–165; Case T–219/99 *British Airways*, n. 10 above, paras. 127–132.

eliminated. This requirement is so essential that without it numerous provisions of the Treaty would be pointless. Moreover, it corresponds to the precept of Article 2 of the Treaty according to which one of the tasks of the Community is 'to promote throughout the Community a harmonious development of economic activities'. Thus the restraints on competition, which the Treaty allows under certain conditions because of the need to harmonise the various objectives of the Treaty, are limited by the requirements of Articles 2 and 3. Going beyond this limit involves the risk that the weakening of competition would conflict with the aims of the Common Market.

25. ... Articles 85 and 86 seek to achieve the same aim on different levels, viz. the maintenance of effective competition within the Common Market. The restraint on competition, which is prohibited if it is the result of behaviour falling under Article 85, cannot become permissible by the fact that such behaviour succeeds under the influence of a dominant undertaking and results in the merger of the undertakings concerned. In the absence of explicit provisions one cannot assume that the Treaty, which prohibits in Article 85 certain decisions of ordinary associations of undertakings restricting competition without eliminating it, permits in Article 86 that undertakings, after merging into an organic unity, should reach such a dominant position that any serious competition is practically rendered impossible. Such a diverse legal treatment would make a breach in the entire competition law which could jeopardise the proper functioning of the Common Market. If, in order to avoid the prohibitions in Article 85, it sufficed to establish such close connections between the undertakings that they escaped the prohibition of Article 85 without coming within the scope of Article 86, then, in contradiction to the basic principles of the Common Market, the partitioning of a substantial part of the Common Market would be allowed. ...

26. It is in the light of these considerations that the condition imposed by Article 86 is to be interpreted whereby in order to come within the prohibition a dominant position must have been abused. The provision states a certain number of abusive practices which it prohibits. The list merely gives examples, not an exhaustive enumeration of the sort of abuses of a dominant position prohibited by the Treaty. As may further be seen from subparagraphs (c) and (d) of Article 86(2), the provision is not only aimed at practices which may cause damage to the consumer directly, but also at those which are detrimental to them through their impact on an effective competition structure, such as is mentioned in Article 3(f) of the Treaty. Abuse may therefore occur if an undertaking in a dominant position strengthens such position in such a way that the degree of dominance reached substantially fetters competition, i. e. that only undertakings remain in the market whose behaviour depends on the dominant one.

27. Such being the meaning and scope of Article 86 of the EEC Treaty, the question of the link of causality raised by the applicants which in their opinion has to exist between the dominant position and its abuse, is of no consequence, for the strengthening of the position of an undertaking may be an abuse and prohibited under Article 86 of the Treaty, regardless of the means and the procedure by which it is achieved, if it has the effects mentioned above.

The decision in *Continental Can* is of seminal importance for Article 82, in terms both of the reasoning employed and the result.

The ECJ's *reasoning* exemplifies its teleological approach. Reliance is placed on the general principles in the Treaty as a guide to the construction of specific Articles. The competition provisions are read as a whole, and the interpretation of Article 82 is strongly influenced by the desire to avoid any 'gap' in the Treaty coverage.

The *result* of the case signals the ECJ's intent that Article 82 should cover situations where the competitive market structure was placed in jeopardy. The Article certainly included classic forms of *behavioural* abuse, which operated directly to the detriment of consumers. It was now clear that it would also embrace *structural* abuse, in the sense of action that weakened the competitive market structure. It was therefore *Continental Can* which made it apparent that Article 82 would cover anti-competitiveness, where the primary injury was to competitors. This construction was reinforced by the Court's negation of the need for any real causal link between the dominance and the impugned action: there did not need to be any proof that it was CC's 'economic muscle' which had forced the merger on a reluctant undertaking.[71] It sufficed that the merger in fact resulted in damage to the competitive market structure.[72]

Continental Can received a mixed reception when it first appeared, with certain commentators being critical of the reasoning and result. The Court has, however, persisted in its general approach as the cases in the following sections will demonstrate.

(b) ABUSE AND REFUSAL TO SUPPLY

(i) *Refusal to Supply: The Basic Principles*

The obligation on a firm in a dominant position to supply to other firms is exemplified by *Commercial Solvents*:[73]

Cases 6 and 7/73 Istituto Chemioterapico Italiano SpA and Commercial Solvents v. Commission
[1974] ECR 223

[Note ToA renumbering: Arts. 3f, 85, and 86 are now Arts. 3(1)(g), 81, and 82]

Commercial Solvents Corporation (CSC) made raw materials, nitropropane and aminobutanol, which were then used to make ethambutol, a drug for tuberculosis. CSC acquired 51 per cent of an Italian company, Istituto, which bought the raw material from CSC and sold it to another Italian company, Zoja, the latter then using it to manufacture ethambutol-based products. Istituto sought to acquire Zoja, but the negotiations were unsuccessful. Istituto then increased its price to Zoja, and Zoja found an alternative source of supply from other customers of CSC. This alternative source of supply then dried up, principally because CSC instructed those to whom it sold the raw material not to sell it on to firms such as Zoja. CSC then stated that it would no longer sell the raw material, but that it would instead integrate vertically downmarket, and use the raw material for its own production of the finished product. When Zoja sought to re-order the raw material from CSC the latter refused to supply.

THE ECJ

25. However, an undertaking being in a dominant position as regards the production of raw material and therefore able to control the supply to manufacturers of derivatives, cannot, just

---

[71] See also Case C–393/92 *Municipality of Almelo* v. *NV Energiebedrijf Ijsselmij* [1994] ECR I–1477. Cf. Case C–333/94 P, *Tetra Pak*, n. 3 above.

[72] P. Vogelenzang, 'Abuse of a Dominant Position in Article 86: The Problem of Causality and Some Applications' (1976) 13 *CMLRev.* 61. For a different view about causality see T. Eilmansberger, 'How to Distinguish Good from Bad Competition under Article 82: In Search of Clearer and More Coherent Standards for Anti-Competitive Abuses' (2005) 42 *CMLRev.* 49.

[73] R. Subiotto and R. O'Donoghue, 'Defining the Scope of the Duty of Dominant Firms to Deal with Existing Customers under Article 82' [2003] *ECLR* 683; DG Competition Discussion Paper, n. 20 above, paras. 207–224.

because it decides to start manufacturing these derivatives (in competition with its former customers) act in such a way as to eliminate their competition which, in the case in question, would amount to eliminating one of the principal manufacturers of ethambutol in the Common Market. Since such conduct is contrary to the objectives expressed in Article 3(f) of the Treaty and set out in greater detail in Article 85 and 86, it follows that an undertaking which has a dominant position in the market in raw materials and which, with the object of reserving such raw material for manufacturing its own derivatives, refuses to supply a customer, which is itself a manufacturer of these derivatives, and therefore risks eliminating all competition on the part of this customer, is abusing its dominant position within the meaning of Article 86. In this context it does not matter that the undertaking ceased to supply in the spring of 1970 because of the cancellation of the purchases by Zoja, because it appears from the applicants' own statement that, when the supplies provided for in the contract had been completed, the sale of aminobutanol would have stopped in any case.

This appears to be a classic case of abusive behaviour: CSC, the dominant firm, teaches Zoja a lesson by making it clear that if the latter seeks an alternative source of supply which later dries up, then Zoja cannot necessarily expect CSC to resume supplies. The case could well have been decided in this way, and this would probably have been justified on the facts. However, the Court's reasoning is broader. It specifically addresses the situation where the refusal to supply is based on a desire by the dominant firm to integrate vertically down into the finished-product market: such a refusal is still deemed an abuse for the purpose of Article 82.

This is more controversial for the reasons given above.[74] A rational firm will seek to enter a new phase of the market downstream only if it believes that it can produce the finished product more efficiently than the incumbent firms. If it is correct then the consumer will benefit by the product being cheaper. If it is wrong then it will suffer accordingly. The effect of such vertical integration may be that existing firms making the finished product will no longer be able to do so if the dominant firm does not have enough of the raw material for its own needs and its rivals'.[75] This exemplifies the tension mentioned earlier as to whether Article 82 is intended to protect consumers or competitors/the competitive market structure. There may be situations where actions by a dominant firm may benefit consumers but be harmful to its competitors. *Commercial Solvents* signals the intent of the Court that, if forced to choose, it will opt to protect the latter.[76]

Refusal by the dominant firm to supply existing customers will therefore be abusive unless there is some objective justification, as will reduction in supplies to firms in a comparable situation in a way which places them at a comparative disadvantage.[77] It has not been easy for dominant firms to satisfy the Court that such justification exists.[78] This is apparent from *United Brands*.

---

[74] See 982–984.

[75] The ECJ was not convinced that CSC could not meet its own needs and those of Zoja: [1974] ECR 223, para. 28.

[76] It may be possible to 'square this circle' by arguing that in the long term the consumer will be better off if there are more competitors at the finished-product-market level; and that if the dominant firm really is more efficient than a firm such as Zoja then the latter will not, in any event, survive.

[77] Case 77/77 *Benzine en Petroleum Handelsmaatschappij BV, British Petroleum Raffinerij Nederland NV and British Petroleum Maatschappij Nederland BV v. Commission* [1978] ECR 1513.

[78] Case T–65/89 *BPB Industries plc and British Gypsum Ltd. v. Commission* [1993] ECR II–389.

Case 27/76 United Brands Company and United Brands Continentaal BV v. Commission
[1978] ECR 207

[Note ToA renumbering: Arts. 3f and 86 are now Arts. 3(1)(g) and 82]

It was alleged that UB had refused to supply to Olesen, a Danish distributor. UB argued that it had refused to continue supplying Olesen because the latter, having failed to secure preferential treatment from UB for the Danish market, then started to sell a competitor's product and to neglect the sale of UB's produce.

THE ECJ

182. [I]t is advisable to assert positively from the outset that an undertaking in a dominant position for the purpose of marketing a product—which cashes in on the reputation of a brand name known to and valued by the consumers—cannot stop supplying a long standing customer who abides by regular commercial practice, if the orders placed by that customer are in no way out of the ordinary.

183. Such conduct is inconsistent with the objectives laid down in Article 3(f) of the Treaty, which are set out in greater detail in Article 86, especially in paragraphs (b) and (c), since the refusal to sell would limit markets to the prejudice of consumers and would amount to discrimination which might in the end eliminate a trading party from the relevant market.

[*The Court then reviewed the reasons given by UB for discontinuing supplies to Olesen. It continued as follows:*]

189. Although it is true, as the applicant points out, that the fact that an undertaking is in a dominant position cannot disentitle it from protecting its own commercial interests if they are attacked, and that such an undertaking must be conceded the right to take such reasonable steps as it deems appropriate to protect its said interests, such behaviour cannot be countenanced if its actual purpose is to strengthen this dominant position and abuse it.

190. Even if the possibility of counter-attack is acceptable that attack must still be proportionate to the threat taking into account the economic strength of the undertakings confronting each other.

191. The sanction consisting of refusal to supply by an undertaking in a dominant position was in excess of what might, if such a situation were to arise, reasonably be contemplated as a sanction for conduct similar to that for which UBC blamed Olesen.

192. In fact UBC could not be unaware of that fact that by acting in this way it would discourage other ripener/distributors from supporting the advertising of other brand names and that the deterrent effect of the sanction imposed upon one of them would make its position of strength on the relevant market that much more effective.

193. Such a course of conduct amounts therefore to a serious interference with the independence of small and medium sized firms in their commercial relations with the undertaking in a dominant position and this independence implies the right to give preference to a competitors' goods.

It is unclear precisely what type of reaction by UB would have been considered to be proportionate and lawful in the light of Olesen's behaviour. It is also unclear whether the rules on refusal to supply apply to new customers, as opposed to existing customers. The case law has certainly come close to condemning such refusals, as has the Commission, subject to certain conditions.[79]

Thus in *Boosey & Hawkes*[80] the Commission found against B & H, which had refused to supply brass-band instruments to a customer which had begun manufacturing in competition with it. The fact that a customer of a dominant producer had become associated with a competitor of that manufacturer would not normally entitle the dominant producer to withdraw all supplies immediately or take reprisals against that customer. This was not, said the Commission, a proportionate response, but it also held that there was no obligation on a dominant firm to subsidize competition to itself and that it could give adequate notice to terminate the pre-existing relationship. In *BPB*[81] the CFI held that, in deciding how to allocate supplies in times of shortage, a firm must use an objective criterion; and that favouring loyal customers, even marginally, over others did not meet this test.

(ii) *Refusal to Supply: The Essential Facilities Doctrine*

There has been considerable debate about Article 82 and the essential facilities doctrine. This is the idea that the owner of a facility which is not replicable by the ordinary process of innovation and investment, and without access to which competition on a market is impossible or seriously impeded, has to share it with a rival.[82] There is some indication of this doctrine in the Court's case law and Commission decisions.

Thus the CFI held that Article 82 applies to a refusal to supply a product which is required by another party to produce a different product, even if the second product is in competition with the first and even if the producer of the first product enjoys an intellectual property right. This was established in *RTE*.[83] RTE was a statutory authority providing broadcasting services, and it reserved the exclusive right to publish a weekly schedule of TV programmes for its channels in Ireland. An Irish company, Magill, sought to publish a weekly guide which would have information on all the available channels. RTE claimed that this infringed its copyright in the weekly schedule for its channels. The CFI held that RTE, by reserving the exclusive right to publish its weekly television programme listings, was preventing the emergence of a new product, namely a general television magazine likely to compete with its own magazine, the *RTE Guide*, and that this constituted a breach of Article 82.

The 'essential facilities doctrine' is also apparent in Commission decisions, as evidenced by the *Sealink* case.[84] Sealink owned the port of Holyhead, and operated a ferry service to Ireland. A rival ferry company claimed that Sealink organized the sailing schedules from Holyhead in the most inconvenient way for the rival company. The Commission held that it was an abuse of Article 82 for the owner of an essential facility to use its power in one market to strengthen its position on another related market. This would occur if it granted its competitors access to

---

79 DG Competition Discussion Paper, n. 20 above, paras. 225–236.

80 Dec. 87/500 [1987] OJ L286/36, [1988] 4 CMLR 67.

81 Case T–65/89, n. 78 above, upheld on appeal, Case C–310/93 P *BPB Industries plc and British Gypsum Ltd. v. Commission* [1995] ECR I–865.

82 Whish, n. 36 above, 668.

83 Cases T–69, 70, and 76/89 *RTE, ITP, BBC v. Commission* [1991] ECR II–485, upheld on appeal, Cases C–241 and 242/91 P *Radio Telefis Eireann (RTE) and Independent Television Publications Ltd. (ITP) v. Commission* [1995] ECR I–743. See also Case T–70/89 *British Broadcasting Corporation and British Broadcasting Corporation Enterprises Ltd. v. Commission* [1991] ECR II–535; Case 238/87 *Volvo AB v. Erik Veng (UK) Ltd.* [1988] ECR 6211.

84 [1992] 5 CMLR 255. See also Dec. 88/589 *London European Airways/Sabena* [1988] OJ L317/47; Dec. 94/19 *Sea Containers Stena SeaLink Ports* [1994] OJ L15/84; *Morlaix (Port of Roscoff)* [1995] 5 CMLR 177.

the related market on terms which were less favourable than those for its own services without any objective justification.[85] There are, however, dangers in the essential facilities doctrine.

D. Ridyard, Essential Facilities and the Obligation to Supply Competitors[86]

It will always be tempting for a liberal-minded competition authority to respond favourably to firms who complain about lack of access to new markets, and there are certain instances where the use of essential facilities can legitimately be used as an aid to market liberalisation. There are many other instances, however, in which an uncritical approach favouring market entry can threaten the incentives to dynamic efficiency that provide the engine for economic and technical progress in workably competitive markets.

... To achieve a better balance, some limiting principles need to be found. ... The approach suggested in this article is to recognise that essential facilities, and the obligations on essential facilities owners that accompany them, should be identified only in circumstances where competition does not and cannot be expected to operate, and with assets that cannot reasonably be subject to effective competition. The fact that it may be inconvenient or costly for competitors to achieve market access by their own devices is not sufficient. Nor is the fact that the asset owner might be enjoying a high return from its policy of refusing to deal with competitors.

Later decisions have indeed taken a more limited view of the essential facilities doctrine. In *Ladbroke* the CFI made it clear that an action for refusal to supply would only be plausible if the product or service being sought was essential for the exercise of the relevant activity. The supply of TV broadcasts concerning horse racing was not essential for the applicant's business of running betting shops.[87] In *ENS*[88] the CFI held that a product or service could not be considered necessary or essential unless there was no real or potential substitute for it. The same cautionary approach is apparent in *Bronner*.

Case C–7/97 Oscar Bronner GmbH & Co. KG v. Mediaprint Zeitungs- und Zeitschriftenverlag GmbH & Co. KG
[1998] ECR I–7791

Bronner published a newspaper that had 3.6 per cent of the market; Mediaprint published newspapers that had 71 per cent of the market. Bronner claimed that Mediaprint had abused its dominant position by not including Bronner's paper in Mediaprint's home delivery service. Mediaprint argued that the establishment of the service was a considerable financial

---

[85] [1992] 5 CMLR 255, para. 41.

[86] [1996] *ECLR* 438, 451–452. See also J. Temple Lang, 'Defining Legitimate Competition: Companies' Duties to Supply Competitors and Access to Essential Facilities' (1994) 18 *Fordham International LJ* 437; P. Areeda, 'Essential Facilities: An Epithet in Need of Limiting Principles' (1990) 58 *Antitrust LJ* 841; M. Bergman, 'Editorial: The Bronner Case—A Turning Point for Essential Facilities' [2000] *ECLR* 59; B. Doherty, 'Just What Are Essential Facilities?' (2001) 38 *CMLRev.* 397; C. Stothers, 'Refusal to Supply as Abuse of a Dominant Position: Essential Facilities in the European Union' [2001] *ECLR* 256.

[87] Case T–504/93 *Tiercé Ladbroke SA* v. *Commission* [1997] ECR II–923.

[88] Cases T–374, 375, 384, and 388/94 *European Night Services Ltd. (ENS)* v. *Commission* [1998] ECR II–3141, paras. 208–209.

investment, and that, although it had a dominant position, it was not bound to subsidize competing companies. The ECJ held that the ruling in the *RTE* case turned on the fact that the information on the TV schedules was indispensable for the publication of the TV guide; that RTE's action prevented the appearance of a new product; and that there was no objective justification. The ECJ then held that access to Mediaprint's home delivery service was not indispensable to Bronner's primary business of newspaper production.

THE ECJ

43. In the first place, it is undisputed that other methods of distributing daily newspapers, such as by post and through sale in shops and at kiosks, even though they may be less advantageous for the distribution of certain newspapers, exist and are used by the publishers of those daily newspapers.

44. Moreover, it does not appear that there are technical, legal or even economic obstacles capable of making it impossible, or even unreasonably difficult, for any other publisher of daily newspapers to establish . . . its own nationwide home-delivery scheme. . . .

45. It should be emphasized in that respect that, in order to demonstrate that the creation of such a system is not a realistic potential alternative and that access to the existing system is therefore indispensable, it is not enough to argue that it is not economically viable by reason of the small circulation of the daily newspaper. . . .

46. For such access to be capable of being regarded as indispensable, it would be necessary at the very least to establish, as the Advocate General has pointed out . . . , that it is not economically viable to create a second home delivery scheme for the distribution of daily newspapers with a circulation comparable to that of the daily newspapers distributed by the existing scheme.

A similarly cautionary approach is apparent in the later *IMS* case.[89] The ECJ held that there were three conditions to be met before a dominant undertaking could be required to grant a compulsory licence of data protected by an intellectual property right: the undertaking that requested the licence must intend to offer new services for which there was consumer demand that were not offered by the dominant firm; there must be no objective justification for the refusal to grant the licence; and the result of the refusal to supply the licence is to eliminate all competition on the relevant market.[90]

The preceding discussion still leaves open the terms on which compulsory access is to be granted. This may well require, as Ridyard has noted, the competition authorities to undertake price regulation of the kind associated with utility regulation, which can be problematic in its own terms.[91]

---

[89] Case 418/01 *IMS Health GmbH & Co. v. NDC Health GmbH & Co. KG* [2004] ECR I–5039.

[90] The Commission did not however seem to follow the same approach in *Microsoft Corp.*, COMP/C–3/37.792. The case is currently under appeal, see Case T–201/04 R *Microsoft Corp. v. Commission* [2004] ECR II–4463, for interim relief proceedings. See also DG Competition Discussion Paper, n. 20 above, paras. 225–242.

[91] D. Ridyard, 'Compulsory Access under EC Competition Law—A New Doctrine of "Convenient Facilities" and the Case for Price Regulation' [2004] *ECLR* 669, 673.

(c) ABUSE AND PRICE DISCRIMINATION

(i) *Price Discrimination: Economic Foundations*

Article 82(c) explicitly prohibits the application of dissimilar trading conditions to equivalent transactions. It is important to understand the economic foundations of this area, since a failure to do so can lead to error.

There is price discrimination where goods are sold or purchased at prices which are not related to differences in costs. Thus, price discrimination can cover the situation in which the same product is sold at different, non-cost-related prices; *and* it can also cover the situation where the goods are sold at the same price, even though there are real cost differences entailed.

Discrimination can occur in a variety of ways. It may be *geographical*, whereby the undertaking prices at different levels for different local markets, and then seeks to insulate one from the other in order to prevent arbitrage (reselling) between them. It may assume the form of *discounts* or *rebates* that are not related to cost differences, but have the objective of tying customers closer to that producer, thereby rendering it more difficult for others to penetrate that market. It may also appear as *predatory pricing*: the dominant firm seeks to protect its dominance by dropping its prices below a certain level in order to deter a would-be entrant to the market, the idea being that it will then raise them again to reap monopoly profits when it has 'seen the other firm off'.

It is common also to distinguish price discrimination according to the nature of the injured party. *Primary-line injury* refers to harm suffered by a competitor at the same level of the market as the dominant firm, as exemplified by loyalty rebates that make it more difficult for a competitor to break into the market. *Secondary-line injury* is concerned with harm to the purchaser of the product. This is exemplified by uniform delivered pricing, whereby goods are sold at the same price irrespective of the fact that one customer is closer to the factory than the other, and therefore transport costs are different in the two instances.

The term 'price discrimination' suggests that differences in the price at which goods are offered are themselves 'bad'. It is, however, not self-evident that price discrimination is in fact 'bad' in economic terms; or the cure may turn out to be worse than the disease. There are three reasons why this is so.

The first concerns *measurement* or *assessment*. All species of price discrimination are dependent upon an assessment of production costs, and these may be difficult to determine. This is particularly problematic in relation to predatory pricing. If a new firm enters the market then the existing dominant firm will respond in some manner, for this is the essence of competition. It is difficult to decide when this response crosses the line between a 'proper' competitive strategy and 'improper' predation. This is because commentators disagree on the test for predation,[92] its application, and upon the empirical likelihood that it will occur.[93] This has led some to argue that legal intervention can be ineffective or worse than the disease.[94] The court may select the wrong criterion. It may choose the 'correct' criterion, but misapply it to the facts. The very existence of the legal rule may, moreover, have an adverse, dampening effect on competition.

The second reason price discrimination is not self-evidently bad relates to *allocative efficiency*. In economic theory monopoly is bad because the monopolist will restrict output to a greater extent than under more normal competitive conditions, with a consequential misallocation of resources within society. The key issue is, therefore, whether this misallocation

---

[92] N. 107 below.
[93] Bork, n. 38 above, 144–159.
[94] *Ibid.*

will be greater under a regime which requires the charging of a single price to all customers, or under one which permits price discrimination. This depends upon whether the price discrimination would have the effect of further restricting output, or whether it might actually lead to an increase in output.

W. Bishop, Price Discrimination under Article 86: Political Economy in the European Court[95]

If a monopolist were able to charge each customer exactly that customer's maximum price, then the monopolist would realise very large profits, but output would be identical to that under perfect competition with not a single sale being sacrificed because of higher price. This is called perfectly discriminating monopoly and is very rare, perhaps non-existent.

Much more important is imperfect price discrimination—different prices in a number of different markets or for different classes of customers. British Rail for example discriminates by offering special discounts to students for no reason other than that most of them would not travel by train otherwise, and a little more revenue is better than none at all when it costs virtually nothing to carry an extra passenger outside peak hours.

In *United Brands* the court condemned imperfect price discrimination when practised on a regional basis so as to divide the common market into a number of sub-markets with different, discriminatory prices. However it is not at all clear that imperfect price discrimination generally reduces output below the level that would prevail under simple monopoly. Whether output under imperfectly discriminating monopoly is nearer the perfectly competitive or further from it will depend upon the facts of each case. Unfortunately in any real case the facts are extremely difficult to ferret out—in practice usually impossible to ascertain at all.

Moreover, as several economists have demonstrated, it is conceivable that price discrimination in practice may reduce economic efficiency, i.e. increase the misallocation of money and resources, even if it increases output as compared with output in the absence of discrimination. Probably the best we can do is to adopt one general rule on price discrimination. Many economists guess that price discrimination is probably on balance efficient, assuming that there will be monopoly anyway. Certainly there is no reason to believe that a rule prohibiting it will promote more efficient allocation of resources. Furthermore it is clear that enforcing the prohibition will lead both enforcers and defendants to incur costs that consume real social resources.

The third reason rules against price discrimination may be undesirable, or the cure may be worse than the disease, relates to *fairness*. This may seem intuitively odd, for many regard price discrimination as unfair. This is however less self-evident than is normally thought. Bishop provides a succinct formulation of the counter-argument.

W. Bishop, Price Discrimination under Article 86: Political Economy in the European Court[96]

The rule in *United Brands* requires any monopolist who hitherto has discriminated in price between national submarkets to discontinue this practice. Henceforth such a monopolist must

---

[95] (1981) 44 *MLR* 282, 287–288. See also Bork, n. 38 above, 394–398; P. Muysert, 'Price Discrimination—An Unreliable Indicator of Market Power' [2004] *ECLR* 353; M. Lorenz, M. Lubbig, and A. Russell, 'Price Discrimination, A Tender Story' [2005] *ECLR* 355.

[96] Bishop, n. 95 above, 288–289, italics in the original.

charge the same price (with due allowance for cost differences). Generally speaking discriminating monopolists will find it profitable to charge higher prices in higher income countries ... than in lower income countries. ... Suppose these firms are now required to charge only one price. Almost certainly the profit maximising price will lie somewhere between the highest and lowest discriminatory prices that such a firm could charge ... consider the effect on income distribution as between high and low income countries. German consumers of (say) bananas get them at a lower price than before. Also some German consumers who did not buy bananas before do buy them now. All these German consumers are better off. Some British consumers who bought before now drop out of the market because the price is too high. Remaining British consumers pay more. All these British consumers are worse off. So, though efficiency effects in this example are ambiguous, distributional effects are quite clear: income is redistributed away from Britain and toward Germany. The general effect of *United Brands* is clear—*it redistributes income away from consumers in the poorer regions of Europe and toward consumers in the richer regions.*

It may be argued that this ignores the importance of the creation of a *single market* in the EC, hence the Court's opposition to divisions along national lines. This is not however a self-evident justification for all aspects of the ECJ's case law. We can lose sight of substance by concentrating upon form or labels. The rationale for a single market in economic terms was to create greater efficiency:[97]

To that end striking down arrangements in which arbitrary national barriers are preserved is a goal of the Community institutions. But that is very different from charging different prices in geographically separated markets, simply because the markets happen to be different countries. It is also very different when the effect of prohibiting the practice is possibly to induce greater misallocation of resources and certainly to redistribute wealth from the poor to the rich. The common European market was set up *as a means to the opposite ends*, so a general appeal to those means cannot justify the decision.

(ii) *Price Discrimination: The Case Law*

Case 27/76 **United Brands Company and United Brands Continentaal BV v. Commission**
[1978] ECR 207

The facts were set out above. UB was accused of price discrimination. It shipped bananas from Central America to Europe. Some of these bore the brand name 'Chiquita', and these tended to fetch a higher price. UB sold the goods to ripeners, who sold them to wholesalers, who in turn sold to retailers. The bananas were landed at two ports, but there were no real differences in unloading costs. The Commission alleged that UB sold the bananas at different prices in different Member States, and that it did so without objective justification. The essence of UB's response was to contend that the price differentials reflected market forces, *viz.* the average anticipated market price in each State; that the Community had not established a single banana market; and that, therefore, it was not possible to avoid differences in the individual supply/demand situations in different countries.

---

[97] *Ibid.*, 288–289, italics in the original.

THE ECJ

227. Although the responsibility for establishing the single banana market does not lie with the applicant, it can only endeavour to take 'what the market can bear' provided that it complies with the rules for the regulation and coordination of the market laid down by the Treaty.

228. Once it can be grasped that differences in transport costs, taxation, customs duties, the wages of the labour force, the conditions of marketing, the differences in the parity of the currencies, the density of competition may eventually culminate in different retail selling price levels according to the Member States, then it follows that those differences are factors which UBC only has to take into account to a limited extent since it sells a product which is always the same and at the same place to ripener/distributors who—alone—bear the risks of the consumers' market.

229. The interplay of supply and demand should, owing to its nature, only be applied to each stage where it is really manifest.

230. The mechanisms of the market are adversely affected if the price is calculated by leaving out one stage of the market and taking into account the law of supply and demand as between the vendor and the ultimate consumer and not as between the vendor (UBC) and the purchaser (the ripener/distributor).

231. Thus, by reason of its dominant position UBC ... was in fact able to impose its selling price on the intermediate purchaser. ...

232. These discriminatory prices, which varied according to the circumstances of the Member States, were just so many obstacles to the free movement of goods and were intensified by the clause forbidding the resale of bananas while still green and by reducing the deliveries of the quantities ordered.

233. A rigid partitioning of national markets was thus created at price levels which were artificially different, placing certain distributor/ripeners at a competitive disadvantage, since compared with what it should have been competition had thereby been distorted.

There is much confusion in this extract, which does not represent the Court's most lucid reasoning. The judgment omits any consideration of the general issue whether price discrimination can be beneficial, and the reasoning is punctuated by mistaken use of concepts. It is, for example, central to the ECJ's judgment that UB would have to take account of the many factors that differentiated the various retail markets only to a limited extent; and that the risks would instead be borne by the distributors/ripeners.[98] This is highly questionable. A manufacturer may well bear the risk of differing demand conditions at the retail level. UB almost certainly did bear these risks. If it had tried to shift these risks to the distributors, then it would have to have given financial inducements to the latter.[99] The Court's references to the markets in which supply and demand is really manifest are equally problematic.[100]

Case 85/76 **Hoffmann-La Roche & Co. AG v. Commission**
[1979] ECR 461

The case turned on certain abusive practices by HLR in the vitamins markets, one aspect of this being HLR's practice of giving rebates.

---

[98] Case 27/76 *United Brands*, para. 228.
[99] Bishop, n. 95 above, 285–286.
[100] *Ibid.*, 284–285.

THE ECJ

89. An undertaking which is in a dominant position on a market and ties purchasers—even if it does so at their request—by an obligation or promise on their part to obtain all or most of their requirements exclusively from the said undertaking abuses its dominant position within the meaning of Article 86 of the Treaty, whether the obligation in question is stipulated without further qualification or whether it is undertaken in consideration of the grant of the rebate. The same applies if the said undertaking, without tying the purchasers by a formal obligation, applies, either under the terms of agreements concluded with these purchasers or unilaterally, a system of fidelity rebates, that is to say discounts conditional on the customer's obtaining all or most of its requirements—whether the quantity of its purchases be large or small—from the undertaking in the dominant position.

90. Obligations of this kind ... are incompatible with the objective of undistorted competition within the Common Market, because ... they are not based on an economic transaction which justifies this burden or benefit but are designed to deprive the purchaser of or restrict his possible choices of sources of supply and to deny other producers access to the market. The fidelity rebate, unlike quantity rebates exclusively linked with the volume of purchases from the producer concerned, is designed through the grant of a financial advantage to prevent customers from obtaining their supplies from competing producers. Furthermore, the effect of fidelity rebates is to apply dissimilar conditions to equivalent transactions with other trading parties in that two purchasers pay a different price for the same quantity of the same product depending on whether they obtain their supplies exclusively from the undertaking in a dominant position or have several sources of supply. ...

91. For the purpose of rejecting the finding that there has been an abuse of a dominant position the interpretation suggested by the applicant that an abuse implies that the use of the economic power bestowed by the dominant position is the means whereby the abuse has been brought about cannot be accepted. The concept of abuse is an objective concept relating to the behaviour of an undertaking in a dominant position which is such as to influence the structure of the market where, as a result of the very presence of the undertaking in question, the degree of competition is weakened and which, through recourse to methods different from those which condition normal competition in products or services on the basis of the transactions of commercial operators, has the effect of hindering the maintenance of the degree of competition still existing in the market or the growth of that competition.

The ECJ thus reiterated the point it made in *Continental Can*: there was no need to prove that the abuse had been brought about by the firm's market power. The concept of abuse was 'objective', and could apply to any behaviour which influenced the *structure* of the market and weakened competition.

The ECJ's antipathy to price discrimination in the form of loyalty rebates emerges clearly in the above extract.[101] This reasoning has been followed in later cases,[102] and it has been held that even a quantity rebate system may be contrary to Article 82 if it is not based on economically justified considerations, more especially if it tends, like fidelity rebates, to prevent a customer obtaining supplies from elsewhere.[103] Particular decisions have however been heavily

---

[101] D. Ridyard, 'Exclusionary Pricing and Price Discrimination Abuses under Article 82—An Economic Analysis' [2002] *ECLR* 286.

[102] Case 322/81 *Michelin*, n. 51 above; Case T–228/97 *Irish Sugar*, n. 35 above, paras. 111–114.

[103] Case C–163/99 *Portugal* v. *Commission* [2001] ECR I–2613; Case T–219/99 *British Airways*, n. 10 above, upheld in Case C–95/04 P *British Airways*, n. 61 above; Case T–203/01 *Michelin*, n. 66 above, paras. 58–62, 95.

criticized,[104] and there has been a more general call for a principled, economic approach to be applied to the pricing policies of dominant firms.[105]

(d) ABUSE AND PREDATORY PRICING

Predatory pricing has already been touched on above. It is now time to focus more specifically on this abusive behaviour. *Akzo* is the leading case.

Case C–62/86 **Akzo Chemie BV v. Commission**
[1991] ECR I–3359

[Note ToA renumbering: Art. 86 is now Art. 82]

Akzo, based in Holland, and ECS, a smaller UK firm, both made organic peroxides. Benzoyl peroxide could be used in both the flour and the plastics markets. ECS was initially engaged in the flour market, but then moved into the plastics market in 1979 and solicited some of Akzo's customers. Akzo had a meeting with ECS at which it threatened that it would take aggressive action on the flour market unless ECS withdrew from the plastics market. ECS ignored the threats, which Akzo then put into operation. Akzo targeted certain of ECS's customers in the flour market, and offered them prices which were below previous rates and below average total cost. Akzo subsidized these low prices by money drawn from the plastics sector. ECS's business fell significantly as a result. The Court quoted the test of abuse from *Hoffmann-La Roche* set out above,[106] and then reasoned as follows.

THE ECJ

70. It follows that Article 86 prohibits a dominant undertaking from eliminating a competitor and thereby strengthening its position by using methods other than those which come within the scope of competition on the basis of quality. From that point of view, however, not all competition by means of price can be regarded as legitimate.

71. Prices below average variable costs (that is to say, those which vary depending on the quantities produced) by means of which a dominant undertaking seeks to eliminate a competitor must be regarded as abusive. A dominant undertaking has no interest in applying such prices except that of eliminating competitors so as to enable it subsequently to raise its prices by taking advantage of its monopolistic position, since each sale generates a loss, namely the total amount of the fixed costs (that is to say, those which remain constant regardless of the quantities produced) and, at least, part of the variable costs relating to the unit produced.

72. Moreover, prices below average total costs, that is to say, fixed costs plus variable costs, but above average variable costs, must be regarded as abusive if they are determined as part of a plan for eliminating a competitor. Such prices can drive from the market undertakings which are perhaps as efficient as the dominant undertaking but which, because of their smaller financial resources, are incapable of withstanding the competition waged against them.

---

104 B. Sher, 'Price Discounts and *Michelin II*: What Goes Around Comes Around' [2002] *ECLR* 482.

105 J. Temple Lang and R. O'Donoghue, 'Defining Legitimate Competition: How to Clarify Pricing Abuses under Article 82 EC' (2002) 26 *Fordham ILJ* 83.

106 See 1012.

The ECJ found Akzo to be in breach of these principles. It had at various times offered prices to ECS's customers that were lower than Akzo's own average total or variable costs, and it had done so to remove ECS from the plastics market. The behaviour of Akzo was particularly blatant. Its unequivocally wrongful intent should not, however, lead us to underestimate the difficulties which a rule against predatory pricing presents for a system of competition policy.

First, there is continuing disagreement about the proper definition of predation in economic terms.[107]

Secondly, the existence of this ground of challenge may do more harm than good. The line between vigorous price competition and illegal predation may be a fine one.[108] A dominant firm may feel that it should not pursue price competition too vigorously, lest this should leave it open to allegations of predatory abuse. This is all the more so given that, on the *Akzo* test, intention is of crucial importance where prices are below average total costs, but above average variable costs.

Finally, there are those who continue to doubt whether a rational firm would engage in predation. The potential gains from successful predation appear straightforward: the dominant firm lowers its prices, takes a loss in the short term, drives out the smaller firm, and then reaps high monopoly profits. The economic reality is much less certain. For predation to be a rational strategy the future flow of profits has to exceed the present losses incurred as a result of the drop in price. This is not theoretically impossible, but it is more difficult to achieve than might initially be thought. Predation is, in this sense, a war of attrition, with the outcome to be determined by the combatants' relative losses and reserves: the 'war will be a *Blitzkrieg* only if the predator has greatly disproportionate reserves or is able to inflict very disproportionate losses'.[109]

There are real obstacles to a successful campaign. The losses during the battle will be higher for the predator than the victim. Any anticipated monopoly profits must be discounted at current interest rates. The predator will, moreover, have to gauge the likelihood of another competitor entering the market, should it seek to reap excessive monopoly profits having disposed of the original combatant.[110] The threat of further predation may constitute a barrier to entry for prospective competitors, but the fact remains that the greater the monopoly profits now being reaped by the predator, the greater the incentive for new entrants.

Whether Akzo was behaving rationally depends whether its present losses were outweighed by future gains.[111] The answer to this is unclear. The losses to the predator from the campaign will however be lower if it can price discriminate, by charging higher prices to its traditional customers, while poaching ECS's customers with lower prices. It appears from the facts that Akzo did this, though how long this strategy could have been maintained is more debatable.

---

[107] See, e.g., P. Areeda and D. Turner, 'Predatory Pricing and Related Practices under Section 2 of the Sherman Act: A Comment' (1975) 88 *Harv LR* 697; F.M. Scherer, 'Predatory Pricing and the Sherman Act: A Comment' (1976) 89 *Harv LR* 869; O. Williamson, 'Predatory Pricing: A Strategic and Welfare Analysis' (1977) 87 *Yale LJ* 284; J. Brodley and G. Hay, 'Predatory Pricing: Competing Economic Theories and the Evolution of Legal Standards' (1981) 66 *Cornell LR* 738; E. Mastromanolis, 'Predatory Pricing Strategies in the European Union: A Case for Legal Reform' [1998] *ECLR* 211.

[108] As recognized by the Commission: DG Competition Discussion Paper, n. 20 above, paras. 94–97; M. Gravengaard, 'The Meeting Competition Defence Principle—A Defence for Price Discrimination and Predatory Pricing' [2006] *ECLR* 658.

[109] Bork, n. 38 above, 147.

[110] *Ibid.*, 149–155.

[111] R. Rapp, 'Predatory Pricing and Entry Deterring Strategies: The Economics of *AKZO*' [1986] *ECLR* 233.

Notwithstanding these difficulties predatory pricing still constitutes abuse under Article 82. Thus in *Tetra Pak*[112] the ECJ held that Tetra Pak, a world leader in the manufacture of aseptic cartons for liquid and semi-liquid food, had abused its dominant position by its pricing policy on non-aseptic cartons. The company had a dominant position on the market for aseptic cartons, and it was held that it had used profits from this market to subsidize sales on the market for non-aseptic cartons, selling the latter at a loss below average variable cost in seven Member States. The ECJ reiterated the holding in paragraphs 72 and 73 of *Akzo*. It was argued that the Commission and CFI should have taken into account the issue whether Tetra Pak had any realistic chance of recouping its losses. This argument was rejected by the ECJ, which held that it must be possible to penalize predation whenever there was a risk that competitors would be eliminated, and that this objective ruled out waiting until such a strategy resulted in the actual elimination of competitors.[113]

(e) ABUSE AND SELECTIVE PRICING

It is clear from cases such as *Irish Sugar*[114] that when judging the legality of a selective pricing policy the CFI and ECJ will take account of the fact that the practice was aimed at eliminating a competitor from the market. This was reaffirmed in the following case.

Cases C–395–396/96 P Compagnie Maritimes Belge Transportes SA, Compagnie Maritime Belge SA, and Dafra Lines A/S v. Commission
[2000] ECR I–1365

The applicants were members of a liner conference that had a dominant position on certain shipping routes in Africa. They were charged, *inter alia*, with lowering their freight rates in order to drive the only competitor from the market.

THE ECJ

117. ... where a liner conference in a dominant position selectively cuts its prices in order deliberately to match those of a competitor, it derives a dual benefit. First, it eliminates the principal, and possibly the only, means of competition open to the competing undertaking. Second, it can continue to require its users to pay higher prices for the services which are not threatened by that competition.

118. It is not necessary, in the present case, to rule generally on the circumstances in which a liner conference may legitimately ... adopt lower prices than those of its advertised tariff in order to compete with a competitor who quotes lower prices. ...

119. It is sufficient to recall that the conduct at issue here is that of a conference having a share of over 90% of the market in question and only one competitor. The appellants have, moreover, never seriously disputed, and indeed admitted at the hearing, that the purpose of the conduct complained of was to eliminate G & C from the market.

---

[112] Case C–333/94 P, n. 3 above. See also Case T–340/03 *France Télécom SA*, n. 6 above.
[113] *Ibid.*, para. 44.
[114] Case T–228/97 *Irish Sugar*, n. 35 above, para. 114.

7. DEFENCES: OBJECTIVE JUSTIFICATION, PROPORTIONALITY, AND EFFICIENCY

Article 82 has no equivalent to Article 81(3). The Court and Commission[115] have however applied the concepts of objective justification and proportionality to provide some flexibility in what would otherwise be too draconian an application of Article 82.[116] Thus if there is an objective justification for the dominant firm's conduct, and it is proportionate, then it will escape condemnation under this Article.[117]

While objective justification and proportionality, therefore, imbue the application of the Article with added flexibility, the application of these concepts is not self-executing. The decision, for example, whether a refusal to supply is objectively justified and proportionate will often reflect certain assumptions concerning the relative importance of protecting competitors and consumers, or the relative significance of single-market integration and consumer welfare.

The Commission has more recently indicated that an efficiency defence should be available under Article 82, provided that the efficiencies outweigh the negative effects of the relevant conduct.[118]

8. REFORM OF ARTICLE 82

In 2005 the Commission undertook a review of Article 82.[119] This was felt to be timely, given the reviews of Article 81 and merger policy, and given also the disquiet about some decisions under Article 82. The review is still ongoing at the time of writing and the outcome is therefore unclear.

The Commission's discussion paper focuses on exclusionary abuses, defined as dominant firm behaviour that can foreclose the market, by denying to existing or potential competitors profitable expansion in or access to markets, completely or partially, thereby harming consumers.[120]

The Commission's overall philosophy as to the purpose of Article 82 is relatively clear. It is to protect consumers, rather than particular competitors. However this requires the safeguarding of the competitive process from foreclosure. This is apparent from the Commission's paper,[121] and from a speech given by the Competition Commissioner.

---

[115] DG Competition Discussion Paper, n. 20 above, paras. 77, 84.

[116] See similar ideas at work in the context of free movement of goods, Ch. 19.

[117] See, e.g., Case 27/76 *United Brands*, n. 4 above; Case T–65/89 *BPB*, n. 78 above; Case T–30/89 *Hilti*, n. 33 above; Case 311/84 *Centre Belge d'Etudes du Marché-Télémarketing (CBEM)* v. *CLT SA* [1985] ECR 3261.

[118] DG Competition Discussion Paper, n. 20 above; Commissioner Kroes, 'Preliminary Thoughts on Policy Review of Article 82', Speech at the Fordham Corporate Law Institute (Sept. 2005), 5, available at http://ec.europa.eu/comm/competition/antitrust/art82/index.html.

[119] DG Competition Discussion Paper, n. 20 above. For comment see Dethmers and Dodoo, n. 28 above; B. Sher, 'The Last of the Steam-Powered Trains: Modernising Article 82' [2004] *ECLR* 243; G. Niels and H. Jenkins, 'Reform of Article 82: Where the Link between Dominance and Effects Breaks Down' [2005] *ECLR* 605; A. Majumdar, 'Whither Dominance' [2006] *ECLR* 161.

[120] DG Competition Discussion Paper, n. 20 above, para. 1.

[121] *Ibid.*, paras. 1, 4, 55–56.

Commissioner Kroes, Preliminary Thoughts on
Policy Review of Article 82[122]

My own philosophy ... is fairly simple. First, it is competition, and not competitors, that is to be protected. Second, ultimately the aim is to avoid consumers harm.

I like aggressive competition—including by dominant companies—and I don't care if it may hurt competitors—as long as it ultimately benefits consumers. That is because the main and ultimate objective of Article 82 is to protect consumers, and this does, of course, require the protection of an undistorted competitive process on the market.

We need to take into account not only short term harm, but also medium and long term harm arising from the exclusion of competitors. . . .

The review has also raised broader issues concerning Article 82, more particularly the extent to which it should be based on legal form or economic effects. The Discussion Paper states that 'in applying Article 82, the Commission will adopt an approach which is based on the likely effects on the market',[123] and this is exemplified to some degree by its treatment of particular instances of exclusionary abuse. Whether this goes far enough for those who advocate an economic-effects approach to Article 82 is less certain. Thus the EAGCP group argues for an economics-based approach, whereby the assessment of cases is not undertaken on the basis of the form of the particular business practice, tying, exclusive dealing, etc., but on assessment of the anti-competitive effects that it generates and the extent to which they are outweighed by efficiency gains.[124] Similar concerns are voiced by Vickers.

J. Vickers, Abuse of Market Power[125]

The law on abuse of market power is far from settled. The law in Europe could now develop in either of two broad directions, with emphasis either on form or on economic effect. Form-based evolution of the law would further develop descriptions of conduct for dominant firms to avoid. Economics-based evolution would clarify underlying principles in terms of actual and potential economic effects, develop practically administrable rules and methods explicitly on the basis of those principles, and apply them to cases.

In the competition between economics-and form-based approaches the former has strong advantages. It can align the law with its economic purpose and in an internally consistent manner. It can prevent form from triumphing over substance at the cost of both allowing detrimental conduct and blocking benign conduct. And it can provide clarity at fundamental, rather than superficial level. These advantages will be realized if European competition law on abuse of dominance becomes more firmly anchored to economic principles, and where those principles are practically applicable by competition lawyers and the courts.

To say that the law on abuse of dominance should develop a stronger economic foundation is not to say that rules of law should be replaced by discretionary decision making based on whatever is thought to be desirable in economic terms case by case. There must be rules of

---

122 N. 118 above, 3.
123 DG Competition Discussion Paper, n. 20 above, para. 4.
124 Report by EAGCP 'An Economic Approach to Article 82' (2005), available at http://ec.europa.eu/comm/competition/antitrust/art82/index.html.
125 (2005) 115 *Economic J* 244, 259.

law in this area of competition policy, not least for reasons of predictability and accountability. So the issue is not rules versus discretion, but how well the rules are grounded in economics. To that end there is great scope for economic analysis and research to contribute to the development of the law on abuse of dominance. To be effective, however, economics must contribute in a way that competition agencies, and ultimately the courts, find practicable in deciding the cases.

9. CONCLUSION

i. It is now generally accepted that Article 82 is to protect consumers rather than particular competitors, and that this requires protection of the competitive process from foreclosure.

ii. Adjudication under Article 82 nonetheless involves difficult problems relating to market definition, the determination of dominance, and the meaning of abuse.

iii. The boundaries of the special responsibility incumbent on dominant firms are not clear from the case law, thereby making it difficult for the dominant firm to know what it is allowed to do.

iv. There is in addition continuing debate as to the extent to which Article 82 should be based on legal form or economic effects, and on the practical, detailed ramifications of a shift from the former to the latter.

v. The enforcement of Article 82 is now subject to the reformed regime discussed in the previous chapter, to which reference should be made.[126]

10. FURTHER READING

(a) Books

Bellamy, C., and Child, G., *European Community Law of Competition* (edited by P. Roth QC and V. Rose, 6th edn., Oxford University Press, 2007)

Bishop, S., and Walker, M., *The Economics of EC Competition Law: Concepts, Application and Measurement* (2nd edn., Sweet & Maxwell, 2002)

Faull, J., and Nikpay, A. (eds.), *The EC Law of Competition* (2nd edn., Oxford University Press, 2007)

Furse, M., *Competition Law of the UK and EC* (5th edn., Oxford University Press, 2006)

Goyder, D., *EC Competition Law* (4th edn., Oxford University Press, 2003)

Jones, A., and Sufrin, B., *EC Competition Law: Text, Cases, and Materials* (2nd edn., Oxford University Press, 2004)

Korah, V., *EC Competition Law and Practice* (8th edn., Hart, 2004)

---

[126] See 999–1001.

Middleton, K., Rodger, B., and MacCulloch, A., *Cases and Materials on UK and EC Competition Law* (Oxford University Press, 2003)

Whish, R., *Competition Law* (5th edn., LexisNexis, 2003)

(b) Articles

Azevedo, J. de, and Walker, M., 'Dominance: Meaning and Measurement' [2002] *ECLR* 363

Doherty, B., 'Just What Are Essential Facilities?' (2001) 38 *CMLRev.* 397

Eilmansberger, T., 'How to Distinguish Good from Bad Competition under Article 82: In Search of Clearer and More Coherent Standards for Anti-Competitive Abuses' (2005) 42 *CMLRev.* 49

Gravengaard, M., 'The Meeting Competition Defence—A Defence for Price Discrimination and Predatory Pricing' [2006] *ECLR* 658

Harbord, D., and Hoehn, T., 'Barriers to Entry and Exit in European Competition Policy' (1994) 14 *International Review of Law and Economics* 422

Heit, J., 'The Justifiability of the ECJ's Wide Approach to the Concept of Barriers to Entry' [2006] *ECLR* 117

Kallaugher, J., and Sher, B., 'Rebates Revisited: Anti-Competitive Effects and Exclusionary Abuse under Article 82' [2004] *ECLR* 263

Kloosterhuis, E., 'Joint Dominance and the Interaction between Firms' [2001] *ECLR* 79

Lorenz, M., Lubbig, M., and Russell, A., 'Price Discrimination, A Tender Story' [2005] *ECLR* 355

Mastromanolis, E., 'Predatory Pricing Strategies in the European Union: A Case for Legal Reform' [1998] *ECLR* 211

Monti, G., 'The Scope of Collective Dominance under Article 82' (2001) 38 *CMLRev.* 131

Niels, G., 'Collective Dominance—More Than Just Oligopolistic Independence' [2001] *ECLR* 168

Rapp, R., 'Predatory Pricing and Entry Deterring Strategies: The Economics of *AKZO*' [1986] *ECLR* 233

Ridyard, D., 'Economic Analysis of Single Firm and Oligopolistic Dominance' [1994] *ECLR* 255

—— 'Essential Facilities and the Obligation to Supply Competitors under UK and EC Competition Law' [1996] *ECLR* 438

—— 'Exclusionary Pricing and Price Discrimination Abuses under Article 82—An Economic Analysis' [2002] *ECLR* 286

Rodger, B., 'Oligopolistic Market Failure: Collective Dominance versus Complex Monopoly' [1995] *ECLR* 21

Sher, B., 'Price Discounts and *Michelin II:* What Goes Around Comes Around' [2002] *ECLR* 482

Stothers, C., 'Refusal to Supply as Abuse of a Dominant Position: Essential Facilities in the European Union' [2001] *ECLR* 256

Subiotto, R., and O'Donoghue, R., 'Defining the Scope of the Duty of Dominant Firms to Deal with Existing Customers under Article 82' [2003] *ECLR* 683

Temple Lang, J., and O'Donoghue, R., 'Defining Legitimate Competition: How to Clarify Pricing Abuses under Article 82 EC' (2002) 26 *Fordham ILJ* 83

Turnbull, S., 'Barriers to Entry, Article 86 EC and the Abuse of a Dominant Position: An Economic Critique of European Community Competition Law' [1996] *ECLR* 96

Vickers, J., 'Abuse of Market Power' (2005) 115 *Economic Journal* 244

Whish, R., 'Collective Dominance', in D. O'Keeffe and A. Bavasso (eds.), *Judicial Review in European Union Law* (Kluwer, 2000), ch. 37

—— and Sufrin, B., 'Oligopolistic Markets and EC Competition Law' (1992) 12 *YBEL* 59

27

COMPETITION LAW: MERGERS

1. INTRODUCTION

Community regulation of mergers was a long time coming.[1] Articles 81 and 82 made no specific mention of mergers. The Commission attempted to fill this gap as early as 1973.[2] While the Member States recognized that some merger control was necessary, they disagreed on the boundary between Community and national merger control, and on the more precise form of Community control. The failure to resolve these issues meant that successive draft merger regulations became a regular feature of the EC.[3] The possibility of a 'final' regulation on mergers came to resemble *Waiting for Godot*.

The ECJ was not idle during this period. It was willing in part at least to fill the gap resulting from legislative inaction. Article 82 was invoked, as we have seen,[4] in *Continental Can*[5] to catch mergers by a firm in a dominant position. The Court took longer to apply Article 81 to mergers. The traditional orthodoxy was that it did not apply to agreements the purpose of which was the acquisition of ownership. However, this orthodoxy was shaken in the *BAT* case, where the ECJ indicated its willingness to consider the application of Article 81 to some instances of share acquisition.[6]

Regulation 4064/89 was finally adopted in December 1989.[7] There have been subsequent amendments and the current regime is to be found in Regulation 139/2004 and accompanying provisions.[8] Most concentrations will now be dealt with under this Regulation, but it may still be possible to use Articles 81 and 82 in certain cases.

2. CENTRAL ISSUES

i. Legal control of mergers is an important component of any regime to regulate competition.

ii. It is important to understand the policy reasons underlying merger control.

---

[1] A. Jones and B. Sufrin, *EC Competition Law: Text, Cases, and Materials* (2nd edn., Oxford University Press, 2004), 854–862; R. Whish, *Competition Law* (5th edn., Butterworths, 2003), 793–799.

[2] Commission Proposal for a Reg. of the Council of Ministers on the Control of Concentrations between Undertakings [1973] OJ C92/1.

[3] See, e.g., [1982] OJ C36/3; [1984] OJ C51/8; [1986] OJ C324/5.

[4] See above, 1021–1022.

[5] Case 6/72 [1973] ECR 215.

[6] Cases 142 and 156/84 *British American Tobacco Co. Ltd. and R. J. Reynolds Industries Inc. v. Commission* [1987] ECR 4487.

[7] [1989] OJ L395/1.

[8] Council Reg. (EC) 139/2004 of 20 Jan. 2004 on the control of concentrations between undertakings (the EC Merger Reg.) [2004] OJ L24/1.

iii. There are jurisdictional, procedural, and substantive aspects to Community merger policy.

iv. Jurisdictional issues cover the types of concentration that are subject to the Merger Regulation and the inter-relationship between merger control at EC and national level.

v. Procedural issues cover matters such as the way in which notice of a proposed merger must be given, and the investigative powers possessed by the Commission.

vi. Substantive issues of merger policy include matters such as the test for determining whether a merger or concentration should be allowed, and the extent to which efficiencies produced by the concentration should be taken into account.

3. MERGER CONTROL: THE POLICY RATIONALE

Mergers can be of three kinds. *Horizontal mergers* are those between companies that make the same products and operate at the same level of the market. *Vertical mergers* are those between companies which operate at different distributive levels of the same product market. *Conglomerate mergers* are those between firms which have no connection with each other in any product market. Horizontal mergers are potentially the most damaging to the competitive process.

(a) ARGUMENTS AGAINST MERGERS

A merger can have a *marked impact on competition.* A horizontal merger may enable the new entity to set price and output in the same manner as a single-firm monopolist, with the same consequences for consumer welfare. In some countries indices are used to measure the reduction of competition brought about by the merger.[9] The impact of vertical mergers on competition is more controversial.[10] A vertical merger is merely one form of vertical integration: a company may relate to those down-market by a number of means ranging from ordinary contract, through exclusive-distribution arrangements, to vertical merger. Such vertical relationships can be potentially anti-competitive, through, for example, foreclosing of outlets to other manufacturers,[11] but commentators also dispute how far these vertical relationships harm competition.[12] This disagreement carries over into the field of vertical merger, since it may, for example, improve the distribution of a branded product and hence promote inter-brand competition. There is also disagreement on the impact of conglomerate mergers on competition. Thus, while some see them as dangerous, allowing, for example, a wealthy firm to cross-subsidize between products to defeat new entrants, others are sceptical whether such mergers involve any detriment to competition.[13]

---

[9] The best known of these is the Herfindahl–Hirschman Index which is used in the USA.

[10] J. Church, 'The Impact of Vertical and Conglomerate Mergers on Competition' (2004), available at http://ec.europa.eu/comm/competition/mergers/studies_reports/studies_reports.html.

[11] G. Abbamonte and V. Rabassa, 'Foreclosure and Vertical Mergers' [2001] *ECLR* 214.

[12] See Ch. 25.

[13] R. Bork, *The Antitrust Paradox* (Basic Books, 1978), ch. 12.

S. Bishop, A. Lofaro, and F. Rosati, Turning the Tables: Why Vertical and Conglomerate Mergers are Different[14]

[T]here should be an economic presumption that non-horizontal mergers are pro-competitive. This conclusion derives from a fundamental difference between horizontal and non-horizontal mergers. Whereas horizontal mergers remove a direct competitive constraint and raise the possibility that post-merger prices will increase to the detriment of consumers, non-horizontal mergers do not. Moreover, the general impact of a non-horizontal merger is to reduce prices as a result of eliminating externalities and other inefficiencies that might have existed pre-merger. While this is not to say that non-horizontal mergers are always pro-competitive, it does indicate an economic presumption (albeit rebuttable) that such mergers are competitively benign.

Another reason for merger regulation is that mergers have been used to strip the *assets of the acquired firm,* and although this may be in the short-term interests of some shareholders, it may not be in the longer-term public interest. Such concerns have been fuelled by empirical research, which indicates that mergers often do not produce the gains expected of them.[15]

Regional policy constitutes a third rationale for merger control. A merger may lead to the rationalization of existing plants, with consequential effects on unemployment and regional vitality. A government may use merger policy as one means of maintaining a balanced distribution of wealth and job opportunities around the country.[16]

(b) ARGUMENTS IN FAVOUR OF MERGERS

Mergers can however have a beneficial impact and enhance economic efficiency in a number of different ways.[17]

Thus mergers can render it easier to reap *economies of scale.* Firms will produce most efficiently when they can maximize economies of scale. These are economies that can be reaped by the firm which is at the optimum size for that type of industry. A certain product may, for example, be made most efficiently with a particular piece of machinery, but this machinery may require a specific turnover before it is economically viable. Mergers are one way in which scale economies can be reaped.

Mergers may also enhance *distributional efficiency.* It may, for example, be more efficient for a manufacturing firm which is seeking to extend its operations down-market into the distributional sphere to merge with an existing distributor, rather than learn the skills of this new area from scratch.

---

[14] [2006] *ECLR* 403, 406.

[15] G. Newbould, *Management and Merger Activity* (Cruthstead, 1970); G. Meeks, *Disappointing Marriage: A Study of the Gains from Mergers* (Cambridge University Press, 1977); A. Hughes, 'Mergers and Economic Performance in the UK: A Survey of the Empirical Evidence 1950–1990', in M. Bishop and J. Kay (eds.), *European Mergers and Merger Policy* (Oxford University Press, 1993), ch. 1.

[16] There may indeed be a conflict between regional policy and competition policy in this respect, particularly where the latter focuses exclusively on the impact of mergers on competition without taking into account other factors.

[17] S. Bishop, A. Lofaro, F. Rosati, and J. Young, 'The Efficiency-Enhancing Effects of Non-Horizontal Mergers' (Office for Official Publications of the European Communities, 2005), available at http://ec.europa.eu/comm/competition/mergers/studies_reports/studies_reports.html.

There is also a considerable literature on the relationship between mergers and *managerial efficiency*.[18] The argument, in brief, is that the threat of a takeover is a spur for management to perform efficiently. On this view the 'market for corporate control' helps to promote economic efficiency: where the shareholders are satisfied with the performance of management they will not wish to sell to another company.

The Merger Regulation recognizes the inevitability and desirability of mergers within the Community. Thus the third recital to the Regulation acknowledges that the dismantling of internal frontiers will result in major corporate reorganization; while the fourth recital states that this is to be welcomed as one means of increasing the competitiveness of European industry on world markets.

4. REGULATION 139/2004: JURISDICTIONAL ISSUES

(a) CONCENTRATION: GENERAL

Regulation 139/2004 will only be applicable if there is a concentration. This issue is dealt with in Article 3(1):

A concentration shall be deemed to arise where a change of control on a lasting basis results from:

(a) the merger of two or more previously independent undertakings or parts of undertakings, or

(b) the acquisition, by one or more persons already controlling at least one undertaking, or by one or more undertakings, whether by purchase of securities or assets, by contract or by any other means, of direct or indirect control of the whole or parts of one or more undertakings.

Article 3(1) must be read in conjunction with Article 3(2):

Control shall be constituted by rights, contracts or any other means which, either separately or in combination and having regard to the considerations of fact or law involved, confer the possibility of exercising decisive influence on an undertaking, in particular by:

(a) ownership or the right to use all or part of the assets of an undertaking;

(b) rights or contracts which confer decisive influence on the composition, voting or decisions of the organs of an undertaking.

Article 3(1) and (2) bring a number of different situations within the ambit of the Regulation, and catch concentrations with a Community dimension irrespective of whether the firms are based in the EU.[19] The Commission has, moreover, made it clear that the determination of whether or not a concentration exists will be based on qualitative rather than

---

[18] See, e.g., F. Easterbrook and D. Fischel, 'The Proper Role of a Target's Management in Responding to a Tender Offer' (1991) 94 *Harv LR* 1161.

[19] Case T–102/96 *Gencor Ltd.* v. *Commission* [1999] ECR II–753.

quantitative criteria, focusing on the notion of control, and that in making this determination it will take account of issues of law *and* fact.[20]

Article 3(1)(a) covers the case of a *complete merger*. Although the Regulation does not define the term merger, it implies the formation of one enterprise from undertakings that were previously distinct. The Commission has, however, made it clear that Article 3(1)(a) can bite in some circumstances where the undertakings retain their separate legal personalities, but create nonetheless a single economic unit.[21]

Article 3(1)(b) captures cases of *change of control*. This is a complex topic, detailed treatment of which can be found elsewhere.[22] The essence of this Article is, however, as follows. A change of control can result in the acquisition of *sole control* by a person or an undertaking. This is exemplified by *Arjomari-Prioux/Wiggins Teape*,[23] where the Commission held that the acquisition of a 39 per cent shareholding in a company was sufficient to give a buyer control, given that the remaining shares were widely dispersed. It is also possible for two or more undertakings to acquire *joint control* over another. Thus in *Northern Telecom/Matra Telecommunications*[24] both companies were held to have acquired joint control over Matra SA, because the consent of both parents was necessary for all important business decisions and financial plans. Cases concerning joint control raise difficult questions of how far the Regulation captures joint ventures.

(b) CONCENTRATION: JOINT VENTURES

Joint venture is not a term of art and covers a wide range of business arrangements, from the establishment of a new corporate entity by two competitors to a joint-purchasing scheme or joint research and development. It is this very breadth of coverage which causes problems for competition systems. There has been debate about whether they should be treated by analogy with cartels, and be regarded as essentially a 'behavioural' problem to be dealt with under Article 81, or as a 'structural' problem, to be dealt with under the Merger Regulation.

The approach in the 1989 Regulation was that the structural/concentrative aspects of joint ventures were dealt with under the Merger Regulation, while behavioural/co-operative aspects concerned with the impact on competition of co-ordination between independent undertakings were considered under Article 81. This however caused real difficulties.[25]

The approach has now been modified so that the concentrative and competitive aspects of joint ventures can be considered within the confines of the Merger Regulation: the former is dealt with through Article 3(4), the latter through Article 2(4)–(5) of the 2004 Regulation. Hence, the Commission's powers of decision contained in Article 8 and the time limits specified in Article 10 apply to determinations made under Article 2(4). Article 3(4) of

---

[20] Commission Notice on the Concept of Concentration under Council Reg. 4064/89 on the Control of Concentrations between Undertakings [1998] OJ C66/5, para. 4. This and a number of other notices will be replaced: see Draft Commission Consolidated Jurisdictional Notice (hereafter DJN), para. 6, available at http://ec.europa.eu/comm/competition/mergers/legislation/legislation.html.

[21] The Concept of Concentration, n. 20 above, para. 7; DJN, n. 20 above, para. 9.

[22] *Ibid.*, paras. 10–87; M. Broberg, 'The Concept of Control in the Merger Control Regulation' [2004] *ECLR* 741.

[23] Case IV/M25 [1991] 4 CMLR 854.

[24] Case IV/M249.

[25] B. Hawk, 'Joint Ventures under EEC Law' *Fordham Corporate Law Institute* (Fordham University, 1991), 575–576.

Regulation 139/2004 provides that:

> The creation of a joint venture performing on a lasting basis all the functions of an autonomous economic entity shall constitute a concentration within the meaning of paragraph (1)(b).

Article 2(4) of the Regulation states that:

> To the extent that the creation of a joint venture constituting a concentration pursuant to Article 3 has as its object or effect the coordination of the competitive behaviour of undertakings that remain independent, such coordination shall be appraised in accordance with the criteria of Article 81(1) and (3) of the Treaty, with a view to establishing whether or not the operation is compatible with the Common Market.

Article 2(5) further provides that:

> In making this appraisal, the Commission shall take into account in particular:
> — whether two or more parent companies retain, to a significant extent, activities in the same market as the joint venture or in a market which is upstream or downstream from that of the joint venture or in a neighbouring market closely related to this market,
> — whether the co-ordination which is the direct consequence of the creation of the joint venture affords the undertakings concerned the possibility of eliminating competition in respect of a substantial part of the products or services in question.

The fact remains that a joint venture will be caught by the Merger Regulation only if it results in the creation of an autonomous economic entity which performs functions on a lasting basis. Guidance on the interpretation of this provision is to be found in the Commission Notice on Full Function Joint Ventures.[26] The Notice is not binding, but provides a useful indication of the Commission's thinking.

Concentrative joint ventures will lead to the creation of the requisite autonomous economic entity. These joint ventures must operate on a market in the same general way as other undertakings on that market. This means that they must have sufficient financial and other resources to function as a business on a lasting basis.[27] Such joint ventures are known as 'full-function' joint ventures. These conditions will not be met where the joint venture only takes over a specific function of the parents' business activities without access to the market, as in the case of joint ventures relating to research and development.[28] The impact of the parent companies' support on the operational autonomy of the joint venture must be determined in the context of the relevant market. It must be decided whether the joint venture carries out functions normally performed by other undertakings on that market.[29]

A full-function joint venture may also have co-operative features, in the sense that the object or effect of the joint venture is the co-ordination of the competitive behaviour of independent undertakings. Co-operative features that threaten to restrict competition will be

---

[26] Commission Notice on the Concept of Full-Function Joint Ventures under Council Reg. 4064/89 on the Control of Concentrations between Undertakings [1998] OJ C66/1; DJN, n. 20 above, paras. 88–104.

[27] Full-Function Joint Ventures, n. 26 above, para. 12; DJN, n. 20 above, para. 90.

[28] Full-Function Joint Ventures, n. 26 above, para. 13; DJN, n. 20 above, para. 91.

[29] Case T–87/96 *Assicurazioni Generali SpA and Unicredito SpA v. Commission* [1999] ECR II–203, para. 73.

evaluated under Article 2(4). The Notice indicates when the Commission believes that the co-ordination of the competitive behaviour of the parent companies may appreciably limit competition.[30] This will not occur if the parent companies transfer their entire business activities to the joint venture. In the converse situation where the parent companies retain their activities in the relevant product and geographic market there is a high probability of such co-ordination.[31] Various intermediate positions are also possible, such as where the parent companies operate in a market upstream or downstream from that of the joint venture.[32]

It is not surprising that it can be difficult to distinguish those joint ventures which will be treated as concentrations for the purposes of Article 3(4).

Case IV/M72 **Re the Concentration between Sanofi and Sterling Drug Inc.**
[1992] 5 CMLR M1

Sanofi (S) and Sterling Drug (SD) are pharmaceutical companies which entered into a series of joint ventures in order to combine worldwide their prescription drug (ethical) activities, and also their European over-the-counter (OTC) activities. The Commission found that the joint ventures were concentrative for the following reasons, but cleared the merger because there was no dominance on the relevant markets.

THE COMMISSION

7. The proposed transaction is a concentration within the meaning of Article 3 of Regulation 4064/89. In arriving at this conclusion the Commission has taken into account the following elements:

— the parties merge, transfer or otherwise lease or license on a permanent basis to operating entities established by the parties their existing production, distribution and marketing assets. All material contracts, government permits and licences . . . will be licensed, transferred or assigned. Employees will be transferred to the operating entities.

— product ranges will be marketed under common trade names. . . .

— with regard to research and development, which is of crucial importance for the ethical business, the parties will continue to carry out their research activities . . . independently. However, they agree to enable each other to participate in the development of future products right from the initial stages of such development. . . .

To this effect a Development Committee is established, in which both parties are equally represented, which will monitor and coordinate all research efforts and which will decide whether or not development should be pursued jointly.

In the event that the committee decides against joint development the parties may not continue development individually, and instead may only assign or license such rights to third parties. With regard to the OTC business, the parties have the choice of carrying out research and development within the 'Alliance' or availing themselves of Sterling Drug's facilities outside the territory:

— new acquisitions will be carried out jointly by the parties,—the new management structure will be fully integrated. Each venture provides for a management entity,

---

[30] Full-Function Joint Ventures, n. 26 above, paras. 16–17.
[31] Case IV/M.088 *Elf Enterprise* [1991] OJ C203/14.
[32] Full-Function Joint Ventures, n. 26 above, para. 18.

which includes a strategic management committee responsible for all strategic management decisions. . . .

. . .

8. The Commission considers that these elements taken together bring about a lasting change in the structure of the undertakings concerned. The operation implies their effective withdrawal from the markets concerned, as they place all their interests in the various joint ventures.

(c) CONCENTRATIONS WITH A COMMUNITY DIMENSION

In order for a concentration to be caught by the Merger Regulation it must have a Community dimension. This is defined by Article 1(2) of Regulation 139/2004:

A concentration has a Community dimension where:

(a) the combined aggregate world-wide turnover of all the undertakings concerned is more than EUR 5000 million, and

(b) the aggregate Community-wide turnover of each of at least two of the undertakings concerned is more than EUR 250 million,

unless each of the undertakings concerned achieves more than two-thirds of its aggregate Community-wide turnover within one and the same Member State.

The reach of Community merger control is extended by Article 1(3). It was felt that concentrations which fell below the thresholds in Article 1(2) could nonetheless be examined under the merger laws of particular Member States, and that this could be costly as well as leading to conflicting assessments in the different legal systems.[33] By extending the reach of Community merger control to catch such concentrations which could have a significant impact in several Member States, it was hoped therefore to ensure that the competitive impact of such concentrations could be considered for the Community as a whole. Article 1(3) provides:

A concentration that does not meet the thresholds laid down in paragraph 2 has a Community dimension where:

(a) the combined aggregate world-wide turnover of all the undertakings is more than EUR 2500 million;

(b) in each of at least three Member States, the combined aggregate turnover of all the undertakings concerned is more than EUR 100 million;

(c) in each of at least three Member States included for the purposes of point (b), the aggregate turnover of each of at least two of the undertakings concerned is more than EUR 25 million; and

(d) the aggregate Community-wide turnover of each of at least two of the undertakings concerned is more than EUR 100 million;

---

[33] DJN, n. 20 above, para. 120.

unless each of the undertakings concerned achieves more than two-thirds of its aggregate Community-wide turnover within one and the same Member State.

The figures in Article 1(2) and (3) can be revised.[34] Turnover is calculated in accordance with Article 5.[35] The test in Article 1(2) and (3) is purely quantitative: it does not in itself indicate that a merger will be regarded as contrary to the Regulation. The substantive criterion is contained within Article 2, considered below. It should also be noted that these definitions can bring many non-EC undertakings within the ambit of the Regulation.[36]

(d) THE RELATION BETWEEN COMMUNITY AND NATIONAL MERGER CONTROL

(i) *The General Principle: 'One-Stop Shop'*

It is obviously undesirable for the same merger to be subject to investigation under differing regimes at Community and national level. It is therefore central to the Merger Regulation that mergers with a Community dimension should, in general, be investigated only by the Commission. Thus Article 21(1) provides that Regulation 139/2004 alone shall apply to concentrations as defined in Article 3;[37] Article 21(2) stipulates that the Commission has sole jurisdiction to take decisions provided for in this Regulation, subject to review by the Community Courts; and Article 21(3) states that, subject to exceptions considered below, no Member State may apply its national legislation to a merger that has a Community dimension.

There are, however, a number of exceptions to this general principle.[38] The Commission published a Notice in 2005 articulating the considerations that should be taken into account when deciding on the application of these exceptions to the one-stop shop principle.[39]

(ii) *Protection of National 'Legitimate' Interests: Article 21(4)*

Article 21(4) allows a Member State to take appropriate measures to protect legitimate interests other than those taken into consideration by the Regulation, provided that they are compatible with Community law. Public security, plurality of the media, and prudential rules are listed as legitimate interests for these purposes. Any other public interest must be notified to the Commission, which must inform the Member State of its decision within twenty-five working days.

(iii) *Referral to the Competent Authorities of the Member States by the Commission: Article 4(4)*

Article 4(4) of Regulation 139/2004 provides that *undertakings may, prior to notification of a concentration,* inform the Commission by reasoned submission that the concentration may

---

[34] Reg. 139/2004, n. 8 above, Art. 1(5).

[35] Commission Notice on Calculation of Turnover [1998] OJ C66/25; DJN, n. 20 above, paras. 150–173.

[36] See, e.g., Case IV/M24, *Mitsubishi Corporation/Union Carbide Corporation* [1992] 4 CMLR M50; Case IV/M69, *Kyowa Bank Limited/Saitama Bank Limited* [1992] 4 CMLR M105.

[37] Subject to exceptions for joint ventures that do not have a Community dimension and which have as their object or effect the co-ordination of competitive behaviour of undertakings that remain independent.

[38] T. Soames and S. Maudhuit, 'Changes in EU Merger Control: Part I' [2005] *ECLR* 57.

[39] Commission Notice on Case-Referral in Respect of Concentrations [2005] OJ C56/2.

significantly affect competition in a market within a Member State that has all the characteristics of a distinct market and should therefore be examined in whole or in part by that Member State.

The Commission transmits this submission to all Member States. The Member State referred to in the submission can then agree or disagree. Unless the Member State disagrees, the Commission can refer the case to that State for the application of its national competition law, where the Commission considers that such a distinct market exists and that competition in that market may be significantly affected by the concentration.

(iv) *Referral to the Competent Authorities of the Member States by the Commission: Article 9*

When the Regulation was being drafted there was concern that a merger might not be regarded as harmful from the Community perspective, but that it could still be detrimental at national level. Article 9(1) provides that the Commission can refer a *notified concentration* to the competent authorities of the Member States. Article 9(2) sets out the conditions.

> Within 15 working days of the date of receipt of the copy of the notification, a Member State, on its own initiative or upon the invitation of the Commission, may inform the Commission, which shall inform the undertakings concerned, that:
>
> (a) a concentration threatens to affect significantly competition in a market within that Member State, which presents all the characteristics of a distinct market, or
>
> (b) a concentration affects competition in a market within that Member State, which presents all the characteristics of a distinct market and which does not constitute a substantial part of the common market.

Article 9(3) states that it is for the Commission to decide whether such a distinct market exists, and also whether there is in reality the relevant threat to competition. The Commission can then either deal with the case itself, or refer the whole or part of the case to the relevant national authorities.[40] The Commission rejected a number of such applications from Member States,[41] but accepted a request from the United Kingdom,[42] and greater use has been made of Article 9 since 1996.[43]

(v) *Referral to Commission at Request of Undertakings: Article 4(5)*

Article 4(5) of the Regulation provides a mechanism for undertakings to suggest that a concentration should be considered by the Commission. It is open to such undertakings to suggest that the Commission should consider a concentration as defined in Article 3, which does not have a Community dimension as defined by Article 1, where the concentration is capable of being reviewed under the national competition laws of at least three Member States. This

---

[40] This is subject to the proviso that the Commission shall so refer the case where the concentration affects competition in a distinct market in a Member State that does not form a substantial part of the common market, if the Commission considers that such a distinct market is affected.

[41] See, e.g., Dec. 91/595, Case IV/M41, *Varta/Bosch* [1991] OJ L320/26; Dec. 93/247, Case IV/M222, *Mannesman/Hoesch* [1993] OJ L114/34.

[42] Case IV/M180, *Streetley plc/Tarmac* [1992] 4 CMLR 343. For examples where the Commission has referred concentrations under Art. 9 see, e.g., *Rheinmetall/British Aerospace/STN Atlas* [1997] 4 CMLR 987; *REW/Thyssengas/Bayernwerk/Isarwerke* [1997] 4 CMLR 23.

[43] Jones and Sufrin, n. 1 above, 886–889.

suggestion can be made by the undertakings before any notification to the competent national authorities. If one Member State disagrees within fifteen working days then the case shall not be referred to the Commission. If no such disagreement is forthcoming, then the concentration is deemed to have a Community dimension and is examined by the Commission; in such instances no Member State applies its national law to the concentration.

(vi) *Referral to Commission at Request of Member States: Article 22*

Article 22 provides that one or more Member States may request the Commission to investigate a concentration as defined in Article 3 that does not have a Community dimension within the meaning of Article 1, where it affects trade between Member States and threatens significantly to affect competition within the territory of the Member State or States making the request. The request may come from the competition authority of the Member State.[44] The Commission can then decide to take action, where it considers that these criteria are met.[45]

The object of this provision was to provide a mechanism for merger control where none existed at national level. It will be rarely used, given that most States now have their own systems of merger control. The Member State that makes a request cannot control or define the scope of the Commission's investigation,[46] and once such a request has been made the Member State can no longer apply its national legislation to the concentration.

(e) A RESIDUAL ROLE FOR ARTICLES 81 AND 82 EC

We have seen how the ECJ used Articles 81 and 82 to control mergers prior to the Merger Regulation. It is therefore necessary to consider the possible scope of application of these Articles now.[47]

As regards the Commission, Article 21(1) of Regulation 139/2004 provides that it alone shall apply to concentrations as defined by Article 3,[48] and that the main implementing regulations concerning Article 81 shall not be applicable. The Regulation cannot however disapply Articles 81 and 82, since these are Treaty provisions, and it may be that the Commission would have power to use these provisions via Articles 84 and 85 EC.[49]

As regards national courts, Articles 81 and 82 have direct effect. It might therefore be possible, for example, for an undertaking opposed to a hostile takeover to seek a preliminary reference under Article 234, claiming that it was in breach of Article 81 or 82, even if the takeover would not come within the Merger Regulation.[50]

5. REGULATION 139/2004: PROCEDURAL ISSUES

(a) PRIOR NOTIFICATION

In order for merger control to be effective it is necessary for the Commission to be informed about any such acquisition. This is covered by Article 4(1), which deals with pre-notification.

---

44 Case T–22/97 *Kesko Oy* v. *Commission* [1999] ECR II–3775.
45 Art. 22(3).
46 Case T–221/95 *Endemol Entertainment Holding BV* v. *Commission* [1999] ECR II–1299.
47 Jones and Sufrin, n. 1 above, 896–898.
48 Subject to the qualification in n. 37 above.
49 Jones and Sufrin, n. 1 above, 897–898.
50 *Ibid.*, 897.

It provides that concentrations with a Community dimension must be notified prior to their implementation, and following the conclusion of the agreement, the announcement of the public bid, or the acquisition of the controlling interest. Article 4(3) imposes an obligation on the Commission to publish those notifications that it considers to fall within the ambit of the Regulation. Failure to comply with the duty to pre-notify can lead to fines under Article 14(2)(a). There is a standard form, known as Form CO, which is used for the notification. This form requires the parties to submit certain information to the Commission, including copies of the documentation bringing about the concentration, copies of the accounts of the parties involved, and copies of any reports which have been prepared for the purposes of the concentration.[51]

(b) SUSPENSION PENDING INVESTIGATION

The effectiveness of merger control also demands that a proposed concentration shall not be completed pending investigation by the Commission. This is dealt with by Article 7(1). This provides for the suspension of a concentration before notification, or until it has been declared to be compatible with the Common Market pursuant to decision under Article 6(1)(b) or Article 8(2), or on the basis of the presumption in Article 10(6). Article 14(2) allows the Commission to impose heavy fines for breach of this obligation. The suspensive effect of notification is, however, qualified by Article 7(3), which allows the Commission to derogate from Article 7(1). The derogation may be made subject to conditions.[52]

(c) INVESTIGATION

There are two stages to the Commission's investigation of notified concentrations.[53] First, there is a preliminary investigation pursuant to Article 6(1) and the Commission can decide that: the concentration is outside the Regulation; it is within the scope of the Regulation, but is not incompatible with the common market; or it is within the scope of the Regulation, there are serious doubts about its compatibility with the common market, and therefore proceedings must be initiated.[54] These decisions must normally be made within twenty-five working days of the notification: Article 10(1). There is also provision for a simplified procedure in certain types of case.[55]

Secondly, the Commission investigates those concentrations where there are serious doubts about their compatibility with the Common Market. The Commission has a number of options, listed in Article 8. It can decide that the concentration or concentrative joint venture is not in fact in breach of the substantive criteria by which such matters are judged, subject to

---

[51] Commission Reg. (EC) 802/2004 of 7 Apr. 2004 implementing Council Reg. 139/2004 on the control of concentrations between undertakings [2004] OJ L133/1, Arts. 2–6, and Annex I.

[52] See, e.g., Case IV/M42, *Kelt/American Express* [1991] 4 CMLR 740.

[53] Merger investigations will be conducted by a unit within Directorate A of DG Competition, which is responsible for Policy and Strategic Support, in conjunction with merger units in Directorates B, C, D, and E, which deal with specific industrial sectors: see http://ec.europa.eu/comm/dgs/competition/index_en.htm; S. Maudhuit and T. Soames, 'Changes in EU Merger Control: Part 3' [2005] *ECLR* 144.

[54] Reg. 139/2004, n. 8 above, Art. 6(2) enables the Commission to decide that a proposed concentration that has been modified no longer raises serious doubts about its compatibility with the Common Market, and that it therefore can be declared to be compatible with the common market. Conditions can be attached and the decision can be revoked if the conditions are not complied with.

[55] Commission Notice on Simplified Procedure for Treatment of Certain Concentrations under Council Reg. 139/2004 [2005] OJ C56/32.

possible modifications.[56] It may determine that the concentration is incompatible with the common market, because it significantly impedes effective competition, in particular by creating or strengthening a dominant position, or because a concentrative joint venture would not benefit from Article 81(3) EC.[57] It may demand the reversal of a concentration in certain circumstances,[58] and has power to take interim measures to restore or maintain effective competition in certain instances.[59] The general time limit for such decisions is ninety working days from the initiation of the proceedings,[60] and if this is not complied with then the merger will be deemed to be compatible with the common market.[61] There are rights to be heard before decisions are made,[62] and the list of parties who can be involved in the proceedings is quite broad.[63] The Commission must consult the Advisory Committee on Concentrations, which consists of one or two representatives from Member States, before any decision is made under Articles 8(1)–(6), 14, and 15.[64]

(d) INVESTIGATION AND ENFORCEMENT

The Commission is given broad powers of investigation and enforcement. It can request information: Article 11; conduct on-site investigations: Article 13; and impose considerable fines: Article 14. A fine of up to 10 per cent of the aggregate turnover of the undertakings concerned may, for example, be imposed where the parties have proceeded with a concentration declared to be incompatible with the common market pursuant to a decision made under Article 8(3).[65]

6. REGULATION 139/2004: THE SUBSTANTIVE CRITERIA

(a) MARKET DEFINITION

Many of the issues encountered in the discussion of Article 82 will be relevant under the Merger Regulation. Thus, it will be necessary to define the relevant market in geographical and product terms, and also in many instances to determine whether there is a dominant position which has been created or strengthened by the concentration.[66] The Commission makes reference to some of the seminal decisions under Article 82 when adjudicating on the Merger Regulation, and the Commission Notice on the definition of the relevant market for the purposes of EC competition law, considered earlier,[67] applies to the Merger Regulation. There

---

[56] *Ibid.*, Art. 8(1)–(2). A decision finding that the concentration is compatible with the common market may also cover restrictions which are directly related and necessary to the implementation of the concentration: Art. 8(1).

[57] *Ibid.*, Art. 8(3).

[58] *Ibid.*, Art. 8(4).

[59] *Ibid.*, Art. 8(5).

[60] *Ibid.*, Art. 10(3). There are a number of exceptions to this basic rule.

[61] *Ibid.*, Art. 10(6), subject to Art. 9.

[62] Art. 18.

[63] Reg. 802/2004, n. 51 above, Art. 11; Case T–290/94 *Kayserberg SA* v. *Commission* [1997] ECR II–2137.

[64] Reg. 139/2004, n. 8 above, Art. 19(3)–(4).

[65] Art. 14(2)(c).

[66] Jones and Sufrin, n. 1 above , 916–931; I. Kokkoris, 'The Concept of Market Definition and the SSNIP Test in the Merger Appraisal' [2005] *ECLR* 209.

[67] See 1011–1012.

must be a causal link between the creation and strengthening of a dominant position and the impact on competition.[68]

(b) THE TEST

The test for determining whether a concentration is compatible with the Common Market is to be found in Article 2(1)–(3) of Regulation 139/2004, which should be read in conjunction with Article 2(4) set out earlier:

> 1. Concentrations within the scope of this Regulation shall be appraised in accordance with the objectives of this Regulation and the following provisions with a view to establishing whether or not they are compatible with the common market.
> In making this appraisal, the Commission shall take into account:
>
> (a) the need to maintain and develop effective competition within the common market in view of, among other things, the structure of all the markets concerned and the actual or potential competition from undertakings located either within or outwith the Community;
>
> (b) the market position of the undertakings concerned and their economic and financial power, the alternatives available to suppliers and users, their access to suppliers or markets, any legal or other barriers to entry, supply and demand trends for the relevant goods and services, the interests of the intermediate and ultimate consumers, and the development of technical and economic progress provided that it is to consumers' advantage and does not form an obstacle to competition.
>
> 2. A concentration which would not significantly impede effective competition in the common market or in a substantial part of it, in particular as a result of the creation or strengthening of a dominant position, shall be declared compatible with the Common Market.
>
> 3. A concentration which would significantly impede effective competition, in the common market or in a substantial part of it, in particular as the result of the creation or strengthening of a dominant position, shall be declared to be incompatible with the common market.

The current formulation in Article 2(2)–(3) differs from that in the earlier Merger Regulation. The original formulation was couched in terms of dominance. Article 2(3) of the 1989 Regulation provided that 'a concentration which creates or strengthens a dominant position as a result of which effective competition would be significantly impeded in the common market or in a substantial part of it shall be declared to be incompatible with the common market'.[69]

Prior to the adoption of the 2004 Regulation there was significant debate as to whether the dominance test contained in the 1989 Regulation should be replaced by a 'substantial lessening of competition test' (SLC), which has been adopted in some other jurisdictions.[70] The Commission argued that there was in reality little real difference between a dominance test and the SLC test,[71] and some academics questioned the desirability of the change.[72] A number

---

[68] Cases C–68/94 and 30/95 *France* v. *Commission* [1998] ECR I–1375, para. 110.

[69] Reg. 4064/89, n. 7 above.

[70] I. Kokkoris, 'The Reform of the European Merger Control Regulation in the Aftermath of the Airtours Case—The Eagerly Expected Debate: SLC v Dominance Test' [2005] *ECLR* 37.

[71] Green Paper on the Review of Council Reg. 4064/89, COM(2001)745/6 final, paras. 160–167.

[72] S. Voigt and A. Schmidt, 'Switching to Substantial Impediments to Competition can have Substantial Costs' [2004] *ECLR* 584.

of academics however advocated the SLC test,[73] as did some Member States,[74] one rationale being that concentrations in oligopolistic markets could harm competition, even where there was no dominance and no tacit co-ordination between the parties.

J. Vickers, Merger Policy in Europe: Retrospect and Prospect[75]

[M]ergers in oligopoly settings can reduce competition through non-co-ordinated effects as well as by co-ordinated effects. . . . If erstwhile competitors A and B merge, the market has lost the competition between A and B. If there was a shortage of surrounding competition, this effect could lessen competition substantially in the market as a whole. For example, with A and B no longer competing, C and D might slacken their competitive efforts in the marketplace.

Thus we had what came to be known as the problem of the gap—i.e. the gap between the policy aim of catching all anti-competitive mergers and the ability to catch them by the concept of dominance even as extended to embrace tacit co-ordination between two or more firms. There were three approaches to the problem of the gap:

- denial at least of its practical importance.
- verbal elasticity—give 'dominance' a sufficiently broad meaning in the context of mergers to cover non-coordinated effects as well as coordinated effects and single firm dominance, and
- change the test from dominance to a direct effect on competition formulation.

The outcome of the reform exercise was the change now embodied in Article 2 of Regulation 139/2004. It is broader than the previous formulation, since a concentration can be prohibited if it significantly impedes effective competition, even if it does not create or strengthen a dominant position. It can therefore catch concentrations that will result in non-co-ordinated effects on oligopolistic markets, even where the firms are not collectively dominant.[76] However Article 2 also states that the significant impediment to competition can arise in particular by creating or strengthening a dominant position, thereby preserving the relevance of the prior case law.[77]

The Commission distinguishes between non-co-ordinated and co-ordinated effects when applying the test in Regulation 139/2004.

Guidelines on the Assessment of Horizontal Mergers[78]

22. There are two main ways in which horizontal mergers may significantly impede effective competition, in particular by creating or strengthening a dominant position:

(a) by eliminating important competitive constraints on one or more firms, which consequently would have increased market power, without resorting to coordinated behaviour (non-coordinated effects);

---

[73] J. Vickers, 'Competition, Economics and Policy' [2003] *ECLR* 95; Z. Biro and M. Parker, 'A New EC Merger Test? Dominance v. Substantial Lessening of Competition' [2002] *Comp L J* 157.

[74] K. Fountoukakos and S. Ryan, 'A New Substantive Test for EU Merger Control' [2005] *ECLR* 277.

[75] [2004] *ECLR* 455, 459.

[76] Reg. 139/2004, n. 8 above, rec. 25.

[77] *Ibid.*, rec. 26; Guidelines on the Assessment of Horizontal Mergers under the Council Reg. on the Control of Undertakings [2004] OJ C31/5, para. 4.

[78] N. 77 above, para. 22.

(b) by changing the nature of competition in such a way that firms that previously were not coordinating their behaviour, are now significantly more likely to coordinate and raise prices or otherwise harm effective competition. A merger may also make coordination easier, more stable or more effective for firms which where were coordinating prior to the merger (coordinated effects).

. . .

(c) APPLICATION OF THE TEST: NON-CO-ORDINATED EFFECTS

Guidelines on the Assessment of Horizontal Mergers[79]

Non-coordinated effects

24. A merger may significantly impede effective competition in a market by removing important competitive constraints on one or more sellers, who consequently have increased market power. The most direct effect of the merger will be the loss of competition between the merging firms. . . .

25. Generally, a merger giving rise to such non-coordinated effects would significantly impede effective competition by creating or strengthening the dominant position of a single firm, one which, typically, would have an appreciably larger market share than the next competitor post-merger. Furthermore, mergers in oligopolistic markets involving the elimination of important competitive constraints that the merging parties previously exerted upon each other together with a reduction of competitive pressure on the remaining competitors may, even where there is little likelihood of coordination between the members of the oligopoly, also result in a significant impediment to competition. The Merger Regulation clarifies that all mergers giving rise to such non-coordinated effects shall also be declared incompatible with the common market.

The Commission then listed the relevant factors in deciding whether significant non-co-ordinated effects would result from a merger: the size of the market share held by the merging firms; whether they were close competitors; the ease with which customers could switch to other suppliers; the ability of the merged entity to hinder expansion by competitors; and whether the merger eliminates an important competitive force. The Commission then considered co-ordinated effects.[80]

The Commission's approach can be conveyed by reviewing some of its decisions. These remain relevant even though made under the previous Merger Regulation, since, as we have seen, dominance is still of importance under the current Merger Regulation. We can begin by considering an instance in which it cleared the merger.

---

[79] N. 77 above, paras. 24, 25, 39.
[80] *Ibid.*, paras. 27–38.

Case IV/M57 **Re the Concentration between Digital Equipment International and Mannesman Kienzle GmbH**
[1992] 4 CMLR M99

Digital Equipment International (DEIL), a wholly-owned subsidiary of Digital Equipment Corporation (DEC), made an agreement with Mannesman Kienzle (MK) to establish a limited partnership under German law, Digital/Kienzle, which was to be owned as to 65 per cent by DEIL and 35 per cent by MK. The new company was to acquire the computer business of MK, which was then to withdraw from the computer industry (except for printers). MK also agreed not to compete with Digital/Kienzle. DEC had less than 10 per cent of the market for personal computers, and this market was, as a whole, relatively fragmented with few firms possessing more than 10 per cent. The proposed concentration did not therefore raise serious doubts about its compatibility with the common market in this sphere. DEC was one of the world's largest suppliers of networked computer systems, but MK was very much smaller. The extract which follows concerns the market for workstations. The merger was cleared under Article 6(1)(b) of Regulation 4064/89.

THE COMMISSION

19. The workstation market is the smallest among the four markets mainly affected, but shows the highest annual growth rate (more than 30 per cent). It is also the most concentrated market with DEC, Hewlett Packard and Sun Microsystems holding an aggregate market share of about 80 per cent. DEC's market share has been in the last three years on average 22 per cent.

20. It is unlikely that the concentration will create or strengthen a dominant position because conditions of competition will not significantly change. The workstation market is a fairly new market which developed out of the PC and small computer market during the last 10 years. High market shares on a new developing market are not extraordinary, and they do not necessarily indicate market power. In fact the development of the market shares of the three leading companies over a period of time shows the dynamic nature of this market. There has been constant change including a change of market leadership.

21. DEC acquires with MK only a relatively small vendor and one which is rather insignificant for the maintenance of competition on this market. . . . Finally, barriers to entry are relatively low for other computer systems manufacturers, especially for those who sell PCs and small multi-user computers. Market entry seems to be feasible even for companies on adjacent markets. . . .

22. Thus, also with regard to the workstation market the concentration does not raise serious doubts as to its compatibility with the Common Market.

At the opposite end of the spectrum we can consider a concentration found to infringe Article 2(3) of the 1989 Merger Regulation.

Case IV/M53 **Re the Concentration between Aérospatiale SNI and Alenia-Aeritalia e Selenia SpA and de Havilland**
[1992] 4 CMLR M2

Aérospatiale and Alenia controlled the world's largest producer of turbo-prop regional aircraft, ATR, and sought to take over de Havilland, which was the world number two in this market.

The Commission found that the product market was regional turbo-prop aeroplanes with between twenty and seventy seats, with sub-markets for aircraft with twenty to thirty-nine seats, forty to fifty-nine seats, and sixty seats and over. The geographical market was the world, excluding China and Eastern Europe.

THE COMMISSION

A. Effect on ATR's Position

27. The proposed concentration would significantly strengthen ATR's position on the commuter markets, for the following reasons in particular:

— high combined market share on the 40 to 59-seat market, and of the overall commuter market
— elimination of de Havilland as a competitor
— coverage of the whole range of commuter aircraft
— considerable extension of customer base.

(a) Increase in Market Shares

. . .

29. ATR would increase its share of the overall worldwide commuter market of 20 to 70 seats from around 30 per cent. to around 50 per cent. The nearest competitor (Saab) would only have around 19 per cent. On the basis of this the new entity would have half the overall world market and more than two and half times the share of its nearest competitor.

30. The combined market share may further increase after the concentration. . . .

Following a concentration between ATR and de Havilland, the competitors would be faced with the combined strength of two large companies. This would mean that where an airline was considering placing a new order, the competitors would be in competition with the combined product range of ATR and de Havilland. . . .

(b) Elimination of de Havilland as a Competitor

31. In terms of aircraft sold, de Havilland is the most successful competitor of ATR. . . .

. . .

The parties argue that if the proposed concentration does not proceed, although de Havilland would not be immediately liquidated, its production might be phased out by Boeing so that de Havilland might in any case be eliminated as a competitor in the medium to long term. Without prejudice as to whether such a consideration is relevant pursuant to Article 2 of the Merger Regulation, the Commission considers that such elimination is not probable. . . .

. . .

(c) Coverage of the Whole Range of Commuter Aircraft

32. The new entity ATR/de Havilland would be the only commuter manufacturer present in all the various commuter markets as defined above.

. . .

(d) Broadening of Customer Base

33. ATR would significantly broaden its customer base after the concentration. On the basis of deliveries to date, the parties state that ATR has currently delivered commuters to 44 customers world-wide and de Havilland has delivered commuters to 36 other customers, giving a combination of 80 customers in all. . . .

The customer base is an important element of market power for aircraft manufacturers since there is at least to some extent a lock-in effect for customers once their initial choice of aircraft is made.

. . .

B. Assessment of the Strength of the Remaining Competition

34. In order to be able to assess whether the new combined entity would be able to act independently of its competitors, in view of its strengthened position, it is necessary to assess the current and expected future strength of the remaining competitors.

[*The Commission evaluated the strength of the other competitors and decided that it was questionable whether they could provide effective competition in the medium to long term.*]

. . .

D. Summary of Effect of the Proposed Concentration on the Commuter Markets

51. The combined entity ATR/de Havilland will obtain a very strong position in the world and Community commuter markets of 40 seats and over, and in the overall world and Community market, as a result of the proposed concentration. The competitors in these markets are relatively weak. The bargaining ability of the customers is limited. The combination of these factors leads to the conclusion that the new entity could act to a significant extent independently of its competitors and customers, and would thus have a dominant position on the commuter markets as defined.

. . .

E. Potential Entry into the Market

53. In general terms, a concentration which leads to the creation of a dominant position may however be compatible with the Common Market within the meaning of Article 2(2) of the Merger Regulation if there exists strong evidence that this position is only temporary and would be quickly eroded because of high probability of strong market entry.

[*The Commission concluded that there was no realistic potential competition in the commuter markets in the foreseeable future.*]

The Commission's decision to block this merger was not accepted unreservedly. The majority of the Advisory Committee on Concentrations agreed with the Commission. The minority disagreed, stating that the Commission 'is not so much protecting competition but rather the competitors to this proposed concentration'.[81] The decision was also criticized by Fox.

E. Fox, Merger Control in the EEC—Towards a European Merger Jurisprudence[82]

First, the Commission seemed to take an ungenerous view of economies likely to be achieved. While it counted economies of scale it seemed to disregard economies of scope; it disregarded the pro-consumer aspects of savings resulting from the merged firm's full line, of opportunities for package buying, and of buyers' opportunities to save costs by concentrating on one firm's technology ('lock-in' effect). The fact that they also yield foreclosing effects simply increases the problem's complexity but does not eliminate the economies' value.

Second, the Commission viewed low pricing, also, only in its anti-competitive light and not in its pro-competitive light. If the merged firm has the incentive to trigger price competition, consumers will, at least in the short run, get a better bargain. . . .

Third, the Commission quickly concluded that the remaining competition would shrink from confrontation. . . . Might the rivals, rather, have been so challenged as to seek new efficiencies and to respond more aggressively to buyers' needs . . .?

---

81 [1992] 4 CMLR M2, 35.
82 B. Hawk (ed.), *Fordham Corporate Law Institute* (Fordham University, 1991), 738–739.

Fourth, the Commission readily adopted a low pricing/monopolization scenario with no mention of a dominant firm/cooperative scenario. Would ATR really engage in all out warfare with the aim of devastating its rivals, or would it more likely engage in leadership conduct inviting cooperative behaviour, with a view towards enjoying less tumultuous life and confronting fewer risks? . . .

Fifth and finally, the commuter aircraft industry is heavily subsidized in Europe and Canada, and moreover, despite subsidies, De Havilland was in seriously weakened financial condition. The Commission did not grapple with the difficult issues raised by either situation.

The Commission later approved a joint venture between Aérospatiale, Alenia, and British Aerospace.[83]

The third example is of a case where the Commission cleared the merger, but only after imposing conditions.

Case IV/M190 **Re the Concentration between Nestlé SA and Source Perrier SA**
[1993] 4 CMLR M17

There were three major suppliers of bottled water in France: Nestlé, Perrier, and BSN. Nestlé sought to take over Perrier and also made an agreement with BSN under which it would sell the Volvic source of Perrier to BSN if it acquired control over Perrier. The Commission held that the merger between Nestlé and Perrier, and the subsequent sale of the Perrier source to BSN, would create a duopolistic dominant position between Nestlé and BSN, which would significantly impede competition in the French bottled water market. This was because they would have a combined market share of 82 per cent; there was no viable Community competitor; the proposed deal would eliminate a major competitor, Perrier, from the market; the market conditions favoured tacit co-ordination; there were high barriers to entry; and the duopolists had acted to deter the entry of a third party to the market. The Commission, nonetheless, cleared the merger on acceptance by Nestlé of the following conditions:[84]

THE COMMISSION

136. Nestlé has offered to modify the original concentration plan as notified by entering into the following commitments:

. . .

In order to meet the requirements of the Commission to facilitate the entry of a viable competitor with adequate resources in the bottled mineral water market or the increase in the capacity of an existing competitor so that in either case such competitor could effectively compete on the French bottled water market with Nestlé and BSN, Nestlé has undertaken that it will make available for sale both brand names and sufficient capacity of water for bottling to such competitor as will permit that competitor to have not less than 3,000 million litres of water capacity per annum.

. . .

---

[83] [1995] 4 CMLR 377.

[84] The extract contains the main condition imposed on Nestlé. There were a number of other related conditions, e.g., that Nestlé would keep the assets of Perrier distinct pending completion of the divestiture required by the Commission.

Nestlé acknowledges that the approval of the purchaser by the Commission is of the essence for the acceptance of its undertaking by the Commission. The establishment of an effective competitor vis-à-vis Nestlé and BSN depends on the strength of the purchaser to develop the sources and brands which will be sold to it. The purchaser must in particular have:

— sufficient financial resources to develop a nation-wide distribution organization and to adequately promote the acquired brands;

and

— sufficient expertise in the field of branded beverage or food products.

. . .

Nestlé is enjoined and restrained from re-acquiring, directly or indirectly, any of the sources or brands which it divests pursuant to this undertaking, for a period of 10 years from the date of this Decision, without the prior written approval of the Commission.

Given that the parties agreed to the conditions set by the Commission there was no reason to appeal the decision to the CFI or the ECJ.[85]

(d) APPLICATION OF THE TEST: CO-ORDINATED EFFECTS AND COLLECTIVE DOMINANCE

The Commission also envisages application of the Merger Regulation in circumstances where there are co-ordinated effects of the concentration.

Guidelines on the Assessment of Horizontal Mergers[86]

Coordinated effects

39. In some markets the structure may be such that firms would consider it possible, economically rational, and hence preferable, to adopt on a sustainable basis a course of action on the market aimed at selling at increased prices. A merger in a concentrated market may significantly impede effective competition, through the creation or the strengthening of a collective dominant position, because it increases the likelihood that firms are able to coordinate their behaviour in this way and raise prices, even without entering into an agreement or resorting to a concerted practice within the meaning of Article 81 of the Treaty. . . .

40. Coordination may take various forms. In some markets, the most likely coordination may involve keeping prices above the competitive level. In other markets, coordination may aim at limiting production or the amount of new capacity brought to the market. Firms may also coordinate by dividing the market, for instance by geographic area or other customer characteristics, or by allocating contracts in bidding markets.

The idea of co-ordinated effects, as exemplified by collective dominance, must be seen against the prior case law.

---

[85] The Commission's decision was challenged by representatives of employees' organizations, but the CFI did not consider the substance of the case: Case T–96/92 *Comité Central d'Entreprise de la Société Générale des Grands Sources* v. *Commission* [1995] ECR II–1213.

[86] N. 77 above, para. 39.

The Commission took the view that the 1989 Merger Regulation covered collective dominance where the concentration created or strengthened a dominant position between the parties to the concentration and another party on that market.[87] This was confirmed by the ECJ and CFI.[88]

Cases C–68/94 and 30/95 **France v. Commission**
[1998] ECR I–1375

K + S and MdK were proposing to enter into a concentration. Both firms operated in the potash and rock salt markets. The Commission was concerned that as a result of this concentration two entities would enjoy a dominant position: K + S/MdK and another firm, SCPA. The applicants argued that the Merger Regulation did not cover collective dominance. They claimed that the wording of the Merger Regulation did not, in contrast to Article 82, speak in terms of 'one or more undertakings', and that the legislative history of the 1989 Merger Regulation showed that it was not meant to cover such cases.

THE ECJ

166. [I]t cannot be deduced from the wording of Article 2 of the Regulation that only concentrations which create or strengthen an individual dominant position, that is a dominant position held by the parties to the concentration, come within the scope of the Regulation. Article 2 . . . does not in itself exclude the possibility of applying the Regulation to cases where the concentrations lead to the creation or strengthening of a collective dominant position, that is a dominant position held by the parties to the concentration together with an entity not a party thereto.

[*The ECJ found that the legislative history was not conclusive, and therefore that the scope of Article 2 should be considered by reference to its purpose and general structure. It considered the recitals to the Regulation and concluded that all concentrations with a Community dimension that could affect the structure of competition within the EC should be within the ambit of the 1989 Regulation.*]

171. A concentration which creates or strengthens a dominant position on the part of the parties concerned with an entity not involved in the concentration is liable to prove incompatible with the system of undistorted competition which the Treaty seeks to secure. Consequently, if it were accepted that only concentrations creating or strengthening a dominant position on the part of the parties to the concentration were covered by the Regulation, its purpose . . . would be partially frustrated. The Regulation would thus be deprived of a not insignificant aspect of its effectiveness, without that being necessary from the perspective of the general structure of the Community system of control of concentrations.

---

[87] Case IV/M190 *Nestlé SA/ Source Perrier SA* [1993] 4 CMLR M17, paras. 112–115.

[88] R. Whish and B. Sufrin, 'Oligopolistic Markets and EC Competition Law' (1992) 12 *YBEL* 59; A. Winckler and M. Hansen, 'Collective Dominance under the EC Merger Control Regulation' (1993) 30 *CMLRev.* 787; D. Ridyard, 'Economic Analysis of Single Firm and Oligopolistic Dominance' [1994] *ECLR* 255; C. Caffarra and K.-U. Kuhn, 'Joint Dominance: The CFI Judgment on Gencor/Lonhro' [1999] *ECLR* 355; R. Whish, 'Collective Dominance', in D. O'Keeffe and A. Bavasso (eds.), *Judicial Review in European Union Law* (Kluwer, 2000), ch. 37.

Case T–102/96 **Gencor Ltd. v. Commission**
[1999] ECR II–753

There was a proposed concentration between two firms in the platinum market. The Commission was concerned that this would lead to a collective dominant position as between them and another firm, the latter being the leading worldwide supplier of platinum and the principal competitor of the two firms that were proposing to concentrate. The CFI followed the ECJ's decision, set out above, and then gave guidance on the relevant factors in judging whether collective dominance existed.

THE CFI

163. In assessing whether there is a collective dominant position, the Commission is therefore obliged to establish, using a prospective analysis of the relevant market, whether the concentration in question would lead to a situation in which effective competition in the relevant market would be significantly impeded by the undertakings involved in the concentration and one or more undertakings which together, in particular because of factors giving rise to a connection between them, are able to adopt a common policy on the market and act to a considerable extent independently of their competitors, their customers and, ultimately, of consumers.

[*The CFI held that the existence of a very large market share could, save for exceptional circumstances be indicative of dominance: paragraph 205.*]

206. It is true that, in the context of an oligopoly, the fact that the parties hold large market shares does not necessarily have the same significance. . . . Nevertheless, particularly in the case of a duopoly, a large market share is, in the absence of evidence to the contrary, likewise a strong indication of the existence of a dominant position.

[*The applicants argued that the Commission had ignored the CFI's decision in* Italian Flat Glass.[89] *They claimed that in that case the CFI had required some structural links, through agreements, licences, and the like, as a pre-condition for a finding of collective dominance. The CFI in* Gencor *rejected this argument: paragraphs 273–275. It held that in* Italian Flat Glass *the structural links were regarded as but one way in which collective dominance could be shown.*]

276. Furthermore, there is no reason whatsoever in legal or economic terms to exclude from the notion of economic links the relationship of interdependence existing between the parties to a tight oligopoly within which, in a market with the appropriate characteristics, in particular in terms of market concentration, transparency, and product homogeneity, those parties are in a position to anticipate one another's behaviour and are therefore strongly encouraged to align their conduct in the market, in particular in such a way as to maximise their joint profits by restricting production with a view to increasing prices. In such a context, each trader is aware that highly competitive action on its part designed to increase its market share (for example a price cut) would provoke identical action by the others, so that it would derive no benefit from its initiative. . . .

277. That conclusion is all the more pertinent with regard to the control of concentrations, whose objective is to prevent anti-competitive market structures from arising or being strengthened. Those structures may result from the existence of economic links in the strict sense argued by the applicant or from market structures of an oligopolistic kind where each undertaking may become aware of common interests and, in particular, cause prices to increase without having to enter into an agreement or resort to a concerted practice.

---

[89] See 1017.

It is clear from *Gencor* that collective dominance within the Merger Regulation can catch oligopolistic collusion, and that the existence of structural links between the relevant firms is not a necessary condition for the concept to apply.

It is also clear from the subsequent *Airtours* case[90] that three conditions are necessary for a finding of collective dominance: there must be sufficient market transparency such that the members of the dominant oligopoly can monitor the behaviour of the other members; the tacit co-ordination must be sustainable over time, with sufficient incentive to comply with the common policy;[91] and the common policy must not be at risk from the foreseeable reaction of competitors and consumers.

The cumulative nature of these conditions, combined with a relatively high standard of proof, means that it may be more difficult for the Commission to rely on collective dominance in the future.[92] However in the *Impala* case, the CFI stated while the three conditions from *Airtours* must be satisfied, they could be 'established indirectly on the basis of what may be a very mixed series of indicia and items of evidence relating to the signs, manifestations and phenomena inherent in the presence of a collective dominant position'.[93]

In any event, Regulation 139/2004 reduces the need to prove collective dominance. It encapsulates, as we have seen, both non-co-ordinated and co-ordinated effects. The former can cover oligopolistic behaviour even where there is no co-ordination or dominance,[94] and thus the fact that it may be more difficult to prove collective dominance will be less important.[95]

(e) CONCENTRATION AND EFFICIENCIES

Prior to Regulation 139/2004 it was unclear whether efficiencies flowing from a concentration could be taken into account. Indeed some argued that the Commission was inclined to hold efficiency gains against the parties.[96] The argument for considering efficiency gains is that relatively modest cost savings can outweigh the impact of price increases when considering allocative efficiency.[97] The issue has now been clarified. Recital 29 of Regulation 139/2004 states:

> In order to determine the impact of a concentration on competition in the common market, it is appropriate to take account of any substantiated and likely efficiencies put forward by the undertakings concerned. It is possible that the efficiencies brought about by the concentration counteract the effects on competition, and in particular the potential harm to consumers, that it might otherwise have and that, as a consequence, the concentration would not significantly impede effective competition, in the common market or in a substantial part of it, in particular as a result of the creation or strengthening of a dominant position. The Commission should publish guidance on the conditions under which it may take efficiencies into account in the assessment of a concentration.

---

[90] Case T–342/99 *Airtours plc* v. *Commission* [2002] ECR II–2585, para. 62.

[91] The importance of this factor was emphasized by Caffarra and Kuhn, n. 88 above, 356–357

[92] The conditions from the *Airtours* case feature in the Horizontal Merger Guidelines, n. 77 above, paras. 41, 49–57.

[93] Case T–464/04 *Impala* v. *Commission* [2006] ECR II–2289, para. 251.

[94] Horizontal Merger Guidelines, n. 77 above, para. 25.

[95] S. Baxter and F. Dethmers, 'Collective Dominance under EC Merger Control—After Airtours and the Introduction of Unilateral Effects is there still a Future for Collective Dominance?' [2006] *ECLR* 148.

[96] F. Jenny, 'EEC Merger Control: Economies as an Antitrust Defense or an Antitrust Attack?', in B. Hawk (ed.), *Fordham Corporate Law Institute* (Fordham University, 1992), 603.

[97] O. Williamson, 'Economics as an Antitrust Defense: The Welfare Tradeoffs' (1968) 58 *Am. Econ. Rev.* 18.

The Commission has published this guidance in the Horizontal Merger Guidelines.[98] Three conditions must be satisfied.

First, the efficiencies must benefit consumers in a substantial and timely manner, and must be passed on to the consumer; the greater the potential anti-competitive effect of the concentration, the greater and more likely must be the efficiency savings. The second condition is merger specificity, which connotes the idea that the efficiencies could not be achieved by less anti-competitive alternatives. The third condition is verifiability: the Commission must be satisfied that the efficiencies are likely to materialize and that they should be sufficiently substantial to outweigh the concentration's potential harm to consumers.

The fact that efficiencies can be considered is to be welcomed. It should nonetheless be recognized that the hurdles to be surmounted in order to 'save' a notified concentration on efficiency grounds are significant.[99]

(f) CONCENTRATIONS AND FAILING FIRMS

The ECJ[100] and Commission[101] have acknowledged that an otherwise problematic merger might be compatible with the common market if one of the merging parties were a failing firm.[102] The central condition is that the deterioration of the competitive structure that follows the merger cannot be said to be caused by the merger, as will be the case where the competitive structure would deteriorate to at least the same extent in the absence of the merger.

Guidelines on the Assessment of Horizontal Mergers[103]

90. The Commission considers the following three criteria to be especially relevant for the application of the 'failing firm defence'. First, the allegedly failing firm would in the near future be forced out of the market because of financial difficulties if not taken over by another undertaking. Second, there is no less anti-competitive alternative than the notified merger. Third, in the absence of a merger, the assets of the failing firm would inevitably exit the market.

(g) THE RELEVANCE OF NON-COMPETITION CONSIDERATIONS

The discussion thus far has focused on the competition inquiry within the framework of Article 2. This leaves for consideration the extent to which industrial or social policy can be taken into account. Regulation 139/2004, recital 23, instructs the Commission to place its appraisal within the general framework of the achievement of the Treaty objectives set out in Article 2 EC and Article 2 TEU. This would arguably allow the Commission to take broader considerations into account.

---

[98] N. 77 above, paras. 76–88.
[99] L. Colley, 'From "Defence" to "Attack"? Quantifying Efficiency Arguments in Mergers' [2004] *ECLR* 342; M. Kocmut, 'Efficiency Considerations and Merger Control—Quo Vadis, Commission' [2006] *ECLR* 19.
[100] Cases C–68/94 and 30/95 *France* v. *Commission* [1998] ECR I–1375.
[101] Case IV/M.2314 *BASF/Pantochim/Eurodiol* IP/01/984; Case IV/M.2876 *Newscorp/Telepiu* IP/03/478.
[102] I. Kokkoris, 'Failing Firm Defence in the European Union: A Panacea for Mergers' [2006] *ECLR* 494.
[103] N. 77 above, para. 90.

The Commission has, nonetheless, taken the view that competition is to be the prime objective of the Regulation.[104] In so far as such issues are taken into account this may be in the College of Commissioners.[105]

(h) REMEDIES

Structural and behavioural remedies are available for breach of the Merger Regulation.[106] The principles that govern the Commission's choice of such remedies are set out in a Commission Notice, which is due to be revised.[107] It is also open to the parties to modify a concentration found to infringe the Merger Regulation and to offer commitments to the Commission.

7. JUDICIAL REVIEW

Commission decisions under the Merger Regulation are reviewable by the Community Courts, subject to the normal conditions, under Article 230.[108] Applicants have to show that there is a decision with legal consequences, and that they have been directly and individually concerned.[109]

The Community Courts have however increased their intensity of judicial review in this area and have imbued review for manifest error with far more vigour than hitherto.[110] This is apparent from decisions such as *Airtours*[111] and *Tetra Laval*.[112] Thus in the latter case the ECJ stated that:[113]

> Whilst the Court recognises that the Commission has a margin of discretion with regard to economic matters, that does not mean that the Community courts must refrain from reviewing the Commission's interpretation of information of an economic nature. Not only must the Community courts, *inter alia*, establish whether the evidence relied on is factually accurate, reliable and consistent but also whether that evidence contains all the information which must be taken into account in order to assess a complex situation and whether it is capable of substantiating the conclusions drawn from it. Such a review is all the more necessary in the case of a prospective analysis required when examining a planned merger with conglomerate effect.

---

[104] Jones and Sufrin, n. 1 above, 974–975.

[105] *Ibid.*, 975–976.

[106] D. Went, 'The Acceptability of Remedies under the EC Merger Regulation: Structural versus Behavioural' [2006] *ECLR* 455.

[107] Commission Notice on Remedies Acceptable under Council Reg. 4064/89 and under Commission Reg. 447/98 [2001] OJ C68/3.

[108] See Ch. 14.

[109] See, e.g., Case T–177/04 *Easy Jet Co. Ltd.* v. *Commission* [2006] ECR II–1931.

[110] Judge B. Vesterdorf, 'Certain Reflections on Recent Judgments Reviewing Commission Merger Control Decisions', in M. Hoskins and W. Robinson (eds.), *A True European, Essays for Judge David Edward* (Hart, 2003), ch. 10.

[111] Case T–342/99 *Airtours plc* v. *Commission* [2002] ECR II–2585.

[112] Case C–12/03 P *Commission* v. *Tetra Laval* [2005] ECR I–987.

[113] *Ibid.*, para. 39.

A similar intensity of review is apparent in more recent cases.[114] Space precludes detailed consideration of this topic, which can be found elsewhere.[115] Suffice it to say for the present that the CFI now engages in very detailed review of Commission decision-making, and that while this is formally undertaken as review for manifest error, it is clear that the meaning of this head of review has been transformed from that evident in prior case law.

8. CONCLUSION

i.   Merger policy necessarily entails choices. These choices relate to all the important aspects of merger control.

ii. In *jurisdictional terms*, Regulation 139/2004 contains more sophisticated provisions designed to ensure that a concentration is investigated by the most appropriate authority at Community or national level.

iii. In *procedural terms*, it reflects the need for prompt notification, coupled with adequate investigative powers, in order that the Community controls can be effective. This is balanced against the need for promptness in the application of the Community's powers, since important business decisions hang in the balance. The specific time limits under the Merger Regulation serve this imperative.

iv. In *substantive terms*, Regulation 139/2004 encapsulates important economic, social, and political choices, exemplified by the modified test for the application of the Regulation, by the explicit inclusion of an efficiency defence, and by the predominance accorded to competition considerations, to the exclusion, in general, of other social considerations.

v.   The Community Courts continue to play an important role in this area, in part through their teleological interpretation of the Merger Regulation, and in part through the increased intensity of judicial review that they apply under Article 230 EC.

9. FURTHER READING

(a) Books

Broberg, M., *The European Commission's Jurisdiction to Scutinise Mergers* (2nd edn., Kluwer, 2003)

Cook, J., and Kerse, C., *EC Merger Control* (4th edn., Sweet & Maxwell, 2005)

Jones, A., and Sufrin, B., *EC Competition Law: Text, Cases, and Materials* (2nd edn., Oxford University Press, 2004), ch. 12

Whish, R., *Competition Law* (5th edn., Lexis/Nexis, 2003), ch. 21

---

[114] Case T–464/04 *Impala*, n. 93 above; Case T–210/01 *General Electric Company* v. *Commission* [2005] ECR II–5575.

[115] P. Craig, *EU Administrative Law* (Oxford University Press, 2006), ch. 13; S. Volcker and C. O'Daly, 'The Court of First Instance's Impala Judgment: A Judicial Counter-Reformation in EU Merger Control' [2006] *ECLR* 589; J. Killick, 'The GE/Honeywell Judgment—In Reality another Merger Defeat for the Commission' [2007] *ECLR* 52.

(b) Articles

Abbamonte, G., and Rabassa, V., 'Foreclosure and Vertical Mergers' [2001] *ECLR* 214

Bailey, D., 'Standard of Proof in EC Merger Proceedings: A Common Law Perspective' (2003) 40 *CMLRev.* 845

Bishop, B., and Caffara, C., 'Merger Control in "New Markets" ' [2001] *ECLR* 31

Bishop, S., Lofaro, A., and Rosati, F., 'Turning the Tables: Why Vertical and Conglomerate Mergers are Different' [2006] *ECLR* 403

Caffarra, C., and Kuhn, K.-U., 'Joint Dominance: The CFI Judgment on Gencor/Lonhro' [1999] *ECLR* 355

Colley, L., 'From "Defence" to "Attack"? Quantifying Efficiency Arguments in Mergers' [2004] *ECLR* 342

Killick, J., 'The GE/Honeywell Judgment—In Reality another Merger Defeat for the Commission' [2007] *ECLR* 52

Kocmut, M., 'Efficiency Considerations and Merger Control—Quo Vadis, Commission' [2006] *ECLR* 19

Kokkoris, I., 'The Reform of the European Merger Control Regulation in the Aftermath of the Airtours Case—The Eagerly Expected Debate: SLC v Dominance Test' [2005] *ECLR* 37

Motta, M., 'EC Merger Policy and the Airtours Case' [2000] *ECLR* 199

Ridyard, D., 'Economic Analysis of Single Firm and Oligopolistic Dominance' [1994] *ECLR* 255

Vesterdorf, Judge B., 'Certain Reflections on Recent Judgments Reviewing Commission Merger Control Decisions', in M. Hoskins and W. Robinson (eds.), *A True European, Essays for Judge David Edward* (Hart, 2003), ch. 10

Vickers, J., 'Competition, Economics and Policy' [2003] *ECLR* 95

—— 'Merger Policy in Europe: Retrospect and Prospect' [2004] *ECLR* 455

Whish, R., 'Collective Dominance', in D. O'Keeffe and A. Bavasso (eds.), *Judicial Review in European Union Law* (Kluwer, 2000), ch. 37

28

THE STATE AND THE
COMMON MARKET

1. CENTRAL ISSUES

i. This chapter is concerned with the way in which the actions of the State itself can infringe the Treaty. The Treaty contains a number of relevant provisions, including Articles 10, 16, 28, 81, 82, 86, and 87–89.

ii. There are valid reasons in principle for controlling state action. Thus, for example, Article 86 is designed to prevent a State from enacting or maintaining in force measures relating to public undertakings, etc., which derogate from other obligations under the Treaty. Some such provision is clearly required in order to prevent a State from evading the proscriptions of the Treaty in so far as these relate to such undertakings. It is equally apparent that the Community must, for example, have some rules concerning the provision of state aids. The control of such aid forms an aspect of the Community's single-market policy: if a State were able to give preferential treatment to its own firms then the very idea of a level playing field would be undermined.[1]

iii. While there are valid reasons for Community controls, the topics discussed within this chapter raise important issues concerning the very nature of the Community. Thus it will be seen that the case law under Article 86 has prompted questions about the extent to which it is possible for a State to entrust certain activities to a public monopoly, or to a private firm which has exclusive rights. The case law concerning state aids, Articles 87–89, raises a plethora of broader issues concerning the way in which Community policy is developed in a particular area, and the appropriate balance between market integration and the attainment of other goals, such as regional policy and Community cohesion.

---

[1] C.-D. Ehlermann, 'The Contribution of EC Competition Policy to the Single Market' (1992) 29 *CMLRev.* 257, 259.

2. THE STATE AND THE MARKET: GENERAL PRINCIPLES

(a) THE GENERAL PRINCIPLE: THE COMPETITION ETHOS

In mixed economic systems it is common for the State to play some role in the market-place. The rationale for this intervention and its legal form may well vary. It has, for example, been common in the past for utilities either to be nationalized, or to have some privileged monopoly or quasi-monopoly status. Recent thinking has tended to favour a more confined role for the State, as manifested in the privatization of nationalized industries and in the deregulation of sectors of the economy. Notwithstanding these changes, there continue to be undertakings which either remain within public ownership or possess a certain privileged status in the market-place.

The basic starting position is Article 295, which states that the Treaty shall in no way prejudice the rules in Member States governing the system of property ownership. The mere fact that certain activities are undertaken in the public or the private sphere is not, therefore, in itself contrary to the Treaty. Article 295 is, however, subject to judicial interpretation, and has been narrowly interpreted so as, for example, not to prevent limitations being placed on intellectual property rights under Community law.[2] Moreover, Article 157 provides that the Community and the Member States shall ensure that the conditions necessary for the competitiveness of the Community's industry exist. The Article is explicitly framed in terms of open and competitive markets. Action to attain this end includes the encouragement of initiative and the development of undertakings throughout the Community, particularly small and medium-sized undertakings.

Thus, while Article 295 can be seen as providing support for Community agnosticism as to the regime of ownership within any particular State, the thrust of much else in the Treaty is against the type of dominance that can accompany public ownership. It is also against the grant of any special, beneficial position to firms, which may have the consequence of distorting competition within the common market.

(b) THE QUALIFICATION: SERVICES OF GENERAL (ECONOMIC) INTEREST

While the general ethos that pervades the Treaty is the free interplay of market forces, this is qualified in certain respects at least by Article 16,[3] which was introduced by the ToA:[4]

> Without prejudice to Articles 73, 86 and 87, and given the place occupied by services of general economic interest in the shared values of the Union as well as their role in promoting social and territorial cohesion, the Community and the Member States, each within their respective powers and within the scope of application of this Treaty, shall take care that such services operate on the basis of principles and conditions which enable them to fulfil their missions.

---

[2] Case 16/74 *Centrafarm BV* v. *Winthrop BV* [1974] ECR 1183.

[3] M. Ross, 'Article 16 EC and Services of General Interest: From Derogation to Obligation?' (2000) 25 *ELRev.* 22.

[4] Art. III–122 CT would have modified Art 16 EC by, *inter alia*, giving the Community power to make laws to define the principles on which services of general interest operate.

Moreover, Article 36 of the Charter of Fundamental Rights[5] provides that the Union recognizes and respects access to services of general economic interest as provided for in national laws and practices, in accordance with the EC Treaty, in order to promote social and territorial cohesion of the EU.

The Commission has addressed the concept of services of general interest on a number of occasions,[6] most recently in its White Paper on services of general interest.[7] This term is not found in the Treaty, the closest formulation being that in Articles 16 and 86(2), which speak in terms of services of general *economic* interest. The concept of services of the general interest was, said the Commission, broader and covered 'both market and non-market services which the public authorities class as being of general interest and subject to specific public service obligations'.[8] Such services were regarded as 'one of the pillars of the European model of society',[9] reflecting Community values and goals based on 'a common set of elements, including: universal service, continuity, quality of service, affordability, as well as user and consumer protection'.[10] For citizens access to such services was perceived as 'an essential component of European citizenship and necessary in order to allow them to fully enjoy their fundamental rights'.[11]

The normal market principles are modified in relation to services of general interest, in the sense that the obligations relating to universal service, continuity, and the like are imposed on those providing the service. This has affected the content of Community legislation and the interpretation accorded to Treaty articles.

In relation to Community legislation, the directives designed to liberalize markets in energy, telecommunications, and the like are not only concerned with the introduction of competition. They also enable or require Member States to impose public-service obligations relating to the security, regularity, quality, and price of supply on suppliers.[12]

In relation to the interpretation accorded to Treaty articles, we shall see below that the undertakings most likely to gain exemption under Article 86(2) are those that have public-service obligations,[13] and that aid granted to offset the cost of public-service obligations on an undertaking will, subject to certain conditions, prevent it from being characterized as state aid under Article 87.[14]

Views on the overall impact of the preceding developments differ. Baquero Cruz argues that some of the legislation on utilities still evinces the relative priority given to competition over services of general interest.[15] Prosser strikes a more positive note when reflecting on developments relating to such services.

---

5 [2000] OJ C364/1.

6 Commission Communication on Services of General Interest in Europe, COM(2000)580 final; Report to the Laeken European Council, Services of General Interest, COM(2001)598 final; Green Paper on Services of General Interest, COM(2003)270.

7 Communication from Commission, White Paper on Services of General Interest, COM(2004)374 final.

8 *Ibid.*, Annex 1.

9 *Ibid.*, para. 2.1.

10 *Ibid.*, para. 2.1.

11 *Ibid.*, para. 2.1.

12 See, e.g., Dir. 2002/22 of the European Parliament and the Council of 7 Mar. 2002 on universal service and users' right relating to electronic communications networks and services (Universal Service Dir.) [2002] OJ L108/51.

13 See 1077–1081.

14 See 1089–1090.

15 J. Baquero Cruz, 'Beyond Competition: Services of General Interest and European Community Law', in G. de Búrca (ed.), *EU Law and the Welfare State: In Search of Solidarity* (Oxford University Press, 2005), 207.

T. Prosser, The Limits of Competition Law, Markets and Public Services[16]

Initially they were seen as something of an irritant, limiting the creation of a full internal market. Now a much more positive view is taken, despite only cautious substantive proposals in the 2004 White Paper. Such services are confirmed an essential element of European citizenship and, rather than the main question being that of how their operation can be restricted and remodelled to become compatible with the single market, it is of how their operation can be improved and made both more efficient and more responsive to social values such as those underlying public service.

3. PUBLIC UNDERTAKINGS AND ARTICLE 86

The interplay between competition and the needs of undertakings that operate services of general economic interest is readily apparent from Article 86, which provides as follows:

1. In the case of public undertakings and undertakings to which Member States grant special or exclusive rights, Member States shall neither enact nor maintain in force any measure contrary to the rules contained in this Treaty, in particular to those rules provided for in Article 12 and Articles 81 to 89.
2. Undertakings entrusted with the operation of services of general economic interest or having the character of a revenue-producing monopoly shall be subject to the rules contained in this Treaty, in particular to the rules on competition, in so far as the application of such rules does not obstruct the performance, in law or in fact, of the particular task assigned to them. The development of trade must not be affected to such an extent as would be contrary to the interests of the Community.
3. The Commission shall ensure the application of the provisions of this Article and shall, where necessary, address appropriate directives or decisions to Member States.

(a) ARTICLE 86(1)

(i) *Public Undertaking and Undertakings accorded Special or Exclusive Rights*

Article 86(1) covers two types of undertaking: public undertakings and those to which Member States have granted special or exclusive rights. These will be examined in turn.

The scope of the term public undertaking was addressed by the ECJ in the *Transparency Directive* case.

Cases 188–190/80 **France, Italy, and the United Kingdom v. Commission**
[1982] ECR 2545

[Note ToA renumbering: Art. 90 is now Art. 86]

The Commission, acting pursuant to Article 90(3), enacted Directive 80/723 on the transparency of financial relations between Member States and public undertakings. The object

---

[16] (Oxford University Press, 2005), 172.

was to make available information on public funds given to public undertakings, and the use to which it had been put. This was necessary to ensure the proper operation of the rules on state aid. Three Member States sought to have the Directive annulled. The ECJ considered the definition of public undertaking contained in the Directive. It acknowledged that the Commission did not set out in the Directive to define 'public undertakings' for the purpose of Article 90, but it nonetheless approved of the definition.

THE ECJ

25. According to Article 2 of the Directive, the expression 'public undertakings' means any undertaking over which the public authorities may exercise directly or indirectly a dominant influence. According to the second paragraph, such influence is to be presumed when the public authorities directly or indirectly hold the major part of the undertaking's subscribed capital, control the majority of the votes, or can appoint more than half of the members of its administrative, managerial or supervisory body.

26. As the Court has already stated, the reason for the inclusion in the Treaty of the provisions of Article 90 is precisely the influence which the public authorities are able to exert over the commercial decisions of public undertakings. That influence may be exerted on the basis of financial participation or of rules governing the management of the undertaking. By choosing the same criteria to determine the financial relations on which it must be able to obtain information in order to perform its duty of surveillance under Article 90(3), the Commission has remained within the limits of the discretion conferred upon it by that provision.

The definition of the term 'public undertaking' in the Transparency Directive is not conclusive, but it was approved by the ECJ. The existence of state influence in one of the above ways will therefore be a sufficient reason for an undertaking to be characterized as public. Thus in *Sacchi*[17] the Italian Broadcasting Authority, RAI, was under the control of a state holding company, IRI; the State was represented in its organs and could intervene in its operations.

Even if an undertaking is not public in the above sense, it will fall within Article 86(1) if a Member State has granted it special or exclusive rights. The rationale is that where the State has relieved an undertaking wholly or partially from the discipline of competition, it must bear responsibility for the consequences. An example would be a nationalized industry that had been privatized, but which continued to have a protected monopoly in the relevant area, or which was accorded certain advantages resulting from the terms on which it had been established.

It is possible for undertakings to be caught by both limbs of Article 86(1). Thus, in *Sacchi*[18] the RAI, as well as being controlled by the State, also possessed a statutory monopoly in relation to broadcasting. In *Muller*[19] the State had power to nominate half of the members of the management and supervisory board of a company that controlled port facilities in Luxembourg. The company itself had certain privileges, including that of being consulted before the development of any other port facilities within a particular area was undertaken.

(ii) *The Obligation Flowing from Article 86(1)*

Article 86(1) requires that a Member State shall neither enact nor maintain in force any measure that is contrary to the Treaty. It constitutes both a standstill obligation, a duty not

---

[17] Case 155/73 [1974] ECR 409.
[18] *Ibid.*
[19] Case 10/71 *Ministère Public of Luxembourg* v. *Muller* [1971] ECR 723.

to enact any such measure, and a positive obligation to remove such a measure that currently exists.

A breach of Article 86(1) presupposes that some other Article of the Treaty has been broken, as exemplified by the specific reference to Articles 12 and 81–89. It would however clearly be possible for a Member State to maintain in force a measure which constituted a breach of some other Treaty Article, such as Article 28. The way in which Article 86(1) operates can be seen from the *Bodson* case.

Case 30/87 **Bodson v. Pompes Funèbres des Régions Libérées SA**
[1988] ECR 2479

[Note ToA renumbering: Arts. 86 and 90 are now Arts. 82 and 86]

French legislation entrusted the provision of external services for funerals (the carriage of the body after it had been placed in the coffin, the provision of hearses, etc.), to local communes. The communes then granted concessions to private undertakings and Pompes Funèbres (PF) held many such concessions. Bodson offered external funeral services at a price significantly lower than that set by PF. PF sought an injunction in the French courts, claiming that Bodson was acting in breach of its exclusive rights resulting from the concession. Bodson argued that PF had abused its dominant position in breach of Article 86 by charging excessive prices. One of the issues before the Court concerned the responsibility of the commune itself under Article 90.

THE ECJ

33. In so far as the communes imposed a given level of prices on the concession holders, in the sense that they refrained from granting concessions for the 'external services' to undertakings if the latter did not agree to charge particularly high prices, the communes are covered by the situation referred to in Article 90(1) of the Treaty. That provision governs the obligations of the Member States—which includes, in this context, the public authorities at the regional, provincial or communal level—towards undertakings 'to which [they] grant special or exclusive rights'. That situation covers precisely the grant of an exclusive concession for the 'external services' for funerals.

34. It follows from that finding that public authorities may not, in circumstances such as those in this case, either enact or maintain in force any 'measure' contrary to the rules of the Treaty.... They may not therefore assist undertakings holding concessions to charge unfair prices by imposing such prices as a condition for concluding a contract for a concession.

(iii) *The ECJ's Expansive Case Law*

We noted above that the Treaty, in formal terms, is agnostic as to whether economic activity is undertaken by the State, or those to whom it has granted special or exclusive rights, as opposed to allowing the free interplay of market forces. A State can therefore choose to grant exclusive rights to a particular undertaking and the normal Treaty rules will apply. Provided that the State itself does not infringe Article 86, and provided that the undertaking does not exercise its exclusive rights so as to constitute an abuse of a dominant position under Article 82, then all will be well. The exclusivity will not, in and of itself, infringe Article 82. On this view Article 86 simply preserves parity, by ensuring that public undertakings or those to whom exclusive rights are granted do not thereby infringe any Treaty provision.

We have, however, also seen that the thrust of the Treaty is more generally in favour of eradicating any impediment to the free movement of goods, and of ensuring that normal competitive principles apply. The result of this competitive contest may lead to a firm that is dominant because of its economic prowess. This is one of the reasons that the Treaty does not proscribe monopoly *per se*. The Treaty is, nonetheless, against artificial barriers to competition. This can produce tensions in relation to public undertakings, or those to whom the State has granted special or exclusive rights, because their privileged position is not the result of economic prowess, but of state grant.

The formal way in which the ECJ resolves these tensions is to recognize that the grant of exclusive rights will not *per se* infringe, for example, Article 82, but that the exercise of such rights may do so if it can be said to be abusive. This is fine in principle, but much depends on the more precise meaning given to the idea of abuse. We have already seen the elasticity of this concept in the discussion of Article 82.[20] The point can be put quite simply: the closer the Court comes to regarding the grant of exclusive rights as abusive in and of itself, the more difficult does it become for a State to choose to organize its economic activities in this manner.

Thus in *Höfner*[21] the ECJ considered the legality of German rules which required certain categories of those looking for work to be placed in contact with potential employers through a state-licensed agency, and the agency was given exclusive powers in the relevant area. The effect of this monopoly was to suppress the activities of independent employment consultants, and contracts they made would be void. The ECJ decided that any state rule that compelled an undertaking to breach Article 86 would be illegal under what is now Article 86(1). It held that the grant of exclusive rights was not *per se* incompatible with Article 86,[22] but that a State would violate Article 86(1) if it placed an undertaking in such a dominant position that the very exercise of these exclusive rights could not avoid being abusive. The ECJ concluded that the Member State had created such a situation, because the state-licensed agency was not in a position to satisfy market demand. Moreover, the exclusivity could affect the nationals of other Member States.[23]

The willingness of the ECJ to characterize a grant of exclusive rights as abusive within Article 86 is also apparent in the following case.

Case C–179/90 **Merci Convenzionali Porto di Genova SpA v. Siderurgica Gabrielli SpA**
[1991] ECR I–5889

[Note ToA renumbering: Arts. 30, 85, 86, and 90 are now Arts. 28, 81, 82, and 86]

Merci enjoyed the exclusive right to organize dock work in the Port of Genoa. It would call upon a dock-work company to unload ships. Siderurgica (S) applied to Merci to have a consignment

---

[20] See Ch. 26.

[21] Case C–41/90 *Höfner and Elser v. Macrotron GmbH* [1991] ECR I–1979.

[22] *Ibid.*, para. 29.

[23] *Ibid.*, para. 34; Case C–55/96 *Job Centre coop. arl.* [1997] ECR I–7119; Case C–258/98 *Criminal Proceedings against Carra* [2000] ECR I–4217; Case C–260/89 *Elliniki Radiophonia Tileorassi AE (ERT) v. Dimotiki Etairia Pliroforissis (DEP) and Sotirios Kouvelas* [1991] ECR I–2925.

of steel unloaded, even though the ship's own crew could have performed the task. Merci called upon the relevant Genoa dock-work company to do the job. Delays arose as a result of strikes. S therefore demanded reimbursement from Merci, claiming that the charges were unfair for the services performed. The ECJ reaffirmed that an undertaking having a statutory monopoly over a substantial part of the common market would be regarded as having a dominant position for the purposes of Article 86. It then continued as follows.

THE ECJ

16. It should next be stated that the simple fact of creating a dominant position by granting exclusive rights within the meaning of Article 90(1) EEC is not as such incompatible with Article 86.

17. However, the Court has had occasion to state, in this respect, that a Member State is in breach of the prohibition contained in these two provisions if the undertaking in question, merely by exercising the exclusive rights granted to it, cannot avoid abusing its dominant position (see Case C–41/90, *Höfner* . . .) or when such rights are liable to create a situation in which that undertaking is induced to commit such abuses (see Case C–260/89, *ERT* . . .).

18. According to Article 86(2)(a), (b) and (c) EEC, such abuse may in particular consist in imposing on the persons requiring the services in question unfair purchase prices or other unfair trading conditions, in limiting technical development, to the prejudice of consumers, or in the application of dissimilar conditions to equivalent transactions with other trading parties.

19. In that respect it appears from the circumstances described by the national court . . . that the undertakings enjoying exclusive rights in accordance with the procedures laid down by the national rules in question are, as a result, induced either to demand payment for services which have not been requested, to charge disproportionate prices, to refuse to have recourse to modern technology, which involves an increase in the cost of the operations and a prolongation of the time required for their performance, or to grant price reductions to certain consumers and at the same time to offset such reductions by an increase in the charges to other consumers.

20. In these circumstances it must be held that a Member State creates a situation contrary to Article 86 EEC where it adopts rules of such a kind as those at issue before the national court, which are capable of affecting trade between Member States as in the case of the main proceedings, regard being had . . . to the importance of traffic in the Port of Genoa.

21. As regards the interpretation of Article 30 requested by the national court, it is sufficient to recall that a national measure which has the effect of facilitating the abuse of a dominant position capable of affecting trade between Member States will generally be incompatible with that Article, which prohibits quantitative restrictions on imports and all measures having equivalent effect (see Case 13/77, *GB-INNO-BM* v *ATAB*) in so far as such a measure has the effect of making more difficult and hence of impeding imports of goods from other Member States.

22. In the main proceedings it may be seen from the national court's findings that the unloading of the goods could have been effected at a lesser cost by the ship's crew, so that compulsory recourse to the services of the two undertakings enjoying exclusive rights involved extra expense and was therefore capable, by reason of its effect on the prices of the goods, of affecting imports.

The ECJ's reasoning is instructive.[24] In paragraph 16 the Court reiterated the proposition that the creation of exclusive rights was not itself abusive within what is now Article 86. This was then qualified in paragraph 17. Exclusivity could entail a breach of what are now Articles

---

[24] See also Case C–320/91 P *Procureur du Roi* v. *Paul Corbeau* [1993] ECR I–2533; Case C–18/93 *Corsica Ferries Italia Srl* v. *Corpo dei Piloti di Genova* [1994] ECR I–1783; Case C–323/93 *Société Civile Agricole du Centre*

86 and 82 either when the exercise of the exclusive rights could not avoid being abusive, or where such rights were liable to create a situation in which the undertaking was induced to commit an abuse. It then applied the latter formulation to the instant case: paragraph 19.

This comes perilously close to regarding the grant of exclusivity as abusive *per se*, albeit through the back door. The reason is to be found in the notion that an undertaking may be induced to commit an abuse in one of the ways identified in paragraph 19. It is, of course, true that an undertaking can be in breach of Article 82 through charging excessive prices, discriminatory prices, and the like. Any firm with the market power attendant upon a dominant position has the potential to do this. Whether it actually chooses to behave in this manner is another matter. The message from the Court is, however, that the very grant of the exclusive rights can create a situation in which the undertaking is induced to commit such abuses.

The meaning of the word 'induce' here is, however, crucial. The ECJ's reasoning comes close to stating that, because the holder of the exclusive right possessed market power which enabled it to price in an abusive manner, therefore it was induced to do so. On this hypothesis it could always be said that the grantee of exclusivity would be induced to price abusively, with the consequence that exclusive rights would, in effect, be rendered illegal *per se*. It might be countered that this is to misread the Court's reasoning, and that it ignores the fact, mentioned at the beginning of paragraph 19, that the holder of the exclusive right had in fact priced in an abusive manner. Yet if this was indeed so then Merci should have been condemned on this basis alone, since nothing was gained by the language of inducement.

The fact that the Court used the language of inducement was not, however, fortuitous. It did so because it wished to make a point about the consequence of forms of economic organization adopted by the State. What is distinctive about the grant of a statutory monopoly is that the grantee obtains a protected sphere of activity, which is immune from the normal rigours of competition. This is by way of contrast to other firms with a dominant position. They must always be looking over their shoulders lest new entrants erode their market power. This is one of the reasons why such a firm may decide not to price too high, since it will act as an incentive for others to enter the market.

The holder of the statutory exclusive right does not have the same rationale for self-restraint, or at least not to the same extent. It is for this reason that such firms may well be induced to charge disproportionate prices, secure in the knowledge that this cannot operate as a carrot to bring others into the market. It is for this reason that the ECJ was particularly concerned about monopoly power in this form. This is readily understandable when looked at from the Community's point of view, but does not alter the fact that the Court's reasoning comes close to regarding the grant of exclusive statutory rights as abusive *per se*.

(iv) The *ECJ's Current Approach*

The general thrust of the ECJ's current approach builds on its jurisprudence in the previous section: the grant of exclusive rights will normally be held *prima facie* to infringe Article 86(1), but the ECJ will then consider whether there is some objective justification for the exclusivity.[25]

---

d'Insémination de la Crespelle v. *Coopérative d'Elevage et d'Insémination Artificielle du Départment de la Mayenne* [1994] ECR I–5077; Case C–242/95 *GT-Link A/S* v. *De Danske Statsbaner (DSB)* [1997] ECR I–4449; Case C–451/03 *Servizi Ausiliari Dottori Commercialisti Srl* v. *Calafiori* [2006] ECR I–2941, para. 23.

25 L. Hancher, Note (1994) 31 *CMLRev.* 105; L. Hancher, 'Community, State and Market', in P. Craig and G. de Búrca (eds.), *The Evolution of EU Law* (Oxford University Press, 1999), ch. 20; D. Edward and M. Hoskins, 'Article 90: Deregulation and EC Law, Reflections Arising from the XVI FIDE Conference' (1995) 32 *CMLRev.* 157; Ehlermann, n. 1 above, 273.

Thus in *Traco*[26] it was held that the grant to Poste Italiana of exclusive rights to carry the post violated Article 86(1). Poste Italiana charged any other postal operator charges equivalent to those paid by customers of Poste Italiana, even though it did not carry the mail. It could not therefore avoid abusing its dominant position, was caught by Article 86(1), and had to seek justification under Article 86(2). In *Ambulanz Glockner*[27] a public body refused to renew the applicant's authorization to provide non-emergency transport services for patients. Two other companies had exclusive rights to provide emergency services for patients. The ECJ assumed that the grant of these exclusive rights could violate Article 82(b), limiting markets, in the sense that only these two companies were allowed to provide non-emergency, as well as emergency, transport services. There was therefore *prima facie* a breach of Article 86(1), and the ECJ then considered justification under Article 86(2).[28]

It is therefore more difficult than hitherto for a State to organize its economic activities by giving special or exclusive rights to particular firms. Agnosticism as to forms of economic organization has been replaced by a more strident belief in the operation of free markets, unless the State can provide special justification for the privileges accorded.

(b) ARTICLE 86(2)

Article 86(2) falls into three parts. It begins by emphasizing that undertakings entrusted with the operation of services of a general economic interest, or which have the character of a revenue-producing monopoly, are subject to the Treaty. It then excludes the application of these rules where the performance of the tasks assigned to such undertakings is liable to be obstructed. This exception is then subject to a proviso that the development of trade must not be affected to such an extent as would be contrary to the interests of the Community.

(i) *The First Step*

The first step is therefore to determine whether an undertaking is of the kind mentioned. Not surprisingly the ECJ has stressed that the category of entrusted undertakings should be strictly defined, since the Article derogates from the rules of the Treaty.[29] The Court will subject claims that a service is of a general economic interest to searching scrutiny. Thus, in the *Merci* case[30] the ECJ rejected the argument that dock work came within this category.

It is, however, not relevant whether the undertaking is public or private, provided that the service entrusted to it has been assigned by an act of a public authority.[31] While it does not seem that this act has to be in any particular legal form, the State must have taken some definite steps to assign the service to the specific undertaking.[32] It has been accepted that undertakings such as utilities serve the general economic interest, as required by Article 86(2). The ECJ also accepted in *Ahmed Saeed* that this Article may apply to airlines obliged by public

---

[26] Case C–340/99 *TNT Traco SpA v. Poste Italiane SpA* [2001] ECR I–4109.

[27] Case C–475/99 *Ambulanz Glockner v. Landkreis Sudwestpfalz* [2001] ECR I–8089.

[28] See also Case C–67/96 *Albany International BV v. Stichting Bedrijfspensioenfonds Textielindustrie* [1999] ECR I–5751; Cases 147–148/97 *Deutsche Post AG v. Gesellschaft für Zahlungssyteme mbH and Citicorp Kartenservice GmbH* [2000] ECR I–825.

[29] Case 127/73 *BRT v. SABAM* [1974] ECR 313; Case C–242/95 *GT-Link*, n. 24 above.

[30] Case C–179/90 *Merci Convenzionali Porto di Genova SpA v. Siderurgica Gabrielli SpA* [1991] ECR I–5889, para. 27; Case C–242/95, *GT-Link*, n. 24 above.

[31] N. 29 above.

[32] Case 7/82 *GVL v. Commission* [1983] ECR 483.

authorities to operate routes that are not commercially viable, but which it is necessary to operate in the general interest.[33]

(ii) The Second Step

The second step in the application of Article 86(2) is to determine whether the exception applies. The ECJ previously held that the exception would apply only if the relevant Treaty prohibitions were incompatible with the performance of the undertaking's assigned tasks.[34]

This is, however, no longer the approach. In *Commission* v. *Netherlands*,[35] the ECJ held that for Article 86(2) to apply it was sufficient if the application of the Treaty rules obstructed the performance, in law or in fact, of the special obligations incumbent on the undertaking. It was not necessary for the survival of the undertaking itself to be under threat. It sufficed to show that the exclusive rights were necessary to enable the holder to perform the tasks of general economic interest assigned to it under economically acceptable conditions. The Member State did not have to prove that no other conceivable measure could enable the tasks to be performed under the same conditions.[36]

The ECJ will nonetheless look closely at claims that the exception applies.[37] Thus in *Merci*[38] the ECJ decided that, even if dock work were to be regarded as of general economic interest, there was no evidence that this demanded modification of the Treaty rules so as to prevent any obstruction in the performance of this task. Similarly in *British Telecom*[39] the Commission had made a decision holding certain practices relating to the transmission of messages to be in breach of Article 82. The ECJ rejected the argument that the measures adopted by BT should be exempted from the competition rules because of Article 86(2), since the claimant had failed to establish that the application of these rules to BT would prejudice the accomplishment of the tasks assigned to it.[40]

The ECJ has been more receptive to use of the exception where the undertaking granted exclusivity has universal service obligations requiring it to perform some tasks that are not in themselves profitable. The only way that it can do this is to have exclusive rights over those parts of the service that are profitable. The fear is that other undertakings will 'cream off' the profitable parts of the relevant business.

Thus, in *Corbeau*[41] the ECJ accepted that the Belgian postal service was an entrusted undertaking, and that some restriction on competition might be necessary to enable it to fulfil the duties it was required to perform. If this were not so then other firms could simply 'cream off' the profitable areas of business, since they would have no corresponding obligation to perform loss-making activities. This did not however serve to exclude all competition. There could, said the Court, be services which could be dissociated from the general public service,

---

[33] Case 66/86 *Ahmed Saeed Flugreisen and Silver Line Reisebüro GmbH v. Zentrale zur Bekämpfung Unlauteren Wettbewerbs eV* [1989] ECR 803, para. 55.

[34] Case 155/73 *Sacchi* [1974] ECR 409; Case 311/84 *Centre Belge d'Etudes du Marché-Télémarketing SA v. Compagnie Luxembourgeoise de Télédiffusion SA and Information Publicité Benelux SA* [1985] ECR 3261.

[35] Case C–157/94 [1997] ECR I–5699; Case C–438/02 *Criminal Proceedings against Hanner* [2005] ECR I–4551, para. 47.

[36] See also Case C–340/99 *TNT Traco*, n. 26 above, para. 54; Case C–67/96 *Albany*, n. 28 above, para. 107.

[37] Case 66/86 *Ahmed Saaed*, n. 33 above, para. 56.

[38] Case C–179/90, n. 30 above, para. 27.

[39] Case 41/83 *Italy* v. *Commission* (*Re British Telecommunications*) [1985] ECR 873, para. 33.

[40] See also Case C–203/96 *Chemische Afvalstoffen Dusseldorp BV v. Minister van Volkshuisvesting, Ruimtelijke Ordening en Milieubeheer* [1998] ECR I–4075.

[41] Case C–320/91 P *Corbeau*, n. 24 above. An analogous argument was unsuccessful in Case T–260/94 *Air Inter SA* v. *Commission* [1997] ECR II–997.

which could be offered by other undertakings without threatening the economic stability needed by the holder of the exclusive right. It was for the national court to determine whether the services in this case came within that category.

In *Albany*[42] a company argued that a Dutch law making affiliation to a supplementary pension scheme compulsory was contrary to Article 86. The ECJ decided that the exclusivity was justified under Article 86(2). The compulsory pension scheme was obliged to accept all workers without a prior medical examination, and contributions did not reflect risk. If the exclusive right of the fund to manage the supplementary pension scheme were removed, then undertakings with young employees in good health engaged in non-dangerous activities would seek more advantageous terms from private insurers. The progressive departure of these 'good risks' would leave the pension fund with an increasing share of 'bad risks'. This would lead to an increase in premiums for these workers, since the fund would not be able to offer pensions at the previous cost.[43]

(iii) *The Third Step*

Even if the exception applies, the third step in Article 86(2) requires that the development of trade must not be affected to such an extent as would be contrary to the interests of the Community. This proviso to the exception has the effect of subjugating Member State interests to those of the Community in the relevant area.

(c) ARTICLE 86(3)

Article 86(3) gives the Commission power to ensure the application of Article 86 through directives or decisions addressed to Member States. It is one of the relatively rare Treaty provisions which confer direct legislative competence on the Commission.[44] The Commission has used its power in Article 86(3) relatively rarely, but the Member States have nonetheless often challenged the competence of the Commission to proceed in this manner. The ECJ has however commonly rejected such challenges.

Thus in the *Transparency Directive* case,[45] the facts of which were set out above, the Member States argued that the Directive could not be enacted under Article 86(3), which, they said, was limited to dealing with a specific situation in one or more Member States. It did not give any more general legislative power to the Commission. The Court rejected this argument: there was no warrant for construing the term 'directive' in Article 86(3) any differently from the same term in Article 249.[46] The parties also contended that the Directive should have been

---

[42] Case C–67/96 *Albany*, n. 28 above, paras. 107–111.

[43] See also Cases C–115–117/97 *Brentjens' Handelsonderneming BV* v. *Stichting Bedrijfspensioenfonds voor de Handel in Bouwmaterialen* [1999] ECR I–6025, paras. 107–111; Case C–340/99 *Traco*, n. 26 above, paras. 54–63; Case C–475/99 *Ambulanz Glockner*, n. 27 above, paras. 57–66; Cases 147–148/97 *Deutsche Post*, n. 28 above, paras. 50–62; Case C–209/98 *Entreprenorforeningens Affalds/Miljosektion (FFAD)* v. *Kobenhavns Kommune* [2000] ECR I–3473, paras. 77–83.

[44] Art. 86 can also be enforced through actions under Art. 226, and the interpretation of Art. 86 can be clarified through Art. 234 references.

[45] Cases 188–90/80 *France, Italy and United Kingdom* v. *Commission* [1982] ECR 2545, paras. 4–15. See also Case C–202/88 *France* v. *Commission* [1991] ECR I–1223; Cases C–48 and 66/90 *Netherlands, Koninklijke PTT Nederland NV and PTT Post BV* v. *Commission* [1992] ECR I–565; Case C–107/95 P *Bundesverband der Bilanzbuchhalter eV* v. *Commission* [1997] ECR I–947; Case C–163/99 *Portuguese Republic* v. *Commission* [2001] ECR I–2613.

[46] Cases 188–90/80, n. 45 above, para. 7.

adopted by the Council pursuant to Article 89. The ECJ disagreed. The specific power to issue directives contained in Article 86(3) was in furtherance of the Commission's duty of surveillance provided for in Article 86. The fact that the rules might have been enacted by the Council under its general power in Article 89 did not preclude the Commission's exercise of power under Article 86(3).[47]

(d) ARTICLE 86 AND NATIONAL COURTS

We must now consider how far the provisions of Article 86 are directly effective. A distinction in this respect must be drawn between Article 86(1) and (2).

It is clear that breach of Article 86(1) is dependent upon a breach of some other Treaty Article. The ability of an individual to invoke Article 86(1) will therefore depend on whether the other Treaty article allegedly broken is directly effective. This is exemplified by the *Merci* case.[48] The ECJ held that Articles 28, 39, and 82 have direct effect when they fall to be considered within the framework of Article 86.

Article 86(2) has, as seen above, three parts: the determination of whether a body is an entrusted undertaking, the application of the exception, and the proviso to the exception. The ECJ has long recognized the competence of national courts to answer the first of these questions. In *SABAM*[49] the ECJ affirmed that a national court has the duty of investigating whether an undertaking which invokes the provisions of Article 86(2) has in fact been entrusted by the Member State with the operation of a service of general economic interest.

There has been more uncertainty about whether a national court can apply the exception. The ECJ's initial response was that Article 86(2) could not be invoked by individuals before national courts since it did not create rights for individuals,[50] but subsequent case law cast doubt on this proposition. The situation has now been clarified by the *ERT* case.[51] The ECJ held that Article 86(2) renders the relevenat undertakings subject to the Treaty, except in so far as it can be shown that those rules are incompatible with the performance of their particular tasks. It was therefore open to a national court to determine whether the practices of such an undertaking were compatible with, for example, Article 82. The national court could also decide whether those practices, if they were contrary to such a provision, could be justified by the needs of the particular task given to the undertaking.[52] The difficulties that this presents for national courts should not, however, be underestimated.[53]

Should an applicant succeed in bringing a case within the exception, the question remains whether a national court is competent to apply the proviso in Article 86(2). It would be difficult for the national courts to perform this task, since they may not have the information on which to make the assessment. On this view it would require a Commission decision made under Article 86(3) to decide the issue.

---

[47] *Ibid.*, para. 14.

[48] Case C–179/90 *Porto di Genova*, n. 30 above, para. 23; Case C–242/95 *GT-Link*, n. 24 above, para. 57; Case C–258/98 *Carra*, n. 23 above, para. 11.

[49] Case 127/73 *BRT v. SABAM*, n. 29 above; Case C–218/00 *Cisal di Battistello Venanzio & C. Sas* v. *INAIL* [2002] ECR I–691, para. 19.

[50] Case 10/71 *Muller*, n. 19 above.

[51] Case C–260/89 *ERT*, n. 23 above, paras. 33–34.

[52] The ECJ adopted the same approach to the tasks of the national courts in the cases mentioned in nn. 28 and 43 above.

[53] See, e.g., the task presented to the national courts in Case C–320/91 P *Corbeau*, n. 24 above, discussed by Hancher, n. 25 above, 119–120.

(e) SUMMARY

i.   Article 86 seeks to reconcile a Member State's interest in using certain undertakings as an instrument of social and/or economic policy with the Community's interest in ensuring compliance with the rules on competition and the internal market.

ii. It is clear that the mere grant of a monopoly or exclusive rights will not infringe Article 86(1). It will do so only when the exercise of the exclusive rights could not avoid being abusive, or where such rights were liable to create a situation in which the undertaking was induced to commit an abuse.

iii. It is equally clear that the ECJ has been ready to find that either of these conditions applies, and that therefore Article 86(1) is applicable.

iv. It is then for the State to provide a justification under Article 86(2). It must be shown that the Treaty rules should be excluded because they would obstruct the performance of the tasks assigned to the undertaking granted exclusive rights. The ECJ will subject such claims to close scrutiny. However, the ECJ has held the exception to be applicable in relation to bodies with universal service obligations or the equivalent thereto. Exclusivity in such instances has been held to be warranted in order that the profitable parts of an activity are not 'creamed off' by the private sector, with the consequence that the body granted exclusive rights is unable, financially, to fulfil its remit.

4. THE STATE, ARTICLES 10, 81, 82, AND 28

The discussion thus far has focused on Article 86. This is not, however, the only Treaty provision relevant to state action and the Community. The Court has also made important decisions on the basis of Articles 10, 81, 82, and 28.[54] The basic principle is that a State may not adopt or maintain in force any measure which would deprive, for example, Article 81 of its effectiveness or prejudice its full and uniform application. A State can be in breach of this obligation either when it requires or encourages undertakings to conclude cartels in violation of Article 81, or when it divests its national provisions of their public nature by, in effect, delegating to the firms the responsibility for taking decisions about the boundaries of competition.[55] This jurisprudence is the means whereby the ECJ has extended the type of obligation imposed on a State by Article 86 to situations where the undertakings are neither public nor enjoy any specially privileged position. The following cases illustrate the Court's jurisprudence.

In *Vereniging van Vlaamse Reisbureaus*[56] a travel agent was prosecuted for violating a professional code of practice incorporated into Belgian law. The code involved horizontal price

---

[54] P.J. Slot, 'The Application of Articles 3(f), 5 and 85 to 94 EEC' (1987) 12 *ELRev.* 179; L. Gyselen, 'State Action and the Effectiveness of the Treaty's Competition Provisions' (1989) 26 *CMLRev.* 33.

[55] The principle was reaffirmed, but not breached, in Case C–2/91 *Wolf Meng* [1993] ECR I–5751; Case C–245/91 *Ohra Schadeverzekeringen NV* [1993] ECR I–5851; Case C–153/93 *Germany* v. *Delta Schiffahrts- und Speditionsgesellschaft mbH* [1994] ECR I–2517; Case C–185/91 *Bundesanstalt für den Güterfernverkehr* v. *Gebrüder Reiff GmbH & Co. KG* [1993] ECR I–5801; Cases C–140–142/94 *DIP SpA* v. *Commune di Bassano del Grappa* [1995] ECR I–3257; Case C–70/95 *Sodemare SA, Anni Azzuri Holding SpA and Anni Azzuri Rezzato Srl* v. *Regione Lombardia* [1997] ECR I–3395; Case C–35/99 *Criminal Proceedings against Arduino* [2002] ECR I–1529; Case C–250/03 *Mauri* v. *Ministero delle Giustizia* [2005] ECR I–1267; Cases C–94 and 202/04 *Cipolla* v. *Fazari*, 5 Dec. 2006.

[56] Case 311/85 *Vereniging van Vlaamse Reisbureaus* v. *Sociale Dienst van de Plaatselijke en Gewestelijke Overheidsdiensten* [1987] ECR 3801.

fixing, a blatant breach of Article 81. The Court also found that the Belgian State was in breach of Article 10, read together with Article 81, by supporting the cartel through its own legal regime.

In *Van Eycke*[57] holders of certain Belgian savings accounts had the benefit of a tax exemption, provided that the bank offered interest rates below that set by the Minister in a Royal Decree. Those who held accounts at banks that gave higher interest rates than that stipulated by the Royal Decree lost the tax exemption, with the consequence that it was unattractive for the banks to offer these higher rates. The effect of this was to limit price competition between banks. The ECJ held that, although the duty in Articles 81 and 82 is directed towards undertakings, the State itself has an obligation, derived from Article 10, not to introduce measures which render the competition Articles ineffective. This would be the case where, for example, national legislation reinforced the effects of existing agreements that were in breach of Article 81; or where the State deprived its own legislation of its official character by delegating to private traders responsibility for taking decisions affecting the economic sphere.[58] More recent attempts to invoke this principle have, however, not been notably successful.[59]

Where the State intervenes not to support an existing agreement which is itself illegal under Article 81, but through an independent measure which undertakings must follow, Article 28 is the most appropriate provision in relation to goods, and Article 49 in the case of services.[60]

5. STATE AIDS: THE SUBSTANTIVE RULES AND ARTICLE 87

(a) THE COMMISSION AND THE DEVELOPMENT OF POLICY

Certain general points should be made clear before discussing the detail of the rules on state aids. First, the Commission, as the initial decision-maker, develops the general policy in this area.[61] Its decisions are subject to judicial review, but the Community Courts are mindful of the complex evaluations of social and economic data involved, and they will not, therefore, substitute their view for that of the Commission. Judicial review is limited to verifying whether the Commission complied with procedural rules, including the provision of reasons, whether the facts on which the decision was based were accurately stated, and whether there has been a manifest error of assessment or misuse of power.[62]

Secondly, the Commission possesses discretion as to the general approach to be taken to state aids. Thus it has, for example, applied a principle of compensatory justification. Before it will approve aid, there must be some contribution by the beneficiary of the aid, over and above

---

[57] Case 267/86 *Van Eycke* v. *NV ASPA* [1988] ECR 4769.

[58] See also Case 229/83 *Leclerc* v. *Au Blé Vert* [1985] ECR 1; Cases 209–213/84 *Ministère Public* v. *Asjes* [1986] ECR 1425; Case C–198/01 *CIF* v. *Autorita Garante della Concorrenza del Mercato* [2003] ECR I–8055.

[59] See the cases in n. 55 above.

[60] Case 229/83 *Leclerc*, n. 58 above.

[61] L. Hancher, T. Ottervanger, and P.J. Slot, *EC State Aids* (3rd edn., Sweet & Maxwell, 2006); A. Evans, *EC Law of State Aid* (Oxford University Press, 1997).

[62] See, e.g., Case T–171/02 *Regione Autonoma della Sardegna* v. *Commission* [2005] ECR II–2123, para. 97; Cases T–228 and 233/99 *Westdeutsche Landesbank Gironzentrale and another* v. *Commission* [2003] ECR II–435, para. 282; Case T–198/01 *Technische Glaswerke Ilmenau GmbH* v. *Commission* [2004] ECR II–2717, para. 97; P. Craig, *EU Administrative Law* (Oxford University Press, 2006), ch. 13.

the normal play of market forces, to the attainment of Community objectives as contained in the derogations from Article 87(3).[63] In general terms, aid can be designed to restructure an undertaking, to rescue an undertaking, or to help it with operating costs. The Commission has provided guidelines on these.[64] The guidelines for restructuring aid stipulate, *inter alia*, that viability is restored, that aid is in proportion to the restructuring costs and benefits, that undue distortions of competition are avoided, and that the restructuring plan is fully implemented. Operating aid relieves an undertaking of expenses that it would normally bear in its day-to-day operations, with no technical or structural alteration in the character of the recipient. It is generally regarded as objectionable by the Commission[65] and the Court,[66] and is normally only authorized to cope with specific regional or sectoral problems.

Thirdly, the Commission can also choose how to develop its substantive policy, whether through formal legislation or through informal rule-making. The Commission has made formal legislation in certain areas. The Council has, pursuant to Article 94, delegated power to the Commission to make regulations exempting types of aid from the requirement of notification, and stipulating that it shall be regarded as compatible with the common market.[67] The Commission has used this power to make formal regulations concerning small and medium-sized enterprises,[68] *de minimis* aid,[69] training aid,[70] aid for employment,[71] and national regional investment aid.[72] Formal legislation has also been made on procedural matters.[73]

Fourthly, the Commission can choose to develop policy, not only through formal legislation but also through individual decisions or informal rule-making. Rules and policy frameworks have been made for particular industrial sectors, and in relation to matters such as regional aid, environmental aid, deprived areas, and aid to promote investment of risk capital in small and medium-sized enterprises.[74] It is lawful for the Commission to structure its discretion through such guidelines, provided that they do not depart from the Treaty rules.[75]

---

[63] *Ibid.*, ch. 3.

[64] Community Guidelines on State Aid for Rescuing and Restructuring Firms in Difficulty [1999] OJ C288/2.

[65] Evans, n. 61 above, 131–138.

[66] Case T–459/93 *Siemens SA* v. *Commission* [1995] ECR II–1675, upheld on appeal in Case C–278/95 P *Siemens SA* v. *Commission* [1997] ECR I–2507; Case T–214/95 *Vlaams Gewest* v. *Commission* [1998] ECR II–717; Case T–190/00 *Regione Siciliana* v. *Commission* [2003] ECR II–5015, para. 130.

[67] Council Reg. 994/98 of 7 May 1998 on the application of Art. 92 and 93 of the Treaty to certain categories of horizontal State aid [1998] OJ L142/1.

[68] Commission Reg. 70/2001 of 12 Jan. 2001 on the application of Art. 87 and 88 of the EC Treaty to small and medium sized enterprises [2001] OJ L10/33. This was extended to cover aid for research and development by Commission Reg. 364/2004 of 25 Feb. 2004 [2004] OJ L63/22.

[69] Commission Reg. 69/2001 of 12 Jan. 2001 on the application of Art. 87 and 88 of the EC Treaty to de minimis aid [2001] OJ L10/30.

[70] Commission Reg. 68/2001 of 12 Jan. 2001 on the application of Art. 87 and 88 of the EC Treaty to training aid [2001] OJ L10/20, as amended by Commission Reg. 363/2004 of 25 Feb. 2004 [2004] OJ L63/20.

[71] Commission Reg. 2204/2002 of 12 Dec. 2002 on the application of Art. 87 and 88 of the EC Treaty to State aid for employment [2002] OJ L337/3.

[72] Commission Reg. 1628/2006 of 24 Oct. 2006 on the application of Art. 87 and 88 of the EC Treaty to national regional investment aid [2006] OJ L302/29.

[73] Council Reg. 659/99 of 22 Mar. 1999 laying down detailed rules on the application of Art. 93 of the EC Treaty [1999] OJ L83/1.

[74] See http://ec.europa.eu/comm/competition/state_aid/legislation/horizontal.html.

[75] Case C–313/90 *CIRFS* v. *Commission* [1993] ECR I–1125, paras. 34–36; Case T–214/95 *Vlaams Gewest*, n. 66 above, para. 89; Case T–149/95 *Ducros* v. *Commission* [1997] ECR II–2031, para. 61; Case C–288/96 *Germany* v. *Commission* [2000] ECR I–8237, para. 62; Case T–171/02 *Regione Autonoma della Sardegna*, n. 62 above, para. 95; Case T–17/03 *Schmitz-Gotha Fahrzeugwerke GmbH* v. *Commission* [2006] ECR II–1139, para. 42.

In *CIRFS*[76] the ECJ accepted that the Commission was bound by the terms of its policy framework,[77] and in *Ijssel-Vliet*[78] it held that Commission guidelines built into a Dutch aid scheme were binding upon the Dutch government. Moreover, in *Vlaams Gewest*[79] the CFI held that the guidelines adopted by the Commission had to be applied in accordance with the principle of equal treatment, with the implication that like cases, as defined in the guidelines, had to be treated alike. Such guidelines are however not formally binding on the Community Courts.[80]

The use of rule-making is not unproblematic, since the variety of instruments used by the Commission can be confusing for users of the system.[81] The reasons for nonetheless employing such policy documents are part practical, part conceptual, and part political.

In practical terms such guidelines help an overburdened administration to cope with an increased workload.[82]

In conceptual terms they have the advantages generally associated with rule-making.[83] They 'reduce Member States' room for manoeuvre in giving aid and the controller's margin of discretion, choice and possible arbitrariness';[84] and they facilitate 'the transparency, legal security and credibility which result from strict and consistent enforcement, to the benefit of governments and industry'.[85]

In political terms, rule-making by the Commission obviates the need for consent in the Council, which is necessary under Article 89 when formal legislation is enacted. Thus Rawlinson, a principal administrator within the state aids directorate, argued that recourse to Article 89 would make policy-making more protracted.[86] However Cananea has pointed to the lack of clarity of certain guidelines, and to the fact that the rights of individuals have not always been properly safeguarded. He has suggested that the time may now be ripe for the passage of a 'Council regulation to cope with the existing lacunae of Community law on state aids'.[87]

(b) ARTICLE 87(1)

Article 87 lays down the test for state aids. It covers aid given to public undertakings within Article 86, subject to Article 86(2), as well as aid given to private firms.[88] Article 87 has three parts. Paragraph (1) establishes the general principle that state aids are incompatible with the common market. Paragraph (2) provides certain exceptions for situations where the aid will be deemed to be compatible with the common market. Paragraph (3) lists certain types of

---

[76] Case C–313/90 *CIRFS*, n. 75 above.

[77] Cf. Case 310/85 *Deufil* v. *Commission* [1987] ECR 901.

[78] Case C–311/94 *Ijssel-Vliet Combinatie BV* v. *Minister van Economische Zaken* [1996] ECR I–5023.

[79] Case T–214/95 *Vlaams Gewest*, n. 66 above, para. 89.

[80] Case C–310/99 *Italy* v. *Commission* [2002] ECR I–2289, para. 52.

[81] Rawlinson, n. 82 below, 59; G. della Cananea, 'Administration by Guidelines: The Policy Guidelines of the Commission in the Field of State Aids', in I. Harden (ed.), *State Aid: Community Law and Policy* (Bundesanzeiger, 1993), 68–69.

[82] F. Rawlinson, 'The Role of Policy Frameworks, Codes and Guidelines in the Control of State Aid', in *ibid.*, 56; Evans, n. 61 above, 408–427.

[83] P. Craig, *Administrative Law* (5th edn., Sweet & Maxwell, 2003), ch. 16.

[84] Rawlinson, n. 82 above, 55.

[85] *Ibid.*, 57.

[86] *Ibid.*, 60; Evans, n. 61 above, 405–408.

[87] Della Cananea, n. 81 above, 74–75.

[88] Case C–387/92 *Banco de Credito Industrial SA (Banco Exterior de Espana SA)* v. *Ayuntamiento de Valencia* [1994] ECR I–877; Case T–106/95 *Fédération Française des Sociétés d'Assurances (FFSA)* v. *Commission* [1997] ECR II–229.

case where the aid may be deemed to be compatible with the common market. Let us then begin with the basic proscription of state aids in Article 87(1):

> Save as otherwise provided in this Treaty, any aid granted by a Member State or through State resources in any form whatsoever which distorts or threatens to distort competition by favouring certain undertakings or the production of certain goods shall, in so far as it affects trade between Member States, be incompatible with the common market.

There are four conditions that must be satisfied before something is classified as aid for the purposes of Article 87. These are cumulative, in the sense that all must be fulfilled before the Member State measure is caught by Article 87.

(i) *The Definition of State Aid: An Advantage Conferred on the Recipient*

Article 87(1) does not define state aid;[89] the ECJ and Commission have, as might be expected, taken a broad view. The rationale for the aid is not relevant at this stage,[90] and substance, not form, is the criterion when defining aid. The essential point is that to constitute aid the measure must confer an advantage on the recipient.

The Commission has provided a full list of the types of aid. These include direct subsidies, tax exemptions,[91] exemptions from parafiscal charges, preferential interest rates, favourable loan guarantees, the provision of land or buildings on special terms, indemnities against losses, preferential terms for public ordering, the deferment of the collection of fiscal or social contributions, and dividend guarantees. This list is illustrative rather than exhaustive.

The ECJ has also made it clear that the concept of aid covers not only positive benefits, such as subsidies, but also measures that mitigate the charges an undertaking would normally bear,[92] such as the supply of goods or services at a preferential rate,[93] a reduction in social security contributions,[94] or tax exemptions.[95]

General measures of economic policy, such as an interest-rate reduction, while benefiting industrial sales, will not in themselves be classified as aid.[96] Thus a non-sectoral measure of general taxation policy remains within the area of state fiscal sovereignty.[97] A measure will nonetheless be classified as aid even if it benefits a whole range of undertakings, as in the case

---

[89] Evans, n. 61 above, 27–46.

[90] Case 173/73 *Italy* v. *Commission* [1974] ECR 709; Case C–241/94 *France* v. *Commission* [1996] ECR I–4187; Case C–251/97 *France* v. *Commission* [1999] ECR I–6639.

[91] Case C–387/92 *Banco de Credito*, n. 88 above; Cases C–182 and 217/03 *Belgium and Forum 187 ASBL* v. *Commission* [2006] ECR I–5479.

[92] Case C–237/04 *Enirisorse SpA* v. *Sotacarbo SpA* [2006] ECR I–2843, para. 42; Case C–222/04 *Ministero dell'Economia e delle Finanze* v. *Cassa di Risparmio di Firenze SpA* [2006] ECR I–289, para. 131; Cases C–393/04 and 41/05 *Air Liquide SA and another* v. *Province de Liege* [2006] ECR I–5293.

[93] Case C–241/94 *France*, n. 90 above; Case C–387/92, *Banco de Credito*, n. 88 above; Case C–39/94 *Syndicat Français de l'Express International (SFEI)* v. *La Poste* [1996] ECR I–3547; Case C–143/99 *Adria-Wien Pipeline GmbH and Wietersdörfer & Peggauer Zementwerke GmbH* v. *Finanzlandesdirektion für Kärnten* [2001] ECR I–8365.

[94] Case C–75/97 *Belgium* v. *Commission* [1999] ECR I–3671.

[95] Case C–6/97 *Italy* v. *Commission* [1999] ECR I–2981.

[96] Case C–143/99 *Adria-Wien*, n. 93 above, para. 35.

[97] Case C–308/01 *GIL Insurance Ltd.* v. *Commissioners of Customs and Excise* [2004] ECR I–4777, para. 78. See however Case C–88/03 *Portugal* v. *Commission* [2006] ECR I–7115.

of a general export aid,[98] though by way of contrast aid for general infrastructure will not generally constitute aid within Article 87.[99] The dividing line between general measures of economic policy and state aids may however be a fine one.[100]

Particular difficulties have arisen where the State takes a shareholding in a private company. In *Intermills*[101] the ECJ made it clear that no distinction could be drawn between aid granted in the form of loans and aid granted in the form of a holding acquired in the capital of an undertaking. Both could be caught by Article 87(1).[102]

Case C–142/87 **Re Tubemeuse: Belgium v. Commission**
[1990] ECR I–959

[Note ToA renumbering: Arts. 92 and 93 are now Arts. 87 and 88]

In 1979 the Belgian Government acquired 72 per cent of the capital holding of Tubemeuse (T), which was in severe financial difficulty following the withdrawal of private shareholders. In 1982 the Commission approved a series of aid measures, but these were not successful and the State then acquired the remaining shares in the firm. Between 1984 and 1986 Belgium initiated a series of measures designed to increase the capital of T. These measures were notified to the Commission, but the Government did not wait for the Commission's approval as required by Article 93(2). The Commission then made a decision that these measures constituted unlawful aid and instructed Belgium to recover the sums. The Belgian Government argued that the measures in 1984–1986 did not constitute state aid, but were rather the normal reaction of any investor whose initial investment (made in 1979 and then in 1982) was at risk. The ECJ reiterated its holding in *Intermills* and then continued as follows.

THE ECJ

26. In order to determine whether such measures are in the nature of State aid, the relevant criterion is that indicated in the Commission's decision, and not contested by the Belgian government, namely whether the undertaking could have obtained the amounts in question on the capital market.

27. In the event, it can be seen from the contested measure taken together with the other documents before the Court that, in addition to the technical difficulties of its plant, which made necessary the extensive modernisation programme in 1982 carried out with the help of the public authorities and authorised by the Commission, the company has, since 1979, had to face structural financial difficulties. Excessively high production costs, continual operating losses, poor liquidity and heavy indebtedness led to the withdrawal of almost all the private shareholders from the undertaking.

---

98 Case C–75/97 *Belgium* v. *Commission*, n. 94 above.

99 Case C–225/91 *Matra* v. *Commission* [1993] ECR I–3203.

100 C. Quigley, 'The Notion of a State Aid in the EEC' (1988) 13 *ELRev.* 242, 252–253.

101 Case 323/82 *Intermills SA* v. *Commission* [1984] ECR 3809.

102 See also Cases 296 and 318/82 *The Netherlands and Leeuwarder Papierwarenfabriek BV* v. *Commission* [1985] ECR 809; Case 40/85 *Belgium* v. *Commission (Re Boch)* [1986] ECR 2321; Case T–16/96 *Cityflyer Express Ltd.* v. *Commission* [1998] ECR II–757; Case T–198/01 *Technische Glaswerke*, n. 62 above, paras. 98–99; Evans, n. 61 above, 56–70.

28. Moreover, it is not contested that the seamless steel tubes sector whose production was intended principally for use in oil exploration, was in a state of crisis, marked by considerable surplus capacity in the producing countries and new production capacity in the developing and State trading countries. Furthermore, the restrictions which the United States imposed on the importation of steel tubes into their territory and the fall in world oil prices, which contributed to a reduction in drilling, led to a fall in demand for the tubes in question and therefore to a substantial reduction in their price and in world production. That is the reason why other Member States sought to reduce their production capacity in that sector.

29. Under those circumstances, there is nothing which suggests any error in the Commission's assessment that Tubemeuse's prospects of profitability were not such as to induce private investors operating under normal market economy conditions to enter into the financial transactions in question, that it was unlikely that Tubemeuse could have obtained the amounts essential for its survival on the capital markets and that, for that reason, the Belgian government's support for Tubemeuse constituted State aid.

The ECJ has continued to apply the same test. When capital is invested by a public investor there must be some interest in profitability in the long term, otherwise the investment will be characterized as aid for the purposes of Article 87(1).[103] It is important to determine whether the private investor would have entered into the transaction on the same terms as the public investor, and if not on what terms it might have done so.[104] The privatization of an undertaking may also give rise to questions concerning state aid, depending upon the terms of the privatization. The Commission has provided guidelines on this issue.[105]

It is, as we have seen, central to the idea of state aid that the recipient gains a financial advantage, directly or indirectly, over its competitors. This will not be so where the assistance is granted to offset public service obligations incumbent on the beneficiary of the aid, provided that the conditions in the *Altmark* case are satisfied.

Case C–280/00 **Altmark Trans GmbH and Regierungspräsidium Magdeburg v. Nahverkehrsgesellschaft Altmark GmbH**
[2003] ECR I–7747

[Note ToA renumbering: Art. 92 is now Art. 87]

THE ECJ

87. [W]here a State measure must be regarded as compensation for the services provided by the recipient undertakings in order to discharge public service obligations, so that those undertakings do not enjoy a real financial advantage and the measure thus does not have the

The ECJ considered the compatibility with Article 87 of state measures that accorded assistance to local transport undertakings.

---

[103] Case C–303/88 *Italy* v. *Commission* [1991] ECR I–1433; Case C–305/89 *Italy* v. *Commission* [1991] ECR I–1635; Case C–42/93 *Spain* v. *Commission* [1994] ECR I–4175; L. Hancher, 'State Aids and Judicial Control in the European Community' [1994] *ECLR* 134, 135–136.

[104] Cases T–228 and 233/99 *Westdeutsche Landesbank*, n. 62 above, paras. 244–246.

[105] Evans, n. 61 above, 70–76.

effect of putting them in a more favourable compettitve position than the undertakings competing with them, such a measure is not caught by Article 92(1) of the Treaty.

88. However, for such compensation to escape classification as State aid in a particular case, a number of conditions must be satisfied.

89. First, the recipient undertaking must actually have public service obligations to discharge, and the obligations must be clearly defined. . . .

90. Second, the parameters on the basis of which the compensations is calculated must be established in advance in an objective and transparent manner, to avoid conferring an economic advantage which may favour the recipient undertaking over competing undertakings.

. . .

92. Third, the compensation cannot exceed what is necessary to cover all or part of the costs incurred in the discharge of the public service obligations, taking into account the relevant receipts and a reasonable profit for discharging those obligations. . . .

93. Fourth, where the undertaking which is to discharge the public service obligations, in a specific case, is not chosen pursuant to public procurement procedure which would allow for the selection of the tenderer capable of providing those services at least cost to the community, the level of compensation needed must be determined on the basis of an analysis of the costs which a typical undertaking, well run and adequately provided with means of transport so as to be able to meet the necessary public service requirements, would have incurred in discharging those obligations, taking into account the relevant receipts and a reasonable profit for discharging the obligations.

The *Altmark* ruling specified that public service compensation would not constitute state aid and hence would not need to be notified *if* the conditions laid down were met.[106] This has enabled the Commission to make a decision[107] and issue a framework[108] specifying in greater detail the requirements to be met if the conditions are to be fulfilled. The Commission is clearly keen to ensure that the ECJ's conditions are strictly adhered to, so that the ruling is not used by Member States to circumvent the application of the state aid rules.

(ii) *Definition of State Aid: 'Member State or through State Resources'*

A second condition for the application of Article 87(1) is that the aid should be granted by a 'Member State or through State resources'. Only advantages granted directly or indirectly through state resources are regarded as aid.[109] It is clear that this can include regional as well as central government.[110] It can also include advantages granted by a public or private body designated or established by the State.[111]

---

106 See also Cases C–34 and 38/01 *Enirisorse SpA v. Ministero delle Finanze* [2003] ECR I–14243; Case C–451/03 *Serrvizi Ausiliari Dottori Commercialisti Srl v. Calafiori* [2006] ECR I–2941; Case C–526/04 *Laboratoires Boiron SA v. Urssaf* [2006] ECR I–7529.

107 Commission Dec. 2005/842/EC of 28 Nov. 2005 on the application of Art. 86(2) EC to State aid in the form of public service compensation granted to certain undertakings entrusted with the operation of services of general economic interest [2005] OJ L312/67.

108 Community Framework for State aid in the form of public service compensation [2005] OJ C297/4.

109 Cases C–52–54/97 *Viscido, Scandella and Terragnolo v. Ente Poste Italiane* [1998] ECR I–2629; Case C–345/02 *Pearle BV and others v. Hoofdbedrijfschap Ambachten* [2004] ECR I–7139; Case T–351/02 *Deutsche Bahn AG v. Commission* [2006] ECR II–1047.

110 Case 323/82 *Intermills*, n. 101 above.

111 See also Case 78/76 *Firma Steinike und Weinlig v. Bundesamt für Ernährung und Forstwirtschaft* [1977] ECR 595; Case 290/83 *Commission v. France (Re Grants to Poor Farmers)* [1985] ECR 439; Case 57/86 *Commission v. Greece* [1988] ECR 2855; Case T–358/94 *Compagnie Nationale Air France v. Commission* [1996] ECR II–2109. There

Cases 67, 68, and 70/85 **Kwerkerij Gebroeders
Van der Kooy BV v. Commission**
[1988] ECR 219

The Commission made a decision that the tariffs charged by Gasunie for gas to certain firms in
the horticultural industry were preferential and constituted aid for the purposes of Article 92.
Gasunie was a company incorporated under private law, but 50 per cent of its shares were held
by the Dutch government, and the tariffs charged by Gasunie were subject to approval by a
government minister. It was argued that the fixing of the tariff did not constitute action by the
Dutch State.

THE ECJ

32. In the first place, the applicants maintain that ... the contested tariff was not imposed
by the Dutch State and cannot be regarded as 'aid granted by a Member State or through State
resources'.

33. They argue that Gasunie is a company incorporated under private law in which the Dutch
State holds only 50% of the share capital and that the tariff is the outcome of an agreement
concluded under private law between Gasunie, Vegin and the Landbouwchap, to which the
Dutch State is not a party.

34. Turning to the point noted by the Commission that the Minister for Economic Affairs has
a right of approval over the tariffs charged by Gasunie, the Dutch Government claims that that
is no more than a retrospective supervisory power which is solely concerned with whether the
tariffs accord with the aims of Dutch energy policy.

35. As the Court has held ..., there is no necessity to draw any distinction between cases
where aid is granted directly by the State and where it is granted by public and/or private bodies established or appointed by the State to administer the aid. In this instance, the documents
before the Court provide considerable evidence to show that the fixing of the disputed tariff
was the result of action by the Dutch State.

36. First of all, the shares in Gasunie are so distributed that the Dutch State directly or indirectly holds 50% of the shares and appoints half of the members of the supervisory board—a
body whose powers include that of determining the tariffs to be applied. Secondly, the
Minister for Economic Affairs is empowered to approve the tariffs applied by Gasunie, with the
result that, regardless of how that power may be exercised, the Dutch Government can block
any tariff which does not suit it. Lastly, Gasunie and the Landbouwschap have on two occasions given effect to the Commission's representations to the Dutch Government seeking an
amendment of the horticultural tariff. . . .

37. Considered as a whole, these factors demonstrate that Gasunie in no way enjoys full
autonomy in the fixing of gas tariffs but acts under the control and on the instructions of the
public authorities. It is thus clear that Gasunie could not fix the tariff without taking account of
the requirements of the public authorities.

38. It may therefore be concluded that the fixing of the contested tariff is the result of action
by the Dutch State and thus falls within the meaning of the phrase 'aid granted by a Member
State'. . . .

can be difficulties about what constitutes a resource granted from the State: Cases C–72–73/91 *Sloman Neptun
Schiffahrts AG* v. *Seebetriebsrat Bodo Ziesmer der Sloman Neptun Schiffahrts* [1993] ECR I–887; Cases C–328 and
399/00 *Italy and SIM 2 Multimedia SpA* v. *Commission* [2003] ECR I–4035.

(iii) *Definition of State Aid: 'Distorts or Threatens to Distort Competition'*

A third condition for the application of Article 87(1) is that the aid should distort or threaten to distort competition by favouring certain undertakings or the production of certain goods.[112] In many cases this will be unproblematic. The grant of, for example, a subsidy will indubitably place the recipient in a more advantageous position. The Court will consider the position of the relevant company prior to the receipt of the aid, and if this has been improved then Article 87 will have been met.[113] It is no 'defence' for the State to argue that the aid is justified because its effect is to lower the costs of a sector of industry which has, in relative terms, higher costs than other industrial sectors.[114] Nor is it possible for a State to contend that its aid should be excused on the ground that other States made similar payments to firms within those countries.[115]

(iv) *Definition of State Aid: Effect on Inter-state Trade*

The final element in Article 87(1) is that there should be an effect on inter-state trade.[116] If aid strengthens the financial position of an undertaking as compared to others within the Community then inter-Community trade will be affected.[117] The relatively small amount of the aid, or the relatively small size of the recipient undertaking, does not as such exclude the possibility that Community trade might be affected.[118] The fact that the aid is given to an undertaking that only provides local transport services does not preclude an effect on inter-state trade, since the aid may render it more difficult for transport undertakings from other Member States to penetrate that market.[119] It is not necessary for the Commission to prove that trade will be affected; it is sufficient to show that trade might be affected.[120]

(c) ARTICLE 87(2)

Article 87(2) lists three types of aid which are deemed to be compatible with the common market.

Article 87(2)(a) states that 'aid having a social character, granted to individual consumers, provided that such aid is granted without discrimination related to the origin of the products concerned' will be compatible with the common market. This Article legitimates aid only if there is no discrimination as to the goods' origin. This limits the occasions when a State will be able to use this provision, since most state aid is directed exclusively to a particular firm within the Member State providing the aid.

Article 87(2)(b) legitimates 'aid to make good damage caused by natural disasters or exceptional occurrences'. The rationale for this exception is self-evident, but its limits are, however,

---

112 Evans, n. 61 above, 76–91.

113 Case 173/73 *Italy* v. *Commission*, n. 90 above.

114 *Ibid.*

115 Case 78/76 *Steinike*, n. 111 above.

116 Evans, n. 61 above, 92–96.

117 Case 730/79 *Philip Morris Holland BV* v. *Commission* [1980] ECR 2671.

118 Case C–142/87 *Belgium* v. *Commission* (*Re Tubemeuse*) [1990] ECR I–959, para. 43.

119 Case C–280/00 *Altmark Trans GmbH and Regierungspräsidium Magdeburg* v. *Nahverkehrsgesellschaft Altmark GmbH* [2003] ECR I–7747, paras. 77–82.

120 Cases T–298, 312, 313, 315, 600–607/97, 1, 3–6, and 23/98 *Alzetta Mauro* v. *Commission* [2000] ECR II–2319, paras. 76–90; Case C–310/99 *Italy* v. *Commission*, n. 80 above, paras. 84–86.

somewhat unclear. While the notion of a natural disaster is reasonably apparent, the meaning of exceptional occurrence is considerably vaguer. The Article is construed strictly and will only be held applicable where the economic disadvantage to the State flows directly from the natural disaster of exceptional occurrence.[121]

Article 87(2)(c) makes provision for the special position of Germany, resulting from the division of the country, in order to compensate for the economic disadvantage caused by that division. It does not however allow full compensation for the new Länder.[122]

(d) ARTICLE 87(3)

The exceptions in Article 87(3) are discretionary: aid which comes within these categories *may* be deemed to be compatible with the common market.

(i) *Article 87(3)(a)*

Article 87(3)(a) states that 'aid to promote the economic development of areas where the standard of living is abnormally low or where there is serious under-employment' may be considered to be compatible with the common market.

There is a connection between this provision and Article 87(3)(c), in that both relate in a general sense to regional development. Article 87(3)(a) can, however, only be used where the problem in an area is especially serious. The Commission has taken the view, upheld by the Court, that the seriousness of the regional problem must be judged in a Community and not a national context.[123] To this end the Commission has published criteria for deciding upon the relative development of different regions as compared to the Community average.[124] Moreover, the Commission can, even under Article 87(3)(a), consider the impact of the aid on the relevant Community markets.[125]

Case 730/79 **Philip Morris Holland BV v. Commission**
[1980] ECR 2671

[Note ToA renumbering: Art. 92(3) is now Art. 87(3)]

The Dutch Government gave aid to a tobacco manufacturer. The Commission found that the aid did not come within Article 92(3)(a),(b), or (c). What follows is an extract from the ECJ's reasoning concerning the general approach to Article 92(3), and its findings on Article 92(3)(a).

THE ECJ

16. According to the applicant it is wrong for the Commission to lay down as a general principle that aid granted by a Member State to undertakings only falls within the derogating

---

[121] Case C–278/00 *Greece* v. *Commission* [2004] ECR I–3997, paras. 81–82.
[122] Cases C–57 and 61/00 P *Freistaat Sachsen and another* v. *Commission* [2003] ECR I–9975; Case C–277/00 *Germany* v. *Commission* [2004] ECR I–3925.
[123] Case 248/84 *Germany* v. *Commission* [1987] ECR 4013, para. 1.
[124] Guidelines on National Regional Aid for 2007–2013 [2006] OJ C54/13, paras. 15–17.
[125] Case C–114/00 *Spain* v. *Commission* [2002] ECR I–7657, para. 81.

provisions of Article 92(3) if the Commission can establish that the aid will contribute to the attainment of one of the objectives specified in the derogations, which under normal market conditions the recipient firms would not attain by their own actions. Aid is only permissible under Article 92(3) of the Treaty if the investment plan under consideration is in conformity with the objectives mentioned in subparagraphs (a), (b) and (c).

17. This argument cannot be upheld. On the one hand it disregards the fact that Article 92(3), unlike Article 92(2), gives the Commission a discretion by providing that the aid which it specifies 'may' be considered to be compatible with the Common Market. On the other hand it would result in Member States being permitted to make payments which would improve the financial situation of the recipient undertaking although they were not necessary for the attainment of the objectives specified in Article 92(3).

18. It should be noted in this connection that the disputed decision explicitly states that the Dutch Government has not been able to give nor has the Commission found any grounds establishing that the proposed aid meets the conditions laid down to enforce derogations pursuant to Article 92(3) of the EEC Treaty.

19. The applicant maintains that the Commission was wrong to hold that the standard of living in the Bergen-op-Zoom area is not 'abnormally low' and that this area does not suffer serious 'under employment' within the meaning of Article 92(3)(a). In fact in the Bergen-op-Zoom region the under-employment rate is higher and the per capita rate lower than the national average in the Netherlands.

. . .

24. These arguments put forward by the applicant cannot be upheld. It should be borne in mind that the Commission has a discretion the exercise of which involves economic and social assessments which must be made in a Community context.

25. That is the context in which the Commission has with good reason assessed the standard of living and serious under-employment in the Bergen-op-Zoom area, not with reference to the national average in the Netherlands but in relation to the Community level.

(ii) Article 87(3)(b)

Article 87(3)(b) states that 'aid to promote the execution of an important project of common European interest or to remedy a serious disturbance in the economy of a Member State' may be considered to be compatible with the common market. This provision covers two types of case.

The first limb has been used for the development of a common standard for high-definition television and environmental protection, but the ECJ takes the wording of Article 87(3)(b) seriously, as is evident from *Glaverbel*.

Cases 62 and 72/87 **Executif Régional Wallon and Glaverbel SA v. Commission**
[1988] ECR 1573

The Belgian Government gave aid to certain glass producers. The applicants argued that the aid could come within Article 92(3)(b), since the new technology made possible by the investment aid would reduce European dependence on American and Japanese producers in the relevant markets.

THE ECJ

21. It should be observed that the categories of aid set out in Article 92(3) . . . 'may' be considered by the Commission to be compatible with the Common Market. It follows that the Commission enjoys a discretion in the matter.

23. . . . The Commission has based its policy with regard to aid on the view that a project may not be described as being of common European interest for the purposes of Article 92(3)(b) unless it forms part of a transnational European programme supported jointly by a number of governments of the Member States, or arises from concerted action by a number of Member States to combat a common threat such as environmental pollution.

In adopting that policy and in taking the view that the investments envisaged in this case did not fulfil the requisite conditions, the Commission did not commit a manifest error of judgment.

24. The two applicants further complain that the Commission failed to give any reasons in the contested decision for its negative assessment. . . .

25. The Court considers that a statement of reasons which is based on a supposedly 'clear' fact must generally be regarded as insufficient. In this case, however, the applicants' arguments cannot be accepted. None of the documents laid before the Court lends any support whatever to the conclusion that the aid at issue might contribute to the implementation of an 'important' project of 'common' European interest. The mere fact that the investments enabled new technology to be used does not make the project one of common European interest; that certainly cannot be the case when, as in this instance, the products have to be sold on a saturated market.

The second limb of this Article concerning serious disturbance to the economy of a Member State will only rarely be used, since the economic problem must afflict the whole of the national economy.[126] More specific problems are dealt with under Article 87(3)(a) or (c).

(iii) *Article 87(3)(c)*

Article 87(3)(c) is in many ways the most significant of the discretionary exceptions. It provides that 'aid to facilitate the development of certain economic activities or of certain economic areas, where such aid does not adversely affect trading conditions to an extent contrary to the common interest' may be compatible with the common market.

It allows aid to be legitimated by reference to the needs of a particular industrial sector,[127] and by reference to economic areas,[128] which the Commission has recognized can have a national, and not just a Community, dimension.[129] Thus Article 87(3)(c) is the provision through which a State can seek to justify aid to a particular depressed region as judged by national criteria.[130] It is still necessary to consider the impact of the aid on Community trade, and its sectoral repercussions at Community level.[131]

---

[126] Cases C–57 and 61/00 P *Freistaat Sachsen*, n. 122 above.
[127] Evans, n. 61 above, ch. 5.
[128] *Ibid.*, ch. 4.
[129] Guidelines, n. 124 above, paras. 21–23.
[130] Case 248/84 *Germany* v. *Commission*, n. 123 above, para. 19.
[131] Cases T–126–127/96 *BFM and EFIM* v. *Commission* [1998] ECR II–3437; Cases T–132 and 143/96 *Freistaat Sachsen*, n. 122 above.

The regional aid must form part of a well-defined regional policy of the State and conform to the principle of geographical concentration. Moreover, given that such aid will benefit regions that are less disadvantaged than those to which Article 87(3)(a) relates, the Commission interprets the geographic scope of the exception and the intensity of the aid strictly, with the consequence that only a small part of the national territory may normally qualify for aid under Article 87(3)(c).[132] The selection of the eligible regions is based on a two-stage process, which considers the maximum population coverage for each Member State and then the selection of the eligible regions.[133]

The Community Courts and Commission have, moreover, made it clear that aid will not normally qualify under this Article unless it is linked to initial investment, to job creation,[134] and/or to a restructuring of the activities of the undertaking concerned.[135] The purpose of the aid must be to develop a particular sector or region and not merely a specific undertaking therein.[136] The ECJ's interpretation of Article 87(3)(c) is evident in *Glaverbel*.

Cases 62 and 72/87 Executif Régional Wallon and Glaverbel SA v. Commission
[1988] ECR 1573

The facts of the case have been given above. It was argued that the Commission had misapplied Article 92(3)(c). The Commission had found that the aid in question, which was for periodic plant renovation, did not satisfy the requirements for the development of the relevant sector without adversely affecting trading conditions to an extent contrary to the common interest.

THE ECJ

31. It is apparent from the points made by the Commission that it based its decision on the view that the investment in question was intended to renovate a float line and that such renovation, which must be carried out periodically, cannot be regarded as designed to facilitate the development of certain economic activities, even if such renovation entails the introduction of new technology. The Commission goes on to consider that, even if such renovation could constitute a new technical development which could be regarded as economic development within the meaning of Article 92(3)(c), it could not warrant an exemption under that provision in the case of the float-glass industry because, in view of the unused capacity in that industry, the aid would affect the position of other undertakings and would thus be contrary to the common interest.

32. It must be stated first of all that that line of reasoning is comprehensible and enables those concerned to ascertain the reasons for the Commission's adverse decision and the Court to review them. The complaint of insufficient reasons must therefore be rejected.

33. As far as the application of Article 92(3)(c) is concerned, it should be observed first of all that the applicants did not challenge the facts on which the Commission relied. In particular,

---

[132] Guidelines, n. 124 above, para. 22.

[133] *Ibid.*, paras. 23–32.

[134] Evans, n. 61 above, 176.

[135] Cases C–278–280/92 *Spain* v. *Commission* [1994] ECR I–4103; Cases T–126–127/96 *BFM*, n. 131 above; Case C–42/93 *Spain* v. *Commission*, n. 103 above; Guidelines, n. 124 above, paras. 1–7, 76–83; Evans, n. 61 above, 186–188.

[136] *Ibid.*, 181–184. The Commission's general approach was approved in Case 248/84 *Germany* v. *Commission*, n. 123 above.

they acknowledged that a float line must be periodically renovated and that, in this instance, the plant in question had to be renovated. . . .

34. It should also be borne in mind that the Commission enjoys a power of appraisal in applying Article 92(3)(c) as well as in applying Article 92(3)(b). It is, in particular, for the Commission to determine whether trading conditions between the Member States are affected by aid 'to an extent contrary to the common interest'. The applicants have supplied no evidence to suggest that in making that assessment the Commission misused its powers or committed a manifest error.

35. It follows from the foregoing that the complaints concerning the alleged infringement of Article 92(3)(c) and the insufficiency of the reasons given in that regard must be rejected.

It should not, however, be thought that the ECJ always upholds the Commission. It will take seriously allegations that the Commission's decision is contradictory or that it has provided insufficient justification for its findings. This is exemplified by the *Intermills* case.[137]

Case 323/82 **Intermills SA v. Commission**
[1984] ECR 3809

The Commission held that aid granted by the Belgian Government in the form of shareholdings did not qualify for exemption, because it was not directly linked to the restructuring of the undertaking, but was rescue aid, intended to allow the undertaking to meet its financial commitments. Such aid could, said the Commission, do serious damage to competition in the Community. The applicants argued that the aid in the form of shareholdings was not rescue aid, and that it was used to finance the closure of unprofitable factories, combined with the conversion of others to products with a better prospect of profitability.

THE ECJ

33. . . . the criticism raised by the applicants appears to be well founded, inasmuch as the contested decision does indeed contain contradictions and does not make clear the grounds for the Commission's action on certain vital points. Such doubts and contradictions relate both to the economic justification for the aid and the question whether the aid was likely to distort competition within the Common Market.

34. First, as regards the economic justification for the aid, the Commission concedes in the statement of reasons on which its decision is based that the restructuring aimed at by the applicants corresponds, as such, to the Commission's own objectives for the European paper industry. That factor seems to be the chief ground on which the Commission recognised the compatibility with the Treaty of the aid granted in the form of low interest loans and advances.

35. On the other hand, the Commission gave no verifiable reasons to justify its finding that the holding acquired by the public authorities in the capital of the recipient undertaking was not compatible with the Treaty. It merely stated that that holding was 'not directly linked to the restructuring operation' and in view of the losses suffered by the undertaking over several

---

[137] See also Case 248/84 *Germany v. Commission*, n. 123 above; Cases 296 and 318/82 *Leeuwarder Papierwarenfabriek*, n. 102 above.

financial years, constituted purely financial 'rescue aid'; ... In making those assessments ... the Commission did not properly explain why its assessment of the restructuring operation in question ... called for such a clear-cut distinction between the effect of the aid granted in the form of subsidised loans and the effect of the aid granted in the form of capital holdings.

...

37. In relation to its claim that the contested aid damages competition in the Common Market, the Commission referred to the provisions of Article 92(1) and to the requirement in Article 92(3), according to which aid may be exempted only if it does not adversely affect trading conditions to an extent contrary to the common interest.

38. As regards the first part of that requirement, the relevant paragraphs of the preamble to the decision merely note the objections raised by the Governments of three Member States, two trade associations and an undertaking in the paper industry. Apart from that reference, the decision gives no concrete indication of the way in which the aid in question damages competition.

39. As regards the second part of the requirement, the Commission, having stated that the aid granted in the form of a capital holding is not directly linked to the restructuring of the undertaking but constitutes 'rescue aid', asserts that such aid 'threatens to do serious damage to the conditions of competition, as the free interplay of market forces would normally call for the closure of the undertaking, allowing more competitive firms to develop'. On that point it must be stated that the settlement of an undertaking's debts in order to ensure its survival does not necessarily adversely affect trading conditions to an extent contrary to the common interest, as provided in Article 92(3), where such an operation is, for example, accompanied by a restructuring plan. In this case, the Commission has not shown why the applicant's activities on the market, following the conversion of its production with the assistance of the aid granted, were likely to have such an adverse effect on trading conditions that the undertaking's disappearance would have been preferable to its rescue.

40. On those grounds, the contested decision must be declared void.

(iv) *Article 87(3)(d) and (e)*

Article 87(3)(d) was added by the TEU. It provides that aid to promote culture and heritage conservation may be compatible with the common market, where such aid does not affect trading conditions and competition in the Community to an extent that is contrary to the common interest.

Article 87(3)(e) constitutes a safety net by providing that such other categories of aid as may be specified by decision of the Council acting by a qualified majority on a proposal from the Commission may be deemed to be compatible with the common market. A number of directives on aid to shipbuilding have been adopted pursuant to this Article.

6. STATE AIDS: THE PROCEDURAL RULES AND ARTICLES 88 AND 89

The procedural rules that apply in this area are derived from the relevant Treaty articles, the case law of the ECJ and CFI, and from Regulation 659/99.[138]

---

138 Council Reg. 659/1999 of 22 Mar. 1999 laying down detailed rules for the application of Article 93 of the Treaty [1999] OJ L83/1.

(a) REVIEW OF EXISTING STATE AIDS

It is readily apparent that the Community has an interest in keeping under review aid granted by Member States, even if the Commission has given the green light to it under Article 87(3). Article 88(1) provides that:

> The Commission shall, in co-operation with Member States, keep under constant review all systems of aid existing in those states. It shall propose to the latter any appropriate measures required by the progressive development or by the functioning of the common market.

There are a number of categories of existing aid. These may be regarded as existing aid because of ECJ case law[139] and Regulation 659/99.[140]

(a) Aid which existed before the entry into force of the Treaty.

(b) Aid which has been given the green light under Article 87(3).[141] Individual disbursement of aid pursuant to a general aid scheme that has been approved by the Commission counts as existing aid, provided that it comes properly within the general scheme.[142]

(c) Aid which has been notified to the Commission pursuant to Article 88(3), where the Commission has taken no action within the requisite time.

(d) Aid that is not recoverable because the limitation period has expired.

(e) Aid deemed to be existing aid because it did not initially constitute aid, and only became so due to the evolution of the common market.[143] Where certain measures become aid following the liberalization of an activity by Community law, such measures are considered existing aid after the date fixed for the liberalization.

(b) THE PROCEDURE FOR NEW STATE AIDS: NOTIFICATION AND PRELIMINARY REVIEW

In order for monitoring of state aids to be effective, it is essential for the Commission to be notified of any aid proposal. Article 88 therefore establishes a two-stage procedure for state aids.

Stage one concerns prior notification of any plan to grant aid and preliminary investigation by the Commission. This is provided for in Article 88(3):

> The Commission shall be informed, in sufficient time to enable it to submit its comments, of any plans to grant or alter aid. If it considers that any such plan is not compatible with the common market having regard to Article 87, it shall without delay initiate the procedure provided for in paragraph 2. The Member State concerned shall not put its proposed measures into effect until this procedure has resulted in a final decision.

---

[139] Case C–44/93 Namur—Les Assurances du Crédit SA v. Office National du Ducroire and Belgian State [1994] ECR I–3829; Cases T–195 and 207/01 Gibraltar v. Commission [2002] ECR II–2309.

[140] Art. 1.

[141] The Commission can review an existing aid scheme and decide that it is no longer compatible with the common market: Reg. 659/99, n. 138 above, Arts. 17–18.

[142] Case C–47/91 Italy v. Commission [1994] ECR I–4635.

[143] Cases T–298 etc./97 Alzetta Mauro, n. 120 above, para. 143.

Member States are therefore under a duty to notify the Commission of any aid prior to granting it.[144] The Member States cannot implement the grant of aid during the period in which the Commission undertakes its initial review of the proposed aid.[145] The Commission must come to some preliminary view within two months. If it does not do so the State is entitled to carry through its aid proposal, after having notified the Commission.[146] The Commission can request further information if it believes that the information supplied is incomplete.[147]

The Commission at this early stage engages in a preliminary review of the aid proposal.[148] It may decide to approve the aid, in which case it notifies the Member State and the latter will implements the aid proposal. The ECJ has emphasized that the preliminary-review procedure is 'meant to be just that'.[149] It is to take no more than two months, and if there are difficulties in reaching a decision within this time then the Commission should proceed to the more complete review in Article 88(2). This is important since other parties are entitled to be consulted under Article 88(2), but have no such rights under Article 88(3).[150]

Moreover, the Commission can resolve a case under Article 88(3) only where it is clear that the aid is compatible with the common market. Where there are serious difficulties in deciding whether aid is compatible with the common market, the fuller investigation under Article 88(2) should be used.[151]

(c) THE PROCEDURE FOR STATE AIDS: DETAILED INVESTIGATION AND ENFORCEMENT

Stage two is based on the assumption that the Commission has not been able to give the green light to the state-aid proposal under Article 88(3). In these circumstances Article 88(2) applies:

> If, after giving notice to the parties concerned to submit their comments, the Commission finds that aid granted by a State or through State resources is not compatible with the common market having regard to Article 87, or that such aid is being misused, it shall decide that the State concerned shall abolish or alter such aid within a period of time to be determined by the Commission.
>
> If the State concerned does not comply with the decision within the prescribed time, the Commission or any other interested State may, in derogation from the provisions of Articles 226 and 227, refer the matter to the Court of Justice direct.

---

[144] Reg. 659/99, n. 138 above, Art. 2.

[145] Case 120/73 *Gebrüder Lorenz GmbH* v. *Germany* [1973] ECR 1471; Case 84/82 *Germany* v. *Commission* [1984] ECR 1451; Reg. 659/99, n. 138 above, Art. 3. The Commission must also be notified of any amendment to the aid proposal: Cases 91 and 127/83 *Heineken Brouwerijen BV* v. *Inspecteur der Vennootschapsbelasting* [1984] ECR 3435.

[146] Case 84/82 *Germany* v. *Commission* [1984] ECR 1451; Reg. 659/99, n. 138 above, Art. 4(5).

[147] *Ibid.*, Art. 5.

[148] *Ibid.*, Art. 4.

[149] Case 120/73 *Gebrüder Lorenz*, n. 145 above; Case 84/82 *Germany* v. *Commission*, n. 146 above; Case T–171/02 *Regione Autonoma della Sardegna*, n. 62 above, paras. 31–32.

[150] *Ibid.*; Case C–198/91 *William Cook plc* v. *Commission* [1993] ECR I–2486; Cases T–195 and 207/01 *Gibraltar* v. *Commission*, n. 139 above.

[151] Case C–367/95 P *Commission* v. *Sytraval and Brink's France Sarl* [1998] ECR I–1719, para. 39; Case C–204/97 *Portugal* v. *Commission* [2001] ECR I–3175, para. 33; Case T–158/99 *Thermenhotel Stoiser Franz Gesellschaft mbh & Co. KG* v. *Commission* [2004] ECR II–1, paras. 59–61.

Article 88(2) applies both to existing aids in relation to which questions have been raised pursuant to Article 88(1), and to new aids that have not been given the green light pursuant to the preliminary investigation under Article 88(3). If an existing aid is found to be incompatible with the common market as the result of a review under Article 88(1) then it will be unlawful from the date set for compliance with that decision. In the case of a new aid, the effect of the decision made under Article 88(2) will be to render permanent the temporary prohibition which flows from Article 88(3), unless the Member State can at some future date show that the circumstances have changed. In either eventuality the procedure described in Article 88(2) comes into operation.

A notice will be placed in the Official Journal inviting parties concerned to submit their comments. The Commission will summarize the relevant issues of fact and law, setting out its doubts about the compatibility of the aid with the common market.[152] The phrase 'parties concerned' covers the undertakings receiving aid and others whose interests may be affected by the grant of the aid, in particular competitors and trade associations.[153] The participation rights of such parties are, however, limited. They cannot engage in an adversarial debate with the Commission in the manner open to the party against which the formal investigation has been initiated.[154] The period for comment will, normally, not exceed one month.[155]

Commission findings pursuant to formal investigations are made by decisions. The Commission may decide that the aid is compatible, or incompatible, with the common market. It may attach conditions to a positive decision.[156] The Commission can revoke its decision where it was based on incorrect information that was a determining factor in the decision.[157] The rationale for the more expedited enforcement process contained in the second paragraph of Article 88(2) is that the Commission has already had the opportunity to make its views known, and because the parties themselves have already been heard. While Article 88(2) therefore provides a speedier method of enforcement against a recalcitrant State, the Court has set itself against any further modification of the enforcement process.[158]

(d) EXCEPTIONAL CIRCUMSTANCES: ARTICLE 88(2), PARAGRAPHS 3 AND 4

The third and fourth paragraphs of Article 88(2) make provision for aid to be granted in certain exceptional circumstances in derogation from the provisions of Article 87. The ECJ has construed this provision narrowly.[159]

> On application by a Member State, the Council may, acting unanimously, decide that aid which that State is granting or intends to grant shall be considered to be compatible with the common

---

[152] Reg. 659/99, n. 138 above, Art. 6.

[153] Case 323/82 *Intermills*, n. 101 above, para. 16; Case C–198/91 *William Cook*, n. 150 above, para. 24; Case C–78/03 P *Commission* v. *Aktionsgemeinschaft Recht und Eigentum eV* [2005] ECR I–10737, paras. 31–37; Case T–395/04 *Air One SpA* v. *Commission* [2006] ECR II–1343, paras. 24–41; Reg. 659/99, n. 138 above, Art. 20(1).

[154] Case C–367/95 P *Sytraval*, n. 151 above, para. 59; Cases 74 and 75/00 P *Falck SpA* v. *Commission* [2002] ECR I–7689, para. 82; Case T–109/01 *Fleuren Compost BV* v. *Commission* [2004] ECR II–127, paras. 40–44; Case T–228 and 233/99 *Westdeutsche Landesbank*, n. 62 above, paras. 123–125.

[155] Reg. 659/99, n. 138 above, Art. 6(1).

[156] *Ibid.*, Art. 7.

[157] *Ibid.*, Art. 9.

[158] Case C–292/90 *British Aerospace plc and Rover Group Holdings plc* v. *Commission* [1992] ECR I–493.

[159] Case C–110/02 *Commission* v. *Council* [2004] ECR I–6333.

market, in derogation from the provisions of Article 87 or from the regulations provided for in Article 89, if such a decision is justified by exceptional circumstances. If, as regards the aid in question, the Commission has already initiated the procedure provided for in the first sub-paragraph of this paragraph, the fact that the State concerned made its application to the Council shall have the effect of suspending that procedure until the Council has made its attitude known.

If, however, the Council has not made its attitude known within three months of the said application being made, the Commission shall give its decision on the case.

(e) ARTICLE 89: IMPLEMENTING REGULATIONS

Article 89 empowers the Council, acting by qualified majority on a proposal from the Commission, and after consulting the Parliament, to make any appropriate regulations for the application of Articles 87 and 88, and in particular to determine the conditions under which Article 88(3) shall apply and the categories of aid exempted from this procedure. Article 89 has been used relatively rarely, and the Commission has sought to rely on soft law and adjudication to develop policy in this area.[160] Article 89 was, however, the basis for the Council regulation empowering the Commission to make regulations about certain categories of aid.[161]

(f) CHALLENGE TO COMMISSION DECISIONS

Challenges to Commission decisions will normally be brought under Article 230 to annul the decision.[162] The most common applicants are the State whose aid has been found to be incompatible with the common market, the undertakings that are the intended beneficiaries of this aid, and competitors. Applicants will have to satisfy the requirements of Article 230 in order to proceed.[163] They will have to show that the action complained of produces legal effects.[164] The time limit of two months will, in general, run from the date when the decision was published in the Official Journal.[165]

The State will, of course, have standing, as will a regional body that set up an aid programme condemned by the Commission.[166] The intended recipient of the aid has been readily admitted to plead the case,[167] and the Court has afforded standing to interveners who have submitted comments to the Commission and who would be likely to suffer harm if the aid

---

[160] Evans, n. 61 above, 405–427.

[161] Council Reg. 994/98 [1998] OJ L142/1.

[162] U. Soltesz and H. Bielesz, 'Judicial Review of State Aid Decisions—Recent Developments' [2004] *ECLR* 133. Actions for failure to act under Art. 232 will be difficult to sustain, since the applicant must show an obligation to act by the Commission: Case T–277/94 *Associazione Italiana Tecnico Economica del Cemento (AITEC)* v. *Commission* [1996] ECR II–351. The Commission must, however, consider diligently whether it should act on a complaint: Case T–95/96 *Gestevision Telecinco SA* v. *Commission* [1998] ECR II–3407. For the use of Art. 241 see Case T–82/96 *Associacao dos Refinadores de Acucar Portugueses (ARAP)* v. *Commission* [1999] ECR II–1889.

[163] In Case C–47/90 *Italy* v. *Commission* [1992] ECR I–4145, the ECJ held that the Commission's decision to open the Art. 88(2) procedure was a reviewable act which could be challenged before the Court.

[164] Case C–400/99 *Italy* v. *Commission* [2001] ECR I–7303, para. 62.

[165] Case T–11/95 *BP Chemicals Ltd.* v. *Commission* [1998] ECR II–3235.

[166] Case T–288/97 *Regione Autonoma Friuli-Venezia Giulia* v. *Commission* [1999] ECR II–1871.

[167] Case 730/79 *Philip Morris*, n. 117 above; Case 323/82 *Intermills*, n. 101 above.

were to be given to the targeted firm.[168] Economic operators that played a significant role in the Article 88(2) procedure have been held to be individually concerned, when they have been affected in their capacity as negotiators.[169] The fact that a party has taken part in the Article 88(2) procedure will not, however, suffice to be accorded standing under Article 230.[170] Moreover, where an undertaking has not exercised its right to submit comments under Article 88(2), it must, in the context of an annulment action, prove that it is individually concerned within Article 230(4). The mere fact that the undertaking is in a competitive relationship with the beneficiary of the aid does not mean that it will be regarded as individually concerned.[171]

An important point concerning the availability of review was affirmed in *William Cook*.[172] We have already seen that interested parties do not have consultation rights under Article 88(3) during the preliminary examination phase, but do have such rights under Article 88(2). This may be problematic if the Commission finds that an aid is compatible with the Common Market under Article 88(3), but an interested party disagrees and believes that the more thorough investigation under Article 88(2) should have been initiated. In *William Cook* the Court held that the *procedural guarantees* in Article 88(2) could, in such a situation, only be properly safeguarded if such parties were able to challenge the Commission's decision before the Court.[173] However, if the applicant seeks to contest the *merits* of the decision appraising the aid, the mere fact that it is a party concerned within Article 88(2) will not suffice to render the action admissible. The applicant must still show individual concern within the *Plaumann* test, as for example where the applicant competitor's market position is substantially affected by the aid to which the decision relates.[174]

The substantive grounds for challenge are set out in Article 230. The legality of a measure is decided on the basis of the facts and law existing when the measure was adopted.[175] It is common for applicants to argue that the Commission's decision is in breach of one of the general principles of Community law, that the reasoning is defective, or that the Commission has misinterpreted the meaning of one of the phrases in the relevant Treaty Articles. However the Court possesses considerable discretion as to the intensity with which it will apply the various grounds mentioned in Article 230. The ECJ will often make reference to the Commission's considerable discretion concerning state aids, and will normally overturn such a decision only if the applicant can show a procedural defect, deficiency of reasoning, factual inaccuracy, a manifest error in assessing the facts, or some misuse of power.[176]

(g) AID THAT HAS NOT BEEN NOTIFIED

The consequences of a failure by a Member State to notify in accordance with Article 88(3) must be separately evaluated in relation to the Commission and the national courts.

---

[168] Case 169/84 *COFAZ v. Commission* [1986] ECR 391; Case C–198/91 *William Cook*, n. 150 above; Case T–380/94 *AIUFFASS v. Commission* [1996] ECR II–2169. Cf. Case T–11/95 *BP*, n. 165 above.

[169] Case C–313/90 *CIRFS*, n. 75 above.

[170] Case C–106/98 *SNRT-CGT, SURT-CFDT and SNEA-CFE-CGC v. Commission* [2000] ECR I–3659.

[171] Case T–11/95 *BP*, n. 165 above.

[172] Case C–198/91 *William Cook*, n. 150 above.

[173] See also Case C–225/91 *Matra*, n. 99 above, Case C–367/95 P *Sytraval*, n. 151 above, paras. 40–41; Case T–158/99 *Thermenhotel*, n. 151 above, para. 73; Case C–78/03 P *Aktionsgemeinschaft Recht und Eigentum*, n. 153 above, para. 35.

[174] *Ibid.*, para. 37; Case T–395/04 *Air One*, n. 153 above, para. 32.

[175] Case T–110/97 *Kneissl Dachstein Sportartikel AG v. Commission* [1999] ECR II–2881.

[176] N. 62 above.

(i) *Non-notification and the Commission*

In relation to the Commission, the ECJ held that failure to notify does not in itself render implementation of the aid unlawful.[177] It held that the Commission has the power, after giving the Member State the opportunity for comment, to issue an interim decision requiring the State to suspend immediately the payment of the aid, pending the outcome of the Commission's determination of whether the aid was compatible with the common market.[178]

If in the light of this request for information the State still refused to supply the requisite material, the Commission could then make an assessment of the compatibility of the aid on the basis of the information available to it. This decision could demand the recovery of aid that had been paid. It was also suggested that the Commission should be able to require immediate repayment of the aid.[179]

These principles have been enshrined in Regulation 659/99. Where the Commission has information from any source regarding alleged unlawful aid, then it must examine it without delay.[180] It can request information from the relevant State. The Commission may, after allowing the State to comment, make a decision requiring the State to suspend the aid until the Commission has taken a decision on its compatibility with the common market. This is termed a 'suspension injunction'.[181] The Commission may, after allowing the State to comment, make a decision requiring the State to recover the aid, pending a decision by the Commission on its compatibility with the common market. This is known as a 'recovery injunction'.[182]

These injunctions may be ordered only where it is clear that there is aid, it is a matter of urgency, and there is a serious risk of substantial and irreparable damage to a competitor. Non-compliance with either type of injunction can lead to an action before the ECJ.[183] The Commission can make its substantive decisions on such aid by way of preliminary review, or by means of the formal procedure. In either eventuality, the normal time limits do not apply.[184] If the Commission decides that the aid is not compatible with the common market, it can issue a 'recovery decision'. This obliges the Member State to take all necessary measures to recover the aid from the beneficiary. This shall not be required if it would be contrary to a general principle of Community law.[185]

(ii) *Non-notification and National Courts*

The position of the national court in relation to aid that has not been notified is somewhat different. The Commission sees national courts and itself as having complementary roles in this area, and its Notice builds upon the ECJ's case law.[186]

The ECJ has established that the duty not to implement aid before notification to the Commission, and before the Commission has undertaken its preliminary investigation under

---

177 Case C–301/87 *France* v. *Commission* [1990] ECR I–307.
178 Case C–75/97 *Belgium* v. *Commission*, n. 94 above.
179 Case C–42/93 *Spain* v. *Commission*, n. 103 above, Jacobs AG; Evans, n. 61 above, 436.
180 Reg. 659/99, n. 138 above, Art. 10(1). The Commission may also re-open a case where aid has been misused: Art. 16.
181 *Ibid.*, Art. 11(1).
182 *Ibid.*, Art. 11(2).
183 *Ibid.*, Art. 12.
184 *Ibid.*, Art. 13.
185 *Ibid.*, Art. 14.
186 Notice on Co-operation between National Courts and the Commission in the State Aid Field [1995] OJ C312/8.

Article 88(3), is directly effective.[187] The ECJ has also held[188] that, although a national court which is enforcing Article 88(3) cannot rule on the compatibility of the aid with the common market, this being for the Commission, the national court should, nonetheless, rule aid to be illegal when it has not been notified as required by this Article. The direct effect of Article 88(3) demanded that the rights of the individual should be protected in this manner. Moreover any later Commission decision which found that the aid was compatible with Article 87 would not be retrospective in effect.

(h) RECOVERY OF UNLAWFUL AID

The Court has, not surprisingly, held that, as a matter of principle, illegal state aids should be repaid, this being the logical consequence of a finding that the aid was unlawful.[189] The peremptory force of this obligation will not easily be deflected by claims that repayment of the aid entails difficulties for the recipient.

Case 52/84 **Commission v. Belgium**
[1986] ECR 89

[Note ToA renumbering: Arts. 5 and 173 are now Arts. 10 and 230]

The Commission had found that the acquisition by a public regional holding company of shares in a firm manufacturing ceramic ware constituted state aid, and ordered that it should be withdrawn since it considered that it was incompatible with the common market. The Belgian Government did not contest this decision, but it stressed the serious social consequences of closing down the undertaking, and it stated that Belgian law did not allow share capital to be refunded except by way of withdrawal of company profits, and no such profits were available. The Government also requested clarification from the Commission of what it meant by 'withdrawal of aid'. The ECJ held that the Belgian Government was outside the time limit for challenging the decision under Article 173. It then proceeded as follows.

THE ECJ

14. In those circumstances the only defence left to the Belgian Government in opposing the Commission's application for a declaration that it failed to fulfil its Treaty obligations would be to plead that it was absolutely impossible for it to implement the decision properly. In this connection it should be noted that the decision demands the withdrawal from the undertaking of a capital holding of 475 million Bfr . . .; that demand is sufficiently precise to be complied with. The fact that, on account of the undertaking's financial position, the Belgian authorities could not recover the sum paid does not constitute proof that implementation was impossible,

---

[187] Case 120/73 *Lorenz*, n. 145 above; Cases 91 and 127/83 *Heineken*, n. 145 above; Case C–143/99 *Adria-Wien*, n. 93 above, paras. 26–27; Case C–295/97 *Industrie Aeronautiche e Meccaniche Rinaldo Piaggio SpA* v. *International Factors SpA* [1999] ECR I–3735; Case C–345/02 *Pearle*, n. 109 above, paras. 30–32.

[188] Case C–354/90 *Fédération Nationale du Commerce Exterieur des Produits Alimentaires* v. *France* [1991] ECR I–5505; Cases C–34 and 38/01 *Enirisorse*, n. 106 above, para. 42.

[189] Case 310/85 *Deufil*, n. 77 above; Case C–277/00 *Germany* v. *Commission*, n. 122 above, paras. 74–76.

because the Commission's objective was to abolish the aid and, as the Belgian Government itself admits, that objective could be attained by proceedings for winding up the company, which the Belgian authorities could institute in their capacity as shareholder or creditor.

. . .

16. It should be added that the fact that the only defence which a Member State to which a decision has been addressed can raise in legal proceedings such as these is that implementation of the decision is absolutely impossible does not prevent that State—if, in giving effect to the decision, it encounters unforeseen or unforeseeable difficulties or perceives consequences overlooked by the Commission—from submitting those problems for consideration by the Commission, together with proposals for suitable amendments. In such a case the Commission and the Member State concerned must respect the principle underlying Article 5 of the Treaty, which imposes a duty of genuine co-operation on the Member States and Community institutions; accordingly, they must work together in good faith with a view to overcoming difficulties whilst fully observing the Treaty provisions, and in particular the provisions on aid. However, in the present instance none of the difficulties referred to by the Belgian Government is of that nature, and that Government made no proposals whatever to the Commission for the adoption of other suitable measures.

The message from the Court was clear. The only exception to the primary obligation to obtain repayment of the illegal aid was where recovery was absolutely impossible, and this was narrowly defined. If the recipient company had to be wound up, so be it. Even where the exception to the primary obligation comes into play, the State is not let off the hook entirely. There is a secondary obligation derived from Article 10, requiring the State to enter into a serious dialogue with the Commission to resolve the problem. The same uncompromising approach is apparent in other cases.[190]

Nor have applicants fared any better by relying on the concept of legitimate expectations. Thus in *Deufil*[191] the ECJ rejected the argument that the existence of a Commission guideline setting out the policy which it intended to adopt in approving state aids in a certain area gave rise to a legitimate expectation that, if a product was not included in the guideline, then aid in relation to that product would not have to be approved. In *Commission v. Germany*[192] the ECJ held that recipients of aid could not have a legitimate expectation that the aid was lawful, unless it had been granted in accordance with the procedure in Article 88. A diligent businessman should normally be able to determine whether that procedure had been followed. Moreover, the Court emphasized that a Member State which had granted aid contrary to the Treaty could not rely on any legitimate expectations of the recipients to justify refusal to recover the sums. Furthermore national concepts such as legitimate expectations could not be relied upon if the effect was to make it impossible to recover the aid, as where the national doctrine set time limits for the revocation of administrative acts. The ECJ has nonetheless recognized that there might be exceptional circumstances where recovery of aid should not be ordered.[193]

---

[190] Case C–142/87 [1990] ECR I–959; Case C–378/98 *Commission* v. *Belgium* [2001] ECR I–5107; Case C–261/99 *Commission* v. *France* [2001] ECR I–2537.

[191] Case 310/85 *Deufil*, n. 77 above.

[192] Case C–5/89 *Commission* v. *Germany* [1990] ECR I–3437; Case C–24/95 *Land Rheinland-Pfalz* v. *Alcan Deutschland GmbH* [1997] ECR I–1591; Case T–171/02 *Regione Autonoma della Sardegna*, n. 62 above, para. 64; Cases T–116 and 118/01 *P & O Ferries (Vizcaya) SA and another* v. *Commission* [2003] ECR II–2957, paras. 201–205, upheld in Cases C–442 and 471/03 [2006] ECR I–4845.

[193] Case C–354/90 *Fédération Nationale*, n. 188 above; Case C–39/94 *SFEI*, n. 93 above.

7. STATE AIDS, MARKET INTEGRATION, AND REGIONAL POLICY

(a) THE RELATIONSHIP BETWEEN ARTICLE 28 AND ARTICLES 87–89

The provisions concerning state aids do not exist in a legal or political vacuum. The ECJ has considered the relationship between them and other Treaty provisions.[194] It is clear that the ECJ's perception of this relationship has broader implications for the balance between market integration and regional policy in the EU.

The most interesting point of interconnection is the relationship between Articles 87–89 and Article 28. The ECJ's approach has altered over time. In *Ianelli & Volpi*[195] it held that if some aspects of aid that might contravene Treaty provisions other than Articles 87–89 were so closely linked to the latter, then it would not be possible to evaluate them separately. However, where certain aspects of an aid scheme were not integral to its operation, then they could be subject to scrutiny under other Treaty provisions. In this sense the Court articulated a severability test.

In its later case law the Court appears to have been more ready to apply Article 28, without too delicate an inquiry into whether the measure caught by this Article was an integral part of the aid scheme or not. In *Commission* v. *France*[196] the Court examined the legality of a measure which gave newspaper publishers tax exemptions on the condition that the papers were printed in France. The Commission argued that this constituted a breach of Article 28. The French Government argued that if its measures constituted aid they should be considered under Article 87, since the tax provisions could not be separated from the general aid scheme for the newspaper industry. The ECJ was unconvinced. It noted that France had never notified its scheme in accordance with Article 88(3). It then proffered the following strong statement of principle:[197]

[I]t should be pointed out that Articles 92 and 94 cannot, as is clear from a long line of cases decided by the Court, be used to frustrate the rules of the Treaty on the free movement of goods or the rules on the repeal of discriminatory tax provisions. According to those cases, the provisions relating to the free movement of goods, the repeal of discriminatory tax provisions and aid have a common objective, namely to ensure the free movement of goods between Member States under normal conditions of competition.... The mere fact that a national measure may possibly be defined as aid within the meaning of Article 92 is therefore not an adequate reason for exempting it from the prohibition contained in Article 30. The argument relating to the Community rules on aid, which the French Republic in any case raised only by way of hypothesis in reply to the observations of the Commission, therefore cannot be accepted.

---

[194] Cases C–149 and 150/91 *Sanders Adour et Guyomarc'h Nutrition Animale* v. *Directeur des Services Fiscaux des Pyrenées-Atlantiques* [1992] ECR I–3899.

[195] Case 74/76 *Ianelli and Volpi SpA* v. *Ditta Paolo Meroni* [1977] ECR 557.

[196] Case 18/84 [1985] ECR 1339. See also Case 249/81 *Commission* v. *Ireland* [1982] ECR 4005.

[197] *Ibid.*, para. 13. References to Arts. 30 and 92–94 should now be read as to Arts. 28 and 87–89.

The Court has persisted with this approach.[198] Thus in *Du Pont de Nemours Italiana*[199] the ECJ considered whether Italian legislation which required that all public bodies obtain at least 30 per cent of their supplies from undertakings established in the Mezzogiorno, where the products were processed, was in breach of Article 28. The referring court asked whether this constituted aid, with the consequence that Article 28 would not be applicable. The ECJ adopted the same 'unitary' view of Articles 28 and 87 as it had done in *Commission* v. *France*: both sets of provisions were designed to ensure the free movement of goods under normal conditions of competition. The fact that a national measure might be considered aid within the meaning of Article 87 did not, therefore, take it outside Article 28. The rule of reason within Article 28 may however legitimate the measure.[200]

The Court's reasoning in these cases has force, but is not unproblematic. It is true that Articles 28 and 87 have in general terms the same objective. Yet the very structure of Articles 87–89 attests to the different way in which fulfilment of this general aim is played out in the context of state aids. These Articles are characterized by the existence of Commission discretion, enabling it to weigh certain social and economic variables in deciding whether aid is compatible with the common market. It is for this very reason that the provisions on state aids are directly effective only to a limited extent. If, in the event of any overlap between Articles 28 and 87, the former is to predominate then it will rule out the type of social balancing which takes place particularly in the context of Article 87(3). Concerns of this nature are apparent in the following extract. The case to which the authors refer is the *Du Pont* decision set out above.

J.F.M. Martin and O. Stehmann, Product Market Integration versus Regional Cohesion in the Community[201]

First of all, one of the grounds on which the Court of Justice justifies its position is that both sets of rules have a common objective, that is to ensure the free movement of goods under normal conditions of competition. Although this is true, it is only partially so. One should not ignore that there is a second objective underlying Articles 92(3) and 93, namely to grant the Commission the possibility to declare compatible with the EEC Treaty those aids which are intended to close the economic, social and regional gaps existing inside the Community. Therefore, the fact that some competition distorting State aids may be permitted to operate proves that certain exceptions to the free movement of goods and to free competition principles are to be admitted. . . .

Secondly, the relation of both sets of rules . . . may have certain undesirable consequences. Whereas this position might be justifiable . . . in those cases in which no prior notification has taken place, applying Article 30 as interpreted in *Dassonville* without engaging in a deeper economic (or other) analysis risks obliterating Articles 92 and 93. After the *Dassonville* definition,

---

[198] In the preceding cases the States in question had not notified the aid in accordance with Art. 88(3). However, in *Du Pont* Italy had notified its scheme to the Commission, but this made no difference to the ECJ's reasoning.

[199] Case C–21/88 *Du Pont de Nemours Italiana SpA* v. *Unità Sanitaria Locale No. 2 di Carrara* [1990] ECR I–889; Case C–351/88 *Laboratori Bruneau Srl* v. *Unità Sanitaria Locale RM/24 de Monterotondo* [1991] ECR I–3641; Case C–156/98 *Germany* v. *Commission* [2000] ECR I–6857, para. 78; Case C–114/00 *Spain* v. *Commission* [2002] ECR I–7657, para. 104.

[200] Case C–379/98 *PreussenElektra AG* v. *Schleswag AG* [2001] ECR I–2099, paras. 70–81.

[201] (1991) 16 *ELRev.* 216, 228–230. References to Arts. 30, 92, and 93 should be read as to Arts. 28, 87, and 88.

almost anything would come under the 'imperium' of Article 30. State aids, by their nature, always have a negative effect on inter-state trade when they strengthen national industry or regions ... If one follows strictly the Court's reasoning of giving priority to the application of Article 30 ... Articles 92 and 93 would lose much of their sense.

Thirdly, from a procedural point of view the Court's reasoning may also bring difficulties. Article 30 is directly applicable while Articles 92 and 93 are not so. ...

From an economic point of view the Court's position leads to favouring rapid market integration—represented by the free movement of goods provisions—to the detriment of regional cohesion—represented by the State aids provisions. ...

(b) THE RELATIONSHIP BETWEEN NATIONAL REGIONAL POLICY AND COMMUNITY REGIONAL POLICY

While there may be concerns at the too-ready application of Article 28, one must be cautious about the more general relationship between national regional-aid policy and that undertaken at the Community level. We must be careful not to condemn the Community for paying insufficient attention to regional problems. Regional[202] and environmental[203] concerns are taken into account within Article 87, and there are Community schemes for regional assistance.

The proper limit of national regional assistance is moreover a contestable issue, since such aid can inhibit market integration. Articles 158 and 159 prioritize greater cohesion within the Community. The attainment of this goal necessitates limits on the grant of aid by the richer Member States to regions that may be poor relative to those States, but not in relation to the Community as a whole. Only in this way will cohesion be possible. It is the larger Member States that spend most on aid to their own industries and regions, and the sums thereby expended exceed the EU's budget for regional policy. The consequence is that 'strict control of State aid in the central, more prosperous, regions is necessary in the interests of cohesion as well as of competition policy'.[204] In a similar vein the Commission has noted the importance of state aid policy for cohesion, 'by preventing a damaging subsidy race between regions, and by creating the right incentives for growth and jobs, in the least developed regions and elsewhere'.[205] However, persuading the richer Member States to increase their contributions to EC spending in the weaker regions is one thing, getting them to refrain in the name of cohesion from spending so much of their own taxpayers' money locally is quite another.

8. STATE AIDS AND REFORM

The Commission instituted a consultation exercise in 2005 designed to reform the state aid regime.[206]

---

[202] F. Wishlade, 'Competition Policy or Cohesion Policy by the Back Door? The Commission Guidelines on National Regional Aid' [1998] *ECLR* 343.

[203] H. Vedder, 'The New Community Guidelines on State Aid for Environmental Protection-Integrating Environment and Competition?' [2001] *ECLR* 365.

[204] A. Petersen, 'State Aid and the European Union: State Aid in the Light of Trade, Competition, Industrial and Cohesion Policies', in Harden (ed.), n. 81 above, 25.

[205] State Aid Action Plan, Less and Better Targeted State Aid: A Roadmap for State Aid Reform 2005–2009, COM(2005)107 final, para. 40.

[206] *Ibid.*

In terms of the substantive coverage of state aids, the Commission reiterated the imperative behind this area of the law, the maintenance of a level playing field between undertakings. It then located the reform exercise within the broader Lisbon agenda[207] of growth and jobs within the EU. The Commission acknowledged that state aid could be legitimate in circumstances of market failure. The more specific reform proposals resonated around that theme. Thus state aid for matters such as innovation, research and development, and risk capital was seen as potentially legitimate where the market failed to provide the requisite incentives to engage in these activities.[208] The Commission was minded to introduce a general block exemption, which could consolidate the existing block exemptions and be applied to other topics, such as aid for research and development.[209] Some of these ideas have already been taken forward.[210]

In terms of the procedure governing state aid, the Commission considered a number of possible improvements, including, *inter alia*, increased efficiency by the Commission in monitoring and enforcement; best practice guidelines; and independent authorities within Member States, which would facilitate enforcement of state aid.

9. CONCLUSION

i.   The Treaty contains a number of Articles that are of especial relevance to the State, and to the way in which it organizes its economic activity. Articles 10, 16, 81, 82, 86, and 87 to 89 are particularly important in this respect.

ii. The Treaty undoubtedly places constraints on state behaviour. Some of this is relatively uncontroversial, such as the control of state aids, and is justified by the need to ensure a level playing field between undertakings. In other areas the Community Courts have had to strike a difficult balance between a State's freedom to organize its economic activities and the impact that this might have on the market, as exemplified by the case law under Article 86. The Community Courts have had to face equally problematic issues concerning the more general relationship between state aids and other provisions of the Treaty, such as those on free movement of goods.

iii. The ECJ and CFI have given a broad reading to the relevant Treaty Articles, have enhanced the competitive process, and demanded a justification from the State for the grant of monopoly or privileged status under Article 86.

iv. However, they have also been more willing, in recent case law to recognize the importance of public-service obligations, and to admit that this is a valid ground for invoking the derogation in Article 86(2). This is reflected in Community legislation on liberalization, which has allowed States to impose such obligations on those providing energy, telecommunications, and the like, and in the proposals for guidelines on state aid to compensate for these obligations. The introduction of Article 16 and the weight accorded to it by the European Council have been of importance in this respect.

---

[207] See above Ch. 5 for discussion of the Lisbon agenda.

[208] State Aid Action Plan, n. 205 above, paras. 25, 27, 30.

[209] *Ibid.*, paras. 35–38.

[210] See, e.g., Community Framework for State Aid for Research and Development and Innovation; Proposal to extend the categories of horizontal aid that can be exempted by amending Reg. 994/98. Both are available at http://ec.europa.eu/comm/competition/state_aid/reform/reform.html.

10. FURTHER READING

(a) Books

Biondi, A., Eeckhout, P., and Flynn, J. (eds.), *The Law of State Aid in the European Union* (Oxford University Press, 2004)

Blum, F., and Logue, A., *State Monopolies under EC Law* (Wiley, 1998)

Buendia Sierra, J., *Exclusive Rights and State Monopolies under EC Law* (Oxford University Press, 1999)

Evans, A., *EC Law of State Aid* (Oxford University Press, 1997)

Hancher, L., Ottervanger, T., and Slot, P.J., *EC State Aids* (3rd edn., Sweet and Maxwell, 2006)

Harden, I. (ed.), *State Aid: Community Law and Policy* (Bundesanzeiger, 1993)

Prosser, T., *The Limits of Competition Law, Markets and Public Services* (Oxford University Press, 2005)

Sauter, W., *Competition Law and Industrial Policy in the EU* (Clarendon Press, 1997)

(b) Articles

Edward, D., and Hoskins, M., 'Article 90: Deregulation and EC Law, Reflections Arising from the XVI FIDE Conference' (1995) 32 *CMLRev.* 157

Ehlermann, C.-D., 'The Contribution of EC Competition Policy to the Single Market' (1992) 29 *CMLRev.* 257

Garcia, E., 'Public Service, Public Services, Public Functions and Guarantees of the Rights of Citizens: Unchanging Needs in a Changed Context', in M. Freedland and S. Sciarra (eds.), *Public Services and Citizenship in European Law* (Clarendon Press, 1998), ch. 4

Hancher, L., 'Community, State and Market', in P. Craig and G. de Búrca (eds.), *The Evolution of EU Law* (Oxford University Press, 1999), ch. 20

Hansen, M., Van Ysendyck, A., and Zuhlke, S., 'The Coming of Age of EC State Aid Law: A Review of the Principal Developments in 2002 and 2003' [2004] *ECLR* 202

Ross, M., 'Article 16 EC and Services of General Interest: From Derogation to Obligation?' (2000) 25 *ELRev.* 22

Soltesz, U., and Bielesz, H., 'Judicial Review of State Aid Decisions—Recent Developments' [2004] *ECLR* 133

INDEX